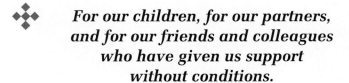

For our children, for our partners,
and for our friends and colleagues
who have given us support
without conditions.

And in memory of our friends and
colleagues, Ted Carr and Doug Guess,
whose positive influence
on the field of disability will
shine for years to come.

❖ Preface ❖

In this seventh edition, we have, as a foundation, many of the same principles about teaching students with severe disabilities that were present in earlier editions because these principles have continued relevance:

- Inclusive schools create new opportunities for *all* students to learn relevant skills and to form supportive social relationships.
- Inclusive schools enable teachers to become better teachers of *all* of their students.
- Teams of people, not isolated individuals, are responsible for designing, implementing, and evaluating educational programs.
- The skills identified for each student to learn should be functional (matching the student's current and future needs), suited to the student's chronological age, and respectful of the student's and family's preferences.
- To be appropriate, instruction must be planned to suit the individual student.
- If special education is merged with general education instead of viewed as a separate educational structure, the diverse talents of both special and general educators will be preserved and instruction for all students will be improved.
- The teaching methods that we use need to be solidly based on research and demonstrated to be effective and appropriate for a variety of students in inclusive settings.

In this seventh edition, as in the sixth, we continue to emphasize that learning is more than increasing specific isolated skills. Learning and supportive efforts should be organized toward the achievement of three outcomes: membership, belonging, and skills. To reach these outcomes, schools need to appreciate the relationship among them and focus on supporting students and their families to follow a vision of a satisfying, meaningful, and personally determined quality of life.

There is great value in building self-determination in our students, as there is for all students; the challenge is to understand the many individualized ways that this characteristic can be developed. For example, teachers can match job training opportunities to students' preferences, and team members can teach their students to make choices and initiate preferred activities. Furthermore, when teams view their students' problem behaviors as having legitimate motivations, then those motivations can drive the development of behavior support planning.

In addition to these principles and foundations, we have incorporated several features into the text to make it more valuable to its readers and more practical for instructors and professors who have adopted it. One of the most effective ways to learn is through examples. Thus, we begin each chapter with case studies of students and then apply chapter concepts to these individuals. Because heterogeneity is characteristic of those with severe disabilities, our examples are diverse and include individuals across the age range—from kindergarten to adult—and with a variety of abilities and disabilities—cognitive, movement, sensory, behavioral, and emotional. As in prior editions, there are activities at the end of each chapter that will help readers apply concepts to individuals and teaching situations. In addition, we have written as we aim to speak—using respectful, people-first language.

New to This Edition

Over the years, this text has gained a reputation for being both comprehensive and current. The aim of earlier editions was to present issues and strategies that were documented as being effective and not to "jump on treatment bandwagons." The seventh edition maintains this reputation. The goal of this revision was to present the latest evidence-based research available

v

with regard to all aspects of educational programs for students with severe disabilities, both intellectual disabilities and autism. It has been and continues to be our aim to align the content of this text with evidence-based strategies. As the field continues to evolve, we strive to have this book evolve. In addition to updating each chapter that is maintained from the sixth edition, the seventh edition of this text includes several new dimensions and a variety of new chapters:

- *Applications to Students on the Autism Spectrum.* Chapters include a case study of a student with autism so that readers can apply their learning specifically to these students.
- *New chapter on Designing and Implementing Instruction for Inclusive Classes.* This chapter, now a part of core Chapters 3, 4, 5, and 6, demonstrates how teams work through the steps of putting individualized teaching programs and supports in place in general education classrooms.
- *New chapter on Supporting Peer Relationships.* This chapter provides a comprehensive review of strategies and supports that teams need in order to promote meaningful opportunities for students to become members of classrooms and schools and to enjoy satisfying relationships with their peers.
- *New chapter on Teaching Functional Communication Skills.* Evidence-based strategies for assessment and intervention are described within a planning framework that is person-centered, focused on multiple modes of communication, and socially responsive.
- *New chapter on Teaching Academic Skills.* This chapter responds to current federal laws that require individualized education plan (IEP) teams to demonstrate how students will participate and progress in the general education curriculum, including reading, math, and science.
- *New chapter on Transitioning from School to Employment.* This chapter gives team members guidelines on the transition process so that their students will be able to access the supports and strategies needed to move into employment and adulthood.
- *PowerPoint® Presentations of Each Chapter.* Each chapter has a PowerPoint® presentation that is prepared by the chapter authors to support instructors in presenting the chapter's key points.
- *Useful Instructor's Manual.* An electronic Instructor's Manual is available to faculty. The manual will include a chapter summary, a review of the case studies, and chapter activities for each chapter. Also included will be a test bank and answer key written by the authors of each chapter.

Organization of the Text

We begin this edition with six chapters that lay the foundation for the rest of the book. The first two chapters focus on basic concepts that are central to the education of students with severe disabilities—inclusion and families. The discussion by Michael Giangreco introduces readers to students with severe disabilities by exploring definitions of severe disabilities and how these definitions and societal perceptions affect the lives of these individuals and their families. Giangreco offers us a historic retrospective of where we've been, how far we've come, and where we need to be heading. Finally, Giangreco helps us to understand what is meant by appropriate education for students with severe disabilities.

Students grow up as members of families, and families are most often the primary advocates for their children throughout life. In Chapter 2, Nina Zuna joins Ann and Rud Turnbull to explore the factors that make successful partnerships between home and school. Two such factors are ongoing, reciprocal communication between home and school and interactions that reflect and respect families from diverse cultural backgrounds.

Chapters 3, 4, 5, and 6, are written by the editors, with Donna Lehr collaborating in Chapter 3, and Rachel Janney taking the lead in Chapter 6. These core chapters set forth the basic strategies and tools that educators use in concert with other team members to plan, teach, and monitor the progress of their students. All other chapters build on this foundation. Four key words sum up the content of this section: assessment, teaching, evaluation, and implementation. We have written this section to equip readers with the strategies and resources on which educators rely.

In Chapter 7, Rob Horner, Rick Albin, Anne Todd, Stephen Newton, and Jeff Sprague set forth the principles of positive behavior support. Using comprehensive case examples, these authors describe how the process of functional behavioral assessment is conducted and used to design effective behavioral support plans that are based on the values of self-determination, respect, and inclusion.

In Chapter 8, Jane Rues and her two coauthors, Carolyn Graff and Marilyn Mulligan Ault, describe the health care procedures required by some students during the school day. This chapter explains how to incorporate special health care procedures into the school day and how educators can contribute to the prevention of related health problems and conditions.

In Chapter 9, Philippa Campbell, an occupational therapist and educator, addresses the related topic of movement disabilities that often are present in our students. Because all team members interact with a student over a range of daily activities, practical knowledge about motor disabilities must be shared. When students with motor disabilities have consistent and conscientious management of their physical needs in their home, school, work, and community environments, they can thrive.

The skills of caring for oneself, toileting, eating, dressing, and grooming are important goals for all individuals regardless of the severity of the disability. In Chapter 10, Martha Snell and Monica Delano provide a comprehensive and current review of effective methods for teaching self-care skills while also showing how these methods apply to specific students.

One of the most important elements that schools can offer students is social relationships with peers. In Chapter 11, Erik Carter illustrates strategies that teams can use to promote membership and a sense of belonging and to build a variety of personal relationships among students in classrooms and schools.

In Chapter 12, June Downing addresses functional communication and the importance of socially responsive environments. She highlights the pervasive influence of communication in all aspects of life, including education, friendships, well-being, and self-determination.

Basic skills in reading, writing, mathematics, and science are increasingly important as states respond to federal laws and policies. In Chapter 13, John McDonnell and Susan Copeland present methods for identifying what academic skills to teach and evidence-based strategies for teaching those skills in inclusive settings.

Chapter 14 guides teachers on the instruction of skills to increase active participation in home and community life. Linda Bambara, Freya Koger, and Audrey Bartholomew begin with a series of guiding values and principles that characterize the outcomes of skill instruction referenced to students' homes and communities. These themes are coupled with instructional methods that have been found to be effective with students who have severe disabilities.

Our special education laws require a clear focus on and preparation for the transition to adulthood. Preparing students for real work in the community is a longitudinal process requiring extensive team effort over the teenage years. In Chapter 15, David Test and Valerie Mazzotti set forth the essential elements of secondary vocational programs that will allow students and their teams to plan the transition from school to adulthood and then to make the transition.

The book closes with Chapter 16, in which Dianne and Phil Ferguson discuss, both as parents and as scholars, the promises that adulthood can offer to individuals with severe disabilities. The Fergusons take us on a remarkable journey across the years with their son Ian and with his friend Douglas. These family stories describe a path that has been "often confusing and frustrating, but also filled with many exciting achievements." The concept of supported adulthood is discussed within the context of current policy, social services, educational practices, and societal expectations.

Acknowledgments

Many people have assisted in the task of developing the seventh edition. First, we are indebted to a small group of students—the children, adolescents, and young adults who add reality to each chapter and whose abilities and disabilities have challenged and shaped our own skills and those of our contributors. Their families and their educators deserve equal gratitude for providing a vast array of teaching ideas, for granting permission to use their photographs, and for giving us extensive examples and information.

Finally, we are grateful for the helpful comments of our reviewers at various stages in the revision process—Joseph Domaracki, Indiana University of Pennsylvania, and Kathleen Gee, California State University–Sacramento. We would also like to thank many of our students who continually inspire our thinking and writing. Recognition also is given to the contributions of production editor Sheryl Langner, photo editor Carol Sykes, editorial assistant Penny Burleson, editor Ann Davis, copy editors Pat Onufrak and Brian Baker, and production managers Niraj Bhatt and Linda Clark. Their combined efforts have been central to the final quality of this text.

Martha E. Snell and Fredda Brown

❖ Brief Contents ❖

❖ Contents ❖

4

Selecting Teaching Strategies and Arranging Educational Environments   **122**

MARTHA E. SNELL AND FREDDA BROWN

5

Measuring Student Behavior and Learning   **186**

FREDDA BROWN AND MARTHA E. SNELL

6

Designing and Implementing Instruction for Inclusive Classes   **224**

RACHEL E. JANNEY AND MARTHA E. SNELL

7

Designing and Implementing Individualized Positive Behavior Support   **257**

ROBERT H. HORNER, RICHARD W. ALBIN, ANNE W. TODD, J. STEPHEN NEWTON, AND JEFFREY R. SPRAGUE

8

Understanding Special Health Care Procedures   304

Jane P. Rues, J. Carolyn Graff, and Marilyn Mulligan Ault

9

Addressing Motor Disabilities   340

Philippa H. Campbell

10

Teaching Self-Care Skills   377

Martha E. Snell and Monica E. Delano

11

Supporting Peer Relationships   431

ERIK W. CARTER

12

Teaching Communication Skills   461

JUNE E. DOWNING

13

Teaching Academic Skills   492

JOHN MCDONNELL AND SUSAN R. COPELAND

14

Building Skills for Home and Community 529

LINDA M. BAMBARA, FREYA KOGER, AND AUDREY BARTHOLOMEW

15

Transitioning from School to Employment 569

DAVID W. TEST AND VALERIE L. MAZZOTTI

16

The Promise of Adulthood   612

Dianne L. Ferguson and Philip M. Ferguson

1

Educating Students with Severe Disabilities
Foundational Concepts and Practices

Michael F. Giangreco

"Learn from yesterday, live for today, hope for tomorrow. The important thing is not to stop questioning."
—ALBERT EINSTEIN

Providing relevant education for students with severe disabilities requires that we learn from our past practices, both the mistakes and the successes, by drawing on the historical bank of foundational concepts and practices available to us. Our contemporary challenge is to apply what we have learned within today's context and to do so with a sense of urgency, because as we ponder, debate, and research the merits of our practices, the children who enter our schools are quickly growing up—they and their families do not have the luxury of waiting. Providing individuals with severe disabilities quality education requires that we adopt conceptually sound, evidence-based practices in our schools and confront assumptions about ability that continually threaten their current and future opportunities.

People identified as having severe disabilities are the epitome of why Einstein's challenge "not to stop questioning" is so important. Less than 40 years ago, many students with severe disabilities had no legal right to attend public schools and many did not—expectations for their educational progress were minimal. Today because of people with disabilities, their family members, and professionals who never stopped questioning, some

people with severe disabilities are doing things that many would have thought to be unimaginable just a few short decades ago. For example, some individuals with severe disabilities are attending supported general education classes with their peers who do not have disabilities, accessing and learning from the general education curriculum, being involved in general education cocurricular activities, engaging in supported employment, transitioning to community-based supported living options, and accessing inclusive post–high school educational opportunities—but, only some.

This chapter presents a series of foundational concepts and practices, past and present, organized into three major sections to encourage us to never stop questioning what people with severe disabilities are capable of learning and our own capacity to change. The first major section addresses the sometimes elusive question "Who are students with severe disabilities?" by examining definitions and how societal perceptions of people with severe disabilities can affect their lives, as well as the reciprocal benefits of interactions among people with and without disability labels. The second major section addresses some of the key areas for optimism and

1

concern for students with severe disabilities. Finally, the bulk of the chapter addresses access to four interrelated aspects of quality education for students with severe disabilities, namely access to (a) inclusive environments, (b) individualized curriculum, (c) purposeful instruction, and (d) necessary supports.

Who Are Students with Severe Disabilities?

Definitions

Although the term *severe disabilities* is used extensively in the professional literature, no single authoritative definition exists. The amendments to the Individuals with Disabilities Education Act (IDEA) (2004), a common source of special education terminology, do not define *severe disabilities*. IDEA and its corresponding Code of Federal Regulations (CFR) (2006) do define 13 distinct disability categories (34 CFR 300.8), several of which reasonably include students considered to have severe disabilities (e.g., autism, deaf-blindness, intellectual disabilities, multiple disabilities, traumatic brain injury), although not all students within these categories have severe disabilities. Consistent with international trends, calls for change from advocacy organizations (e.g., Self Advocates Becoming Empowered [SABE]), and the leadership of the American Association on Intellectual and Developmental Disabilities (AAIDD), throughout this chapter the term *intellectual disabilities* is used to replace the outdated term *mental retardation* (Schalock, Luckasson, & Schogren, 2007).

Not surprisingly, many definitions describing individuals with severe disabilities focus on deficits such as intellectual, orthopedic, sensory, behavioral, and functional impairments; unfortunately, such definitions tell us very little about them as people (McDonnell, Hardman, & McDonnell, 2003). What can be said with some confidence is that individuals with severe disabilities include a widely heterogeneous group in terms of their disability characteristics, capabilities, and educational needs. Their nondisability characteristics (e.g., interests, preferences, personalities, socioeconomic levels, cultural heritage) are as diverse as those found in the general population. Sometimes people with severe disabilities are described as having *low-incidence* disabilities because it is estimated that less than 1% of the general population has severe disabilities

(see Chapter 3 for specific incidence and prevalence information).

Although all students, with and without disabilities, need supports, students with severe disabilities typically require more and different supports in order to pursue their educational goals and participate in their daily lives. Consistent with this focus on supports, the international organization TASH (formerly The Association for Persons with Severe Handicaps) has identified the persons for whom it advocates as those

> who require ongoing support in one or more major life activities in order to participate in an integrated community and enjoy a quality of life similar to that available to all citizens. Support may be required for life activities such as mobility, communication, self-care, and learning as necessary for community living, employment, and self-sufficiency. (TASH, 2000)

Similarly, the American Association on Intellectual and Developmental Disabilities (AAIDD, 2010) has shifted away from describing people on the basis of the severity of their intellectual disability (e.g., mild, moderate, severe, profound) and toward a multidimensional classification system (e.g., intellectual abilities, adaptive behavior, health, participation, context) that also categorizes people on the basis of the pattern and intensity of the support they need. The AAIDD classification system is consistent with broader, multidimensional models of human functioning, such as the International Classification of Functioning, Disability and Health (World Health Organization, 2001), that stress providing contextually necessary supports which allow for participation that accounts for a person's abilities, adaptive behavior, and health characteristics (Wehmeyer et al., 2008).

Snell (2003) reminds us that in addition to their collective diversity and need for lifelong supports, individuals with severe disabilities share a fundamental human trait: "the capacity to learn" (p. 2210). Although this may seem too obvious to mention, as recently as the early 1980s there were heated debates in the professional literature about whether individuals with the most severe disabilities were capable of learning and how such judgments affected their right to be educated. While some questioned the educability of children with the most severe disabilities and the wisdom of educating them (Kaufman & Krouse, 1981), others offered persuasive arguments favoring the pursuit of education for every child, regardless of the perceived severity of their disability (Baer, 1981). As Baer pointed out, in addition to the potential benefits associated with students learning skills that will be useful to them, approaching *all* students as capable of learning provides us with the opportunity to extend our own understanding of teaching and learning:

> *To the extent that we sometimes finally succeed in teaching a child whom we have consistently failed to teach in many previous efforts, we may learn something about teaching technique.... Too often, in my opinion, we teach children who are not only capable of teaching themselves, but eager to do so; in their wisdom, they cheat us of learning completely how the trick is done because they do some of it for us and do it privately. It is when they cannot do much if any of it for us that we get to find out how to do all of it ourselves, as teachers. (p. 94)*

The stance favoring education for *all* was then— and continues to be—consistent with the federal *zero-reject* principle embedded in IDEA. The zero-reject provision established that *all* school-aged children, regardless of the severity of their disability, are entitled to a free, appropriate public education (Turnbull, Stowe, & Huerta, 2007). The zero-reject principle was tested in the case of *Timothy W. v. Rochester School District* (1989). In this case, a student with severe, multiple disabilities had been denied admission to his local public school because school officials deemed him too severely disabled to benefit from education. Although the federal district court agreed with the school, the U.S. Court of Appeals for the First Circuit overturned the lower court's ruling and strongly affirmed the zero-reject principle as a core component of IDEA. Furthermore, the Court of Appeals affirmed the notion that education is defined broadly to include "not only traditional academic skills, but also basic functional life skills." The court recognized that

> *...educational methodologies in these areas are not static, but are constantly evolving and improving. It is the school district's responsibility to avail itself of these new approaches in providing an educational program geared toward each child's individual needs. The only question for the school district to determine, in conjunction with the child's parents, is what constitutes an appropriate individualized education program (IEP)....* (Timothy W. v. Rochester School District, *1989, p. 973*)

Societal Perceptions and Expectations

Frequently, people with severe disabilities are defined primarily, sometimes exclusively, by their disability characteristics. This has been referred to as *disability spread,* defined as the tendency to make broad inferences, assumptions, and generalizations about a person on the basis of disability stereotypes within the society (Dembo, Leviton, & Wright, 1975). Some common stereotypes portray persons with disabilities as sick, subhuman, a menace, an object of pity, an object of charity, or a holy innocent (Wolfensberger, 1975). As pointed out by Van der Klift and Kunc (2002), "When disability is seen as the largest component of a person, much of what is unique and human about him or her is obscured" (p. 25). Biklen and Mosley (1988) explained that people with disabilities may not think of themselves in ways that put their disability characteristics at the forefront of their self-perception, instead "preferring to identify with members of particular religious groups, as certain kinds of workers, employees of particular companies, or as fans of particular sports teams" (p. 155).

Opportunities for Interaction and Reciprocal Benefit

Because people with severe disabilities require ongoing supports, the ways in which they are perceived and subsequently treated by others can have a major impact on the quality of their lives. While it is quite certain that disability spread adversely affects people with disabilities, some suspect that far too many people without disabilities are missing out on potentially important relationships with people with disabilities because of this artificial, socially constructed barrier to interaction (Bogdan & Taylor, 1989). If you accept the notion that personal relationships are among a small set of the most defining characteristics that influence the quality of a person's life, then disability spread is a problematic issue for those with and without disabilities alike (Siperstein, Parker, Bardon, & Widaman, 2007; Taylor & Bogdan, 1989).

As you continue to read this chapter and the rest of this book about people who have the label of *severe disabilities,* you are encouraged to think about how these individuals are *like all other people, like some other people,* and *uniquely like no other people.* Keep in mind that first and foremost we *all* are human beings—someone's child, someone's sibling, someone's classmate, or someone's friend. It is true that some people are born with or acquire disability characteristics that are considered so severe in today's society as to require extensive or pervasive supports. However, our collective attitudes and responses to a person's disability characteristics can influence how much of a barrier those characteristics are to leading a regular, or hopefully, enviable life. As an Nth Degree T-shirt worn by a self-advocate says, "Your attitude just might be my biggest barrier" (Wilkins, 2003).

Reasons for Optimism and Concern

From an historical perspective, our current times are among the best for individuals with severe disabilities, at least thus far. I write this with the full recognition that our current *best* is relative and is quite a long way from *good* for far too many people labeled as having severe disabilities. The next two subsections highlight a set of key reasons for optimism about the education of students with disabilities followed by a set of continuing concerns. This framework is designed to build on success while recognizing that much remains in need of attention.

Reasons for Optimism

Table 1–1 highlights areas for optimism about our present and future. Such optimism about our collective potential to make a positive difference in the lives of students with and without disabilities is an essential ingredient of the creative problem solving necessary to tackle such important challenges.

First, nowhere is progress more evident or reason for optimism more warranted than with regard to *inclusive educational opportunities*. Across the country, students with severe disabilities increasingly are

TABLE 1–1
Areas for Optimism

1. Inclusive education
2. School reform and restructuring
3. Access to the general education curriculum
4. Alternative assessment in statewide accountability systems
5. Transition to adult life (e.g., postsecondary education, supported employment, community living)
6. Positive behavior supports
7. Peer supports
8. Self-determination

accessing general education classrooms; such options were rare or nonexistent just two or three decades ago. The literature now is replete with examples, strategies, and research focusing on inclusive schooling across the age span (Downing, 2008; Hunt & Goetz, 1997)—from early childhood and elementary education (Grisham-Brown, Hemmeter, & Pretti-Frontczak, 2005; Janney & Snell, 1997), through middle and high schools (Fisher, Sax, & Pumpian, 1999; Kennedy & Fisher, 2001; Villa, Thousand, Nevin, & Liston, 2005). Table 1–2 lists key elements of inclusive education.

Inclusion-oriented people seek to establish an ethic that welcomes all children into their local schools and simultaneously pursues a range of individually meaningful learning outcomes through evidence-based practices (Habib, 2007). Although prompted by the needs of students with disabilities, the concept of inclusive

TABLE 1–2
Elements of Inclusive Education

1. *All* students are welcomed in general education. The first placement options considered are the general education classes in the school that the students would attend if they did not have a disability.
2. Disability is recognized as a form of human diversity. Hence, students with disabilities are accepted as individuals and are not denied access because of their disabilities.
3. Appropriate supports are available, regardless of disability label or severity. Given their portability, supports are provided in typical environments instead of sending students to specialized settings to receive supports.
4. The composition of the classrooms in which students are educated reflects the naturally occurring proportion of students with and without disabilities (referred to as *natural proportions*). Therefore, the percentage of students without disabilities in each class is substantially higher than the percentage of students with disabilities.
5. Students, irrespective of their developmental or performance levels, are educated with peers in the same age groupings available to those without disability labels instead of with younger students. Students with disabilities need not function at or near the same academic level as their classmates (although some do) to benefit from a chronologically age-appropriate, inclusive placement.
6. Students with and without disabilities participate in shared educational experiences while pursuing individually appropriate learning outcomes with the necessary supports. Educational experiences are designed to enhance valued life outcomes that seek an individualized balance between both the academic-functional and the social-personal aspects of schooling.
   Inclusive education exists when each of the previous six characteristics occurs on an ongoing, daily basis.

(Adapted from Confronting Obstacles to Inclusion-Giangreco, Carter, Doyle, & Suter, in press) education is broader. It seeks to promote equity, opportunity, and social justice (Hasazi & Shepherd, 2009). These outcomes are relevant for any student across a range of diversity characteristics (e.g., race, culture, primary language, socioeconomic level), as well as any student who simply is having difficulty becoming part of the classroom's learning community.

Second, inclusive schooling increasingly is being linked with broader *school reform and restructuring* efforts designed to improve educational opportunities for *all* students, such as the Schoolwide Applications Model (SAM) (Sailor, 2002; Sailor & Roger, 2005) and Whole Schooling (Peterson, 2004). Third, curricular options for students with severe disabilities have extended beyond functional life skills to include greater alignment and *access to the general education curriculum* (Browder & Spooner, 2006; Dymond, Renzaglia, Gilson, & Slagor, 2007; Jorgensen, McSheehan, & Sonnenmeier, 2009; Udvari-Solner, Thousand, & Villa, 2002; Wehmeyer, 2006). Correspondingly, a fourth area for optimism is that students with severe disabilities are now being included in statewide accountability systems using *alternative assessment* approaches (Browder et al., 2004; Klienert & Kearns, 2001) (see Chapter 3). This helps ensure that the educational progress of students with disabilities is monitored within schoolwide improvement efforts.

Fifth, a significant volume of literature exists on promising practices for *transition to adult life* (Thoma, Bartholomew, & Scott, 2009) leading to *supported employment* (Wehman, Inge, Revell, & Brooke, 2007) and supported *community living* (Taylor, 2006) (see Chapters 15 and 16). Emerging examples exist that describe *college options* for young adults with disabilities (Doyle, 2003; Feldman, Fialka, & Rossen, 2006; Grigal & Hart, 2009).

Sixth, further cause for optimism comes from the rapidly developing technology of *positive behavior support* (Brown & Michaels, 2006; Freeman et al., 2006; Horner, Sugai, Todd, & Lewis-Palmer, 2005) (see Chapter 7). Increasingly, teams are conducting functional assessments of student problem behavior in an effort to better understand the functions of those behaviors and their communicative intent. Behavior support plans are being developed and implemented by teams to teach students social, communication, and other functional skills as a way to replace problem behaviors (Durand & Merges, 2001). Within the positive behavior support framework, change does not focus exclusively on an individual's problem behaviors but instead more comprehensively on changing environmental conditions

that may be contributing to a person's challenging behaviors. Positive behavior supports use evidence-based strategies not only to reduce problem behaviors (e.g., aggression, self-injury, property destruction) but also to "build prosocial behavior, document durable change, generalize across the full range of situations an individual [has] encountered, and produce access to a rich lifestyle" (Carr et al., 1999, p. 4).

Seventh, drawing upon peers to lend support to students with severe disabilities has emerged as a prominent area of research because it is central to social and academic classroom success (Carter, Cushing, & Kennedy, 2009; Janney & Snell, 2006). Peers without disabilities can effectively provide an array of supports to their classmates with disabilities in ways that enhance educational experiences. Increasingly, school personnel are recognizing the benefits of peer supports instead of the common response of relying too heavily or unnecessarily on extra adult supports (e.g., one-to-one teacher assistants) (Carter, Sisco, Melekoglu, & Kurkowski, 2007) (see Chapter 11).

Finally, the focus on family involvement has expanded beyond parental involvement to include *self-determination* by individuals with disabilities. Self-determination is pursued by teaching individuals the skills needed to make decisions about their own lives, providing them with opportunities to make decisions, and then honoring their decisions (Wehmeyer, 2005). As succinctly summarized in self-advocacy circles, "Nothing about me without me!"

Reasons for Concern

Although the eight areas for optimism presented in the previous section are encouraging trends, the field of special education is not at a stage of development where the curricular, instructional, and support needs of students with severe disabilities are consistently and sufficiently addressed. Table 1–3 lists six continuing areas of concern.

TABLE 1–3
Areas for Continuing Concern

1. Inconsistent access to inclusive classrooms
2. Questionable quality of curriculum and instruction
3. Too many families are frustrated by the lack of professional responsiveness
4. Continued use of aversive procedures
5. Challenging working conditions for special educators
6. Limited postschool options

First, inclusive educational opportunities have remained relatively static, and *inconsistent access to inclusive classrooms* continues to plague public school systems, especially for students with severe disabilities. Primary placement in general education means that a student with a disability receives 80% or more of his or her instruction in a general education classroom with appropriate supports. The U.S. Department of Education (2007) indicates that for all students with disabilities (ages 6–21) in U.S. states, including the Bureau of Indian Education (BIE) and outlying areas, 57% have their primary placement in general education classrooms. This represents an increase of only about 1% per year over the past decade (Giangreco, Hurley, & Suter, 2009). As of 2007, only four states (Alabama, Nebraska, North Dakota, and Rhode Island) and three outlying areas (American Samoa, the Northern Mariana Islands, and Puerto Rico) reported including more than 70% of all students with disabilities (ages 6–21) in general education classes as their primary placement. Conversely, in Hawaii and the District of Columbia, the overall placement rates in general education classes remain below 20%. The overall lack of change nationally obscures some trends of concern. Fewer than half of the states report that the general education classroom is the primary placement for more than 60% of their students with any type of disability. Several states that formerly had overall general class placement rates above 70% have reported declines in general class placement that now leave them below 70% (e.g., Colorado, Idaho, Kansas, Massachusetts, Minnesota, Ohio, South Dakota, Vermont).

A closer look at categories most likely to include students with severe disabilities (e.g., autism, deaf-blindness, intellectual disabilities, multiple disabilities, and traumatic brain injury) depicts a more stark reality. For example, rates of placement in general education classes as the primary placement for students with intellectual disabilities are dismal—only 16% nationally. The rates are below 10% in 17 states and the District of Columbia and a scant 11% to 30% in 27 other states. The general education class placement rates for students with intellectual disabilities in four states (Alabama, Connecticut, Kentucky, and Nebraska) and Puerto Rico range from 35% to 46%. Only one state exceeded 50% general education class placement rates for students with intellectual disabilities—Iowa (57%). Data for New Hampshire and Vermont, which have historically had rates exceeding 50%, were not reported in the 2007 federal data because of a government

practice that currently precludes reporting in certain small number categories (U.S. Department of Education, 2007). Unfortunately, the odds that any particular student with a severe disability will be included in a general education class currently depends, in large part, on where that student lives and what disability category has been assigned to him or her. Although placement does not equal inclusion, it is a telling indicator of access to general education environments and a first step toward inclusive opportunities.

As we move slowly closer to realizing the promises of the IDEA and toward an educational system that supports access to general education curriculum and environments for students with disabilities, serious questions remain about whether progress is simply too slow (Brown & Michaels, 2003):

> *How long should educators accept that in many locations across the country the more "primitive" steps toward inclusion continue to be accepted and reinforced? Can they afford to wait another decade . . . ? In the meantime, what happens to children, especially those with the most severe disabilities . . . ? Is it acceptable for the education field to praise its progress when generations of these students continue to be excluded? (p. 240)*

Second, even in situations where access to inclusive environments is better, the *questionable quality of the curriculum and instruction* for students with severe disabilities in general education classrooms continues to be a serious and ongoing issue. Being physically present in settings with same-age peers who do not have disabilities is necessary, but not sufficient, to be included. Too many students with severe disabilities who are placed in general education classes are subjected to undesirable conditions, such as being (a) separated within the classroom (e.g., taught primarily by a paraprofessional apart from classmates), (b) taken through the motions of a lesson or activity without having appropriately targeted learning outcomes (i.e., not learning much of value or importance to them), or (c) presented with lesson content that is inconsistent with their abilities or learning and communication characteristics. Such practices obviously limit a student's learning opportunities and may contribute to internalized (e.g., withdrawal, lack of responsiveness) or externalized (e.g., self-stimulation, aggression, tantrums) problem behaviors.

The very concept of inclusive education has become distorted because fragmented, partial, or low-quality implementation efforts have been mislabeled as "inclusive" (Davern et al., 1997). Clashing ideological views among special education scholars have increased confusion about exactly what inclusive education is, and what should be done about it (Brantlinger, 1997).While public debates continue to be waged regarding the *least restrictive environment* provision of IDEA, years pass, and the lives of real children and their families are adversely affected.

Third, *too many families are frustrated by the lack of professional responsiveness* to their children's educational needs (Soodak & Erwin, 2000).While some educators interact with parents and students as consumers and embrace them as partners in the educational process, others still resist, preferring to retain the role of professional as *expert*. Family members, friends, and persons with disabilities themselves also have expertise and knowledge concerning issues such as an individual's likes and dislikes, understanding of behavioral challenges, rest/sleep patterns, idiosyncratic communication, personal history, and other important information that may contribute to educational and service planning. It is when the respective expertise of professionals and families are combined that teams have the opportunity to experience the synergy that comes from true collaboration (Harry, 2008) (see Chapter 2).

Fourth, concern exists about the *continued use of aversive procedures* to manage challenging behaviors. Shockingly (pun intended), in an era when electric cattle prods are becoming a thing of the past in American agriculture, some students with severe disabilities continue to be subjected to an arsenal of aversive procedures and punishments (e.g., contingent electric shock, restraints, seclusion, noxious smells, white noise, physical assaults) in the name of "treatment," resulting in lost learning opportunities, degradation, psychological trauma, physical injury, and, in a small number of cases, even death (Gonnerman, 2007; National Disability Rights Network, 2009; U.S. Government Accountability Office, 2009).This problem persists despite the availability of effective, positive alternatives (e.g., Bambara & Kern, 2005; Janney & Snell, 2008) (see Chapter 7).

Fifth, *challenging working conditions for special educators* contribute to the concerns about the education of students with severe disabilities. Of particular alarm is the national shortage of qualified special educators, as well as the need to train and retain more of them (Billingsley, 2003). The shortages interfere with students with disabilities receiving an appropriate, quality education (McLeskey, Tyler, & Saunders, 2002). Kozleski, Mainzer, and Deshler (2000) highlighted some of the key factors contributing to special educators leaving the field (e.g., excessive paperwork, large caseloads, lack of administrative support).The field needs a full and capable cadre of special educators to team up with parents, related services providers, and teachers. As so eloquently stated by Brown, Farrington, Ziegler, Knight, and Ross (1999), "because learning is so difficult for students with significant disabilities, they are in dire need of continuous exposure to the most ingenious, creative, powerful, competent, interpersonally effective, and informed professionals" (p. 252).

Finally, *limited postschool options* adversely affect young adults with severe disabilities. As noted in a past report of the National Council on Disability on the implementation of IDEA, "After years of public education, youth with severe disabilities all too often exit school unemployed, without basic skills, lonely, isolated from peers, and disenfranchised from the larger society" (Giangreco & Snell, 1996, p. 100). Unfortunately, this statement is as true today as it was in 1996.While some students with severe disabilities are accessing meaningful postschool opportunities, many are not (Certo, Luecking, Murphy, Brown, Coury, & Belanger, 2008).

If you are interested in improving the lives of people with severe disabilities through education, there is plenty to motivate you to act, regardless of whether you see this point in time as the glass half full or half empty. For those of you motivated by positive news, there is a continually growing set of examples and body of literature documenting steady progress to encourage your continuing contributions to these efforts. Regardless of what "fuels your fire"—the slow pace of progress or ongoing injustices facing people with severe disabilities—there is plenty of motivation to act and work to do!

Access to Quality Education

The remainder of this chapter offers foundational information and ideas about access to quality education for students with severe disabilities in four main areas: (a) access to inclusive environments, (b) access to individualized curriculum, (c) access to purposeful instruction, and (d) access to necessary supports. All of these components of quality education and others are given in-depth attention in the subsequent chapters.

Access to Inclusive Environments

The least restrictive environment (LRE) provision of the IDEA regulations, which has been in place since the Act's inception in 1975 (Rebhorn & Smith, 2008), clearly establishes that "to the maximum extent appropriate, children with disabilities . . . are educated with children who are nondisabled" (34 CFR 300.114). The LRE provision states that "special classes, separate schooling, or other removal of children with disabilities from the regular educational environment occurs only if the nature or severity of the disability is such that education in regular classes with the use of supplemental aids and services cannot be achieved satisfactorily" (34 CFR 300.114).

Ironically, it has been this second part of the LRE provision that, at times, has been used to justify the continued segregation of students with the most severe disabilities. Across the country, far too many students who are designated as having severe disabilities are automatically placed in self-contained special education classes or schools, sometimes requiring them to travel far greater distances each day than their siblings and neighbors to attend school as they are bussed to regional programs.

Federal support of the LRE provisions retains a strong preference for placement in general education classes for students with disabilities, including those with severe disabilities (Rebhorn & Smith, 2008). As the U.S. Department of Education wrote in the regulation's "Analysis of Comments and Changes," the Act

presumes that the first placement option considered for each child with a disability is the regular classroom in the school that the child would attend if not disabled, with appropriate supplementary aids and services to facilitate such placement. Thus, before a child with a disability can be placed outside of the regular educational environment, the full range of supplementary aids and services that could be provided to facilitate the child's placement in the regular classroom setting must be considered. (CFR, 2006, p. 46588)

The act goes on to state the following:

In all cases, placement decisions must be individually determined on the basis of each child's abilities and needs and each child's IEP, and not solely on factors such as category of disability, severity of disability, availability of special education and related services, configuration of the service delivery system,

availability of space, or administrative convenience. (CFR, 2006, p. 46588)

Further evidence of federal support for LRE provisions for students with severe disabilities is found in a jointly submitted amicus curiae (Friend of the Court) brief; the U.S. Department of Justice (Office of Civil Rights) and the U.S. Department of Education wrote in support of a student with severe disabilities (named Spike) to be educated in the general education classroom with supplemental supports and aids. In part, the government's stance, which was ultimately affirmed by the U.S. Court of Appeals (3rd Circuit), stated,

The district court correctly held that the placement in a LSS (Life Skills Support) classroom that Valley Grove proposed would not educate Spike in the least restrictive environment, as required by the IDEA, properly analyzing the case pursuant to the IDEA and this Court's precedent. Contrary to the decision of the Appeals Panel, and Valley Grove's argument, the IDEA does not require that Spike be able to perform at or near the grade level of non-disabled students before placement in the regular class can be considered the LRE for him. Congress expressed a strong preference in favor of educating children with disabilities in an inclusive manner and an integrated environment and requires States accepting IDEA funds to educate children with disabilities in the least restrictive environment (i.e., with their nondisabled peers in the regular classroom) to the maximum extent appropriate. States and school districts are not asked to determine whether LRE is an appropriate policy but rather to determine how a child can be educated in the LRE. Thus, school districts must determine how a child can be educated in the regular class with the use of supplementary aids and services. Valley Grove did not even attempt to make the necessary determination of how Spike could be educated in the LRE. Indeed, Valley Grove argues instead that, directly contrary to IDEA regulations, Spike must be removed from his age-appropriate regular classroom solely because his educational level is below that of the class. (U.S. Department of Justice, 2002, pp. 13–14)

IDEA is clear that the default placement—in other words, the starting point—for *all* students with disabilities is the regular education classroom with appropriate supports. Teams that are responsible for making placement decisions must make those decisions in ways that are consistent with the LRE provisions of the law. This means discarding many of the common reasons students with severe disabilities are denied access to general education classes. IDEA *does not* say that students with disabilities should be denied access to general education classes

- if they have a particular label (e.g., autism, intellectual disabilities) or require extensive supports,
- if their skills are discrepant from their classmates,
- if they are pursuing different learning outcomes than their classmates,
- just because it hasn't been done that way before in the school,
- if it is administratively inconvenient or if needed services are not currently in place,
- if they require supports or accommodations, or
- if the adults in the school are unaccustomed to the characteristics presented by the students.

Despite trends toward greater access to regular class placements, too many students with severe disabilities remain unnecessarily segregated in special education schools and classes; some are even segregated *within* general education classes. Yet, for every student with a severe disability who remains educationally segregated there are other students with similar attributes, abilities, and needs who are successfully included and learning relevant skills. This suggests that whether a student with a severe disability is meaningfully included may have less to do with his or her characteristics and more to do with the attitudes, skills, structure, and practices of the adults responsible for providing education (Giangreco, Carter, et al., in press).

Placement teams should shift away from asking "Who is appropriate to exclude?" It would be more constructive and consistent with IDEA to ask "How can we change our practices so that more students with disabilities can be successfully included and educated?" By approaching this challenge proactively, people with varying philosophical orientations can, it is hoped, come together around the simple purpose of ensuring that students' lives should be better because they went to our schools.

Access to Individualized Curriculum

IDEA provides a potent framework to enhance the lives of students with disabilities through *special education* and the development of an *individualized education program (IEP)*. Special education is defined as "specially designed instruction, at no cost to parents, to meet the unique needs of a child with a disability" (20 U.S.C. § 1400 (2004); IDEA, sec. 602(29)). Specially designed instruction means "adapting . . . content, methodology, or delivery of instruction to meet the unique needs of the child that result from the child's disability; and to ensure access of the child to the general education curriculum" (34 CFR 300.39 [3]).

As described in the IDEA, special education is a service, not a place (Taylor, 1988). At its heart, special education refers to the *individualized* ways in which we provide instruction to students in an effort to respond to their unique learning characteristics resulting from their disability. Sometimes individualization means (a) *changes in curriculum* to account for a student's present level of performance or special learning needs, (b) *adaptations to the delivery of instruction* (e.g., sensory, physical, behavioral, environmental) that allow a student to have access to learning opportunities, or (c) use of *different instructional methods* applied to the general education curriculum or to individually determined learning outcomes that extend beyond the general education curriculum.

Individualized Participation Options Within General Education

One of the most basic barriers for students with severe disabilities accessing special education within general education settings is the difficulty that some people have conceptualizing how to retain overall curricular and instructional integrity for all members of the classroom. People who may not fully understand the value, importance, or logic of including a student with a severe disability in a general education classroom ask reasonable questions such as "How does it make sense for a student with a severe cognitive disability to be in a fifth-grade class when he can't do fifth-grade work?" Such legitimate questions deserve answers. Placing a student in an age-appropriate general education classroom *does* make sense when we shed the notion that the student must participate at the same level or necessarily should have the same learning outcomes as his or her classmates without disabilities. The question isn't whether the student performs at grade level, but whether his or her individual needs can be met within the general class context with special education plus supplemental supports and aids.

The participation of students with severe disabilities within general education classes and activities can be broadly characterized along two dimensions: (a)

FIGURE 1–1

Inclusion Options Within General Education Environments and Activities

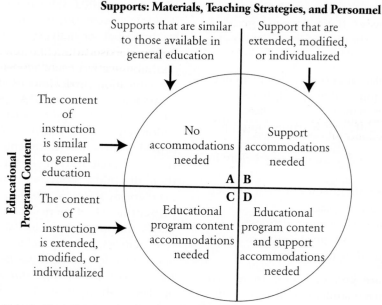

(Adapted from Giangreco, Cloninger, & Iverson, 1998)

their *educational program content* (i.e., individualized curriculum, IEP annual goals with corresponding benchmarks or short-term objectives, and designated learning outcomes from the general education curriculum) and (b) their *supports,* namely, what is provided to assist the student in accessing and pursuing achievement of his or her educational goals (e.g., assistive technology, materials, adaptations, learning strategies, related services). As shown in Figure 1-1, this can be conceptualized as four basic options for including students with severe disabilities (or any student for that matter) within typical class activities; each is described in the sections that follow. During the course of a school day, even sometimes within a single activity, an individual student will move among these different options, depending on the nature of the activity and his or her individual needs. This approach requires deliberate collaboration among teachers, special educators, and related services providers (Chapter 6 in this text; Janney & Snell, 1997; Snell & Janney, 2000).

Option A: No Accommodations Required

Option A exists when a student is participating in the same activity with students without disabilities in the same way, with the same content, and at the same level of difficulty. It should be noted, however, that supports

(e.g., teacher, classmates, classroom equipment) that are typically available can and do vary widely from class to class or school to school.

The participation of students with severe disabilities can be characterized as Option A during certain parts of the day. If Option A existed all of the time, the student would not be in need of special education nor would he or she be characterized as having severe disabilities (i.e., extensive or pervasive support needs). For example, in a primary classroom, when the teacher is reading a story to the class, the student with severe disabilities may not require specialized instruction or specialized supports. The teacher may position the child close by so that the teacher can show each page and respond if the student's attention wanders, or the teacher may have a peer sit nearby in case the student starts to lose his or her balance while seated on the floor with the rest of the class. However, these types of simple supports are not specialized to the level of considering them "special education." Indeed, these types of supports are typically given in classrooms to many students who are not labeled with a disability.

It is important to recognize times when a student with a severe disability can participate within Option A because (a) it provides opportunities for the teacher to interact with a student who has disabilities in typical (nonspecialized) ways, (b) it allows classmates to see that the student doesn't always need extraordinary help, and (c) it allows the student to avoid unnecessary supports that may inadvertently interfere with peer interaction or teacher engagement. Many students with severe disabilities have one-to-one paraprofessional support while they are in general education class activities (Suter & Giangreco, 2009). There can be a tendency to provide such support, even at times when it is not needed. Using the previous example, having the student with a severe disability sit beside or on the lap of the paraprofessional not only may be unnecessary, but also may have unintended negative consequences such as stigmatization, unnecessary dependency, interference with peer interactions, and interference with teacher engagement (Giangreco, Yuan, McKenzie, Cameron, & Fialka, 2005). The extensive use of one-to-one paraprofessional supports is a critical issue in special education for students with developmental disabilities, and emerging research is suggesting potential alternatives to overreliance on paraprofessionals (Carter et al., 2007; Giangreco, Broer, & Suter, in press). Therefore, teams should continually look for Option A opportunities by considering how naturally available supports can be utilized (Nisbet, 1992).

Option B: Support Accommodations Required

Option B exists when a student with a disability requires extended, modified, or otherwise individualized supports while pursuing substantively the same general education program. For example, in order for a student with deafness or blindness to access the general education program, he or she may require signing from an interpreter or the use of tactile materials as necessary supports. Similarly, a student with severe orthopedic or multiple disabilities might require a tape recorder and adapted switch to "take notes" during a high school class.

Option C: Educational Program Content Accommodations Required

Option C exists when a student requires extension, modification, or individualization of the content of the general education program but *does not* require specialized supports. For example, the teacher might adjust (a) the amount (e.g., 4 new vocabulary words instead of 10), (b) the level (e.g., posing less complex questions), or (c) the type of content (e.g., 1:1 correspondence instead of fractions). Across each of these possibilities, once the content adjustment is made, the student does

not require other specialized supports—although, like Option A, natural supports might be provided.

Option D: Educational Program Content and Support Accommodations Required

Option D exists at times when a student needs extension, modification, or individualization of both the general education program content and the supports to participate.

> *Following a small-group geometry lesson on calculating the angles of various types of triangles, the teacher has planned a variety of activities for students to practice what they learned during the lesson. For Jamie, a student with severe and multiple disabilities, the content of the lesson and follow-up activities have been focused on discriminating triangles from other shapes; this represents individualization in the content of the general education math program. Making such discriminations also supports his communication; he is learning to extend his ability to discriminate beyond actual objects to symbolic representations. Additionally, instead of being asked to complete a paper-and-pencil task, he requires tactile materials that he can hold and feel, visual cues to highlight the three sides of the triangles, and individualized prompting and feedback on his performance; these represent support accommodations. So, for this math activity, Jaime receives both program and support accommodations (Option D).*

Within both options C and D, teams may employ the *principle of partial participation* (Baumgart et al., 1982). This principle asserts that it is important for individuals with severe disabilities to participate in whatever parts of activities they can, even if they cannot participate in every aspect and that they "can acquire many skills that will allow them to function, at least in part, in a wide variety of least restrictive school and nonschool environments and activities" (Baumgart et al., 1982, p. 19). Ferguson and Baumgart (1991) remind us that, like any principle, partial participation can be misused. They identified passive participation, myopic participation, piecemeal participation, and missed participation as common error patterns that have occurred when people have attempted to apply the principle of partial participation. Partial participation is designed to foster socially valued roles for people with disabilities that have a positive influence on their image and personal competencies. Consider Kendra, a middle school student with multiple disabilities who has severe oral–motor problems (e.g., difficulty chewing and swallowing).

Many foods that Kendra is helped to eat fall out of her mouth. When in the noisy, bustling cafeteria, she seems particularly distracted. Her parents identified eating in busy environments as a priority because the family often eats in these types of public places.

School personnel, however, were concerned that eating in the cafeteria was socially problematic for Kendra and would detract from how she was perceived by others. So since she moved into this school district a year ago, she has been eating lunch in a private area while working on goals to improve her eating and drinking skills with a paraprofessional. Unfortunately, this practice, while intended to be respectful of her, took an all-or-nothing approach. A subgroup of Kendra's educational team, including her mother, special education teacher, and occupational therapist, came up with a plan that was designed to respect her dignity while also providing her with access to the cafeteria with classmates.

The Principle of Partial Participation was key to various aspects of their plan that systematically shifted from eating alone to eating with peers in the cafeteria. First, recognizing that Kendra quickly became fatigued and her eating skills deteriorated as time went on, they decided that instead of having Kendra eat her entire lunch in one 20-minute sitting, she was offered two 10-minute mini-meals spread out over 40 minutes. During the regularly scheduled lunch period for her class, she spent only 5 minutes in a private area working on her eating and drinking goals with a paraprofessional. The remaining 15 minutes was spent in the cafeteria with her peers, eating only foods that she could easily manage and hanging out just like everyone else in the middle school cafeteria. After she had been going to the cafeteria for a couple of weeks and seemed more comfortable, the amount of time that she spent there was gradually increased. Kendra's parents and occupational therapist identified a specific set of foods that she was able to chew and swallow most effectively without spilling. She would still lose food occasionally; this would also allow her peers to learn that some people eat differently and for the adults to model that it's not a big deal. Kendra continued to work on eating more challenging, messy foods in private. The team recorded data on both her eating goals and social interactions—they met regularly to
discuss Kendra's progress. As time passed, they gradually shifted her eating to the cafeteria completely, although she still didn't eat her entire meal during the scheduled lunchtime. The team used partial participation by offering her only certain foods in the cafeteria and using only part of the time for eating; these modifications in the usual lunch routine allowed Kendra to be more fully part of the life of the school.

It is often the case that Option D (program content and support accommodations required) will be necessary, at least part of the time, for students with severe disabilities because of their extensive or pervasive support needs. Teams are encouraged to consider when options A, B, or C are possibilities and to be conscious of not overusing Option D if less intrusive options are appropriate.

Understanding how the participation of a student with severe disabilities can be characterized using these options can help some team members conceptualize the inclusion and meaningful participation of these students. Equally as important, some general education teachers experience uncertainty when they are unclear about the nature of a student's participation in their class and their role with the student. These teachers want to know what is expected of the student in their classroom and what is expected of them as teachers. Clarifying the options for participation in a variety of class activities can help alleviate teachers' anxieties and establish a firm foundation on which to establish inclusion, thus retaining curricular and instructional integrity.

Inclusion options C and D often lead teams to ask an important question: "How can individualized curricular content be addressed appropriately in the classroom when students without disabilities are pursuing different curricular content?" Lack of clarity about this issue can lead to one of the most common anxiety-producing questions asked by classroom teachers: "How do you expect me to incorporate an individualized curriculum for a student with disabilities while teaching the rest of my class?" Unfortunately, all too often the solution to this challenge is for a paraprofessional to operate a parallel educational program in the back or side of the classroom. Such an approach minimizes the potential benefits of participation in a general education class. Delegating primary instructional responsibilities to a paraprofessional also may relegate students with disabilities, presumably the students with the most significant learning challenges, to receiving their instruction from the least prepared personnel, who

TABLE 1–4
Components of Multilevel Curriculum/Instruction and Curriculum Overlapping

Shared Components
1. Lessons include a diverse group of same-age learners (e.g., advanced, those with disabilities, at grade level, at-risk).
2. Learning occurs within a shared activity or experience within a regular class activity.
3. Each learner has individually appropriate learning outcomes at an appropriate level of difficulty.

Distinct Components	
Multilevel Curriculum/Instruction	**Curriculum Overlapping**
4. All learning outcomes are within the same curricular area (e.g., science or math or social studies) and students are responsible for more or less of them in terms of amount and complexity.	4. Learning outcomes for the target student come from a different curricular area (e.g., communication, socialization, or personal management) from those of other classmates (e.g., science, communication, math, or social skills).
Variations:	
(a) Same topical subject matter in same curricular area	
(b) Different topical subject matter in same curricular area	

(Adapted from Giangreco, 2007)

tend to be undertrained and undersupervised (Giangreco & Broer, 2005). Two alternatives include *multilevel curriculum/instruction* and *curriculum overlapping* (Giangreco, 2007). See Table 1–4 for shared and distinct components of these two related approaches.

Multilevel Curriculum/Instruction

There are two requirements of multilevel curriculum/instruction. First, it occurs when a student with disabilities and peers without disabilities participate together in a shared activity such as a science lab experiment. Second, each student has individually appropriate learning outcomes that may be at any of multiple levels (i.e., below, at, or above grade level), all within the same curricular area (Campbell, Campbell, Collicott, Perner, & Stone, 1988; Peterson & Hittie, 2010). While one student may be learning at a basic knowledge or comprehension level, another student simultaneously may be working at a more advanced level.

Imagine second-grade students playing a small-group social studies board game designed by their teacher and a special educator to learn about their neighborhood, town, and state. The teachers have prepared a set of 10 game cards for each student that targets individual learning outcomes. For three students (at grade level), the game cards require applying knowledge about the roles of community helpers (e.g., police, firefighters, store clerks, postal workers) by moving game pieces to respond to scenarios on the cards (e.g.,

"Move your player to the place where you might go if you wanted to send a card to your grandmother for her birthday."). For another student who has autism and has occasionally gotten lost or separated from his family, game cards have the student answer questions about himself and where he lives (e.g., last name, street address, phone number, where his parents work). A third student (who is performing above grade level) is using map skills such as north, south, east, and west to respond to questions (e.g., "If you started at the bookstore, went two blocks north and one block east, where would you be?"). In this example, all of the students have individualized social studies learning outcomes, pertaining to different content/subject matter, within a shared activity.

By definition, multilevel curriculum/instruction involves individually appropriate learning outcomes that may be at any of multiple levels (i.e., below, at, or above grade level) and can include variations across subject content.

In one seventh-grade social studies class focusing on American history from the Revolution through the Civil War, the topic is the same for Joseph, a student with disabilities, and his classmates without disabilities. But his level of learning outcomes is adapted to suit him (e.g., historical people, places, events). In Joseph's algebra class, however, the subject content for Joseph is different from that for many of his classmates, focusing on counting and basic compu-tation (e.g., adding is a variation within the subject content). In this case, the level and quantity of the learning outcomes would be adapted as well. In both classes, Joseph is working on individualized learning outcomes within the same curricular content area as his classmates, just at a different level.

Curriculum Overlapping

Curriculum overlapping starts in the same way as mul-tilevel curriculum/instruction; a student with disabili-ties and peers without disabilities participate together in a shared activity where each student has individu-ally appropriate learning outcomes. Curriculum over-lapping differs in that the learning outcomes being pursued within a shared activity come from two or more different curricular areas; this is unlike the multi-level curriculum/instruction examples, where they were all within the same curricular area.

In a middle school biology class, students are grouped in teams of three for lab activities. They are assembling a model of a human heart. Two students have goals related to the identification, anatomy, and physiology of the human heart. The third stu-dent, who has severe intellectual disabilities, partici-pates in helping to assemble the model heart but is working on communication and social skills (e.g., taking turns, following instructions, responding to yes/no questions, maintaining socially acceptable behavior for longer periods of time).

Curriculum overlapping is appropriate to use when there are large differences between the level of learn-ing outcomes being pursued by most of the students in a class and the student with a severe disability. Before employing curriculum overlapping, the team should consider whether the student could pursue the same learning outcomes as the rest of the class or whether either of the two multilevel curriculum/instruction variations are viable options; this helps to ensure that we do not underestimate students with severe disabilities.

In a middle school math class, six students are arranged in a circle for a game that involves throw-ing and catching a beach ball covered with numbers to practice multiplication. The game starts by having one student call a classmate by name and then toss the ball: "Terry, I'm throwing the ball to you." After

catching the ball, the student is asked to multiply the two numbers that are touched by his or her thumbs. All of the students have math learning outcomes ex-cept for Jesse, a student with intellectual disabilities and extensive support needs. Jesse participates in the same activity but has a series of nonmath goals. He is learning to orient himself toward a person who calls his name, react to the tossed ball by moving his arms to attempt a catch, match to a sample by point-ing to a photograph of a classmate in the group, and then orient himself toward that person before being assisted to toss the ball.

At times, both multilevel curriculum/instruction and curriculum overlapping can be used within the same activity. By pursuing more than one learning out-come within class activities, students with severe dis-abilities are provided with numerous opportunities to learn and practice skills. There is some research that has demonstrated the effectiveness of embedding indi-vidually determined learning outcomes within general class activities (McDonnell, Johnson, Polychronis, & Risen, 2002). At times, it may be necessary to plan an alternate activity if a student needs to work on a high-priority goal that doesn't lend itself to being incorpo-rated into the multilevel curriculum/instruction or curriculum overlapping options. For example, a high school student with severe disabilities may need spe-cific, alternative instruction on a skill that doesn't read-ily lend itself to available high school curriculum, such as how to safely cross various types of intersections to travel to a community-based work or recreation site. At other times, students' privacy needs dictate the need for alternatives, such as when a student is learning to use the toilet or some dressing skills.

The Curricular Balancing Act

Ensuring access to a relevant, individualized curriculum for a student with severe disabilities also requires a bal-ancing act in at least two ways. First, a sound curricu-lum establishes a *balance between focus and breadth.* Providing access to a breadth of learning outcomes that includes, but is not limited to, general education cur-riculum ensures that students with disabilities will have opportunities that may have been denied them in the past. A sound curriculum establishes a clear focus, based on a reasonably small set (e.g., five to eight goals and related objectives) of the highest educational prior-ities agreed to by the team; these are documented as IEP goals (Giangreco, Cloninger, & Iverson, 1998).

Historically, curricula for students with severe disabilities have emphasized the identification of *chronologically age-appropriate and functional skills* needed to function in current and future environments (Brown, Nietupski, & Hamre-Nietupski, 1976; Brown et al., 1979). While these foundational concepts remain contemporary 35 years after they were first articulated in the professional literature, variations on the themes have been expanded. Today, the basis for selecting IEP goals and objectives for students with severe disabilities has shifted to place a greater emphasis on determining which goals and objectives are most likely to result in positive lifestyle improvements. Research is beginning to tackle elusive concepts such as identifying, validating, and increasing the indices of "happiness" in individuals with extensive and pervasive support needs (Lancioni, Singh, O'Reilly, Oliva, & Basili, 2005). By asking parents who have children with disabilities and people with disabilities themselves what does or would contribute to living a "good life," we can better identify and select goals and objectives that will contribute to the development of *valued life outcomes* (Giangreco et al., 1998) such as the following:

- Being safe and healthy
- Having a home now and in the future
- Having meaningful relationships
- Having choices and control that matches one's age and culture
- Participating in meaningful activities in various places with various people

The Perez family has three children. Their youngest, Juanita, has severe disabilities and is in first grade. Juanita's special education teacher, Ms. Brown, worked collaboratively with the team, including Mr. and Mrs. Perez, to identify the highest priorities for Juanita from the family's perspective. These priorities would be translated into IEP goals and objectives to be focused on during the school year. These priorities included (a) expressing "more," (b) making a selection when given options, (c) responding to yes/no questions using eye gaze, (d) calling others to her using a switch and recorded message, and (e) using a switch to activate leisure devices (e.g., digital music player, battery-operated toys). The team cross-referenced each of these priorities to one or more valued life outcomes. For example, being able to activate toys was designed to give Juanita

more choices and control and was hoped to be a point of connection that might serve to extend her relationships with other children her age. The team also considered a set of additional learning outcomes to establish the breadth of Juanita's educational program. They did this by systematically looking at the general education curriculum in each subject area, as well as functional skill categories, to decide which learning outcomes would make the most sense for Juanita. As a result, they selected a series of additional functional skills (in addition to the family's highest priorities), such as imitating skills used in daily life, eating finger foods, drinking through a straw, and increasing the amount of time that she could sustain attention to a task. From the general education curriculum, they started with skills such as recognizing symbols, distinguishing between shapes, writing her name using an adapted stamp, and using a variety of art media, among others.

Second, a sound curriculum *balances the assessed level of appropriateness with a measure of challenge.* An age-old tenet of instruction is that a student's learning outcomes should be selected at an *appropriate level of difficulty* on the basis of assessment data. Targeted learning outcomes should be reasonably attainable yet challenging, although not so challenging as to be unattainable or frustrating. Although it is logical to select instructional targets on the basis of the student's current level of performance and known learning characteristics, quality instruction should *provide ample opportunities for students to surprise us with their capabilities.*

Therefore, we should never presume to know the upper limits on a student's abilities, especially if the student has not been sufficiently exposed to a concept or skill or has not received ongoing, competent instruction using research-based interventions. This is consistent with Donnellan's (1984) *criterion of the least dangerous assumption,* which asserts that "in the absence of conclusive educational data, educational decisions should be based on assumptions which, if incorrect, will have the least dangerous effect on the student" (p. 142). For example, if an individual with a severe disability is nonverbal and does not have a fluent alternative or augmentative method of language or communication, it would be most dangerous to assume that he or she does not understand much, if any, of what is said to or near him or her. It would be less dangerous to assume that he or she understands everything being said to or near him or her. Similarly, it would be most dangerous to prevent the student's exposure to a general education curriculum and least dangerous to provide not only exposure but also instruction.

Juanita's team did not select any science learning outcomes for her because they felt that the concepts were too advanced for her and because they were not able to adequately assess her science learning given her challenges with expressive communication. Recognizing that this could be a dangerous assumption given the challenge of knowing how much Juanita understands, they decided to include her in science class and start with curriculum overlapping so that the learning outcomes that she focused on during science class were primarily communication and social skills. By including her in the science activities and exposing her to instruction in this area along with her classmates, they are providing her with opportunities that would not deny the possibility that she understands more than they were currently able to discern. At least at the outset, accountability for learning during science class will focus on the nonscience communication and social skills. Over time, on the basis of the teacher's observations during science class activities, Juanita's additional learning outcomes may be expanded in the future to include science class outcomes.

Access to literacy instruction is a prime example of how curricular balance and applying the criterion of the least dangerous assumption have changed both the educational opportunities available to students with severe disabilities and the corresponding professional practices (Erickson & Koppenhaver, 1995). Historically, literacy instruction has been extremely limited for individuals with moderate or severe disabilities (e.g., teaching functional sight words). Conventional wisdom suggested that our limited teaching time should be spent almost exclusively on teaching functional life skills instead of selected academics. To date, professionals have had some initial success teaching literacy skills to students with severe disabilities—increasingly, this option is being explored. Many now recognize that every child, regardless of the severity of his or her disability, can begin to work on some early literacy skills. Some students, many of whom people previously would have not considered teaching literacy skills, are developing skills in reading and writing (Browder & Spooner, 2006;

Downing, 2005; Erickson, Koppenhaver, Yoder, & Nance, 1997). This has occurred because of a change in attitude, followed by opportunity, and effective instruction.

In Juanita's case, the team agreed that as a first grader she was much too young to forgo literacy instruction. Instead, they made a conscious effort to expose her to books in English and Spanish because her family is bilingual. Daily, she was shown books, read to, assisted to turn the pages, and otherwise shown the wonders of stories and reading. At the same time, she worked on skills such as (a) directing and sustaining attention to objects, books, activities, or interactions; (b) establishing consistent response modes (e.g., pointing, eye gaze, activating a switch); (c) differentiating or discriminating among various objects, photos, or symbols; or (d) matching to a sample. While everyone was hopeful that these efforts would provide important foundations for literacy, they agreed that working on these skills was worthwhile regardless of whether Juanita's literacy proficiency ever reached the heights of functional reading. Her pursuit of important early literacy skills would likely have generalized implications for the development of related skills in domains such as communication, social skills, and recreation.

Although access to the general education curriculum is designed to give students opportunities to learn a wide variety of new skills, exposure to new curricular content can initiate curiosity about a topic that can become a lifelong interest and a point of connection to others regardless of an individual's skill level. We all know people who are not great musicians but who love music. You may know someone who is not particularly versed in science but through exposure to astronomy has become fascinated with the moon and stars. Such interests can hold great meaning to people. Consider the letter (see Box 1–1) written by a parent to two high school English teachers about her daughter, Erin, who had a passion for theater. Erin had Down syndrome.

Access to Purposeful Instruction

Over the past several decades, the field of educating students with severe disabilities has relied extensively on the use of systematic instructional methods to pursue meaningful curricular outcomes because of their strong theoretical foundation and documented

Box 1–1 But What About Shakespeare?

Dear Peggy and Jim,

Erin attended the State Thespian Conference with the Drama Club this past weekend. I was one of the chaperones. I wanted to share that on Friday night the all-state play was *The Tempest*, and when Erin heard that it was by Shakespeare she was all excited. She knows him by name. Then on Sunday morning, there was a comedy on the works of Shakespeare where three male characters do short versions (of course made to be outrageously funny) of all of Shakespeare's plays. Erin insisted on attending after she heard that it was about Shakespeare. The actors spent the most time on *Romeo and Juliet* and Erin loved it!

On Saturday night, we saw one of the best musical presentations I have ever seen, even professionally, of *Les Miserable*. Now, of course, Erin says she has to get the CD. This was her first time to see the play. She was mesmerized, but then we all were—just a phenomenal performance by a high school or any group. Suddenly, at intermission, she said that this was about what she had learned in history class and made that connection.

This reinforces for me again the need for all students to access the general education curriculum, even if they can't describe all the nuances of what they are learning about. I doubt very much that Erin would have gotten any Shakespeare or other great literary pieces in the special ed classroom for students with cognitive and developmental disabilities. That would have been unfortunate. Theatre has also helped Erin to continue to make connections with great literature she has learned about in class. She still watches *The Crucible* all the time—the movie version and a video of Westerville South High School's performance last year.

Please remember this when you are planning for smaller learning communities. All students, with any disability label, must be part of the mix. Please don't let anyone assume that any student cannot get something out of a lesson.

Thank you both for giving Erin the opportunity to access great literature!

Sincerely,

Barb McKenzie

(Reprinted with permission from McKenzie [2008, pp. 36–37].)

effectiveness (Alberto & Troutman, 2009; Snell & Brown, 2006). This set of instructional methods, such as chaining, shaping, prompting, time delay, and error correction (see Chapter 4), offered a bright spot in a special education system that was all too often characterized by unnecessarily low expectations, too much instructional downtime, limited access to peers without disabilities, and questionable curricula. Use of these and other systematic instructional methods played a major role in documenting the wide range of skills and functional routines that people with severe disabilities could learn if offered consistent, quality instruction. In fact, the use of these methods was instrumental in helping to establish, once and for all, the belief in the "educability" of people perceived as having the most profound disabilities.

Ironically, as students with severe disabilities have gained more access to general education classes with higher expectations, peers without disabilities, and a broader curriculum, new questions have been raised about the integrity of their instruction. The field is wrestling with the challenge of how to utilize the time-tested, evidence-based, systematic instructional approaches in new and contextually viable ways (Logan & Malone, 1998; McDonnell et al., 2002). In part, this has included a shift from individual instruction and small homogeneous groups to mixed-ability groupings where there is only one student with a disability with classmates who do not have disabilities.

Consider the case of Lisa, a high school student with severe disabilities. In the past, although she was included in general education classes, typically she was separated from the rest of the class for individualized instruction with a paraprofessional who implemented a systematic instructional plan that had been developed by a special educator. Although this plan had certain positive features (e.g., use of systematic instructional procedures, attention to functional skills), the lessons had no contextual relevance to the classrooms where they were being delivered. This resulted in Lisa's not being a true member of the classroom community because she had no substantive involvement with the classroom teachers or peers. When the team began planning ways to embed important learning outcomes for Lisa into class activities (e.g., multilevel curriculum/instruction, curriculum overlapping) and creating opportunities for classmates to help each other learn, Lisa actually had more real opportunities for learning than ever before. The team met on a regular basis in an effort to evaluate how their plans were working and to continually explore ways to use the best of the validated instructional approaches in a more natural and contextually grounded manner.

As teams pursue quality instruction, it is important to remember that the principles of teaching and learning do not change because a child gets a disability label or because those who were once in a special class are now supported in a general class (see Box 1–2). Many doors have been opened for people with severe disabilities using foundational principles of instruction, and these remain critical for learning in inclusive settings. As with all strategies, however, the specific and changing learning environments and individual learning needs of each student will shape how strategies are used and adjusted to fit the evolving context. (For more on this topic, see Chapter 6.)

Know Each Student's Characteristics

Quality instruction always starts by making sure you know your students. This means more than being familiar with their disability diagnosis, although that is important to understand. It means understanding their cognitive, physical, and sensory characteristics that

affect instruction. It also means being cognizant of their social/emotional traits (e.g., temperament, behaviors), motivations, preferences and dislikes, interaction patterns, and creative attributes. Understanding such aspects of your students supports *individualization*, a hallmark of special education, and encourages the development of instructional approaches that build on each student's strengths and preferences.

Select Meaningful Learning Outcomes

Quality instruction really matters only if it is applied to meaningful learning outcomes. Highly effective instruction applied to irrelevant, nonfunctional, or chronologically age-inappropriate learning outcomes is a waste of the student's time as well as your own. Effective teams establish and maintain a positive sense of urgency about their work without simultaneously creating undue stress on the student or team. They know that, relatively, they have precious little time to teach, so their curricular selections and instructional intensity matter. Although many of the curricular aspects related to instruction were mentioned earlier in this chapter (e.g., functionality, age appropriateness, balance of breadth and focus), there are a few additional considerations when selecting meaningful learning outcomes.

Consider the frequency with which a learned skill will be used both now and in the future. Clearly, skills that are used frequently and have current and future utility generally are more important than those which are used infrequently or won't be useful in the future. Selecting meaningful learning outcomes is always a judgment. Sometimes, skills with a lower frequency of use can be extremely important for being safe (e.g., street crossing, evacuating a building in response to an alarm) or for personal preferences (e.g., the leisure skills that one enjoys, predictable environments, unstructured time). For individuals with the most severe or multiple disabilities, a major consideration is the extent to which

 ## Box 1–2 Principles of Quality Instruction

1. Know each student's characteristics
2. Select meaningful learning outcomes
3. Establish shared expectations among team members
4. Create a motivating learning environment
5. Select effective teaching methods
6. Provide sufficient and consistent learning opportunities
7. Use data to make instructional decisions

a learned skill will allow a person to control his or her environment (Brown & Lehr, 1993). For example, learning to use an adapted microswitch may allow a person with severe or multiple disabilities to activate a wide variety of electrical or electronic devices across a range of locations and activities (e.g., communication, cooking, leisure, work).

Establish Shared Expectations Among Team Members

As curricular and instructional planning continues, team members need to establish shared expectations. From a logistical standpoint, ensuring that team members strive toward being on the same wavelength regarding philosophy, curriculum, and instruction can be a challenge simply because students with severe disabilities typically have teams with numerous members. Such teams often include parents, teachers, special educators, paraprofessionals, and related service providers such as speech-language pathologists, physical therapists, occupational therapists, orientation and mobility specialists, and school psychologists. When teams are too large, it poses challenges in selecting meeting times and communicating. Team membership often changes substantially each school year, with parents and students being the members most likely to remain on the team for extended periods.

Having the perspectives of a variety of members can be an asset to a planning team. Managing the group's size and diversity of input is important for enhancing the productivity of the group and avoiding the stereotypical problems of team meetings, such as (a) being unclear about the purpose of the meeting, (b) going off on tangents, (c) having the meeting dominated by one or more members, or (d) leaving the meeting feeling as if it was a waste of time. Effective interactions among members can be facilitated through a variety of collaborative teamwork practices (Snell & Janney, 2005; Thousand, Villa, & Nevin, 2006). Establishing shared expectations means that all members should (a) know the student's learning-related characteristics, (b) be aware of the student's priority learning outcomes (e.g., IEP goals), (c) be aware of the breadth of learning outcomes that are targeted for instruction (e.g., general education curriculum), (d) know when learning outcomes will be addressed throughout the school day, (e) know what general supports or accommodations need to be made for the student, (f) know the student-specific instructional procedures and adaptations, and (g) know what information should be collected on the student's progress.

It is critical that all team members clearly understand the distinction between a *learning outcome* and a *general support*. A learning outcome is a goal or objective that the team has targeted for the student to learn, such as "pointing to a desired food item on a communication board" or "finding one's own locker." This requires the student to respond and is designed to change a student's behavior (e.g., the acquisition of a new skill). A general support, on the other hand, refers to what will be provided for a student so that he or she may have access to education, participate in school, and pursue identified learning outcomes. On IEP documents, the terms used to describe general supports vary from place to place (e.g., accommodations, modifications, supports, management needs). General supports tend to fall into one of six main categories (Giangreco et al., 1998):

1. Personal needs (e.g., support to eat, catheterization, provide medication)
2. Physical needs (e.g., reposition at least hourly, regular management of braces)
3. Teaching others about the student (e.g., teach staff and classmates about the student's augmentative communication, teach staff seizure management procedures)
4. Sensory needs (e.g., auditory amplification system, tactile materials, large-print materials,)
5. Providing access and opportunities (e.g., environmental modifications, access to cocurricular activities, access to materials in the student's native language, computer access,)
6. Other general supports (those not clearly addressed in any other category) (e.g., class notes are to be recorded, extended time to complete tasks, communication with the family)

Distinguishing between general supports and learning outcomes is important because too often goals and objectives listed on IEPs for students with severe disabilities are written as passive general supports (e.g., reposition at least hourly) instead of active learning outcomes (Downing, 1988; Giangreco, Dennis, Edelman, & Cloninger, 1994).

The volume, range, and complexity of information that teams exchange in the process of establishing shared expectations require practical documentation in addition to the IEP. There are a variety of ways that a team's shared expectations for a student can be clarified. First, a one- or two-page *program-at-a-glance* is a simple and concise way to summarize a student's learning outcomes and general supports for daily use (Giangreco et al., 1998). The *program-at-a-glance* consists of a simple listing of (a) a student's annual goals (sometimes in an abbreviated format), (b) other learning outcomes that are targets of instruction (e.g., general education learning outcomes) organized by curricular content areas, and (c) general supports that need to be provided to or for the student, also organized by categories (e.g., physical needs, sensory needs, teaching others about the student).

A second way to clarify the team's shared expectations are in lesson or program plans that explicitly describe how a student with a severe disability will pursue his or her learning outcomes within typical class activities. Such plans can also be effective reminders of basic information such as (a) operational definitions of target skills; (b) how to arrange the environment to facilitate learning (e.g., seating arrangement, materials); (c) methods for introducing tasks; (d) what to do if the student doesn't respond in a reasonable length of time, responds incorrectly, or responds correctly; and (e) student performance data gathered and a schedule for gathering such information. Ensuring that all team members understand how to respond under these varying circumstances is critical to achieving instructional consistency.

Third, general supports can be effectively documented through photographs or video clips, such as (a) how to safely transfer a student to and from their wheelchair and other places (e.g., stander, toilet, floor), (b) how a student should be appropriately positioned in his or her wheelchair, or (c) specialized feeding techniques. When using photo or video documentation for program support or communication purposes, it is important to receive explicit written permission from the family that describes the types of images that you would like to collect and the range of purposes for which the images may be used and with whom they may be shared.

Create a Motivating and Welcoming Learning Environment

Although it may seem obvious, the importance of *creating a motivating and welcoming learning environment* for all students cannot be underestimated. Establishing a sense of belonging is considered a key building block for effective learning (Kunc, 2000). Researchers have demonstrated that the quality of the relationships and rapport between individuals with developmental disabilities and their caregivers can be an important variable that influences behavior. Magito McLaughlin and Carr (2005) found that when the assessed relationships were poor, the level of problem behaviors was higher. Conversely, when the relationships were good, the level of problem behaviors was lower. As rapport improved, problem behaviors decreased. Studies of students with severe disabilities in elementary and middle schools highlight the limitations of part-time participation in general classes and the importance of participating in shared experiences (Schnorr, 1990, 1997). In order for students with disabilities to develop meaningful relationships with peers who do not have disabilities and to have access to a broad range of meaningful learning outcomes, they must share learning experiences with peers on an ongoing basis.

Select Effective Teaching Methods

Part of instructional access involves selecting effective teaching methods as a starting point for intervention. Students with disabilities often respond favorably to many of the same teaching methods that are common and effective for students who do not have disabilities. Some of these common methods include modeling and demonstration, repeated practice, guided discovery, participatory activities, using educational games or play, using positive and negative examples, giving corrective feedback, or cooperative group learning approaches. Challenges arise when students do not progress adequately when you have relied on typical instructional methods. In such cases, it is often necessary to be more precise in the application of methods; break the skills down into smaller components; or use different instructional methods, such as task analysis, chaining, shaping, and time delay (see Chapters 4, 5, 6, 10, 12, 13, and 14). Consider how Tom learned a new skill because of the use of a systematic instructional procedure and its impact on his life:

> *Tom had a traumatic brain injury that resulted in severe physical, cognitive, and sensory disabilities, including cortical visual impairment, loss of language, and the inability to walk, sit up independently, or use his arms and hands. Tom was fed primarily through a gastrostomy tube, although his parents had worked with him so that he could eat soft foods and drink by mouth. His only consistent, voluntary skill was some head movement from side to side when supported from behind, the ability to*

open and close his mouth, and some chewing. Tom communicated primarily through vocalizations. For example, he made a groaning sound that everyone easily recognized as discomfort. This usually meant that it was time to get him out of his wheelchair for a while. At a meeting when Tom was 14 years old, his parents were asked for their input into Tom's IEP goals for the year. Tom's father said, "I don't care what he learns; I just want to know that he can learn." Building on Tom's strengths, the team decided to teach Tom to respond to the verbal instruction "Open up" so that he would open his mouth to receive food, drink, and medicine, and have his teeth brushed. The team knew that Tom currently didn't respond to "Open up" or any other instruction, but he did open his mouth wide when his lower lip was touched lightly (e.g., by a spoon with food). Some team members wondered if he was actually responding to the lip touch or something else, such as the air movement of something coming toward him, smell, or cues from some residual vision. Their assessment convinced them that it was the touch cue only that caused him to open his mouth. They decided to use an instructional procedure called "time delay." This was started by simultaneously pairing the cue that they knew Tom responded to (i.e., touching his lip with a spoon) with the cue that they wanted him to respond to (i.e., the verbal instruction "Open up"), followed by giving him a spoonful of fruit yogurt. This simultaneous pairing is known as a zero delay because there is no time delay between the presentation of both cues. This was done numerous times throughout the day when Tom would normally be expected to open his mouth in an effort to help Tom to make the connection between the two cues. After this had been done for a few days, a one-second time delay was inserted between the cues. The teacher would say "Open up," then wait one second before touching his lip. Over the next couple of weeks, the time delay between asking Tom to "Open up" and touching his lip was gradually increased in one-second intervals, always followed by a small bite to eat or a sip to drink. When the time delay was increased to five seconds, Tom opened his mouth to accept the food before his lip was ever touched—he had responded to the instruction! He soon was opening his mouth immediately and consistently following the request. Time delay had been successfully used to transfer control from the one cue to another. Some people might think that this didn't matter much, but it did!

For the first time in years, people who worked with Tom were excited and encouraged that he had learned a new skill. People interacted with him differently, more positively, as someone capable of learning. They were anxious to find out what else Tom could learn. Tom will always need substantial support, but this small change had a big impact. Once it was clear that he could respond to the "Open up" cue, the staff was sensitive to considering that Tom might keep his mouth closed as a way to indicate that he no longer wanted more to eat. Increasingly, the team was more aware of subtle behaviors that might have communicative intent.

Provide Sufficient and Consistent Learning Opportunities

Once instructional methods have been selected, with the individual student's learning characteristics in mind, the team needs to ensure that sufficient and consistent learning opportunities are provided for the student. A *scheduling matrix* (Giangreco et al., 1998) provides a way for the team to ensure that the student's IEP goals and additional learning outcomes are incorporated into the daily or weekly schedule. A scheduling matrix is set up as a simple grid. Listed across the top are regularly occurring class activities (e.g., arrival, language arts, math, science, physical education, lunch, recess). Listed down the left side of the matrix are IEP goals and other targeted learning outcomes (see Chapters 4 and 6 examples). It can be helpful to note the amount of time devoted to each activity. For example, arrival may be only 10 to 15 minutes at the beginning of the day, whereas a full hour might be devoted to language arts. The time frame is important to know because the number of learning outcomes that can reasonably be addressed will vary accordingly. Because daily schedules often change (e.g., on one day math is at 9:00 a.m., and on a different day it is at 10:30 a.m.), when using a scheduling matrix it is not crucial to arrange the general class activities in a specific order according the schedule. The team examines the matrix, determines which learning outcomes will be addressed in each class, and marks those locations on the matrix. The match between the learning outcomes and the class where they will be taught will be the same regardless of what time the class occurs or on which day of the week. In this way, the scheduling matrix can then be used to clarify which of a student's learning outcomes can be embedded within all classes (e.g., express greetings and farewells, respond to yes/no questions, follow instructions, make choices when presented with options) and which will be targeted to specific classes or activities that make the most sense.

> *During computer class, Joshua will engage in individual active leisure by activating single-response software on a computer using an adapted microswitch. During language arts, he will identify photos and symbols, summon others, and do classroom jobs.*

Providing sufficient and consistent learning opportunities requires persistence and creativity on the part of team members to embed opportunities for learning within class activities. Although the team wants to provide a reasonable level of planned consistency because students with severe disabilities often present a very unique constellation of learning characteristics, team members need a certain level of instructional flexibility. They need room to explore new approaches and combinations of approaches and to capitalize on unscheduled, teachable moments.

Use Data to Make Instructional Decisions

Along with this flexibility comes accountability in the form of data collection. Just as we collect data and examples of work completed by students who do not have disabilities in order to monitor and document progress and be accountable for our teaching, teams have a responsibility to do the same for students with severe disabilities (see Chapter 5). Individualized data provide essential information for making reasoned instructional decisions (Farlow & Snell, 2005).

As we think about collecting data on student learning, it is important to remember that performance related to specific IEP goals and objectives is only part of what is necessary. Regardless of the extent of student progress, it is important for each priority goal to be evaluated on the basis of its real impact on a person's life. Wolf's (1978) classic article introduced the field of applied behavior analysis to the assessment of *social validity*. Wolf argued that we must augment objective observable measures of behavior with the subjective perspectives of consumers if we are to achieve outcomes of social importance. He suggested that we evaluate (a) the social significance of the goals being sought, (b) the social appropriateness of the procedures being used, and (c) the social importance of the effects. The concept of social validity acknowledges that a student's attainment of an established goal is not

necessarily synonymous with its importance or with meaningful changes in the student's life.

> *Maria is learning a set of social skills (e.g., responding to the presence of others, greeting, taking turns) with the intent that the attainment of these skills will contribute to establishing or extending friendships with her peers. Merely knowing that she has acquired those skills is a good first step, but it is incomplete until we determine whether her relationships with peers have changed for the better and whether her improved skills contributed to those socially important changes.*

Sometimes, socially important outcomes can occur even when target skills are not achieved. There may be circumstances where a student does not progress much in the development of the targeted skill, but where the nature of the instructional arrangement (e.g., peer involvement in typical class activities) leads to improvement in valued life outcomes because something in the environment has changed (e.g., access to typical settings, attitudes of classmates). Improvements in valued life outcomes for individuals with severe disabilities can be enhanced by a combination of skill acquisition on their part, as well as changes in the environment, especially the attitudes and actions of the people in those environments.

Access to the Necessary Related Services and Supports

As described earlier, one of the defining characteristics of people with severe disabilities is that they require extensive or pervasive supports. A primary mechanism within IDEA to provide support is through the provision of *related services*:

> *The term related services means transportation, and such developmental, corrective, and other supportive services (including speech-language pathology and audiology services, interpreting services, psychological services, physical and occupational therapy, recreation, including therapeutic recreation, social work services, school nurse services designed to enable a child with a disability to receive a free appropriate public education as described in the individualized education program of the child, counseling services, including rehabilitation counseling, orientation and mobility services, and medical services, except that*

such medical services shall be for diagnostic and evaluation purposes only) as may be required to assist a child with a disability to benefit from special education, and includes the early identification and assessment of disabling conditions in children. (20 U.S.C. § 1400 (2004); IDEA, sec. 602(26)(A))

For many students with severe disabilities, special education services alone are not sufficient for them to receive an appropriate education; in such cases, the provision of related services is essential. The availability and array of related services recognizes the reality that no single discipline embodies the varied knowledge and skills necessary to effectively support the education of the full range of students with disabilities. One of the primary challenges of providing related services is ensuring that a student receives the appropriate supports, yet at the same time being careful that those services do not inadvertently interfere with the student's access to the least restrictive environment, appropriate curriculum, or effective instruction.

Team Decisions About Related Services

Too often, related services for students with severe disabilities are based on separate, discipline-specific goals and perspectives. Such scenarios highlight that merely assigning a group of individuals to the same student does not make them a team. It is the way that these individuals interact that ultimately distinguishes whether they are accurately referred to as a *group of individuals* or a *team*.

When making team decisions about related services, it is helpful to acknowledge that all decision making is based on underlying assumptions and values. Sometimes these are clearly understood and agreed to by team members. It is when they are unclear or conflicting that it becomes problematic because it increases the probability that team members will be working at cross-purposes, sometimes without even realizing why this is happening. Although honest disagreements about values will certainly exist among some team members, it is preferable that disagreements are out in the open and that members strive toward identifying shared values that can be used to guide their decisions. Having shared values can assist members in evaluating proposed actions as being consistent or inconsistent with the team's approach. Listed in the sections that follow are three common value systems that teams might encounter. The first two are

inconsistent with sound educational practices; the third is suggested as a desirable alternative.

More Is Not Necessarily Better. Some team members continually advocate for *more* related services. If one session of a therapy is recommended, they think that two would be better, and three better yet. The *more-is-better* approach is misguided because it confuses quantity with value. Although rooted in benevolent intentions, the more-is-better approach can have unintended, negative consequences for students by interfering with participation in other school activities. What is the student missing when he or she is spending time receiving a service that someone has advocated for but is not necessary? Providing more services than necessary may do the following:

- Decrease the time available for participation in activities with peers who do not have disabilities.
- Disrupt class participation and membership by removal from class activities.
- Cause disruption in acquiring, practicing, or generalizing other important skills.
- Cause inequities in the distribution of resources, with some students remaining unserved or underserved.
- Overwhelm families with an unnecessarily large number of professionals.
- Result in stigmatization by the provision of special services.
- Create unnecessary or unhealthy dependencies.
- Unnecessarily complicate communication and coordination among team members.

The Fallacy of Return on Investment. Another misguided value system, called *return on investment,* places a high value on serving students who have a favorable history and prognosis for being "fixed"—those who are likely to contribute the most, economically, to society. The return-on-investment approach fails to recognize the many noneconomic contributions made by people, including those with the most severe disabilities.

The return-on-investment value orientation is based on a curative mentality that sends negative messages to children with disabilities and their families. Imagine what it might be like to continually get the message "You are not okay the way you are. In order to be okay, your disability has to be fixed and you need to be more like us (people without disabilities)." Increasingly, self-advocates are asking that their disabilities be viewed as a form of natural human diversity and that others' efforts be less about "fixing" a person's disabilities and more about accepting individuals for who they are and providing necessary and self-determined supports.

In addition, a return-on-investment approach tends to discriminate against individuals with the most severe disabilities. It problematically seeks to justify the differential valuing of people and the services that they receive on the basis of the severity of their disability characteristics. Anytime that schools sanction practices that imply that some students are more worthy of staff time and resources than other students, there is a serious problem. All children are worthy, although they have differing needs.

Only as Specialized as Necessary. An alternative value system is referred to as *only as specialized as necessary*—providing enough but not too much. This value orientation is based on the notion that, like other things people *need* (e.g., food, water, sleep, sunshine, time with others), our aim should be to get what we need in balance with all of the other items that we need, instead of simply getting the greatest amount possible. This balance requires individualization when determining the appropriate type and amount of service for each student. This determination will be a collective best judgment of team members. The conceptual basis for this value system has a legal foundation in a U.S. Supreme Court precedent (*Board of Education of the Hendrick Hudson Central School District v. Rowley*, 1982).

The only-as-specialized-as-necessary approach seeks to identify and draw on natural supports, including those which currently exist and are available to students without disabilities (e.g., guidance counselor, teachers, school nurse, peers, supported study halls). In cases where more specialized services are necessary, ongoing data should be collected to document the impact of the services while the team continues to explore alternatives that would allow students with disabilities to receive needed supports in the most natural and sustainable way possible. This approach supports the provision of needed services and acknowledges the contributions made by various disciplines but takes precautions to avoid the inherent drawbacks of providing well-intentioned but unnecessary services.

It is important to recognize that the only-as-specialized-as-necessary approach does not automatically mean that "less is always best" or "only a little is plenty." Some

advocates have voiced concern that this approach might be misused to justify the denial of needed services; this certainly is not its intended use. When used as intended, the only-as-specialized-as-necessary approach results in students receiving needed services. Furthermore, it is meant to be a value orientation agreed to by the team, which includes the family. In sum, it is most important that teams understand the value orientations held by their members and that they work toward a shared value system that will contribute to making educationally sound support service decisions. (See Chapter 6 for further discussion of the only-as-specialized-as-necessary approach.)

Educational Relevance and Necessity

When considering a value orientation such as the only-as-specialized-as-necessary approach within the context of the IDEA definition of related services, teams must ask themselves challenging questions about the educational relevance and necessity of a proposed service. *Educational relevance* exists when a proposed service can be explicitly linked with a component of a student's educational program (e.g., IEP goals, general education curriculum).

> *Lisa, an occupational therapist, has made various recommendations to support the handwriting skills of Adam, a student with autism, based on her evaluation of him. If handwriting is included as a goal or objective on Adam's IEP or is part of the general education for which the student needs special education, then the recommended occupational therapy supports are educationally relevant.*

Educational relevance alone is not sufficient to warrant the provision of services; services must also be *educationally necessary.* A service is educationally necessary if, after establishing its educational relevance, the team determines that the service is essential. In many cases, IEP teams are asking the wrong questions, such as "Could the proposed related service help?" When this question is posed, the answer is almost always "Yes." But this is not the question that the IDEA poses in the definition of a related service. The question may be more appropriately posed like this: "If the student does not receive a proposed related service, is there reason to believe that he or she will not (a) have access to an appropriate education or (b) experience educational benefit?" This question requires a higher standard of accountability to answer

"Yes" than the one asking whether it could help. If a team does answer "Yes," it clearly suggests educational necessity.

Consider two potentially problematic scenarios in relation to Ms. Reeve and her daughter Jana, who has multiple disabilities. In the first scenario, Jana goes to a private clinic for an evaluation and a clinic consultant recommends that Jana receive music therapy once a week as a related service. In the second scenario, a physical therapist, who contracts with the school, recommends therapeutic horseback riding for Jana twice a week. First, consider the following question to assist your team in determining whether a proposed related service is educationally necessary: "Will the absence of the service interfere with the student's access to or participation in his or her educational program this year?" If the team answers "Yes" to the aforementioned question, then the service under consideration probably *is* educationally necessary. However, if the team answers "Yes" to any of the following questions, the service under consideration probably *is not* educationally necessary (Giangreco, 2001):

- Could the proposed service be addressed appropriately by the special educator or classroom teacher?
- Could the proposed service be addressed appropriately through core school faculty or staff (e.g., school nurse, guidance counselor, librarian, physical education teacher, bus drivers, cafeteria staff, custodians)?
- Has the student been benefiting from his or her educational program without the service?
- Could the student continue to benefit from his or her educational program without the service?
- Could the service appropriately be provided during nonschool hours (as established in the 1984 U.S. Supreme Court decision, *Irving Independent School District v. Tatro*, 1984)?
- Does the proposed service present any undesirable or unnecessary gaps, overlaps, or contradictions with other proposed services?

So while it is reasonable to assert that therapeutic horseback riding or music therapy, as examples, may have positive benefits for some students, it much harder to make the case that they are *educationally necessary* related services and without them a student would be unable to receive an appropriate education. It can be particularly challenging for external clinics and consultants to make appropriate decisions about necessary related services when they are unfamiliar with the student's educational program content or the specific educational context, or to make those decisions in isolation without knowing the roles of the teacher, special educator, or other related service professionals. Because both music and recreational activities (e.g., horseback riding) do hold potential benefits, teams should explore participation and support in general education music classes and extracurricular options such as chorus, band, or orchestra. Similarly, other classmates who are involved in horseback riding typically do so after school or on weekends, not at school; weekends would be potentially appropriate times for youth with disabilities to participate in these activities with appropriate supports.

If the team asked the question "Could these services help?" it could be quite easy to answer "Yes." It would be more difficult to answer "Yes" if the question was asked a different way: "If the student does not receive music therapy or therapeutic horseback riding as a related service, is there reason to believe that he or she will not be able to receive an appropriate education?" This aspect of educational relevance is rooted in the Supreme Court's decision in *Board of Education of the Hendrick Hudson Central School District v. Rowley* (1982). In that case, the court established that if a student was receiving educational benefit without the service, it was evidence that the service was not needed, even though providing the service might help. In such cases, schools are not required to provide the proposed service.

In the example of Jana, the school might not agree to provide therapeutic horseback riding or music therapy as related services if (a) Jana was receiving educational benefit without the service, (b) the service wasn't deemed necessary for Jana to receive educational benefit, or (c) the service could be appropriately provided during nonschool hours, in accordance with the reasoning presented in both the Rowley and Tatro cases. Jana's team might plan to provide opportunities to experience music as part of a general education music class with supports; while the family might arrange horseback riding as a recreational activity with peers. In all situations, IEP teams are charged with making individual decisions about the need for related services; therefore, the full range of related services may be considered, which includes therapeutic recreation. This type of scrutiny of service provision presents many gray areas and points of potential conflict among team members, which is why it is so important to continually build a shared understanding as a team.

Ultimately, unnecessary services take away from, instead of improve, a student's educational program. Conversely, well-conceived and well-executed related services can make a substantial contribution to a student's educational program, as Jamal's case illustrates.

Jamal is a student with multiple disabilities, including deaf-blindness. The related service providers on his team have worked closely with the special educator, his classroom teacher, and his parents to ensure that his related services are both educationally relevant and necessary. The physical and occupational therapists have selected and modified equipment (e.g., specialized seating, arm/hand supports, adapted computer interface) that allows Jamal to access many learning opportunities. The speech-language pathologist has developed an augmentative communication system and corresponding instructional approaches that create opportunities for Jamal to communicate more effectively with teachers and peers. The vision and hearing specialists have adapted materials and learning environments (e.g., tactile labels, individualized amplification) to allow Jamal to access the general education curriculum.

These are only a few of the many ways that educationally relevant and necessary related services can be imperative for some students with disabilities. Making team decisions is not always easy, but it is important.

Summary

Regardless of your role on the team, how you approach the task of educating students with severe disabilities depends substantially on the attitudes and dispositions you bring to this important task. One of the best places to look for encouraging and affirming perspectives is the families who have accepted their child with a severe disability unconditionally. That leads me to my colleague and friend, Susan Yuan, who has three children, all of whom are now adults. Her youngest, Andreas, has Angelman's syndrome. In an essay (Yuan, 2003), she wrote about "seeing with new eyes" by using metaphors to help people think differently about individuals with severe disabilities. Her metaphor regarding Andreas was that of a bicycle. Yuan likened her earlier parenting experiences with her two older daughters to riding a basic bike with wide tires, no gears, and a coaster brake. She knew basically

what to expect and was able to figure it out. When Andreas was born, one of Yuan's first reactions was "There is no way I could be a good mother to him!" He wasn't like the bike that she was accustomed to riding.

Sticking with the bicycle metaphor, we find that, to many people in our society, the constellation of characteristics presented by Andreas would lead them to think of him as a bike that was broken or missing some parts. Such a perspective leads to many of the traditional ways that our society limits opportunities and provides services for people with disabilities. You don't take a broken bike out for a ride on the recreation path; first you try to fix it. If it can't be fixed, some consider discarding it. Others become sentimental or hopeful and put the bike in the garage and tinker with it now and then; but their expectation is that it will never be a bike they can really ride or fully enjoy.

Instead of thinking of Andreas as a broken bike, Yuan extended the metaphor by coming to think of him as a fancy Italian racing bike, with many gears, hand brakes, and racing handlebars. This bike wasn't broken; she just hadn't learned to ride it yet. She came to see this new bike as more complex, more sensitive, more responsive than a typical bike. On top of it all, it was a tandem bike that both parents would need to learn to ride together, move together, and get in sync. Yuan closed her essay this way:

Though I may not be ready for the Tour de France, I have become quite comfortable and capable with my own fancy, complex bicycle, known in the metaphorical world as my son, Andreas. Yes, he has his own unique characteristics, idiosyncrasies, peculiarities—don't we all! As I enter the 30th year of an incredible journey, I am still tinkering with the gears, appreciating that this bike has a mind of its own, and enjoying the ride. (2003, p. 210)

As you proceed with your learning and your practice, part of the work is the struggle to find a balance between attending to the undoubtedly special needs of individuals with severe disabilities and their right to live regular lives. As a community of educators, we know quite a lot about what we think makes for effective education, but there is so much that we don't know or simply don't do regularly enough. A key aspect of this work is creativity and unwavering persistence. By combining these elements, we have a reasonable chance for making the kinds of individual, collective, and incremental breakthroughs that can make a difference in people's lives.

References

Alberto, P. A., & Troutman, A. C. (2009). *Applied behavior analysis for teachers* (8th ed.). Upper Saddle River, NJ: Merrill/Pearson Education.

American Association on Intellectual and Developmental Disabilities. (2010). *Mental retardation: Definition, classification, and systems of supports* (11th ed.). Washington, DC: Author.

Baer, D. (1981). A hung jury and a Scottish verdict: "Not proven." *Analysis and Intervention in Developmental Disabilities, 1*(1), 91–98.

Bambara, L. M., & Kern, L. (2005). *Designing positive behavior supports.* New York: Guilford.

Baumgart, D., Brown, L., Pumpian, I., Nisbet, J., Ford, A., Sweet, M., et al. (1982). Principle of partial participation and individualized adaptations in educational programs for severely handicapped students. *Journal of the Association for the Severely Handicapped, 7*(2), 17–27.

Biklen, S. K., & Mosley, C. R. (1988). "Are you retarded?" "No, I'm Catholic": Qualitative methods in the study of people with severe handicaps. *Journal of the Association for Persons with Severe Handicaps, 13,* 155–162.

Billingsley, B. S. (2003). *Special education teacher retention and attrition: A critical analysis of the literature* (COPSSE Document No. RS-2). Gainesville, FL: Center on Personnel Studies in Special Education, University of Florida. Retrieved January 25, 2009, from http://www.coe.ufl.edu/copsse/docs/RS-2/1/RS-2.pdf

Board of Education of the Hendrick Hudson Central School District v. Rowley, 102 S. Ct. 3034 (1982).

Bogdan, R., & Taylor, S. J. (1989). Relationships with severely disabled people: The social construction of humanness. *Social Problems, 36,* 135–147.

Brantlinger, E. (1997). Using ideology: Cases of nonrecognition of the politics of research and practice in special education. *Review of Educational Research, 67*(4), 425–459.

Browder, D., Flowers, C., Ahlgrim-Delzell, L., Karvonen, M., Spooner, F., & Algozzine, R. (2004). The alignment of alternate assessment content with academic and functional curricula. *Journal of Special Education, 37,* 211–223.

Browder, D. M., & Spooner, F. (Eds.). (2006). *Teaching language arts, math, & science to students with significant cognitive disabilities.* Baltimore: Paul H. Brookes.

Brown, F., & Lehr, D. H. (1993). Making activities meaningful for students with severe multiple disabilities. *Teaching Exceptional Children, 25*(4), 12–16.

Brown, F., & Michaels, C. A. (2003). The shaping of inclusion: Efforts in Detroit and other urban settings. In D. Fisher & N. Frey (Eds.), *Inclusive urban schools* (pp. 231–243). Baltimore: Paul H. Brookes.

Brown, F., & Michaels, C. A. (2006). School-wide positive behavior support initiatives and students with severe disabilities: A time for reflection. *Research and Practice for Persons with Severe Disabilities, 31,* 57–61.

Brown, L., Branston, M. B., Hamre-Nietupski, S., Pumpian, I., Certo, N., & Gruenewald, L. (1979). A strategy for developing chronologically age-appropriate and functional curricular content for severely handicapped adolescents and young adults. *Journal of Special Education, 13,* 81–90.

Brown, L., Farrington, K., Ziegler, M., Knight, T., & Ross, C. (1999). Fewer paraprofessionals and more teachers and therapists in educational programs for students with significant disabilities. *Journal of the Association for Persons with Severe Handicaps, 24,* 249–252.

Brown, L., Nietupski, J., & Hamre-Nietupski, S. (1976). The criterion of ultimate functioning and public school services for severely handicapped students. In M. A. Thomas (Ed.), *Hey, don't forget about me! Education's investment in the severely, profoundly, and multiply handicapped* (pp. 2–15). Reston, VA: Council on Exceptional Children.

Campbell, C., Campbell, S., Collicott, J., Perner, D., & Stone, J. (1988). Individualized instruction. *Education New Brunswick—Journal of Education, 3,* 17–20.

Carr, E. G., Horner, R. H., Turnbull, A., Marquis, J. G., McLaughlin, D. M., McAtee, M. L., et al. (1999). *Positive behavior support for people with developmental disabilities: A research synthesis.* Washington, DC: American Association on Mental Retardation.

Carter, E. W., Cushing, L. S., & Kennedy, C. H. (2009). *Peer support strategies for improving all students' social lives and learning.* Baltimore: Paul H. Brookes.

Carter, E. W., Sisco, L. G., Melekoglu, M., & Kurkowski, C. (2007). Peer supports as an alternative to individually assigned paraprofessionals in inclusive high school classrooms. *Research and Practice for Persons with Severe Disabilities, 32,* 213–227.

Certo, N. J., Luecking, R. G., Murphy, S., Brown, L., Courey, S., & Belanger, D. (2008). Seamless transition and long-term support for individuals with severe intellectual disabilities. *Research and Practice for Persons with Severe Disabilities, 33,* 85–95.

Code of Federal Regulations. (2006). 34 CFR Parts 300 and 301: *Assistance to states for the education of children with disabilities and preschool grants for children with disabilities: Final rule.* Retrieved March 3, 2009, from http://idea.ed.gov/download/finalregulations.pdf

Davern, L., Sapon-Shevin, M., D'Aquanni, M., Fisher, M., Larson, M., Black, J., et al. (1997). Drawing the distinction between coherent and fragmented efforts at building inclusive schools. *Equity and Excellence in Education, 30*(3), 31–39.

Dembo, T., Leviton, G. L., & Wright, B. A. (1975). Adjustment to misfortune: A problem of social-psychological rehabilitation. *Rehabilitation Psychology, 22,* 1–100.

Donnellan, A. (1984). The criterion of the least dangerous assumption. *Behavior Disorders, 9,* 141–150.

Downing, J. (1988). Active versus passive programming: A critique of IEP objectives for students with the most severe disabilities. *Journal of the Association for Persons with Severe Handicaps, 13,* 197–210.

Downing, J. E. (2005). *Teaching literacy to students with significant disabilities: Strategies for the K-12 inclusive classroom.* Baltimore: Paul H. Brookes.

Downing, J. E. (2008). *Including students with severe and multiple disabilities in typical classrooms: Practical strategies for teachers* (3rd ed.). Baltimore: Paul H. Brookes.

Doyle, M. B. (2003). "We want to go to college too": Supporting students with significant disabilities in higher education. In D. L. Ryndak &

S. Alper (Eds.), *Curriculum development for students with disabilities in inclusive settings* (pp. 307-322). Boston: Allyn & Bacon.

Durand, V. M., & Merges, E. (2001). Functional communication training: A contemporary behavior analytic intervention for problem behaviors. *Focus on Autism and Other Developmental Disabilities, 16,* 110-119, 136.

Dymond, S. K., Renzaglia, A., Gilson, C. L., & Slagor, M. T. (2007). Defining access to the general curriculum for high school students with significant cognitive disabilities. *Research and Practice for Persons with Severe Disabilities, 32,* 1-15.

Erickson, K., & Koppenhaver, D. (1995). Developing a literacy program for children with severe disabilities. *Reading Teacher, 48*(8), 676-684.

Erickson, K. A., Koppenhaver, D. A., Yoder, D. E., & Nance, J. (1997). Integrated communication and literacy instruction for a child with multiple disabilities. *Focus on Autism and Other Developmental Disabilities, 12,* 142-150.

Farlow, L. J., & Snell, M. E. (2005). Making the most of student performance data. In M. L. Wehmeyer & M. Agran (Eds.), *Mental retardation and intellectual disabilities: Teaching students using innovative and research-based practices* (pp. 27-77). Upper Saddle River, NJ: Merrill/Prentice Hall.

Feldman, R., Fialka, J. (Producers), & Rossen, P. (Director/Producer). (2006). *Through the same door: Inclusion includes college* [Motion picture]. (Available from Dance of Partnership Publications at http://www.danceofpartnership.com/index.htm)

Ferguson, D. L., & Baumgart, D. (1991). Partial participation revisited. *Journal of the Association for Persons with Severe Handicaps, 16,* 218-227.

Freeman, R., Eber, L., Anderson, C., Irvin, L., Horner, R., Bounds, M., et al. (2006). Building inclusive school cultures using school-wide positive behavior support: Designing effective individual support systems for students with significant disabilities. *Research and Practice for Persons with Severe Disabilities, 31,* 4-17.

Fisher, D., Sax, C., & Pumpian, I. (1999). *Inclusive high schools.* Baltimore: Paul H. Brookes.

Giangreco, M. F. (2001). *Guidelines for making decisions about I.E.P. services.* Montpelier: Vermont Department of Education. Retrieved June 24, 2009, from http://www.uvm.edu/~cdci/iepservices/pdfs/decision.pdf

Giangreco, M. F. (2007). Extending inclusive opportunities. *Educational Leadership, 64*(5), 34-37.

Giangreco, M. F., & Broer, S. M. (2005). Questionable utilization of paraprofessionals in inclusive schools: Are we addressing symptoms or causes? *Focus on Autism and Other Developmental Disabilities, 20,* 10-26.

Giangreco, M. F., Broer, S. M., & Suter, J. C. (in press). Guidelines for selecting alternatives to overreliance on paraprofessionals: Field-testing in inclusion-oriented schools. *Remedial and Special Education.* Advance online publication. doi:10.1177/0741932509355951

Giangreco, M. F., Carter, E. W., Doyle, M. B., & Suter, J. C. (in press). Supporting students with disabilities in inclusive classrooms: Personnel and peers. In R. Rose (Ed.), *Confronting obstacles to inclusion: International responses to developing inclusive schools.* London: Routledge.

Giangreco, M. F., Cloninger, C. J., & Iverson, V. S. (1998). *Choosing outcomes and accommodations for children: A guide to educational planning for students with disabilities* (2nd ed.). Baltimore: Paul H. Brookes.

Giangreco, M. F., Dennis, R. E., Edelman, S. W., & Cloninger, C. J. (1994). Dressing your IEPs for the general education climate: Analysis of IEP goals and objectives for students with multiple disabilities. *Remedial and Special Education, 15*(5), 288-296.

Giangreco, M. F., Hurley, S. M., & Suter, J. C. (2009). Personnel utilization and general class placement of students with disabilities: Ranges and ratios. *Intellectual and Developmental Disabilities, 47,* 53-56.

Giangreco, M. F., & Snell, M. E. (1996). Severe and multiple disabilities. In R. Turnbull & A. Turnbull (Eds.), *Improving the implementation of the Individuals with Disabilities Education Act: Making schools work for all of America's children* (pp. 97-132). Washington, DC: National Council on Disability.

Giangreco, M. F., Yuan, S., McKenzie, B., Cameron, P., & Fialka, J. (2005). "Be careful what you wish for . . .": Five reasons to be concerned about the assignment of individual paraprofessionals. *Teaching Exceptional Children, 37*(5), 28-34.

Gonnerman, J. (2007). School of shock. *Mother Jones.* Retrieved February 23, 2009, from http://www.motherjones.com/politics/2007/08/school-shock

Grigal, M., & Hart, D. (2009). *Think college: Postsecondary education options for students with intellectual disabilities.* Baltimore: Paul H. Brookes.

Grisham-Brown, J., Hemmeter, M. L., & Pretti-Frontczak, K. (2005). *Blended practices for teaching young children in inclusive settings.* Baltimore: Paul H. Brookes.

Habib, D. (Director/Producer). (2007). *Including Samuel* [Motion picture]. (Available from Dan Habib at http://www.includingsamuel.com)

Harry, B. (2008). Collaboration with culturally and linguistically diverse families: Ideal versus reality. *Exceptional Children, 74,* 372-388.

Hasazi, S., & Shepherd, K. (2009). Leading beyond labels: The role of the principal in leading through a social justice framework for students with disabilities. In R. G. Johnson (Ed.), *A twenty-first century approach to teaching social justice: Educating for both advocacy and action* (pp. 91-106). New York: Peter Lang.

Horner, R. H., Sugai, G., Todd, A. W., & Lewis-Palmer, T. (2005). Schoolwide positive behavior support. In L. M. Bambara & L. Kern (Eds.), *Individualized supports for students with problem behaviors* (pp. 359-390). New York: Guilford Press.

Hunt, P., & Goetz, L. (1997). Research on inclusive educational programs, practices, and outcomes for students with severe disabilities. *Journal of Special Education, 31,* 3-29.

Individuals with Disabilities Education Act, 20 U.S.C. § 1400 (2004), sec. 602(26)(A).

Individuals with Disabilities Education Improvement Act of 2004, PL 108-446, 20 U.S.C. §§ 1400 et seq.

Irving Independent School District v. Tatro, 104 S. Ct. 3371 (1984).

Janney, R., & Snell, M. E. (1997). How teachers include students with moderate and severe disabilities in elementary classes: The means and meaning of inclusion. *Journal of the Association for Persons with Severe Disabilities, 22,* 159-169.

Janney, R., & Snell, M. E. (2006). *Teacher's guides to inclusive practices: Social relationships and peer support* (2nd ed.). Baltimore: Paul H. Brookes.

Janney, R., & Snell, M. E. (2008). *Teacher's guides to inclusive practices: Behavioural support* (2nd ed.). Baltimore: Paul H. Brookes.

Jorgensen, C. M., McSheehan, M., & Sonnenmeier, R. (2009). The beyond access model: Promoting membership, participation, and learning for students with disabilities in the general education classroom. Baltimore: Paul H. Brookes.

Kauffman, J. M., & Krouse, J. (1981). The cult of educability: Searching for the substance of things hoped for; the evidence of things not seen. *Analysis and Intervention in Developmental Disabilities, 1*(1), 53-60.

Kennedy, C. H., & Fisher, D. (2001). *Inclusive middle schools.* Baltimore: Paul H. Brookes.

Kleinert, H. L., & Kearns, J. F. (2001). *Alternative assessment: Measuring outcomes and supports for students with disabilities.* Baltimore: Paul H. Brookes.

Kozleski, E., Mainzer, R., & Deshler, D. (2000). Bright futures for exceptional learners: An action agenda to achieve quality conditions for teaching and learning. *Teaching Exceptional Children, 32*(6), 56-69.

Kunc, N. (2000). Rediscovering the right to belong. In R. A. Villa & J. S. Thousand (Eds.), *Restructuring for caring and effective education: Piecing the puzzle together* (2nd ed., pp. 77-92). Baltimore: Paul H. Brookes.

Lancioni, G. E., Singh, N. N., O'Reilly, M. F., Oliva, D., & Basili, G. (2005). An overview of research on increasing indices of happiness of people with severe/profound intellectual and multiple disabilities. *Disability & Rehabilitation, 27*(3), 83-93.

Logan, K., & Malone, D. M. (1998). Instructional contexts for students with moderate, severe, and profound intellectual disabilities in general education classrooms. *Education and Training in Mental Retardation and Developmental Disabilities, 33,* 62-75.

Magito McLaughlin, D., & Carr, E. G. (2005). Quality of rapport as a setting event for problem behavior: Assessment and intervention. *Journal of Positive Behavior Interventions, 7*(2), 68-91.

McDonnell, J., Hardman, M., & McDonnell, A. (2003). *An introduction to persons with moderate and severe disabilities: Educational and social issues* (2nd ed.). Boston: Allyn & Bacon.

McDonnell, J., Johnson, J. W., Polychronis, S., & Risen, T. (2002). Effects of embedded instruction on students with moderate disabilities enrolled in general education classes. *Education and Training in Mental Retardation and Developmental Disabilities, 37,* 363-377.

McKenzie, B. (2008). *Reflections of Erin: The importance of belonging, relationships, and learning with each other.* Seaman, OH: Art of Possibility Press.

McLeskey, J., Tyler, N., & Saunders, S. (2002). *The supply and demand of special education teachers: The nature of the chronic shortage of special education teachers.* Gainesville: Center on Personnel Studies in Special Education, University of Florida.

National Disability Rights Network. (2009). *School is not supposed to hurt: Investigative report on abusive restraint and seclusion in schools.* Washington, DC: Author. Retrieved May 25, 2009, from http://www.napas.org/sr/SR-Report.pdf

Nisbet, J. (Ed.). (1992). *Natural supports in school, at work, and in the community for people with severe disabilities.* Baltimore: Paul H. Brookes.

Peterson, J. M. (2004). Whole schooling tool kit [CD-ROM]. Detroit: Whole Schooling Consortium, Wayne State University. Available online at http://www.wholeschooling.net

Peterson, J. M., & Hittie, M. M. (2010). *Inclusive teaching: The journey towards effective schools for all learners* (2nd ed.). Columbus, OH: Merrill.

Rebhorn, T., & Smith, A. (2008, April). LRE decision making (Module 15). *Building the legacy: A training curriculum on IDEA 2004.* Washington, DC: National Dissemination Center for Children with Disabilities. Available online at http://www.nichcy.org/training/contents.asp

Sailor, W. (Ed.). (2002). *Whole-school success and inclusive education: Building partnerships for learning achievement and accountability.* New York: Teachers College Press.

Sailor, W., & Roger, B. (2005). Rethinking inclusion: Schoolwide applications. *Phi Delta Kappan, 86*(7), 503-509.

Schalock, R. L., Luckasson, R. A., & Schogren, K. A. (2007). The renaming of mental retardation: Understanding the change to the term intellectual disability. *Intellectual and Developmental Disabilities, 45,* 116-124.

Schnorr, R. (1990). "Peter? He come and he goes . . .": First graders' perspectives on a part-time mainstream student. *Journal of the Association for Persons with Severe Handicaps, 15,* 231-240.

Schnorr, R. (1997). From enrollment to membership: "Belonging" in middle and high school classes. *Journal of the Association for Persons with Severe Handicaps, 22,* 1-15.

Siperstein, G. N., Parker, R. C., Bardon, J. N., & Widaman, K. F. (2007). A national study of youth attitudes toward the inclusion of students with intellectual disabilities. *Exceptional Children, 73,* 435-455.

Snell, M. E. (2003). Education of individuals with severe and multiple disabilities. In J. W. Guthrie (Ed.), *Encyclopedia of education* (2nd ed., pp. 2210-2213). New York: Macmillan.

Snell, M. E., & Brown, F. (2006). *Instruction of students with severe disabilities.* Upper Saddle River, NJ: Pearson.

Snell, M. E., & Janney, R. J. (2000). Teachers' problem solving about young children with moderate and severe disabilities in elementary classrooms. *Exceptional Children, 66,* 472-490.

Snell, M. E., & Janney, R. (2005). *Teacher's guides to inclusive practices: Collaborative teamwork* (2nd ed.). Baltimore: Paul H. Brookes.

Soodak, L. C., & Erwin, E. J. (2000). Valued member or tolerated participant: Parents' experiences in inclusive early childhood settings. *Journal of the Association for Persons with Severe Handicaps, 25,* 29-41.

Suter, J. C., & Giangreco, M. F. (2009). Numbers that count: Exploring special education and paraprofessional service delivery in inclusion-oriented schools. *Journal of Special Education, 43,* 81-93.

TASH. (2000, March). TASH resolution on the people for whom TASH advocates. Retrieved April 22, 2010, from http://www.tash.org/IRR/resolutions/res02advocate.htm

Taylor, S. J. (1988). Caught in the continuum: A critical analysis of the principle of the least restrictive environment. *Journal of the Association for Persons with Handicaps, 13,* 41-53.

Taylor, S. J. (2006). Supporting adults to live in the community: Beyond the continuum. In S. M. Pueschel (Ed.), *Adults with Down syndrome* (pp. 173-182). Baltimore: Paul H. Brookes.

Taylor, S. J., & Bogdan, R. (1989). On accepting relationships between people with mental retardation and non-disabled people: Towards an understanding of acceptance. *Disability, Handicap & Society, 4,* 21-36.

Thoma, C. A., Bartholomew, C. C., & Scott, L. A. (2009). *Universal design for transition: A road map for planning and instruction.* Baltimore: Paul H. Brookes.

Thousand, J. S., Villa, R. A., & Nevin, A. I. (2006). The many faces of collaborative planning and teaching. *Theory into Practice, 45,* 239-248.

Timothy W. v. Rochester School District, 559 EHLR 480 (D.N.H. 1988), 875 F.2d 954 (1st Cir. 1989), cert. denied, 493 U.S. 983 (1989).

Turnbull, H. R., Stowe, M. J., & Huerta, N. E. (2007). *Free appropriate public education: The law and children with disabilities* (7th ed.). Denver: Love Publishing.

Udvari-Solner, A., Thousand, J. S., & Villa, R. A. (2002). Access to the general education curriculum for all. In J. S. Thousand, R. A. Villa, & A. I. Nevin (Eds.), *Creativity and collaborative learning: The practical guide to empowering students, teachers, and families* (2nd ed., pp. 85-103). Baltimore: Paul H. Brookes.

U.S. Department of Education. (2007). *Table 2-2: Students ages 6 through 21 served under IDEA, Part B, by disability category, educational environment and state: Fall 2007* [Data file]. Available online from Individuals with Disabilities Education Act (IDEA) Web site: https://www.ideadata.org/PartBdata.asp

U.S. Department of Justice. (2002). Brief for the United States as amicus curiae supporting appellee and urging affirmance in the case of Girty v. School District of Valley Grove on appeal from the United States District Court for the Western District of Pennsylvania to the U.S. Court of Appeals for the Third Circuit. Retrieved April 10, 2007, from http://www.usdoj.gov/crt/briefs/girty.pdf

U.S. Government Accountability Office. (2009). *Seclusion and restraints: Selected cases of death and abuse at public and private schools and treatment centers.* Washington, DC: Author. Retrieved May 24, 2009, from http://gao.gov/products/GAO-09—719T

Van der Klift, E., & Kunc, N. (2002). Beyond benevolence: Supporting genuine friendship in inclusive schools. In J. S. Thousand, R. A. Villa, & A. I. Nevin (Eds.), *Creativity and collaborative learning: The practical guide to empowering students, teachers, and families* (2nd ed., pp. 21-28). Baltimore: Paul H. Brookes.

Villa, R., Thousand, J., Nevin, A., & Liston, A. (2005). Successful inclusive practices in middle and secondary schools. *American Secondary Education Journal, 33*(1), 33-50.

Wehman, P., Inge, K. J., Revell, W. G., & Brooke, V. A. (2007). *Real work for real pay: Inclusive employment for people with disabilities.* Baltimore: Paul H. Brookes.

Wehmeyer, M. L. (2005). Self-determination and individuals with severe disabilities: Re-examining meanings and misinterpretations. *Research and Practice for Persons with Severe Disabilities, 30,* 113-120.

Wehmeyer, M. L. (2006). Beyond access: Ensuring progress in the general education curriculum for students with severe disabilities. *Research and Practice for Persons with Severe Disabilities, 31,* 322-326.

Wehmeyer, M. L., Buntinx, H. E., Lachapelle, Y., Luckasson, R. A., Schalock, R. L., Verdugo, M. A., et al. (2008). The intellectual disability construct and its relation to human functioning. *Intellectual and Developmental Disabilities, 46,* 311-318.

Wilkins, D. (2003). Your attitude. Retrieved April 22, 2010, from http://www.thenthdegree.com/advocacy.asp#YOUR%20ATTITUDE

Wolf, M. M. (1978). Social validity: The case for subjective measurement, or how applied behavior analysis is finding its heart. *Journal of Applied Behavior Analysis, 11,* 203-214.

Wolfensberger, W. (1975). *The origin and nature of our institutional models.* Syracuse, NY: Human Policy Press.

World Health Organization. (2001). International classification of functioning, disability, and health (ICF). Geneva: Author.

Yuan, S. (2003). Seeing with new eyes: Metaphors of family experience. *Mental Retardation, 41,* 207-211.

Fostering Family–Professional Partnerships

Nina Zuna
Ann Turnbull
Rud Turnbull

❖ ❖ ❖ ❖ ❖   **Introducing the Campbell Family, an African-American Family**   ❖ ❖ ❖ ❖ ❖

Loretta Campbell is determined that her son Jamal, 13, will be included in all school activities with his classmates who do not have disabilities. Her determination, however, encounters obstacles. "It has not always been easy to make this happen; I guess you could say that it has been more of a learning process over the past 10 years." Hard going? Yes. Late-night e-mails and frequent telephone calls to Jamal's teachers prove how hard it is.

Transition exacerbates the challenge. Jamal has just entered middle school; the relative protectiveness of elementary school and its curriculum are things of the past. At a time when nearly all students are acutely self-conscious and socially sensitive, Jamal's autism and intellectual disability inhibit his ability to establish friendships easily. But this has not stopped him from being curious about the many items that his peers possess, particularly items related to the Dallas Cowboys football team, a given because the Campbell family used to live in Dallas. However, they recently moved to Arlington, Texas, to be closer to family after Jamal's father left the household.

Has Ms. Campbell's insistence on inclusion been worth the effort? Yes. Clearly, Jamal enjoys the routine of going to school, and, with the support of his peers, he has just mastered finding his way to all six of his classes in his middle school. He spends 80% of his day in general education classrooms and the remaining 20% in a resource room with other special education students to complete unfinished assignments and to develop self-management skills.

Ms. Campbell didn't want to send all the e-mails and make all the telephone calls. She had to. Jamal's teachers in elementary school and his new teachers in middle school were concerned about the academic challenges that middle school would present for Jamal. Many of them urged her to consider having Jamal spend the majority of his time in a resource room and then reassess his readiness for full inclusion at a later date. Although Ms. Campbell felt that Jamal could be successful in the new middle school and in general education classes, she, too, shared those concerns. Jamal would be in a new school, with a new routine, and instead of being in one classroom all day, he would have to transition to six classrooms throughout the day. She also knew that Jamal had difficulty with transitions, was slow to establish friendships, and exhibited behavioral problems when faced with increased academic demands. However, she remembered how successful he had been the past 2 years in a fully inclusive elementary school when he had peer mentors who had similar interests. Ms. Campbell trusted her instincts and the evidence of Jamal's elementary school progress and advocated for Jamal's inclusion in all aspects of middle school. Nine months have passed and Jamal's success has exceeded everyone's expectations. While on spring break, Jamal indicated that he would rather be at school than at home!

Ms. Campbell is pleased with the progress that Jamal has made and is justifiably satisfied with her advocacy for his inclusion.

But she's worn out. "This is hard work; I am tired both physically and emotionally from convincing teachers to do what I feel is right for my son. I don't think that they understand everything my family has gone through in addition to my long work hours and caring for three children as a single mom. To tell you the truth, I am not sure that I will be able to keep up this level of advocacy for the future transitions that lie ahead for Jamal. I am also very concerned about Jamal's life after high school. I want him to have the same opportunities that he has now, but I just can't think that far into the future right now. Planning one year in advance is as much as I can handle at this moment."

Just what has her family "gone through"? Ms. Campbell's father battled liver cancer for a year and died during Jamal's last year in elementary school; grieving and advo-cacy are not exactly compatible—each sapped her energy and neither allowed much room for the other. Ms. Campbell has two other children, Shelia, 17, and Donnell, 15. Also, Jamal's father left the household when Jamal was only 7 years old. Ms. Campbell doesn't talk about it much, but says that it was for the best. She now relies on her mother, Sandra (or Ma Ma Sandy as her grandchildren affectionately call her), and close friends for emotional and practical support. Indeed, this past year has been quite challenging for the Campbell family; however, with the support of friends and extended family, they are managing. The passing of the children's maternal grandfather has caused increased stress and sadness for Ms. Campbell. The older children, while sad, are coping; however, Jamal is demonstrating increased behavioral challenges as he struggles to understand the passing of his grandfather. Ms. Campbell's mother remains stoic, but is beginning to show signs of depression, mourning the loss of her husband.

❖ ❖ ❖ ❖ ❖   **Introducing the Gonzalez Family, an Hispanic-American Family**   ❖ ❖ ❖ ❖ ❖

Coming to America! Those three words tell the life stories of nearly everyone in this country. Almost all of us are immigrants, some of us more recent than others. These three words—"Coming to America"—certainly tell the story of the Gonzalez family.

Coming to America meant economic opportunity for the family. Manuel came here from Mexico, leaving his wife Lucille and two children, Isabella, seven, and Maria, six, behind. Here, he worked as a migrant farmer until he became a citizen. His citizenship assured, he sought more permanent work and now has a job with a company that builds new homes in Wichita, Kansas. With citizenship and a good job in hand, Manuel brought Lucille, Isabella, and Maria to Wichita. Why Wichita? Because Lucille's sister, brother-in-law, and niece live there and they encouraged Lucille and Manuel to join them. At last, the family is together again. At least most of the family is together. Manuel's and Lucille's brothers and sisters still live in Mexico. "We aren't entirely a family until all of us are in one place, together," laments Manuel. Will they be able to come to America? "They want to, but immigration is hard, especially now that there's a recession."

Coming to America also meant educational opportunity, especially for Isabella. She had insufficient oxygen when she was born and was diagnosed at birth as having cerebral palsy. She later acquired two other diagnoses: epilepsy and severe intellectual disability.

Although some general education programs and schools for children without disabilities in Mexico are beginning to accommodate children with disabilities, they are mostly for children with more mild disabilities. Isabella was rejected for admission to a regular school; its faculty regarded her disability as being too significant for them to address. Instead, she received most of her services from a specialized school and from medical personnel. After arriving in Wichita two years ago, Isabella has attended an early childhood Life Skills classroom for children, K–3. In Mexico, she had always attended school in a segregated setting; there, very few staff knew how to provide individualized teaching to address her cerebral palsy and learning issues. Here, education is different.

Isabella uses a wheelchair; has limited speech, with mostly words that only the Gonzalez family understands; and has frequent seizures. Isabella loves to be around other children and attends several classes (e.g., music, art, P.E.) with her peers without disabilities, but Mr. and Mrs. Gonzalez wish that there were more opportunities for her to be included in school; they understand that it is important for her teachers to emphasize academic training for all students, but they want more social opportunities for their daughter. They have asked themselves, why don't the teachers recognize that Isabella enjoys being with children who don't have disabilities? Why can't the teachers help Isabella develop more of her social skills? And why do they leave it up to Mrs. Gonzalez to make sure that Isabella has opportunities to be with children without disabilities in her neighborhood and church?

Coming to America meant even more than employment and educational opportunities. It meant adjusting to a new culture, a new language, and a new lexicon of school terminology. In their native culture, Mr. and Mrs. Gonzalez had learned to defer to educators. Here, deference is not so much the norm; partnership and advocacy are. In Mexico, Spanish was the common language; here, English is. In Mexico, the school terminology was different from what it is here; there's "special-education speak," as Mr. Gonzalez put it—and he speaks English better than Lucille, having been here longer.

But language remains a barrier, especially now that Isabella is beginning to have more frequent seizures. On a daily basis she has petit mal seizures (i.e., frequent eye blinks and mouth tremors) that last only a few seconds. Mr. and Mrs. Gonzalez worry about whether Isabella's teachers even notice these slight and frequently repeated seizures, much less appreciate the toll that they take on her body. At other times, she has grand mal seizures that are so severe that her whole body trembles and she gets caught in the straps of her wheelchair. Mr. and Mrs. Gonzalez are concerned that the school is not properly addressing her needs or, worse yet, no one will see her when the big seizures occur. Speaking in Spanish, Mrs. Gonzalez explains the challenge: "There is not a translator every time I just want to pick up the phone and talk to her teacher or tell her on Monday morning how her weekend had been. We always have to schedule for a translator."

Two Families and Two Windows for Understanding Families in Special Education

The Campbell and the Gonzalez families offer us two windows through which we can gain a clearer understanding about the relationship of special education for students with severe disabilities and the nature of family life. The first window lets us look at the law governing special education and relationships between eductors and parents. The second window lets us consider the family systems perspective, a framework through which professionals can understand families' preferences, strengths, and needs.

Individuals with Disabilities Education Act: Parental Rights and Responsibilities

The ultimate purpose of the Individuals with Disabilities Education Act (IDEA) has always been to create a combined federal, state, and local system that would provide all students with disabilities a free appropriate public education (FAPE) in the least restrictive environment. To secure that outcome, Congress created a framework within which educators and the parents of children with disabilities can be partners. The U.S. Supreme Court, in *Schaffer v. Weast* (2005), has said that the "cooperative process . . . between parents and schools" is at the core of IDEA. In this chapter, we discuss that "cooperative process" by examining the partnership as it can exist under the six principles of IDEA (Turnbull, Stowe, & Huerta, 2007). For the sake of brevity, we use the word *parent* to refer to the parents and other family members that IDEA covers, unless we indicate otherwise. We also use the acronym *LEA* to refer to local educational agencies and *SEA* to refer to state educational agencies.

IDEA's Six Principles

Figure 2–1 illustrates IDEA's six principles and their relationships to each other. The principles are zero reject, nondiscriminatory evaluation, appropriate education, least restrictive environment, parent and student participation in shared decision making, and procedural due process. In this chapter, we have focused on the partnership that parents and professionals can create under IDEA. Accordingly, Figure 2–1 presents the parent–professional partnership as the hub for the other five principles.

Zero Reject is a rule that requires educators to offer FAPE to all age-eligible students with disabilities. It's a principle that is easy to understand: *All* means all. The type or severity of the student's disability is irrelevant. *All* includes Jamal and Isabella; their multiple disabilities do not result in exclusion but instead make it all the more important for them to be educated.

IDEA connects the zero-reject principle to parental rights and responsibilities in several ways. The first relates to the ages of the children. Under IDEA's early intervention provisions (referred to as Part C of IDEA), families and their infant or toddler children may receive a large number of services (set out in an individualized family support plan [IFSP]) designed to develop

FIGURE 2–1
Process for Implementing IDEA's Six Principles in Educational Decision Making

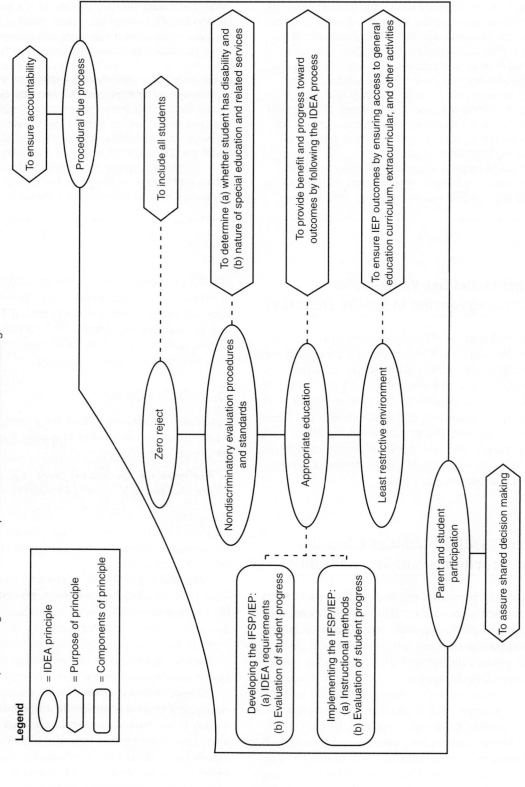

Legend

⬭ = IDEA principle

⬡ = Purpose of principle

▭ = Components of principle

To ensure accountability

Procedural due process

To include all students

To determine (a) whether student has disability and (b) nature of special education and related services

To provide benefit and progress toward outcomes by following the IDEA process

To ensure IEP outcomes by ensuring access to general education curriculum, extracurricular, and other activities

Zero reject

Nondiscriminatory evaluation procedures and standards

Appropriate education

Least restrictive environment

Developing the IFSP/IEP:
(a) IDEA requirements
(b) Evaluation of student progress

Implementing the IFSP/IEP:
(a) Instructional methods
(b) Evaluation of student progress

Parent and student participation

To assure shared decision making

the children's capacities, minimize their potential for developmental delays, and enhance families' capacities to work with their children. If families consent to early intervention, they can benefit from and influence the nature and extent of the early intervention services that they are offered.

Isabella was living in Mexico at the time of her birth so she did not receive early intervention services from IDEA; however, she and her family were referred to medical specialists within her hospital shortly after her birth because the doctors and nurses knew immediately that she had cerebral palsy resulting from lack of oxygen at birth. During her early years, she received medical care from her family doctor, nurses, and physical therapists in Mexico.

Jamal's journey was quite different.

Jamal had numerous ear infections during the first 18 months of his life; his doctors attributed his developmental and speech delays to his medical issues. When he was 26 months old, Jamal seemed to lose what little language he had and began to engage in odd behaviors such as lining up all of the coins in their change jar and spinning forks on the kitchen floor. He promptly was referred to early intervention and received services when he was 28 months old. These services ended when he was 36 months old. He then was evaluated and qualified for services under Part B of IDEA. His diagnosis is autism.

IDEA has changed since Jamal received his early intervention services. At that time, services ended when a child turned three. Now, SEAs have the option to offer early intervention until the child is eligible to enter kindergarten or elementary school; the option exists if the child has qualified for IDEA preschool services (20 U.S.C. § 1419) and the parent chooses to have the child remain in early intervention (20 U.S.C. § 1435(c)(1)). A parent may not want to elect that option; in that case, the child leaves Part C services (early intervention) and enters Part B services (preschool and beyond).

Part B serves children ages 3–21 who have any one of 10 types of disabilities and need special education and related services to progress in the general education curriculum (20 U.S.C. § 1402(3) (A)). Here, services are free; under Part C, services might be free or low cost, depending on a family's income. A second connection between FAPE and family concerns is related to the word *free*. *Free* means that neither the Campbells nor the Gonzalezes may be required to use private insurance benefits to pay for their children's education. They may use their insurance benefits to pay for services that their children need but that the schools do not provide (typically, medical services).

Mr. Gonzalez has health insurance for his family through his employer, but he, like other families, wants to use his insurance benefits only when absolutely necessary; he does not want to exceed the maximum benefits under his policy, especially now that Isabella's seizures are occurring more often and seem to be more significant than in the past. Yet he also recognizes that her seizures affect her education and that he may have to get help from physicians that he cannot get from her teachers.

A third connection between FAPE and families is related to school-imposed discipline. Since the U.S. Supreme Court decided in *Honig v. Doe* (1988) that IDEA limits the power of LEAs to discipline students with disabilities, the issue of school discipline has been a controversial issue. Discipline and behavioral challenges continue to be a focus of IDEA, with school safety being necessary for effective teaching and learning (20 U.S.C. §§ 1401(c), 1414(a)–(d), and 1415(k)). These provisions are important to the Campbell family.

Jamal has recently begun to engage in increased challenging behavior. While most of his behavior is self-injurious (e.g., hitting and pinching himself), he has been sent home on several occasions for aggressive behavior towards his peers (e.g., lunging, pushing, and hitting), causing his mother, a single parent, to leave work each time that the school called about his behavior.

Just what do the discipline provisions mean for Jamal? Under IDEA, an LEA has the authority to remove a child with a disability who violates a code of student conduct from the child's current placement to an appropriate interim alternative educational setting or another setting, or suspend the child for not more than 10 school days (20 U.S.C. § 1415(k)). At the same time, IDEA also protects the child's right to an education by giving the child's LEA the option of providing services during the 10-day period. So, Jamal could be out of school for up to 10 days for a school-code infraction, which would mean 10 days of lost income for the family.

If the LEA removes the child for more than 10 school days or changes the child's placement as a form of discipline, the LEA must (a) continue to provide special education and related services, (b) conduct a functional behavior assessment and develop and implement (or modify and implement) a (new or existing) behavioral intervention program designed to address the behavior for which the LEA has disciplined the child, and (c) determine whether the child's behavior (for which the child is being disciplined) is a manifestation of the child's disability (20 U.S.C. § 1415(k)).

Educators agreed that Jamal's behavior was a manifestation of his autism. However, they failed to comply with the IDEA requirement to review his current behavioral intervention plan and modify it as necessary to address these new behavioral concerns.

What if they had complied? The school would have been required to consider—only consider—whether to use positive behavioral supports to address his behavior or even behavior that impairs his and other students' ability to learn (20 U.S.C. §§ 1414(d)(3)(B) and 1415(k)(1)(D)). That's all—just consider. They could have used those supports, used them in conjunction with other interventions, not used them at all, or even not used any different interventions. Inasmuch as Congress declared that the use of positive behavior supports and evidence-based interventions are strategies for making sure that all students receive FAPE (20 U.S.C. § 1401(c)(5)(F)), Jamal's teachers certainly should not only consider but also use positive behavior supports. IDEA presumes that they will; it does not command them to do so, but it pushes them in that direction.

Nondiscriminatory Evaluation is a rule that requires educators to eliminate bias on the basis of a student's language, culture, or other traits as they (a) determine whether the student has a disability and (b) specify what kind of special education and related services the student should receive if the student has a disability (20 U.S.C. § 1414(a)–(c)).

Educators and parents alike have the right to request an initial evaluation of a student. If educators want to evaluate a student, whether for an initial evaluation or for a reevaluation, they must secure the consent of the student's parents. Parents may consent or refuse to consent. If the school has taken reasonable measures to secure parental consent for an initial evaluation (e.g., by using certified mail, registered mail, telephone, fax, or a home visit) and if the parents have failed to respond, the school may try to persuade the parents to consent by using mediation or another method of resolving disputes (see Procedural Due Process, p. 42) or it may simply decline to conduct an initial evaluation. In that event, the school is not required to provide special education and is not liable if it does not because the parents have opted out of special education.

In partnering with families to conduct evaluations, educators have the responsibility to

- Provide notice of the evaluation;
- Conduct the evaluation using a variety of assessment tools and strategies;
- Ensure that the assessments are not culturally biased and are valid and reliable;
- Review existing data, including evaluations and information provided by the parents of the child;
- Include the parent in the determination of eligibility and educational need;
- Provide the parent with a copy of the evaluation report and documentation concerning their child's eligibility (or lack of eligibility) for special education (20 U.S.C. § 1414(a)–(c)); and
- Conduct the evaluation within 60 days after the child is referred for evaluation.

Not all evaluations are done by a student's educators. Parents such as Ms. Campbell and Mr. and Mrs. Gonzalez have a right to secure (at their own expense) an independent evaluation—one done by qualified professionals not employed by the student's school district—and to require that the school's evaluation team consider it. Parents also may recover the cost of an independent evaluation from the LEA if the LEA's evaluation is not appropriate according to a due process hearing officer or court or if the reevaluation was ordered by a due process hearing officer or court. This means that team evaluations may not be completely influenced by only LEA members.

As much as their culture teaches them to defer to educators and as much as they do not want to use Mr. Gonzalez's health insurance, Mr. and Mrs. Gonzalez may want to secure an independent evaluation if Isabella's educators fail to assess her needs and strengths in her native language, as IDEA requires, or do not have a specialist physician (such as a neurologist) evaluate her to determine the causes of, and interventions for, her seizures.

Educators and families have flexibility with respect to reevaluations. They may jointly decide whether it is necessary to conduct a reevaluation to determine whether a student still qualifies for educational and related services. If they decide to forgo a reevaluation when one otherwise would occur (three years after the preceding one), they may do so. If, however, the parent or teacher requests a reevaluation, educators should invite the parents to share their perspectives and rationale for why they believe a reevaluation is important. In some instances, parents may pinpoint problems that educators have not yet recognized. Not surprisingly, the Campbells and Gonzalezes may welcome the option to waive the three-year evaluation; they would have one less meeting to attend, and because both Jamal and Isabella have lifelong disabilities, the emphasis now is on appropriate education, not evaluating again for no constructive purpose.

If the parents refuse to consent to a reevaluation, the school may not conduct one and may use mediation or other methods for resolving disputes. If the school wants to do a reevaluation but cannot secure parental consent, it may nevertheless do a reevaluation if it can demonstrate that it took reasonable action to secure parental consent and the parents have failed to respond (20 U.S.C. § 1414(c)(3)).

Appropriate Education is a rule that requires educators to comply with all IDEA processes and thereby benefit the student (*Board of Education of the Hendrick Hudson Central School District v. Rowley*, 1982). The linchpin for an appropriate education is the student's IFSP (for infants and toddlers, from birth to age 3) or individualized educational program (IEP) (for students ages 3–21). The IEP may be revised as often as necessary. Normally, it is revised annually; however, some states may have been approved to pilot a multiyear IEP. Figure 2–2

FIGURE 2–2
Required Contents of Individualized Educational Plan (IEP)

The IEP is a written statement for each student, ages 3–21. Whenever it is developed or revised, it must contain the following statements:
1. The student's present levels of academic achievement and functional performance, including
   - How the student's disability affects the student's involvement and progress in the general curriculum (for students 6–21)
   - How a preschooler's disability affects the child's participation in appropriate activities (for children 3–5)
   - A description of the benchmarks or short-term objectives for students who take alternate assessments that are aligned to alternate achievement standards
2. Measurable annual goals, including academic and functional goals, designed to
   - Meet each of the student's needs resulting from the disability in order to enable the student to be involved in and make progress in the general curriculum
   - Meet each of the student's other educational needs that result from the disability
3. How the student's progress toward annual goals will be measured and when periodic reports on the student's progress on, and meeting of, annual goals will be provided
4. The special education and related services and supplementary aids and services, based on peer-reviewed research to the extent practicable, that will be provided to the student or on the student's behalf and the program modifications or supports for school personnel that will be provided for the student to
   - Advance appropriately toward attaining the annual goals
   - Be involved in and make progress in the general curriculum and participate in extracurricular and other nonacademic activities
   - Be educated and participate in those three types of activities with other students with disabilities and with students who do not have disabilities
5. An explanation of the extent, if any, to which the student will not participate with students who do not have disabilities in the regular class and in extracurricular and other nonacademic activities
6. Any individual appropriate accommodations that are necessary to measure the student's academic and functional performance on state- and district-wide assessments; if the IEP team determines that the student will not participate in a regular state- or district-wide assessment or any part of an assessment, an explanation of why the student cannot participate and the particular alternate assessment that the team selects as appropriate for the student
7. The projected date for beginning the special education, related services and supplemental aids and services, and modifications and the anticipated frequency, location, and duration of each
8. Beginning no later than the first IEP that will be in effect after the student turns 16, and then updated annually, a transition plan that must include
   - Measurable postsecondary goals based on appropriate transition assessments related to training, education, employment, and, where appropriate, independent living skills
   - A statement of transition services, including courses of study, needed to assist the student to reach those postsecondary goals
   - Beginning no later than 1 year before the student reaches the age of majority under state law (usually at age 18), a statement that the student has been informed of those rights under IDEA that will transfer to the student from the parents when the student comes of age

Note: From *Exceptional Lives: Special Education in Today's Schools* (p. 53) (6th ed.), by Ann P. Turnbull, Rud Turnbull, and Michael L. Wehmeyer, copyright 2010. Reprinted by permission of Pearson Education, Upper Saddle River, NJ.

displays the required content for an IEP. For students, like Jamal and Isabella, who take alternate assessments, their IEP must include short-term objectives. These objectives are typically used as benchmarks to gauge progress toward meeting the annual goals. Students also have a right to related services if, like Jamal and Isabella, the services are necessary to ensure that the student receives FAPE. Parents, too, may benefit from related services. A few related services of interest to families include

- Family training, counseling, and home visits (e.g., PBS training for Ms. Campbell);
- Parent counseling and training;
- Psychological services;
- Coordination of services for infants and toddlers and their families;
- Social work services;
- Speech-language pathology services; and
- Assistive technology and services (such as Isabella Gonzalez may need).

IDEA's IFSP and IEP requirements enable families and professionals to work together as partners in planning and implementing the student's appropriate education. In addition to considering the evaluation data, the strengths of the child, and the concerns of the parents, IDEA requires that the educational team, when developing an IEP, consider the academic, developmental, and functional needs of the child (20 U.S.C. § 1414(d)). For example,

Isabella Gonzalez's upper-body spasticity makes it difficult for her to eat and, indeed, for her parents to take her with them when they go out to eat. With appropriate adaptations and specialized feeding equipment, the family could enjoy their mealtimes together, whether at home or out in the community. By addressing Isabella's feeding needs through assistive technology and occupational therapy, educators and other professionals directly address her functional needs.

An LEA must take certain steps to ensure that one or both of the student's parents are members of any group (including the IEP team) that makes decisions on the child's educational placement. These steps include advance notice of the meeting, mutually convenient scheduling of the meeting (taking into account Mr. Gonzalez's long working hours), and arranging for interpreters for parents who are deaf or non-English speaking, such as Mrs. Gonzalez. If a parent cannot attend the meeting, he or she may participate through video conferencing or telephone conference calls, again with interpreters as needed. Not surprisingly, Ms. Campbell and Mrs. Gonzalez have attended every IEP meeting related to their own child.

Unfortunately, Mr. Gonzalez has not been able to attend all of the meetings because of his long work hours and erratic work schedule. Should Isabella's teachers have asked him to participate by telephone? Of course, but they didn't; they did not consider that he, like most people, have a cell phone.

The LEA may have an IEP meeting without a student's parents only when it can document that it attempted unsuccessfully to have them participate. The documentation should include detailed records of telephone calls, copies of letters to and from the parents, and the results of any visits to the parents' homes or places of work.

Parents are not necessarily "voting" members of IFSP and IEP teams because IDEA does not direct how a team is to make decisions (e.g., whether members vote or reach decisions through other means). Clearly, however, professional members of the team must take the parents' perspectives into account in all decision making and must give the parents a copy of the IFSP/IEP. Taking the Gonzalez family's culture into account means, for example, allowing Isabella to learn the Spanish names for her family members before learning the English names.

Parents may invite other family members or other individuals knowledgeable about their child to attend the IFSP and IEP team meetings. This provides parents with supportive allies and the entire team with additional information. For example,

Ms. Campbell's mother has attended in the past, as has Jamal's brother, Donnell. Ms. Campbell said that "having other children at a meeting can be very enlightening. Plus, I think it's helpful to hear their opinions because, a lot of times, they come up with better ideas on how to solve a problem with Jamal than the adults do."

Mrs. Gonzalez has been accompanied by her sister, Alice, when her husband is unable to attend. Not only is Alice Isabella's aunt, but she is also her godmother and is very close to Isabella.

Having supportive allies, such as family members, attend IEP meetings with the family can be helpful because an IEP is a legal document that contains many important details about how a child's educational program is to be delivered. The information may be overwhelming at times for families.

The presence of a large number of school personnel at meetings can also be overwhelming. And indeed, a large number may also be inefficient for a school. IDEA (20 U.S.C. § 1414(d)(1)) allows for an otherwise required member of the IEP team to be excused if the parent and school agree that the member's attendance is not necessary because his or her area of the curriculum or service is not being modified or discussed. Furthermore, team members whose attendance is necessary for FAPE may be excused if both the school and the parent agree and the excused members submit written recommendations for the IEP.

Educators should be cautious about their own "excused absences." School efficiency is one thing; student outcomes are quite another and are far more important. Schools must also consider the impression that an absence might convey. Might Ms. Campbell or the Gonzalez family regard an absence as a lack of concern or dedication to their child? Consider how you would feel if a member of your health care team submitted a written statement about your health progress (or lack thereof) and next steps for how to care for your condition, but was not there in person to describe how your care plan should be implemented.

Nearly all infants and toddlers (birth up to age three) leave early intervention programs and enter early childhood education programs. That is why their IFSPs must describe the steps that will be taken to ensure a smooth transition and to involve the parents in transition planning. Infants and toddlers who do transition to early childhood programs may now carry their IFSPs with them with their parents' and educators' consent. Their teachers and parents do not have to develop an IEP for them; they may simply adopt and amend, as appropriate, the child's IFSP. This portability provision is important for both the infant and the parents. The infant is assured that there will be no disruption in services and thus no loss of a beneficial program, and the parents continue to have an IFSP plan that includes services for them. (Unlike IEPs, IFSPs include services for families.) Basically, the portability provisions recognize that the IFSP approach

is solid and that the benefits of early intervention should be sustained over time.

There are also important IEP considerations for older students. When students turn 16, their IEPs must describe appropriate, measurable postsecondary school goals and provide a description of transition services to prepare them for future education, employment, and independent living, as appropriate (see Chapter 15 for a discussion of transitions).

It's not too early for Ms. Campbell to start thinking about where Jamal will live when he becomes an adult—maybe with her, maybe with his brother Donnell. Nor is it too early for Mr. and Mrs. Gonzlaez to think about the work that Isabella might do; they already have decided that she will live at home with them.

Furthermore, when a student attains the age of majority (usually age 18), the student, if legally competent (i.e., able to make and communicate personal decisions), is entitled to exercise his or her IDEA rights independent of parental oversight. Indeed, a year before coming of age, a student is entitled to a notice concerning what rights will transfer to him or her upon attaining the age of majority. This provision means that parents need to begin to consider, at least a year before the student's age of majority, how to ensure that the student knows about IDEA rights and is capable of exercising them. A curriculum in self-determination or self-advocacy (including knowledge of rights, responsibilities, and decision-making processes) is especially important. Jamal would currently benefit from a curriculum that focuses goals and objectives on skills related to self-determination (Wehmeyer & Field, 2007). Later we will learn that self-determination skills can also be encouraged in very young children, such as Isabella.

Least Restrictive Environment is a rule which assures that, to the maximum extent appropriate, each child with a disability will be educated with children who do not have disabilities—that is, in the regular educational environment (20 U.S.C. § 1412(a)(5)). The LRE rule creates a rebuttable presumption in favor of placement in regular educational environments. This presumption enables Jamal and Isabella to potentially have access to education in the general curriculum—to be included (i.e., to have an inclusive education).

A "presumption" is a rule of law that drives individuals into a predetermined result. For example, there is a presumption of innocence when an individual is charged by the state with a crime. The presumption (of innocence) drives the judge or jury to favor the accused. The presumption, however, is rebuttable. That is, it may be set aside if the facts so warrant. Thus, the state may have sufficient evidence to convict the accused; the presumption of innocence is then rebutted by the facts.

Under IDEA, the presumption is that the student will be educated with students who do not have disabilities. That presumption, however, may be set aside when the student's needs are so great that, even with related services and with supplementary aids and services, the child cannot be educated satisfactorily in the regular educational environment (20 U.S.C. §§ 1412 and 1414(a)–(d)). When setting aside the presumption, educators may place a student into one of several settings along a continuum of services, including resource rooms, special education classes, separate schools, and institutions and hospitals (20 U.S.C. § 1412).

IDEA does not define "the regular educational environment." Instead, it uses such terms as *general curriculum* and *regular class* (20 U.S.C. § 1414(b)–(d)). IDEA defines *general curriculum* to mean the academic, extracurricular, and other school activities available to students without disabilities (20 U.S.C. § 1414(d)(1)(A)). Jamal and Isabella both benefit from the presumption, Jamal more so than Isabella. Jamal has received the majority of his academic instruction in the same classrooms as peers who do not have disabilities, albeit through an adapted curriculum and with the benefit of a paraprofessional.

> *Remember how important it is to Ms. Campbell for Jamal to be included? And that Jamal's teachers were not as committed as she; indeed, they were skeptical? Perhaps unlike them, she had a vision for Jamal that extended far beyond his years at school. She wants him to be able to live independently and work in the community after high school graduation. She is right to assume that the skills that he gains from his inclusive experiences will prepare him for his transition to the adult world.*
>
> *Isabella, however, has attended a life skills classroom, with inclusion in homeroom, lunch, recess, music, art, and P.E. Why? Supposedly, it is because the extent of her disabilities is so great that she would not benefit from inclusion. Or at least that's the reason her teachers give.*

This brings us to a consideration of the teachers' perspectives. Which student needs are so great that the student should not be in the same environment as students without disabilities of the same age? In Jamal's case, there are few—certainly, his behavior is a factor, but only if the school fails to use PBS and to provide social-skills training, as it should. In fact, he's a good candidate to be an assistant football manager, which would provide natural opportunities for building and refining his social skills.

> *Isabella's health-related needs are a legitimate factor to consider with respect to the academic program. But what prevents her from participating in some extracurricular or other school events? Only her teachers' failure to understand that, at home, Mrs. Gonzalez arranges for Isabella's peers without disabilities to be part of the Gonzalez family.*

The role of the LRE rule is to increase academic and other kinds of inclusion because inclusion benefits not only the student with a disability but also peers who do not have disabilities (Hunt & McDonnell, 2007; Leyser & Kirk, 2004). There are times when educators may not know or cannot accurately measure the educational benefits that all children receive through inclusion. And that is why both Jamal and Isabella have the right to participate in all other school activities, such as field trips, assemblies, social occasions, and after-school programs, often with the support of peers who volunteer to be in their respective circles of friends.

Similarly, IDEA provides that infants and toddlers in early intervention programs will receive services in "natural environments," namely, those in which peers without disabilities participate, to the extent appropriate for the child with a disability (20 U.S.C. §§ 1432(4)(G) and 1436(d)(5)). Four settings comply with the "natural environments" rule: (a) the child's home, (b) full- or part-time participation in preschool programs operated by public agencies (e.g., Head Start), (c) segregated private schools (in which there are only children with disabilities) or integrated private schools (in which there are children with and without disabilities), and (d) classes in general education elementary schools (with children who do not have disabilities).

These options are justified on the basis that the child's needs are valued more greatly than the child's placement. There is no federal mandate for early intervention programs, and thus compliance with the natural-environments rule is shaped by the laws, policies, and practices of state and local agencies. The natural-environments rule is a rebuttable presumption similar to the LRE rule for children ages 3–21 and is interpreted and applied in the same manner as that rule.

The rebuttable nature of the natural-environments rule is made explicit by the language of the statute itself, providing that separate settings such as hospitals are permissible only when the child requires extensive medical treatment (20 U.S.C. § 1436(d)(5)). Were these settings (such as hospitals) impermissible, the natural-environments rule would be an irrebuttable presumption, and no placement would be allowed except in an integrated setting.

According to IDEA's structure and logic, the placement decision may not be made until after the child has been given a nondiscriminatory evaluation. Section 1414 (a)–(c) provides for the initial evaluation (subsection a), reevaluation (subsection b), and additional requirements for initial evaluations and reevaluations. Section 1414(d) then provides for the IEP. Section 1414's structure—evaluation precedes IEP, and IEP specifies program and placement—is also logical: Section 1414(d), the IEP provisions, begins by stating the contents of the student's IEP, including "present levels of academic achievement and functional performance." Information about those attributes of the child derives directly from the evaluation. Accordingly, the IEP team uses the evaluation data to write the IEP, determine program and related services, and determine placement and supplementary aids and services. Parents are members of that team and thus have a role in deciding how the LRE rule applies to their child.

Parent and Student Participation in Shared Decision Making is the fifth of IDEA's six principles. When Congress reauthorized IDEA in 2004, it declared that children's education can be made more effective by strengthening the parents' roles and responsibilities (20 U.S.C. § 1401(c)(5)(B)). We have described the ways in which parents may participate in their child's nondiscriminatory evaluation, IEP development, and least restrictive setting planning. There are, however, still other ways for parents to participate as partners with educators.

Parents have the right to have access to their children's school records and to limit the distribution of those records to only those persons who have "a need to know." They also have the right to access the school district's general records about special education, such as the records that show how many students receive special education services and the amount of money that the district receives and spends on special education. Obviously, they do not have the right to see other students' records. In addition, parents generally have the right to see the state's special education plan, receive public notice of hearings on the plan, and comment on the plan. They are entitled to serve on the state advisory council on special education, and they must constitute the majority of the council's membership. Finally, parents of infants and toddlers are entitled to serve on the state's interagency coordinating council on early intervention and must constitute a majority of the membership of the council.

Most of all, however, parents have a right to participate in evaluation and IEP team meetings, and their children, whatever their age and however challenging their disabilities may be, also have a right to be members of the IEP team "whenever appropriate." When is it appropriate? Basically, whenever parents and educators decide that it is.

Jamal has been included in general education classrooms with his peers for the past several years; however, only recently, with his transition to middle school, were Jamal's opinions solicited. This was so because his mother stated that she would like for him to attend his IEP meeting to have a chance to ask questions and give his opinions about his transition from elementary to middle school. While his role was minimal at this IEP meeting, his first ever, he was able to share what it meant for him to "work and have fun" with his friends. Ms. Campbell was very proud of the advocacy role her son played at such a young age. Jamal practiced his "IEP speech" at home with his mother and siblings using his communication board.

There are strategies that educators can use to increase student participation in decision making. Educators can assist their students in (a) developing a portfolio of their work and information about their goals; (b) preparing a PowerPoint presentation about their needs, preferences, and goals; or (c) developing a recordable storybook about their achievements and their ideas about future goals to pursue.

It is essential for other IEP team members to listen with respect to the student's contributions, ask questions, and incorporate the contributions as collaborative decisions are made. A student's mere presence at a meeting can cause educators and parents to emphasize the student's strengths, not simply to describe the student's needs; Jamal's presence prompted educators to consider his strengths. Investigating multiple ways for students to participate in decision making is especially important, particularly for students who have limited communication (such as Jamal and Isabella).

Ensuring parents' full participation in educational decision making might require additional effort, especially with parents from culturally and linguistically diverse backgrounds, as well as from European American backgrounds, who might not agree that it is important for their child's voice to be heard. Cultural values strongly influence who families consider to be appropriate decision makers and the extent of autonomy that might be extended to someone who is not yet an adult. That may be the case with Mr. and Mrs. Gonzalez, who are still bound to many Mexican traditions and mores.

Having Isabella participate and express her own desires about her education is a new experience for them. Mr. Gonzalez states, "We typically make the decisions for all of our children because we know what is in their best interests—we've been through the hardships. We know what the world expects and we have an obligation to guide our children in these ways."

We encourage educators to ask families about their thoughts on student input and to reach agreement on what is appropriate for a particular student's participation.

Procedural Due Process

Procedural due process is a technique whereby parents and educators may hold each other accountable for assuming that the student receives a free appropriate public education. One element of accountability involves parental consent to the initial evaluation, a reevaluation, and the student's placement into special education. Without parental consent, educators have only limited options with respect to the child's education.

To ensure that parents are adequately informed in order to give consent, IDEA requires educators to give two types of notice to parents. The first notice is a "notice of action." Educators must give parents a notice before they take any action to change or refuse to change a student's identification (his or her classification as having a disability), evaluation, placement, or provision of a free appropriate public education (20 U.S.C. § 1415(b)(3)). The notice of action must (a) describe what the educators propose or refuse to do, (b) explain why they propose or refuse to take a certain action, (c) describe the parents' right to protest what the educators want to do and where they may obtain a copy of their rights, (d) describe the sources from

which parents may obtain information with regard to understanding the notice and their rights, (e) explain the options that the educators considered but rejected and why they rejected other options for educating the student, and (f) describe other factors relevant to their decision.

The second notice is a "rights notice"—basically, a notice regarding the parents' and student's rights to due process and procedural safeguards (20 U.S.C. § 1415(d)(1)). This notice must inform parents of their rights to (a) an independent nondiscriminatory evaluation; (b) prior written notice (the "notice of action"); (c) parental consent; (d) access to the student's records; (e) opportunities, timelines, and processes for filing a complaint; (f) where the child will receive an education during any ongoing hearings on the educators' plans for the child; (g) the parents' right to place their child in a private school program; (h) the parents' right to a full hearing to resolve any grievances; and (f) the parents' right to appeal an adverse judgment at the hearing, to take other legal action, and to recover the fees that they paid to their lawyers.

Both notices must be written in language that the general public can understand and must be provided in the parent's native language (if not English). If the parents do not speak English, the educators must take steps to ensure that the notice is translated into the parents' native language, the parents understand the content of the notice, and there is written evidence that the requirements related to language and understanding have been met.

It is best for Isabella's teachers to be sure to provide her parents with a notice in both English and Spanish; Mr. Gonzalez does well with English, but Mrs. Gonzalez does not.

What if parents are dissatisfied with the educational services that educators are providing their child? They have several options. They may file a complaint with the state education agency; they may file a complaint with the U.S. Department of Education, Office of Civil Rights; or they may file a request for a due process hearing (a mini-trial to determine whether the educators are acting consistently with IDEA and providing a free appropriate public education to the student).

IDEA states that any party may present a complaint. If the parents choose to exercise their due process hearing rights, they (or the attorney representing them) must notify their child's local education agency and state education agency, and include in the notice

(a) their child's name and residence, and the name of the school that their child attends; (b) a description of the nature of the problem with their child and the facts related to that problem (i.e., the action that the LEA proposes to take); and (c) a resolution of the problem (20 U.S.C. 1415(b)(7)(A)).

State education agencies are required to develop a model form to assist parents in filing complaints. If parents are represented by a lawyer, the lawyer must give this notice or face the possibility that his or her fees will be reduced (if he or she is entitled to recover the fees from the LEA). A parent may not bring a complaint or sue an LEA for an alleged violation that occurred two years before the time the parent files the complaint (20 U.S.C. Sec. 1415(b)(6)(B)). The two-year rule is known as a *statute of limitations* and requires a parent to act promptly so that the facts about the complaint will be "fresh" and the remedy, if any, will address the present needs of the child. The due process hearing is like a civil trial, with both the parents and the LEA having the right to be represented by lawyers and to produce evidence. The losing party may appeal to a state-level hearing officer and then to the courts. If the parents prevail (win), they may recover the fees that they paid to their lawyers.

Unfortunately, research indicates that many parents are dissatisfied with some aspect of their child's educational program. In a national, random sample survey of parents of students with disabilities, 31% of the parents of students with severe disabilities reported that they had considered suing the school or had threatened to sue because of their disappointment in the quality of the services provided to their child (Johnson, Duffett, Farkas, & Wilson, 2002). More than twice as many parents of students with severe disabilities indicated their consideration of suing than did parents of students with mild disabilities. These data should be of concern to every teacher of students with severe disabilities.

If one-third of parents are dissatisfied to the point of considering suing, it is essential that we learn more from parents about their preferences concerning educational partnerships. As you complete this chapter, you will learn about the family systems approach, which is a way that you can begin to understand the individual strengths and needs of families as a basis for forming the most effective partnership possible. It is a far better investment of time and energy to focus on building effective partnerships instead of spending time involved in a lawsuit.

Summary of the Six Principles

Through each of its six principles, IDEA strengthens parents' rights. Five principles (zero reject, nondiscriminatory evaluation, appropriate education, least restrictive environment, and parent and student participation in shared decision making) establish a framework within which parents acquire rights in order to affect their children's education; the due process principle establishes a mechanism by which parents can hold the LEA accountable for complying with IDEA.

Assisting Families in Becoming Educational Advocates

One way that educators can assist families in becoming educational advocates is to ensure that families are equal partners in making decisions with regard to their children's education. To make informed decisions, families need to have up-to-date information about their child's disability, special education policy, and evidenced-based practices. There are several resources that educators can share with families, many of which educators will also find helpful in increasing their own understanding of educational policy and practices.

Parent Training and Resource Centers

An extensive national resource network exists for parents called the Parent Training and Information Centers (PTIs). Currently, there are 71 PTIs funded by the U.S. Department of Special Education, Office of Special Education and Rehabilitative Services. Each state has at least one PTI, and some states have two or more. Each PTI must have a private, nonprofit status. Typically, PTIs are directed by parents of children with disabilities, and under IDEA, the majority of the staff must be parents. PTIs vary in their specific activities, although they all share the same primary purpose of preparing parents to be effective advocates in educational decision making. They provide a broad range of workshops, conferences, other training opportunities, and even one-to-one assistance to families. Many PTIs have IDEA information in languages other than English and have staff who are from diverse cultural and linguistic groups. Teachers should refer families of students in their classrooms to their respective state PTIs.

In addition to PTIs, Community Parent Resource Centers (CPRCs) are useful resources for traditionally underserved families. Whereas PTIs typically have statewide mandates, CPRCs are located in communities and are characterized by cultural and linguistic diversity.

CPRCs focus on parents with low incomes, parents of children who are English-language learners, parents who live in "empowerment zones" (federally designated urban areas that are eligible for additional federal assistance), and parents who have disabilities. CPRCs offer intensive, culturally relevant support to families. Currently, the U.S. Department of Education funds 32 CPRCs. Both PTIs and CPRCs can be valuable resources to educators and to the families that they serve.

There is a national technical assistance program for the PTIs and CPRCs that is a part of the Minnesota PTI; this program is known as PACER (Parent Advocacy Coalition for Educational Rights) Center. This national network—the Technical Assistance Alliance for Parent Centers—provides information and ongoing staff development, technology access, and a range of other informational resources for the national PTI and CPRC networks. On the Web site of the Technical Assistance Alliance for Parent Centers (http://www.taalliance.org), you can find many helpful resources, including a list of the names, addresses, and contact information for all of the PTIs and CPRCs by state (http://www.taalliance.org/ptidirectory/pclist.asp).

Educators should ensure that parents are aware of these resources and encourage parents to contact their state PTI, as well as the Alliance, to learn about training opportunities and obtain printed information developed specifically for families. For example, the PATH program in Texas is the PTI that would serve the Campbell family. There are only two CPRCs in Texas and neither one is close to the Campbell family. In this situation, several schools might work with the closest CPRC to develop a central resource center in one of the schools to house training materials, books, videos, and contact information for other community resources (e.g., the social security office, mental health centers, employment centers, drug treatment centers, safe shelters) that might be helpful. Schools could also assist families with developing a support group to meet the needs of families who face additional challenges related to poverty or a child's specific disability (e.g., autism, Down syndrome).

Offering your school as a host site for a support group or assisting with the announcement of a support group by the local media are two examples of supporting families in this endeavor. One of the best ways that schools and professionals can advocate for families is to demonstrate that they care about the unique concerns and needs of families by inviting them to their school and making resources readily available to them.

Assisting families in becoming educational advocates also requires that educators understand how families from different cultures and backgrounds view education. This knowledge affects how educators should teach children from culturally and linguistically diverse backgrounds and how they should partner with families to develop culturally relevant educational programs. We encourage professionals to explore this next set of national resources in order to learn more about working with children and families from culturally and linguistically diverse backgrounds: (a) the National Center for Culturally Responsive Education Systems (NCCRESt), (b) the National Institute for Urban School Improvement (NIUSI), and (c) the Council for Exceptional Children's (CEC) Division on Culturally and Linguistically Diverse Exceptional Learners. Although there are many resources available from each of these organizations, we will highlight only one resource from each.

National Center for Culturally Responsive Education Systems (NCCRESt)

NCCRESt provides a brief PowerPoint presentation entitled *Complicating Inclusivity and Dis/ability: Exploring the Relationship Between Families' Social Capital and Their Expectations of the Educational System*. It is a helpful resource for thinking more critically about how social class affects how families partner with professionals within educational systems. In this presentation, Kozleski and colleagues (2008) note that more often than not, it is White families who insist that their child be in inclusive settings because they have experienced success in general education settings. Many parents of children from culturally diverse backgrounds who grew up in impoverished neighborhoods with poor school systems have not experienced success when making the same request. This resource can be accessed at http://nccrest.org/presentations/presentations_2008.html

Unlike many families whose educational experiences were rocky, Ms. Campbell is a strong advocate for her son Jamal. She bases her motives on her own troubled life of getting pregnant while still in high school, working at minimum wage, and experiencing domestic violence. As a result of these experiences, she instilled in all of her children the importance of obtaining a good education to "take care of yourself." Despite the fact that Jamal has a disability, she feels that his education is just as important as the education of her children without disabilities.

As you review the NCCRESt resource, consider how some of the families with whom you work might come to the table with negative perceptions about schools or feel unsure of how to enter the school culture. How might you help them respond in an empowered manner as Ms. Campbell has? How might you help them trust the educational services at your school?

The National Institute for Urban School Improvement Web Site

On the NIUSI Web site, educators can learn how Benito Martinez Elementary School in El Paso, Texas, which serves primarily Latino students, received exemplary academic status from the Texas state education agency, reached out to partner families to meet the needs of all of its students, and created a strong community culture. This resource can be found at http://www.urbanschools.org/publications/on_the_move.html.

Like many of the families at Benito Martinez Elementary School, the Gonzalez family still struggles with understanding English and the policies that affect the education of their daughter. One way that educators could demonstrate respect and understanding for the Gonzalez family is to ensure that translators are available for IEP meetings and parent–teacher conferences. Notes home to the Gonzalez family from the teacher could be translated easily to Spanish using any of a number of free online translators such as Google Translate. While each family may have different reasons for integrating their culture within their child's educational program, educators must take time to understand and honor a family's culture when partnering with families.

Council for Exceptional Children

Finally, the CEC has a wealth of resources for educators to keep abreast of IDEA policy, professional practices, and research. One resource that educators may find helpful is the Professional Practice Topic Center, which houses information on a range of practice areas. We invite educators to explore the practice topics on cultural and linguistic diversity found at http://www.cec.sped.org/Content/NavigationMenu/NewsIssues/TeachingLearningCenter/ProfessionalPracticeTopicsInfo/?from=tlcHome.

CEC also has a separate division for educators to partner with other professionals, parents, and researchers to stay informed about meeting the needs of students from culturally and linguistically diverse backgrounds and their families. More information about this division can be found at http://www.cec.sped.org/Content/NavigationMenu/AboutCEC/Communities/Divisions/Division_for_Culturally_and_Linguistically_Diverse_Exceptional_Learners__DDEL_.htm.

Parental Participation. Inviting parents to be a part of the school culture is an excellent way to ensure that families are informed decision makers. This may be achieved in a variety of ways. Schools can inform families about special disability workshops in the district and local community. This will help families keep abreast of the latest disability resources and practices. School administrators can extend invitations to families to be involved in formal school meetings, such as the Parent Teacher Association or school governance councils. These activities might be a welcome opportunity for some families, but they could also be a burden for families who work several jobs or long hours.

It is important to be aware of how and to what extent parents choose to be involved in their children's education and to understand other issues that may prevent their involvement. Some parents may participate in educational partnerships to implement all six IDEA principles; however, even with the resources and training available, other parents may opt for a less active role. Parents of students with disabilities are a heterogeneous group with different preferences, strengths, and needs, just as are the parents of children not identified with disabilities. The assumption that many parents want to be involved has led some professionals to assume that all parents want to be involved.

However, parental participation in the decision-making process may be detrimental to some parents and extremely helpful to others (Turnbull, Turnbull, Erwin, & Soodak, 2006). Similar to parents of children without disabilities, some parents of children with disabilities have many other critical day-to-day concerns that may prevent participation, other parents do not value or feel confident about schools, and still other parents believe that all educational decision making is the teacher's job.

Research over the past 30 years indicates that many parents have consistently participated passively in educational decision making (Able-Boone, 1993; Goldstein, Strickland, Turnbull, & Curry, 1980; Harry, Allen, & McLaughlin, 1995; Turnbull et al., 2006). However, educators should consider whether passive participation is a family's choice or whether a family has had negative school experiences in the past that make them hesitant to be partners. As we learned earlier, Ms. Campbell is an active participant in her son's education instead of being a passive participant as is typical for many families with similar educational backgrounds.

Interpreting special education policy can be challenging for both professionals and families. The National Association of State Directors of Special Education sponsors Web-based training on IDEA policy for educators and administrators (http://www.ideainfo.org). They provide extensive information that can enable professionals to continue to expand their knowledge of IDEA's requirements and the effective implementation of those requirements.

In this section, we have shared several resources for assisting parents, and assisting teachers in assisting parents, to become stronger educational advocates for their children. We also shared resources to help educators recognize and appreciate a family's culture, strengths, and needs while assisting them to become educational advocates. The next section reviews the progress that has been made in working with families within a family systems perspective.

A Family Systems Perspective

A system is defined as a "set(s) of elements standing in inter-relation among themselves and with the environment" (Bertalanffy, 1975, p. 159). Systems theory assumes that a system can be understood only as a whole. A familiar saying is that "the whole is greater than the sum of its parts." Professionals can enhance their understanding of the Campbell and Gonzalez families by understanding and applying a family systems perspective.

Systems theory has been applied to family sociology and family therapy in terms of how families interact as a whole system. Prior to the family systems approach within the field of special education, educators were concerned primarily about the education of the child within the context of the school setting (i.e., what happens between the hours of 8:00 a.m. and 3:00 p.m.). Instead, family systems theory encourages professionals to think about the child within the context of the whole family and how each family member interacts with and affects all other family members across multiple settings. When professionals understand a student's life within multiple contexts (e.g., school, home, community), multiple roles (e.g., child, sibling, grandchild, nephew), and multiple interactions (e.g., child–parent, child–grandparent, child–sibling), they can develop more meaningful educational programs.

When utilizing a family systems perspective to develop an IEP, professionals and families should con-

sider the connections between the home and school environments. Some issues that educators might introduce for team discussions are (a) Which communication skills could be taught that are applicable to both home and school settings? (b) How might behavioral goals for a school setting be shared with families to enhance appropriate behavior at home and in the community? (c) Which daily living skills are applicable to both home and school settings (e.g., toileting, hygiene, dressing, eating)? and (d) Which practical skills (e.g., following instructions, making decisions, navigating directions) can be practiced in school, home, and community settings? An excellent way for educators to begin these conversations with families is to let families know that they are interested in developing academic, behavioral, and social goals for the student that will be meaningful across multiple settings and with many different people. You might begin these conversations by asking families about their typical daily routines (e.g., mealtimes, family chores), leisure activities (e.g., shopping, children's ball games, movies), and cultural events (e.g., cultural and religious celebrations).

By having discussions about these topics, practitioners and families can develop more meaningful IEP goals that will benefit not only the student (i.e., goals for at home and at school) but also the family (i.e., increasing the child's participation in meaningful family routines). This is an important step in relationship building with families because families often lament that service providers do not understand both the joys and challenges of raising a child with a disability (Rodger, Keen, Braithwaite, & Cook, 2008). Listening to families' stories is an excellent way for educators to have a balanced view of the influence of disability on families; their partnership must not be one of sympathy, but instead it should contribute to the empowerment of families. If you are still learning about the families with whom you work, you may find it helpful to read other families' stories to gain personal perspectives about disability from the voices of families. The Beach Center on Disability Web site houses family stories and hosts a Community of Practice where families, educators, and researchers share stories, information, and support (http://www.beachcenter.org).

Raising a child with a disability can be stressful at times (Brobst, Clopton, & Hendrick, 2009; Guralnick, Hammond, Neville, & Connor, 2008); however, some research indicates that raising a child with a disability is no more stressful than the challenges of raising children in general (Lightsey & Sweeney, 2008; Lundeby & Tossebro,

2008). Educators need to understand how the child with a disability affects all family members (e.g., siblings, grandparents, aunts, uncles). The Campbell and Gonzalez families help us to understand both of these perspectives. As you recall from Jamal's opening vignette, the Dallas Cowboys are Jamal's favorite football team.

Jamal and his older brother Donnell have a tradition of eating chicken wings and drinking Root Beer floats every time they watch the Dallas Cowboys play on TV. Jamal loves his brother very much, although he has yet to speak these words; however, the bond between these two brothers is obvious. Ms. Campbell and Jamal enjoy their Saturday afternoon walks to the dog park where Jamal gets to pet every dog that lets him! The afternoon walk allows Ms. Campbell to have a much needed break from her long hours at work and to spend time with Jamal doing an activity in which he rarely displays any problem behavior.

The Gonzalez family practices Roman Catholicism. Isabella loves to attend church; it is the one place where she seems to be most happy, moving to the music and chanting along with the responsorial prayers in her own special way. Isabella is also an avid TV watcher. Her sister is only one year younger than she; both of them look forward to their Saturday mornings together when they watch their favorite cartoons.

However, neither the Campbell nor Gonzalez family is without challenges.

When Jamal's routine is disrupted, his screams and self-abusive hits are almost unbearable for all family members to witness. They all generally know how to intervene to help Jamal communicate, but sometimes it can be very stressful, particularly when these behaviors occur in public places. After the children's grandfather passed away, Jamal's behaviors intensified and sometimes nothing they try seems to calm him down.

Similarly, the Gonzalez family also faces some challenges.

They are often frightened by Isabella's seizures. They have continued to intensify as she ages despite her being on numerous medications. Both Mr. and Mrs. Gonzalez are afraid that something might happen to her when she is sleeping so they have often traded off nights to watch her sleep when she is having frequent seizures. This has left them exhausted the next day. Because of the long hours Mr. Gonzalez works, Mrs. Gonzalez is usually the one that volunteers to watch Isabella through the night. Isabella is also exhausted the next morning and rarely can participate in educational activities the day after a night of seizures. One of her doctors has recommended brain surgery to reduce the number and intensity of the seizures; another doctor suggested the placement of a vagal nerve stimulator in her upper chest to control her seizures. The thought of brain surgery on their daughter is frightening.

Both the Campbell and Gonzalez families could benefit from receiving information to assist them with some of their concerns. The Campbell family would benefit from information on behavioral support for Jamal, particularly for crisis situations that occur in public places. Challenging behavior can serve one function or many functions; additionally, problem behavior may occur in one context (e.g., home) and not in another context (e.g., school) or vice versa. Families and professionals should work together to understand the complexity of behaviors and jointly develop appropriate behavioral interventions that will benefit the child across multiple settings. (See Chapter 7 for more details on positive behavior support.) The Gonzalez family might appreciate information about obtaining on-call respite care to assist with nighttime support when Isabella's seizures are severe. Their teachers could work with school nurses and social workers to develop a list of community resources that would be helpful for not only the Campbell and Gonzalez families but also for other families of children with disabilities who attend their school. Both the Campbell and Gonzalez families have multiple needs, but their teachers would not have known about these needs unless they engaged in conversations that addressed the effect of the child with a disability within the context of the whole family. Educators must listen carefully to families when they describe their child's life within the context of their families' everyday lives. McNaughton and colleagues (2008) provide excellent suggestions to help educators hone their listening skills: (a) listen intently and utilize empathy to acknowledge parents' concerns, (b) ask open-ended questions, (c) take notes during the conversation, (d) utilize the notes to summarize parent's concerns, and (e) develop a first step to address the concern.

The application of family systems theory to special education requires educators to understand the connections between families and schools. We alluded to this earlier when we stressed the importance of educators understanding the multiple roles and contexts in which their students live and learn. The family systems approach takes into account the well-being of all family members across all domains of a family's life. It does not single out education or developmental milestones as the priority for children and youth who have disabilities. Furthermore, it recognizes the support needs of parents and siblings (such as Jamal's brother and sister), and the importance of other family members (such as Isabella's aunt and uncle).

As we continue to explore family systems theory, we ask you as educators to consider the following questions: Who is the consumer of services delivered by special education professionals and other related professionals? In the past, the student has been viewed as the sole consumer. The family systems approach identifies the entire family as the consumer of services. This approach also seeks to have a much broader view instead of education or skill development only. Figure 2–3 depicts the family systems framework that we will be discussing in the remainder of this chapter. The components of the framework and their interrelationships within the family system are as follows:

1. *Family characteristics* describe the entire family as a unit (e.g., size and form, cultural background, socioeconomic status, geographic location), the family's personal characteristics (e.g., health, coping styles), and the family's special challenges (e.g., poverty, abuse). These characteristics are the underlying input to the system that shapes the way in which the family interacts.
2. *Family interaction* is the hub of the system, the process of interaction among individual family members and subsystems. Subsystem interactions are influenced by, and in turn influence, what family members do to respond to individual and collective family needs.
3. *Family functions* are the output of the interactional system. On the basis of its characteristics (the input), the family interacts (the process) to produce responses that fulfill family affection, self-esteem, economic, daily care, socialization, recreation, and educational needs.
4. *Family life cycle* introduces the element of change into the family system. As the family moves through time, developmental and nondevelopmental changes alter the family's characteristics and needs; these, in turn, produce changes in the way that the family interacts.

FIGURE 2–3
Family Systems Framework

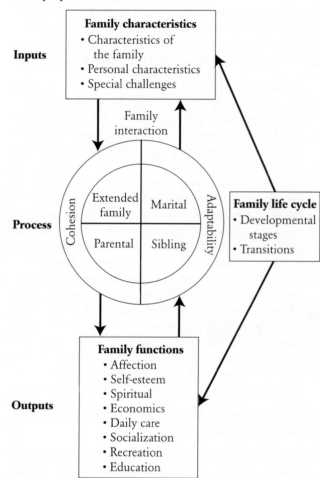

Source: Turnbull, A. P., Summers, J. A., & Brotherson, M. J. (1984). *Working with families with disabled members: A family systems approach* (p. 60). Lawrence: University of Kansas, Kansas Affiliated Facility. Adapted by permission.

The family systems framework enables educators to recognize each family's complexity and uniqueness. Each family is composed of so many attributes that it can interact in an almost endless variety of ways. A family is not a static entity; it is constantly changing and also resists change. As a result, families and educators may have different views about educational goals and how to partner in order to develop these goals.

To have only one way of interacting with families, one type of policy or program, or one idea of how families "should be" would not value the diversity that exists within families. What may be suitable for the Campbell family may not be suitable for the Gonzalez family. For example, Mrs. Gonzalez wants Isabella to live at home with her and her husband throughout her adult life, whereas Ms. Campbell has the vision that Jamal will live in his own apartment initially, possibly with his older brother Donnell, or perhaps supported by a caregiver who is also his roommate. Understanding families within a family systems context enables educators to peer into the window of a family's dreams, joys, and challenges and enables them to understand how a family's values, customs, and religious affiliation influence their decisions.

Each of these four components—characteristics, interaction, functions, and life cycle—provides a different perspective from which educators can understand the many factors that shape families lives and how these factors interact with the family member's exceptionality, the services that families receive, the professionals they encounter, and their everyday life experiences. The following sections briefly address each of the four components outlined in Figure 2–3 and highlight issues relevant to special educators. For a more comprehensive description of these elements, see Turnbull et al. (2006).

Family Characteristics

As practitioners consider the range of students they serve, they are often struck by the increasingly diverse students in their caseload and, accordingly, the diverse number of families with whom they partner to develop educational programs. This diversity greatly influences not only how professionals interact with the child in the school setting but also how professionals understand the impact that a child with a severe disability has on a family and a family's responses to meeting their child's needs. For practitioners to effectively educate their students, they need to understand and respond to various family characteristics. We focus on three types of family characteristics: (a) the characteristics of the family as a whole, (b) the personal characteristics of each family member, and (c) the characteristics of the special challenges that a family faces.

The Characteristics of the Family

Families vary in areas such as size, form (e.g., dual vs. single parents, original vs. blended family), culture, socioeconomic status, and geographic location. Obviously, although the Campbell and Gonzalez families have much in common, they also differ from each other in many ways. For example, there are many more

Gonzalez family members than Campbell family members who reside in their respective household. In this section, we focus on culture as illustrative of variations in family characteristics.

Culture provides a framework through which individuals and families form a sense of group identity (Gollnick & Chinn, 2002). It involves many considerations, including race, ethnicity, geographical location, religion, income, sexual orientation, gender, disability, and occupation. People often equate culture with race or ethnicity, but culture is a much broader concept. For example, the Campbell family is African American, and in most states large proportions of African Americans reside in poorer, inner-city neighborhoods. In contrast, the Gonzalez family is of a different race and has a different cultural heritage; the Gonzalezes are Hispanic, specifically, Mexican. However, the Gonzalez and Campbell families have limited incomes; each family lives in an inner-city neighborhood and shares the concern of increased crime and drugs where they live.

In contrast, their cultures are quite different. Ms. Campbell and her family are devout Baptists, while the Gonzalez family is Roman Catholic, attending mass in their native language of Spanish. Each has strong ties to their extended family; however, the Gonzalez family includes several members of their extended family in one household. These cultural differences can be substantial, but they are by no means bound to be so, especially when families and practitioners work together to share and understand how culture infuses their everyday lives.

To gain insight into the importance of culture, Mrs. Gonzalez describes a difference of opinion that she had with Isabella's teacher concerning an IEP goal that the teacher recommended for Isabella.

Isabella's teacher was conducting a unit on families. Part of the lesson was to learn about family member composition (e.g., mother, father, brother, sister, aunt, uncle). Isabella is taught English in school; however, Isabella's teacher did not understand the importance of teaching Isabella some Spanish words. Mrs. Gonzalez explained that in her culture young children often affectionately call their aunts and uncles tía *and* tío, *the Spanish words for aunt and uncle, respectively. Although Isabella's sister, who does not have a disability, knows English, she still does not use the English words aunt and uncle. Mrs. Gonzalez felt that the teacher's original goal, therefore, would not honor their cultural heritage and would make*

Isabella stand out instead of blend in with the other young children in their family and in their church. Because it takes Isabella a long time to learn new words, Mrs. Gonzalez thought it would be more important for her to learn the Spanish words first. In addition to honoring Isabella's cultural heritage, this would also allow the other children in Isabella's classroom to appreciate her culture.

Culture influences marriage ceremonies, religious beliefs and practices, rites of passage (e.g., a bar or bat mitzvah), holiday celebrations, holy day observations, rituals surrounding death and burial, a person's perception of his or her relationship to the world, political beliefs, attitudes toward independence and work, and, in general, parenting practices (e.g., the extent to which it is appropriate for children and youth to be self-determining). For example, self-determination is a value which suggests that people should be the primary causal agents in their life decisions and that acting autonomously is not only appropriate but also preferred (Wehmeyer, 2007). A study of cultural diversity and application of self-determination principles reveals that some families emphasize values such as family unity and permanence, interdependence, and protectiveness much more than self-determination (A. P. Turnbull & Turnbull, 1996). While this still holds true for most collectivist cultures (e.g., Asian, Latino, Native American), more recent evidence suggests that this trend may be changing. Students of different cultures are now more frequently being provided opportunities to develop self-determination skills within home and school environments (Frankland, Turnbull, Wehmeyer, & Blackmountain, 2004; Zhang & Benz, 2006).

Not all families uniformly agree with the principles of self-determination for their children; on the contrary, there is tremendous variability within cultures, as well as among cultures. Consider the child of parents who value interdependence over self-determination. How might you work with parents to develop self-determination and transition goals for students that are aligned with families' cultural values? From a European American perspective, it can be easy to assume that appropriate goals are employment, independent living, and community contribution (Hanson, 2004). The Gonzalez family, for example, sees work in Isabella's future but not living on her own in an apartment or house.

Members of the Gonzalez family say that Isabella is la joya de la familia ("the jewel of the family"). She is surrounded by family and will continue to live with family members as long as they are here to care for her. Her aunt and uncle are also her godparents and will obtain custody of her and her siblings should anything happen to both Mr. and Mrs. Gonzalez.

While you need to be aware of cultural differences, you also need to be careful not to stereotype families on the basis of this awareness. To say that all people of color, in comparison to the dominant European American culture in the United States, value family unity and permanence, interdependence, and protectiveness is contrary to the real-life experiences of many individuals in these groups. You should always strive to enhance cultural self-awareness and cultural competence so that you can, in turn, create partnerships with families that are respectful of their cultural values (Harry, Klingner, & Hart, 2005; Lynch & Hanson, 2004; Zhang & Benz, 2006), as well as respectful of their individual family characteristics.

Personal Characteristics

Personal characteristics include the aspects of a member's disability, each family member's mental and physical health status, and individual life management skills. The characteristics of a child's disability contribute to shaping the impact of the child's needs and strengths on the family system and the ability of the family system to be responsive. In contrast to Jamal, Isabella has multiple disabilities (a combination of cerebral palsy, intellectual disability, and epilepsy), but that does not mean that their families' needs, related to disability, differ. Both need knowledge about the nature and extent of disability and the likely trajectory of their child's development and future.

The characteristics of a child's disability include many factors, such as the nature of the disability, the extent or degree of the disability, the time of onset, and future prognosis. A child with medically complex needs often requires a family to make adaptations in daily routines, such as providing ongoing assistance, purchasing special equipment, and interacting frequently with medical personnel (Carnevale, Rehm, Kirk, & McKeever, 2008; Shattuck & Parish, 2008).

Specific disabilities also have their own unique challenges. Families of children with autism have frequently noted that providing additional services, particularly behavior services in the home for their child, has created a financial strain on their family (Sharpe & Baker, 2007). Children with problem behavior can place inordinate demands on family members and create stress during activities both within and outside the home (Lucyshyn et al., 2007). A child with a later onset of disability (e.g., disability caused by an accident during his or her school years) can cause major family readjustments. Stanford and Dorflinger (2009) suggest that families which suddenly experience a child's disability adjust in phases: (a) initial shock, yet relief that their child is alive; (b) confusion and anxiety during the initial rehabilitation and recovery phase; (c) mourning the loss of the child they had prior to the accident; and (d) acceptance of the disability and planning for the future.

Regardless of the particular nature of the disability, children and youth also provide a broad array of positive contributions to their families, including happiness and fulfillment, strength, personal growth, an expanded social network, career or job growth, and pride in accomplishments (Hastings, Beck, & Hill, 2005; King, Baxter, Rosenbaum, Zwaigenbaum, & Bates, 2009; Scorgie & Sobsey, 2000). Thus, for professionals to understand the impact of a child with a severe disability, they will need to understand both the child's demands on the family and the child's contributions to the family. Some people assume that a severe disability always produces greater stress on the family than a mild disability. King and colleagues (2009) report several positive findings from parents about the impact of their child with a disability on their family:

"I think he's just helped us become more rounded, more accepting, more aware ... that life out there is a challenge and different, and to appreciate the little things." (p. 57)

"We've learned [that] you celebrate the little things and I think that's the one thing other people miss out on.... [Our child] makes little steps, and so we transfer that to celebrating the little things." (p. 57)

"My dreams and my hopes are that they reach their potential, that they have all the supports to reach their potential." (p. 56)

According to Ms. Campbell, "Jamal has contributed to the family by teaching his older siblings about responsibility, compassion, and patience." Grandma Sandy particularly likes Jamal's smile, his inquisitiveness, and infectious laughter. Ms. Campbell enjoys the times when Jamal shows affection and the connection between them is obvious. Thus, while the family experiences challenges related to caring for Jamal,

they also experience joy from their relationships with him. And just as Jamal has affected his family positively, Isabella's love of music unites the Gonzalez family, particularly during church services.

Religion is very important to the Gonzalez family; to see Isabella rock her body to the beat of the music at church not only demonstrates Isabella's happiness but also brings much joy to their family. Her parents say that this is one way that they can connect with her as a family.

Professionals should be encouraged to understand the impact of disability within the context of each family's situation and in light of the family's values and perceptions.

Special Challenges

The final aspect of family characteristics is related to the special challenges that families face. Families face many challenges other than a child's exceptionality, from less extreme ones (e.g., moving to a new community, changing jobs, or having a new baby) to more extreme challenges (e.g., the death of a family member, which happened in the Campbell family). Additional extreme challenges include substance abuse, exposure to violence, having a family member who is incarcerated, having teenage parents, having parents with an intellectual disability, and living in poverty. Because so many culturally diverse families experience poverty and our nation is increasingly becoming more ethnically diverse, we highlight poverty as an important topic to be shared with professionals.

Poverty challenges many families, especially those whose children have disabilities. Families that live in poverty are more likely to be in poor health; have less access to health care services; and have babies who are born with a low birth weight, which is linked to later disability. Furthermore, ethnicity continues to be a distinguishing characteristic that determines who lives in poverty. In the 2006–2007 school year, higher percentages of African American, Hispanic, and American Indian/Alaskan Native students attended schools in areas of high poverty in comparison with White or Asian/Pacific Islander students (Planty et al., 2009).

Poverty can also have an impact on families' experiences with accessing community resources and their interactions with service providers (Silverstein, Lamberto, DePeau, & Grossman, 2008). Silverstein and colleagues (2008) set out to examine low-income parents' experiences with adversity and stress, but during their qualitative interviews they realized that many of these parents also talked about their struggles with navigating community and social service systems and interacting with professionals whose job it was to help them. Silverstein et al. reported four important themes that would be helpful for professionals in school settings to understand, namely, (a) external requirements and value systems; (b) the locus of control as the powerful driver of mood; (c) feeling judged, intrusion on privacy, and too many people involved; and (d) receiving formulaic recommendations.

We share two quotes from families in the research study by Silverstein et al. (2008) that illustrate two of these themes and ask educators to reflect on their own socioeconomic status and values as they internalize the comments that these parents share. The first parent speaks about her feeling of being overwhelmed with too many people involved in her family's life. She exclaims that there are

"[a] lot of voices telling you what to do . . . the case manager tell you to do that, and the house manager tell you to do this, then a lot of appointments, downtown appointments, and then appointment for the case manager, the house manager, and then nutrition here, nutritionist, and then the 2 more social workers here and my case manager here. Can you imagine how many people I have to deal with? It was probably 6, 7 people." (p. 1145)

Another parent commented on her concern about being judged; she states,

"As soon as we got to the door of the classroom, she would start crying. It was like, okay, we're doing this every day. I'm not sure what to do. But I can't yell at you [the child] because it's like that's not helping you. And then if I'm yelling at you as well, the teachers are going to look at it as if I'm threatening you, or I'm hitting her before she goes to school. And they used to think that. So at times I would keep her at home or at least try and talk to the teacher and at least to try and coach her . . . And after a while, it's like okay, I have to withdraw her because she's not going to stop crying until she can feel like she's comfortable." (p. 1146)

If you knew that these voices came from the parents of students who you teach now or will teach in the future, how would these situations change the ways in which you would partner with families?

Both the Campbell family and the Gonzalez family struggle to make ends meet.

Ms. Campbell only occasionally receives child support payments and is too tired to fight the system or her ex-husband to collect these dollars regularly.

The Gonzalez family is on and off of welfare benefits, depending on Mr. Gonzalez's ability to stay employed in the construction business. For the past few years, the housing market has been in a slump, forcing them to once again collect welfare benefits, including food stamps for exchange at a grocery store.

Many families indicate that receiving information about their child with a disability and about family issues is their number one need. To address families' special challenges, it would be helpful for educators to develop a community resource file by working closely with other school professionals (e.g., social worker, nurse, psychologist, music therapist) so that they are prepared to respond to families' information and resource needs. This file will also be helpful when planning for family and disability resource fairs at your school. Grant and Ray (2010) provide an excellent example of how to create a community resource file for families. They suggest that resources be arranged by topical area (e.g., physical/medical needs, parenting support) and provide enough detail so that families can determine whether the resource will be helpful. For example, the entry should include the name of the resource (e.g., Salvation Army), the contact information (e.g., address, telephone number), the purpose of the resources (e.g., to provide clothes, food, appliances), and helpful notes (e.g., the agency is willing to do school presentations but needs two weeks' notice).

Family Interaction

Family–professional partnerships typically are mother–professional relationships. But do not assume, as many do, that *mother* and *family* are synonymous terms. The members of some families are related by blood or marriage, whereas others are related by preference (e.g., a close family friend who is regarded as a family member). The family is a unit of interaction. Each family member is affected by the child's disability, and the child is affected by each family member. The goal of educators should be to form a partnership with multiple family members who have an interest in supporting the child's education, including mother, father, siblings, and extended family members.

You should keep in mind that any interaction with the child or other member ripples throughout the entire family. A home visit can be a very positive experience, or it can create family stress because of the perception of having one's privacy violated or because of the need to alter the schedule of activities or responsibilities. Scheduling a parent conference to discuss the child's progress can create an argument between two working parents about which one will take time off from employment. The behavior of the child with a disability may cause siblings to be embarrassed by their brother or sister in the presence of their friends.

Working on a child's social skills can enhance a sibling relationship, particularly if the siblings are close in age and attend the same school. This will help to reduce any embarrassment that siblings may feel about their brother or sister with a disability. Requesting that parents follow through on instructional programs at home can strengthen their relationship with their child but may also create major tension.

> *Just how much time does Ms. Campbell have for being a "follow-through" educator for Jamal, given that she is a single mother also raising his two older siblings?*
>
> *How much time do Mr. and Mrs. Gonzalez have for raising Isabella, given that Mr. Gonzalez works long hours in construction and is physically tired at the end of the day? As a result, Mrs. Gonzalez maintains the home, cuts the lawn, and has even learned to do minor repairs in the home. Each works long hours to make ends meet.*

What support does either family have to be highly involved parents, assuming that the family wants to perform that role? The tensions between parent and child can then spill over into a marriage; sibling interactions; and interactions with extended family, neighbors, bosses, and coworkers. Interaction with any member of the system has implications for all members. From the perspective of family interaction, two major concepts are critical: (a) family subsystems and (b) family cohesion and flexibility in order to maintain balance.

Family Subsystems (4)

The family systems framework highlights four major subsystems within traditional nuclear families:

1. Marital subsystem—marital partner interactions
2. Parental subsystem—parent and child interactions
3. Sibling subsystem—child and child interactions
4. Extended family subsystem—entire family or individual member interactions with relatives, friends, neighbors, and professionals

Variations in subsystems exist in many families, such as single parents, stepparents, families with one child or many children, families with extensive extrafamilial subsystems (such as the Gonzalez family), and families that consist of people who are not related by blood or marriage to each other but who perform the same roles as people who are related by blood and marriage. We will highlight information on marital and sibling subsystems.

Marital Subsystem

There is a common assumption that children with disabilities—particularly severe disabilities—place their parents at greater risk for serious marital problems. Risdal and Singer (2004) conducted a metasynthesis of 13 studies on marital adjustment in the families of children with and without disabilities. These researchers found a small effect size, indicating that families of children with disabilities experienced a small negative impact on marital adjustment in comparison to families of children without disabilities. These authors suggest that this is a positive finding given that the literature has tended to report that "children with disabilities cause severe family strain in almost all families" (Risdal & Singer, 2004, p. 101).

Raising a child with a disability can be stressful, although it does not necessarily imply that serious marital problems will occur (Brobst, Clopton, & Hendrick, 2009; Urbano & Hodapp, 2007). While Brobost and colleagues (2009) found that parents who have children with autism experience more parental stress and a higher intensity of behavior problems than parents of children who do not have developmental disorders, they also found that respect for one's spouse was the most significant predictor of relationship satisfaction for both couples of children with and without disabilities, over and above variables such as parental stress or the level of the child's disability. This finding demonstrates that one of the values associated with strong marriages—having respect for one's spouse—stood out as the most salient predictor regardless of whether the couple had a child with a disability or not. Given that most marital research on couples who have children with disabilities tends to examine the negative aspects of marriages such as parental stress or marital dissatisfaction, this study is important because it provides insight into the positive factors that affect marital satisfaction, not just factors related to the child with a disability.

However, when marital problems do occur, both the type of disability and time may be factors that affect the marital subsystem. Urbano and Hodapp (2007) found that families of children with Down syndrome were less likely to divorce than families of children with other disabilities or no disability. Still, of the families that did divorce, more than 30% of the divorces occurred in the first two years of the child's life for families of children with Down syndrome in comparison with only 17% of families of children without disabilities. What we do know is that a strong marriage makes a big difference in the family's overall quality of life. At the same time, it is also important to remember that many single parents also experience strong family well-being (Turnbull et al., 2006). Ms. Campbell has one of those families, as evidenced by her close ties to her own mother and her siblings, particularly her brother, who is a father figure for her children.

Research is resulting in better ways to reduce parental stress in families who have children with disabilities (Guralnick, Hammond, Neville, & Connor, 2008; Paczkowski & Baker, 2008). Guralnick and colleagues (2008) found that one of the strongest predictors of both child-related stress and parent-related stress was the level of parenting support received. For both of these outcome variables, lower levels of parenting support received at Time 1 (average age of the child was five years old) was associated with higher levels of child and parent stress at Time 2 (two years later). In this study, parenting support was defined as "amount of and satisfaction with support specific to advice about problems with their child with developmental delay" (p. 1143). Paczkowski and Baker (2008) found that mothers' positive beliefs about the family situation were associated with lower parental stress and mothers' positive beliefs were also a mediator between child behavior and parental stress for families of children with developmental delay who were under three years of age.

Each of these studies provides insight into how practitioners might partner with families to provide support. Providing parental support by sharing information and resources, such as helping the Campbell family implement positive behavioral support in community settings, is one way to let families know that you care about their well-being outside of the classroom. Even a short note to the parent to share positive news

about the child may be just the thing that a parent needs to hear after a long day at work.

Mrs. Gonzalez says, "Knowing that my little Isabella is happy at school eases my mind at home; I worry, you know, that no one will like her and she will be so sad. Just reading in her communication book that she smiled a lot at lunchtime makes my day!"

Professionals can also support families' marital well-being by listening and responding to parents' preferences for the support that they themselves need in caring for their son or daughter. For example, when Mrs. Gonzalez indicates that there is stress because of the long hours that her husband is working, Isabella's teacher might ask the social worker to contact the Gonzalez family occasionally to check on their need for respite care. Educators working with the Gonzalez family should be especially cognizant of the long hours that Mr. Gonzalez works by scheduling meetings at times when both parents can attend.

Finally, professionals should be respectful of alternative family lifestyles. Parents of children with severe disabilities, similar to those of children without disabilities, may be in same-sex relationships. Same-sex relationships may occur in families in which parents have been in heterosexual relationships, had children, and then have taken those children into same-sex partnerships, legal unions, or marriages. Some children in same-sex marriage are adopted or are born through in vitro fertilization. Although we have not been able to find research that specifically addresses children and youth with severe disabilities in these relationships, reviews of literature on the well-being of children who grow up with same-sex parents consistently show that children develop positively in terms of psychological, intellectual, behavioral, and emotional development (Fitzgerald, 1999; Tasker, 1999). There are many steps that you can take to welcome children from these families into schools and to welcome their parents as well. Some suggestions from Lamme and Lamme (2002) include the following:

- Provide electronic and library resources on diverse families, including same-sex parents.
- Promote a respectful school environment, and ensure that harassment related to homophobic issues is not acceptable within the school culture.
- Just as you might sponsor African American, Hispanic, or women's history month, also consider celebrating Gay Pride Week.

Sibling Subsystem

Some studies about siblings have found that brothers and sisters of siblings with disabilities have a higher incidence of emotional problems, lower self-esteem, and greater responsibility for household chores (Fisman, Wolf, Ellison, & Freeman, 2000). Other studies have found that the opposite is true (Cuskelly & Gunn, 2003; Hannah & Midlarsky, 1999). The values that Ms. Campbell wants to pass on to her children include acceptance of differences and compassion for others. She is happy that Donnell and Shelia are learning these values through interactions with Jamal. Ms. Campbell speaks of the unconditional acceptance that Jamal's siblings show Jamal, saying,

> It's just normal to them. This is who he is. I have always appreciated that in them. . . . They like to go in his room and watch movies—but they watch them with him, they don't ignore him. They all eat popcorn together. During football games, Jamal's brother, Donnell, will roughhouse with the NERF football; Jamal just breaks out in uncontrollable laughter. I think that's what I like the most—seeing them do things that typical siblings do.

For Isabella's family, however, there is not only her younger sister but also her cousin, aunt, and uncle who live in the household with them. While this is temporary for now, until her uncle can find a job, they still function as one big family. In Isabella's eyes, it is as if she has two siblings.

A national resource for siblings is a program called Sibshops, which has the goal of providing information and emotional support for brothers and sisters. You can learn more about this program on their Web site (http://www.siblingsupport.org), as well as help parents locate a Sibshop near them. If your community does not sponsor Sibshops, you might consider collaborating with families, educators, adults with disabilities, and other community citizens to start a Sibshop program.

Meyer and Vadasay (2007) have recently revised their very popular workbook on establishing a Sibshop in order to guide you through the steps for developing this program in your community. An evaluation of the Sibshop program with school-age siblings found that siblings were able to talk more about the positive and negative aspects of having a brother or sister with a disability and they were able to identify more specifically how their sibling's disability affected their life in four areas: school, home, play, and the future (D'Arcy,

Flynn, McCarthy, O'Connor, & Tierney, 2005). In addition to the beneficial outcomes of participating in sibling programs (Conway & Meyer, 2008), research also suggests that there are many positive benefits to having a sibling with a disability, such as increased empathy, patience, social justice, and acceptance of differences (Dykens, 2005; Stoneman, 2005).

An especially helpful way to become sensitive to sibling issues is to listen to sibling perspectives. We share a perspective from a sibling whose younger brother has multiple disabilities and significant health concerns (see Figure 2–4). This sibling indicates not only the meaning that her brother gives to her life but also, as others have noted, her own personal growth of increased empathy and acceptance of differences. Siblings can be invited to IEP conferences or to discussions with teachers or related service providers outside of the IEP conference. Another possibility for gaining information is to read the perspectives of siblings that are often provided in the newsletters of family organizations and in a book featuring the perspectives of 45 siblings ranging in age from 4 to 18 (Meyer, 1997). Sometimes, siblings may get frustrated when their schedule is affected by the support needs of their sibling with a disability. For example, Jessica,

FIGURE 2–4
Sibling Perspective

My little brother's nickname is "Happy Boy" because he always smiles and laughs, even in his sleep! He always makes me happy because his smiles and laughs are so contagious. If it wasn't for him I would never understand people with special needs. He is the best brother I could ever have, and I love him more than anything in the whole wide world!

nine years old, has an older brother with autism. She comments,

"In some ways, my life is different from kids who have a normal brother, because most of my schedule revolves around Danny. Sometimes I can't go to special activities because my mother has no one to watch Danny and can't take me. I think parents, teachers, and doctors should have more understanding for siblings, because they go through difficult experiences with their brothers or sisters." (Meyer, 1997, p. 27)

Establishing Balance: Cohesion and Flexibility

Family therapists have identified two dimensions in establishing balance in family relationships: cohesion and flexibility. Cohesion is the emotional bonding that family members have toward one another (Olson & Gorall, 2006). Green (2007) highlighted one mother's experiences of the impact that their child with a disability had on the closeness of her relationship with her spouse.

"One of the changes I've seen in (my husband) is he is more helpful to me . . . with my children than ever before . . . we share roles and it's great and . . . I don't know that it would have happened if there hadn't been the problem with (our son) . . . I think my husband and my relationship is probably grounded a lot deeper than it was before . . ." (p. 159)

Researchers propose that balanced families (i.e., high cohesion and high flexibility) will experience greater satisfaction with their family system than unbalanced families (i.e., low cohesion and low flexibility) (Olson, Gorall, & Tiesel, 2007). Lightsey and Sweeney (2008) provide additional insight into the importance of family cohesion and its relationship to family satisfaction. In their research, they found that not only did family cohesion directly predict family satisfaction, but it also significantly altered the original relationship between family stress and family satisfaction. In both of these studies, we learn that when families experience strong cohesion, stress is no longer a strong predictor of family satisfaction. Family cohesion mediates this relationship, acting like a buffer between the two.

So what can educators do to enhance family cohesion? One way that families can experience greater cohesion is to understand the value of each family member's contributions to the family's well-being and the importance of that person's insights in the family decision-making process. Educators could ask families to describe how certain programs would affect their family well-being and routines (e.g., positive behavior support, respite, music therapy, circle of friends). Educators could also enhance family cohesion by ensuring that all family members (e.g., Isabella's aunt, uncle, and cousin) are active participants in the decision-making process.

Because Isabella's aunt and uncle are also her godparents and would be responsible for her care if anything should happen to Mr. and Mrs. Gonzalez, including them in long-term planning, such as through a MAPs process (see Chapter 3), would be appropriate. Ensuring that all family members have a voice could also be accomplished by inviting siblings to IEP meetings or by connecting a parent by phone to meetings if the parent cannot attend in person.

Mothers, in particular, may feel greater family cohesion when they are supported in the everyday routines of raising their children. It is easy to feel overwhelmed if one parent is staying up all night with the child with a disability (the Gonzalez family) or if the same family member always has to deal with a child's challenging behavior (Jamal's siblings). School counselors and social workers may be helpful by suggesting fun ways that all family members can support each other by embedding simple interventions within the everyday routines of a family's life (Pretti-Frontczak, Barr, Macy, & Carter, 2003).

We urge you to help families experience a balanced life instead of one that is singularly focused on the child with the disability. You can do this by connecting them with community resources, referring them to professionals to address immediate concerns, and helping their child build a social support network. In order for families to have highly cohesive lives, they need to learn to not only rely on each other but also to reach out for supports to maintain balance in their lives. If you recall Ms. Campbell's comments in Jamal's opening vignette, she indicated that her body and mind are tired; she is unsure of how much longer she will be able to keep up her level of advocacy to ensure that Jamal continues to receive appropriate services. It is easy to see that Ms. Campbell has been a "one-woman show," ensuring that things get done on the home front, while juggling her job and partnering with the school to achieve the outcomes for Jamal that she values.

Although she has support from her extended family, she still feels guilty about asking for assistance because

she knows that everyone has his or her own life, too. When Ms. Campbell lost her dad, she kept a lot of her emotions in check so that she could support her mother. After all, her mother was also grieving from the loss of her husband, and Ms. Campbell did not want to burden her mother with additional stress.

How might educators support Ms. Campbell and her family during such a difficult time? A teacher might work with the school counselor to locate resources and books not only for Jamal but also for his siblings to help them cope with the death of a close family member. Another resource could be the use of virtual peer support groups on the World Wide Web, where the older siblings could talk with other peers who are coping with the death of a family member. Finally, the social worker might spend extra time with Jamal at school to help him use his communication board to express his feelings about the death of his grandfather and to develop a story about appropriate ways for dealing with his feelings.

Family flexibility is defined as "the quality and expression of leadership and organization, role relationship rules and negotiations" (Olson, Gorall, & Tiesel, 2007, p. 2). Many families establish interaction patterns. For example, a mother may assume responsibility for bathing, dressing, feeding, and toileting a child with severe physical disabilities. This pattern may become so ingrained that she is unable to leave town for a vacation or a visit with extended family or even to have a break from these duties. If the mother is ill or an emergency arises, a family crisis related to parents' roles is likely to occur. One way to help families achieve successful interactions is to encourage them to develop an array of alternatives and options consistent with their cultural values. For families who believe that it is too much trouble to teach others how to care for their children, you might be able to persuade people who are willing to provide caregiving to come to your classroom for tips from you on how they might best provide support. This would prevent parents from having to provide this orientation for those who might be able to help them.

Family Functions

Families exist to serve the individual and collective needs of their members. Attending to family functions is one way to characterize how families serve their needs. Family functions can be characterized in many ways. Figure 2–5 highlights these functions and some of the tasks performed by family members to meet them.

FIGURE 2–5
Family Functions and Tasks

1. *Affection:* Developing intimate personal relationships, expressing sexuality, giving and receiving nurturance and love, and expressing emotions
2. *Self-esteem:* Establishing self-identity and self-image, identifying personal strengths and weaknesses, and enhancing belonging and acceptance
3. *Economic support:* Generating income and handling family finances, paying bills, earning allowances, and handling insurance matters
4. *Daily care:* Purchasing food, preparing meals, providing health care, maintaining the home, providing transportation, and taking general safety measures
5. *Socialization:* Fostering individual and collective friendships, developing social skills, and engaging in social activities
6. *Recreation:* Developing and participating in hobbies or clubs, setting aside everyday demands, and going on vacations
7. *Education:* Participating in school-related activities, continuing education for adults, doing homework, providing for career development, and developing a work ethic

Family functions are not independent of one another. One function may facilitate another function, such as when a family member's participation in recreational activities leads to increased socialization and increased self-esteem from mastering a new hobby. On the other hand, one function may impede progress in another function area. For example, economic hardship may affect a family's ability to meet routine care needs (e.g., nutrition, transportation, health care), in turn impinging on a parent's or child's self-esteem.

A son or daughter with a disability can affect a family in negative, neutral, and positive ways. In the next two sections, we highlight the effects on the economic and socialization functions of families. For a thorough discussion of all family functions, see Turnbull et al. (2006).

Economic Needs

All families must have income and a way to spend the money earned to meet food, clothing, shelter, and other needs. The presence of a son or daughter with a severe disability can create excess expenses (Shattuck & Parish, 2008). Some of the devices and services for a child with a severe disability may include adaptive feeding utensils; special clothing; lift-equipped vans; bathroom adaptations, such as support and safety bars; ongoing medications required for seizures and other physiological needs; body braces; voice synthesizers; hearing aids; adaptive seating equipment; ongoing evaluations by specialists; specially adapted furniture; hospital beds; respirators; suctioning equipment; adaptive exercise equipment; remote control devices for televisions, radios, and lights; positioning equipment, such as prone standers; adaptive toys; and adaptive mobility devices, such as walkers and crutches. Many devices require ongoing servicing and periodic replacement. Even families fortunate enough to have the best health insurance coverage find that the cost of buying and maintaining many adaptive devices and medical services is not fully covered. Mrs. Gonzalez comments,

Isabella is a very active girl; she enjoys participating in many outdoor activities and P.E. class with her peers. Isabella will be nine years old soon, and we feel that she would be a good candidate for a power wheelchair; however, our insurance company will only pay for a manual chair. Even with multiple requests and notes from her doctor, our insurance company refuses to pay for a power chair at her age. We desperately want her to keep up with her friends at school and a power chair would give her more independence. We know that she has the determination to learn to use a power chair, but we struggle to pay our bills some months, and purchasing a power chair is only an option for rich people.

The economic impact on families varies with the nature and extent of the child's disability and, of course, with the family's own resources. (Predictably, the Gonzalez household's financial resources are meager.). When the housing market is good, the Gonzalez family feels secure; however, these past few years have been quite difficult. The costs associated with providing for the needs of one family member can limit the funds available for the other family members. Parents and other family members may forgo attending to their own needs in order to afford services for the child with a severe disability. Family members may become resentful, particularly siblings who might not understand the financial responsibilities of maintaining a household. Parents may know that a child could benefit from the purchase of a special piece of equipment and not be able to afford it, like the power wheelchair for Isabella.

The presence of a family member with a disability may prevent parents from obtaining employment because of the level of care and supervision required.

This was the case for Mrs. Gonzalez. She found that she was unable to work outside of the home after Isabella was born. She explained, "I have found it literally impossible to work. Isabella has had several surgeries related to her contractions due to her severe cerebral palsy. You can't say [to an employer], 'I'd like to work, but I need Tuesday afternoons and every other Friday off,' so Isabella and I spent all the time going to doctors and therapy and I just have never gone back to work ... We still haven't found it possible for me to do that."

In 2007, it was estimated that more than 37 million families live in poverty, which represents about 12% of the U.S. population (U.S. Census Bureau, 2008). It is helpful for educational teams to be knowledgeable about community resources in order to help families ease their financial burden and to improve their quality of life. The largest source of support for families is currently Title XIX of the Social Security Act, Home and Community-Based Services (HCBS) (Braddock, Hemp, & Rizzolo, 2008). First authorized in 1981, the HCBS waiver was increasingly available to families who have children with disabilities under the age of 18 and also available to adults with disabilities living in community settings (Braddock et al., 2008). HCBS funding enables families to exercise control over how HCBS funds are spent. Studies consistently report high levels of satisfaction on the part of families and an increase in quality of life (Heller, Factor, Hsieh, & Hahn, 1998; Melda, Agosta, & Smith, 1995).

Braddock et al. (2008) have provided an ongoing national profile of family support funding for the past two decades. Although there has been a continuous expansion of family support initiatives since the 1980s, only 5% of the national budget for developmental disability services is devoted to family programs. However, on a positive note, the reimbursement for family support services through the Medicaid HCBS waiver increased from 62% in FY 2004 to 70% in FY 2006; furthermore, 15 states financed 90% of their family support services through the Medicaid HCBS waiver (Braddock et al., 2008). Eleven states paid for family support services through state funding sources. Understanding how to help families access HCBS funding to pay for items such as respite care, personal attendants, therapies, and adaptive medical equipment can help to alleviate some of the financial burdens associated with raising a child with a disability. Both the Gonzalez and Campbell families would benefit from respite services through Medicaid HCBS, and Isabella might be able to obtain a power wheelchair.

One of the most exciting economic developments for families is the current effort by the federal government's Centers for Medicare and Medicaid Services to provide participant-directed funding (Braddock et al., 2008; Parish, Pomeranz-Essley, & Braddock, 2003; Weiner, Tilly, & Alecxih, 2002). Now being implemented in approximately half of the states for adults, this approach puts far more control into the hands of individuals with disabilities and their trusted allies for using funds to pursue community inclusion, productivity, and independence. Despite many issues that remain to be resolved, including the flow, accountability, and outcomes of participant direction, research has documented substantial positive outcomes for families when they experience control of funding (Caldwell, 2007; Neely-Barnes, Marcenko, & Weber, 2008).

Because states differ in how family support and participant-directed programs are administered, we encourage families and professionals to contact state PTIs (Web site addresses are included earlier in the chapter) to find out about the state family support resources available, as well as any other programs that provide financial resources to families. The local Social Security Office can provide information about eligibility criteria for receiving Supplemental Security Income (SSI) and Social Security Disability Insurance (SSDI). In many states, people who qualify for SSI are also eligible for Medicaid funds to meet medical expenses. In sum, professionals can provide financial information to families in many ways (Turnbull et al., 2006):

- Identify appropriate community contacts and provide parents with the names and telephone numbers of persons to contact regarding estate planning, disability benefits, or family subsidies.
- Provide information on financial planning and government entitlement funds, such as SSI, as part of a family resource library.
- Encourage parents who have been successful in obtaining financial resources or who have completed financial planning to provide assistance to other parents who have financial questions.
- Provide information to help families investigate scholarships and financial aid.

Socialization Needs

Often, professionals tend to focus on developing academic and behavioral goals for their students. However, parents are often disappointed that their sons and daughters with severe disabilities have limited friendships. Children with disabilities, particularly children with autism, like Jamal, have social impairments that severely affect their ability to develop meaningful friendships. Including socialization goals on students' IEPs is one way to address this need. The good news is that in the past two decades there has been an increasing number of studies that are investigating social interventions in order to guide educators toward effective teaching methods (Kroeger, Shultz, & Newsom, 2007; Matson, Matson, & Rivet, 2007; Owen-DeSchryver, Carr, Cale, & Blakely-Smith, 2008). However, for children with autism, like Jamal, systematic evaluation of social skills treatment packages is still lacking (Williams-White, Keonig, & Scahill, 2007). Nonetheless, Williams-White and colleagues (2007) share promising instructional strategies that educators can use to benefit peer relationships. These strategies address ways to (a) increase social motivation, (b) increase social initiations, (c) improve appropriate social responses, (d) reduce interfering behaviors, and (e) promote skill generalization.

The use of peer models is one way that Jamal's teachers could help Jamal increase his social initiations and social responses.

One of Jamal's teachers noticed his keen interest in football so she contacted the parents of two students in Jamal's class, who also love sports, to ask if their children could be peer models for Jamal in a more formal way. After the parents and students gave consent, Jamal's teacher contacted the social worker to devise a training program for the peers. The peers received information about autism and were provided with training to increase Jamal's social interactions in a variety of school settings (e.g., classroom, lunch, class transitions).

An excellent peer modeling program for increasing social opportunities and inclusion is called Peer Buddies (Hughes & Carter, 2006). These authors provide a step-by-step guide on how to implement a peer buddy program in your school. (See Chapter 11 for additional details on enhancing social relationships for children with disabilities.)

Webster and Carter (2007) conducted an extensive review of studies examining social relationships and friendships in children with and without developmental disabilities. While they report that this is an under-investigated topic, a few studies in their review provide excellent information that educators may find helpful when facilitating friendships between children with and without disabilities (Freeman & Kasari, 2002; Lee, Yoo, & Bak, 2003). In terms of demographic characteristics, Freeman and Kasari (2002) report that the playmates of children with Down syndrome who were similar in chronological age and gender were associated with higher levels of responsive and interactive play. Lee, Yoo, and Bak (2003) indicated that the friendships of typically developing children use more verbal interaction and visual social exchange, while friendships between typically developing peers and children with disabilities tended to have more physical interactions. In terms of factors that children without disabilities mentioned as being important in developing friendships with their peers with disabilities, Lee and colleagues (2003) report that the greatest response from children was the opportunity to spend time with a peer with a disability (33%), followed by teacher encouragement to help and understand a child with a disability (17%). Other responses included willingness to teach or help a child with a disability (11%) and closer placement to a child with a disability (11%).

However, it is imperative that educators are mindful that sometimes what can seem like friendships for children with severe disabilities are really helping relationships (e.g., peer tutoring and behavioral monitoring). Despite research indicating that peers used in helping or academic support roles are useful ways to initiate friendships, we remind educators to evaluate whether the characteristics of true friendships are also present in these relationships. Friendships typically revolve around companionship (e.g., going places together, participating in school activities, engaging in sports and activities), emotional support (e.g., tending to feelings, expressing affection and caring, enhancing self-esteem), and instrumental support (e.g., providing information, practical help, or advocacy) (A. P. Turnbull, Blue-Banning, & Pereira, 2000a). In addition to what professionals can do to directly facilitate friendships, they also can encourage parents to consider being facilitators of friendship.

Mrs. Gonzalez has made it a point to invite children from their neighborhood to their house to spend time with Isabella and to develop a friendship with her. She teaches the children a few basic Spanish words so that they may connect with Isabella from her own cultural perspective. Mrs. Gonzalez has learned to be thrifty with her money and enjoys going to garage sales to stock their home with a variety of typical children's games. She believes that it will be helpful for Isabella to learn to play these games so that she might play more easily with other children when opportunities arise.

Not all parents have the time to orchestrate friendships for their child with a disability, as Mrs. Gonzalez does. Therefore, team members should brainstorm about the many different settings and individuals who would be available to facilitate friendship development. A broad range of people can be friendship facilitators, including general and special education teachers, related service providers, paraprofessionals, family members, community citizens, and classmates (Calloway, 1999; Meyer, Park, Grenot-Scheyer, Schwartz, & Harry, 1998; A. P. Turnbull, Pereira, & Blue-Banning, 2000b). Many teachers have used the "Circle of Friends" approach with success for students with disabilities (Thousand, Villa, & Nevin, 2000). Circle of Friends is a social skills training approach used to encourage friendships between students with disabilities and their peers without disabilities.

From a family systems perspective, it is important to recognize that although you may perceive friendships to be very important, families may have other priorities. In some situations, families may believe that friendships are just as important as, or even more important than, you think they are, but the family may have no unclaimed minutes in which to take on one more responsibility.

The Family Life Cycle

Families differ in characteristics, and those differences influence interaction patterns that affect the family's ability to meet its functional needs. Each family is a unique unit that changes as it goes through the stages and transitions of the family life cycle. Two dimensions of the family life cycle that are important for educators to understand include (a) life-cycle stages and (b) life-cycle transitions.

Life-Cycle Stages

The family life cycle has been described as a series of developmental stages that are periods of time in which family functions are relatively stable (Carter & McGoldrick, 2005). Researchers and theorists disagree concerning the number of life-cycle stages that exist. Some have identified as many as 24 stages, although others have identified as few as 6 (Turnbull et al., 2006). The number is not as important as the tasks that families are responsible for accomplishing at each stage. Six stages are identified here: (a) birth and early childhood, (b) elementary school years, (c) adolescence, (d) early adulthood, (e) middle adulthood, and (f) aging. Many tasks facing the families of adolescents are different from those facing the families of preschoolers, as the Campbell family illustrates.

Now that Jamal is in middle school, he also is about to change physically and perhaps emotionally. The impending changes raise discomfiting issues. Who, for example, will teach him about the changes in his pubescent body and appropriate times for private moments? What roles are appropriate for educators with respect to his adult physical changes? In middle school, Jamal has many more teachers; luckily, he has two male teachers, history and natural science. How

might male school personnel be included in educational planning meetings? How might Jamal's uncle also be included in these discussions? Jamal has displayed inappropriate self-touching during school in the past; given that his hormones are changing, how should the family and school address these issues in a proactive manner? What concerns might his family have about his teachers, who were relative strangers the year before, assisting with sexual issues? These are sensitive issues for both the school and the family, but are life-cycle needs that must be addressed given Jamal's past inappropriate behavior in school.

Table 2–1 identifies possible parental issues encountered during the first four life-cycle stages, which are the stages in which families and educators have the most contact.

TABLE 2–1

Possible Parental Issues Encountered at Four Life-Cycle Stages

Life-Cycle Stage	Possible Parental Issues
Early childhood (ages 0–5)	Obtaining an accurate diagnosis Informing siblings and relatives Locating support services Clarifying a personal ideology to guide decisions Addressing issues of stigma Identifying positive contributions of exceptionality Participating in IFSP/IEP conferences Learning about IDEA rights and responsibilities
Elementary school (ages 6–12)	Establishing routines to carry out family functions Adjusting emotionally to implications of disability Clarifying issues of inclusive practices Participating in IEP conferences Locating community resources Arranging for extracurricular activities Establishing positive working relationships with professionals Gathering information about educational services available to the family and the child Setting great expectations about the future for their child Understanding different instructional strategies
Adolescence (ages 13–21)	Adjusting emotionally to possible chronicity of disability Identifying issues of emerging sexuality Addressing possible isolation and rejection by peers Planning for career and vocational development Arranging for leisure-time activities Dealing with physical and emotional changes of puberty Planning for postsecondary education Planning for the transition from school to adult life Addressing issues of preferred postschool outcomes
Adulthood (from age 21)	Addressing the need for preferred living situations Adjusting emotionally to adult implications for intensive support Addressing the need for socialization opportunities outside the family Initiating career choice or vocational program Adjusting to how the changes of adult life will affect family decision making

Inclusion. Although some families' tasks and issues tend to be stage specific, others permeate all stages. An example of the latter is advocating for inclusive experiences. Many families strongly favor inclusion (Leyser & Kirk, 2004; Peck, Staub, Galluci, & Schwartz, 2004; Soodak et al., 2002) and are the major advocates for their children in obtaining inclusive experiences starting during the early childhood stage and continuing throughout the life span.

> *For Ms. Campbell, inclusion is a very important issue. She continues to work hard to ensure that her son has the supports which he needs in order to be included as much as possible with his peers without disabilities.*

As inclusion advocates, families often invest tremendous energy at each stage to access experiences that enable their children to be in typical settings:

1. *Birth and early childhood:* Participating in the nursery within their religious organization, attending neighborhood and community playgroups and child care, and participating in community recreation programs designed for young children
2. *Elementary school years:* Attending neighborhood schools and being placed in general education programs, taking advantage of typical extracurricular activities such as Scouts and community recreation, and developing friendships with classmates with and without disabilities
3. *Adolescence:* Attending inclusive secondary schools, participating in extracurricular activities consistent with preferences, and enjoying friendships and dating
4. *Early adulthood:* Participating in supported employment, developing a home of one's own, and participating in community activities consistent with preferences

Families who commit themselves early to inclusion and advocate for inclusive experiences across the life span often spend a great amount of time and energy educating others, making logistical and support arrangements, and troubleshooting when special issues arise. Educators, who strongly favor inclusion, are also advocates; their advocacy takes place primarily at the school level, educating general education teachers and related service personnel about the importance of integrating specialized instruction into typical settings to ensure that their students have opportunities to access the general education curriculum.

Special educators must employ a specialized skill set across a variety of areas to successfully implement inclusive practices (Fisher, Frey, & Thousand, 2003). Fisher and colleagues provide an excellent framework to understand the roles and skill sets required of inclusive educators. The roles that special educators assume at inclusive schools require that they have knowledge across a broad array of areas such as instruction, assessment, communication, leadership, and record keeping. The specific topical areas in which specialized skill sets are required include (a) collaborative teaming and teaching, (b) curricular and instructional modifications, (c) assistive technology, (d) positive behavior support, and (e) personal supports. For an additional resource for learning more about the skill set of special educators, we recommend the CEC publication *What Every Special Educator Must Know* (Council for Exceptional Children, 2008).

Self-Determination Skills. A second pervasive issue across the life span is development of self-determination skills. Researchers in the self-determination field describe self-determination as being composed of the following four essential characteristics: self-realization, self-regulation, psychological empowerment, and autonomous actions (Wehmeyer, 2007; Wehmeyer, Abery, Mithaug, & Stancliffe, 2003). These skills help children and youth with severe disabilities to live their lives according to their own personal values and preferences. Although the major emphasis within the special education field has been on development of self-determination skills at the adolescent level (Test, Fowler, Wood, Brewer, & Eddy, 2005), it is critically important for families and educators to recognize that the foundation of self-determination starts during the birth and early childhood stage and evolves throughout the entire life span (Brotherson, Cook, Erwin, & Weigel, 2008; Erwin et al., 2009). However, some educators and families may be unsure of how to enhance their child's self-determination skills, particularly when children are young. Shogren and Turnbull (2006) provide practical strategies that professionals and families may find useful to enhance self-determination in young children with disabilities in the school and home settings. These strategies include (a) placing artwork and photos at the child's eye level, (b) setting up a private area that the child can call his or her own, (c) using routines to ensure predictability and consistency, (d) having a childproof area that allows for safe exploration so that the child can develop a sense of control over the environment, (e) allowing for age-appropriate risk taking, (f) being careful to not over-protect the child with disabilities relative to his or her siblings and peers, and (g) setting up social and environmental reinforcers for appropriate behavior (Shogren & Turnbull, 2006).

From the earliest years, families and professionals must clarify their values and priorities related to self-determination and recognize that its development is a long-term life-cycle issue (Palmer & Wehmeyer, 2002; Turnbull et al., 2006). Clarification is important now for the Campbell family and Jamal's teachers; his entry into middle school is a good time to discuss these matters, especially because Ms. Campbell is already concerned about Jamal's future after high school but is unsure of how to proceed in planning for the future. While IDEA requires transition planning to begin when Jamal is 16 years old, it is still not too early to ensure that Jamal's current curriculum and IEP goals are preparing him to lead a self-determined life after high school graduation.

Isabella's teachers may want to discuss with the Gonzalezes their culturally based expectations for Isabella's independence, given that their family functions in a more interdependent manner. Mrs. Gonzalez comments, "Isabella is a very strong-willed little girl despite her mobility issues. She often dictates with her behavior how the family should do things." Isabella's teacher might share with the Gonzalez family appropriate ways that Isabella can express her preferences and needs. Her teacher has had much success using a visual schedule and Alpha Talker™ at school.

Both of these strategies could be implemented in the home so that Isabella can appropriately act in a self-determined manner.

Life-Cycle Transitions

Transitions represent the periods of change as families move from one developmental stage to another. One way to think about life-cycle stages and transitions is that stages are similar to plateaus and that transitions resemble peaks and valleys that divide those plateaus. Because transitional times represent changes in expectations and often in service systems, they typically are the times that families identify as the most challenging (Rous, Hallam, Harbin, McCormick, & Jung, 2007; Winn & Hay, 2009; Ytterhus, Wendelborg, & Lundeby, 2008). These transitions may involve movement from the

intensive care nursery to the home and community, from early intervention to preschool, from preschool to kindergarten (La Paro, Kraft-Sayer, & Pianta, 2003), from elementary to middle school (as for Jamal Campbell), from middle school to high school, and from high school into adulthood (Bambara, Wilson, & McKenzie, 2007; Mank, 2007).

Cultural values strongly influence life-cycle issues:

In Mexican culture, la Quinceañera is the celebration of a girl's 15th birthday to mark her passage from young girl to womanhood. The celebration also takes place in conjunction with a religious ceremony in which the young girl renews her religious vows to the Catholic church (Pizarro & Vera, 2001). While this celebration is still several years away for Isabella, her mother has already mentioned the significance of this event for all young girls in her culture and says that Isabella will celebrate this life event as well.

Thus, it is critically important to understand transitions from a cultural point of view.

One example of how educators can embrace cultural life cycles is to incorporate these special events within instruction. Lychner (2008) is a music educator; he provides several examples of how to celebrate students' multicultural heritage, including important life-cycle transitions, within the context of the classroom using music as a medium. Another example is to use children's storybooks and journaling exercises. With respect to stories, numerous children's texts are available for use in the classroom to teach students about important cultural life-cycle transitions. One text, in particular, *Remembering my Roots and Living my Traditions,* is a story about two young siblings who travel to their home country, Mexico, for the summer. One dialogue between the siblings tells the story about their attendance at their cousin's Quinceañera. When Isabella is older, her teachers might also invite Mrs. Gonzalez to the classroom to share her story about her own Quinceañera celebration.

Different cultures have various kinds of rituals that they consider appropriate, such as baptism, first communion, bar or bat mitzvah, graduation, and voting. Because these rituals serve as symbols of ongoing development for the family, they help reorient family perspectives toward changes that are occurring throughout the transition. A special challenge for families who have a child with severe disabilities is that the child often does not have access to many of these rituals and therefore does not have the experience of transition. Educators can support families by encouraging and supporting the inclusion of their child in these rituals. (See Chapter 16 for a discussion of symbols of adulthood.)

Some families may believe that their children should not participate in rituals because of their disability. For example, a mother may think that her child cannot benefit by having religious confirmation experiences. Perhaps you might convene parents whose children have been confirmed and parents who fear that the experience might be unrealistic for their child. Leaders in a religious community might not encourage parents because they may never have had the experience of including a person with a severe disability. Sharing resources with religious leaders or inviting them to the IEP meeting (of course, with parental consent) to learn about classroom adaptations might be a welcomed gesture to assist with adaptations in religious classes. Educators might also learn helpful tips from the religious leaders as well.

An excellent and inspiring example of a child's inclusion in religious confirmation experiences is the film documentary, *Praying with Lior* (www.prayingwithlior.com). This film chronicles the experiences of a child with Down syndrome during his bar mitzvah. On the Web site, educators will find a schedule for nationwide showings of this film. School districts and other organizations may also purchase the video for educational purposes to teach about inclusion and family dynamics. A key point is that many parents are led to believe that normal events are unrealistic for their children with disabilities. The more you can share positive examples and foster a partnership of reliable allies to create inclusive experiences related to family rituals, the more likely it will be that the child will truly belong as part of that celebration. In addition to participation in celebrations and rituals, there are many other ways that professionals can collaborate with families in enhancing successful transitions. Table 2–2 includes ideas for how professionals can help families improve their child's transitions.

TABLE 2–2
Approaches for Professionals to Enhance Successful Transitions

Early Childhood
- Provide parents with resources and tips to assist with child separation anxiety (e.g., books parents can read to their child about the first day of school; leaving the child with others for short periods).
- Provide information about various preschools in the community to assist parents with decision making.
- Encourage participation in "Parent to Parent" programs, in which veteran parents are matched in one-to-one relationships with parents who are just beginning the transition process.
- Familiarize parents with possible school (elementary and secondary) programs, career options, or adult programs so that they have some knowledge about future opportunities.

Childhood
- Provide parents with an overview of curricular options.
- Ensure that IEP meetings provide an empowering context for family collaboration.
- Encourage participation in "Parent to Parent" matches, workshops, or family support groups to discuss transitions with others.

Adolescence
- Assist families and adolescents in identifying community leisure-time activities.
- Incorporate into the IEP skills that will be needed in future career and vocational programs.
- Visit or become familiar with a variety of career and living options.
- Develop a mentor relationship with an adult with a similar disability and with an individual who has a career that matches the student's strengths and preferences.

Adulthood
- Provide preferred information to families about guardianship, estate planning, wills, and trusts.
- Assist family members in transferring responsibilities to the individual with the exceptionality, other family members, or service providers, as appropriate.
- Assist the young adult or family members with career or vocational choices.
- Address the issues and responsibilities of marriage and family with the young adult.

Summary

Historically, family–professional partnerships have not been as positive and productive as they could have been. IDEA has established ground rules for both educational professionals and parents in their interactions with each other. Associated with each of the six major principles of the law—zero reject, nondiscriminatory evaluation, appropriate education programs, least restrictive environment, parent and student participation in shared decision making, and due process—are requirements for family–professional partnerships.

IDEA alone does not ensure collaboration among parents and professionals. Parents and educators alike must work within the guidelines to develop partnerships to meet families' individual needs and preferences. The preferred educational roles of the parents and other family members vary across families. Likewise, the level of involvement sought by different family members fluctuates.

Professionals must be encouraged to view students within the broader context of family life. A family systems perspective recognizes the true complexity of families and offers a framework for understanding the characteristics, interactions, functions, and life-cycle issues of families.

The challenge is exciting. Providing individuals who have severe disabilities with the academic, social, emotional, and vocational skills necessary to meaningfully participate in society is a complex task. It requires innovative efforts by families and professionals working toward shared goals. The possibilities are boundless, and the benefits for persons with disabilities are unlimited if all parties apply their energies and imaginations in a partnership of progress.

Suggested Activity: A Tale of Two Families

The Angelino Family

The Angelino family has five children and a sixth is on the way. The children are ages 14 (girl), 12 (boy), 10 (girl), 7 (boy), and 6 (girl). They all attend a nearby parochial school. Mr. Angelino owns a butcher shop that had been his father's and that was begun by his grandfather, who emigrated from Italy in 1904. The butcher shop at one time had upstairs living quarters for the family, but about 10 years ago the family moved into a large, Victorian-style house about a block away.

Mr. Angelino's youngest brother once came back from college with ideas about expanding the business and marketing the family's secret recipe for Italian sausage, but Mr. Angelino (the oldest son) decided against it because it would take too much time away from the family. He is fond of saying, "We ain't rich, but we got a roof over our heads, food in our bellies, and each other. What more could we want?" This youngest brother is the only one in the family with a college education, and he is also the only one who scandalized the family by marrying a non-Catholic. Mr. Angelino uses his little brother as an example of the detrimental effects of "too much education."

Both Mr. and Mrs. Angelino come from large families; most of their brothers and sisters still live in the "Little Italy" section of this large eastern city. All grandparents are dead, with the exception of Mrs. Angelino's mother (Mama). Mama lives in the home with them and is very frail. One of Mrs. Angelino's brothers or sisters is sure to stop by nearly every day, bringing children, flowers, or food, for a visit with Mama. They often take Mama for rides or to their homes for short visits, depending on her health, and help with her basic care.

Life with the Angelinos can be described as a kind of happy chaos. Kids are always running in and out of the butcher shop, where the older brothers and male cousins are often assigned small tasks in return for a piece of salami or some other treat. The old house is always full of children—siblings and cousins—from teenagers to toddlers. Children are pretty much indulged until they reach age 9 or 10, at which time they are expected to begin taking responsibility, which is divided strictly along traditional gender-role lines. Child care, cooking, and cleaning are accomplished by the women—older sisters or cousins, aunts, or mothers. Evening meals are a social event. There is nearly always at least one extended family member or friend at the table, and everyone talks about the events of the day, sometimes all at once, except when Mr. Angelino has something to say, at which point everyone stops to listen. Mr. Angelino is obviously a very affectionate father, but he expects his word to be obeyed. Bedtimes, rules about talking at the table, curfews, and other rules are strictly enforced. This situation is beginning to cause conflict with the oldest daughter, who wants to date and spend more time with her friends from school. Mrs. Angelino is often sympathetic to her children's requests, but her husband has the final say.

All in all, life in the Angelino home is warm, close, and harmonious. Mrs. Angelino, as she approaches her eighth month of pregnancy with this last "surprise" child, shares her contentment with her priest: "I don't know what I have done to deserve so many blessings from the Good Lord."

The McNeil Family

Mr. and Mrs. McNeil have been married for two years, and she is expecting their first child. Mr. McNeil is the youngest partner in a prestigious law firm in a midwestern city. Everyone considers him upwardly mobile and thinks that it is phenomenal that he achieved a partnership only three years out of law school. Mrs. McNeil has a degree in interior design. She worked full time for a while for a decorating firm in another city. After she married, Mrs. McNeil moved to this city, where she has a part-time, on-call job with an exclusive architectural firm. She has ambitions of starting her own business.

Mr. McNeil is an only child. His parents live on the East Coast. They are both successful in business—his father is a banker and his mother is a real estate broker. They have always demanded perfection from their son, and he seems to have lived up to their expectations. Mrs. McNeil has one younger sister. Her parents live on the West Coast. They are both professionals; her father is a college professor and her mother is a social worker. Mrs. McNeil's family has always been very close. She calls her parents about once a week, and the family occasionally has conference calls with the parents and the two siblings to decide some important issue or to relay some big news. Mrs. McNeil's parents place no demands on her except that she be true to herself. They often tell her how proud they are of her accomplishments.

Both sets of parents are experiencing grandparenthood for the first time with Mrs. McNeil's pregnancy. They are thrilled. It sometimes seems to the McNeils that their parents vie with each other over the gifts that they give them. The McNeils refuse the more extravagant gifts to make the point that they are indeed making it on their own, and they have discussed some strategies for disengaging themselves from so much contact with their parents.

The McNeils' avant-garde apartment is the scene of much entertaining with his law firm colleagues and her artistic friends and decorating clients. Although their social spheres overlap somewhat, each has separate groups of friends and pursues individual interests. They call this "giving each other space," and they consider it to be an important strength in their marriage. The McNeils believe strongly in supporting each other's careers and in sharing family responsibilities; they divide cooking and cleaning in a flexible manner, according to whoever has the time. They are also attending Lamaze classes together and are looking forward to sharing childbirth.

Exercise

The babies who Mrs. Angelino and Mrs. McNeil are expecting will have severe cognitive and physical disabilities.

1. Use the family systems framework to predict the preferences, strengths, and needs of both families in terms of characteristics, interaction, function, and life cycle.
2. The Angelinos and the McNeils have different cultural values. How would you characterize the cultural values of each family? How do you think these cultural values influence what they consider to be appropriate self-determination for each of the parents (mother and father), as well as for their children with and without a disability? (Assume that the McNeils will have more children, who do not have a disability.)
3. Given their views on appropriate levels of self-determination, identify two ways that you might work with each family in addressing self-determination within a culturally responsive framework.

References

Able-Boone, H. (1993). Family participation in the IFSP process: Family or professional driven. *Infant–Toddler Intervention, 3*(1), 63–71.

Bambara, L. M., Wilson, B. A., & McKenzie, M. (2007). Transition and quality of life. In S. L. Odom, R. H. Horner, M. E. Snell, & J. Blacher (Eds.), *Handbook of developmental disabilities* (pp. 371–389). New York: Guilford Press.

Bertalanffy, L. von. (1975). General system theory. In B. D. Ruben & J. Y. Kim (Eds.), *General systems theory and human communication* (pp. 6–20). Rochelle Park, NJ: Hayden.

Board of Education of the Hendrick Hudson Central School District v. Rowley, 458 U.S. 176, 102 S. Ct. 3034 (1982).

Braddock, D., Hemp, R., & Rizzolo, M. C. (2008). *The state of the states in developmental disabilities*. Washington, DC: American Association on Intellectual and Developmental Disabilities.

Brobst, J. B., Clopton, J. R., & Hendrick, S. S. (2009). Parenting children with autism spectrum disorders: The couple's relationship. *Focus on Autism and Other Developmental Disabilities, 24*(1), 38–49.

Brotherson, M. J., Cook, C. C., Erwin, E. J., & Weigel, C. J. (2008). Understanding self-determination and families of young children with disabilities in home environments. *Journal of Early Intervention, 31*(1), 22–43.

Caldwell, J. (2007). Experiences of families with relatives with intellectual and developmental disabilities in a consumer-directed support program. *Disability & Society, 22*(6), 549–562.

Calloway, C. (1999). 20 ways to . . . promote friendship in the inclusive classroom. *Intervention in School and Clinic, 34*(3), 176–177.

Carnevale, F. A., Rehm, R. S., Kirk, S., & McKeever, P. (2008). What we know (and do not know) about raising children with complex continuing care needs. *Journal of Child Health Care, 12*(1), 4–6.

Carter, E. A., & McGoldrick, M. (2005). *The expanded family life cycle: Individual, family, and social perspectives* (3rd ed.). Boston Pearson/Allyn & Bacon.

Conway, S., & Meyer, D. (2008). Developing support for siblings of young people with disabilities. *Support for Learning, 23*(3), 113–117.

Council for Exceptional Children. (2008). *What every special educator must know: Ethics, standards, & guidelines* (6th ed.). Arlington, VA: Author.

Cuskelly, M., & Gunn, P. (2003). Sibling relationships of children with Down syndrome: Perspectives of mothers, fathers, and siblings. *American Journal on Mental Retardation, 108*(4), 234–244.

D'Arcy, F., Flynn, J., McCarthy, Y., O'Connor, C., & Tierney, E. (2005). Sibshops: An evaluation of an interagency model. *Journal of Intellectual Disabilities, 9*(1), 43–57.

Dykens, E. M. (2005). Happiness, well-being, and character strengths: Outcomes for families and siblings of persons with mental retardation. *Mental Retardation, 43*(5), 360–364.

Erwin, E. J., Brotherson, M. J., Palmer, S. B., Cook, C. C., Weigel, C. J., & Summers, J. A. (2009). How to promote self-determination for young children with disabilities: Evidenced-based strategies for early childhood practitioners and families. *Young Exceptional Children, 12*(2), 27–37.

Fisher, D., Frey, N., & Thousand, J. (2003). What do special educators need to know and be prepared to do for inclusive schooling to work? *Teacher Education and Special Education, 26*(1), 42–50.

Fisman, S., Wolf, L., Ellison, D., & Freeman, T. (2000). A longitudinal study of siblings of children with chronic disabilities. *Canadian Journal of Psychiatry, 45*, 369–375.

Fitzgerald, B. (1999). Children of lesbian and gay parents: A review of the literature. *Marriage & Family Review, 29*(1), 57–75.

Frankland, H. C., Turnbull, A. P., Wehmeyer, M. L., & Blackmountain, L. (2004). An exploration of the self-determination construct and disability as it relates to the Diné (Navaho) culture. *Education and Training in Developmental Disabilities, 39*, 191–205.

Freeman, S. F. N., & Kasari, C. (2002). Characteristics and qualities of the play dates of children with Down syndrome: Emerging or true friendships. *American Journal on Mental Retardation, 107*(1), 16–31.

Goldstein, S., Strickland, B., Turnbull, A. P., & Curry, L. (1980). An observational analysis of the IEP conference. *Exceptional Children, 46*(4), 278–286.

Gollnick, D. M., & Chinn, P. C. (2002). *Multicultural education in a pluralistic society* (6th ed.). Upper Saddle River, NJ: Merrill/Pearson Education.

Grant, K. B., & Ray, J. A. (2010). *Home, school, and community collaboration: Culturally responsive family involvement.* Thousand Oaks, CA: Sage.

Green, S. E. (2007). "We're tired, not sad": Benefits and burdens of mothering a child with a disability. *Social Science & Medicine, 64*(1), 150–163.

Guralnick, M. J., Hammond, M. A., Neville, B., & Connor, R. T. (2008). The relationship between sources and functions of social support and dimensions of child- and parent-related stress. *Journal of Intellectual Disability Research, 52*(12), 1138–1154.

Hannah, M. E., & Midlarsky, E. (1999). Competence and adjustment of siblings of children with mental retardation. *American Journal on Mental Retardation, 104*(1), 22–37.

Hanson, M. J. (2004). Families with Anglo-European roots. In E. W. Lynch & M. J. Hanson (Eds.), *Developing cross-cultural competence: A guide for working with children and their families* (3rd ed.). Baltimore: Brookes.

Harry, B., Allen, N., & McLaughlin, M. (1995). Communication versus compliance: African-American parents' involvement in special education. *Exceptional Children, 61*(4), 364–377.

Harry, B., Klingner, J., & Hart, J. (2005). African American families under fire: Ethnographic views of family strengths. *Remedial and Special Education, 26*(2), 101–112.

Hastings, R. P., Beck, A., & Hill, C. (2005). Positive contributions made by children with an intellectual disability in the family: Mothers' and fathers' perceptions. *Journal of Intellectual Disabilities, 9*(2), 155–165.

Heller, T., Factor, A., Hsieh, K., & Hahn, J. E. (1998). The impact of age and transitions out of nursing homes for adults with developmental disabilities. *American Journal on Mental Retardation, 103*, 236–248.

Honig v. DOE, 484 U.S. 305 (1988).

Hughes, C., & Carter, E. W. (2006). *Success for all students: Promoting inclusion in secondary schools through peer buddy programs.* Boston: Pearson.

Hunt, P., & McDonnell, J. (2007). Inclusive education. In S. L. Odom, R. H. Horner, M. E. Snell, & J. Blacher (Eds.), *Handbook of developmental disabilities* (pp. 269–291). New York: Guildford Press.

Individuals with Disabilities Education Act Amendments of 2004, 20 U.S.C. § 1400 et seq.

Johnson, J., Duffett, A., Farkas, S., & Wilson, L. (2002). *When it's your own child: A report on special education from the families who use it.* New York: Public Agenda.

King, G., Baxter, D., Rosenbaum, P., Zwaigenbaum, L., & Bates, A. (2009). Belief systems of families of children with autism spectrum disorders or Down syndrome. *Focus on Autism and Other Developmental Disabilities, 24*(1), 50–64.

Kozleski, E. B., Engelbrecht, P., Hess, R., Swart, E., Eloff, I., Oswald, M., et al. (2008). Where differences matter: A cross-cultural analysis of family voice in special education. *The Journal of Special Education, 42*(1), 26–35.

Kroeger, K. A., Schultz, J. R., & Newsom, C. (2007). A comparison of two group-delivered social skills programs for young children with autism. *Journal of Autism and Developmental Disorders, 37*(5), 808–817.

Lamme, L. L., & Lamme, L. A. (2002). Welcoming children from gay families into our schools. *Educational Leadership, 59*, 65–69.

La Paro, K. M., Kraft-Sayre, M., & Pianta, R. C. (2003). Preschool to kindergarten transition activities: Involvement and satisfaction of families and teachers. *Journal of Research in Childhood Education, 17*(2), 147-158.

Lee, S., Yoo, S., & Bak, S. (2003). Characteristics of friendships between children with and without mild disabilities. *Education and Training in Developmental Disabilities, 38*(2), 157-166.

Leyser, Y., & Kirk, R. (2004). Evaluating inclusion: An examination of parent views and factors influencing their perspectives. *International Journal of Disability, Development and Education, 51*(3), 271-285.

Lightsey, O. R., Jr., & Sweeney, J. (2008). Meaning in life, emotion-oriented coping, generalized self-efficacy, and family cohesion as predictors of family satisfaction among mothers of children with disabilities. *The Family Journal, 16*(3), 212-221.

Lucyshyn, J. M., Albin, R. W., Horner, R. H., Mann, J. C., Mann, J. A., & Wadsworth, G. (2007). Family implementation of positive behavior support for a child with autism: Longitudinal, single-case, experimental, and descriptive replication and extension. *Journal of Positive Behavior Interventions, 9*(3), 131-150.

Lundeby, H., & Tossebro, J. (2008). Family structure in Norwegian families of children with disabilities. *Journal of Applied Research in Intellectual Disabilities, 21*(3), 246-256.

Lychner, J. A. (2008). Instrumental music experiences from Mexico: Connect with your students of Mexican heritage and provide multicultural experiences with instrumental music from Mexico. *Music Educators Journal, 94*(4), 40-45.

Lynch, E. W., & Hanson, M. J. (Eds.). (2004). *Developing cross-cultural competence: A guide for working with young children and their families*. Baltimore: Paul H. Brookes.

Mank, D. (2007). Employment. In S. L. Odom, R. H. Horner, M. E. Snell, & J. Blacher (Eds.), *Handbook of developmental disabilities* (pp. 390-409). New York: Guildford Press.

Matson, J. L., Matson, M. L., & Rivet, T. T. (2007). Social-skills treatments for children with autism spectrum disorders: An overview. *Behavior Modification, 31*(5), 682-707.

McNaughton, D., Hamlin, D., McCarthy, J., Head-Reeves, D., & Schreiner, M. (2008). Learning to listen: Teaching an active listening strategy to preservice education professionals. *Topics in Early Childhood Special Education, 27*(4), 223-231.

Melda, K., Agosta, J., & Smith, F. (1995). *Family support services in Utah: Striving to make a difference*. Salem, OR: Human Services Research Institute.

Meyer, D. (Ed.). (1997). *Views from our shoes: Growing up with a brother or sister with special needs*. Bethesda, MD: Woodbine House.

Meyer, D., & Vadasy, P. (2007). *Sibshops: Workshops for siblings of children with special needs* (Rev. ed.). Baltimore, MD: Paul H. Brooks.

Meyer, H., Park, H. S., Grenot-Scheyer, M., Schwartz, I. S., & Harry, B. (1998). *Making friends: The influences of culture and development*. Baltimore: Paul H. Brookes.

Neely-Barnes, S. L., Marcenko, M. O., & Weber, L. (2008). Community-based, consumer-directed services: Differential experiences of people with mild and severe intellectual disabilities. *Social Work Research, 32*(1), 55-64.

Olson, D. H., & Gorall, D. M. (2006). FACES IV & the Circumplex model. Retrieved May 5, 2009, from http://www.facesiv.com/pdf/3.innovations.pdf

Olson, D. H., Gorall, D. M., & Tiesel, J. W. (2007). FACES IV & the Circumplex model: Validation study. Retrieved May 5, 2009, from http://www.facesiv.com/pdf/2.development.pdf

Owen-DeSchryver, J. S., Carr, E. G., Cale, S. I., & Blakeley-Smith, A. (2008). Promoting social interactions between students with autism spectrum disorders and their peers in inclusive school settings. *Focus on Autism and Other Developmental Disabilities, 23*(1), 15-28.

Paczkowski, E., & Baker, B. L. (2008). Parenting children with developmental delays: The role of positive beliefs. *Journal of Mental Health Research in Intellectual Disabilities, 1*(3), 156-175.

Palmer, S. B., & Wehmeyer, M. L. (2002). *Self-determined learning model for early elementary students: A parent's guide*. Lawrence: Beach Center on Disability, University of Kansas.

Parish, S. L., Pomeranz-Essley, A., & Braddock, D. (2003). Family support in the United States: Financing trends and emerging initiatives. *Mental Retardation, 41*(3), 174-187.

Peck, C. A., Staub, D., Gallucci, C., & Schwartz, I. (2004). Parent perception of the impacts of inclusion on their nondisabled child. *Research and Practice for Persons with Severe Disabilities, 29*(2), 135-143.

Pizarro, M., & Vera, E. M. (2001). Chicana/o ethnic identity research: Lessons for researchers and counselors. *The Counseling Psychologist, 29*(1), 91-117.

Planty, M., Hussar, W., Snyder, T., Kena, G., KewalRamani, A., Kemp, J., et al. (2009). *The Condition of Education 2009* (NCES 2009-081). Washington, DC: National Center for Education Statistics, Institute of Education Sciences, U.S. Department of Education.

Pretti-Frontczak, K. L., Barr, D. M., Macy, M., & Carter, A. (2003). Research and resources related to activity-based intervention, embedded learning opportunities, and routines-based instruction: An annotated bibliography. *Topics in Early Childhood Special Education, 23*(1), 29-40.

Risdal, D., & Singer, G. H. S. (2004). Marital adjustment in parents of children with disabilities: A historical review and meta-analysis. *Research and Practice for Persons with Severe Disabilities, 29*(2), 95-103.

Rodger, S., Keen, D., Braithwaite, M., & Cook, S. (2008). Mothers' satisfaction with a home-based early intervention programme for children with ASD. *Journal of Applied Research in Intellectual Disabilities, 21*, 174-182.

Rous, B., Hallam, R., Harbin, G., McCormick, K., & Jung, L. A. (2007). The transition process for young children with disabilities: A conceptual framework. *Infants and Young Children, 20*(2), 135-148.

Schaffer v. Weast, 126 S. Ct. 528 (2005).

Scorgie, K., & Sobsey, D. (2000). Transformational outcomes associated with parenting children who have disabilities. *Mental Retardation, 38*(3), 195-206.

Sharpe, D. L., & Baker, D. L. (2007). Financial issues associated with having a child with autism. *Journal of Family and Economic Issues, 28*(2), 247-264.

Shattuck, P. T., & Parish, S. L. (2008). Financial burden in families of children with special health care needs: Variability among states. *Pediatrics, 122*(1), 13-18.

Shogren, K. A., & Turnbull, A. P. (2006). Promoting self-determination in young children with disabilities: The critical role of families. *Infants & Young Children, 19*(4), 338-352.

Silverstein, M., Lamberto, J., DePeau, K., & Grossman, D. C. (2008). "You get what you get": Unexpected findings about low-income parents' negative experiences with community resources. *Pediatrics, 122*(6), 1141-1148.

Soodak, L. C., Erwin, E. J., Winton, P., Brotherson, M. J., Turnbull, A. P., Hanson, M. J., et al. (2002). Implementing inclusive early childhood education: A call for professional empowerment. *Topics in Early Childhood Special Education, 22*(2), 91.

Stanford, L. D., & Dorflinger, J. M. (2009). Pediatric brain injury: Mechanisms and amelioration. In C. R. Reynolds & E. Fletcher-Jansen (Eds.), *Handbook of clinical child neuropsychology* (pp. 169-186). New York: Springer.

Stoneman, Z. (2005). Siblings of children with disabilities: Research themes. *Mental Retardation, 43*(5), 339-350.

Tasker, F. (1999). Children in lesbian-led families: A review. *Clinical Child Psychology and Psychiatry, 4*(2), 153-166.

Test, D. W., Fowler, C. H., Wood, W. M., Brewer, D. M., & Eddy, S. (2005). A conceptual framework of self-advocacy for students with disabilities. *Remedial and Special Education, 26*(1), 43-54.

Thousand, J. S., Villa, R. A., & Nevin, A. I. (2000). *Creativity and collaborative learning: The practical guide to empowering students, teachers, and families.* Baltimore: Paul H. Brookes.

Turnbull, A. P., Blue-Banning, M., & Pereira, L. (2000a). Successful friendships of Hispanic children and youth with disabilities: An exploratory study. *Mental Retardation, 38*(2), 138-155.

Turnbull, A. P., Pereira, L., & Blue-Banning, M. (2000b). Teachers as friendship facilitators. *Teaching Exceptional Children, 32*(5), 66-70.

Turnbull, H. R., Stowe, M. J., & Huerta, N. E. (2007). *Free appropriate public education: The law and children with disabilities* (7th ed.). Denver: Love Publishing Company.

Turnbull, A. P., & Turnbull, H. R. (1996). Self-determination within a culturally responsive family systems perspective: Balancing the family mobile. In L. E. Powers, G. H. S. Singer, & J. A. Sowers (Eds.), *On the road to autonomy: Promoting self-competence in children and youth with disabilities* (pp. 195-220). Baltimore: Paul H. Brookes.

Turnbull, A. P., Turnbull, H. R., Erwin, E., & Soodak, L. (2006). *Families, professionals, and exceptionality: Positive outcomes through partnerships and trust* (5th ed.). Upper Saddle River, NJ: Merrill/Pearson Education.

Urbano, R. C., & Hodapp, R. M. (2007). Divorce in families of children with Down syndrome: A population-based study. *American Journal on Mental Retardation, 112*(4), 261-274.

U.S. Census Bureau. (2008). U.S. Census Bureau News (CB 08-129). Retrieved April 20, 2009, from http://www.census.gov/Press-Release/www/releases/archives/income_wealth/012528.html

Webster, A. A., & Carter, M. (2007). Social relationships and friendships of children with developmental disabilities: Implications for inclusive settings. A systematic review. *Journal of Intellectual & Developmental Disability, 32*(3), 200-213.

Wehmeyer, M. L. (2007). *Promoting self-determination in students with developmental disabilities.* New York: Guilford Press.

Wehmeyer, M. L., Abery, B. H., Mithaug, D. E., & Stancliffe, R. J. (2003). *Theory in self-determination: Foundations for educational practice.* Springfield, IL: Charles C. Thomas Publisher.

Wehmeyer, M. L., & Field, S. L. (2007). *Self-determination: Instructional and assessment strategies.* Thousand Oaks, CA: Corwin Press.

Weiner, J. M., Tilly, J., & Alecxih, L. M. B. (2002). Home and community-based services in seven states. *Health Care Financing Review, 23*(2), 89-114.

Williams-White, S., Keonig, K., & Scahill, L. (2007). Social skills development in children with autism spectrum disorders: A review of the intervention research. *Journal of Autism and Developmental Disorders, 37*(10), 1858-1868.

Winn, S., & Hay, I. (2009). Transition from school for youths with a disability: Issues and challenges. *Disability & Society, 24*(1), 103-115.

Ytterhus, B., Wendelborg, C., & Lundeby, H. (2008). Managing turning points and transitions in childhood and parenthood—insights from families with disabled children in Norway. *Disability & Society, 23*(6), 625-636.

Zhang, D., & Benz, M. R. (2006). Enhancing self-determination of culturally diverse students with disabilities: Current status and future directions. *Focus on Exceptional Children, 38,* 1-12.

Overview to
Chapters 3, 4, 5, and 6

The next four chapters untangle the complex process of developing and delivering instructional programs for students with severe disabilities. Even after reading these chapters, it will be evident that this process is not straightforward and requires the efforts of a team. Many steps are involved in the process, starting with determining a student's eligibility for special education services, identifying his or her priority goals and objectives for an individualized education program (IEP), identifying the needed supports and teaching strategies to best teach what is on the IEP, determining how the student's progress will be evaluated, and finally putting the educational program into action and monitoring the student's learning. Each student is unique, so the process requires individualization, and the result—the educational program—is exclusive to that student. To help explain the material in these four chapters, we apply many of the concepts to three students: Marc, Jacob, and Christine. These students differ in their ages, abilities and disabilities, behavioral characteristics, and instructional goals, as well as in the supports that are needed to realize their goals.

❖ ❖ ❖ ❖ ❖   **Marc, Jacob, and Christine**   ❖ ❖ ❖ ❖ ❖

Marc, *who just turned six, has a history of problem behavior; he does not speak more than a few words, nor does he initiate greetings or play with peers. But Marc will greet people with a wave when prompted and does ask some adults to play tag. His tantrums have greatly decreased as he has learned to work within defined expectations, but he does not tolerate eating in the cafeteria and he spends much of his day in the resource room.*

Jacob *is a member of a fourth-grade class. His classmates know that he has more difficulty completing classwork than they do, but they also have seen that memory strategies, like his personal daily schedule and calendar with picture reminders, a number line, and a calculator, help him to remember.*

Christine, *like many others with severe disabilities, has spent most of her school years attending self-contained classrooms with little opportunity to interact with nondisabled peers at school. As a result, she does not have friends in school, does not take part in social activities with peers, and lacks the social skills that are characteristic of older teens.*

To make meaningful differences in the lives of students like Marc, Jacob, and Christine, their teams have to address skill development but also must think beyond this goal. We agree with Billingsley and his colleagues that teams should structure their planning and teaching to aim for three crucial student outcomes: skills, membership, and relationships in inclusive school settings (Billingsley, Gallucci, Peck, Schwartz, & Staub, 1996). The outcomes for which team members aim influence the curriculum and the methods that they use (Snell, 2007). Attending school alongside peers without disabilities creates options and opportunities that do not exist in separate special education classrooms. Inclusion also changes teachers' roles in many ways and requires dynamic teamwork (Snell & Janney, 2005). We recognize that while the number of schools practicing meaningful inclusion has increased in recent years, the majority of students with severe disabilities still experience very isolated lives apart from typical classmates, are detached from peers in community activities and at work, and are accompanied primarily by their family members or by paid companions (Brown & Michaels, 2003; Hunt &

McDonnell, 2007). It is true that these patterns of segregated association and education are currently balanced in our country by laws to prevent discrimination against persons with disabilities and to create the less restrictive educational environments. Still, the widespread prevalence of their isolation seems to be maintained both by beliefs that separation is better and by rigid traditions, such as special buildings and classrooms, programs designed for labeled groups of people, and the methods that school systems use to place students with disabilities. Another strong force, one that blocks movement toward inclusion, is the confusion that comes with inexperience and the anticipation of change. Paraphrasing Norm Kunc (1983): Don't confuse "I don't know how to do it" with "it's not a good idea." The next four chapters—and much of the entire book—are written to address this confusion and to teach readers how to meaningfully educate students with severe disabilities in inclusive school settings.

Before you get started reading chapters 3 through 6, read some more about 6-year-old Marc, 9-year-old Jacob, and 20-year-old Christine:

Marc

In April of his kindergarten year, Marc had just turned six. He is a lively boy with diagnoses of autism and developmental delay. He participates actively in many school activities at his neighborhood elementary school. While he still spends much of his time in the resource room with his special education teacher Ms. Wharton and several assistant teachers, he is now able to work with his peers on some kindergarten activities, including morning circle, some table work, recess, and physical education—about 30% of the school day. When his team meets, the kindergarten teacher Ms. Kwan provides regular updates on the literacy and math work that she is teaching and on Marc's performance in kindergarten activities. Next year, he will spend more than half of his time supported in first grade, including lunch. Marc communicates mainly through pictures symbols and sometimes with problem behavior. He has started to use single words and phrases to ask for help ("milk," "zip,"), to request favorite activities like tag and going outdoors ("go out"), to greet others, and to protest activities that he wants to stop (e.g., loud intercom announcements). He enjoys computer activities and will play alone with blocks or LEGO® for long periods of time. Marc follows a picture schedule throughout the day, which involves getting a pictured item from his schedule, matching it to the activity location in the room, completing the task, and then going back to the schedule for the next pictured item. He has learned to respond to some single schedule words on a list in place of pictures. He uses a structured work system where he completes kindergarten work, such as matching sounds to pictures and writing letters, first with one-to-one instruction, then independently

in the resource room, and finally in the kindergarten classroom. Next year, he will transition more of his work skills to the first-grade classroom.

Marc does not eat in the cafeteria yet at school, but his team is working on this now with the goal that he will be eating alongside his peers before the end of the school year. Just last week, with a picture schedule of the steps involved, he was able to go through the line, get his food, punch in his payment number (from a model), and return to his classroom to eat. Marc also has expanded his food repertoire from earlier this year and eats more of the school lunches, but does not consistently use utensils. Marc is not yet toilet trained. His team is currently gathering baseline data to assess the times that he is most likely to eliminate and will start instruction during summer school. He washes his hands using a picture schedule to prompt him, wipes instead of blows his nose, and is becoming more skilled at buttoning his clothes and pants. Because Marc's teeth are not healthy and he resists tooth brushing, his team has developed a plan with his family and the regional autism specialist, Ms. Soroka-Smith, to gradually desensitize his dislike of tooth brushing. They will use a social narrative about tooth brushing, along with a task analysis of easy to difficult steps that progress from getting used to various brushes and toothpastes away from the sink, shifting to the sink area, tolerating some teeth being brushed, and gradually increasing the amount of time that his teeth are being brushed. Marc's team members are excited about the progress that he has made during the year, and they expect that his involvement with his kindergarten and first-grade class will increase the likelihood that he will develop relationships with other children his age.

Jacob

Jacob is nine years old and is in fourth grade at his neighborhood elementary school. He qualifies for special education under the classification of intellectual disability and requires limited to extensive supports in academic areas but only limited supports in functional, daily living skills. Jacob has significant behavioral support needs, which currently are being effectively addressed through a comprehensive plan for Positive Behavioral Support (PBS). Whereas in past years Jacob had spent more than half of the school day in the resource room (either to prevent episodes of problem behavior or to interrupt them), he now spends the majority of his school day with his class. Jacob has a foundation of basic reading and math skills, which has been built through direct instruction coupled with repeated practice and practical applications. He has a good store of general knowledge and many interests (e.g., animals, vehicles, video games), which at times can be so strong that behavior problems result when his access to those interests is thwarted. His teachers (Ms. Bowers, the fourth-grade teacher, and Ms. Fuentes, the special education teacher) work closely with his occupational therapist, his speech and language pathologist, and his parents to plan and implement a supported learning program that enables Jacob to learn meaningful academic and functional skills. His PBS plan calls for numerous prevention strategies, including movement breaks scheduled into the day and the use of social narratives to prepare for upcoming activities. These strategies, along with interventions to teach self-control skills, have been effective in greatly decreasing problem behaviors such as crying and screaming, lying on the floor, and throwing or destroying materials.

Jacob is very active and curious, and has a mind of his own; it can be difficult to engage him in any task not of his own choosing for very long. The primary challenge in adapting reading, math, and content area lessons for Jacob is not finding meaningful ways for him to participate, but instead finding ways to maintain his engagement and participation for more than 10 minutes or so. A second primary challenge is his strong negative reaction (in the form of active and passive refusals) to most writing tasks. A third challenge is that Jacob does not follow classroom rules and routines unless the classroom teacher's cues to the class are supplemented with personalized verbal and visual prompts directed specifically at Jacob. He needs organizational skills and skills for participating in large groups. Jacob's peer relationships are fairly good, although he is hypersensitive to any sort of perceived slight and his classmates sometimes tire of dealing with his emotional needs. His teacher uses class meetings for peer problem solving for the entire class and addresses most of Jacob's social difficulties in this context, as well as through on-the-spot interventions to repair poor interactions.

Christine

Christine, who turned 20 last spring, is actively involved in the transition from school to adulthood. She has a winning personality and often jokes with others, but she also has clear views and preferences with regard to her daily and weekly activities, her friends, and her life. Her school day is divided between the community and the post–high school program, which is held at a nearby university.

Because she has cerebral palsy, she uses a wheelchair for much of the day and uses a variety of means to communicate: sounds; facial expressions; gestures; words; yes-or-no responses; and a computerized, portable communication device. Christine has limited vision, which, along with her cerebral palsy, means that she must often depend on others for help. It is her communication skills that enable her to have ongoing active involvement in "running her life" by making choices, indicating her preferences, expressing her feelings, and sharing her perspective with her family, friends, and the team. Her communication device, a DynaVox™, has a low-volume auditory scanning system that allows Christine to listen and then select her response with a hand-operated switch; she is learning to efficiently select the relevant category of responses from a menu of communication categories, organized with options that fit her daily life. She scans the choices and makes a selection, activating a spoken response. It has taken Christine and her team a long time to identify, refine, and use this complex system, and the system continues to grow to reflect the changes and growth in Christine's life.

Christine's IEP is geared toward her transition needs: finding a job that she likes and can be actively involved in, learning the job and its related skills (e.g., interacting with others, understanding job responsibilities, taking care of her personal needs at the work site), using community services and leisure options, and getting ready to exit school services and enter the adult services system. She also participates in the university drama club and the pep group and eats often at several campus locations. Christine is involved with Best Buddies™ (http://www.bestbuddies .org), a national organization that helps universities and other groups match typical persons with persons who have an intellectual disability for the purpose of friendship. The Best Buddies™ group at the university has been in place for several years; students engage in activities (e.g., athletic and music events, pizza and movie parties, and just hanging out) in buddy pairs and in small groups during the academic year. Her special education teacher, Ms. Rowyer, works closely with Mr. Fuller, the faculty advisor for the drama club, and also with the Best Buddies™ organizer on campus to ensure that these activities are successful for Christine.

References

Billingsley, F. F., Gallucci, C., Peck, C. A., Schwartz, I. S., & Staub, D. (1996). "But those kids can't even do math": An alternative conceptualization of outcomes for inclusive education. *The Special Education Leadership Review, 3,* 43–56.

Brown, F., & Michaels, C. A. (2003). The shaping of inclusion: Efforts in Detroit and other urban settings. In D. Fisher & N. Frey (Eds.), *Inclusive urban schools* (pp. 231–243). Baltimore: Paul H. Brookes.

Hunt, P., & McDonnell, J. (2007). Inclusive education. In S. L. Odom, R. H. Horner, M. E. Snell, & J. J. Blacher (Eds.), *Handbook on developmental disabilities* (pp. 269–291). New York: Guilford Press.

Kunc, N. (1983). Integration: Being realistic isn't realistic. *Canadian Journal for Exceptional Children, 1*(1).

Snell, M. E. (2007). Advances in instruction. In S. L. Odom, R. H. Horner, M. E. Snell, & J. Blacher (Eds.), *Handbook on developmental disabilities* (pp. 249–268). New York: Guilford Press.

Snell, M. E., & Janney, R. E. (2005). *Practices for inclusive schools: Collaborative teaming* (2nd ed.). Baltimore: Paul H. Brookes.

3

Conducting and Using Student Assessment

Fredda Brown
Donna Lehr
Martha E. Snell

The Importance of Assessment

Assessment plays a critical role in the planning, implementation, and evaluation of educational programs for all students with disabilities. Assessment is used to determine who is eligible for educational support and services, what and how students are taught, and the effectiveness of educational interventions. Because each of these components of educational programming for students is so important, and assessment outcomes influence these critical components, great care must be taken to ensure that the assessment process used is appropriate and produces meaningful and usable results.

This need for appropriate assessment has been emphasized in numerous policies affecting special education practices. The Council for Exceptional Children (CEC) (2004), in their Policy on Assessment and Accountability acknowledges the "important role that standardized and other student assessments play in documenting educational accountability, and in ensuring [that] sound educational decisions are made toward achieving the highest possible academic standards" (p. 70). The regulatory language regarding assessment and evaluation in the Individuals with Disabilities

Education Act (IDEA), the federal law governing special education practices, requires that it be "comprehensive and detailed" (Yell, 1998). It specifies that

- a variety of instruments must be used;
- no one single measure or instrument should be used to determine eligibility for services or educational programming;
- assessments must be technically sound, valid, and reliable;
- assessments must address cognitive, behavioral, physical, and developmental factors;
- assessments must be nondiscriminatory with regard to culture, race, language, or method of communication; and
- assessments must be conducted by trained assessors (20 U.S.C. §§ 1412(a)(6)(B) and 1414(b)(1)–(3)).

Additionally, the No Child Left Behind Act of 2001 (NCLB) is focused on the important role of assessment in determining the progress of schools, districts, and states in meeting the goal of having all students reach proficiency in key academic areas. NCLB specifies that all students, including those with severe disabilities, must be assessed annually in reading and math in grades 3–8 and once in high school. In science, students must be assessed once in grades 3–5, once in grades 6–9, and once in grades 10–12. NCLB emphases the importance of designing valid and reliable assessments that do not discriminate against students on the basis of culture, language, or disability (20 U.S.C. § 6311(b)(3)) and requires the development of alternative assessments that are appropriate for the population of students with severe disabilities (34 CFR 200).

There are unique challenges in meeting these requirements for students with severe disabilities. This is a small population of students, with great variability in their characteristics. Some have motor impairments, some have communication impairments, and some have social skill deficits. All have intellectual impairments—but to greatly varying degrees. Some of these students have sensory impairments that affect vision and/or hearing, and some have complex health care needs. How do we determine what students can and cannot do when they do not readily let us know what they are capable of through typical means? How do we assess this population of students so that we collect meaningful information on which to found educational decisions? We intend to answer these questions in this chapter.

Factors Related to Meaningful Assessment

Meaningful assessment in the education of students with severe disabilities is dependent on several variables. Most importantly, it depends on the understanding that assessment is a process, not a product. Additionally, it requires the careful selection of instruments and procedures that (a) are technically adequate, (b) match the belief and views of those engaged in the assessment process, (c) match the intent of the assessment, and (d) are conducted in a manner that is appropriate for individual students.

Assessment Is a Process

Meaningful assessment is not a single event; it is a process. The purpose of assessment is not to obtain a score; instead, its purpose is to derive objective data on which educational decisions can be founded. Any single test should be seen as just one part of a comprehensive process of assessment designed to learn about each student's strengths and needs. The assessment of students with severe disabilities requires an interdisciplinary

team effort at all phases of the assessment process, including selecting the assessments, conducting the assessments, interpreting the results, and determining program priorities. It is not possible to rely solely on commercially available assessments; no single commercially available assessment is capable of capturing this information for the wide range of learners with severe disabilities, as noted in both IDEA and NCLB. Thus, educational program teams must design assessment processes for each individual learner, and these processes must include a variety of instruments, from a variety of informants, that must yield relevant data. These assessment data are carefully considered by educational team members on an ongoing basis throughout each student's education.

Technically Adequate Instruments and Procedures

Standardized tests, prior to being published, typically undergo extensive research to ensure that the test itself is well constructed, that it accurately measures what it purports to measure, and that it consistently and reliably measures the same construct over time. Accuracy is determined on the basis of test validity and test reliability.

Test Validity

Test validity refers to the extent to which a test measures what it is supposed to measure. For example, imagine that the goal is to assess a student's ability to add numbers and this is what transpires:

Christine is presented with a sheet of paper that says, "If your friend gave you three stickers and you already had two, how many stickers would you have altogether?" The teacher waits; the student does not respond. The teacher prompts her to read the question. Christine still does not answer.

Can we conclude that Christine cannot add? Of course not; it may be that the student cannot read. In addition to being asked to add quantities, the student was also asked to read and to read words describing quantities. This test is measuring the student's ability to read first and to add second, and thus is not a valid approach for assessing this student's math abilities. Consider an additional example regarding Christine.

Christine's team would like to assess her receptive language skills. But the speech and language pathologist typically uses a test that requires pointing to objects and pictures. The team knows that the test results would not be a valid measure of communication because Christine, who has cerebral palsy, has great difficulty using her hands. She also has limited vision. The team then concludes that although the test manual indicates that the test has good validity, it does not have validity for Christine.

Instead of measuring Christine's receptive language, this test would be measuring her motor skill of pointing to visual stimuli and the visual acuity skills of seeing the test item. Thus, this test lacks *validity* for this student, and the particular type of validity it lacks is *content validity.*

Content validity is also lacking if a test does not sample a broad enough range of skills to determine whether competency is sufficient. If the self-help domain of a particular test includes only basic toileting, dressing, and eating skills, but omits all grooming skills, the test would be an insufficient measure of self-help capabilities. The test would then be judged invalid for many students whose personal care skills extend beyond the basics.

Criterion-related validity refers to the extent to which scores on a test agree with (concurrent validity) or predict (predictive validity) some given criterion. A test is considered to have concurrent validity if performance on that particular test is related to performance on another similar test. For example, it is not necessary to test students using two different IQ tests, such as the Wechsler Intelligence Scale for Children III (WISC III) and the Stanford–Binet, because psychometric research has demonstrated that the scores are likely to be similar. A test that has predictive validity can be used to reasonably predict future behavior, much in the way that test scores like, for example, SATs or GREs are used to predict success in undergraduate and graduate studies.

Reliability

Test reliability refers to the extent to which an instrument is *consistent* in measuring whatever it purports to measure. If an assessment is repeated within a short interval of time, a student should receive the same score or rating. Reliability is usually measured by some form of reliability coefficient, ranging from 0 to 1, or by the standard error of measurement derived from it. Salvia and Ysseldyke (2007) state that tests should have reliability coefficients greater than .90 whenever their results are used to make decisions regarding individual students, while scores used simply for administrative reporting in groups can have lower reliability coefficients (greater than .60).

It is important to remember that reliability does not address the content of what is being assessed, only its consistency. A teacher may reliably measure a student's ability to "place pegs in a pegboard within 1 minute" as part of an assessment of vocational readiness. Such a measure may be reliable (consistent) over time, and two evaluators may agree on the student's test performance (interrater reliability). Yet, many argue that the skill of placing pegs in a pegboard has no relationship to vocational preparation. Thus such a test, while possibly reliable, is not a valid assessment of vocational readiness. Validity, not reliability, addresses the purpose or the content of what is being measured.

Assessment That Reflects Changing Beliefs and Views

Assessments that professionals perceive as appropriate and meaningful are strongly influenced by the teams' views regarding what is important to assess, and is influenced by existing philosophies. This is plainly illustrated by the changing focus of assessment in response to the evolving definition of mental retardation, now referred to as intellectual disability (Schalock et al., 2009). In 1983, mental retardation was defined as "significantly subaverage general intellectual functioning *existing concurrently* [emphasis added] with deficits in adaptive behavior" (Grossman, 1983, p. 1). This definition revised earlier definitions that did not include the criteria of adaptive behavior (Heber, 1959, 1961). The addition of the concept of adaptive behavior acknowledged that measurement of intelligence was insufficient to define mental retardation and that adaptive behavior was the other critical characteristic for defining this disability. This change expanded the types of instruments used to diagnose mental retardation (intellectual disability) by adding a new dimension to assessment, that is, the measurement of an individual's adaptation to environmental demands.

Since the 1990s, an ecological viewpoint has become the basis for defining individuals with disabilities. The definitional focus was shifted from a deficit orientation to a support orientation (Luckasson et al., 2002). TASH (formerly the Association for Persons with Severe Handicaps) defined individuals with severe disabilities as follows:

These persons include individuals with disabilities of all ages, races, creeds, national origins, genders and sexual orientation who require ongoing support in one or more major life activities in order to participate in an integrated community and enjoy a quality of life similar to that available to all citizens. Support may be required for life activities such as mobility, communication, self-care, and learning as necessary for community living, employment and self-sufficiency. (TASH Resolution on the People for Whom TASH Advocates, available at http://www.tash.org/IRR/resolutions/res02advocate.htm)

TASH chose to move away from defining people by specific personal characteristics and instead characterized these individuals with disabilities in relation to societal attitudes and treatment. Individuals with severe disabilities are further described by TASH as being those who are characterized as follows:

- Are most at risk for being excluded from the mainstream of society;
- Are perceived by traditional service systems as being most challenging;
- Are most likely to have their rights abridged;
- Are most likely to be at risk for living, working, playing, and/or learning in segregated environments;
- Are least likely to have the tools and opportunities necessary to advocate on their own behalf;
- Historically have been labeled as having severe disabilities; and
- Are most likely to need ongoing, individualized supports in order to participate in inclusive communities and enjoy a quality of life similar to that available to all citizens (TASH Mission, http://www.tash.org/WWA/WWA_mission.html).

In 1992, the American Association on Mental Retardation (AAMR) again revised its definition to reflect changing views about individuals with intellectual disabilities and the importance of support.

Mental retardation refers to substantial limitations in present functioning. It is characterized by significantly subaverage intellectual functioning, existing concurrently with related limitations in two or more of the following applicable adaptive skill areas: communication, self-care, home living, social skills, community use, self-direction, health and safety, functional academics, leisure, and work. Mental retardation manifests before age 18. (Luckasson et al., 2002, p. 1)

In this definition, an individual's disability still was considered related to intellectual *and* adaptive behavior, but also was influenced by the context within which he or she lived—the immediate social setting,

the neighborhood, the community, and the culture and supports provided in these contexts. Application of this definition led to the practice of assessing the level and type of individualized *supports* needed by the person to function in the home, school, and community. The assessment process was expanded: The diagnosis of mental retardation by assessing a person's general intellectual functioning and adaptive behavior was to be followed by the identification of that person's needed supports in their everyday environments.

More recently (in 2002 and 2009), the definition was changed to reflect contemporary knowledge of adaptive behavior assessment (Luckasson et al., 2002; Schalock et al., 2009). Still a debated construct, adaptive behavior is now measured as an expression of an individual's conceptual, social, and practical adaptive skills. In 2007, the term *mental retardation* was replaced by intellectual disability because it was more consistent with international terminology and was less offensive to persons with the disability (Schalock et al., 2007), and the organization changed its name to reflect this thinking—American Association on Intellectual and Developmental Disabilities (AAIDD). The current definition and its assumptions reflect contemporary knowledge of assessment, diagnosis, and support:

Intellectual disability is characterized by significant limitations both in intellectual functioning and in adaptive behavior as expressed in conceptual, social, and practical adaptive skills. This disability originates before age 18. (Schalock et al., 2009, p. 1)

The accurate application of this definition of intellectual disability depends on five assumptions:

1. Limitations in present functioning must be considered within the context of community environments typical of the individual's age peers and culture.
2. Valid assessment considers cultural and linguistic diversity as well as differences in communication, sensory, motor, and behavioral factors.
3. Within an individual, limitations often coexist with strengths.
4. An important purpose of describing limitations is to develop a profile of needed supports.
5. With appropriate personalized supports over a sustained period, the life functioning of the person with intellectual disability generally will improve. (Schalock et al., 2009, p. 1)

These assumptions influence the focus of assessment—from assessment of the individual, to assessment of the individual in relationship to the supports needed to participate in the natural environment. AAIDD's *Supports Intensity Scale* (2004) promotes the identification of those resources and strategies (e.g., individuals, money or other tangible assets, assistive devices, instruction, friendships) that enable individuals with developmental disabilities to live meaningful lives in integrated community settings. According to Thompson et al. (2004), this assessment approach calls for us to

a. identify, describe, and understand people in regard to their pattern and intensity of support needs, and
b. focus on planning and service delivery on providing supports that reduce the gap between an individual's level of personal competence and the demands of the settings in which the person participates (p. 6).

This assessment approach is founded, not on a philosophy of deficits, but instead on the philosophy of personalized support: People with intellectual disabilities have *support needs* that should be identified and used to guide planning and service delivery. The assessment process, consequently, focuses not just on the individual student, but also on the environment, a clear example of the way in which our beliefs affect the focus and process of assessment.

Assessment That Matches Intent

The purpose of the assessment and the ways in which the assessment data are to be used also determine which instruments are appropriate. Different types of assessments provide different types of information. Just as teachers should select an educational intervention to match the particular targeted skills, so should teachers select assessment instruments and procedures to match the purpose of the assessment. Failure to do so results in an invalid assessment, as described previously.

Assessments are used to gain information for the purposes of screening, diagnosis and eligibility, program planning and placement, curriculum and program development, and evaluation of instructional effectiveness. Different assessment instruments and strategies are used for each of these purposes.

Screening
Screening is designed as a broad and quickly administered measure used to determine whether students are significantly different from their peers and require

further evaluation. Medical personnel, psychologists, and other professionals use screening instruments with young children who are delayed in their development to determine whether a more in-depth evaluation is needed and to determine eligibility for special programs or related services (e.g., speech, physical, or occupational therapy). Screening may begin as early as the prenatal period, with the use of chorionic villus sampling, amniocentesis, and alpha-fetal protein screening to determine the presence of certain chromosomal and genetic disorders, and ultrasound to determine the presence of structural anomalies. Immediately following birth, screening procedures may be used to check for obvious disabling conditions or genetic and metabolic disorders and the physiological and behavioral status of the newborn. The Apgar scoring system (Apgar, 1953; Apgar & Beck, 1973) is used to quickly evaluate a newborn's heart rate, respiration, reflexes, muscle tone, and general appearance at 1 minute, 5 minutes, and 10 minutes after birth. The Neonatal Behavioral Assessment Scale (NBAS), informally known as the Brazelton, after its creator (Brazelton & Nugent, 1995), is used to assess newborns and infants up to 2 months relative to 27 behavioral measures. These general measures assess an infant's alertness, activity level, self-quieting activity, smiles, sleep patterns, and specific behaviors (e.g., the newborn's response to environmental stimuli, such as a light, sounds, and a pinprick on the bottom of the foot). The Apgar test and the NBAS alert medical personnel to newborns who are in distress and signal the need for immediate intervention and follow-up with more refined evaluations of the health status of the infants.

Screening instruments for infants and older children vary in terms of the range of skills included. The Denver Developmental Screening Test (Frankenburg et al., 1990) and the Developmental Profile 3 (DP-3; Alpern, 2007) cover a variety of domains of development, such as personal and social, fine and gross motor, language, and self-help. Other frequently used screening instruments for young children include the Bayley II Developmental Assessment (Bayley, 2005) and the Battelle Developmental Inventory (2nd ed.) (Newborg, 2004). Some screening instruments focus on only one domain of interest, such as vision or hearing. Traditional visual acuity screening tests, such as the well-known Snellen chart or Sloan chart, which require reading letters at various sizes that represent various distances from the chart, or the Lea symbols or Allen cards, which use pictures, cannot be adequately administered to students with severe disabilities because of the complex verbal instructions and the cognitive discriminations required (U.S. Preventive Services Task Force, 2004). Instead, screening my be accomplished by focused observers who notice behaviors such as blinking, moving closer to objects, tilting of the head, or squinting. Additionally, vision care clinicians can use more formalized procedures, as well as technical equipment, to check the physical structure of the eye and its responsiveness to light. Some clinicians and teachers who specialize in visual quality-of-life assessment, whereby they analyze the ability of students with severe disabilities to fully participate and the supports that are necessary for them to do so, should be a part of this process.

Diagnosis and Eligibility

Some assessments are designed for the purposes of testing the child in order to identify the disorder and the possible cause of the delay or disorder, and to make eligibility, classification, and placement decisions (Salvia & Yesseldyke, 2007). Determination of classification and eligibility is made by the assessment team or the IEP team, which makes its decision on the basis of evidence from several sources, as required by IDEA. IDEA specifies that multifaceted assessment be used for the purpose of determining eligibility for special education services. Once a delay or a disability is suspected, either through screening or observation, diagnostic testing is conducted to learn more specific information about the delay or disability. The primary measures used to diagnose individuals with severe disabilities are intelligence tests and tests of adaptive behavior (Snell, 2003). Typically, these tests are administered by psychologists, education specialists, and/or therapists. Accurate psychological testing is difficult because of potential movement, vision, hearing, and communication challenges, as well as possible problems with cooperation during the assessment sessions (Snell, 2003).

Many tools have been developed to identify students on the autism spectrum. The Gilliam Autism Rating Scale (GARS) (Gilliam, 1995), for example, was designed for use by parents, teachers, and other professionals to help identify and diagnose autism in individuals ages 3–22 and to estimate the severity of the problem. Other tools that are easily used to determine where a child falls on the autism spectrum include the Checklist for Autism in Toddlers (CHAT) (Baron-Cohen, Allen, & Gillberg, 1992) and the Childhood Autism Rating Scale (CARS) (Schopler, Reichler, & Rochen-

Renner, 1998). The Autism Diagnostic Observation Schedule (ADOS) (Lord, Rutter, DiLavore, & Risi, 1999) and the Autistic Diagnostic Interview–Revised (ADI–R) (Lord, Rutter, & Le Couteur, 1994) require more specialized training and experience working with students with autism and related disorders.

Curriculum and Program Development

A major purpose of assessment is to gather information that is useful for the development of an appropriate educational program. This phase of the assessment process is usually coordinated by the teacher, who directly observes and assesses the student and also collects pertinent information from parents, psychologists, and therapists.

Some assessment instruments are more suited than others for the purpose of determining curriculum content. These assessments provide meaningful information about what should be taught to students. Other instruments, such as intelligence tests, are inappropriate for this purpose; they are designed to measure general intelligence and should not be used to determine instructional goals and objectives. In contrast, ecological inventories of functional environments (discussed later in this chapter) are informal instruments that lead to the identification of critical age-appropriate functional skills for students with severe disabilities and translate readily into curricular content. Assessment instruments should be carefully inspected to determine their intended purposes.

Evaluation of Instructional Effectiveness

To enable program planners to determine whether instructional programs are producing the desired results, assessment of instructional effectiveness must also be conducted frequently. For example, is the communication intervention effective in increasing the number of self-initiated requests that the student makes? Is the antecedent intervention effective in decreasing the amount of time that the student engages in self-stimulatory behavior, and conversely, is it effective in increasing the amount of time that the student is meaningfully engaged? It is not enough to develop an educational program for a student; teams must be accountable for the impact of the educational program on the student and his or her family. Evaluation of instructional effectiveness includes examining the progress that the student is making, the impact of the educational program on the student's quality of life, and an evaluation of the total educational program.

Evaluation of student progress is a critical form of educational measurement. Teachers are required to include in each student's IEP a statement of how progress toward each of the specified objectives will be measured and the extent to which that progress is sufficient to enable the student to achieve the annual goals. (See Chapter 5 for a review of measurement strategies.) Additionally, some experts stress the importance of evaluating broader student outcomes, such as those related to improvement in a student's quality of life. Because of the subjective nature of this concept, there are wide variations in opinion on exactly what should be measured. There is, however, growing consensus about what constitutes the core quality-of-life dimensions. These include emotional well-being, interpersonal relationships, material well-being, personal development, physical well-being, self-determination, social inclusion, and human rights (Schalock, 1997).

The quality of the program itself (e.g., educational, residential, vocational) in which students receive an education is another important focus for assessment. Assessment of this nature could be used to aid program personnel and administrators in thinking about the quality of the environment and the supports that they provide. For example, what opportunities are available for interaction with nondisabled peers? What is being done to encourage support for, and the participation of, families in the school program? These are broader dimensions of program evaluation that must be considered so that we know that instruction is taking place within a meaningful context. This topic is discussed more fully in the section on Assessment of Program Quality.

Alternate statewide assessments are specialized types of assessments designed to evaluate program effectiveness by assessing students with the most significant cogntive disabilities relative to statewide academic curriculum standards. IDEA requires that all students, including those with severe disabilities, "have access to, participate in, and make progress in the general curriculum" (U.S. Department of Education, 2003). NCLB requires that all states establish high standards and develop statewide tests to measure students' progress in meeting those standards. Students with severe disabilities must be included in statewide accountability systems. Because many students with severe disabilities are not able to participate in general statewide assessments, even with accommodations, each state has developed alter-

nate methods of assessing those students. The data from students taking the alternate assessment are combined with data from all of the other students in the state, and these data are used to determine whether *adequate yearly progress* (also referred to as AYP) is being made by students with and without disabilities. More information about the way in which academic performance is assessed is discussed later in the chapter.

Methods of Assessment

The way in which students with severe disabilities are assessed also affects the accuracy of the information derived from the assessment process. There are three basic methods for gathering assessment information: direct testing, observation, and interviewing. Each of the methods provides different information and has its own advantages and disadvantages. Additionally, variables, such as the location of the testing or observation and the student's or interviewer's familiarity and comfort level with each other, will affect the information gained from the assessment.

Direct Testing

Direct testing is a method of data collection that requires the teacher to provide the student with an arranged opportunity to respond to specific stimuli. The teacher presents the student with certain materials or instructions to determine whether the student can perform the target behavior.

> *Marc's teacher takes him into the bathroom and then asks him to wash his hands. His teacher then observes what steps of the task he performs and records his performance on a task analysis data collection sheet.*

The contrived, on-demand nature of this process allows the teacher to assess whether the student demonstrates the steps involved in hand washing, but does not allow observation of some key skills. For example, we would not know whether Marc was able to wash his hands without being verbally prompted to do so. Does he wash his hands when they are dirty, after he uses the bathroom, or before he eats, or only when told to? Direct testing can provide useful information, but the contrived nature of such testing must be considered.

Observation in the Natural Environment

To the greatest extent possible, testing should occur in the environment where the skill is naturally used and under natural conditions—at the appropriate times, in natural settings, with typical distractions, and using the natural materials. This is especially important for children with severe disabilities whose performance may be very different in unfamiliar settings, with unfamiliar examiners, and using unfamiliar materials (Nelson, van Dijk, McDonnell, & Thompson, 2002). The major advantage of assessing a student in the natural environment is that the teacher may observe more typical performance of the target skill and a wider range of related behaviors than in the more contrived testing situation previously described. In other words, the assessment will better represent the student's routine performance of a task. The teacher can see whether the student demonstrates associated skills, such as movement to the location of the activity, initiation of the skill, ability to find solutions to problems that arise in the natural environment, and social behaviors.

In the example of Marc and his hand-washing skills discussed earlier, the teacher assessed Marc in a natural setting where hand washing typically occurs. If the materials used in this activity are the same as those used at home, the results may well relate to how he washes his hands at home and provide some more valid information than that which can be gained through direct testing in the classroom. Furthermore, if the teacher waited to see whether Marc initiated the skill after he used the bathroom, she would have been able to determine whether he knew the appropriate time to initiate hand washing.

Consider another example. Jacob's teacher wants to assess his skill in handling money. His teacher gathers initial information on his skill level in the fourth-grade classroom. She keeps in mind, however, that Jacob's performance in the classroom may be different from what it would be in the school store when buying supplies or at the school book fair when purchasing a book (e.g., there are many students mulling around the book fair; a parent and not the teacher is requesting money). If Jacob demonstrates the desired skill in the classroom, his teacher will then conduct a second, more contextually valid assessment of the skill in these school settings.

To increase the value of data gathering in the natural environment, observations should sample a range of relevant settings (e.g., classroom, home, playground, bathroom) at the appropriate times (e.g., before or after lunch, morning, afternoon) and using a variety of arrangements (e.g., group, one-to-one, free play). Because each of these variables may influence the student's performance, observations over several days is the preferred method to obtain data that accurately represent the student's ability.

Christine and a peer from her drama club, along with the teaching assistant, went to the mall to find a certain type of makeup that they needed for an upcoming production. Her special education teacher and her teaching assistant planned to assess several of Christine's skills and routines while at the mall (e.g., purchasing from a store, ordering and eating in the food court). Her teacher knew Christine's skills when ordering and eating lunch in the school cafeteria; however, she was interested in determining her skill at the food court, where there were many unknown variables. For example, at the food court, Christine would not know the food server, the waiting line would be made up of people whom she did not know, and different food choices would be available, some of which would not match the food options on her communication device.

The disadvantages of observing in the natural environment are that the behavior to be assessed may not occur at the time of the observation or the natural observation conditions may be dangerous. For example, a teacher may take a student into the community to assess the appropriateness of his response to strangers. The ideal way of assessing this would be to take the student to a mall and observe his behavior if a stranger were to approach him; however, there is a good chance that no stranger will approach the student on that particular day at that particular time. Furthermore, purposely allowing a student to be in a vulnerable situation where a stranger may approach is obviously unethical and potentially dangerous!

Interviews

Interviews of others who know the student well is a third way to collect information about a student. Interviews may follow a formal or standardized test format and provide norms against which to judge responses. For example, the Adaptive Behavior Scales (2nd ed.) (Lambert, Nihira, & Leland, 1993) and the Vineland Adaptive Behavioral Scales (2nd ed.) (Sparrow,

Balla, & Cicchetti, 2005) are two assessments of adaptive behavior that obtain information through interviews. O'Neill et al. (1997) also use an interview format for one component of their comprehensive assessment of problem behaviors. Informal interviews, however, are often more useful for teachers. An interview with family members, for example, is the method by which teachers understand parental priorities for a child's skill instruction and learn more about a student's current performance of skills, communication abilities, and preferences.

Interviews may be with family members, staff from a supported living arrangement (if the student does not live at home), current and past teachers, the student, a friend of the student, or any other person who knows the student well. The major advantage with interviews is that the information provided by the informants is likely to reflect the student's typical performance in natural settings with naturally occurring cues and consequences. The major disadvantage is that the interview data may be more subjective than direct observation and, consequently, less accurate. Interviewing family members is an informative strategy for finding out about the activities in which a family engages, parents' preferences for particular activities, and the student's likes and dislikes. Used in conjunction with the other types of information gathering, educators can become more knowledgeable about the student's home environment. This method is also a constructive way of involving parents in the program and letting them know that their input is critical for the development of a sound educational program. It is important, however, that the interview process and the information gathering be done in a culturally sensitive manner and be respectful of families from diverse cultural backgrounds (Harry, 2008). Including families in the functional behavioral assessment process and the collaborative development of behavior intervention plans is recognized as being key in behavioral support; development of behavior intervention plans that are contextually compatible with family routines and practices contributes greatly to success (Albin, Lucyshyn, Horner, & Flannery, 1996; Moes & Frea, 2000).

If family members, for whatever reason, are not available for a face-to-face interview, other strategies should be implemented to facilitate meaningful participation. Some families may be more available for a phone interview, and others may prefer to complete and return a written questionnaire. If a written questionnaire is used, it should be simple to complete, not lengthy, presented in the family's native language, and culturally sensitive. This brief questionnaire should be designed to assess the family's ideas and priorities concerning their child's present and future needs at home, at school, and in the community. Variables such as student preferences and dislikes, the family's routines, and the child's participation in these routines are important to assess and will be critical for the development of a meaningful educational program.

There are some general strategies that teachers can use to make the most of informal interviews:

- Plan interview questions ahead of time and individualize them to suit the interviewee and the situation.
- Listen more and talk less so that you gain the most information from the respondent. *Silence is okay— let the respondent think.* Restate their answers to confirm/clarify your understanding ("Do you mean that . . . ?").
- Start with broad questions ("Tell me how Jacob communicates with you") and then narrow the focus if you do not learn what you need to learn ("How does Jacob indicate that he is bored?").
- Avoid leading questions that suggest a particular answer ("Don't you think that it is important that Jacob improve his writing skills?").
- Take good notes (or record them with permission) so that you can retain all of the information obtained during an interview.

Types of Assessments

There are many types of assessments that are used for students with severe disabilities. In this section of the chapter, we will discuss different types of norm-referenced and criterion-referenced assessments, and how these tests are best used. ***Norm-referenced tests*** are used to determine the extent of the deviation from the norm and are standardized around the average score of the normative group so that half of the sample scores are above the average score and half are below it (Lewis & Russo, 1998). These measures usually compare the performance of students with disabilities to nondisabled students of the same age. Norm-referenced measures allow the evaluator to determine whether a given student can perform the same skills as the majority of the students in the normative sample. In contrast, ***criterion-referenced tests*** compare a student's performance to a predetermined set of behaviors and skills of interest and level of mastery (criterion), regardless of the performance of other students. They are designed and used to determine what a student knows or does related to a preset list of skills or standards. This type of test is often used as a guide in curriculum planning and its use will lead to the identification of skills that the student needs to learn. In this section, a variety of assessments are discussed, some of which are norm referenced, some criterion referenced, and some both. The ways in which each assessment is (or should be) used, as well as its benefits and limitations, are presented.

IQ Tests

The IQ test, along with adaptive behavior scales, is typically used in the diagnosis of intellectual disability during the eligibility process. Some frequently used IQ tests are the Bayley Scales of Infant Development III (Bayley, 2005), the McCarthy Scales of Children's Ability (McCarthy, 1972), the Stanford–Binet Intelligence Scales (5th ed.) (Roid, 2003), the Wechsler Intelligence Scale for Children (4th ed.) (Wechsler, 2003), and the Wechsler Preschool and Primary Scale of Intelligence–Revised (Wechsler, 2002).

IQ tests are designed to measure learning ability, or "intellectual capacity." "Intelligence," however, is a construct that one infers from a person's performance (Salvia & Ysseldyke, 2007), so the practice of assigning numeric values to a construct (e.g., an IQ score) and using these numbers to make important decisions is questionable to many professionals. Intelligence tests sample behaviors such as discrimination, generalization, motor behavior, vocabulary, inductive reasoning, comprehension, sequencing, detail recognition, understanding of analogies, abstract reasoning, memory, and pattern completion (Salvia & Ysseldyke, 2007).

There are many problems in administering IQ tests to students with disabilities and in applying the test results. First, because few, if any, standardized intelligence tests include students with severe disabilities in their normative samples, the more severe an individual's disability, the less appropriate are their norms for interpreting an individual's performance. Further, because the items on the IQ test may be too advanced for students with severe or profound disabilities, some clinicians may turn to infant intelligence tests. The inappropriateness of intelligence tests is then further exacerbated by the lack of age appropriateness.

(Evans, 1991; Gaylord-Ross & Holvoet, 1985). Evans (1991) reflects as follows:

> *Extrapolation of scores or the derivation of IQ scores from scales designed for use with infants or for other special purposes is an especially hazardous practice that provides some continued professional expectation that scores can be meaningfully assigned to people falling within the lower ranges. (p. 40)*

Another major disadvantage is the misuse of the results obtained from intelligence tests. It is inappropriate to make decisions about individual students and services on the basis of IQ tests, or to use them to measure student progress.

Developmental Scales

Developmental scales are founded on research designed to identify the typical sequence of development of large groups of individuals in areas including motor, communication and language, social skills, self-care skills, and so on. Test items on developmental scales are typically written in observable terms so that the presence or absence of a skill in various areas of development can usually be determined reliably. When used for educational assessment, the items that a student can and cannot do are identified. The first items that a student cannot do are then targeted for intervention. They follow a *developmental approach* and give information on functioning in various skill areas, and because skills are listed chronologically, they may provide direction for the next skills to be taught, especially for young children. Student progress on the measures can then be noted by periodic administration of the instrument.

Using this approach, prevalent in the early 1970s (Browder et al., 2004), the mental age (MA) of a student was determined by comparing his or her skills to the age at which a normally developing child acquired those skills. Developmental scales, when used to target instruction, are then considered criterion referenced because the educational needs of persons with severe disabilities were then thought to be best met by focusing on the skills expected for a person with the same mental age as derived from the developmental assessment (Browder et al., 2004). Justification for this approach rests on at least three assumptions: (a) normal development constitutes the most logical ordering of behaviors, (b) many behaviors within normal development are prerequisite behaviors, and (c) behaviors acquired by a nondisabled child are appropriate measures for an individual with a disability who is at the same developmental level (Guess & Noonan, 1982).

There are, however, many problems with applying the developmental approach to students with severe disabilities and using normative scales as criterion-referenced tests in order to determine curriculum. For students with sensory or movement disabilities, test items must be adapted so that the disability does not prevent the assessment of the actual skill being evaluated. Additionally, this approach assumes, first, that there are set sequences for the development of skills for all children and, second, that the sequences of behavior typical of nondisabled students are relevant for students with severe or multiple disabilities. Both assumptions are problematic. Typical children do not always follow the same sequence of skill development when, for example, learning to walk or talk. Children with disabilities also may develop in a different sequence or may skip skills typically demonstrated by normally developing students or suggested by developmental tests. Prostheses or environmental adaptations may render demonstration of typical developmental sequences unnecessary. For example, White (1985) pointed out that although head control is a prerequisite for normal walking, it is not a prerequisite for use of a motorized wheelchair. Therefore, although the student may have failed the "head control" item included in an assessment, the evaluator should not stop probing higher level gross motor skills. Given individualized adaptations, this student may score on many other more advanced skills while not demonstrating earlier more basic skills. Or, similarly, a student may not demonstrate eye contact, but still engage in social interactions.

Furthermore, because the developmental approach assumes that certain behaviors must be present before other behaviors can be acquired, the results may influence some teachers to instruct students on skills that are neither age appropriate nor functional for adapting to their daily environments (Guess & Noonan, 1982), which may lead to lower expectations. For example, a 15-year-old student who has severe disabilities may fail the item "points to parts of the doll" on the Bayley Scales of Infant Development (Bayley, 2005), an item that is usually passed by babies by the time they are 26 months. Instruction on this skill would require materials that are not appropriate for a 15-year-old student, and it is a skill that would have little relevance for that student. Focus on these types of assessment items would naturally have an impact on our expectations of students. Linehan, Brady, and Hwang (1991) found that assessment reports created on the basis of developmental measures led respondents to have lower expectations for individuals with severe disabilities than did reports created on the basis of functional, ecological approaches in which everyday skills are examined.

Another potential danger is that skills are sometimes not assessed within the context of functional routines. For example, take the skill of grasping—generally considered to be an important skill. However, unless grasping is related to a functional application, it has little meaning and may not be demonstrated. Grasping of a brush during grooming, a spoon while eating, or a toy during play provides more contextually relevant assessment information than does the grasping of a 2-inch wooden dowel during a contrived direct testing context. Likewise, "scans objects" is important when it is related to materials used in daily routines (e.g., scan the workbooks to find the one with your name on it, scan the DVDs to find one that you like) and may not be demonstrated "on demand."

Some developmental test items are included on instruments simply because of their high reliability at certain ages, such as the classic item of "imitating a bridge built with three 1-inch cubes." However, what ability this item actually is meant to test is not clear (White, 1985). If used to assess the fine motor ability of a student, then a child who has little fine motor control or is unable to manipulate a prosthetic device would obviously fail the item. However, if the intent is to assess imitation, then some alternative strategy must be developed to allow the child to demonstrate this cognitive ability given his or her physical capabilities.

It is important that teachers understand that just because an item is on an assessment, it does not mean that it is something that should be targeted for instruction. For example, the skill "builds tower of three blocks" is an item that is commonly found on developmental scales. Before considering instruction on such an item, the teacher must question the purpose for assessing this particular skill. Is it to determine the motor ability of the student, whether the student can play with blocks, whether the student can imitate actions, or simply because tower building (like bridge building) is another reliable milestone of development often found in early childhood measures? If a specific rationale for the assessment of that particular item (e.g., motor ability) is determined, then the teacher must decide whether this basic function is a relevant instructional objective for the student. If the teacher concludes that the play function of the item is relevant, the teacher should translate the item into a form that is meaningful for the student's age and specific environment (i.e., age-appropriate materials and functional context). The teacher must be cautious, however, to select skills for instruction that are both needed by the student and possible to teach by the educational team during a school year.

Some developmental instruments relate more directly to the program development component of the assessment process. These instruments are accompanied by curriculum guides. Some of these assessments include the Assessment, Evaluation, and Programming System (AEPS®) for Infants and Children (Bricker, 2002); the Carolina Curriculum for Preschoolers with Special Needs (Johnson-Martin, Attermeier, & Hacker, 2004); Learning Accomplishment Profile (LAP) (Nehring, Nehring, Bruni, & Randolph, 1992); and SCERTS (Prizant, Wetherby, Rubin, Laurent, & Rydell, 2006). Although these instruments were developed with instructional implications in mind, a teacher must still carefully evaluate the relevance of particular test items for each student. The student's age, interests, motor or sensory disabilities, and home and community environments must be considered in the decision-making process.

Siegel-Causey and Allinder (1998) suggest that assessment practices founded on norm-referenced tests are often "limited in their ability to document and provide instructionally relevant information on those aspects of children's lives most valued by parents and practitioners, specifically children's membership in inclusive settings, their social relationships with nondisabled children, and development of competence in relevant functional skills" (p. 173). Regardless of the well-known problems with using IQ and other norm-referenced tests with individuals who have disabilities, the practice continues. It is our position that IQ tests have no value in planning educational programs for students with disabilities, while norm-referenced developmental measures may have *general programming value only for younger children* with disabilities and only when used in combination with consideration of the student's age, interests, motor and sensory abilities, and home and community environments.

Focus of Assessment

As previously discussed, assessments are designed for different purposes (e.g., screening, eligibility and placement, curriculum planning, and program evaluation). IQ tests are designed to assess general intellectual functioning, and developmental scales are often used to assess students in the areas of motor skills development, language development, and social skill development. Instruments and processes that are designed to assess adaptive behavior and academic skills, as well as the role of environmental assessment, will be discussed in the next section.

Assessment of Adaptive Behavior

IQ tests and other norm-referenced assessments focus on conceptual intelligence, while adaptive behavior scales focus on the skills that a person typically displays as he or she engages in routine tasks in the daily environment (Thompson et al., 2004). *Adaptive behavior* is defined as "the collection of conceptual, social, and practical skills that have been learned by people in order to function in their everyday lives" (Luckasson et al., 2002, p. 73). It is important to consider the individualized nature of adaptive behavior and the connection between an individual's adaptive behavior and his or her chronological age and sociocultural context, both of which influence opportunities, motivation, and performance of adaptive skills (Luckasson et al., 2002).

> *The social, academic, and behavioral expectations for Christine, who is 20 years old, are very different than the expectations for Marc, who is 6 years old. In addition, the fact that Marc lives in an urban area, where there are many stores, public transportation, streetlights, and so on, will shape the types of skills that should be assessed as he becomes older. Christine, who lives in a more suburban setting, will need to learn different ways to travel and get along in her environment.*

The concept of adaptive behavior has encouraged educators to assess behaviors that have relevance to a student's functioning in society. Measures of adaptive behavior are usually checklists of skills required to function in the daily environment. For example, the Adaptive Behavior Scale–School (3rd ed.) (Lambert et al., 1993) includes the domains of independent functioning, physical development, economic activity,

TABLE 3–1

Correspondence Among Three Dimensions of Adaptive Behavior and Empirically Derived Factors on Existing Measures

Instrument	Conceptual Skills	Social Skills	Practical Skills
AAMR Adaptive Behavior Scale–School and Community (Lambert, Nihira, & Leland, 1993)	Community self-sufficiency	Personal-social responsibility	Personal self-sufficiency
Vineland Adaptive Behavior Scales (Sparrow, Balla, & Cicchetti, 2005)	Communication	Socialization	Daily living skills
Scales of Independent Behavior–Revised (Bruininks, Woodcock, Weatherman, & Hill, 1996)	Community living skills	Social interaction and communication skills	Personal living skills
Comprehensive Test of Adaptive Behavior–Revised (Adams, 2000)	Language concepts and academic skills; Independent living	Social skills	Self-help skills; Home living

Source: Luckasson et al. (2002). *Mental retardation: Definition, classification, and systems of supports* (10th ed.). Washington, DC: American Association on Mental Retardation.

language development, numbers and time, prevocational or vocational activity, self-direction, responsibility, and socialization. These scales can provide information that can contribute, at least in part, to the identification of needed functional skills and areas in which to concentrate instruction (Siegel-Causey & Allinder, 1998).

However, adaptive behavior measures have been criticized on several counts. First, adaptive behavior is difficult to measure because the concept remains vague and inadequately defined, making interpretation subjective (Greenspan, 1999). Although more than 200 adaptive behavior measures have been developed in the past two decades, most disagree on the construct of adaptive behavior (Thompson, McGrew, & Bruininks, 1999). Second, although these measures focus on the skills required in daily living, they often do not assess an individual's ability to adapt to changing circumstances. An item such as "able to catch a bus to work" may assess a skill necessary for functioning in the work world, but it does not address the individual's ability to solve the problem that would arise if the correct bus failed to come on time (Evans & Brown, 1986). Third, the high correlation between adaptive behavior and IQ leads many educators to conclude that adaptive behavior measures and IQ tests may be measuring the same abilities (Adams, 1973; Baumeister & Muma, 1975). Fourth, the information obtained from most current tests of adaptive behavior do not indicate much more about the severity of the problem or its cause than do more simplified screening instruments (Gaylord-Ross & Holvoet, 1985). Fifth, for some students with severe and multiple disabilities, the gap between current and expected performance may be so

great that the focus may inappropriately shift to deficits instead of strengths (Nelson et al., 2002).

Table 3–1 describes the domains, or content areas, covered by four frequently used scales that measure adaptive behavior. In this table, Luckasson et al. (2002) analyze the domains according to the three-dimensional framework of conceptual, social, and practical skills. Some adaptive behavior scales include computer components that provide options such as direct scoring, visual profiles of the student's performance across domains, identification of priority areas, items missed, and items successfully passed. These scales include the Inventory for Client and Agency Planning (ICAP) (Bruininks, Hill, Weatherman, & Woodcock, 1986); the Scales of Independent Behavior, Revised (SIB-R) (Bruininks, Woodcock, Weatherman, & Hill, 1996); and Vineland Adaptive Behavior Scales, 2nd edition (Sparrow et al., 2005).

Assessment of Academic Performance

Comprehensive assessment of students with severe disabilities includes assessment in all areas of development, including academic skills. The following sections provide a brief discussion of the types of assessments that are used to assess academic skills, including the alternate assessment of students on statewide academic standards.

Because there are no formal assessments of academic skills specifically designed for students with severe disabilities, teachers often use instruments designed for typical students. For example, the Brigance Diagnostic Inventory of Early Development II (Brigance & Glascoe,

2004) and the Brigance Comprehensive Inventory of Basic Skills–Revised (Brigance & Glascoe, 1999) are frequently used assessments of the academic skill performance of typically developing children between the ages of birth to 7 years and 5–13 years, respectively. These tests are designed to assess students' skills in a number of areas, including reading and math. The assessments are both criterion referenced (i.e., they assess skills such as printing uppercase letters in sequence and reading numerals) and norm referenced (i.e., the student's performance on the assessment is compared to that of others) and can be administered directly to a student by a teacher or paraprofessional who carefully follows the directions regarding administration specified in the manual. When these assessments are used with students with severe disabilities, as they sometimes are, the information gained is often invalid and unreliable, and can lead to the identification of skills to be taught that are not critical to the development of functional academic skills. The artificiality of the testing situation, the one-time assessment opportunity, the extent to which assessment relies on the typical sequences of development of academic skills, and the lack of consideration of the functionality of the skills assessed can affect the meaningfulness of the information derived from these assessments. (See also previous section, Developmental Scales.)

Commercially available guides or checklists can aid assessment of academic skill development in students with severe disabilities via direct observations. For example, Assessing and Monitoring Progress of Functional Skills (AMPFS; Valletutti, Bender, & Baglin, 2008) is a checklist of skills designed for teachers to determine a "continuing point-in-time measure" of students' progress in functional reading, writing, and math (p. 7). Teachers observe, date, and rate skills as being not evident, emerging, with assistance, or independent and then, on the basis of interactions with team members, select priority skills for instruction. *The Syracuse Community-Referenced Curriculum Guide* (Ford et al., 1989), also designed specifically for students with severe disabilities, includes scope and sequence charts of skills in functional goal areas. Applied academic skills are organized by age and embedded within functional areas such as safety and health (e.g., middle school and high school: uses phone to obtain emergency help) and budgeting and planning (middle school: manages allowance). Teachers use these charts to gain an understanding of what skills are considered to be important to target for instruction and as a curriculum-referenced checklist to identify what skills students presently have on the basis of teacher observation of prior demonstration of those skills. Teacher-made skills checklists are an additional method of assessing academic skills frequently used. Teachers, either individually or as part of curriculum development committees, identify functional academic skills that are considered to be critical, develop checklists for those skills, and then consider students' skills relative to those checklists.

Assessent of Student Performance on State-Adopted Standards

The academic skills of students with severe disabilities are also being assessed in today's schools through systems of assessment that are specifically designed to evaluate the progress of students (and their programs) in meeting each state's academic content standards. The states are required to assess *all* of their students, including students with severe disabilities, relative to state-adopted standards (Elementary and Secondary Education Act, 1994; IDEA, 1997). Lawmakers recognized, however, that students with severe disabilities are unable to demonstrate their acquisition of academic skills through the use of the general statewide tests, typically paper-and-pencil tests, even with accommodations. Consequently, the states were required to develop *alternate assessments* for their students with severe disabilities; alternate assessments have their own achievement standards and methods of assessment. Considerable variation exists, however, in the academic areas assessed, the ways that the skills are described, and the methods of assessment utilized (Browder et al., 2003; Thompson & Thurlow, 2001).

Initially, many states based their alternate assessments on the measurement of students' skills in functional domains such as self-care, domestic, and community living skills (Thompson & Thurlow, 2001). This gradually has shifted to the content of the assessment being linked to each state's academic standards and the assessment being conducted on those same academic areas that are assessed for students without disabilities. For example, while many states have delineated *standards* in the areas of reading, writing, mathematics, history, science, technology, the arts, health, and other areas, statewide *assessments* may be limited to the areas of reading, writing, and mathematics. Consequently, alternate assessments are limited to those areas as well, and alternate achievement standards are being developed for each area assessed.

No Child Left Behind allows states to decide the method of assessment used to determine student progress on the alternative achievement standards.

> *An alternate assessment may include materials collected under a variety of circumstances, including (1) teacher observation of the student; (2) samples of student work produced during regular classroom instruction that demonstrate mastery of specific instructional strategies; and (3) standardized performance tasks produced in an "on-demand" setting, such as completion of an assigned task on test day. These are not requirements. They are only examples of different types of alternate assessments. States have considerable flexibility in designing the most appropriate format for alternate assessments. (U.S. Department of Education, 2005, p. 15-16)*

As an example, the Pennsylvania Alternate System of Assessment (PASA) identified the critical essence of each of the standards in reading and mathematics and translated them into functional applications of the skills relevant to students with severe disabilities. The PASA is an individually administered test given each spring to students by their teacher or another certified test administrator who knows the student well. Test administration can be adapted so that even students with the most severe disabilities can participate in the assessment and receive a score. The test, administered to students in the equivalent of grades 3–8 and 11, consists of 25 test items related to reading standards; 25 test items related to math standards; and, for students in grades 4, 8, and 11, approximately 25 test items related to science standards. Each test item represents an authentic, relevant, and age-appropriate skill related to reading, mathematics, or science. There are three levels of difficulty for each content area. Level A contains the least complex reading-, math-, or science-related skills. Level B consists of intermediate skills, and Level C consists of the most complex skills. The PASA is designed to be a snapshot of a student's typical performance on a small sample of academic skills derived from the Pennsylvania Academic Standards. Student performance is recorded via video or narrative notes and is submitted for scoring. Teams of scorers (composed of practicing teachers, administrative school personnel, and college/university faculty) are trained to use a six-point scoring rubric to evaluate student performance. Once scoring has been completed,

aggregated results are submitted to the state for inclusion with scores from the Pennsylvania System of School Assessment PSSA. In addition, PASA reports are generated at the state, home district, service provider, and student levels (http://www.pasaassessment.org).

> *Last spring when Jacob was in third grade, his teacher used the PASA test booklet that she received to assess Jacob on 25 reading skills on the basis of the state's alternate achievement standards. Jacob was assigned to take the "C" level of the reading test based on his teacher's description of his skills. While assessing him, she followed the script specified in the test booklet and used the materials provided, but adapted them as needed in order to use wording and materials that were familiar to Jacob. For the first test item, she placed cards printed with the words* soap, dish, sharp, nap, *and* letter *on the table directly in front of him and then she read each of the words. She asked him to find the word that started with the sound /s/. He pointed to the word* dish, *instead of* soap, *so she repeated the prompt and gave him another chance to respond. He made the correct selection on the second try. For the next test item, she read a three-word sentence, which was printed on a card and placed in front of him, and asked him a question about the sentence. Another item asked the student to read the word that she pointed to in a simple sentence. He read it incorrectly, so the teacher helped him sound out the word.*
>
> *While she administered the test, an aide served as videographer, recording what the test administrator and Jacob did during the test. Jacob's actions, as recorded, were later scored by a team at the scoring conference.*

In contrast, Massachusetts uses a portfolio model that includes "materials collected annually by the teacher and student. Evidence for the portfolio may include work samples, instructional data, videotapes, and other supporting information" (Massachusetts Comprehensive Asseesment System Alternate Assessment (MCAS–Alt), http://www.doe.mass.edu/mcas/alt). Teachers are required to submit evidence of student performance on specific standards and specific strands, which must include data charts with a minimum of eight data points, along with two additional pieces of primary evidence from the student's work. Examples of primary evidence are described as data charts, work samples, videos, photographs, or audiotapes that correspond to the data charts. Portfolios are then submitted to the state and, like the PASA, are scored by teams using a specific scoring rubric. The MCAS–Alt scoring rubric is used to describe the complexity of the skill demonstrated (at acess level, modified, on grade level), the accuracy of the performance, the breadth of knowledge and skills, and the level of independence.

Roeber (2002) also noted that some states use criterion-referenced checklists to assess students on their achievement of academic standards. The checklists are used to guide teachers in observing or recalling student performance on specific academic skills that are linked to the state standards. Roeber (2002) pointed out that while checklists have the advantage of being easy to use, they may not yield reliable data. Some states use checklists as one part of a multicomponent assessment of students' academic skills.

Assessing the Relationship Between the Individual and the Environment

The final area of assessment focus is on the relationship between an individual and his or her specific environmental demands. Similar to criterion-referenced tests, environmental assessment strategies examine the environment to determine the skills and supports needed by the individual. In this case, however, instead of using commercially prepared instruments, strategies are individually applied to assess environments that are determined to be relevant to a particular student. Consequently, the procedure is individualized. The first purpose of environmental assessments is to identify the functional routines and activities required across relevant settings, such as home, school, work, and community. The second purpose is to measure or estimate a student's performance on the specific routines and activities found within those settings. Environmental assessments will be the focus of the remainder of this chapter.

Putting It All Together for Meaningful Assessment

Environmental Assessment

We have reviewed many issues related to the use of standardized measures for students with developmental disabilities. The most critical point is that these measures often provide little useful data for educational

programs, while nonstandardized, or alternative, assessment procedures, also referred to as *environmental assessment,* provide more relevant and useful data regarding educational programs and a student's achievement of desired outcomes (Browder, 2001; Knowlton, 1998; Siegel-Causey & Allinder, 1998). Environmental assessment focuses on the relationship between an individual and specific environmental demands. Before describing specific environmental assessment strategies, it is useful to consider three characteristics that increase the validity of the environmentally based assessment process. First, meaningful assessment should be multidimensional in its focus (i.e., the assessment should tap a variety of content areas that are relevant to typical individuals of the same chronological age as the target student and are valued by the educational team, the family, and the student being assessed). Second, meaningful assessment should include feedback from a variety of informants (i.e., individuals who know the student well (such as parents and teachers), as well as the student him or herself, to the greatest extent possible). Third, meaningful assessment should reflect the natural environments and contexts in which the student typically participates.

Multidimensional Outcomes

The assessment process is only as meaningful as the behavior or skill outcomes that are identified and measured. In order for assessment outcomes to be relevant to the individual, they must be inclusive of a range of dimensions—because each individual's life is multidimensional—and each dimension must be important. For many years, the acquisition of functional skills (e.g., brushing teeth, identifying a cup) was considered to be the sole outcome of educational programs. This focus then expanded to include social inclusion and self-determination. Finally, with the new requirements of NCLB, access to the general curriculum was added to the range of meaningful outcomes that must be assessed (Browder et al., 2004). It is clear that the assessment of functional skill acquisition or just academic development, while important, is not sufficient to demonstrate a meaningful or comprehensive educational experience. Billingsley, Gallucci, Peck, Schwartz, and Staub (1996) argue that this narrow focus "fails to acknowledge the breadth of outcomes that may contribute to the ability of students to lead fulfilling lives" (p. 44). These authors developed a three-part framework to represent the important outcomes for students with severe disabilities (see Table 3-2). If

TABLE 3–2
Definitions of Outcome Categories

Membership	Relationships	Skills
Belonging to a group (treated as a member, accommodations made to include, shared rituals and symbols)	Patterns of interaction that typically develop among peers	Behavioral competencies that develop over time and are the traditional focus of special education
Role in small group Student plays an essential role in multiple groups throughout the school day.	**Play/companionship** Student engages in reciprocal social interactions with peers.	**Social/communication skills** Student learns ways to interact with peers appropriately, to engage cooperatively, to be understood through a system of communication, and to attend to and understand others, even if only in part.
Class membership Student is involved in class activities, takes turns with class responsibilities, participates in class privileges, and is active in class routines.	**Helper** Student offers or provides appropriate levels of help to peers.	**Academic skills** Student learns basic skills or facts in reading, writing, math, science, and social studies.
Friendship cliques Student is a stable member of a consistent group of friends.	**Peer/reciprocal** Student engages in reciprocal task-related interactions with peers.	**Functional skills** Student learns practical routines such as dressing, eating, mobility, putting things away, grooming, making purchases, safe street crossing, and so on.
School membership Student is involved in school-wide activities, attends assemblies, and other school functions.	**Adversarial** Student is involved in negative interactions with one or more peers.	
Outside of school activities Student is a regular participant in extracurricular activities and clubs. Necessary accommodations are present.		

Note: Adapted, with permission, from Billingsley et al. (1996), p. 47.

assessment is to be meaningful, it must include some focus on each type of outcome.

One domain of the conceptual framework is *membership* (belonging) in formal and informal groups in the classroom and in the school community. Membership can take at least five forms: (a) a role in a small group, (b) class membership, (c) friendship cliques, (d) school membership, and (e) activities outside of school. A second domain of the conceptual framework refers to the variety of personal *relationships* formed with other children. Billingsley et al. identified five major patterns of interaction: (a) play or companionship, (b) "helpee," (c) helper, (d) peer partner, and (e) adversarial. A third domain of the framework is *skills*. This part of the model focuses on such traditional skill areas as the use of appropriate social or communication skills; academic skills, such as reading, writing, and math; and functional skills that increase the student's degree of independence and control over the environment.

Taken together, the three components can be used to plan for a comprehensive assessment process, organize assessment information, and determine whether the appropriate range of assessments were conducted. For example, if assessments were conducted for a student that covered the areas of skill acquisition and relationships but did not include any information about membership, the assessment would be incomplete. Marc's preschool team mistakenly omitted several important areas of assessment:

When Marc was in preschool, he attended a self-contained classroom in a building with other special education preschool classrooms. His educational team carefully assessed his communication and academic skills. These findings were useful in understanding how his skills compared with other preschoolers and in identifying what he knew and did not know. However, the team failed to assess any aspects of membership because the school's organization did not allow for any inclusion with typical peers. The team also did not assess his relationships with others, even though Marc's autism was an indicator that relationships with other would be a priority area. Consequently, their assessment results fell short in reflecting all of the outcomes that were considered to be important for learners with severe disabilities. Marc's IEP had an array of academic and communication objectives but none that pertained to social interactions, relationships, or participation in groups with peers.

Inclusion of Important Informants

IDEA formally identifies individuals who must participate on an evaluation team, including the student's parents; at least one of the student's general education teachers (if the student is or may be participating in a general education setting); at least one special education teacher; a representative of the school district who is qualified to provide or supervise instruction; an individual who can interpret the instructional implications of evaluation results; at the parents' or school's discretion, other individuals who have knowledge or special expertise; and the student (when appropriate) (H. R. Turnbull & A. P. Turnbull, 2000). Participants in an environmental assessment may include these evaluation team members but at times may involve other individuals. Professionals and others who know the student well are expected to offer information about the student's behavior and performance in a variety of the student's natural environments. Who these people are will vary according to the abilities and disabilities, age, characteristics, and needs of the student (Orelove, Sobsey, & Silberman, 2004; Silberman & Brown, 1998). For example, a bus driver is not likely to be an "informant" on a developmental assessment but may be important in the environmental assessment of a students' traveling routines.

Special education law has long encouraged student participation, when appropriate, but student participation in educational planning has been more the exception than the practice (Wehmeyer & Sands, 1998). Trends in educating students with disabilities emphasize the involvement of each student in critical elements of the educational process. Accomplishing this for students with severe disabilities is often a challenge because participation requires effective methods of communication (Gothelf & Brown, 1998). A variety of strategies, however, are available for gaining student input from those who have difficulty communicating. For example, a teacher can (a) observe nonverbal forms of communication (e.g., which activities appear to be most engaging for the student and which instructional strategies seem to be the most effective and comfortable for the student), (b) interview people who know the student well, and (c) observe the

student's behavior in a variety of environments and contexts (F. Brown, Gothelf, Guess, & Lehr, 1998; Gothelf & Brown, 1998; Silberman & Brown, 1998). These types of strategies support student participation in the educational planning process.

During one-to-one instruction, Ms. Soroka-Smith (the autism specialist) reported that Marc would intermittently cry and throw his materials on the floor. She and his special education teacher, Ms. Wharton, decided to more closely observe Marc's behavior to determine what he might be communicating with his behavior. For one week, they kept track of variables such as when the behaviors occurred, in which activities they occurred, and how long he would participate before the onset of the behaviors, as well as how they responded to his behavior. They discovered that the disruptive behaviors typically occurred during the same two one-to-one sessions and would occur after about five trials into the session. The two sessions in which the behavior occurred were the writing of the letters of the alphabet and matching sounds to pictures. They also noted that both teachers tended to end the session once Marc became disruptive. The two teachers made several hypotheses about what Marc might be expressing about his curriculum. They decided to try several program changes in these two activities to test their hypotheses and note Marc's response to them: (a) shorten the sessions, (b) take a brief break after three trials, and (c) change the materials to more meaningful and preferred stimuli (e.g., the first letters of the names of his favorite toys). By noting Marc's response to these changes, they would be testing their hypotheses. Consequent changes in his programs, and potentially his goals, would thus reflect Marc's contribution to his educational program.

Focus on Natural Environments and Contexts

Standardized assessments are conducted in settings that are, to the greatest degree possible, free from distractions (McLoughlin & Lewis, 1994), including, for example, special testing areas or therapy rooms. These practices are used to get as pure a reading as is possible on the individual's responses to test items. In contrast, environmental assessments have a different mission: to explore the individual's performance in settings in which he or she routinely participates. Thus, environmental assessment will be conducted, to the greatest degree possible, in those routine locations, which will include all of the distractions that are typically found there (Silberman & Brown, 1998), and interviews will focus on gaining information concerning the individual's behavior and performance in those settings.

Problems with response generalization and stimulus overselectivity further necessitate assessing performance in everyday settings using materials that are natural to the context. Some children like Marc may be able to perform a skill in natural contexts but not in a contrived setting.

> *Marc was tested for "verbal imitation" in the speech therapy room. Sitting directly across from Marc, his therapist presented a verbal cue (e.g., "Say ball"), hoping to elicit an imitation of her verbal stimulus. Marc made only a few correct responses to the list of words and frequently left his seat during testing. Observations made during music time in his kindergarten class, however, indicate that during songs such as* "Old MacDonald Had a Farm," *Marc will imitate the teacher or his peer's choice of animal sounds. His mother also has reported that, at home, Marc will imitate his older sister's verbalizations of excitement (e.g.,* "wow," "cool," "way to go") *when they watch videos together.*

Other times, the student may be able to perform a skill in contrived settings, but not in the natural settings. This is particularly likely when skills have been taught only in the isolated setting.

> *In the special education classroom, Marc was successfully taught to sort objects of the same color and shape (e.g., reds go in the red pile and blues in the blue pile; triangles go in the triangle bin and squares in the square bin). However, when his kindergarten teacher observed him putting away toys after free play, Marc did so randomly instead of putting the foam blocks with the other foam blocks and the wood blocks in the wood block bin.*

Because we are interested in assessing the student's performance in typical routines, assessment is most valid in those natural settings, using those materials that are natural to those settings and with all of the distractors associated with those settings. Not only is it informative to know what the student can or cannot do, but it is critical to consider the reason for failure. Downing and Demchak (2008) suggested that when a student cannot perform an item on an assessment, we should determine whether the student is actually unable to perform the skill, lacks motivation in that

context, or has no reason to perform the skill when requested. This information is important to the design and modification of educational programs.

Environmental Assessment Strategies

This next section reviews a variety of assessment strategies that focus on the relationship between an individual and specific environmental demands. Environmental assessment strategies examine the environment to determine the skills and supports needed by the individual. The purposes of environmental assessments are to identify the functional routines and activities required across relevant settings, such as home, school, work, and community, and to measure or estimate a student's performance of the specific routines and activities found within those settings. Specifically, we will be examining task analytic assessment, ecological assessment, a brief look at the assessment of problem behavior (see Chapter 7 for a comprehensive review), assessment of preference and choice, and assessment of program quality.

Task Analytic Assessment

Task analysis is one of the mainstays for in designing instructional programs for students with all levels of disability. It is a strategy that breaks complex activities, tasks, or skills into smaller, teachable units, the product of which is a series of sequentially ordered steps (Cooper, Heron, & Heward, 2007). Indeed, many of us depend on task analysis in our daily lives to learn new skills, such as following a recipe for a complicated dish, using a map to go someplace that we have never been, or following directions to put together a piece of furniture. But for individuals with disabilities, task analysis has been a foundational approach for assessment and teaching. For example, Taber, Alberto, Seltzer, and Hughes (2003) taught six secondary-school-age students with cognitive disabilities to use a cell phone if and when they become lost in the community (e.g., at the grocery store, the large discount department store, or the main street of a rural downtown area). One of their task analyses was designed to teach the student to answer his or her cell phone to get assistance:

1. Press the top-left (blue) button to turn on the phone.

2. Place phone in pocket, on belt, or in hand.
3. When the phone rings, remove the phone from pocket or belt (if in hand, hold up to visually check that it's ringing).
4. Press "yes" (or the blue button) to answer the phone.
5. Put phone to ear and say, "Hello."
6. Listen for directions.
7. Verbally describe the location and the surroundings.
8. Stay put.
9. Continue to speak to the caller until found.
10. Once found, press "no" (or red) button to hang up.

Once a task analysis is created, it can be used to assess a student's performance and then, along with chaining strategies, it can be used to teach the student to engage in the activity. (See Chapter 4 for a review of task analysis as an instructional strategy.)

There are some strategies, however, that can further increase the relevance and utility of task analytic assessment. The Component Model of Functional Life Routines (F. Brown et al., 1987) identifies areas of concern in the standard application of task analysis for assessment. First, most task analyses are designed with a very limited scope of skills. Traditionally, tasks are broken down within the context of observable motor skills (e.g., pick up the hairbrush, bring brush to head, brush down the hair on the left side of the head) and do not identify related skills associated with meaningful performance of an activity in the natural environment (e.g., choosing a hairstyle, what to do if you have a knot in your hair). Most activities, as they are typically performed by individuals in real settings, include skills such as initiating the activity, socializing during the activity, communicating about the activity, problem solving as needed, making choices related to the activity, and monitoring the quality of the activity. These skills that are frequently excluded from task analysis could enable students (especially those with severe physical disabilities) to have more control over the routine (i.e., exercise more self-determination).

Second, the beginning and ending points of behavioral chains are often arbitrary or inconsistent, and may not require students to engage in the task in the way that their nondisabled peers typically do. As we design task analyses to assess a student's performance of important tasks and routines, it is important to consider natural cues in the environment and the ways that typ-

ical people perform tasks. For example, it is preferable for a student to respond to a natural environmental cue (e.g., the sound of the lunch bell) instead of responding to a teacher's verbal cue (e.g., "it's time to go to lunch"). Similarly, in many task-analyzed activities, students with disabilities are often not expected to end a task in the way that their nondisabled peers do. For example, ending a task may mean putting away the materials that were used (e.g., putting the game into the box and back on the shelf); for other students, especially those who do not have the physical ability to put away materials, ending a task may mean indicating when they would like the activity to end. Task analytic assessment should include the expectation of performing in ways that reflect typical performance and/or allow meaningful participation so that skills are more functional and complete.

Third, because the usual division of an activity into smaller steps focuses on the motor aspects of the activity, teachers often focus on participation in just those components of the activity. For a student with multiple disabilities, such as Christine, this would mean that partial participation in activities would center on physical expectations and outcomes (e.g., lifting the brush to her head). This may present an obstacle for Christine, preventing her from participating in a way that she finds meaningful or satisfying (e.g., choosing to wear a hair ribbon or a barrette). Partial participation should allow the student greater control, or self-determination, over personal routines and activities (F. Brown & Lehr, 1993).

For a student like Marc who can physically participate extensively in the routine, teachers should identify an appropriate range of skills to more closely represent mastery. For example, the Adaptive Behavior Scales–Public School Version (Lambert et al., 1993) breaks down "washing hands and face" into the following components: (a) washes hands and face with soap and water without prompting, (b) washes hands with soap, (c) washes face with soap, (d) washes hands and face with water, and (e) dries hands and face. Would successful performance of these four parts imply that the student has mastered this skill? These core skills do not sample the range of behaviors necessary for functional use of the routine. To use this skill in the natural environment, Marc would also be expected to know, for example, when his hands needed to be washed, to check to make sure that they are clean, and to know where to find more soap when the soap runs out.

The Component Model of Functional Life Routines (F. Brown et al., 1987; F. Brown & Lehr, 1993) outlines several ways in which an individual can meaningfully participate in activities. Performing the basic motor, or *core*, skills is only one of three ways that participation can occur in any given routine. *Extension skills* expand on the core skills and create a more comprehensive routine and thus provide a more meaningful evaluation of student competence. Extension skills include (a) initiation, (b) preparation, (c) monitoring the quality, (d) monitoring the tempo, (e) problem solving, and (f) terminating.

Extension skills provide options for meaningful participation in the activity without extensive physical requirements. For example, Christine cannot eat independently, but she can independently initiate a routine by pointing to her communication board or indicating that she wants more to eat or that she is finished eating. Christine can also monitor the quality of the routine by indicating that her blouse is dirty from lunch and needs to be changed, even though she may not be able to independently change her own blouse.

Enrichment skills are not critical to independent performance of a routine. They do, however, add to the quality of the routine and, as such, may be considered to be equally as important as the skills already mentioned. If educators are concerned with the quality of students' lives, then their assessment procedures should reflect this concern. Enrichment skills include expressive communication, social behaviors, and choice. If one were doing class recycling, commenting on the activity may not be crucial to accomplishing the task, but it may make this task a more pleasant experience and also offers functional practice of the communication skill. Choosing between two or more feasible alternatives (e.g., which book to read, read a book or listen to music, what hairstyle to wear) is also not crucial to the performance of a routine, but it adds to the quality of a student's experience, as well as providing more control over daily life.

Each resulting skill in a component analysis represents a meaningful unit of behavior; all items are relevant to the demands of the natural environment and are particularly important for students with severe physical disabilities. Students like Christine often "bottom out" on many assessments because core motor skills are the usual focus. In interpreting a core skill assessment, a teacher may conclude that the student should begin to learn the specific motor movements of the skill as determined by a detailed task analysis.

Using the component model, however, the student may be able to engage in other, more meaningful and more satisfying aspects of the routine.

Before going to meet her friends at the campus food court, Christine's friend Anna takes her into the restroom where they "check their look in the mirror." Anna asks Christine whether she would like her to comb her hair for her. Christine indicates "yes" or "no" on her Dynavox. If Christine replies "yes," Anna will comb her hair for her. They feel that this is not the time for Christine to practice combing her hair— she just wants to make sure that her hair looks the way she wants it to look. After Anna combs her hair, she prompts Christine to look in the mirror and let her know whether it's okay with her. After they are both satisfied, Christine uses her Dynavox to thank Anna for helping her with her hair.

With the component model, team members not only assess relevant items and score meaningful dimensions of behavior, but also include these items as relevant goals in the student's educational program. The items identified using this approach are closely aligned with the mission of Billingsley et al.'s (1996) outcome framework: to identify those skills that would facilitate the individual's membership and belonging in settings that are valued by the individual, family members, and other members of his or her community.

Figure 3–1 is an example of the component model applied to the activity of "plays a game with a peer and an adult," which was identified as an objective for Jacob. In addition to delineating meaningful units of behavior, the format depicted in Figure 3–1 can be used to record a baseline and to assess progress during instruction. Note that in this analysis of the activity, "performs basic steps of the game" is only one of a total of 11 steps. This implies that playing the game itself is only one part of the activity and that there are many other ways that we are expecting Jacob to participate. If playing the game (e.g., following the rules of the game) were the goal, this step would be further task-analyzed.

Ecological Inventories

Ecological inventories are a type of informal environmental assessment that require teachers to consider areas of instruction arranged in "domains of adult functioning," or skill categories (L. Brown et al., 1979). These domains may include domestic, leisure, community,

FIGURE 3–1

Task Analysis of "Plays Game with Peer and Adult" Using The Component Model of Functional Life Routines

Student: _Jacob_

Age: _9_   Date: _____

Domain: _Leisure_

Routine: _Plays game with peer and adult_

Plays Game with Adult	Yes	No	NA	With Adaptations	Comments
1. Lets you or peers know in some way it is time to play game (*initiate*)					
2. Selects game of choice					
3. Selects peer(s) to play with (*choice*)					
4. Arranges play area, gets materials, or arranges with others for things to be done (*prepare*)					
5. Performs basic steps of the game (*core*)					
6. Attempts to improve skills or increase enjoyment for self or others (*monitor quality*)					
7. Spends appropriate amount of time engaged in game (*monitor tempo*)					
8. If a problem arises (e.g., can't find game piece) will take action to remove problem (*problem-solve*)					
9. Puts away materials, arranges for others to put away, or lets other know he is done playing (*terminate*)					
10. Expresses or communicates about any aspect of the activity (e.g., enjoyment, request) (*communication*)					
11. Responds appropriately with peers during game, such as sharing and taking turns (*social*)					

Note: Adapted with permission from Brown, F., Evans, I. M., Weed, K. A., & Owen, V. (1987). Delineating functional competencies: A component model. *Journal of the Associations for Persons with Severe Disabilities, 12*(2), 122.

school, and vocational areas. The domestic domain includes skills performed in and around the home, such as self-care, clothing care, housekeeping, cooking, and yard work. In the leisure domain are spectator or participant skills that may take place in the community, at school, or at home. The community domain includes skills such as crossing the street, using public transportation, shopping, eating in restaurants, and using other public facilities. The vocational domain includes skills involved in attaining meaningful employment, some of which occur in the middle school and high school settings, but most of which take place in community locations. Historically, the activities and skills identified under each of the four domains (i.e., domestic, leisure, community, and vocational) were used to develop the school program for a student with severe disabilities. With neighborhood-inclusive schools being the standard for best practices, the school domain is also examined to determine the school-specific routines (e.g., eating in a cafeteria, using a locker, attending an assembly) that should be assessed for a particular student.

Lou Brown and his colleagues (L. Brown et al., 1979) refer to their assessment strategy as a "top-down" approach to skill building. That is, they begin with the requirements of independent adult participation within each domain. This practice helps to ensure the identification of skills that are functional. The ecological approach differs from the developmental approach, in which instructional objectives are chosen from the "bottom up," starting with skills that are normally performed by infants and proceeding to those considered more advanced. When IEP goals and objectives address skills that are functional for a person, the chances that those skills, once learned, will be used and thus naturally maintained are increased. Because learning is often slow and skill loss through disuse is predictable for students with severe disabilities, target skills that meet the criterion of functionality can facilitate good conditions for skill retention.

Ecological inventories are tailored to encourage skill generalization in several ways. First, functionality is defined for each student by a variety of individuals familiar with this student and the student's current and potential home, school, community, leisure, and work environments. Second, we typically will see some redundancy in skills and activities that are required across environments (e.g., using the bathroom occurs in many different settings). Skills that are required more often will be given a higher priority than those required less often; higher priority skills will be more naturally supported by teachers, peers, and coworkers in those environments.

Another advantage of using ecological inventories over commercially prepared tests is their flexible content (L. Brown et al., 1979). The content is not predetermined; instead, it depends on each student's life circumstances. Considering the variability in students and their environments and their subsequent demands, individually determined assessment content is an asset. For example, the demands and activities in

urban settings are quite different from those in rural settings. Certainly, recreational options in various communities differ greatly, as do the leisure preferences of students and their families. The age and family culture of the student also will be determining factors in the types of environments and activities in which they engage. If one's goal is to assess a student's ability to adapt within a particular environment, the content of the assessment should reflect the unique requirements of the community and family context.

According to L. Brown et al. (1979), there are five phases of the ecological inventory process:

1. Identify the curriculum domains.
2. Identify and survey current and future natural environments.
3. Divide the relevant environments into subenvironments.
4. Inventory these subenvironments for the relevant activities performed there.
5. Determine the skills required for performance of the activities.

The teacher, working with school staff and family members, proceeds through each phase in order.

Curriculum Domains

For many students, all five domains (i.e., domestic, leisure, school, community, and vocation) are relevant. However, teachers and parents need not concern themselves with the vocational domain until the middle school years. Instead of the traditional academic or developmental categories, curriculum domains are used because they (a) represent the major life areas, (b) lead to the selection of practical skills, and (c) emphasize the functional goals of self-sufficiency. However, use of curriculum domains does not mean that communication, motor, social, or academic skills are forgotten. Instead, the domains are used as contexts in which to embed and teach those skills.

Most often, the ecological inventory focuses on elementary, middle school, high school, and beyond. However, when considering very young children, many professionals do not feel that it is appropriate to predict possible adult environments (Lehr, 1989). Several educators describe application of the *criterion of the next environment* for preschool children. For young children, the skills that are identified should focus on social behavior and skills needed for the next environment, such as an inclusive kindergarten. Figure 3–2 shows the different domains identified for Jacob and Christine, reflecting the differences in their ages;

FIGURE 3–2

Examples of Domains, Environments, and Subenvironments for Jacob and Christine

Jacob:

Domain	Domestic	School	Community	Leisure
Environments	**Apartment**	**4th Grade**	**Grocery store**	**Park**
Subenvironments	Elevator	Classroom	Shopping cart area	Benches
	Kitchen	Bathroom	Food aisles	Playground
	Bathroom	Hallway	Deli counter	Baseball field
	Bedroom	School yard	Cashier	Water fountain
	Fire escape	Main office	Parking lot	Basketball court

Christine:

Domain	Domestic	School	Community	Leisure	Vocational
Environments	**Private house**	**University campus**	**Recycle center**	**Movie theatre**	**Library**
Subenvironments	Kitchen	Classrooms	Parking lot	Ticket booth	Check out desk
	Bathroom	Student union	Cans and plastic area	Concession stand	Hallways
	Bedroom	Bookstore	Paper area	Theatre	Restroom
	Den	Library	Bottles area	Bathroom	Break area
	Yard	Restrooms	Office	Video games	Stacks

Note: Adapted with permission from Silberman, R. K., & Brown, F. (1998). Alternative approaches to assessing students who have visual impairments with other disabilities in classroom and community environments. In S. Z. Sacks & R. K. Silberman (Eds.), *Educating students who have visual impairments with other disabilities* (p. 81). Baltimore: Paul H. Brookes.

Jacob's assessment will reflect four domains, and Christine, who is older, is expected to participate in all five domains.

Current and Future Natural Environments

The next step requires the teacher to identify and examine the environments in which the student currently lives, learns or studies, works, and plays. Although it is difficult to predict future environments, it is necessary to identify them as early as possible. For Jacob, who is nine years old, several environments are relevant—his own home (an apartment), the babysitter's home, various shops in his neighborhood, doctor's offices, the neighborhood park, and his school building. A future environment will be the middle school in his neigh-

borhood. In contrast, Christine's relevant environments at age 20 include her home, the university campus, the various job sites that she is sampling (e.g., the library), and the different facilities in the community in which she and her family participate (e.g., the recycling center). Figure 3–2 reflects variations in the types of environments identified for assessment for Jacob, who lives in a more urban setting, and Christine, who lives in a suburban environment.

Subenvironments

Further division is necessary to identify the physical areas, or subenvironments, most likely to be frequented in each environment for the student. Because Jacob and Christine live in different environments (i.e., an apartment versus a private house), it follows that the subenvironments will also be different. For example, Jacob uses an elevator, while Christine has access to a backyard. The diversity in these two students' ages, living environments, and a variety of other variables underscore the need for assessments that will be sensitive to individual lifestyles. Figure 3–2 shows examples of subenvironments for Jacob and Christine.

Relevant Activities

What are the essential activities that occur in these subenvironments? Because there are potentially an endless number of possible activities that could occur, teachers must consider a variety of factors as they determine which activities are most relevant—for example, (a) activities that are considered to be mandatory for successful participation in the various environments, (b) the number of times an activity is needed in other subenvironments in which the student participates, (c) the student's current skills, (d) the student's preferences and interests, (e) the priorities of the family,

(f) the specific physical characteristics of the setting in which the activity will occur, (g) the potential for the student's meaningful partial participation in the activity, and (h) the contribution of this activity to the student's relationships and belonging. Figure 3–3 provides examples of activities found in one subenvironment of the school domain for Jacob and one environment of the leisure domain for Christine.

Skills Required

This step requires that activities be broken down into teachable units, or task analyzed. A task analysis (described earlier in Task Analytic Assessment and in more detail in Chapter 4) is a detailed description of each behavior needed to accomplish a complex behavior (Alberto & Troutman, 2008). As task analysis relates to assessment, the student is asked to perform a selected task or activity, and the student's performance on each component is recorded (see Chapter 5 for examples of evaluating performance on task-analyzed activities). The teacher then knows which components of the chain need to be addressed (e.g., taught, environmental

FIGURE 3–3

Examples of Activities in One Subenvironment in the School Domain for Jacob and Christine

	Jacob	Christine
ENVIRONMENT	**SCHOOL**	**HIGH SCHOOL**
Subenvironment	**Classroom**	**Homeroom**
Activities	Morning group	Pledge to flag
	Snack	Attendance
	1:1 discrete trial instruction	Hand in notices
	Centers	Pack new notices
	Toileting and handwashing	Review day's schedule
	Recess	
	Music group	

Adapted with permission from Silberman, R. K. & Brown, F. (1998). Alternative approaches to assessing students who have visual impairments with other disabilities in classroom and community environments. In S. Z. Sacks & R. K. Silberman (Eds.). *Educating student who have visual impairments with other disabilities* (p. 82). Baltimore: Paul H. Brookes.

FIGURE 3–4

Blank Form for an Environmental Inventory

Student:
Environment:
Date:
Informants:
Methods:

Domain:	Performance Level			Component Skills					Comments
	(Check one)			(Check skills that are displayed)					
Subenvironments/Activity									

modifications made). Although each skill is separated for measurement and teaching, the teacher must not lose sight of the activity or clusters of related skills that must be performed together in the natural environment. For Christine, the "Communicate food and drink order" step at the concession stand (see Figure 3–3) includes many related skills: knowing when it is her turn to order, selecting the desired items on her Dynavox, placing her food and drink order with the cashier, paying for her order, and communicating "thank you" to the cashier.

Examples of Ecological Inventories. We are not recommending any one format for completing an ecological inventory because ecological inventories should be individualized to assess the variables deemed critical by the educational team. Figure 3–4 is an example of an environmental inventory format. This inventory does not specify the type of scoring used to measure the core skills (e.g., the performance level of the activity or routine), nor does it specify the type of component skills that will be measured. The inventory should be individualized according to variables such as the context; the student's age, strengths, and needs; and the component skills identified by the team as being important. For some students, a dichotomous performance score of "yes" or "no" may be appropriate; for others, the team may be interested in the level of prompt needed for the student to complete the activity (e.g., verbal, model, physical assistance). Assessment of component skills will also vary according to the needs of the individual student. Problem solving and initiation may be critical skills for one student; assessing social and communication skills throughout the school day may be of interest with regard to another student.

Figure 3–5 shows a section of the ecological inventory that Marc's teacher completed to examine the subenvironments and activities involved from the time of his arrival at school through "centers" time. The activities typically expected of other children in his class in each of the subenvironments (e.g., hallways, bathroom, morning group) were listed down the left side of the form. The team was interested in assessing Marc's performance in these activities using a three-part scoring system (i.e., assistance needed for most steps, some steps, or independent performance), so these are indicated across the top of the form. The team was also interested in Marc's performance of a variety of component skills.

It was decided by Marc's team that, in addition to assessing his basic performance of the activities, assessment of several component skills would be revealing. Discussion focused on Marc's inconsistent initiation and termination of activities in both the special education class and the kindergarten. Termination was of particular interest to his teachers, who reported that sometimes Marc would get upset when he was asked to leave one activity and begin another. On the other hand, Marc would terminate too quickly when he did not care for the activity or the interaction. Marc's parents were especially interested in their son exhibiting social and interaction skills with others, so these skills also were assessed within activities. Finally, everyone agreed that assessing Marc's choice making and communication skills would address his IEP goals and foster self-determination and cognitive development. The team felt that it would be especially critical to assess choice and communication within the context of his daily activities because much instruction in these areas occurred in one-to-one and therapeutic settings.

The ecological inventory strategy is an important step in curriculum development for students with severe disabilities; however, it can be very time consuming. What strategies might the team use to make the process more efficient and still identify functional outcomes that can be considered as IEP goals? Often there are multiple students in a given school whose IEP process will benefit from this assessment. Thus, teams might first develop a general environmental inventory in a computer file for a particular school setting, including common subenvironments and activities. When applied to a specific student, the inventory would then be individualized. As the student changes grades, computer files can simply be reviewed with the team and revised; entirely new inventories need not be designed until there is a change in the school setting.

When designing ecological inventories, it is important to remember that the general process does not take into consideration the subjectivity of the assessors. Although the process very much ensures identification of skills that are functional for the individual, the skill sequences identified by two raters may be substantially different. For example, a teacher who has had extensive training in communication may identify numerous communication opportunities within her ecological inventory. A second teacher who has had extensive experience teaching students with multiple

FIGURE 3–5

Sample from Environmental Inventory for Jacob

Student: Jacob
Environment: Preschool
Date: October 2009
Informants: Parents, preschool teacher, teaching assistant, speech therapist, 1:1 instructor
Methods: Interview and observation

Domain: School	Performance Level (Check one)			Component Skills (Check skills that are displayed)					Comments
Subenvironment/Activity	Assist on most steps	Assist on some steps	Independent	Initiates	Relates social skills	Makes choices	Terminates	Communicates	
Parking lot and building entrance									
• Enters			X	X					
• Greets children	X								
• Greets adults	X								
Hallways									
• Greets others	X								
• Hangs up coat		X		X		X	X		
Bathroom									
• Toilets		X		X			X		Terminates too quickly
• Washes hands		X				X	X		Terminates too quickly
• Checks appearance		X					X		Terminates too quickly
Morning group									
• Sits in place		X				X			
• Interacts with others	X				X		X		Terminates too quickly; only interacts with Melinda

FIGURE 3–5 (*Continued*)

Domain: School	Performance Level (Check one)			Component Skills (Check skills that are displayed)					Comments
Subenvironments/Activity	Assist on most steps	Assist on some steps	Independent	Initiates	Relates social skills	Makes choices	Terminates	Communicates	
Morning group continued									
• Follows instructions	X								
• Uses materials	X								Doesn't want to terminate
• Initates actions		X							
• Raises hand for attendance		X							
Centers									
• Follows schedule		X				X			Seems to enjoy looking at schedule and choosing
• Shares with others	X					X		X	Shares only with certain peers; terminates quickly
• Uses materials		X							Doesn't want to terminate
• Switches centers following bell cue		X							Hard to switch activities once he is involved in one
• Interacts with others	X				X		X	X	Terminates too quickly; interacts easily with Melinda

disabilities may focus on the physical demands of an environment.

Teachers need to be sure that ecological inventories identify not only the observable activities and skills that are associated with competent performance in natural environments, but also related skills (e.g., extension and enrichment skills) that may not be quite so apparent. In addition to communication and motor skills, subtle social skills, such as smiling at a waitress and having eye contact with the cashier at a restaurant, may not be consistently identified. Although not always critical to the performance of the routine, these behaviors may nonetheless be crucial to socially appropriate performance of an activity. Similarly, some language competencies may not be observable because they do not occur at that specific place or at the time of the activity. For example, "attending a school assembly" or "going to a movie" may be identified as an activity within the school domain and will be divided into its component parts, but "communicating about the assembly" or the movie later in the day or "sitting by a friend at the assembly" or "inviting a friend to a movie" probably would not be identified in an inventory.

Applications of Ecological Inventory. Several authors have formalized the ecological inventory approach by providing more structure or by systematizing the approach within the context of life domains.

The *Functional Assessment and Curriculum for Teaching Students with Disabilities* is a multiple-volume guide to functional curriculum across multiple domains: self-care, motor skills, household management, living skills (Bender, Valletutti, & Baglin, 2008); communication and literacy preparation (Valletutti, Bender, Hoffnung, & Baglin, 2008); functional academics (Valletutti et al., 2008); interpersonal skills, vocational skills, and leisure-time skills (Bender, Valletutti, & Baglin, 2008). Each of the four volumes uses a simple checklist assessment approach. Teams rate student skills on behaviors in the domains of interest using a four-point rating scale: not evident, emerging, with assistance, and independent. Once the team selects the priority skills, IEP objectives are written, instructional procedures are identified, and an assessment strategy is specified to monitor student progress.

The *Syracuse Community-Referenced Curriculum Guide for Students with Moderate and Severe Disabilities* (Ford et al., 1989) is a curriculum guide that uses the ecological approach. This guide focuses on the four domains of (a) self-management and home

living, (b) vocational, (c) recreation and leisure, and (d) general community functioning. Also included in this guide are sections on functional academic skills (e.g., reading, writing, money handling, time management) and embedded skills (e.g., social, communication, motor). Each scope and sequence chart lists the major goal areas of the domain and examples of the sequence of possible activities relevant to students as they progress through the school years. Thus, the goal (or function) remains the same over time, but the form of the activity in which students participate may differ (e.g., a child in kindergarten may learn to prepare a simple snack, a high school student may learn to plan a menu).

Choosing Options and Accommodations for Children (COACH) (Giangreco, Cloninger, & Iverson, 1998) is another assessment and planning tool. COACH is a comprehensive curriculum guide that helps the team develop annual goals and objectives, and determine general supports and accommodations that the student needs to participate in the educational program. There are a wealth of forms to facilitate assessment, implementation, and evaluation of priority goals and objectives. COACH offers a comprehensive system for helping the educational team move from assessment and identification of objectives to implementation and evaluation of the educational plan within the context of the general education program.

Functional Behavioral Assessment of Problem Behaviors

A comprehensive assessment of problem behaviors is the cornerstone for developing effective and positive behavioral strategies. Recent efforts to reduce severe problem behaviors, such as self-injury, aggression, and property damage, have focused on assessment of the variables that predict and functionally maintain behavior. In other words, the relationship between the inappropriate behavior and the environment becomes the focus of the assessment. The term *functional behavioral assessment* refers to the process used to identify the antecedent and consequent events that occasion and maintain problem behavior (Lennox & Miltenberger, 1989). (See Chapter 7 for an in-depth description of functional assessment and the development of positive behavior support programs.)

Many problem behaviors are attributed to specific pragmatic intents (i.e., the behavior serves a specific function for the individual and is a form of communication for the individual). Durand (1990) classifies controlling variables into four categories, or functions, for the individual: (a) social attention (the behavior elicits attention for the individual), (b) escape (the behavior results in the individual's being removed from an unpleasant situation), (c) access to tangible consequences (the behavior results in access to reinforcing events or materials), and (d) sensory feedback (the behavior provides or reduces auditory, visual, or tactile stimulation). O'Neill et al. (1997) suggest that problem behaviors serve the two major functions of obtaining desired events (e.g., internal stimulation, attention, activities or objects) or escaping/avoiding undesirable events (e.g., internal stimulation, attention, tasks or activities).

Once the function of the behavior is determined (e.g., escape from difficult tasks), the student should be provided with and instructed on a more appropriate way of communicating the same message (e.g., show picture symbol to obtain assistance instead of hitting oneself to escape the difficult task). In other words, the behavior taught to the individual should be functionally equivalent to the problem behavior (Durand & Carr, 1991; Haring & Kennedy, 1990). This strategy has been termed *functional communication training* (Durand & Merger, 2001).

Functional behavioral assessment indicated that some of Marc's tantrums, which were typically accompanied by throwing materials and falling to the ground, resulted in his "escape" from nonpreferred activities (especially writing). His teachers, the speech and language therapist, and his parents scheduled a meeting to design a program to teach him how to indicate that he needed a break from nonpreferred activities, both at school and at home. The goal would be for Marc to refuse to participate or to terminate an activity in a socially acceptable way instead of using tantrum behavior to escape from or avoid the activity. Two agenda items were identified for their meeting. First, they wanted to decide how to change the writing task (e.g., use a slant board to make writing easier; use a built-up pencil; give him a choice of writing implements). Second, they wanted to decide which form of communication would best allow him to communicate that he needed a break. It would be important to give Marc a way to indicate "break" that would be quick, easy to execute, and easily understood by others (e.g., a card printed with the word break or a picture of a stoplight).

When a student engages in problem behaviors, it is critical to examine a variety of educational and curricular variables that might be associated with the behaviors (Bambara & Kern, 2005; Dunlap, Kern-Dunlap, Clarke, & Robbins, 1991; Knoster, 2000). This process is often a challenge for the team as they proceed with functional behavioral assessment, but it is a critical component of the development of an educational program for students who engage in behaviors that interfere with learning.

A comprehensive functional behavioral assessment should provide information concerning the function of the behavior, as well as other environmental variables that maintain the behavior. The range of possible variables that may contribute to the presence of problem behavior is as wide, varied, and unique as are the students themselves. There are a variety of comprehensive assessments and program development guides to help teams through this process (e.g., Bambara & Kern, 2005; Carr et al., 1994; Crone & Horner, 2003; Durand, 1990; Janney & Snell, 2008; O'Neill et al., 1997). From a summary of variables that are included in a variety of published functional behavioral assessments, F. Brown (1996) identified four major areas that teams should assess: *environmental variables* (e.g., when and where is it most and least likely to happen, in what activities is it most and least likely to occur, who is present), *communication variables* (e.g., whether the student has the skills to communicate in a more appropriate way, whether others understand the student's communicative attempts), *choice/control variables* (e.g., whether the student is thwarted from doing preferred activities, whether the student values the activities in which he or she is involved), and *teaching/instructional variables* (e.g., whether tasks are too difficult or not sufficiently challenging, whether team members are adequately prepared to implement the behavior support plan, whether prompting strategies are too intrusive).

An exciting area that has an emerging research base is the impact that the quality of the environment and social relationships have on problem behaviors. Although, as a field, we have for some time placed great value and importance on relationships and the quality of the environment, Carr and his colleagues have been systematically exploring this relationship. Carr, Ladd, and Schulte (2008) suggest that "function does not exist in a vacuum; it is embedded in and influenced by specific contexts that involve physical, activity/routine, social, and biological factors" (p. 92). These researchers then recommend that assessment of problem behavior should also include assessment of the context in which the person participates. Regarding social relationships, Magito McLaughlin and Carr (2005) found that when rapport between the individual with the disability and the caregiver was good, levels of problem behaviors were reduced; conversely, when rapport was low, problem behaviors were high. Furthermore, these researchers found that when rapport was improved, the individual's task completion also improved.

Four strategies frequently used to conduct functional analysis include (a) informant assessment or interview, (b) rating scales, (c) direct observation, and (d) systematic manipulation of controlling variables (or analog assessments). Analog assessments "involve the manipulation of various antecedents and consequences that are presumed to be important and observing their effect on an individual's problem behavior" (Durand, 1990, p. 66). (See Chapter 6 for a comprehensive description of each strategy.) As an example, we can apply one component of the process—manipulation of controlling variables—to Marc, who sometimes exhibits tantrum behaviors (e.g., cries, throws materials, falls to the ground).

Through the functional assessment process, Marc's tantrums were hypothesized to be motivated by a desire to escape from the activities during which they occurred. To test this hypothesis, his special education teacher set up a time (e.g., Monday during writing) when Marc would be allowed to "escape" each time he began a tantrum (i.e., Ms. Wharton would reinforce the tantrum by allowing him to escape). This would be repeated on Wednesday and Thursday. Data from those days would be compared with data from Tuesday and Friday, when escape by tantrum would not be reinforced (i.e., his teacher would attempt to redirect him back to his activities). If the data revealed a greater number of tantrums on Monday, Wednesday, and Thursday, then Ms. Wharton could conclude that the tantrum may be a function of the escape that it produces; that is, the tantrum behavior increases when it is reinforced by escape from the activity. Ms. Wharton could use this information to design or revise current instructional strategies. As described previously, she and others from the team might design a functional communication training program to teach Marc to escape in a more appropriate way (e.g., indicate the need for a break).

Furthermore, Ms. Wharton might examine Marc's scheduled activities that are associated with tantrum behavior to determine whether they are (a) needed, (b) preferred or disliked, and (c) on an appropriate level of difficulty. Some activities associated with Marc's tantrums might not be necessary and could be eliminated from his schedule. However, other activities associated with his problem behavior might not be dispensable, so Ms. Wharton would need to investigate further. Are certain activities too difficult, and if so, should they be simplified, or should Marc be taught to request help? Are the activities simply disliked? If so, Ms. Wharton could make one or several program improvements: (a) teaching Marc to request periodic breaks, (b) preceding the problematic activities with simpler activities, (c) allowing Marc to schedule when he will complete the nonpreferred activities, or (d) following participation in nonpreferred activities with a choice of preferred activities (i.e., positive reinforcement for participation in nonpreferred activities).

Functional behavioral assessment of behavior problems is an important element of assessment that teachers should use when developing support plans for students who exhibit serious behavior problems. The assessment process should involve the entire educational team because functional assessment requires a study of a student throughout his or her daily activities.

Assessment of Student Preferences and Choices

Everyone, regardless of his or her level of disability, has preferences; thus, the opportunity to express one's preferences and to make and enjoy choices is important to everyone. Expressing preferences, however, can be very challenging for individuals who do not communicate in traditional ways (Brown, Gothelf, Guess, & Lehr, 1998). The educational team plays an important role in acknowledging efforts aimed at the expression of preference and self-determination, teaching the individual to more effectively communicate these preferences, and adjusting goals and objectives to respect the individual's preferences. Consistent with this basic life quality tenet, by law, educational and rehabilitation programs for persons with disabilities must reflect the use of an individual's preferences and allow choice making (Hughes, Pitkin, & Lorden, 1998). While related, *choice* and *preference* do not mean the same thing.

Choice can be observed when an individual acts to get or engage in something as an opportunity occurs, but a *preference is something consistently chosen* and is observed only by its effect on the individual over time. Preferences, like reinforcers, certainly can change with age, options, and satiation; higher preference activities can become less preferred or even nonperferred, depending on these and other factors. "While choice is an observable behavior, preference, on the other hand, is inferred from the act of choice" (Hughes et al., 1998, p. 299). We usually assume that choices reflect an individual's preferences, although they may not always do so.

Assessment Procedures

There is an abundance of research on the assessment, or identification, of reinforcers and preferences and the effects of offering opportunities for choice making to individuals with severe disabilities (e.g., Bambara, Ager, & Koger, 1994; Hughes et al., 1998; Ivanic & Bailey, 1995; Kern et al., 1998; Lohrmann-O'Rourke, Browder, & Brown, 2000). This research has demonstrated that increasing choice-making opportunities is associated with increases in appropriate behavior and decreases in inappropriate behavior (Kern et al., 1998). Cannella, O'Reilly, and Lancioni (2005) conducted an extensive review of the research literature on choice interventions and preference assessments and found 30 studies published between 1996 and 2002. These researchers found that studies fell into four categories: (a) integrating choice opportunities into daily contexts, (b) assessing the impact of choice making on behavior, (c) assessing preferences, and (d) evaluating the effectiveness of various formats for assessing preferences. Like Kern et al. (1998), Cannella et al. (2005) found a significant amount of research that supported the positive impact of choice on appropriate and inappropriate behaviors. Furthermore, they found that there were a variety of assessment formats that could be used to identify reinforcing stimuli.

Knowing what an individual prefers is important for several reasons. First, and foremost, when we know what an individual prefers, we can include these preferred stimuli in a variety of everyday routines. This will naturally create a more satisfying environment, thus contributing to quality of life (Brown, Gothelf, Guess, & Lehr, 1998). Second, preferred stimuli may be used to reinforce target behaviors or skills. This approach involves using preferred stimuli as a conse-

quence to reinforce students contingent on specific target behaviors; the outcome is that the strength or quality of the behavior is likely to improve.

Third, offering opportunities to choose between preferred activities or events may increase students' active involvement and promote their motivation during instruction (Hughes et al., 1998). A student's control in an activity is increased when he or she is asked to select the task, the materials (e.g., markers or colored pencils), the location, the classmates with whom to participate, or the order of the tasks. Mechling, Gast, and Cronin (2006) found that two adolescents with autism completed work tasks more quickly when they selected their reinforcers (from a choice of computer-displayed videos of themselves) than when teachers selected tangible reinforcers for them from a pool of known reinforcers. Increased involvement and motivation are good reasons to individually assess the activities, events, and objects that each student prefers and to offer many opportunities for choices within the context of daily routines throughout the day (Bambara, Koger, Katzer, & Davenport, 1995; F. Brown, Belz, Corsi, & Wenig, 1993). Choosing is better than just being given preferred activities or reinforcers by someone else.

Fourth, offering opportunities to choose among preferred activities or events increases a student's control over variables in their environment, which has been associated with a reduction in problem behaviors. For example, Carlson, Luiselli, Slyman, and Markowski (2008) worked with a 13-year-old girl and a 5-year-old boy, both on the autism spectrum, who engaged in public disrobing and urinary incontinence. The researchers used an intervention that offered each student several opportunities to change their clothes each day; if they chose to change, they were then offered a choice of two preferred clothing articles from which to select. Carlson et al. found a reduction in both public disrobing and incontinence to almost zero.

The hierarchy of most to least preferred activities, people, or items for individuals often varies over time (e.g., during the day, across days, across years). Because most students with severe disabilities cannot verbally inform us of these changes, initial comprehensive assessments should be followed by intermittent (or even daily) mini-assessments to determine what activities or items are currently preferred (Mason, McGee, Farmer-Dougan, & Risley, 1989; Roane, Vollmer, Ringdahl, & Marcus, 1998). As an alternative to mini-assessment, others suggest that always offering a choice of items and letting the student, instead of the teacher, select the activity or item is a more efficient way to ensure that the activities chosen are reinforcing (Horner & Carr, 1997).

In the following section, we review several comprehensive and mini-assessment methods that have been successful in identifying the preferences of students who have severe disabilities (Lohrmann-O'Rourke & Browder, 1998). It is important to remember, however, that assessment of preferences, just like all assessments, must be appropriate to the skill level of the student. Lee, Nguyen, Yu, Thorsteinsson, Martin, and Martin (2008) found that the effectiveness of a preference assessment depends, in part, on both the presentation modality of the items (e.g., objects, pictures) and on the individual's discrimination skills (e.g., visual discrimination, matching skills). For example, if a student does not understand picture representations and has limited verbal comprehension, it would be difficult to assess their activity preferences during a traditional one-to-one testing situation. Other formats would need to be employed (e.g., parental input).

Indirect Assessment

Indirect preference assessments rely on the opinion of others who know the individual well and involve the use of structured and unstructured interviews or checklists (Hagopian, Long, & Rush, 2004). Many teachers find it helpful to interview parents or others who know the student well to help them identify potential reinforcers. This type of indirect assessment could be very helpful, but should be considered just one step in assessing the student's preferences. Green et al. (1988) found that interviews do not usually identify reliable preferences when not used in combination with direct observation. However, as previously described, this type of assessment may be critical for assessing activities that are difficult to represent in classroom settings, and for students with more limited comprehension and discrimination skills.

Direct Assessment

Direct preference assessments involve systematically exposing the individual to stimuli for a brief period and then recording the person's approach or level of engagement with the stimuli (Hagopian et al., 2004). The accuracy and efficiency of preference assessment is likely to be enhanced if indirect assessments are conducted first to get an idea of a student's preferences

and then direct observations of the student are made during opportunities to interact with or choose from a pool of potentially interesting activities, foods, or objects. The outcome is a set of potential reinforcers (e.g., those which were approached 80% of the time), which also may be rank ordered from highly preferred to less preferred, not preferred, or avoided. Piazza et al. (1996) asked caregivers of four children with severe and profound disabilities to generate a list of potential reinforcers; these items were then used to create a direct preference assessment that was implemented with the participants. The results of the study showed that those items that were assessed as highly preferred by the children did function as reinforcers for the participants, and those that were deemed lower preference during the assessment did not act as reinforcers. This study demonstrates the importance and effectiveness of using both indirect assessment (e.g., caregiver input) to identify potential reinforcers and direct assessment. Usually, one of three methods are used for systematic, comprehensive assessment of preferences: approach–avoidance (e.g., Pace, Ivancic, Edwards, Iwata, & Page, 1985), forced choice (e.g., Fisher, Piazza, Bowman, & Amari, 1996), or free operant.

The *approach–avoidance* method involves presenting single items to a student and waiting for a short, standard length of time (e.g., about five seconds) for a student response. Just what constitutes an approach or an avoidance response must be defined individually for each student. Examples of approach responses are making eye contact with the item, moving toward the item, touching the item, and making a positive vocal expression. Avoidance responses may include behavior such as pushing the item away, making a movement away from the item, and making a negative vocalization. If the student approaches the item, that item is made available for another short interval (e.g., 5 seconds). If the student does not approach the item, it is removed, and shortly after the student is given an opportunity to sample the activity with prompts (e.g., help Marc turn on a tape recorder to play music). Following any opportunities to sample an activity, the student is given another approach opportunity with the same activity; if the student approaches it, an additional five seconds is given to allow engagement with that item. Another variation of this approach involves free access to a group of 10 or more potentially reinforcing items that involve various types of stimuli and social attention (e.g., tactile: Koosh ball; play: ball; drink: water, cola; social: praise, hugs) (Dyer,

1987). Any items that are consumed are replenished, and social attention is provided intermittently. An observer watches and rates the individual's approach and avoidance responses to each item or event.

Using the *forced-choice* method, items are presented in pairs, and each item in the pool of potential reinforcers is presented randomly with every other item. The same general procedures used in the approach–voidance method are used, except that items are presented in sets of two. The findings from this method may be more consistent than when items are presented alone, but the method can be time consuming. Kreiner and Flexer (2009) used a forced-choice computer software program to assess the age-appropriate leisure preferences of transition age students with severe and multiple developmental disabilities. In the Preferences for Leisure Attributes (PLA) program, two pictures of leisure activities are displayed on the screen side-by-side and the student selects the picture of his choice using any of a variety of responses (e.g., using a touch screen, using a mouse, pointing to the screen while the facilitator uses the mouse to point). Following the selection, another set of pictures are displayed, and the student again chooses; this continues until all choices have been made. The computer program compiles the data regarding the critical attributes of the selected stimuli (e.g., sports or arts, individual or group activities, level of motor skills required, level of physical activity required). These data then inform caretakers about what type of activities to make available to the student and what skills to develop so the individual can more fully participate in and enjoy their preferences. Unless students accurately associate the leisure options with the picture, the assessment is not valid.

Roane et al. (1998) used a *free-operant* method to assess preferences. According to this method, the student selects freely from a group of potentially like items. To conduct a free-operant assessment, a pool of 5 to 10 or more age-appropriate, potentially liked items are placed around the edge of a table. The student is guided around the table and is shown each item; new items are sampled or demonstrated. Once the teacher is prepared to record the student's choices, the student is allowed to have free access to the table for five minutes. No items are removed or replaced and no requests or prompts are given. The teacher simply records the frequency or duration that each item is manipulated or held. This approach also can be used on a regular basis to refresh the list of preferences when new items are added. This method was reported as taking less time and resulting in less student misbehavior, but still identifying items that students found to be reinforcing. When teachers do not control the presentation of various stimuli, as in the forced-choice assessment format, but provide free access, students appear more likely to participate willingly.

Considerations for Assessing Preferences

While the assessment methods we describe were used with students who have severe disabilities, these students demonstrated intentional behavior (see Chapter 11) and typically did not have motor or sensory limitations such as Christine's. Because our current methods for assessing preferences with students who have severe disabilities are less inclusive of students with extensive motor and sensory limitations, team members must make adjustments to these approaches when they are used with any particular student (Green & Reid, 1996; Ivancic & Bailey, 1995):

- The student's approach and avoidance response should be identified in observable terms: Be clear on what means *like* and *dislike*.

  Christine does not visually seek out items associated with preferred activities but smiles and sometimes laughs when engaged in activities that she enjoys. Marc does not show emotions in this way, but instead persists in the activities that he likes and cries when they are removed or when he cannot have access to them.

- Potential preferred items and activities need to be presented so that the student is aware of them. This is often referred to as "reinforcer sampling."

  Depending on the activity, Christine's team members tell her the name of the activity, let her experience any movement involved, hear noise associated with the activity, and feel objects involved in the activity.

- Items or activities should be sampled in ways that are meaningful to the student.

  Simply telling Marc about a new activity (e.g., "Marc, you can play with the water table today") will not provide a meaningful sample. Marc needs to be directed/encouraged to watch others use the water table and be encouraged to try it himself before his preference is assessed.

In designing and conducting preference assessments, there are also many considerations pertaining to the social validity of the assessment process. The following guidelines can increase the social validity of the assessment and its application to inclusive settings (Lohrmann-O'Rourke, Browder, & Brown, 2000):

- Assessments should be conducted in settings and within contexts that are as natural as possible.
- Assessments should be conducted by individuals who know the student well.

A behavioral consultant recently hired by Marc's school was interested in determining Marc's preferences. Using a forced-choice format, he systematically presented a variety of stimulus items to Marc. Marc avoided contact not only with the behavioral consultant but with all of the items presented by the consultant. The consultant concluded that the results did not measure Marc's preference for the stimuli that were being assessed but his level of comfort with the consultant. Plans were made to have his teacher learn how to conduct the assessment.

- Stimuli presented to the individual should be valued by the individual and represent a range of stimuli that reflect events or activities preferred by individuals who do not have disabilities.

When his teacher presented the stimulus pairs to Marc, the consultant was able to judge Marc's approach-avoidance to each item. Ms. Wharton was concerned, however, that although these items were chosen and thus were assumed to be preferred, perhaps they did not represent the events and activities that Marc seemed to enjoy most (e.g., DVDs, computer time, "high fives").

- In addition to identifying potential reinforcers, the results of preference assessments should provide information that will contribute to the improvement of daily life (i.e., noncontingent access to preferred events).

When it was determined that music was a potential reinforcer for Marc, some team members suggested that the opportunity to listen to music be contingent upon Marc's performance during group activities. But other team members thought that because we now know how much Marc likes music, he should have more access to music and that music should be a context in which he learns other skills. After much discussion, the team decided that there should be more music in Marc's life!

Assessment of Program Quality

The emphasis in this chapter, thus far, has been on assessment of students for the purpose of individual program design. It is important to remember, however, that individual students participate within the broader context of a classroom, school, district, and state. Assessment of the quality of services at each of these administrative levels is important. How well are students served by the class, school, district, state, or even country? Data collected to answer these questions include demographic information related to the number of students served, the settings in which they are served, the gender and racial characteristics of the population, student scores on statewide assessments, and so on.

Program quality assessment is important, not only for students, schools, districts, and states, but also for individual teachers attempting to develop and implement high-quality educational programs for their students. Teachers do not function within a vacuum—the quality of the support in their school and district will influence what can be accomplished in their own classrooms. Teachers may or may not feel supported by their school. The term "teacher efficacy" refers to the extent to which a teacher feels that he or she can have an impact on student performance; in other words, a teacher's belief in his or her own capacity to influence how well students learn (Soodak, Podell, & Lehman, 1998; Tschannen-Moran, Hoy, & Hoy, 1998). The quality of the school environment, district policies and regulations that are student centered, and ongoing professional development can all have a positive impact on teacher efficacy.

Following are three examples of instruments that have been developed to focus, not on the individual student, but on the broader context in order to determine the quality of the environment and the supports. Each of these evaluations helps schools and educators identify areas of strengths and needs, and allows the tracking of progress over time toward achieving program improvements.

Autism Program Quality Indicators (APQI)
APQI (Crimmins, Durand, Theuer-Kaufman, & Everett, 2001) is a self-review and program improvement guide for schools and programs serving students with autism spectrum disorders. The intent of the manual is to provide benchmarks of quality programs that are associated with positive outcomes for these students. Schools

can then self-evaluate their programs and identify areas of strengths and areas where they need further development. Seven categories of APQI relate to the educational process for students (i.e., Individual Evaluation, Development of the IEP, Curriculum, Instructional Activities, Instructional Methods, Instructional Environments, and Review and Monitoring of Progress and Outcomes), and seven categories focus on broader program characteristics and supports (i.e., Family Involvement and Support; Inclusion; Transitions across Settings; Challenging Behavior; Community Collaboration; Personnel; and Program Evaluation).

Program Quality Measurement Tool (PQMT)

The PQMT (Cushing, Carter, Clark, Wallis, & Kennedy, 2009) was developed for administrators and educators to evaluate their programs for students with severe disabilities regarding research-based practices, especially in the area of inclusive education. The PQMT contains 44 indicators, organized into three sections. The local education agency section includes indicators related to district-level support and policies regarding inclusion; the school building section contains indicators regarding values, integration, school climate, and policies and support; and the student section addresses practices related to assessment, planning, monitoring, and instructional practices.

School-Wide Positive Behavior Supports

The School-Wide Evaluation Tool (SET) (Sugai, Lewis-Palmer, Todd, & Horner, 2001) is a program assessment instrument used to evaluate a school's environment regarding the use of positive proactive school-wide discipline procedures (see Chapter 7). The purpose of the instrument is to support the school in developing environments in which students are safe, are learning important social skills, and that allow and encourage academic achievement (Horner et al., 2004). This research-validated instrument assesses and evaluates the extent to which a school is implementing School-wide Positive Behavior Supports (SW-PBS) and whether the efforts are actually resulting in positive changes in the school environment. Positive changes refer to improvement in school safety and culture. The SET consists of 28 items organized into the following seven subscales, which represent the key features of SW-PBS:

1. School-wide behavioral expectations are defined.
2. Expectations are taught to all children in the school.
3. Rewards are provided for adhering to the expectations.

4. A consistently implemented continuum of consequences for problem behavior is put in place.
5. Problem behavior patterns are monitored and the information is used for ongoing decision-making.
6. An administrator actively supports and is involved in the effort.
7. The school district provides support to the school in the form of functional policies, staff training opportunities, and data collection options (Horner et al., 2004, p. 5).

Prioritizing Skills from Assessment Information

Usually many more skills and activities are identified in the assessment process as being relevant for a student than can possibly be taught. Following the assessment process, the team must select which skills and activities will become the core of the individualized educational program. Prioritizing skills and activities is an important step because it defines the activities in which the student will participate for the upcoming year. A team approach is critical in this step of the educational process. Rainforth, York, and MacDonald (1997) reflect that "it is natural for service providers to see priorities from the vantage [point] of their own discipline. A collaborative and consensual approach to determining priorities may be the most difficult aspect of designing the IEP, since it frequently requires one or more team members to let go of what they view as important from their discipline's perspective" (p. 160).

One area in which all team members are likely to have consensus is regarding the priority of those skills that contribute to the student's quality of life. When professionals view each student with disabilities as having all the feelings, hopes, and needs of their more typical peers, focus on the assessment and evaluation of small skill changes seems inadequate. As described throughout this chapter, assessment should reflect a range of meaningful outcomes for the individual, the school, the family, and the community (Billingsley et al., 1996; Meyer & Janney, 1989). These types of skills must be considered high priority, including skills related to one's social life (the activities performed with other people) (Kennedy, Horner, & Newton, 1990); skills that increase the individual's control and choices in their daily life (F. Brown, 1991; Meyer & Evans, 1989); and skills that contribute to social and physical integration, family participation, and physical accessibility. In the sections that follow, we first discuss person-centered strategies that support the identification of high-priority skills associated with a good quality of life. We then discuss additional criteria that influence the selection of skills considered to be necessary for a given person.

Person-Centered Approaches

Person-centered planning is an approach that emerged in the mid-1980s to allow us to better understand the experiences of people with developmental disabilities and more respectfully and effectively support them to expand those experiences to achieve a desired quality of life (Cohen, 1998; Holburn, 2002; Holburn & Vietze, 2002; O'Brien, O'Brien, & Mount, 1997). This approach is qualitatively different from traditional educational, diagnostic, and standardized assessment approaches because it shifts the focus of control from the interdisciplinary team to the person with disabilities and his or her family, and it is their hopes and dreams that are assessed, which are then used to determine and direct the educational program and supports (Knowlton, 1998; Sands, Bassett, Lehmann, & Spencer, 1998; A. P. Turnbull et al., 1996). Kincaid (1996) suggests that person-centered planning activities share a commitment to seeking five essential goals, outcomes, or valued accomplishments in the individual's life: (a) being present and participating in community life, (b) gaining and maintaining satisfying relationships, (c) expressing preferences and making choices in everyday life, (d) having opportunities to fulfill respected roles and to live with dignity, and (e) continuing to develop personal competencies.

Two widely used person-centered planning tools—the McGill Action Planning System, or Making Action Plans (MAPS), and Personal Futures Planning—will be discussed here. MAPS (Forest & Lusthaus, 1989; Pearpoint, Forest, & O'Brien, 1996; Vandercook, York, & Forest, 1989) involves having typical students who know the individual well participate in several planning sessions. In MAPS, the individual and members of the individual's inner circle discuss several questions: (a) What is the individual's history? (b) What are your dreams for this person? (c) What is your nightmare about him or her (e.g., fears about the future)? (d) Who is this person? (e) What does he or she like? (f) What are his or her strengths, gifts, and talents? (g) What are his or her needs? (h) What would an ideal day for him or her look like? (i) What do we need to make this ideal real?

MAPS serves as a guide for the individual's circle of friends to identify critical areas of focus. The group meets regularly with the facilitating teacher or school staff and the target individual, informally evaluating actions, discussing improvements and new ideas, and continuing to support the target individual. Sometimes when elementary-school-age students are involved, the nightmare question is omitted (Snell & Janney, 2000).

In Personal Futures Planning (Mount & Zwernik, 1988), a facilitator trained in the planning process leads a group of key people through planning steps. The key people may be related to the target individual as close friends, family members, staff, or others with whom the person spends a lot of time. Whenever possible, the target individual is included in the planning process; advocates or spokespersons may be present to help the target person communicate. The first task of the group is to write a personal profile for the target individual. Personal profiles consist of three kinds of information about the individual: (a) history, (b) accomplishments, and (c) preferences and desires. The second task, a second meeting, addresses the individual's future plans. During the third task, the same participants proceed through seven steps: (a) review the personal profile, (b) review the trends in the environment that may affect the individual, (c) find desirable images of the future, (d) identify obstacles and opportunities, (e) identify strategies to implement the plan, (f) identify actions to get started, and (g) identify any needs for system changes.

At age 18, before Christine made the transition to the post–high school program at the nearby university, her parents and the rest of her educational team were joined by a few of her friends from the university and two high school students who knew her well to complete a person-centered plan. They hoped that the plan would help them further focus all their efforts on Christine's interests and life. The first activities took most of the afternoon and involved describing (a) who was at the meeting; (b) the people in Christine's life; (c) the places that she frequents— home, work, school, and in the community; (d) her history; (e) her health issues; (f) her preferences; (g) what promotes respect and what detracts from the respect given by others; (h) strategies that work and those which don't; (i) the team's hopes and fears about Christine; (j) barriers and opportunities; and (k) the themes of her life (Kincaid, 1996). The group was pleased with their efforts and they acquired a lot of new and important information regarding Christine's and her family's thoughts on priorities for the next year.

Criteria for Prioritizing Skills

There are many criteria to be considered when prioritizing objectives from assessment information. However, no single objective can meet all the criteria, and certainly some objectives may meet only a few but are still critical (e.g., an objective that meets health or medical needs). The relative importance of each criterion varies from student to student, especially given variations in family values, lifestyles, and perspectives (Rainforth et al., 1997). The following are questions that should be asked when selecting IEP objectives:

Does the objective reflect the student's chronological age, culture, preferences, and profile of strengths and needs? The student must be recognized as an individual with a chronological age and level of physical maturity, a culture, a family history and context, preferences (including likes and dislikes), and personal strengths and needs. Many students have clear strengths in their adaptive skills and in other personal abilities.

Because Christine's vision and spoken communication are very limited, her family, team members, and friends have learned that several strategies are important. For example, it is best when peers, parents, and teachers tell her what will happen next in simple terms; follow familiar routines while avoiding surprises when possible; avoid strategies that rely only on vision; and read her body language. She is very social and enjoys being around others when these simple guidelines for interaction are respected. This profile of strengths and needs for Christine has guided the team in selecting work sites for her to sample, and the profile also suggested some preparatory steps for each site. As an example, the team guessed that Christine would enjoy (a) assisting in checking out books at a nearby elementary school library and (b) being a greeter at Walmart. They hypothesized this because both jobs allowed active engagement and offered many social opportunities.

Does the objective focus on functional skills and lead to meaningful routines and activities? Another guideline for selecting IEP objectives is

functionality, or skill usefulness, a measure of how necessary and important a skill is to a particular person, given his or her current and future environments. Applying the functionality guideline to learning objectives means that no generic bank of IEP objectives can be universally taught. What is functional for one person often is not functional for another person. Functionality and need must be individually defined. Applying the functionality guideline also means looking to the near and distant future and planning for upcoming expectations and stages in the student's life cycle: entering preschool, moving into elementary school, starting middle school and becoming an adolescent, going to high school, taking a job, moving away from home, retiring, and facing death.

For example, in identifying objectives for his current IEP, Marc's teachers and parents must consider what skills are needed to prepare him for participating in first grade next year. By using assessment strategies that involve family, friends, present and upcoming teachers, or program staff, a team will be able to understand their students' present lives and formulate ideas about future expectations, possibilities, and hopes.

Can the student participate in the activity in a meaningful way? A student may be able to learn an activity so that it can be performed in its entirety in the natural environment. For these students, the appropriate range of participation necessary for competent performance of the skill in relevant contexts should be ensured (e.g., by initiation, problem solving, quality monitoring). Many students, however, are not able to attain independence in important, needed, or enjoyed skills or activities. Some of the cognitive and motor requirements of tasks may appear to present insurmountable obstacles for an individual student. However, partial participation (Baumgart et al., 1982) can open the door to many possibilities for including that student instead of excluding him or her because "she (or he) will never be able to do that!" Adaptive or prosthetic aids, adapted materials, rule or schedule adaptations, and personal assistance strategies are ways in which a student can meaningfully participate in an activity (Baumgart et al., 1982).

Meaningful participation can also be facilitated by focusing on extension and enrichment skills. For example, initiating, monitoring quality, terminating, choosing, social interacting, and communicating are ways to participate in a routine that do not require extensive motor participation (F. Brown et al., 1987; F. Brown & Lehr, 1993).

Does the objective reflect the student's personal and social needs? Planning an IEP by "functional" guidelines alone may mean that personal and social domains are slighted and that supports are viewed narrowly to include only teachers, therapists, and educational materials. This guideline stresses the importance of the relationships and membership domains. Regardless of the presence or the degree of a disability, children, adolescents, and adults need friends to participate in activities in a way that increases self-esteem. In fact, the presence of a disability may increase the need for supportive friends. Objectives that facilitate friendships, supports, and membership in the school and community should be given high priority.

Developing and Writing IEPs

Following the comprehensive assessment process and the prioritization of goals, the team will meet to work on development of the IEP. There are many variations in the IEP forms and procedures used by school systems and by teachers and, ultimately, in the specificity and utility of their contents. Still, all IEPs should be accurate road maps created collaboratively for a particular student by an educational team; IEPs must actively guide team members throughout a school year, not sit passively in file cabinets. IEP goals set the general direction for instruction and give a basis for developing detailed instructional plans, but they need not be detailed enough to be considered the equivalent of an instructional plan (Bateman & Herr, 2003). IEPs are agreements among team members on the focus and decisive elements that will become a particular student's educational program for a year unless changed by team consensus. This means that goals and objectives should be both measurable and specific enough to translate into classroom instruction. As specified in the Individuals with Disabilities Education Act (2004) in Sec. 614(d)(1)(A)(i), the IEP must include "a statement of the child's present levels of academic achievement and functional performance, including how the child's disability affects the child's involvement and progress in the general education curriculum." Furthermore, for "children with disabilities who take alternate assessments aligned to alternate achievement standards,

a description of benchmarks or short-term objectives" continues to be required in IEPs.

What Is a High-Quality IEP?

"The IEP is a firm, legally binding commitment of resources" by a school system and thus must be written with great care (Bateman & Linden, 1998, p. 60). Resources range widely from basic to specialized services and supports. Basic resources include buildings, transportation, professional and paraprofessional staff, instructional materials, and staff development; more specialized services and supports include related services personnel, educational programs designed to teach specific objectives, curriculum modifications, training on and support for collaborative teams and positive behavior support, augmentative and alternative communication devices, transportation to job settings in the community, and job coaches. The IEP is a document in which a student's many unique needs are addressed in a highly individualized way.

To develop an IEP, teams work together to assess and reach consensus in the following areas:

- *Unique needs and characteristics:* On the basis of assessment information, what are a student's unique educational needs or characteristics that the IEP should address?
- *Present level of performance (PLOP):* For each unique need, how is the student currently performing?
- *Educational services:* What will the educational team and district do, and what services will be furnished in response to each unique need or characteristic? When will these services begin? What will be their frequency, location, and duration?
- *Annual goals and objectives:* What student accomplishments (written as measurable goals and objectives) address these needs and link to that student's present level of performance? What student accomplishments will verify that the services provided are effective (Bateman & Linden, 1998, p. 100)?

The IEP constitutes the educational team's and district's design for providing special education, related services, supplementary aides and services, assistive technology, program modifications, and personnel support. IEP goals and objectives are written to be indicators of learning and program evaluation. Measuring goals and objectives enables a school to judge whether the services and educational program are successful.

Another essential element of the IEP concerns transition. IDEA requires IEP teams to include transition planning, in the form of an individualized transition plan (ITP), in the first IEP that will be in effect when the child turns 16 years of age. ITPs may well include interagency linkages between the school and adult services. Transition services are "a coordinated set of activities," not a haphazard plan, aimed at fostering movement from school to postschool life. These services include instruction; related services; community experiences; the development of employment and adult living skills; and, as is often needed with most students who have severe disabilities, the acquisition of daily living skills and functional vocational assessment. Thus, the focus of the IEP changes during the teen years to include the transition to the postschool years: higher education (for some students), adult life, and work (see Chapter 15).

Listed among the "worst sins" of an IEP are five failures: (a) failure to individualize; (b) failure to address all of a student's educational needs; (c) failure to specify needed services; (d) failure to write clear, meaningful, and measurable goals and objectives; and (e) failure to clearly describe a student's present levels of functioning (Bateman & Linden, 1998, p. 88). When teams write IEP objectives on the basis of inquiry in the four areas listed earlier, many of these failures can be prevented. The next section will trace the steps that IEP teams take to design and implement instructional programs.

Writing IEPs

Define the Student's Unique Characteristics and Needs in Everyday Terms

To write an IEP for a student, a team first needs to identify the student's characteristics and needs. The results from the ecological inventory will reflect the student's skill characteristics and serve as the team's primary guide for defining a student's needs. The team meets and agrees on activities and skills that are important to a particular student in the specific environments in which he or she participates—school, home, and, if older, in the community and at work as well. Next, the special education teacher usually takes the lead in interviewing other team members about the student's participation and ability in activities and skills performed in these environments. Interview results are recorded on an ecological inventory form (see Figures 3-4 and 3-5) with ratings of performance level and component skills (e.g., initiation, has related social skills, communicates) and comments about perfor-

mance or priority. The ecological inventory usually yields many student needs, along with the other assessments discussed in this chapter.

Marc has distinctive ways of communicating that often are difficult to understand. His tantrums seem to say that he is not happy with what's happening, but adults and peers don't always know what he needs or wants. The team agrees that understandable communication with familiar people is a primary need at home and at school. This is also clearly reflected in his assessment.

Prioritize Student's Needs and Recognize Strengths

Next, the team meets again to discuss the ecological inventory assessment results with the goal of determining the student's priority needs for the upcoming year. This can be done more efficiently as a group prior to the IEP meeting but also can be coordinated by the special education teacher through separate interactions with team members. Figure 3-6 lists some criteria that teams will consider when deciding what needs are most important; they will ensure that the skills (a) reflect the student's chronological age and preferences, (b) mirror the family's culture, (c) focus on functional skills that lead to meaningful participation, (d) be useful across activities and settings now and in the future, and (e) facilitate interactions with nondisabled peers.

As the team focuses on a student's needs, the student's strengths and preferences should not be forgotten. Teaching with preferred activities or materials will enhance a student's motivation to participate and learn. Expecting students to use their skill strengths means that skills are not forgotten and that teachers can build on these strengths to teach more complex behaviors.

Christine's team identified paid jobs and volunteer work as a priority need. They also know that she enjoys participating in the care of cats and dogs. This preference is one that her team will use as they identify potential work and volunteer settings for her to sample during her final two years of high school.

Define the Student's Present Level of Performance

In one section of the IEP, the team describes the student's *present level of performance* (PLOP) for each unique area of need. Because the PLOP defines the starting point or baseline for measuring the year's progress, it must be stated in measurable terms:

To determine whether Jacob has improved with regard to his IEP goals by June, his team clearly states

FIGURE 3–6

Examples of Criteria Used for Setting Priorities

Student: _____

Person(s) completing form: _____

Date: _____

List each activity or objective that is being considered for instruction.

Rate each activity or objective using: 3 = strongly agree with statement; 2 = agree somewhat with statement; 1 = disagree somewhat with statement; 0 = disagree strongly with statement

Criteria	Activity/Objective									
1. Can be used in current environments										
2. Can be used in future environments										
3. Can be used across environments and activities										
4. Facilitates interactions with nondisabled peers										
5. Increases student independence										
6. Is chronologically age-appropriate										
7. Student can meaningfully participate										
8. Student rates as high priority or highly preferred										
9. Family rates as high priority										
10. Improves health or fitness										
11. Meets a medical need										
12. Promotes a positive view of the individual										
13. Student shows positive response to activity										
14. Supported by related service staff										
15. Student can achieve, accomplish, or control a meaningful part of the activity										
Total										

Note: Adapted with permission from Dardig, J. D., & Heward, L. (1981). A systematic procedure for prioritizing IEP goals. *The Directive Teacher, 3,* 6–7, and Helmstetter, E. (1989). Curriculum for school-age students: The ecological model. In F. Brown & D. H. Lehr (Eds.), *Persons with profound disabilities: Issues and practices* (p. 254). Baltimore: Paul H. Brookes.

his skill level at the beginning of the school year. His team first reaches consensus on his unique needs, defines his PLOP for each need, and sets an annual goal. Later they will identify any needed specialized services, as well as short-term objectives or benchmarks to get Jacob from his PLOP to his annual goal. (Table 3–3)

Identify the Educational Supports and Services That Address a Student's Needs

The team also determines any specialized educational services or other "developmental, corrective, or supportive services" that "are required to assist a child with a disability to benefit from special education" (34 CFR 300.16). While some potential services are listed in the law, it is not an inclusive list, and teams will use this guideline to make their decision (Bateman & Linden, 1998). Teams must define clearly in the IEP how much time will be committed to each service (frequency, and duration), where services will be provided, and when services will begin. Specialized services are broad and include special education, related services, and supplementary aids and services, among others. Special education includes direct instruction (e.g., one to one, small or large group), instructional support (e.g., providing assistance in a routine, monitoring transitions), and consultation among staff (e.g., planning, problem solving, collecting data, coaching staff). Related services include occupational, physical, and communication therapy and consultation, as well as vision and mobility services and adaptive physical education. Special education and related services may be provided in the context of a general education classroom (i.e., services are pulled into the classroom) or provided apart from the general education classroom (e.g., services are given when the student is pulled out of the general education classroom, given in a resource room, in the community, or in a self-contained classroom). Other specialized educational services that may be determined by the IEP committee include supplementary aids, modifications, personnel support, accommodations, and staff training and teamwork. All services must be provided by the school (or contracted out) at no cost to the parent and are chosen on the basis of the student's needs, not on the availability of those services in the school district.

Write Measurable Annual Goals and Identify the Intermediate Short-Term Objectives or Benchmarks

The assessment and prioritization steps that come before writing the goals and objectives ensure that IEPs will focus on needed skills that are viewed by all team members as being meaningful to, and suitable for, the student. When teams write goals and objectives, the focus changes to "measurability," a requirement of IDEA. All goals, objectives, and benchmarks must be measurable; however, the amount of time required to achieve

TABLE 3–3

Three Examples from Jacob's IEP

Unique Needs	Present Level of Performance	Specialized Educational Service	Annual Goals
Follow class routines and schedule	Lacks organizational skills and usually needs prompting to the next activity.	Special education teacher	Will follow class routines and procedures from classroom teachers' cues and makes use of a picture schedule to attend daily school activities on his own, 4 of 5 days.
Social communication	Jacob's peer relationships are fairly good, although he is hypersensitive to any sort of perceived slight and his classmates sometimes tire of dealing with his emotional needs.	Speech and language pathologist	Will use simple sentences, augmented by picture system or devices, to express needs, feelings, ask questions, make choices, yes/no, greetings, in 5 routines each day, for 4 of 5 days.
Maintain engagement in academic activities	It can be difficult to engage him in any task not of his own choosing for more than 5 to 10 minutes.	Special education teacher	When given a choice of materials to work with (e.g., pens, paper) and a timer, Jacob will set the timer and engage in academic activity for 15 minutes, for 4 of 5 days.

them differs (Bateman & Herr, 2003). Goals are written to be reached within the school year, while objectives and benchmarks are written to be reached in 6 to 9 weeks. The PLOP is the starting point for identifying goals and objectives; it is linked to an annual goal by short-term objectives or benchmarks as shown in the formula that follows. The fourth element in this formula is any specialized educational services (e.g., special education, related services) provided through the IEP that helps move a student's performance from its present level to the goal level:

PLOP → objective → objective → objective → objective → Goal

↓

Special Education and Related Services

For Jacob, these elements work together to achieve priority skills.

Jacob's team has identified telling time to the quarter hour as an annual goal on his IEP. He will be given daily special education services during math instruction in the general education setting and individual instruction twice weekly. The teams identify the PLOP-to-goal sequence in this manner:

PLOP: Jacob tells time to the hour and half hour and recognizes numbers from 1 to 12.

Short-term objectives:

When the big hand points to "3," he will say "quarter after" and the hour (e.g., "quarter after 2") without error in 9 out of 10 opportunities.

When the big hand points to "9," he will say "quarter to" and the hour (e.g., "quarter to 3") without error in 9 out of 10 opportunities.

Goal: He will tell time to the quarter hour without prompts in 9 out of 10 opportunities during his daily activities.

Goals and objectives are written so that they (a) specify the target behavior in observable terms and (b) identify a simple criterion that tells how well the student must perform to meet the goal or objective (e.g., four out of five opportunities, for a distance of 50 yards, all the time, with no errors, and without prompting or assistance). Sometimes the conditions for performance will need to be stated explicitly (e.g., given a face or digital clock set at various times, Jacob

will tell the time to the minute), but other times this is unnecessary (e.g., the picture schedule is assumed when it is stated that Marc will use a picture schedule). While it can be challenging for teams to make all goals and objectives measurable, it is essential.

Summary

Assessment is a complex but critical component of program development. If used wisely, information gathered from assessments becomes the cornerstone of program development. Although there are no easy formulas for the selection of an appropriate assessment process for any one student, this chapter reviews the advantages and disadvantages of a variety of assessment strategies and describes how they can best be applied. The assessment process determines whether the outcomes that are identified and measured are meaningful. Focusing solely on academic development or skill development, as was done historically, is not sufficient. Assessment outcomes should also be referenced to the domains of relationships and membership. Involvement in person-centered planning strategies is an excellent way to guide teams and ensure that they focus on those elements that will contribute to the quality of an individual's life.

The chapter discusses developmental approaches to assessment, assessments of adaptive behavior, environmental assessment approaches, assessments of program quality and quality of life, and variables to consider when prioritizing skills for instruction. Teachers must know the appropriate uses—and be aware of the inappropriate uses—of a wide range of assessments and assessment strategies. Information resulting from the assessment process is prioritized and developed into appropriate goals and objectives; these then form the foundation of the IEP. In the next chapter, you will continue to follow Marc, Jacob, and Christine to see how teaching methods are designed.

Suggested Activities

1. Select one student in your class and carefully examine the assessments that are in his or her file.
   a. How many norm-referenced tests and criterion-referenced tests do you see?
   b. Are there any environmental assessments?

c. Are there any questionnaires eliciting input from this student's family?

d. If the student has problem behaviors, are there any functional behavioral assessments?

2. Select a different student and carefully examine the instructional objectives targeted on his or her IEP. How do the objectives compare with the following four criteria?

a. Do the objectives reflect the student's chronological age, culture, preferences, and profile of strengths and needs?

b. Do the objectives focus on functional skills and lead to meaningful routines and activities?

c. Do the objectives reflect the student's personal and social needs?

d. Can the student participate in the activities in a meaningful way?

References

Adams, J. (1973). Adaptive behavior and measured intelligence in the classification of mental retardation. *American Journal of Mental Deficiency, 78,* 77–81.

Alberto, P.A., & Troutman, A. C. (2008). *Applied behavior analysis for teachers* (5th ed.). Upper Saddle River, NJ: Merrill/Pearson.

Albin, R. W., Lucyshyn, J. M., Horner, R. H., & Flannery, K. B. (1996). Contextual fit for behavioral support plans: A model for "goodness of fit." In R. L. Koegel, L. K. Koegel, & G. Dunlap (Eds.), *Positive behavioral support: Including people with difficult behavior in the community* (pp. 81–98). Baltimore: Paul H. Brookes.

Alpern, G. (2007). *Developmental Profile III.* Los Angeles: Western Psychological Services.

Apgar, V. (1953). A proposal for a new method of evaluation of the newborn infant. *Current Researches in Anesthesia and Analgesia, 32,* 260–267.

Apgar, V., & Beck, J. (1973). *Is my baby all right?* New York: Trident Press.

Bambara, L. M., Agar, C., & Koger, F. (1994). The effects of choice and task preference on the work performance of adults with severe disabilities. *Journal of Applied Behavior Analysis, 27,* 555–556.

Bambara, L. M., & Kern, L. (2005). *Individualized supports for students with problem behaviors: Designing positive behavior plans.* New York: Guilford Press.

Bambara, L. M., Koger, F., Katzer, T., & Davenport, T. (1995). Embedding choice in daily routines: An experimental case study. *Journal of the Association for Persons with Severe Handicaps, 20,* 185–195.

Baron-Cohen, S., Allen, J., & Gillberg, C. (1992). Can autism be detected at 18 months? The needle, the haystack, and the CHAT. *British Journal of Psychiatry, 161,* 839–843.

Bateman, B. D., & Herr, C. M. (2003). *Writing measurable IEP goals and objectives.* Verona, WI: Attainment Company/IEP Resources.

Bateman, B. D., & Linden, M.A. (1998). *Better IEPs* (3rd ed.). Longmont, CO: Sopris West.

Baumeister, A. A., & Muma, J. R. (1975). On defining mental retardation. *Journal of Special Education, 9,* 293–306.

Baumgart, D., Brown, L., Pumpian, I., Nisbet, J., Ford, A., Sweet, M., et al. (1982). Principle of partial participation and individualized adaptations in educational programs for severely handicapped students. *Journal of the Association for the Severely Handicapped, 7,* 17–27.

Bayley, N. (2005). *Bayley Scales of Infant Development III.* San Antonio, TX: Psychological Corporation.

Bender, M., Valletutti, P. J., & Baglin, C. A. (2008a). *A functional assessment and curriculum for teaching students with disabilities: Interpersonal, competitive job-finding, and leisure-time skills* (3rd ed.). Austin, TX: PRO-ED.

Bender, M., Valletutti, P. J., & Baglin, C. A., (2008b). *A functional assessment and curriculum for teaching students with disabilities: Self-care, motor skills, household management, and living skills* (3rd ed.). Austin, TX: PRO-ED.

Billingsley, F. F., Gallucci, C., Peck, C. A., Schwartz, I. S., & Staub, D. (1996). "But those kids can't even do math": An alternative conceptualization of outcomes for inclusive education. *Special Education Leadership Review, 3,* 43–55.

Brazelton, T. B., & Nugent, J. K. (1995). *Neonatal behavioral assessment scale* (3rd ed.). London: MacKeith.

Bricker, D. (2002). *Assessment, Evaluation, and Programming System (AEPS®) for infants and children.* Baltimore: Paul H. Brookes.

Brigance, A., & Glascoe, F. P. (1999). *Brigance Comprehensive Inventory of Basic Skills–Revised.* North Billerica, MA: Curriculum Associates.

Brigance, A. & Glascoe, F. P. (2004). *Brigance Diagnostic Inventory of Early Development II.* North Billerica, MA: Curriculum Associates.

Browder, D. M. (2001). *Curriculum and assessment for students with moderate and severe disabilities.* New York: Guilford Press.

Browder, D., Spooner, F., Ahlgrim-Delzell, L., Flowers, C., Algozzine, B., & Karvonen, M. (2004). A content analysis of the curricular philosophies reflected in states' alternate assessment performance indicators. *Research and Practice for Persons with Severe Disabilities, 28,* 165–181.

Browder, D. M., Spooner, F., Algozzine, R., Ahlgrim-Delzell, L., Flowers, C., & Karvonen, M. (2003, Fall). What we know and need to know about alternate assessment. *Exceptional Children, 70,* 45–61.

Brown, F. (1991). Creative daily scheduling: A nonintrusive approach to challenging behaviors in community residences. *Journal of the Association for Persons with Severe Handicaps, 16,* 75–84.

Brown, F. (1996). Variables to consider in the assessment of problem behaviors. *TASH Newsletter, 22,* 19–20.

Brown, F., Belz, B., Corsi, L., & Wenig, B. (1993). Choice diversity for people with severe disabilities. *Education and Training in Mental Retardation, 28,* 318–326.

Brown, F., Evans, I. M., Weed, K. A., & Owen, V. (1987). Delineating functional competencies: A component model. *Journal of the Association for Persons with Severe Handicaps, 12,* 117–124.

Brown, F., Gothelf, C. R., Guess, D., & Lehr, D. H. (1998). Self-determination for individuals with the most severe disabilities: Moving beyond chimera. *Journal of the Association for Persons with Severe Handicaps, 23,* 17-37.

Brown, F., & Lehr, D. (1993). Meaningful outcomes for students with severe disabilities. *Teaching Exceptional Children, 4,* 12-16.

Brown, L., Branston, M. B., Hamre-Nietupski, S., Pumpian, I., Certo, N., & Gruenewald, L. (1979). A strategy for developing chronological-age-appropriate and functional curricular content for severely handicapped adolescents and young adults. *Journal of Special Education, 13,* 81-90.

Bruininks, R. H., Hill, B. K., Weatherman, R. F., & Woodcock, R. W. (1986). *Inventory for Client and Agency Planning (ICAP).* Riverside, CA: DLM Teaching Resources.

Bruininks, R. H., Woodcock, R. W., Weatherman, R. F., & Hill, B. K. (1996). *Scales of Independent Behavior-Revised (SIB-R).* Riverside, CA: DLM Teaching Resources.

Cannella, H. I., O'Reilly, M. F., & Lancioni, G. E. (2005). Choice and preference assessment research with people with severe to profound developmental disabilities: A review of the literature. *Research in Developmental Disabilities, 256,* 1-15.

Carlson, J. I., Luiselli, J. K., Slyman, A., & Markowski, A. (2008). Choice-making as intervention for public disrobing in children with developmental disabilities. *Journal of Positive Behavior Interventions, 10,* 86-90.

Carr, E. G., Ladd, M. V., & Schulte, C. F. (2008). Validation of the contextual assessment inventory for problem behavior. *Journal of Positive Behavior Interventions, 10,* 91-104.

Carr, E. G., Levin, L., McConnachie, G., Carlson, J. I., Kemp, D. C., & Smith, C. E. (1994). *Communication-based intervention for problem behavior.* Baltimore: Paul H. Brookes.

Cohen, S. (1998). *Targeting autism: What we know, don't know, and can do to help young children with autism and related disorders.* Berkeley: University of California Press.

Cooper, J. O., Heron, T. E., & Heward, W. L. (2007). *Applied behavior analysis* (2nd ed.). Upper Saddle River, NJ: Pearson/Merrill Pearson.

Council for Exceptional Children. (2004). Policy on assessment and accountability. *Teaching Exceptional Children, 36,* 70-71.

Crimmins, D. B., Durand, V. M., Theuer-Kaufman, K., & Everett, J. (2001). *Autism program quality indicators: A self-review and quality improvement guide for schools and programs servicing students with autism spectrum disorders.* Albany, NY: New York Office of Vocational and Special Education Services for Individuals with Disabilities, State Education Department.

Crone, D. A., & Horner, R. H. (2003). *Building positive behavior support in schools: Functional behavioral assessment.* New York: Guilford Press.

Cushing, L. S., Carter, E. W., Clark, N., Wallis, T., & Kennedy, C. H. (2009). Evaluating inclusive educational practices for students with severe disabilities using the Program Quality Measurement Tool. *The Journal of Special Education, 42,* 195-208.

Downing, J. E., & Demchak, M. A. (2008). First steps: Determining individual abilities and how best to support students. In J. E. Downing (Ed.), *Including students with severe and multiple disabilites in typcial classrooms: Practical strategies for teachers* (2nd ed., pp. 49-90). Baltimore: Paul H. Brookes.

Dunlap, G., Kern-Dunlap, L., Clarke, S., & Robbins, F. R. (1991). Functional assessment, curricular revision, and severe problem behaviors. *Journal of Applied Behavior Analysis, 22,* 387-397.

Durand, V. M. (1990). *Severe behavior problems: A functional communication training approach.* New York: Guilford Press.

Durand, V. M., & Carr, E. G. (1991). Functional communication training to reduce challenging behavior: Maintenance and application in new settings. *Journal of Applied Behavior Analysis, 24,* 251-264.

Durand, V. M., & Merger, E. (2001). Functional communication training: A contemporary behavior analytic intervention for problem behaviors. *Focus on Autism and Other Developmental Disabilities, 16,* 110-119.

Dyer, K. (1987). The competition of autistic stereotyped behavior with usual and specially assessed reinforcers. *Research in Developmental Disabilities, 8,* 607-626.

Elementary and Secondary Education Act of 1965, as amended by the Improving America's Schools Act of 1994, P.L. 103-382 (1994).

Evans, I. M. (1991). Testing and diagnosis: A review and evaluation. In L. H. Meyer, C. A. Peck, & L. Brown (Eds.), *Critical issues in the lives of people with severe disabilities* (pp. 25-44). Baltimore: Paul H. Brookes.

Evans, I. M., & Brown, F. (1986). Outcome assessment of student competence: Issues and implications. *Special Services in the Schools, 2*(4), 41-62.

Fisher, W. W., Piazza, C. C., Bowman, L. G., & Amari, A. (1996). Integrating caregiver report with a systematic choice assessment to enhance reinforcer identification. *American Journal on Mental Retardation, 101,* 15-25.

Ford, A., Schnorr, R., Meyer, L., Davern, L., Black, J., & Dempsey, P. (1989). *The Syracuse community-referenced curriculum guide for students with moderate and severe disabilities.* Baltimore: Paul H. Brookes.

Forest, M., & Lusthaus, E. (1989). Promoting education equality for all students: Circles and maps. In S. Stainback, W. Stainback, & M. Forest (Eds.), *Educating all students in the mainstream of regular education* (pp. 43-57). Baltimore: Paul H. Brookes.

Frankenburg, W. K., Dodds, J., Archer, P., Bresnick, B., Maschka, P., Edelman, N., et al. (1990). *The DENVER II.* Denver: Denver Developmental Materials, Inc.

Gaylord-Ross, R. J., & Holvoet, J. (1985). *Strategies for educating students with severe handicaps.* Boston: Little, Brown.

Giangreco, M. F., Cloninger, C. J., & Iverson, V. S. (1998). *Choosing outcomes and accommodations for children (COACH): A guide to educational planning for students with disabilities* (2nd ed.). Baltimore: Paul H. Brookes.

Gilliam, J. E. (1995). *Gilliam Autism Rating Scale (GARS).* Austin, TX: PRO-ED.

Gothelf, C. R., & Brown, F. (1998). Participation in the education process: Students with severe disabilities. In M. L. Wehmeyer & D. J. Sands (Eds.), *Making it happen: Student involvement in education planning, decision making, and instruction* (pp. 99-121). Baltimore: Paul H. Brookes.

Green, C. W., & Reid, D. H. (1996). Defining, validating, and increasing indices of happiness among people with profound multiple disabilities. *Journal of Applied Behavior Analysis, 29,* 67-78.

Green, C. W., Reid, D. H., White, L. K., Halford, R. C., Brittain, D. P., & Gardner, S. M. (1988). Identifying reinforcers for persons with profound handicaps: Staff opinion versus systematic assessment of preferences. *Journal of Applied Behavior Analysis, 21,* 31-43.

Greenspan, S. (1999). What is meant by mental retardation? *International Review of Psychiatry, 11,* 6-18.

Grossman, H. J. (Ed.). (1983). *Classification in mental retardation.* Washington, DC: American Association on Mental Deficiency.

Guess, D., & Noonan, M. J. (1982). Curricula and instructional procedures for severely handicapped students. *Focus on Exceptional Children, 4,* 1-12.

Hagopian, L. P., Long, E. S., & Rush, K. S. (2004). Preference assessment procedures for individuals with developmental disabilities. *Behavior Modification, 28,* 668-677.

Haring, T. G., & Kennedy, C. H. (1990). Contextual control of problem behaviors in students with severe disabilities. *Journal of Applied Behavior Analysis, 23,* 235-243.

Harry, B. (2008). Family-professional collaboration with culturally and linguistically diverse families: Ideal vs. reality. *Exceptional Children, 72*(3), 372-388.

Heber, R. (1959). *A manual on terminology and classification in mental retardation.* Willimantic, CT: American Association on Mental Deficiency.

Heber, R. (1961). Modifications in the manual on terminology and classification in mental retardation. *American Journal of Mental Deficiency, 65,* 499-500.

Holburn, S. (2002). How science can evaluate and enhance person-centered planning. *Research and Practice for Persons with Severe Disabilities, 27,* 250-260.

Holburn, S., & Vietze, P. M. (2002). *Person-centered planning: Research, practice, and future directions.* Baltimore: Paul H. Brookes.

Horner, R. H., & Carr, E. G. (1997). Behavioral support for students with severe disabilities: Functional assessment and comprehensive intervention. *Journal of Special Education, 31,* 84-104.

Horner, R. H., Todd, A. W., Lewis-Palmer, T., Irvin, L. K., Sugai, G., & Boland, J. B. (2004). The School-Wide Evaluation Tool (SET): A research instrument for assessing school-wide positive behavior support. *Journal of Positive Behavioral Interventions, 6*(1), 3-12.

Hughes, C., Pitkin, S. E., & Lorden, S. W. (1998). Assessing preferences and choices of persons with severe and profound mental retardation. *Education and Training in Mental Retardation and Developmental Disabilities, 33,* 299-316.

Individuals with Disabilities Education Act (IDEA) Amendments of 1997, P.L. 105-17, 20 U.S.C. 1401 *et. seq.*

Ivanic, M. T., & Bailey, J. S. (1995). Current limits to reinforcer identification for some persons with profound disabilities. *Research in Developmental Disabilities, 17,* 77-92.

Janney, R., & Snell, M. E. (2008). *Teachers guides to inclusive practices: Behavioral support* (2nd ed.). Baltimore: Paul H. Brookes.

Johnson-Martin, N. M., Attermeier, S. M., & Hacker, B. (2004). *The Carolina Curriculum for Preschoolers with Special Needs.* Baltimore: Paul H. Brookes.

Kennedy, C. H., Horner, R. H., & Newton, J. S. (1990). The social networks and activity patterns of adults with severe disabilities: A correlational analysis. *Journal of the Association for Persons with Severe Handicaps, 15,* 86-90.

Kern, L., Vorndran, C., Hilt, A., Ringdahl, J., Adleman, B., & Dunlap, G. (1998). Choice as an intervention to improve behavior: A review of the literature. *Journal of Behavioral Education, 8,* 151-169.

Kincaid, D. (1996). Person-centered planning. In L. K. Koegel, R. L. Koegel, & G. Dunlap (Eds.), *Positive behavioral support: Including people with difficult behavior in the community* (pp. 439-465). Baltimore: Paul H. Brookes.

Knoster, T. P. (2000). Practical application of functional behavioral assessment in schools. *Journal of the Association for Persons with Severe Handicaps, 25,* 201-211.

Knowlton, E. (1998). Considerations in the design of personalized curricular supports for students with developmental disabilities. *Education and Training in Mental Retardation and Developmental Disabilities, 33,* 95-107.

Kreiner, J., & Flexer, R. (2009). Assessment of leisure preferences for students with severe developmental disabilities and communication difficulties. *Education and Training in Developmental Disabilities, 44,* 280-288.

Lambert, N., Nihira, K., & Leland, H. (1993). *Adaptive Behavior Scale-School.* Austin, TX: PRO-ED.

Lee, M. S. H., Nguyen, D., Yu, C. T., Thorsteinsson, J. R., Martin, T. L., & Martin, G. L. (2008). Discrimination skills predict preference assessment methods for adults with developmental disabilities. *Education and Training in Developmental Disabilities, 43,* 388-396.

Lehr, D. (1989). Educational programming for young children with the most severe disabilities. In F. Brown & D. Lehr (Eds.), *People with profound disabilities: Issues and practices* (pp. 213-238). Baltimore: Paul H. Brookes.

Lennox, D. B., & Miltenberger, R. G. (1989). Conducting a functional assessment of problem behavior in applied settings. *Journal of the Association for Persons with Severe Handicaps, 14,* 304-311.

Lewis, S., & Russo, R. (1998). Educational assessment for students who have visual impairments with other disabilities. In S. Z. Sacks & R. I. Silberman (Eds.), *Educating students who have visual impairments with other disabilities* (pp. 39-71). Baltimore: Paul H. Brookes.

Linehan, S. A., Brady, M. P., & Hwang, C. (1991). Ecological versus developmental assessment: Influences on instructional expectations. *Journal of the Association for Persons with Severe Handicaps, 16,* 146-153.

Lohrmann-O'Rourke, S., & Browder, D. M. (1998). Empirically based methods to assess the preferences of individuals with severe disabilities. *American Journal on Mental Retardation, 103,* 146-161.

Lohrmann-O'Rourke, S., Browder, D. M., & Brown, F. (2000). Guidelines for conducting socially valid systematic preference assessments. *Journal of the Association for Persons with Severe Handicaps, 25,* 42-53.

Lord, C., Rutter, M., DiLavore, P. C., & Risi, S. (1999). *Autism Diagnostic Observation Schedule.* Los Angeles: Western Psychological Services.

Lord, C., Rutter, M., & LeCouteur, A. (1994). Autism Diagnostic Interview-Revised: A revised version of a diagnostic interview for caregivers of individuals with possible developmental disorders. *Journal of Autism and Developmental Disorders, 24,* 649-685.

Luckasson, R., Borthwick-Duffy, S., Buntinx, W. H. E., Coulter, D. L., Craig, E. M., Reeve, A., et al. (2002). *Mental retardation: Definition, classification, and systems of supports* (10th ed.). Washington, DC: American Association on Mental Retardation.

Magito McLaughlin, D. M., & Carr, E. G. (2005). Quality of rapport as a setting event for problem behavior: Assessment and intervention. *Journal of Positive Behavior Interventions, (7),* 68-91.

Mason, S. A., McGee, G. G., Farmer-Dougan, V., & Risley, T. R. (1989). A practical strategy for ongoing reinforcer assessment. *Journal of Applied Behavior Analysis, 22,* 171-179.

McCarthy, D. (1972). *McCarthy Scales of Children's Abilities.* New York: Psychological Corporation.

McLoughlin, J. A., & Lewis, R. B. (1994). *Assessing special students* (4th ed.). Upper Saddle River, NJ: Merrill/Pearson.

Mechling, L. C., Gast, D. L., & Cronin, B. A. (2006). The effects of presenting high-preference items, paired with choice, via computer-based video programming on task completion of students with autism. *Focus on Autism and Other Developmental Disabilities, 21,* 7-13.

Meyer, L. H., & Evans, I. H. (1989). *Nonaversive intervention for behavior problems: A manual for home and community.* Baltimore: Paul H. Brookes.

Meyer, L. H., & Janney, R. E. (1989). User-friendly measures of meaningful outcomes: Evaluating behavioral interventions. *Journal of the Association for Persons with Severe Handicaps, 14,* 263-270.

Moes, D. R., & Frea, W. D. (2000). Using family context to inform intervention planning for the treatment of a child with autism. *Journal of Positive Behavior Interventions, 2,* 40-46.

Mount, B., & Zwernik, K. (1988). *It's never too early, it's never too late: A booklet about personal futures planning.* St. Paul, MN: St. Paul Metropolitan Council.

Nehring, A. D., Nehring, E. F., Bruni, J. P., & Randolph, P. L. (1992). *Learning Accomplishment Profile–Diagnostic standardized assessment.* Lewisville, NC: Kaplan School Supply.

Nelson, C., van Dijk, J., McDonnell, A. P., & Thompson, K. (2002). A framework for understanding young children with severe multiple disabilities: The van Dijk approach to assessment. *Research and Practice for Persons with Severe Disabilities, 27,* 97-111.

Newborg, J. (2004). *Battelle Development Inventory* (2nd ed.) Chicago: Riverside.

No Child Left Behind Act of 2001, Pub. L. No. 107-110, 115 Stat. 1425.

O'Brien, J., O'Brien, C. L., & Mount, B. (1997). Person-centered planning has arrived . . . or has it? *Mental Retardation, 35,* 480-488.

O'Neill, R. E., Horner, R. H., Albin, R. W., Sprague, J. R., Story, K., & Newton, J. S. (1997). *Functional assessment and program development for problem behavior: A practical handbook* (2nd ed.). Pacific Grove, CA: Brooks/Cole.

Orelove, F. P., Sobsey, D., & Silberman, R. K. (2004). *Educating children with multiple disabilities* (4th ed.). Baltimore: Paul H. Brookes.

Pace, G. M., Ivancic, M. R., Edwards, G. L., Iwata, B. A., & Page, T. J. (1985). Assessment of stimulus preference and reinforcer value with profoundly retarded individuals. *Journal of Applied Behavior Analysis, 18,* 249-255.

Pearpoint, J., Forest, M., & O'Brien, J. (1996). MAPS, Circles of Friends, and PATH: Powerful tools to help build caring communities. In S. Stainback & W. Stainback (Eds.), *Inclusion: A guide for educators* (pp. 67-86). Baltimore: Paul H. Brookes.

Piazza, C. C., Fisher, W. W., Hagopian, L. P., Bowman, L. G., & Toole, L. (1996). Using choice assessment to predict reinforcer effectiveness. *Journal of Applied Behavior Analysis, 29,* 109.

Prizant, B., Weatherby, A. M., Rubin, E., Laurent, A. C., & Rydell, P. J. (2006). *The SCERTS® Model: A comprehensive educational approach for children with autism spectrum disorders.* Baltimore: Paul H. Brookes.

Rainforth, B., York, J., & MacDonald, C. (1997). *Collaborative teams for students with severe disabilities: Integrating therapy and educational services* (2nd ed.). Baltimore: Paul H. Brookes.

Roane, H. S., Vollmer, T. R., Ringdahl, J. E., & Marcus, B. A. (1998). Evaluation of a brief stimulus preference assessment. *Journal of Applied Behavior Analysis, 31,* 605-620.

Roeber, E. (2002). *Setting standards on alternate assessments* (Synthesis Report 42). Minneapolis: University of Minnesota, National Center on Educational Outcomes. Retrieved April 16, 2004, from http://education.umn.edu/NCEO/OnlinePubs/Synthesis42.html

Roid, G. H. (2003). *Stanford-Binet Intelligence Scales* (5th ed.). Chicago: Riverside.

Salvia, J., & Ysseldyke, J. E. (2007). *Assessment in special and inclusive education* (10th ed.). Boston: Houghton Mifflin.

Sands, D. J., Bassett, D. S., Lehmann, J., & Spencer, K. C. (1998). Factors contributing to and implications for student involvement in transition-related planning, decision making, and instruction. In M. L. Wehmeyer & D. J. Sands (Eds.), *Making it happen: Student involvement in education planning, decision making, and instruction* (pp. 25-44). Baltimore: Paul H. Brookes.

Schalock, R. L. (1997). Reconsidering the conceptualization and measurement of quality of life. In R. L. Schalock (Ed.), *Quality of life: Vol. 1. Conceptualization and measurement* (pp. 123-139). Washington, DC: American Association on Mental Retardation.

Schalock, R. L., Borthwick-Duffy, S., Bradley, V., Buntinx, W., Craig, E. M., Coulter, D. L., et al. (2009). *Intellectual disability: Definition, classification, and systems of supports* (11th ed.). Washington, DC: American Association on Intellectual and Developmental Disabilities.

Schalock, R. L., Luckasson, R. A., & Schogren, K. A., With Borthwick-Duffy, S., Bradley, V., Buntinx, W., Craig, E. M., Coulter, D. L., Gomez, S. C., et al. (2007). The renaming of mental retardation: Understanding the change to the term intellectual disability. *Intellectual and Developmental Disabilities, 45,* 116-124.

Schopler, E., Reichler, R., & Rochen-Renner, B. (1998). *The Childhood Autism Rating Scale (CARS).* Los Angeles, CA: Western Psychological Services.

Siegel-Causey, E., & Allinder, R. M. (1998). Using alternative assessment for students with severe disabilities: Alignment with best practices. *Education and Training in Mental Retardation and Developmental Disabilities, 33,* 168-178.

Silberman, R. K., & Brown, F. (1998). Alternative approaches to assessing students who have visual impairments with other disabilities in classroom and community environments. In S. Z. Sacks & R. K. Silberman (Eds.), *Educating students who have visual impairments with other disabilities* (pp. 73–98). Baltimore: Paul H. Brookes.

Snell, M. E. (2003). Education of individuals with severe and multiple disabilities. *Encyclopedia of education* (2nd ed., pp. 2210–2213). New York: Macmillan Reference USA.

Snell, M. E., & Janney, R. E. (2000). *Practices for inclusive schools: Social relationships and peer support.* Baltimore: Paul H. Brookes.

Soodak, L. C., Podell, D. M., & Lehman, L. R. (1998). Teacher, student, and school attributes as predictors of teachers' responses to inclusion. *The Journal of Special Education, 31,* 480–497.

Sparrow, S. S., Balla, D. A., & Cicchetti, D. V. (2005). *Vineland Adaptive Behavior Scales, 2nd ed.* Circle Pines, MN: American Guidance Service, Inc.

Sugai, G., Lewis-Palmer, T., Todd, A., & Horner, F. H. (2001). *School-wide Evaluation Tool.* Eugene: University of Oregon.

Taber, T. A., Alberto, P. A., Seltzer, A., & Hughes, M. (2003). Obtaining assistance when lost in the community using cell phones. *Research and Practice for Persons with Severe Disabilities, 28,* 105–116.

Thompson, J. R., Bryant, B. R., Campbell, E. M., Craig, E. M., Hughes, C. M., Rotholz, D. A., et al. (2004). *Supports Intensity Scale: Users manual.* Washington, DC: American Association on Mental Retardation.

Thompson, J. R., McGrew, K. S., & Bruininks, R. H. (1999). Adaptive and maladaptive behavior: Function and structural characteristics. In R. L. Schalock (Ed.), *Adaptive behavior and its measurement: Implications for the field of mental retardation* (pp. 15–42). Washington, DC: American Association on Mental Retardation.

Thompson, S., & Thurlow, M. (2001). *2001 State special education outcomes: A report on state activities at the beginning of a new decade.* Minneapolis: University of Minnesota, National Center on Educational Outcomes.

Tschannen-Moran, M., Hoy, A. W., & Hoy, W. K. (1998). Teacher efficacy: Its meaning and measure. *Review of Educational Research, 68*(2), 202–248.

Turnbull, A. P., Blue-Banning, M. J., Anderson, E. L., Turnbull, H. R., Seaton, K. A., & Dinas, P. A. (1996). Enhancing self-determination through group action planning. In D. J. Sands & M. L. Wehmeyer (Eds.). *Self-determination across the life span* (pp. 237–256). Baltimore: Paul H. Brookes.

Turnbull, H. R., & Turnbull, A. P. (2000). *Free appropriate public education: The law and children with disabilities* (6th ed.). Denver: Love Publishing.

U.S. Department of Education. (2003, December 9). *Federal Register, 68*(236), 68698.

U.S. Department of Education. (2005). Alternate achievement standards for students with the most significant cognitive disabilities: Non-regulator guidance. Washington, DC: Author.

U.S. Preventive Services Task Force. (2004). Screening for visual impairment in children younger than age 5 years: Recommendation statement. *Annuals of Family Medicine, 2*(3), 263–266.

Valletutti, P. J., Bender, M., & Baglin, C. A. (2008). *A functional assessment and curriculum for teaching students with disabilities: Functional academics* (3rd ed.). Austin, TX: PRO-ED.

Valletutti, P. J., Bender, M., Hoffnung, A. S., & Baglin, C. A. (2008). *A functional assessment and curriculum for teaching students with disabilities: Nonverbal communication, oral communicatin, and literacy preparation* (3rd ed.). Austin, TX: PRO-ED.

Vandercook, T., York, J., & Forest, M. (1989). The McGill Action Planning System (MAPS): A strategy for building the vision. *Journal of the Association for Persons with Severe Handicaps, 14,* 205–215.

Wechsler, D. (2002). *Wechsler Preschool and Primary Scale of Intelligence–Revised.* San Antonio, TX: Psychological Corporation.

Wechsler, D. (2003). *Wechsler Intelligence Scale for Children (WISC-IV).* San Antonio, TX: Psychological Corporation.

Wehmeyer, M. L., & Sands, D. (Eds.). (1998). *Making it happen: Student involvement in education planning, decision making, and instruction.* Baltimore: Paul H. Brookes.

White, O. R. (1985). The evaluation of severely mentally retarded individuals. In B. Bricker & J. Filler (Eds.), *Severe mental retardation: From theory to practice* (pp. 161–184). Reston, VA: Council for Exceptional Children.

Yell, M. (1998). *The law and special education.* Upper Saddle River, NJ: Merrill/Pearson.

4

Selecting Teaching Strategies and Arranging Educational Environments

Martha E. Snell
Fredda Brown

In this chapter, we explain and illustrate a glossary of evidence-based teaching strategies that teams may select from when designing teaching programs. Some strategies will directly influence instructional methods, while other strategies pertain more to the classroom environment and organization. Chapter 5 describes complementary approaches for measuring student progress, and Chapter 6 explains a team process for planning and implementing instructional programs.

This chapter organizes teaching strategies in a manner recently suggested by Copeland and Cosbey (2008–2009), using the Response to Intervention (RtI) framework. RtI is a multitiered decision model for evaluating student progress and adding instructional support when students are not learning. In this model, less specialized teaching interventions are used before more specialized interventions are added. The logic behind RtI is similar to the logic of School-wide Positive Behavior Support; both are best illustrated by a triangle that represents all students in a school setting. Most students will respond successfully and learn needed skills when Tier 1 or "universal" teaching interventions are applied on a classroom-wide (and school-wide) basis.

These Tier 1 or universal interventions constitute the base of the triangle and tend to be effective with roughly 60 to 80% of students. Universal interventions or teaching strategies are those that have a proven track record and, when implemented correctly, will be effective for most students. However, when students respond less favorably to universal teaching approaches and their performance reflects less–than-expected gains, their teams reexamine their instruction plans and make improvements, sometimes adding more specialized interventions. These more specialized strategies are referred to as Tier 2 strategies and are estimated to be needed for about 15% of students. When additional specialized interventions are needed (for about 5% of students), Tier 3 strategies are identified following a precise assessment of the reasons for failure.

Using RtI logic means that educational teams follow several guidelines:

- Every student in a general education classroom gets the basic universal teaching interventions.
- Student performance data are used to judge the need for more specialized interventions.

- Intervention is additive so that when data indicate a need for more specialized interventions, the team selects additional methods, services, or supports.
- More specialized methods do not require a change in the teaching setting because location and methods are independent.
- The need for more specialized methods in one academic area does not necessarily indicate the need for more specialized methods in other academic areas; the selection of the teaching intervention relies on student performance data.

This chapter begins with five principles that influence teams as they plan instruction (see Figure 4–1); then we shift to describing teaching strategies. Using the logic that Copeland and Cosbey (2008–2009) set forth, we roughly categorize teaching strategies into two groups:

- Strategies that are effective with a wide range of students, including those with disabilities (Universal)
- Strategies that are effective with students who have severe disabilities (Specialized)

The first group, *universal approaches,* which are akin to Tier 1 approaches, have been applied in general education classrooms and are generally less specialized. These approaches include, for example, information sharing, classroom rules, cooperative learning, and universal design. The second group, *specialized*

FIGURE 4–1
Teaching Methods That Are Effective with Students Who Have Extensive Support Needs

Principles to Guide Instruction

Work as Collaborative Teams
Reach Consensus on What to Teach
Understand How Stage of Learning Affects Instruction
Reach Agreement on How Students Will be Taught
Monitor Student Learning with Performance Data

"Universal" Teaching Strategies That Are Effective with a Wide Range of Students

- Information about students
- Materials and universal design
- Instructor
- Schedule for instruction
- Teaching arrangements
- Prevention strategies
- Peer-mediated instruction and peer support
- Individualized adaptations: Accommodations and modifications
- Self-management

Less to more specialized

Specialized Teaching Strategies That Are Effective with Students Who Have Severe Disabilities

- Visual modality strategies
- Task analysis and chaining
- Elements of teaching discrete trials
- Stimulus and response prompting
- Consequence strategies
- Arranging teaching trials

approaches (akin to Tiers 2 and 3), rest primarily on research conducted with students with disabilities in special education settings. These methods are more focused on small group and individualized instruction and offer added support when universal approaches are ineffective. Among these more specialized approaches are systematic response prompting and error correction, embedded instruction, and instructional approaches that are more intensive (e.g., pivotal response training, Treatment and Education of Autistic and Communication-handicapped Children [TEACCH] methods). When teams plan teaching methods for a particular student that are highly specialized, the probability is greater that the student will require someone besides the general education teacher to do the teaching, will be less likely to be taught as part of the group amid peers, and more likely to be taught separate from the group. In contrast, if the teaching methods for students with disabilities are the same as, or overlap with, those used with peers, then separation is less likely.

Principles to Guide Instruction

All students, including those with disabilities, should be attending age-appropriate school settings and spending much, if not all, of their day in general education with the supports needed to learn. The educational programs for individual students with disabilities are designed with individualized instructional goals and supports. Thus, the educational program for one student will look very different than the program for another student.

> *In comparison to Jacob, who is in fourth grade, Marc, who is in kindergarten, spends less time and requires different supports to participate and learn in general education. Both students, however, are learning functional skills and academic skills, while also coping with challenging behavior and learning effective ways to communicate.*
>
> *Christine, who is in a post–high school program located on a university campus, spends time around typical peers at lunch and in a drama club, but spends much of her day preparing for the job she will hold once she graduates. Successful communication with others is a primary focus for Christine.*

The following five principles will guide teams as they develop individualized, inclusive, and effective educational supports for students.

Work as Collaborative Teams

Designing educational programs to teach students needed skills requires that team members consider many factors and make numerous decisions. Decisions are made at numerous points, but only after team members share their different perspectives on the student, engage in relevant discussion and problem solving, and then reach consensus as a team (Friend & Cook, 2010). When decisions are made by majority vote or by experts or authority figures without reaching consensus, the team will not be equally invested in the decisions or the outcomes. Nonconsensual decisions tend to reflect a narrower range of information and risk being of poorer quality (Snell & Janney, 2005). Teams must be mindful of their interpersonal health, as well as their working efficiency, as one affects the other. At times, teams under stress or in conflict will need to seek ways to strengthen themselves, to improve the communication between members, and to develop their decision-making capacity.

Reach Consensus on What to Teach

Teams must use a reasoned and collaborative process to identify what should be included in a student's individualized educational program (IEP) (see Chapter 3). Working as a team, members draw on their separate areas of expertise as parents, special education teachers, general education teachers, speech and language pathologists (SLPs), occupational therapists (OTs), physical therapists (PTs), and, at times, school nurses, adaptive physical educators, mobility trainers, and consultants in deaf-blindness and autism. Teams start IEP planning by gathering assessment data on students using tools that less often are norm-referenced tests and more often are informal interviews and observations. These assessments are planned and carried out with the aim of identifying the student's unique needs and characteristics. The team studies these results and selects goals and objectives from three types of skills:

Basic Skills: These skills are behaviors that contribute to participation in inclusive environments, including toileting, eating, and dressing skills; mobility and getting around; reaching and grasping; communicating; making choices; following routines; classroom survival skills; working with classmates; and self-directed learning.

Academic Skills: These skills are knowledge and abilities that are drawn from the general education curriculum in reading, writing, math, science, and social studies and are adapted to suit the student's needs and learning traits.

Functional Skills: These skills pertain to everyday life, including domestic, recreational, community, and vocational skills, and may incorporate academic skills.

Team members then work together to identify the student's present level of performance (PLOP) in these targeted skill areas so that individualized goals and objectives can be written that are appropriate to the student. The IEP will (a) contain measurable annual goals that can be achieved in a year, (b) identify the intermediate, short-term objectives or benchmarks leading from the PLOP to the goal level, and (c) specify the educational supports and services that address the student's needs.

Understand How the Stage of Learning Affects Instruction

For *all* individuals, learning appears to move through different stages related to one's grasp of the target skill (Browder, 2001; Liberty, 1985). Thus, the ways we teach students who are just beginning to learn a skill will differ somewhat from the ways we teach students who are more experienced. As shown in Figure 4–2, a student's stage of learning for a given skill will reflect the extent of his or her experience and current performance, and should be evident from reading the PLOP. The learning stage has a powerful influence on how a student is taught (see Table 4–1).

Acquisition Stage: Typically, skills in this stage are new skills, performed with accuracy varying from 0% to about 60% of the steps performed correctly (Farlow & Snell, 1995, 2005). The focus of early learning is usually on approximate performance of the core steps of a skill. But, as discussed in Chapter 3, teaching may be expanded to include some extension and enrichment skills, such as initiating the task, preparing for the task, terminating the task, and making choices within the task (Brown, Evans, Weed, & Owen, 1987). Teaching simpler versions of skills makes sense during acquisition, when the tendency to make errors is great.

When Marc was first learning to use a schedule in preschool, his teachers made a vertical set of shelves, one shelf for each major morning activity. On the shelves, they placed single objects that were used in the activity. Marc carried the object to the activity and placed it in a designated spot. Objects were changed for the afternoon so fewer objects were visible at a time. Later, picture symbol cards were added; finally, the objects were eliminated.

For some students, the core skills may not represent the initial priority; instead, their acquisition focus may be on extension or enrichment skills. For example, a student like Christine, who has limited ways to participate in the motor aspects (core steps) of an activity, may more meaningfully begin with learning to initiate (e.g., selecting the hairbrush option on her speaking communication device to request that someone brush her hair) or choosing among several options (e.g., selecting a preferred snack from several options on her communication device to indicate her choice).

FIGURE 4–2
Stages of Learning

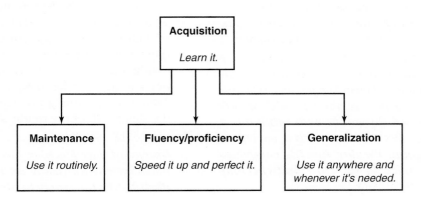

TABLE 4–1

Teaching Focus and Characteristics of the Learning Stages

Acquisition Stage	Maintenance Stage	Fluency/Proficiency Stage	Generalization Stage
Teach beginning performance of skill while keeping errors low	Expect regular use of skill while promoting perfection through habitual use	• Speed performance up to its typical rate • Perfect the skill so that it suits the student's age	Teach student to adapt performance with changes in task, setting, materials, or people
Characteristics of Learner at Each Stage			
• Student may perform none or up to about half of the task • May need to cue or prompt initiation • May need a low-error prompt system • Possibly break skill down into smaller components • Give frequent positive feedback	• Student performs more than half of the task • "Schedule it" and expect student to perform • Add to the skill to make it more functional (e.g., initiates, prepares) • Enrich skill with communication, choice, or social behaviors • Drop all intrusive requests • Fade intrusive prompt • Shift attention to natural cues and prompts • Thin out reinforcement • Shift to natural reinforcement	• Student performs more than half of the task • Add realistic speed and quality criteria • Add to skill to make it more functional (e.g., monitors speed and quality) • Enrich skill with communication, choice, or social behaviors • Drop all intrusive requests • Fade intrusive prompt • Shift attention to natural cues and prompts • Thin out reinforcement • Shift to natural reinforcement	• Student performs more than half of the task • Vary settings • Vary instructors, supervisors, others • Vary materials • Vary conditions and teach problem solving • Enrich skill with communication, choice, or social behaviors • Drop all intrusive requests • Fade intrusive prompt • Shift attention to natural cues and prompts • Thin out reinforcement • Shift to natural reinforcement

Probably most research on skill instruction has addressed the initial learning of core skills during the acquisition stage. Despite the importance of the three later stages of learning to building competence, we seem to focus on them less often and understand them less well than we do the acquisition stage. Table 4–1 identifies several teaching characteristics that are common to the maintenance, fluency, and generalization stages. During the later stages of learning, teachers must gradually "pull away" from the learner, thereby giving less direct supervision, while emphasizing natural forms of reinforcement and error correction. Students are taught to self-monitor performance in the absence of external reinforcement, supervision, and assistance.

Marc has learned to get his daily schedule each morning when he arrives in the resource room. Once he checks with his teacher for any schedule symbols to move or new symbols to add, he goes to his kindergarten classroom. With minimal reminders, he uses his schedule with a variety of teachers throughout the day, moving completed symbols to the back of the card and checking what's next.

Maintenance Stage: Skills in this stage, while still imperfect, are good enough to use with some level of independence. The adage "practice makes perfect" applies to this stage and reminds us of two things: (a) forgetting is best remedied through regular and expected use; and (b) functional skills, because they are needed, offer extensive opportunities for practice. Maintenance is a stage that many teachers forget or at least find difficult to implement because it requires shifting from an active teaching role (e.g., prompting, praising) to a less active role by distancing themselves and giving intermittent attention. Researchers have found that when students cannot predict teachers' supervision of their work on a task that they know fairly well, they attend better and complete more of the task (Dunlap & Johnson, 1985). Maintenance is an important stage of learning. Teachers who address maintenance learning will expect the student to use the skill for all of the routines during the day when that skill is needed.

Instead of only teaching Jacob to tell time during math instruction using an unplugged clock and flash cards, his teachers also will have him use this skill at the end of every class activity, by asking him what time it is.

Fluency or Proficiency Stage: This stage uses the catchphrase "speed it up and perfect it." Students may be taught to monitor the tempo (the rate and duration) of the task performed (e.g., Can I count out the money fast enough so that I don't hold up the line of customers? Am I taking too long to empty the dishwasher?). Other students focus on improving the quality of task performance (e.g., Is the floor clean enough? Did I write my name at the top and staple the top left corner of my report?). Still other students work on both the tempo *and* quality of skills while also improving accuracy.

Jacob is learning to look at the clock at the end of each activity, report the time quickly and accurately, and then identify the next activity on his pocket schedule.

Generalization Stage: The goal of this stage is to learn to "use it anywhere and whenever it is needed." In this stage, students are exposed to more variations in task materials and environments. They particularly need to learn problem solving because natural stimuli change and adaptations in their responses are required.

Jacob will be taught to tell time using the variety of analog clocks that exist at home and school, including clocks with an incomplete array of numbers or numbers that are not Arabic numerals.

Reach Agreement on How Students Will Be Taught

Determining how to teach what is on the IEP is a team process. When selecting teaching methods, teams will consider students' stage of learning with regard to the target skill and students' preferences and dislikes. Also, teams will review their students' learning history to assess what *has been* effective and what *might be* effective with particular students. To design educational programs, teams select and combine ideas that are not only practical and efficient, but also substantiated, logical, consistent with current knowledge, and likely to realize change in the desired directions.

The principle of parsimony (Etzel & LeBlanc, 1979) provides an uncomplicated rule for teams making decisions about how to teach their students: *Select the simplest but still effective approach.* First, the principle cautions educators against selecting questionable methods that are not founded on evidence. Second,

when team members are faced with several teaching approaches that all work, the principle advises them to choose the least complicated approach. Often more than one adult fills the teacher role and sometimes peers do so as well. Thus, the methods must be acceptable to all and be uncomplicated enough to be consistently applied.

Furthermore, teams will follow the guiding principle of using methods that are "only as specialized as necessary," thereby avoiding stigmatizing materials and approaches that are not age- or grade-appropriate or that draw unfavorable attention to the student. If it is necessary to make adaptations for some students, the adaptations should be designed to be as nonintrusive as possible for the student and as user-friendly as possible for the teaching team.

Marc's team adapted materials to simplify the demands of handwriting: he uses a stencil to help keep his letters in a smaller space and a small typing device to quickly spell out words that would take too long to print.

Jacob's team adapted the expectations in spelling by selecting fewer spelling words from the class's weekly list. For the class's astronomy unit, the team identified just the core concepts that he would learn.

Because of her visual limitations, Christine's team adapted the way that her job coach, teachers, and peer tutors presented new material to her or presented choices. They supplemented their verbal instructions with large images on a laptop or by giving demonstrations within her visual range. Thus, once at her library job, the job coach demonstrated the book scanner and her two switches; then they practiced this with the job coach role-playing a student checking out a book. When her peer tutor arrived for lunch, she began by showing Christine large images on her laptop of the campus grill lunch options while naming them.

When needed adaptations follow the "only as specialized as necessary" rule, they will not emphasize the student's differences, will mesh better with ongoing classroom instruction, and be easier for team members to use.

Monitor Student Learning with Performance Data

The principle of teams using student performance data to judge progress will be discussed in depth in Chapter 5 and illustrated in Chapter 6. Because data-based decision making is another guiding principle for teams, it is briefly mentioned here. Before each objective is taught, teams will assess the student's *baseline performance* using informal *probes* (or tests); baseline performance reflects the student's ability with regard to the target skill before teaching begins. Baseline probe performance is used as a rough guide for judging the student's progress on the same skill over the course of teaching. Teams compare *probe performance during baseline* with *probe performance during intervention* roughly every 1 to 2 weeks for skills taught frequently. Teams also can gather *teaching performance data*—information on how students perform the target skill during instruction when prompts and reinforcers are readily available. These data can further inform team members about the student's reactions to, comfort with, and performance under the teaching strategies that are being used and whether instruction can shift from the acquisition stage of learning to the maintenance, fluency/proficiency, or generalization stages. Performance measured under probe conditions (no prompts or reinforcement) typically yields a more conservative picture of the student's skill level than performance measured under teaching conditions when prompts and reinforcements are readily available.

"Universal" Strategies That Are Effective with a Wide Range of Students

This section will describe basic or universal strategies that have been successfully applied in general education settings with typical students and with students with disabilities. When well planned, a teaching program will involve strategies that create a positive learning environment, make use of appropriate learning materials and supports, and involve teaching methods that are suited both to the student (the stage of learning and preferences) and to the target skill. Some approaches described are *antecedent strategies* in that they dictate the organization, mechanics, procedures, and style of teaching, and thus concern the educational setting, materials, content, directions, teaching arrangement, and methods that teachers use to motivate student learning. Other strategies focus more on the *consequences* that teachers provide to students (reinforcement and error correction) or on some combination of antecedents and consequences. Teaching strategies range from simple to complex. Simpler antecedent methods include having a logical and consistent schedule of

instruction or providing all team members with information on the student's preferences, learning challenges, accommodations, and goals for teaching. Ordinary and simpler consequent strategies include giving students positive reinforcement for their improvements on target skills, providing opportunities to use their target skills, giving immediate corrective feedback, and offering a higher ratio of positive reinforcement to individual students than corrective feedback (e.g., the four-to-one rule) (Knoster, 2008).

Earlier we described "universal" approaches as methods that were demonstrated as being successful in general education settings with most students. These teaching strategies may include antecedent or consequent elements or both.

For Jacob's team, the primary challenge was adapting fourth-grade reading, math, and content area lessons in ways that would maintain his engagement and participation for more than 10 minutes or so. The team decided to build on his preferences (video games, animals, and "anything on wheels") while avoiding his dislikes (loud noises, crowds, and handwriting of any kind), which often triggered problem behavior. Using interesting content to teach academics was also appealing to many of his classmates, so a "Math on Wheels" group was started and "My Favorite Things" reading clubs were initiated. Jacob's fourth-grade teacher called on the school district's assistive technology consultant who introduced a wealth of academic video games to the fourth- and fifth-grade team and set up the school computers so that these games could be accessed. Jacob's team now had many strategies that would lengthen his learning engagement while also benefiting and appealing to his classmates.

Information About Students

Including students in general education often increases the number of adults who work with a student. Thus, it is important that all adults teaching a particular student understand that student's program objectives, learning characteristics, and any pertinent health information. We have found two student information summaries to be helpful for team members: (a) the Student Information Form (see Figure 4–3) and (b) the Program-at-a-Glance form (see Figure 4–4) (Janney & Snell, 2004; Snell & Janney, 2005). Often, IEPs are many pages long and may not be printed out or made available

FIGURE 4–3
Student Information Form for Marc

Student Information Form (Confidential)		
Student: Marc	**Grade:** K	**School year: 2008–2009**
Disability: Autism, developmental delay		

Current Teachers: *SE teacher (Joan Wharton), Kindergarten teacher (Lilly Kwan), Autism Specialist (Diane Soroka-Smith), SLP (Mary Cornell), OT (Ginger Smith), Teaching Assistants (Rita Ramirez, Sally Washington)*	**Last Year's Teachers:** *Head Start briefly, then transferred to Multiple Disabilities classroom*
Special Education & Related Services _x_ Academics: *All areas; currently spends about 10% of his time in kindergarten academics with peers and special education supports; rest of academic instruction in resource room* _x_ Speech/Language: *20 minutes × 2 days (pull-in)* _x_ Occupational Therapy: *20 minutes × 2 days (pull-in)* __ Physical Therapy: _x_ Aide Support: *Language arts, math, transitions, school/classroom routines, self-help/care, lunch, specialties* _x_ Sp. Ed. Instruction: *4 hours for 5 days a week. He spends most of his day in a resource classroom, but a total of 20% of his day with kindergarten class (Physical Education, assemblies); next year he will spend about half his time in first grade.* _x_ Sp. Ed Consultation: *20 minutes × 2 days*	**Likes/Interests** *Loves DVDs, Mr. Potato Head, Sponge Bob, figure toys and acting out familiar DVD scenes, computer* **Dislikes** *Making transition from desired activity, any classroom intercom announcements that are loud, other loud noises [but will go to assemblies]; announcements (says "No, shut up" – covers ears)*
Medical/Health Information Medication: *Takes Clonadine for sleeping at night* Allergies Diabetes Seizures Medical/physical needs **Special physical or self-help needs:** *He is not toilet trained, requires help blowing his nose, buttoning, and using fasteners. He is resistant to having his teeth brushed; has dental caries.*	**See guidance counselor/principal for other relevant confidential information?** __ yes _x_ no **Behavior Support Plan?** __ yes _x_ no **Testing:** State/District Accommodations __ yes _x_ no *Will not determine until end of second grade* Alternate Assessment __ yes __ no
Learns Best by: _x_ Seeing (picture/video/graphic organizer) _x_ Teacher or peer modeling (esp. video modeling) _x_ Hands on, labs, projects _x_ Multisensory (all of the above)	**Learning and Behavioral Strengths/High-Skill Areas** *He uses gestures, pictures, some spoken and printed words to express what he wants or needs. He is beginning to use some words and phrases to request or reject activities.*

Adapted from *Teachers' guides to inclusive practices: Modifying schoolwork* (2nd ed.), by R.E. Janney and M.E. Snell, 2004, Baltimore: Paul H. Brookes. Reprinted with permission.

because of legal requirements. Yet all members of the team need a succinct summary of the student's targeted goals and objectives. The Program-at-a-Glance form is meant to be a one-page confidential listing of briefly stated IEP objectives, accommodations and adaptations, self-management needs, and any special needs or comments. After the information on these two forms is shared at an initial face-to-face meeting, the completed forms are provided to relevant classroom teacher(s), specialty teachers, and instructional aide(s).

Materials and Universal Design

Materials must be suited to students and must facilitate learning. While this strategy seems to be obvious, suitable materials have great potential to enrich instruction

FIGURE 4–4
Marc's Program-at-a-Glance

Student: Marc	Date: September 2009
IEP Goals	**IEP Accommodations**
Social/Communication	*Receive special education support/instruction with academics, daily routines, transitions, communication, peer interactions*
Use gestures and words, augmented by picture system to express needs, feelings, make choices, yes/no	
Respond to choice questions augmented with pictures	*Modified curriculum goals*
Functional Skills	*Weekly curricular adaptations by special education and general education teachers*
Follow class routines and procedures from classroom teacher's cues	
School arrival, departure, lunch routines	*Instruction on classroom tasks follows a structured work system and then is transitioned to kindergarten*
School/classroom jobs	
Math	*Daily home/school communication log*
Rote count 1–10	*Educational team familiar with and uses all augmentative communication methods*
Identify numerals 1–10	
Count out objects 1–10	*Behavior redirection*
Language Arts	*Breaks scheduled as requested in designated location in school*
Match letters to pictures	
Write letters	*Visual schedule and other visual supports*
Follows picture	
Read schedule words	
Content Areas	
Key vocabulary/concepts for each unit	
Academic/Social Management Needs	**Comments/Special Needs**
Peer planning at beginning of year and as needed	*Toileting schedule every hour*
Visual supports: schedule, now/next, count down system to end activities, communication picture glossary, rule scripts to clarify rules for an activity	*Anecdotal records for IEP progress*
	Core team meetings weekly; whole team monthly
	Share autism information with all team members/relevant staff

Adapted from *Teachers' guides to inclusive practices: Modifying schoolwork* (2nd ed.), by R.E. Janney and M.E. Snell, 2004, Baltimore: Paul H. Brookes. Reprinted with permission.

and inappropriate materials can stifle learning and stigmatize students. Teaching materials (including school furniture, room arrangement, and school architecture) that possess several characteristics may promote learning and eliminate negative side effects. Most obvious among these characteristics are that the materials must be *matched to the learner's ability to use them,* including books adapted for meaningful use; work activities that are linked to a student's understanding and ability to respond; and even desks and chairs that are the correct height and have any needed postural supports, as well as pencils that the student can grip and use.

A second characteristic concerns *age-appropriateness,* or whether teaching materials are linked to a certain age group that matches the age of the students being taught. Many typical students will reject materials

that they perceive as being unsuitable for their age, and students who use age-inappropriate materials may be socially rejected by their peers who notice the mismatch. Sometimes teachers must make concerted efforts to either design or to locate materials that are suited to a student's ability and to his or her chronological age. Several other characteristics with regard to instructional materials are important: (a) the student's preference for materials and their general appeal to others, and (b) the variety and availability of suitable materials for teaching and for individual student manipulation (e.g., in science experiments, manipulatives for individual use in math).

When materials and curricula reflect a collective or common *universal design,* they are usable by more people. For example, curb cuts accommodate not only wheelchairs, but also bikes, strollers, and shopping carts. Telephones with larger and lighted numbers are easier for all to use. Reading material that is available digitally (instead of only in a textbook format) can be converted easily to other languages, made larger for viewing, printed in Braille, and read aloud by a screen reader (Center for Applied Special Technology, 2004). Programs such as IntelliTools® Classroom Suite (http://www.intellitools.com/classroom_suite/documentation_tutorials.aspx), which provides a universally designed academic support program for math, social studies, science, and language arts, were created for use by all students, both with and without disabilities, and can be accessed by mouse, IntelliKeys® keyboard, or a switch.

The logic behind universal design is that materials and curricula should be created from the start to have alternative ways of being accessed so more individuals can participate successfully with fewer teacher modifications and prompts. Universal design was applied to redesign the high school science curriculum by Dymond and colleagues (2006) so that students with mild to severe disabilities could learn alongside their peers without disabilities. Changes were made in the instructional delivery, the organization of the classroom, the ways in which students participate, class materials, and assessment methods; both staff and all students gave positive evaluations of these changes. Universal design requires us to think differently—not just as teachers but also as publishers, architects, car manufacturers, computer programmers, and others. Because universal design increases accessibility, it can reduce the need for prompts.

After Mr. Evans, the middle school science teacher, met Jacob on his visit to the school at the beginning of his fifth-grade school year, he decided to go ahead with a universal design approach for the science lab. He had been inspired by his colleague Ms. Rayfield, who had had a student with limited vision in her geography class this year. She'd read about universal design and decided to rearrange her classroom so that every student had a direct line of vision to the chalkboard and the classroom maps. Using the same logic and some ideas that he learned from Jacob's teacher, Mr. Evans decided to create simple word/picture directions which he knew that all of his students would benefit from. Using the Boardmaker® Plus! *software program (Mayer-Johnson, Inc., http://store.mayer-johnson.com/us/review/product/list/id/133/category/13/#customer-reviews), Mr. Evans uploaded*

photos from the science lab to use in Boardmaker. With advice from the middle school reading consultant, Mr. Evans labeled the science equipment and work stations, took pictures of sequenced steps in planned experiments that students would carry out that fall, illustrated the directions for each experiment, and added pictures of all of the materials that students would need to gather before starting an experiment. Finally, he added simplified directions with photographic illustrations for cleanup and safety (e.g., wearing safety glasses, disposal of chemicals). When the new school year started, he introduced picture labels first to students, followed by teaching the word/picture directions.

The Instructor

Teaching plans are ultimately the responsibility of the special education teacher with input from other team members. The plan denotes what is taught, when, where, with which classmates, and by which adult, as well as how learning is evaluated. When the student is taught in the general education classroom or during scheduled activities like P.E., teaching programs must mesh with classroom schedules, planned activities, available staff, and feasible grouping arrangements to take advantage of the opportunities for learning with and around peers.

Collaborative Teamwork

Teams have many options for determining who will teach: the general or special education teacher, a paraprofessional, related services staff, and peers. The more cohesive the team, the more likely it is that the teaching plans will fit into ongoing school activities and suit multiple instructors. If cooperative learning groups are used in classrooms, peers will help teach each other. In addition, older students (typical or with disabilities) in a cross-age tutoring program may be taught to serve as the tutor of younger students (typical or with disabilities). All adults who teach also need to be involved in team conversations about the student's progress so that any problems can be solved together. When instructors communicate as a team, having multiple instructors can be beneficial because it (a) encourages students to generalize their learning across people, (b) provides the team with broader experience in teaching the student, and (c) prevents overinvolvement of instructors with students or their isolation from peers.

Several researchers have studied students in inclusive elementary classrooms and have found that the individual who taught (e.g., general or special educator, paraprofessional, another student) made little difference in the student's level of academic response (Hunt, Soto, Maier, Muller, & Goetz, 2002; Logan, Brakeman, & Keefe, 1997; McDonnell, Thorson, & McQuivey, 1998). What does seem to influence a student's academic response in these classrooms is a combination of factors: (a) whether there is team collaboration on students' objectives and educational supports; (b) the arrangement used: the rate of engagement is slightly higher when the number of students are fewer (cooperative group or small group or one-to-one instruction versus whole-class instruction); (c) whether instruction is directed toward the student (i.e., the student is given opportunities to respond, is given materials, and is given feedback), which seems to improve a student's rate of response; and (d) having individualized instruction: Academic responses increase when the teaching method is tailored to the student.

Rethinking the One-to-One Assignment of Paraprofessionals

A practice often used by schools and IEP teams is to pair students who have more extensive support needs with paraprofessionals for much of the day. Dymond and Russell (2004) confirmed this practice; they found that students with severe disabilities in grades 3–5 spent less time included in general education than younger students and, when included, they were more likely to be supported by a paraprofessional than a special education teacher. When a single teaching assistant spends much of the school day with a single student, problems can result. Giangreco, Edelman, Luiselli, and MacFarland (1997) studied this staffing practice and identified eight undesirable patterns that may develop when teaching assistants are in the exclusive role of assisting a single student. Teaching assistants may do the following:

1. Obstruct the general educator's role by having complete control in implementing the student's program;
2. Isolate the student from classmates by removing or distancing the student from other students and activities;
3. Promote dependency on adults;
4. Affect peer interactions negatively by their constant proximity and their sometimes protective approach;

5. Use less-than-competent teaching;
6. Encourage a loss of personal control by failing to promote choice making or peer interaction;
7. Be insensitive to the student's gender, for example, by taking male students into female bathrooms; and
8. Distract classmates, for example, by involving the student in activities that differ from classmates.

Schools and educational teams are advised to rethink their practices and policies concerning the use of paraprofessionals so that these problems are prevented. Experts who have written about pairing paraprofessionals with students who need support have made some suggestions about addressing these potential difficulties (Carter, Sisco, Melekoglu, Kurkowski, 2007; Doyle, 2008; Giangreco et al., 1997; Hall, McClannahan, & Krantz, 1995; Snell & Janney, 2005). We list seven of these suggestions :

1. It is important to broaden the responsibilities of general education classroom teachers so that they are centrally involved in the supervision of special education teaching assistants.
2. Classroom teachers and paraprofessionals should have basic training in systematic instruction, including ways to promote peer interaction.
3. Classroom teachers should feel ownership of the students with disabilities in their classrooms so that they are invested in their instruction and their learning.
4. Paraprofessionals need job descriptions that set forth their responsibilities and the line of supervision. When their responsibilities include participation on the student's planning team, paraprofessionals have input and can benefit from team thinking.
5. Students' schedules should be designed so that they are truly integrated into class activities and peer interactions, using adaptations as needed to promote meaningful involvement; *simply being present with an assistant does not constitute meaningful inclusion.*
6. Peer support interventions (described later in this section) offer a proven alternative to the use of one-to-one, adult-delivered support and redefine their role as supporters of a network of peers (Carter et al., 2007).
7. Finally, for students who need more personal assistance and the support of a paraprofessional, several practices may reduce the possibility of isolation: (a) assign two assistants to a single student, each for part of the day, and let assistants rotate among other students; (b) assign assistants to classrooms instead

of to students; (c) vary a student's support so it rotates among team members; and (d) design teaching arrangements so that team members reduce one-to-one instruction and increase instruction in pairs or small groups of students with mixed abilities.

Christine receives support and instruction at a variety of locations both on campus and off. She has different teachers in these different settings: two paraprofessionals, a job coach, the drama teacher, and her special education teacher. Three peers lend informal support and friendship instead of formal instruction. Her physical and occupational therapists and her speech-language pathologist all provide input on a consultative basis, teaching only to demonstrate to others. The special educator and the job coach also supervise all of those who teach.

Schedule for Instruction

Classrooms need to have planned and predictable schedules from the first day of school. The schedule for students with disabilities will reflect the schedule for the general education classroom(s) where they are members and any additional instruction at other locations. A matrix of IEP objectives by scheduled general education activities is useful for planning when, where, and how often instruction takes place. Figure 4–5 indicates "Yes" when certain IEP objectives can be taught to Marc during kindergarten and "No" when IEP objectives do not mesh well with class routines.

Marc, who has a diagnosis of autism, will be 6 years old in the spring of his kindergarten year. His preschool program was self-contained, but he is now included, with the needed supports, in his neighborhood elementary school. Marc participates actively in many school activities. While he still spends much of his time in the resource room, he is able to work with his peers for some kindergarten activities, including arrival, morning circle, some table work in language arts, and recess for about 30% of every day. Next year, he will spend more than half of his time supported in first grade, including lunch and more academics.

Like their peers, students with severe disabilities learn both inside and outside the classroom: in hallways, other classrooms, and the cafeteria; outside the

school on playgrounds; at the bus loading areas; and in the community. As these students grow older and their IEP objectives include skills or activities not targeted for typical students, their instruction will expand into alternative settings beyond the general education classroom. As a general rule, some alternate teaching settings away from the general education classroom but in the school (with or apart from peers) are necessary during the later elementary and middle school years.

Instead of participating in the afternoon kindergarten activities, Marc receives one-to-one instruction in the resource room on grade-level academics and self-care skills, and in learning school routines more independently (e.g., lunch, library, fire drills). The goal for next year is for Marc to spend most of the day with his first-grade class.

Jacob spends more than half of his day with his fourth-grade class, but receives short daily instructional sessions, one-to-one, in the resource room on handwriting and language arts. These are two areas where he has particular difficulties in the fourth-grade curriculum. The success of his positive behavior support plan has meant that Jacob's time in general education is fairly free from the tantrums that he often had from kindergarten through last year.

During the middle school, high school, and post–high school years, as the instructional focus for students with severe disabilities shifts to include more functional academic, community, and job-related skills, the alternative teaching settings expand to include stores, offices, libraries and other public buildings, streets and sidewalks, restaurants, and work settings in the nearby community. Teams still must plan for general education classes or school activities that maximize students' continued contact with peers.

Christine spends the bulk of her school week learning vocational skills in community settings, but she participates in the Best Buddies Chapter on the university campus, where her post–high school class is located. With the support of a teaching assistant and several of her classmates, she is active in the university drama club.

Teaching Arrangements

Most students with severe disabilities, much like their typical peers, can acquire the ability to learn in groups and can also benefit from observing others learn. While there is clear research support for teaching

FIGURE 4–5
Program Planning Matrix for Marc

Program Planning Matrix												
Student: *Marc*			Class: *Kwan / K; Wharton / Sp Ed*						Date: *September 2009*			
IEP GOALS	**Class Schedule**											
	Arrival: K	*Circle: K*	*Language skills: K*	*Guided: K*	*Small Gp: K*	*Recess: K*	*Resource Rm*	*Lunch*	*Resource Rm*	*Adapted PE*	*Resource Rm*	*Departure*
Communication, Social, Behavior												
Use pictures or words to express needs, make choices	YES	YES	YES	YES	YES	YES	YES	YES	YES	YES	YES	YES
Respond to and initiate interactions with peers	YES	YES	NO	YES	YES	YES	NO	YES	NO	NO	NO	YES
Use self-control strategies with cues and support	YES	YES	YES	YES	YES	YES	YES	YES	YES	YES	YES	YES
Functional Skills and School Participation												
Follow class procedures from classroom teacher's cues (line up, sit on rainbow rug)	YES	YES	YES	YES	YES	YES	YES	YES	YES	YES	YES	YES
Arrival/departure routines; toileting routine	YES	NO	YES	NO	NO	YES	NO	YES	NO	YES	NO	YES
Participate in individual work (5 min.), small and large groups (10 min.)	NO	YES	YES	YES	YES	YES	YES	NO	YES	YES	YES	NO
Language Arts												
Match sounds to pictures	YES	YES	YES	NO	NO	NO	NO	NO	YES	NO	YES	NO
Write letters	NO	NO	YES	YES	YES	NO	YES	NO	YES	NO	YES	NO
Follow picture schedule	YES	YES	YES	YES	YES	YES	YES	YES	YES	YES	YES	YES
Recess/Break Time/Socialization												
Keep proximity with classmates	YES	YES	YES	YES	YES	YES	NO	YES	NO	YES	NO	YES
Cooperative play with classmates, use playground/PE equipment	YES	NO	NO	NO	YES	YES	NO	YES	NO	YES	NO	NO

Adapted from *Teachers' guides to inclusive practices: Modifying schoolwork* (2nd ed.), by R.E. Janney and M.E. Snell, 2004, Baltimore: Paul H. Brookes. Reprinted with permission.

students with severe disabilities in various-sized, homogeneous groups (from two to five) in special education settings, there has been far less research conducted on teaching these same students along side their peers without disabilities (e.g., Collins, 2007; Wolery, Ault, & Doyle, 1992). Likewise, little research exists on the effects of varying instructional arrangements and instructors in general education classrooms on learning for students with severe disabilities. One exception is a study by Carter and his colleagues

(Carter, Sisco, Brown, Brickham, & Al-Khabbaz, 2008). They found that in inclusive secondary classrooms teacher proximity had two predictable effects on students. When teachers were close to students with disabilities, students interacted far less often with peers than when teachers were at a distance; however, students' academic engagement increased when teachers were close.

The task of teaching is more complicated whenever instruction is differentiated to suit a mix of ability levels. However, it also is true that most small groups of students, with or without disabilities, reflect a range of ability and that differential instruction can only improve what the group members will learn. Teaching arrangements (one to one, student pairs, small groups, or large groups) should be chosen carefully to suit the student, the skill objective, and the setting. When students experience difficulties in remaining with a small group, or in attending or learning, the team must identify the difficulties and build the skills.

One-to-One Instruction
On a practical level, one-to-one instruction has *not* proven to be as beneficial to students with severe disabilities as many educators have thought (Carter et al., 2007; Giangreco, Halvorsen, Doyle, & Broer, 2004). Historically, the rationale for one-to-one instruction has been to minimize distractions and thus enable stimulus control (Rotholz, 1987). Some confuse the notion of *individualized* instruction for students with *individual* instruction, but they are not synonymous. Individualized instruction is teaching designed to suit a specific student and can be delivered in a variety of teaching arrangements, while individual instruction usually means that one adult teaches one student.

One disadvantage of one-to-one instruction is the increased probability of failure to generalize. Skills mastered by students with autism and other severe disabilities in one-to-one arrangements do not automatically generalize to larger groups of students (Koegel & Rincover, 1974) or to people other than the original teacher (Rincover & Koegel, 1975). Another disadvantage is that the student is excluded from being with other pupils, which means that the student does not learn how to participate in a group and loses many opportunities for peer-to-peer teaching, peer reinforcement, social interaction, and learning by observing peers (Farmer, Gast, Wolery, & Winterling, 1991; Stinson, Gast, Wolery, & Collins, 1991). In contrast, small

group instruction allows opportunities to experience taking turns, waiting, and imitating others—skills that have practical value in everyday life. Finally, one-to-one instruction is not cost effective in terms of teacher time. It results in increased downtime (i.e., noninstructional time) for students. Thus, one-to-one instruction should be reserved for teaching tasks in which (a) privacy is required, (b) other students cannot easily be included (e.g., job training), (c) an older student (or a peer) teaches a student in a supervised tutoring program, and (d) short-term intensive instruction is needed during part of the day for a specific skill. Figure 4–6 shows Marc following short-term, intensive instruction.

If a student cannot work in a group, there should be IEP objectives directed toward that goal. Teams will want to consider several old but proven strategies that build these skills by varying the teaching arrangement, including tandem instruction, sequential instruction, concurrent instruction, and combination instruction (see Table 4–2).

Small Group Instruction
Having the ability to learn in a group of two or more students is important for several reasons (Collins, Gast, Ault, & Wolery, 1991; Wolery et al., 1992): (a) most teaching in general education happens in groups, both small and whole class; (b) teaching in groups is more efficient for teachers and creates less noninstructional time for students; (c) group instruction, when conducted skillfully, provides opportunities for students to learn by observing others; and (d) group instruction allows students to interact with peers and creates occasions for teaching peer interactions skills. General education and special education teachers must make several decisions when planning small group instruction. Is the goal academic learning, social interaction among group members, or both? What will the composition of the group be (e.g., ability levels, group size)? What skills will be taught and what materials are needed to teach those skills? What will be the actual physical arrangement? When students with severe disabilities are included in a small group with typical peers, the team must differentiate instruction so that all members can understand the task, perform, and learn. The specific objectives taught will differ across group members, but it is beneficial when the academic content (e.g., math, language arts) or teaching focus (e.g., learning volley ball in the gym) is the same for all students. When the academic content is the same (e.g., adding and counting amounts), *multilevel instruction*

FIGURE 4–6
Several weeks ago, Marc was learning to match hour times on a clock to written times during one-to-one structured teaching. Because Marc now does this task independently, using a Now–Next word schedule to guide his work, He is ready to complete the task in kindergarten. Once he has completed the time-matching task, he knows that "motor" comes next, which means using the swing. While swinging, he engaged in a social routine—requesting that his teacher "tag" him, which is followed by a tag and laughter.

TABLE 4–2
Methods to Build Group Participation Skills

Tandem Instruction
Instruction begins with a one-to-one arrangement, and then other students are added gradually, one at a time, until there is a group. With students who appear to have difficulties, use simple requests or visuals to "sit quietly," "put your hands down," or "look at this." Gradually fade continuous reinforcement for staying with the group and participating. Koegel and Rincover (1974) found that while slowly increasing the group size from one to eight students, attending skills were shaped along with students' ability to tolerate less reinforcement. However, the same attending skills can be shaped in the context of the group itself. Thus, tandem instruction can be used part of the day while the same student participates in some groups for short periods at other times of the day—a strategy that reduces the disadvantages of gradually fading out one-to-one teaching (Rincover & Koegel, 1975). This approach is good for students with little experience working in groups (Collins, Gast, Autl, & Wolery, 1991; Wolery et al., 1992).

Sequential Instruction
Students are taught in a sequential manner (each student gets one turn, while others wait their turn) (Brown, Holvoet, Guess, & Mulligan, 1980). Reinforcing group members who are engaged and attend to others as they take a turn increases the possibility for observational learning (e.g., Fickel, Schuster, & Collins, 1998). Alternatively, the waiting time can be replaced with another activity for students who are less skilled at waiting, although these students will have less opportunity to learn by observing others. When sequential instruction is used, it is better to give turns contingent on being ready or contingent on being prompted to be ready instead of simply giving turns in sequence and risking giving turns to students who are inattentive or misbehaving. Thus, turns should not be given in strict sequential order.

Concurrent Instruction
Direct instruction is provided to an entire group, with individuals responding or with the group responding in unison (Reid & Favell, 1984). When the diversity of a group is increased, teachers must adjust their presentation of content so that all students can understand (e.g., use words, signs, and concrete objects to describe the task or concept being taught) and allow a variety of response levels and modes so that all students can participate.

Combination Groups
In many classrooms, it is not unusual to address a concept within the whole group, give instructions for an activity that applies the concept, and then divide into smaller groups of mixed or similar ability levels to carry out the activity. Ideally, groups will have cooperative activities geared to individual abilities and goals. The teacher also may provide instruction to one group at a time or teach each group using turn taking (sequential). Students who have difficulty working in a group may be faded gradually into a group (tandem model) from a one-to-one teaching arrangement with peers or special educators in the same classroom as Koegel and Rincover (1974) did with students who have autism. Likewise, students first may be taught to work independently for brief periods on an academic task related to the grade curriculum (e.g., cutting out 10 words and matching them to 10 pictures), after which they join a small group where individualized instruction is continued during turn taking (Rincover & Koegel, 1975). The latter example is a combination of tandem and sequential models.

will need to be planned so that each student is learning at a level that is commensurate with his or her current skills. With the learning task adjusted to suit students in the group, the teaching materials also may differ across students. (The teaming process to plan multilevel instruction and adaptations is described in detail in Chapter 6.)

Wolery et al. (1992) describes two variations for teaching groups of students: *Intra-sequential* arrangement involves the teacher presenting teaching trials to each student one at a time, but not programming any student-to-student interaction within the group. In the *intersequential* arrangement, the teacher makes use of observation learning and prompts students to attend to each other during instruction, to provide assistance as needed, and to praise each other. Both approaches require that the teacher be situated within reach of the students to present materials, to prompt, and to provide corrective feedback. The intersequential approach requires that students be able to see each other, thus suggesting a circular arrangement, either seated in chairs or on the floor, or standing, depending on the task. Research presented next (enhanced group instruction and observation learning) lends support to the intersequential approach. Table 4–2 describes several other variations for building students' skills to learn in small groups: tandem, sequential, concurrent, and combination.

By studying the amount of peer interaction and academic engagement of middle and high school students with intellectual disabilities, Carter and his colleagues (2008) made some discoveries that are important to this discussion. When in small groups without direct special education support versus other arrangements (whole group arrangements or independent work), students with disabilities interacted 2 to 3 times more often with their typical peers. But when a general or special educator was nearby, there was considerably less social interaction. However, students with disabilities showed substantially more *academic engagement* (e.g., attending to instruction and materials, responding on task) when these same teachers were in close proximity during small group arrangements or one-to-one teaching. They concluded that teaching students with severe disabilities in small groups alongside their typical peers was still the best intervention for promoting peer interaction and learning. Furthermore, drawing on other research, they recommended that the goal of increasing meaningful social interactions might best be achieved through peer support interventions.

When peers are equipped to support their classmates with disabilities both socially and academically, reliance on paraprofessionals can be reduced and substantial improvements in social interactions can occur (Carter et al., 2007).

Enhanced Group Instruction

Enhanced group instruction (EGI) (Kamps, Dugan, Leonard, & Daoust, 1994; Kamps, Leonard, Dugan, Boland, & Greenwood, 1991), which uses an intersequential approach, has been found to effective in promoting responding and learning in small groups of students with intellectual disabilities and autism. Teachers working with groups of three to five students made tasks interesting and promoted learning by (a) requesting frequent student-to-student responses, (b) using fast-paced and random trials, (c) rotating materials and concepts taught, (d) using multiple examples of each concept taught (a minimum of three sets per concept), and (e) using individualized sets of materials for each student. These strategies meant that students were handling learning materials and actively and repeatedly responding to the teacher and to classmates on task concepts. As a result, they focused on the target stimuli, participated in the target response, and were reported as being interested in the group activity. While all of the students in these studies had disabilities, many of these group strategies for making instruction interesting and focused are often used in heterogeneous groups in general education classrooms and appear to have the same effects with a diverse array of students (Hunt, Staub, Alwell, & Goetz, 1994; Snell & Janney, 2000; Tomlinson, 2001). To the extent that enhanced group instruction makes teaching more effective for *all* learners, it has the features of a *universal design* in that it benefits most, if not all, students.

Observation Learning

It is not surprising that students with severe disabilities can learn by watching others. Researchers have shown positive learning effects from intersequential arrangements where one student observes another student acquire academic skills (e.g., spelling one's name, adding, using a calculator, identifying community signs) and nonacademic skills (e.g., sharpening a pencil) (Brown & Holvoet, 1982; Doyle, Gast, Wolery, Ault, & Farmer, 1990; Singleton, Schuster, & Ault, 1995; Stinson et al., 1991; Whalen, Schuster, & Hemmeter, 1996). In these studies, which involved only pairs or small groups of students with disabilities, students not only learned the skills that they were taught directly, but also acquired some of their classmates' skills that they had only observed or that had been presented to them incidentally. Learning through observation in small groups works well when group members have the same type of task (e.g., identifying over-the-counter medications) but are taught with different materials (e.g., each student learns two different medications) instead of all having the same materials.

> *Christine's teacher, Ms. Rowyer, places two other students together with Christine when teaching them to identify community words. They look at videos that have been taken of familiar locations in the community—locations that all of the students are learning to use more independently (e.g., several grocery stores and fast-food restaurants, two discount stores, and the video store). The videos show closeups of frequently encountered words that are also target sight words that they are learning to locate, read, and act upon. When starting a new set of words, Ms. Rowyer shows and also gives them each a different word card (Christine's words are written in large font), names the words, and states their meanings. They review these responses and then watch the video segment where the three words are naturally displayed. Ms. Rowyer uses time-delay prompts to teach them to match the words to her identical card, name the words, and state their meanings. Then they switch words and repeat the process.*

Learning through observation in small groups also works well when typical classmates model functional tasks for students with severe disabilities while stating each step that they perform (e.g., spelling their name with letter tiles, using a calculator) (Werts, Caldwell, & Wolery, 1996).

> *During kindergarten, Marc's teacher often groups Marc with two peers to help teach him routines such as putting things in his cubby and getting ready for snack time. Jacob and Meredith are good models; they make sure that Marc is watching and then perform one small step at a time as they tell him with words and gestures what they are doing.*

Cooperative Learning Groups

Strategies to promote cooperation among students working toward a group goal have had widespread application in regular education programs (Johnson & Johnson, 1997). Many of the strategies for successful group instruction are evident in cooperative learning groups, with the added advantage that students learn to cooperate with others while shifting competition with others to competition with oneself (Snell & Janney, 2000). Slavin (1991) defines cooperative learning methods as "instructional techniques in which students work in heterogeneous learning teams to help one another learn academic material" (p. 177). In contrast to the group arrangements just described, cooperative learning groups work more independently from the teacher. However, cooperative learning groups receive instructions on the purpose of the activity, have ongoing supervision, interact with the teacher, and require a great deal of teacher planning.

> *Marc's kindergarten teacher makes frequent use of cooperative groupings. The cooperative activities are changed daily and involve art (making a mural together), music and dance, building with blocks or other materials, science, cooking, or games. The small groups are balanced so that children who need extra assistance and those who are more independent are spread out among the groups. Group membership changes several times over the school year. Following simple directions given by Ms. Kwan, the kindergarten teacher, the students move with their group to the activity, get settled, receive instructions, participate together, finish the activity, and clean up. After instructions or a demonstration of the activity, Ms. Wharton, the special education teacher, and Ms. Kwan rotate among the groups and help group members decide who will do what to contribute to the activity. For example, Marc, who likes to put things in their places, is often given responsibility for putting materials away for his group. Marion and Charles, each with delayed language, are in different groups; they enjoy passing out items to group members and benefit from naming group members, so they are often given such tasks.*

Several examples of cooperative learning groups have involved students with severe disabilities in general education classrooms. Dugan and colleagues demonstrated that fourth graders with autism could learn skills such as word recognition, peer interaction, and academic engagement alongside their peers in social studies cooperative groups (Dugan, Kamps, Leonard, Watkins, Rheinberger, & Stackhaus, 1995). Hunt et al. (1994) taught second graders to use positive feedback and prompts to assist classmates with movement, cognitive, and communication disabilities to respond in cooperative groups. The students with disabilities rotated to new cooperative groups in the classroom every 8 to 10 weeks. Not only did peers achieve their academic objectives even when serving as mediators, but target students also learned motor and communication objectives that were embedded within the cooperative activity and generalized these skills to new groups, peers, and activities. While the typical students focused on learning geometry from shapes and money skills, their classmates with disabilities worked on communication and motor IEP objectives because the group activity allowed many opportunities for requesting turns and moving task materials. Both studies support the use of cooperative learning groups as a means for promoting meaningful inclusion of students with severe disabilities in general education classrooms.

Group Instruction Guidelines

Group instruction has many benefits over one-to-one instruction but may be challenging to some students. Several simple methods can maximize student motivation for working in groups:

1. Individualize instruction so that all group members actively participate. This means that the same concept will be taught at varying levels of complexity suited to individual students, while also allowing for different response modes and using modified materials if needed.
2. Keep the group instruction interesting by (a) keeping turns short, (b) giving everyone turns, (c) making turns contingent on student attending, (d) giving demonstrations, and (e) using a variety of task materials that can be handled by the students.
3. Encourage students to listen and watch other group members as they take their turns and praise them when they do so. Actively involve students in the process of praising and prompting others.
4. Attend to students during instruction and provide task-specific praise that students can understand and individualized reinforcement. Also, use group reinforcement contingencies so that the group is reinforced on the basis of all members' combined performance.
5. Allow students to participate in demonstrations and handle materials related to the skill/concept being taught.

6. Keep waiting time to a minimum by controlling group size, teacher talk, and the length of each student's turn.
7. Prompt cooperation and discourage competition among group members.

Prevention Strategies

In recent years, there has been widespread support for the positive effects on students' discipline and achievement of a three-tiered model for School-wide Positive Behavior Support (Bradshaw, Koth, Thornton, & Leaf, 2009; Horner, Sugai, Smolkowski, Eber, Todd, & Esperanza, 2009; Horner, Sugai, Todd, & Lewis-Palmer, 2005; Irvin, Tobin, Sprague, Sugai, & Vincent, 2004; McIntosh, Chard, Boland, & Horner, 2006; Taylor-Greene et al., 1997). In Tier 1 (primary prevention), the Positive Behavior Interventions and Supports (PBIS) model promotes strategies that teachers can use with *all* students to reduce the probability of inattentive and disruptive behavior. Clear expectations are provided for all students on what constitutes appropriate behavior within the school environment and how students are rewarded for meeting behavioral expectations, thus contributing to a positive school climate. As in the universal tier of RtI, the primary prevention tier will be effective for most students in the school. Tier 2, secondary prevention, is aimed at those students in the school who need more focused behavioral support. Finally, Tier 3 (tertiary prevention) addresses the needs of those few students in a school who require comprehensive behavioral support (see Chapter 7 and http://www.PBIS.org).

PBIS is a comprehensive and systematic approach to School-wide Behavior Support. There are also a wealth of individual evidence-based prevention strategies that are effective in supporting students to achieve improvements in both behavior and academics. Several of these preventative approaches, including the use of engaging, age-appropriate materials, predictable classroom schedules, and a variety of teaching arrangements, have already been described. Several additional prevention strategies are explained in Table 4–3.

Peer-Mediated Instruction and Peer Support

There is a long history in special education of engaging peers of all ages to intervene and assist with the teaching of skills to their classmates with disabilities. Phil Strain (Strain & Odom, 1986) is one of the

TABLE 4–3

Common Prevention Strategies

Strategy	How It Works	Support for This Approach
Offer choices	• Offering students choices appears to improve their motivation, performance, behavior, and day-to-day experiences. • Student protests may decrease and task initiations increase when choices are given in place of direct imperatives. • Teachers can offer choices at the beginning of, during, or after completing a task: (a) "Which of several activities/chores do you want to work on?" (b) "Where do you want to do this activity?" (c) "Who would you like for a work partner?" (d) "When do you want to take a break?" and (e) "What do you want to do during the break or after you are done?" • Students can be taught to make choices if they do not know how. • There is evidence of the differential effects of making a choice over being given preferred items; the act of choosing is reinforcing as it appears to lead to more active task involvement.	Brown (1991); Green, Reid, Rollyson, & Passante (2005); Kern, Vorndram, Hilt, Ringdahl, Adelman, & Dunlap (1998); Mechling, Gast, & Cronin (2006); Heller, Stafford, Alberto, Fredrick, & Helfin (2002); Moes (1998); Vaughn & Horner (1997)
Develop and use rules	• Establish and post a small number of rules that focus on essential classroom behaviors, and identify expected behaviors. • Rules must be understood by students and identify expected behavior. • Teach the expected behaviors across class routines through modeling, reminders, and reinforcement. • Enforce rules and behavior expectations consistently and through positive feedback.	Bradshaw, Koth, Thornton, & Leaf (2009); Horner, Sugai, Todd, & Lewis-Palmer (2005)
Facilitate transitions	• Provide a warning before the end of the activity. • Establish rules and classroom procedures for specific transitions (e.g., out of one activity and into the next activity or class, to lunch, to and from the bus, fire drills). • Teach transition procedures by creating opportunities and giving positive feedback. • Transitions are facilitated with (a) precorrection—staff remind students to walk, keep hands and feet to self, and use a quiet voice *just before* entering the transition area (rules specific to the transition)—and (b) active supervision—move around (vary your position), look around (scan all areas, especially in the distance), and interact with students (greet, chat briefly, use hand signals, give feedback on behavior, praise, send the student back if he or she breaks a rule).	Colvin, Sugai, Good, & Lee (1997); Cote, Thompson, & McKerchar (2005)
Establish rapport, positive interactions	• Work to make interactions with students enjoyable, satisfying, and interesting. The goal is for teachers to have warm, open, and balanced relationships with students and to share experiences and enjoy each others' company. • There is some agreement that good rapport between teachers and students is associated with low problem behavior in students.	Carr, Levin, McCon-nachie, Carlson, Kemp, & Smith (1994); McLaughlin & Carr (2005)

early researchers on peer-mediated instruction with preschoolers; the focus that he and his colleagues addressed was social interactions, teaching peers to initiate interactions during play and then monitoring their efforts and the target child's responses. Since then, many researchers have applied this basic concept of involving peers to support their classmates with disabilities. Recent work demonstrates the effectiveness of peer support arrangements as an alternative to relying completely on support and instruction from adults (Carter et al., 2007; Hughes, Rung, Wehmeyer, Agran, Copeland, & Hwang, B., 2000).

Peer Tutoring

Students without disabilities have been found to be effective instructors and social supports for their peers with severe disabilities in both one-to-one and two-to-one arrangements (two peers with one student with disabilities) (Carter & Kennedy, 2006). Not surprisingly, students with severe disabilities were found to have significantly more interactions when working with peers than when working with paraprofessionals or special educators (Carter et al., 2007). Peer support has also been shown to be a vehicle for students with disabilities to access the general education curriculum (Carter, Cushing, Clark, & Kennedy, 2005; McDonnell, Mathot-Buckner, Thorson, & Fister, 2001). For example, when peer tutors learned to use enhanced group instruction (Kamps, Walker, Locke, Delquadri, & Hall, 1990) to teach word reading, their tutees made as much progress as they did when taught one-to-one or in small groups by teachers or paraprofessionals. Other researchers demonstrated that adolescents who were underachievers could learn to be as effective as special educators in getting their tutees to engage in class tasks while also improving their own engagement (Shukla, Kennedy, & Cushing, 1998).

Many effective peer tutoring programs have been reported from preschool to high school in which peers have been taught to tutor classmates with disabilities on communication, social skills, physical education, and academic skills (Carter & Kennedy, 2006; Carter et al., 2007; Collins, Branson, Hall, & Rankin, 2001; Gilberts, Agran, Hughes, & Wehmeyer, 2001; Hughes et al., 2000; McDonnell, Johnson, & McQuivey, 2008; Ward & Ayvazo, 2006). Peer tutoring programs become more acceptable when they are balanced with efforts to promote friendships and nonhelping reciprocal relationships between classmates and peers with disabilities and when they are unobtrusively supervised and supported by adults (Carter, Cushing, & Kennedy, 2009; Janney & Snell, 2006).

Developing peer tutoring programs that promote equal relationships among students can be a challenge. Strategies that can help avoid the problem of one-way teaching among peers include class-wide or reciprocal peer tutoring and peer assistance with cooperative groups, in which dyads or groups of three students take turns teaching each other (one student may have a disability) (Delquadri, Greenwood, Whorton, Carta, & Hall, 1986; Dugan et al., 1995; McDonnell et al., 2001). Another way to avoid having *peers* be teachers is to pair older students, one or more grades older, as the tutors of younger students; with this arrangement, one-way teaching is less of an issue because there is no peer relationship between the tutor and the tutee, but instead there is a mentoring relationship.

Twice a week, Jacob looks forward to sessions with his seventh-grade tutor, Steve. After checking in at the tutoring office and getting the lesson plan and Jacob's record book, Steve takes Jacob to a tutoring station in the library. There they review what Jacob has done over the past few days in his classes: getting around the school, carrying out tasks without being distracted, and using picture or word guides to remember task steps. Then Jacob reads the task for that day from his schedule (return old class books and pick up new class books from the library), reviews the steps, gets the materials, and completes the task with reminders as needed from Steve. Afterward, Jacob self-evaluates with Steve's input. Before returning to the middle school next door, Steve shows the tutoring supervisor Jacob's record; once a month, Steve is observed by the tutoring supervisor.

With the goal of increasing the amount of meaningful time spent in general education classrooms for students with disabilities, McDonnell and his colleagues (2001) demonstrated the success of an intervention package that involved reciprocal peer tutoring and multielement curricula with accommodations. Six middle school students (three with moderate/severe disabilities, three without) were involved, along with the rest of the middle school classes, in prealgebra, physical education, and history. Classes were organized into reciprocal peer tutoring teams that included three students, each at different skill levels (above average, average, and below average); some teams included a student with a moderate or severe intellectual disability. All team members were taught to serve in tutor, tutee, and observer roles. Thus, each member of the tutoring teams learned to present instructional cues, to praise, and to correct errors. The multielement curricula involved special and general education teachers who were developing objectives for students with disabilities within the general education curriculum (prealgebra, physical education, and history) and also were identifying needed accommodations so that these students could learn related content alongside their peers. Examples of accommodations included a requiring reduced number of problems, allowing the student to dribble a basketball with the right hand instead of alternating between the right and left hands, and pointing to indicate the answer instead of speaking or writing. The researchers measured students' weekly test scores and coded their academic response and competitive behaviors (e.g., aggression, disruption, talking off task, inattention, noncompliance, self-abuse). The combined intervention (multilevel curriculum, accommodations, and reciprocal peer tutoring) appeared to lead to improved rates of academic response and reduced rates of competitive behavior in all three students. The peers without disabilities demonstrated benefits received from the peer tutoring program as shown by their test scores.

Peer Support Programs

In contrast to peer tutoring, peer support is less formal and more broadly directed toward social interaction and friendship, but also may focus on improving classroom engagement and task focus (e.g., looking at the teacher, asking questions about assignments, making comments in class). Recent less formal versions of peer support tested by Carter and his colleagues (2005, 2007) in secondary schools have been demonstrated to increase positive interactions between students with disabilities and their peers in general education settings and to improve academic engagement. In fact, interactions and engagement have been shown to be higher with support from peers than from adults (Carter et al., 2007). Also, the use of two peers to support one student was shown to yield even more improvements in academic involvement and social interaction than did the use of a single peer to support a student (Carter et al., 2005).

Several steps are involved in creating peer support programs in secondary school settings. First, peers and the students whom they support are carefully recruited with team input. Second, peer supports are trained and put into place in the general education classroom. Finally, peer supports are monitored by adults for the quality of support with retraining given as needed (Carter & Kennedy, 2006). Peer support may include a variety of activities carried out during class time, small group instruction, transitions, and breaks. Peers are taught to lend support for a partner's social IEP goals (e.g., taking conversational terms, initiating interaction), to promote their participation in class activities (e.g., cuing them to get needed materials, asking partners to work together on assignments, explaining assignments), to give partners a lot of positive reinforcement for participating and corrective feedback as needed, and to encourage their partners to interact with them and with other classmates. (These strategies are described in more depth in Chapter 11.)

Individualized Adaptations: Accommodations and Modifications

A crucial approach that is used by both general and special educators involves adapting instruction for individual students so that they achieve their expected educational goals. For students with high support needs, team members must work together to find adaptations that can resolve learning problems:

> *Because handwriting was slow and tedious for Marc and often resulted in tantrums, the team wanted to simplify the task. The occupational therapist suggested using a slant board to position materials and a hard plastic template with ½- by 1-inch openings for him to write the letters in. He also was taught to use a small keyboard printer to quickly produce words and phrases instead of writing them by hand.*

Adaptations is a broad term that encompasses both accommodations and modifications. Adaptations occur informally whenever teachers (a) adjust their method of delivery because they see that one or more students seem to be lost (e.g., they move closer to a student while repeating the directions), (b) change their expectations of how students respond (e.g., "First tell me and then write it") in order to improve students' participation, or (c) examine and modify the academic goals or performance criteria for students on the basis of their performance. *Accommodations* are adjustments that the IEP team makes to a student's school program that do not significantly change the curriculum level or performance criteria; instead, accommodations enable a student to access curriculum content or to demonstrate learning without changing curriculum goals (e.g., Jacob's extra time on his tests, Christine's adapted computer mouse and moving her desk close to the board). In contrast, *modifications* alter curriculum goals and performance criteria.

> *Jacob's team modified his fourth-grade curriculum goals and performance criteria for science: Jacob will show understanding of several primary concepts from the science unit on weather by matching pictures with simplified terms and definitions. Jacob's classmates are expected to explain all of the concepts using unit terminology.*

Students with severe disabilities typically will have many IEP accommodations and modifications that support their learning. For these students with more extensive support needs, it is best to have a more organized approach for teachers to work together to identify and implement needed individualized adaptations. Chapter 1 provided an overview of this collaborative process. In Chapter 6, we review and illustrate a model for designing schoolwork and individualized supports for students who are members of inclusive classrooms (Janney & Snell, 2004). This model depends on ongoing teamwork among special and general educators, paraprofessionals, related services professionals, and family members. The goal of teams is to meaningfully include those students who are active participants both socially and instructionally as members of general education classrooms. The model includes a process for planning three types of adaptations: curricular (individualize the learning goal), instructional (individualize the methods and materials), and alternative (individualize the goal, the methods/materials, *and* the activity).

Self-Management

Self-management procedures and student-directed learning strategies have many variations. These procedures are highly flexible and can be individualized to suit different students, behaviors, and settings. The common purpose of these approaches is "to enable students to modify and regulate their own behavior" (Agran, King-Sears, Wehmeyer, & Copeland, 2003, pp. 3-4). These approaches teach students to take a more active role in their own learning. Variations of self-management strategies include the following:

> *Antecedent Cue Regulation and Picture Cues:* Students learn to use visual, tactile, or auditory guides to remind them of the steps in a task, such as a work sequence, or to improve engagement in the classroom (Mechling, 2007).

> *For her job as a greeter at Walmart, Christine's job coach created a small photo guide that would be displayed on a plasticized sheet placed on her lap tray and also displayed on her DynaVox™ communication device. Initially, the 12 photos were large and were used one at a time to prompt each step of her role as a greeter at Walmart (e.g., job preparation, the ride to the store, check-in). Now she uses the photo grid by herself to remind her of each job step.*

> *Self-instruction:* Students learn to give themselves verbal cues as they are carrying out a targeted task in order to complete each step in the task at work or school (e.g., Agran & Moore, 1994).

> *Because Jacob had become highly dependent on prompting in two routines, his teachers designed a self-instruction task analysis of the steps involved in arriving at school and getting ready to go home. They used a did–next–now procedure to teach both routines. He learned to do each step as he verbalized in a did–next–now format: "I did put my backpack in my locker; I need to give my check-in sheet to Ms. Bowers; I'm going to give my check-in sheet to Ms. Bowers." Now he uses this approach to cue himself through the steps of both routines.*

> *Self-monitoring:* Students who self-monitor have learned to (a) observe their own behavior, (b) judge whether or not they have performed a targeted behavior, and (c) determine whether their performance met agreed-upon criteria (e.g., learning to discriminate following teachers' directions in general education classrooms) (Agran, Sinclair, Alper, Calvin, Wehmeyer, & Hughes, 2005).

> *Jacob's team thought that he could learn several necessary classroom behaviors better by using a self-monitoring system instead of being instructed*

Self-Monitoring Device

Jacob's car moves	──────▶			
	Get my binder ❑	Say Hi to Ms. Bowers ❑	Get in my seat fast ❑	**Computer time**
Ted's car moves	──────▶			
	Get my binder ❑	Say Hi to Ms. Bowers ❑	Get in my seat fast ❑	**Computer time**
Mitch's car moves	──────▶			
	Get my binder ❑	Say Hi to Ms. Bowers ❑	Get in my seat fast ❑	**Magazine time**

by Ms. Connors, the fourth-grade teaching assistant. The behaviors (taking his binder from his backpack, greeting Ms. Bowers as the other students did, and being in his seat when the bell rang) were ones that two of his classmates also needed to learn, so all three boys were involved in the project. Ms. Bowers met with Jacob and his classmates to discuss and design the simple recording form that they set up like a race car track. The students learned to pick a race car and move it forward when whenever they performed the classroom skills and checked the box. Each student learned to record accurately and liked earning a favorite activity like computer time or time to read race car magazines that they had brought from home.

Self-evaluation: Students learn to compare their own performance of a behavior to a desired level of performance (e.g., self-evaluating social responses) (Koegel, Koegel, Hurley, & Frea, 1992).

Marc was slow eating his lunch. Ms. Wharton, his special education teacher, timed him and his classmates over several days to see how long they took. Marc took 45 minutes and his classmates took 20 to 30 minutes. Marc's team set his goal at 30 minutes, but established successive time goals of 44, 41, 38, 35, 32, and 30 minutes. Ms. Wharton showed Marc a small visual timer and challenged him to eat faster before the red on the timer disappeared. Before lunch, Marc selected a desired activity to put on his schedule, and if he "beat the clock," he could participate in that activity.

Self-reinforcement: Students learn to compare their own performance of a targeted behavior to an agreed-upon level and administer a reinforcing consequence if they met the criterion. The reinforcement can be as simple as self praise ("I finished my work!") (Moore, Agran, & Fodor-Davis, 1989).

As part of the fourth-grade classroom behavior self-monitoring program, Jacob and his two classmates learned to take their checklists to Ms. Bowers at lunchtime and say "I got my binder, said hello, and got in my seat on time!"

Koegel and Koegel and their colleagues have applied self-management instruction to individuals with autism as a means for reducing problem behavior and increasing appropriate replacement behaviors (Koegel, Koegel, Boettcher, Harrower, & Openden, 2006). They suggest using a series of steps to design self-management programs and to involve students *at every step* as a means for encouraging commitment to a shared goal of positive behavior change (Keogel, Koegel, & Carter, 1999):

- Define the target behavior.
- Identify functional reinforcers that the student will work toward earning.
- Design a self-monitoring method or device that is appealing and can be learned by the student (e.g., placing a check mark next to a picture that represents a target behavior, using a wrist counter).
- Teach the student to use the method until he or she does so accurately (identify opportunities, set up opportunities, teach using prompts, fade prompts).
- Determine whether the student's use of self-management results in the desired behavior change; if not, problem solve and improve the procedures.
- Validate whether the student is using the device in natural environments.

Sometimes the variations in the self-management methods applied are not very distinct or may be intentionally combined (e.g., antecedent cues, self-evaluation, and/or self-reinforcement). For example, Agran and his colleagues (2005) taught middle school students with moderate to severe disabilities in general education classrooms to self-monitor their following of teachers' directions. Students first learned to discriminate directions from nondirections, then they learned to self-record their direction through the use of modeling and guided practice, and, finally, they learned to self-monitor through role-play (Agran et al., 2005). As a result of the intervention, all of the students made rapid improvements in following teachers' directions in class and educators agreed that their progress was significant and valuable. In another secondary school example, Hughes and her colleagues applied an antecedent cue regulation approach to teach high school students with intellectual disabilities to use a stimulus like money placed in their hands or a picture prompt card to direct themselves to carry out a relevant behavior (e.g., thanking the cashier, keeping the head upright, completing assignments, and initiating a conversation; Hughes, Copeland, Agran, Wehmeyer, Rodi, & Presley, 2002). Teaching sessions started with hearing a rationale for learning the behavior and then involved modeling, direct instruction, guided practice, and corrective feedback; after two or three teaching sessions, the students mastered self-management.

Finally, middle school students, taught by peer tutors, learned to self-monitor their performance of teacher-selected classroom survival skills (e.g., be in the classroom and seated when the bell rings, bring appropriate materials, greet teachers and peers, ask and answer questions) (Gilberts et al., 2001). Whenever they performed the classroom skills in their general education classroom, students learned to place check marks by survival skill words and pictures on a simple recording form; once they became accurate in self-recording, their performance of these survival skills greatly improved. When students are taught to self-manage their own behavior, they are less dependent on others and may have mastered improved engagement, better work completion, and appropriate social behavior.

Specialized Teaching Strategies That Are Effective with Students Who Have Severe Disabilities

This section will describe specialized teaching approaches that have been shown to be successful with students who have severe disabilities. Some examples of specialized strategies include visual supports, embedded instruction, chaining methods, and low error prompting procedures. These approaches, as a group, tend to have stronger research support with learners who have extensive disabilities than do the universal approaches. Many of these approaches rely on the use of discrete teaching trials whose elements we will explain in detail. While the research supporting most of these strategies has been conducted in special education classrooms or even separate school settings, most of these strategies are "portable" and all have been applied successfully to support students who are included in general education settings.

While both universal and specialized strategies range from the simpler to the more complex, specialized strategies, as a group, are often quite dissimilar from the methods used with typical students, and not all of these approaches may fit well in the general education setting without some adaptation. These specialized approaches often depend on direct and systematic instruction and require an understanding of the discrete teaching trial and its elements: (a) giving a task request, (b) waiting for a response, (c) giving assistance as needed, (d) reinforcing correct responses, and (e) providing feedback with regard to errors.

Jacob spends part of his school day in the resource room either to prevent behavioral episodes or to interrupt them. His Positive Behavior Support plan calls for numerous prevention strategies, including movement breaks scheduled throughout the day and the use of social narratives to prepare for upcoming activities. These strategies, along with interventions to teach self-control skills, have been effective in greatly decreasing problem behaviors such as crying and screaming, lying on the floor, and throwing or destroying materials.

Specialized approaches often look different, may require more teacher effort, and may not blend easily with general education teaching procedures. Educators, therefore, must be cautious when planning to use specialized approaches with specific students in inclusive settings. The *only-as-specialized-as-necessary* criterion (discussed more in Chapter 6) emphasizes the need to keep teaching strategies and adaptations both *nonintrusive for the student* and *user-friendly for the teaching team*. The goal for applying this criterion is to acknowledge that (a) students do not want to be singled out for extra assistance or adapted treatment all of the time and (b) students who need specialized interventions can still participate in typical activities and ordinary relationships. Thus, when teams apply the strategies described in this section in general education settings, they will use the teaching strategy with a student only when it is needed and when less intrusive approaches have not been successful, taking care that the strategy does not stigmatize the student and is not overburdening for team members to use. A second guide for selecting specialized teaching strategies, mentioned earlier in the chapter, is the principle of parsimony (Etzel & LeBlanc, 1979)—*select the simplest but still effective approach*—which reminds us that teaching strategies should be based on prior evidence.

Visual Modality Strategies

With the increased interest in effective teaching methods for students with autism and students with limited verbal skills, researchers have begun to study the use of visual supports to replace or supplement teachers' verbal cues. More recently, the use of several types of video models have been reported and have been found to be effective antecedent strategies that may accompany other teaching approaches.

Visual Supports

There are many different applications for using symbols to support students' understanding of their school day and activities outside of school. Visual symbols, such as objects and pictures have the characteristic of being concrete and permanent, instead of fleeting, like verbal requests or even signs and gestures. Object and picture symbols have been demonstrated to be highly effective, especially for students whose verbal understanding or expression is limited. (The use of visual symbols for communication is discussed in more detail in Chapter 12.)

Visual Schedules. Among the most prevalent forms of visual support are *schedules* that use real objects, tangible symbols, picture symbols, or even words to represent regularly scheduled events during a student's school day. Mirenda and her colleagues differentiate between schedules that represent the activities in a day or a partial day (called *between-task schedules*) and schedules that represent the steps or subactivities within a single activity (called *within-task schedules*) (Mirenda, MacGregor, & Kelly-Keough, 2002). Both between- and within-task schedules are constructed following similar guidelines. Many give credit to Stillman and Battle (1984), as well as to Eric Schopler and his colleagues in the TEACCH program, for setting forth the use of visual schedules to structure routines for individuals with autism (e.g., Schopler, Brehm, Kinsbourne, & Reichler, 1971). The TEACCH checklist for individualizing visual schedules that is shown in Table 4-4 provides teachers with six key elements for creating visual schedules and teaching their use; items within each element are ordered from simple to more complex

TABLE 4–4
TEACCH Checklist for Individualization of Visual Schedules

Form of Representation
Object that will be used in an activity
Object that is symbolic of an activity/area
Photograph
Icon
Picture/word combination
Single word
Phrases or sentences

Length of Schedule
One item at a time, signifying transition
Two items, signifying a first–then sequence
Three or four items, up to an hour
2 hours
½ day
Full day

Presentation Format
One item at a time
Left to right sequence
Top to bottom sequence
Multiple rows

Ways to Manipulate the Schedule
Carry object to be used
Carry visual cue to be matched (in basket, box, pocket, on VELCRO®)
Turn over visual cue on schedule as completed
Mark off visual cue on schedule as completed

Location of the Schedule
Teacher takes schedule information to student
Stationary schedule in central, neutral location on table
Stationary schedule in central, neutral location on shelf or wall
Portable schedule: "Pull-off" segment of schedule
Portable schedule: On clipboard
Portable schedule: In notebook

Initiation of the Use of the Schedule
Teacher takes schedule information to student
Student goes to schedule with transition symbol: From same room, schedule within view
Student goes to schedule with transition symbol: From a variety of locations
Student travels to schedule using verbal cue: From same room, schedule within view
Student travels to schedule using verbal cue: From a variety of locations
Student spontaneously checks schedule

Compiled by Susan Boswell, Division TEACCH, UNC-Chapel Hill; for more information: http://www.teacch.com/

(Mesibov, Shea, & Schopler, 2004). Teams must identify the method for representing activities on a schedule in ways that students can understand (e.g., matching the actual object used in the activity to words naming the activity). (Figure 4–7 shows a student using his symbolic object schedule and then learning to make activity choices using symbolic objects.) The schedule length can be a single activity or can contain representations of activities that last an entire day. The schedule items (objects, icons, etc.) must be arranged in some way and designed so that they can be manipulated by the student. The teacher may give schedules directly to beginning students, but students will need to learn either to go to a set location in the classroom to find their schedule or to use a portable schedule. Finally, learning to initiate schedule use can range from teachers prompting students to use their schedule to students spontaneously checking their schedules. (Figure 4–8 shows Kyle using his schedule spontaneously.)

In the TEACCH system, visual schedules are coordinated with a *structured work/activity system* for helping students understand the beginning, the end, and the content of a task. The structure uses visual symbols (or objects) to help students grasp answers to questions such as the following:

- What task(s) will I do? (Symbols represent the tasks in a teaching session.)
- How much work is required? (The number of symbols indicate the number of work tasks.)
- How can I monitor my progress? (The symbols are removed in order once completed.)
- When am I done? (When all symbols are removed from the activity board, the task is done.)
- What happens next? (Students may refer to a final break activity symbol, or to their between-task schedule, for the next task.)

(Figure 4–9 illustrates a structured activity system used by an occupational therapist.)

Activity Boards, Rule Scripts. There are numerous variations on the theme of supporting students using visuals (Beukelman & Mirenda, 2005; Downing, 2005). *Activity boards* contain a small number of symbols related to a specific activity and thus supply the visual vocabulary needed for a student to communicate and for adults and peers to augment their verbal input when they communicate with the student. *Augmented input* means that communication partners augment or couple their spoken word communication with the communication forms that the student uses (e.g., tangible symbols, picture symbols, signing, touching symbols on a speaking communication device). Augmented input helps reinforce the meaning of the student's communication forms or symbols (for more on this, see Chapter 12).

FIGURE 4–7

Toby has learned to use a picture schedule. From the top box, he selects a small ball that is a symbol for a combined communication and physical therapy session in the gym. The second box has an object that symbolizes art class with his peers, while the third represents toileting. Once in the gym, Toby works with his SLP to make an activity choice as he learns to associate objects that are symbolic of an activity with the activity itself (choosing from the swing or the roller).

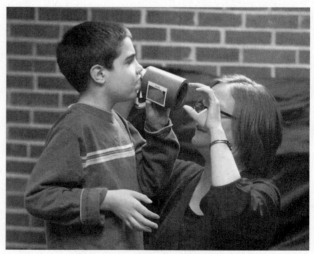

FIGURE 4–8

Kyle uses a picture schedule to guide his morning, icons and pictures arranged from top to bottom. Kyle has completed a work session and now goes to the computer for 5 minutes; after the computer, he will join his kindergarten class. While at the computer, his teacher uses a "count down" visual to help him understand how much time he has left on the computer.

Mirenda and her colleagues (2002) describe several useful approaches that can help prevent problem behavior just before and during an activity. For example, a *within-task symbol script* might be created to represent the required steps in a nonpreferred or difficult task, such as having one's hair washed during bath time (see Figure 4–10). *Rule scripts,* another visual support strategy, may be designed to clarify the rules related to how an activity is conducted instead of the activity's sequence of steps (e.g., rules for eating

FIGURE 4–9

An occupational therapist, Ms. Helene, works with Valerie to assess her sensitivity to fine motor tasks. She uses a structured activity system to organize the assessment. They start by reviewing symbols for the four tasks, and then Valerie will take the first symbol and match it to the first task. When she is finished, she puts that symbol in a "Finished" pocket on the back of the card. This approach helps Valerie know what tasks will be performed, how much work is required, how to monitor her progress, when she is finished, and what happens next.

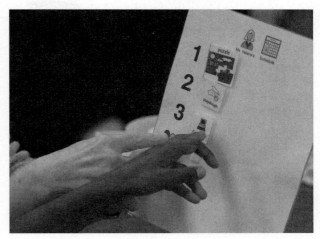

properly, rules for walking in the hallway during transitions). Figure 4–11 shows the approach Mirenda and her colleagues (2002) used to teach a child during a trip to a museum whether or not she could touch various exhibits.

FIGURE 4–10

When hair washing caused severe tantrums, a within-task symbol script was devised to teach Kelti the sequence for washing hair: what came first, second, and third, and when it was finished. Initially, her parents used the script with role-play before bath time and omitted hair washing; later they used the script before bath time and during the hair-washing routine picture without tantrums (Mirenda, MacGregor, & Kelly-Keough, 2002).

FIGURE 4–11

Haley's "Can I Touch?" rule script, was used to clarify the rules concerning whether or not she could touch various items in stores and at other community locations. She practiced the script at various community locations and then used it in a museum to determine whether she could touch an exhibit. The script helped Haley learn that she could sometimes touch things, but not always, which meant that she had more control and did not run away when someone told her "No" (Mirenda, MacGregor, & Kelly-Keough, 2002).

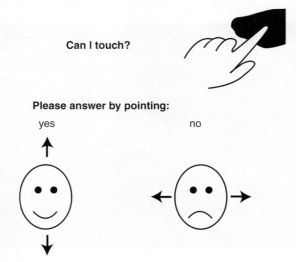

Can I touch?

Please answer by pointing:

yes   no

Social Narratives. *Social narratives* are short accounts of activities that may cause difficulty for students. Social narratives usually consist of pictures and simple words that state what to do, instead of focusing on what not to do, and that are written in first person to take the student's perspective. Typically, social narratives are read to students as a means of rehearsing what they should do in that activity. Social narratives are more flexible versions of Social Stories™ (Gray & Garand, 1993), but take a similar approach. The evidence behind this general approach is supportive even when the guidelines for writing Social Stories are not systematically followed or when additional cuing elements are added (e.g., Delano & Snell, 2006; Kuoch & Mirenda, 2003; Lorimer, Simpson, Myles, & Ganz, 2002; Thiemann & Goldstein, 2001).

> *Marc's teachers designed a five-page narrative to help him learn what he needed to do at circle time in kindergarten. The pages read as follows:*
>
> *Page 1: My name is Marc [his picture]. I am in kindergarten. I go to two classes—Ms. Rachel's and Ms. Kwan's.*

> *Page 2: I sit on the rainbow rug in Ms. Kwan's room [picture of rainbow rug with Marc and classmates sitting on it].*
>
> *Page 3: Everyone is quiet on the rainbow rug [picture symbol of quiet]. Everyone sits criss-cross-apple-sauce on the rainbow rug [picture symbol of sitting criss-cross].*
>
> *Page 4: I will try to be quiet on the rainbow rug. I will try to sit criss-cross-apple-sauce on the rainbow rug [picture].*
>
> *Page 5: My teachers will be very happy if I do not talk when I am sitting on the rainbow rug. I will talk in Ms. Joan's room. I will talk in Ms. Kwan's room when I am not sitting on the rainbow rug.*

There are several teaching considerations for using visually cued instruction and visual supports such as schedules, activity boards, symbol-structured activity systems, rule scripts, social narratives, and so forth:

- Use objects or symbols that the student associates with familiar routines or activities or can readily learn to associate.
- Use vocabulary that matches the student's comprehension skills or that may be understood when coupled with familiar routines.
- Rely primarily on the objects or symbols to represent the concept instead of using a lot of spoken words.
- Augment your spoken words by pointing to the symbols that match your words (augmented input).
- Provide feedback when symbols within the visual support are used correctly, stating the key word(s) ("Right, P.E.'s finished").

Video Modeling

Capitalizing on the strength of observational learning, video modeling is an intervention in which brief videos are used to teach specific skills. There is evidence of their effectiveness for teaching students with disabilities of all ages a variety of skills, including play, social communication, academics like spelling and reading, self-care (grooming, brushing teeth), and functional routines (ordering fast food, cooking) (Delano, 2007). Video modeling may be used alone or in combination with other teaching methods. This strategy has been shown to be particularly helpful in teaching students with autism, perhaps because of the emphasis on visual modeling over verbal instruction and because instruction involves less adult control (Charlop-Christy, Le, & Freeman, 2000). There is emerging evidence that video modeling promotes generalization and enables children with autism to acquire skills faster than in vivo modeling, when teachers use model prompts with students (Charlop-Christy et al., 2000). Videos can be created in several different ways: basic video modeling, video self-modeling, point-of-view video modeling, and video prompting (Cox, Delano, Sturgill, Franzone, & Collet-Klingenberg , 2009).

Basic Video Modeling.

The most common form, basic video modeling, simply requires that a peer or adult be taped as they perform a target skill. Usually these videos are short and do not have narration, thus making them easy to create and use. When the video is loaded onto a classroom computer, students can easily watch the video prior to the teaching session. After watching the video, the student is prompted to perform the target skill. Most of the video-modeling research with students on the autism spectrum has used this basic approach (e.g., D'Ateno, Mangiapanello, & Taylor, 2003; Nikopoulous & Keenan, 2003, 2004). An advantage of video modeling over live modeling is that steps which a student found to be difficult during baseline testing can be video-taped more slowly, with a closer view, as was done by Charlop-Christy et al. (2000) when teaching elementary school-aged students with autism cooperative play, emotion labels, greetings, brushing their teeth, and face washing.

Video Self-modeling.

The videos used in self-modeling show the student him or herself performing the target skill. While such tapes may be very motivating to students, making the tapes requires careful editing so that any assistance given to the student is not apparent in the videotape. (Chapter 10 describes these approaches in more detail.) What is important for teachers to know is that there may be little or no difference in effectiveness between basic video modeling and video self-modeling. Sherer and colleagues compared video self-modeling with basic video modeling in which a peer served as a model (Sherer, Pierce, Paredes, Kisacky, Ingersoll, & Schreibman, 2001). Their results suggest that students learned the task at similar rates regardless of which video-modeling approach was used. While more research would be helpful to confirm these findings, teachers should proceed as if the two methods are similar in effectiveness, thus saving time by not needing to prepare video self-modeling tapes.

Other Video-Modeling Approaches.

Two additional types of videos have been used successfully in video-modeling instruction. *Point-of-view video modeling* (Hine & Wolery, 2006) shows the performance that a learner sees when successfully carrying out the task. Thus, during taping, the camera is held just behind a pair of hands performing the task. Point-of-view taping avoids the issue of whether the performer is the student or someone else because the performer is not seen. With *video prompting*, the task and the taping are broken down into steps as a sequence of short video clips. Instruction involves having the student watch the first video clip of the first task step and then perform that behavior, moving through each video clip/task step in order. Researchers have used this approach to teach elementary school-aged students with disabilities to zip jackets, clean glasses, and put on a watch (Kamlesh, 2008) and to teach adults daily living skills (Cannella-Malone, Sigafoos, O'Reilly, de la Cruz, Edrisinha, & Lancioni, 2006). In the latter study (Cannella-Malone et al., 2006), researchers compared the effectiveness of video prompting with video modeling to teach six adults with developmental disabilities to set a table and put groceries away. While video prompting consisted of 10 separate video clips, one for each step of the task analysis, shot from the perspective of the performer (like point-of-view video modeling), the video-modeling tape showed *all* of the steps of the task analysis in one film that was taped from the perspective of the spectator. The findings showed that video prompting led to rapid acquisition, but video modeling was not effective. Because the video perspective was confounded with the type of video, it may be that the perspective from which the videos are filmed also contributes to the effectiveness of the intervention. More research will help isolate the value of video perspective apart from video-modeling type.

Our experience has been that teachers are comfortable with creating simple video-modeling sequences, that these videos may be created and played back on handheld devices such as video iPods™ (Cihak, Fahrenkrog, Ayres, & Smith, 2010), that their students enjoy watching them, and that the low-effort approach seems to contribute to student learning.

Task Analysis and Chaining

Chained and Discrete Response Skills

The types of behaviors that students are taught can be divided roughly into two groups: discrete behaviors and multiple-step behaviors. Target skills that involve a single, isolated response with an obvious beginning and end are called *discrete behaviors;* these behaviors are individually distinctive and can stand alone (e.g., naming familiar people, making numeral/quantity matches, reading words, identifying pictures). Target skills that consist of many behaviors chained together in sequence (e.g., sweeping the floor, playing UNO®, eating at a fast-food restaurant, brushing one's teeth, operating a CD player, counting out combinations of coins to pay for a product) are viewed as being *multiple-stepped responses or chained behaviors.* When chained behaviors are targeted for instruction, teams will need to complete a task analysis of the responses that are performed to complete the activity.

Examine Marc's goals and decide whether they are discrete or contain multiple steps:

> Following the use of the toilet, Marc will wash his hands by completing 8 of the 10 task steps independently.

> During lunchtime at school, Marc will complete 10 of the 12 steps independently: get in line, go to the cafeteria, move through the cafeteria line, get utensils, select three of the five food options, put them on his tray, enter his payment code using a match cue, carry his tray to the table, eat, empty his trash, get in line, and return to the classroom.

> When asked to circle a word (e.g., nap, mop, map) that matches a picture (e.g., of a mop) on a worksheet, Marc will correctly circle the word on 75% of the worksheet for two probes in a row.

> When given a slant board to hold his papers and a template to limit the range of writing, Marc will print all of the letters of the alphabet from a model 100% of the time on two probes in a row.

If you identified the first two goals as multiple-stepped behaviors and the last two as discrete behaviors, you are correct. His team members will write task analyses for the first two skills that will guide both assessment and teaching. His teachers might teach all of the task steps in order (total task chaining) or they may "chunk" the steps and teach them as clusters of steps. Alternately, they could teach just one step in the sequence at a time in a forward or backward order (forward and backward chaining, respectively). Typically, the last response is followed by reinforcement, either natural (e.g., completing a task and enjoying the outcome, such as making popcorn, getting the help that

was requested) or artificial (e.g., teacher praise, participation in a preferred activity), or both.

Discrete behaviors may be taught separately from the task in which they are used (e.g., reading prices) or taught as a step within a larger chain of functionally related behaviors (e.g., reading prices during the task of getting a snack from a vending machine). The distinction between discrete and multiple-stepped behaviors is not always clear. Many discrete behaviors can be divided into steps. For example, reading words involves a sequence of behaviors: look at the word, make the initial letter sound, and blend the initial letter sound with the medial and final sounds to say the word. How teams decide to view a target behavior depends on the behavior and the student, and this view influences instruction and measurement.

While the discrete behaviors do not require a task analysis, the team needs to agree on the skill and any prerequisites skills (often called a *skill sequence*).

> Before teaching Christine to read new functional words that she would encounter often, she learned to match targeted words and then to match the new words to pictures of that word. Then she was taught to read the words. Her teachers used a sequence of discrete behaviors: match identical words, match words to pictures, read the words.

Discrete behaviors are likely to be taught in a ladder fashion, gradually making the task expectations harder. Students advance from simpler objectives to more difficult or complex objectives, progressing toward their goal. Academic discrete behaviors like naming and counting often are taught in this manner using skill sequences—a listing of related skills arranged from simple to more difficult that are taught *separately*, in order, over a predetermined period. Table 4–5 sets forth a longer skill sequence that starts with the kindergarten-level focus and spans several grade levels, including Jacob's current IEP objectives for counting out combinations of coins to match prices. Many of the skills are discrete, while some may be more logically taught as a chain of responses.

> After several years of money instruction, Jacob has mastered steps 1 through 12; he is now working on counting quarters and soon will learn to count combinations of all coins. His teachers schedule regular application of these skills in school, where he makes small purchases. For example, skills 7 and 12 require Jacob to count out a given amount of money, which

TABLE 4–5
Skill Sequence for Using Coins to Make Purchases

1. Identification of pennies and stating their value (discrete responses)
2. Counting pennies by ones (chained response) and identifying the total amount (discrete)
3. Identification of nickels and stating their value (discrete responses)
4. Identification and stating the values of nickels and pennies in a mixed order (discrete responses)
5. Counting nickels by fives (chained response) and identifying the total amount (discrete)
6. Counting combinations of pennies and nickels (counting by fives and then continuing to count by ones) (chained response) and stating the total amount (discrete response)
7. Counting combinations of pennies and nickels to yield a written or stated price (chained response, as in making purchases)
8. Identification of dimes and stating their value (discrete responses)
9. Identification and stating the values of dimes, nickels, and pennies in a mixed order (discrete responses)
10. Counting dimes by 10s (chained response) and identifying the total amount (discrete response)
11. Counting combinations of pennies, nickels, and dimes (counting by 10s and then continuing to count by fives and then ones) (chained response) and stating the total amount (discrete response)
12. Counting combinations of pennies, nickels, and dimes to match a written or stated price (chained response, as in making purchases)
13. Identification of quarters and stating their value (discrete responses)
14. Identification and stating the values of nickels and pennies in a mixed order (discrete responses)
15. Counting quarters by 25s (chained response) and identifying the total amount (discrete response)

is required for paying library fines (5 cents per day), buying his school lunch ($1.00) or milk (20 cents), and buying pencils (25 to 35 cents) and paper (2 to 5 cents) in the school store.

Task Analysis

Analyzing a task and breaking it down into teachable steps for a student is not a trivial process. Consider how Marc's teachers planned for his active participation in the morning arrival routine.

Before teaching Marc the morning arrival routine, Ms. Wharton, the special education teacher, worked with the school's autism specialist. They watched other children perform the task and then analyzed the steps. They identified both the responses that they wanted Marc to learn and the relevant stimulus that Marc needed to learn to attend to (see Table 4–6). Ms. Wharton also asked Marc's kindergarten teacher, Ms. Kwan, to use the preliminary task analysis and to observe students upon their arrival to double-check the steps. Ms. Wharton piloted the task analysis for Marc to be sure that the steps made sense for him. When she found that some of the steps were too hard for him to do alone (e.g., Step 2: Open the door to the building), she modified those steps by adding adult/peer assistance or by dividing one step into two steps: (a) Take off jacket, and (b) Hang jacket on

TABLE 4–6
Initial Task Analysis of the Sequence of Stimuli and Responses Involved in Marc's Arrival Routine

Stimulus	Response
• Bus stops, driver opens door, kids get up	Get out of bus
• See school door	Open and walk through door
• See lobby and hallway to the left	Walk through lobby and down hallway
• See blue classroom door on the right	Open door and go in
• See teacher (hear/see greeting)	Greet teacher by waving
• See coat rack and other students removing their backpacks and jackets	Find empty space, take off backpack
• See other students putting backpack into cubby	Place backpack in cubby
• See other students hanging up their jackets	Remove jacket, hang on empty hook
• Jacket and backpack are put away (smiles and praise from teacher)	Go to schedule
• See activity cards arranged vertically	Take top card for centers, match to activity
• Teacher rings start bell	Go to schedule
• See activity cards arranged vertically	Take top card for circle, match to activity
• See rainbow rug, peers, and Ms. Kwan	Sits on rug

the hook. Marc's mother, who was familiar with the arrival routine, then looked at the task analysis and added her own ideas. Because Marc could perform very little of the task during the initial pilot, the two teachers anticipated that Marc would be in the acquisition stage of learning and thus left the main focus of the task analysis on the core steps of the task. The SLP suggested the enrichment skill of communicating a greeting.

Figure 4–12 shows the final task analysis of Marc's arrival routine with 17 steps that reflect the validation

process. The team decided to extend the task to include the two morning activities in kindergarten. The form allows team members to record teaching and testing data and note anecdotal comments to explain Marc's performance.

Teams will be more successful if task analyses are carefully developed through a process:

1. Select a needed skill by using ecological inventory results to identify a functional and age-appropriate skill that is an important target for a particular student (see Chapter 3).

FIGURE 4–12
The Team's Task Analysis Data Collection Form for Marc's Morning Arrival Routine

Teachers: Walton, Kwan **Instructional cue:** Arrival at school by school bus; Bus stops, kids stand up
Student: Marc **Settings:** Bus arrival area, sidewalk, lobby, hallway, classroom **Target:** Morning arrival routine
Day(s): Daily at arrival **Stage of learning:** Acquisition **Teaching method:** Constant time delay (0, 4 seconds)
Probe schedule: First Tuesday each month **Baseline/Probe method:** Multiple opportunity task analytic assessment (4-sec. latency)

Dates →	9/21	9/22	9/23	9/24	9/27	9/28	9/30	10/1	10/4	10/5
Delayed prompt →			0	0	4	4	4	4	4	
Task Steps ↓										
1. Get off bus	−	−	√	√	√	√	√	√	+	+
2. Open and walk through door (help OK)	−	−	√	√	√	√	√	√	√	−
3. Walk down the hallway (thru lobby to left)	+	−	√	√	√	√	√	√	√	
4. Open Ms. Kwan door, go in	−	−	√	√	√	√	√	√	√	−
5. Wave to Ms. Kwan*	−	−	√	√	√	√	√	+	+	+
6. Find empty cubby, take off backpack	−	−	√	√	+	+	+	+	+	+
7. Put backpack inside cubby (on floor)	+	−	√	√	√	+	+	+	+	+
8. Take off jacket	−	−	√	√	√	√	√	√	+	−
9. Hang it up (empty hook)	−	−	√	√	√	√	+	√	+	−
10. Go to your schedule get card (first card)	+	+	√	√	√	+	+	+	+	+
11. Go to _____ and get started (first card)	−	−	√	√	√	√	√	√	√	
12. Go to schedule get rainbow rug card (when teacher rings bell)	−	−	√	√	√	√	√	√	√	−
13. Go sit on rainbow rug (criss-cross)	−	+	√	√	√	√	+	+	+	+
14. Listen and do _____ (use circle schedule)	−	−	√	√	√	√	√	√	√	√
15. Go to schedule get Ms. Wharton's room card (when circle done)	−	−	√	√	√	√	+	+	+	+
16. Find Ms. Kwan, say good-bye*	−	−	√	√	√	√	√	√	+	+
17. Go to Ms. Wharton's room	−		√	√	√	+	√	+	√	−
Total independent	3	2	0	0	1	4	6	7	10	8
Baseline/Teach/Probe	B	B	T	T	T	T	T	T	T	P

Date	Teacher	Anecdotal Comments
9/23	JW	Waited for help most steps
9/25	JW	Sleepy, ear infection meds
10/4	LK	He's more sure
10/5	LK	Great probe!

[Located on back of task analysis]

Materials: Arrival schedule, backpack, Jacket
Latency Period: 0 sec., 4 sec.
Criterion: 10 of 15 steps correct (67%) for 3 of 5 teaching days

Recording Key: Test: + correct, − incorrect; Teach: + unprompted correct, √ prompted correct (gestural/partial physical prompt), − unprompted/prompted error; NR no response *Social enrichment steps

2. Define the target skill simply, including a description of the settings and materials most suited to the natural performance of the task.

3. Perform the task and observe peers performing the task, using the chosen materials in the natural settings while noting the steps involved.

4. Adapt the steps to suit the student's disabilities and skill strengths; employ as needed the principle of partial participation, the only-as-specialized-as-necessary rule, and component analysis to design a task analysis that is both age appropriate and functional.

5. Validate the task analysis by having the student perform the task, but provide assistance on steps that are unknown so that performance of all of the steps can be viewed.

6. Revise the task analysis so that it works; explore adding simple, nonstigmatizing adaptations to steps that appear to be unreasonable in an unadapted form.

7. Write the task analysis on a data collection form so that steps (a) are stated in terms of observable behavior; (b) result in a visible change in the product or process; (c) are ordered in a logical sequence; (d) are written in second-person singular so that they could serve as verbal prompts (if used); and (e) use language that is not confusing to the student, with the performance details that are essential to assessing performance enclosed in parentheses.

Approaches for Teaching Chained Tasks

Chaining refers to learning to perform a sequence of functionally related responses in an approximate or exact order to complete a more complex routine or task (e.g., clearing a table of dirty dishes, making a sandwich, brushing one's teeth, printing one's name, or completing an addition problem). Many of the skills that we perform and that we teach students to perform consist of a chain of small component responses linked together. Learning the sequence of responses involves performing each discrete behavior of the chain in sequence and in close temporal succession. When responses in the chain are learned, each response becomes the discriminative stimulus for the next response in the chain. Reinforcement is provided by others or by the act of completing the steps or the task itself, particularly if a preferred activity follows task completion.

When she first started teaching Marc to zip his jacket, Marc's occupational therapist would connect the zipper plackets, put Marc's fingers on the zipper

pull, start the movement, and then encourage Marc to pull the zipper up an inch. When he did, he was enthusiastically praised. Over several weeks, a few more steps earlier in the chain were added so that he now grasps the zipper pull by himself right after the therapist connects the zipper.

Each component of the chain becomes a conditioned reinforcer for the previous response and a discriminative stimulus for the next response in the chain.

By December, when Jacob would count out a mixed pile of coins, he sometimes stopped, started over, or just paused and self-corrected, but he usually finished with the total amount, saying, for example, "That's 85 cents!"

To teach behavior chains, the cluster of responses is first divided into an ordered list, or task analysis, of separate teachable behaviors. The number of steps into which a chain is divided varies for different students and skills. Because chaining may proceed forward (like Jacob's coin counting) or backward (like Marc's zipping task) across the sequence of behaviors, or may involve instruction across all steps concurrently, a team must select the manner in which it will teach the task components (i.e., *forward or backward chaining, or total task*). The chaining approach selected and the teaching procedures used depend on how fast the student learns under various teaching conditions, the length and complexity of the chain, the opportunity to perform the chain, and the component responses already known. (Refer to Chapter 5 for more examples of task analytic assessment.) The three basic chaining strategies (i.e., total task, forward, and backward) that teams choose from when planning teaching programs are described in Figure 4–13.

Elements of Discrete Teaching Trials

A discrete teaching trial "consists of a concise and consistent instruction or question, the child's response, and a specific consequence, the nature of which is determined by the child's response" (Schreibman, 2000, p. 374). Learning trials form the basis of all systematic instruction, regardless of the type of student or the skill taught. "Teaching is a process of organizing student experience so that target behaviors come under the control of new and different stimulus conditions"; this is a process that involves establishing and

FIGURE 4–13
Chaining Approaches

Description	Examples	Considerations for Use
Response Chaining: Total Task		
• Task analyze steps and measure baseline performance. • Instruction begins by starting with the first step in the chain and teaching each successive step in order until the chain of responses is completed. • All steps that need instruction are taught in order and concurrently during each performance of the chained routine. • Reinforcement is given quickly (e.g., praise) after each response for corrections and improved performances, and again at the end of the chain (e.g., a short leisure break).	• Has been used successfully with all sorts of chained tasks: self-care; mobility; daily living; community, vocational, and social interactions; and some multiple-step academic routines.	• Works best if the chain is not too long (chained tasks can be subdivided) or a single training trial can be too lengthy. • Main advantage are that all teaching opportunities are used (each step is taught each time) and that the task is completed. • May produce faster learning than other chaining methods. May be combined with repeated training just on difficult step(s) of a routine, although this is usually rather unnatural. • This seems to be a more natural approach than the other options.
Response Chaining: Forward Chaining		
• Task analyze steps and measure baseline performance. • Begin instruction by starting with the student performing any learned steps in order up to the first unmastered response, at which point instruction occurs. Reinforcement is given quickly after the training step, while more extensive reinforcement may be given after the last step in the chain is completed. • The remainder of the chain may be either completed by the teacher or by the student with assistance, but the routine should be finished before another training opportunity occurs. • Once this segment of the chain is mastered, through additional trials, instruction shifts to the next unmastered step, while prior learned steps are performed in sequence but without assistance.	• Useful with many self-care routines (grooming tasks, dressing, using the toilet). • May suit many home management and vocational tasks. Appropriate for some chained academic tasks (e.g., use of number line, telephone dialing, calculator use). (Not as useful in school or community setting when assistance through the unlearned part of the task is more obvious and may be stigmatizing.)	• Usually combined with prompting to teach the target step, as well as shaping across the entire chain. • May work better than the total task for some learners who have multiple disabilities or for longer tasks. Initial mastery of single responses in the chain may be faster but slower overall. • Replace with backward chaining when task has an especially reinforcing end. • Replace with total task if chain is performed less often; may want to switch to total task after half of the steps are learned. • May need to create more training opportunities or learning will be slow. • Involves a lot of teacher effort to complete unlearned portion of task.
Response Chaining: Backward Chaining		
• Task analyze steps and measure baseline performance. • Instruction begins by either completing or helping the student perform the entire chain of behavior up until the last step of the chain, at which point instruction occurs.	• Useful with many self-care routines (grooming tasks, dressing, using the toilet).	• Similar to forward chaining. The main advantages over forward chaining and total task are that the student is being assisted through the task, completes the task quickly, and gets reinforcement early in learning.

FIGURE 4–13 (*Continued*)

Description	Examples	Considerations for Use
Response Chaining: Backward Chaining		
• After additional opportunities and when the student has mastered the last step, teaching shifts to the next-to-last step of the chain, but the student is expected to perform the last step(s) unassisted. • Reinforcement is given quickly after the training step, while more extensive reinforcement occurs only after the last step in the chain is completed. As the remaining steps are taught, learned, and added in a backward order, the entire chain is performed, and the learner is reinforced.	• May suit many home management and vocational tasks. Appropriate for some chained academic tasks (e.g., use of number line, telephone dialing, calculator use). (Not as useful in school or community setting when assistance through the unlearned part of the task is more obvious and may be stigmatizing.)	• Usually combined with prompting to teach the target step, as well as shaping across the entire chain. • May work better than total task for some learners who have multiple disabilities or for longer tasks. Initial mastery of single responses in chain may be faster but slower overall. • Replace with total task if chain is performed less often; may want to switch to total task after half of the steps are learned. • May need to create more training opportunities or learning will be slow. • Involves a lot of teacher effort to complete unlearned portion of task.

transferring stimulus control over repeated learning trials (Wolery et al., 1992, p. 202). A discrete teaching trial can be represented as follows:

$$\text{Discriminative stimulus} \longrightarrow \text{Student response} \longrightarrow \text{Consequence for response}$$

When teaching trials are presented back to back, a pause is provided at the end of one trial and before the next trial to make each trial discrete from the next; this pause is called an *intertrial interval.* As we discuss in a later section, trials can be clustered together, or *massed* (also called *repeated practice*), so that many trials are presented on the same target skill (e.g., as in teaching Jacob to read vocabulary words) or can be *distributed* so that single trials are presented at a time when they are more natural to performing the task (e.g., teaching Marc to wash his hands after using the toilet and to change his socks after gym). *Contextualized* teaching means teaching at a time that is natural to the task, while *noncontextualized* teaching takes place apart from the natural application of the skill (e.g., pull-out speech sessions, in which the student is removed from the general education classroom to a therapy setting and follows instructions on making pretend purchases at a table in the classroom rather than in a real store).

Learning is most likely to occur (a) when the target behavior is reinforced in the presence of the desired

stimulus, and (b) when the target behavior is performed but not reinforced whenever the desired stimulus is not present. For example, as drivers, we have learned that driving (the target behavior) through green traffic lights (the desired stimulus) is legal, but driving (the target behavior) through red traffic lights (the incorrect stimulus) is not within the law and might result in an injury or a fine. In this case, the green light is the discriminative stimulus for driving through the intersection. This type of *discrimination training* is how we learned the names of our relatives (e.g., "Mama" and "Daddy"); to identify numbers, colors, and feelings; and to carry out complex behaviors like playing Monopoly® or tennis, reading books, and conducting titration experiments in chemistry class.

When students with high support needs are taught, in contrast to students *without* disabilities, teachers must attend closely to the elements of the teaching trial because it is important to keep student errors to a minimum. Making errors during initial instruction has been shown to slow learning, even with an error correction procedure (Ault, Wolery, Doyle, & Gast, 1989). Planning teaching trials so that students learn new responses fairly quickly without making many errors requires an awareness of the elements and the selection of strategies that support learning. Teachers might modify the expected student response so that it is a simpler version of the goal and then shape performance over time. Educators also need to be aware of the number of teaching trials provided (whether repeated or distributed), knowing that a higher frequency of correct responses to the desired stimuli facilitates learning. Attention is always paid to the consequences so that reinforcement is made contingent on successive approximations to the goal response—that is, students are reinforced for improvements in the target skill over time, even if they are only slight improvements. Learning is best when reinforcement is provided immediately and often during early learning; the frequency of reinforcement is faded in the later learning stages and the goal is to shift to natural forms of reinforcement. Often, some type of assistance or prompt that is known to be understood by the student (e.g., point cue, model, physical assist) is inserted between the discriminative stimulus and the student response; this often increases the likelihood that the student will make the correct response.

Discriminative stimulus $\rightarrow$ Prompt $\rightarrow$ Student response $\rightarrow$ Consequence for response

Discriminative Stimuli

Learning is the process of understanding how to behave (student response) in the presence of specific and changing signals or stimuli (discriminative stimuli) in the environment.

> *When Marc was three years old, he learned that at lunchtime in the presence of food at the kitchen table (discriminative stimuli), if he made the "eat" or "drink" sign (student response), his mom quickly gave him food. When Marc was given food he did not like, he also learned that making a pouting face and giving a negative vocalization meant that his mom would often take the food away.*

Marc's use of certain responses in the presence of food and drink have been reinforced for so long that he has learned which responses lead to food. A discriminative stimulus (also referred to as an S^D) is a relevant aspect of a task or situation in the presence of which a par-

ticular behavior is frequently reinforced. As shown below, discriminative stimuli can include aspects of a task setting, teacher requests, materials, the time of day, the student's physical state, and other relevant contextual stimuli.

Discriminative Stimuli	Examples
Task setting	Sink in the bathroom Sand table Swings at the playground
Teacher requests	"Everyone line up in front of the room." "It's time to take out your workbooks." "Who can tell me whether it's sunny or rainy?"
Materials	Picture schedule Workbook Spoon
Time of day	Students lining up in front of class at dismissal Bell signaling the end of math class Clock says 1:10—time to go to the resource room
Student's physical state	Empty stomach Full bladder Headache
Other relevant contextual stimuli	Fire alarm Overheated classroom Nonworking hearing aide

Initially, a parent's or teacher's reminders and assistive prompts are the stimuli that control a student's response. But once the task-discriminated stimuli are learned, they come to control the student's response and, therefore, prompts from others are not needed. For example, when Marc was two years old, his teachers and parents created opportunities to teach him to use several functional signs; he was initially given prompts (known as S^Ds) to teach him to associate signing with eating:

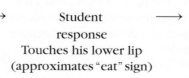

S^D (To be learned)	$\longrightarrow$	S^D (Known)	$\longrightarrow$	Student response	$\longrightarrow$	Consequence for response
Marc is hungry, at table, empty plate, with preferred food smells and food visible		Mom gets close to Marc and models the sign for "eat"		Touches his lower lip (approximates "eat" sign)		"You want food? Here you go!"

Teaching involves shifting the control from teacher-supplied stimuli (request and prompts) to natural task stimuli. For most students, the goal is to respond to the presence of natural cues instead of teacher-applied stimuli, such as requests and prompts.

One of Marc's kindergarten goals was independent hand washing. Initially, teachers and parents asked him to wash his hands at the appropriate times and then prompted him through the steps. His team expected that, over time, with repeated opportunities, he would learn (a) to discriminate the stimuli of dirt, food, or art supplies on his hands and respond by heading to a sink to wash them, and (b) to complete the task without prompts. Because the goal was for natural task stimuli to control his behavior, his teachers incorporated them into the teaching plan.

In February, Christine started sampling a job at an elementary school library close to campus. The job was checking out books. Initially, she did not understand what to do when someone asked her to check out a book or placed a book on the counter. After instruction from her job coach, she became alert to critical stimuli which "told" her that it was time to press the book scanning switch. Signals which indicated that a book was ready to be checked out included a child asking to check out a book, followed by the thud of the book against the metal end of the slanted book holder. She learned to activate the scanner switch and listen for the beep indicating that the book was scanned; however, if there was no beep, the book had not been put in the holder correctly (with the bar code positioned up and under the scanner). The absence of a beep was a different stimulus, which she learned to respond to by pushing her communication device to say, "Oops! Can you put the book in the right way?"

Instructional Cues

Teaching in natural settings and at natural times promotes the use of environmental cues. Initially, for most tasks in the acquisition stage of learning, an *instructional cue or request* is needed to signal the beginning of instruction and the target behavior. Instructional cues are not meant to be verbal prompts, but are used simply to initiate instruction in situations where the relevant contextual stimuli may not be initially discriminated by the student. Instructional requests need to be carefully planned:

1. State requests so that the student easily understands them (e.g., show visual symbol and say "Wash your hands").
2. Phrase them as requests ("Read this," "Tie your shoes,"), not questions ("Can you read this?" Do you want to tie your shoes?").
3. Provide requests only when the student is attending.
4. Give requests only once at the beginning of the task instead of repeating requests over and over.
5. Pair the request with relevant, natural task stimuli: times of day, materials, and settings.
6. Fade instructional requests when the student starts to notice relevant task stimuli or once the student reaches the advanced stages of learning (i.e., maintenance, fluency, and generalization).

Stimulus and Response Prompting

Prompting is an important antecedent strategy used to "get responses going" and to prevent errors. The behavior must occur before it can be shaped to a criterion level through instruction. Various types of assistance given just prior to the response in an instructional trial increases the likelihood that the learner will perform the desired behavior or will perform a better approximation. Thus, prompts can make learning more efficient because teachers need not wait for the target behavior to occur so that it can be reinforced. However, the behavior is not considered to have been learned until all prompts are eliminated or faded out. Initially, prompts are given to obtain a student response, but then are faded to shift control of the student's response from the prompt stimuli to the natural or relevant stimuli. There are two general classes of prompt procedures: Prompts that are associated primarily with the task stimuli (materials) are called *stimulus prompts or stimulus modification procedures,* while prompts associated with the response are called *response prompts*.

Stimulus Prompts

Stimulus prompts, or stimulus modification procedures, involve manipulating the relevant and irrelevant task stimuli and gradually changing the teaching stimuli from simpler to more challenging levels. Stimulus modification procedures are used by teachers to increase the chance of a correct response. A classic example of this approach are the stimulus-fading procedures used by Gold (1972) involving color coding of several key parts of bicycle brake pieces to make the assembly task easier for workers with disabilities. Given color-coded parts, the workers simply matched the colors of the parts to be joined. Eventually, the color coding was faded or eliminated.

While stimulus prompts are more time consuming to prepare and use than response prompts, they have the advantage of being used by students independently, without the need to have a staff member present. Prompting students to be successful during instruction by modifying the curriculum, class materials, and work directions are important strategies for teaching in the general education classroom. When making modifications in class materials, they must be slowly faded from simple to more difficult discriminations. The change in the stimulus must be so gradual that the new step will likely be achievable for the student.

> *Marc's letter-writing worksheets started out with dotted letters. The dotted letters were then gradually lightened and eliminated so that Marc was writing more and more of the letters on his own.*

While, most examples of these methods reduce errors to a minimum and have excellent research support, they also require that the student have accurate vision to be effective and may demand extensive preparation of teaching materials (Wolery et al., 1992). Computer-assisted versions of stimulus modification procedures may be an efficient option to teacher-made materials and have been applied to reading instruction for students with severe disabilities (Browder, Wakeman, Spooner, Ahlgrim-Delzell, & Algozzine, 2006).

Two commonly used stimulus modification procedures include stimulus fading and stimulus superimposition. *Stimulus fading* involves the pairing of an irrelevant stimulus (e.g., color or size) with a relevant stimulus (e.g., the word on the red card matches the picture shown, the big object matches the picture shown) and the gradual fading of the irrelevant stimulus (e.g., background color, object size). *Stimulus superimposition* involves the placement of a known stimulus (e.g., a picture) over another that is not known (e.g., the word for the picture) in a manner that both the known stimulus (the picture) and the stimulus to be learned (the word) can be viewed. Slowly, the intensity, clarity, or salience of the known stimulus (the picture) is modified until it is not visible, leaving only the originally unknown stimulus (the word) visible. This is exemplified by learning to read flash cards that

are prepared in four sets: set 1 has cards with a picture superimposed over the word, sets 2 and 3 have cards with the pictures faded out to different degrees, and set 4 has cards with only words. Instruction starts with set 1, the superimposed cards, progresses to set 2 and then 3 (each level of the faded picture cards), and ends with set 4, the word cards. Both stimulus fading and stimulus superimposition are used to teach an association between two stimuli, one known or familiar but irrelevant to the target skill (location, color, picture) and the other unknown but relevant (word, number). A simple application of stimulus modification procedures can be used to teach with a variety of task materials, allowing the student to become accustomed to changes in the irrelevant stimulus dimensions. Researchers like Kamps and her colleagues (Kamps et al., 1991, 1994) not only rotated materials often during small group instruction, but also used multiple exemplars—a minimum of three sets of materials per concept taught—to promote students' attention to the relevant task stimuli and away from the irrelevant task stimuli (color, size).

Response Prompts

Response prompts are actions taken by the teacher before a student responds (or after an error) to increase the probability of a correct response. Response prompts are "portable" in that they are readily available whenever the teacher is present and they do not require extensive materials as do stimulus prompts. Most response prompts used during the early stages of learning require a teacher to perform them close to the student or on the student, but there are many options for "teacher-free" response prompts when students learn to use picture guides to task steps, audio- or videotaped instructions, or computer-generated response prompts (refer back to the sections on visual supports and video modeling). Teacher-free response prompts such as these seem to be more successful in the later stages of learning, but this is not a hard-and-fast rule!

Typical response prompts that teachers provide directly to students include verbal instructions, gestures or pointing movements, models (stating the answer, showing a picture symbol), and physical assists. Unlike cues added to permanently remind students (e.g., Christine's use of picture cues to self-manage her memory of her Walmart job steps), response prompts are faded. All response prompts given by teachers need to be faded as students learn to respond to stimuli from the natural task context, to stimuli caused by their own task performance, or to other relevant internal stimuli (Wolery et al., 1992; Wolery & Gast, 1984). To do this, teachers must draw students' attention to natural stimuli by doing the following:

- Match verbal prompts with the actual words used in the setting where the skill ultimately will be performed:

  At her library job, Christine's teachers use the words "scanner" and "beep" because that's what the library staff and the students say.

- Emphasize the type of prompt most prevalent in the natural setting:

  When Jacob missed the teacher's directions, his peer support classmate tells him to watch what he and the others seated nearby are getting and to just do the same thing.

- When a student skips an important task step, call attention (with gestures, words, and positioning) to the step that occurred just before the missed step so that the student attends to the relevant natural stimuli:

  Marc pulled up his pants, flushed the toilet, and then started to leave the bathroom when the teacher called him back, positioned him facing the sink, and said, "What's next?"

- Use natural prompts and correction procedures whenever possible during maintenance, fluency, and generalization:

  Christine has learned to listen for the scanner beep after she activates the switch in order to judge whether the library book was placed in the book holder correctly.

- Teach students performing in the later learning stages to ask for assistance when prompts are faded:

  While learning to return the classroom's books to the library, Jacob performs well enough that his instructors assist only if there is a possibility of danger. He knows that if he needs help, he must ask for it.

Types of Instructional Prompts

Prompts come in many forms (e.g., words, visual demonstrations, physical movement) and are often combined. Prompts differ in the amount of assistance that they provide, the student skills required, and their intrusiveness. Teams should choose single prompts or combinations of prompts that suit the skill and setting, and the student's preferences, abilities, and stage of learning. The prompts in Figure 4–14 are arranged roughly in order from difficult to easy, with prompts that require more student skill to be effective first and prompts that require less student skill to be effective last.

Response Latency

In terms of giving instructional prompts, *response latency* can be defined as the period allowed for a student to respond without assistance or to respond before being giving a prompt. Without the opportunity to self-initiate, students may become prompt dependent and fail to learn the target response. The length of the response latency period depends primarily on the student; the student's stage of learning; and, in part, the response, or task step. For many students without significant movement difficulties and for many tasks, a latency of 3 to 5 seconds often suits them during the acquisition stage of learning. For many prompting procedures, the full latency is provided before any assistance is given to allow the student time to perform on their own. If a student does not respond during the latency period, the teacher gives a prompt and waits for the latency period again to allow the student time to respond to the prompt. If the student makes an error before the latency period is over, it is important to immediately and gently interrupt the error with a prompt (if none had been given yet) or with a prompt that provides more assistance if a prompt had been given but was not successful.

When Marc is standing by the coat hooks, Ms. Kwan watches and waits about 5 seconds to see whether he will take off his jacket. When he does not do so or starts to, but then stops, she gets close to him, directs his attention to a peer nearby, and uses point cues to indicate that his jacket should be taken off and hung on a hook. If he does not initiate the action after about 5 seconds, she uses a combined gestural and physical prompt (she points to his peer and the hook, then tugs gently at his jacket) and then waits about 5 more seconds for him to initiate the action before giving a full physical prompt.

FIGURE 4–14
Definitions, Examples, and Pros and Cons of Common Response Prompts

Definition and Examples	Pros and Cons
Spoken or Signed Prompts	
• Words or manual signs that tell the student how to respond ("Spray the mirror"); not the same as instructional cues (e.g., "Clean the bathroom") or directions • Match to fit student's comprehension of words/signs and the amount of prompt needed (e.g., nonspecific prompts like "What's next?" may be good later in learning but provide little information)	**Pros:** Can be given to a group and used from a distance. Do not require visual attention; involve no physical contact. **Cons:** Must be heard and understood by student and followed. Level of complexity varies considerably. May be hard to fade.
Pictorial or Written Prompts	
• Pictures or line drawings that tell the student how to perform a behavior; pictures may show the completed task or one or more steps in the task; words may accompany pictures if student can read • May be used as permanent prompts that are not faded • Level of abstraction needs to fit student (e.g., photos, drawings, line drawings, letters, numbers, words)	**Pros:** Can be used unobtrusively; do not require reading. Can promote independence even when used as permanent prompts. Standard symbols may help maintain consistency. **Cons:** Pictures may be poorly drawn or taken; if lost, pictures may not be replaceable. Some actions are difficult to illustrate. Must be seen and understood by student and followed. Level of abstraction varies.
Gestural Prompts	
• Movements made to direct a person's attention to something relevant to a response • Pointing toward the desired direction; tapping next to the material needed	**Pros:** These are unobtrusive, more natural cues. Can be given to a group and used from a distance; requires no physical contact. **Cons:** Must be seen and understood by student and followed.
Model Prompts	
• Demonstrations of the target behavior that students are expected to imitate • Models often involve movement (showing a step in shoe tying) but may involve no movement, as in showing a finished task (show one place set at a table and match to sample) or be verbal ("Sign 'want ball'") • Models may be complete (show entire step) or partial (show part of the step); if the model is done on a second set of materials, it need not be undone • Model prompts usually match task steps	**Pros:** No physical contact with person is needed; can be used with a group and given from a distance. Versatile: Models suit many target behaviors. Complexity of the model can be adjusted to suit student's level of performance. Others can be effective models on a planned or incidental basis; modeling can be unobtrusive. **Cons:** Require students to attend (see, feel, or hear the model) and to imitate. If model is too long or complex, imitation will be difficult.
Partial Physical Prompts	
• Brief touching, tapping, nudging, or lightly pulling or pushing a student's hand, arm, leg, trunk, jaw, etc. • Used to help a student initiate a response or a sequence of responses • Follow the rule: "As little as necessary"	**Pros:** Give some control over student responding with little physical contact. Useful when vision is limited. **Cons:** Can be intrusive; some students do not like to be touched; can't be used at a distance. Care must be taken not to injure or throw student off balance.

FIGURE 4–14 (*Continued*)

Definition and Examples	Pros and Cons
Full Physical Prompts	
• Full guidance through a behavior, often involving hand-over-hand assistance (as in using a spoon or smoothing a bed-spread) or movement of the trunk and legs (as in assisting crawling or walking forward) • Physical prompts should match task steps • Follow the rule "As little as necessary" while being sensitive to any student movement and easing physical control; does not involve force	**Pros:** Allows total control over response, thereby reducing errors. These are useful when vision is limited. **Cons:** Highly intrusive, unnatural, and stigmatizing in public; some students do not like to be touched; can't be used at a distance. Care must be taken not to injure through tight holding, to force compliance with a movement, or to throw student off balance.

Adapted from *Teaching students with moderate to severe disabilities* (pp. 38–41) by M. Wolery, M. J. Ault, and P. M. Doyle (1992), New York: Longman. Adapted with permission.

S^D (To be learned)	Latency $\longrightarrow$	S^D (Known) $\longrightarrow$	Student Response $\longrightarrow$	Consequence for response
Marc has his jacket on and is standing by the coat hooks among the other students who are just arriving.	Ms. Kwan waits 5 seconds for Marc to begin taking off his jacket.	Ms. Kwan kneels close and directs his attention to a peer in his line of vision who is removing and hanging his jacket. She then points to Marc's jacket and to the empty hook and tugs gently on his jacket.	Marc removes his jacket and hangs it on a hook, but not securely.	"Great! You hung up your jacket, Marc!" Ms. Kwan rearranges the jacket.

If a student seems to require more time to initiate a response, the teacher must determine the student's natural response latency by timing the student as he or she performs a known task involving similar movements. The time that it takes for the student to "get the response going" on those known tasks should be roughly the latency period used in teaching.

Because of her cerebral palsy, Christine is aware of the need to move before she can actually make a required move. Her teachers use response latencies longer than 5 seconds for responses that involve her hands and arms.

Prompt Fading

Fading is the gradual changing of the prompt stimuli that control a student's performance, to less intrusive and more natural prompt stimuli, and finally, to only natural task stimuli. Prompt fading also may be conducted by inserting time between the stimulus to be learned and the controlling stimulus (prompt), as is done in time-delay strategies, so that students learn to perform in the presence of natural task stimuli and prior to being prompted. Regardless of the fading approach, the goal is to fade prompts without noticeably increasing

student errors or depressing student performance. Fading of prompts is not an exact science (Demchak, 1990). Often, teams must observe a student's performance and adjust their methods so that fading is not too fast (thus keeping errors low) and not too slow (thus keeping motivation for the task high).

Prompts are faded in many ways. First, the number of prompts provided can be gradually reduced in several phases: (a) model and verbal prompts, (b) only verbal prompts, and (c) all prompts eliminated. Most fading approaches involve decreasing the amount of information provided by a prompt: (a) pointing to materials with a complete verbal reminder of a step, (b) only pointing to the materials, (c) saying "What's next?," and (d) giving no prompt. Additionally, the amount of physical control can be reduced over successive teaching opportunities: (a) full hand-over-hand assistance, (b) three-finger assistance, (c) one finger assistance, and (d) no physical assistance. Although it is important to transfer behavior control from training prompts to natural cues quickly, removal of prompts too quickly is certain to hamper successful transition. Fading is most successful when it is planned and completed systematically. Making observations of students performing without any prompts (i.e., by *probing their performance*) is the best way to judge whether students can carry out the task without assistance. Once all prompts have been faded and the student continues to make the correct response, learning or independent performance has been demonstrated.

Prompting Systems

Prompts may be used singularly, in combination, or as part of a specific prompting system. Some prompt systems employ a hierarchy; in other words, prompts are arranged either in order from most to least intrusive, called *most-to-least prompting* (e.g., physical–model–

verbal), or in order from least to most intrusive, often called a *system of least prompts* or *least-to-most prompting* (e.g., verbal–model–physical). Several other prompt systems (time delay, graduated guidance, and simultaneous prompts) have also been shown to be highly successful for teaching a variety of self-care, play, vocational, academic, and daily living skills during the acquisition stage of learning to students who have severe disabilities. These prompt systems have specific rules for their use and work differently to shift stimulus control from the prompt stimuli to the relevant task stimuli.

Figure 4–15 sets forth a description of prompt systems ordered roughly from the easiest to use and

FIGURE 4–15
Commonly Used Response Prompt Systems and Considerations for Use

Description of Prompt System	Supportive Research and Considerations for Use
Constant Time Delay	
• Select prompt that controls the response and determine how many trials will be given at 0-second delay. • During initial requests to respond, the prompt is given at the same time as the request (0-second delay), making early trials look like simultaneous prompting. • After a trial, several trials, or session(s), the delay between the task request and the prompt is lengthened to 4 seconds (or longer). If the student does not respond correctly in 4 seconds, the prompt is given. • Initially reinforce prompted correct responses, later differentially reinforce. • Always reinforce unprompted correct responses. • Continue giving delayed prompts until learning occurs (responds correctly without the prompt over several trials). • If errors occur, interrupt with the prompt; after several consecutive errors, reintroduce 0-second delay for one trial or more. • Response fading is part of the procedure as students learn that anticipating the delayed prompt enables faster reinforcement and/or completion of the task.	*Supportive Research:* There is strong evidence of success for both chained responses (Dogoe & Banda, 2009) and discrete responses, including a range of academic skills (Browder, Ahlgrin-Delsell, Spooner, Mims, & Baker, 2009) and functional tasks (Dogoe & Banda, 2009). *Considerations:* Initially, student does not have to wait for assistance. Easier to use than progressive delay or prompt hierarchy. Only one prompt or two combined prompts (verbal 1 model) are used; prompt(s) must work for student. Requires practice in using; need to count off the delay silently. Responses made before 4 seconds (correct anticipations) should receive more reinforcement than prompted responses. If an error is repeated, use progressive delay, change program, or simplify task. When teaching chained tasks, delay can be used with forward or backward chaining or when a total task format is used. *Recommended Use:* Use during early to late acquisition as well as other phases, but change to a less intrusive prompt. Good with chained or discrete tasks; equally effective but easier to use than progressive delay and more efficient than increasing assistance system. Peers have been successful using delay to teach chained tasks to students with moderate and severe disabilities (Godsey, Schuster, Lingo, Collins, & Kleinert, 2008).
Simultaneous Prompting	
• Request that student perform the target behavior while prompting at the same time. Model prompts are often used. • Reinforce both prompted correct and independent correct responses. • Before every training session, give an opportunity to perform without prompting (probes) (or following a set number of trials) to determine when to fade prompts.	*Supportive Research:* There is broad support with wide range of students with/without disabilities and tasks (Morse & Schuster, 2004). Successful with discrete behaviors (reading aisle headers) (Parker & Schuster, 2002) and chained tasks (hand washing and dressing for young students) (Sewell, Collins, Hemmeter, & Schuster, 1998). *Considerations:* Student does not have to wait for a prompt. Procedure is relatively easy to use. Must use probes to determine when to fade prompt.

Description of Prompt System	Supportive Research and Considerations for Use
Simultaneous Prompting	
• Fading of prompts occurs when probes alert teacher to stop prompting, prompting is stopped, and student continues to respond correctly.	*Recommended Use:* Use during early to late acquisition phase. Seems to work well when student cannot use less intrusive prompts. Good evidence that learned skill is maintained and generalized (Morse & Schuster, 2004).
System of Least-to-Most Prompting (Increasing Assistance)	
• Select a response latency and two to four different prompts that suit the student and the task; arrange prompts in an order from least assistance to most assistance (e.g., verbal, verbal 1 model, verbal 1 physical). • Student is asked to perform the task and allowed the latency period to respond. • Whenever a correct response (or a prompted correct) is made, reinforcement is given and the next training step/trial provided. • If student makes an error or gives no response, the first prompt in the hierarchy is given and the latency period is given. If the student again makes an error or gives no response, the next prompt is given and the latency period is given, and so on through the last level of prompt. • Errors are interrupted with the next prompt. • The last prompt should be adequate to produce the response. • Prompt fading generally occurs as students learn to respond to less intrusive prompts and then become independent. Simply put, the method involves telling student what to do, showing student what to do, and finally helping student to do the task.	*Supportive Research:* There is extensive support with both discrete and chained responses; less support with students who have multiple, severe disabilities and with basic self-care tasks. In comparison with delay, outcomes are the same or less efficient (errors, time to criterion, etc.). It is more efficient to use a *prescriptive* (individually suited) set of prompts than the traditional three (verbal, model, physical), but may be more difficult for staff (Wolery et al., 1992). *Considerations:* While hierarchies of verbal, model, and physical prompts are most prevalent, many options for simpler hierarchies exist (gestural, gestural + partial physical, gestural + full physical). Requires a lot of practice to use consistently but versatile across tasks. May be intrusive and stigmatizing. Some question the amount of time between task stimuli and response, and the change of response modalities across different prompts. Can be used with forward or backward chaining or when a total task format is used. *Recommended Use:* If learning is in the acquisition stage, avoid more than two levels of prompt. If learning is in the fluency stage, this is more efficient than decreasing assistance. Reduce intrusiveness of prompts for use in later learning phases.
Progressive Time Delay	
• This is similar to constant delay, except that delay interval is gradually increased from 0 to 8 or more seconds. • Determine delay levels and how many trials will be given at each level; plan error approach. • During initial requests to respond, the prompt is given at the same time as the request (0-second delay), making early trials look like simultaneous prompting. • After a trial, several trials, or session(s), the delay between the task request and the prompt is lengthened by 1- to 2-second increments up to 8 (or more) seconds, where delay remains until student learns. • Errors and corrections are handled as in constant delay, except delay may be reduced partially or completely when the student makes errors and then increased gradually or quickly when the student responds without errors. . • Response fading is part of the procedure as students learn that anticipating the delayed prompt enables faster reinforcement and/or completion of the task.	*Supportive Research:* Extensive history of support for discrete behaviors; good for chained responses across a range of students with disabilities and tasks (Wolery et al., 1992). *Considerations:* Same as for constant delay. Progressive time delay is more difficult to use, particularly with chained tasks. Reducing and then increasing the delay for repeated errors is also complex. Produces fast learning with few errors. Better than constant delay for students who have difficulty waiting because the delay is gradually increased and the ability to wait is shaped. Can be used with forward or backward chaining or when a total task format is used. *Recommended Use:* Use during the early to late acquisition stages; good with chained or discrete tasks; equally effective with constant delay but less easy to use and less efficient (requires more trials to achieve criterion). More efficient than increasing the assistance system.

(*continued*)

FIGURE 4–15 (*Continued*)

Description of Prompt System	Supportive Research and Considerations for Use
System of Most-to-Least Prompting (Decreasing Assistance)	
• Select a response latency and two to four different prompts that suit the student and the task; arrange prompts in an order from most to least assistance (e.g., verbal 1 physical, verbal 1 model, verbal). • The first prompt should be adequate to produce the response. • Determine the criterion for progressing to a less intrusive prompt (e.g., so many minutes of training at each level, a certain number of corrections in a row). • Student is asked to perform the task and allowed the latency period to respond. Whenever a correct response (or a prompted correct) is made, reinforcement is given, and the next training step/trial is provided. • Prompt fading generally occurs when teachers substitute less intrusive prompts for more intrusive ones and students learn to respond to less intrusive prompts and then become independent.	*Supportive Research:* There is convincing support for use with students who have severe disabilities and a range of skills (self-care, mobility, following directions). *Considerations:* Teachers must plan how to fade prompts and implement these plans, or students may become prompt dependent. Can be used with forward or backward chaining or when a total task format is used. *Recommended Use:* It may be better for teaching basic skills to some students in the acquisition stage than is a least-to-most prompting system. Works well when student cannot use less intrusive prompts (e.g., cannot follow verbal direction or imitate, or does not wait for prompts) and makes many errors. Helps teach students to wait longer latency periods, after which constant time delay or a system of least prompts may be used (Collins, 2007). Good when target task is chained and requires fluent movement. Less useful in later stages of learning.
Graduated Guidance	

• Select a general procedure to use:
  a. Gradually lighten physical assistance from full hand over hand, to partial, to light touch, to shadowing. Shadowing means that the teacher's hands are close to the student's involved body part (hand, arm) but not in contact, ready to assist.
  b. Hand-to-shoulder fading, which uses a full physical prompt, is applied at the hand and then faded to the wrist, forearm, elbow, upper arm, shoulder, and then to shadowing; hand-to-shoulder fading has been accompanied by ongoing verbal praise and tactile reinforcement, with concrete reinforcers given at the end of a task chain.
  c. Reduce the amount of pressure from initial full hand-over-hand assistance, to two-finger assistance, to one-finger guiding, and then to shadowing.
• Prompts are delivered simultaneously with the task request so that the student's movements through the task are continuous.
• Begin fading when there is evidence that the student can perform with less assistance: (a) sensing the student's assistance with the response through tactile cues, (b) improved performance (less help or no help) during probe trials, (c) student initiates the task, or (d) after what seems like an adequate amount of training.
	Supportive Research: This is supported by mostly older research in institutional groups and self-care tasks with intensive training methods. There are several more recent school applications (Collins, Gast, Wolery, Holcombe, & Leatherby, 1991; Denny, Marchand-Martella, Martella, & Reilly, 2000; Reese & Snell, 1990).
	
	Considerations: This is typically used with chained tasks, a total task format, no latency period, and intensive training, but can be used without intensive training. A latency period may be used to help judge when fading is appropriate (Reese & Snell, 1990). While the procedure is not complex (physical prompt only and then fading), it requires many teacher judgments about when to fade prompts; may not be systematic. Prompts may be faded too quickly, causing errors. Can be highly intrusive because only physical prompts are used.
	
	Recommended Use: Use during early to later acquisition stages only and after other, less intrusive systems have not worked. It is a fairly easy but physically intrusive prompting method that should only be used when other less intrusive procedures have not been successful (Collins, 2007).

potentially the least intrusive to the most difficult to use and the most intrusive. Still, *no prompt systems are easy to use;* each requires practice for teachers to become fluent users. One of the main advantages of these systems, if used correctly, is that students gener-

ally learn with few errors. The prompt systems we describe have varying histories of published research success with students who have moderate to high support needs. The reader is referred to several other general sources for more detail on these methods and their use with students (Ault et al., 1989; Collins, 2007; Schuster, Morse, Ault, Doyle, Crawford, & Wolery, 1998; Wolery et al., 1992) and to specific reviews of research using time delay (Browder, Ahlgrim-Delzell, Spooner, Mims, & Baker, 2009; Dogoe & Banda, 2009) or simultaneous prompting (Morse & Schuster, 2004).

The prompt system, the prompts, and the response latency that a team selects for teaching a student should be chosen to suit that student's skills. For example, teams will need to consider how long a student can wait for assistance, how well the student follows spoken or signed requests, whether the student imitates models or responds to pointing, whether the student tolerates physical touch, and also the student's preferences and dislikes for assistance (Demchak, 1990). Perhaps the most efficient approaches for learners in the acquisition stage are simultaneous prompting, constant time delay, and *prescriptive* increasing of assistance, or the system of least prompts with individualized prompts (see Figure 4–15).

In later stages of learning (i.e., maintenance, fluency/proficiency, and generalization), these same prompt systems also can be used if the prompt intensity is lessened. Thus, a teacher might use indirect verbal prompts (such as "What's next?" or the confirmation "That's right," or the command "Keep going" if a student pauses too long) on time delay or as part of a hierarchy of two or three prompts (the least intrusive prompt system). More extensive prompts used during acquisition might be replaced by unobtrusive cues or gestures that the student understands (e.g., the teacher looks in the direction of the correct choice or the next step nods toward materials needed in the missed step, gives hand motions to go faster).

Researchers have found that constant time delay is one of the most effective and efficient prompting methods and also is versatile across a range of academic, communication, and practical skills that involve either discrete behaviors or a chain of behaviors (Browder et al., 2009; Dogoe & Banda, 2009; Wolery et al., 1992). For example, time delay yielded fewer errors and less disruptive behavior than did the system of least prompts when young children with autism were taught academic tasks (e.g., matching pictures to objects, receptive identification of objects, numeral identification, word reading) (Heckman, Alber, Hooper, & Heward, 1998). Clearly, teams must select prompt procedures to suit individual students and

then monitor each student's progress as instruction progresses.

Applications of Prompt Systems: Constant Time Delay. Using time delay with discrete behavior skills is perhaps easier than with chained responses. Many discrete academic skills (e.g., social responses, reading, math) have been taught using constant time delay; a review by Browder et al. (2009) suggests that the use of time delay to teach literacy to students with severe disabilities qualifies as an evidence-based practice.

Marc's team identified telling time on the hour as an expected kindergarten skill that also was functional for him to learn. After conferring with Ms. Kwan, his kindergarten teacher, Ms. Wharton, his special education teacher, created materials to teach him to match clock picture times to numbers and words (3 o'-clock) and vice versa. As with many of his other skills, the team used a three-step progression: It started acquisition instruction using one-to-one teaching in the resource room using time delay, progressed to maintenance or independent use of the skill (as shown in Figure 4-6), and finally taught Marc to generalize the skill to kindergarten lessons on telling time. When Ms. Wharton used time delay, it looked like this:

Zero Time Delay

TEACHER: [She places two clock face cards showing different times (12:00 and 2:00) on the table in front of Marc and then shows him the number/word time card: 12 o'clock.] "Match 12 o'clock" [She immediately points to the matching clock using a touch cue at a 0-second delay.]

MARC: Picks up the number/word time card and places it below the correct matching clock face card.

TEACHER: "Right, 12 o'clock. Good!" [Teacher repositions the two face clocks and repeats for a second trial, again using a touch cue at a 0-second delay.]

MARC: Picks up the number/word time card and places it below the correct matching clock face card.

TEACHER: "Right, 12 o'clock. Good!" [Teacher conducts another trial but shows Marc the 1 o'clock number/word time card and places two clock face cards, one showing 1:00, on the table.]

4-Second Delay

After several successful zero-delay trials on 12 o'clock and 1 o'clock, the teacher pauses 4 seconds before giving the touch cue, hoping that Marc would try to answer before her cue:

TEACHER: [She places two clock face cards showing different times (12:00 and 4:00) on table in front of Marc and then shows him the number/word time card: 12 o'clock.] "Match 12 o'clock." [She waits 4 seconds to see whether Mark will give the correct response; he does not and so she gives him a touch cue.]

MARC: Picks up the number/word time card and places it below the matching clock face card.

TEACHER: "Right, 12 o'clock."

TEACHER: [Teacher repositions the two face clocks and repeats the trial.] "Match 12 o'clock." [She again waits 4 seconds before giving a touch cue if needed.]

MARC: *Before* the card is shown, Marc responds by matching the number/word time card to the clock.

TEACHER: "That's right, 12 o'clock!"

The teacher continued trials at a 4-second delay until Marc was able to match the first two number/word timecards independently and then started two additional times at a 0-second delay, while intermittently reviewing the learned times at a 4-second delay. She lengthened the delay for the second set of number/word time cards to 4 seconds until they were mastered, after which she added a third set, while continuing to intermix and review the times that had been learned. If Marc missed matching a known time, she would repeat the trial at zero delay and then follow with a 4-second delay trial. Each day, they started by reviewing the known number/word time cards at a 4-second delay, but after weekends and vacations, review was set back to a 0-second delay. Eventually, Marc was able to match all time cards to clock pictures; at this point he worked on this task independently (as shown in Figure 4–6) and his one-to-one learning focused on matching single pictures of a clock with an on-the-hour time to a choices of three time cards (e.g., 12 o'clock, 4 o'clock, and 9 o'clock).

Timed delay also is effective in teaching chained responses, but it may seem a bit more complicated. For example, Jacob's team agreed that it was important for Jacob to follow regular school routines. The team wrote an IEP goal with objectives that focused first on the morning classroom routine, then on departure, and last on preparation for lunch. His first objective was "Jacob will accurately complete the morning routine within 10 minutes on two consecutive weekly probes." After watching his peers perform the same routine over several days, the team task analyzed the routine into 10 steps:

1. Respond to peer's greeting.
2. Place backpack on desk; unpack agenda and homework folder.
3. Find locker; hang up backpack.
4. Take off outerwear and hang in locker.
5. Return to desk.
6. Take out homework, put in wire basket.
7. Make lunch choice.
8. Sharpen two pencils, if needed.
9. Fill in day and date on schedule and agenda.
10. Begin morning work.

Because Jacob had responded well to constant time delay with other tasks, the team selected that method and used it for all 10 steps, teaching each step of the task in order every morning (a total-task approach). Teaching occurred days each week during natural opportunities, with probes conducted once a week by either his special education teacher, Ms. Fuentes, or a teaching assistant, Ms. Connors. They used gestural prompts (point to or manipulate materials, point to picture symbols) or quiet verbal prompts to watch peer models ("Look at what Ty is doing. You do it, too."). They did not use any other verbal prompts for two reasons. Jacob was less attentive to verbal prompts and verbal prompts called attention to the fact that Jacob was being taught. For the first 2 days, they used zero time delay. During zero-delay trials, instruction moved quickly as the teacher prompted the first step as soon as Jacob was in the classroom among peers, then reinforced his greeting with a smile or a thumbs-up gesture, and immediately prompted the next step by gesturing to his backback and showing a symbol for "agenda". Teaching was fast paced and Jacob responded to each prompt. After 2 days of zero-delay trials, Ms. Fuentes delayed her prompt for 4 seconds for the first step and waited for 4 seconds after Jacob completed each step before giving a prompt. After long weekends and vacations, teachers used zero delay for a single day (assuming that he may have forgotten the routine); if he made four or more step errors in one session, they again used zero delay. The team's goal was to increase his unprompted correct responses.

Wolery et al. (1992) give helpful general rules about using zero-delay trials:

- When all students in a group are learning the same skill, fewer zero-delay trials are needed because they can learn from each other.
- When multiple behaviors are being taught (e.g., if Marc had to both match and state the time, and in chained tasks), more trials at zero delay are needed.
- Students with past success in learning by time delay may need fewer zero-delay trials.
- Younger students with less familiarity with direct instruction may need more zero-delay trials.

The goal is that teachers use as few zero-delay trials as they can, but that teachers not delay the prompt until the student consistently responds correctly for zero-delay trials (Wolery et al., 1992).

Applications of Prompt Systems: System of Least Prompts.

Marc's teachers are using a system of least prompts to teach him to use the bathroom in the resource room. They teach across all steps in the task, a technique known as a total-task approach. They start by giving him a 3-second latency period to respond. If he does not respond or if he makes an error, they use a gestural prompt (point to the item associated with the step) and wait 3 more seconds. If this does not work, they give a gestural and a physical prompt (point and gently assist him through the beginning of the step). Given the importance of selecting prompts that suit the student and the task, his teachers decided that these two levels of prompts suited him better than did verbal prompts or full physical prompts. Marc usually completed steps with partial physical prompts, but often resisted full physical prompts. Marc's instruction on the first three teaching steps [1. Goes into the bathroom; 2. Opens the door, goes in (teacher closes the door); 3. Grabs his pants, pulls them down, and sits on the toilet] looked like this:

TEACHER: Shows Marc the toilet symbol on his schedule. [Instructional cue, waits a 3-second latency period]

Marc continues sitting. [Response: No response]

Teacher gets close to him and in his view, and points toward the bathroom. [Gestural prompt]

Marc looks in that direction but does not move. [Response: Prompted approximation, but incomplete]

Teacher tugs gently on his sleeve and points toward the bathroom. [Gestural and partial physical prompt]

Marc gets up and moves to the bathroom door. [Response: Prompted correct on first task step]

TEACHER: "Good job, Marc!"

Marc continues into bathroom and stops by the toilet. [Response: Unprompted correct on second task step]

TEACHER: "Good, you're by the toilet!"

Marc stands without taking further action for the entire latency. [No response]

Teacher points to his loose elastic waistband pants. [Gestural prompt]

Marc grabs his pants, pulls them down, and sits on the toilet. [Prompted correct on third step]

TEACHER: "Good pulling pants down, Marc!" [Pats him on the shoulder]

After he sits for 2 minutes (or less if he eliminates), instruction continues on each remaining task step.

While the prompt systems just described are effective and systematic ways to teach students with high support needs, they are not simple approaches and they often look different from teaching methods used in general education classes. These two examples emphasize the importance of (a) determining whether such a specialized approach is needed, (b) selecting the specific prompt method and the prompts used to suit the student and the task, and (c) practicing the method until team members are consistent and comfortable in its use.

General Guidelines for Using Structured Prompts and Cues

To effectively use prompts or prompt systems with students, team members should follow several guidelines:

1. Select the least intrusive prompt(s) that is effective for the student and the task.
2. Select a prompt(s) that suits the student; combine prompts if necessary.
3. Choose natural prompts that are related to the target behavior (e.g., responses that involve movement may be best prompted with a gesture or

partial physical prompt, verbal responses may be prompted with verbal prompts).

4. Highlight natural prompts (e.g., call attention to the bell signaling the transition to the next class or to peers gathering their books and papers).
5. Generally wait a latency period (e.g., 3 seconds) before and after the prompt so that learners have a chance to respond without assistance. (Or, with systems like time delay and simultaneous prompting, shift to a delayed prompt or use a prompt-free probe so that the student has an opportunity to respond without assistance.)
6. Avoid repeating a prompt for the same response. Instead, if a prompt does not work, try more assistance.
7. Prompt only when the student is attending.
8. Devise a plan to fade prompts as soon as possible.
9. Do not introduce prompts unnecessarily.
10. Reinforce a student for responding correctly to a prompt during early acquisition; later, encourage learning through differential reinforcement.

Consequence Strategies

We will discuss several general consequence strategies in this section, including (a) the presentation of *positive reinforcement* for an appropriate response, (b) planned ignoring (also know as *extinction*) when students do not respond in appropriate ways, and (c) the use of corrective feedback. What is considered *appropriate responding* changes depending on the teaching objective and the student's present level of performance or stage of learning for the targeted skill. In early learning, an appropriate response often includes approximate performance of target behaviors and improvements in being attentive to task stimuli. For students who have mastered some of the task and are in later stages of learning, we would expect correct performance more than half of the time, and would be teaching students to extend their performance to include, for example, initiating and terminating the task, assessing their own performance of the task, performing across settings and variations in materials, and performing at the appropriate speed. The rules or contingencies that we apply for providing planned consequences are adjusted to suit the goals for a student's learning.

We do not address consequence strategies that are punitive in this chapter. Technically, *punishment* includes anything that reduces the probability of a behavior occurring (e.g., presenting nonpreferred

comments or activities, or contingently removing positive reinforcers following a response); however, a broader nontechnical definition of punishment extends to a variety of harmful categories that cause humiliation, fear, pain, temporary loss of ability, and prolonged loss of freedom or pleasure (Singer, Gert, & Koegel, 1999). Such aversive methods are not regarded as acceptable teaching or discipline strategies on both moral and educational grounds.

This reasoning regarding punitive consequences was applied by the members of Marc's team as they planned his teaching program for using the bathroom:

> *After task analyzing the steps involved in toileting, Marc's team decided that it would use constant time delay with a prompt that paired pointing to and showing a picture of the next step. The team members decided to teach all of the steps in the bathroom chain each time he used the bathroom (total task chaining), but to use backward chaining to teach hand washing. They made the decision to use backward chaining for hand washing because Marc did not like to get his hands wet. They felt that teaching one step at a time would allow for slower exposure to difficult steps and would be less "punishing" for him. They decided that they definitely would not use full physical assists because Marc does not like to be touched most of the time and would find this punishing, especially with regard to the steps of the task analysis related to getting his hands wet.*

Positive Reinforcement

Positive reinforcement occurs when preferred consequences (called *positive reinforcers*) are given contingent on a behavior *and*, as a result, there is an increase in the performance of that behavior over consecutive teaching opportunities. Thus, *to reinforce* means to strengthen behavior by increasing its frequency, duration, or intensity. Positive reinforcement is involved not only in shaping and chaining, but also in all the prompting methods discussed in the previous section. For example, shaping involves the reinforcement of successive approximations of a goal response. Instructors provide praise and other reinforcers for better and better performance over time. Shaping is a strategy inherent in most teaching methods that use positive reinforcement; systematic prompting procedures all involve shaping or a gradual increase in the teacher's expectations or criteria for reinforcement over repeated teaching opportunities. This practice acts to improve the student's response. This interdependent or contingent arrangement between behaviors and consequences (also involved in chaining and error correction) lets teachers build behaviors purposefully.

Reinforcers versus Preferences. What is reinforcing for one person will not necessarily be reinforcing for another, particularly with students who have more extensive disabilities; therefore, the activities and objects that an individual student finds reinforcing must be determined through informal assessment involving observation (see Chapter 3). The term *preference* is newer than the term *reinforcer,* but they are often used as synonyms. Preferences, like reinforcers, can be determined through direct observation. The distinction between the two terms seems to relate more to who is in control: the adult (e.g., teacher, therapist, parent) who provides reinforcement, or the student who has a preference for something. Traditionally, reinforcement is manipulated by adults for the purpose of increasing the frequency or intensity of a target behavior. In contrast, the opportunity to experience a preferred event may be made available in the context of everyday routines through choice making offered by an adult or peer (e.g., choice of activity, location, peers) or may be self-initiated by the student, as with self-reinforcement. When preferences are experienced in this way, they are more under the control of the individual student than the teacher. *Preference*, as a concept, is more consistent with fostering self-control or self-determination than is reinforcement. We use the terms as loose synonyms, but recognize that opportunities to choose and indicate preferences encourage self-determined behavior, while the tight control of reinforcers by others may not.

Types of Reinforcement. Although reinforcers—preferred activities and objects—have unlimited range and vary from tangible items and activities to abstract thoughts of self-approval, all reinforcers are either primary (unlearned or unconditioned) or secondary (learned or conditioned). The first category includes the universal or automatic reinforcers to which everyone responds (although not continuously) without instruction. Primary reinforcers for someone who is feeling hungry, thirsty, or cold include food, drink, and warmth, respectively. Primary reinforcers serve to return a person who is physically uncomfortable to a state of comfort. Secondary reinforcers develop reinforcing value through their

association with primary reinforcers. Secondary reinforcers begin as neutral stimuli, but with repeated pairings with already existing reinforcers, they take on their own reinforcing value.

> *Marc has learned to enjoy playing with blocks with his classmates because it involves putting things in order and creating large structures, which are activities that he already enjoys.*
>
> *Christine began listening to rock music for pleasure because listening to music was something that her peers liked. Also, her paycheck from work is now a secondary reinforcer because she has learned that her money buys CDs and other enjoyable items.*

Secondary reinforcers commonly used in educational settings include attention, approval, favorite activities, check marks, stickers, and tokens. It is important to couple simple but specific praise with known reinforcers so that praise acquires reinforcing value for students. The goal is for students to not only enlarge their options for reinforcement, but also to replace artificial, primary, or age-inappropriate reinforcers for those that are naturally occurring and suited to their chronological age. Self-reinforcement, of course, is the ultimate goal.

Reinforcement Schedules. Schedules of reinforcement indicate the frequency and pattern with which a student's responses are reinforced. Reinforcement may be given according to the number of responses performed (*ratio schedules*) or the passage of time in relation to the performance (*interval schedules*). Reinforcement schedules may be founded on an absolute, predetermined number of responses (which are then called *fixed ratio schedules*) or an absolute, predetermined amount of time (which are then called *fixed interval schedules*). An FR:5 schedule is a fixed pattern of reinforcement for every fifth correct response, an FR:2 schedule is a fixed pattern of reinforcement for every second correct response, and so forth. The presentation of one reinforcer for every occurrence of the target response is a *fixed ratio schedule* of 1, or FR:1. This is more commonly called *continuous reinforcement*. All other schedules may be generally referred to as *intermittent reinforcement*.

Variable ratio schedules produce a changing, nonfixed number of reinforcements, but offer reinforcement on a schedule that is an average of the reinforcement pattern selected. If a teacher specified a variable ratio schedule of reinforcement of VR:5, reinforcement will be delivered an *average* of every fifth correct response. This VR:5 pattern may consist of giving reinforcement after three, seven, two, and then eight occurrences of a target behavior. These numbers average out to reinforcement every fifth correct response. Variable schedules of reinforcement in classrooms are less predictable to students than are fixed schedules and thus produce more stable rates of behavior.

For *interval schedules,* the first target response is reinforced that occurs after a regular period of a *fixed* number of seconds or minutes (fixed interval, or FI) or a *variable* or average number of seconds of minutes (variable interval, or VI). In many classrooms, reinforcement schedules are time based (at the end of a class period) and teacher dispensed; feedback and social praise may be as meager as once every 10 minutes. In a classroom of 25 students, this converts to an even thinner reinforcement schedule. Classroom reinforcement schedules are more likely to be variable than fixed. Teachers may provide opportunities for students to choose a preferred activity when they judge the quality or quantity of work as "good enough" or after they judge that sufficient time has passed. Because "enough" and "sufficient" tend to change over time, a variable schedule results.

Because of the powerful influence of reinforcement schedules on behavior, teachers should apply several rules for scheduling reinforcement when planning instruction:

- During the acquisition stage of learning, more instances of behavior should be encouraged by the continuous provision of small amounts of contingent reinforcement (e.g., a smile and task-specific praise, fulfilling a request, sorting words read correctly into the "Awsome" pile, a "high five" or a "Yes!") instead of larger amounts of reinforcement given less often.

One of Marc's mathematics objectives was linked to the Kindergarten Standards of Learning and also had a functional focus: Recognize a penny, nickel, dime, and quarter and determine the value of a collection of pennies and/or nickels whose total is 10 cents or less. When Marc was first learning to count out amounts of pennies, his teaching assistants made a "big deal" of his performance by cheering each and every time that he was right (FR:1).

- After a higher rate of more accurate behavior has been established (later in the acquisition stage), reinforcers should be faded slowly from a continuous to an intermittent schedule, which requires more behavior for each reinforcement. This strengthens the behavior as the student learns to tolerate periods of nonreinforcement instead of abruptly giving up and not responding when reinforcement is not forthcoming.

After Marc was correctly counting out pennies on a frequent basis, his teachers still cheered him on, but not as much (e.g., FR:5).

- Over time, fixed schedules of reinforcement may produce uneven patterns of behavior because the student can predict roughly how far away the next reinforcement is on the basis of the last instance. Behaviors on fixed schedules can extinguish quickly following reinforcement because the students recognize the absence of reinforcement.

To increase her students' sense of responsibility for keeping their classroom neat, Ms. Bowers, Jacob's fourth-grade teacher, and the class instituted "Clean Teams"—groups of students who have assigned responsibilities for various parts of the classroom. Initially, Ms. Bowers conducted Friday "Clean Team" inspections and gave awards, which meant that the room was clean on Friday but not the rest of the week. She then realized she should not have such a predictable reward schedule.

- Variable schedules generally produce more even patterns of behavior than do fixed schedules because the individual cannot predict the occasions for reinforcement. Behaviors that have been reinforced by variable reinforcement schedules are also more resistant to extinction, so they are more durable if reinforcement stops for a given length of time.

Now, Ms. Bowers performs random spot checks and gives awards to "Clean Teams," and the room stays pretty neat.

- Reinforcers must be reassessed periodically (Lohrmann-O'Rourke, Browder, & Brown, 2000; Mason, McGee, Farmer-Dougan, & Risley, 1989; Roane, Vollmer, Ringdahl, & Marcus, 1998) so that they continue to be reinforcing to the student. It is also wise to offer students the opportunity to choose their reinforcer from a group of preferred activities/items; this way, teachers can be more confident that an activity/item is actually reinforcing.

For a while, Marc would almost always select Mr. Potato Head as a reinforcer. However, after a few weeks, he seemed to tire of this toy and all of the other selections that he was offered on the basis of his earlier reinforcer assessment. His teacher decided to conduct another reinforcer assessment to determine a wider selection of choices that he might like better at this time.

- Reinforcers must be suited to the student's chronological age, the activity, and the learning situation. Aim for replacing less appropriate reinforcers with ones that have more availability in the natural environments encountered by the student.

None of the team members wanted to use food to reinforce Marc, even though his mother reported that food reinforcers had been successful at home. They talked about what activities he liked, what the other five-year-old boys liked, and what he could easily do at school. They shared this list with his mother, then tried each activity out with Marc, giving him a "sample" first and then letting him choose. He showed clear preferences for Lego® toys, stories on CD-ROM, bouncing on the large plastic Hoppity Hop™ ball, and spinning in the net swing.

- The more immediately a reinforcer is presented following the performance of the behavior, the greater will be its effect.

Marc's teachers and his peers respond quickly when he uses his picture symbols or word approximations to initiate a request or interaction. As a result, he is using both forms more and more to communicate requests.

- Satiation results from the overuse of a reinforcer, and its reinforcing effect may be reduced. To avoid satiation, teams should (a) explore new reinforcers with students; (b) preserve the special quality of objects or activities selected as reinforcers; (c) use intermittent reinforcement because it requires fewer reinforcers for more behavior and reflects more natural schedules; and (d) whenever possible, give students opportunities to choose preferred activities instead of selecting and presenting reinforcers to students.

Because Marc responded positively to simple praise from his teachers, they decided to quietly say "Good!" after each step performed with or without assistance

during early learning. Marc also chose a preferred activity to add to his schedule after each toileting/hand-washing trial, and he reviewed this selection before the teaching trial began.

Planned Ignoring

When teachers intentionally withhold reinforcement following a student's behavior they are using a practice called *extinction*. When teachers have good rapport with students, they can be more confident that the student enjoys their attention. In these cases, simply ignoring a student's behavior by withholding attention constitutes extinction and may have a reductive effect on the ignored behavior. However, because ignoring alone is less likely to teach the student what to do, it is usually coupled with reinforcement or some type of support or assistance for appropriate behavior. For example, errors made during skill instruction can be ignored while offering the student another opportunity to perform the behavior or skill step, perhaps with some assistance provided. As another example, a teacher may ignore a student for calling out during a group lesson and prompt the student to raise his hand when it is likely that he knows the correct answer. Many of the prompt procedures described earlier incorporate planned ignoring for errors along with immediate presentation of a prompt.

Christine is learning to use her DynaVox™ communication device. This speaking device is really a computer that must be programmed with categories and vocabulary to suit her daily routines. Instruction is complicated because Christine's vision is poor so she must listen as each pictured option is named by the device through an earphone that she wears. When teaching her to go to the menu page and listen as the choices are scanned and named, Christine must select on the second cycle through the menu the item that matches her schedule for that day (e.g., Tuesday's schedule is morning instruction, library work site, lunch, drama club, Walmart work site, preparation for tomorrow, and home). When she clicks on the wrong menu item, Ms. Rowyer does not say anything, but instead stops the scanner so that it won't go to the wrong choice, repeats the request to click on "morning instruction," and restarts the scanner, ready to use a "listen" prompt right before the correct item is scanned and named. Ms. Rowyer has found that ignoring errors and repeating the trial with assistance makes instruction successful and less complicated for Christine.

Problem behavior can also be subjected to the extinction strategy in an effort to reduce its occurrence. This is discussed more in Chapter 7. Using extinction as the only means for reducing problem behavior is often ineffective because (a) it must be consistently used even when students might increase their rate of problem behavior in response to being ignored, and (b) no models for appropriate behavior are provided. Thus, extinction is typically used in combination with intentional instruction of the correct response or the appropriate behavior.

Response to Errors

To maintain a reinforcing environment for learning, it is important to minimize the potential for student errors. If there are many errors, instruction may need to be improved or the target behavior may need reexamination. When teachers provide repeated error correction, instruction may become aversive to students, as well as inefficient. While teachers plan instruction so that errors are minimized, when they do occur, the teacher may ignore them, provide specific feedback so that students are made aware of the errors, or gently interrupt and correct them in several ways. It is important to handle errors in a way that promotes learning.

Types of Errors. Errors include incorrect responses, problem behavior, and nonresponses. Incorrect responses can be missed steps in a chained response (e.g., not getting silverware or milk when going through the lunch line, skipping several key steps when washing dishes), discrimination errors in a discrete behavior (e.g., signing "eat" instead of "help," or reading "men" instead of "women"), or error responses that are not related to the target response (e.g., playing with the flash cards, looking away from the task, and attending to peers). In contrast, *nonresponse* may simply consist of the student waiting longer than the response latency, stopping in the middle of a chained response, not trying the task at all, or looking away from the task because of distraction or boredom. What the teacher does to respond to errors depends on both the type of error (e.g., incorrect response, problem behavior, nonresponse) and the student's skills (e.g., performance on the target task, ability to understand teacher feedback, and preferred ways of having mistakes dealt with).

Errors that involve problem behavior often are motivated by the student's interest in escaping from the task for some reason or needing assistance because the task is too difficult. Teams need to study the situation, determine the cause, and improve the teaching plan. For example, the teaching session may be too long, may involve lots of error correction and little success, may provide no student choice, or may be boring. (Chapter 7 addresses this assessment process.) In particular, when academic skills are involved, teams must have a process for making adaptations, which may include adjusting the method of delivery, changing how a student responds, or modifying the academic goals or performance criteria for a student on the basis of his or her performance. Students with severe disabilities typically will have many IEP accommodations and modifications that support their learning and thus improve the probability that they will respond successfully. (Chapter 6 describes and illustrates a model for making adaptations.)

The cause of errors that involve nonresponse, such as problem behavior errors, also needs to be analyzed. When some students are motivated to escape from a task that is too long, involves too much waiting, or is somehow boring to the student, they do so by withdrawing, not attending, not responding, or being easily distracted. Other students are challenged by a tendency to be highly distracted even when teaching is carefully planned to be motivating. Usually, preventing errors by improving the motivation to participate is the best means for addressing nonresponse errors.

For errors that involve incorrect discrimination, teachers can use one or more strategies: (a) ignore errors and not give any reinforcement (planned ignoring or extinction), (b) provide clear and immediate feedback to students ("No, that's not right; try again"), (c) follow up errors with assistance, or (d) have students participate in correcting their own errors. The last two approaches are examples of error correction. Technically, error correction procedures are response-prompting procedures—teachers prompt students to make the correct response (Wolery et al., 1992). However, the timing differs in that error correction is conducted *after* the student responds and has made an error, while response prompting is provided *before* the student's response. The example in the last section involved Christine's teacher using two of these strategies to address her errors when learning to operate her DynaVox™ device: strategy (a) ignoring her error, and strategy (c) following up each error with assistance to complete the missed response.

Most prompt systems that we discussed earlier in this chapter have built-in methods for preventing and for handling errors; however, teams still need to decide what approach works best with a given student and task.

When adults use words to correct Marc's errors, he does not attend or react. He is often resistant when physical corrections are attempted. But gesture cues are often effective (e.g., pointing to materials involved or moving materials associated with the missed step into his view). Thus, for the toileting sequence, they used constant time delay with a prompt that paired pointing to and showing a photo of him doing the next step. He had no problem when the prompt was given at a 0-second delay, but he sometimes failed to use the prompt when it was delayed 4 seconds. At these times, they used gentle physical assistance (as little as possible) to get him to complete the step, and on the next trip to the bathroom, they gave the prompt at a 0-second delay for the step that had been missed.

Jacob becomes resistant if teachers verbally point out his errors. The word no *seems to be a stimulus for anger. His teachers have found better ways to prevent and to address his mistakes during early learning*

tasks. First, they start by getting his attention or pausing for him to get ready. Second, they use a systematic prompt strategy, such as time delay for academic tasks and least prompts for chained tasks, because these methods make prompts available before errors typically occur. So if he fails to respond or makes an error, they say nothing, provide assistance instead, and then praise his efforts. Finally, his teachers have learned that interspersing known responses with new responses is a great way to motivate him. Thus, when working on new words, problems, or routines, they add items, questions, or steps that review the responses that he already knows well.

Figure 4–16 gives descriptions of ways to handle errors and lists considerations for their use. When a student has learned more than half of a skill and moves into the fluency, maintenance, or generalization stage, less structured and less informative error correction procedures should be used. Because the student is now more proficient at the skill, errors are less frequent and may be caused by distraction or carelessness instead of by not knowing what to do.

FIGURE 4–16
Strategies for Handing Incorrect Response Errors and Considerations for Their Use

Strategy	Considerations for Use

• During acquisition, it may be best to gently interrupt errors with a prompt (as in most prompt systems).
 • After an error, provide feedback (pause, hold up index finger, say "Not quite") and give another immediate opportunity to perform while increasing the assistance (as in a system of least prompts).
 • Gently stop an error and wait to see if the student will self-correct. Direct the student's attention to relevant task stimuli, add prompts as needed. Reinforce any self-corrections.
 • Later in learning, it may be good to follow some errors by waiting for the student to self-correct; if this does not occur, give assistance to correct the error.
 • Simplify those responses that are frequently missed or performed incorrectly.
 • Gently interrupt errors and provide several immediate opportunities to practice the missed response (or steps in a chained task) that are frequently missed.
	• Incorrect responses can be missed steps in a chain or discrimination errors. Repeated error correction is aversive for most students and inefficient. Analyze performance data to decide how to improve instruction. Also, consider the student's stage of learning and motivation for the task.
	 • Sometimes improving the antecedents may be necessary to reduce errors:
	   a. Improve the task analysis of the steps frequently missed.
	   b. Select a simpler version of the same skill.
	   c. Use backward chaining to teach these steps.
	   d. Use simpler prompts (gestural model instead of verbal).
	   e. Replace a prompt hierarchy with a single prompt system (constant time delay, simultaneous prompts).
	   f. Provide a visual cue (permanent prompt) such as a picture sequence.
	   g. Use stimulus prompts like color coding temporarily.
	 • During the later learning stages, allowing or prompting students to self-correct lets the students experience the natural stimuli resulting from the error and learn ways to improve the situation. Self-correction needs to be used carefully in order not to endanger or embarrass the student.

For some math, reading, and spelling tasks, Jacob and his classmates are working on improving their accuracy and speed. Teachers have students (a) correct their own worksheets, giving them time to redo the items that they missed; and (b) count the number of items that they got correct during flash card drills or timed math fact tests, and enter the number on their personalized bar graph.

When students have moved beyond acquisition into the advanced stages of learning, one of the following procedures may be chosen:

1. The student who makes an error or hesitates may be given a few seconds to self-correct. Some errors, if uninterrupted, will provide natural learning opportunities for students. If a correction is not forthcoming, then one of the other procedures can be tried.
2. The error may be acknowledged (holding up an index finger, saying "Oops" or "Not quite") without providing negative or harsh feedback. The teacher then requests another try at the same step ("Try it again"). If a second error results, some assistance is given. Efforts to soften the acknowledgment of an error, however, should not result in confusing or ambiguous feedback. For example, smiling and saying "That was a great try" in response to an error can be misinterpreted by the student as praise. Many students tune more into facial expression and tone of voice than to the specific words spoken. Thus, being neutral instead of animated is important.
3. A minimal prompt ("What's next?") or a verbal rehearsal of the last step correctly performed ("You just finished getting the plates, now what's next?") may be provided as soon as the error is stopped. If the student stops before a step has been completed, the teacher may offer confirmation and urge the student to continue ("That's right, keep going").

There are many other methods for correcting errors; however, to be effective, error correction procedures must reflect the following characteristics:

- Be suited to the learner's age, level of understanding, and preferences;
- Be suited in the amount of assistance and reinforcement (if any) to the student's stage of learning for that task;
- Be applied immediately and consistently, but unemotionally;

- Be nonstigmatizing, humane, and socially valid, and do not endanger the student;
- Provide enough help to correct the error quickly, but not so much as to create dependency on the teacher;
- Be followed by additional opportunities to respond to the task or step; and
- Encourage and reinforce independence.

Precautions. Some precautions must be taken with error correction so that it is not punishing to students. Facial expression, tone of voice, and the actual correction methods need to be matched to students' preferences. While it is important throughout learning that students discriminate making errors from making correct responses, error correction should not be aversive or reinforcing, but instead neutral and informative. When there are repeated errors, it is critical that the team examine performance data gathered during skill probes and also training trials to better understand possible reasons for the errors. For example, some task steps may be too difficult and simplifying the steps in the task analysis might improve the student's performance. At other times, it may be that the type of chaining strategy needs to be revised (e.g., change from a total task approach to a backward chaining strategy). Another option is to add extra instruction on just the difficult steps. Depending on the student, the teacher might ask the student whether he or she needs a prompt ("Need help?") and allow the student to choose self-correction or assistance. Another option that reduces the probability of errors is to replace a prompt hierarchy with a single prompt system (time delay, simultaneous) or with a most-to-least approach like graduated guidance. Adding temporary stimulus prompts (such as color coding or putting a large X on a shirt label) also is a way to help students discriminate difficult steps like identifying the front and the back of a T-shirt while dressing. Teachers also might teach students to use a series of photos of the steps that will offer permanent reminders. Finally, teachers can make digitized videos that model the task and show difficult steps in slow motion or close up.

There are also numerous ways to improve a teaching plan that can reduce a particular student's errors: (a) changing the prompting system (e.g., changing to time delay or simultaneous prompts), (b) increasing or reducing the response latency (before the prompt) or the time allowed to complete a task step, (c) using a simpler prompt that does not require understanding words (gestural/model instead of verbal), (d) increasing motivation for task participation and refreshing the reinforcing consequences, or (e) giving choices (select task, choose order of task completion). The approaches used will be individually selected to suit the student.

Arranging Teaching Trials

Earlier we noted that when students are provided instruction on a targeted skill, planned teaching often consists of one or more instructional trials. Each discrete trial contains the elements described earlier: (a) the discriminative stimulus to be learned, followed by (b) a latency period, (c) a known discriminative stimulus or prompt, (d) the student response, and (e) the teacher's consequence for that response.

Distributed or Massed Trial Instruction

There are a number of options for arranging teaching trials. Teaching trials may be clustered and taught in a massed manner with short intertrial intervals (as in applied behavior analysis discrete trial training). Teaching trials also may be distributed over time with minutes or hours between teaching trials (as in incidental teaching). Distributed teaching has been credited with being more effective in producing generalization of skills than massed trial teaching; yet massed trial teaching is credited with faster learning during acquisition.

The teaching setting often influences the intensity of trials (massed versus distributed trials) during instruction. Teaching trials may be presented within meaningful contexts (contextualized) or may be presented at times and in places that are not logically connected to the skill and may be removed from the natural environment. When teaching trials are clustered together, or *massed*, so that many trials are presented on the same target skill (e.g., as in teaching Jacob to read vocabulary words or asking Marc to repeatedly use the bathroom), trials typically are not contextualized and generally do not conform to the natural performance of the skill. However, there are some exceptions. Some skills and routines offer natural repeated teaching opportunities, such as learning to eat with a spoon, putting toys away, clearing tables in a cafeteria, and filling salt and pepper shakers in a restaurant job. Similarly, when teaching skills during natural or contextualized opportunities (e.g., greeting others, toileting), teaching trials are more often distributed over an activity or a day instead of massed with repeated opportunities to teach. If we consider teaching Marc to hang up his jacket, a massed trial approach would involve asking him to repeat the behavior several times in a row—not a very natural way to perform this skill. In a more natural context, the opportunities that Marc has to put his backpack and coat away occur only upon arrival at school; thus, his teaching trials are both distributed and contextualized.

Intensive teaching or using repeated trials is not uncommon when teaching academic skills. For example, reading and writing instruction in small groups offer students many opportunities to respond in a single 15-minute session. Massed discrete trial instruction has been shown to be successful in teaching some skills to some students during acquisition (e.g., communication in children with autism; Lovaas & Taubman, 1981) and toileting skills (Richmond, 1983). However, despite agreement that discrete trial instruction can be effective for teaching skills to children with autism, it has many limitations. Researchers and practitioners have been critical of the unnatural intensity of such teaching, the lack of generalization for skills taught in this intensive manner, the reliance on tangible reinforcers that are not available under natural conditions, and the difficulty of using an approach that requires one-to-one adult–student interactions (Charlop-Christy & Carpenter, 2000). Recent reviews of early intensive behavioral interventions (EIBI) for children with autism have found that effectiveness is highly variable at the individual level with the child's IQ at the beginning of training being predictive of how effective this intervention has been for preschoolers with autism (Howlin, Magiati, & Charman, 2009).

Another complication with massed trial instruction is its association with pull-out instruction. While massed trial instruction on academic skills can be used in some small group instruction, generally this approach means removing the student from peers with pull-aside, one-to-one instruction in the general education classroom or taking the student to another setting. Using massed trials also often means that natural conditions must be simulated so that repeated trials can be conducted (e.g., asking Marc to take off and hang up his backpack and coat four times upon arrival, after which the natural cues of arrival have long since passed).

As we discuss further in Chapter 6, there are times when intensive instruction is appropriate. There are several criteria that should be met if teams decide to use *remedial or compensatory instruction* (the term that we use for massed trial instruction) for basic skills. First, teachers must be skilled in using direct instruction with prior training to implement a research-based model or program (e.g., discrete trial instruction, functional communication training, certain commercial reading programs) and be able to evaluate student progress. Intensive one-to-one teaching sessions may also be directed toward motor, speech, and communication goals. Second, remedial instruction should be truly specialized; be prescriptive; and yield measurable, noticeable, and valued gains (e.g., functional communication training, pivotal response treatment, discrete trial instruction, structured teaching). Third, remedial instruction should be conducted with careful team planning so that (a) skills transfer and generalize to general classroom activities, (b) students' time away from their peers does not interfere with their class membership, and (c) students' removal from the general education classroom is planned so that it is not disruptive and does not occur at times when valued activities are scheduled.

Contextualized or Decontextualized Instruction
Teaching in context means that the relevant stimuli for the skill being taught are present and that teachers can take advantage of naturally reinforcing consequences. Contextualized instruction appears to be more effective overall for students with severe disabilities because it promotes skill generalization. Methods that address naturalistic or contextualized communication instruction have received a lot of attention by researchers in an effort to overcome the difficulties that discrete trial instruction yields (e.g., poor generalization, segregated instruction) (Snell, Chen, & Hoover, 2006). The incidental teaching approach (McGee, Krantz, Mason, & McClannahan, 1983; McGee, Morrier, & Daly, 1999) involves discrete trial instruction in the natural classroom setting with teaching initiated whenever the student shows an interest in an activity or item during regularly scheduled activities. Both student-preferred items and the natural consequence of communicating—such as giving the student what he or she asks for—are offered as the reinforcers for communication. Another approach is milieu teaching (Kaiser, Hancock, & Nietfield, 2000; Kaiser, Ostrosky, & Alpert, 1993), which builds on student interests and uses carefully planned instructional trials embedded into natural and created opportunities for communication. Both incidental and milieu teaching use time delay to prompt correct responses, but milieu teaching also makes use of models and a procedure that involves a least-to-most prompt hierarchy. Because one downside to distributed trial instruction is that there

may not be enough opportunities to teach, teachers can increase the number of trials under natural circumstances. For example, the environment can be arranged to create opportunities for teaching the target skill, such as adding preferred items (e.g., toys, play equipment, games, books), giving choices, withholding help to give students the opportunity to request assistance, and so forth. (See Chapter 12 for more on environmental arrangements.) Another approach for addressing inadequate distributed teaching opportunities is to increase the number of trials during each natural opportunity. Modified incidental teaching incorporates two practice trials following every trial taught during a natural opportunity to communicate (Charlop-Christy & Carpenter, 2000).

Some of the targeted skills for students with severe disabilities are *functional skills* that cannot be completed within regularly scheduled class activities. Apart from self-care skills, such instruction is less frequent for elementary and middle school students. However, during the high school and postsecondary years, students will have many functional skills targeted on their IEP and transition plans (e.g., learning to make purchases in stores, learning specific job skills). These skills are best taught using contextualized instruction in a real setting that is natural to the skill. Thus, teams will need to plan for community-based instruction.

Embedding Instruction Within Activities
Embedding instruction means inserting teaching trials into ongoing schedules "without breaking the flow of the routine or the ongoing activity" (Schepis, Reid, Ownbey, & Parsons, 2001, p. 314). This strategy is also referred to as activity-based instruction. Much instruction on functional skills and physical education is somewhat naturally embedded into the actual activity—for example, teaching students to set tables, throw balls, or open lockers (Fetko, Schuster, Harley, & Collins, 1999). But more recently, embedding has been applied to academic skills in general education settings (McDonnell et al., 2008). While embedding is sometimes used with typical students, its use with students who have severe disabilities must be more systematic to yield learning. Generally, with embedding, the teacher provides teaching trials to students in a distributed manner over time instead of massed in a short amount of time. One caution is that an adequate number of teaching opportunities should be scheduled to yield learning. Knowing what is adequate requires conducting periodic probes of the skill to see how well the student performs.

Younger students have been successfully taught a range of skills (speaking, cutting, putting things away, following instructions) through embedded teaching opportunities applied during play, meals, recess, and self-care (Shepis et al., 2001). With older students, general and special education teachers, as well as paraprofessionals, have embedded instruction during general education classes, school transitions, and class breaks (Johnson, McDonnell, Holzwarth, & Hunter, 2004; McDonnell, Johnson, Polychronis, Riesen, Jameson, & Kercher, 2006), while parents and others have embedded their instruction on restaurant use during community-based instruction (Sowers & Powers, 1995). Embedding can make efficient use of otherwise noninstructional time, but should not be used to the exclusion of social interaction with peers.

Some researchers have suggested that learning through embedded instruction may be as good as learning through small group instruction. McDonnell et al. (2006) taught paraprofessionals how to teach middle school students with moderate intellectual disabilities scientific concepts and vocabulary (e.g., the cell is a basic unit of living things) and history (e.g., a citizen is a member of a country) during general education classes. They compared two approaches—embedded instruction and instruction in small groups—and found that students learned equally well whether taught embedded instruction within activities or directly in small groups; students also generalized their knowledge to classroom teachers. While there is no specific guiding research, embedded trials can also supplement instruction in small groups. The key is to monitor learning through regular data collection.

When and how do you embed instruction? First, teachers identify the material to be taught during embedded trials; then they identify the opportunities for instruction that do not interfere with classroom operations or schedules; finally, they specify and use the teaching procedure. Team members can embed instruction in a number of ways:

• Instruction on academics can be embedded into opening or closing activities, activity transitions, and breaks:

Several trials are given to Jacob on his weekly vocabulary words while students are settling into their seats.

• As "rehearsal" trials before an activity where those skills will be needed:

Several trials are given to Marc on today's day and month during his transition to kindergarten circle time.

• Instruction on communication skills can be embedded into functional routines, either occurring naturally or created:

When Christine was younger, her teachers gave her embedded instruction on using a communication device during specific situations to request (a) help on tasks that were too difficult or where needed materials were missing; (b) a snack when presented with a pair of food items, one preferred and one nonpreferred; or (c) a break after being engaged longer than usual in a work activity. (Johnson et al., 2004)

• As "instruction on the way" with regard to behavior, schedule, and upcoming activity:

Marc's assistant teacher reviews cafeteria rules with him before leaving class and as he enters the lunch line.

Embedded instruction itself involves one or several discrete trials (Johnson et al., 2004):

Using the fourth-grade reading curriculum, Jacob's teachers identified three sets of five words that would be useful to him. These words were ones that his peers were learning, but also were words likely to be encountered or used by him. Then they determined six times each day when several instructional trials could be embedded and taught one set at a time. At these times, the teaching assistant or the classroom teacher would present Jacob with two words, one the target word and the other a distracter word, and ask him to "Touch ___," naming the target word. The instructor used a touch prompt (touching the correct word card) and constant time delay so that prompts were given initially with no delay; Jacob always imitated correctly. Errors were followed by "no" and the trial was repeated with physical assistance. Once he responded correctly on all zero-delay trials two consecutive times, the delay before giving the prompt was increased to 4 seconds. The goal was to provide 15 trials for each word daily.

Teams will want to answer several questions when deciding whether to use embedded instruction:

• Is there adequate opportunity to use embedded instruction trials without interfering with the student's interaction with peers or classroom routines?

- Is the student motivated to learn during activities?
- What students and skills are best taught this way?
- How will you prompt and handle errors? Embedding does not specify these strategies, only when skills are taught.

Summary

Teaching students with severe disabilities effectively involves many steps and decisions. The advantage that teams have is that there many effective and promising strategies to select from. Students with significantly differing abilities need instructional experiences that not only focus on appropriate educational goals and objectives, but also reflect effective and efficient teaching techniques. To keep errors to a minimum during early learning and also to facilitate skill generalization, teams must plan instruction so that the structure, the support, and the stage of learning are properly balanced regardless of the location where teaching occurs. But to promote skill maintenance, fluent and proficient performance, and generalization of skills, teams must adjust their teaching procedures to reduce structure, fade prompts, and shift the student's attention to the natural cues and stimuli that must come to control their behavior.

Special education teachers cannot accomplish the best practices described in this chapter if they work alone. Collaboration and problem solving among educators, administrators, and parents are the primary means for successfully including students who have disabilities. While teaching in inclusive schools makes planning more complicated, the outcomes are richer. Only inclusive settings allow the benefits of normalized social contexts and linkage with the general education curriculum.

Suggested Activities

1. Use the table that follows to evaluate the school program that you work in or are familiar with. If possible, gather a focus group of educators and an administrator and involve them in this evaluation process. First, work together and use the following grid to rate your school on the following five school practices using a scale from 0 (not present) to 4 (school-wide evidence of its practice):
   a. Students' IEP objectives address priority skills and some are linked to the general education curriculum.
   b. Students' IEPs include teaching and testing accommodations that facilitate their progress in learning.
   c. Collaborative teaming is ongoing and supported by school staff and administrators. Teams plan for individualized adaptations, use problem solving, and reach consensus among team members. Relevant team members are involved.
   d. All students are members of general education classrooms alongside age peers; their membership is valued.
   e. Instruction is planned, individualized, and makes use of strategies that are supported by the literature.

Conduct Needs Assessment of Best Practices and Complete Issue–Action Problem-Solving Form					
Supportive practice	Not present	Spoken about but not practiced	Some evidence of its application	Good evidence of its application	School-wide evidence of its application
List below:	0	1	2	3	4

Then, with the focus group, rank order the practices (issues) that need improvement in your school and brainstorm the actions needed to tackle each priority issue. Use the following issue–action problem-solving form:

Issue	Action	Taken by whom	Taken when

2. Examine the IEP of a student with more extensive support needs. If the student is being included with his or her peers in general education activities, observe the student over one or several days and check how adequately his or her IEP objectives are being addressed. Complete a matrix for this student by listing IEP objectives down the left side and the class schedule across the top. Indicate with check marks the activities during which it would be logical to teach each objective (see Figure 4–5 as an example). Note when (or if) pull-out instruction is being used. Explore how inappropriate instances of pull-out instruction might be replaced with adaptation of classroom activities.

If the student is not included in general education activities, observe a class (or classes) in which it might be suitable for the student to be included. Complete a matrix as you did previously and then explore the steps needed to include the student in that class.

Note: For the student applications, we give thanks to Rachel Dickinson, Jeanne Pfaff, Diane Talarico-Cavanaugh, Heather Grunden, and Gay Singletary of Charlottesville, Albemarle County, and Greene County Public School Systems.

References

Agran, M., King-Sears, M. E., Wehmeyer, M., & Copeland, S. (2003). *Teachers' guides to inclusive practices: Student-directed learning.* Baltimore: Paul H. Brookes.

Agran, M., & Moore, S. C. (1994). *How to teach self-instruction of job skills.* Washington, DC: American Association on Mental Retardation.

Agran, M., Sinclair, T., Alper, S., Cavin, M., Wehmeyer, M., & Hughes, C. (2005). Using self-monitoring to increase following-direction skills of students with moderate to severe disabilities in general education. *Education and Training in Developmental Disabilities, 40,* 3–13.

Ault, M. J., Wolery, M., Doyle, P. M., & Gast, D. L. (1989). Review of comparative studies in instruction of students with moderate and severe handicaps. *Exceptional Children, 55,* 346–356.

Buekelman, D. R., & Mirenda, P. (2005). *Augmentative and alternative communication* (3rd ed.). Baltimore: Paul H. Brookes.

Bradshaw, C., Koth, C., Thornton, L., & Leaf, P. (2009). Altering school climate through school-wide positive behavioral interventions and supports: Findings from a group-randomized effectiveness trial. *Prevention Science, 10,* 100–115.

Browder, D. M. (2001). *Curriculum and assessment for students with moderate and severe disabilities.* New York: Guilford Press.

Browder, D., Ahlgrim-Delzell, L., Spooner, F., Mims, P. J., & Baker, J. N. (2009). Using time delay to teach literacy to students with severe developmental disabilities. *Exceptional Children, 75,* 343–364.

Browder, D., Wakeman, S. Y., Spooner, F., Ahlgrim-Delzell, L., & Algozzine, B. (2006). Research on reading instruction for individuals with significant cognitive disabilities. *Exceptional Children, 72,* 392–408.

Brown, F. (1991). Creative daily scheduling: A non-intrusive approach to challenging behaviors in community residences. *Journal of the Association for Persons with Severe Handicaps, 16,* 75–84.

Brown, F., Evans, I. M., Weed, K. A., & Owen, V. (1987). Delineating functional competencies: A component model. *Journal of the Association for Persons with Severe Handicaps, 12,* 117–124.

Brown, F., & Holvoet, J. (1982). The effect of systematic interaction on incidental learning of two severely handicapped students. *Journal of the Association of the Severely Handicapped, 7*(4), 19–28.

Brown, F., Holvoet, J., Guess, P., & Mulligan, M. (1980). The individualized curriculum sequencing model (III): Small group instruction. *Journal of the Association of the Severely Handicapped, 5,* 352–367.

Cannella-Malone, H., Sigafoos, J., O'Reilly, M., de la Cruz, B., Edrisinha, C., & Lancioni, G. (2006). Comparing video prompting to video modeling for teaching daily living skills to six adults with developmental disabilities. *Education and Training in Developmental Disabilities, 41,* 344–356.

Carr, R. G., Levin, L., McConnachie, G., Carlson, J. I., Kemp, D. C., & Smith, C. E. (1994). *Communication-based intervention for problem behavior.* Baltimore: Paul H. Brookes.

Carter, E. W., Cushing, L. S., Clark, N. M., & Kennedy, C. H. (2005). Effects of peer support interventions on students' access to the general curriculum and social interactions. *Research and Practice for Persons with Severe Disabilities, 30,* 15–25.

Carter, E. W., Cushing, L. S., & Kennedy, C. H. (2009). Peer support strategies for improving all students' social lives and learning. Baltimore: Paul H. Brookes.

Carter, E. W., & Kennedy, C. H. (2006). Promoting access to the general curriculum using peer support strategies. *Research and Practice for Persons with Severe Disabilities, 31,* 1–9.

Carter, E. W., Sisco, L. G., Brown, L., Brickham, D., & Al-Khabbaz, Z. A. (2008). Peer interactions and academic engagement of youth with developmental disabilities in inclusive middle and high school classrooms. *American Journal on Mental Retardation, 113,* 479–494.

Carter, E. W., Sisco, L. G., Melekoglu, M. A., & Kurkowski, C. (2007). Peer supports as an alternative to individually assigned paraprofessionals in inclusive high school classrooms. *Research and Practice for Persons with Severe Disabilities, 32,* 213–227.

Center for Applied Special Technology. (2004). Universal design for learning. Retrieved November 24, 2009, from http://www.cast.org.

Charlop-Christy, M. H., & Carpenter, M. H. (2000). Modified incidental teaching sessions: A procedure for parents to increase spontaneous speech in their children with autism. *Journal of Positive Behavior Interventions, 2,* 98–112.

Charlop-Christy, M. H., Le, L., & Freeman, K. (2000). A comparison of video modeling with in vivo modeling for teaching children with autism. *Journal of Autism and Developmental Disorders, 30,* 537–552.

Cihak, D., Fahrenkrog, C., Ayres, K. M., & Smith, C. (2010). The use of video modeling via a video iPod and a system of least prompts to improve transitional behaviors for students with Autism Spectrum Disorders in the general education classroom. *Journal of Positive Behavior Interventions, 12,* 103–115.

Collins, B. C. (2007). *Moderate and severe disabilities: A foundational approach.* Upper Saddle River, NJ: Pearson.

Collins, B. C., Branson, T. A., Hall, M., & Rankin, S. W. (2000). Teaching secondary students with moderate disabilities in an inclusive academic classroom setting. *Journal of Developmental and Physical Disabilities, 13,* 41–59.

Collins, B. C., Gast, D. L., Ault, M. J., & Wolery, M. (1991). Small group instruction: Guidelines for teachers of students with moderate to severe handicaps. *Education and Training in Mental Retardation, 26,* 18–32.

Collins, B. C., Gast, D. L., Wolery, M., Halcombe, A., & Leatherby, J. (1991). Using constant time delay to teach self-feeding to young students with severe/profound handicaps: Evidence of limited effectiveness. *Journal of Developmental and Physical Disabilities, 3,* 157–179.

Colvin, G., Sugai, G., Good, R. H., & Lee, Y. (1997). Using active supervision and precorrection to improve transition behaviors in an elementary school. *School Psychology Quarterly, 12,* 344–363.

Copeland, S. R., & Cosbey, J. E. (2008–2009). Making progress in the general curriculum: Rethinking effective instructional practices. *Research and Practice in Severe Disabilities, 33*(4), 214–227.

Cote, C. A., Thompson, R. H., & McKerchar, P. M. (2005). The effects of antecedent interventions and extinction on toddlers' compliance during transitions. *Journal of Applied Behavior Analysis, 38,* 235–238.

Cox, A. W., Delano, M. E., Sturgill, T. R., Franzone, E., & Collet-Klingenberg, L. (2009). *Video Modeling.* Chapel Hill: National Professional Development Center on Autism Spectrum Disorders, Frank Porter Graham Child Development Institute, University of North Carolina.

D'Ateno, P., Mangiapanello, K., & Taylor, B. (2003). Using video modeling to teach complex play sequences to a preschooler with autism. *Journal of Positive Behavior Interventions, 5*(1), 5–11.

Delano, M. (2007). Video modeling interventions for individuals with autism. *Remedial and Special Education, 28,* 33–42.

Delano, M., & Snell, M. E. (2006). The effects of social stories on the social engagement of children with autism. *Journal of Positive Behavior Interventions, 8,* 29–42.

Delquadri, J., Greenwood, C. R., Whorton, D., Carta, J. J., & Hall, R. V. (1986). Classwide peer tutoring. *Exceptional Children, 52,* 535–542.

Demchak, M. (1990). Response prompting and fading methods: A review. *American Journal on Mental Retardation, 94,* 603–615.

Denny, M., Marchand-Martella, N., Martella, R. C., Reilly, J. C., Reilly, J. F., & Cleanthous, C. C. (2000). Using parent-delivered graduated guidance to teach functional living skills to a child with Cri du chat syndrome. *Education and Treatment of Children, 23,* 441–454.

Dogoe, M., & Banda, D. R. (2009). Review of recent research using constant time delay to teach chained tasks to persons with developmental disabilities. *Education and Training in Developmental Disabilities, 44,* 177–186.

Downing, J. E. (2005). Teaching communication skills to students with severe disabilities (2nd ed.). Baltimore: Paul H. Brookes.

Doyle, M. B. (2008). *The paraprofessional's guide to the inclusive classroom: Working as a team* (3rd ed.). Baltimore: Paul H. Brookes.

Doyle, P. M., Gast, D. L., Wolery, M., Ault, M. J., & Farmer, J. A. (1990). Use of constant time delay in small group instruction: A study of observational and incidental learning. *Journal of Special Education, 23,* 369–385.

Dugan, E., Kamps, D., Leonard, B., Watkins, N., Rheinberger, A., & Stackhaus, J. (1995). Effects of cooperative learning groups during social studies for students with autism and fourth-grade peers. *Journal of Applied Behavior Analysis, 28,* 175–188.

Dunlap, G., & Johnson, J. (1985). Increasing the independent responding of autistic children with unpredictable supervision. *Journal of Applied Behavior Analysis, 18,* 227–236.

Dymond, S. K., Renzaglia, A., Rosenstein, A., Chun, E. J., Banks, R. A., Niswander, V., et al. (2006). Using participatory action research approach to create a universally designed inclusive high school science course: A case study. *Research and Practice for Persons with Severe Disabilities, 31,* 293–308.

Dymond, S. K., & Russell, D. L. (2004). Impact of grade and disability on the instructional context of inclusive classrooms. *Education and Training in Developmental Disabilities, 39,* 127–140.

Etzel, B. C., & LeBlanc, J. M. (1979). The simplest treatment alternative: The law of parsimony applied to choosing appropriate instructional control and errorless-learning procedures for the difficult-to-teach child. *Journal of Autism and Development Disorders, 9,* 361–382.

Farlow, L., & Snell, M. E. (1995). *Making the most of student performance data* (AAMR Research to Practice Series). Washington, DC: American Association on Mental Retardation.

Farlow, L. J., & Snell, M. E. (2005). Making the most of student performance data. In M. L. Wehmeyer, & M. Agran. (Eds.), *Evidence-based practices for teaching students with mental retardation and intellectual disabilities* (pp. 27–54). Upper Saddle River, NJ: Merrill/Pearson.

Farmer, J. A., Gast, D. L., Wolery, M., & Winterling, V. (1991). Small group interaction for students with severe handicaps: A study of observational learning. *Education and Training in Mental Retardation, 26,* 190–201.

Fetko, K. S., Schuster, J. W., Harley, D. A., & Collins, B. C. (1999). Using simultaneous prompting to teach a chained vocational task to young adults with severe intellectual disabilities. *Education and Training in DevelopmentalDisabilities, 34,* 318-329.

Fickel, K., Schuster, J.W., & Collins, B.C. (1998). The effectiveness of simultaneous prompting with a small heterogeneous group of middle school students when taught different tasks using different stimuli. *Journal of Behavioral Education,* 8, 219-244

Friend, M., & Cook, L. (2010). *Interactions: Collaboration skills for school professionals* (6th ed.). Upper Saddle River, NJ: Merrill/Pearson.

Giangreco, M. F., Edelman, S. W., Luiselli, T. E., & MacFarland, S. Z. C. (1997). Helping or hovering? Effects of instructional assistant proximity on students with disabilities. *Exceptional Children, 64,* 7-18.

Giangreco, M.F., Halversen, A.T., Doyle, M.B., & Broer, S.M. (2004). Alternatives to overreliance on paraprofessionals in inclusive schools. *Journal of Special Education Leadership,* 17, 82-90.

Gilberts, G. H., Agran, M., Hughes, C., & Wehmeyer, M. (2001). The effects of peer delivered self-monitoring strategies on the participation of students with severe disabilities in general education classrooms. *Journal of the Association for Persons with Severe Handicaps, 26,* 25-36.

Godsey, J. R., Schuster, J. W., Lingo, A. S., Collins, B. C., & Kleinert, H. L. (2008). Peer-implemented time delay procedures on the acquisition of chained tasks by students with moderate and severe disabilities. *Education and Training in Developmental Disabilities, 43,* 111-122.

Gold, M.W. (1972). Stimulus factors in skill training of the retarded on a complex assembly task: Acquisition, transfer, and retention. *American Journal of Mental Deficiency, 76,* 517-526.

Gray, C.A., & Garand, J. D. (1993). Social stories: Improving responses of students with autism with accurate social information. *Focus on Autistic Behavior, 8*(1), 1-10.

Green, C.W., Reid, D.W., Rollyson, J. H., & Passante, S. C. (2005). An enriched teaching program for reducing resistance and indices of unhappiness among individuals with profound multiple disabilities. *Journal of Applied Behavior Analysis, 38,* 221-233.

Hall, L. J., McClannahan, L. E., & Krantz, P. J. (1995). Promoting independence in integrated classrooms by teaching aides to use activity schedules and decreased prompts. *Education and Training in Mental Retardation and Developmental Disabilities, 30,* 208-217.

Heckman, K. A., Alber, S., Hooper, S., & Heward, W. L. (1998). A comparison of least-to-most prompts and progressive time delay on the disruptive behavior of students with autism. *Journal of Behavioral Education,* 8, 171-201.

Heller, K.W., Stafford, A. M., Alberto, P.A., Fredrick, L. D., & Helfin, L. J. (2002). Preference variability and the instruction of choice making with students with severe intellectual disabilities. *Education and Training in Mental Retardation and Developmental Disabilities, 37,* 70-88.

Hine, J., & Wolery, M. (2006). Using point-of-view video modeling to teach play to preschool-ers with autism. *Topics in Early Childhood Special Education, 26*(2), 83-93.

Horner, R., Sugai, G., Smolkowski, K., Todd, A., Nakasato, J., & Esperanza, J. (2009). A randomized, wait-list controlled effectiveness trial assessing school-wide positive behavior support in elementary schools. *Journal of Positive Behavior Interventions, 11,* 133-144.

Horner, R. H., Sugai, G., Todd, A. W., & Lewis-Palmer, T. (2005). Schoolwide positive behavior support. In L. M. Bambara & L. Kern (Eds.), *Individualized supports for students with problem behaviors: Designing positive behavior plans* (pp. 359-390). New York: Guilford Press.

Howlin, P., Magiati, M., & Charman, T. (2009). Systematic review of early intensive behavioral interventions for children with autism. *American Journal on Intellectual and Developmental Disabilities, 114,* 23-41.

Hughes, C., Copeland, S. R., Agran, M., Wehmeyer, M., Rodi, M. S., & Presley, J. A. (2002). Using self-monitoring to improve performance in general education high school classes. *Education and Training in Mental Retardation and Developmental Disabilities, 37,* 262-272.

Hughes, C., Rung, L. L., Wehmeyer, M. L., Agran, M., Copeland, S. R., & Hwang, B. (2000). Self-prompted communication book use to increase social interaction among high school students. *Journal of the Association for People with Severe Handicaps, 25,* 153-166.

Hunt, P., Soto, G., Maier, J., Muller, E., & Goetz, L. (2002). Collaborative teaming to support students with augmentative and alternative communication needs in general education class-rooms. *Augmentative and Alternative Communication, 18,* 20-35.

Hunt, P., Staub, D., Alwell, M., & Goetz, L. (1994). Achievement by all students within the context of cooperative learning groups. *Journal of the Association for Persons with Severe Handicaps, 19,* 290-301.

Irvin, L.K., Tobin, T.J., Sprague, J.R., Sugai, G., & Vincent, C. G. (2004). Validity of office discipline referral measures as indices of school-wide behavioral status and effects of school-wide behavioral interventions. *Journal of Positive Behavior Interventions,* 6, 131-147.

Janney, R. E., & Snell, M. E. (2004). *Teachers' guides to inclusive practices: Modifying schoolwork* (2nd ed.). Baltimore: Paul H. Brookes.

Janney, R. E. & Snell, M. E. (2006). *Teachers' guides to inclusive practices: Social relationships and peer support* (2nd ed.). Baltimore: Paul H. Brookes.

Johnson, D.W., & Johnson, F.W. (1997). *Joining together: Group theory and skills* (6th ed.). Upper Saddle River, NJ: Prentice Hall.

Johnson, J.W., McDonnell, J., Holzwarth, V. N., & Hunter, K. (2004). The efficacy of embedded instruction for students with developmental disabilities enrolled in general education classes. *Journal of Positive Behavior Interventions, 6,* 214-227.

Kaiser, A. P., Hancock, T. B., & Nietfeld, J. P. (2000). The effects of parent-implemented enhanced milieu teaching on the social communication of children who have autism [Special issue]. *Journal of Early Education and Development, 4,* 423-446.

Kaiser, A. P., Ostrosky, M. M., & Alpert, C. L. (1993). Training teachers to use environmental arrangement and milieu teaching with nonvocal preschool children. *Journal of the Association for Persons with Severe Handicaps, 18*(3), 188-199.

Kamlesh, R. (2008). Technology to teach self-help skills to elementary students with mental disabilities. *Journal of the Indian Academy of Applied Psychology, 34,* 201-214.

Kamps, D. M., Dugan, E. P., Leonard, B. R., & Daoust, P. M. (1994). Enhanced small group instruction using choral responding and student interaction for children with autism and developmental disabilities. *American Journal of Mental Retardation, 99,* 60-73.

Kamps, D. M., Leonard, B. R., Dugan, E. P., Boland, B., & Greenwood, C. R. (1991). The use of ecobehavioral assessment to identify naturally occurring effective procedures in classrooms serving students with autism and other developmental disabilities. *Journal of Behavioral Education, 1,* 367–397.

Kamps, D. M., Walker, D., Locke, P., Delquadri, J., & Hall, R. V. (1990). A comparison of instructional arrangements for children with autism served in a public school setting. *Education and Treatment of Children, 13,* 197–215.

Kern, L., Vorndran, C. M., Hilt, A., Ringdahl, J. E., Adelman, B. E., & Dunlap, G. (1998). Choice as an intervention to improve behavior: A review of the literature. *Journal of Behavioral Education, 8,* 151–169.

Knoster, T. (2008). *The teacher's pocket guide for effective classroom management.* Baltimore: Paul H. Brookes.

Koegel, L. K., Koegel, R. L., Boettcher, M. A., Harrower, J., & Openden, D. (2006). Combining functional assessment and self-management procedures to rapidly reduce disruptive behaviors. In R. L. Koegel & L. K. Koegel (Eds.), *Pivotal response treatments for autism* (pp. 245–258). Baltimore: Paul H. Brookes.

Koegel, L. K., Koegel, R. L., Hurley, C., & Frea, W. D. (1992). Improving social skills and disruptive behavior in children with autism through self-management. *Journal of Applied Behavior Analysis, 25,* 341–354.

Koegel, R. L., Koegel, L. K., & Carter, C. M. (1999). Pivotal teaching interactions for children with autism. *School Psychology Review, 28,* 576–594.

Koegel, R. L., & Rincover, A. (1974). Treatment of psychotic children in a classroom environment: I. Learning in a large group. *Journal of Applied Behavior Analysis, 7,* 45–59.

Kuoch, H., & Mirenda, P. (2003). Social Story interventions for young children with autism spectrum disorders. *Focus on Autism and Other Developmental Disabilities, 18,* 219–227.

Liberty, K. A. (1985). Enhancing instruction for maintenance, generalization, and adaptation. In C. Lakin & R. H. Bruininks (Eds.), *Strategies for achieving community integration of developmentally disabled citizens* (pp. 29–71). Baltimore: Paul H. Brookes.

Logan, K. R., Brakeman, R., & Keefe, E. B., (1997). Effects of instructional variables on engaged behavior of students with disabilities in general education classrooms. *Exceptional Children, 63,* 481–497.

Lohrmann-O'Rourke, S., Browder, D. M., & Brown, F. (2000). Guidelines for conducting socially valid systematic preference assessments. *Journal of the Association for Persons with Severe Handicaps, 25,* 42–53.

Lorimer, P. A., Simpson, R. L., Myles, B. S., & Ganz, J. B. (2002). The use of social stories as a preventative behavioral intervention in a home setting with a child with autism. *Journal of Positive Behavior Interventions, 4,* 53–60.

Lovaas, O. I., & Taubman, M. T. (1981). Language training and some mechanisms of social and internal control. *Analysis and Intervention in Developmental Disabilities, 1,* 363–372.

Mason, S. A., McGee, G. G., Farmer-Dougan, V., & Risley, T. R. (1989). A practical strategy for ongoing reinforcer assessment. *Journal of Applied Behavior Analysis, 22,* 171–179.

McDonnell, J., Johnson, J. W., & McQuivey, C. (2008). *Embedded instruction for students with developmental disabilities in general education classes.* Alexandria, VA: Division of Developmental Disabilities, Council for Exceptional Children.

McDonnell, J., Johnson, J. W., Polychronis, S., Riesen, T., Jameson, M., & Kercher, K. (2006). Comparison of one-to-one embedded instruction in general education classes with small group instruction in special education classes. *Education and Training in Developmental Disabilities, 41,* 125–138.

McDonnell, J., Mathot-Buckner, C., Thorson, N., & Fister, S. (2001). Supporting the inclusion of student with moderate and severe disabilities in junior high school general education classes: The effects of classwide peer tutoring, multi-element curriculum, and accommodations. *Education and Treatment of Children, 24,* 141–160.

McDonnell, J., Thorson, N., & McQuivey, C. (1998). The instructional characteristics of inclusive classes for elementary students with severe disabilities. *Journal of Behavioral Education, 8,* 415–437.

McGee, G. G, Krantz, P. J., Mason, D., & McClannahan, L. E. (1983). A modified incidental-teaching procedure for autistic youth: Acquisition and generalization of receptive object labels. *Journal of Applied Behavior Analysis, 16,* 329–338.

McGee, G. G., Morrier, M. J., & Daly, T. (1999). An incidental teaching approach to early intervention for toddlers with autism. *Journal of the Association for People with Severe Disabilities, 24,* 133–146.

McIntosh, K., Chard, D., Boland, J., & Horner, R. (2006). A demonstration of combined efforts in school-wide academic and behavioral systems and incidence of reading and behavior challenges in early elementary grades. *Journal of Positive Behavior Interventions, 8,* 146–154.

McLaughlin, D. M., & Carr, E. G. (2005). Quality of rapport as a setting event for problem behavior: Assessment and intervention. *Journal of Positive Behavior Inventions, 7,* 68–91.

Mechling, L. C. (2007). Assistive technology as a self-management tool for prompting students with intellectual disabilities to initiate and complete daily tasks: A literature review. *Education and Training in Developmental Disabilities, 42,* 252–269.

Mechling, L. C., Gast, D. L., & Cronin, B. A. (2006). The effects of presenting high-preference items, paired with choice, via computer-based video programming on task completion of students with autism. *Focus on Autism and Other Developmental Disabilities, 21,* 7–13.

Mesibov, G. B., Shea, V., & Scholper, E. (2004). *The TEACCH approach to autism spectrum disorders.* New York: Springer.

Mirenda, P., MacGregor, T., & Kelly-Keough, S. (2002). Teaching communication skills for behavioral support in the context of family life. In J. M. Lucyshyn, G. Dunlap, & R. W. Albin, (Eds.), *Families and positive behavior support: Addressing problem behaviors in family contexts* (pp. 185–207). Baltimore: Paul H. Brookes.

Moes, D. R. (1998). Integrating choice-making opportunities with teacher-assigned academic tasks to facilitate the performance of children with autism. *The Journal for the Association of Persons with Severe Handicaps, 23,* 319–328.

Moore, S. C., Agran, M., & Fodor-Davis, J. (1989). Using self-management strategies to increase the production rates of workers with severe handicaps. *Education and Training in Mental Retardation, 24,* 324–332.

Morse, T. E., & Schuster, J. W. (2004). Simultaneous prompting: A review of the literature. *Education and Training in Developmental Disablities, 39,* 153–168.

Nikopoulous, C. & Keenan, M. (2003). Promoting social initiation in children with autism using video modeling. *Behavioral Interventions, 18,* 87-108.

Nikopoulous, C., & Keenan, M. (2004). Effects of video modeling on social initiations by children with autism. *Journal of Applied Behavior Analysis, 37*(1), 93-96.

Parker, M. A., & Schuster, J. W. (2002). Effectiveness of simultaneous prompting on the acquisition of observational and instructive feedback stimuli when teaching a heterogeneous group of high school students. *Education and Training in Mental Retardation and Developmental Disabilities, 37,* 89-104.

Reese, G., & Snell, M. E. (1990). Putting on and removing coats and jackets: The acquisition and maintenance of skills by children with severe multiple disabilities. *Education and Training in Mental Retardation, 26,* 398-410.

Richmond, G. (1983). Shaping bladder and bowel continence in developmentally retarded pre-school children. *Journal of Autism and Developmental Disorders, 13,* 197-205.

Rincover, A., & Koegel, R. L. (1975). Setting generality and stimulus control in autistic children. *Journal of Applied Behavior Analysis, 8,* 235-246.

Roane, H. S., Vollmer, T. R., Ringdahl, J. E. & Marcus, B. A. (1998). Evaluation of a brief stimulus preference assessment. *Journal of Applied Behavior Analysis, 31,* 605-620.

Rotholz, D. A. (1987). Current considerations on the use of one-to-one instruction with autistic students: Review and recommendations. *Education and Treatment of Children, 10,* 271-278.

Schepis, M. M., Reid, D. H., Ownbey, J., & Parsons, M. H. (2001). Training support staff to embed teaching within natural routines of young children with disabilities in an inclusive preschool. *Journal of Applied Behavior Analysis, 34,* 313-327.

Schopler, E., Brehm, S. S., Kinsbourne, M., & Reichler, R. J. (1971). Effect of treatment structure on development in autistic children. *Archives of General Psychiatry, 24,* 415-421.

Schreibman, L. (2000). Intensive behavioral/psychoeducational treatments for autism: Research needs and future directions. *Journal of Autism and Developmental Disorders, 30,* 373-381.

Schuster, J. W., Morse, T. E., Ault, M. J., Doyle, P. M., Crawford, M. R., & Wolery, M. (1998). Constant time delay with chained tasks: A review of the literature. *Education and Treatment of Children, 21,* 74-106.

Sewell, T. J., Collins, B. C., Hemmeter, M. L., & Schuster, J. W. (1998). Using simultaneous prompting within an activity-based format to teach dressing skills to preschoolers with developmental delays. *Journal of Early Intervention, 21,* 132-145.

Sherer, M., Pierce, K. L., Paredes, S., Kisacky, K. L., Ingersoll, B., & Schreibman, L., (2001). Enhancing conversation skills in children with autism via video technology: Which is better, "self" or "other" as a model? *Behavior Modification, 25,* 140-158.

Shukla, S., Kennedy, C. H., & Cushing, L. S. (1998). Adult influence on the participation of peers without disabilities in peer support programs. *Journal of Behavioral Education, 8,* 397-413.

Singer, G. H. S., Gert, B., & Koegel, R. L. (1999). A moral framework for analyzing the controversy over aversive behavioral interventions for people with severe mental retardation. *Journal of Positive Behavior Interventions, 1,* 88-100.

Singleton, K. C., Schuster, J. W., & Ault, M. J. (1995). Simultaneous prompting in a small group instructional arrangement. *Education and Training in Mental Retardation and Developmental Disabilities, 30,* 218-230.

Slavin, R. E. (1991). Cooperative learning and group contingencies. *Journal of Behavioral Education, 1,* 105-115.

Snell, M. E., Chen, L. Y., & Hoover, K. (2006). Teaching augmentative and alternative communication to students with severe disabilities: A review of intervention research 1997-2003. *Research and Practice for Persons with Severe Disabilities, 31,* 203-214.

Snell, M. E., & Janney, R. J. (2000). Teachers' problem solving about young children with moderate and severe disabilities in elementary classrooms. *Exceptional Children, 66,* 472-490.

Snell, M. E., & Janney, R. E. (2005). *Teachers' guides to inclusive practices: Collaborative teaming* (2nd ed.). Baltimore: Paul H. Brookes.

Sowers, J., & Powers, L. (1995). Enhancing the participation and independence of students with severe physical and multiple disabilities in performing community activities. *Mental Retardation, 33,* 209-220.

Stillman, R., & Battle, C. (1984). Developing prelanguage communication in the severely handicapped: An interpretation of the Van Dijk method. *Seminars in Speech and Language, 5,* 159-170.

Stinson, D. M., Gast, D. L., Wolery, M., & Collins, B. C. (1991). Acquisition of nontargeted information during small-group instruction. *Exceptionality, 2,* 65-80.

Strain, P. S., & Odom, S. L. (1986). Peer social initiations: Effective intervention for social skill development of exceptional children. *Exceptional Children, 52,* 543-552.

Taylor-Greene, S., Brown, D., Nelson, L., Longton, J., Gassman, T., Cohen, J., et al. (1997). School-wide behavioral support: Starting the year off right. *Journal of Behavioral Education, 7,* 99-112.

Thiemann, K. S., & Goldstein, H. (2001). Social stories, written text cues, and video feedback: Effects on social communication of children with autism. *Journal of Applied Behavior Analysis, 34,* 425-446.

Tomlinson, C. A. (2001). *How to differentiate instruction in mixed-ability classrooms* (2nd ed.). Alexandria, VA: Association for Supervision and Curriculum Development.

Vaughn, B. J., & Horner, R. H. (1997). Identifying instructional tasks that occasion problem behavior and assessing the effects of student versus teacher choice during these tasks. *Journal of Applied Behavior Analysis, 30,* 299-312.

Ward, P., & Ayvazo, S. (2006). Classwide peer tutoring in physical education: Assessing its effects with kindergartners with autism. *Adapted Physical Education Quarterly, 23,* 233-244.

Werts, M. G., Caldwell, N. K., & Wolery, M. (1996). Peer modeling of response chains: Observational learning by students with disabilities. *Journal of Applied Behavior Analysis, 29,* 53-66.

Whalen, C., Schuster, J. W., & Hemmeter, M. L. (1996). The use of unrelated instructive feedback when teaching in a small group instructional arrangement. *Education and Training in Mental Retardation and Developmental Disabilities, 31,* 188-202.

Wolery, M., Ault, M. J., & Doyle, P. M. (1992). *Teaching students with moderate to severe disabilities.* New York: Longman.

Wolery, M., & Gast, D. L. (1984). Effective and efficient procedures for the transfer of stimulus control. *Topics in Early Childhood Special Education, 4,* 57-77.

5

Measuring Student Behavior and Learning

Fredda Brown
Martha E. Snell

Why Measure Student Behavior?

To evaluate the impact of a school program on a student, educators must formulate specific strategies for measurement. Four basic reasons for developing measurement strategies are (a) to document what has occurred, (b) to identify the variables responsible for the occurrence (Zirpoli & Melloy, 2008), (c) to understand when and why learning is occurring or not occurring, and (d) to be accountable (Alberto & Troutman, 2009). Measurement strategies enable teachers to better predict future performance, and prediction helps teams decide whether program modifications are necessary. Furthermore, knowledge of measurement strategies allows educators to better understand the findings and implications of published research and determine their relevance to teaching practices (Alberto & Troutman, 2009). Kennedy (2005) points out that human memory is fallible—what people think they see, or remember seeing, is often dramatically different from what actually occurred. Objectively and directly measuring behavior is necessary to make the best decisions regarding our students' education.

Teachers are now required to use strategies that have been demonstrated to be effective (i.e., those

founded on evidence). However, using evidence-based strategies is only the first step. Teachers must then be accountable for student outcomes; they must demonstrate either that their students are benefiting from these strategies or that they are making data-based program modifications to try to improve the outcomes.

Using an Evidence Base to Guide Instruction

Being accountable for student outcomes has become increasingly important and has now been explicitly stated in educational policy and law, including the No Child Left Behind (NCLB) Act of 2002 and the Individuals with Disabilities Education Act (IDEA) of 2004. These federal mandates were adopted to ensure the quality of instruction and outcomes for all students with disabilities. One requirement of these regulations is that evidence-based practices be used to guide classroom practice (Odom et al., 2005; Wang & Spillane, 2009). The term *evidence-based practice* refers to educational programs or instructional procedures that have been determined to reliably produce positive student outcomes (Tankersley, Harjusola-Webb, & Landrum, 2008). Recently, there has been much discussion in the field concerning what constitutes an evidence basis

(Horner et al., 2005; Odom et al., 2005; Tankersley et al., 2008). There are at least two considerations that must be examined in order to understand this issue (Spooner & Brown, in press): (a) experimental methodologies with adequate strength to identify research meeting quality criteria (Odom et al., 2005; Tankersley et al., 2008) and (b) the number of quality research studies necessary to establish an evidence basis (Horner et al., 2005). Although large-group randomized trials are considered to be "the gold standard" of research methodologies, most of the research focusing on students with severe disabilities has used single-subject experimental designs, and researchers in this field regard such designs as a valid methodology (McDonnell & O'Neill, 2003).

There have been several suggestions regarding the number of single-subject studies required to establish an evidence base. For example, Horner et al. (2005) recommends that a practice have a minimum of five studies that (a) meet acceptable methodological criteria; (b) have been published in peer-reviewed journals; (c) have been conducted by at least three different researchers, across at least three different geographical locations; and (d) include a total of at least 20 participants. In addition to rigorous research support, the National Autism Center's National Standards Project (2009) includes criteria related to the values and preferences of parents, care providers, and individuals with autism spectrum disorders (ASDs), including a consideration of (a) the side effects of the treatment, (b) whether the treatment is aligned with the values of family members, and (c) whether the individual with ASD is in agreement with the specific treatment. Interestingly, there is no evidence basis for determining criteria for what constitutes an evidence basis! It might be generally agreed on, however, that the more successful demonstrations of an educational practice, the more confidence we would have in a true functional relationship between that practice and student performance (Tankersley et al., 2008). Oliva, Brown, and Gilles (2010) also suggest that for strategies that are more contentious or controversial, the criteria for establishing an evidence basis should be even more rigorous.

Accountability Through Evaluation

Using evidence-based strategies is the foundation of good practice. However, just because a teacher uses an evidence-based strategy does not ensure that a given student will benefit from it. Ongoing evaluation of individual student progress is an integral part of the teaching–learning process. Teachers must develop expertise in collecting data on their students' learning and making changes in instruction on the basis of an analysis of those data (Ryndak, Clark, Conroy, & Stuart, 2001). With an increasing focus on educating students with severe disabilities alongside their typically developing peers in general education settings, data collection strategies become even more of a challenge. Each teacher must balance the need for data to make instructional decisions and to evaluate program effectiveness with the needs of the regular classroom. Although many teachers question the value of data and find data difficult to manage, it is widely accepted that teachers make better instructional decisions when they found them on student performance data (Farlow & Snell, 2005; Janney & Snell, 2004; Zirpoli & Melloy, 2008).

Teachers need to be accountable for two levels of measurement: process measures and outcome measures (Haring & Breen, 1989). *Process measures* focus on precise, small units of behavior, such as the individual responses within a complex chain or performance of the entire chain (e.g., a task analysis for using a vending machine, the frequency of positive interactions with peers) (Haring & Breen, 1989). Process measures data are important in the evaluation of instructional programs; they guide routine decision making regarding program modifications. *Outcome measures* do not provide this level of detailed information for behaviors that occur within a situation. Instead, these measures offer information regarding the general effects of a program on a person's quality of life. Outcome measures include, for example, a student's performance on individualized education plan (IEP) objectives at the end of a school year, test scores, or the development of friendships. Process measures, which focus on a specific, discrete target behavior, lack the breadth necessary to assess the broader impact of interventions (Storey, 1997) and typically represent only temporary changes in a controlled setting. Outcome measures offer a more meaningful measurement, reflecting a range of significant outcomes for the individual, school, family, and community (Meyer & Janney, 1989). As described in Chapter 3, a broad outcome framework, such as the one described by Billingsley, Gallucci, Peck, Schwartz, and Staub (1996), which includes the domains of skills, membership, and relationships, is necessary for representing a meaningful educational experience for students with severe disabilities.

It is critical that administrative, teaching, and related service practitioners evaluate student progress with outcome data (Snell, 2003). According to Haring and Breen (1989), outcome measures that reflect the success of an inclusive education program include acceptance, friendships, and social participation. Social participation includes the role of the student in the social network, the number of after-school outings with nondisabled friends, and the time spent in social interactions with nondisabled peers.

Meyer and Evans (1993) included in their criteria for successful outcomes of behavioral interventions those which are related to self-determination and quality of life, such as less restrictive placements, greater participation in integrated school experiences, subjective quality-of-life improvements (e.g., happiness, satisfaction, choices, and control), improvements perceived by significant others, and expanded social relationships and informal support networks. Carr (2007) encapsulates these important quality-of-life outcomes as happiness and personal satisfaction and proposes that these hard-to-define variables must be our vision for the future.

Think about the case of a young man who lived in a facility where he received contingent electric shock for the self-injurious behavior of scratching (Gothelf & Brown, 1998). He wore a shock device 24 hours per day at his school program and in his group home. After many thousands of shocks, his self-injury was significantly reduced although not entirely. Using the process measure of "rate of scratching" as the only measure of success, it could be concluded that the contingent electric shock was effective. However, this man's program was judged as being far from effective, not only because it applied an unacceptable strategy, but also because there was little impact on the quality of his life. Consider the following outcomes that accompanied the behavior reduction: (a) wearing a shock device 24 hours per day, (b) the inability to manage his own behavior without the shock device, (c) going to school and living in a group home with individuals who all had severe behavior problems, (d) having no control over daily activities (e.g., what to eat, when to go to bed or wake up), (e) limited social interaction with individuals without disabilities, (f) limited social interaction with unpaid individuals, (g) self-reports of being unhappy, (h) no control over his future, and (i) living a great distance away from his family. Outcome measures would reveal just how limited this intervention was for this young man.

Measurement not only must accurately describe current performance on priority skills, but also must reach beyond this traditional assessment of isolated skill increases or behavior reduction to assess the outcomes that make a significant difference in the individual's life. Meyer and Janney (1989) state, "In contrast to a limited outcome such as a temporary change in one target behavior in a controlled clinical setting, an expanded definition of effectiveness would require evidence of a range of more meaningful outcomes for child, school, family, and community" (p. 263). In the previous example of the young man who participated in an aversive program, meaningful outcomes would include, for example, self-management of his behavior, living in his own home and near his family, designing his own daily routines, pursuing and acquiring a job of his preference, and selecting his own personal care assistants.

Much of this chapter explains how to describe, measure, and graph student behavior and learning with admittedly more focus on process measures and less on outcome measures. However, it is not sufficient to just measure behavior; measurement must be meaningful. Albert Einstein had a sign in his office that read: *Not everything that can be counted counts, and not everything that counts can be counted.* So, before we get to the details, we will begin with a discussion of basic foundations and principles for selecting measurement strategies and making measurement meaningful.

Foundations of Meaningful Measurement

Before reviewing strategies for measuring and graphing student behavior and learning, it is important to understand the nature of meaningful and accurate data. Data, if wisely used, can provide information that is critical to the development, evaluation, and revision of instructional efforts (Farlow & Snell, 1994; Zirpoli & Melloy, 2008, 5e). However, measurements of behavior change are of little importance if they do not provide meaningful information. Three characteristics of student performance data must be present in order for a measurement system to be meaningful: (a) data must reflect important behavior, (b) data must be contextually appropriate, and (c) data must be sufficiently accurate and reliable.

Measurement of Important Behaviors

Data should reflect important and significant behaviors. Simply being accurate and reliable is not sufficient. For example, a teacher can accurately measure the number of times that Jacob was able to complete a preschool puzzle; however, because a preschool puzzle is not age appropriate for Jacob, who is in the fourth grade, it would not be a meaningful measurement. Teams should consider a series of questions to determine whether their measurement strategies are meaningful:

- Do these data measure behaviors or skills that are valued by the student, his or her parents, and the community or society?
- Do these data reflect the qualitative changes that we hope to see in this student?
- Are the types of changes or the amount of change in the student significant?

Many efforts have been made to describe the criteria for evaluating the validity and importance of behavior changes. Researchers and clinicians have used the following five criteria to evaluate the success of behavioral change efforts: (a) statistical significance, (b) clinical significance, (c) social validity, (d) educational validity, and (e) quality of life.

Statistical Significance

Experimental or *statistical significance* involves comparing behavior during or following an intervention with what it was prior to the intervention and asking whether that difference is beyond what might be expected by chance (Kazdin, 1976). Often, statistical analysis is used to evaluate the success of an intervention in a research study, but it is not sufficient as the sole criterion for evaluating change, nor is it practical for teams to apply in school.

Clinical Significance

Therapeutic or *clinical significance* is the importance of the change achieved in the behavior (Kazdin, 1976), or the comparison between the change in behavior that has occurred and the level of change required for the individual to more adequately function in society (Risley, 1970). In other words, if the result of an intervention makes no improvement in the student's life (e.g., enabling him or her to eat independently), even though there is statistical significance, the change does not meet the criterion of clinical significance.

Social Validity

Social validity also refers to the significance of a change in an individual's life. In an analysis of the development of applied behavior analysis, Baer, Wolf, and

Risley (1987) stated, "We may have taught many social skills without examining whether they actually furthered the subject's social life; many courtesy skills without examining whether anyone actually noticed or cared; many safety skills without examining whether the subject was actually safer thereafter; many language skills without measuring whether the subject actually used them to interact differently than before; many on-task skills without measuring the actual value of those tasks; and, in general, many survival skills without examining the subject's actual subsequent survival" (p. 322).

Social validity is a concept that addresses qualitative aspects of the educational program. It focuses on the acceptability of the educational goals, the appropriateness of the procedures used to influence behavior, and the social importance of the behavior change (Cooper, Heron, & Heward, 2007; Kazdin, 1977; Wolf, 1978). Social validation procedures can be used to determine whether the learned behavior is functional or meaningful (Kazdin, 1980). There are two methods for determining social validity. *Social comparison* contrasts the student's performance with the performance of the student's nondisabled peers. This standard checks against imposing unnecessarily rigorous performance criteria or stopping instruction before the student reaches a socially acceptable level of performance.

At Marc's team meeting, the psychologist suggested that a behavioral objective be developed to teach him to sit in his seat and keep his hands in his lap and his feet on the floor for 15 minutes. His general education teacher, Ms. Kwan, questioned the objective, saying "I'm not sure any of the children in the class can sit like that for 15 minutes!" Ms. Wharton, Marc's special education teacher, suggested that they observe Marc during a variety of kindergarten activities and record data on a few typically developing children to determine the range of their attending duration and the "styles of sitting" displayed by the other students. Ms. Kwan agreed that observing peers would help set a more appropriate goal for Mark's paying attention in class.

The second method used to determine social validity is *subjective evaluation*. In this method, the opinions of significant people, because of their expertise or familiarity with the student, are used to judge the significance of the behavior change. For example, Binnendyk and Lucyshyn (2009) evaluated the effectiveness of a family-centered positive behavior support plan to reduce food refusal behavior in a six-year-old child with autism. The child in the study ate very few foods, and his family was concerned about his health, as well as the problem behaviors that would result when they tried to prompt him to eat new foods (e.g., spitting out food, vomiting, self-injury). After ruling out any organic causal factors for the food intolerance, the researchers worked with the child's mother to implement a behavior support plan based on a comprehensive functional assessment, family assessment, and preference assessments. The mother learned to implement the multicomponent behavior plan (e.g., visual strategies, eating schedule, contingent praise, stimulus fading, prompting), which resulted in improvements in the child's eating behavior and food consumption. In this study, the researchers were not only concerned with improving the child's eating, but also with his family's experience in implementing the procedure and the impact of the program on the family's quality of life. The child's mother evaluated the intervention goals, procedures, and outcomes using a 10-item instrument. The results of the social validity ratings indicated that the mother consistently believed that the goals, procedures, and outcomes were acceptable, and that there were improvements in family interaction, parenting, health and safety, family resources, and supports. Measuring social validity was critical in this study; if the family had not been comfortable with the strategy and had not seen a positive impact on the family's well-being, they would not likely persist in the implementation of the strategies.

Whalon and Hanline (2008) looked at the social validity of a reading and language intervention for children with autism. In this study, three students with autism, seven and eight years of age, were taught to ask questions about the book that their teacher was reading to a small group, which included their general education peers. Social validity data were collected via interviews of the children with autism, their parents, and their general education peers. Parents were interviewed to determine whether they noticed changes in their child's reading and social behavior, and whether they thought that the intervention was important. Also, videos of the first intervention session and the last session were shown to the parents, and they were asked to describe any changes that they noted in their children's reading and language skills. The children with autism and their general education peers were individually interviewed and were asked about the usefulness of the intervention and whether they experienced any changes in their relationships with each other. The results of the social validity measures indicated that the children with autism thought that the intervention helped them to better understand what they read. Their general education peers reported that they thought that the intervention was helpful, they enjoyed the sessions, and they had more interactions with their peers with autism. Finally, the parents thought that the intervention was helpful for improving both reading and language skills. These studies emphasize the value that social validity data has in understanding the significance of intervention effects on individuals.

Educational Validity

Voeltz and Evans (1983), in response to the narrow ways in which special education outcomes have been evaluated, offered the term *educational validity* to describe a more inclusive set of criteria for program evaluation for individuals with severe disabilities. To demonstrate educational validity, three criteria must be met. First, *internal validity* criteria must be met. That is, teachers should feel confident that the behavior change occurred as a function of the educational intervention.

> *Marc's team reached a consensus that although they did not want to set an objective that he sit in his seat for 15 minutes, having him sit in his seat long enough to complete a short activity would be a valuable goal. Ms. Wharton, familiar with the literature on the positive impact of choice on activity participation, suggested that their intervention be based on providing Marc with more choices of activities to determine whether this strategy would increase the length of time that he sat in his seat. Following intervention, Ms. Wharton was happy to report to the team that the use of more choices seemed to be effective— Marc was sitting for longer periods. His mother, however, questioned this finding when she shared with the team that she does not think that he feels very well because of spring allergies and that, in general, he seems to be lethargic and sitting more. Ms. Wharton then wondered whether the change in Marc's in-seat behavior was a function of his new choice program or spring allergies.*

Second, the criterion of *educational integrity* should be demonstrated. Educational integrity refers to the implementation of the procedures. It answers the question, "Did the educational intervention occur as specified in the treatment plan?" This is an important question to ask. Consider trying to analyze why a new intervention is not working. If we are not sure whether the various team members are implementing the strategy in the same way, we cannot determine whether it is the program that is not effective or whether it is just the inconsistent teaching. The final criterion is the *qualitative significance* (social validity) of the behavior change. Teams must question whether the behavior change benefited the student and was considered to be valuable by significant others in the student's natural environment (Voeltz & Evans, 1983).

Quality of Life

In addition to the qualitative aspects of social and educational validity, other criteria are increasingly being suggested as critical in the evaluation of program success. Meyer and Evans (1989) delineate eight possible outcomes to evaluate the effectiveness of a teaching program:

- Improvement in target behavior
- Acquisition of alternative skills and positive behaviors
- Positive collateral effects and the absence of side effects
- Reduced need for and use of medical and crisis management services for the individual or others
- Less restrictive placements and greater participation in integrated community experiences
- Subjective quality-of-life improvement—happiness, satisfaction, and choices for the individual
- Perceptions of improvement by the family and significant others
- Expanded social relationships and informal support networks

Certain measurement procedures in community settings promote less-than-normalized lifestyles and interactions, thus detracting from the individual's quality of life. For example, the teaching staff may be so interested in recording the prompting levels necessary to complete a leisure activity that they forget to notice whether anyone is having fun (Brown, 1991; Brown & Lehr, 1993). Professionals are recognizing that critical components of program evaluation are choice and control over one's life (e.g., Bambara, & Koger, 1996; Bannerman, Sheldon, Sherman, & Harchik, 1990; Brown & Lehr, 1993; DiCarlo & Vagianos, 2009; Kern & Clarke, 2005; Knoster & Kincaid, 2005; Mechling, Gast, & Cronin, 2006).

It is critical that each individual, to the greatest degree possible considering the child's age, have control over the activities in which he or she participates, retain the option to refuse participation, and maintain control over the sequence in which the activities take place and the times at which the activities occur (see also Chapter 3). Opportunities for self-determination are also associated with better postschool outcomes (McGlashing-Johnson, Agran, Sitlington, Cavin, & Wehmeyer, 2003; Wehmeyer & Schwartz, 1997). Interestingly, Agran, Snow, and Swaner (1999) found that although most of the special education professionals who they surveyed supported the notion that self-determination was an important outcome, they did not necessarily include IEP goals related to self-determination. Inclusion of these goals on the IEP would better ensure the team's commitment to self-determination.

Evaluating the educational impact on quality-of-life factors is important if we are to take seriously our commitment to effecting meaningful change in the student's life. However, measurement of the qualitative components of life is often challenging. For example, limited cognitive and communication skills make it difficult for educators and even families to understand a student's vision of quality of life (Brown, Gothelf, Guess, & Lehr, 1998). Holburn (2002) points out that often the strategies that are used to improve students' quality of life (e.g., person-centered planning) and the collateral outcomes of these strategies (e.g., community inclusion, improved relationships) are difficult to measure but nonetheless necessary.

Thus, recent trends look beyond simple quantitative reports of progress (e.g., acquisition of isolated skills) and see each individual within the context of a meaningful life. Measurement strategies must support the evaluation of these important outcomes.

Measurement That Is Contextually Appropriate

It is critical that a full range of student data be collected and it is equally important that we are unobtrusive in its collection, storage, and use. Always remember that evaluation information is confidential. It should be available only to the student, family members, and the professionals who are directly involved in the student's program. Just as a typical student's report card is never publicly displayed, neither should a student's progress graphs or data records be displayed for others to see. Graphs and data sheets should be organized and stored in record files that are accessible only to teaching staff.

Unobtrusive collection of data can be a challenge for teachers. It is easy to envision a data-collecting teacher or school psychologist armed with a clipboard, stopwatch, and portable video camera to record a student's performance. When teaching staff are so obtrusive in their data collection efforts, they call unnecessary attention to their students and may inadvertently stigmatize them (Test & Spooner, 1996). Professionals need to choose data collection strategies that are unobtrusive but that still provide sufficient information to determine program effectiveness (Test & Spooner, 1996).

There is an obvious need for data collection strategies that are user friendly (Meyer & Janney, 1989) and that do not require significant sacrifices of teachers' time (Zirpoli & Melloy, 2008). According to Meyer and Janney (1989), user-friendly methods are those that can be managed in real classrooms and that are reflective of meaningful outcomes (not just isolated behaviors). Walther-Thomas, Korinek, McLaughlin, and Williams (2000) suggest the KISS principle for inclusive classrooms: *K*eep *it s*imple yet *s*ensitive.

Behavior measurement must be relatively accurate and must provide relevant information. However, the accuracy and relevance of data need not depend on obvious or bulky recording equipment, an excessive number of adult observers, or measurement procedures that interfere with teaching or learning within the community or school setting. Typically, teaching staff (and sometimes peer tutors) collect data as they teach or record data after an instructional session, basing the data on the permanent products left over as a result of a student's performance (e.g., counting the number of clean cafeteria tables). Additional observers usually are not needed or available.

The methods selected for directly measuring behavior in teaching settings should be as simple and time-saving as possible (e.g., the frequency or event counts for carefully selected and distinct periods or a count of permanent products). Typically, teachers avoid methods that require extensive observation time (e.g., frequency counts taken across an entire day) and avoid measurement equipment that interferes with teaching (e.g., a portable tape recorder and headset for an interval measurement). Teachers must make some compromises in order to obtain the maximum amount of information with the least effort and time commitment.

Minimizing the obtrusiveness of data collection typically can be accomplished with a little imagination and some brainstorming. In some cases, typical measurement methods are used but the equipment is simpli-

fied. For example, a teacher who knows a task analysis fairly well can make notes on index cards or on small "sticky notes". Some teachers may want to keep 3- by 5-inch cards readily available for reference (e.g., in their pockets), noting the specific step number (correct or prompted) on the card as the student performs the task. Sticky notes can be stuck to purses or watches, and hash marks can record the frequency of a target behavior. Wrist or key-chain counters, calculators, or quiet counters also can be used to keep frequency counts unobtrusively and to time the duration of target behaviors. Some teachers have made simple bead-counter bracelets using leather or silky shoestrings and 19 plastic beads arranged in two differently colored groups of 9 and 10 each; the bead arrangement enables counting by 1s in the first group and by 10s in the second group for a possible total count of 109 before resetting the beads. In those instances when behaviors require the use of interval observations, teachers or psychologists may use headsets and precounted-interval tapes on portable cassette recorders fairly unobtrusively, but this works only if the activity does not require the observer to instruct or interact with the student.

In other cases, teachers reduce the obviousness of their evaluation procedures by using less traditional measures. Meyer and Janney (1989) suggest a wide range of measurement tools that they call "user friendly." For example, once Marc can enter his classroom reliably and safely in his "arrival program," the teacher may simply measure two products that result from Marc's performance of the entire arrival chain: (a) whether his coat or sweater is hung on a hook and (b) whether Marc is participating in the activity that he placed by his photo on the activity choice chart. This measure would be taken 10 minutes after his arrival. Other examples include using measurements of weight gain to evaluate the effectiveness of a program to reduce rumination and vomiting and using ratings of spillage to evaluate the success of a feeding program. Communication logs between home and school may be examined to ascertain a family's perception of student improvement and satisfaction with an instructional program. The list of examples for user-friendly measures depends on the imagination of teachers and family members with regard to alternative ways to evaluate learning.

Measurement That Is Accurate and Reliable

When a team has decided that a change in a student's behavior is a goal (e.g., increase social interactions, decrease inappropriate verbalizations, extend the use of sign language to peers), one of the first steps in the process is to define the behavior. A precise description of the behavior is necessary to ensure that the teacher is consistently observing the same behavior, that others are observing the same thing, and that there is continuity of instruction (Alberto & Troutman, 2009). For example, if "improve manners" is a goal, it is unlikely that the student, parents, teachers, teaching assistants, and therapists automatically agree on what "appropriate manners" are. To some, appropriate table manners mean sitting up straight, arms off of the table, napkin in lap, and chewing with one's mouth closed. Others, however, may feel that some of these components are unnecessarily formal. Indeed, for some students, eating with their mouths closed is physically unrealistic.

To prevent ambiguity, an *operational definition* of the target behavior is created; that is, the behavior must be described in a way that is observable and measurable. Agreement on what constitutes a behavior is critical to the development of reliable and valid measurement and evaluation systems. The description of a behavior must be specific enough to allow two or more observers to read the definition and make the same judgment about the occurrence or nonoccurrence of the behavior (Alberto & Troutman, 2009; Baer, Wolf, & Risley, 1968). Table 5–1 compares terms that are vague and descriptions that are observable and measurable. These terms represent a sample of the goals that were determined for Marc and Christine. The concepts of "functional" and "meaningful" behaviors should not be confused with the standard of describing behaviors in observable and measurable ways. Designing an operational definition to objectively describe a behavior does not ensure that the definition is functional or meaningful to an individual. For example, the statement "When shown either a red or blue block, Christine will point to the red or blue block placed in front of her" is observable and measurable. It is not, however, a meaningful activity for Christine, as it is neither age appropriate nor functional.

If data are not accurate and reliable, it would be impossible to make confident judgments or decisions about a student's progress on his or her goals and objectives. Later in this chapter, we will discuss interrater reliability (i.e., whether the target behavior is being recorded accurately) and procedural reliability (i.e., the degree to which the instructional procedures are implemented accurately).

Quantitative Measures

Teams must know whether each student's instructional program is effective in helping the student achieve his or her IEP objectives. Many teachers resist data collection because they feel as if they cannot afford the time. However, such teachers may find four months into the school year that their intervention is not working. Students cannot afford to participate in ineffective interventions for four months! Frequent and ongoing data collection provides ongoing feedback about the student's progress and reveals important information that can guide program improvement.

TABLE 5–1
Vague Versus Observable Descriptions of Behavior

Student	Vague	Observable
Marc	Interacts appropriately with peers	Waves "hi" to peers when he enters the classroom in the morning
	Has improved his grooming	Washes hands before meals
		Asks for assistance to tie his shoes
	Has increased his academic skills	Identifies numerals 1 through 10
		Matches letters to pictures
Christine	Has shown an increase in her community participation	Goes to the grocery store with a peer once each week to purchase snacks for drama class
		Uses her Dynavox to request directions and answer questions in the grocery store
	Understands her job responsibilities	Completes a sequence of job tasks that are recorded on the communication device
		Requests help when needed during job tasks

Rationale

Research has shown that instructional decisions are enhanced by the use of data and that such decisions positively influence student performance (Farlow & Snell, 1994; Fuchs & Fuchs, 1986; Holvoet, O'Neil, Chazdon, Carr, & Warner, 1983; Utley, Zigmond, & Strain, 1987; White, 1986). Nearly 25 years ago, Fuchs and Fuchs (1986) demonstrated that teachers were more effective when they used student performance data instead of subjective judgment when making instructional decisions. These researchers also found greater improvement in student performance when the teachers used graphed data instead of ungraphed data to make decisions. In another classic study, Utley et al. (1987) established that teachers and teachers in training made more accurate judgments about student performance when they used data (graphed, ungraphed, or both) than when they based their judgments on observation. These findings are still regarded as guidelines for teachers' use of student performance data.

When teachers begin to measure individual student performance, other advantages become obvious. Precise measurement of behavior allows teams to see even small changes in the behavior, giving everyone the message "Keep up the good work!" This encourages the continued use of promising instructional programs. Continuing an instructional strategy is frustrating when one does not feel that any progress is being made. Student performance data also allow the team to determine when a program is not as effective as planned so that they can design modifications and not let precious instructional time be wasted.

Student performance data can enhance communication with others in the same ways as precise definitions of behavior. Saying, on the basis of intuition, that someone is "doing better in cooking" or "seems to be initiating interactions more frequently" is vague, subjective, and possibly inaccurate. Making a statement such as "Christine uses her communication board to greet the cashier with only two verbal prompts" or "Jacob now waves hello when he enters the classroom in the morning four out of five days each week" communicates clearer and more objective messages.

Measurement Strategies

In this section, we review several ways to measure student performance. The strategy selected should suit the behavior to be measured and the situation. Some of the strategies are easy to use and require little time

away from the usual routine; other strategies, however, take more planning and time. These more complex strategies may be used when a challenging situation in the classroom warrants additional measurement precision. Table 5-2 summarizes these measurement strategies: (a) permanent products, (b) frequency recording, (c) percentage, (d) rate, (e) duration, (f) task analytic measurement, and (g) interval recording and time sampling.

Permanent Products

Many behaviors have a concrete result, or product, that lasts. Unlike behaviors that must be directly observed when they occur, behaviors that result in a product or physical outcome can be evaluated after the individual has performed the behavior. For example, Marc's parents need not sit by his bed all night long to observe toileting accidents. Instead, evidence of accidents can be observed by looking at or touching the child's sheet in the morning. Jacob's teacher can simply look at his computer journal to check for the number and length of sentences written. Permanent product measures provide opportunities to detect error and quality patterns (e.g., particular words or sounds that may be problematic for Jacob). Because measurement of permanent products does not require continuous observation, it is convenient for classroom use.

Frequency Recording

Some behaviors are transitory and must be measured as they occur. Frequency recording measures the number of times that a behavior (appropriate or inappropriate) occurs within a specified period (e.g., the number of times that a student throws his or her work materials onto the floor during a 30-minute work session, the number of times that the student greets people appropriately throughout the school day). Frequency has been used to measure many types of behaviors. For example, Cosbey and Johnston (2006) used a naturalistic approach to teach three children with severe multiple disabilities to use a voice output communication aid (VOCA) to request access to preferred items and/or peers during play activities. The researchers recorded the frequency of unprompted responses (i.e., the student independently activated the VOCA in the presence of peers), as well as prompted and generalized responses.

In order to have meaningful frequency data, it is necessary to specify the length of time and to compare data from the same length of time only. For example, a

TABLE 5–2
Measurement Procedures That Are Appropriate for Classrooms

Description of Measurement	Advantages	Disadvantages	Examples of Behaviors Measured
Permanent products Direct measurement of the lasting and concrete results of a target behavior	• Does not require continuous observation • Permits analysis of products for error patterns	• Behavior must have a tangible result • No immediate feedback	• Appropriate behaviors (e.g., the number of newsletters folded and stapled) • Inappropriate behaviors (e.g., the number of buttons ripped from clothing)
Frequency recording The number of times a behavior occurs within a specified period	• Is useful with a wide variety of discrete behaviors • Can be easily accomplished in the classroom • May be converted to a rate	• Necessitates continuous attention during the observation period • Yields less accurate results with high-rate behaviors or behaviors of varying duration • Inappropriate for behaviors of long duration	• Appropriate behaviors (e.g., spontaneous requests for materials needed, initiation of greetings) • Inappropriate behaviors (e.g., talking out, hitting, incorrect sorting)
Percentage The number correct compared with the number of opportunities (or intervals)	• Useful when the number of opportunities varies across sessions • Can be used to report task analytic measurements, duration, interval, and time-sampling data	• Cannot distinguish the number of opportunities from the score • Cannot be used if there is no ceiling on the number of opportunities	• Appropriate behaviors (e.g., independent eating, correct signing) • Inappropriate behaviors (e.g., hitting, self-injury, cursing, etc., if measured through interval recording or time sampling)
Rate The frequency of a behavior and its relationship to time expressed as a ratio	• Useful when the number of opportunities varies across sessions • Reflects proficiency	• Cannot determine the total time of the observation period	• Appropriate behaviors (e.g., vocational tasks completed per minute, social interactions per hour) • Inappropriate behaviors (e.g., callouts per class period)
Duration The total amount of time in which a targeted behavior occurs in a specified observation	• Yields a precise record of the length of the occurrence of a behavior • May be used to record the duration of each occurrence of a behavior	• Necessitates continuous attention during the observation period • Requires a stopwatch for optimum accuracy • Inappropriate for frequent behaviors of short duration	• Appropriate behaviors (e.g., attending to lesson, completion of hygiene routine) • Inappropriate behaviors (e.g., tantrums, stereotypical behavior, out-of-seat behavior)
Task analytic measurement A record of the performance of each step in a sequence of behaviors that make up a task	• Useful for most skills in the domestic, vocational, leisure, and community domains • May be used to guide instruction • Enables a measurement of each behavior that makes up a skill • Can be summarized as a percentage or a number of steps	• Requires a good task analysis of the skill being measured • Not suitable for measuring inappropriate behaviors • May focus too much on motor skills, neglecting the qualitative aspects of the task	• Appropriate behaviors (e.g., making the bed, playing a CD, assembly tasks, preparing a snack)

(continued)

TABLE 5–2 (*Continued*)

Description of Measurement	Advantages	Disadvantages	Examples of Behaviors Measured
Interval recording A record of the occurrence of behavior within each of the time intervals within a single observation	• Requires less effort than continuous frequency or duration methods • Does not require as precise a definition of a unit of behavior • Applicable to a wide range of behaviors	• Provides an estimate only • The size of the interval must be appropriate for the behavior frequency • Accuracy is facilitated by timers or tape-recorded countings of intervals	• Appropriate and inappropriate behaviors (i.e., any of the behaviors listed for frequency or duration)
Whole interval Records whether behavior occurred continuously throughout each of the intervals within the observation session	• Useful when it is important to know that the behavior is not interrupted	• Underestimates the magnitude of the target behavior	• Appropriate behaviors (e.g., on-task behaviors, engagement in play) • Inappropriate behaviors (e.g., out-of-seat behavior, tantrums)
Partial interval Records whether behavior occurred at any time within the interval	• Useful for behaviors that may occur during fleeting moments • Applicable to behaviors of longer duration • Applicable to high-frequency behaviors	• Overestimates the magnitude of the target behavior	• Appropriate behaviors (e.g., social interactions) • Inappropriate behaviors (e.g., out-of-seat behavior, hitting, hand biting, tantrums)
Momentary time sampling Records whether behavior occurred at the moment each of the intervals ends	• Useful for behaviors that tend to persist for a while • Does not require continuous observation • Can be used with more than one student at a time	• Must sample at frequent and relatively short intervals	• Appropriate behaviors (e.g., on-task behaviors, engagement in play) • Inappropriate behaviors (e.g., tantrums, off-task behaviors)

teacher may report that her student bit his hand 15 times on Monday but only 5 times on Tuesday. This certainly sounds like excellent progress. However, if the teacher observed the student for 3 hours on Monday but only for 1 hour on Tuesday, it is not possible to conclude whether there was any progress.

Behaviors measured in this way should be readily divided into discrete units, with a clear beginning and end, and should be easily visible and countable. For example, stereotypical behavior, such as hand waving, may occur at such a high rate that it is impossible to count each instance accurately. Attempting a frequency count of vocalizations may also be difficult if each vocalization does not have a clear beginning and a clear end. For these two examples, another measurement method (such as duration or interval) should be selected in place of frequency.

Finally, behaviors measured in this way should be relatively uniform in length and not occur for long periods. For example, a parent may report that her child sucked his thumb only two times. This is not helpful information if each occurrence of thumb sucking lasts 45 minutes! The frequency, in this case, does not reflect the amount of behavior. Other measures, such as duration, would be more appropriate for such behaviors. Frequency recordings would accurately measure Jenny's correct coin and value identification and the number of times that Timothy waved to his teacher and peers.

Percentage

A percentage score can be used when a behavior can occur a fixed number of times in an observation session instead of an undetermined number of times.

Percentage is calculated by dividing the number of behaviors observed by the number of opportunities to perform that behavior. This type of measure is used frequently in the general education system to evaluate mastery of academic concepts (e.g., percentage of words correctly spelled, percentage of math problems correctly completed). Marc's teacher used a percentage to measure social interactions when she counted how many times he passed the materials to his neighbor when it was his turn; on one day, she recorded correct responses for two out of the five opportunities occurring during the morning song, or 40% of the opportunities. Percentages can also be used to measure the number of intervals in which a behavior occurred (Christine correctly completed 8 out of 10, or 80%, of book checkouts).

Many educators use percentages to measure performance on task-analyzed activities. For example, Mechling and Stephens (2009) taught four young adults (ages 19 to 22 years) to independently complete task-analyzed (nonmicrowave) cooking tasks (e.g., preparing hot chocolate, chocolate pudding, ravioli, tuna, french fries) using self-prompting strategies. These researchers compared the use of static picture recipes and video prompting strategies, measuring performance by the percentage of task-analyzed steps completed independently. The results demonstrated that all of the students made substantial gains with both the static picture and the video prompting interventions, although the video prompting resulted in the most gains.

Percentage measures are not appropriate when the number of opportunities to perform a behavior is not fixed or controlled. For example, it is inappropriate to write an objective that states that Christine will "greet her peers 80% of the time" if her teacher cannot determine the number of opportunities that she has to greet her peers.

Rate

Rate can be used to determine the frequency of a behavior and its relationship to time. A rate is expressed by the ratio of the number of behaviors divided by the unit of time (e.g., Jacob got out of his seat three times in the 15-minute writing task, or 0.2 times per minute). In vocational training situations, for example, a goal may be to increase the number of cleaning tasks completed in a certain amount of time (e.g., from washing 5 windows in 30 minutes, or 0.17 per minute, to 10 windows in 30 minutes, or 0.33 per minute).

Rate is also a helpful measure when the observation time of a session varies (e.g., to measure the number of spoonfuls of food that Christine eats per minute with her self-feeder when the length of the lunchtime varies). Using an adaptation of prelinguistic milieu teaching, Brady and Bashinski (2008) increased the intentional communication skills (i.e., gestures and vocalizations) of nine students with deaf-blindness. These researchers measured the frequency of the communication acts and then, because of variations in the length of the sessions, converted these measures to rate per minute. Another advantage of using rate to measure performance is that rate reflects both accuracy and speed, or fluency of performance, instead of just accuracy (Billingsley & Liberty, 1982).

Duration

A duration recording is used if the focus is the amount of time that an individual is engaged in a specific behavior or activity. Sometimes it is desirable for a person to increase the amount of time engaged in an activity (e.g., brushing teeth, exercising, studying), and sometimes it is desirable for an individual to decrease the amount of time spent in an activity (e.g., watching television, displaying self-injurious behavior). Duration measures the total amount of time in which a targeted behavior occurs within a specified time.

Delano and Snell (2006) evaluated the effects of social stories on the duration of appropriate social engagement (and the frequency) of four social skills in three elementary school-age students with autism. The intervention consisted of individualized social stories, responding to comprehension questions, and a 10-minute play session with nondisabled peers. The researchers found that all three students increased their duration of social engagement. Harvey, Baker, Horner, and Blackford (2003) used duration of sleep to explore the presence of sleep problems in individuals with intellectual impairments who were living in community settings. They found that while the duration of sleep for the individuals in their sample was similar to those without disabilities, the quality of sleep was different (e.g., waking up in the middle of the night) as a function of the interaction between the level of the disability and the use of medications.

Duration can be recorded in three ways: (a) as total duration, (b) as percentage of time, and (c) by measuring each occurrence. Using the *total duration* method, the teacher records the total amount of time that the individual spent engaged in the behavior during the observation period. For example, Marc's teacher may be interested in measuring the amount of time that he spends in appropriate play with peers during recess. Before starting the duration measurement, the teacher must operationally define appropriate play for Marc, making sure that it is possible to clearly determine the onset and termination of the behavior. The teacher can then measure the behavior using a stopwatch that is unobtrusively carried in her pocket. All that the teacher has to do is to start the stopwatch when Marc begins playing with his peers. As soon as he stops playing (e.g., participates instead in self-stimulatory behavior), the teacher stops the stopwatch. The teacher starts and stops the stopwatch accordingly for the course of the recess period. The amount of time accumulated on the stopwatch at the end of the period reflects the total duration.

A *percentage of time* can be derived by simply dividing the total time engaged in the activity by the length of the playtime. For example, Marc may have played with his peers for a total of 5 minutes during a 15-minute playtime. The following equation represents the process for determining the percentage of time:

$$\frac{\text{Total duration of behavior}}{\text{Length of observation period}} = \frac{5 \text{ minutes}}{15 \text{ minutes}} = 33\%$$

Although the duration measure is simple and accurate (if the behavior is clearly defined), another piece of information makes the duration measure even more informative: the frequency of each occurrence. For example, we know that Marc participated in playing with his peers for 5 minutes (or 33% of recess); however, we do not know whether he played for 5 minutes in a row or if he played for only 30 seconds at a time but kept returning to the play area. Such information may be valuable in determining the type of intervention to use with Marc to increase his interactions during recess. The method of *measuring each occurrence* provides this information, although it is more time consuming than the previous two methods. To measure the occurrences, the teacher would start the stopwatch when Marc started to play with a peer, turn the stopwatch off when he stopped playing, and then record the duration on a data sheet. The teacher would then return the stopwatch to zero. When Marc started to play again, the teacher would start the stopwatch and have it continue until he stopped playing. When Marc stopped again, the teacher would record this duration, and so on. (Alternatively, the teacher could record on the stopwatch in an accumulating manner as before, but

record the frequency of instances of playing, which might be easier to do). At the end of the observation period (e.g., 15 minutes), the teacher would have a record of total duration (e.g., 5 minutes), as well as a count of the number of times that Marc started and stopped playing (e.g., eight times). In this case, the goal would be to increase the duration of time that Marc spent playing and to decrease the number of times that he got distracted from playing.

Task Analytic Measurement

Task analytic measurement focuses on a student's performance on a sequence, or chain, of behaviors during teaching or during testing. This type of measurement is the most frequently used method of instruction and evaluation of student performance on routines or complex activities. To implement task analytic measurement, a teacher conducts a task analysis (see Chapter 4), designs a data sheet to record student performance, and then records the student's performance on each of the steps delineated in the task analysis (or some portion of the steps if using backward or forward chaining).

During teaching, there are a variety of ways in which the teacher may record student performance: by recording a plus (+) or minus (−), by recording the prompt level (e.g., verbal or physical prompt) required for the student to complete the step, or by using another type of measure (e.g., the amount of time to complete a step). If the teacher is using a total task-chaining strategy (see Chapter 4), then all of the steps in the task analysis are scored. If the teacher is using a partial participation strategy or using forward chaining or backward chaining, then only the steps that the student is working on are scored. Table 5–3 shows a task analysis for the skill of making a peanut butter sandwich. Because Jacob can participate extensively in this type of activity, his teacher, Ms. Fuentes, chose to use a total task-chaining strategy and a least-to-most prompting procedure. But, as Jacob's behavior has clearly indicated that he prefers not to be guided and touched in this way, her team decided to teach Jacob using just the verbal and model prompts. It was agreed that if Jacob did not complete a step of the task analysis independently after a verbal prompt or a model, which was typically sufficient, the teacher would simply complete that step for him and allow him the opportunity to perform the next step of the sequence. Jacob's mother said that she would also practice this skill with him when he gets home from school.

TABLE 5–3
Jacob's Task Analysis for Making a Peanut Butter Sandwich

Name: Jacob   **Teacher:** Ms. Fuentes

Activity: Making a peanut butter sandwich

Materials: Peanut butter, bread, butter knife, plate, napkin

Record number that indicates amount of assistance: 3 – Independent, 2 – Verbal, 1 – Model, 0 – Teacher completes

Routine Steps	Dates			
	9/06	9/13	9/27	10/04
1. Initiate snack by going to resource room	3	3	3	3
2. Go to refrigerator	2	2	2	2
3. Get out peanut butter	2	2	2	2
4. Put peanut butter on counter	2	2	3	3
5. Get bread from bread box	1	1	1	1
6. Put bread on counter	2	2	2	3
7. Get butter knife	1	1	1	2
8. Get plate	1	1	1	1
9. Put knife and plate on counter	3	3	2	3
10. Open bread bag	1	1	1	2
11. Remove two slices of bread and put on plate	3	3	3	3
12. Open peanut butter jar	0	0	0	0
13. Scoop out peanut butter with knife	1	1	2	1
14. Spread peanut butter on one slice	3	3	3	3
15. Repeat until preferred thickness	3	3	3	3
16. Put other slice on top	1	2	1	2
17. Put knife in sink	1	1	1	2
18. Put peanut butter away	2	2	2	2
19. Get napkin	1	2	2	2
20. Bring sandwich and napkin to table	3	3	3	3
Total	36/60 (60%)	38/60 (63%)	38/60 (63%)	43/60 (72%)

In general, Jacob's data reflect that he is slowly moving toward the criterion: At the beginning of the week, he achieved 60%, and at the end of the week, he achieved 72%. Keeping track of the individual steps of his task analysis allows more detailed analysis that can contribute to constructive program modifications. Looking at individual steps on his data sheet reveals a few steps that seem to be problematic for him. Jacob is unable to open the peanut butter jar (Step 12) and consistently requires *models* to complete Step 5 (getting bread from the bread box) and Step 8 (getting a plate). This information will allow her team to consider some modifications or adaptations for these steps. For example, should Jacob be provided with a rubber gripper that might make opening the jar easier? Or should he be taught instead to ask someone for assistance to open the jar? Could the bread box and the plates be moved closer to him to make accessing them easier? Or might pictures be helpful as a prompt to remind Jacob of where the items that are needed are kept?

Table 5–4 shows another task analysis for the same activity, but this time for Christine, who is expected to participate partially in the activity instead of performing

all of the steps. Christine is scored on eight steps of the task and her teacher (or peer for Step 2) completes the steps that are marked with an X. Extension and enrichment skills (e.g., initiation, social skills, monitoring skills) are skills where Christine can likely achieve independence. These components allow for meaningful participation in, and control of, the activity even though she cannot perform most of the motor components of the task (see Chapters 3 and 4). The prompt procedure for Christine includes physical assistance.

During testing, task analytic measurement can be carried out by using either a *single-opportunity* or a *multiple-opportunity* method. The easiest, although

TABLE 5–4
Christine's Task Analysis for Making a Peanut Butter Sandwich

Name: Christine   **Teacher:** Ms. Washington

Activity: Making a peanut butter sandwich

Materials: Peanut butter, bread, butter knife, plate, napkin, meal preparation overlay for communication board

Record number that indicates amount of assistance: 5 – Independent, 4 – Verbal, 3 – Model, 2 – Partial physical, 1 – Full physical, X – Teacher or peer completes

Routine Steps	Dates				
	10/07	10/08	10/09	10/10	10/11
1. Initiate snack by activating communication device					
2. Peer assists her into home economics class	X	X	X	X	X
3. Press switch when "peanut butter" is scanned on communication device					
4. Press switch when "bread" is scanned on communication device					
5. Teacher gets items, puts them on counter	X	X	X	X	X
6. Press switch when "knife" is scanned on communication device					
7. Press switch when "plate" is scanned on communication device					
8. Press switch when "napkin" is scanned on communication device					
9. Teacher gets items, puts them on counter	X	X	X	X	X
10. Teacher makes sandwich	X	X	X	X	X
11. Teacher gives her a sample of sandwich and asks whether sandwich is OK	X	X	X	X	X
12. Press switch when "yes/no" is scanned on communication device					
13. Teacher fixes sandwich as necessary	X	X	X	X	X
14. Press switch when "thank you" is scanned on communication device					
Total					

less informative, method is the single-opportunity method. This approach is carried out as follows:

1. Conditions (including materials) are arranged as planned in the instructional program.
2. The instructional cue (if any) is given when the student is attending.
3. The student's response to each step in the task analysis is recorded until an error occurs.
4. The following rules can be used to handle errors, periods of no response, and inappropriate behavior:
   - Testing is stopped after the first error and all remaining steps are scored as errors.
   - After a specified latency period of no response (e.g., 3 seconds), testing is stopped and all remaining steps are scored as errors.
   - After a specified period of inappropriate behavior (e.g., 10 seconds of stereotypical behavior) or after a single inappropriate response (e.g., throwing the soap or the towel), testing is stopped and all remaining steps are scored as errors.

For many tasks, the steps performed are scored as correct if they correspond to the task description, regardless of the order in which they are carried out, as long as the result is satisfactory. For example, it is not important whether Marc pulls his right or left arm out of his coat first. However, for many other tasks (e.g., certain assembly tasks), performing each step in order is crucial to the successful completion of the activity. In tasks where order is important, the first step out of sequence is scored as an error. In addition, when the rate of performance is important (as specified in the criteria or standards), the maximum length of time allowed is specified.

Once each week, Ms. Bowers probed Jacob's performance with regard to packing his book bag. Using the single-opportunity method, Ms. Bowers observed Jacob following two instructional cues. First, she gave the entire class the instruction that they need to get their things together to go to music. Second, she told Jacob, as she always did before activity changes, to check his picture schedule to see what the next class is and what he needs to take with him. Following the natural cue of the other students in the class, he began to gather some things together. Ms. Bowers scored a plus (+) on her data sheet for the first three steps: (a) taking out his book bag, (b) unzipping it, and (c) putting in his pencils. After these first three steps of the task analysis, Jacob stood up to join his

friends in the front of the room. Ms. Bowers scored a minus (−) on her data sheet to indicate that he did not independently perform the fourth step of putting his music book into his bag. According to the single-opportunity testing method, all remaining steps were scored with a minus (−). Ms. Bowers then proceeded to implement teaching by giving him a verbal prompt for the missed step.

The single-opportunity method generally is completed quickly. It provides a conservative estimate of the student's skills. Less instructional time is wasted because teaching can begin immediately after the first error. Furthermore, learning is less likely to occur during testing; therefore, the single-opportunity method provides a more accurate estimate of the effect of instruction. However, a disadvantage of the method is that performance on task analytic steps that occur after the first error are not measured because testing is terminated at this point. Thus, probes or tests taken during the baseline phase do not initially reflect learning on later steps, and performance is underestimated. If a teacher is using backward chaining (i.e., teaching the last step first), the single-opportunity probe does not reflect any progress until training advances to the earlier steps in the chain. Therefore, in such cases, the multiple-opportunity probe produces more information.

The multiple-opportunity method uses the following steps:

1. Conditions are arranged as planned in the instructional program.
2. The instructional cue (if any) is given when the student is attending.
3. The student's responses to each step in the task analysis are recorded as correct or incorrect (i.e., performed correctly or not performed at all).
4. Whenever an error occurs after a specified period of no response or inappropriate behavior, the step is completed by the teacher. Instead of the probe ending, the student is given an opportunity to engage in the next step in the chain. Thus, performance on every step can be assessed.

With both assessment approaches, feedback is not provided to the student with regard to performance of the targeted skill. The withholding of feedback differentiates between the conditions of testing (which represent the most difficult conditions specified in the objective) and the conditions of teaching (when prompts and reinforcement are available). For some students, noncontingent reinforcement may be made available (i.e., reinforcement for something other than performance of the task or generic praise like "Keep up the hard work!") to hold their interest during assessment.

Interval Recording

To use interval recording, the observer divides an observation session into short, equal intervals, and the occurrence of the behavior within each interval is recorded. Some observers build in a brief period (e.g., 5 seconds) for recording between-observation intervals that can increase accuracy (Alberto & Troutman, 2009). Interval recording is useful for those behaviors which do not have discrete start or stop times and which vary in length, are continuous (i.e., of longer duration), or occur with high frequency (Alberto & Troutman, 2009). Interval recording has been used to measure both appropriate behaviors (e.g., peer social initiations and interactions in inclusive settings) and inappropriate behaviors (e.g., out-of-seat, stereotypical, aggressive) in schools and other community settings.

There are two types of interval recording strategies: whole interval and partial interval. In *whole-interval* strategies, the observer notes whether the given behavior occurred continuously throughout the interval. For example, Cox, Gast, Luscre, and Ayres (2009) used a 10-second whole-interval recording system to measure the impact of weighted vests on the in-seat behaviors of students with autism and severe disabilities; that is, the researchers observed whether in-seat behavior occurred throughout the *entire* 10-second interval. This is also what Christine's teacher used to measure her participation in drama rehearsals.

Christine's drama teacher thought that she was losing interest in the play. Lately, rehearsals were quite tedious, often focusing on just one or two students while the other students sat and read or did homework from other classes. In order to assess Christine's interest, her teacher asked Christine's teaching assistant to conduct a whole-interval recording for 5 minutes, once at the beginning of the class, once in the middle of the class, and once toward the end of the class. Each of the 5-minute periods was divided into 30 brief intervals of 10 seconds. The teaching assistant noted whether Christine was engaged throughout each 10-second interval in either watching the play or interacting with others. Christine's teacher found that Christine was mostly inattentive to the play and had few interactions with her peers during

these times. The first observation at the beginning of the class revealed that she was engaged for 10 out of 30 intervals (or 33%). In the middle of the class, she was engaged for 5 out of 30 intervals (or about 17%); at the end of the class, it was only 2 out of 30 intervals (or 6%). Christine's engagement decreased as the class period progressed. Christine's teacher, the teaching assistant, and two of her friends decided that they needed to make sure that Christine had something to do during these downtimes.

In *partial-interval* recording, the observer notes whether the behavior occurs *at all* during the interval instead of whether it occurs continuously throughout the interval. Once a behavior is observed and noted on the data sheet, further observation is not required for the remainder of that interval. Exactly how many times the behavior occurs during each interval is not recorded. Thus, interval recording provides an estimate of the occurrence of behavior. Because of this, interval size must be carefully chosen, only limited conclusions can be drawn from the data, and the data must be interpreted cautiously (Alberto & Troutman, 2009).

Marc seems to be by himself more and more during unstructured times of the day (e.g., free play), not interacting with other children. His special education teacher, Ms. Wharton, decides that they will use a partial-interval recording to get a better idea of how much time Marc is spending alone during these times. Ms. Wharton selects a 10-minute period in the middle of the 9:30 a.m. free play and a 10-minute period during the 11:30 a.m. free play. Then she divides each of these observation sessions into 10 equal 1-minute intervals. Ms. Wharton records a plus (+) in the 1-minute box if Marc has any type of interaction with another student during the interval and a minus (−) if there is no interaction.

Figure 5–1 shows that Marc had interactions with other children in 2 of the 10 intervals during early morning free play (or 20%). The data do not tell us, however, if Marc had two very brief interactions with other children or spent a full 2 minutes interacting with them. Marc had interactions with other children in 6 out of the 10 intervals (60%) during the 11:30 a.m. free play.

If Ms. Wharton repeated this observation for a week, following implementation of an instructional strategy to increase interactions, she may still find no change in the data. However, it is possible that Marc is having a

FIGURE 5–1
Partial Interval Recording Form for Marc's Peer Interactions

Name:	Marc	Teacher:	Ms. Wharton
Date:	November 2	Behavior:	Peer interaction
Code:	(+) peer interaction; (–) no peer interaction		

9:30 Free Play

10 minutes

Minutes	1	2	3	4	5	6	7	8	9	10
	–	+	–	–	–	+	–	–	–	–

Total: 20%

11:30 Free Play

10 minutes

Minutes	1	2	3	4	5	6	7	8	9	10
	–	+	+	+	–	+	+	–	+	–

Total: 60%

Comments: *Seemed to initiate and sustain interactions when musical toys are involved. When other children got loud, Marc seemed to move away.*

significantly greater number of interactions with his peers, but because the interactions were clustered within two or three of the intervals, the progress cannot be seen. In this case, the results of the interval recording may be misleading.

Data from the 11:30 a.m. free play show a higher percentage of peer interaction (60% of the intervals). Continued recording will reveal either that this is an unusual day or that it is typical for Marc to interact more with his peers during free play. Knowing this, Ms. Wharton can analyze that period to determine what variables might be contributing to the increased level of peer interaction. Comments on the data sheet suggest, for example, the possibility that when other students are loud, their noise may inhibit Marc from interacting with them. Ms. Wharton can now investigate further the role that noise plays in Marc's peer interactions.

Selection of the appropriate interval method should be guided by the characteristics of the behavior and the goals of intervention. If the behavior is brief and the goal is to have the behavior occur on a consistent but not necessarily continuous basis (such as Marc's interactions), the partial-interval method must be used or the behavior will not be detected. Other behaviors, such as attention to a task, appropriately occur in a more continuous manner. Such behaviors are best measured by the whole-interval strategy.

When measuring behaviors targeted for reduction, it is best to use the method that provides the most rigorous information. For example, if you were using the whole-interval method to record the extent of self-injurious behavior, the teacher would check the interval only if the self-injury occurs for the entire length of the interval. This would mean that it was possible for the data to reflect no occurrences when, in fact, the student engaged in extensive self-injury, but not *continuous* self-injury. In this situation, the partial-interval method would be more appropriate.

The length of the interval depends on both the behavior being observed (its average length and frequency) and the observer's ability to record the behavior. Interval length usually is measured in seconds (e.g., 5, 10, 30 seconds). The more frequent the behavior, the smaller the interval for observation should be so that the data yield a more accurate representation of behavior.

If large intervals (e.g., 15 minutes) were used with partial-interval recording to measure Christine's frequent behavior of smiling, for example, 100% would be the typical result. In other words, it is almost certain that Christine would smile at least once during every 15-minute interval. This is not informative because it does not provide information about the density of the behavior (e.g., whether Christine smiled 5 times or 150 times).

For behaviors that occur infrequently, the partial-interval method can have longer intervals. For example, because Jacob infrequently initiates interactions with his peers, observing for 30-second intervals makes no sense. It is not likely that Jacob will display the behavior within 30 seconds. However, if the interval is too large, any instance of the behavior can artificially inflate the percentage of intervals. Thus, if Jacob interacts only two times within an hour but the intervals are 30 minutes long, then, statistically, Jacob interacted for 100% of the intervals! This certainly does not reflect the quality of Jacob's behavior. Five-minute intervals might be more appropriate.

Interval recording cannot be done casually, because a teacher's total attention must be directed toward watching the student and timing the intervals during the entire observation period. The teacher must know when to move from one interval to the next. It can be challenging to teach and collect interval data at the same time (Alberto & Troutman, 2009). A watch or clock with a second hand can be used to time the intervals, but checking the time interrupts the observer's concentration; a portable tape recorder with a tape of prerecorded intervals and earplugs may eliminate this problem, although it is somewhat obvious. For longer intervals (e.g., 3 to 5 minutes), inexpensive egg timers and kitchen timers have been used. Still, teachers must be sensitive to the environment and should be as unobtrusive as possible. For example, it would be distracting to have a beep sound every 10 seconds when observing Christine attending to her drama class.

Time Sampling

Time sampling is a type of interval measure that can be used more practically in teaching settings. As in the whole- or partial-interval recording strategy, a specified observation period (e.g., 30 minutes) is divided into smaller units (e.g., 5-minute intervals). However, unlike interval recording, where a teacher observes the behavior throughout the entire interval, the teacher observes the student only at the *end* of the interval. Time sampling usually uses longer intervals (minutes) than does interval recording (seconds). The teacher records on the data sheet whether the student was engaging in the target behavior at the end of each interval. For example, Reinhartsen, Garfinkle, and Wolery (2002) investigated the effect of child choice of toys versus teacher choice of toys on the engaged and problem behaviors of three 2-year-old boys with autism in an inclusive preschool classroom. Using a time-sampling strategy, these researchers divided the play period into small intervals of time (30 seconds) and observed the children's behaviors at the end of every 5 seconds. The researchers found that when children chose the toys to play with, there was an increase in engaged time and fewer problem behaviors for two of the three boys.

Implementation of time sampling can be done flexibly. Instead of continuously observing and recording at the end of each interval, the teacher can set up random intervals within an observation period. For example, the teacher may decide on an observation period of 1 hour and preselect six random times to observe (instead of exactly every 10 minutes).

It is also possible to use time sampling throughout the day and pre-identify observation times. For example, Ms. Wharton could choose to use time sampling (instead of interval recording) to record Marc's interactions with peers throughout the 3-hour day at school (e.g., free play, snack, lunch, circle time). This strategy is relevant if the goal is for Marc to increase interactions with his peers across many activities, not just during playtime.

Because time sampling does not require continuous observation, teaching and data collection can occur simultaneously (Alberto & Troutman, 2009; Maag, 2003). In addition, because the observation is so quick (e.g., whether the behavior was occurring or not occurring at that moment), teachers can use the strategy with more than one student at a time (Schloss & Smith, 1998). For example, a teacher could record the on-task behavior of a group of students at the end of every 2-minute interval during independent seat work. Every 2 minutes, the teacher would look up and see which of the students were or were not engaged in their independent work (as previously defined by the teacher). She would record a plus (+) for those who were engaged and a minus (−) for those who were not engaged.

Like interval recording, however, time sampling provides only an estimate of the behavior. In fact, for low-frequency and short-duration behaviors, time sampling is even less accurate than interval recording. The less frequent or briefer a behavior, the shorter the interval must be. (Because a teacher is checking at the end of the interval only, he may miss the behavior if it does not occur frequently or if it is of short duration.) Thus, time sampling is most appropriate for measuring behaviors that occur frequently and are of long duration.

Organizing Student Performance Data

At this point, we have introduced you to the importance of measuring student behavior and to a variety of quantitative strategies to objectively record behavior. However, if these data are not organized and used, it will be the same as not collecting any data at all. The following section will provide examples of data sheets on which you can record data and then will instruct you on how to visually display, or graph, the data so that the team can understand each student's progress on their IEP goals and objectives.

Designing Data Sheets

Data sheets allow teachers to systematically record data from their observations (e.g., frequency data, task analytic data, interval data). It is important to record this information in a format that will promote subsequent data analysis. For example, some student performance data can provide information for error analyses (e.g., which steps of the task analysis are consistently missed; see Table 5–3), and most data can be converted into graphs for visual analysis.

The basic elements of a data sheet are (a) the student's name; (b) the observer's name; (c) the date, time, and location of the observation; (d) the length of the observation; (e) the behavior(s) observed and, if necessary, a brief observable description of each; (f) adequate space for data recording (e.g., room for a 15-step task analysis or ten 2-minute intervals); (g) a scoring code; (h) a data summary; and (i) comments (see Figure 5–1 and Tables 5–3 and 5–4). In addition to

providing the range of information necessary to make effective instructional decisions, a data sheet can also assist in functional behavioral assessment (Brown, 1991) (see Chapter 6 for a discussion of functional behavioral assessment). For example, for the time-sampling procedure used to measure Marc's interactions with his peers throughout the day, his teacher could specify the time of day and the activity in which the data were measured. With this type of information, it is possible to analyze the events or variables (e.g., activities, the time of day, different peers, materials) contributing to the presence or absence of peer interaction. Adding an extra column on the data sheet for recording the incidence of any inappropriate behavior may enable the teacher to see a trend in the relationship between an inappropriate behavior and the time of day or the type of activity.

Graphing Your Data

Analysis of information on a data sheet may provide important details about performance during an instructional session (e.g., specific steps performed correctly or missed on a task analysis, number of interactions at the beginning versus the end of free play). However, significant limitations are encountered if such data are left in this raw form. For example, it is difficult to interpret or analyze behavioral data from a data sheet alone, especially when weeks of data are considered. Behavioral data can be most effectively interpreted and analyzed when they are graphed. Furthermore, graphing data soon after the observation period provides the teacher with immediate feedback regarding performance (Cooper et al., 2007) instead of waiting and possibly missing opportunities to modify the program as needed. Graphs allow teachers to more easily detect trends in a student's progress and thus to make more effective program decisions. When trends are positive, many teachers also find that graphs are reinforcing because they are a continual source of feedback.

Although some teachers initially feel apprehensive or intimidated by graphs, most soon discover that graphs are actually simple to design and read (Hojnoski, Gischlar, & Missall, 2009). A graph is made up of two axes (see Figure 5–2). The *abscissa,* or the *x-axis,* is the horizontal line. The abscissa usually represents the time frame of a measurement (e.g., each data point reflects the data from a day, week, or month). The *ordinate,* or the *y-axis,* is the vertical line. It is labeled with the target behavior being measured

FIGURE 5–2
Basic Components of a Graph

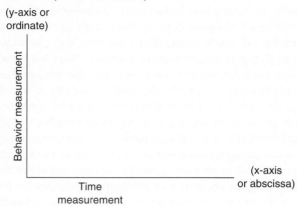

(e.g., peer interaction, the number of words read) and the measurement that was used (e.g., duration, frequency, percentage of intervals). For example, on a graph of Marc's interval data for interactions with his peers, his teacher might label the abscissa as "school dates" and the ordinate as "the percentage of 1-minute intervals of interaction with peers."

Converting Data

Before any points can be plotted on the graph, data must be converted into a single numeric form for each data point. Frequency data can be tallied and presented as the total number in a given period (e.g., the number of times that Marc correctly looked at the named peers during the morning group). Total duration data may be presented as the total number of seconds or minutes during which a behavior occurred within a given period (e.g., the number of minutes spent in a 15-minute leisure activity). Duration data that are collected using the method of measuring each occurrence can be presented as a duration (the number of minutes spent interacting with peers during morning free play) or as a frequency (the number of peer interactions during morning free play), or both ways if the teacher thinks that such a presentation would be helpful. Interval or time-sampling data can be converted into the number or percentage of intervals in which the behavior occurred.

Converting task analytic data, which involves multiple steps and may have a range of scoring codes, is a little more complex. There are a number of ways to summarize the data. First, a common approach is to summarize data as the number of steps that the student performed independently during the baseline and intervention phases out of the total number of steps. Second, data may be converted to the percentage of total steps performed independently during the baseline and intervention phases. Third, as in the example of Jacob's 20-step task analysis for making a peanut butter sandwich (see Table 5–3), data may be summarized in terms of the amount of assistance required to complete a step, with no assistance given during probes. As described previously, Jacob did not need physical prompts within an activity. Because of this, his teacher used a four-component prompt hierarchy (0 – Teacher completes, 1 – Model, 2 – Verbal, 3 – Independent). The steps for converting Jacob's task analytic data into a single numeric form for graphic presentation are as follows:

1. *Determine the most points that Jacob can earn during each session:* The teacher multiplies the number of steps in the task analysis (20) by the number of points possible in each step (3) for a total of 60 possible points that can be earned. For probes, when no prompts are provided, Jacob's performance is either 0 (the student does not perform correctly) or 3 (the student completes the task independently).
2. *Add the number of points earned in the session:* Jacob scored a total of 36 points (out of a possible 60) on September 6.
3. *Calculate the percentage:* Divide the number of points earned (36) by the total number of points possible (60) to calculate the performance percentage (in this case, 60%).
4. *Plot the data:* Plot the performance percentages on the graph.

Setting Up a Graph

Once raw data have been converted into a single number to be graphed, it is easy to plot the data point. First, be sure to label the ordinate or vertical line (the *y*-axis) with the behavior being measured and the type of measurement being used (e.g., percentage of independent vacuuming, number of verbalizations during lunch). Next, divide the ordinate into equal intervals that cover the possible range of data (e.g., 0% to 100%, 0 to 50). If there are no definite upper and lower limits, the range should extend from the baseline level to the target level, with some extra space added at both ends to allow for variability.

Data points within each phase of a program (e.g., baseline, intervention, reinforcer change) are connected by straight lines, but they should not be connected across the vertical lines that indicate a phase change (e.g., the change from the baseline to the intervention phase). Each program phase is separated by a broken vertical line and should be labeled at the top of the graph to indicate the intervention used (e.g., baseline, picture prompting, peer model). Data points that represent probe data should be distinct from data points that represent teaching data because the conditions are very different. For example, a teacher might use open data points for the probe data and closed data points for training data. To enhance the effectiveness of a graph for data analysis, date the graph along the abscissa (*x*-axis) using the same time intervals as the data (e.g., daily, weekly, monthly). Figure 5-3 lists every week for 3 months because probe data will be recorded for making a peanut butter sandwich on a weekly basis. It is important to delineate the dates before recording to allow automatic skipping of spaces for missing sessions. Because missed sessions can have a detrimental effect on a student's performance, it is important to be able to see these gaps in time. Note that no data are recorded for September 20 in Figure 5-3. Jacob's teacher should investigate the reason for the absence of data collection and the effect of this absence on his performance.

Plotting Data Points

Figure 5-3 shows 4 days of data taken from Jacob's data sheet. To plot data, place each data point (i.e., the total for the session) at the intersection of the session date (on the abscissa) and the level of performance (on the ordinate). Note the space between the dates of

September 13 and September 27; it is best to skip the space to indicate the missed session. However, all consecutive sessions in a given phase (according to the scheduled plan of intervention) are connected.

Many teachers find it useful to distinguish between graphs that reflect behavior targeted for acceleration versus graphs that reflect behavior targeted for deceleration. To distinguish between these behaviors, some teachers use a dot to represent acceleration data and an X for deceleration data. This strategy makes successful and unsuccessful trends even more obvious during data analysis. It also allows two related data paths to be plotted on the same graph. Figure 5-4 shows a graph for Marc that uses dots for acceleration data (the percentage of intervals with the appropriate peer interactions during free play) and Xs for deceleration data (the number of times that he grabbed toys from peers). Note that Figure 5-4 uses two ordinates to identify the two targeted behaviors (i.e., peer interactions and the frequency of grabbing) with the two different measurement strategies (i.e., percentage and frequency). Figure 5-4 reflects a successful program. That is, the appropriate behavior (peer interactions) shows an increasing trend and the inappropriate behavior (grabbing) shows a decelerative trend.

Computer-Generated Graphs

Computer-generated graphs have a variety of advantages, including easy storage of data, analysis capabilities, dissemination capabilities (although this can also be a potential danger because of privacy and confidentiality),

FIGURE 5–3

Four Days of Graphed Probe Data for Jacob Making a Peanut Butter Sandwich

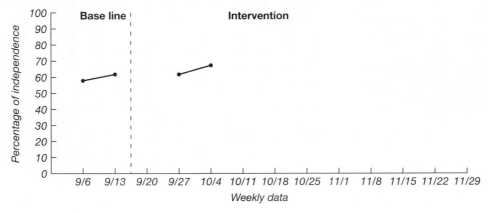

FIGURE 5–4

Use of Graph to Show Marc's Progress and Program Changes During Free Play

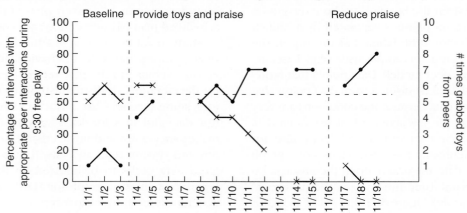

and professional presentations of data at team meetings. More and more teachers and other professionals are using computers to generate their graphs instead of using a pencil and paper. Hojnoski et al. (2009) describe (in a nine-step task analysis) how to use Microsoft® Excel® 1997 to create line graphs. Microsoft 2007 has made some changes in the procedures; there are many tutorials online. Descriptions are also available to chart single-subject designs (see Barton, Reichow, & Wolery, 2007).

Using Self-Graphing Data Sheets

Some teachers find that it is efficient to combine the data recording sheet and the graph. This has been done to measure prompting levels (Alberto & Schofield, 1979), task sequences (Holvoet, Guess, Mulligan, & Brown, 1980), and task analysis (Bellamy, Horner, & Inman, 1979). Plotting data from a task analysis in this manner has been referred to as an upside-down or self-graphing format (Test & Spooner, 1996). Figure 5–5 is a self-graphing data sheet for recording progress on hair

FIGURE 5–5

Self-Graphing Data Sheet for Hair Brushing

Program: Brush hair   Student: Jacob   Teacher: Ms. Fuentes

Task analysis

11. Puts brush away	X	X	X	X	11	11	11	11	11	11	11	11	11	11
10. Check hair for neatness	X0	X0	X0	X0	10	10	10	10	10	10	10	10	10	10
9. Brush left back of head	9	9	9	9	9	9	9	9	9	9	9	9	9	9
8. Brush left side of head	8	8	⑧	⑧	8	8	8	8	8	8	8	8	8	8
7. Brush front	7	X	X	V	7	7	7	7	7	7	7	7	7	7
6. Brush right side of head	X6	X6	6	6	6	6	6	6	6	6	6	6	6	6
5. Brush right back of head	5	5	5	5	5	5	5	5	5	5	5	5	5	5
4. Pick up brush	X	4	4	4	4	4	4	4	4	4	4	4	4	4
3. Selects desired materials	X3	3	3	3	3	3	3	3	3	3	3	3	3	3
2. Locates brushing materials	2	2	2	2	2	2	2	2	2	2	2	2	2	2
1. Initiates brushing	X	X	X	X	1	1	1	1	1	1	1	1	1	1
	9/2	9/9	9/16	9/23										

Key: ╱ = independent
       ╳ = needs assistance

brushing. (See Chapter 15 for another example of a self-graphing data sheet.)

A self-graphing data sheet can be used to record data by making a slash (/) through the step number if the student responds independently and an X through the step number if the student needs assistance to complete the step. At the end of the session, add the number of slashes and then circle the number correct for the day. A graph is formed by connecting the circles over a number of days.

Saving Ungraphed Data

When raw, or ungraphed, data of performance on a multiple-stepped task are summarized and graphed, a certain amount of information is lost. For example, teachers who look at a graph on the accuracy of Jacob's sandwich making would know about his overall progress on the task across sessions, but they would not know the specific information available on his data sheet, such as which steps he missed or did correctly on a given day or if these missed or correct steps were consistent across days.

Teachers should preserve ungraphed data because response-by-response information may help them make decisions about program implementation when progress is poor (Farlow & Snell, 1994; Snell & Lloyd, 1991). Even with non–task analytic or discrete data (e.g., the number of correct greetings made by Timothy at preschool), graphed summaries lose some of the information that can be preserved on the data collection sheets. For example, Timothy's teacher analyzed the ungraphed data to determine whether his performance is better in the early part of the morning or in the later part of his school day, or if he greeted certain peers or adults more frequently than others.

Frequency of Data Collection

Early in the development of current data-based teaching models, it was fairly common to hear the advice that data should be collected each time an instructional activity was implemented. In fact, data collection practices that were recommended for teachers were similar to those used by researchers. Although this may now sound excessive, it was an important phase, as it afforded educators additional understanding of the learning process of students with severe disabilities and increased knowledge of data analysis and evaluation. As educational strategies have become more integrated and community based, data collection procedures have also changed to better fit these settings (Test & Spooner, 1996). In contexts where teachers of nondisabled peers are not recording data, conspicuous data collection procedures do not enhance an integrated view of a student with severe disabilities. Smith (1990) points out that data collection should be neither obtrusive nor intrusive. Measures that are most appropriate for inclusive community settings are ones that do not interrupt instruction, take minimal time to complete, are unobtrusive and do not stigmatize the individual, and provide both objective and subjective observations.

Just how often a teacher should take data is a subject of great debate. Holvoet et al. (1983) point out the irony in this debate—the arguments about data collection do not appear to be data based. A teacher may find a wide variety of suggestions when reading the literature (e.g., collect data once each day, every time the skill is practiced, or once a week). For example, a teacher can collect trial-by-trial data or collect probe data, and the teacher may not be the only one collecting data (Alberto & Troutman, 2009). Most discussions of the frequency of data collection, however, suggest that once a skill is in the maintenance, fluency, or generalization stage of learning, data collection could be reduced (Farlow & Snell, 2005).

Although there are still no definitive answers to the question of exactly how much data are needed to make accurate instructional decisions, the following guidelines can assist teachers in deciding how frequently to collect data:

- Higher priority objectives (i.e., those related to the health and safety of the individual or others) warrant daily data collection (Browder, 1991). Daily data collection not only is more sensitive to changes in the trend but also contributes to an important functional assessment of the behavior (Brown, 1991).
- Lower priority objectives, or objectives that are scheduled for instruction on a less-than-daily basis (e.g., grocery shopping), may be evaluated less frequently (e.g., once every 1 or 2 weeks) (Browder, 1991).
- Implementation of a new program requires frequent data collection. For the first 2 weeks of the instructional program, data could be collected daily or at every teaching session if the lessons are not held at least once a day. When the student has shown steady progress (e.g., 2 weeks of data), data collection could be reduced to weekly (Farlow & Snell, 1994).

- Skills being taught to replace problem behaviors can be measured in the same way as any other new program (e.g., initially, data are collected daily; then, following progress, collection is reduced to weekly); however, these probes should be carried out in the context of relevant situations, persons, and environments (Meyer & Janney, 1989).
- Data that show progress as planned, with a clear accelerating trend, may be evaluated less frequently (Snell & Lloyd, 1991), such as on a weekly basis (Farlow & Snell, 1994).
- Data that do not show progress as planned or that are variable warrant evaluation on a continual basis (Snell & Lloyd, 1991), minimally twice a week and ideally on a daily basis (Farlow & Snell, 1994).
- Anecdotal records or logs can be used once or twice weekly to record general information concerning a student's overall daily performance and to systematically assess responses to program efforts and any conditions that might affect a student's learning (e.g., tasks or activities that the student enjoys, tasks or activities that the student does not enjoy) (Farlow & Snell, 1994; Meyer & Janney, 1989). Such logs may be useful supplements to more precise, quantified data.

Data Analysis for Better Decision Making

Team members can learn a lot from their graphed data. However, teams need to make sure that the data they collect are accurate. Only if data are accurate can the team be confident that data analysis will help improve the educational program. The remainder of this chapter discusses the importance of accurate data, the use of different types of data, and then provides strategies for analyzing classroom data and ways in which this information can most effectively help teachers make instructional decisions.

Measures of Accuracy

Because important decisions are made on the basis of data, team members must have confidence in the data they collect. Consider the following example where the relationship between accurate data collection and effective program evaluation is obvious.

Data recorded by Jacob's teaching assistant indicate that he can prepare his snack with only two verbal prompts. However, when his teacher assists Jacob in

this activity, she finds that Jacob needs not only significant verbal prompts but also gestural cues. The discrepancy in these data may be because Jacob is not accustomed to preparing his snack with his teacher. If this is the case, then certain programmatic changes can help Jacob generalize his snack preparation skills in the presence of others. However, it is also possible that someone is not recording Jacob's data accurately. If this is the case, changes focusing on generalization would not be appropriate. Efforts should instead focus on increasing the accuracy and reliability of the data collection.

Interobserver (or Interrater) Reliability

Interobserver reliability is assessed to determine whether the target behavior is being recorded accurately (Miltenberger, 2008) and is the most commonly used indicator of measurement quality in applied behavior analysis (Cooper et al., 2007). One way to ensure that data are accurate or reliable is to have two independent observers record the behavior of a student at the same time, compare the two observations, and mathematically determine the extent of agreement of the data. The percentage of interobserver reliability can be calculated by dividing the number of agreements between the two observers by the number of agreements plus disagreements and multiplying by 100. The result of this calculation is a *percentage of agreement:*

$$\frac{\text{Agreements}}{\text{Agreements} + \text{Disagreements}} = \frac{\text{Percentage of}}{\text{Agreements}}$$

For example, two teachers use a partial-interval recording to observe the presence of a specified behavior. A 5-minute observation period is divided into ten 30-second intervals. Each time that they observe the target behavior, they record an X in the correct cell. The results of the observation are as follows:

30-second intervals	1	2	3	4	5	6	7	8	9	10
Teacher 1		X	X		X		X		X	X
Teacher 2		X	X	X	X		X		X	X

According to this formula, the reliability between the two teachers is as follows:

$$\frac{9 \text{ agreements}}{9 \text{ agreements} + 1 \text{ disagreement}} = \frac{9}{10}$$

$$= 90\% \text{ agreement}$$

Generally, a reliability coefficient of 0.80, or 80%, is considered to be acceptable. Poor interrater reliability should prompt the team to improve agreement among its members in ways such as clarifying the behavioral definition of the behavior being observed, offering further training for the staff collecting the data, or simplifying the observational system (Schloss & Smith, 1998).

Procedural Reliability

Procedural reliability (also referred to as treatment integrity, treatment fidelity, and fidelity of intervention) is the degree to which program procedures are implemented accurately. Procedural reliability asks the question: Did the teacher follow the instructional plan? If we do not assess the accuracy of the implementation of a program and a student is not experiencing success, then we could not determine whether it was actually the intervention that was ineffective (Hojnoski et al., 2009; Lane & Beebe-Frankenberger, 2004). In an extensive discussion of procedural reliability, Billingsley, White, and Munson (1980) point out that all relevant variables in a program must be evaluated. Program components such as delivery of reinforcers, use of prompts, program setup, antecedent events, and consequent events should be examined (Billingsley et al., 1980). A behavioral checklist for each intervention procedure can be designed, and the teacher can check off each component used (Kerr & Nelson, 2009). Lane and Beebe-Frankenberger (2004) suggest designing checklists for the specific instructional components expected to be implemented by the educator. This checklist would then be used to assess whether the procedure was being followed. The following are some specific questions to consider when assessing procedural reliability:

- Is the instructional plan implemented as frequently as planned?
- Does the instructor use the correct sequence and timing of instructional prompts?
- Does the instructor deliver the appropriate consequences?
- Are instructional cues delivered in the manner designated in the program plan?
- Were all of the necessary instructional materials available?
- Was the program implemented in the correct environment?

Procedural reliability can be calculated in much the same way as interobserver reliability. Billingsley et al. (1980) offer the following formula:

$$\text{Procedural reliability (\%)} = \frac{(TA \times 100)}{TT}$$

In this formula, TA is the number of teacher behaviors in accordance with the program plan, and TT is the total number of teacher behaviors that could have been performed in accordance with the program plan. As an example, Christine was supposed to participate in the library with her nondisabled peers eight times each month (twice each week) but participated only six times last month. Applying this formula to the intervention frequency gives the procedural reliability:

$$\text{Procedural reliability (\%)} = \frac{6 \times 100}{8} = 75\%$$

Teams must feel confident that instruction is having the desired effect on student performance. It is also helpful to know that an intervention is responsible for the change in the student's performance, not just the passage of time or some other event. Sometimes simple, single-subject designs (e.g., reversal, changing criterion) can help teachers feel more confident about the effect of their instruction or the impact of various changes on the educational environment.

Jacob's parents informed his teacher that he was going to be placed on a new medication for a few weeks and that she should be observant to determine whether she noticed any changes in Jacob's on-task behavior. Ms. Fuentes decided to draw a vertical change line on his "on-task" graph to mark the beginning of the medication. At the end of 3 weeks, Ms. Fuentes was informed that they would be discontinuing the medication; she then drew another vertical line to indicate the discontinuation of the medication. At this point, Ms. Fuentes was able to inform the team that during the time that he was taking the medication, Jacob's on-task behavior improved and that when it was discontinued, the behavior returned to premedication levels. The physician represcribed the medication, and Ms. Fuentes drew another change line and, within a week, saw that the on-task behavior once again increased.

Ms. Fuentes used what is called an ABAB, or reversal design, to monitor the changes in Jacob's behavior as a result of the changes in his medication regime made by his family and doctor. After seeing an initial increase in the behavior following the medication, Ms. Fuentes was not confident that it was actually the medication that was responsible for the change in behavior. After all, at around the same time, she added more picture cues to his instruction; perhaps it was the picture cues that helped Jacob stay on task. However, because the behavior decreased *each time* that the medication was withdrawn and increased *each time* that it was prescribed, Ms. Fuentes and the team were more confident that the medication was, at least in part, responsible for the change in Jacob's on-task behavior.

Although an in-depth discussion of single-subject experimental designs (e.g., reversal, multiple baseline, changing criterion) is not possible in this text, we recommend further reading in this area. There are a number of texts that provide comprehensive reviews of single-subject designs (e.g., Alberto & Troutman, 2009; Cooper et al., 2007; Kennedy, 2005; Kerr & Nelson, 2009; Maag, 2003; Miltenberger, 2008; Zirpoli & Melloy, 2005). We will limit our later discussion to the simplest classroom design that is nonexperimental in nature (i.e., the baseline-intervention, or AB, design).

Types of Data

There are many sources of information that are available to teachers that will help them determine whether students are benefiting from instructional programs. For example, anecdotal records that teachers maintain can be a useful supplement to the quantitative data that is the focus of this chapter. These records may include staff notes on unusually excellent or unusually poor student performance, or comments sent by the teacher to the home, or from the family to the school. Different levels of quantitative evaluation can occur for each objective identified on an IEP. Test conditions and training conditions provide two contexts for obtaining valuable data (Farlow & Snell, 1994).

Probes or Testing Data
Testing or probing means that a person's performance is checked under criterion conditions (i.e., conditions that as closely as possible use natural contexts, cues, and consequences); that is, those conditions under which we ultimately want the behavior to be performed. Thus, the teacher typically provides no prompting or teaching assistance, no reinforcement for task success or improvement, and no corrections. The goal of testing is to learn about a student's current performance under criterion conditions (specified in the objective), not to teach the student. Thus, testing is "an evil necessity": Students do not learn when tested, but testing

must be done as frequently as needed to get an accurate picture of the student's performance under criterion conditions. Because students do not learn during testing, teams should limit the amount of "test to teaching" data. The "one to five or less" rule of thumb can be used to keep testing infrequent (gather test data once every 5 days or every 2 weeks when teaching occurs daily).

Teaching Data
In contrast, teaching data can be recorded whenever the student is taught or less often. Under teaching conditions, data are recorded while a student is assisted, as needed, to keep responding; the student is within the instructional context (e.g., he or she is provided with instructional feedback, given corrections for errors, provided with appropriate reinforcement). Learning is the goal of teaching, so conditions are planned to promote improvement in performance and to advance the student through the various stages of learning.

Because of the absence of prompts and reinforcement during probes, a student's performance is typically less proficient than under teaching conditions. Probe data thus represent conservative measures of learning but may more accurately represent a student's performance in natural, unaided situations. Probe data taken for a skill before a teaching program is initiated are called *baseline data*.

> *When Christine was first learning how to use her communication board to greet the cashier in the grocery store, her teacher initially tested her at the grocery store (i.e., she was given a baseline probe, or test). Probe data showed that Christine was unable to activate the correct greeting symbol. Instruction was implemented to teach her this skill during daily sessions at school in which her teacher recorded her performance during instruction (teaching data). When Christine went to the grocery store, her teacher again recorded probe data to determine how she was performing the skill in the natural context. When Christine performed some, but not all, of the steps, her teacher noted this and then immediately began teaching to prevent any more difficulty.*

Obtaining a Baseline

In order to objectively determine whether a student is progressing with regard to a particular objective, we must first know what the student's skills were prior to our intervention. This is done by conducting a *baseline* measurement. The baseline is the period when no intervention or teaching is occurring. Baseline data measure the behavior (the dependent variable) before intervention (the independent variable) is initiated. In other words, the baseline phase of measurement describes a student's performance under the naturally occurring conditions in his or her environment without instructional manipulation.

Ms. Wharton used interval recording to measure Marc's interactions with his classmates during two unstructured periods for 3 days (Figure 5-1 shows the recording on 1 day). Because Ms. Wharton observed Marc under natural conditions, without intervening in any way, these 3 days are considered to be a baseline. After implementation of an intervention program to increase Marc's interactions with his classmates, Ms. Wharton will compare the baseline data with the intervention data to determine whether there was an increase in peer interactions. Ms. Wharton was particularly interested in the effect of the intervention on Marc's behavior during the 9:30 a.m. free play.

A teacher should be cautious about how long a baseline condition is in effect. Generally, the rule is to continue baseline measurement until there is a stable trend in the data. It is considered unethical, however, to continue a baseline measurement in certain situations. First, if a behavior is dangerous, it is unacceptable to wait for a stable trend before beginning treatment. Many times, a teacher can find other forms of data to use as a baseline (e.g., incident reports, daily logs). Second, many students have little or no behavioral activity related to the target objective (e.g., sign language for a student who has never used sign language). Again, it is considered unethical to delay instruction for an extended period of time when a student clearly cannot perform the behavior. Teachers must remember that the baseline does not refer to the absence of a program or to downtime; instead, the baseline refers to the time before a given program is implemented or the time when a particular program is withdrawn or stopped. Third, if the direction of the baseline trend is opposite to the direction of the desired trend (e.g., the number of peer interactions are decreasing, aggression is increasing), collection of baseline data should be discontinued and intervention initiated. When this type of trend occurs, something in the baseline condition is either extinguishing the behavior (e.g., the absence of intermittent teacher praise for playing with others was once reinforced and was withdrawn during the baseline period) or reinforcing the behavior (e.g., a lack of teacher-implemented consequences for aggressive behavior allows the student to get attention from the other students).

Baseline–Intervention Design

Comparing a baseline condition (A) with an intervention condition (B) is called an AB, or baseline–intervention, design. This design is referred to as a nonexperimental design because no conclusive demonstration of a cause–effect, or functional, relationship between the intervention and the observed changes in behavior is possible. Because there is no withdrawal of the intervention or replication of treatment effects, rival hypotheses f based on factors that are not controlled by the teacher may have caused the changes in the behavior (e.g., the student may have matured over time, a new student joined the class, a parent has been working on the skill at home).

Marc's teachers decide to implement an intervention to increase his interactions during the 9:30 a.m. free play. Intervention consisted of seating Marc in proximity to two of his outgoing, friendly classmates, Sam and Mario, and praising the students for all interactions. Marc's interactions with his peers increased. However, Ms. Wharton wondered whether it was the new intervention (i.e., praise and environmental manipulation) that increased the peer interaction or if, perhaps, it might be the new action figures that Sam was bringing to school.

Given the lack of experimental control, the AB design rarely is used by researchers, but it is appropriate for monitoring student performance within teaching settings, particularly when proven teaching strategies are used. Sometimes, however, it is possible for teams to use a reversal design (ABAB), as described earlier when Jacob's teacher had the opportunity to assess his behavior under medication and without medication.

When teams are familiar with a student's typical learning patterns and are aware of various events that affect performance, they can usually judge treatment effects with a considerable degree of certainty. Because student performance is monitored before teaching occurs (during the baseline phase) and during different phases of teaching, the AB design provides an objective (although not scientifically conclusive) description of a student's behavior before, during, and after teaching.

If a student's performance during the baseline phase progresses in the same direction as is expected during the intervention, teachers have difficulty interpreting the intervention data. That is, unless the intervention has a great effect, it is difficult to judge whether the change in the data (from the baseline phase to the intervention phase) is the result of the intervention or simply a continuation of the trend seen during the baseline phase. Because of this difficulty, teachers typically wait until the baseline performance is relatively stable before starting intervention; however, in some instances, as discussed previously (e.g., dangerous behavior), teachers may not wait for a stable baseline or may not take a baseline measurement at all before beginning intervention.

An AB design is shown in Figure 5-6. This example shows an increase in Christine's engagement during drama club after intervention. Intervention consisted of having her sit closer to peers, having the teaching assistant move to the back of the room to do paperwork, teaching her peers how to communicate with her, and programming her communication device with vocabulary suited to the class.

Graphing Conventions

As described earlier, the main purpose of converting raw data to graphs is to provide a visual summary of the student's performance and progress. These interpretations guide program modification. The ability to accurately interpret graphs is enhanced by the use of certain graphing conventions. Four major graphing conventions are shown in Figure 5-4:

- *Broken vertical lines,* or phase changes, represent changes in the instructional program. These can include planned programmatic changes (e.g., a change from baseline to intervention measurement, a modification of the task analysis or materials, a change in the time or setting of the instruction, or a change in the reinforcement or prompt). Broken vertical lines can also be used to indicate situations or events that might indirectly or incidentally affect the student's performance. These events include, for example, changes in medication, staff changes, or a new student joining the class.
- *Broken horizontal lines* (a criterion line) can be used to indicate the criterion for the program. This criterion should match the criterion stated in the behavioral objective of the program. Seeing this line

FIGURE 5–6

An AB Design for Evaluating the Effects of Intervention on Christine's Engagement During Drama Club (with and without a mean line)

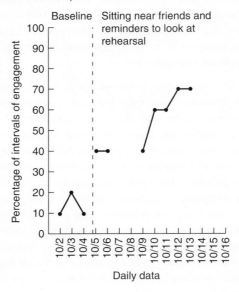

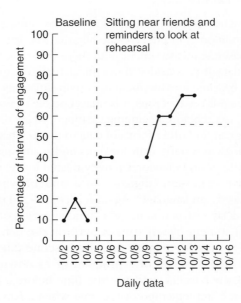

on the graph gives the team a quick visual reminder of what the goal of the program is and where the student is in relation to the goal.

- *Connect data points* only for consecutive days within a phase. Data points should not be connected across phase change lines or across missed data days (e.g., a student absence or a missed session). This allows a clear picture of the effect of the program change but also allows the team to note the gaps in instructional opportunities and its effect on performance.

- *Show the expected trend.* Teams can quickly note whether a graph represents a successful or an unsuccessful program effort by using an X to represent behavior that is to be decreased and dots to represent skill building. This graphing convention also allows multiple data paths on one graph (e.g., increasing toy play and decreasing self-stimulatory behavior during free play).

Marc's teacher graphed his progress in increasing peer interactions in his 9:30 a.m. free play. Ms. Wharton decided that it would be helpful not just to note his progress for this social interaction skill, but also to analyze the impact of the intervention on Marc's behavior of grabbing toys from his peers. She drew a criterion line across the graph at 70% because the objective was to have Marc engage in appropriate peer interactions for 70% of the intervals during the free play (this percentage was based on her observations of other children in the class playing together). When Marc reached the criterion level for peer interactions and there was also a significant decrease in his grabbing of toys, Ms. Wharton decided that she should reduce the amount of praise she was giving to Marc and his peers so that it would be more typical of the frequency of praise she provided to other children in the class. To indicate this program change, she drew a broken vertical line on the graph. She was happy to note that the appropriate peer interactions remained high and that the grabbing behavior remained at zero (see Figure 5-4).

Visual Analysis

Visual inspection of a graph is most frequently used to evaluate the effects of classroom data (Alberto & Troutman, 2009; Hojnoski et al., 2009). That is, certain characteristics and comparisons of the data paths (e.g., data from the baseline compared with data from the first phase of instruction) are examined to judge the effectiveness of the instructional strategy. Sometimes, the effects of a program are so strong that the impact is obvious by just looking at ("eyeballing") the graph. In these situations, when the graph itself lets you know all that you need to know, you are using visual analysis. For example, the top panel of Figure 5-6 shows a very distinct difference between the baseline and the intervention. It is easy to see on this graph a

positive change both in the trend (an accelerating data path) and the level of change (performance of 10% and 20% during baseline, which then jumped to 40% and higher during intervention). As described above, however, an AB design is not an experimental design, and it is possible that confounding variables may be contributing to the change in behavior.

When such strong changes in behavior are not so obvious, teachers and researchers often find that their efforts in analyzing the trends on a graph are aided by several simple visual aids—mean line, aim line, and trend line.

Mean Lines

An easy visual addition to a graph to help analyze intervention effects is looking at the mean (i.e., the average) of each phase and comparing these lines. This can be done by calculating the mean of the data points in each phase and drawing a horizontal broken line that corresponds to that value on the ordinate scale (Alberto & Troutman, 2009). For example, we could calculate the average of the baseline for Figure 5-6 in the following manner:

1. Add the baseline data point values:

$$10\% + 20\% + 10\% = 40\%$$

2. Divide the total by the number of days:

$$\frac{40\%}{3} = 13.3\%$$

3. Draw a horizontal broken line across the baseline phase at 13%.

The same would be done for the intervention:

1. Add the intervention data point values:

$$40\% + 40\% + 40\% + 60\% \\ + 60\% + 70\% + 70\% = 380\%$$

2. Divide the total by the number of days:

$$\frac{380\%}{7} = 54.28\%$$

3. Draw a horizontal broken line across the intervention phase at 54%.

The bottom panel of Figure 5-6 shows the difference in the two horizontal lines and is an additional visual representation of the success of the intervention. Mean lines can be particularly helpful in detecting change when the difference in the levels of behavior between phases is obvious.

Aim Lines

The aim line is a more sophisticated version of the criterion line that is calculated from a student's data collected during the baseline assessment or after several days of training. Usually, the aim line starts at the initial performance level of the student when you begin instruction and extends over the instructional period to the criterion level and date that you have set in the instructional objective (Farlow & Snell, 1994, 2005). This progress-monitoring visual aid is drawn onto a graph early in a program and allows the team to compare actual progress to their expectations for progress. Although they might look quite complicated, aim lines are simple to draw and easy to interpret. Aim lines result from connecting two points made by (a) the intersection of the middate and the mid-performance of the first 3 training days (or the last 3 baseline days) and (b) the intersection of the criterion performance with the goal date of accomplishment (i.e., the aim date).

In March, Jacob's team was concerned about his organizational skills and how they would affect him in fifth grade when following the schedule was even more important. Specifically, they wanted him to learn a four-step task analysis for following his schedule: (a) Look at his schedule and state the next activity, (b) gather the needed materials, (c) go to the appropriate location and participate, and (d) leave when done and return to his classroom. First, the team revised his schedule so that it reflected the 15 activities that he needed to do each day, including two bathroom breaks so that he would not skip going, which had resulted in accidents. Then, Ms. Bowers met with him and showed him the plan for the revised schedule to determine the changes that he might suggest. Jacob wanted the schedule to fit into his notebook and not be so obvious to his classmates, and he did not want VELCRO® symbols because they were too "noisy," but he agreed that the new schedule would help him to remember. The final version of his schedule consisted of 15 small picture/word symbols that were slipped into clear plastic pockets from left to right and top to bottom on one page. This way, the schedule symbols could be adjusted during his check-in each morning, if necessary. Then the team developed a teaching program and a data collection sheet and schedule (see Figure 5-7). Prior to recording the baseline data, Ms. Bowers gave Jacob the new schedule and various staff members (depending on where he was) recorded his per-formance over 3 days, withholding all prompts. The team wanted to determine whether the schedule alone would be enough. On his first day of the baseline period (see Figure 5-7), he used his schedule independently for 8 out of the 15 activities, which indicated that he needed instruction in addition to the schedule.

Table 5-5 shows Jacob's data for the entire program. Gray lines are probes, while unshaded lines are training data. Figure 5-8 shows a graph of these data. Jacob's teachers drew an aim line on the graph at the beginning of his program for the purpose of guiding their judgments about his progress. Look at the aim line in the graph and let's review how his teachers drew it on the graph.

Jacob's first three teaching data points in Table 5-5 show that he scored 50%, 60%, and 73%, respectively, during the first 3 days of teaching (March 26, 27, and 30); this was a gradual improvement over his baseline performance.

Ms. Fuentes, Jacob's special education teacher, was in charge of entering the data onto a graph for the team. After the first three training data points had been graphed, she drew the aim line. She began by setting the anchor (beginning point) for the aim line at the intersection of the second day of teaching, or mid-date (March 27), and his mid-performance, which was 60% (i.e., the middle value of the three percentages). The aim line endpoint was set at the intersection of the criterion performance that was expected for Jacob (i.e., 100%) and the goal date for learning pennies (April 24). Jacob's teacher then drew a straight line connecting these two points.

The selection of the aim criterion reflects the team's expectations for the student. Jacob's team wanted him to master schedule use and his baseline performance indicated that he was independent about half of the time. Thus, they set his criterion at 100%. The selection of an aim date is influenced by several factors, including the school's typical evaluation periods (e.g., every 9 weeks), the urgency (or time line) for learning the skill, the difference between current performance and the criterion, and the speed of learning on similar tasks in the recent past. Aim dates should not be excessively distant from implementation dates and may be set to correspond to the more frequent marking periods used in general education (e.g., 9 to 12 weeks). Jacob's team chose the third week in April,

FIGURE 5–7

Jacob's Schedule Use Program and Data Collection Sheet

Student Name: Jacob

Days: Daily

Settings: Classroom, hallways, playground, lunchroom, gym, music room, computer lab, resource room, library

Instructional Cue: "Jacob, check your schedule."

Latency: 5 seconds (probes and teaching)

Baseline/Probe Method: Multiple opportunity task analytic assessment; don't repeat cue

Probe Schedule: Every Wednesday

Teaching Method: System of Least Prompts: verbal; verbal + gestural; verbal + physical

Recording Key:

   Probe codes: ✓ independent on all steps, - incorrect/no response on one or more steps

   Teach codes:
   + Attended to activity with prompting or independently (some of 4 steps needed prompting, some independent)
   − Needed prompts on all steps

Materials: Visual schedule in his notebook, academic materials for scheduled activity in desk, classroom, or backpack

Objective: Jacob will use his schedule, identify the activity, get the needed materials, do to the activity and participate, and leave the activity when it is finished for all 15 daily activities.

Date: 23 March baseline Staff: MM	Arrival, Check-in	A.M. Work	Language Arts	Guided*	Specialty**	Recess	Restroom	Math	Lunch	Science/Social Studies	Writers' Workshop	Shared Reading	Restroom	Check-out	Departure
1. Look at schedule, name activity	✓	−	✓	−	✓	−	−	✓	−	✓	−	✓	✓	✓	✓
2. Get any needed materials.	✓	−	✓	−	✓	−	−	✓	−	✓	−	−	✓	✓	✓
3. Go to activity.	✓	−	✓	✓	✓	−	−	✓	−	✓	−	−	✓	✓	✓
4. Leave activity, return to class.	✓	−	✓	−	✓	−	−	✓	✓	✓	−	−	✓	✓	✓
Summary score: 8/15 = 53%	✓	−	✓	−	✓	−	−	✓	−	✓	−	−	✓	✓	✓

*Resource Room

**Monday: Music; Tuesday and Thursday: P.E.; Wednesday: Library; Friday: Computer

Note: Credit is given to Mandy McKee for this adaptation of her instructional program.

---

as they hoped to have this skill in place before the fourth graders started their state assessment testing.

Trend Lines

A trend line roughly averages the direction and slope of a student's performance when the performance is uneven, variable, or difficult to interpret by just look-ing at the graph. A trend indicates the direction of graphed data, as well as the slope, or steepness, of the data path. A trend can be of three general types:

1. *Ascending trends* have an upward slope on a graph and indicate improvement (or learning) when the behavior graphed is a skill or adaptive behavior. (If

TABLE 5–5
Data for Jacob's Program for Using a Schedule

Date	Arrival, Check-In	Morning Work	Language Arts	Guided	Specialty	Recess	Restroom	Math	Lunch	Science/Social Studies	Writers' Workshop	Shared Reading	Restroom	Checkout	Departure	Total Independent	Percentage Correct During the Day
23-Mar	✓	−	✓	−	✓	−	−	✓	−	✓	−	−	✓	✓	✓	8	53
24-Mar	✓	−	✓	−	✓	−	✓	✓	−	✓	✓	−	✓	−	✓	9	60
25-Mar	✓	−	−	−	✓	−	−	✓	−	✓	✓	−	✓	−	✓	7	47
26-Mar	+	−	−	−	+	−	+	+	−	+	Early release					5	50
27-Mar	+	+	+	−	+	−	−	+	−	+	+	−	+	−	+	9	60
30-Mar	+	−	+	−	+	+	+	+	−	+	+	−	+	+	+	11	73
31-Mar	+	−	−	+	+	−	+	+	+	+	+	−	+	+	+	11	73
1-Apr	✓	−	✓	✓	✓	✓	−	✓	−	✓	✓	−	✓	✓	✓	11	73
3-Apr	+	Late arrival				−	+	+	−	+	+	−	+	+	+	8	73
Spring break: 4-Apr through 13-Apr																	
14-Apr	+	−	+	+	+	+	+	+	+	+	+	−	+	−	+	12	80
15-Apr	✓	−	−	−	✓	−	✓	✓	✓	✓	✓	−	✓	−	✓	9	60
16-Apr	+	−	−	+	+	+	+	+	+	+	+	−	+	−	+	11	73
17-Apr	+	Late arrival							+	+	+	−	+	−	+	6	75
20-Apr	+	Late arrival						+	+	−	+	−	+	+	+	7	70
21-Apr	+	Field trip +								+	+	−	+	+	+	7	88
22-Apr	✓	−	+	−	✓	−	✓	✓	✓	✓	✓	−	✓	✓	✓	11	73
23-Apr	+	−	−	+	+	+	+	+	+	+	+	−	+	−	+	11	73
24-Apr	+	−	−	+	+	+	+	+	+	+	+	−	+	−	+	11	73

Shaded data are probe data

Probe codes: ✓ Independent on all steps, − Incorrect/No response on one or more of the four task steps

Teach codes: + Attended to activity with prompting or independently (some of four steps needed prompting, some were independent)
−Needed prompts for all steps

Note: Credit is given to Mandy McKee for this adaptation of her instructional program.

the goal of the program is to reduce a behavior, the ascending trend would be interpreted as regression, or deterioration.)

2. *Flat trends* have either no slope or a very slight upward or downward slope. When the behavior graphed is a skill or an adaptive behavior, flat trends indicate no learning or improvement.

3. *Descending trends* have a downward slope and indicate regression, or deterioration, when the behavior graphed is a skill or an adaptive behavior. (If the

FIGURE 5–8

Percentage of Class Activities Attended by Jacob During the School Day

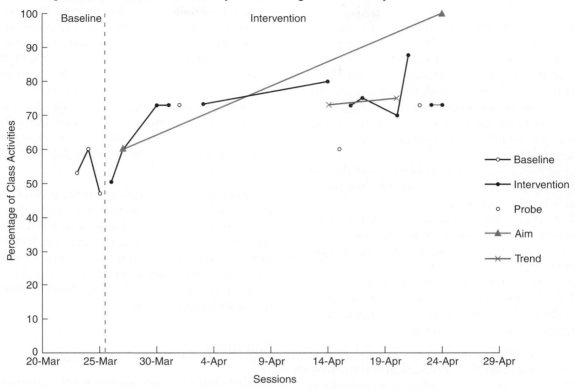

Note: Credit is given to Mandy McKee for this adaptation of her instructional program.

goal of the program is to reduce a behavior, the downward slope would be interpreted as indicating improvement.)

When the trend of graphed teaching data is not obvious or uniform, trend lines help teachers summarize and interpret the fluctuating, or variable, nature of performance (Tawney & Gast, 1984). Some researchers have defined an ascending slope as 30° or more in the positive direction and a descending slope as 30° or more in the negative direction (DeProspero & Cohen, 1979).

When the trend is obvious, there is no need to draw a trend line, but when a student's progress is below the aim line for three out of five consecutive data points and the trend is not obvious, a teacher should pencil in a trend line to define the trend. If the line indicates that the trend on a target skill is flat or descending (for skill-building programs), then the team should further analyze the data and other relevant information to decide whether specific program modifications are needed.

Jacob stayed above the aim line until spring break (April 4). When he returned, his performance varied, *but was below the aim line even after a week of teaching. Ms. Fuentes drew a trend line to help summarize his performance (see Figure 5-8).*

There are several ways to draw trend lines, including the "quickie split-middle trend line" (White & Haring, 1980), which can be drawn simply and clarifies the general direction of change in the data, as well as the relative rate of change (reflected in the slope). Although teachers may collect test (probe) data intermittently and add them to the same graph using differently coded lines or points, teaching or training data constitute the primary information used to make judgments about day-to-day progress (Browder, 1991; Farlow & Snell, 1994; Haring, Liberty, & White, 1980). Teachers should draw a trend line using the following six steps (see Figure 5-8):

1. Take the last 6 to 10 days of teaching data collected and draw a vertical line to divide the data in half.
2. Look at the first half of the data (the first three, four, or five data points) and locate the middle date. Draw a small vertical line through this data point.

- If an odd set of data points is considered (e.g., three or five), draw the line through the middle date.
- If an even set of data points is considered (e.g., four), just sketch a pencil line between the dates for the second and third data points.

3. Look at the middle performance level and draw a short horizontal line through this data point. The middle performance level is not the average of the performances for the data points in the set of three to five data points. It is simply the middle performance value.
   - For an odd number of data points, select the middle value (e.g., for 10%, 15%, and 12%, the middle performance value is 12%).
   - For an even number of data points, select a value halfway between the two middle data points (e.g., for 15%, 10%, 15%, and 11%, the middle value between 11 and 15 is 13%).
4. Extend the two lines until they intersect.
5. Repeat this process for the other half of the data.
6. Then draw a line connecting the two points of intersection from both halves of the data.

Once the trend line is drawn, visually judge whether the trend is ascending, flat, or descending. If the trend is flat or descending, teachers should hypothesize or determine why and make program modifications on the basis of the hypotheses or explanations. If the trend is ascending but not fast enough, teachers may (a) make changes in the program (e.g., modify the materials or prompts, change the reinforcer) to try to speed progress, or (b) adjust the aim line by lowering the criterion or moving the date further into the future. Alternately, teachers may do nothing to the program and look for other explanations for the student's reduced progress.

Jacob's trend line was drawn using 6 days of training data starting with April 3 and ending with April 20. Ms. Fuentes divided the data into two groups: the first three data points and the last three. For the first 3 days (April 3, 14, and 15: 73%, 80%, 60%, respectively), the middle date was April 14 and the middle value was 73%. For the last 3 days (April 16, 17, and 20: 73%, 75%, 70%, respectively), the middle date was April 17 and the middle value was 73%. She connected the two points that resulted by drawing a line. The trend was very slightly ascending, but practically flat. The team members discussed their options because Jacob had stopped making progress. They could lower the criterion from 100%, move the aim date to May, or improve the program. They decided to keep the criterion at 100% because this was a skill that he really needed. They also decided to move the aim date to the end of May, giving more time and a more gradually ascending aim line. Finally, they decided to improve the program in two ways: (a) As a way to help motivate Jacob, they added two other classmates to the program who also had problems following the schedule, and (b) they added high-fives to the reinforcement from each teacher following steps 1 through 3 and following Step 4 if completed correctly.

Teams may decide to use computer-generated graphs instead of hand-drawn ones. Graphs can be fairly easily drawn and data added using Microsoft Excel and the step-by-step guide of Carr and Burkholder (1998). In addition, trend lines and aim lines can be constructed, although a somewhat different version of the quickie split-middle trend line (White & Haring, 1980) is produced with this program.

Summary

Teachers must evaluate each student's progress in his or her school program. Frequent and meaningful data collection that is individualized allows teachers to effectively design, evaluate, and modify their instructional strategies. This chapter discusses quantitative measurement strategies, as well as outcome measures, that focus on an individual's quality of life. For measurement to be useful and meaningful, it must be reliable (accurate) and it must measure behaviors and skills that are considered by the individual and significant others to be socially valid; that is, the behaviors and skills measured must have a positive impact on the quality of the student's life. Measurement and evaluation strategies must be designed and implemented in ways that respect each student's privacy and participation in integrated and community-based environments.

Suggested Activities

1. Select one student in your class and examine the current measurement strategies used for each IEP objective.
   a. For each objective that includes a measurement strategy, consider whether that strategy is the

most appropriate one to use. Would a different strategy be more meaningful?

b. For each objective that does not include a measurement strategy, describe an appropriate and manageable strategy that could be used.

2. For this same student, design a graph for each instructional objective not currently displayed in graphic format.

References

Agran, M., Snow, K., & Swaner, J. (1999). Teacher perceptions of self-determination: Benefits, characteristics, strategies. *Education and Training in Mental Retardation and Developmental Disabilities, 34,* 291–301.

Alberto, P. A., & Schofield, P. (1979). An instructional interaction pattern for the severely handicapped. *Teaching Exceptional Children, 12,* 16–19.

Alberto, P. A., & Troutman, A. C. (2009). *Applied behavior analysis for teachers* (8th ed.). Upper Saddle River, NJ: Merrill/Pearson.

Baer, D. M., Wolf, M. M., & Risley, T. R. (1968). Some current dimensions of applied behavior analysis. *Journal of Applied Behavior Analysis, 1,* 91–97.

Baer, D. M., Wolf, M. M., & Risley, T. R. (1987). Some still-current dimensions of applied behavior analysis. *Journal of Applied Behavior Analysis, 20,* 313–327.

Bambara, L. M., & Koger, F. (1996). *Opportunities for daily choice-making* (AAMR Research to Practice Series: Innovations). Washington, DC: American Association on Mental Retardation.

Bannerman, D. J., Sheldon, J. B., Sherman, J. A., & Harchik, A. E. (1990). Balancing the right to habilitation with the right to personal liberties: The rights of people with developmental disabilities to eat too many doughnuts and take a nap. *Journal of Applied Behavior Analysis, 23,* 79–89.

Barton, E. E., Reichow, B., & Wolery, M. (2007). Guidelines for graphing data with Microsoft® PowerPoint®. *Journal of Early Intervention, 29,* 320–336.

Bellamy, G., Horner, R., & Inman, D. (1979). *Vocational habilitation of severely retarded adults: A direct service technology.* Baltimore: University Park Press.

Billingsley, F. F., Gallucci, C., Peck, C. A., Schwartz, I. S., & Staub, D. (1996). "But those kids can't even do math": An alternative conceptualization of outcomes for inclusive education. *Special Education Leadership Review, 3,* 43–55.

Billingsley, F. F., & Liberty, K. A. (1982). The use of time-based data in instructional programs for the severely handicapped. *Journal of the Association for the Severely Handicapped, 7,* 47–55.

Billingsley, F. F., White, O. R., & Munson, R. (1980). Procedural reliability: A rationale and an example. *Behavioral Assessment, 2,* 229–241.

Binnendyk, L., & Lucyshyn, J. M. (2009). A family-centered positive behavior support approach to the amelioration of food refusal behavior: An empirical case study. *Journal of Positive Behavior Interventions, 11,* 47–62.

Brady, N. C., & Bashinski, S. M. (2008). Increasing communication in children with concurrent vision and hearing loss. *Research and Practice for Persons with Severe Handicaps, 33,* 59–70.

Browder, D. M. (1991). *Assessment of individuals with severe disabilities: An applied behavior approach to life skills assessment* (2nd ed.). Baltimore: Paul H. Brookes.

Brown, F. (1991). Creative daily scheduling: A nonintrusive approach to challenging behaviors in community residences. *Journal of the Association for Persons with Severe Handicaps, 16,* 75–84.

Brown, F., Gothelf, C. R., Guess, D., & Lehr, D. (1998). Self-determination for individuals with the most severe disabilities: Moving beyond chimera. *Journal of the Association for Persons with Severe Handicaps, 23,* 17–26.

Brown, F., & Lehr, D. (1993). Making activities meaningful for students with severe multiple disabilities. *Teaching Exceptional Children, 25,* 12–16.

Carr, E. G. (2007). The expanding vision of positive behavior support: Research perspectives on happiness, helpfulness, hopefulness. *Journal of Positive Behavior Interventions, 9,* 3–14.

Carr, J. E., & Burkholder, E. O. (1998). Creating single-subject design graphs with Microsoft® Excel®. *Journal of Applied Behavior Analysis, 31,* 245–251.

Cooper, J. O., Heron, T. E., & Heward, W. L. (2007). *Applied behavior analysis* (2nd ed.). Upper Saddle River, NJ: Pearson Merrill Prentice Hall.

Cosbey, J. E., & Johnston, S. (2006). Using a single-switch voice output communication aid to increase social access for children with severe disabilities in inclusive classrooms. *Research and Practice for Persons with Severe Disabilities, 31,* 144–156.

Cox, A. L., Gast, D. L., Luscre, D., & Ayres, K. M. (2009). The effects of weighted vests on appropriate in-seat behaviors of elementary-age students with autism and severe to profound intellectual disabilities. *Focus on Autism and Other Developmental Disabilities, 24,* 17–26.

DiCarlo, C. F., & Vagianos, L. (2009). Using child preferences to increase play across interest centers in inclusive early childhood classrooms. *Young Exceptional Children, 12*(4), 31–39.

Delano, M., & Snell, M. E. (2006). The effects of social stories on the social engagement of children with autism. *Journal of Positive Behavior Interventions, 8,* 29–42.

DeProspero, A., & Cohen, S. (1979). Inconsistent visual analyses of intrasubject data. *Journal of Applied Behavior Analysis, 12,* 574–579.

Farlow, L. J., & Snell, M. E. (1994). *Making the most of student performance data* (AAMR Research to Practice Series: Innovations). Washington, DC: American Association on Mental Retardation.

Farlow, L. J., & Snell, M. E. (2005). Making the most of student performance data. In M. L. Wehmeyer & M. Agran (Eds.), *Evidence-based practices for teaching students with mental retardation and intellectual disabilities* (pp. 27–54). Upper Saddle River, NJ: Merrill/Pearson.

Fuchs, L. S., & Fuchs, D. (1986). Effects of systematic formative evaluation: A meta-analysis. *Exceptional Children, 53,* 199–208.

Gothelf, C. R., & Brown, F. (1998). Participation in the education process: Students with severe disabilities. In M. L. Wehmeyer & D. J. Sands (Eds.), *Making it happen: Student involvement in education planning, decision making, and instruction* (pp. 99-121). Baltimore: Paul H. Brookes.

Haring, N. G., Liberty, K. A., & White, O. R. (1980). Rules for data-based strategy decisions in instructional programs: Current research and instructional implications. In W. Sailor, B. Wilcox, & L. Brown (Eds.), *Methods of instruction for severely handicapped children* (pp. 159-192). Baltimore: Paul H. Brookes.

Haring, T. G., & Breen, C. (1989). Units of analysis of social interaction outcomes in supported education. *Journal of the Association for Persons with Severe Handicaps, 14,* 255-262.

Harvey, M. T., Baker, D. J., Horner, R. H., & Blackford, J. U. (2003). A brief report on the prevalence of sleep problems in individuals with mental retardation living in the community. *Journal of Positive Behavior Interventions, 5,* 195-200.

Hojnoski, R. L., Gischlar, K. L., & Missall, K. N. (2009). Improving child outcomes with data-based decision making: Graphing data. *Young Exceptional Children, 12*(4), 15-30.

Holburn, S. (2002). How science can evaluate and enhance person-centered planning. *Research and Practice for Persons with Severe Disabilities, 27,* 250-260.

Holvoet, J., Guess, D., Mulligan, M., & Brown, F. (1980). The individualized curriculum sequencing model (II): A teaching strategy for severely handicapped students. *Journal of the Association for the Severely Handicapped, 5,* 337-351.

Holvoet, J., O'Neil, C., Chazdon, L., Carr, D., & Warner, J. (1983). Hey, do we really have to take data? *Journal of the Association for the Severely Handicapped, 8,* 56-70.

Horner, R. J., Carr, E. G., Halle, J., McGee, G., Odom, S., & Wolery, M. (2005). The use of single-subject research to identify evidence-based practice in special education. *Exceptional Children, 71,* 165-179.

Janney, R., & Snell, M. E. (2004). *Modifying school work* (2nd ed). Baltimore: Paul H. Brookes.

Kazdin, A. E. (1976). Statistical analysis for single-case experimental designs. In M. Hersen & D. Barlow (Eds.), *Single-case experimental designs: Strategies for studying behavior change* (pp. 265-316). New York: Pergamon.

Kazdin, A. E. (1977). Assessing the clinical or applied importance of behavior change through social validation. *Behavior Modification, 1,* 427-452.

Kazdin, A. E. (1980). *Behavior modification in applied settings.* Homewood, IL: Dorsey Press.

Kennedy, C. H. (2005). *Single-case designs for educational research.* Boston: Pearson/Allyn and Bacon.

Kern, L., & Clarke, S. (2005). Antecedent and setting event interventions. In L. M. Bambara & L. Kern (Eds.), *Individualized support for students with problem behaviors: Designing positive behavior plans* (pp. 201-236). New York: Guilford Press.

Kerr, M. M., & Nelson, C. M. (2009). *Strategies for managing behavior problems in the classroom* (6th ed.). Upper Saddle River, NJ: Merrill/Pearson.

Knoster, T., & Kincaid, D. (2005). Long-term supports and ongoing evaluation. In L. M. Bambara & L. Kern (Eds.), *Individualized support for students with problem behaviors: Designing positive behavior plans* (pp. 303-333). New York: Guilford Press.

Lane, K. L., & Beebe-Frankenberger, M. (2004). *School-based interventions: The tools you need to succeed.* Boston: Pearson/Allyn & Bacon.

Maag, J. W. (2003). *Behavior management: From theoretical implications to practical applications* (2nd ed.). San Diego: Singular.

McDonnell, J. J., & O'Neill, R. (2003). A perspective on single/within subject research methods and "scientifically based research." *Research and Practice for Persons with Severe Disabilities, 28,* 138-142.

McGlashing-Johnson, J., Agran, M., Sitlington, P., Cavin, M., & Wehmeyer, J. (2003). Enhancing the job performance of youth with moderate to severe cognitive disabilities using the self-determined learning model of instruction. *Research and Practice for Persons with Severe Disabilities, 28,* 194-204.

Mechling, L. C., Gast, D. L., & Cronin, B. A. (2006). The effects of presenting high-preference items, paired with choice, via computer-based video programming on task completion of students with autism. *Focus on Autism and Other Developmental Disabilities, 21,* 7-13.

Mechling, L. C., & Stephens, E. (2009). Comparison of self-prompting of cooking skills via picture-based cookbooks and video recipes. *Education and Training in Developmental Disabilities, 44,* 218-236.

Meyer, L. H., & Evans, I. M. (1989). *Non-aversive intervention for behavior problems: A manual for home and community.* Baltimore: Paul H. Brookes.

Meyer, L. H., & Evans, I. M. (1993). Meaningful outcomes in behavioral intervention: Evaluating positive approaches to the remediation of challenging behaviors. In J. Reichle & D. P. Wacker (Eds.), *Communicative alternatives to challenging behavior: Integrating functional assessment and intervention strategies* (pp. 407-428). Baltimore: Paul H. Brookes.

Meyer, L. H., & Janney, R. (1989). User-friendly measures of meaningful outcomes: Evaluating behavior interventions. *Journal of the Association for Persons with Severe Handicaps, 14,* 263-270.

Miltenberger, R. (2008). *Behavior modification: Principles and procedures* (4th ed.). Pacific Grove, CA: Brooks/Cole.

National Autism Center. (2009). *National standards project: Findings and conclusions.* Randolph, MA: Author.

Odom, S. L., Brantlinger, E., Gersten, R., Horner, R. H., Thompson, B., & Harris, K. (2005). Research in special education: Scientific methods and evidence-based practices. *Exceptional Children, 71,* 137-148.

Oliva, C. M., Brown, F., & Gilles, D. (2010). *Contingent electric shock for challenging behavior: An exploration of external validity.* Manuscript submitted for publication.

Reinhartsen, D. B., Garfinkle, A. N., & Wolery, M. (2002). Engagement with toys in two-year-old children with autism: Teacher selection versus child choice. *Research and Practice for Persons with Severe Disabilities, 27,* 175-187.

Risley, T. R. (1970). Behavior modification: An experimental-therapeutic endeavor. In L. A. Hamerlynck, P. O. Davidson, & L. E. Acker (Eds.), *Behavior modification and ideal health services* (pp. 103-127). Calgary, Alberta, Canada: University of Calgary Press.

Ryndak, D. L., Clark, D., Conroy, M., & Stuart, C. H. (2001). Preparing teachers to meet the needs of students with severe disabilities: Program configuration and expertise. *Journal of the Association for Persons with Severe Handicaps, 26,* 96-105.

Schloss, P. J., & Smith, M. A. (1998). *Applied behavior analysis in the classroom* (2nd ed.). Boston: Allyn & Bacon.

Smith, M. D. (1990). *Autism and life in the community: Successful interventions for behavioral challenges.* Baltimore: Paul H. Brookes.

Snell, M. E. (2003). Applying research to practice: The more pervasive problem? *Research and Practice for Persons with Severe Disabilities, 28,* 143-147.

Snell, M. E., & Lloyd, B. H. (1991). A study of the effects of trend variability, frequency, and form of data on teachers' judgments about progress and their decisions about program change. *Research in Developmental Disabilities, 12,* 41-61.

Spooner, F., & Brown, F. (in press). Educating students with significant cognitive disabilities: Historical overview and future projections. In J. M. Kauffman & D. P. Hallahan (Eds.), *Handbook of special education.* New York: Routledge.

Storey, K. (1997). Quality of life issues in social skills assessment of persons with disabilities. *Education and Training in Mental Retardation and Developmental Disabilities, 32,* 197-200.

Tankersley, M., Harjusola-Webb, S., & Landrum, T. J. (2008). Using single-subject research to establish the evidence base of special education. *Intervention in School and Clinic, 44,* 83-90.

Tawney, J., & Gast, D. (1984). *Single subject research in special education.* New York: Merrill/Macmillan.

Test, D. W., & Spooner, F. (1996). *Community-based instructional support* (AAMR Research to Practice Series: Innovations). Washington, DC: American Association on Mental Retardation.

Utley, B. L., Zigmond, N., & Strain, P. S. (1987). How various forms of data affect teacher analysis of student performance. *Exceptional Children, 53,* 411-422.

Voeltz, L. H., & Evans, I. M. (1983). Educational validity: Procedures to evaluate outcomes in programs for severely handicapped learners. *Journal of the Association for the Severely Handicapped, 8,* 3-15.

Walther-Thomas, C., Korinek, L., McLaughlin, V. L., & Williams, F. T. (2000). *Collaboration for inclusive education: Developing successful programs.* Boston: Allyn & Bacon.

Wang, P., & Spillane, A. (2009). Evidence-based social skills interventions for children with autism: A meta-analysis. *Education and Training in Developmental Disabilities, 44,* 318-342.

Wehmeyer, M. L., & Schwartz, M. (1997). Self-determination and positive adult outcomes: A follow-up study of youth with mental retardation or learning disabilities. *Exceptional Children, 63,* 245-255.

Whalon, K., & Hanline, M. F. (2008). Effects of a reciprocal questioning intervention on the question generation and responding of children with autism spectrum disorder. *Education and Training in Developmental Disabilities, 43,* 367-387.

White, O. R. (1986). Precision teaching—precision learning. *Exceptional Children, 53,* 522-534.

White, O. R., & Haring, N. G. (1980). *Exceptional teaching* (2nd ed.). New York: Merrill/Macmillan.

Wolf, M. M. (1978). Social validity: The case for subjective measurement or how applied behavior analysis is finding its heart. *Journal of Applied Behavior Analysis, 11,* 203-214.

Zirpoli, T. J., & Melloy, K. J. (2008). *Behavior management applications for teachers* (5th ed.). Upper Saddle River, NJ: Merrill/Pearson.

6

Designing and Implementing Instruction for Inclusive Classes

Rachel E. Janney
Martha E. Snell

The focus of this chapter is the design and implementation of instruction to teach the goals targeted by students' individualized educational program (IEP) teams. Teaching teams must select and combine ideas that not only are consistent with current knowledge, but also are practical and efficient. We will describe a model whereby teams can plan instruction for students with severe disabilities and apply those plans in inclusive classrooms.

The material in this chapter is founded on several assumptions and beliefs about the nature of the task being undertaken and what it takes to do it right. Several of these assumptions and beliefs are set forth here, while others appear throughout the chapter. One assumption is that designing a comprehensive, state-of-the-art educational program for a student with severe disabilities requires a team to plan several different types of learning activities, as well as the services and supports required to meet the student's physical, health, behavioral, and other needs. A student's IEP goals may include the areas of academics, functional skills, and developmental skills (e.g., social-behavioral, communication, motor skills). The learning activities designed to teach these goals will involve different

professionals and use a variety of student groupings, learning environments, instructional formats, methods, and materials (see Chapter 5). Thus, team-developed plans may include (a) task analytic teaching guides, (b) lesson plans for direct teaching of targeted academic or developmental skills, (c) plans for how class academic tasks will be adapted for the student, and (d) less structured guidelines for supporting the student's incidental learning. In addition, planning must address other supports—physical, social, and access supports (see Chapter 1)—that are needed in order for the student to participate in nonacademic activities (e.g., lunch, assemblies, field days), classroom routines (roll call, lunchtime preparation), and organizational procedures (e.g., how and when to turn in homework and class work, when to sharpen pencils). A second assumption is that the numerous decisions that teams must make to create and implement these teaching plans should be explicit, founded on sound rationales, and made by team consensus.

One key belief about the task of designing instruction is the *principle of partial participation,* which states that even if full participation in a given activity is not a realistic goal for a student, this does not mean that a student cannot be actively and meaningfully involved (Baumgart et al., 1982). In order for students with severe disabilities to be meaningfully involved in all school and classroom activities, teachers and support personnel must first agree that the principle of partial participation is a valid guideline for their work and, second, have systems for putting this principle into practice. A second key belief, captured by the words *only as specialized as necessary,* is that adaptations must be as nonintrusive as possible for the student and as user-friendly as possible for the teaching team. That is, adaptations should differ as little as possible from typical programming and, as is inherent in the *principle of parsimony* (Chapter 4; Etzel & LeBlanc, 1979), teams should select the simplest yet effective approach.

The Pyramid of Support/ Response-to-Intervention Logic

As represented in Figure 6–1, the foundation or base of support for inclusive education consists of an inclusive culture in the school and classroom. Above this base is a second level of support: the use of effective, accommodating curricular and instructional practices in the classroom put into place by collaborative teams. This dual foundation minimizes the need for individualized adaptations. That is, the combination of a school and classroom culture that is established with a sense of community and that emphasizes the value of diversity, *plus* the use of curriculum approaches and instructional strategies that are known to be effective in enhancing achievement for a wide range of students, can greatly ease the task of developing adaptations for individual

FIGURE 6–1
The Pyramid of Support

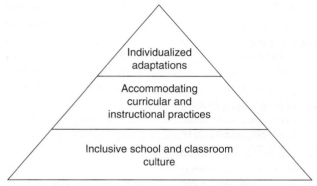

Adapted from *Teachers' guides to inclusive practices: Modifying schoolwork* (2nd ed.), by R. Janney and M. E. Snell, 2004, Baltimore: Paul H. Brookes. Reprinted with permission.

students. The Individuals with Disabilities Education Act (IDEA) incorporates a similar logic in its response-to-intervention (RTI) requirements. Response-to-intervention specifies that before students are admitted into special education, less specialized interventions must be implemented in an effort to remediate learning and behavior problems. In other words, universal or whole-school interventions and group interventions should be applied before individualized interventions.

The model for adapting schoolwork that is described in this chapter presupposes the existence of the base of support created by the existence of an inclusive culture in the school and classroom, and the use of effective, accommodating teaching practices in the classroom. We understand that inclusive practices are not fully in place in all schools. Indeed, many—if not most—schools are on a developmental trajectory toward the implementation of inclusive practices (Williamson, McLeaskey, Hoppey, & Rentz, 2006), but these schools may be lacking some of the assumptions, values and beliefs, collaborative teaming structures, instructional practices, and other elements that make inclusive education work. We would not want a school to wait until its culture and all of its teaching practices are accommodating for all students before providing inclusive experiences to individual students with disabilities within that school. However, when a school does not have inclusive practices in operation, that school needs to create an action plan aimed at improving *all* of the necessary elements for inclusive education, not only the element that encompasses effective ways to modify schoolwork for diverse learners (see Janney & Snell, 2004, for a Team Survey of Inclusive Practices that can aid schools in identifying the elements of inclusive education that need further development in their own schools).

The principles of instructional design and delivery presented in this chapter *do not* apply only to inclusive schools. Even in settings that are not inclusive (e.g., self-contained special education classrooms or resource rooms), students' special education programming should be only as specialized as necessary. This means that students' individualized learning goals will stem from or be aligned with the general education curriculum framework, materials will be age appropriate, and instructional strategies will be adapted only enough to enable success. No matter what the setting, collaborating teams of teachers, specialists, and other relevant personnel should design and deliver systematic instruction and then collect and analyze progress data according to the techniques and principles described in this chapter. Some of the team planning and communication strategies that we describe and illustrate are more essential in inclusive settings; however, the instructional planning and progress monitoring strategies apply in any educational setting that serves students with severe disabilities.

Collaborative Teaming for Ongoing, Day-to-Day Planning and Delivery of Instruction

The ways that teachers plan and deliver instruction are related, in part, to the type of program and the age/grade structure in a school. Inclusive schools use a variety of program types (such as grade-level teams and instructional departments), which influence staffing arrangements. Those arrangements are seldom static, but often change from one year to the next. What these staffing arrangements have in common is that administrators and teachers have devised some way to unify special and general education teachers and support staff into integrated educational teams. It is important to assign special education teachers to students located in a *narrower band of grades* and in *one or a few school settings*. Although this approach will result in a caseload that reflects a mix of students with disabilities categories, this approach also will avoid the impossible situation of special educators being allocated caseloads of students for whom they cannot logistically provide instruction or consultation. For example, if a special education teacher is assigned 12 students with severe disabilities who are enrolled in 12 different classrooms, this means that he or she must team with 12 different teachers at multiple grade levels and possibly in multiple schools. The corresponding scenario from the classroom teacher's perspective is that he or she must team with multiple special educators, each of whom is an IEP manager for one or more students in the classroom. Instead, special education teachers assigned to students in a narrower band of grades and in one or a few schools can be linked to integrated teams as follows:

- For elementary schools: Grade-level teams or clusters of grade levels, in which special education teachers team with the classroom teachers for that grade level or cluster

- For middle schools: Interdepartmental teams, houses, pod, or families in which special education teachers are members of specific teams
- For high schools: Grade-level plus subject area(s) teams that include a special education teacher

Regardless of the specific staffing configuration in a school, the processes described in this chapter involve a number of personnel, with some personnel participating more in planning and some participating more in implementing instruction. We do not assume that special educators will undertake full-time co-teaching with general educators in the classroom, but we do assume (a) collaborative teaming with one or more general education teachers who are on the IEP team (typically, with one grade-level classroom teacher for elementary school, but with more for middle and high school), (b) a special education teacher who serves as an IEP manager and provides some instruction to the student, and the likelihood of (c) some special education aide support and some involvement by related service specialists.

Team members need to adopt three practices in order to work together effectively and to meet students' needs in inclusive settings (Doyle, 2008; Snell & Janney, 2005):

- *Clear roles and responsibilities:* Team members must delineate who has primary responsibility for the student's instruction in each goal area, who adapts materials, who sends notes home, and so on. These and other responsibilities should be distributed among team members and clearly articulated to avoid gaps and overlaps in services and supports. Using a Team Roles and Responsibilities form such as the one shown in Figure 6–2 can facilitate the collaborative teaming process.
- *Agreed-upon systems and strategies for making and communicating decisions about instruction and supports:* These systems are designed to (a) document decisions, (b) facilitate educational integrity—teachers must plan instruction even if an instructional aide delivers it, and (c) make teaming an expected part of the school culture (i.e., "This is how we do it here").
- *Team meeting skills:* Necessary skills include assigning leadership roles and rotating them (e.g., facilitator, recorder, timekeeper), writing and following ground rules, using meeting agendas, using problem-solving strategies to make decisions, recording decisions, taking time to process, and celebrating successes.

FIGURE 6–2

Team Roles and Responsibilities Form for Jacob

Team Roles and Responsibilities Form

Student: Jacob   **Date:** September 2009

Teaching and Support Team Members:

Bowers   **Classroom Teacher**   Conners   **Instructional Assistant**

Fuentes **Special Education Teacher**   Ms. Johnson   **Parent**

Key: x = Primary responsibility
         input = Input into implementation and/or decision making

Roles and Responsibilities	Who Is Responsible?			
	Classroom teacher	Special education teacher	Instructional aide	Parent
Developing lesson and unit plans	x	input		
Developing Individualized Adaptations Plan	input	x	input	input
Providing instruction (with accommodations and modifications):	x	x	input	
• Communication, social, behavior	input	x	input	input
• Functional skills and school participation	input	x	input	input
• Academics: Basic skills	input	x	input	input
• Academics: Content areas	x	input	input	input
Adapting instructional materials	x (reading) input (other subjects)	input (reading) x (other subjects)	input	
Assigning grades/report card	x	input	input	
Monitoring progress on IEP goals	input	x (reports, IEP)	input (data log)	
Assigning duties to and supervising instructional aides	x (daily)	x (long term)		
Training instructional aides	input	x		
Scheduling/facilitating team meetings: a. IEP team b. Core instructional team	a. input b. x	a. x b. input		
Daily communication with parents	x	input	input	
Communication/collaboration with related services	input	x (service coordinator)	input (notes, logs)	
Facilitating peer relationships and supports	x (lunch bunch)	x (peer planning)	Input	

Source: Adapted from *Teachers' guides to inclusive practices: Modifying schoolwork* (2nd ed.), by R. Janney and M. E. Snell, 2004, Baltimore: Paul H. Brookes. Reprinted with permission.

School systems differ in their preferred and/or required ways of specifying services on the "free, appropriate public education" (FAPE) section of the IEP, and your teams should, of course, follow those guidelines. However, as an instructional team, it will be important to distinguish among the various special education service delivery methods that are used in an inclusive context. In a resource or self-contained program model, special education teachers and related service providers deliver most of a student's special education services directly to the student. In an inclusive program model, a wider array of methods may be used to deliver those services so that a student may receive full-time special education services, but also be fully included in general education. These methods include:

- *Special education instruction,* which is a direct service delivered by a special education teacher. Such instruction may be delivered using various instructional arrangements, including collaborative-teaching, small-group instruction, or individual instruction. (Note that special education instruction does not require or infer that the instruction is "pull-out." Special education is a "portable" service, not a place!)
- *Special education consultation,* which is an indirect service, provided by a special educator to other team members for purposes such as co-planning, providing information, locating or preparing adapted materials, collecting and analyzing data, and training or coaching paraprofessionals.
- *Special education instructional aide support,* which is a direct service from a paraprofessional and is planned and monitored by a special educator.
- *Related services,* which may include services from a speech-language pathologist (SLP), occupational therapist (OT), and physical therapist (PT). These services may be delivered via *direct service* to the student or via *consultation with other team members.* The direct service may be pull in or pull out.

It is important to remember that *special education* does not mean instruction delivered by a special education teacher; instead, it is defined in the Individuals with Disabilities Education Act Amendments of 2004 as "specially designed instruction . . . to meet the unique needs of a child with a disability." Although *co-teaching* by a general education and a special education teacher is one way to ensure that students receive full-time special education within a regular class, the reality is that many, if not most, inclusive classrooms are not co-taught all day. Instead, instructional teams must use problem solving to determine the parts of students'

special education and related services that can be delivered effectively through indirect services (consultation), instructional aide support, and/or the use of accommodations that don't require special personnel (Snell & Janney, 2000). Students with severe disabilities often receive their special education services through a combination of methods. Marc, Jacob, and Christine, the case students in Chapters 3–6, all qualify for full-time special education services; however, on the basis of their varying needs and characteristics and the learning priorities targeted by their teams, their IEPs reflect differing combinations of service delivery methods (see Table 6–1).

A Model for Making Individualized Adaptations

Often, students with severe disabilities require planned adaptations to participate meaningfully in classroom activities and lessons with their peers in general education. Teacher educators and researchers have conceptualized several models or frameworks that describe the process of making these individualized adaptations. Here, we briefly summarize a comprehensive model that builds on other adaptative approaches (e.g., Giangreco, Cloninger, & Iverson, 1998; Jorgensen, 1998; Sailor, Gee, & Karasoff, 2000; Udvari-Solner, 1995; Villa & Thousand, 2000) and suits students with many types of special education needs who are members of general education classes (Janney & Snell, 2004). Using such a model is particularly useful because it provides a *process,* including a series of guidelines and decision-making rules that can be used to address a range of student needs. Also, having a model gives teams a *common language* to use when discussing their work and the tasks that are required of them.

Criteria for Making Individualized Adaptations

When teams decide that a student needs individualized adaptations to the typical educational program, those adaptations should be made systematically and for a purpose. Ideally, the most effective adaptations meet two important criteria: (a) they facilitate both social and instructional participation in class activities, and (b) they are only as specialized as necessary. The criterion of both *social and instructional participation* highlights the belief that although one goal of inclusive education is for all students with disabilities to belong socially to their schools and classroom groups,

TABLE 6–1
Special Education and Related Services for Jacob, Marc, and Christine

| Student | Special Education and Related Services | | | |
	Special Education Instruction	Special Education Consultation	Special Education Aide Support	Related Services
Marc (age 5), kindergarten	• 4 hours x 5 days (pull out) • 30 minutes x 5 days for morning activities (pull-in direct instruction)	20 minutes x 2 days for progress monitoring, record keeping, developing adaptations, aide training and supervision, teacher consultation	2 hours x 5 days for morning circle, some table work, recess, P.E., specialties, school/class routines, self-care	Speech-Language therapy: 20 minutes x 2 days (pull-in resource room) Occupational therapy: 20 minutes x 2 days (pull-in P.E., resource room) Autism specialist: consult alternate weeks
Jacob (age 9), fourth grade	• 30 minutes x 5 days for language arts (co-teaching 2 days, pull-out direct instruction 3 days) • 30 minutes x 5 days for social-behavioral skills (pull-in co-teaching)	15 minutes x 5 days for progress monitoring, record keeping, developing adaptations, aide training and supervision, teacher consultation	5¼ hours x 5 days for math, content areas, specialties, recess, school/class routines, self-help	• Speech-Language therapy: 20 minutes x 1 day (pull-in direct service, within small-group activities) • Occupational therapy: consult once per marking period
Christine (age 20), post–high school program at community college	• 30 minutes x 5 days for drama club, functional academics for work and daily routines (co-teaching 2 days, pull-out direct instruction 3 days) • 30 minutes x 5 days for work-site skills (pull-in direct instruction)	30 minutes x 5 days for progress monitoring, record keeping, developing adaptations, aide training and supervision, teacher consultation, and AAC and adaptive equipment maintenance	5½ hours x 5 days at work site, drama club, Best Buddy activities, lunch, self-help, daily routines	• Physical therapy: every 4 weeks checks her equipment; consults with work site weekly • Occupational therapy: weekly consult • Speech-Language therapy: weekly consult on communication device

the achievement of academic and functional competence should not be sacrificed. When students with significant disabilities are included in general education classrooms, neither instructional nor social participation should be forfeited, although teams will, at times, be challenged to negotiate the tension between the two. It is inadequate to merely be present for "socialization" or for "exposure to the general curriculum," or to participate by moving through the activity; students should be actively involved and making meaningful progress (Carter, Hughes, Guth, & Copeland, 2005).

The *only-as-specialized-as-necessary* criterion underscores the need to keep adaptations nonintrusive for the student and user-friendly for the teaching team. In applying the only-as-specialized-as-necessary criterion, the goal is to recognize that no one wants to be singled out for extra assistance or adapted treatment all of the time, nor should receiving such treatment when necessary deprive a person of opportunities to engage in typical activities and ordinary relationships.

Furthermore, adaptations that are overly technical or specialized may not suit the context; may not be implemented; and, therefore, may do little to aid students in achieving their educational goals.

*When **Marc** completes sound–letter matching worksheet activities in kindergarten, he uses peel-off labels for the letters instead of writing the letters with a pencil, something he still has difficulty with. This simple adaptation enabled Marc to participate more actively than when his teacher or instructional aide wrote the letters for him or physically assisted him through writing the letters.*

***Jacob** cannot write a complete paragraph to describe what he learned on the field trip to the science museum, but he can fill in words and phrases to complete sentence stems such as "The most interesting thing that I learned at the science museum was _____" on a writing "frame" created by his special education teacher for such activities. Jacob's* *team felt that using the writing frame resulted in more instructional participation than would otherwise occur with options such as having him dictate his paragraph to a teacher or a peer who acts as a scribe; in addition, the writing frame was easy for Jacob's special education teacher to create, and enabled Jacob to participate with his peers in discussing the field trip.*

Christine*'s job in the library is to oversee students as they scan their books. Her speech pathologist and job coach have devised two small switches that allow her to quickly direct students, depending on whether the book scanner beeps successfully ("Thanks, enjoy the book") or not ("Oops, you need try again"). Christine's DynaVox™ device, while an effective communication device for most other situations, slowed her down in giving these frequently used messages.*

Types of Adaptations: Curricular, Instructional, and Alternative

Figure 6–3 represents a model for making individualized adaptations. Before we describe the model, a note about terminology is in order. In this chapter, we use the term *adaptations* as an overarching term that en-

compasses both accommodations and modifications. *Accommodations* are adjustments to the school program that do not substantially change the curriculum level or performance criteria; they enable a student to access curriculum content or to demonstrate learning without changing curriculum goals (e.g., adapted computer mouse, extra time on a test, desk close to the board). *Modifications,* however, alter curriculum goals and performance criteria (e.g., Jacob will show his understanding of several primary concepts from the science unit on weather by matching pictures with simplified terms and definitions, while classmates must explain them using unit terminology). Students with severe disabilities typically have numerous IEP accommodations and modifications that address support needs related to the instructional program. Students also have other support needs related to accessing and benefitting from educational opportunities, such as assistive technology, assistance with physical management and self-care, behavioral supports and interventions, and related services (see Chapters 7–9), but this chapter focuses primarily on support needs related to the instructional program.

Next we describe three types of adaptations: curricular, instructional, and alternative. Meeting the

FIGURE 6–3

A Model for Making Individualized Adaptations

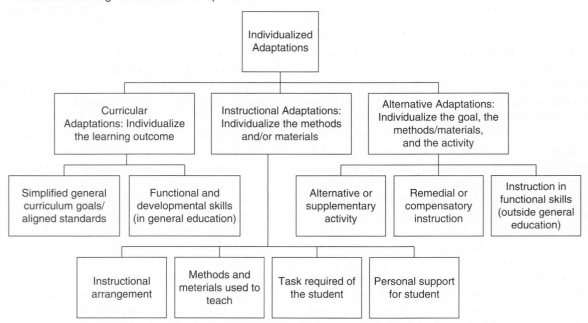

Source: Adapted from *Teachers' guides to inclusive practices: Modifying schoolwork,* by R. Janney and M. E. Snell, 2000, Baltimore: Paul H. Brookes. Reprinted with permission.

criteria of only-as-specialized-as-necessary and social-and-instructional participation is aided by differentiating among these three types of adaptations.

Curricular Adaptations: Individualize the Learning Goal

The term *curriculum* refers to *what* is taught: the knowledge, skills, and processes that are the instructional goals and targeted learning outcomes for students. For students with severe disabilities, the curriculum is often modified. The core general curriculum can be adapted in two ways: (a) by simplifying it—reducing the difficulty or number of learning goals—and (b) by altering the curriculum to incorporate functional learning priorities that are relevant to students' everyday lives:

1. *Simplified curriculum goals* are academic learning targets that are drawn from the general curriculum but are reduced in complexity or number. Simplified academic goals may be chosen from several sources, depending on a number of variables, including the state's approach to delineating general education learning standards and the standards used in alternate assessments, and the school system's curriculum philosophy. In addition to meeting state requirements for completing alternate assessments, academic goals for students with severe disabilities should align with their classmates' goals, be useful now and in the future, and have high acquisition probability. (Chapter 13 elaborates more on the teaching of academic skills.)
2. *Alternative curriculum goals* emphasize the *functional skills* that will enable students to accomplish the activities of daily life that are typical for their age, gender, and culture. Alternative curriculum

goals target age-appropriate activities in five domains: (a) school, (b) domestic (or home living) and self-help, (c) vocational, (d) general community use, and (e) recreational. Alternative goals also include the motor, social, and communication skills required to accomplish those targeted functional activities. In addition, problem-solving, self-management, and social interaction skills that are not functional in the strictest sense of the word, but are necessary for interacting successfully with other people, must be taught if students are to become contributing members of their families, schools, and communities (Ford, Davern, & Schnorr, 2001).

Table 6–2 gives illustrations of these two subtypes of curricular adaptations for Marc, Jacob, and Christine. *How are appropriate curricular adaptations chosen?* The learning goals that a team targets for a student with severe disabilities comprise an individualized set of these *simplified* and *alternative curriculum goals* (meaning functional routines and social, communication, and motor skills). Educators continue to debate the extent to which the education of students with severe disabilities should emphasize simplified academic skills or alternative functional skills from the general curriculum (Clayton, Burdge, & Kleinert, 2001; Ward, Van De Mark, & Ryndak, 2006). We suggest that students' IEP teams should gather input from parents, teachers, and students to determine an individualized balance between academic and functional skills, or a "blended curriculum."

It is important to understand that students' learning goals should not bear an across-the-board designation as "adapted/modified," nor should students be placed in a "functional" or "alternative" curricular track. Instead, a student's learning goals in certain subject areas may

TABLE 6–2
Subtypes and Illustrations of Curricular Adaptations

Subtypes of Curricular Adaptations	Illustrations for Three Students		
	Marc (Kindergarten)	**Jacob (Fourth Grade)**	**Christine (Post–Secondary School)**
Simplified Academic Skills	Counts objects 1–10	Reads/writes/spells high-frequency and functional words (increase by 100 words)	Selects her name from others regardless of fonts and sizes
Alternative (Functional and Developmental) Skills	Uses gestures and words, augmented by picture system, to express needs, feelings, make choices, yes/no	Follows class procedures from classroom teachers' cues (organization, materials, transitions, and so on)	Uses work check-in and check-out system at three work sites (i.e., store, library, veterinary office)

be adapted by simplifying the general education goal, while, in other subject areas or domains, the goals may be made more functional. The balance between academic and functional skills in a student's IEP changes over time and is likely to tilt toward the functional side as a student grows older.

A case also can be made for including curriculum content that is merely culturally relevant and/or personally interesting. In other words, a well-rounded educational program will include **need-to-know** as well as **nice-to-know** learning goals. Giangreco and his colleagues (1998) stress the need to balance "depth of curriculum" (the essential learning priorities that should be mastered) with "breadth of curriculum" (the goals that enhance belonging and participation with peers and the school community). Ford and colleagues (2001) assert that curricular relevance can be maintained by taking two steps. First, teams should target high-priority learning outcomes from the *foundational skills* that are needed to "successfully navigate the tasks of daily living, problem solving, and contributing to society" (p. 215). Second, these priorities are taught throughout the day, within the rich and varied activities available in inclusive classrooms.

Although the perception persists among some that students with modified curricular goals cannot be educated effectively in general classes, both the IDEA and evidence gleaned from educational research contradict this notion. The IDEA states that "a child is not removed from education in age-appropriate regular classrooms solely because of needed modifications in the general curriculum" (34 CFR 300.116). Researchers have demonstrated that students with severe disabilities can accomplish individualized learning goals within general education contexts (e.g., Hunt, Soto, Maier, & Doering, 2003; Hunt, Soto, Maier, Muler, & Goetz, 2002; Johnson, McDonnell, Holzwarth, & Hunter, 2004; McDonnell, Mathot-Buckner, Thorson, & Fister, 2001). Students should not to be identified or tracked by their curriculum goals. Instead, members of the instructional team should know what students' priority goals or objectives are for each learning activity. Relevant members of the instructional team need to understand whether a lesson will use (a) *multilevel instruction*—students' learning goals are all from the same subject area, but vary in difficulty, or (b) *curriculum overlapping*—students are learning together in shared activities, but a student with a disability has goals that are drawn from a different subject area or domain (see Chapter 1).

Instructional Adaptations: Individualize the Methods and/or Materials

The term *instruction* refers to *how* the student is taught (i.e., the teaching *methods*). Teaching methods include, for example, the instructional arrangements, the methods and materials used to convey the content, and the ways that students practice what they are learning and demonstrate progress. Some teaching methods and strategies are known to be effective for most learners. Indeed, the premise of our approach to teaching in inclusive classrooms is that instructional planning should begin by considering the instructional methods that will encompass the similarities across all students instead of first planning for students without IEPs and then adapting for individual students. The principle of *universal design* for learning (Rose & Meyer, 2002), along with the response-to-intervention logic incorporated into the IDEA suggest that evidence-based teaching practices be utilized on a class-wide basis instead of limiting the focus to making adaptations or creating interventions for specific students.

Even when universal design is used, teachers often must alter aspects of their teaching methods and materials to enable individual students with severe disabilities to participate fully and to benefit from typical lessons. The intrusiveness of an adaptation sometimes depends on the particular student and the situation, but, *in general, adapting what the teacher does tends to be less intrusive than adapting what the student does.* Listed next, in order from least to most intrusive, are four aspects of instruction that can be adapted to enable students with disabilities to participate fully and to benefit from classroom lessons:

1. *The instructional arrangement* (i.e., the grouping of teachers and students)
   - use peer partners;
   - while classmates work in groups of 4–6, place a targeted student in a group of 3; and
   - group a targeted student with particular peers who know him or her well, share similar interests, or have complementary learning strengths and needs.
2. *The methods and materials used to convey the lesson content to the students*
   - use more visuals—maps, pictures, or drawings;
   - use concept maps and other nonlinguistic representations (cause–effect, compare–contrast, hierarchy);
   - use models, demonstrations, simulations, and role plays;

- use concrete materials prior to visual representations or symbolic representations;
- check for understanding more frequently, using methods that require active responses;
- provide differentiated reading material;
- provide large-print books and enlarged written materials; and
- add pictures or symbols to text.

3. *The task required of the student*
   - provides written or pictorial task steps;
   - uses the same materials but completes fewer items (e.g., on a math worksheet, does only half of the page);
   - uses the same materials but in a different way (e.g., on a math worksheet, circles numerals named by the teacher instead of completing math problems);
   - adapts reading demands—listens or watches DVDs instead of reading; and
   - adapts writing demands—completes story frames, draws pictures, or fills in the blanks instead of writing sentences/paragraphs; dictates to a scribe and then types on a computer.

4. *The personal assistance provided to the student*
   - provides additional prompts to prevent errors;
   - gives immediate feedback and encouragement; and
   - completes some of the task steps.

Table 6–3 provides examples of how these four aspects of instruction were adapted for Jacob.

The topic of *personal assistance* warrants additional discussion. Modifying instructional programming by adding increased *adult* support is an adaptation that should be considered with great care. Research has shown that adult proximity can interfere with the development of social relationships and peer supports (Giangreco, Edelman, Luiselli, & MacFarland, 1997; Janney & Snell, 1996). Recent research on peer support in general education classrooms has demonstrated that students with moderate to severe intellectual disabilities experience beneficial effects such as increased academic engagement and peer interactions. Peer support also was shown to have promoted better outcomes in engagement and interactions than did adult support (Carter, Sisco, Melekogu, & Kurkowski, 2007).

TABLE 6–3

Subtypes and Illustrations of Instructional Adaptations from Least to Most Intrusive

Subtypes of Instructional Adaptations	Illustrations for Jacob
Change the instructional arrangement	• During guided reading, while most students work in groups of five or six, Jacob is placed in a group with just two other students who read at a similar level.
Change the teaching methods and materials used to convey content to the students	• While Jacob's fourth-grade teacher explains erosion, the special educator completes a concept map on the Smart board; Jacob has a copy of the completed concept map at his desk. • For guided reading, Jacob and his classmates read leveled readers—four different books on the same topic, each suited to a specific group's reading level. • Colored highlighting tape is used on Jacob's science and social studies textbooks: topic sentences are red, targeted vocabulary terms are yellow, and definitions are blue.
Change the task required of the student by making it easier, reducing the amount, adapting the format	• When the class does a science investigation, Jacob's fourth-grade teacher lists the steps to follow on the Smart board; she prints a copy of the steps for Jacob so that he has them nearby. • Jacob uses a story frame for book summaries; the frame provides spaces in which to fill in the title, the author's name, the characters, the setting, and so on. Jacob draws a picture of the outcome of the story. • Jacob's classmates have 10, 12, or 15 spelling words per week; Jacob is assigned 5 high-frequency words or words with a particular spelling pattern.
Change the level of personal assistance provided to the student—either from peers or from adults	• During science projects, an adult prompts Jacob to watch his classmates and do what they are doing. • When an activity requires cutting intricate or small shapes, a peer or an adult offers to do the cutting for Jacob. • All adults working with Jacob give frequent thumbs-ups, "high fives," and verbal encouragement when Jacob is participating and following rules.

We offer the following guidelines regarding individualized personal assistance from an adult:

- Keep personal assistance only as specialized as necessary. That is, lend assistance during specific activities or task steps instead of at all times of day, for each and every activity. A student may need extensive adult support to use the restroom or to complete a writing task, yet be able to participate in shared stories or a science learning center with peer support and indirect adult supervision, or perhaps independently. Many students need extra help to get organized and begin an activity, but then the adult can withdraw that assistance once the student is actively engaged. Often, strategies can be developed that lessen the dependence on adults to initiate activities, such as the use of picture cues or teaching the student to observe natural cues in the environment. Like other adaptations, personal assistance should be gradually lessened over time.
- Make sure that personal assistance does not interfere with social and instructional participation. Ensure that adults facilitate and prompt, but do not do things for the student. Adults who provide one-to-one support should take care to reference natural cues and corrections (e.g., the adult should refer the student to the classroom teacher's instructions and feedback instead of repeating the teacher's instructions), and lessen their prompts.
- Teach peers how to assist in natural ways. Provide informal lessons for peers on how to interact respectfully, help without doing things for the targeted student, offer choices, use communication systems, and so on (Carter et al., 2005; Carter & Kennedy, 2006; Janney & Snell, 2006).
- Teach peers how to assist in more structured ways. Peers may teach through peer tutoring methods or assist through peer support networks. Rely on methods shown to achieve good effects (Carter, Cushing, Clark, & Kennedy, 2005; Carter et al., 2007; Janney & Snell, 2006; McDonnell et al., 2001; also see Chapter 11).

Alternative Adaptations: Individualize the Goal, the Methods/Materials, and the Activity

Alternative adaptations include activities that are coordinated with classroom instruction but are designed to address individualized learning priorities using methods and/or materials that *differ* from those of classmates. Sometimes class lessons are just too long and students can participate for only part of the time and thus need an alternative activity for the remaining time. Other times, a student's team determines that the student needs direct instruction from a specialist in a small-group or one-to-one format in areas such as reading or writing. (There also may be times when a team has yet to determine a way to integrate a student's learning goals or support needs into ongoing class activities, and what is really needed is better problem solving.) These alternative adaptations may be implemented within the general classroom setting or elsewhere, depending on considerations such as the way the level of noise and activity in the surrounding environment affect the student's focus and motivation. Functional skill instruction that goes beyond teaching the student to accomplish typical school and classroom routines (e.g., arrival and departure, lunch, using the restroom) is also considered an alternative adaptation. Such instruction takes place in the criterion environment for that student at least part of the time, and thus may occur in the classroom or elsewhere in the school or community. The challenge is to coordinate alternative adaptations with the general education class to (a) avoid activities that are stigmatizing and separate, and (b) time these alternative adaptations so that important general education activities are not missed: "Educational priorities should be pursued through schedules and locations that are respectful of the student's membership in a learning community" (Ford et al., 2001, p. 220).

In Chapter 1, Giangreco describes four inclusion options within general education environments and activities: (a) no accommodations required, (b) support accommodations required, (c) program content accommodations required, and (d) program content and support accommodations required. The model that we are explaining for making adaptations follows that same logic, but it adds "alternative adaptations," some of which may be consistent with the "program content and support accommodations required" option, but some of which are not, as they may be delivered outside of general education environments. Teams may decide that some alternative adaptations for a student are better implemented outside the classroom (e.g., study hall, multipurpose room, or resource room), but these decisions must be balanced with an overall schedule that does not interfere with that student's class membership. Adaptations for given students will change over time as students gain new skills and team members learn more about how to teach and support the student.

This category of adaptations includes three types of instructional activities:

1. *Alternative or supplementary activities* are designed to (a) prime the student for instruction, or (b) extend/reinforce previous instruction. To be only as specialized as necessary, such activities should match class lesson topics or themes, and are implemented before or after the targeted student participates in a portion of a class activity. For example, if a student is not able to participate in an entire whole-class lesson and does an alternate activity for part of the time, the alternate activity should involve the same subject area that classmates are studying. Or, if the class lesson is part of a thematic unit, the student could do an alternate activity that relates to the same unit theme.

2. *Remedial or compensatory instruction* in basic skills requires the use of direct instruction by a teacher trained to implement and monitor a research-based model or program (e.g., discrete trial instruction, functional communication training, certain commercial reading programs). Motor, speech, and communication goals also may be the focus of intensive one-to-one teaching sessions. To be acceptable under our adaptations model, such instruction should be truly specialized, prescriptive, and yield noticeable and highly valued gains (e.g., functional communication training, pivotal response treatment, discrete trial instruction, structured teaching). It also should be conducted with consideration for issues related to transfer and generalization of skills to general classroom activities. Remedial instruction can be especially important for younger students whose skill deficits may be more easily remedied.

3. *Instruction in functional skills* that cannot be completed within ongoing, regularly scheduled class activities. Such instruction is relatively rare for elementary and middle school students but becomes more frequent during high school and the post–secondary years (e.g., learning to make purchases in stores, job sampling).

Alternative adaptations are the most specialized adaptations and should be selected judiciously, with careful consideration of the costs and benefits with regard to the student's social and academic needs. Some alternative adaptations (e.g., a priming activity that will help to prevent behavior problems) may be part of an individualized plan for positive behavioral support (PBS). Often, alternative adaptations are used temporarily until the

team can determine a less intrusive adaptation, or until the student learns new skills that enable fuller participation in ongoing class lessons and activities.

Although the teams teaching and supporting Marc, Jacob, and Christine were intent on including these students in every way possible with their same-age peers, all three teams still implemented one or more alternative adaptations, not because including the student was too difficult for the teachers, but because, in good faith and on the basis of good data, the teams determined that the students would be better served socially and academically at this time by these alternative adaptations.

Jacob's fourth-grade teacher presents large-group science lessons in which she lectures and guides students through the use of interactive notebooks (Young, 2003). (Interactive notebooks are created for students to record, organize, and process new material; the teacher guides students in making outlines, illustrating content graphically, and exploring their opinions about new content.) Jacob participates in the first half of the whole-class lesson using an adapted version of the interactive notebook process. His notebook already has some skeleton notes in it so that he can fill in the blanks and circle or highlight key terms and definitions. He also is provided with graphic organizers and pictures that other students draw for themselves. During the second half of the science lesson, he goes to a learning center in the classroom where there are several activities related to the topic: a sort board, picture books, flash cards with vocabulary words and definitions, and computer quizzes. Classmates utilize the center when they finish their assignments and have choice time. (Alternative or supplementary activity)

Jacob's reading and writing skills are below what his teachers and the school psychologist estimate that they could be on the basis of assessments of his cognitive ability. Although a sight word approach had been used previously in his reading instruction, a reading assessment conducted by the special education teacher showed that Jacob was able to apply some phonetic strategies. Jacob was beginning to enjoy reading for the first time and was clearly motivated by the guided reading used by his fourth-grade teacher, and the team wanted to accelerate his reading progress. Jacob's team decided (with Jacob's input) on the following approach: Three days each week, instead of missing guided reading, Jacob participates in the first 20 minutes of Writers' Workshop in fourth grade and then goes to the library for 20 minutes of individualized reading instruction in a prescriptive reading program with his special education teacher. He returns to the classroom in time for the "sharing" portion of Writers' Workshop. (Remedial or compensatory instruction)

*   **Marc** receives two sessions each week of intensive communication instruction on a one-to-one basis outside the classroom with the speech-language therapist, but the rest of his communication instruction is done in the classroom among classmates and in the context of ongoing activities. (Remedial or compensatory instruction)*

*   **Christine**, a 20-year-old, spends much of each school day away from the post–high school program in order to learn needed community skills and to prepare for a job when she graduates next year. She works 1½ hours each day at a library helping with book checkout; she will be employed there during the summer and possibly after graduation. In addition, Christine serves as a greeter at a large department store. In both settings, the bathrooms are different and pose challenges for her. Christine takes time from the job (pull out) when her physical therapist visits; together with the teaching assistant they determine the adaptations needed for Christine to get in, use, and get out of the restroom. Then the physical therapist consults with Christine's teacher weekly to check on her progress. (Instruction in functional skills)*

When alternative adaptations are used,

- sessions should be short and timed to match natural transitions in the class schedule;
- include peers when possible and appropriate;
- be coordinated with classroom content and themes;
- provide intensive, individualized instruction or other specialized services; and
- be monitored and adjusted to be more normalized and less intrusive as the student makes gains.

Although alternative adaptations are more specialized—and even may be somewhat intrusive—they do not have to jeopardize class membership. Individualized instruction becomes more ordinary when these conditions are in place: (a) the school is truly inclusive in both philosophy and practice; (b) all students are regularly involved in a variety of groupings, with a variety of adults and peers, in a variety of places; (c) special educators are viewed as teachers and helpers for the entire class; (d) the student is a full member of the classroom group; and (e) the only-as-specialized-as-necessary guidelines are followed.

Using the Model to Develop Individualized Adaptations

Applying this model to plan for the inclusion of students in general education, team members follow four steps. Figure 6-4 lists the steps and the corresponding planning tools described and illustrated in this section.

Step 1. Gather and Share Information About the Student(s) and the Classroom

Before school starts or during the first month, the team collects and shares information about the student(s) and the classroom. All team members must know or have easy access to essential information from the student's IEP (i.e., special education and related services; IEP goals and accommodations; academic, social, and management needs). This information can be recorded on a *Program-at-a-Glance* form (see Figure 6-5) and *Student Information Form* (see Figure 6-6). These forms are provided to relevant classroom teacher(s), specialty teachers, and instructional aide(s) after the information is shared at an initial face-to-face meeting. Figure 6-5 shows that, in addition to brief synopses of Jacob's IEP goals, Jacob's team was alerted about his

FIGURE 6–4
Steps and Tools for Making Individualized Adaptations

Step 1. Gather and Share Information
  a. About the Student
    ☐ Program-at-a-Glance (see Figure 6–5)
    ☐ Student Information Form (see Figure 6–6)
  b. About the Classroom
    ☐ Ecological Assessment of Class Activities (see Figure 6–7)

Step 2. Determine When Adaptations Are Needed
    ☐ Program Planning Matrix (see Figure 6–8)

Step 3. Plan and Implement Adaptations: First General, Then Specific, Then Alternative
    ☐ Individualized Adaptations Plan (see Figure 6–10)
    ☐ Weekly Plan for Specific Adaptations (see Figure 6–11)

Step 4. Monitor and Evaluate
    ☐ Program plans, data collection forms, problem analysis worksheets (see Figures 6–13, 6–14, and 6–15, respectively)
    ☐ Team Evaluation of Student Adaptations (see Figure 6–16)

Source: Adapted from *Teachers' guides to inclusive practices: Modifying schoolwork* (2nd ed.), by R. Janney and M. E. Snell, 2004, Baltimore: Paul H. Brookes. Reprinted with permission.

FIGURE 6–5
Program-at-a-Glance for Jacob

Program-at-a-Glance	
Student: Jacob	**Date:** September 2009

IEP Goals (see IEP for measurable goal statements and objectives/benchmarks)	**IEP Accommodations and Modifications**
Social/communication • Use simple sentences to express needs, feelings, ask/answer questions, make choices, relate recent events • Respond to and initiate interactions (e.g., greetings, requests) with peers • Use self-control strategies with cues and support *Functional skills and class participation* • Follow class procedures from classroom teachers' cues (organization, materials, transitions, etc.) • School arrival, departure, lunch routines • School/classroom jobs • Participate in individual work to 10 minutes, small and large groups (including specialties) to 20 minutes *Math* • Write numbers 0–100 • Compare ($<$, $=$, $>$) whole numbers to 100 • $+$ and $-$ to 50, concrete objects • Time to 15 minutes (analog, digital) • Counting out combinations of coins to match prices • Measurement: pounds, inches and feet, cups and quarts • Basic geometric figures • Basic bar and line graphs *Language arts* • Comprehension questions, fiction and nonfiction (purpose, setting, characters, event sequences) • Read/write/spell high-frequency and functional words (increase by 100 words) • Write three-sentence paragraph • Collect information from print, media, online *Science/Social studies* • 3–4 key vocabulary/concepts for each unit • Conduct investigations (predict, observe, conclude; cause and effect; measurements)	• Receive special education support/instruction for academics, daily routines, transitions, social-communication • Modified curriculum goals • Weekly curricular and instructional adaptations by special education and general education teachers • Science and social studies texts read aloud or with computer text reader, and/or summaries provided • Math, science/social studies test read aloud • Additional scheduled movement breaks • Daily home/school homework planner and communication log • Educational team familiar with and uses PBS plan • Visual daily schedule • Visual organizer/checklists for task steps of multistep activities, investigations
	Behavior/Social management needs • Peer planning at beginning of year and as needed • Visual schedule • Clear time limits and beginnings/endings to activities and assignments • See PBS plan; share key strategies with all relevant teachers and staff. **Comments/Special needs** • Anecdotal records for IEP progress • Core team meetings biweekly; whole team monthly

Source: Adapted from *Teachers' guides to inclusive practices: Modifying schoolwork* (2nd ed.), by R. Janney and M. E. Snell, 2004, Baltimore: Paul H. Brookes. Reprinted with permission.

IEP accommodations, which include the use of a daily home/school homework planner and communication log, and visual organizers or checklists for multistep activities and investigations, and his behavior/social management needs, which include the need for clear time limits and clear beginnings and endings to activities. Figure 6-6 shares crucial information about Jacob's learning and behavioral strengths (general knowledge, math, and sense of humor), learning and behavioral liabilities (hyperactivity, difficulty sustaining attention, and anxiety), likes and interests (anything on wheels, video games, animals), dislikes (writing, loud noises, crowds), and how he learns best (a multisensory approach).

Information About the Classroom
Knowing when to adapt and what kind of adaptations will be needed require familiarity with the academic, social, physical, and behavioral demands of the classroom. In order for a student with significant disabilities to be meaningfully included, all team members need to understand the classroom's structure and culture. The team needs to assess how the classroom operates,

FIGURE 6–6
Student Information Form for Jacob

Student Information Form		
Student: Jacob (9 years)	**Grade:** 4	**School Year:** 2009–2010

Disability: Mental retardation (requires limited to extensive support in most skill areas; academic and social-behavioral needs are more significant than functional skill needs)

Current Teachers: Bowers (fourth grade) Fuentes (special ed.)	**Last Year's Teachers:** Kohn (third grade) Carhart (special ed.)

Special Education and Related Services _x_ Academics: *All areas* _x_ Speech/Language: *20 minutes x 2 days* _x_ Occupational Therapy: *Consult* __ Physical Therapy: _x_ Aide Support: *4.5 hours x 5 days for math, content areas, transitions, school/classroom routines, self-help* _x_ Special Ed. Instruction: *45 minutes x 5 days for language arts and social skills* __ Special Ed. Consultation: *15 minutes x 5 days*	**Learning and behavioral strengths/high skill areas:** General knowledge Math Sense of humor (likes to joke, laugh) **Learning and behavioral liabilities/areas of concern:** Hyperactive, difficulty sustaining attention to an activity not of his choosing for more than 8–10 minutes. When bored or afraid of making mistakes, becomes anxious, cries, lies on floor. When dislikes assigned task, makes disruptive noises, uses materials for "play." (See PBS plan for details.)
Special health, physical, or self-help needs: Uses restroom with minimal supervision; needs help with zippers, buttons, and flushing toilet (it scares him). Very picky eater; usually packs lunch. Eats with minimal assistance opening packages and cleaning up self and table/area.	**See guidance counselor/principal for other relevant confidential information?** __ yes _x_ no **Behavior Support Plan?** _x_ yes __ no **Testing:** State/District Accommodations __ yes _x_ no Alternate Assessment _x_ yes __ no
Learns best by __ Seeing (picture/video/graphic organizer) __ Teacher or peer modeling __ Hands on, labs, projects _x_ Multisensory approach (all of the above)	**Likes/Interests** Anything on wheels: cars, trucks, bikes Video games Animals **Dislikes** Writing of almost any kind or amount Loud noises, loud music Crowded areas

Source: Adapted from *Teachers' guides to inclusive practices: Modifying schoolwork* (2nd ed.), by R. Janney and M. E. Snell, 2004, Baltimore: Paul H. Brookes. Reprinted with permission.

including organizational routines and procedures, types of instructional activities, behavior expectations and contingencies, and homework and testing practices. Early in the school year or semester, the special education teacher gathers this information through observation and interviews. In middle and high schools, information must be gathered for each class in which a targeted student participates; in elementary school, the main classroom, as well as specialties such as music, art, and physical education, need to be assessed. Procedures for using the cafeteria and other common areas of the school, as well as behavior expectations for various school environments, also should be considered.

There are no rules for how detailed this information should be, or even how much of it must be written down. If teams of classroom teachers and special education teachers have collaborated in the past, much of this information will be known without doing a formal assessment. But if the team is newly formed, the special education teacher and other support personnel should become familiar with these classroom variables and record any information that needs to be analyzed by the team. Although the task of gathering this information for the first time may sound daunting, remember that, in all likelihood, the special educator will be using the information about the classroom context to develop adaptations for *other* students with IEPs as well, not only for the student with extensive support needs, such as those addressed in this book.

In-depth Information About Class Activities and Participation

When a student has extensive support needs and a significant portion of his or her classroom participation is embedded social, motor, and communication skills (as for Marc and Christine), the assessment process will include more detailed descriptions of class activities and the student's level of participation in them. The special educator or other trained staff member conducts an *Ecological Assessment of Classroom Activities,* which is a detailed observation of the targeted student's performance on each step of lessons and routines during which the extent of the student's participation and/or instructional benefit is in question. These observations yield valuable information that the team uses to identify the skills needed by the student and adaptations that could be provided to increase the student's participation.

Figure 6-7 shows an Ecological Assessment of Classroom Activities for Christine. The observation was conducted and recorded by a teaching assistant who had been taught to use the assessment procedure by Christine's IEP manager. The assessment was recorded during the second meeting of the drama club when club routines and procedures were already in place (e.g., sign in near the stage; socialize during refreshments and before call to order; when faculty advisor or club leader starts talking, get quiet and come to order; review club business; decide on acting activities; participate in activities; socialize; and depart). Christine's core team examined and discussed the findings at their next meeting. The observation provided useful ideas for the team on ways to improve Christine's participation through additional skills and adaptations.

After implementing skill instruction and adaptations for a period of time, a repeated observation of the same activity can be conducted to determine whether the student's level of participation has increased.

Step 2. Determine When Adaptations Are Needed

The purpose of adaptations is to enable the targeted student to participate as much as possible in all class activities while also pursuing individual learning priorities. In Step 2 of the planning process, the team looks at all of the activities throughout the school day that must

be adapted. The team decides when to teach functional skills or other individualized learning priorities.

The *Program Planning Matrix* is a form used to plot a student's IEP goals against the class's daily schedule. It is especially valuable for students whose learning priorities include functional skills, social-communication skills, and other skills that should be used throughout the day. The matrix is useful for identifying when and where a student's individualized learning priorities will be taught and for determining the times for the student to receive special supports and services such as heath care, movement breaks, therapies, or mobility training.

As shown on Jacob's Program Planning Matrix in Figure 6-8, the student's IEP goals are listed in the left-hand column and the daily schedule of subjects and activities is listed across the top row (for a middle school or high school student, the daily schedule of classes is listed). Cells are marked with an "x" or other symbol to indicate the IEP goals that will be addressed during corresponding class activities. Jacob's goals include simplified academic goals, as well as goals for functional skills and social-communication skills. Obviously, Jacob's adapted language arts, math, science, and social studies goals are addressed when the class is scheduled to work on the same subject matter, although at a different level of difficulty. Jacob's functional skill goals that are related to his participation in school and classroom routines are also relatively easy to enter on the matrix because they are addressed at naturally occurring times throughout the day. He engages in arrival, departure, and classroom job routines when those activities are scheduled for the entire class, although he receives instruction and support not provided for most of his classmates.

Jacob also has social and communication goals (e.g., to initiate and respond to greetings from peers and adults) that neatly correspond with typical fourth-grade instructional activities and which should be addressed at multiple times throughout the day instead of in the context of just one subject or activity. The matrix assists Jacob's team to identify the most *appropriate* opportunities for providing Jacob with direct or embedded instruction in social-communication skills, as well as helping to ensure that the team provides *adequate* instructional opportunities in these goals throughout the day.

The Program Planning Matrix also can be used to schedule the delivery of program supports (in contrast to the learning goals) that are delivered during the day.

FIGURE 6–7

An Ecological Assessment of Christine in Drama Club

Ecological Assessment of Classroom Activities	
Class: Drama Club	**Student:** Christine
Day/Time: Alternate Thursdays 4:00–6:00	**Instructional Assistant:** Ms. Washington
Club President: Paul	**Date:** 9/16/09 (second meeting)
Faculty Adviser: Mr. Fullen	**Time:** 4:00–6:00

Key to Participation: + social and instructional participation; +/– missing either social or instructional participation; missing both social and instructional participation

Typical Sequence of Steps/Procedures	Target Student Participation	Participation: +, +/–, –
1. Students file in several at a time, most socializing from prior acquaintance.	1. Christine is wheeled to a location away from other students.	1. –
2. Students sign in on the club attendance notebook located on the stage.	2. Ms. Washington goes to the attendance book and signs Christine in.	2. –
3. Students get a drink and chips from the meeting refreshment area and then mingle and socialize.	3. Ms. Washington wheels Christine to the refreshment area and pours a drink for Christine into her sport cup on her tray. Several students talk to Christine but do not understand how to pause for her to respond.	3. +/–
4. Club president calls the group to order and reviews club business, seeks discussion and membership vote on several fund-raising issues.	4. Christine is quiet and looks at Paul but does not participate in voting.	4. –
5. Mr. Fullen takes ideas for drama activities and group decides to focus first on some warm-up exercises (voice and movement) and then on improvisation exercises.	5. Christine is quiet and looks in Mr. Fullen's direction. She laughs with others when he shows some improvisations.	5. +/–
6. Group is divided into five stations for different improvisations; groups rotate after about 10 minutes.	6. Ms. Washington wheels Christine to one group, close enough so that she can hear and see the larger movements of the students. Christine is attentive to students who act, laughs at the right times, but does not participate.	6. +/–
7. Paul gives club announcements and ends meeting.	7. Christine is attentive to Paul.	7. +
8. Students talk and socialize, leaving in small groups or individually.	8. Several students go to Christine after the meeting and make conversation. Christine listens but is not successful in communicating with her AAC device.	8. +/–

Skills Needed to Increase Participation	Adaptations Needed to Increase Participation
1. Teach peers how to interact with Christine.	1. Position Christine by peers before meeting starts.
2. Raise hand to signal teacher for response or turn and to vote.	2. Adapt sign-in procedure; maybe have peer sign in for her.
3. Able to access and use DynaVox categories programmed.	3. Assistant provides some translation of Christine's remarks or intent as needed; direct others to talk to Christine or prompt Christine to respond.
4. Practice and adapt improvisations to suit Christine; teacher involves class in obtaining suggestions.	4. Program DynaVox with vocabulary suited to club activities.
	5. Position Christine close to demonstrations and use extra lighting to improve her perception.

Source: Form adapted from *Teachers' guides to inclusive practices: Modifying schoolwork* (2nd ed.), by R. Janney and M. E. Snell, 2004, Baltimore: Paul H. Brookes. Reprinted with permission.

Supports such as movement breaks, toileting, and physical therapy can be listed in the left-hand column, below the student's IEP goals, and a symbol or color code can be added to the cells that correspond to the time during the daily activity schedule when those supports should be provided.

An additional use for the matrix is described in the following section, which details Step 3 of the adaptations process. The cells on the matrix can be coded (using color or symbols) to indicate whether the corresponding activity requires planning and preparation of adapted methods and/or materials.

FIGURE 6–8
Program Planning Matrix for Jacob

Program Planning Matrix												
Student: Jacob	**Class:** Bowers/Fourth									**Date:** September 2009		
IEP GOALS	**Class Schedule**											
	Arrival	Morning Work	Language Skills	Guided	Specialty*	Recess	Math	Lunch	Science/Social Studies	Writers' Workshop	Shared Reading	Departure
Communication, Social, Behavior												
Use simple sentences to express needs, feelings, ask/answer questions, make choices, relate recent events	x	o	x	x	o	x	o	x	x	x	x	x
Respond to and initiate interactions with peers	x	x	x	x	x	x	o	x	x	o	x	x
Use self-control strategies with cues and support	x	o	o	o	x	x	o	x	o	x	o	o
Functional Skills and School Participation												
Follow class procedures from classroom teacher's cues	x	x	x	x	x	x	x	x	x	x	x	x
Arrival/departure, lunch routines, classroom jobs	x							x				x
Participate in individual work to 10 minutes, small and large groups to 20 minutes		x	o	x	x		x		x	o	x	
Math												
Write numbers 0–100 **(S)**							x		o			
Compare (=, <, >) whole numbers to 100 **(S)**							x		o			
Add and subtract to 50, concrete objects **(S)**							x					
Time to 15 minutes (analog, digital) **(S)**	x				x		x		x			x
Measurement: pounds, inches and feet, cups and quarts **(S)**							x		x			
Basic bar and line graphs (across curriculum) **(S)**		x					x		x			
Language Arts												
Readable handwriting for name, date, high-frequency words, and phrases **(S)**	x	x	x	o				x	o	x		
Comprehension questions, fiction and nonfiction (fact/fantasy, purpose, setting, characters, events) **(S)**			x	x						x	x	
Write 3-sentence paragraph **(S)**		x		x						x		
Read/write/spell high-frequency and functional words **(S)**		x		x					x	x		
Collect information from print, media, online **(S)**		x		x	x				x			
Science and Social Studies												
Conduct investigations (predict, observe, conclude; cause and effect; measurements; graphs) **(S)**									x			
Key concepts and vocabulary from each unit **(S)**			x						x			

*Monday: Music; Tuesday and Thursday: P.E.; Wednesday: Library; Friday: Computer
KEY: x = Instruction provided, o = Opportunistic teaching; **(S)** Specific adaptations to class activities and materials may be needed

Source: Adapted from *Teachers' guides to inclusive practices: Modifying schoolwork* (2nd ed.), by R. Janney and M. E. Snell, 2004, Baltimore: Paul H. Brookes. Reprinted with permission.

Step 3. Plan and Implement Adaptations: First General, Then Specific

Using the assessment information gathered in Step 1 and the Program Planning Matrix developed in Step 2, the team now plans the adaptations that should be used throughout the day for the student. The team creates an *Individualized Adaptations Plan,* which summarizes the curricular, instructional, and any alternative adaptations that will be implemented. One way to make the process of creating effective adaptations more efficient is to divide it into two stages. First, focus on general adaptations that enable the student to participate in typical classroom routines and instructional activities. Then, focus on more specific adaptations that apply to particular content and intermittently occurring activities. These two stages are not strictly sequential; however, general adaptations are broader, more global supports than specific adaptations, which tend to be narrower and more time limited. (See Table 6–4.)

General Adaptations

General adaptations are those that apply to predictable aspects of classroom activities, including daily routines (e.g., arrival, bathroom use), organizational procedures (e.g., handling paperwork, sharpening pencils, seeking help, making transitions), and regularly used instructional formats (e.g., guided reading groups, interactive science notebooks, math journals). General adaptations, by necessity, include the alternate and augmentative ways that students communicate with others and others communicate with students.

General adaptations are, in essence, routine ways of scaffolding the focus student's social and instructional participation in the class. General adaptations capitalize on the fact that classroom teachers have a set of routines and learning rituals that they use regularly. General adaptations are patterns or formats for adapting those organizational practices and learning rituals. They are designed and then applied for a period of time—for a marking period, semester, or until the student no longer needs the adaptation; the instructional team does not need to re-invent them from week to week.

Marc has an activity communication board for each activity in which he participates. The communication boards have picture symbols for the steps of the activity and/or any needed vocabulary. Whenever Ms. Kwan, Marc's kindergarten teacher, interacts with Marc, she touches his picture symbols on his daily schedule and on his activity communication boards while she

TABLE 6–4

Components of a Model for Making Adaptations That Are Only as Specialized as Necessary

Prerequisites to the model	The classroom is truly inclusive (i.e., age-appropriate general education class, collaborative between general and special education, welcoming culture).
	Accommodating, evidence-based teaching practices are in place (e.g., active learning, multiple modalities, small groups, systematic lesson structure, graphic organizers, data-based decision making).
Three types of adaptations	**Curricular adaptations:** Alter the learning goals for the student. Include the student's IEP goals in initial, class-wide planning:
	• Simplified goals from the general curriculum and/or alternate/aligned learning standards, and
	• Functional and developmental skill goals.
	Instructional adaptations: Alter the methods or materials:
	• Consider changing the instructional arrangement (e.g., smaller group, particular peers, cooperative learning).
	• Consider changing the teaching methods and/or materials.
	• Consider changing the task required of the student.
	• Consider providing additional personal support from peers and from adults.
	Alternative adaptations: Change to an alternative activity that is coordinated with classroom instruction. The activity is often conducted before or after part of a related class activity and includes peers if possible and appropriate.
	• Alternative or supplementary activity (often used temporarily)
	• Remedial or compensatory instruction in basic skills or other individualized learning priorities
	• Instruction in age-appropriate functional skills (other than typical school and class routines) at school or in the community
Two stages for creating adaptations	**General adaptations:** Formats for adapting predictable types of activities and routines. These are usually adaptations to goals, methods, materials, and personal support.
	Specific adaptations: Time-limited adaptations for a specific lesson, activity, or unit; matches class lesson content.

Source: Adapted from *Teachers' guides to inclusive practices: Modifying schoolwork* (2nd ed.), by R. Janney and M. E. Snell, 2004, Baltimore: Paul H. Brookes. Reprinted with permission.

speaks softly; this procedure helps Marc understand her messages.

Jacob has five spelling words each week (his classmates have 10 or more), only one of which is a new, unknown word. Like his classmates, he has a spelling packet, with one page assigned per day, but Jacob's packet is created using a number of general adaptations: (a) larger spaces for writing (or tracing) the words, (b) fill-in-the-blank items instead of writing complete sentences, (c) crossword puzzles with larger grids, and (d) spelling flash cards to cut out and take home.

Christine, at age 20, spends most of her school week learning vocational skills in community settings, but she participates in the drama club on the university campus where her post–high school class is located. When Mr. Fuller calls roll at club meetings, Christine responds "here" by smiling and lifting her head up high, a response that is faster than using her Dynavox.

Because general adaptations help to establish the student's participation in class routines and learning activities, they should be put in place as soon as possible at the beginning of the school year. High-priority general adaptations include plans for the use of communication devices and systems, visual supports such as individual schedules, and strategies for supporting students when they participate in routines such as arrival, departure, lunch, and restroom use. When school and classroom routines are targeted for instruction, an *Instructional Program Plan* with a task analysis and teaching guide is created. These plans for task analytic instruction, which are discussed later in this chapter in the section on monitoring and evaluating instruction, and also in Chapters 4 and 10—can be considered as general adaptations, too; once they are planned and put into practice, they do not require additional collaborative team planning unless performance data reveal either difficulties that should be addressed or mastery of the routine.

Specific Adaptations

When general adaptations are in place, teams can then focus on the *specific adaptations* for changing class content. In contrast to general adaptations, *specific adaptations* apply to a particular lesson or activity and require more short-term planning in order to match the content being taught. The timeline for creating specific adaptations depends on the number of teachers involved and their usual planning methods;

however, specific adaptations usually are planned and created weekly (e.g., for spelling words, math skills) or for each unit (e.g., for science and history/social studies). In middle school and high school, the increasing complexity of the curricula and the growing number of paper-and-pencil tasks often necessitate weekly planning.

Ms. Bowers, Jacob's fourth-grade teacher, uses guided reading groups several days each week. Ms. Bowers, Ms. Fuentes (the special education teacher), an instructional assistant, and a student teacher each teach a group. Each group reads a leveled reader that belongs either to a literary genre (e.g., historical fiction, fables) being studied or is related to a current content area theme (e.g., Colonial Virginia, animal adaptations). During guided reading, while the other students work in groups of five or six, Jacob is placed in a group with only two other students. Ms. Bowers selects two students who know Jacob well and who read at a similar level. Ms. Fuentes, the special educator, instructs Jacob's group and is able to give the extra visual prompts and immediate feedback that Jacob needs to stay focused and motivated. These general adaptations to the instructional methods will stay in force until Jacob is able to participate more independently in a group with more members. In addition to reading aloud, students do a practice activity. They might complete a table on the basis of the features of the genre being studied, or fill in a compare-and-contrast diagram showing how the material relates to other texts that they have read. On the basis of Jacob's language arts goals, the team has decided on several general adaptations that will be used for these sorts of tasks (e.g., letting Jacob write words or phrases instead of sentences, providing models from which Jacob copies, and adding lines to any unlined worksheets). During their weekly collaborative planning, the two teachers discuss the specific adaptations required for the week, which pertain to the content of the guided reading sessions (e.g., which of the defining characteristics of the genre Jacob will learn or how the terminology used to teach a reading strategy will be simplified).

Marc attends his kindergarten class about 30% of the day, which includes morning circle and some table work. Along with his classmates, Marc is learning to connect letters and their sounds (e.g., F is for fish) and write the letter. Marc started the year refusing to hold a pencil or to be guided by a teacher. His team, with advice from the OT, introduced a slant board, a choice of writing tools, a stencil that helps him keep the pencil in a smaller space (see Figure 6-9), and teaching activities from the Handwriting Without Tears® *program. As an alternate to handwriting because his writing is still very slow, Marc was taught to use a small typing/printing device to type out letters and words. Two weeks in advance, Ms. Kwan, his kindergarten teacher, discusses her weekly plans and shares the worksheets for handwriting and letter-sound lessons with Ms. Wharton, his special education teacher. All new worksheets and letter-matching activities are first taught one-to-one in the resource room and then Marc learns to complete them independently in the resource room. Finally, he completes the same letter-sound activity in kindergarten with minimal support from a teaching assistant; the teachers' expectations for his handwriting are less than for his peers. Each week his work in the resource room changes to reflect the specific upcoming language arts lesson.*

Several general adaptations are in place to support **Christine***'s participation in the drama club, including positioning strategies and ways to use her DynaVox. However, the specific topics for improvisations and sources for line-reading activities for each club session must be analyzed to determine the specific adaptations that will enable Christine's participation. The drama club faculty advisor, Mr. Fuller, meets weekly with Christine's teacher, Ms. Rowyer, to review what is coming up on the club's schedule. The club generated drama activities at the beginning of the semester and revisits this schedule every month. The club always starts with warm-up exercises (voice and movement), but the first few weeks will be devoted to improvisational exercises. On the basis of the ecological inventory (see Figure 6-7) from Christine's first few days with the club, it was clear that others did not understand how she could communicate with them. She was attentive and took in much of the interactions, but when others greeted or talked to her, they did not wait long enough for her to respond with facial expressions or with her DynaVox assistive and adaptive computing (AAC) device. Because the next club meeting was going to continue with improvisations, Ms. Rowyer took notes on the necessary vocabulary to be added to her device. Mr. Fuller shared activities that the group might engage in and they generated ideas for how Christine could be involved. Later that week*

before the club meeting, Mr. Fuller got a lesson from Christine and Ms. Washington, the instructional aide, on how her device worked; they practiced by engaging in some improvisations to stimulus pictures. He and Christine decided to do some improvisations together for the group to show how Christine expresses herself.

Notice that Jacob's Program Planning Matrix (see Figure 6–8) includes notations about which of his IEP goals require specific adaptations. Whereas instruction in functional skill routines and developmental skills that are embedded throughout the day is founded largely on general adaptations (e.g., procedures for using his visual schedule, or the task analysis and teaching guide for completing the morning routine), instruction in simplified academic goals is likely to require specific adaptations to match the content being taught in class lessons. This practice is illustrated below for Marc, who uses a communication board (general adaptation) that is updated each week with vocabulary needed for upcoming lessons and activities (specific adaptation).

Marc's functional goals for communication are embedded throughout his school day. He uses a series of small activity communication boards matched to each activity; each board has removable picture symbols that he points to or removes and shows to express himself. His speech therapist spends 20 minutes on Tuesdays and Thursdays with him in the resource room; the focus is on expanding his symbol vocabulary and encouraging his emerging speech. Before these sessions in the resource room, the speech therapist checks with Marc's kindergarten teacher about vocabulary that Marc will need for upcoming lessons and activities, and then makes these words and symbols the focus of Marc's pull-out instruction. The activity communication board is a general adaptation; the picture symbols needed for the activity at hand (e.g., the alphabet or number lesson, the art project, the game being played at recess) are specific adaptations.

Conceptualizing the process of developing adaptations as occurring in two stages—general and specific—makes the task more efficient because it allows teaching teams to focus their short-term planning on the content of upcoming lessons. Teams also need to revisit general adaptations as the student's performance improves and/or as problems arise. But

FIGURE 6–9
Marc checks his schedule: (a) He learns to do kindergarten worksheets first with his teaching assistant in the resource room. (b) Then he learns to do them on his own (c, d). (e) Finally, he completes the activities in the kindergarten room alongside peers.

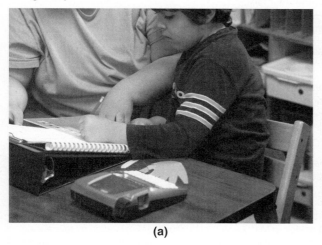

(a)

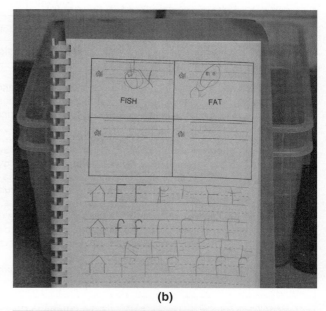

(b)

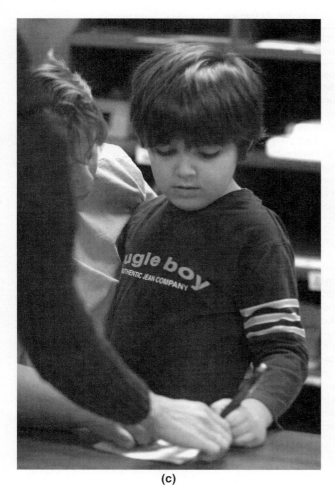

(c)

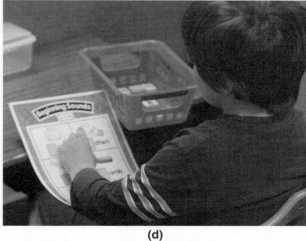

(d)

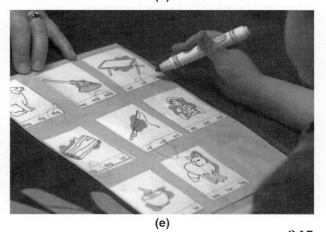

(e)

FIGURE 6–10

Sample of Jacob's Individualized Adaptations Plan

<table>
<tr><td colspan="5" align="center">**Individualized Adaptations Plan**</td></tr>
<tr><td colspan="2">**Student:** Jacob</td><td colspan="2">**Class/Grade:** Fourth grade</td><td>**Date:** January 10, 2009</td></tr>
<tr><td colspan="2">**Classroom Teacher:** Bowers</td><td colspan="3">**Special Education Teacher:** Fuentes</td></tr>
<tr><td colspan="5">

Curriculum Adaptations
- Jacob's math and reading/language arts goals are simplified and stress functional applications of basic skills. His science and social studies goals are from the fourth-grade learning standards, but are significantly simplified and reduced in number.
- Jacob has additional, individualized goals in functional skills (daily living, school and classroom participation), social-communication skills, and self-control skills.

</td></tr>
<tr><td colspan="5">

General Instructional Adaptations to Use Throughout the Day
- Use visual prompts (models, demonstrations, manipulation of materials, gestures) more than verbal prompts. Avoid using repeated verbal prompts or corrections. Give only as much assistance as needed to achieve success. Encourage Jacob to get help from peers when appropriate (e.g., how to spell a word, assistance with cutting).
- Give a lot of encouragement for participation and following rules. Work toward greater independence and delayed feedback. Establish his participation, then say, for example, "I'm going to help some other students. Raise your hand if you have any questions."
- Cue Jacob to listen when Ms. Bowers gives instructions. If Jacob does not follow Ms. Bowers' instructions, prompt Jacob by referencing natural cues (e.g., "Listen to Ms. Bowers," "What were Ms. Bowers' directions?" "What are your classmates doing now?") (Do not simply repeat Ms. Bowers' directions.)
- Throughout the day, emphasize organization and good work habits. Jacob should write his name and the date on all assignments, get out and put away materials, and throw away his own trash.

</td></tr>
<tr><td colspan="5" align="center">**Adaptations to Class Schedule and Activities**</td></tr>
<tr>
<td>**Class Activity**</td>
<td>**IEP Goals**</td>
<td colspan="2">**General Adaptations (Instructional and Alternative)**</td>
<td>**Specific Adaptations**</td>
</tr>
<tr>
<td>9:00–9:15 Morning routine: check-in, get organized, do morning work</td>
<td>
- Independence in morning routine
- Readable handwriting for name, date, high-frequency words
- Follow class routines and procedures from classroom teachers' cues
</td>
<td colspan="2">
- Jacob arrives a few minutes early to avoid noisy hallways. Complete arrival routine following task analysis and brief teaching guide. Use picture cues to make lunch choice. For homework agenda, Jacob copies month, day, and date from a peer's agenda.
- Have personal schedule on Jacob's desk. If Jacob does not independently check off activities throughout the day, prompt him first by pointing to the box, then by handing him a pencil.
- Morning work: For word searches, highlight first letters and reduce number of words, or have peer do some with him. For activity sheets: Help with cutting, use plastic box for crayons so they don't roll off his desk.
</td>
<td>
- Aide places pictures for daily lunch choices beside the computer.
- Ms. Bowers writes morning work and any special events on Jacob's schedule.
</td>
</tr>
<tr>
<td>9:15–10:15 Language arts</td>
<td>
- Read/write/spell high-frequency and functional words
- Readable handwriting for name, date, high-frequency words and phrases
- Basic comprehension questions
- Write 3-sentence paragraph.
- Collect information from print, media, online
</td>
<td colspan="2">
- Word study: 5 spelling words per week (4 known and 1 unknown). Spelling packet follows format for class packet, but is adapted with larger print, more space to write. Add a page for tracing words and make spelling flash cards. Aide gives Jacob spelling test on Fridays.
- Guided reading: Jacob's group is limited to three; Ms. Bowers chooses students and selects books close to his instructional level. Ms. Fuentes teaches Jacob's group.
- For written activities related to the reading selection:
- Jacob writes words/phrases instead of sentences. Use cloze method (fill in the blanks) and use whiteboard to provide models. If paper is unlined, provide line guide to place underneath.
- Use nonwriting options to complete part of the task if needed: (a) draw or cut out pictures, (b) write choices for Jacob to circle, (c) provide word strips to cut apart and glue onto the page, and (d) complete task cooperatively with other students.
</td>
<td>
- Spelling words are selected by Ms. Fuentes and Ms. Bowers at weekly conference. Ms. Fuentes makes spelling packet.
- Pictures and cloze method activities planned and created weekly.
</td>
</tr>
</table>

FIGURE 6–10 (*Continued*)

Class Activity	IEP Goals	General Adaptations (Instructional and Alternative)	Specific Adaptations
10:45–11:40 Math	• Write numbers 0–100 • Compare (<, =, >) numbers to 100. • + and − to 50, concrete objects • Time to 15 minutes • Count and use coins and bills to $10 • Measurement: pounds, inches and feet, cups and quarts • Basic geometric figures • Basic bar and line graphs	• For large group lessons, Jacob partially participates in lessons on numbers, measurement, geometry, and graphing. Provide visuals and manipulatives as needed. • For individual practice activities: When possible, modify math journal pages to suit his objectives. If not, Jacob works in individualized math journal. • For center rotation activities: Give gestural prompts and alert Jacob to watch peer models. If he is not completing tasks, do fewer rotations, then an alternative activity. • Tests are modified to focus on Jacob's goals. Written test items are supplemented with hands-on applications. • **Alternative adaptation:** Occasionally (e.g., when class lesson is working on algebra), Jacob works one-to-one with teacher or aide on functional math skills such as money. Crate with suitable activities is found on the math shelf. • **Alternative adaptation:** 10-minute movement break at about 11:00. Breaks are noncontingent. See PBS plan.	• Ms. Bowers and Ms. Fuentes discuss alternative adaptations in weekly planning meeting. • Class tests adapted by Ms. Fuentes and administered by aide.
12:45–1:50 Science and social studies	• Simplified goals focusing on key terms/concepts for each unit • Conduct investigations (predict, observe, conclude; cause and effect; measurements)	• Textbook: Main ideas and key concepts are highlighted. For silent reading, a peer or adult reads with Jacob. • Interactive notebooks: Jacob puts a box around each paragraph and highlights key words. When illustrating is required, provide pictures to cut and paste. Assist Jacob to get out, organize, use, and put away his materials (e.g., notebook, ruler, pencil, highlighters, glue stick). • Small group projects: Ms. Bowers places Jacob in a group of 3–4 suitable peers. • Tests are simplified to match Jacob's goals, but are based on the template used for the class test. • **Alternative adaptation:** After approximately 15 minutes of work in interactive notebook or other large-group lesson, Jacob goes to science or social studies center. Use pictures of center activities to make a schedule for three activities—two teacher choices and one student choice. Options: Sorting board for unit concepts and vocabulary, flash cards, activity sheets, and computer quizzes.	• Ms. Bowers and Ms. Fuentes choose key concepts for each unit. Ms. Bowers prints any pictures needed for interactive notebook. • Aide highlights textbook. • Ms. Fuentes, using the class test as a template, simplifies tests.

Source: Adapted from *Teachers' guides to inclusive practices: Modifying schoolwork* (2nd ed.), by R. Janney and M. E. Snell, 2004, Baltimore: Paul H. Brookes. Reprinted with permission.

having a store of general adaptations on which to build makes the task of determining specific adaptations more manageable.

Individualized Adaptations Plans
The Individualized Adaptations Plan includes

• a summary of the general adaptations (curricular, instructional, and alternative) that should be in place and implemented regularly for each type of instructional activity and routine,
• notes indicating the times/activities for which specific adaptations (curricular, instructional, and

alternative) must be planned on a more short-term basis,
• links to the student's IEP goals (both simplified academic and functional or embedded skills), and
• information about the logistics of implementation—who is responsible for the adaptation and when.

There are a number of ways to organize and format an adaptations plan. Figure 6–10, which shows part of Jacob's Individualized Adaptations Plan, illustrates one possibility. Jacob's plan includes some general instructional adaptations to be used throughout the day, as well as detailed descriptions of how each subject and routine in his fourth-grade class's daily schedule is adapted. The main section of the plan is created in a tabular format, with four columns to detail (a) the class schedule or activities, (b) the student's IEP objectives/benchmarks for each activity, (c) the general adaptations made in procedures and materials to teach or support the student in that activity, and (d) the specific adaptations that will need to be created weekly. Because Jacob is in elementary school, his adaptations plan covers the entire school day; secondary school students typically have a plan for each course in which they are enrolled.

Jacob's IEP manager takes primary responsibility for writing his adaptations plan, but it is founded on team problem solving and decision making. A paper copy of the plan is kept in a notebook with other plans and records to document Jacob's performance. The classroom teacher, special educator, and instructional aide make notes directly on the paper copy of the plan of what works and difficulties that arise. The plan is updated every four to six weeks in a computer file; the changes made as the plan evolves provide evidence of both Jacob's skill gains and the team's increased ability to facilitate Jacob's independence and participation in fourth grade.

Teams also must devise a way to record and communicate decisions about specific adaptations. One method is to detail specific adaptations on the classroom teacher's daily or weekly planning form. An example of this approach to planning is illustrated in Figure 6–11. Ideally, the classroom teacher and special educator would meet to note any specific adaptations directly in the classroom teacher's plan book and then make a photocopy for the student's adaptations notebook. Alternatively, if the special educator and classroom teacher are not able to meet face to face, the classroom teacher can provide a copy (photocopy or electronic) of the class's weekly plans to the special educator, who inserts the specific adaptations and then shares the document with relevant team members. This weekly plan gives only the adaptations for the week's particular lessons and activities; the general adaptations detailed on Jacob's Individualized Adaptations Plan (see Figure 6–10) are not reiterated.

Step 4. Monitor and Evaluate

The fourth step of the model requires that team members monitor and evaluate student learning.

Responsible teaching is not possible without some written documentation, but if paperwork takes too much time, teaching suffers. Especially when multiple adults, including teachers, related services staff, and instructional aides, are responsible for implementing a student's educational program, guidelines should be readily available for teaching students and monitoring their progress using simple data collection forms. Although plans for some lessons and activities that require limited curricular and/or instructional adaptations can be incorporated into an Individualized Adaptations Plan and weekly lesson plans for the class, certain adaptations require more specialized planning and evaluation. Written programs (e.g., lesson plans, program formats, or teaching guides) are called for when curricular and instructional adaptations are extensive and constitute a specialized teaching methodology that requires systematic, accurate delivery and evaluation. Most often, when some of the more systematic teaching methods examined in Chapter 4 are used to teach IEP goals, written programs should be developed. Such programs would be needed for teaching the functional routines required for participation in an inclusive classroom, as well as for alternative adaptations designed to teach functional skills or to remediate academic needs. Written programs should specify the essential elements: (a) the student, (b) objective(s) or benchmark(s), (c) start and aim dates, (d) teaching time and setting, (e) instructor(s), (f) arrangement, (g) materials, (h) evaluation procedures and schedule, and (i) teaching procedures (e.g., instructional cues, prompt and fading methods, error correction procedure, reinforcers, and a rough schedule). Written programs also may give general instructions for changing procedures during later stages of learning. When teaching programs are briefly described with this level of detail, there are several advantages:

- Successful program methods can be used again with the same student (and modified for others), while those that yield little or no learning can be modified more precisely.
- Programs are more likely to be implemented consistently regardless of who teaches.

It also is important to remember that although instructional assistants may provide instruction and collect data, instructional planning and evaluation are the responsibility of qualified teachers.

FIGURE 6–11

Part of a Weekly Plan for Specific Adaptations for Jacob

Plans for Andi Bowers Week of 11/20/09		
	Monday	**Tuesday**
9:00–9:15	**Morning Routine** – Check in, get organized – Morning work: Thanksgiving word search *Jacob: Reduce number of words, highlight initial letters*	**Morning Routine** – Check in, get organized – Morning work: Thanksgiving greeting card for a school helper *Jacob: Make card for his bus driver. Jacob dictates his message, fills in blanks for date, names, greeting, and closing.*
9:15–10:15	**Language Arts** – Introduce historical fiction: characteristics, compare with realistic fiction and fantasy – Guided reading: Four groups—two focus on immigrants coming to America, two on First Americans. Write summaries. *Jacob: Preview vocabulary and repeating lines that he can read. Provide storyframe for his summary.*	**Language Arts** – Morning spelling packet, one page – Morning guided reading: Continue historical fiction. Complete summaries; two groups share summaries and do Venn diagrams to compare stories *Jacob: Make sure that he can share at least one item from summary. Peel-and-stick labels for his Venn diagram.*
10:15–10:45	**Art**	**P.E.**
10:45–11:40	**Math** Multiplying 2-digit numbers: – Large group: Review partial sums and lattice methods – Practice using individual whiteboards – Independent work: pp. 34–35, digit x 2 digit *Jacob: During large group, count and group items for tomorrow's Measurement Centers. During independent work, p. 22 in his math journal.*	**Math** Measurement Centers: Estimate then measure; work in cooperative groups with assigned roles to complete booklet 1. Weight—pounds and ounces 2. Liquid volume—ounces, cups, pints, quarts 3. Length—feet, inches to fourths *Jacob: Group with Jay, Frankie, Delia. Role of "Checker." Enlarge checklist of steps. Focus on pounds, cups, feet.*
11:40–12:05	**Recess and Cleanup**	**Recess and Cleanup**
12:10–12:40	**Lunch**	**Lunch**
12:45–1:45	**Science/Social Studies** – Review of Virginia's First Inhabitants—Powhatan, Teton Sioux, Pueblo – Comparison matrix with region, homes, occupations, transportation *Jacob: Cut and paste pictures with captions onto his matrix. Make sure that he raises his hand to offer at least one answer.*	**Science/Social Studies** – States of matter—interactive notebooks – Concept organizer with definitions, examples of physical properties and physical changes *Jacob: Circle terms and underline definitions in his notebook. Focus on states of water (solid/ice, liquid/water, steam/gas). Cut and paste pictures to match states of matter. Go to Science Center when finished.*

Monitoring Student Performance

Monitoring student performance means keeping reliable records of students' accomplishments both just before teaching begins (baseline performance) and also once instruction gets under way. Having some baseline data along with intervention data allows progress to be assessed. As described in Chapter 5, student performance can be measured during instruction by gathering *teaching data* and during testing by gathering *probe data*. Both teaching and probe data are informative and can be used to make improvements in a teaching program if students are not progressing as expected.

When student performance is graphed, several visual elements can help teams visually analyze a student's progress (see Chapter 5). *Aim lines* establish a visual guide on the graph of the student's expected performance over time; aim lines suggest how fast learning should progress if the student is to achieve the desired performance by a goal date. *Trend lines* can be added to graphs if the student's performance is up and down and its slope (ascending, descending, or flat) over time is not easily understood. The purpose of gathering student performance data and visually analyzing the data is twofold: (a) to monitor the implementation of adaptations, and (b) to make data-based decisions that resolve any problems.

Jacob's team has completed a task analysis data collection form for his morning routine (see Figure 6–12) that lists the target behaviors in order, along with the instructional cue and the recording key. The form is used to record baseline performance, as well as the results of teaching trials and probe (or testing) trials. His team can use information recorded on this form to detect day-to-day progress and to identify particular steps that may appear either to be mastered or to be consistently difficult. Dated anecdotal notes recorded on the back of the form help the team to hypothesize whether changes in performance result from learning, from problems with the teaching plan, or from problems in the classroom or at home. Using this type of form encourages teams to found their decisions on data and be consistent in their teaching, making it easier for Jacob to learn when multiple instructors participate. Staff members also refer to the brief teaching guide (see Figure 6–13), which describes the teaching procedures that they use with Jacob, including the constant time delay method and the types of prompts (see Chapter 5). The teaching guide also indicates the social/communication skills and aligned academic learning standards (in this case, Virginia's Aligned Standards of Learning) that are embedded within this functional routine.

Notice that the steps of Jacob's morning routine are listed in reverse order on the task analysis form (see Figure 6–12) so that the first step is at the bottom of the table and the last step, Step 10, is at the top. This self-graphing form allows his teacher to convert the task analytic data into a bar graph so that data do not have to be transferred to a separate graph for visual analysis. The y-axis of a graph represents the measurement of the target behavior and the x-axis represents the time frame of the measurement. On the task analysis form, the numbered rows on the left side of the table become the vertical, or y-axis, of the graph and the bottom horizontal line of the table becomes the x-axis. The x-axis is already labeled with the dates on which performance data were taken, and the y-axis now represents the number of steps in the task where the student performed independently. To create a histogram, or bar graph, of the results, simply count the number of steps completed independently and shade that day's column up to the corresponding number on the y-axis. For example, on 9/17 Jacob performs four steps independently and that column is shaded up to 4 on the horizontal axis, while on 9/24 he gets five steps correct and that column is shaded up to 5. (Alternatively, a line graph can be made by plotting points in the columns instead of using shading to create a histogram.) On Figure 6–12, only the columns in which testing (not teaching) data were recorded are shaded. The graph shows that Jacob's progress in completing his morning work is ascending and meets program criteria on 10/29 with 2 consecutive days at 100% independent performance.

If probe and teaching data are to be useful to teams, they must be accurate (interobserver agreement). Likewise, teams need to know whether programs are being carried out as planned (procedural fidelity). To achieve these types of accuracy, all team members who are involved in teaching a particular program first should work together to review the written program directions (for probing and for teaching) for clarity. Second, team members can use role-play, practice and feedback, and in-class coaching to teach each other to use new procedures effectively and consistently (Schepis, Reid, Ownbey, & Parsons, 2001). Observing videos taken of team members demonstrating the probing or teaching procedures also can be a helpful training technique.

FIGURE 6–12

Task Analysis for Jacob's Morning Routine

Task Analysis Instructional Program Plan																			

Student: Jacob   **Teachers:** Bowers, Fuentes, Conners (aide)   **Routine:** Morning routine

Setting: Classroom   **Days and Time:** Daily, 9:00–9:10   **Start Date:** 9/01/09

Probe Schedule: Every Thursday   **Baseline/Probe Method:** Multiple opportunity task analytic assessment (4-second latency)

Recording Key: Test: + correct, − incorrect
Teach: + unprompted correct, ✓ prompted correct (gestural prompt), − unprompted/prompted error, NR no response
Write anecdotal comments on back of form.

Task Steps	Dates																		
	9/1*	9/2*	9/3	9/8	9/10	9/15	9/17	9/22	9/24	9/29	10/1	10/6	10/8	10/13	10/15	10/20	10/22	10/27	10/29
Baseline/Teach/Probe →	B	B	T	T	T	T	P	T	P	T	P	T	P	T	P	T	P	T	P
Total Independent Steps →	0	0	0	1	2	4	4	4	5	5	6	6	8	8	9	9	10	10	10
10. Begin morning work	−	−	✓	✓	✓	+	−	✓	−	✓	+	✓	−	✓	+	+	+	+	+
9. Fill in day and date on schedule and agenda	−	−	✓	✓	✓	✓	−	✓	−	✓	−	✓	−	✓	−	✓	+	+	+
8. Sharpen two pencils, if needed	−	−	✓	✓	✓	✓	−	✓	−	✓	−	+	+	+	+	+	+	+	+
7. Make lunch choice	−	−	✓	+	✓	✓	+	+	+	+	+	+	+	+	+	+	+	+	+
6. Take out homework, put in wire basket	−	−	✓	✓	✓	✓	−	✓	−	✓	−	✓	+	+	+	+	+	+	+
5. Return to desk	−	−	−	✓	✓	✓	+	+	+	+	+	✓	+	+	+	+	+	+	+
4. Take off outerwear and hang in locker	−	−	✓	−	+	+	−	✓	+	+	+	+	+	+	+	+	+	+	+
3. Find locker; hang up backpack	−	−	✓	✓	✓	+	+	+	+	+	+	+	+	+	+	+	+	+	+
2. Place backpack on desk; unpack agenda and homework folder	−	−	✓	✓	✓	✓	−	✓	−	✓	−	✓	+	+	+	+	+	+	+
1. Respond to peer's greeting	−	−	✓	✓	+	+	+	+	+	+	+	+	+	+	+	+	+	+	+

Once a program is implemented by team members, the special education teacher will want to make informal observations to ask the following questions:

- Is the program being carried out as planned? Are needed supports provided? Are the individualized adaptations made as planned? Is instruction given as scheduled? (See Procedural Reliability in Chapter 5.)
- Are the adaptations only as specialized as necessary?
- Does the team consistently record and examine the student's performance data?

- Are probe and teaching data accurate? (See Interobserver Agreement in Chapter 5.)

Evaluating Student Progress

Teams will regularly meet and review the student's progress by looking at performance data and anecdotal notes, and by sharing their perspectives. During this phase of teaching, the team's focus is primarily on one crucial question: *Does the student have social and instructional participation that is adding up to mastery and accomplishment?* To answer this question, team members will

FIGURE 6–13
Brief Teaching Guide for Jacob's Morning Routine

Brief Teaching Guide	
Student: Jacob	**Routine:** Morning routine
Teacher(s): Fuentes (Monday); aide (Tuesday–Friday)	**Start Date:** 9/01/09
Start Date for Objective 1: 9/01/09	**Aim Date for Objective 1:** 11/01/09
IEP Goal: Jacob will complete regularly scheduled classroom routines (Objective 1: Morning; Objective 2: Departure; Objective 3: Preparation for lunch) 100% steps correct on two consecutive weekly probes **Objective 1:** Jacob will accurately complete the morning routine within 10 minutes on two consecutive weekly probes. **Related/Embedded IEP Goals** (social, communication, motor, or functional academic goals related to this routine): 1. Communication-Social: Greet and respond to greetings from teachers and peers. **Aligned Standards of Learning, if any, related to this routine:** 1. Recognize and write numerals 0–100 (Math—Number Sense 9). 2. Tell time to the quarter hour using analog and digital clocks (Math—Measurement 15).	
Time: 9:00–9:10 A.M.	**Setting(s):** Classroom
Stage of Learning: Acquisition	**Arrangement:** One-to-one, naturalistic
Teaching Days: Mon., Tues., Wed., Fri.	**Test Day:** Thursdays (Multiple opportunity: Test every step)
Materials: Daily schedule sheet placed on desk; backpack, two pencils, homework folder, and agenda	
Teaching Procedure: Constant time delay (0, 4 seconds) across total task	
Prompts: Gestural (point to or manipulate materials, point to picture prompts) or verbal prompt to watch peer model ("Look what Ty is doing. You do it, too."). Do not use any other verbal prompts.	
Cue: "It's time to unpack and get organized."	
Description of Teaching Procedures: For first 2 days, use zero time delay; then delay prompt 4 seconds. Use zero time delay for 1 day after long weekends, vacations, or on all steps following four or more error steps in one session. The goal is to increase his unprompted correct responses.	

- check student performance data on IEP objectives/benchmarks,
- consider continuing a program if performance is at or better than the aim line,
- consider changing a program if performance is below the aim line or highly variable,
- if anecdotal data and graphed data do not agree, identify potential reasons and observe to verify the reason for the disagreement, and
- check anecdotal notes on social participation and make needed improvements.

The team will also want to informally assess the social validity of the teaching program by asking whether all team members and others (e.g., student, peers) are satisfied with the teaching program and with the student's learning outcomes.

One of Marc's mathematics objectives was linked to the Kindergarten Standards of Learning and also had a functional focus: Recognize a penny, nickel, dime, and quarter and determine the value of a collection of pennies and/or nickels whose total is 10 cents or less (Virginia SOL, K.7 Measurement). He received instruction both in the resource room and alongside his classmates in kindergarten. Additionally, his special education teacher provided many practical opportunities (some real and some contrived) to use pennies (and later nickels) to make small purchases at school. The first objective in the program was to teach penny. They started the program on 9/13 with an aim date of 9/28. Using a simple dated grid, the team kept track of the number of correct purchases made with pennies out of 10 opportunities during teaching and during probes. These data were converted to percentages and then graphed.

Graph A in Figure 6-14 shows that Marc scored 10%, 10%, and 20% during the first 3 days of teaching pennies. They set the first endpoint for the aim line at the intersection of the second day of the program, or middle date (9/17), and his mid-performance, which was 10% (i.e., the middle value of the three percentages). The aim line endpoint was set at the intersection of the criterion performance expected of Marc (i.e., 80%) and the goal date for pennies (9/28). (See Chapter 5 for an explanation of aim lines.) Marc's teacher then drew a straight line between these two endpoints.

When Marc's performance continued to be irratic and below the aim line after a week of teaching, they decided to pencil in a trend line (see graph B in Figure 6-14). Marc's team drew a trend line using data from the first seven days of training. (See Chapter 5 for a description of trend lines). They divided these data into two groups—the first three

data points and the last four. For the first three days, the middle date was 9/17 and the middle value was 10%; for the next four days, the middle date was halfway between 9/23 and 9/24, and the middle value was 15 (halfway between 10 and 20). They connected the two points that resulted and drew a line. The trend was slightly ascending, although almost flat. They decided to improve the program because this progress seemed to be too slow for Marc (see graph B in Figure 6-14).

Marc's team looked at the problem analysis worksheet (see Figure 6-15) and checked several possible issues that might be contributing to his slow progress (numbers 20 and 27). They hypothesized that involving peers would help motivate him. After changing the aim date to 10/11, lowering the criterion performance, and including two classmates in the sessions, his progress improved and reached and passed criterion (see Graph C in Figure 6-14).

Marc's and Jacob's teams used regularly gathered student performance data to monitor and evaluate their progress. When the level of learning was not what they had expected, team members engaged in problem solving.

FIGURE 6–14

Marc's Performance During a Month of Instruction on the Objective of Making Purchases at School Using Pennies for Totals of 10 Cents or Less

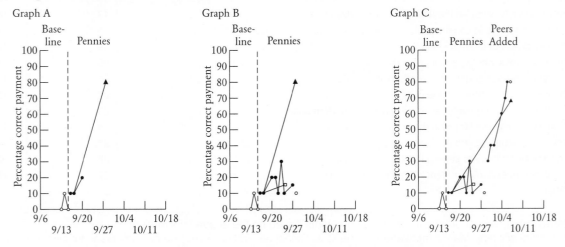

Graph (A) shows his performance during baseline and the first 3 days of teaching (up to September 20) when his teacher drew an aim line. Graph B shows his performance up to September 28 when the team decided to draw a trend line to better determine his slope of progress. Graph C shows his progress after making a program improvement (adding peers) up until when he reached aim on October 6. (Assistance on these graphs is credited to Marci Kinas-Jerome and Corey Jerome.)

FIGURE 6–15

Program Analysis Worksheet Completed on Marc's Objective for Making Purchases with Pennies

Problem Analysis Worksheet

Student: _____   Time Period: _____
Program: _____
Team Members present at meeting: _____

Directions: Put a check (√) by the statement that you feel describes the data collected during the latest review period. If you suspect the statement describes the data, but you need more data to address the issue, check the second column. (Check only one column.)

			Seems to be true	Need more data
1. The trend of the data is:	Ascending	1.	√	NMD
	Flat			
	Descending			
2. The data are:	Not variable	2.	√	NMD
	Variable			
3. The level of the data is:	Low	3.	√	NMD
	Moderate			
	High			
4. Student performance is related to medication		4.		NMD
5. Student has experienced a temporary environmental change/problem/stress		5.		NMD
6. The data may not be reliable		6.		NMD
7. The staff are not implementing the program reliably		7.		NMD
8. The trend or level of variability has changed since the last review		8.		NMD
9. The student used to perform the skill at higher levels		9.		NMD
10. The data pattern indicates that variability is random		10.		NMD
11. The data pattern indicates that variability is cyclical		11.		NMD
12. Test data conflict with the instructional data		12.		NMD
13. Test scores tend to be greater than instructional scores		13.		NMD
14. Errors typically occur on the same step(s) of the task analysis		14.		NMD
15. Student is not progressing through prompt levels		15.		NMD
16. Errors typically occur on the first trials of the day/session		16.		NMD
17. Errors typically occur on the latter trials of the day or session		17.		NMD
18. Errors occur more in some settings or with specific staff		18.		NMD
19. Student does not attempt the task		19.		NMD
20. Student is reluctant to participate in the task		20.	√	NMD
21. Student responds negatively to certain levels of prompts		21.		NMD
22. Student does not attend to the cues		22.		NMD
23. Student is receiving reinforcement for incorrect performance		23.		NMD
24. Student exhibits similar problems in other programs		24.		NMD
25. Interfering behaviors are present...		25.		NMD
26. Problem behaviors are staying the same or increasing		26.		NMD
27. The program excludes student interaction with peers		27.	√	NMD
28. Other:		28.		NMD

State team's hypothesis about the instructional problems based on the above information:
Involving peers will help Marc's motivation for the task. Select several kindergarten classmates to involve who would benefit from the applied purchasing activities. Change the aim date from September 28 to October 11 and lower criterion.

Source: From *Making the Most of Student Performance Data,* by L. J. Farlow and Martha E. Snell, 1994, Innovations: Research to Practice Series, Washington, D.C.: American Association on Mental Retardation. Copyright 1994 by American Association of Mental Retardation. Adapted with permission.

Summary

The adaptations model described in this chapter provides a framework for undertaking the process of designing and implementing instructional programs for students with severe disabilities who are members of general education classes. The model emphasizes the use of collaborative team problem solving to make adaptations that will lead to academic, functional, and social success for students. Table 6-3 provides a review of the components of the model, including prerequisites, the elements of class lessons and activities that can be adapted (from least to most intrusive), and the two stages—general and special—in which individualized adaptations are developed. The model is designed to guide instructional teams to create adaptations that will meet the two primary criteria of enabling social and instructional participation that yields meaningful progress and being only as specialized as necessary. Throughout this chapter, we have provided illustrations of the planning forms used by teams to record and share decisions about a targeted student's instructional program. Teams should adapt these tools to suit their students, any circumstances that are particular to their schools, and their own planning styles. However, we recommend that teachers in a school adopt a set of planning formats that are used schoolwide, with other student-specific or team-specific forms included as needed. This approach enhances communication among teachers and facilitates students' transition from one grade level to the next.

Suggested Activities

1. Look at Figures 6-5 (Program-at-a-Glance) and 6-6 (Student Information Form) and compare with the confidential information sharing procedures that your school uses. What are the differences? How do you think that your school's procedures could be improved?
2. Identify a student (a) with extensive support needs whose classroom participation primarily involves embedded social, motor, and communication skills, and (b) whose extent of classroom participation is questionable. Have a team member conduct an *Ecological Assessment of Classroom Activities* (Figure 6-7) of this student to understand his/her performance on each step of lessons and routines.

Use the information with other team members to identify skills that could be taught and activity adaptations that would lead to more active involvement by the student.

3. Involving other team members, complete a program planning matrix (Figure 6-8) for a student to plot his/her IEP goals against the class's daily schedule. Examine the results with the team to identify (a) when and where a student's individualized learning priorities can be taught more efficiently and effectively, and (b) to determine the times for the student to receive special supports and services such as heath care, movement breaks, therapies, or mobility training.

Identify a student whose IEP is appropriate for applying the model to develop individualized adaptation. Use the four steps listed in Figure 6-4 and the corresponding forms to develop individualized adaptations for this student that will enable meaningful inclusion that results in socialization with peers and learning of needed skills.

Note: For the student applications, we give thanks to Rachel Dickinson, Diane Talarico-Cavanaugh of Piedmond Regional Education Program and Greene County Public School Systems.

References

Baumgart, D., Brown, L., Pumpian, I., Nisbet, J., Ford, A., Sweet, M., et al. (1982). Principle of partial participation and individualized adaptations for severely handicapped students. *Journal of the Association for Persons with Severe Handicaps, 7,* 17-27.

Carter, E. W., Cushing, L. S., Clark, N. M., & Kennedy, C. H. (2005). Effects of peer support interventions on students' access to the general curriculum and social interactions. *Research and Practice for Persons with Severe Disabilities, 30,* 15-25.

Carter, E. W., Hughes, C., Guth, C., & Copeland, S. R. (2005). Factors influencing social interaction among high school students with intellectual disabilities and their general education peers. *American Journal on Mental Retardation, 110,* 366-377.

Carter, E. W., & Kennedy, C. H. (2006). Promoting access to the general curriculum using peer support strategies. *Research and Practice for Persons with Severe Disabilities, 31,* 1-9.

Carter, E. W., Sisco, L. G., Melekoglu, M. A., & Kurkowski, C. (2007). Peer supports as an alternative to individually assigned paraprofessionals in inclusive high school classrooms. *Research and Practice for Persons with Severe Disabilities, 32,* 213-227.

Clayton, J., Burdge, M., & Kleinert, H. L. (2001). Integrating alternate assessment with ongoing instruction. In H. L. Kleinert & J. F. Kearns (Eds.), *Alternate assessment: Measuring outcomes and supports for students with disabilities* (pp. 77-87). Baltimore, MD: Paul H. Brooks.

Doyle, M. B. (2008). *The paraprofessional's guide to the inclusive classroom: Working as a team* (3rd ed.). Baltimore: Paul H. Brookes.

Etzel, B. C., & LeBlanc, J. M. (1979). The simplest treatment alternative: The law of parsimony applied to choosing appropriate instructional control and errorless-learning procedures for the difficult-to-teach child. *Journal of Autism and Developmental Disorders, 26,* 361–382.

Ford, A., Davern, L., & Schnorr, R. (2001). Learners with significant disabilities: Curricular relevance in an era of standards-based reform. *Remedial and Special Education, 22*(4), 215–222.

Giangreco, M. F., Cloninger, C. J., & Iverson, V. S. (1998). *Choosing outcomes and accommodations for children: A guide to educational planning for students with disabilities* (2nd ed.). Baltimore: Paul H. Brookes.

Giangreco, M. F., Edelman, S., Luiselli, T. E., & MacFarland, S. (1997). Helping or hovering? Effects of instructional assistant proximity on students with disabilities. *Exceptional Children, 64*(1), 7–18.

Hunt, L., Soto, G., Maier, J., & Doering, K. (2003). Collaborative teaming to support students at risk and students with severe disabilities in general education classrooms. *Exceptional Children, 69,* 315–332.

Hunt, P., Soto, G., Maier, J., Muler, E., & Goetz, L. (2002). Collaborative teaming to support students with augmentative and alternative communication needs in general education classrooms. *Augmentative and Alternative Communication, 18,* 20–35.

Individuals with Disabilities Education Act Amendments of 2004, PL 108-446; so U. S. C. §§ 1400 *et seq.*

Janney, R. E., & Snell, M. E. (1996). How teachers use peer interactions to include students with severe disabilities in elementary classrooms. *Journal of the Association for Persons with Severe Handicaps, 21,* 72–80.

Janney, R., & Snell, M. E. (2004). *Teachers' guides to inclusive practices: Modifying schoolwork* (2nd ed.). Baltimore: Paul H. Brookes.

Janney, R., & Snell, M. E. (2006). *Teachers' guides to inclusive practices: Social relationships and peer support* (2nd ed.). Baltimore: Paul H. Brookes.

Johnson, J. W., McDonnell, J., Holzwarth, V. N., & Hunter, K. (2004). The efficacy of embedded instruction for students with developmental disabilities enrolled in general education classes. *Journal of Positive Behavior Interventions, 6*(4), 214–227.

Jorgensen, C. M. (1998). *Restructuring high schools for all students: Taking inclusion to the next level.* Baltimore: Paul H. Brookes.

McDonnell, J., Mathot-Buckner, C., Thorson, N., & Fister, S. (2001). Supporting the inclusion of students with moderate and severe disabilities in junior high school general education classes: The effects of classwide peer tutoring, multi-element curriculum, and accommodations. *Education and Treatment of Children, 24*(2), 141–160.

Rose, D. H., & Meyer, A. (2002). *Teaching every student in the Digital Age: Universal design for learning.* Alexandria, VA: Association for Supervision and Curriculum Development.

Sailor, W., Gee, K., & Karasoff, P. (2000). Full inclusion and school restructuring. In M. E. Snell & F. Brown (Eds.), *Instruction of students with severe disabilities* (5th ed., pp. 1–29). Upper Saddle River, NJ: Merrill/Pearson.

Schepis, M. M., Reid, D. H., Ownbey, J., & Parsons, M. H. (2001). Training support staff to embed teaching within natural routines of young children with disabilities in an inclusive preschool. *Journal of Applied Behavior Analysis, 34,* 313–327.

Snell, M. E., & Janney, R. (2005). *Teachers' guides to inclusive practices: Collaborative teaming* (2nd ed.). Baltimore: Paul H. Brookes.

Snell, M. E., & Janney, R. E. (2000). Teachers' problem solving about young children with moderate and severe disabilities in elementary classrooms. *Exceptional Children, 66,* 472–490.

Udvari-Solner, A. (1995). A process for adapting curriculum in inclusive classrooms. In R. Villa & J. Thousand (Eds.), *Creating an inclusive school* (pp. 110–124). Alexandria, VA: Association for Supervision and Curriculum Development.

Villa, R. A., & Thousand, J. S. (2000). *Restructuring for caring and effective education: Piecing the puzzle together* (2nd ed.). Baltimore: Paul H. Brookes.

Ward, T., Van De Mark, C. A., & Ryndak, D. L. (2006). Balanced literacy classrooms and embedded instruction for students with severe disabilities. In D. M. Browder & F. Spooner (Eds.), *Teaching language arts, math, and science to students with significant cognitive disabilities* (pp. 125–170). Baltimore: Paul H. Brookes.

Williamson, P., McLeaskey, J., Hoppey, D., & Rentz, T. (2006). Educating students with mental retardation in general education classrooms. *Exceptional Children, 72,* 347–361.

Young, J. (2003, January). Science interactive notebooks in the classroom. *Science Scope 26*(4), 44–47.

7

Designing and Implementing Individualized Positive Behavior Support

Robert H. Horner
Richard W. Albin
Anne W. Todd
J. Stephen Newton
Jeffrey R. Sprague

In this chapter, we provide an introduction to positive behavior support (PBS), a description of the core procedures that make PBS effective, and examples of how this approach is applied with students who require individualized behavior support plans. Over the past years, PBS has developed from an approach to providing individualized behavioral support for persons with severe disabilities and problem behaviors living in the community to a three-tiered model of prevention and intervention that addresses school discipline and all students' behavior support needs at the level of the entire school (Dunlap, Sailor, Horner, & Sugai, 2009). PBS is a core element of education today and has been implemented in thousands of schools across the United States and abroad. Emerging research literature documents the positive impact of implementing the three-tired PBS model on schools' disciplinary problems and academic outcomes (Bradshaw, Koth, Thornton, & Leaf, 2009; Horner et al., 2009; Horner, Sugai, Todd, & Lewis-Palmer, 2005; Irvin, Tobin, Sprague, Sugai, & Vincent, 2004; McIntosh, Chard, Boland, & Horner, 2006; Taylor-Greene et al., 1997).

This chapter focuses on procedures for implementing individualized, function-based support with students who engage in high levels of problem behavior. The chapter outlines specific research-validated practices and systems, but is guided by a small number of core assumptions. The first is that the goal of effective behavior support is to reduce problem behavior while also improving the quality of life experienced by the target individual. Social behavior is important (see Chapter 11) because problem behavior can serve as a major barrier to valued relationships and the acquisition of academic competence. Behavior support should both reduce the barriers posed by problem behaviors and open up opportunities for engaging in more valued activities. A second assumption is that behavior support should be guided as much as possible by the values and goals of the person receiving support. While the practices that are employed in PBS should be founded on sound science, the application of those practices should be consistent with the values and goals of the individuals (and families) most directly affected by the support. Finally, our description of behavior support assumes that individualized support efforts are always influenced by the social and societal context in which they are used. A great deal has been written about the role of societal values in educational and community support (see also Chapters 2 and 16), but we also believe that the social culture of a school affects the impact of behavior supports. The use of individualized PBS is more effective in schools that have established a school-wide social culture that emphasizes clear, consistent, positive, and safe

behavioral expectations for *all* of its students. The extent of this effect is not well documented empirically, which is why we list it here as a basic assumption that guides the practices and systems described below.

Throughout the chapter, we refer to two students, Maya and Eric, and to the activities that their support teams conducted to illustrate the various features and procedures that constitute individualized, function-based PBS. Let's meet Maya.

❖ ❖ ❖ ❖ ❖   **Maya**   ❖ ❖ ❖ ❖ ❖

Maya is seven years old, lives at home with her family, and has Down syndrome, moderate to severe intellectual disabilities, and autism. Maya lives with her two middle school-age brothers and both birth parents, and recently entered first grade at her neighborhood elementary school. She enjoys fish, has an aquarium, and wants to work with fish or in a pet store when she grows up. Maya takes care of most of her dressing and personal care needs and enjoys helping in the kitchen and listening to music with her brothers and friends. She names the letters of the alphabet, follows two-step directions, uses icons and photos to "read," counts items up to 10, identifies the numbers 1 through 5, and writes her first name. Maya also engages

in problem behaviors that are becoming increasingly intense and currently threaten her continued participation in regular school settings. The major concern is that in situations where Maya is not receiving social attention from peers, she will yell at her peers and then sometimes hit them. Maya's behavior can escalate to dangerous levels. She also has a history of sticking her tongue out, spitting, and throwing objects when she has had very little peer attention. At the same time, Maya has difficulty during transitions as a result of people getting too close to her. She yells at her peers and hits them when agitated during transition periods such as waiting in line and passing through the hallway.

Twenty or thirty years ago, Maya most likely would have been placed in a segregated school with a minimalist curriculum and behavior support that likely included the delivery of highly aversive events (e.g., physical punishment, restraint, and isolation). Today, the Individuals with Disabilities Education Act of 2004 (U.S. Department of Education, 2009) and current U.S. Department of Education standards (Shavelson & Towne, 2002) require research-validated strategies that provide Maya with access to the least restrictive environment possible and help her to meet her individualized education program (IEP) goals. To meet this responsibility, schools now have access to technological behavioral and academic supports that are designed to address the needs of all students. PBS is a key element of this technology (Sailor, Dunlap, Sugai, & Horner, 2009).

PBS is about designing or redesigning environments and systems of support to prevent or minimize the development and occurrence of problem behavior. Its purpose, however, is not simply to decrease problem behavior; instead, the purpose of PBS is to increase

personally valued and desired lifestyle outcomes such as improved learning, academic success, access to friends and social networks, continued educational opportunities, employment, and involvement in the full range of school and community activities. PBS is a broad approach to providing support that is grounded in the strong values provided by advocates of normalization (Nirje, 1969; Wolfensberger, 1983), self-determination (Wehmeyer & Schwartz, 1997), and person-centered planning (Holburn & Vietze, 2002; Kincaid, 1996; O'Brien, O'Brien, & Mount, 1997). Dunlap, Sailor, Horner, and Sugai (2009) describe the core features of PBS as (a) application of research-validated behavioral science; (b) integration of multiple intervention elements to provide ecologically valid practical support; (c) commitment to substantive, durable lifestyle outcomes; and (d) implementation of support within organizational systems that facilitate sustained effects.

The goal of PBS is to invest in understanding the vision and strengths of each individual and to use this information to craft an environment that promotes socially adaptive behaviors while simultaneously making problem behaviors irrelevant, inefficient, and ineffective:

- Making a problem behavior *irrelevant* means reducing or eliminating the need to engage in a problem behavior by proactively creating effective environments.
- Making a problem behavior *inefficient* means teaching a person appropriate replacement behaviors that serve the same function as the problem behavior but that are even more efficient in producing desired outcomes.
- Making a problem behavior *ineffective* means *not allowing* the person to get what he or she wants through problem behavior.

This goal represents a significant shift in perspective from a vision of behavior support as a process that "changes the person" or emphasizes delivering consequences that will guide a person toward adapting to an established setting (e.g., classroom, residential setting). Within the PBS approach, consequences that follow both appropriate and problem behaviors remain

important. However, the major focus is on procedures and strategies that are designed to *prevent* the occurrence of problem behaviors (Bambara & Kern, 2005; Carr et al., 1994; Crone & Horner, 2003). This focus on prevention is seen in the PBS approach's emphasis on removing or modifying stimuli that promote or evoke problem behavior (e.g., changing activity schedules, tasks, and the social contexts associated with problem behavior) and investing in teaching new skills, such as communication and social skills, that can replace problem behavior (Carr et al., 1999; Dunlap & Carr, 2007; Kern & Clarke, 2005).

Carr (1994, 2000) offered an important insight into PBS when he encouraged those who design supports to focus as much, or more, on what happens *between* bouts of problem behavior (i.e., when the person is doing well) as they do on what is happening *during* a bout of problem behavior. Using information about situations where the person is successful can provide valuable guidance for identifying how to organize support in more difficult situations. To illustrate the implications of this idea, meet our second student, Eric.

✤ ✤ ✤ ✤ ✤ Eric ✤ ✤ ✤ ✤ ✤

Eric is a 15-year-old young man with autism and severe intellectual disabilities who was at risk of being excluded from his school because he would scream, pull at his own hair, and scratch at staff when he was asked to shift from one activity to another. Eric has some speech, but primarily uses a symbol communication system for much of his "formal" communication. Eric does not like change or new situations. He also is allergic to grass and tree pollens, which contribute to his challenges during parts of the year. Earlier efforts to provide clear positive and negative consequences (e.g., token economies, dense schedules of reinforcement) had been ineffective.

Eric's team decided to try a PBS approach. His teachers looked carefully at the situations where he behaved well and considered the differences between the situations where he was successful and those that were difficult for him. In Eric's case, the process of functional behavioral assessment (described in detail later in this chapter), a central feature of PBS, made it clear that when his day followed highly predictable routines, he did well. When he was asked to shift from his routine (even to preferred activities), he found the process highly aversive and engaged in dangerous behaviors. His problem behaviors were maintained over time because periodically

Eric was successful in getting his predictable routine reinstated. Eric's behavior support plan emerged as a combination of schedule redesign to prevent problem situations, teaching him new ways to request predictability, systematic consequences to prevent problem behaviors from being rewarded, and clear rewards for moving through his daily events. To provide predictability without succumbing to the trap of continually repeating a narrow daily routine, the staff taught Eric to use a picture communication system to review current activities and label what activity would come next. New activities could be introduced as long as they had a picture, were reviewed in advance, and were to be followed by a preferred activity. The staff also learned to give Eric precorrection prompts (i.e., a prompt for an appropriate response that is delivered just before the individual experiences a context or cue that has reliably evoked a problem behavior in the past) 1 to 3 minutes before an activity change. Finally, staff made sure that Eric received his allergy medication during the spring and early summer pollen season. Together, these efforts resulted in an 85% reduction in his problem behavior, the opportunity to remain in his neighborhood school, and the ability to sustain important social relationships with peers.

The Cascading Model of Individualized PBS

In many ways, the process of implementing individualized PBS is a cascade of steps, each step building from its predecessor. Figure 7–1 offers an overview of this process and provides the organizing structure for describing the specific practices and organizational systems for each step. We begin with a review of the entire process and then provide more detailed implementation recommendations and supporting research for each step. The delivery of PBS in schools utilizes a team-based approach that involves multiple staff who represent a variety of roles (e.g., regular and special education teachers, administrators, behavior specialists, counselors, educational assistants, and related service providers) (Horner, Sugai, Todd, & Lewis-Palmer, 2005; Todd, Horner, Sugai, & Colvin, 1999; Todd, Horner, Sugai, & Sprague, 1999). Readers should keep in mind that completing the steps presented in Figure 7–1 is a team responsibility, and not that of any single individual within a school.

Step 1: Define the problem behavior. The cascade of activities begins when a problem behavior (or set of problem behaviors) is identified. If the problem behavior is of sufficient severity as to require a formal plan of support, then an assessment is conducted. Note that from the beginning, problem behavior is (a) defined as problematic because it serves as a barrier to important lifestyle goals, including health, safety, and inclusion; (b) clustered into classes of behavior that are maintained by the same consequences (e.g., obtain attention, allow escape from an aversive activity); and (c) organized according to daily routines when it is most likely to occur (e.g., transitions, mealtime, toileting, reading period), so the challenge shifts from simply reducing the problem behavior to providing the support needed so that the person is successful within his or her daily routines. PBS focuses not just on reducing problem behavior but also on building the skills that result in success for routines that are difficult for the individual.

Step 2: Conduct an assessment for behavior support planning. Two types of assessments provide

FIGURE 7–1
Cascading Model of Behavior Support

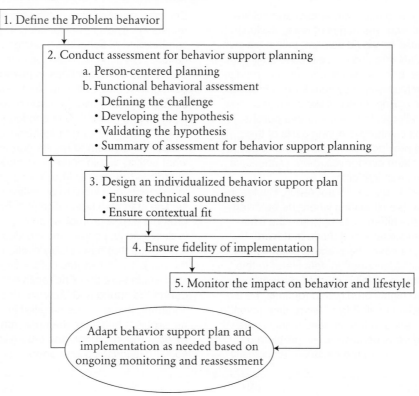

information to guide individualized PBS. Use of a *person-centered planning process* defines the personal goals and preferences of the individual and his or her family and also identifies important elements, strengths, and gaps in the individual's life. A *functional behavioral assessment* provides a clear statement that defines (a) exactly what the problem behavior(s) looks like, (b) when it is most and least likely to occur, and (c) why the problem behavior keeps occurring. This information may be obtained from a review of the student's history; from active interviews with advocates, the student, and those who support the student; from direct observation in natural situations; from more structured observation; and, on occasion, from functional analysis.

Step 3: Design an individualized behavior support plan. The assessment information is used to construct a support plan. A major feature of PBS is that the unique knowledge gleaned from the assessment process should directly guide the content of the support plan. The term *function-based support* is used to reflect the fact that the procedures used are linked to the function(s) of problem behaviors. A process known as *competing behavior analysis* (Crone & Horner, 2003; O'Neill et al., 1997) is useful for moving from assessment results to a formal behavior support plan. PBS plans that result from this process are characterized by (a) clear operational definitions of the problem behavior(s), (b) a formal summary of the assessment outcomes, (c) specific strategies for altering the environment to prevent problem behaviors, (d) teaching objectives for building the desired skills that replace the problem behaviors, (e) strategies for ensuring that desired behaviors are rewarded, (f) strategies for minimizing the rewards associated with problem behaviors, (g) consequences for problem behaviors (if necessary), (h) strategies for minimizing the danger caused by severe problem behaviors (if necessary), and (i) formal procedures for assessing and adapting the support plan and implementation over time.

Step 4: Ensure fidelity of implementation. To increase the likelihood that behavior support plans are implemented as written, emphasis is placed on (a) a clear description of the implementation process (who will do what and when) and (b) consideration of contextual fit (i.e., the extent to which those individuals who are expected to provide support have the skills, resources, and support to be successful) (Albin, Lucyshyn, Horner, & Flannery, 1996).

Step 5: Monitor the impact on behavior and lifestyle. For PBS to have a substantive impact on not just problem behavior but also on the options that are available for a desirable lifestyle, ongoing monitoring of plan effects is needed. PBS is not a brief intervention that "fixes" or "corrects" a person, but instead it includes *ongoing* support as needed. Effective support plans monitor and adapt plan procedures and implementation over time. For example, the procedures used to produce an initial change in behavior may need to be modified to sustain that behavior change over an extended period of time.

In the following sections, we will follow Maya and Eric through the cascade of PBS steps, with more detailed descriptions of the specific procedures that result in effective support. These examples help highlight the relevance of each step in the cascade of PBS steps.

Define the Problem Behavior

The individualized PBS process begins when a student is identified as having a problem behavior(s) that requires more attention and support than is provided for the vast majority of students within the broader context of school-wide and classroom behavior support systems (Sugai, Horner, & Gresham, 2002). In particular, individualized PBS is used for students whose behavior raises concerns regarding the health and safety of the student, peers, school staff, or others; interferes significantly with the student's educational program or the education of others; or places the student at risk for losing an inclusive educational placement and being placed in a more restrictive or segregated setting. Consider Maya, who was entering a regular elementary school but whose problem behavior put her at risk for exclusion from that school because of concerns about Maya's and other students' safety.

> *Maya had a history of engaging in problem behavior that the elementary school staff knew about from her history and files, and from the transition process that was implemented to facilitate Maya's move from preschool to elementary school. The elementary school staff was concerned about Maya's serious problem behaviors, which included hitting other students, spitting, and sticking out her tongue. There also was concern that Maya's behaviors were becoming increasingly frequent and intense, and that sometimes her behavior escalated out of control, especially*

during transition periods, less structured activities, and in lunch and recess lines. From the very beginning of the school year, the staff was alerted to Maya's behavior. Behavioral incidents in the hallways did occur and were noted. After the first month of first grade, the staff also noted that Maya had begun to put her head down on the table during reading and math instruction. If Maya was to be supported successfully in her new elementary school, it was clear to Maya's teachers that an individualized behavior support plan would be needed. A behavior support team was created for Maya and the process of designing and implementing a behavior support plan was initiated.

Conduct Assessment for Creating a Behavior Support Plan

Before a Behavior Support Plan (BSP) can be developed for a student who exhibits problem behavior, an assessment is initiated. In supporting students with disabilities, it is advisable that two types of assessment be completed: (a) person-centered planning and (b) a functional behavioral assessment. A school's PBS team should have the capacity to complete these assessments or ready access to that capacity (e.g., through access to district-level specialists or resources).

Person-Centered Planning

A central feature of PBS is the recognition that the outcomes of behavior support should include not just the elimination or reduction of problem behavior but also an improvement in adaptive behavior and overall quality of life (Dunlap et al., 2009; Lucyshyn, Horner, Dunlap, Albin, & Ben, 2002; Newton & Horner, 2004; Schalock & Alonso, 2002). To be successful, the outcomes that result from behavior support must be referenced to the personal values of the student receiving the support and his or her family.

This focus on quality of life, personal values, and outcomes has resulted in persons with disabilities, their families, and teachers and other professionals working to create processes for defining a person's values and desired lifestyle, and for rallying the support required to achieve that vision. For example, the many varieties of person-centered planning are designed to ensure that the person and those closest to the person both (a) define a high-quality lifestyle from their personal perspectives, and (b) discuss and develop broad strategies for creating the conditions that will enable that lifestyle (Holburn & Vietze, 2002; Kincaid, 1996).

Person-centered planning assists support teams to identify a "vision" for the student and to place behavior support into the broader contexts of the student's life and personal goals.

The design of behavior support for Maya began with her support team conducting a Personal Futures Plan meeting (Mount, 1994). The meeting was led by a trained facilitator from the district office and guided to the greatest degree possible by Maya's family and Maya herself. Also participating were three elementary school staff (Maya's teacher, the vice principal, and the school behavior specialist), Maya's preschool teacher, Maya's aunt, and Maya's longtime home care provider. This group of people developed the following long-term goals, or "vision," for Maya: (a) high school graduation; (b) living in an apartment with a friend; (c) employment in a fish or pet store; (d) skills in cooking, clothing care, basic household chores, money management, personal care, and time management; (e) joining a community group; and (f) maintenance of good physical health through diet and exercise. With these long-term goals in mind, the team worked on a set of goals for Maya to meet by the end of first grade, which included reading functional sight words, identifying numbers, counting and sorting, conversational skills, and behavior self-management. These goals provided Maya's support team with a common vision for Maya and for what they wanted and needed to accomplish with Maya's IEP and a BSP.

Teachers and others providing support to students with problem behaviors should be mindful that the development and implementation of any BSP should occur within the context of the broader lifestyle considerations that emerge during person-centered planning processes. There are seven foundational issues that should always be considered when developing an individualized BSP: (a) communication options, (b) mobility, (c) predictability, (d) opportunities for choice, (e) social interactions and networks, (f) activity patterns, and (g) health and physiology. In addition to building a vision for a student, person-centered planning processes provide the opportunity to identify whether any of these foundational considerations need to be addressed in developing a BSP for that student. Although not formally an assessment, person-centered planning provides essential information for developing an individualized BSP that will meet all of a student's support needs.

Because the goals and aspirations of students and families may change over time, it is desirable that person-centered planning be more than a one-shot process, particularly as students approach their postschool lives. When students have the kinds of lives that they want, their problem behaviors may decrease, and PBS can be initiated to address any lingering or "residual" problem behaviors (Risley, 1996). In dealing with such problem behaviors and in supporting a student in the quest to obtain a more desired life, the initiation of functional behavioral assessment will be vital (Holburn, Jacobson, Vietze, Schwartz, & Sersen, 2000).

Functional Behavioral Assessment

Functional behavioral assessment (FBA) is a central feature of PBS. FBA is a process for gathering information about problem behavior and the environmental conditions that predict and maintain it (Crone & Horner, 2003; O'Neill et al., 1997). The goal of FBA is to improve the effectiveness and efficiency of the BSP. The process of FBA involves gathering information about the problem behavior, the situations where problem behavior is most and least likely to occur, and the consequences that reward and maintain the problem behavior. This information is typically gathered through multiple methods, including interviews; rating scales; checklists; reviews of records and files; direct observation under natural conditions; and, at times, formal processes such as structured descriptive assessment (English & Anderson, 2006) or functional analysis (Iwata, Dorsey, Slifer, Bauman, & Richman, 1982/1994). Not all of these methods are necessarily used within a single FBA. The nature of the problem behavior, its scope of occurrence, severity, complexity, or resistance to intervention attempts, as well as the contexts in which problem behavior occurs, will influence decisions regarding the methods used in conducting an FBA. A major outcome of FBA is a hypothesis statement (also referred to as a summary statement) that identifies the function(s) (i.e., the purpose) that the problem behavior serves for the person. FBA helps us understand why problem behavior occurs (i.e., it identifies the variables that are associated with the problem behavior). The details of FBA procedures and outcomes are described in the following sections of this chapter.

A functional behavioral assessment of Maya's behavior was conducted through file reviews, interviews, and direct observations led by the behavior specialist on Maya's team. Situations were categorized where Maya was most likely and least likely to engage in hitting, spitting, and sticking her tongue out. Through functional assessment interviews with Maya's former and current teachers and her family, and through systematic observations of her behavior during the school day, Maya's team identified two broad categories of routines/activities where her problem behaviors were most likely to occur; the first category involved hallway transition periods and other unstructured routines (e.g., lunch and recess). Despite these behaviors, she still seemed to want peer attention. Maya's problem behaviors were preceded by low levels of peer attention and were followed by and seemingly rewarded by immediate access to peer attention. The other category was during academic instructional periods (e.g., reading and math), in which Maya was often "too tired" to participate and put her head on the table to nap. The team hypothesized that the curriculum may be too difficult for Maya.

FBA is neither a process for producing a diagnosis nor a process for determining whether a behavior problem is a manifestation of a disability (Carr et al., 1994; Sugai, Lewis-Palmer, & Hagan-Burke, 1999–2000). The focus of FBA is on understanding the relationship between environmental events and the problem behavior, and how to change the environment, not the student. A medical approach would likely focus on identifying deficits in the *child,* but an approach founded on FBA focuses on identifying deficits in the *environment* (i.e., the conditions that establish and maintain problem behavior). FBA and PBS emphasize the engineering of effective environments as the key to producing desired behavior change.

FBA is less concerned with the fundamental etiology of problem behavior (i.e., how it originated) and more concerned with the environmental conditions (i.e., the consequences) that *currently* maintain the behavior. The conditions under which a problem behavior initially develops may be very different from the conditions that currently maintain it. For example, Guess and Carr (1991) suggested that some forms of severe self-injury may have begun as simple forms of self-stimulation (or responses to short-term illness), only later to develop into complex and destructive behaviors that are maintained by their social consequences. O'Reilly (1997) found that a 26-month-old girl's self-injurious behavior was correlated with the presence of recurrent otitis media (an ear infection that produces ear pain, ear fullness, or hearing loss). Naturally, such behavior would draw the attention of any caring parent. Thus, although the behavior began as a reaction to ear pain, it was ultimately emitted in the absence of ear pain because of a parent's contingent attention. FBA and PBS (a) use a behavioral approach instead of a medical approach; (b) focus on environmental conditions that set up, trigger, and maintain problem behaviors instead of on diagnostic labels; and (c) remediate deficient environments instead of "fix" or "cure" students with problem behaviors.

Why Conduct an FBA?

The main reason for conducting an FBA is to increase the efficiency and effectiveness of BSPs. In addition, the Individuals with Disabilities Education Act of 2004 maintained the requirements that schools use FBA and PBS under certain conditions, as mandated in the 1997 amendments to the Individuals with Disabilities Education Act. If a student's problem behavior or "misconduct" has been found to have a direct and substantial relationship to his or her disability, the IEP team needs to conduct an FBA, unless one has already been conducted, and write a BSP, unless one already exists. If a BSP already exists, then the IEP team needs to review the plan and modify it, as necessary, to address the behavior. Also, when a student with a disability is removed from his or her current placement because of problem behavior, the student should receive an FBA, behavioral intervention services, and modifications that are designed to address the behavior so that it does not recur (U.S. Department of Education, 2009).

The mandate in the 1997 amendments to the Individuals with Disabilities Education Act to use FBA in schools triggered thoughtful reviews and questions about (a) the extent to which school personnel have the technical capability to implement effective FBA and PBS (e.g., Ervin et al., 2001; Scott et al. 2004); (b) the degree to which FBA and PBS demonstrate external validity across the full range of settings, students, and behaviors that constitute a school-based application (e.g., Nelson, Roberts, Mathur, & Rutherford, 1999; Scott et al., 2004); (c) the social validity of FBA (e.g., Reid & Nelson, 2002); and (d) the extent to which interventions founded on FBA can be demonstrated to be more effective than interventions not derived from FBA (e.g., Gresham et al., 2004). These were important issues that triggered further research to determine whether the federal government's confidence in FBA and PBS is warranted. The results of this research are emerging.

For example, two meta-analyses of behavior intervention and PBS research have found that the presence of pretreatment FBA was associated with the increased effectiveness of an intervention (Didden, Duker, & Korzilius, 1997; Marquis et al., 2000). Marquis et al. found strong differences in the percentage of problem behavior reduction resulting from PBS interventions when FBA was conducted and used in planning the intervention. They concluded, "These results indicate that doing an assessment and using it to plan the PBS intervention probably results in a better outcome" (p. 161).

Further support for the beneficial effect of using FBA to plan interventions was provided in two studies involving students with problem behaviors in general education settings (Ingram, Lewis-Palmer, & Sugai, 2005; Newcomer & Lewis, 2004). These two studies compared interventions that were logically derived from a preceding FBA (i.e., were "FBA indicated") to interventions that were either "contraindicated" by FBA or not tied to an FBA hypothesis. In both studies, the interventions that were logically linked to an FBA produced substantial reductions in problem behavior in comparison to commonly used interventions that were not linked to FBA.

Finally, relevant to the question of whether FBA is doable by typical school personnel is a study by Bergstrom, Horner, and Crone (cited in Crone, Hawken, & Bergstrom, 2007). This study found that following training and limited technical assistance, school-based teams (a) independently developed FBA hypotheses that were later confirmed to be accurate by a researcher who independently conducted a functional analysis; (b) independently developed and implemented BSPs founded on the preceding FBA that significantly reduced students' disruptive behavior and increased their on-task behavior; and (c) completed the FBA processes in a relatively short time, accurately implemented the interventions, and rated the interventions as being high in acceptability.

In addition to informing decisions regarding the selection of effective behavior support procedures, FBA provides the conceptual logic needed to make multicomponent support plans work as intended. Many problem behaviors necessitate multicomponent support plans (e.g., modifying the curriculum, teaching new skills, reinforcing alternative behavior, extinguishing problem behavior). However, the complexity of multicomponent interventions can increase the difficulty of implementation. Without the conceptual logic provided by an FBA, there is a danger that an individual intervention procedure that appears sound when examined in isolation may be revealed as being illogical when considered as a component of an integrated intervention package. FBA helps ensure that the multiple elements of an intervention work together instead of at cross-purposes.

> *Recall Eric, who was at risk of being excluded from his school because he would scream, pull his hair, and scratch at staff when he was asked to shift from one activity to another. When Eric was requested to alter his typical routine in an unpredictable manner, he found the process highly aversive and he engaged in these dangerous behaviors that often resulted in his predictable routine being reinstated. On the basis of this knowledge, his staff could have chosen to "extinguish" the problem behavior by not allowing his predictable routine to be reinstated, hoping to reduce the problem behavior by withholding the reinforcer. Although this might have worked and made some programmatic sense as an isolated support strategy, it also could have resulted in dangerous situations. The staff instead chose to use a package of integrated procedures that combined (a) redesigning Eric's schedule to prevent problem situations, (b) teaching him new ways to request predictability, (c) introducing systematic consequences to prevent problem behaviors from being rewarded, and (d) providing clear rewards to Eric as he moved through his activities.*

The conceptual logic underlying FBA and the emerging research results that demonstrate the effectiveness and utility of FBA argue for continued research and application. Founding interventions on the function of problem behavior instead of attempting to overpower problem behavior through the application of interventions involving arbitrary contingencies of positive and negative consequences appears to be a fruitful approach to helping students overcome problem behavior.

Six Outcomes of FBA

Broadly considered, FBA produces information that results in six outcomes: (a) a description of the student's problem behavior and daily routines; (b) identification of consequence conditions that maintain the problem behavior; (c) identification of antecedent conditions that set the occasion for (or "trigger") the problem behavior, as well as antecedent conditions that *do not* trigger the problem behavior; (d) identification of setting events that make the problem behavior more sensitive (or less sensitive) to the maintaining conse-

quences and their associated antecedents; (e) production of a written hypothesis that synthesizes the foregoing information into a testable summary statement about the problem behavior; and (f) direct observations of the student during typical daily routines for the purpose of tentatively confirming (or disconfirming) the hypothesis (O'Neill et al., 1997).

Who Is Involved in FBA?

Depending on the school or district and its policies, the person (or persons) with the responsibility for conducting or leading an FBA may be a school psychologist, behavior specialist, counselor, special educator, teacher, or some other member of a PBS team. However, FBA involves a team process with many team members sharing responsibilities. Typically, the process for achieving the six FBA outcomes begins with interviews of school personnel and others who are most knowledgeable about the student's problem behavior (e.g., persons who have actually witnessed the student's problem behavior). The informants may include current and former teachers, instructional assistants, a bus driver, a school nurse, parents, and, if possible, the student him or herself. A review of existing records and data also may be undertaken.

Various manuals and accompanying forms and questionnaires have been developed to aid in conducting interviews that identify problem behaviors, daily routines, and the problem behaviors' triggering antecedents and maintaining consequences (e.g., Crone & Horner, 2003; O'Neill et al., 1997; see Dunlap & Kincaid, 2001, for a review of FBA manuals). As we note in the Validating the Hypothesis section, there are also several instruments that can be used to facilitate direct observation of the student during his or her daily routines. However, even as we present such instruments in the following pages, we believe that it is more important to understand the concepts that underlie the use of the instruments than to understand how to complete a specific questionnaire or form.

Regardless of the instruments used, it is useful to think of FBA as proceeding in three phases: (a) defining the challenge, (b) developing the hypothesis, and (c) validating the hypothesis. Completing these phases is a necessary precursor to developing an effective and efficient BSP.

Defining the Challenge

This phase of FBA is concerned with achieving the first FBA outcome—a description of the student's problem behavior and daily routines. A successful behavior support effort cannot be initiated until those involved reach agreement about the nature of the problem behavior. This is best accomplished by first defining the problem behavior in operational terms. An operational definition specifically describes what the student is doing when he or she is said to be engaging in a "problem behavior." A problem behavior that is described as "anger" or "frustration" lacks the clarity of a description such as "hitting," "refusing to follow the teacher's instructions," or "throwing textbooks." Operational definitions help ensure that those who are called on to implement the BSP are operating with a common understanding of the behavioral challenge. There are many tools that assist teams in identifying and defining problem behavior, identifying daily routines, and organizing problem behavior by daily routines. Two examples of tools are the Request for Assistance form (presented in Figure 7-2) and the Functional Assessment Checklist for Teachers and Staff (FACTS, Part A) (presented in Figure 7-3). Maya's team used both of these tools in defining the challenge.

A sample Request for Assistance form was completed by Maya's teacher, Ms. Craig, in collaboration with the school behavior specialist, Ms. Schwartz, on 10/17/08, to initiate a referral for assistance from the school's PBS team with Maya's problem behaviors. This request for assistance was the impetus to formalize convening a behavior support team in the hope that they could ultimately develop a BSP that would help Maya learn different ways to communicate instead of communicating by using problem behaviors. On the Request for Assistance form, Maya's problem behaviors initially were identified by her teacher as aggressiveness, poor attention span, poor work completion, and disruptiveness.

Later, on 10/21/08, Ms. Schwartz used Part A of a tool called the Functional Assessment Checklist for Teachers and Staff (FACTS) to begin an FBA interview with Ms. Craig and the school's learning specialist, Mr. Martinez. During these interviews, Maya's problem behaviors were more specifically defined as hitting peers, sticking out her tongue, spitting, and putting her head down.

In addition to identifying and operationally defining problem behavior(s), defining the challenge also involves identifying the student's typical daily routines and determining the occurrence of problem behavior(s) in those routines. Routines are sequences of behavior

that are a usual part of daily life that result in socially important outcomes. For example, eating breakfast, traveling to school, participating in morning circle, engaging in recess activities, and transitioning from one school activity to the next are common routines for students. A routine involves a predictable sequence of events that results in predictable outcomes. A challenge of PBS is to ensure that a student is not excluded from typical routines because of problem behavior but instead is provided with behavioral support that results in the problem behavior being rendered irrelevant, ineffective, or inefficient during those routines.

We strongly recommend that an FBA describe the student's full daily routines and identify those routines where the student's problem behavior is most likely and least likely to occur. For students, a daily routine can be described in terms of the daily schedule of school activities. Part A of the FACTS (see Figure 7-3) incorporates this as Step 4, providing a section to record the daily routines, rate the likelihood of problem behavior within each routine, and identify the specific problem behavior(s) that occurs within each routine.

During the course of leading the FBA interview for Maya, Ms. Schwartz recorded Maya's school routines/schedule directly on Part A of the FACTS (see Figure 7-3). Organizing Maya's problem behaviors within the context of daily routines helped Maya's team to understand that her problem behaviors were most likely to occur during two broad types of situations: (a) hallway transition periods (including transitions to and from the school bus area) and activities with minimal structure and waiting lines (e.g., lunch, recess), and (b) academic instruction that was too difficult. The specific problem behaviors identified were sticking out her tongue, hitting, and spitting, which occurred during the first type of situation, and putting her head down, which occurred during the second type of situation. By organizing the behaviors in this way, Maya's team could see that there were two separate issues that needed to be addressed.

Developing the Hypothesis

Once the student's problem behavior has been operationally defined and organized within the contexts of his or her typical daily routines, we focus on gathering information that will lead to developing a hypothesis about when and why the problem behavior occurs. To gather the information required to arrive at a hypothesis, the person responsible for conducting the FBA will

FIGURE 7–2
Request for Assistance Form

Request for Assistance

Student's name: Maya   Referred by: Moira Craig   Date: 10/17/2008

Student ID #: 1596   DOB: 04/16/2001   Grade: 1   IEP: (Y) N

Student strengths in academic areas: Student strengths in social skills:
    Identifies numbers 1–5   *Likes peers*
    Alphabet names   *Likes board games and cards (at table, not on floor)*
    Counts items 1–10

1. Check the areas of concern:

Academic	Problem Behaviors	Communication	Personal Care	Health	Contributing Factors
✓ reading	✓ aggressive	✓ language	__ dressing	__ visual acuity	✓ curriculum
✓ math	__ noncompliant	__ fluency	__ hygiene	__ visual tracking	__ trauma
__ spelling	✓ poor attention	✓ articulation	✓ organization	__ hearing	__ personal loss
__ writing	✓ work completion	__ voice	__ glasses	__ physical	__ anxiety
__ study skills	__ withdrawn	__ ELL	__ other _____	__ seizures	__ peers
__ other _____	✓ disruptive	__ other _____		__ medication	__ family
	__ poor attendance			__ gross/fine motor	__ other _____
	__ other _____			__ other _____	

2. Check the strategies tried so far and circle those that were effective:

General Review	Modify Environment	Modify Presentation	Modify Curriculum/ Homework	Modify Expectations
__ review cum file	__ change seating arrangement	__ pre-teach	✓ change task size	__ group product
✓ talk with parents	__ provide quiet space	✓ give extra practice	__ change color	__ individual product
__ talk with previous teacher	✓ provide a larger space	__ guided practice	__ provide computer	✓ make it easier
✓ seek peer help	__ encourage work breaks	__ change pacing	__ provide calculator	__ give more time
__ classroom assessment	__ other _____	__ give extra feedback	__ use visuals/ manipulatives	✓ tutor/mentor
__ other _____		__ provide patterns	__ change instruction	__ alternative response
		__ vary materials	__ provide a model	✓ emphasize quality over quantity
		__ increase instruction time	__ other _____	__ other _____
		__ planned positive reinforcer		
		__ other _____		

3. Requested team members: Moira Craig (first-grade teacher), Vance Tilman (educational assistant), Lacey Reimeriz (Maya's mom), and Trudy Schwartz (behavior specialist)

4. Parent contacted by ✓ phone, __ conference, __ letter on 10/20/2008 (date)

5. What do you hope to gain from this meeting?   __ spec. ed. referral   ✓ suggestions/support
        ✓ behavior plan   __ other _____

6. When completed, place this form in Mindy's (office assistant) mailbox

> **Teacher(s) brings the following information to meeting:**
> Work samples, assessment scores, reading rate/accuracy, office referral forms, incident reports, and any other data

(continued)

FIGURE 7–2 (*Continued*)

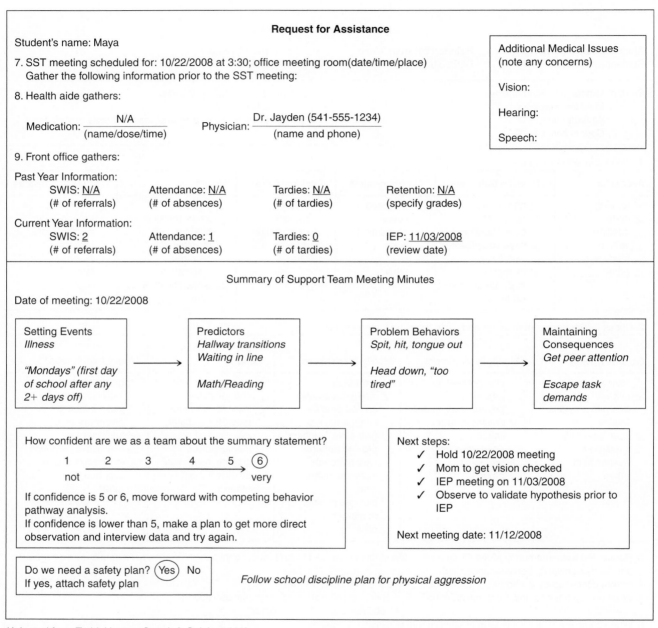

Request for Assistance

Student's name: Maya

7. SST meeting scheduled for: 10/22/2008 at 3:30; office meeting room(date/time/place)
   Gather the following information prior to the SST meeting:

8. Health aide gathers:

   Medication: ___N/A___   Physician: __Dr. Jayden (541-555-1234)__
                (name/dose/time)   (name and phone)

Additional Medical Issues (note any concerns)
Vision:
Hearing:
Speech:

9. Front office gathers:

Past Year Information:
| SWIS: N/A | Attendance: N/A | Tardies: N/A | Retention: N/A |
| (# of referrals) | (# of absences) | (# of tardies) | (specify grades) |

Current Year Information:
| SWIS: 2 | Attendance: 1 | Tardies: 0 | IEP: 11/03/2008 |
| (# of referrals) | (# of absences) | (# of tardies) | (review date) |

Summary of Support Team Meeting Minutes

Date of meeting: 10/22/2008

Setting Events		Predictors		Problem Behaviors		Maintaining Consequences
Illness	→	*Hallway transitions*	→	*Spit, hit, tongue out*	→	*Get peer attention*
"Mondays" (first day of school after any 2+ days off)		*Waiting in line* *Math/Reading*		*Head down, "too tired"*		*Escape task demands*

How confident are we as a team about the summary statement?

    1   2   3   4   5   ⑥
   not   very

If confidence is 5 or 6, move forward with competing behavior pathway analysis.
If confidence is lower than 5, make a plan to get more direct observation and interview data and try again.

Next steps:
✓ Hold 10/22/2008 meeting
✓ Mom to get vision checked
✓ IEP meeting on 11/03/2008
✓ Observe to validate hypothesis prior to IEP

Next meeting date: 11/12/2008

Do we need a safety plan? (Yes) No
If yes, attach safety plan   *Follow school discipline plan for physical aggression*

(Adapted from Todd, Horner, Sugai, & Colvin, 1999)

continue interviewing the school personnel and others who are most knowledgeable about the student's problem behavior. Depending on the time available, this may involve simply continuing with the same interview that produced the operational definition of the student's problem behavior and a description of his or her daily routine. Typically, it is useful to talk with at least two people who have daily contact with the student and

have witnessed the problem behavior. As noted, it may also be appropriate to interview the student if he or she can participate in an interview effectively.

Interviews, Checklists, and Rating Scales. Several interview instruments, checklists, and rating scales are available for gathering the information required to complete this phase of the FBA. Structured interviews

FIGURE 7–3
Functional Assessment Checklist for Teachers and Staff (FACTS, Part A)

Functional Assessment Checklist for Teachers and Staff (FACTS, Part A)

Step 1 Student/Grade: **Maya, Grade 1**   Date: **10/21/2008**
Interviewer: **Trudy Schwartz**   Respondent(s): **Moira, Vance**

Step 2 **Student Profile:** Please identify at least three strengths or contributions that the student brings to school.
Likes being around people; loves fish and aquarium; likes music

Step 3 **Problem Behavior(s): Identify problem behaviors**

___ Tardy	✓ Fight/Physical Aggression	✓ Disruptive	___ Theft
___ Unresponsive	___ Inappropriate Language	___ Insubordination	___ Vandalism
✓ Withdrawn	___ Verbal Harassment	✓ Work not done	___ Other _____
	✓ Verbally Inappropriate	___ Self-injury	

Describe problem behavior(s): **Hits peers, spits, sticks tongue out, puts head down on desk**

Step 4 **Identifying Routines: Where, when, and with whom problem behaviors are most likely**

Schedule (Times)	Activity	Likelihood of Problem Behavior	Specific Problem Behavior
8:20	Bus to class	Low 1 2 3 4 5 High ⑥	Spitting at and hitting others
8:30	Morning meeting	1 2 ③ 4 5 6	Tongue out
8:50	Reading	1 2 3 ④ 5 6	Head down, "too tired"
9:45	Groups	① 2 3 4 5 6	
10:15	Recess	1 2 3 4 ⑤ 6	Spit, hit, tongue out
11:00	Math	1 2 3 ④ 5 6	Head down, "too tired"
11:45	Lunch and Recess	1 2 3 4 ⑤ 6	Spit, hit
12:30	Projects	1 ② 3 4 5 6	Tongue out
1:15	P.E./Music/Library	① 2 3 4 5 6	
1:45	Afternoon meeting	1 ② 3 4 5 6	Tongue out
2:10	Class to bus	1 2 3 4 5 ⑥	Spit, hit

Step 5 **Select 1–3 Routines for further assessment: Select routines based on (a) similarity of activities (conditions) with ratings of 4, 5, or 6, and (b) similarity of problem behavior(s). Complete the FACTS, Part B, for each routine identified.**
Hallway transitions, recess, lunch, and recess (combining routines for Part B because their features are similar: unstructured, peers present, may be crowded or waiting in line)

(Adapted from March, Horner, Lewis-Palmer, Brown, Crone, Todd, et al., 2000)

(Crone & Horner, 2003; O'Neill et al., 1997); checklists, such as the FACTS (Crone & Horner, 2003; March et al., 2000) and the Functional Analysis Checklist (Van Houten & Rolider, 1991); and rating scales, such as the Motivation Assessment Scale (Durand, 1988), organize information about problem behaviors, antecedent stim-uli (including setting events), and consequences to help determine behavioral function. Comprehensive interview forms (e.g., O'Neill et al., 1997) also solicit information about the student's repertoire of adaptive behavior, particularly behavior that may serve to replace the problem behavior; his or her communication skills;

the quality of the support environment; and the success (or failure) of previous support plans. Interviews have the advantage of (a) being relatively low in cost, (b) allowing for the inclusion of multiple people who have important information about the student, and (c) providing a rich array of information that can be used to structure more detailed analyses of problem behavior.

An FBA interview concerning a complex, challenging pattern of behavior may take anywhere from 45 minutes to 2 hours. However, when problem behavior is not too complicated, an efficient FBA interview, such as the FACTS, may be completed in 20 minutes. The time required to complete an interview can vary considerably, depending not only on the complexity of the problem but also on the number of people participating in the interview and their knowledge of the student, talkativeness, and level of agreement. Using a structured interview or a checklist helps keep the process focused. Consistent with the outcomes of this phase of FBA, the interview should produce, at a minimum, the following: (a) identification of consequent conditions that maintain the problem behavior; (b) identification of antecedent conditions that set the occasion for (or "trigger") the problem behavior, as well as

antecedent conditions that *do not* trigger the problem behavior; and (c) identification of setting events, if any, that make the problem behavior more (or less) sensitive to the maintaining consequences and their associated antecedents.

Identification of Consequent Conditions That Maintain the Problem Behavior. An important aspect of behavior-environment relationships is the consequence(s) produced by a person's behavior, including problem behavior. Behavior is useful in that it serves a *function* for the person. We assume that any behavior that occurs repeatedly is serving some useful function (i.e., is producing an outcome that is reinforcing to the person).

Behavior may serve two major functions (i.e., produce two major outcomes): (a) *obtaining* something that is desirable, or (b) *avoiding or escaping* something that is undesirable. In more technical terms, obtaining desirable things is referred to as *positive reinforcement* and escaping or avoiding undesirable things is referred to as *negative reinforcement* (if such consequences result in continued occurrences of the behavior). Figure 7-4 provides a framework for

FIGURE 7–4
Functions of Behavior

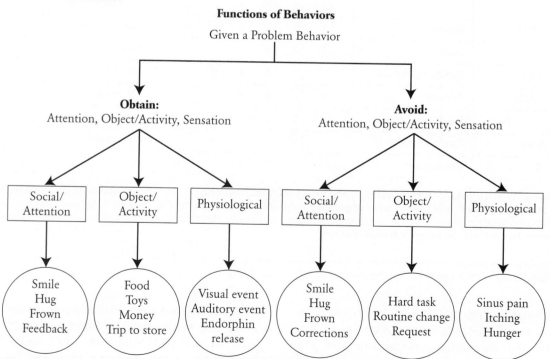

From *Functional assessment and program development for problem behavior* (2nd ed.), page 13, by R. E. O'Neill, R. H. Horner, R. W. Albin, J. R. Sprague, K. Storey, & J. S. Newton, 1997, Pacific Grove, CA: Wadsworth. Copyright 1997 by Wadsworth, a part of Cengage Learning, Inc. Reprinted with permission.

organizing the possible functions of problem behaviors into six categories (three under "Obtain" and three under "Avoid"). Events that may be obtained or avoided may require interactions that involve other persons or things (i.e., are socially mediated events), or may be internal (i.e., physiological) to the person with problem behavior and not require the presence of others. Some problem behaviors may serve multiple functions (Day, Horner, & O'Neill, 1994).

Developing a hypothesis about the function of problem behavior(s) on the basis of the information collected in an interview(s) is a critical outcome of the FBA process and is essential for developing an effective and efficient BSP. Some FBA interview forms, such as the Functional Assessment Interview from O'Neill et al. (1997) and Part B of the FACTS (presented in Figure 7-5), provide a place on the form to record a hypothesis that identifies the function of a problem behavior. Part B of the FACTS is completed for each different type of routine associated with a high likelihood of problem behavior (i.e., a rating of 4, 5, or 6) as indicated in Part A.

Using Part B of the FACTS, Ms. Schwartz and Maya's team found that during the "hallway transitions" portion of Maya's routines (e.g., traveling to and from the school bus to her classroom, and to lunch and recess), her problem behaviors were maintained by getting peer attention and by getting peers to give her more space when crowded. This is noted in the Summary of Behavior section, Step 6 in Part B of the FACTS.

Identification of Antecedent Conditions That Do and Do Not Trigger the Problem Behavior.

Interview questions will inquire about routines during which the problem behavior(s) occurs, including *when, where,* and *with whom* it occurs and the *specific activities or events* within the routine that may trigger the problem behavior. It is useful to identify any aspect of a routine that may serve as a trigger (e.g., particular academic demands, free time, transitioning to the next routine, types of prompts). Interview questions should also solicit information about routines that do not evoke problem behavior. Note, for example, that Part A of the FACTS (see Figure 7-3) provides a place to identify the likelihood of problem behavior across all routines, including those where problem behaviors do not occur or are unlikely to occur.

The FBA interview concerning Maya produced findings about antecedent conditions that trigger—and do not trigger—her problem behaviors. Using Part A of the FACTS, Ms. Schwartz inquired about the likelihood that Maya would engage in problem behaviors during specific time periods in her daily routine. The FACTS shows that the likelihood of Maya's engaging in problem behaviors was rated as "high" in the context of the following routines: transitioning from the bus to the classroom, lunch and recess, and transitioning from the classroom to the bus. Each of these routines involved a hallway transition for Maya and a relatively unstructured period of time; some routines also involved waiting in line with peers. In contrast, the likelihood of Maya's engaging in problem behavior was rated as relatively low during the following routines: morning and afternoon meetings, groups, projects, P.E., music, and library. After completing Part A, Maya's team completed Part B of the FACTS for the hallway transition routines (combining transitioning to and from the bus with lunch and recess because of the similarity of the latter to the transition routines). Step 4 in Part B of the FACTS indicates that hallway transitions and unstructured time periods where peers are present are environmental features that are predictors (antecedent triggers) for Maya's problem behaviors.

Identification of Setting Events.

Setting events are conditions that temporarily alter the value of reinforcers that maintain problem behaviors. For example, sleep deprivation is a setting event that may make some tasks more aversive than usual and decrease the value of the social praise obtained by doing these tasks. The result is that sleep deprivation may increase the value of escaping from boring tasks (e.g., via tantrums) (Durand, 1990). Having spent a period of time alone may be a setting event that increases the value of social attention, and thereby increases the likelihood of problem behaviors that result in peer or teacher attention. Setting events help explain why on some days an instructional session goes well and on other days the same instructional session occasions problem behavior.

Eric did not like shifting from his routine to another activity and asking him to do so was a trigger for problem behavior. However, Eric did not always engage in problem behavior when he was asked to shift to another activity. On some days, Eric would shift without exhibiting problem behavior. However, on

FIGURE 7–5
Functional Assessment Checklist for Teachers and Staff (FACTS, Part B)

Functional Assessment Checklist for Teachers and Staff (FACTS, Part B)

Step 1 Student/Grade: **Maya, Grade 1**   Date: **10/24/2008**
Interviewer: **Trudy Schwartz**   Respondent(s): **Moira and Vance**

Step 2 **Routine/Activities/Context:** Which routine (only one) from the FACTS, Part A is assessed?

Routine/Activities/Context	Problem Behavior(s)
1. Hallway transitions (bus to class, class to bus)	1. Spitting and hitting, Sticking tongue out

Step 3 **Provide more details about the problem behavior(s):**

What does the problem behavior(s) look like? **Tongue out and giggle, spit toward peers' feet, hit peers with fist**
How often does the problem behavior(s) occur? **Moderate to high frequency (lower in other routines)**
How long does the problem behavior(s) last when it does occur? **Until peer gives attention and moves out of Maya's way**
What is the intensity/level of danger of the problem behavior(s)? **Moderate to high; can escalate**

Step 4 **What are the events that predict when the problem behavior(s) will occur? (Predictors)**

Related Issues (Setting Events)		Environmental Features	
✓ illness	✓ other: first day after	___ reprimand/correction	___ structured activity
___ drug use	weekend or long break	___ physical demands	✓ unstructured time
✓ negative social: too crowded		___ socially isolated	___ tasks too boring
___ conflict at home		✓ with peers	___ activity too long
___ academic failure		✓ Other: hallway transitions	___ tasks too difficult

Step 5 **What consequences appear most likely to maintain the problem behavior(s)?**

Things That Are Obtained		Things Avoided or Escaped From	
___ adult attention	✓ Other: more space	___ hard tasks	✓ Other: bumped;
✓ peer attention		___ reprimands	crowded in hall
___ preferred activity		___ peer negatives	
___ money/things		___ physical effort	
		___ adult attention	

SUMMARY OF BEHAVIOR
Step 6 **Identify the summary that will be used to build a plan of behavior support.**

Setting Events and Predictors	Problem Behavior(s)	Maintaining Consequence(s)
Hallway transitions, especially Mondays and after breaks	Hitting and spitting, tongue out	Get peer attention; get space when crowded

Step 7 **How confident are you that the Summary of Behavior is accurate?**

Not very confident					Very confident
1	2	3	4	5	(6)

Step 8 **What current efforts have been used to control the problem behavior?**

Strategies for Preventing Problem Behavior		Strategies for Responding to Problem Behavior	
___ schedule change	Other: reminders, monitor	___ reprimand	Other:
___ seating change		✓ office referral	(for hitting)
✓ curriculum change		___ detention	

(Adapted from March, Horner, Lewis-Palmer, Brown, Crone, Todd, et al., 2000) *days when pollen counts were very high and his allergy was acting up (and he had not taken his allergy medication), Eric was much more likely to engage in problem behavior when asked to shift to another activity. Eric's allergy was a setting event for his problem behavior. It did not trigger problem behavior by itself, but it did increase the likelihood of problem behavior when Eric was asked to shift to another activity.*

The design of behavior support is improved when information about powerful setting events is available and is used to design support procedures that address relevant setting events and their effects. Because setting events may be distant in time (i.e., they may have occurred earlier in the day or the night before) and may not have clearly visible effects or indicators, asking interview questions about potential setting events may be the best way to learn about them. Thus, using the FBA interview to gather information about general medical status, social interaction patterns, daily activities, and other possible setting events that may increase (or decrease) the person's sensitivity to the previously identified maintaining consequences and their associated triggering antecedent conditions is an important aspect of the FBA interview.

Maya's team identified breaks from school (e.g., a weekend, a holiday), illness, and being too crowded as being possible setting events for Maya's problem behaviors. These also were recorded in Part B of the FACTS in Step 4.

Other Information of Interest. Depending on the time available for the interview, gathering additional information can ultimately prove to be useful when developing the BSP. For example, it will be useful to inquire about appropriate behavior that is already part of the student's repertoire, particularly behavior with which the student may be able to secure the maintaining consequence currently gained via the problem behavior. For example, a student may have demonstrated that she can ask for help or ask for a break from an activity by signing or signaling. If the student appears to be engaging in tantrums to escape difficult academic tasks, the support team could include a prompt in the BSP for the student to use the sign or signal to ask for a break (and then provide the break) as an alternative to escaping from the task via a tantrum. If the student does not already have a usable signal, a teaching

component designed to help the student acquire this important skill could be included in the BSP.

In thinking about appropriate alternative behaviors, communication is the single most important skill to be considered for students with severe problem behaviors. Different theories have been proposed to explain why this is so, but the consistent conclusion is that effective support requires understanding the ways in which a person communicates important information to others in the environment. PBS plans often include teaching or enhancing communication skills; therefore, it is essential to inquire about the communication skills that a person currently uses (Donnellan, Mirenda, Mesaros, & Fassbender, 1984).

Eric had experience using a symbol system to communicate simple requests. His support team recognized that this type of communication response could be used as an alternative behavior to replace Eric's problem behavior. Their hypothesis was that Eric's problem behavior was maintained by avoiding shifts between activities. He often was allowed to remain in activities when he was asked to shift to another activity. What Eric needed was a better way, an acceptable way, to communicate that he wanted to stay with his current activity (and thereby avoid a shift). The team determined that they could teach Eric to request more time by pointing to a symbol in a communication book.

It may also prove wise to use the interview as an occasion to identify reinforcers that will be effective with the student (e.g., objects, events, activities). Prior to developing the BSP, one may want to assess the student's preferences with regard to reinforcing objects, events, and activities. Such assessments typically involve exposing the student to a variety of potential reinforcers, for example, edibles, toys/objects, entertainment (e.g., music, TV, movies), games, outings, domestic and personal care activities, and various forms of social attention and sensory stimulation (Green, Reid, Canipe, & Gardner, 1991; Pace, Ivancic, Edwards, Iwata, & Page, 1985; see also Chapter 3).

Interviews with Maya's teachers and parents indicated that Maya thrived on peer attention, even though it seemed that by hitting and spitting at peers, she did not want their attention. Maya wanted peer attention AND enough physical space in order to be comfortable. Maya's desire to get peer attention was incorporated into her support plan by arranging for her to have a peer mentor with her during unstructured times on the bus and at school. Having a peer mentor during routines that were difficult for Maya meant that she had regular access to peer attention with no crowding, and did not need to engage in problem behavior (i.e., problem behavior was made irrelevant).

Finally, one may also want to ask about the history of the student's problem behavior (e.g., how long it has persisted), the various programs and interventions that have been used to manage the behavior, and the degree of success achieved by implementing those programs. Learning about the types of supports that have been attempted and their effects can provide clues about the things that influence problem behaviors. For example, if a time-out program was tried in the past and had the effect of *increasing* the frequency of a behavior, this might indicate that the behavior is motivated by escaping or avoiding situations or demands. In many cases, it may be hard to obtain clear and reliable information about what has been tried and how well it worked or did not work; however, it is usually worthwhile to make the attempt.

Produce a Written Hypothesis as a Testable Summary Statement. At this point, one should be in a position to synthesize the previously gathered information into a testable hypothesis statement about the problem behavior. The hypothesis statement describes the relationship among the setting events, the triggering antecedents, the behaviors of concern, and the maintaining consequences. This hypothesis is tentative until it is validated as described below.

Ms. Schwartz's hypothesis statement regarding Maya's problem behavior is recorded in Step 6 on Part B of the FACTS (Summary of Behavior) (see Figure 7–5). She has noted that Maya is likely to stick her tongue out at peers, spit at them, or hit them during hallway transitions (particularly on Mondays after a weekend break from school and when the halls are crowded) with the maintaining consequence (function) being to gain peer attention while also getting enough physical space, if needed. Ms. Schwartz and her colleagues have a very high degree of confidence in this tentative hypothesis; they gave it a rating of 6 on a six-point scale in Step 7.

Table 7–1 provides samples of other hypothesis statements derived from hypothetical FBA interviews. These statements are broken down into setting events, immediate antecedents, problem behaviors, and maintaining consequences as follows: When Sarah is getting no attention during the morning circle (the immediate antecedent), she is likely to shout profanities and throw things (the problem behaviors) to get attention from her peers (the maintaining consequence). The longer that she has gone without direct attention, the more likely she is to engage in shouting profanities (the setting event).

Validating the Hypothesis

Once a testable tentative hypothesis statement has been produced, the final stage of the FBA can occur—validating the hypothesis. Because the hypothesis statements will ultimately guide the development of a BSP and because it is often difficult to define hypothesis statements with a high degree of confidence, it is necessary to validate (test) the accuracy of the hypothesis.

TABLE 7–1
Sample Hypothesis Statements from Hypothetical FBA Interviews

1. When Monica is asked to do independent seat work (the immediate antecedent), she is likely to tear up materials and hit her teacher (the problem behaviors) to escape from the task demands (the maintaining consequence). This process is more likely if she has had a negative interaction with the teacher earlier in the day (the setting event).
2. When Jolene is prompted to stop using the computer (the antecedent), she is likely to fall to the floor and scream (the behavior). The problem behaviors are maintained by keeping access to the computer (the consequence), and the likelihood is greatest when Jolene has had limited time on the computer earlier in the day (the setting event).
3. In situations with low levels of activity or attention at home or school (the antecedent), Dan will rock and begin to chew his fingers (the behavior). These behaviors appear to be maintained by self-stimulation (the consequence).
4. When Bishara is asked to dress himself or do other nonpreferred self-care routines (the antecedent), he will begin to slap his head (the behavior). Head slaps appear to be maintained by getting to escape from the self-care routines (the consequence) and are even more likely if he is not feeling well or has had limited opportunities to engage in preferred activities in the recent past (the setting events).
5. When Anya begins to have difficulty with a reading or math assignment (the antecedent), she will put her head down, refuse to respond, and/or close her book (the behaviors). Anya's refusal is maintained by avoiding the assignment (the consequence) and is far more likely to occur if she has had less than 5 hours of sleep the previous night (the setting event).

Three strategies for validating hypothesis statements are (a) direct observation of the student in the context of the relevant routines under natural conditions (e.g., simply observe while the teacher presents a math lesson); (b) structured descriptive assessment, where specific conditions are set up and observed within otherwise natural routines (e.g., ask the teacher to present difficult material while observation occurs); and (c) formal functional analysis manipulations where mini-experiments are conducted to demonstrate a functional relationship between the problem behavior and environmental events (e.g., antecedent conditions and consequences for the behavior are systematically manipulated in a controlled setting). Conducting a structured descriptive analysis or a functional analysis requires relatively greater degrees of skill. The easiest, least dangerous, and most common strategy for confirming a hypothesis is direct observation under naturally occurring conditions or during routines.

Direct Observation. Direct observation of behavior has long been a cornerstone of applied behavior analysis (e.g., Baer, Wolf, & Risley, 1968). The antecedent, behavior, consequence (ABC) chart (Bijou, Peterson, & Ault, 1968) was an early method for supplementing interview data with direct observation. ABC charting involves watching the student and recording, in narrative style, information about the problem behavior and its antecedent and consequent events. The narrative approach used in ABC charting is limited in that its narrative style does not lend itself to gathering measures of observational reliability, can be difficult to use when observing high-frequency behaviors, and often uses subjective language. Finally, ABC charting may tell us little about conditions that are associated with the *absence* of problem behavior because ABC charting is event driven and occurs only when problem behavior occurs.

An extension of the ABC chart, called scatter plot analysis, was developed by Touchette, MacDonald, and Langer (1985) and elaborated by Doss and Reichle (1991). A scatter plot is a grid that allows one to record the occurrence of problem behavior (via a shorthand behavior code) within designated time intervals (e.g., hour or half-hour periods) across multiple days. The scatter plot has the advantage of documenting both when problem behaviors occur and when they do not occur. Touchette et al. documented that by focusing on the features of those periods when problem behavior was observed, interventions that altered those periods resulted in a reduction in problem behavior.

An adaptation of the scatter plot observation form that also incorporates elements of ABC charting is the Functional Assessment Observation form (O'Neill et al., 1997). This system for conducting direct observations allows for the identification of events that reliably occur just prior to problem behaviors and events that occur just after problem behaviors. By identifying these relationships, one can infer antecedent events that trigger problem behaviors and consequence events that maintain the problem behaviors. When the contents of the form are structured in accordance with information previously gained via interviews (e.g., identified problem behavior, antecedents, consequences, routines), the form can be a useful tool. However, it should be noted that direct observation systems seldom focus on distant setting events (e.g., setting events that occur earlier in another setting, such as a fight at home or on the way to school, or lack of sleep the previous night).

Although direct observation methods are more objective and precise than interviews, their results must also be viewed with caution. Given that simple direct observation does not involve manipulation or control of targeted variables, the data demonstrate correlations, not causal relationships, between environmental events and behavior. An example will illustrate the potential risk of relying solely on direct observation data to design a BSP. Consider the case of a student who engages in severe head hitting. A record of direct observations showed that when the student hit her head, the teacher usually went to her side, provided a reprimand, and attempted to redirect her to play with a toy. Multiple direct observations of this series of events suggested that the student's head hitting was maintained by the teacher's attention. However, a later, more extensive analysis indicated that the student had chronic sinus infections and that head hitting lessened the pain from the infections. In this case, attempts to replace head hitting with requests for attention would have been ineffective. However, medication to relieve the sinus pain was effective. Multiple factors can affect problem behavior, and care is needed when developing and confirming FBA hypotheses.

Studies have documented that carefully conducted direct observations can be used to confirm hypotheses developed from FBA interviews and as the basis for designing effective BSPs (Borgmeier & Horner, 2006; Carter & Horner, 2007, 2009; Filter & Horner, 2009; Mace & Lalli, 1991; March & Horner, 2002; Repp, Felce, & Barton, 1988; Sasso et al., 1992), while others have demonstrated that less accurate findings also may work (Lerman & Iwata, 1993). The full range of appropriate applications of direct observation methods has not been documented across settings, participants, and qualifications of personnel. Further investigations are needed to delineate appropriate applications of direct observation versus experimental analysis methods (e.g., functional analysis). However, at this time, it appears that interviews followed by direct observations designed to confirm (or disconfirm) hypotheses can lead to useful conclusions about the antecedents and consequent events that control the problem behavior (McIntosh et al., 2008). The relatively low cost, effort, and skill required to conduct interviews and direct observations offer a practical alternative to functional analysis for many practitioners.

It is important that direct observation procedures be structured to provide clear and useful information while not overburdening those responsible for collecting the data. The results of an FBA interview should be used to guide the direct observations. Observations and an observation data form should focus on the behaviors and environmental conditions identified during the interview process (O'Neill et al., 1997). Maya's team used the Functional Assessment Observation form (O'Neill et al., 1997) to collect data (see Figure 7-6).

FIGURE 7–6
Functional Assessment Observation Form

Functional Assessment Observation Form

Name: **Maya**

Starting Date: 10/27/2008   Ending Date: 10/27/2008

Time	Tongue out	Spit	Hit	Head down	Demand/request	Difficult task	Transitions/Hall	Interruption	Alone (no attention)	Less structured activities	Attention	Desired item/Activity	Self-Stimulation	Demand/request	Activity (transitions)	Person	Other/don't know	Sit alone	Comments: (if nothing happened in period, write initials)
8:20 Hall	2	1, 3	3			1, 2, 3					1, 2, 3							3	
8:50 Reading				4, 5	4, 5									4, 5					
10:15 Recess																			TS
11:00 Math				6, 7	6, 7									6, 7					
11:45 Lunch Recess	8, 9, 10	8, 9, 10			8, 10					9	8, 9, 10								
1:15 Music																			TS
2:10 Hall		11, 12	11, 12		11, 12						11, 12								
Totals																			

Events: ~~1~~ ~~2~~ ~~3~~ ~~4~~ ~~5~~ ~~6~~ ~~7~~ ~~8~~ ~~9~~ ~~10~~ ~~11~~ ~~12~~ 13 14 15 16 17 18 19 20 21 22 23 24 25
Date: 10/27/2008

On 10/27/08, the next Monday after completing the FACTS, Ms. Schwartz collected direct observation data to validate (or disconfirm) the team's tentative hypothesis that Maya is likely to stick her tongue out at peers, spit at them, and/or hit them during hallway transitions (particularly on Mondays after a weekend break from school) for the function of gaining their attention, as well as to make an initial assessment on task difficulty and problem behavior during math and reading. To collect the data, Ms. Schwartz used the Functional Assessment Observation form. Data were collected for the entire school day across all of Maya's routines. Ms. Schwartz observed Maya in all of her routines in order to confirm that problem behaviors occurred in routines and conditions where they were expected, on the basis of the team's hypothesis, and did not occur in the routines in which they were not expected.

A quick overview of the other aspects of the structure of the Functional Assessment Observation form may be helpful. The first group of columns on the form lists the problem behaviors.

For Maya, these problem behaviors are sticking out her tongue, spitting, hitting peers, and putting her head down.

The second group of columns lists the hypothesized predictors (the antecedent triggers) for the problem behaviors.

In Maya's case, generic predictors, such as "Demand/ Request" and "Difficult Task," have been supplemented with more specific predictors, such as "Transitions/ Hall" and "Less Structured Activities."

The next set of columns lists the perceived functions of the problem behavior, organized into two subgroups: (a) Get/Obtain and (b) Escape/Avoid. Within each of these subgroups are listed the generic functions of problem behavior (e.g., get attention or a desired activity/item; self-stimulation; escape/avoid a demand/request, activity, or person). Finally, the last set of columns provides a place to record the actual consequences of a problem behavior (i.e., the specific consequent events that occurred when the problem behavior occurred).

In Maya's case, being made to sit alone was an actual consequence that she experienced when she hit another student.

On the Functional Assessment Observation form, problem behaviors are recorded as events instead of frequency counts. A single event includes all instances of a problem behavior of a given type (e.g., spitting) that are separated by no more than a 3-minute time gap. Counting behavior events is easier than trying to count every instance of a behavior, particularly with problem behaviors that have hard-to-determine beginnings and endings. Each time a problem behavior event occurs, the data collector records the sequence number of the event (e.g., 1 for the first event that occurred, 2 for the second event that occurred, and so on) in each of the relevant columns of the form.

Maya's first problem behavior event (i.e., Event 1) occurred between 8:20 a.m. and 8:50 a.m. while she was making a hallway transition and included her spitting at a peer (note the 1 in each of those columns). The data collector has also recorded that the predictors for Event 1 were transitions and hall (note the 1 in each of those columns) and that the perceived function of the event was getting attention (note the 1 in that column). There was no consequence delivered for Event 1. During this same time period, two other distinct problem behavior events occurred (i.e., events 2 and 3). Event 3 involved Maya's spiting and hitting a peer again, and the data collector has recorded the predictors as "Transitions and hall," the perceived function as "Getting attention," and the actual consequence as "Maya's being made to sit alone."

Note also that when no problem behavior events occur during an observed portion of a student's routine, the observer simply writes his or her initials in the final column of the form. This makes it clear that although an observation did occur, no problem behavior occurred.

The data on Maya's direct observation form show that she experienced no problem behaviors during recess and her music class.

In all, Maya engaged in 12 problem behavior events on 10/27/08, the last of which occurred about 2:10 p.m. when she was making a hallway transition to the bus. At the bottom of the form, the data collector has drawn a slash mark through events 1 through 12, drawn a vertical line after the number 12, and written the date as 10/27/08. Thus, a quick check reveals that 12 behavioral events occurred on 10/27/08. If the same form were to be used to collect data on the following day, 10/28/08, the first behavioral event on that date would be recorded as event 13.

Validation (or disconfirming) of the tentative hypothesis can be undertaken once sufficient data have been collected. O'Neill et al. (1997) recommend collecting data until 15–20 behavior events are observed. However, confirmation or disconfirmation of a hypothesis can be done with fewer events if clear patterns of behavior are evident.

There is confirmation that the FBA interview correctly identified Maya's problem behaviors in that no problem behaviors other than those that were revealed in the interview had been recorded. Maya engaged in four behavioral events that involved sticking her tongue out (events 2, 8, 9, and 10), seven events that involved spitting (events 1, 3, 8, 9, 10, 11, and 12), three events that involved hitting a peer (events 3, 11, and 12), and four events that involved putting her head down (events 4, 5, 6, and 7). Except for events 1 and 2, occurrences of sticking her tongue out, spitting and hitting included multiple problem behaviors (sticking her tongue out and spitting; spitting and hitting), which may be an indication that this cluster of behaviors serves the same function.

The tentative hypothesis coming out of the FBA interviews was that Maya was more likely to engage in problem behaviors during hallway transitions (particularly on Mondays after a weekend break from school) than at other times in order to gain peer attention. A review of the data for 10/27/08 (a Monday) indicates that of the 12 behavioral events, seven (58%) occurred during hallway transitions (i.e., events 1, 2, 3, 8, 10, 11, and 12). This provides support for the hypothesis, although the data also reveal that a similar behavioral event occurred during lunch, which is a less structured activity (Event 9). For all eight events, the form shows that the perceived function was getting attention, thus providing confirmation for that portion of the tentative hypothesis.

In summary, Maya's direct observation data provide confirmation of the tentative hypothesis regarding problem behavior during hallway transitions and less structured activities. The observations also confirm that Maya's BSP needs to reflect the appropriate curriculum level and adaptations to address her putting her head down during reading and math.

In developing such a plan, it will be important to consider the prevailing environmental conditions during transitions, when the probability of her problem behaviors appears to be low.

There are many forms for collecting direct observation data. The key issue is that direct observation systems can be used to validate tentative FBA hypotheses developed through interview procedures. In cases where the hypothesis is at least reasonably confirmed, development of a related BSP can be initiated. In cases where the hypothesis is at least temporarily disconfirmed, the direct observations will either provide enough information to revise the hypothesis statement accordingly or launch another round of focused information gathering from additional informants, followed by another round of direct observations. Ideally, successive rounds of information gathering will be sharpened until a final round of direct observations succeeds in tentatively confirming the final hypothesis statement.

Where problem behaviors and environmental conditions are so complex that a series of direct observations fail to result in a reasonably confirmed hypothesis, or where BSPs that have been implemented with fidelity nevertheless fail to produce reductions in problem behavior, it may be necessary to conduct more formalized behavioral assessment procedures such as a structured descriptive analysis or a functional analysis. These procedures require more behavioral expertise than direct observation. Functional analysis, in particular, should not be undertaken lightly as it requires time and a high level of behavioral skills, and can present significant safety risks.

Structured Descriptive Assessment. In a structured descriptive assessment (SDA), specific antecedent conditions previously shown or suspected to produce problem behavior are systematically presented to a focus student by the teacher (or a typical caregiver) within an otherwise natural context or environment (English & Anderson, 2006). For example, a teacher may systematically vary academic content, instructional procedures, or levels of attention within a lesson taught in the classroom. Consequences for behavior are not manipulated in an SDA, and teachers and caregivers are instructed to respond to problem behaviors as they normally would in the natural setting.

The structured format of presenting antecedents within an SDA provides more frequent opportunities to assess environment–behavior relationships than are likely to occur during typical direct observations that rely solely on natural occurrences of antecedent conditions. Because SDA involves systematic manipulation and frequent occurrences of specific antecedents, data on student behavior during an SDA may reveal clearer patterns of behavior for confirmation of hypotheses about problem behavior. Because SDA is conducted by a natural caregiver (the teacher) in a natural setting (the classroom), the results of an SDA may have improved applicability and validity for a specific student within his or her natural setting and routines. A common criticism of functional analysis, described next, is that it is often conducted in analog and contrived settings by highly trained specialists who may be unknown to or unfamiliar with the focus student (English & Anderson, 2006).

Functional Analysis. Within applied behavior analysis, functional analysis refers to the explicit manipulation of variables in order to demonstrate a functional relationship between an environmental event and a behavior. As such, a functional analysis is a mini-experiment. The conceptual foundation for functional analysis has been described by Bijou et al. (1968), Carr (1977), and Skinner (1953), among others.

In a highly influential study, Iwata and colleagues (1982/1994) demonstrated what has become the classic methodology for conducting a functional analysis—*the manipulation of consequent variables*. They examined, in an analog setting (i.e., a controlled setting created specifically for the functional analysis), the relationship between self-injury and various consequent events (e.g., contingent attention, contingent escape from academic demands, being alone, and unstructured play/control). This study conclusively demonstrated the wisdom of deriving interventions on the basis of the function (or purpose) of a problem behavior, instead of merely imposing the arbitrary contingencies of reinforcement or punishment on problem behavior in a trial-and-error approach designed to overpower the problem behavior regardless of its function. The functional analysis conducted by Iwata et al. revealed that some participants engaged in high rates of self-injury only when self-injury resulted in escape from difficult tasks, other participants engaged in self-injury only when the behavior resulted in adult attention, and still others engaged in self-injury under all conditions.

Despite the success and widespread use of functional analysis by researchers, its "ecological validity" has sometimes been questioned. In their review, Hanley, Iwata, and McCord (2003) note that functional analysis is usually conducted under well-controlled conditions in settings that may not entirely duplicate the settings in which the problem behavior occurs (e.g., a functional analysis might be conducted in the corner of a classroom instead of in the midst of typical classroom activities). Nevertheless, functional analysis is not limited to contrived analog settings. Variations in the basic analog protocol have been demonstrated in schools and communities (Durand & Carr, 1991; Lalli, Browder, Mace, & Brown, 1993; Lang et al., 2008; Northup et al., 1995; Sasso et al., 1992; Sprague & Horner, 1992; Umbreit, 1995), clinical outpatient settings (Wacker, Steege, Northup, Reimers, et al., 1990), and homes (Arndorfer, Miltenberger, Woster, Rortvedt, & Gaffaney, 1994; Lucyshyn, Albin, & Nixon, 1997; Lucyshyn et al., 2007).

Regardless of the setting in which functional analysis is conducted, it is a complex procedure that is currently much more likely to be conducted by a trained behavior analyst than by a teacher. A particularly cautionary aspect of functional analysis is that, by its very nature, it evokes problem behavior. That is, in manipulating successive consequent variables, the behavior analyst is searching for the reinforcer for the problem behavior and the antecedent condition that reliably triggers the problem behavior by setting the occasion for delivery of the reinforcer (e.g., a difficult academic task that reliably evokes problem behavior because of a history of the problem behavior resulting in escape from the task). A functional analysis that targets, for example, aggression or self-injury is not to be undertaken lightly because the analysis will cause those problem behaviors to occur. Despite these cautions about functional analysis, there has been at least one demonstration of a methodology that effectively taught teachers to use functional analysis in actual elementary-level classroom settings (Moore et al., 2002) in which the target problem behavior was that students yelled out during class.

There are some variations in how functional analysis is conducted that could perhaps be adapted to increase the likelihood of its use by typical intervention agents, such as teachers. For example, Wacker and his colleagues (Northup et al., 1991; Wacker, Steege, Northup, Reimers, et al., 1990; Wacker, Steege, Northup, Sasso, et al., 1990) have developed a *brief functional analysis protocol* that involves an analog assessment phase followed by a "contingency reversal" phase. During the analogue assessment phase, functional analysis conditions (e.g., attention, escape) are alternated in rapid sessions (5 to 10 minutes per session, two or three consecutive sessions per condition) to identify the maintaining consequences (i.e., the function) of problem behavior. In the subsequent contingency reversal phase, the participant is taught an appropriate response that produces the maintaining consequence identified in the analog assessment phase (e.g., how to say "Come here, please" to gain attention). The effect on problem behavior of reinforcing or not reinforcing this new appropriate response is then tested in a series of contingency reversals. This brief functional analysis procedure can result in the identification of maintaining consequences (functions) for problem behavior during the course of a 90-minute evaluation.

As an example of the brief functional analysis methodology, consider Figure 7–7. During the analog assessment phase, the hypothetical student's rate of aggression is high during the attention condition

sessions (when the student is provided with attention that is contingent on engaging in aggression but otherwise ignored) and his rate of requesting attention or assistance is low. During the escape condition sessions (when the student is prompted/assisted through a difficult academic task and allowed to escape the task contingent on engaging in aggression), his rates of both problem behavior and requesting attention or assistance are low. The analog assessment phase suggests that aggression is maintained by getting attention. This hypothesis is further tested during the contingency reversal phase conditions. The first condition of the contingency reversal phase replicates the analog assessment condition that tested attention as the maintaining consequence. However, prior to the onset of this condition, the student is taught to sign "Come here, please" and attention is given to the student contingent on his signing. During this condition, the student's rate of aggression is low and his rate of signing is high. This condition is then reversed to replicate the analog condition in which only aggression produces

FIGURE 7–7
Example of Brief Functional Analysis

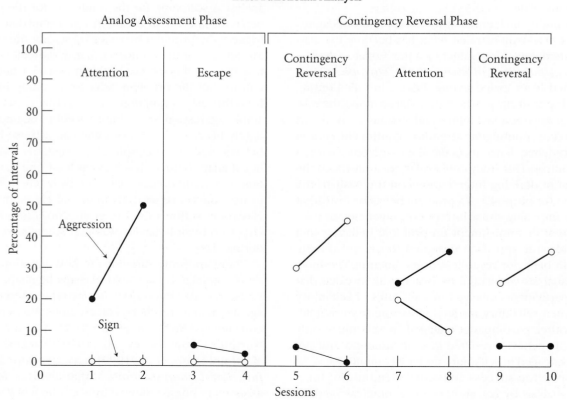

attention and then reversed one final time to assess the rate of aggression when attention is again delivered contingent on the student's appropriate signing. The contingency reversal phase confirms that aggression was maintained by attention and demonstrates that providing an appropriate replacement behavior to get attention reduces aggression substantially.

Another possibility for increasing the likelihood that functional analysis could be conducted in schools is the option of focusing on the *manipulation of antecedent variables* instead of consequence variables. This is sometimes referred to as a *structural analysis* (Axelrod, 1987). Structural analysis involves a focus on discovering a relationship between an antecedent condition and a behavior. This typically is done using a single-subject withdrawal (ABAB) design approach. Manipulating antecedent conditions, while holding consequence conditions constant, may be much easier, and more natural, for teachers (e.g., Vollmer & Van Camp, 1998; Wacker, Berg, Asmus, Harding, & Cooper, 1998). Many curricular, instructional, and other antecedent variables (e.g., type of task, task difficulty, level of attention, choice) can be, and have been, manipulated in school settings to identify relationships between antecedents and problem behavior (Carr & Durand, 1985a; Dunlap, Kern-Dunlap, Clarke, & Robbins, 1991).

Structural analysis is similar to structured descriptive assessment in its manipulation of antecedent conditions, but the two procedures differ in two important ways. The first difference is in how consequences are handled during the assessment sessions. In structural analysis, consequences are held constant across conditions and may be different from the consequences that would typically occur in natural contexts. In an SDA, there is no emphasis on holding consequences constant, and teachers (caregivers) are instructed to provide the consequences that would typically follow problem behavior. The second difference relates to the procedures for implementing each type of assessment. SDA is implemented by a teacher or caregiver who is the natural support provider, someone who is familiar to the focus student, and is implemented in a natural environment. Although structural analysis could be conducted by a teacher or natural caregiver, most published examples of structural analyses have been conducted by behavior specialists or researchers, instead of by teachers or typical caregivers. Structural analysis also is often conducted in a pull-out or contrived setting, instead of in the natural setting as is the procedure for an SDA.

Although functional analysis is considered to be "the gold standard" for defining the maintaining function of problem behaviors, we recommend that functional analysis should be attempted (a) only with the support of a trained behavior analyst, and (b) only when other methods of FBA do not provide a clear set of validated hypothesis statements.

Summary of Assessment for Behavior Support Planning

In completing the assessment processes that precede development of a BSP, you will have engaged in person-centered planning and will have conducted an FBA. The FBA will have produced six outcomes: (a) description of the student's problem behavior and daily routines; (b) identification of consequence conditions that maintain the problem behavior; (c) identification of antecedent conditions that set the occasion for (or "trigger") the problem behavior, as well as antecedent conditions that *do not* trigger the problem behavior; (d) identification of setting events that make the problem behavior more sensitive (or less sensitive) to the maintaining consequences and their associated antecedents; (e) production of a written hypothesis that synthesizes the foregoing information into a testable statement about the problem behavior; and (f) direct observations of the student during typical daily routines for the purpose of tentatively confirming (or disconfirming) the hypothesis (O'Neill et al., 1997). If necessary, you may also have requested the help of a trained behavior analyst in conducting a functional analysis.

Use Assessment Information to Design an Individualized Behavior Support Plan

Once the assessment phase of the PBS process has been completed, you are ready for the next three steps in the cascading model: (a) design an individualized BSP, (b) ensure the fidelity of its implementation, and (c) monitor the impact of the BSP on behavior and lifestyle. At this point in the support process, the six outcomes for a functional assessment should be completed and a person-centered vision of broader lifestyle goals for the focus student should be agreed on by the support team. The information gathered in the functional assessment and person-centered planning processes provide the foundation for the BSP. However, as the development and implementation of the BSP progresses, it is important to remember that the functional assessment and person-centered planning processes are ongoing. Each of these assessment processes should be performed on a recurring basis because the student's BSP affects both appropriate and problem behaviors and is likely to result in changes in lifestyle, routines, and living environments.

An individualized BSP provides a guide for the behavior of those persons who provide support (e.g., teachers, parents, classroom assistants, specialists). We often think of a BSP as the plan for changing the behavior of a student with problem behaviors. In fact, although it is designed for a focus student, a BSP actually describes changes and behaviors that we as teachers, administrators, family members, friends, and peers will make happen and occur. A multicomponent BSP is a blueprint for designing and maintaining effective environments that render problem behaviors irrelevant, inefficient, and ineffective. The changes that we make in the physical setting, the daily schedule, what we teach, the way we teach, and the way we respond to appropriate and problem behaviors are what will produce changes in the behaviors of the student. It is through changes in our behavior that we effect changes in the behavior of students with problem behaviors. As such, written BSPs should be clear in describing the exact changes expected in the behavior of those who will implement the plan and in the settings in which the plan will be implemented. In the following sections, we describe important features of a positive BSP.

A Positive BSP Should be Technically Sound

In designing an individualized PBS, it is essential that a BSP be *technically sound* (Crone & Horner, 2003; Horner, 1999; O'Neill et al., 1997). Technically sound means that the procedures in the support plan are logically linked to functional assessment hypotheses and also are grounded in the basic principles of human behavior and biomedical sciences (Alberto & Troutman, 2009; Carr et al., 2002). Interventions that are technically sound are also evidence based. Research or clinical application data should exist that support the effectiveness and logic behind each procedure used in a plan (e.g., Carr & Carlson, 1993).

A Positive BSP Should be Contextually Appropriate

In addition to being technically sound, a BSP should be *contextually appropriate* (Albin et al., 1996; Horner,

1999; Lucyshyn, Kayser, Irvin, & Blumberg, 2002). Contextually appropriate refers to how well support plan procedures "fit" their implementers and settings. The term *contextual fit* (or *goodness of fit*) has been used to describe the compatibility between a BSP and the values, skills, and resources of BSP implementers, both at home and at school (Albin et al., 1996). Contextual fit influences the selection of procedures within a BSP, as well as whether the plan procedures are put in place, are implemented with fidelity, and are implemented for extended periods of time (Moes & Frea, 2000; Sandler, 2001). To be effective, PBS plans must be implemented with fidelity by typical support providers in natural school, home, and community settings, often for extended time periods. The contextual fit of the BSP is as important to its effectiveness as is the technical soundness of the plan.

A Positive BSP Should be a Collaborative Team Endeavor

We strongly recommend that a collaborative team process be used in the design, implementation, evaluation, and modification of the plan. The team should include all of the key stakeholders involved in supporting a student with problem behaviors, including teachers and school staff who will implement the plan, family and friends, the student with problem behaviors (when appropriate), school and other administrators who must support the BSP implementation process, and any others (e.g., behavior or related services specialists, respite providers) involved in supporting the student (Crone & Horner, 2003; Scott, Anderson, Mancil, & Alter, 2009; Todd, Horner, Sugai, & Colvin, 1999). Benazzi, Horner, and Good (2006) found that the composition of school teams had an effect on both the technical soundness and contextual fit of BSPs. Teams consisting of regular school personnel plus a behavior specialist produced BSPs with the best combination of technical adequacy and contextual fit in comparison to BSPs developed by behavior specialists alone (low contextual fit) or teams of school personnel without a behavior specialist (low technical adequacy).

A collaborative team process also provides the framework for a support approach that is dynamic and capable of responding to changing support needs. The behavior support needs of persons with severe problem behaviors are likely to be long term in nature. Support should be designed with longevity in mind and with the expectation that the nature of the support will change as the person's skills, needs, and preferences change. Sustained plan implementation, ongoing monitoring of effects, and timely adaptation and modification of plan procedures and features are essential elements of effective, comprehensive behavior support. A collaborative team process involving all key stakeholders facilitates high-quality performance of these elements.

Todd, Horner, Sugai, and Colvin (1999) described a team-based approach to PBS in schools that utilizes two levels of teams. The first level is a core school-wide PBS team that consists of a school administrator, someone with behavioral expertise, and a representative sample of school staff (i.e., teachers and others). The core team has responsibility for coordinating and managing all aspects of behavior support within a school, including both school-wide and individual student systems of support. The core team serves as a resource for the school and staff in the area of behavior support. The second team level involves "action teams" that are formed to conduct the individualized PBS process. Each student who requires a BSP would have his or her own action team. Each action team would consist of a member (or members) from the school's core PBS team (e.g., a school behavior specialist), the student's teacher(s), the student's parents/family, and any other school or community members who are involved in the student's life or are interested in participating (e.g., a counselor, social worker, speech/language therapist, physical therapist, school bus driver, probation officer, respite care provider). In this two-level model, the core team is responsible for receiving and managing staff requests for assistance with students' behavioral problems; forming and supporting action teams; and assisting as needed in the design, implementation, and evaluation of BSPs. The action team is responsible for conducting person-centered planning and FBA, developing and implementing an individualized BSP, supporting the student and teachers in support plan implementation, ensuring fidelity of implementation, and collecting data to evaluate support plan effectiveness (Crone & Horner, 2003).

Maya's school had instituted a school-wide PBS system that identified three expectations for all students: Be respectful, be responsible, and be safe. School staff had translated these expectations into specific student behaviors that were expected in the various settings (e.g., hallways, cafeteria, classrooms, bus loading zone, playground) and activities (e.g., entering school, at assemblies, during fire drills and after-school functions) that make up a school day. Importantly, staff had taught these expected behaviors to all students, so that students at Maya's school knew what behaviors were expected of them. In addition, Maya's school had strategies for monitoring students and rewarding them for performing expected behaviors (e.g., the school held a weekly raffle on Fridays and students received raffle tickets to acknowledge appropriate behaviors).

Although Maya participated in the school-wide system, by itself, the school-wide system was not sufficient to meet Maya's behavior support needs. Maya required more individualized support. That is why Ms. Schwartz, the behavior specialist, initiated the individual student behavior support system in Maya's school by completing a Request for Assistance form. With this request for assistance, an action team was set up for Maya that included Ms. Schwartz, Maya's teacher, Maya's educational assistant, and Maya's mother. This action team set about the task of further assessing Maya's behavior and designing, implementing, and monitoring a BSP.

A Positive BSP Should be Comprehensive

The goal of PBS is to have a broad, positive impact on the life of a person with disabilities and challenging problem behaviors (Carr et al., 2002; Horner, 1999). Successful behavior support should translate into real differences in a person's life across all contexts in which behavior support needs are present (e.g., home, school, respite care, community). The following three features characterize a comprehensive BSP:

1. *All problem behaviors performed by the focus person are addressed:* The need for behavior support often is prompted by the occurrence of a few intense problem behaviors. Teachers and families have noted, however, that high-frequency occurrences of low-intensity behaviors (e.g., whining, refusal) may be as disruptive, problematic, and damaging to the student and those around him or her as higher-intensity aggression, self-injury, and property damage (Horner, Diemer, & Brazeau, 1992; Turnbull & Ruef, 1996). Research also indicates the value of organizing support around all of the problem behaviors that are maintained by the same function (e.g., all behaviors that produce attention, all

behaviors that are maintained by escape from tasks) (Sprague & Horner, 1992, 1999). Both our current understanding of behavioral theory and the goal of producing change that has a broad impact argue for focusing behavior support on the full range of problem behaviors that a person performs instead of on just one or two high-intensity behaviors.

2. *A comprehensive support plan is implemented across all relevant settings and times of the day:* Just as addressing all problem behaviors is important, so, too, is implementation of behavior support procedures across the relevant scope of a person's entire day. In the past, it was not unusual for individual behavioral interventions to be implemented for limited periods of time, across limited settings or situations. The research literature shows clearly that a single intervention procedure can have a dramatic effect in reducing severe problem behavior across brief periods in specific contexts. However, to achieve a true lifestyle impact, behavior support must produce broad and lasting effects across the relevant range of contexts, conditions, activities, and routines that a person with severe problem behaviors experiences in the course of the day. A challenge for individualized PBS is to develop comprehensive support strategies that can be implemented and sustained across the entire day and the full range of conditions encountered (Horner, 1999).

3. *A comprehensive support plan blends multiple procedures:* It would be unusual for a single intervention procedure to address the full spectrum of problem behaviors exhibited by an individual with severe problem behaviors and to cover the full range of settings where problems occur. Comprehensive support will more likely involve the use of a multicomponent support plan. For example, strategies for curricular revision and schedule modification may be used to minimize contact with highly aversive events; instructional procedures will build new skills; and consequences throughout the day will be modified to increase the rewards associated with communication and learning, and decrease the rewards that follow problem behaviors. Collectively, these multiple changes result in an environment that minimizes and redirects access to problem events, builds new skills, and provides constructive feedback that both promotes appropriate behavior and minimizes the rewards for problem behavior.

A Positive BSP Should be Sustainable

PBS has moved the delivery of behavioral intervention for persons with severe problem behaviors from specialized and restrictive settings to regular, integrated community settings. A challenge facing families, schools, and community support providers today is to deliver effective behavior support in typical homes, schools, and community settings for as long as such support is needed. Individualized PBS plans, in most instances, will be implemented by the "typical persons" (e.g., family members, friends, teachers, classroom assistants, paid caregivers) who live and work in those settings. To be effective over the long term, BSP implementation must be sustainable (i.e., capable of being implemented with reasonable fidelity by typical persons for extended periods of time).

We have two recommendations for facilitating sustained implementation of a BSP across all relevant settings and contexts in a student's life for extended periods. First, the BSP must continue to have good contextual fit over time. As the BSP is implemented and changed over time, team members should continue to monitor it for contextual fit. Second, it is important that BSP procedures can be relatively easily embedded and implemented within the typical routines and activities that make up the student's daily life at school, at home, and in the community. If BSP procedures require teachers, families, or other support providers to make substantial changes in their daily or other regular routines and activities as part of plan implementation, then the BSP procedures are much less likely to be implemented across all contexts and times of day, and implementation is much less likely to be sustained over time.

Competing Behavior Analysis

Competing behavior analysis (CBA) is completed before writing an individualized BSP because it provides a conceptual bridge for moving from functional assessment information to the design of a multicomponent BSP (Crone & Horner, 2003; Horner & Billingsley, 1988; O'Neill et al., 1997). Conducting a CBA provides a framework to logically link the multiple intervention procedures and support strategies of a multicomponent BSP to information collected in the FBA. Thus, CBA is a strategy for producing a BSP that is technically sound. A separate CBA should be completed for each response class of problem behaviors identified in an FBA. If a student performs one set of problem behaviors (e.g., throws and destroys materials) to escape difficult tasks and another set (e.g., calls out, pounds desk) to get attention, then two CBAs will be completed, one for each set of behaviors (i.e., each response class). If one set of behaviors serves multiple functions (Day et al., 1994), then a separate CBA should be completed for each function.

The process for conducting a CBA involves four basic steps: (a) summarize the FBA information to construct a hypothesis statement for each response class of problem behaviors; (b) identify appropriate desired and alternative replacement behaviors and the contingencies associated with them; (c) identify potential intervention procedures, across four support strategy categories (i.e., setting event, antecedent, behavior teaching, and consequence strategies), that promote the occurrence of appropriate behaviors and make problem behaviors irrelevant, ineffective, and inefficient; and (d) select the set of strategies from the options proposed that are technically sound, likely to result in behavior change, and are a good contextual fit (Crone & Horner, 2003; O'Neill et al., 1997). Figure 7–8 provides an example CBA form for Eric that illustrates the first two steps described next.

Summarizing FBA information to construct a summary statement for a response class involves listing, from left to right, the setting event(s), the immediate antecedents (predictors), the problem behavior(s) in the response class, and the maintaining consequence(s) that have been identified in the FBA. The maintaining consequence(s) for problem behavior indicates (or suggests) the function of the problem behavior (refer to Figure 7–4 for a listing of potential functions). In Figure 7–8, the functional assessment summary statement for Eric indicates that he screams, pulls his hair, and scratches at the staff (the problem behaviors) when he is asked to shift from one activity to another (the immediate antecedent). Eric's problem behaviors, at least sometimes, lead to a maintaining consequence of his getting to stay in his current activity (i.e., getting to escape/avoid having to shift). Screaming, pulling his hair, and scratching staff are more likely to occur when Eric is in new or unpredictable situations or when he suffers from his pollen allergy (the setting events). The consequence that occurs for Eric's problem behavior suggests that the function of his problem behaviors is escape from transitions, which he finds aversive. This information is diagrammed in the middle path of Eric's CBA form (see Figure 7–8).

The second step in completing a CBA is to identify two appropriate behaviors that will "compete" with

FIGURE 7–8
Competing Behavior Analysis for Eric: First Two Steps

Student Name: Eric

Behavior Support Plan: Competing Behavior Analysis

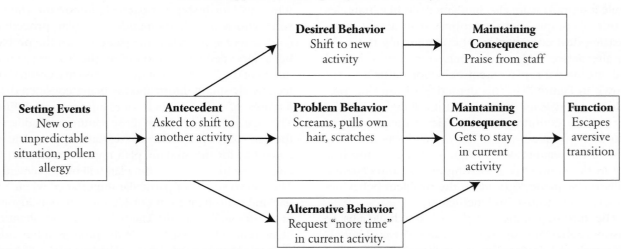

From *Functional assessment and program development for problem behavior* (2nd ed.), page 71, by R. E. O'Neill, R. H. Horner, R. W. Albin, J. R. Sprague, K. Storey, & J. S. Newton, 1997, Pacific Grove, CA: Wadsworth. Copyright 1997 by Wadsworth, a part of Cengage Learning, Inc. Reprinted with permission.

the problem behavior path. Two questions can be asked: (a) Given that the setting event(s) and predictor(s) have occurred, what is the appropriate *desired behavior* that you want the student to perform in that situation? and (b) Given that the setting event(s) and predictor(s) have occurred, what would be an acceptable *alternative replacement* behavior that the student could perform in order to produce the *same consequence* as the problem behavior(s)?

For Eric, the desired behavior is that he transition from activity to activity when asked without incident. The current (actual) maintaining consequence for shifting without incident for Eric is teacher praise and acknowledgment for "acting like an adult." An acceptable alternative replacement behavior for Eric is that he requests more time to stay in the current activity using an appropriate communication response (e.g., a symbol requesting "More time, please"). His team reasoned that requesting to stay in the current activity is an appropriate response that produces the same maintaining consequence as the problem behavior (i.e., Eric escapes the transition). When he asks appropriately to stay in the current activity, Eric will receive additional time in the activity (e.g., 2 more minutes). This is not what the staff wants Eric to do, but it is preferable to his problem behavior and is an acceptable option as the staff works on other strategies in Eric's plan to get him to transition without incident upon request (i.e., the desired behavior).

An important aspect of alternative replacement behaviors is that they may serve as short-term solutions while a support team also implements other strategies within a comprehensive support plan aimed at increasing desired behaviors and eliminating the need for alternative replacement behaviors. Eric's desired and alternative replacement behavior paths also are shown in Figure 7–8. This depiction of the CBA provides support team members with a literal picture of the current contingencies for Eric in the context of transitions from activity to activity and sets the occasion for the team to define what to change or manipulate in the context (e.g., setting events, antecedents, skills, consequences) to make the problem behaviors irrelevant, ineffective, and inefficient.

The third step in the CBA process is to build a list of possible behavior support procedures. The goal here is not simply to look for a single intervention that would eliminate the problem behavior(s), but to identify a range of strategies and procedures that would reduce

the likelihood of problem behavior(s) and increase the likelihood that either or both of the competing behaviors (i.e., desired or alternative replacement) would occur. A multicomponent support plan might address the setting events (e.g., for Eric, designing a schedule to reduce the unpredictability of activities), the immediate antecedents (e.g., asking Eric to shift activities only after first presenting a reminder that a transition was coming), the behaviors (e.g., teaching Eric to ask for more time on an activity), and the consequences (e.g., increasing reinforcers for the desired behavior of shifting to new activities throughout the day, ensuring that the problem behavior does not result in escaping the transition but that requesting more time does). A comprehensive BSP will have multiple components that address the full range of variables that influence which behaviors occur from among the alternatives available. This third step often involves a process of first creating a menu of potential intervention and support strategies from which support team members can then select the best options and procedures for their situation. In this way, the resulting plan is more likely to be both technically sound (i.e., consistent with both the FBA and the CBA) and have good contextual fit (i.e., strategies are identified that work best for the team members and the context) (Albin et al., 1996; Crone & Horner, 2003; O'Neill et al., 1997).

The fourth step in building a BSP involves reviewing the list of potential strategies and selecting specific procedures that the team identifies as likely to be effective, doable, and an appropriate fit with their skills, values, schedules, resources, and administrative support system. This fourth step is extremely important. The persons who will be implementing the plan procedures (and, where appropriate, the student with the problem behaviors) decide on and define the features (procedures) of the BSP. The first three steps have ensured that technically sound information is being considered. The features of effective behavior support are defined. The final step adds form to those features and addresses the issue of the plan being contextually appropriate and a good fit for the student, plan implementers, and the context (settings) where the plan will be implemented. This fourth step is of particular importance when a behavioral consultant from outside the school is involved in the design of support. The behavioral consultant can be of tremendous assistance in the process of functional assessment and coordination of the competing behavior model. The final selection of the specific strategies that make up a behavior plan, however, must be done with the very active participation of persons who know the student best and who will be implementing the final plan. Support team consensus that a plan's procedures are doable, consistent with the team members' values and skills, in the best interest of the student, and likely to be effective is key in moving forward toward implementation of the plan. Figure 7-9 presents a complete CBA for Maya that illustrates the completion of all four steps.

FIGURE 7–9

Complete Competing Behavior Analysis for Maya

Student name: Maya

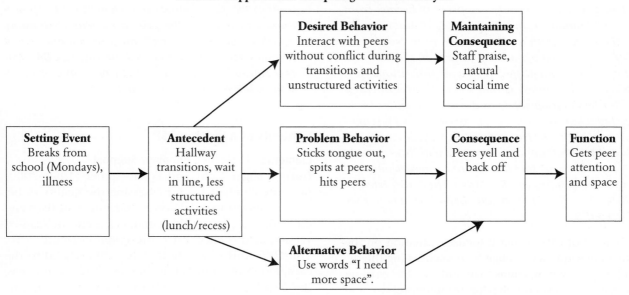

Behavior Support Plan: Competing Behavior Analysis

Identify and List Potential Intervention Strategies; Circle Strategies to be Implemented in BSP

(*Make problem behavior irrelevant*)	(*Make problem behavior inefficient*)		(*Make problem behavior ineffective*)
Setting Event Strategies	Antecedent Strategies	Behavior Teaching Strategies	Consequence Strategies
⊙ Call peer on phone on Sunday night	⊙ Provide pictorial schedule and review for social times	⊙ Teach how to use pictorial schedule as a conversation book	⊙ Ask peers to ignore inappropriate behavior
⊙ Provide peer mentor during unstructured times	⊙ Staff and peers prompt use of communication book	⊙ Teach peers about conversation book	⊙ Peers ask Maya to use communication book (low-level problem) or notify staff (high-level problem)
• Check curriculum difficulty and necessary adaptations	⊙ Precorrect to use words before all transitions	⊙ Teach to say "I need more space"	⊙ Remove from setting if hitting occurs
	⊙ Increase hall monitoring by staff		⊙ Increase social times throughout the day
	• Precorrect to ask for help when task is too hard		

From *Functional assessment and program development for problem behavior* (2nd ed.), page 75, by R. E. O'Neill, R. H. Horner, R. W. Albin, J. R. Sprague, K. Storey, & J. S. Newton, 1997, Pacific Grove, CA: Wadsworth. Copyright 1997 by Wadsworth, a part of Cengage Learning, Inc. Reprinted with permission.

The functional assessment hypothesis statement for Maya could be stated as follows:"During lunch, hallway transitions, and less structured activities, Maya engages in sticking her tongue out, hitting, and spitting at peers, with these behaviors being maintained by Maya's receiving attention from her peers and getting physical space, in the forms of yelling back and backing away when she does the behaviors. Maya's problem behaviors are even more likely when two setting events are present: breaks from school (Mondays) and illness." This is diagrammed as the middle path on Maya's CBA form (see Figure 7-9). The desired behavior for Maya in the problematic routines identified (hallway transitions, less structured activities) is that she talks and interacts with peers appropriately and without conflict. In assessing what consequences were currently present to maintain this desired behavior, Maya's team concluded that talking appropriately with peers would produce natural social time and interactions that would be reinforcing for Maya. They also tried to praise her for appropriate behavior when they observed it.

A benefit of CBA is that it focuses attention on the existing consequences available to maintaining the desired behavior. Often, teams may find that the existing reinforcers for desired behavior are unimpressive and inadequate, particularly relative to the maintaining consequence for the problem behavior.

The alternative replacement behavior identified by Maya's team was teaching Maya to use a communication book to initiate and conduct a conversation with peers and also to indicate "I need space, please back up" when feeling crowded. This behavior would produce the peer attention and space that Maya desired. Maya's peers also would be taught about the communication book and how it worked with Maya.

The third step in the CBA for Maya had the support team identify several potential intervention procedures and support strategies that could be used to make Maya's problem behavior irrelevant, inefficient, or ineffective. These procedures and strategies are organized as the setting event, the antecedent, teaching, and consequence manipulations. We encourage teams to identify several potential options within each category of manipulations first, and then consider and select the procedures to be included in a multicomponent BSP.

After identifying a variety of potential support plan components, Maya's team carefully reviewed and discussed the procedures that they had identified and selected the ones that they would include in Maya's plan. In determining which procedures to implement, Maya's team considered how effective they thought each procedure would be with Maya; whether they had the skills, resources, and capacity to implement the procedure with high fidelity; how comfortable they were with implementing the procedure; and whether the procedure was reasonably doable within Maya's academic program and school routines. The strategies circled on Maya's CBA form (see Figure 7-9) were selected by her team for inclusion in her multicomponent BSP.

Contents of a Written BSP

Elements of Effective Behavior Support

Horner, Sugai, Todd, and Lewis-Palmer (1999–2000) presented a checklist for assessing the quality of behavior support that delineates 10 features of BSPs and the planning process that produces them. An adapted version of this checklist is presented in Figure 7–10. The 10 features include the elements related to the completion of an FBA, the support planning process, the development and features of a written support plan, and the evaluation and assessment of the plan and its effects. In this section, we use the checklist as a guide for describing key elements of a written BSP, as well as elements to be addressed in the support planning process even if they do not need to be included in the written BSP.

The elements of a written positive BSP are organized around the goal of creating an effective environment that promotes and supports appropriate behavior and makes problem behavior irrelevant, inefficient, and ineffective. Accomplishing this goal typically necessitates development and implementation of a multicomponent support plan that focuses on proactive strategies for prevention and teaching, as well as on reactive strategies for responding to both appropriate and problem behaviors. The actual format, length, and style of a written BSP may vary. Instead of focusing on a particular form or format to use, we shall focus on the information presented in a written plan and on the processes described.

1. *Define the academic and lifestyle context for behavior support:* A written BSP should begin with a

FIGURE 7–10
Checklist for Assessing the Quality of Behavior Support Planning

---

BSP for <u>Maya Reimeriz</u>

Does the Plan (or Planning Process) have these features?

1. ✓ Define academic and lifestyle context for behavior support
2. ✓ Operational description of problem behaviors
3. ✓ Problem routines identified
4. ✓ Functional assessment hypotheses stated
5. Intervention/Foundational Issues (issues that cut across routines)
    a. __ health and physiology
    b. ✓ communication
    c. __ mobility
    d. ✓ predictability
    e. __ control/choice
    f. ✓ social relationships
    g. __ activity patterns
6. Intervention/Prevention Strategies (make problem behavior irrelevant)
    a. __ schedule
    b. ✓ curriculum
    c. ✓ instructional procedures
7. Intervention/Teaching Strategies (make problem behavior inefficient)
    a. ✓ replacement skills
    b. ✓ new adaptive skills
8. Intervention/Consequence Strategies
    Extinction (make problem behavior ineffective)
    a. ✓ minimize positive reinforcement
    b. ✓ minimize negative reinforcement
    Reinforcement (make appropriate behavior more effective)
    a. ✓ maximize positive reinforcement
    Negative Consequences (if needed)
    a. __ negative consequences contingent on problem behavior
    Safety/Emergency Intervention Plan (if needed)
    a. ✓ clear plan for what to do if/when crisis behaviors occur
9. Evaluation and Assessment
    a. ✓ define the information to be collected
    b. ✓ define the measurement process
    c. ✓ define the decision-making process
10. Ensure Contextual Fit
    a. ✓ values
    b. ✓ skills
    c. ✓ resources
    d. ✓ administrative system
    e. ✓ perception that the program is in best interests of the student

---

Adapted from Horner, Sugai, Todd, and Lewis-Palmer (1999–2000), reprinted by the permission of the publisher (Taylor & Francis Group, http://www.informaworld.com)

brief summary of the person-centered goals and vision that guide the BSP and the support team's planning efforts and decisions. This summary may also describe the connection between the BSP and the desired or projected personal outcomes for the student. Whenever a BSP is proposed and developed, there should be a rationale for the plan and objectives for the plan's components that are directly related to the health, safety, and lifestyle of the focus student). This summary places the BSP within the broader context of the student's life.

2. *Include an operational description of the problem behaviors:* Clear definitions of problem behaviors, stated in observable and measurable terms, are an important initial step in designing a BSP. Clear definitions assist a support team in reaching agreement on the nature and severity of the problems faced. Definitions or descriptions of problem behaviors should focus both on individual behaviors (e.g., screaming, hitting, talking out, throwing objects) and on response classes (i.e., the groups of behaviors that are maintained by the same consequences). It is rare that a student engages in only one problem behavior. More likely, a student engages in several behaviors that work together and are members of a response class. In some cases, behaviors in a response class may occur in very predictable patterns, such as an escalating sequence (Albin, O'Brien, & Horner, 1995) that can and should be identified as part of operationally describing the problem behaviors.

3. *Identify the problem routines:* An important consideration in describing problem behaviors is to define the behaviors within the routines and contexts in which they occur (Lucyshyn et al., 2002; O'Neill et al., 1997). Too often, problem behaviors are described or defined as if they were characteristics or traits of the person (e.g., he's aggressive, he's a biter, she's noncompliant). Defining problem behaviors within the routines in which they occur (e.g., Maya's problem behaviors occur during transitions and activities with minimal structure but do not occur in predictable and highly structured activities) emphasizes that a student's behavior must be understood in relationship to the context in which it occurs (i.e., antecedent stimuli, setting events, and consequences). Defining problem behavior within routines assists the support team in understanding the function of the behavior, the environmental variables affecting and controlling the behavior, and the scope of behavior problems (e.g., whether behavior problems are limited to a single

routine or a small number of routines or are present across a large number and broad range of routines), as well as in identifying patterns of problem behavior (e.g., finding similar problem behaviors or the absence of problem behaviors across routines with similar features).

4. *State the functional assessment hypotheses:* For each response class of problem behaviors identified in the FBA, a hypothesis statement should be presented that identifies setting events, antecedents/predictors, the behaviors in the response class, and the maintaining consequences and function. The hypothesis statement(s) provides the basis for a CBA and the subsequent generation of potential intervention procedures. For response classes that have multiple functions, a separate summary statement should be produced for each function that identifies the different setting events and predictors for each different maintaining consequence (i.e., function). Having the functional assessment hypothesis statements presented at the beginning of a written BSP serves as a reminder for plan developers and implementers of the underlying basis for the plan's procedures and goals. Hypothesis statements may be written in the BSP in sentence format or in a table format that presents the components of a hypothesis statement (setting events, antecedents, problem behaviors, consequences, and function). Both formats were illustrated in examples provided earlier in this chapter.

5. *Specify the intervention/foundational issues (issues that cut across routines):* One of the roots of PBS is the recognition that problem behaviors may result from and communicate, intentionally or unintentionally, the absence of or failure of living environments to provide basic foundational features in a person's life. These features cut across specific routines, activities, and settings. They include a person's health and physiological status, ability to communicate, mobility, predictability of environments, control and choices exercised by the person, social relationships, and activity patterns. These features must be addressed in the behavior support planning process. Some of them (e.g., mobility) may not be equally important or reflected within a written BSP for all persons. However, for each of the features that are relevant for a focus person, the written BSP should describe the importance of the feature and the strategies and procedures of the plan that address the feature. This should be communicated within the written plan.

For Eric, the predictability of the environment is a major factor in his problem behavior and ensuring predictability is a guiding objective for his BSP.

For Maya, the ability to communicate effectively and appropriately is a foundational issue and a guiding factor in her support plan.

6. *Specify the intervention/prevention strategies:* Prevention strategies help to make problem behavior irrelevant. The guiding question in planning for prevention is "How can we redesign environments (e.g., classroom, school, home) proactively to eliminate or minimize, as much as possible, the occurrence of problem behaviors?" In many cases, immediate antecedents that trigger problem behavior or setting events that increase the likelihood of problem behavior when triggers are present can be removed or modified. Setting events that increase appropriate behavior may be added (e.g., building rapport with a student may make your praise more rewarding and your error corrections less aversive). Other common goals for prevention strategies are making the environment as predictable as possible and providing opportunities for choice or other means for accommodating individual preferences. There are three specific environmental manipulations that are used in schools: (a) *Schedules are restructured* in order to modify or avoid antecedent stimuli that evoke problem behavior and remove setting events that increase the likelihood of problem behaviors or minimize their effects with neutralizing routines when they do occur (Horner, Day, & Day, 1997; Horner, Vaughn, Day, & Ard, 1996), including positive reinforcers for appropriate behavior so that the positives far outweigh the negatives (e.g., at least a 4:1 to 6:1 ratio of positives to negatives). (b) *Curricular content is adapted* to ensure that it is at an appropriate level for individual learners and is relevant (e.g., age and context appropriate), useful (e.g., functional), interesting, and stimulating (Ferro, Foster-Johnson, & Dunlap, 1996). (c) *Instruction is appropriately designed, paced, and adapted for individual learners* (Munk & Repp, 1994).

7. *Specify the intervention/teaching strategies:* Teaching strategies help make problem behaviors inefficient by teaching students (a) appropriate replacement skills that are functionally equivalent to problem behaviors as identified within the CBA, and (b) new adaptive skills that we want or expect them to perform as identified within the CBA. Academic and social skill deficits often are associated with increased levels of

problem behavior or, at least, put students at risk for problem behavior (Gresham, 2002). Adaptive skills to be taught may include academic, social, community and independent living, leisure, recreational, self-management, and coping skills. Adaptive skills are often (or should be) the focus of long-term objectives on an IEP.

Appropriate replacement skills constitute an intermediate step toward the performance of adaptive skills. A replacement skill within the CBA framework is an appropriate behavior that will produce the same maintaining consequence as the problem behavior, thereby acting as a replacement skill. The term *functional equivalence* is used in describing replacement skills because they produce the same maintaining consequence as the problem behavior (Carr, 1988). Frequently, the alternative skill identified for teaching in a BSP is an appropriate communication response.

> *Eric engaged in problem behavior to avoid transitioning to another activity. The alternative behavior identified for Eric in his CBA was an appropriate communication response—using a symbol to request more time in the current activity and thus avoiding the transition temporarily. The staff honored the communication alternative immediately, but also included a reminder that a shift still would occur (e.g., "OK, Eric, you can have 2 more minutes and then we'll shift to...."). Meanwhile, the team continued to work on other strategies to make transitions less aversive for Eric.*

The teaching of an alternative communication response is an intervention known as *functional communication training* (FCT) (Carr & Durand, 1985a; Carr et al., 1994; Durand, 1990). FCT is a well-researched and empirically documented procedure that builds on the idea that problem behavior frequently serves a communicative purpose, particularly for persons with disabilities who may have limited communication skills and repertoires (Carr & Durand, 1985b, 1987). Teaching appropriate communication skills through FCT can have a rapid and long-lasting effect in reducing problem behavior to a zero or near-zero level (Berotti & Durand, 1999; Carr & Durand, 1985a; Durand & Carr, 1991, 1992). The basic steps for applying FCT include the following (see Carr et al., 1994, for a more complete description of FCT procedures):

a. Identify the function of the problem behavior through FBA. To use FCT, it is essential to know whether the function of the problem behavior is to obtain desired reinforcers (e.g., attention, tangible materials or items, preferred activities, comfort) or to escape or avoid activities, items, or situations that the student finds aversive (e.g., things that are difficult, boring, painful, effortful, disliked).

b. Identify a request response to teach the student. This should be an appropriate response that will serve as a replacement behavior for the problem behavior. The request response may be a verbal response; a manual sign; a gesture; the use of a card with a printed symbol, word, or picture; the use of an augmentative and alternative communication (AAC) device; or any other response that allows the student to communicate a message to others. The request response should be easy for the student to learn (perhaps a response that is already in his or her repertoire) and easy for others to perceive and interpret (or learn to interpret). The request response should match the function of the problem behavior (e.g., getting attention: "I want to play," getting more time on an activity: "More time, please," escaping a difficult task: "I want a break" or "Help me, please").

c. Engage the student in an activity or context related to the problem behavior and teach the student to use the alternative communication response. Do this by prompting the student to use the communication response before a problem behavior occurs and then immediately honoring the communication response (e.g., prompt the student to ask for help and immediately provide help when the student asks). Fulfilling the communicated request immediately is very important, particularly when first teaching the response, so that the student learns that the appropriate request works even more efficiently than does the problem behavior. Teachers often rely on naturally occurring contexts for opportunities to teach alternative communication responses. However, naturally occurring opportunities to teach an alternative response may not occur frequently enough to produce rapid acquisition of the alternative, particularly if there is a history of avoiding such situations with a student with problem behavior. Teachers may need to set up opportunities to prompt, teach, and reward appropriate alternative communication responses. Care must be taken to ensure both safety and effective instruction.

In addition to communication responses, functionally equivalent replacement skills may include self-management skills (e.g., self-scheduling to produce predictability or self-recruited feedback to produce teacher attention), self-control or coping responses (e.g., relaxation training to reduce stressful arousal), social skills (e.g., a social initiation response that produces peer attention), and appropriate responses to produce stimulation similar to that produced by problematic self-stimulation behavior.

8. *Specify the intervention/consequence strategies:* Consequence strategies help to make problem behavior ineffective. They also are used to increase the performance of desired behaviors. Consequence strategies are reactive, with the consequences being delivered after a response (behavior) has occurred. Traditionally, consequence strategies have served as the mainstay for applied behavior analysis and behavior management. While PBS emphasizes proactive and teaching strategies in providing behavior support, consequence strategies still play an important role and are likely to be included in a multicomponent BSP. This is particularly true with students because schools have a long history of relying on consequence strategies to change behavior. Many school discipline policies spell out specific consequences (often negative consequences such as office referrals, suspension, or expulsion) that apply to all students for infractions of school rules (e.g., fighting, possession of weapons or drugs, disrespect shown to teachers).

The principles of human behavior identify three consequence procedures that are applied in the process of behavior support: (a) positive consequences (reinforcement), (b) negative consequences (punishment), and (c) extinction (withholding reinforcement). There has been much discussion and debate regarding whether any punishment procedure is acceptable within PBS (Horner et al., 1990; Repp & Singh, 1990). A goal of PBS is to minimize, if not eliminate, the use of negative consequences to control persons and their behaviors. The use of severe punishments and heavy reliance on punishment procedures are not acceptable in providing individualized PBS. Procedures that cause or rely on pain, tissue damage, and humiliation should never be used, and those that seclude, restrict, or restrain students may also be unacceptable and require substantial review and consideration. It is our experience and belief, however, that some negative consequences, including procedures that fit the *technical definition* of punishment, are a natural part of learning and life and, therefore, may be

an appropriate part of a multicomponent positive BSP (Horner et al., 1990; Kern, 2005). The procedures that we believe to be acceptable are mild procedures that would be typical of what is found in public schools and considered to be acceptable for children of the same age who do not have disabilities. Examples of negative consequences that may be included in a BSP are mild reprimands, negative feedback, or error corrections (e.g., being told "No" or "Hitting is unacceptable," being made to stop and walk when running in the hall), redirection involving minimal or no physical contact, reasonable response cost or loss of activity (e.g., the blocks are put away when you throw them at classmates, computer time is lost when you push classmates to get to the computer first), and some mild forms of time-out (e.g., you have to sit on the bench for a minute because you were roughhousing during recess).

School-based support teams need to carefully consider, plan, and regularly review the use of appropriate consequences, both positive and negative, in a BSP. Increasingly, state and local education agencies have clear policies that guide and that may prohibit or restrict the use of intrusive punishment procedures, seclusion, and restraint (U.S. Government Accountability Office, 2009). School teams and families of students with problem behaviors should be familiar with state and local district policies, and individualized BSPs should be in compliance with those policies.

Extinction. Extinction is the withholding of reinforcement for a behavior that has been reinforced in the past. Extinction is used in a BSP to make problem behaviors ineffective. One objective for a BSP is to minimize the extent to which problem behaviors continue to produce the desired reinforcers for a student. Putting problem behavior "on extinction" is a procedure that will reduce the occurrence of problem behavior. However, implementers of extinction should anticipate the possibility of an increase in problem behavior—an *extinction burst*—when the procedure is first implemented. An extinction burst raises particular concerns if the problem behavior being placed on extinction is dangerous. It is important to keep in mind that problem behavior may be maintained by either positive reinforcement (e.g., getting adult or peer attention, obtaining desired activities or objects) or negative reinforcement (e.g., escape or avoidance of aversive tasks or demands, having teachers or peers stay away or leave you alone). This will be identified in the FBA process and an appropriate extinction procedure can be designed and implemented.

Extinction is a challenging intervention to be implemented logistically and can be problematic when implemented alone because it may result in an escalation of problem behavior (Shukla & Albin, 1996). In a comprehensive BSP, an extinction contingency for problem behavior is typically used in combination with prompts and reinforcers for an alternative replacement behavior such as a functional communication response. The idea is to prompt and teach a replacement behavior that is effective and immediately reinforced, while at the same time making problem behavior ineffective by eliminating or reducing the reinforcement that it receives by using extinction.

> *Maya sticks her tongue out and hits and spits at her peers during hallway transitions and at other times to get their attention and to get them to give her more space. These behaviors are positively reinforced by Maya's getting what she wants in response to her actions. The team realizes that placing Maya's problem behavior on extinction would require getting Maya's peers to not attend to her or give her space when she performs the behaviors. This strategy would be extremely difficult to carry out (i.e., getting all of the students to not attend to Maya when she sticks her tongue out at them) and could lead to dangerous situations because Maya escalates to hitting when her lower intensity problem behaviors do not produce the outcome that Maya wants.*

A better procedure is to teach an alternative replacement behavior, such as a communication response.

> *Maya's team decided to teach her to use her picture schedule as a conversation book to get appropriate peer social attention. Maya will be taught to approach peers to initiate a conversation with the picture schedule. Maya's peers also will receive a brief instructional session on how they should respond when Maya approaches them with the conversation book. During Maya's instruction, with staff supervision, fellow students acting as confederates will prompt Maya to approach and use her con-*

> *versation book. Maya will receive immediate peer attention for using the conversation book. Should Maya stick out her tongue during instruction, student confederates will not respond to her, and the teacher guiding the instruction will prompt her to use the conversation book.*

Positive Consequence Procedures. Positive reinforcement for desired and appropriate replacement behaviors is included in a BSP to help make those behaviors more effective and efficient, which also makes problem behaviors relatively more inefficient. As noted in the Competing Behavior Analysis section of this chapter, the presumed maintaining consequences for desired behaviors are too often inadequate to compete successfully with the maintaining consequences for problem behaviors. The CBA helps show support teams when existing positive consequences are not strong enough and do not provide sufficient incentive to support the performance of desired behaviors. An essential component in a BSP is the regular delivery of strong positive reinforcement in terms of both the quality and the schedule of reinforcers, contingent on the occurrence of the desired appropriate behaviors. Reinforcers for desired behavior must be strong enough and delivered with sufficient frequency to compete successfully with the consequences that maintain the problem behaviors. For some students, it may be necessary to identify effective reinforcers through systematic reinforcer or preference assessments (Durand, Crimmins, Caulfield, & Taylor, 1989; Green et al., 1991; Roane, Vollmer, Ringdahl, & Marcus, 1998).

A commonly heard comment regarding the frequency of positive reinforcement is that a student needs or demands too much positive reinforcement. The issue is often that teachers and other support providers have difficulty delivering reinforcers frequently enough to meet students' needs. Self-management strategies offer one solution for this problem. Students may be taught to self-monitor their behavior and then to self-recruit reinforcement or feedback from staff (Mank & Horner, 1987; Smith & Sugai, 2000; Todd, Horner, & Sugai, 1999). A self-management approach to delivering positive reinforcement reduces the demand on staff to constantly monitor student performance and remember to deliver frequent reinforcers, while at the same time increasing the independence and self-determination of the student. The student self-monitors and then cues staff that a reinforcer or feedback of some type should now be delivered.

Negative Consequence Procedures. As noted previously, mild negative consequence procedures may be included in a multicomponent BSP when they are (a) used to make the plan effective and beneficial for a student with a problem behavior, (b) appropriate for the student and the contexts in which they are used, and (c) implemented ethically and reasonably. For example, mild negative consequences are sometimes used instead of extinction to help make problem behavior ineffective or inefficient. In these cases, negative consequences may be used in combination with prompting and reinforcing or teaching an appropriate alternative behavior, such as a functional communication response. In some cases, school or district policies may delineate negative consequences that will be included and implemented for all students in a school regardless of whether they have an individualized BSP or IEP.

> *Maya's team and her parents agreed to follow the school discipline policy with regard to fighting and physical aggression. If Maya hits another student, she will be escorted to the administrator's office and her parents will be contacted.*

If negative consequences are included in a BSP, clear guidelines for their use must be included in the written BSP. Behavior(s) that results in the delivery of negative consequences should be clearly defined. Students and staff should be informed about school disciplinary policies and how, when, and what negative consequences will be implemented. A significant problem with the use of negative consequences in schools is inconsistent and confusing implementation (Mayer & Sulzer-Azaroff, 2002). Support teams should use the least intrusive negative consequence that they expect to be effective and should carefully monitor implementation and the effects, including the side effects, of negative consequences. Teams also should consider the risks that a student faces from problem behavior when selecting the consequences for that behavior. The consequences used should not increase the risks to a student (e.g., delivering reprimands for a mild problem behavior may trigger escalation to much more dangerous problem behavior [Albin et al., 1995]). Finally, negative consequences that cause pain, tissue damage, or humiliation should never be used (Horner et al., 1990).

Safety or Emergency Intervention Plan. An emergency/crisis plan should be included in the multicomponent BSP for any student with severe problem behaviors who engages in (or has some likelihood of engaging in) high-intensity self-injurious, aggressive, or destructive behaviors that threaten his or her safety and health or the safety and health of others. The purpose of an emergency/crisis plan is to protect people from harm, not to teach or change behavior. An emergency/crisis plan should (a) precisely define what constitutes an emergency/crisis; (b) describe in detail the specific intervention procedures to be implemented, including procedures designed to defuse and de-escalate crisis behavior, as well as procedures to deal with crisis behaviors directly once they occur; (c) define specific criteria for ending implementation of any intrusive or restrictive emergency procedures (e.g., criteria for ending an emergency restraint procedure); (d) describe in detail specific procedures for data collection related to the emergency/crisis; (e) detail reporting procedures to be followed and identify who should be informed; (f) describe training and caregiver support procedures designed to the maintain capacity to respond effectively to emergency/crisis behaviors; and (g) describe debriefing, feedback, and other follow-up procedures to be implemented after implementation of emergency/crisis intervention. Readers interested in learning more about behavioral crisis prevention and management are referred to Carr et al. (1994) and Colvin (2004).

9. *Specify the evaluation and assessment procedures:* The written BSP should include descriptions of data collection procedures, including forms and directions for using them, and procedures for ongoing monitoring and evaluation of plan effects (see Figure 7-1, Step 5 of the cascading model). The evaluation plan will specify the behaviors to be tracked, the form(s) to be used, procedures for summarizing and sharing the information collected, and the person(s) responsible for each of the evaluation activities. A process for regular review and analysis of evaluation information should be identified so that timely decisions can be made regarding ongoing implementation and modification of plan procedures. An effective strategy is to set a regular meeting schedule for the support team to review plan effects and any issues that arise in relationship to plan implementation.

Maya's support team created a plan for monitoring and evaluating Maya's progress on her BSP. This evaluation plan identified data collection procedures and timelines, and was attached to Maya's written BSP (see Figure 7–11).

10. *Ensure contextual fit:* A BSP will be effective only if it is implemented with consistency and fidelity. Ensuring contextual fit is an element of the support planning process that may not show up in the written BSP but is important for ensuring the fidelity and sustainability of plan implementation (Albin et al., 1996). Factors to be considered when assessing the contextual fit of a BSP are (a) the values of the implementers, (b) the skills of the implementers, (c) the resources available for BSP implementation,

FIGURE 7–11

Sample Behavior Support Plan for Maya with Implementation Action Plan and Evaluation Plan

---

Behavior Support Plan for Maya

Student: Maya Reimeriz   **Adoption Date:** 10/29/2008
Date: 11/17/2008   **DOB:** 06/14/2001
Contacts: Mrs. L. Reimeriz (541-555-6789)—Mother
Action Team: Ms. Craig (First Grade Teacher), Ms. Schwartz (Behavior Specialist), Mr. Tilman (Educational Assistant), Mrs. Reimeriz (Mother)

Vision and Rationale for Support

Maya is 7 years old and lives at home with her parents and two older brothers. She has Down syndrome and moderate to severe intellectual disabilities (see student file for test scores) and autism. Her parents are very committed to Maya's inclusion in regular education classes and school settings. Maya enjoys fish, has an aquarium, and hopes to work at a fish or pet store. A personal futures plan for Maya was completed in September and produced the following goals: (a) high school graduation; (b) apartment living with a friend; (c) employment in a fish or pet store; (d) skill development in cooking, clothing care, basic household chores, money mangement, personal care, and time mangement; (e) joining a community group; and (f) maintenance of good physical health through diet and exercise. Currently, Maya reads below the first-grade level, follows step-by-step directions by reading icons and photos, counts to 10, identifies numbers 1 through 5, and copies two- and three-word phrases. She takes care of most of her dressing and personal care needs. Maya enjoys talking and listening to music with peers. Her mother notes that she likes to help with cooking.

Maya engages in problem behaviors that are becoming increasingly intense and frequent. Her behaviors currently threaten her continued participation in regular school settings. The major concern is that in situations where Maya feels crowded, she will spit and/or hit to get peer attention. The hitting is becoming more frequent and conflicts with peers are becoming more intense. She also sticks her tongue out at people and spits at people (although she rarely hits them with spit). Maya's parents and school staff are concerned for her future. In addition, Maya is increasingly tuning out on instruction by putting her head down on her desk during math and reading. Her team agrees that her life at school and at home will be greatly improved by learning new social and communication skills to replace her problem behaviors.

Team Agreements

✓ Maya will receive her education in the neighborhood elementary school.
✓ Maya's behavior support plan will be based on functional assessment outcomes.
✓ Maya's support plan will be implemented and evaluated on a consistent and regular basis for a specified period of time (i.e., the school year).
✓ Behavior support for Maya is a high priority because with age, aggressive and inappropriate behaviors may become more frequent, disruptive, and problematic and may put her and those around her at even more risk.

Description of Problem Behaviors

1. Sticking tongue out: Maya sticks her tongue out of her mouth as she orients her face toward peers. Tongue protrudes clearly as she faces peer. Licking her lips and having her mouth relaxed and open (tongue not visible) are not examples of sticking tongue out.
2. Spitting: Maya spits in the direction of her peers. Spitting includes actual fluid being spit out or the imitation and intent to look as if fluid will be spit out. Spit does not need to hit someone to count as spitting.

(continued)

FIGURE 7–11 (*Continued*)

3. Hitting peers: Hitting peers is defined as Maya striking (i.e., making contact with any degree of force) or attempting to strike (i.e., swinging at or punching at someone with no contact) peers with an open hand or fist. Accidentally bumping someone or tapping someone's shoulder to get their attention are not examples of hitting peers.
4. Head down: Maya folds her arms on her desk or lap and puts her face down. Putting her face down to look away, briefly, is not an example of head down.

Maya's behaviors often happen in a sequence. When she sticks her tongue out, her peers usually say something and step closer. When peers get closer to Maya or don't respond to her sticking out her tongue, she often spits at the closest peer(s). If peers challenge her or yell back at her, she may hit them. If Maya is particularly agitated about being crowded, she may spit and hit from the very beginning.

Summary of FBA and Hypothesis Statement

The functional behavioral assessment included the completion of a Request for Student Support Team Assistance; the FACTS, Parts A and B; and a full day of direct observation on a Monday using the Functional Assessment Observation Form (O'Neill et al., 1997). From this process, the team identified two routines where Maya's problem behaviors were most likely to occur: (a) hallway transition periods, waiting in line, and activities with minimal structure (e.g., lunch, recess, large-group activities); and (b) instructional demands when the work is too difficult. Maya's team identified that Maya's "hallway" problem behaviors were preceded by low levels of peer interaction and attention or feeling crowded and were rewarded by immediate access to peer attention (peers make comments and yell back at her), and that problem behaviors during academic instruction were preceded by curricular demands that were too difficult, and were maintained by escaping from task completion. Maya's problem behaviors were found to be more likely on Mondays and if she was ill. The team agrees that Maya's problem behaviors are maintained primarily by getting peer attention during hallway transitions and by escaping task demands during instructional periods. A diagram of the summary hypothesis statement for Maya is included on her Competing Behavior Analysis form (see attached form). *[Note that this form, which is included as Figure 7–8 in this chapter, would be attached as part of the written behavior support plan.]* The team also will check appropriate levels of curriculum for reading and math. Curricular adaptations will be made as appropriate.

General Intervention Plan for Maya

Overview: The main goals of Maya's behvior support plan will be to (a) reduce the unpredictability of when Maya will have opportunities to have access to and interactions with peers by providing her with a picture schedule, (b) teach Maya to use her picture schedule as a conversation book so that she can approach peers and initiate a conversation in an appropriate and respectful manner, (c) provide Maya with a peer mentor during less structured activities so that she will get peer attention naturally and not have to engage in her problem behavior routine to get it, and (d) teach and prompt Maya to say "I need more space" when she feels crowded. To help make the conversation book work for Maya, the team has agreed to spend 15 to 20 minutes explaining it to the other students and explaining how they should respond when she approaches them with it. During academic instruction, adaptations to new skill instruction and to independent seatwork assignments include a quick review of previous skills before instruction of new skills and breaking one assignment into three or four mini-assignments.

Maya's school discipline policy states that the consequence for physical aggression and fighting is problem solving with the administrator in the office and notification of the parents/guardians. The team and her parents agreed to follow the school discipline policy for fighting and physical aggression and Maya will be escorted from the situation to the administrator's office and her parents will be contacted should she engage in such behavior.

Specific Procedures for Maya: Specific elements of Maya's behavior support plan are identified on the attached Competing Behavior Analysis form.

Action Plan for Implementation of Maya's BSP: BSP implementation action plan is attached.

Safety Plan

Note: If emergency behavior management procedures are necessary, attach safety plan as separate sheet.

FIGURE 7–11 (*Continued*)

				Evaluation Decision • Monitor • Modify • Discontinue
Behavior Support Plan for Maya: Implementation Action Plan				
Tasks	**Person Responsible**	**By When**	**Review Date**	
Prevention: **Make problem behavior irrelevant (environmental redesign)**				
Identify and schedule peer mentors Identify appropriate academic level and needs	Ms. Craig Ms. Schwartz	10/30	11/15	
Teaching: **Make problem behavior inefficient (teach new skills)**				
Teach use of communication book Teach to use words "I need help" or "I need space"	Ms. Schwartz Ms. Schwartz	10/30	11/15	
Extinction: **Make problem behavior ineffective (minimize reward for problem behavior)**				
Explain Maya's communication book and how to respond to it to students	Ms. Schwartz	10/30	11/15	
Reinforcement: **Make desired behavior more rewarding**				
Ensure that Maya has opportunities for social interaction with peers where there is plenty of physical space	Ms. Craig and Mr. Tilman	10/30	11/15	
Safety: **Ensure the safety of all (what to do in dangerous situations) (if needed)**				
Use school discipline policy for hitting—send to vice principal and document incident on SWIS-ODR	Ms. Craig informs staff	10/27	11/15	

Behavior Support Plan for Maya: Evaluation Plan

Behavioral Goal (Use specific, observable, measurable descriptions of goal)

What is the short-term behavioral goal?

Teach Maya to use the communication book to approach peers in the hallway. Maya will approach peers in the hallway with her communication book at least once per transition for 5 consecutive days.

Expected date: 2/01/2009

What is the long-term behavioral goal?

Maya will interact appropriately with her peers in all school settings (classrooms, hallways, etc.) for 4 weeks with no incidences of tongue out, spitting, or hitting.

Expected date: 6/01/2009

Evaluation Procedures

Data to be Collected	Procedures for Data Collection	Person Responsible	Timeline
Is Plan Being Implemented? Peer mentor Use of the communications book Use of the words schedule	 Check in with teachers Observations in the halllway Observations at bus and in hallway	 Rachel Trudy and Vance Vance and teachers	 Daily for 2 weeks Daily for 2 weeks Daily for 2 weeks
Is Plan Making a Difference? Number of conversations with peers Number of incidents Office discipline referrals for hitting Academic performance	 Observations in hallway Reports from staff SWIS system Progress monitoring data	 Trudy and Vance Trudy compiles Trudy checks Trudy	 Daily for 2 weeks Weekly for first month Check weekly to start Check every 3 days

Plan review date: Weekly review for first month, then adjust as needed.

and (d) the administrative support provided for BSP implementation. In addition, the extent to which the BSP is perceived by implementers as being in the best interests of the focus student and its perceived effectiveness are considerations for contextual fit and the fidelity and sustainability of BSP implementation.

BSP Implementation Plan

A written implementation plan provides a guide for getting the procedures and features of a multicomponent BSP into place and operational. This is an often-overlooked element of effective behavior support. Unfortunately, there are many cases in which excellent BSPs have been developed but never fully implemented. Developing an implementation plan as part of the overall process of providing individualized PBS facilitates both initial and sustained implementation of multicomponent BSP procedures. The implementation plan identifies responsibilities and timelines for the activities required to make BSP procedures happen (e.g., who will obtain or develop needed materials and forms and when). The implementation plan also might describe procedures for implementing each of the various components of the BSP, including identifying the sequence in which BSP procedures will be implemented, setting target dates and timelines for implementation, and monitoring and review. The implementation plan can be used to identify any resources needed for plan implementation, the training needs of those who will implement plan procedures, and strategies for meeting those training needs. Just as the multicomponent BSP itself is the product of a collaborative team process, an implementation plan also should reflect the consensus of the support team.

The implementation plan can also serve as a guide and provide aids (e.g., checklists, one-page summaries) to ensure the ongoing fidelity of the implementation of BSP procedures (Lucyshyn & Albin, 1993), fulfilling Step 4 in the model of behavior support (see Figure 7–1). Team and caregiver support strategies and procedures for sustaining long-term implementation of a support plan also can be incorporated into the implementation plan. Procedures for sustaining a collaborative team process over time and for maintaining the team's focus on their vision and goals for a focus student's lifestyle are essential for the long-term delivery of effective, comprehensive behavior support.

Examples of a written BSP, an implementation plan, and an evaluation plan for Maya are presented in Figure 7–11.

Individual Behavior Support in a Whole-School Context

A basic assumption throughout this chapter is that investing in individualized, function-based behavior support will be most useful when the individual student's procedures are part of a larger, whole-school approach. The essential logic is that (a) investing in whole-school PBS will result in students expecting appropriate behavior from each other and will reduce the problem behaviors that arise from student–student conflict; and (b) behavior changes resulting from intensive, individualized support will be more likely to be maintained when the individualized supports occur within a whole-school context that acknowledges positive behavior and limits the rewards for problem behavior.

Over the past 12 years, more than 9,500 schools across the United States have adopted school-wide PBS practices. These schools report a reduction in problem behaviors, an improved organizational climate, and enhanced academic gains (Bradshaw et al., 2009; Horner et al., 2009). A common feature of these efforts is the direct teaching of school-wide behavioral expectations such as "Be respectful," "Be responsible," and "Try your best." Students are taught basic behavioral skills and to expect these skills from everyone around them. When this has been accomplished, recent research indicates that students are less likely to prompt problem behavior and less likely to reward behaviors such as bullying and teasing (Ross & Horner, 2009). There is insufficient research to document the large-scale impact of school-wide PBS on the frequency or effectiveness of individualized student supports. Preliminary results, however, suggest that one underemphasized component in intensive, individualized PBS is implementation within a school-wide system that supports both the use of function-based procedures and student gains that are achieved as a result of individualized support plans.

Summary

PBS is among the most exciting developments in the support technology available to children and adults with severe disabilities. Problem behaviors have long been a major obstacle to important living, educational, and employment opportunities. For too long, we have assumed that to be part of typical environments, a person first needed to acquire appropriate behaviors. We now have learned that appropriate behaviors are best learned when appropriate supports are delivered *in typical contexts.* The procedures associated with PBS provide the means for assessing and designing support that will both reduce problem behaviors and develop the constellation of skills that is needed to have a real impact on how a person lives.

This chapter provides (a) a structure for understanding problem behaviors; (b) a set of procedures for conducting assessments that can transform chaotic, painful, and confusing situations into understandable, logical patterns that can be addressed; and (c) a process for building individualized PBS plans that will be both effective and doable.

The science of behavior analysis has defined an important set of mechanisms that describe how human beings learn from their environment. This science has been transformed into teaching and support procedures that have the potential to produce important changes in the behavior of children and adults with disabilities. PBS is the joining together of this science with the fundamental beliefs about the way that persons with disabilities should be part of our society. The challenge is to use the science with precision and the beliefs with distinction. Those implementing PBS need the self-discipline to learn the science before they venture to change someone else's behavior, the wisdom to learn the values so that they apply the technology with discretion, and the humility to work collaboratively and to continually assess the impact of interventions on the lives of those who receive support.

Suggested Activities

1. Look at Figure 7–1 and compare the steps listed with those your school uses to address students' challenging behavior. What are the differences? Do you think that your school's procedure could be improved?.
2. Identify a student's problem behavior(s) that the team considers in need of intervention. Complete a Request for Assistance Form (Figure 7–2). Discuss information gathered with the student's team and determine if a functional behavioral assessment (FBA) and behavior support plan (BSP) are needed.
3. For a student whose behavior(s) the team considers in need of a BSP, follow the steps described in this chapter to conduct an FBA:
   a. Name and define the problem behavior.
   b. Use the Functional Assessment Checklist for Teachers & Staff (FACTS; Figures 7–3, 7–5) to interview relevant people on the problem behavior

   c. Select and use an suitable device to observe the behavior
      i. ABC chart (gives rough view of relevant antecedents and consequences)
      ii. Scatter plot (requires a predictable schedule; gives little information on the relevant consequences, but helps to identify times that problem behavior occurs and does not occur)
      iii. Functional Assessment Observation form (Figure 7–6)
   d. Use the FBA information gathered to achieve 6 outcomes:
      • Identify student's problem behavior and daily routines;
      • Identify consequence conditions that maintain the problem behavior;
      • Identify antecedent conditions that set the occasion for (or "trigger") the problem behavior, as well as antecedent conditions that *do not* trigger the problem behavior;
      • Identify setting events, if any, that make the problem behavior more sensitive (or less sensitive) to the maintaining consequences and their associated antecedents;
      • Write an hypothesis that synthesizes the foregoing information into a testable summary statement about the problem behavior; and
      • Directly observe the student during typical daily routines to tentatively confirm (or disconfirm) the hypothesis.
4. Examine the FBA results for a student with challenging behavior. Use these findings to conduct a competing behavior analysis (Figures 7–8 and 7–9) for this student.

References

Alberto, P.A., & Troutman, A. C. (2009). *Applied behavior analysis for teachers* (8th ed.). Upper Saddle River, NJ: Merrill/Pearson.

Albin, R. W., Lucyshyn, J. M., Horner, R. H., & Flannery, K. B. (1996). Contextual fit for behavior support plans: A model for "goodness-of-fit." In L. K. Koegel, R. L. Koegel, & G. Dunlap (Eds.), *Positive behavioral support: Including people with difficult behavior in the community* (pp. 81–98). Baltimore: Paul H. Brookes.

Albin, R. W., O'Brien, M., & Horner, R. H. (1995). Analysis of an escalating sequence of problem behaviors: A case study. *Research in Developmental Disabilities, 16,* 133–147.

Arndorfer, R. E., Miltenberger, R. G., Woster, S. H., Rortvedt, A. K., & Gaffaney, T. (1994). Home-based descriptive and experimental analysis of problem behaviors in children. *Topics in Early Childhood Special Education, 14*(1), 64–87.

Axelrod, S. (1987). Functional and structural analysis of behavior: Approaches leading to reduced use of punishment procedures. *Research in Developmental Disabilities, 8,* 165–178.

Baer, D. M., Wolf, M. M., & Risley, T. G. (1968). Some current dimensions of applied behavior analysis. *Journal of Applied Behavior Analysis, 1,* 91-97.

Bambara, L. M., & Kern, L. (2005). *Individualized supports for students with problem behaviors: Designing positive behavior plans.* New York: Guilford Press.

Benazzi, L., Horner, R. H., & Good, R. H. (2006). Effects of behavior support team composition on the technical adequacy and contextual fit of behavior support plans. *Journal of Special Education 40*(3), 160-170.

Berotti, D., & Durand, V. M. (1999). Communication-based interventions for students with sensory impairments and challenging behavior. In J. R. Scotti & L. H. Meyer (Eds.), *Behavioral intervention: Principles, models, and practices* (pp. 237-250). Baltimore: Paul H. Brookes.

Bijou, S. W., Peterson, R. F., & Ault, M. H. (1968). A method to integrate descriptive and experimental field studies at the level of data and empirical concepts. *Journal of Applied Behavior Analysis, 1,* 175-191.

Borgmeier, C., & Horner, R. H. (2006). An evaluation of the predictive validity of confidence ratings in identifying accurate functional behavioral assessment hypothesis statements. *Journal of Positive Behavior Interventions, 8,* 100-105.

Bradshaw, C., Koth, C., Thornton, L., & Leaf, P. (2009). Altering school climate through school-wide positive behavioral interventions and supports: Findings from a group-randomized effectiveness trial. *Prevention Science, 10,* 100-115.

Carr, E. G. (1977). The motivation of self-injurious behavior: A review of some hypotheses. *Psychological Bulletin, 84,* 800-816.

Carr, E. G. (1988). Functional equivalence as a mechanism of response generalization. In R. H. Horner, R. L. Koegel, & G. Dunlap (Eds.), *Generalization and maintenance: Lifestyle changes in applied settings* (pp. 194-219). Baltimore: Paul H. Brookes.

Carr, E. G. (1994). Emerging themes in the functional analysis of problem behavior. *Journal of Applied Behavior Analysis, 27,* 393-399.

Carr, E. G. (2000). Reconceptualizing functional assessment failures: Comments on Kennedy. *Journal of Positive Behavior Interventions, 4,* 205-207.

Carr, E. G., & Carlson, J. I. (1993). Reduction of severe behavior problems in the community using a multicomponent treatment approach. *Journal of Applied Behavior Analysis, 26,* 157-172.

Carr, E. G., Dunlap, G., Horner, R. H., Koegel, R. L., Turnbull, A. P., Sailor, W., et al. (2002). Positive behavior support: Evolution of an applied science. *Journal of Positive Behavior Interventions, 4,* 4-16, 20.

Carr, E. G., & Durand, V. M. (1985a). Reducing behavior problems through functional communication training. *Journal of Applied Behavior Analysis, 18,* 111-126.

Carr, E. G., & Durand, V. M. (1985b). The social-communicative basis of severe behavior problems in children. In S. Reiss & R. Bootzin (Eds.), *Theoretical issues in behavior therapy* (pp. 219-254). New York: Academic Press.

Carr, E. G., Horner, R. H., Turnbull, A. P., Marquis, J. G., McLaughlin, D. M., McAtee, M. L., et al. (1999). *Positive behavior support for people with developmental disabilities: A research synthesis.* Washington, DC: American Association on Mental Retardation.

Carr, E. G., Levin, L., McConnachie, G., Carlson, J. I., Kemp, D. C., & Smith, C. E. (1994). *Communication-based intervention for problem behavior: A user's guide for producing positive change.* Baltimore: Paul H. Brookes.

Carter, D. R., & Horner, R. H. (2007). Adding functional behavioral assessment to First Step to Success: A case study. *Journal of Positive Behavior Interventions, 9,* 229-238.

Carter, D. R., & Horner, R. H. (2009). Adding function-based behavioral support to First Step to Success: Integrating individualized and manualized practices. *Journal of Positive Behavior Interventions, 11,* 22-34.

Colvin, G. (2004). *Managing the cycle of acting-out behavior in the classroom.* Eugene, OR: Behavior Associates.

Crone, D. A., Hawken, L. S., & Bergstrom, M. K. (2007). A demonstration of training, implementing, and using functional behavioral assessment in 10 elementary and middle school settings. *Journal of Positive Behavior Interventions, 9,* 15-29.

Crone, D. A., & Horner, R. H. (2003). *Building positive behavior support in schools: Functional behavioral assessment.* New York: Guilford Press.

Day, H. M., Horner, R. H., & O'Neill, R. E. (1994). Multiple functions of problem behaviors: Assessment and intervention. *Journal of Applied Behavior Analysis, 27,* 279-289.

Didden, R., Duker, P. C., & Korzilius, H. (1997). Meta-analytic study on treatment effectiveness for problem behaviors with individuals who have mental retardation. *American Journal on Mental Retardation, 101,* 387-399.

Donnellan, A. M., Mirenda, P. L., Mesaros, R. A., & Fassbender, L. L. (1984). Analyzing the communicative functions of aberrant behavior. *Journal of the Association for Persons with Severe Handicaps, 9,* 201-212.

Doss, S., & Reichle, J. (1991). Replacing excess behavior with an initial communicative repertoire. In J. Reichle, J. York, & J. Sigafoos (Eds.), *Implementing augmentative and alternative communication* (pp. 215-237). Baltimore: Paul H. Brookes.

Dunlap, G., & Carr, E. G. (2007). Positive behavior support and developmental disabilities: A summary and analysis of research. In S. L. Odom, R. H. Horner, M. E. Snell, & J. Blacher (Eds.), *Handbook of developmental disabilities* (pp. 469-482). New York: Guilford Press.

Dunlap, G., Kern-Dunlap, L., Clarke, S., & Robbins, F. R. (1991). Functional assessment, curriculum revision, and severe behavior problems. *Journal of Applied Behavior Analysis, 24,* 387-397.

Dunlap, G., & Kincaid, D. (2001). The widening world of functional assessment: Comments on four manuals and beyond. *Journal of Applied Behavior Analysis, 34,* 365-377.

Dunlap, G., Sailor, W., Horner, R. H., & Sugai, G. (2009). Overview and history of positive behavior support. In W. Sailor, G. Dunlap., G. Sugai, & R. H. Horner (Eds.), *Handbook of positive behavior support* (pp. 3-16). New York: Springer.

Durand, V. M. (1988). The Motivation Assessment Scale. In M. Hersen & A. Bellack (Eds.), *Dictionary of behavioral assessment techniques* (pp. 309-310). Elmsford, NY: Pergamon.

Durand, V. M. (1990). *Severe behavior problems: A functional communication approach.* New York: Guilford Press.

Durand, V. M., & Carr, E. G. (1991). Functional communication training to reduce challenging behavior: Maintenance and application in new settings. *Journal of Applied Behavior Analysis, 24,* 251-264.

Durand, V. M., & Carr, E. G. (1992). An analysis of maintenance following functional communication training. *Journal of Applied Behavior Analysis, 25,* 777-794.

Durand, V. M., Crimmins, D. B., Caulfield, M., & Taylor, J. (1989). Reinforcer assessment I: Using problem behavior to select reinforcers. *Journal* of the Association for Persons with Severe Handicaps, 14, 113-126.

English, C. L., & Anderson, C. M. (2006). Evaluation of the treatment utility of the analog functional analysis and the structured descriptive assessment. *Journal of Positive Behavior Interventions, 8,* 212-229.

Ervin, R. A., Radford, P. M., Bertsch, K., Piper, A. L., Ehrhardt, K. E., & Poling, A. (2001). A descriptive analysis and critique of the empirical literature on school-based functional assessment. *School Psychology Review, 30,* 193-209.

Ferro, J., Foster-Johnson, L., & Dunlap, G. (1996). The relationship between curricular activities and the problem behavior of students with mental retardation. *American Journal on Mental Retardation, 101,* 184-194.

Filter, K. J., & Horner, R. H. (2009). Function-based academic interventions for problem behavior. *Education and Treatment of Children: Special Issue on Practical Applications of Functional Analysis, 32,* 1-20.

Green, C. W., Reid, D. H., Canipe, V. S., & Gardner, S. M. (1991). A comprehensive evaluation of reinforcer identification processes for persons with profound multiple handicaps. *Journal of Applied Behavior Analysis, 24,* 537-552.

Gresham, F. M. (2002). Teaching social skills to high-risk children and youth: Preventive and remedial strategies. In M. A. Shinn, H. M. Walker, & G. Stoner (Eds.), *Interventions for academic and behavior problems II: Preventive and remedial approaches* (pp. 403-432). Bethesda, MD: National Association of School Psychologists.

Gresham, F. M., McIntyre, L. L., Olson-Tinker, H., Dolstra, L., McLaughlin, V., & Van, M. (2004). Relevance of functional behavioral assessment research for school-based interventions and positive behavioral support. *Research in Developmental Disabilities, 25,* 19-37.

Guess, D., & Carr, E. G. (1991). Emergence and maintenance of stereotypy and self-injury. *American Journal on Mental Retardation, 96,* 299-319.

Hanley, G. P., Iwata, B. A., & McCord, B. E. (2003). Functional analysis of problem behavior: A review. *Journal of Applied Behavior Analysis, 36,* 147-185.

Holburn, S., Jacobson, J. W., Vietze, P. M., Schwartz, A. A., & Sersen, E. (2000). Quantifying the process and outcomes of person-centered planning. *American Journal on Mental Retardation, 105,* 402-416.

Holburn, S., & Vietze, P. M. (2002). *Person-centered planning: Research, practice, and future directions.* Baltimore: Paul H. Brookes.

Horner, R. H. (1999). Positive behavior supports. In M. L. Wehmeyer & J. R. Patton, (Eds.), *Mental retardation in the 21st century* (pp. 181-196). Austin, TX: PRO-ED.

Horner, R. H., & Billingsley, F. F. (1988). The effect of competing behavior on the generalization and maintenance of adaptive behavior in applied settings. In R. H. Horner, G. Dunlap, & R. L. Koegel (Eds.), *Generalization and maintenance: Lifestyle changes in applied settings* (pp. 197-220). Baltimore: Paul H. Brookes.

Horner, R. H., Day, H. M., & Day, J. (1997). Using neutralizing routines to reduce problem behaviors. *Journal of Applied Behavior Analysis, 39,* 601-614.

Horner, R. H., Diemer, S. M., & Brazeau, K. C. (1992). Educational support for students with severe problem behaviors in Oregon: A descriptive analysis from the 1987-1988 school year. *Journal of the Association for Persons with Severe Handicaps, 17,* 154-169.

Horner, R. H., Dunlap, G., Koegel, R. L., Carr, E. G., Sailor, W., Anderson, J., et al. (1990). Toward a technology of "nonaversive" behavioral support. *Journal of the Association for Persons with Severe Handicaps, 15,* 125-132.

Horner, R., Sugai, G., Smolkowski, K., Todd, A., Nakasato, J., & Esperanza, J., (2009). A randomized control trial of school-wide positive behavior support in elementary schools. *Journal of Positive Behavior Interventions, 11*(3), 113-144.

Horner, R. H., Sugai, G., Todd, A. W., & Lewis-Palmer, T. (1999-2000). Elements of behavior support plans: A technical brief. *Exceptionality, 8,* 205-216.

Horner, R. H., Sugai, G., Todd, A. W., & Lewis-Palmer, T. (2005). Schoolwide positive behavior support. In L. M. Bambara & L. Kern (Eds.), *Individualized supports for students with problem behaviors: Designing positive behavior plans* (pp. 359-390). New York: Guilford Press.

Horner, R. H., Vaughn, B., Day, H. M., & Ard, B. (1996). The relationship between setting events and problem behavior. In L. K. Koegel, R. L. Koegel, & G. Dunlap (Eds.), *Positive behavioral support: Including people with difficult behavior in the community* (pp. 381-402). Baltimore: Paul H. Brookes.

Ingram, K., Lewis-Palmer, T., & Sugai, G. (2005). Function-based intervention planning: Comparing the effectiveness of FBA indicated and contra-indicated interventions plans. *Journal of Positive Behavior Interventions, 7,* 224-236.

Irvin, L. K., Tobin, T., Sprague, J., Sugai, G., & Vincent, C. (2004). Validity of office discipline referral measures as indices of school-wide behavioral status and effects of school-wide behavioral interventions. *Journal of Positive Behavioral Interventions, 6,* 131-147.

Iwata, B. A., Dorsey, M. F., Slifer, K. J., Bauman, K. E., & Richman, G. S. (1982/1994). Toward a functional analysis of self-injury. *Journal of Applied Behavior Analysis, 27,* 197-209.

Kern, L. (2005). Responding to problem behavior. In L. M. Bambara & L. Kern (Eds.), *Individualized supports for students with problem behaviors: Designing positive behavior plans* (pp. 275-302). New York: Guilford Press.

Kern, L., & Clarke, S. (2005). Antecedent and setting event interventions. In L. M. Bambara & L. Kern (Eds.), *Individualized supports for students with problem behaviors: Designing positive behavior plans* (pp. 201-236). New York: Guilford Press.

Kincaid, D. (1996). Person-centered planning. In L. K. Koegel, R. L. Koegel, & G. Dunlap (Eds.), *Positive behavior support: Including people with difficult behavior in the community* (pp. 439-465). Baltimore: Paul H. Brookes.

Lalli, J. S., Browder, D. M., Mace, F. C., & Brown, D. K. (1993). Teacher use of descriptive analysis data to implement interventions to decrease students' problem behavior. *Journal of Applied Behavior Analysis, 26,* 227-238.

Lang, R., O'Reilly, M., Machalicek, W., Lancioni, G., Rispoli, M., & Chan, J. M. (2008). A preliminary comparison of functional analysis results when conducted in contrived versus natural settings. *Journal of Applied Behavior Analysis, 41,* 441-445.

Lerman, D. C., & Iwata, B. A. (1993). Descriptive and experimental analysis of variables maintaining self-injurious behavior. *Journal of Applied Behavior Analysis, 26,* 293-319.

Lucyshyn, J. M., & Albin, R. W. (1993). Comprehensive support to families of children with disabilities and behavior problems: Keeping it "friendly." In G. H. S. Singer & L. E. Powers (Eds.), *Families, disability, and empowerment* (pp. 365–407). Baltimore: Paul H. Brookes.

Lucyshyn, J. M., Albin, R. W., Horner, R. H., Mann, J. C., Mann, J. A., & Wadsworth, G. (2007). Family implementation of positive behavior support with a child with autism: A longitudinal, single-case experimental and descriptive replication and extension. *Journal of Positive Behavior Interventions, 9,* 131–150.

Lucyshyn, J. M., Albin, R. W., & Nixon, C. D. (1997). Embedding comprehensive behavioral support in family ecology: An experimental, single-case analysis. *Journal of Consulting and Clinical Psychology, 65,* 241–251.

Lucyshyn, J. M., Horner, R. H., Dunlap, G., Albin, R. W., & Ben, K. R. (2002). Positive behavior support with families. In J. M. Lucyshyn, G. Dunlap, & R. W. Albin (Eds.), *Families and positive behavior support: Addressing problem behavior in family contexts* (pp. 3–43). Baltimore: Paul H. Brookes.

Lucyshyn, J. M., Kayser, A. T., Irvin, L. K., & Blumberg, E. R. (2002). Functional assessment and positive behavior support at home with families: Designing effective and contextually appropriate behavior support plans. In J. M. Lucyshyn, G. Dunlap, & R. W. Albin (Eds.), *Families and positive behavior support: Addressing problem behavior in family contexts* (pp. 97–132). Baltimore: Paul H. Brookes.

Mace, F. C., & Lalli, J. S. (1991). Linking descriptive and experimental analysis in the treatment of bizarre speech. *Journal of Applied Behavior Analysis, 24,* 553–562.

Mank, D. M., & Horner, R. H. (1987). Self-recruited feedback: A cost-effective procedure for maintaining behavior. *Research in Developmental Disabilities, 8,* 91–112.

March, R. E., & Horner, R. H. (2002). Feasibility and contributions of functional behavioral assessment in schools. *Journal of Emotional and Behavioral Disorders, 10,* 158–170.

March, R., Horner, R. H., Lewis-Palmer, T., Brown, D., Crone, D., Todd, A. W., et al. (2000). *Functional Assessment Checklist for Teachers and Staff (FACTS)*. Eugene: Department of Educational and Community Supports, University of Oregon.

Marquis, J. G., Horner, R. H., Carr, E. G., Turnbull, A. P., Thompson, M., Behrens, G. A., et al. (2000). A meta-analysis of positive behavior support. In R. M. Gerston & E. P. Schiller (Eds.), *Contemporary special education research: Syntheses of the knowledge base on critical instructional issues* (pp. 137–178). Mahwah, NJ: Lawrence Erlbaum Associates.

Mayer, G. R., & Sulzer-Azaroff, B. (2002). Interventions for vandalism and aggression. In M. R. Shinn, H. M. Walker, & G. Stoner (Eds.), *Interventions for academic and behavior problems II: Preventive and remedial approaches.* Silver Spring, MD: National Association of School Psychologists.

McIntosh, K., Borgmeier, C., Anderson, C., Horner, R. H., Rodriguez, B., & Tobin, T. (2008). Technical adequacy of the Functional Assessment Checklist for Teachers and Staff FBA intervention measure. *Journal of Positive Behavior Interventions, 10,* 33–45.

McIntosh, K., Chard, D., Boland, J., & Horner, R. (2006). A demonstration of combined efforts in school-wide academic and behavioral systems and incidence of reading and behavior challenges in early elementary grades. *Journal of Positive Behavior Interventions, 8,* 146–154.

Moes, D. R., & Frea, W. D. (2000). Using family context to inform intervention planning for the treatment of a child with autism. *Journal of Positive Behavior Interventions, 2,* 40–46.

Moore, J. W., Edwards, R. P., Sterling-Turner, H. E., Riley, J., DuBard, M., & McGeorge, A. (2002). Teacher acquisition of functional analy-

sis methodology. *Journal of Applied Behavior Analysis, 35,* 73–77.

Mount, B. (1994). Benefits and limitations of personal futures planning. In V. J. Bradley, J. W. Ashbaugh, & B. C. Blaney (Eds.), *Creating individual supports for people with developmental disabilities* (pp. 97–108). Baltimore: Paul H. Brookes.

Munk, D. D., & Repp, A. C. (1994). The relationship between instructional variables and problem behavior: A review. *Exceptional Children, 60,* 390–401.

Nelson, J. R., Roberts, M. L., Mathur, S. R., & Rutherford, R. B., Jr. (1999). Has public policy exceeded our knowledge base? A review of the functional behavioral assessment literature. *Behavioral Disorders, 24,* 169–179.

Newcomer, L. L., & Lewis, T. J. (2004). Functional behavioral assessment: An investigation of assessment reliability and effectiveness of function-based interventions. *Journal of Emotional and Behavioral Disorders, 12,* 168–181.

Newton, J. S., & Horner, R. H. (2004). Emerging trends in methods for research and evaluation of behavioral interventions. In E. Emerson, T. Thompson, T. Parmenter, & C. Hatton (Eds.), *International handbook of methods for research and evaluation in intellectual disabilities* (pp. 495–515). New York: Wiley.

Nirje, B. (1969). The normalization principle and its human management implications. In R. Kugel & W. Wolfensberger (Eds.), *Changing patterns in residential services for the mentally retarded* (pp. 179–195). Washington, DC: President's Committee on Mental Retardation.

Northup, J., Broussard, C., Jones, K., George, T., Vollmer, T. R., & Herring, M. (1995). The differential effects of teacher and peer attention on the disruptive classroom behavior of three children with a diagnosis of attention deficit hyperactivity disorder. *Journal of Applied Behavior Analysis, 28,* 227–228.

Northup, J., Wacker, D., Sasso, G., Steege, M., Cigrand, K., Cook, J., et al. (1991). A brief functional analysis of aggressive and alternative behavior in an outclinic setting. *Journal of Applied Behavior Analysis, 24,* 509–522.

O'Brien, C. J., O'Brien, J., & Mount, B. (1997). Person-centered planning has arrived or has it? *Mental Retardation, 35,* 480–484.

O'Neill, R. E., Horner, R. H., Albin, R. W., Sprague, J. R., Storey, K., & Newton, J. S. (1997). *Functional assessment and program development for problem behavior: A practical handbook* (2nd ed.). Pacific Grove, CA: Brooks/Cole.

O'Reilly, M. (1997). Functional analysis of episodic self-injury correlated with recurrent otitis media. *Journal of Applied Behavior Analysis, 30,* 165–167.

Pace, G. M., Ivancic, M. R., Edwards, G. L., Iwata, B. A., & Page, T. J. (1985). Assessment of stimulus preference and reinforcer values with profoundly retarded individuals. *Journal of Applied Behavior, 18,* 249–256.

Reid, R., & Nelson, J. R. (2002). The utility, acceptability, and practicality of functional behavioral assessment for students with high-incidence problem behaviors. *Remedial Special Education, 23,* 15–23.

Repp, A. C., Felce, D., & Barton, L. E. (1988). Basing the treatment of stereotypic and self-injurious behaviors on hypotheses of their causes. *Journal of Applied Behavior Analysis, 21,* 281–289.

Repp, A. C., & Singh, N. N. (1990). *Perspectives on the use of nonaversive and aversive interventions for persons with developmental disabilities.* Pacific Grove, CA: Brooks/Cole.

Risley, T. R. (1996). Get a life! In L. K. Koegel, R. L. Koegel, & G. Dunlap (Eds.), *Positive behavioral support: Including people with difficult behavior in the community* (pp. 425–437). Baltimore: Paul H. Brookes.

Roane, H. S., Vollmer, T. R., Ringdahl, J. E., & Marcus, B. A. (1998). Evaluation of a brief stimulus preference assessment. *Journal of Applied Behavior Analysis, 31,* 605–620.

Ross, S. W., & Horner, R. H. (2009). Bully prevention in positive behavior support. *Journal of Applied Behavior Analysis, 42,* 747–759.

Sailor, W., Dunlap, G., Sugai, G., & Horner, R. H. (Eds.). (2009). *Handbook of positive behavior support.* New York: Springer.

Sandler, L. (2001). *Goodness-of-fit and the viability of behavioral support plans: A survey of direct care adult residential staff.* Unpublished doctoral dissertation, University of Oregon, Eugene.

Sasso, G. M., Reimers, R. M., Cooper, L. J., Wacker, D., Berg, W., Steege, M., et al. (1992). Use of descriptive and experimental analyses to identify the functional properties of aberrant behavior in school settings. *Journal of Applied Behavior Analysis, 25,* 809–821.

Schalock, R., & Alonso, M. A. V. (2002). *Handbook on quality of life for human service practitioners.* Washington, DC: American Association on Mental Retardation.

Scott, T. M., Anderson, C., Mancil, R., & Alter, P. (2009). Function-based supports for individual students in school settings. In W. Sailor, G. Dunlap, G. Sugai, & R. H. Horner (Eds.), *Handbook of positive behavior support* (pp. 421–441). New York: Springer.

Scott, T. M., Bucalos, A., Liaupsin, C., Nelson, C. M., Jolivette, K., & DeShea, L. (2004). Using functional behavior assessment in general education settings: Making a case for effectiveness and efficiency. *Behavioral Disorders, 29,* 189–201.

Shavelson, R. J., & Towne, L. (Eds.). (2002). *Scientific research in education.* Washington, DC: National Academy Press.

Shukla, S., & Albin, R. W. (1996). Effects of extinction alone and extinction plus functional communication training on covariation of problem behaviors. *Journal of Applied Behavior Analysis, 29,* 565–568.

Skinner, B. F. (1953). *Science and human behavior.* New York: Macmillan.

Smith, B. W., & Sugai, G. (2000). A self-management functional assessment-based behavior support plan for a middle school student with EBD. *Journal of Positive Behavior Interventions, 2,* 208–217.

Sprague, J. R., & Horner, R. H. (1992). Covariation within functional response classes: Implications for treatment of severe problem behavior. *Journal of Applied Behavior Analysis, 25,* 735–745.

Sprague, J. R., & Horner, R. H. (1999). Low-frequency, high-intensity problem behavior: Toward an applied technology of functional analysis and intervention. In A. C. Repp & R. H. Horner (Eds.), *Functional analysis of problem behavior: From effective assessment to effective support* (pp. 98–116). Belmont, CA: Wadsworth.

Sugai, G., Horner, R. H., & Gresham, F. (2002). Behaviorally effective school environments. In M. R. Shinn, G. Stoner, & H. M. Walker (Eds.), *Interventions for academic and behavior problems: Preventive and remedial approaches* (pp. 315–350). Silver Spring, MD: National Association for School Psychologists.

Sugai, G., Lewis-Palmer, T., & Hagan-Burke, S. (1999–2000). Overview of the functional behavioral assessment process. *Exceptionality, 8,* 149–160.

Taylor-Greene, S., Brown, D., Nelson, L., Longton, J., Gassman, T., Cohen, J., et al. (1997). School-wide behavioral support: Starting the year off right. *Journal of Behavioral Education, 7,* 99–112.

Todd, A. W., Horner, R. H., & Sugai, G. (1999). Self-monitoring and self-recruited praise: Effects on problem behavior, academic engagement, and work completion in a typical classroom. *Journal of Positive Behavior Interventions, 1,* 66–76, 122.

Todd, A. W., Horner, R. H., Sugai, G., & Colvin, G. (1999). Individualizing school-wide discipline for students with chronic problem behaviors: A team approach. *Effective School Practices, 17*(4), 72–82.

Todd, A. W., Horner, R. H., Sugai, G., & Sprague, J. R. (1999). Effective behavior support: Strengthening school-wide systems through a team-based approach. *Effective School Practices, 17*(4), 23–37.

Touchette, P. E., MacDonald, R. F., & Langer, S. N. (1985). A scatter plot for identifying stimulus control of problem behavior. *Journal of Applied Behavior Analysis, 18,* 343–351.

Turnbull, A. P., & Ruef, M. (1996). Family perspectives on problem behavior. *Mental Retardation, 34,* 280–293.

Umbreit, J. (1995). Functional analysis of disruptive behavior in an inclusive classroom. *Journal of Early Interventions, 20,* 18–29.

U.S. Department of Education (2009, August). *Building the legacy: IDEA 2004.* Retrieved August 19, 2009, from http://idea.ed.gov/explore/view/p/%2Croot%2Cstatute%2C

U.S. Government Accountability Office. (2009). *Seclusions and restraints: Selected cases of death and abuse at public and private schools and treatment centers.* Testimony before the Committee on Education and Labor, U.S. House of Representatives, May 19, 2009. Available at http://www.pbis.org/seclusion/restraint/gao_report.aspx

Van Houten, R., & Rolider, A. (1991). Applied behavior analysis. In J. L. Matson & J. A. Mulick (Eds.), *Handbook of mental retardation* (pp. 569–585). New York: Pergamon.

Vollmer, T. R., & Van Camp, C. M. (1998). Experimental designs to evaluate antecedent control. In J. K. Luiselli & M. J. Cameron (Eds.), *Antecedent control: Innovation approaches to behavioral support* (pp. 87–111). Baltimore: Paul H. Brookes.

Wacker, D. P., Berg, W. K., Asmus, J. M., Harding, J. W., & Cooper, L. J. (1998). Experimental analysis of antecedent influences on challenging behavior. In J. K. Luiselli & M. J. Cameron (Eds.), *Antecedent control: Innovation approaches to behavioral support* (pp. 67–86). Baltimore: Paul H. Brookes.

Wacker, D. P., Steege, M., Northup, J., Reimers, T., Berg, W., & Sasso, G. (1990). Use of functional analysis and acceptability measures to assess and treat severe behavior problems: An outpatient clinic model. In A. C. Repp & N. Singh (Eds.), *Perspectives on the use of aversive and nonaversive interventions for persons with developmental disabilities* (pp. 349–359). Pacific Grove, CA: Brooks/Cole.

Wacker, D. P., Steege, M. W., Northup, J., Sasso, G., Berg, W., Reimers, T., et al. (1990). A component analysis of functional communication training across three topographies of severe behavior problems. *Journal of Applied Behavior Analysis, 23,* 417–429.

Wehmeyer, M., & Schwartz, M. (1997). Self-determination and positive adult outcomes: A follow-up study of youth with mental retardation and learning disabilities. *Exceptional Children, 63,* 256.

Wolfensberger, W. (1983). Social role valorization: A proposed new term for the principle of normalization. *Mental Retardation, 21,* 234–239.

This research was supported by the Office of Special Education Programs, U.S. Department of Education (H326S980003). Opinions expressed herein are those of the authors and do not necessarily reflect the position of the U.S. Department of Education, and such endorsements should not be inferred. For additional information regarding the contents of this chapter, contact the first author (robh@uoregon.edu).

8

Understanding Special Health Care Procedures

Jane P. Rues
J. Carolyn Graff
Marilyn Mulligan Ault

Students with special health care needs are similar to all other students in terms of their right to an appropriate education in the least restrictive environment, with full family participation. The presence of special health care needs, estimated at 13.9% for all children and 16% for children 6–11 years of age (U.S. Department of Health and Human Services, 2007), requires additional accommodations in the educational setting. This is best accomplished by training educational staff in the knowledge and skills needed to manage these procedures at school.

❖ ❖ ❖ ❖ ❖   **Liz**   ❖ ❖ ❖ ❖ ❖

Mark Vontz is not surprised when he learns that a student enrolling in his class next year has special health care needs. He has become accustomed to looking out for a variety of his students' needs over his seven years of teaching fifth- and sixth-grade math and science. In the past, he has encountered several medical situations, one that had taken him to the emergency room with a student. The episode that most clearly taught him the necessity of proper training and support resulted from the near death of a student during his fifth year of teaching. On a spring field trip to gather water quality samples, a student was stung by a bee. While Mr. Vontz was removing the stinger, the student moved rapidly through the stages of anaphylactic shock. He was able to call for emergency medical services (EMS) on his cell phone and arrange to meet an ambulance on the way to the hospital.

More typical issues surrounding health care occurred throughout the years, including medication administration, burns and wounds, and allergies. Mr. Vontz feels quite confident that he is prepared to handle any health-related condition, or if he doesn't know about a particular condition, he can learn from trained professionals how to best be prepared.

During the past seven years of teaching, Mr. Vontz's school has actively moved toward the practice of full inclusion for all children. Children with a range of disabilities have been enrolled in his classroom and he enjoys the challenge of including them in science and math activities with their more typical peers. He feels that he is a contributing member of a team who is trying to determine how the math and science content could be taught in a way that will be meaningful in their lives. With the support of a consulting teacher, he feels positive about his efforts and their results. Now he is being presented with the challenge of including a student with severe cognitive disabilities who also uses a wheelchair to navigate around the building and within his classroom. He has dealt with children who had these conditions before, but not any children who have had multiple needs. He knows he has to be prepared. This child, Liz, has her nutritional needs met by

being fed through a gastrostomy tube. Mr. Vontz knows that the aide will assist the child with these tube feedings. He will, however, have a significant role on the team that is planning for her full inclusion. He and all of her other teachers have to understand her nonverbal communication not only about how she expresses herself in academic and social situations, but also about the very critical basics, such as how she indicates hunger and thirst, knowledge of her oral and non-oral nutritional needs and how to respond, and how to integrate the needs of the health care procedure into her educational activities.

Throughout their careers, teachers encounter students who need a variety of special health care procedures to promote and maintain health (Boulet, Boyle, & Schieve, 2009; Clair, Church, & Batshaw, 2007; Nageswaran, Silver, & Stein, 2008). The emphasis in this chapter is on quality health care in the educational setting, with suggestions for integrating health care needs into the educational program, and the role of prevention. It focuses on special health care procedures that are common across a number of health conditions and is organized to reflect a continuum of classroom use—from procedures used more frequently to those used infrequently. The first group of procedures includes a general body of knowledge and a group of skills referred to as "health and safety procedures." These procedures include infection control, cardiopulmonary resuscitation, and first aid. The second group includes routine procedures that are identified as "routine prevention procedures," which include teeth and gum care, skin care, and bowel care. The third group includes procedures that are needed less frequently; they are identified as "specialized health care procedures." These include seizure monitoring, medication administration, growth monitoring, nutrition supplementation, and management of food intake. The final section addresses procedures that occur infrequently and that teachers may or may not be expected to participate in their implementation. These procedures, referred to as "low-incidence health care procedures," include non-oral feeding, atypical elimination, respiratory management, glucose monitoring, and shunt care. Each section addresses what is involved in the implementation of the procedure, why this particular knowledge and skills are necessary, and where to go for further information and training. Both the Internet and the school nurse are important informational resources for teachers and their respective roles are also addressed.

Using the Internet

The Internet is one of the most valuable options available to educators and parents to quickly access current information on most health conditions or procedures. It offers many sources of information about (a) specific disabilities and the characteristics associated with these disabilities; (b) typical (and alternative) medical treatments; and (c) opportunities to learn from and confer with other individuals who have a specific disability, are family members of children with that disability, or are teaching others with the disability.

Information About Specific Disabilities

The Internet is an accessible and powerful tool commonly used to gather information about health care conditions. The range of information requires that the reader be discerning in determining the value of the information; criteria are available for evaluating a Web site (see *The Good, the Bad, & the Ugly,* http://lib.nmsu.edu/instruction/eval.html) and should be used routinely by educators and families. The information found in this chapter or through reputable Internet sites will allow you to ask relevant and informed questions of parents of students with disabilities who are newly enrolled in your class. This information can also be helpful in ascertaining when certain behaviors may be part of a disability. For example, a student receiving a certain medication may experience dryness of the mouth or lethargy. Knowing this and using the tips that parents, educators, and health care providers have shared to address this problem can certainly make the education of a child more effective.

Many Web sites now provide options for consumers: Information is organized by the category of reader (professionals or parents) or by topic (e.g., education, leisure, health and wellness) and the readability better reflects the audience range. A good medical dictionary (http://www.medterms.com) is always useful and talking with the parents may help clarify many of the less familiar terms. Learning the terms allows clearer and more professional communication when you wish to ask questions of parents or experts either personally or via e-mail.

Medical Treatments

An educator may be interested in what medical treatments are associated with different disabilities. For example, knowing what types of medications are typically prescribed and the intended effect and possible side effects of the medication may help the educator be a more informed observer in the classroom. If surgeries are scheduled for a student, knowing more about those surgeries and what type of care the student may need upon returning to school may make this experience go more smoothly for both. In addition to the parents and the hospital discharge planners, educators can access general information online at http://www.aap.org/healthtopics/hospitalcare.cfm, http://www.aap.org/healthtopics/populunique.cfm, http://www.aap.org/healthtopics/specialneeds.cfm, http://www.cincinnatichildrens.org/svc/alpha/c/special-needs/resources/discharge.htm#hospital, and http://www.caregiving.org/pubs/brochures/familydischargeplanning.pdf.

An educator can also search for information by using a search engine and typing in the name of the treatment (e.g., spica cast) or medication (e.g., phenytoin [Dilantin]). Sites where you can start your investigation include: The Virtual Hospital®: http://www.uihealthcare.com/vh/index.html, the Connecticut Children's Center Patient Education Guides: http://patiented.aap.org/, MedlinePlus®: http://www.nlm.nih.gov/medlineplus, drug information: http://www.nlm.nih.gov/medlineplus/druginformation.html, ipl2 (medical texts for health professionals): http://www.ipl.org, and the National Center for Complimentary and Alternative Medicine: http://nccam.nih.gov.

There are also Internet sites, developed and operated by parents, that focus on disabilities. Often, these sites have information about alternative treatments for various conditions that may not be endorsed by the medical community nor founded on research. When looking at alternative treatment literature, be sure to read both the pros and the cons so that you are an informed reader. You should not make recommendations about alternative treatments, but you could provide information from both sides of a controversy to a family or team searching for ideas, which, of course, should be reviewed by the appropriate health care professionals.

Opportunities to Confer with Others

A useful option available on the Internet is the opportunity to easily correspond with experts about specific areas where more information is needed. Most Web pages dedicated to a health condition and those sponsored by departments of education or special education also provide links to a resource person. Often, the regional children's hospital provides Web pages that address a range of services (e.g., clinics that serve children with cerebral palsy, feeding clinics). These sites provide the educator with access either personally by phone, by accompanying the student and the family to a clinic, or through e-mail contact with these local experts.

Quality Health Care and Teaching

The process of establishing quality health care in the educational setting means a commitment to (a) integrating special health care needs into the student's ongoing educational program, and (b) actively preventing the development of health-related problems or conditions. This commitment must be made by the educational staff, as well as the administrative personnel, and supported through the provision of necessary training, the accessible location of the classroom or instructional setting within the school building, and the availability of backup support personnel. The student's team, composed of teachers, staff members, and related service personnel, is an important vehicle for discussions on how to incorporate special health care procedures in the classroom; the parents, as members of the team, are helpful in identifying appropriate educational strategies and in determining how to explain aspects of the procedure to the student's peers while maintaining the student's dignity. A team model can be effective, efficient, accountable, and proactive because each team member is responsible for implementing the goals throughout the school day using incidental and embedded teaching and partial participation.

✥ ✥ ✥ ✥ ✥	**Tommy**	✥ ✥ ✥ ✥ ✥

Tommy, a student with autism, will be attending kindergarten this year at Liz's school. He struggles with chronic constipation and limited food choices; his parents are concerned that the constipation may create behavior problems in class (as a result of cramping and bloating) and his restricted food choices may make snack and lunchtime a struggle for the staff. His current weight for his height is below the third percentile for his chronological age. His teacher and parents want to be proactive in working with Tommy and have already requested a consultation with the multidisciplinary team to develop an intervention program that could be implemented at home and at school.

Integrating Health Care Needs

The first commitment, addressing both the educational and health requirements of students in the school, confirms the willingness of teachers to address the needs of the whole student. The fact that a student has a gastrostomy tube (i.e., a tube inserted through the wall of the abdomen in order to deliver food and fluids), a tracheostomy (i.e., an opening at the base of the throat that facilitates breathing), or is catheterized (i.e., a tube inserted into the bladder to drain urine) can add to instead of subtract from situations that provide the content or occasion for instruction.

At least three instructional strategies facilitate the incorporation of health-related procedures into the educational day. These include incidental teaching, embedded skill teaching, and partial participation (see Chapter 4). Briefly, incidental teaching is a procedure during which a teacher follows a student's initiation in identifying an interest or a need. Once the teacher has responded to the signal or initiation presented by the student, the opportunity to practice specific skills is provided. Incidental teaching, usually described in the context of language instruction, can also be applied when responding to a student's need for special health care procedures. On the basis of an initiation from a student (e.g., facial expression and an increase in body movement, pointing via eye gaze, or upper-extremity movement to a picture of the desired item), the teacher can provide, for example, humidified oxygen or a tube feeding.

Tommy's parents have worked hard this past year to identify signals that indicate that Tommy has to use the bathroom. They are anxious to share this information with the team and develop an intervention program that will decrease his chronic constipation and increase his food choices while increasing his weight.

Embedded teaching suggests that multiple skills, addressing many different goals, can be taught simultaneously. Critical skills such as language, reach and grasp, relaxation, and head control can be practiced in conjunction with daily health care procedures. For example, prior to administering medication, the student assumes an erect sitting posture, reaches and touches the glass of water to indicate readiness, and visually tracks the pill as it is poured from the bottle. With assistance from the teacher, the student brings the spoon (with the pill and applesauce) to her mouth. She then chooses more applesauce or water to make sure that she has completely swallowed the pill.

With partial participation, the third instructional strategy, teachers support the student's involvement in a health-related activity as an educational objective. With this approach, the student is not required to independently perform a health care procedure but may practice and participate in many important component skills that are part of a special health care procedure; these can contribute to greater independence, control, and self-determination. Participating in components of a procedure, such as grasping a toothbrush and spitting after teeth and gum care, visually fixating and swallowing during medication administration, or communicating the need for position changes, all represent meaningful participation and contribution to health care procedures.

Mr. Vontz plans to implement a sequence in his math class that will allow Liz to keep an inventory of her medical supplies. This includes sorting and counting the tubes, formula bottles, and bags. As part of a math activity related to sets, fractions, and projections, Liz will keep a weekly total of her nutritional intake so that she can project her formula needs for the next week for the school nurse.

Preventing Additional Health Care Problems

In addition to meeting the current needs of students, teachers must participate in efforts designed to prevent the development of further health-related problems. Problems may result from complications from an already identified condition (e.g., contractures resulting from cerebral palsy) or from conditions not related to any currently identified problem (e.g., food refusal because of gastroesophageal reflux). Health-related activities and procedures that may prevent future problems include careful hand washing, adequate nutrition and hydration, cardiovascular exercise and physical fitness, changes in instructional environments and materials, and access to the outdoors and sunshine.

A School Nurse's Role

Since the inception of school nursing, the role of school nurses in managing students with chronic health problems has continued to expand (American Nurses Association, 2005). Early on, school nurses focused on protecting the entire student population from the spread of common disease by screening for contagious diseases, immunizing students, and implementing basic health instruction in the schools (Walker & Jacobs, 1984). Today, school nurses monitor immunizations; ensure that students with infectious illnesses are excluded from school as necessary; provide health education to students, staff, families, and the community; screen hearing and vision; administer or supervise the administration of medication; and participate as the health expert on individualized education program (IEP) teams (American Academy of Pediatrics, 2008; National Association of School Nurses, 2002). A school nurse may not have specific knowledge or skill in the implementation of certain procedures such as catheterization, tracheostomy suctioning, or gastrostomy tube feedings. But given his or her background and training, the school nurse is the most qualified member of the team to function as the coordinator of school health services (American Academy of Pediatrics, 2008) and to take a major role in identifying resources, training, and monitoring special health care procedures for individual students (Students with Chronic Illnesses, 2003).

As the number of students with special health care needs in educational settings has increased, school nurses have expanded their contribution to the school team's plan. An important component of the overall plan is the individualized health care plan (IHP), which is developed by the school nurse to meet the needs of students whose health needs affect their daily functioning (National Association of School Nurses, 2008). The IHP can be incorporated into the IEP when the

health care issues are related to the educational needs of the student. The IHP serves as legal protection by showing that proper plans and safeguards, such as an emergency care plan, are in place for any student with a condition that has the potential for developing into a medical emergency.

Guidelines that stress the need for school leaders to establish emergency response plans to deal with life-threatening medical emergencies in children have been published by the American Academy of Pediatrics (2004) and the American Heart Association (2005). These guidelines include goals for developing an efficient and effective campus-wide communication system for each school with local EMS; establishing and practicing a medical emergency response plan (MERP) involving school nurses, physicians, athletic trainers, and the EMS system; identifying students at risk for life-threatening emergencies and ensuring the presence of individual emergency care plans; training staff and students in first aid and cardiopulmonary resuscitation; equipping the school for potential life-threatening emergencies; and implementing lay rescuer automated external defibrillator programs.

Health and Safety Procedures

These procedures contribute significantly to the overall health and safety of all students, but particularly for young children and youth with severe or profound disabilities. These procedures include infection control, cardiopulmonary resuscitation, and first aid. The procedures (a) have a broad range of applications across many different settings, and (b) require that all staff members who have direct contact with students be skilled in their application.

Infection Prevention and Control

The purpose of infection prevention and control is to prevent the transmission of disease to students and school personnel. Infections occur when organisms enter the body and find an environment that allows them to grow and spread. Some infections, such as the common cold, are an expected part of childhood. Other infections, such as AIDS or tuberculosis, which occur in the general public, present minimal risk in the schools if proper control procedures are followed.

What Is Involved

Infection prevention and control refers primarily to the efforts of public health and school officials to prevent the initial occurrence of infection. Secondarily, it refers to efforts to prevent the spread of an already established infection. Proper immunization, before school enrollment, is the major method of infection control. The schedules for childhood immunizations established by the Centers for Disease Control and Prevention (CDC) are listed on their Web site at http://www.cdc.gov/vaccines/recs/schedules/child-schedule.htm. Current data indicate that nearly 90% of all U.S. children are immunized by the time they attend elementary school (U.S. Department of Health and Human Services, 2008).

Infection prevention and control also involves using proper procedures to prevent the spread of infection to students, as well as educators. When a student is identified as having an infection, consultation with the school nurse and the primary health care provider is necessary to determine whether the child should remain in or return to the classroom. If the student remains, then specific procedures designed to prevent the spread of infection without unnecessarily stigmatizing the student must be followed. Because certain students are more susceptible to infections than others, efforts must be made to maintain or promote the health of the student with the infection, as well as those students who are potentially exposed. Frequent hand washing, particularly as the teacher moves from physical contact with one student to another, is a critical and effective intervention for infection prevention and control in the classroom.

There are some viruses that may be present for varying lengths of time but present no symptoms. These include, but are not limited to, cytomegalovirus (CMV), herpes virus, hepatitis A and B viruses, and HIV. Preventing the spread of these infections requires a clear understanding of how infections are transmitted. For example, a child may have acquired a CMV infection early in life. The virus will leave the body through saliva or urine only at certain times, with no sign that this is occurring. School policy may require that disposable gloves be used whenever feeding or changing the child's diaper if such a level of support is required. Because there is a risk to pregnant women, health authorities also recommend that pregnant staff persons working with infants and children be informed of the risk of getting CMV, the potential effects on their unborn child, and ways to reduce the risk of infection (Centers for Disease Control and Infection, 2008). Neither HIV nor hepatitis B virus (HBV) transmission has been documented from exposure to bodily fluids commonly encountered in school, such as

feces, nasal secretions, sputum, sweat, tears, urine, and vomitus. Extreme care procedures should be applied in dental or oral care settings in which saliva might be contaminated with blood. (See Centers for Disease Control and Infection at http://www.cdc.gov/oralhealth/infectioncontrol/) and http://www.cdc.gov/hiv/resources/factsheets/hcwprev.htm.

Classroom Applications

The best way to prevent the spread of infection in the classroom is for all students and staff to use appropriate sanitation procedures. (See the School Network for Absenteeism Prevention (SNAP), at http://www.itsasnap.org/index.asp.) The most simple and effective procedure is to engage in proper hand washing, which includes lathering hands with warm running water and soap. Figure 8–1 presents one description of proper

FIGURE 8–1
Proper Hand-Washing Technique and Guidelines for When to Wash

- Wet your hands with warm, running water and apply liquid soap or use clean bar soap. Lather well.
- Rub your hands vigorously together for at least 15 to 20 seconds.
- Scrub all surfaces, including the backs of your hands, wrists, between your fingers, and under your fingernails.
- Rinse well.
- Dry your hands with a clean or disposable towel.
- Use a towel to turn off the faucet.

Proper hand washing should always occur *after*

➢ blowing your nose with a tissue;
➢ covering your mouth/nose when you cough or sneeze;
➢ food preparation;
➢ touching cuts or sores;
➢ contact with an ill child;
➢ feeding a child (or supporting a child to eat); and
➢ all toileting activities, including contact with diapers.

Hand washing should occur *before*

➢ handling food;
➢ setting the table;
➢ eating or feeding a child;
➢ treating a scrape, cut, or wound; and
➢ taking care of someone who is sick.

Source: Adapted from Centers for Disease Control and Prevention. (2008). *An ounce of prevention campaign.* Campaign was created by the National Center for Infectious Diseases, Coordinating Center for Infectious Diseases of the Centers for Disease Control and Prevention in partnership with Reckitt Benckiser, Inc., the makers of LYSOL® Brand Products. Download educational materials at www.cdc.gov/ounceofprevention.

hand-washing techniques and guidelines for when they should be implemented. Sanitation procedures also involve the proper washing of school items, such as toys and teaching materials, with disinfectants before the items are shared. This is particularly true if items are mouthed, if saliva is present outside the mouth (e.g., on the hands or clothing), or if sneezing or coughing onto materials is common. For the most effective implementation of sanitation procedures, classrooms should be equipped with or have access to toileting and hand-washing areas that are separate and distinct from food preparation areas. The teacher is responsible for promoting and maintaining a clean classroom environment.

Where to Go for Further Information or Training
Local health departments and hospitals can be contacted for additional information. The Centers for Disease Control and Prevention (http://www.cdc.gov/), the American Academy of Pediatrics (http://www.aap.org), and the American Academy of Family Physicians (http://www.aafp.org) provide information and guidelines about infectious diseases, methods of transmission, and strategies for prevention.

Cardiopulmonary Resuscitation

Cardiopulmonary resuscitation (CPR) is an *emergency* procedure used when breathing or breathing and pulse have ceased. The American Heart Association adopted new CPR science guidelines in 2005, which are the basis for teaching CPR. CPR training is required for certification and what follows is general procedural information.

What Is Involved
The three basic rescue skills of CPR are opening the airway, restoring breathing, and restoring circulation. CPR applied immediately upon discovery of a casualty and sustained until more advanced life support arrives is the key to saving lives. Teachers should be trained and recertified every two years in the CPR procedures associated with the ages of the students who they teach. Separate procedures have been developed for infants (birth to one year of age), children (one to eight years of age), and adults (eight years of age through adult).

CPR guidelines updated in 2005 recommend the use of an automated external defibrillator (AED) as a part of treating cardiorespiratory arrest in adults and children older than eight years (American Heart Association, 2005). The AED is used to restore a normal heartbeat in a student whose heart has suddenly stopped beating. The AED provides an electrical shock to the heart to help restore a normal rhythm.

If the student appears to be choking, identify whether the airway is completely obstructed by determining whether the student can speak or cough. If the student can do either of these, do not interfere with the student's attempts to force out the object that is blocking the airway. If the student is unable to speak or cough, CPR is to be performed.

Classroom Applications
Difficulty breathing is a frequent medical emergency for children. The need for resuscitation may result from injuries; suffocation caused by toys, food, or plastic covers; smoke inhalation; and infections, especially of the respiratory tract, among other conditions. The majority of situations that result in the need for CPR in children are preventable; therefore, instructional settings and routines must be established to ensure the presence of environments that are safe and that foster independence.

Although any individual may need CPR, students with severe disabilities have characteristics that increase the likelihood. Heart defects, seizure disorders, aspiration of fluids and/or food, tracheostomies, or excess fluids in the mouth are examples of these characteristics. Eating characteristics that may result in the need for an emergency response are inadequate chewing and/or swallowing that can result in students aspirating portions of their meals. Children, ages three years and younger, are particularly at risk because of their tendency to place objects in their mouths, poor chewing ability, and narrow airways compared with those of older children (Altkorn et al., 2008).

All teachers and staff at Mr. Vontz's school routinely update their CPR and first aid certification. Students who use wheelchairs require a slightly more involved response from staff should resuscitation be needed. Mr. Vontz's principal has made sure that the local hospital provides one-to-one training in a response protocol for a student in a wheelchair, particularly for resuscitation and CPR. Most first aid situations do not require a different response for students who use or do not use a wheelchair.

Teachers and other professionals who interact on a regular basis with students who have disabilities should be routinely certified in CPR. Although significant injuries are rare in children who receive CPR, occurring in 3% of cases (Bush, Jones, Cohle, & Johnson, 1996; Ryan, Young, & Wells, 2003), if a student is injured during the procedure, the state's Good Samaritan laws usually protect that person. The Good Samaritan doctrine is a legal principle that prevents a rescuer who has voluntarily helped a victim in distress from being successfully sued for "wrongdoing."

Where to Go for Further Information or Training

The American Heart Association (http://www.americanheart.org), local hospitals, the Red Cross (http://www.redcross.org), school districts, and other local agencies routinely conduct CPR and management of airway obstruction classes. A course, Heartsaver CPR in Schools, is offered through the American Heart Association to train students and teachers on the chain of survival and the warning signs of heart attack, cardiac arrest, stroke, and choking.

First Aid

First aid refers to emergency care that is given before regular medical aid can be obtained. The first aid procedures administered in most schools are not life-saving situations, yet unmanaged or improperly managed, these situations can become life threatening with serious consequences. The most frequent reasons for school-based emergency medical services are falls, other trauma (e.g., fracture or dislocation), and medical illness (e.g., breathing difficulty, seizures, and other illnesses) (Knight, Vernon, Fines, & Dean, 1999). Because these events often occur when the teacher is the first available source of assistance, first aid training should be required of all school staff and should be taught by competent and certified health care professionals.

Students may need first aid at some point in their school career, such as for an episode of asthma, an allergic reaction to food, or a reaction to medication. Students with special health care needs may present additional challenges for school staff because their symptoms may be subtle and difficult to recognize or they may have difficulty communicating. For example, a student may experience a headache, nausea, or fever, but is unable to describe these symptoms to others. Parents can provide their input on body language, facial expressions, and changes in appetite, which may be indicators of an illness in their child.

Tommy's parents are excellent members of his team. Although Tommy has difficulty communicating orally, *his parent are able to provide school staff with body language and physical activity cues that indicate stomach cramping and discomfort.*

What Is Involved

Planning. An emergency plan and procedures for school staff to follow should include not only the school setting and available resources in that setting, but also settings away from the school campus (e.g., traveling to and from school by bus or when on a field trip). The plans and procedures for a school should be consistent with the policies established by the school district and with state laws and regulations for school staff. Procedures could include, for example, assignment of the persons responsible for calling EMS; calling the student's parents; accompanying the student to the emergency room, physician's office, or other location in order to receive emergency care; and attending to the needs of the other students who witnessed the event that resulted in a need for first aid.

School staff should have phone numbers for contacting the student's parents during the school day, along with the names and phone numbers of persons to contact when the parents are not available. Additionally, the name and phone number of the student's health care professional should be easily available for school staff who are responsible for using this information. Phone numbers for the school nurse, school administrator, ambulance, police department, fire department, paramedics, poison control center, and hospital emergency room should be posted at each telephone in the school. A list of the steps to be followed in an emergency should also be posted near all telephones.

Students with special health care needs may require emergency care for acute life-threatening complications that are unique to their chronic conditions. These students should be identified, with student and parental permission, and emergency plans developed (American Academy of Pediatrics, 2004; Porter, Haynie, Bierle, Caldwell, & Palfrey, 2006). Copies of this plan should be kept in easily accessible places at the child's home, school, and any other location where the child regularly spends time. The plan should include provisions for any special training that will be needed by emergency medical personnel, family members, school personnel, or other persons who may be called on to provide emergency care for the child. An Emergency Information Form for Children with Special Needs can be accessed at http://pediatrics.aappublications.org/cgi/reprint/104/4/e53. An emergency care plan should also be a part of the student's IHP and IEP. The New Mexico Department of Health has a collection of documents in their *School Health Manual* for use when developing and implementing a plan for the inclusion of children and youth who require specialized health care procedures in an educational setting. Figure 8–2 represents a portion of these documents adapted for Liz. The IHP could also serve as part of the educational plan for children who are hospitalized for either elective or emergency care. Although students with multiple

FIGURE 8–2
Sample Individualized Health Care Plan for Liz

Student's Name: **Liz Harmon**	DOB: **2/14/99**	School: **Border Star**	School Nurse: **Jane Roland, RN**
Date of IHP: **9/08/2009**	Physician: **M. Couch, MD**	Ph#: **913-545-2676**	

Nursing Diagnosis/ Concern	Educational Goal	Plan of Action	By Whom/ When
Potential for seizures at school	Student will maintain optimal health, safety, and well-being during the school day	Kind of seizure: **Grand mal** Usual frequency of seizures: **1–2/month** Date of last seizure: **7/28/99** Events that may precipitate a seizure: ☒ **Illness, not receiving meds, fatigue** ☐ Student will be monitored for signs of seizure activity, including: ☒ **Mealtime, outdoor activities, symptoms of cold, cough** ☐ If seizure activity is noted, the seizure management procedures will be followed to maintain open airway and prevent injury. Other nursing interventions specific to this student during seizure: ☒ **Maintain change of clothes** ☐ Student's privacy will be maintained during a seizure at school. All seizure activity will be recorded on individualized student log. Student will be allowed to rest after a seizure, if necessary. ☐ Rest in classroom ☒ Rest in nurse's office ☒ Parent will be called and student will go home Parent/guardian will be called if seizure is unusual or lasts more than **8** minutes. **CALL 911 EMERGENCY MEDICAL SERVICES** if seizures are continuous (status epilepticus) or if:	School personnel/ Ongoing basis
Potential need for medication management for seizures	Student will cooperate with medical treatment plan during school day.	Student will come to the nurse's office for supervised administration of the following medication(s) according to written physician's orders: **Mediation(s)**　　**Dose**　　**Time** Phenobarbital　　20mg/1 tsp of elixir　　12–12:30	Student/ School nurse/ As ordered by physician
Knowledge deficit and loss of self-esteem related to seizure disorder	Student will increase/maintain self-esteem and effective seizure management at school.	Student will be given information and health counseling related to seizure disorder and management appropriate to level of understanding. ☒ Classroom presentations will be given on seizure disorders as appropriate and when requested. ☐ Student's medical condition will be discussed with him/her as needed to ensure that appropriate level of knowledge is being maintained. ☐ Classroom teacher will be provided information, support, and consultation regarding management of this student's health needs.	School nurse/ Ongoing or as requested

FIGURE 8–2 (Continued)

Nursing Diagnosis/ Concern	Educational Goal	Plan of Action	By Whom/ When
Potential change in medical status	Student will collaborate, in an age-appropriate manner, with the facilitation of his/ her optimal health and safety necessary for classroom activities	Parent/guardian will provide the school nurse with a copy of the current medical report or the physician's annual statement OR when changes occur in medical status. The school nurse will call the student's doctor to obtain current medical information verbally when this is necessary to mange the student's condition at school.	Parent or guardian School nurse/ As needed
This IHP will be reviewed annually by the school nurse with the parent/guardian and appropriate instructional assistants. It will be revised as needed. The school nurse will, in collaboration with the parent/guardian, train and supervise all school personnel who are assigned responsibility for implementing any part of this health plan.	IHP will be updated annually, or as necessary, to meet the student's needs.	Review Date: RN's Initials: Parent's Initials: 1. 9/09/09 JR MH 2. 3. 4. 5. 6. 7.	School nurse/ Annually or as needed

Source: Adapted from *New Mexico school health manual*, 2009, funding and content by New Mexico Department of Health, Public Health Division, Health Services Bureau, Office of School Health, 300 San Mateo Blvd., Suite 902, Albuquerque, NM 87108; available at www.nmschoolhealthmanual.org

disabilities usually have higher rates of illness and hospitalization, survey results indicated that only 1 in 46 students had a plan for delivering educational services during an absence from school (Borgioli & Kennedy, 2003).

An emergency identification bracelet or necklace should be worn, or an emergency information card with the student's name and blood type should be carried to identify any serious condition (e.g., diabetes, epilepsy, hemophilia) or allergies (reactions to medications or insect stings) that the student has. Use of personal emergency identification is especially important as students grow older, become more independent, and are less supervised by persons who are aware of their potential need for immediate intervention.

Certain supplies are necessary when administering first aid and these are usually available in the office of the school nurse. Disposable gloves should be used when staff come in contact with bodily

secretions, including urine, blood, mucus drainage, or saliva. The special health care needs of an individual student may dictate additional items (e.g., blood sugar testing apparatus) that can be kept in a designated location for the student or be with the student at all times.

Although medications are frequently part of a first aid supply, they cannot be given without written permission from the student's physician and parents. The exact procedure depends on the policies of the local school district and state laws and regulations.

Deciding Whether Emergency Attention Is Needed. Guidelines on when to contact medical professionals may be in place for an individual student, but unexpected emergencies can occur and must be handled immediately. During an emergency situation, such as severe bleeding, shock, sudden unconsciousness, or anaphylaxis, EMS is contacted to take the student to a hospital. When contacting emergency room staff or EMS for assistance in determining the seriousness of the student's condition, school staff should minimally provide the following information: (a) the student's specific complaints or symptoms; (b) when the symptoms began; (c) what makes the pain or condition better or worse; (d) what the student was doing when the injury or illness occurred; (e) what changes have occurred since the onset of the injury or illness; (f) what, if anything, the student has swallowed; and (g) what medication(s) the student has been taking. When a student is known to have a health problem such as a severe, acute systemic allergic reaction that can potentially result in a life-threatening situation, inform the emergency room staff and paramedics as allowed by the student's parents. The Asthma and Allergy Foundation of America (http://www.aafa.org) advises students who are prone to anaphylaxis to have an "allergy action plan" on file at school and at home in case of an anaphylactic emergency; AAFA also provides a Plan form online.

First Aid in the Classroom

First aid procedures must be conducted with appropriate regard to the danger of cross infection. Hand washing is the single most effective way to prevent the spread of infections and has been repeatedly shown to reduce overall infection risks (Pittel, 2001). Before and after providing the aid, wash hands with soap and water or use an alcohol-based hand rub. Many school districts recommend that school staff wear gloves when in contact with blood or bodily secretions that may contain blood. Concerns about transmission of HIV, HBV, and other organisms that may be present in the blood have resulted in changes in policies in school districts. Authorities have emphasized that any transmission of HIV or HBV most likely involves exposure of skin lesions or mucous membranes to blood and possibly to other bodily fluids of an infected person.

Where to Go for Help

Resources include the local hospital and emergency room staff; health departments; trained EMS; and, in some communities, fire and/or police departments. Web sites with information on first aid training and procedures include http://www.redcross.org and http://www.americanheart.org. A poison control center can be reached at 1-800-222-1222 or http://www.aapcc.org.

Routine Prevention Procedures

Routine prevention procedures are those that tailored toward routine care, including procedures conducted during an ordinary school day for students with special health care needs. These procedures include teeth and gum care, skin care, and bowel care.

Teeth and Gum Care

Teeth and gum care include oral hygiene, preventive dental care, and good nutrition and eating habits. Teeth and gum care are included in the curriculum because families of children with special health care needs identify oral health care as the most common unmet health need (U.S. Department of Health & Human Services, 2007). Additionally, oral health is integral to the general health of the student and routine, effective oral hygiene will decrease dental caries, periodontal disease, and the possibility of aspiration caused by food particles that remain undetected in the mouth.

Oral Hygiene and Preventive Dental Care

Many factors, such as an improperly formed jaw or teeth, prolonged dependence on a feeding bottle, lack of stimulation from chewing, inadequate cleaning of the teeth and gums, infrequent dental care, and the side effects of medications, can result in unhealthy and malformed teeth and gums. Children with oral-motor problems are also at an increased risk of dental caries, particularly "baby bottle" tooth decay because the bottle is often the primary source of nutrition well beyond 12 to 18 months of life. Rigorous attention to diet and oral hygiene is required to maintain healthy teeth and gums. A healthy diet includes the following major food groups: bread, cereal, rice, and pasta; vegetables and fruit; milk, yogurt, and cheese; and meat, poultry, fish, dry beans, eggs, and nuts.

Establishing a schedule of routine dental care includes guidance on brushing the teeth and flossing, dental development, fluoride, oral habits, and proper diet. For the student with special health care needs, regular attention to oral hygiene at an early age will establish a routine that is associated with eating for the child and the feeling of having a clean mouth, and will desensitize the oral-motor area for the child with increased sensitivity to touch in and around the mouth. The American Dental Hygienists' Association (http://www.adha.org) is a resource for oral hygiene.

Classroom Adaptations

Anticipatory guidance provided through the school can facilitate an interchange on the provision of developmentally appropriate, preventive oral health information and care. The development of a routine of oral hygiene, independent or assisted, that is ongoing and consistent both at home and at school will help (a) prevent periodontal disease by maintaining healthy teeth and gums, (b) promote a healthy diet and good eating habits, and (c) promote correct speech habits and a positive body image (Perlman, Friedman, & Fenton, 2007).

Brushing the teeth is performed after meals and snacks; flossing is performed at least once a day at either home or school. Gloves should be used when completing any oral hygiene procedure. Although the student may initially require complete assistance with brushing the teeth and flossing, task analysis and prompting (see Chapter 4) are useful strategies for increasing independence. Occupational and physical therapists can assist with positioning for oral hygiene.

Occasionally, a child with a severe physical disability and poor oral-motor skills has a bite reflex. This involuntary reflex often occurs when a spoon, toothbrush, or other object is placed in the child's mouth. If this is a problem when cleaning the teeth, a soft mouth prop/rest can be used to gently keep the mouth from closing (see http://www.specializedcare.com/shop/pc/viewCategories.asp?idCategory=18). This will protect the child's teeth and the individual who is assisting the child with oral hygiene. Brushing the teeth can then be carried out with this device holding the mouth slightly open.

Additional Resources

The American Dental Association provides two excellent online resources for families and educators: *Oral Health Care Guide* and *A Caregivers Guide to Good Oral Health for Persons with Special Needs.* (See the American Dental Association Web site at http://www.ada.org/; see also http://media.specialolympics.org/soi/files/healthy-athletes/Special%20_Smiles_Good_Oral_Health_Guide.pdf.) Information can also be obtained from local dentists, the local health department, or the following Web sites: American Academy of Pediatric Dentistry (http://www.aapd.org) and National Institue of Dental and Craniofacial Research (http://www.nidcr.nih.gov/OralHealth/Topics/DevelopmentalDisabilities/DentalCareEveryDay.htm).

Skin Care

The most appropriate skin care program in the schools focuses on the prevention of skin breakdown and development of pressure sores. Risk factors for skin breakdown in children include (a) paralysis, (b) lack of sensation or feeling, (c) high activity, and (d) immobility (Samaniego, 2003). Because some students spend the majority of their day in a wheelchair, braces, or splints and are dependent on others for changing their position, it is critical that skin care and skin monitoring be systematically addressed in the classroom. Four objectives must be considered when promoting healthy skin: (a) keeping the skin clean and dry, (b) maintaining proper nutrition, (c) reducing shear or friction (two surfaces rubbing against one another) when transferring or repositioning the student, and (d) reducing periods of continuous pressure on parts of the body across the day.

Clean, dry skin is a necessary requirement for healthy skin. A primary skin care program should include efforts to reduce or eliminate incontinence, establish a regular toileting schedule, establish catheterization, or establish frequent routines for checking and changing diapers and cleansing the skin to reduce prolonged exposure of the skin to feces or urine. Moisture, stool, and frequent and excessive washings cause a decrease in the skin's ability to tolerate friction, leaving it more vulnerable to chafing by diapers and clothing (Jeter & Lutz, 1996). This exposure can also result in the softening or maceration of the skin. Maceration of the skin by urine and feces adds to the excoriating (skin cutting) effects of the decomposing substances in the urine and the infective organisms present in the feces on already damaged tissue, increasing the likelihood that sores will develop (Jeter & Lutz, 1996).

Butler (2006) recommends the maintenance of adequate nutrition and hydration as an important strategy in the prevention of pressure sores. Adequate nutrition and hydration allows the body to develop healthy skin and more resistance to bacteria and pressure sores, and supports healing when a sore has developed.

Optimal levels of activity also must be encouraged as part of a proactive skin care program. Inactivity can result in increased opportunities for the student to experience pressure on the skin surfaces. Pressure occurs when the skin and subcutaneous tissue is squeezed between an underlying bony prominence and a hard surface, such as a bed or a chair. Unrelieved pressure on the skin squeezes tiny blood vessels that supply the skin with nutrients and oxygen. Sliding down in a chair or bed (friction or shear force) can stretch or bend blood vessels. When skin is starved of nutrients and oxygen for too long, the tissue dies and a pressure ulcer forms (Bryant & Doughty, 2000). In a national survey of children's health care institutions, Baldwin (2002) found that the sacrum/coccyx was the most frequent site for pressure ulcers, heels the second, followed by the occipital region (the back of the head). Certain parts of the body sustain more weight when sitting and lying and are considered pressure-sensitive areas (e.g., the back of the head, the heels, bony prominences along the spinal column, or the buttocks). A change in position should occur *about every one to two hours* for those students with severe physical disabilities in order to relieve continuous pressure, as well as to increase blood circulation (Butler, 2006). Preventing mechanical injury to the skin from friction and shearing forces during repositioning and transfer activity is important and may require two people and/or assistive devices (e.g., transfer boards to protect the skin).

The student, whether active or inactive, may also experience pressure from braces, shoes, or sitting in a wheelchair. The same concern about pressure resulting from inactivity applies to pressure resulting from ill-fitting equipment. The skin underneath braces and splints or in contact with wheelchair seats should be checked daily to identify persistent red spots. If the spots do not fade within 20 minutes after the pressure is relieved, the health care worker should be notified of (a) ill-fitting equipment, and (b) the potential for the development of a pressure sore.

Classroom Adaptations

The student's skin should be examined daily by the teacher or designate, emphasizing the areas of the body that are susceptible to the development of pressure sores. The school health care worker or the primary care physician should write a general health plan for the student at risk for skin problems. The plan should address the need for routine position changes, cleansing, maintenance of nutrition, and use of barrier lotions or oils on the skin.

Additional Resources

The student's family and physician can provide guidance to the educational staff on the prevention or treatment of skin problems. The enterostomal therapist from a local hospital can provide assistance in caring for the student's skin and the physical and occupational therapist can help identify positions that will prevent prolonged pressure on a few skin areas. (See also http://www.healthychildren.org/English/Pages/default.aspx, the American Academy of Pediatrics Web site at http://www.healthy children.org/English/health-issues/conditions/skin/Pages/default.aspx, and http://www.healthfinder.gov, a general health information locator provided by the U.S. government).

Bowel Care

The purpose of bowel care is to increase awareness of factors that may affect the elimination schedule and to promote the overall health of a student. Constipation occurs in 23% of all children (Loenig-Baucke, 2007) and 26% to 50% of children with cerebral palsy and other significant developmental disorders (Sullivan, Lambert, Ford-Adams, Griffiths, & Johnson, 2000; Tse, Lueng, Chan, Sien, & Chan, 2000). Increased or decreased muscle tone affects coordination of the anal muscles or the muscles of the pelvic floor, making it more difficult for the student to have regular bowel movements. These muscle tone differences are often compounded by insufficient fiber and water consumption, delayed transit time through the colon (Park, Park, Cho, Na, & Cho, 2004), and immobility and certain medications. Symptoms of constipation can include behavior problems, apparent abdominal pain, decreased appetite, gassiness, vomiting, and a swollen abdomen (Fishman & Bousvaros, 2006).

> *Tommy's team, which is composed of the school nurse, occupational therapist, teacher, psychologist, district dietician, and the child's family physician, has developed a plan to increase calories and food groups, in particular, fiber and fat; increase acceptance of new tastes and textures; increase fluid intake; and increase physical activity. A food diary will be kept to log intake and the school nurse will monitor Tommy's weight on a bimonthly basis. The food diary will also be used to monitor bowel movements at home and at school. Data on behavior problems will be recorded to see whether the expected reduction in cramping and bloating will descrease the incidence of such problems (see Chapters 3 and 7).*

Factors that contribute to optimal bowel function include a diet high in fiber, adequate fluid intake, a regular daily schedule for elimination, an established plan for toilet training (if applicable), an environment that is conducive to elimination, proper positioning for elimination, and daily physical activity or exercise (Eisenberg, Zuk, Carmeli, Katz-Leurer, 2009; Elawad & Sullivan, 2001; Fishman & Bousvaros, 2006; Park et al., 2004; Tse et al., 2000).

Fiber and Fluid Intake

Diet, particularly fluid and fiber content, is often the first line of intervention for managing the toileting process (Sullivan-Bolyai, Swanson, & Shurtleff, 1984). Fiber is found in raw fruits and vegetables, whole-grain breads, and cereals. When the student has difficulty chewing and swallowing, an increase in fiber content may be difficult to achieve. Student should progress from blended, pureed, or baby foods as rapidly as possible. Unfortunately, commercial baby foods contain very little fiber. To supplement the low fiber content, table foods can be placed in a baby food grinder or food processor to obtain the best texture for the student with oral-motor impairment. Serving bran cereal for breakfast or mixing unprocessed bran in food each day can supply additional fiber.

Studies have demonstrated that even when families are instructed on how to increase fiber intake, follow-up reveals that their children still consume less than the recommended fiber intake (McClung, Boyne, & Heitlinger, 1995). Dietary management requires intensive and ongoing counseling to be effective. The student's physician or other health care professional may recommend a dietitian for this purpose. Most children need between 1 and 2 quarts of fluid each day, preferably unsweetened juice and water. Prune juice has a natural laxative effect and can be combined with another fruit juice to be more readily accepted by the student if he or she dislikes the taste. Thickening liquids with items such as infant cereals, blended fruit, or unflavored gelatin may change the consistency of the liquid to be more easily accepted by the student with oral-motor problems. Frequent opportunities to drink small amounts of fluid are often scheduled throughout the day to better meet the liquid needs of a student who has difficulty swallowing.

In a study of children with severe neurological disorders, increased intake of fiber in the diet resulted in increased frequency of bowel movements, improved consistency of stool, and fewer episodes of pain during bowel movements. The transit time or movement of stool through the colon and rectum among children with an increased fiber intake did not increase (Staiano et al., 2000). Neurological disorders and related disturbances in the motor function of the colon may contribute to diminished colon motility and transit time. Opportunities for increased and independent participation in daily activities have been shown to reduce constipation in children with cerebral palsy (Eisenberg et al., 2009).

Classroom Applications

Normal bowel function promotes a normal schedule of elimination. This developing or existing pattern may be incorporated into a student's ongoing or new toilet-training program. Stimuli or activities that aid in or detract from the process of defecation should be identified through discussion and collaboration with the family and school personnel. These include (a) promoting a normal schedule of elimination by placing the student on the toilet for approximately 10 minutes after meals and snacks to take advantage of the gastro-colic reflex that usually occurs 15 to 30 minutes after meals, (b) proper positioning of the student to increase the student's overall muscle tone (e.g., a squatting position), (c) using adapted equipment (e.g., toileting chairs), and (d) promoting physical activity and exercise to help the fecal material move through the large intestine toward the rectum.

Where to Go for Further Information or Training

Each individual has unique patterns of bowel function and the student with a disability brings additional complications to the issue of bowel control. These complications can include oral-motor impairment, resulting in inadequate intake of fiber and fluids; medications that alter the consistency, color, and frequency of bowel movements; decreased levels of activity that result in improper emptying of the intestines; inadequate innervation of the rectal sphincters; and the inability to recognize the urge to defecate.

These problems, if not addressed, affect the student's participation in the curriculum because of either discomfort from chronic constipation or increased frequency of bowel movements. Both of these conditions will limit participation and interfere with bowel-training programs. The physical or occupational therapist can provide a plan for positioning the student during meals and elimination. The dietitian is an important source of information on incorporating fiber in the meals and should work with the occupational therapist on developing an eating plan that addresses both dietary needs and the oral-motor skills of the student.

The student's physician can be helpful in solving problems with diarrhea, constipation, and skin irritation. When diet and adequate fluids are not enough, the physician may recommend supplemental fiber, laxatives, medications, or occasional suppositories and enemas. Atypical bowel elimination procedures (ileostomy and colostomy) are discussed later in this chapter.

Specialized Health Care Procedures

There are a number of specialized health care procedures that are often required for students with severe or profound disabilities. These procedures require monitoring during the school day and include seizure monitoring, administration of medication, and nutrition monitoring and supplementation.

Seizure Monitoring

Seizure monitoring provides a record of the frequency of seizures during the school day and assists the parents and health care professionals to evaluate the effectiveness of the seizure medications. A plan for monitoring seizures during the school day, shown in Figure 8-3, allows us to carefully observe and summarize information about a student's seizures. Systematic observations over time help us distinguish behaviors that are and are not related to the seizure, communicate these observations to the parents and the physician, and physically protect the child during a seizure.

A seizure is sudden, abnormal bursts of electrical activity in the brain, resulting in a temporary change in behavior. This change in electrical activity may be limited to one area of the brain or may begin in one area and spread to other areas of the brain. If the electrical disturbance is limited to only part of the brain, then the result is a partial seizure. For example, the child may experience stiffening or jerking of one arm or leg. If the electrical disturbance affects the entire brain, the result is a generalized seizure, also referred to as a tonic-clonic or grand mal seizure.

Epileptic seizures, including febrile seizures, occur in 0.5% to 1% of children; of the 300,000 new cases that develop each year, up to 40% occur in children and adolescents under age 18 (Boss, 2002; Epilepsy Foundation, 2010). Among U.S. children between 3 and 17 years of age with two or more developmental disabilities, 55% have seizures occurring with developmental disabilities such as attention deficit disorder/ attention deficit hyperactivity disorder, cerebral palsy, learning disability, intellectual disability, and stuttering (Boulet et al., 2009). Children with cerebral palsy and other health and developmental problems are less likely to "grow out of their seizures" and less likely to achieve optimal control with anticonvulsants (Carlsson, Hagberg, & Olsson, 2003; Singhi, Jagirdar, Khandelwal, & Malhi, 2003). Thus, the monitoring of students' seizures has been identified as one of the major health-related procedures performed by the classroom teacher (Weinstein & Gaillard, 2007) (see Figure 8-3).

Normally, a seizure lasts from 30 seconds to 3 minutes (Weinstein & Gaillard, 2007); recording the duration of a student's seizure provides a record of the "typical" length of the seizure. A series of consecutive seizures with no recovery of consciousness that last longer than 30 minutes is called status epilepticus; this condition is life threatening and requires immediate medical care (Boss, 2002). The Epilepsy Foundation of America (2008) considers a seizure to be an emergency when the student (a) has a seizure longer than five minutes, (b) has repeated seizures without regaining consciousness, (c) is injured or has diabetes, (d) has a first-time seizure, (e) has breathing difficulties, and (f) has a seizure in the water. Rectal medication to control a student's seizure should be administered by a school nurse and delegated only when allowed by existing state laws and school district policy (National Association of School Nurses, 2003a).

Classroom Applications

Timely and comprehensive seizure monitoring requires the teacher to be prepared with a systematic approach to collecting behavioral data. Adequate preparation for meeting the needs of students with epilepsy requires that the educational staff work closely with the family to gain all of the necessary information, such as the types of seizures to be prepared for, as well as typical behaviors seen before, during, and after a seizure.

Collaboration among school, family, and health care providers will increase the usefulness of seizure monitoring; for example, school staff who are aware of medication changes can provide feedback to the family and physician on changes in the frequency and intensity of seizures. This information is critical, particularly if the physician is in the process of evaluating the student's prescription and dosage. An increase in the number of seizures per day or per week may indicate that the

FIGURE 8–3
Seizure Monitoring Form EPILEPSY FOUNDATION®
Not another moment lost to seizures

Seizure Observation Record				
Student Name:				
Date and Time				
Seizure Length				
Pre-Seizure Observation (Briefly list behaviors, triggering events, activities)				
Conscious (yes/no/altered)				
Injuries (briefly describe)				
Muscle Tone/Body Movements	Rigid/clenching			
	Limp			
	Fell down			
	Rocking			
	Wandering around			
	Whole body jerking			
Extremity Movements	(R) arm jerking			
	(L) arm jerking			
	(R) leg jerking			
	(L) leg jerking			
	Random Movement			
Color	Bluish			
	Pale			
	Flushed			
Eyes	Pupils dilated			
	Turned (R or L)			
	Rolled up			
	Staring or blinking (clarify)			
	Closed			
Mouth	Salivating			
	Chewing			
	Lip smacking			
Verbal Sounds (gagging, talking, throat clearing, etc.)				
Breathing (normal, labored, stopped, noisy, etc.)				
Incontinent (urine or feces)				
Post-Seizure Observation	Confused			
	Sleepy/tired			
	Headache			
	Speech slurring			
	Other			
Length to Orientation				
Parents Notified? (time of call)				
EMS Called? (call time and arrival time)				
Observer's Name				

student is not receiving medication as prescribed or that the student is in need of a change in medication as a result of a change in the student's metabolism or altered utilization of the medication. Careful, accurate reporting of seizure activity to parents and health care providers should result in improved seizure management. The Epilepsy Foundation (http://www.epilepsyfoundation.org) provides sample Seizure Action Plan forms (see Figure 8–4) that can be customized to meet a student's specific needs.

Liz has a seizure disorder that is controlled with medication. At Mr. Vontz's request, her parents shared with the team the characteristics of Liz's seizures at an IEP meeting. This allowed Mr. Vontz to be prepared when Liz had a seizure at school. Liz stiffened in her chair as the students were getting ready to go out to the playground. Mr. Vontz quickly released the seat belt and placed Liz on the floor with her coat underneath her head. He moved the desks out of the way and sent another student to get assistance. Although he had forgotten to time it, Liz's tonic-clonic seizure was brief. Mr. Vontz had a change of clothing for Liz (who had lost bladder control during the seizure), which he gave to the school nurse. Liz normally sleeps for several hours after a seizure in the school nurse's office.

Understanding the behaviors that occur before, during, and after a seizure will help the staff prepare the school areas accordingly. For example, a student may become somewhat drowsy approximately two hours after the administration of a seizure medication, which is generally around 9:30 a.m. In this instance, the teacher needs to plan for activities that require less interaction and participation from the student at this time of the day. A student who produces large amounts of secretions during a seizure needs for a suction machine or bulb syringe to be available in the classroom in order to remove secretions from the mouth.

The potential for injury to the student during a seizure is a concern for all school staff. Students whose seizures are not well controlled can experience a head injury as a result of a seizure-related fall. Often, these students wear a lightweight helmet to protect their head. Efforts should be made to make this protective device as age appropriate and unstigmatizing as possible. Because there is a possibility of physical harm to the child or school staff while a student is being held or restrained, the student must *never* be restrained during a seizure.

Additionally, the school environment must be as safe as possible for students with seizures. Objects (e.g., furniture, equipment, or toys) that could cause an injury should be portable and easy to remove during a student's seizure. Pathways and instructional environments should be wide and free of unnecessary objects (i.e., unused wheelchairs or storage boxes) to minimize the chance of injury during a fall.

Additional Resources

The Epilepsy Foundation sponsors a wide variety of programs and activities for persons with epilepsy, as well as workshops and training for staff and educational materials developed for school personnel working with students with epilepsy. Local affiliates can be located by searching for a locally based Epilepsy Foundation at http://www.epilepsyfoundation.org

The Administration and Monitoring of Medication

The general purpose of administering medication is to relieve symptoms, to treat an existing disease, or to promote health and prevent disease. Because most medications require administration throughout the day, many students would be unable to attend school unless the administration of medication was provided.

Preparation for Administering Medication

Before administering any medication, the policies of the school district with regard to approval or consent for the administration of medication must be reviewed. The American Academy of Pediatrics (2003) has issued a policy statement to guide prescribing physicians, as well as school administrators and health staff, on the administration of medications to children at school. In addition to prescribed medications, the statement also addresses over-the-counter products, herbal medications, experimental drugs that are administered as part of a clinical trial, emergency medications, and the principles of student safety. The administration of any prescribed medication requires a written statement from the parent and the physician that provides the name of the drug, the dose, the approximate time that it is to be taken, and the reason that the medication is needed. In the absence of trained medical staff, the school principal or designee (e.g., a teacher) will be trained to administer medication to students. Secure storage for the medication is also a requirement (National Association of School Nurses, 2003b). A physician's written approval may also be

FIGURE 8–4
Seizure Action Plan

Seizure Action Plan

EPILEPSY FOUNDATION®
Not another moment lost to seizures™

Effective Date: _____

THIS STUDENT IS BEING TREATED FOR A SEIZURE DISORDER. THE INFORMATION BELOW SHOULD ASSIST YOU IF A SEIZURE OCCURS DURING SCHOOL HOURS.

Student's Name: _____   Date of Birth: _____

Parent/Guardian: _____   Phone: _____ Cell: _____

Treating Physician: _____   Phone: _____

Significant Medical History: _____

SEIZURE INFORMATION:

Seizure Type	Length	Frequency	Description

Seizure triggers or warning signs:_____

Student's reaction to seizure:_____

BASIC FIRST AID: CARE & COMFORT:
(Please describe basic first aid procedures)

Does student need to leave the classroom after a seizure?   YES   NO
If YES, describe process for returning student to classroom.

EMERGENCY RESPONSE:
A "seizure emergency" for this student is defined as:

Seizure Emergency Protocol: *(Check all that apply and clarify below)*

☐ Contact school nurse at _____

☐ Call 911 for transport to _____

☐ Notify parent or emergency contact

☐ Notify doctor

☐ Administer emergency medications as indicated below

☐ Other _____

Basic Seizure First Aid:
✓ Stay calm & track time
✓ Keep child safe
✓ Do not restrain
✓ Do not put anything in mouth
✓ Stay with child until fully conscious
✓ Record seizure in log
For tonic-clonic (grand mal) seizure:
✓ Protect head
✓ Keep airway open/watch breathing
✓ Turn child on side

A Seizure is generally considered an Emergency when:
✓ A convulsive (tonic-clonic) seizure lasts longer than 5 minutes
✓ Student has repeated seizures without regaining consciousness
✓ Student has a first time seizure
✓ Student is injured or has diabetes
✓ Student has breathing difficulties
✓ Student has a seizure in water

TREATMENT PROTOCOL DURING SCHOOL HOURS: (include daily and emergency medications)

Daily Medication	Dosage & Time of Day Given	Common Side Effects & Special Instructions

Emergency/Rescue Medication _____

Does student have a **Vagus Nerve Stimulator (VNS)**?   YES   NO
If YES, Describe magnet use_____

SPECIAL CONSIDERATIONS & SAFETY PRECAUTIONS: *(regarding school activities, sports, trips, etc.)*

Physician's Signature: _____   Date: _____

Parent's Signature: _____   Date: _____

required for over-the-counter medications. Any administration of a medication should be recorded using a log similar to that shown in Figure 8-5.

Administering Medications

The method of administration depends on the developmental age of the student and the student's ability to chew and swallow. For students who are not yet sitting independently or for those who have difficulty retaining food or fluid in the mouth, the student is usually supported in a sitting position. A smaller student may be held; a larger student may remain in a wheelchair or chair (Algren & Arnow, 2007). When holding or supporting a student, maintain a relaxed position to decrease the chances of choking. This may be achieved by ensuring that the student's neck is flexed, the shoulders are rounded, and the student is in a slightly forward position.

The medication is carefully measured and placed in the student's mouth with a spoon, plastic dropper, or plastic syringe (of course, a syringe without a needle). If the dropper or syringe is placed alongside the

FIGURE 8-5
Medication Monitoring Form

Medication Information Form

Name _____ Age _____

Route _____

Administration Analysis:

Date	Medication	Dosage Indicated	Time Received	Full dosage Received at Time Prescribed		Initials
_____	/ _____	_____	_____	Y	N	_____
_____	/ _____	_____	_____	Y	N	_____
_____	/ _____	_____	_____	Y	N	_____
_____	/ _____	_____	_____	Y	N	_____
_____	/ _____	_____	_____	Y	N	_____
_____	/ _____	_____	_____	Y	N	_____
_____	/ _____	_____	_____	Y	N	_____
_____	/ _____	_____	_____	Y	N	_____
_____	/ _____	_____	_____	Y	N	_____
_____	/ _____	_____	_____	Y	N	_____
_____	/ _____	_____	_____	Y	N	_____
_____	/ _____	_____	_____	Y	N	_____

Maintenance/Episodic Meds and Side Effects	Possible Interactions of Medications
M/E 1. _____	1. _____ & _____ = _____
M/E 2. _____	2. _____ & _____ = _____
M/E 3. _____	3. _____ & _____ = _____
M/E 4. _____	4. _____ & _____ = _____
M/E 5. _____	5. _____ & _____ = _____
M/E 6. _____	6. _____ & _____ = _____

student's tongue, the dropper or syringe should be discarded after use. If the dropper or syringe is reused, it should be washed and rinsed thoroughly and allowed to dry completely. The medication is given slowly to ease swallowing and avoid choking. For a student with tongue thrust, it may be necessary to rescue medication from the student's lips or chin and readminister it. If the student uses a sucking response in order to take in liquid, the medication can also be slowly pushed into a nipple while the student is sucking (Algren & Arnow, 2007).

If the student is able to swallow a tablet, the medication may be placed on the middle of the tongue. The student can then swallow it with juice or water. Because of the possibility of aspiration (the pulling of the tablet or secretions into the lungs), a whole tablet should not be given until the student is about five years old or demonstrates the necessary oral-motor control to safely swallow the tablet. Students who cannot swallow tablets may accept crushed tablets mixed with a flavorful syrup. The crushing and mixing of a medication with syrup or another liquid should be approved by the student's health care provider and pharmacist (Woo & Bloser, 2004).

Classroom Applications

Medication given during the school day must be made available at the school and labeled with the student's name, dosage, frequency of administration, and the prescribing physician's name. A system for recording and documenting when the medication was administered must be established. Finally, the school district's policy should be reviewed to determine who can administer the medication in the school setting. Although medications are often administered in the school nurse's office, there may be some unique administration scheduling requirements (e.g., medications must be given with food) that could result in the medications being given in the lunchroom. Regardless of the location, the nurse or designate must identify the best location to promote student participation while ensuring privacy. The "Five Rights" of medication administration are applicable regardless of who administers the medication: The person administering the medication makes certain that the *right dose* of the *right medication* is given to the *right student* at the *right time* by the *right route* (Potter & Perry, 2008). These guidelines are used every time a medication is given. A few minutes of double-checking a medication or writing down the routine procedure can prevent a serious error that can

result in unfortunate experiences for the school staff, the student, and the family.

Where to Go for Further Information or Training

School staff can find more information on the administration of medication by first consulting with the school nurse (National Association of School Nurses, 2004a). Administering medication is a task for licensed nurses and is delegated to others when school policy and state laws allow. Nurses in the school, the physician's office, public health department, or local hospital can provide assistance on methods of administration, the side effects and toxic effects of medications, and setting up a medications log for the student. The occupational and physical therapists can provide guidance on proper positioning for the administration of medication and suggestions with regard to oral or motor problems that hinder the administration of medication. A pharmacist and the student's physician can provide information about the student's medication (e.g., side effects, toxic effects, and interactions with other medications). Continuing education is available through online courses (HealthSoft, Inc., 2007) and through local and state agencies that serve individuals with developmental disabilities.

Growth Monitoring, Nutritional Supplementation, and the Management of Food Intake

The well-nourished child grows at an expected rate, is resistant to illness, and has the energy to take advantage of social and educational opportunities. Adequate nutrition is critical to achieving a child's potential for brain and physical development. A review of the literature by Fung et al. (2002) indicates that a feeding dysfunction is significantly associated with poor health and nutritional status in children with moderate to severe cerebral palsy. Even children with only a mild feeding dysfunction that requires chopped or mashed foods may be at risk for poor nutritional status. Children and adolescents with moderate to severe cerebral palsy are also at significant risk for fractures because of the prevalence of low bone mineral density (BMD) (Henderson, Kairalla, Barrington, Abbas, & Stevenson, 2005). Interestingly, the prevalence of obesity in ambulatory children with cerebral palsy has risen over the last decade from 7.7% to 16.5%, an increase that is similar to what is seen in the general pediatric population in the United States. Children with a lesser degree of involvement were twice as likely as children with greater involvement to become obese (Rogozinski et al., 2007). To initiate appropriate intervention, the school team must be aware of students at risk for nutritional problems and the simple screening methods used to identify these children.

Growth Monitoring Procedures

Growth is a sensitive measure of health, nutritional status, and development. We can monitor the nutritional status of a student by measuring his or her growth. Trends revealed through repeated height and weight measurement can be used to detect growth abnormalities, monitor nutritional status, or evaluate the effects of nutritional or medical interventions (see Figure 8-6). Growth measurements must be made accurately and recorded correctly at least three times a year. In addition to weight and height measurements, body mass index (BMI) is calculated to provide information about a student's growth. The BMI expresses the relationship between height and weight. It is of particular impor-

tance in monitoring many students with profound disabilities because these students frequently do not grow at the same rate as other individuals of the same age. Growth monitoring will also provide objective data on changes in linear growth and/or weight in the event that questions regarding growth attenuation are raised in relation to a child who is nonambulatory and has multiple disabilities. Growth attenuation is a controversial medical technique used to limit or decrease growth and is discussed briefly in Box 8-1.

Monitoring Nutritional Supplementation and Food Intake

Many children with multiple or profound disabilities experience difficulty eating. This may be the result of chronic health problems, early negative oral experiences (e.g., tube feedings, intubation, suctioning), neurological problems, fatigue during meals, or a combination of these factors. The special education teacher, trained to be an observer of behavior, can play

FIGURE 8–6
Growth Monitoring Form

Growth Monitoring Form

Name: Tommy Purcell **DOB:** 11/18/2003 **Age:** 5 years 10 months

Special Considerations: Restricted food choices, chronic constipation, thin, avoids certain food textures, no current meds

I. AT RISK FOR GROWTH PROBLEMS
Weight for height is < 5% or > 95% OR if there is no weight gain over a 9-month period

FALL: <u>9/28/09</u>   WINTER: _____   SPRING: _____
    (Date)   (Date)   (Date)

Height: 41″   Height: Height:
Weight: 32 lbs.   Weight: Weight:
Ht/Wt%: < 3%   Ht/Wt%:   Ht/Wt%:
(Plot on growth chart)

II. AT RISK DUE TO MEALTIME CHARACTERISTICS
Refer if two or more of these characteristics apply:

_____ Meal lasts longer than 40 minutes

___X___ Student displays discomfort during or after meal, such as
    ___X___ excessive crying, whining, or other signs of discomfort
    _____ frequent gagging, coughing, choking

___X___ Meal consistently contains items from only two of the six food groups or contains less than the suggested amounts of food for the student's height

___X___ Drinks less than 4–6 glasses of fluid per day

III. CHECK MEDICATION INFORMATION FORM FOR ANY MEDICATION THAT COMPROMISES NUTRIENTS AND/OR SUPPRESSES APPETITE

Box 8–1 The Controversy over Growth Attenuation

Growth attenuation is an elective medical treatment that involves administering estrogen to cause closure of the epiphyses of the bones, resulting in a reduced adult height. Since the 1960s, this treatment has been performed primarily on children who growing toward an adult height that is considered unacceptably excessive by their parents and physicians. This issue came to the public's attention in 2006, when physicians reported in the journal *Archives of Pediatric & Adolescent Medicine* on the case of a six-year-old girl with profound disabilities whose parents asked that estrogen be prescribed to their daughter in order to limit her growth so that she would grow no taller than 4'6". The parents wanted to continue caring for their daughter at home but did not feel that they could do so if she grew too large for them to lift (Gunther & Diekema, 2006).

The specialists involved in her care agreed that there would be no significant future improvement in her cognitive or neurologic status. They concluded that "After extensive consultation between parents and physicians, a plan was devised to attenuate growth by using high-dose estrogen and to reduce the long-term complications of puberty in general, and treat adverse effects in particular, by performing pretreatment hysterectomy" (Gunther & Diekema, 2006, p. 1014).

The case set off a storm of controversy, with advocates for persons with disabilities condemning the treatment. Advocates view the choices that these parents made as a failure of society to provide adequate support to people with disabilities and their families (ADAPT Youth, 2007; American Association on Intellectual and Developmental Disabilities, 2007a; Disability Rights Education and Defense Fund, 2007; TASH, 2007). They argued that the decision was given for the convenience of the caregivers, not for the well-being of the child.

With regard to this issue, the American Association on Intellectual and Developmental Disabilities published *Board Position Statement: Growth Attenuation Issue* (http://www.aamr.org/content_173.cfm?navID=31 and TASH published *Resolution on Unnecessary and Dehumanizing Medical Treatments* in 2007 (http://www.tash.org/IRR/resolutions.html). In addition, thoughtful overviews of this complex issue can be found at http://bioethics.seattlechildrens.org. The Growth Attenuation Symposium presentation and discussion can both be found at http://www.seattlechildrens.org/research/initiatives/bioethics/events/growth-attenuation-children-severe-disabilities/.

Classroom Adaptations and Applications

A variety of growth charts are available for assessing the growth of children. The growth charts revised in 2000 by the National Center for Health Statistics (http://www.cdc.gov/growthcharts) can be used to assess the growth of most children and should be a permanent part of a child's record. Recognizing that children with disabilities may have different growth expectations than children without disabilities has prompted the development of separate growth charts for children with Down syndrome, Prader-Willi syndrome, Turner syndrome, and achondroplasia dwarfism (http://depts.washington.edu/nutrpeds/fug/growth/specialty.htm). Generally, these data are recorded and plotted by the school nurse or dietitian, but any member of the team can be trained to measure and record a child's growth. A referral to a dietitian should be made if any of the following occur: (a) the weight for an age is at or below the 5th percentile or at or above the 95th percentile, (b) the length/height for an age is at or below the 5th percentile, or (c) the BMI is at or below the 5th percentile or at or above the 85th percentile.

> *Tommy's current weight for his height (or BMI) is below the 3rd percentile for his chronological age. The intervention plan developed by the multidisciplinary team addresses increasing calories and food groups, in particular, fiber and fat. The school nurse monitors Tommy's weight and height with bimonthly measurements to determine the effects of these nutritional modifications on growth and promptly provides feedback to his teacher and parents. Tommy's rate of weight gain has improved and the increase in fat and fiber has resulted in more regular bowel movements and a decrease in behavioral outbursts related to cramping and bloating.*

Additional Resources

A registered dietitian can be contacted through a local medical center, hospital clinic, county or state extension service, or state or local chapter of the American Dietetic Association at http://eatright.org. The request should be made for dietitians who work with children who have special health care needs or profound disabilities. An additional resource is the University of Iowa Children's Hospital at http://www.uihealthcare.com/topics/medicaldepartments/pediatrics/index.html; educational materials on pediatric nutrition can be found at http://www.uihealthcare.com/topics/nutrition/catnutr.html.

an important role in monitoring the child's eating abilities and behaviors, food intake, and preferences.

Because the process of mealtime or eating extends well beyond the school day, it is critical that the school and family work together and exchange information about changes in eating behavior or volumes of food consumed. Specific behaviors to be monitored include (a) whether a meal lasts less than 10 minutes or longer than 40 minutes; (b) behaviors such as excessive whining, crying, or signs of discomfort, including frequent gagging, coughing, or choking; and (c) whether the meal consistently contains items from only two of the six food groups (e.g., fats, oils, and sweets; milk, cheese, and yogurt; meat, poultry, fish, beans, eggs, and nuts; vegetables; fruits; and bread, cereal, rice, and pasta) or contains either more or less than the suggested amounts for the student's height and weight.

Recording the foods eaten at each meal and the student's responses to the various textures, tastes, and consistencies can provide the family and the school with important information about preferences and differential oral-motor responses to the various foods. The effect of body position, particularly the head and trunk, on the student's ability to eat should also be documented because these observations can provide information that is important to the identification of simple positional interventions or lead to appropriate referrals. Some students with multiple or profound disabilities are tube fed or receive a combination of tube and oral meals. For these youngsters, it is important to monitor over time the amount and types of food ingested both orally and through the tube.

Increasing Caloric Intake. It is a myth that "failure to thrive" is a necessary part of having a disability. The reason for a student's BMI being less than desired is often because the child does not get enough calories. Simply increasing the amount of food to increase weight gain is often unsatisfactory because of impaired oral-motor function or the effects of fatigue. Frequent illness or infection may also decrease a child's appetite, as do certain medications.

There are several techniques for increasing the number of calories that a student ingests when not enough food is consumed in order to maintain an appropriate rate of growth. The addition of fats (a particularly concentrated source of calories), evaporated milk, wheat germ, or eggs in the preparation of foods increases the caloric and nutrient intake without requiring the student to eat more food. A regular meal pattern with two or three high-calorie snacks per day is also recommended to promote weight gain.

Increasing Fluid Intake. Adequate fluid intake is essential for maintaining health. Children with oral or motor problems often have difficulty with consuming sufficient liquids. This may be caused by an inability to communicate thirst; problems with hand-to-mouth coordination; or problems with sucking, swallowing, and/or heavy drooling. Many students with oral-motor difficulties are able to consume thickened liquids more successfully than thin liquids. Products commonly used to thicken thin liquids include pureed fruit, baby cereal, yogurt, dehydrated fruits and vegetables, mashed potato flakes, gelatin (added to warm liquids), or commercially available products designed specifically for thickening foods. Fruits and vegetables such as canned fruit, watermelon, cucumbers, and squash are also excellent sources of water.

Low-Incidence Health Care Procedures

Procedures that occur with low frequency (i.e., less than 25% of students with disabilities) are identified in this chapter as *low-incidence health care procedures*. These procedures require additional equipment and specialized training. This section describes the low-incidence procedures for various non-oral methods for providing nutrients, atypical methods for the elimination of feces and urine, respiratory management, and shunt care.

Non-Oral Feeding Procedures

Gastrostomy and nasogastric tube feedings are two methods for providing nourishment other than by mouth. Either of these may be necessary if the student cannot eat enough food orally to get needed nutrients and fluids. Research has shown that children with moderate to severe motor impairment who were tube fed were taller and had greater body fat stores than orally fed subjects with similar motor impairment (Fung, et al., 2002). A *gastrostomy tube (G-tube)* extends through the abdomen into the stomach. This tube allows liquid nutrients to move into the stomach when a student is unable to eat or to eat adequate amounts of food by mouth. Gastrostomy tubes are used for long periods of time or on a permanent basis. Some students may have a G-tube and not require feedings through the tube during school hours. Their tubes may be used to supplement oral intake or be used when the student is ill or oral intake is not adequate. A *jejunostomy tube (J-tube)* extends through the abdomen into the jejunum, or the second part of the small intestine. Students with a G-tube or J-tube whose oral-motor skills allow and who are not at risk for aspiration may be able to eat and drink by mouth. This allows students to continue activities that will promote oral-motor skills during mealtimes with their peers. Some students may receive their tube feeding after eating food by mouth in the cafeteria. The G-tube or J-tube is usually covered by the student's clothing. Students' participation in activities such as physical education and sports depends on their individual skills, not on the presence of a G-tube or J-tube.

A *nasogastric tube (N-G tube)* extends through the nose, down the throat and esophagus, and into the stomach. Some students have N-G tubes placed for each feeding, while others have tubes inserted for several weeks at a time. An N-G tube is typically a short-term solution to assist a student who is unable to meet his or her nutritional needs by mouth. Because this may be related to an illness or hospitalization, school staff are less likely to have contact with students who have N-G tubes.

What Is Involved

Liquid nutrients can be given as formula or regular food carefully blended to be administered through the tube. Feedings are either continuous (liquid nutrients slowly drip through the feeding tube over the entire day or night) or intermittent (larger amounts of liquid nutrients are given during five to eight feedings each day). The amount of liquid nutrients given through the tube varies for each student and must be determined by the student's health care professional. In addition to formula or blended food, the student's health care professional will recommend a specific amount of water to be given each day.

Students may be fed by *gravity drip, pump, or syringe*. A student who is fed by gravity drip has a container of formula hanging 8 to 24 inches above the level of the stomach. A clamp is used to regulate the flow of the formula. Students may receive nutrients by gravity drip continuously or intermittently. However, most students receive the formula by a pump that automatically regulates the flow of liquid nutrients into the gastrostomy tube. The pump may be electric or battery operated. The student may receive the nutrients by a third method—syringe. A large syringe is attached

to the end of the feeding tube and liquid nutrients are poured into the syringe. When the remaining liquid nutrients have flowed into the bottom of the syringe tip, the appropriate amount of water is poured into the syringe and flows into the feeding tube to clear the tube of any remaining formula. Liquid is never forced through the tube.

Instead of a G-tube, which extends out of the student's stomach through the abdomen and is secured beneath the clothing, the student may have a *button gastrostomy*. This is a short tube that fits against the skin on the abdomen and has a small plug that can be removed for feeding. The button G-tube fits snugly against the student's skin and is not as noticeable to others or to the student. Tubing connected to the pump can be placed into the button opening, allowing liquid nutrients to flow into the stomach or jejunum (i.e., the first 10 inches of small intestine). When the student has received the proper volume of formula, the tubing is disconnected and the opening is closed by the small plug attached to the button gastrostomy tube.

Classroom Applications

Regardless of the method of ingestion, food intake should occur during the mealtime or snack time of peers. Students should participate in their meals in as typical a manner as possible to promote the development of mealtime skills and to have the opportunity to engage in the social interactions that occur at mealtime.

Generally, students are in a seated or upright position during a tube feeding and remain in that position for 30 to 60 minutes after all of the formula has entered the stomach. Oral stimulation activities can be carried out as the student receives formula through the tube and oral hygiene should be provided at the end of a feeding; particularly if a student cannot eat food or drink by mouth. If eating by mouth becomes a possibility, it is important to introduce the food that can be eaten orally before the formula is given so that hunger works as a stimulus for eating.

If a child's N-G tube or G-tube comes out during the school day, a clean gauze pad or clean cloth is placed over the opening. The school nurse, as well as the student's parents, may be trained to replace the tube, so an extra tube is kept at school. It is important to replace a G-tube within 2 hours or before the next feeding. If a J-tube comes out, the student's physician must replace it. The student's peers should understand the purpose of the tube and any equipment such as the pump and connecting tubing so that they will avoid accidentally pulling on the tube.

Where to Go for Further Information or Training

Nurses in the local hospital, the pediatrician's office, the public health office, or a home health agency can provide information on the intake of nutrients by tube. Dietitians in the local hospital or health department can provide information about many formulas given by tube. Medical supply companies may provide information and training in the use of the equipment (e.g., G-tube, connecting tubing, and pump). The following are several Web sites that provide illustrations and instructions on the care of a feeding tube: http://www.cincinnatichildrens.org/health/info/abdomen/home/g-tube-care.htm and http://www.nuh.com.sg/healthinfo/gastrointes/PEG/3_caring_gastros.asp

Atypical Elimination Procedures: Bowel or Intestinal Ostomy Care

Atypical elimination procedures address methods of eliminating feces and urine that require some type of assistive device or special procedure. While the goal is independent performance of these procedures, students with severe and multiple disabilities generally require assistance. In these situations, partial participation goals are appropriate.

What Is Involved

An *ostomy* is a surgically created opening in the body for the discharge of bodily waste; there are two main types—*colostomy* and *ileostomy*. When the opening is created from the bowel or intestine and leads to the abdominal surface, a student is able to eliminate feces from the bowel without using the rectum. A *colostomy* refers to an opening created when a portion of the colon or large intestine is removed and the remaining colon is brought to the surface of the abdomen. An *ileostomy* refers to an opening in some portion of the ileum (the lower part of the small intestine) into the abdomen. Feces are eliminated through this opening and collected in a small pouch or bag. The pouch tightly adheres to the skin around this opening on the abdomen, called a *stoma*. Because there is no control over when feces move into the pouch, feces collect in the pouch during the school day. This is especially true when a student has an ileostomy. The fecal material passing through the stoma is liquid or of a pasty consistency and contains digestive enzymes that can be irritating to the skin. Ostomy care involves procedures to collect feces in an odor-free manner and to keep the skin and stoma healthy and free of irritation.

Ostomy care should be conducted in an area that is private and allows a student to be in the best position for emptying or replacing the pouch. This may be a sitting or reclining position. Extra supplies for changing the pouch should remain at school at all times, along with an extra change of clothes (Porter et al., 2006). A procedure for ostomy care should be developed by the student's parents, the school nurse, the teacher, and other school staff that respects the student's right to privacy, but includes the student's participation in the procedure to the greatest extent possible. Effort is made to prevent skin irritation around the ostomy and beneath the pouch, to eliminate odors due to gas accumulation in the pouch, and to prevent loosening of and leakage from the pouch. Careful attention must be given to hand washing before and after the ostomy pouch is drained or changed. School staff must wear gloves during these two procedures.

Classroom Applications

Although a colostomy or ileostomy pouch is usually changed at home, a student may require a pouch change at school. A bag may become loose or leak as a result of activity or unintentional pulling on the pouch. A student may also develop diarrhea or excessive gas. Changing of the pouch is recommended between meals, not right before meals, because the signs and smells of the ostomy may reduce the student's appetite.

Ostomy care may be done by the student, the school nurse, or other school staff who are properly trained. Some students may require distraction during ostomy care to keep their hands from exploring the pouch and stoma. However, other students may be able to participate in the ostomy care by holding supplies and helping clean the stoma area, or they may carry out the procedures themselves (Algren & Arnow, 2007). Parents can offer school staff suggestions about the ways in which a student can participate in ostomy care.

School staff who have regular contact with the student should receive specific training about the colostomy or ileostomy and potential problems. Understanding how to manage problems allows students to continue classroom activities with little interruption. The goal is to promote as much independence and participation as possible.

Where to Go for Further Information or Training

Information and literature on colostomy or ileostomy care can be obtained from United Ostomy Associations of America (http://www.uoaa.org), the International Ostomy Association (http://www.ostomyinternational .org/), and the American Cancer Society (http://www .cancer.org).

Atypical Elimination Procedures: Clean Intermittent Catheterization

Students who have defects of the spinal cord, such as spina bifida or myelomeningocele, may also have neurological impairment of the bladder (*neurogenic bladder*), which results in little or no control over emptying the bladder. Typically, the bladder stretches as it fills with urine until full, when nerve signals cause the bladder to contract and empty. Usually, a person can delay bladder emptying and control the occurrences of urination. A neurogenic bladder may overstretch or contract frequently or irregularly, resulting in constant dribbling or incomplete evacuation. *Clean intermittent catheterization* is a procedure used to empty the bladder and is most frequently used in students with neurogenic bladder.

Clean intermittent catheterization involves the insertion of a catheter through the urethra (the passageway between the bladder and the opening to the outside of the body) into the bladder and is usually done every two to four hours during the day. The area chosen to carry out the procedure should provide privacy and have a sink in order to allow proper cleansing before and after the procedure.

During the catheterization, the student may sit on the toilet, stand, or lie down. The urine, if not emptied directly into the toilet, should be collected in a container. After thorough hand washing, the area around the opening to the urethra is cleansed with soap and water. Nonlatex gloves are worn (Porter et al., 2006).

Classroom Applications

Clean intermittent catheterization is a health or related service that must be provided to students who require this procedure during the school day (Individuals with Disabilities Education Improvement Act, 2004). In an important decision issued by the U.S. Supreme Court (*Irving Independent School District v. Tatro,* 1984), clean intermittent catheterization was identified as a related service that should be provided during school hours and be included in the child's educational program when needed (Glucksman, 1984; Vitello, 1986).

A student with a neurogenic bladder has little or no control over the process of emptying the bladder and needs assistance in controlling the release of urine during the school day. The teacher who is involved in this process should encourage the student to participate in his or her own urinary catheterization as much as possible. The extent of participation in catheterization will depend on the student's fine motor control to manipulate the catheter and clothing, and, of course, the student's motivation. Students should be encouraged to participate as much as possible by washing their hands, holding equipment, or participating in whatever activities are appropriate (McCormick, Mackey, & Wilson, 2007). Collaboration with the family will support consistency of procedures and generalization.

When students are unable to control their bladder, they may not achieve complete dryness, so protective clothing may be used. Students may also experience leakage when laughing, coughing, or sneezing. An extra set of clothes may be kept at school in case of an accident.

Where to Go for Further Information or Training

Nurse specialists in clinics, urologists, and hospitals serving children with myelomeningocele can provide information and assistance in this area. Guidelines for clean intermittent catheterization from the American Academy of Pediatrics can be accessed at http://www .healthychildren.org/English/health-issues/conditions/ chronic/Pages/Clean-Intermittent-Catheterization.aspx? nfstatus=401&nftoken=00000000–0000-0000–0000- 000000000000&nfstatusdescription=ERROR%3a+No +local+token, from the University of Iowa Health Care's Center for Disabilities and Development at http:// www.medicine.uiowa.edu/cdd/patients/cic.asp, and from Toronto's Hospital for Sick Children at http:// www.aboutkidshealth.ca/HealthAZ/Clean-Intermittent- Catheterization-CIC-Step-By-Step-Instructions-for-Boys .aspx?articleID=10379&categoryID= (for boys) or http:// www.aboutkidshealth.ca/HealthAZ/Clean-Intermittent- Catheterization-CIC-Step-By-Step-Instructions-for-Girls .aspx?articleID=10380&categoryID= (for girls).

Respiratory Management: Tracheostomy Care

Respiratory management involves procedures to maintain an adequate oxygen level in the bloodstream; it is the process of helping students maintain respiration or breathing. Typically, respiratory management procedures in school involve tracheostomy care, suctioning, supplemental oxygen, and assisted ventilation.

What Is Involved

A *tracheostomy* is a surgically created opening into the trachea. It is created when there is an obstruction in the respiratory tract that prevents the movement of oxygen through the trachea; it allows for long-term as-sisted ventilation and a way to remove aspirated oral secretions by suctioning (Porter et al., 2006). A hollow plastic or Silastic® tube, called a *tracheostomy tube,* is placed in this opening and secured by cotton ties or other ties around the neck. The student can then breathe through the trachea instead of through the mouth or nose.

Care of the tracheostomy so that air can move freely includes removal of secretions from the student's trachea, cleaning the tracheostomy tube, care of the skin around the tube, changing the tracheostomy ties, and changing the tracheostomy tube. Changing a tra-cheostomy tube and cleaning the old tube should be done at home. The skin around the tube is cleaned at least once daily and more often as needed. The student may wear a bib or dressing around the tube to collect secretions coming out of the tube. When the bib is soiled, it is changed during the school day. School staff should carefully examine the skin around the tube for any signs of redness or irritation. Staff should wear gloves and wash their hands carefully before and after tracheostomy care at a sink that is not used for food preparation. Proper hand washing (see Figure 8–1) is an effective method for minimizing the risk of infection.

Classroom Applications

Although the overall number of tracheostomies being performed on children is decreasing, the length of time that tracheostomies remain in place is increas-ing (Carron, Derkay, Strope, Nosonchuk, & Darrow, 2000; Wetmore, Thompson, Marsh, & Tom, 1999). Parents are routinely trained to care for a child with a tracheostomy at home. When school staff know that a student will have a tracheostomy tube placed, one or more of the school staff should also be trained with the parents before the student's discharge from the hospital. Even though a teacher may not be designated as the person who is routinely responsible for chang-ing the tube, all classroom personnel should be able to respond in an emergency. Supplies should always be available at school. In addition to learning tracheostomy care, school staff should be trained in CPR for a student with a tracheostomy.

Students may use a speaking valve that allows the stu-dent to speak as a result of a positive pressure closure

valve that opens only when the student breathes in to allow air to enter the tracheostomy tube. After the stu-dent has breathed in, the positive closure mechanism shuts, forcing air out through the vocal cords, nose, and mouth, thus creating speech (Passy, 1986). The Passy-Muir speaking valve is used with infants and children to promote speech and language development.

Other students in the classroom may be curious about the tracheostomy. They should be informed about the purpose of the tracheostomy tube and its im-portance to the child. They may need reminders not to touch, pull on, or put objects into the tube. The student may wear light clothing to cover the tube or a small pouch known as an "artificial nose" over the opening of the tracheostomy tube, particularly during cold weather. As the student breathes in and out through the "artificial nose," the air is warmed and humidified. This device can prevent tracheal spasms caused by cold air or irritation of the trachea by dust particles. Play near water, such as a swimming pool or stream, is restricted to avoid accidentally getting water in the opening of the tracheostomy tube. Care should also be taken to avoid any talc products, such as baby powder, and fumes, such as paint, varnish, or hair spray (Hueckel & Wilson, 2007).

Where to Go for Further Information or Training

Qualified persons, such as nurses and respiratory ther-apists who have taught the student's parents, can teach tracheostomy care. CPR for a person with a tra-cheostomy requires specialized devices and training. For more information, go to the American Home Portal Web site (http://www.medicalhomeportal.org/issue/tracheostomy-in-children) or Aaron's Tracheostomy Page (http://www.tracheostomy.com).

Respiratory Management: Suctioning

Suctioning is the removal of secretions from the respi-ratory tract to allow breathing. Suctioning may be done through the nose (nasopharyngeal), mouth (oropharyngeal), or trachea. Suctioning in the school setting is most likely to be done through the mouth by the school nurse or designated staff trained in this pro-cedure. A suction catheter (attached to a suction ma-chine by connected tubing), a bulb syringe, or a DeLee suction catheter may be used to remove secretions from the mouth. These devices produce a suctioning sound when in operation. Because of its unusual sound, it is important to introduce both the machine and its operation to the student's peer group.

What Is Involved

Suctioning is carried out when a student is unable to remove secretions effectively and requires assistance in moving the secretions from a certain area of the body. Signs that a student may need suctioning include audible secretions, symptoms of obstruction, and signs of oxygen deficiency. Large amounts of secretion in the mouth may be visible and can be removed by suctioning. Positioning the student on one side allows secretions to move out of the mouth to be suctioned more easily.

Secretions removed with a bulb syringe should be expelled onto a disposal tissue before a second attempt is made to remove additional secretions. Gloves should be worn and care must be taken to avoid skin contact with the secretions. Thorough hand washing before and after suctioning is essential.

Where to Go for Further Information or Training

Resources include home health nurses, nurses in local hospitals, respiratory therapists, and the American Lung Association at http://www.lungusa.org. School nurses may use guides such as the basic skills checklists prepared by Porter et al. (2006) in order to train school staff.

Respiratory Management: Oxygen Supplementation

Oxygen supplementation is necessary if the current level of oxygen in the body is inadequate because of respiratory or cardiac conditions. Oxygen is given through a nasal catheter (a small catheter placed into one nostril), nasal prongs or cannulae (two small hollow, plastic prongs that fit into the student's nostrils), a face mask (a plastic mask that fits over the student's mouth and nose), or a trachea mask (a plastic mask that fits loosely over the student's tracheostomy tube). Nasal prongs are the most frequently used method of administering oxygen to children.

What Is Involved

Oxygen should not be given over a prolonged period of time without humidification because it can dry up secretions and mucous membranes. The flow rate of oxygen is not changed unless ordered by the student's primary care provider. Occasionally, a student needs to have more oxygen during mealtimes or certain activities. The student's primary care provider must prescribe this change in flow rate. Indications that the student has an inadequate supply of oxygen include difficulty breathing, irritability, increased respiration, fatigue, pale color, cyanosis (i.e., bluish lips and nail beds), or an increase in the heart rate.

Classroom Applications

Most likely, a student will receive oxygen from a portable oxygen tank that is attached to a wheeled device or wheelchair and is carried by or with the student. Because oxygen is highly combustible, precautions should be taken to avoid using highly flammable substances while oxygen is being administered. Areas where oxygen is being used should be marked with large, easily read warning signs. Administration of oxygen may be a necessary part of a student's health care plan.

Liz's oral-motor skills had been improving throughout the school year, so she had begun accepting small amounts of pureed food before formula was given through her gastrostomy tube. However, her respiratory status became a problem after an episode of pneumonia. Liz continued accepting small amounts of pureed food, but needed oxygen during and after mealtimes. She also experienced breathing problems when she became excited or stressed. Her classmates learned to recognize her distress and need for oxygen and would bring Liz's distress to the teacher's attention.

Where to Go for Further Information or Training

Respiratory therapists and pediatric nurses in a local hospital and home health care staff may provide information about the administration of oxygen. Medical equipment supply companies provide information about the oxygen tank, humidifier, and tubing. The student's physician is a resource for school staff when questions arise about oxygen supplementation. The American Thoracic Society's Patient Education Series (http://www.thoracic.org) offers helpful information on oxygen therapy for children.

Respiratory Management: Mechanical Ventilation

Mechanical ventilation is required when the student is unable to breathe in or breathe out adequately; oxygen supplementation is accomplished using the student's current breathing pattern. Students may be dependent on a ventilator as a result of conditions such as neurological damage, muscle weakness, or severe pulmonary disease (Porter et al., 2006). Respiratory management in the schools involves monitoring the equipment needed to allow breathing and the ability to intervene in emergency situations.

What Is Involved

Although there are many different types of ventilators, the most common is a *positive pressure ventilator*. This ventilator breathes for the student by forcing air into the lungs, usually through a tracheostomy tube. Noninvasive positive pressure ventilation (NPPV) is used with children and includes a nasal or oral mask attached to the ventilator. Types of NPPV are (a) continuous positive airway pressure, and (b) bilevel positive airway pressure (Cheifetz, 2003). A student may require ventilation only during sleep and can attend school with oxygen supplementation. Other students may require ongoing ventilation and attend school with the constant attention of a private nurse or other health care professional.

Classroom Applications

Students require assisted ventilation for a variety of reasons: fatigue from the increased work of breathing, periods when breathing does not occur spontaneously, or periods when conditions restrict or prevent adequate ventilation. Students who require ventilator assistance, as well as their parents, are often anxious when others become responsible for managing this aspect of their daily routine. Anxiety can increase the student's respiration and possibly lead to hyperventilation. Training school staff about the ventilator and what to do in case of an emergency can increase the student's and parents' confidence in the staff and decrease their anxiety.

Staff members must feel confident and secure in the procedures that they are using, have a clear understanding of all aspects of the procedures, and have a plan to follow if problems arise. A nurse or respiratory therapist who has received specialized training for managing mechanical ventilation should perform the care. A trained caregiver should be available to the student in the classroom and in transit to and from the school. In addition to knowing how to care for the student and the ventilator, these trained persons must know how to provide CPR for the student with a tracheostomy. Backup electrical power should be available for a mechanical ventilator at all times. A resuscitation bag, a spare tracheostomy tube, suction supplies, and other necessary equipment and supplies should always be with the student.

Where to Go for Further Information or Training

Respiratory therapists, home health care staff, nurse specialists working with the student in the hospital, and the student's physician can provide information to develop and implement an overall plan for a student's respiratory management.

See also http://www.healthfinder.gov, provided by the U.S. government, and Allergy & Asthma Network, Mothers of Asthmatics at http://www.aanma.org, a nonprofit organization that helps families overcome and maintain control of asthma, allergies, and related conditions. Online information is also available at Cincinnati Children's Hospital Medical Center (http://www.cincinnatichildrens.org), Gillette Children's Hospital (http://www.gillettechildrens.org), and the University of Minnesota Amplatz Children's Hospital (http://www.uofmchildrenshospital.org).

Glucose Monitoring

Glucose monitoring is a procedure used to identify the amount of glucose (sugar) present in the blood and is carried out by the school nurse for students who have diabetes. This is a disorder in which carbohydrates are unable to be used because of inadequate production or use of insulin, resulting in excessive amounts of glucose in the student's blood and urine.

Type 1 diabetes occurs when insulin is not produced, resulting in problems getting glucose into the cells of the body. Between 5% to 10% of Americans with diabetes have Type 1 diabetes. Type 2 diabetes results from the body's failure to use insulin properly, along with a relative deficiency of insulin in the body. Around 90% to 95% of Americans with diabetes have Type 2 diabetes. Type 1 diabetes occurs more frequently in children, but an increasing number of children are developing Type 2 diabetes. Therapeutic management of Type 1 diabetes includes (a) medication (insulin therapy), (b) blood glucose monitoring, (c) nutrition, and (d) exercise (Cerasuolo, 2007). Students with Type 1 diabetes usually require testing of blood glucose levels three or four times per day, which will likely affect the classroom routine. The number of times that a student's blood glucose level is checked will depend on whether the student takes insulin or another diabetic medication, has a hard time controlling blood glucose levels, has severe low blood glucose levels or ketones from high blood glucose levels, or has low blood sugar levels without warning signs (http://www.diabetes.org). Another test used to measure blood glucose levels is glycosylated hemoglobin (hemoglobin A1$_c$). This test reveals overall glucose control over the prior 2 to 3 months and serves as a "report card" (Bayne, 1997) on dietary and insulin management.

What Is Involved

Glucose monitoring is taught to students and their parents as a method of achieving optimal control of blood glucose levels and can be carried out relatively easily during the school day. The student's fingertip is pricked with a lancet or spring-activated lancet by the student, school nurse, or designate. When a drop of blood forms, the blood is allowed to drop from the student's finger onto a special reagent strip. The strip is placed into a special meter. A reading of the student's glucose level appears on the meter's screen. If this device is not used, the color of the reagent strip can be compared with the color blocks on the reagent container; this method results in a probable range of glucose levels. Using a reagent strip and comparing the color change against a color chart is the least expensive method of testing. As more advanced technology leads to improvements in glucose monitoring equipment, it is important to follow the directions that come with the child's device (Cerasuolo, 2007).

Classroom Applications

A team approach to management includes informing teachers, school staff, the student's peer group, bus drivers, and others who interact with the student about diabetes. The student may wear a MedicAlert® bracelet or necklace to provide identification that could be lifesaving. The teacher and peer group can play a role in helping the student manage his or her disease by providing sugar-free treats or other appropriate foods during holiday and birthday celebrations. Careful monitoring provides accurate, current information on the student's glucose level and allows treatment of levels that are too high or too low. Foods can be given to provide extra glucose, foods can be limited, or insulin can be given. Glucose levels that are too high or too low can affect a student's ability to perform in the classroom. It is desirable for some students to test their blood glucose levels before lunch and when signs or symptoms of abnormal levels are present; however, monitoring of blood glucose levels should be individualized and determined by the student's status, health care provider, and parents (American Association of Diabetes Educators, 2000, 2007).

When glucose levels are too high, insulin may need to be given. Because students with disabilities may not communicate symptoms of low or high glucose levels, parents can be extremely helpful in identifying behaviors which indicate that glucose levels are not within the desired range. The school nurse, or the person designated by the school nurse, monitors the student's glucose levels. When possible, the student should have some responsibility to assist with monitoring. The student's IEP and IHP will reflect the efforts of the school nurse and teacher to monitor the student's glucose levels and minimize the interruptions related to glucose monitoring during the student's school day.

Where to Go for Further Information or Training

Information about diabetes can be obtained through diabetes educators, nurses who work with children who have diabetes, and dietitians in local hospitals. American Diabetes Association local affiliates can be contacted for more information (http://www.diabetes.org). Additional resources include Juvenile Diabetes Research Foundation International (http://www.jdf.org), the American Association of Diabetes Educators (http://www.aadenet.org), MedicAlert® Foundation International (http://www.medicalert.org/), and the National Institute of Diabetes and Digestive and Kidney Diseases (NIDDK) (http://www2.niddk.nih.gov). Other online resources include the following: http://www.childrenwithdiabetes.com, http://www.cincinnatichildrens.org/svc/alpha/d/diabetes/resources.htm, and http://www.seattlechildrens.org/our_services/endocrinology/resources.asp.

Shunt Care

Hydrocephalus is a condition in which the accumulation of excess amounts of fluid in the cerebral ventricles results in enlargement of the ventricles, which can eventually lead to enlargement of the head and subsequent brain damage. Some causes of hydrocephalus are Arnold-Chiari malformations, brain tumors, Dandy-Walker syndrome, and meningitis (McCormick et al., 2007). A student with hydrocephalus may have a shunt that drains excess cerebrospinal fluid from the ventricles of the brain into another part of the body. Shunt care almost exclusively involves procedures to identify when the shunt has malfunctioned.

What Is Involved

Surgical placement of a shunt allows fluid to leave the cerebral ventricles and to move to (a) the peritoneal cavity (ventriculoperitoneal, or VP, shunt), or (b) the right upper chamber (atrium) of the heart (ventriculoatrial, or VA, shunt) for elimination by the body. If a shunt becomes obstructed or malfunctions, fluid begins to build up, creating increased pressure in the brain. Signs of shunt malfunction in students include headache, vomiting or change in appetite, neck pain, change in upper extremity strength and hand function, deterioration in school performance, swelling along the shunt tract, lethargy or irritability, and seizures (Jacobs, 2006).

Classroom Applications

School staff must be aware of the student's usual behavior, level of activity, and responses. This knowledge will help the school team note changes which may indicate that the shunt is not working. Lethargy, nausea, and vomiting are common signs of shunt malfunction, but idiosyncratic behaviors are best identified through discussion with the student's parents. There are generally no restrictions on a student's activities, with the exception of exclusion from contact sports when there is a high risk of head injury. Physicians' recommendations about restrictions in contact sports vary as reported by Blount et al. (2004).

Where to Go for Further Information or Training

The student's physician (pediatrician or family physician, neurologist, neurosurgeon) and a nurse specialist who works with children who have neurological disorders can provide additional information. The student's parents can be exceptional resources by providing information about the student's usual behavior and behavior that can be expected when the shunt is not functioning properly. National organizations include the Hydrocephalus Association (http://www.hydroassoc.org), the National Hydrocephalus Foundation (http://www.nhfonline.org), and the Spina Bifida Association of America http://www.spinabifidaassociation.org

Issues in Providing Special Health Care

Participation in Integrated Settings

In the past, the rationale for placement of students who require complex special health care procedures in restricted, segregated settings was that the resources (personnel and equipment) were more efficiently, economically, and reliably provided if all students requiring special health care procedures

at school were in close proximity. Separation from peers, however, is in opposition to current efforts toward both integration and inclusion. A large body of research has identified effective instructional options for inclusive classrooms, including the use of specific educational contexts (e.g., grouping strategies), techniques, curricula, and assessment methods. Use of these strategies appears to facilitate the academic and social success of both students with and without disabilities (Katz & Mirenda, 2002).

Proponents of inclusion of children with special health care needs support the position that if a student has been discharged from a hospital to the home and non-nursing personnel can accomplish the necessary special health care procedures in the home, it is also possible to provide these same procedures in the school setting (American Academy of Pediatrics, 2007; Porter et al., 2006). Medically, there does not appear to be a reason for school segregation.

When Liz was born and the degree of her disabilities became increasingly clear, her parents were very much afraid that Liz would not have the same educational and social opportunities and experiences growing up that her sisters had. The family liked their neighborhood, their school, and their community. They felt that Liz should be a part of all of this, just as her sisters were. Since birth, Liz had been receiving services through the school district, with home visits from infant and early childhood teachers. When Liz turned six, she started in a segregated school, but soon the district moved her to an inclusive placement in Liz's neighborhood school. Although often challenging, the process of including Liz with her peers was and is being accomplished. Her parents, again, were faced with the familiar fears and concerns when Liz had the G-tube placed. The school personnel, although initially hesitant, were willing to "give it a try." Liz's parents worked closely with the district's health care coordinator to develop a plan for her health management at school. Together, they developed a strategy to address the technical skills that are needed by school personnel, as well as any emotional or philosophical supports that might be provided to the school as they begin to participate in this new health care procedure. Aside from a few days missed because of colds and one case of diarrhea, Liz's attendance has been very good.

Inclusion is a major objective of legislation such as the Individuals with Disabilities Education Act (IDEA) and the Americans with Disabilities Act. All students, including students with disabilities and health care needs, have a right to participate in a regular classroom with appropriate supports during the school day. The responsibility of school districts to provide necessary health services to students with disabilities has been upheld in court cases such as the *Tatro* case (Vitello, 1986) and *Cedar Rapids Community School District v. Garrett F.* (Katsiyannis & Yell, 1999). In the *Tatro* case (http://supreme.justia.com/us/468/883/), a "three-part test" was adopted by the U.S. Supreme Court in which services that affect the educational and health needs of a student must be provided under IDEA if (a) the student's disability requires special education services, (b) the service is necessary to assist the student in benefiting from special education, and (c) a nurse or other qualified person who is not a physician can provide the service.

Environmental Concerns in Educational Settings

Children are at greater risk of harm when exposed to environmental hazards such as toxic chemicals than adults because of their developing body, higher metabolic rates, and behavior. Students with disabilities can be predisposed to greater harm from exposure to toxic chemicals because of certain behaviors and challenges that they face (Graff, Murphy, Ekvall, & Gagnon, 2006). Students with disabilities may have behaviors (e.g., hand-to-mouth activity, mouthing, chewing) that persist past a developmentally appropriate age. They may have difficulty communicating symptoms related to exposure and school staff and parents may attribute a symptom or problem to the child's disability instead of to toxic chemical exposure. For example, a student with a severe disability may experience respiratory distress from exposure to pesticides or cleaning products, and the school staff and parents unknowingly attribute the symptoms to the student's disability. Students are at risk if they are unable to move themselves away from irritating fumes or those who spend long period of time indoors can be at increased risk of harm from environmental tobacco smoke. Students who spend large amounts of time on the floor may be at greater risk for exposure to fertilizers, pesticides, formaldehyde, and mold. Students who engage in pica can be at risk for exposure to lead. School staff should be alert to potentially toxic chemicals in the school environment and opportunities for students with disabilities to be exposed, and take action to minimize the risk of exposure.

The National Association of School Nurses (2004b) identified 14 environmental toxins that can impair the health of students. A fact sheet developed by the American Association on Intellectual and Developmental Disabilities (2007) stresses the importance of considering potential environmental hazards that students with disabilities may be exposed to during the school day. Internet resources for additional information include http://www.cehn.org, http://www.epa.gov/iaq/schools, and http://www.healthyschools.org/

Children in Pain

Pain is a substantial problem in the pediatric population, conservatively estimated to affect 15% to 20% of children (Goodman & McGrath, 1991). Children and their families experience significant emotional and social consequences as a result of pain and disability. Specifically, children who complained often of aches and pains used more health services, missed more school, and experienced more psychological and academic problems (Campo, Comer, Jansen-McWilliams, Gardner, & Kelleher, 2002).

Definition of Pain

Acute pain follows injury to the body and generally disappears when the injury heals. It is often associated with objective physical signs of autonomic nervous system activity, such as increased heart rate and respiration. Chronic pain, in contrast, is rarely accompanied by signs of sympathetic nervous system arousal (the classic fight or flight response). The lack of objective signs may prompt the inexperienced clinician to say that the patient "does not look like" he or she is in pain (American Pain Society, 1999). Careful and thorough assessments are necessary when communication with the child may be problematic, as may be the case with children who are cognitively impaired, severely emotionally disturbed, or impaired in sensory or motor modalities. Cultural and language differences between the child and the health care professional also require additional resources (e.g., interpreter) during assessment. When such patients are unable to report pain, credible assessment usually can be obtained from a parent or another person who knows the child well (American Academy of Pediatrics, 2001).

The student's behaviors, expressions, fears, and sources of comfort provide objective information about the student's experience of pain. The different ways that a child or youth may express pain are very individual. For example, if experiencing a fracture, a student may guard an arm or try not to bear weight on a leg. The student may hold his or her head or stomach, a common response for all persons with stomachaches or headaches, or wince when swallowing or breathing. Often, however, the pain is not localized, or the child is not able to localize the pain or protect an area of the body. In these instances, the only indication that the student is in pain is the student's different behavior.

Instruments have been developed to assess behavior changes associated with pain, yet few instruments exist for assessing pain in students with disabilities, who express themselves nonverbally. The Non-Communicating Children's Pain Checklist (Breau, McGrath, Camfield, & Finley, 2002) and the Pain Indicator for Communicatively Impaired Children (Stallard et al., 2002) are used to assess pain in children with cognitive and communication impairments, respectively. School staff must rely on their own observations and knowledge about the student, along with information provided by the student's family, to make an objective interpretation about a student's experiences with pain.

Children Who Are Dying

When a student's condition is expected to worsen or when death is expected within months or years, four options are available. These include (a) focusing on skill training that will maintain the child's present skills as long as possible; (b) teaching skills that are needed in order to compensate for lost ability; (c) aiding the student, family, school, and other students in dealing with increasing deterioration; and (d) lessening the likelihood of secondary complications, such as pain or additional impairment. These options are founded on the assumptions that it is important for the student's life to be as normal as possible and that part of a child's normal life includes going to school. Some or all of these options may be selected, depending on the student's condition and family preferences. It is especially important that families, school staff, and health professionals work closely together during this time.

School staff can gain understanding of the degenerative illness and feel more comfortable with the student by meeting with the parents and medical staff to (a) learn about the student's condition, (b) learn what the student can and cannot do, and (c) clarify how to recognize and respond to emergencies (American Academy of Pediatrics, 1999). When a student dies, school staff members are dealing not only with their own feelings, but also with the feelings of classmates,

families, and other staff members. It is important to discuss a student's death openly and allow others to express their feelings.

Withholding Treatment

Sometimes, the families of students with special health care needs have made a decision to limit resuscitative efforts by signing a Do Not Attempt Resuscitation (DNAR) order for their child. Despite recent attention to in-school DNAR orders, an assessment of state laws and school policies revealed that 80% of the school districts sampled did not have policies, regulations, or protocols for dealing with student DNARs. Similarly, 76% either would not honor student DNARs or were uncertain about whether they could. Frequent contradictions between school policies and state laws also existed (Kimberly, Forte, Carroll, & Feudtner, 2005). Consequently, children living with life-shortening conditions who have DNARs may not have these orders honored if cardiopulmonary arrest were to occur on school premises. Coordinated efforts are needed to harmonize school district, state, and federal approaches in order to support the rights of children and families to have important medical decisions honored. The American Academy of Pediatrics (2000) recommends that physicians and parents meet with relevant school personnel to explain the child's medical condition and the goals of care, and to hear the concerns of other parents and school personnel. It also urges that all parties be realistic, flexible, and ready to negotiate. Thoughtful discussion will assist us in recognizing and understanding the values involved, our respective roles and responsibilities, and the process through which decisions are made or changed.

Summary

To establish quality health care in an educational setting, teachers must (a) incorporate special health care procedures into the educational day, and (b) actively prevent the development of related health problems and conditions. Procedures that should be a part of training for all classroom personnel include infection control, first aid, and CPR. Teachers also should have readily available information concerning the special health care needs of students. This information should minimally include (a) seizure information, with the type, frequency, and response; (b) medication information, with the type, purpose, schedule of administration, and possible side effects or interactions; (c) emergency contact numbers for family members, the medical facility of choice, and the primary health care provider; and (d) specific protocols for the implementation of special health care procedures for individual students, the person primarily responsible for implementing the procedures, designated backups, and the dates of training of school staff for the implementation of the procedures.

The student's health care needs are best addressed through collaboration among the school, the family, and health care professionals. When it is clear to everyone, including the student, why a particular procedure is required, the student's health and ability to participate in the educational process is enhanced through inclusion of the procedures in the IHP and/or IEP. Creativity and consistency in implementation and monitoring can be an outcome. It is hoped that this chapter will provide team members with the information and resources needed to serve students with a variety of health care conditions comfortably and safely.

Suggested Activities

1. Complete training in CPR with an emphasis on children and a basic Red Cross first aid course.
2. Monitor the BMI of a student for whom you feel normal growth is at risk. Plot growth with the school nurse or dietitian over several months and determine whether the student's weight in relationship to height places the student below the 5th percentile. Determine whether growth is occurring at an acceptable rate.
3. Spend approximately two hours participating in a specialty pediatric clinic, such as a cerebral palsy, spina bifida, or feeding clinic. Learn to implement a special health care procedure for a student with whom you are familiar. Develop at least two or three instructional skills that are appropriate for the student to practice during implementation of the special health care procedure.
4. The U.S. Environmental Protection Agency developed the Indoor Air Quality (IAQ) Tools for Schools (TfS) Program in order to reduce exposure to indoor environmental contaminants in schools through the voluntary adoption of sound indoor air quality management practices. Visit the Web site (http://www.epa.gov/iaq/schools) and download a kit for implementation within your school.

References

ADAPT Youth. (2007). ADAPT Youth appalled at parents surgically keeping disabled daughter childlike. Retrieved January 18, 2007, from http://www.adapt.org/adaptpr/index.php?mode=A&id=253;&sort=D

Algren, C. L., & Arnow, D. (2007). Pediatric variations of nursing interventions. In M. J. Hockenberry, & D. Wilson (Eds.), *Wong's Nursing Care of Infants and Children* (8th ed., pp. 1083–1139). St. Louis, MO: Mosby Elsevier.

Altkorn, R., Chen, X., Milkovich, S., Stool, D., Rider, G., Bailey, C. M., et al. (2008). Fatal and non-fatal food injuries among children (aged 0–14 years). *International Journal of Pediatric Otorhinolaryngology, 72,* 1041–1046.

American Academy of Pediatrics. (1999). Emergency preparedness for children with special health care needs. *Pediatrics, 104,* 53.

American Academy of Pediatrics (2000). Do not resuscitate orders in schools. Committee on School Health and Committee on Bioethics. *Pediatrics, 105,* 878–879.

American Academy of Pediatrics. (2001). The assessment and management of acute pain in infants, children, and adolescents. *Pediatrics, 108,* 793–797.

American Academy of Pediatrics. (2003). Guidelines for the administration of medication in school. *Pediatrics, 112*(3), 697–699.

American Academy of Pediatrics. (2004). Response to cardiac arrest and selected life-threatening medical emergencies: The medical emergency response plan for schools. A statement of healthcare providers, policy makers, school administrators, and community leaders. *Pediatrics, 113,* 155–168.

American Academy of Pediatrics. (2007). Provision of educationally related services for children and adolescents with chronic diseases and disabling conditions. *Pediatrics, 119*(6), 1218–1223.

American Academy of Pediatrics, Council on School Health. (2008). Role of the school nurse in providing school health services. *Pediatrics, 121*(5), 1052–1056.

American Association of Diabetes Educators. (2000). Management of children with diabetes in the school setting. *The Diabetes Educator, 26,* 32–35.

American Association of Diabetes Educators. (2007). AADE Position Statement: Individualization of diabetes self-management education. *The Diabetes Educator, 33,* 45–59.

American Association on Intellectual and Developmental Disabilities. (2007a). Unjustifiable non-therapy: A response to Gunther and Diekema (2006) and to the issue of growth attenuation for young people on the basis of disability. Retrieved January 11, 2007, from http://www.aaidd.org/content_173.cfm?navID=31

American Association on Intellectual and Developmental Disabilities. (2007b). AAIDD Fact Sheet: Students with disabilities in schools. Retrieved June 26, 2009, from http://www.aaidd.org/ehi/media/Health_Schools_Fact_Sheet_2003_202007.pdf

American Heart Association. (2005). Overview of CPR. *Circulation, 112,* IV-12–IV-18.

American Nurses Association and the National Association of School Nurses. (2005). *School nursing: Scope and standards of practice.* Washington, DC: American Nurses Association.

American Pain Society. (1999). *Principles of analgesic use in the treatment of acute pain and cancer pain* (4th ed.). Glenview, IL: Author.

Baldwin, K. M. (2002). Incidence and prevalence of pressure ulcers in children. *Advances in Skin & Wound Care, 15,* 121-124.

Bayne, C. G. (1997). How sweet it is: Glucose monitoring equipment and interpretation. *Nursing Management, 28*(9), 52, 54.

Blount, J. P., Severson, M., Atkins, V., Tubbs, R. S., Smyth, M. D., Wellons, J. C., et al. (2004). Sports and pediatric cerebrospinal fluid shunts: Who can play? *Neurosurgery, 54*(5), 1196-1198.

Borgioli, J.A., & Kennedy, C. H. (2003). Transitions between school and hospital for students with multiple disabilities: A survey of causes, educational continuity, and parental perceptions. *Research and Practice for Persons with Severe Disabilities, 28,* 1-6.

Boss, B. (2002). Concepts of neurologic dysfunction. In K. L. McCanse & S. E. Huether (Eds.), *Pathophysiology* (pp. 438-549). St. Louis, MO: Mosby Elsevier.

Boulet, S. L., Boyle, C.A., & Schieve, L.A. (2009). Health care use and health and functional impact of developmental disabilities among U.S. children, 1997-2005. *Archives of Pediatric and Adolescent Medicine, 163,* 19-26.

Breau, L. M., McGrath, P. J., Camfield, C. S., & Finley, G. A. (2002). Psychometric properties of the Non-communicating Children's Pain Checklist-Revised. *Pain, 99*(1-2), 349-357.

Bryant, R.A., & Doughty, D. (Eds.). (2000). *Acute and chronic wounds: Nursing management* (2nd ed.). St. Louis, MO: Mosby Elsevier.

Bush, C. M., Jones, J. S., Cohle, S. D., & Johnson, H. (1996). Pediatric injuries from cardiopulmonary resuscitation. *Annals of Emergency Medicine, 28,* 40-44.

Butler, C. (2006). Pediatric skin care: Guidelines for assessment, prevention, and treatment. *Pediatric Nursing, 32,* 443-450.

Campo, J. V., Comer, D. M., Jansen-McWilliams, L., Gardner, W., & Kelleher, K. J. (2002). Recurrent pain, emotional distress, and health service use in childhood. *Journal of Pediatrics, 141*(1), 76-83.

Carlsson, M., Hagberg, G., & Olsson, I. (2003). Clinical and aetological aspects of epilepsy in children with cerebral palsy. *Developmental Medicine and Child Neurology, 45*(6), 371-377.

Carron, J. D., Derkay, C. S., Strope, G. L., Nosonchuk, J. E., & Darrow, D. H. (2000). Pediatric tracheotomies: Changing indications and outcomes. *Laryngoscope, 110,* 1099-1104.

Centers for Disease Control and Prevention. (2008). *Cytomegalovirus (CMV): People who work with infants and children.* Retrieved June 26, 2009, from http://www.cdc.gov/cmv/daycare.htm

Cerasuolo, K. (2007). The child with endocrine dysfunction. In M. J. Hockenberry & D. Wilson (Eds.), *Wong's Nursing Care of Infants and Children* (8th ed., pp. 1676-1729). St. Louis, MO: Mosby Elsevier.

Cheifetz, I. M. (2003). Invasive and noninvasive pediatric mechanical ventilation. *Respiratory Care, 48*(4), 442-458.

Clair, E., Church, R. P., & Batshaw, M. L. (2007). Special education services. In M. L. Batshaw, L. Pellegrino, & N. J. Roizen (Eds.), *Children with disabilities* (6th ed.). Baltimore: Paul H. Brookes.

Disability Rights Education and Defense Fund. (2007). Modify the system, not the person. Retrieved January 10, 2007, from http://www.dredf.org/news/ashley.shtml

Eisenberg, S., Zuk, L., Carmeli, E., & Katz-Leuer, M. (2009). Contribution of stepping while standing to function and secondary conditions among children with cerebral palsy. *Pediatric Physical Therapy, 21,* 79-85.

Elawad, M.A., & Sullivan, P. B. (2001). Management of constipation in children with disabilities. *Developmental Medicine & Child Neurology, 43,* 829-832.

Epilepsy Foundation of America. (2008). *Seizure action plan.* Retrieved June 26, 2009, from http://www.epilepsyfoundation.org/programs/schoolnurse/upload/seizure-action-plan.pdf

Epilepsy Foundation of America. (2010). *About Epilepsy and Seizures: Epilepsy and seizure statistics.* Retrieved May 22, 2010, from http://www.epilepsyfoundation.org/about/statistics.cfm on

Fishman, L. N., & Bousvaros, A. (2006). Gastrointestinal issues. In I. L. Rubin & A. C. Crocker (Eds.), *Medical care for children and adults with developmental disabilities* (pp. 307-324). Baltimore: Paul H. Brookes.

Fung, E. B., Samson-Fang, L., Stallings, V. A., Conaway, M., Liptak, G., Henderson, R. C., et al. (2002). Feeding dysfunction is associated with poor growth and health status in children with cerebral palsy. *Journal of the American Dietetic Association, 102,* 361-373.

Glucksman, J. (1984, November). Clean intermittent catheterization—The law. *Spina Bifida Spotlight,* 1-2.

Goodman, J. E., & McGrath, P. J. (1991). The epidemiology of pain in children and adolescents: A review. *Pain, 46,* 247-264.

Graff, J. C., Murphy, L., Ekvall, S., & Gagnon, M. (2006). In-home toxic chemical exposures and children with intellectual and developmental disabilities. *Pediatric Nursing, 32,* 596-603.

Gunther, D. E., & Diekema, D. S. (2006). Attenuating growth in children with profound developmental disability: A new approach to an old dilemma. *Archives of Pediatric & Adolescent Medicine, 160,* 1013-1017.

HealthSoft, Inc. (2007). *A caring approach to teaching medication administration tasks.* Retrieved June 26, 2009, from http://healthsoftonline.com/hsi/mycourses.asp

Henderson, R., Kairalla, J., Barrington, A., Abbas, R., & Stevenson, R. (2005). Longitudinal changes in bone density in children and adolescents with moderate to severe cerebral palsy. *The Journal of Pediatrics, 146,* 769-775.

Hueckel, R., & Wilson, D. (2007). The child with disturbance of oxygen and carbon dioxide exchange. In M. J. Hockenberry & D. Wilson (Eds.), *Wong's nursing care of infants and children* (8th ed., pp. 1273-1313). St. Louis, MO: Mosby Elsevier.

Individuals with Disabilities Education Improvement Act of 2004, 20 U.S.C. 1400 et seq., P.L. 108-446.

Jacobs, R.A. (2006). Spina bifida. In I. L. Rubin & A. C. Crocker (Eds.), *Medical care for children and adults with developmental disabilities* (pp. 139-153). Baltimore: Paul H. Brookes.

Jeter, K. F., & Lutz, J. B. (1996). Skin care in elderly, dependent, incontinent patients. *Advances in Wound Care, 9*(1), 29-34.

Katsiyannis, A., & Yell, M. (1999). Education and the law: School health services: Cedar Rapids Community School District v. Garrett F. *Preventing School Failure, 44*(1), 37-38.

Katz, J., & Mirenda, P. (2002). Including students with developmental disabilities in education classrooms: Social benefits. *International Journal of Special Education, 17,* 25-35.

Kimberly, M. B., Forte, A. L., Carroll, J. M., & Feudtner, C. (2005). Pediatric do-not-attempt-resuscitation orders and public schools: A national assessment of policies and laws. *American Journal of Bioethics, 5,* 59-65.

Knight, S., Vernon, D. D., Fines, R. J., & Dean, N. P. (1999). Prehospital emergency care for children at school and nonschool-based locations. *Pediatrics, 103*(6), e81.

Loening-Baucke, V. (2007). Prevalence rates for constipation and faecal and urinary incontinence. *Archives of Disease in Childhood, 92,* 486-489.

McClung, H. J., Boyne, L., & Heitlinger, L. (1995). Constipation and dietary fiber intake in children. *Pediatrics, 96,* 997-1000.

McCormick, B. M., Mackey, W. L., & Wilson, D. (2007). Conditions caused by defects in physical development. In M. J. Hockenberry & D. Wilson (Eds.), *Wong's nursing care of infants and children* (8th ed., pp. 422-498). St. Louis, MO: Mosby Elsevier.

Nageswaran, S., Silver, E. J., & Stein, R. K. (2008). Association of functional limitation with health care needs and experiences of children with special health care needs. *Pediatrics, 121*(5), 994-1001.

National Association of School Nurses. (2002). *School health nursing services role in health care: Role of the school nurse* (Issue Brief). Silver Spring, MD: National Association of School Nurses. Retrieved June 25, 2009, from http://www.nasn.org/Default.aspx?tabid=279

National Association of School Nurses. (2003a). *The role of the school nurse caring for a student requiring a rectal medication for seizures* (Position Statement). Silver Spring, MD: National Association of School Nurses.

National Association of School Nurses. (2003b). *Medication administration in the school setting* (Position Statement). Silver Spring, MD: National Association of School Nurses.

National Association of School Nurses. (2004a). *Rescue medications in school* (Position Statement). Silver Spring, MD: National Association of School Nurses.

National Association of School Nurses. (2004b). *School health nursing services role in health care: Environmental concerns in the school setting* (Issue Brief). Silver Spring, MD: National Association of School Nurses. Retrieved June 26, 2009, from http://www.nasn.org/Default.aspx?tabid=270

National Association of School Nurses. (2008). *Individualized Healthcare Plans (IHP)* (Issue Brief). Silver Spring, MD: National Association of School Nurses. Retrieved June 25, 2009, from http://www.nasn.org/Default.aspx?tabid=226

Park, E. S., Park, C. I., Cho, S., Na, S., & Cho, Y. S. (2004). Colonic transit time and constipation in children with spastic cerebral palsy. *Archives of Physical Medicine and Rehabilitation, 85,* 453-456.

Passy, V. (1986). Passy-Muir tracheostomy speaking valve. *Otolaryngology and Head and Neck Surgery, 95,* 247-248.

Perlman, S. P., Friedman, O., & Fenton, S. J. (2007). *A caregiver's guide to good oral health for persons with special needs.* Washington, DC: Joseph P. Kennedy, Jr. Foundation for the Benefit of Persons with Intellectual Disabilities.

Pittel, D. (2001). Improving adherence to hand hygiene: A multidisciplinary approach. *Emerging Infectious Diseases, 7,* 234-240.

Porter, S., Haynie, M., Bierle, T., Caldwell, T. H., & Palfrey, J. S. (2006). *Children and youth assisted by medical technology in educational settings: Guidelines for care* (2nd ed.). Baltimore: Paul H. Brookes.

Potter, P. A., & Perry, A. G. (2008). *Fundamentals of nursing* (7th ed.). St. Louis, MO: Mosby Elsevier.

Rogozinski, B. M., Davids, J. R., Davis, R. B., Christopher, L. M., Anderson, J. P., Jameson, G. G., et al. (2007). Prevalence of obesity in ambulatory children with cerebral palsy. *Journal of Bone and Joint Surgery, 89,* 2421-2426.

Ryan, M. P., Young, S. J., & Wells, D. L. (2003). Do resuscitation attempts in children who die, cause injury? *Emergency Medicine Journal, 20,* 10-12.

Samaniego, I. A. (2003). A sore spot in pediatrics: Risk factors for pressure ulcers. *Pediatric Nursing, 29*(4), 278-282.

Singhi, P., Jagirdar, S., Khandelwal, N., & Malhi, P. (2003). Epilepsy in children with cerebral palsy. *Journal of Child Neurology, 18*(3), 174-179.

Staiano, A., Simeone, D., Giudice, E. D., Miele, E., Tozzi, A., & Toraldo, C. (2000). Effect of the dietary fiber glucomannan on chronic constipation in neurologically impaired children. *The Journal of Pediatrics, 136,* 41-45.

Stallard, P., Williams, L., Velleman, R., Lenton, S., McGrath, P. J., & Taylor, G. (2002). The development and evaluation of the Pain Indicator for Communicatively Impaired Children (PICIC). *Pain, 98*(1-2), 145-149.

Students with chronic illnesses: Guidance for families, schools, and students. (2003). *Journal of School Health, 73*(4), 131-132.

Sullivan, P. B., Lambert, B., Ford-Adams, M., Griffiths, P., & Johnson, A. (2000). The prevalence and severity of feeding and nutritional problems in children with neurological impairment: Oxford Feeding Study. *Developmental Medicine & Child Neurology, 42,* 674-680.

Sullivan-Bolyai, S., Swanson, M., & Shurtleff, D. B. (1984). Toilet training the child with neurogenic impairment of bowel and bladder function. *Issues in Comprehensive Pediatric Nursing, 7*(1), 33-43.

TASH. (2007). Attenuating growth. Retrieved January 18, 2007, from http://www.tash.org/IRR/resolutions.html

Tse, P. W., Leung, S. S., Chan, T., Sien, A., & Chan, A. K. (2000). Dietary fibre intake and constipation in children with severe developmental disabilities. *Journal of Paediatrics and Child Health, 36*(3), 236-239.

U.S. Department of Health and Human Services, Health Resources and Services Administration, Maternal and Child Health Bureau. (2007). *The National Survey of Children with Special Health Care Needs chartbook, 2005-2006.* Rockville, MD: Author.

U.S. Department of Health and Human Services, National Center for Health Statistics. (2008). *The 2007 National Immunization Survey.* Hyattsville, MD: Centers for Disease Control and Prevention.

Vitello, S. J. (1986). The Tatro case: Who gets what and why. *Exceptional Children, 52*(4), 353-356.

Walker, D. K., & Jacobs, F. H. (1984, Winter). Chronically ill children in school. *Peabody Journal of Education, 61*(2), 28-76.

Weinstein, S. L., & Gaillard, W. D. (2007). Epilepsy. In M. L. Batshaw, L. Pellegrino, & N. J. Rozien (Eds.), *Children with disabilities* (6th ed., pp. 439-460). Baltimore: Paul H. Brookes.

Wetmore, R., Thompson, M., Marsh, R., & Tom, L. (1999). Pediatric tracheostomy: A changing procedure? *Annals of Otology, Rhinology, and Laryngology, 108,* 695-699.

Woo, T. M., & Blosser, C. G. (2004). Medications. In C. E. Burns, A. M. Dunn, M. A. Brady, N. B. Starr, & C. G. Blosser (Eds.), *Pediatric primary care: A handbook for nurse practitioners* (3rd ed., pp. 1263-1320). St. Louis, MO: Saunders.

9

Addressing Motor Disabilities

Philippa H. Campbell

Quality programs for individuals with motor disabilities include both instructional programs and physical management routines. Instructional programs work to develop specific movements for use in performing functional outcomes in communication, mobility, socialization, work, and learning. For example, teaching an individual to stand and move with assistance from a chair to a toilet, a sofa, or the floor requires an instructional program. However, individuals with motor disabilities also require conscientious management of their physical needs while in their home, school, work, and community environments. Lifting, carrying, positioning, feeding, toileting, dressing, and other similar routines must be managed when a person is not able to do the routine independently or may not be independent in all settings. Physical management routines allow adults (or peers) to use therapeutic procedures for the muscles, bones, and joints, and compensate for the overall motor limitations that may be present. Lifting a child from an adaptive chair can be done in ways that promote relaxation or in ways that make a child stiff, uncomfortable, or fearful. A child may sit comfortably in an adaptive chair or may sit uncomfortably with poor positioning in an ill-fitting chair. Occupational therapists and physical therapists, together with family members, teachers, and others, can ensure that the easiest and most efficient ways are used to manage physical care needs in all settings. How students' needs are addressed depend on their age and size, the degree and type of motor disability, the setting, and the person who will be carrying out the routine. In addition to the team, there are many useful Internet resources, such as the Web site for the American Academy for Cerebral Palsy and Developmental Medicine (http://www.aacpdm.org) or United Cerebral Palsy http://www.ucp.org).

This chapter provides an overview of the guidelines used to accommodate the physical care needs of individuals with motor disabilities so that they will be able to participate as fully as possible in activities in everyday settings. Two children, Susan, a six-year-old kindergartener, and Mackenzie, a high school freshman, are described here and are used as examples to illustrate the ways in which general handling and care routines are individualized for specific children and circumstances.

❖ ❖ ❖ ❖ ❖   **Susan**   ❖ ❖ ❖ ❖ ❖

At age six, Susan, who has been diagnosed as having cerebral palsy with spastic quadriplegia, remains dependent on caregivers for all of her care. Susan likes a lot of activities that other kindergartners enjoy, such as being read stories, making art projects, and playing with toys. Susan might like to be as independent as other children, but

340

severe stiffness in her arms and legs prevents such independence. Susan needs extensive assistance while eating, dressing, and bathing as well as when she is lifted and carried from place to place. Susan attends kindergarten and, when her mother is working, is cared for in a community day care center. At school and the child care center, Susan receives special education and therapy services through her local school district. These specialists help the educational and child care program staff and Susan's family manage her care and maximize her participation.

Much of the assistance provided to small children by adults in physical management routines will be necessary for Susan throughout her life. However, over time and with the help of her family and team members, Susan will learn to take part in daily care routines and to perform other routines independently. For example, Susan participates in dressing and bathing, and her mother, teacher, and the child care workers are helping Susan learn to eat without assistance. The team's goal is to use resources and methods to manage Susan's physical care routines, help her participate fully in activities and routines, and promote her ability to become as independent as possible.

❖ ❖ ❖ ❖ ❖   **Mackenzie**   ❖ ❖ ❖ ❖ ❖

Mackenzie has been receiving special education and a variety of related services for the past 14 years. "Mac" was diagnosed with cerebral palsy at 6 months and began receiving early intervention services shortly thereafter. Now, at 15 years old, she is a veteran of numerous orthopedic surgeries, and just last year, selective dorsal rhizotomy surgery was done to help lower the muscle tone in her legs. The surgery improved the ease with which Mac's care needs can be addressed and allowed her to stand with considerable support and assistance.

Mac attends her local high school where she is enrolled in many classes with her peers. She also participates in other classes to learn community skills, such as riding public transportation and ordering food in a restaurant. Her high school peers have grown up with Mac, who has attended regular schools since kindergarten, and many of her peers are sensitive to her needs. One of her friends assists her during lunchtime each day in the cafeteria. Another friend spends time with her during swimming. A paraeducator has been assigned to work with Mac and other students with special needs. The paraeducator assists Mac in the bathroom and in moving her from one piece of equipment to another. The paraeducator follows team recommendations and helps by making special adaptations and modifying materials so that Mac can do her schoolwork with her peers. Mac is able to get around the school independently using a power chair. She communicates her wants and needs with a communication device and uses a computer with a switch to participate in her classes. Mac receives occupational, physical, and speech and language therapy. Her team, which includes her teacher, parents, therapists, and lots of friends, recognizes her many strengths and has established individualized educational program (IEP) goals that will enable her to be as independent as possible upon graduation.

Key Concepts in Understanding Motor Disability

Most types of pediatric physical disability are identified during infancy or early childhood. Children who have the most severe physical disabilities are likely to be diagnosed at or shortly after birth, while those with mild physical disabilities or those with some forms of genetically based physical limitations may not be identified until their toddler or preschool years or sometimes later in school. Physical disability also may be the result of an accident or injury that may occur at any time during childhood; it may be the only disability that the child has or it may be accompanied by other disorders, such as vision or hearing impairment, intellectual disability, or other types of learning disorders (see Batshaw, 2002). As a result of the physical or combined disability, children may have difficulties with physical development, learning, or performance.

> *Susan has a physical disability that is influencing her participation during many kindergarten activities (art, motor, snack time, and transitions), as well as her performance of self-care routines and communication.*

Movement Abilities, Adaptation, and Participation

Motor disability may range from severe to mild and may involve the whole body (i.e., arms, legs, head, trunk) or only parts of the body (e.g., one side or both legs). When the motor disability is severe, the whole body is more likely to be involved than when the disability is mild or moderate (Palisano et al., 1997). When motor disability is mild to moderate, there is a greater chance that children will learn to perform the same motor skills that typically developing children master during their early years. Children with mild to moderate disability will learn basic gross motor skills, such as sitting, crawling, and walking, although they may look different or be less coordinated than children without motor disability or may achieve skills at a later time than typical children. Children with severe motor disability may never be able to perform these basic skills because the degree of motor impairment may prevent them from doing so. Severe motor disability may not just affect gross motor skills like mobility, but may also influence whether a child is able to learn to eat independently, play with toys, hold a pencil, manage clothing, or use the bathroom independently. Severe motor disability impacts performance in many different areas (Dormans & Pellegrino, 1998).

Throughout the childhood years, whether at home, in school, or in community settings, participation in typical activities and routines must be promoted no matter how severe the motor disability. *Activities* include all of the academic, leisure, and social events that occur for students of a particular age and grade level during and after school; *routines* are more basic events that are often associated with completing basic self-care tasks and include the assistance of others as needed to manage a routine (e.g., lifting, helping the student to use the bathroom, helping someone eat). When a motor disability limits the performance of skills, participation in typical settings is ensured through accommodations, adaptations, assistive technology, or other strategies. The terms *accommodation* and *adaptation* are often used interchangeably, but both terms relate to physical accessibility, or program modifications that are made to promote access and participation. *Accessibility* results from environmental adaptations (or modifications) that allow an individual with a disability to enter into and use a particular setting. Designing a bathroom with wider doors, grab bars, a higher toilet, special water spigots, or other modifications makes it possible for people with physical disabilities to go into and use the bathroom facilities. Program adaptations allow an individual with a disability to participate in the activities and routines of a particular environment or setting by changing the ways in

which information is presented. A museum that provides exhibit information in braille has made program modifications to allow people with visual disabilities to enjoy the exhibits. A teacher who tapes a paper to the desk of a student with a physical disability so that the student may still write, draw, or paint on the paper has adapted the activity for the student. Simple adaptations, such as a picture board that a student may use to communicate by pointing to pictures or placing a non-slip mat under a plate so it won't move during eating, are considered to be within the definition of assistive technology or may simply be seen as adaptations. *Assistive technology* includes a variety of items, ranging from items that are readily available and used by people with or without disabilities to those that have been developed specifically for use by individuals with disabilities. Simple adaptations of readily available items are often classified as "low tech," while those that are specific to individuals with disabilities are defined as "high tech" (Best, Bigge, & Heller, 2004; Campbell, Milbourne, & Wilcox, 2008; Mistrett, 2001). Assistive technology can help individuals perform specific skills in a different way than is typically done. Communication devices, referred to as alternative and augmentative communication (AAC) devices, enable students who cannot speak to communicate using another means. The device may be as simple as pictures or symbols pasted onto cardboard (an example of a low-tech assistive device) or as complicated as a computerized device that both speaks and writes (an example of a high-tech device). Accommodations, adaptations, and assistive technology all enable children with disabilities to fully participate in typical home, school, and community activities. For example, a child with a physical disability who is unable to run may still be able to participate in a community baseball program (such as Little League) by using an adaptation to hit the ball or by "running" bases by moving a wheelchair.

> *Mac is improving her skills in using her power wheelchair during times when ninth graders are changing classes. She and another student leave class a little earlier than the others so that Mac has more time to get to the next class. Her student helper walks along with her and provides assistance when she has difficulty negotiating through doorways or steering around obstacles in the halls.*

When motor disability is severe and limits performance of self-care skills, the basic needs of an individual must be managed in the environments or settings where the person spends time (Campbell, 1995). For a child to participate in baseball, strategies for managing eating, toileting, and other care needs during the baseball game and in the settings where baseball takes place must be identified. Often such care falls on parents, other family members, or hired personal care assistants; a child may be permitted to participate only with family members or a personal care assistant present. There are many reasons why children may be required to participate only if adults are present, and these include perceived safety, liability and risk management, and the view that the child needs more assistance than may actually be the case. A better alternative involves good planning and instruction for the people who spend time with an individual in a particular setting. For example, the places where baseball takes place may be assessed to determine the accommodations and adaptations necessary for meeting an individual's eating, drinking, and toileting needs. People who are at the community games, such as the coaches or perhaps an older high school student who wishes to volunteer or, depending on age and the situation, the friends and peers of the child, may be taught the best ways of addressing individual needs during baseball games and practice. Assistance in determining strategies for management of care is generally provided by the occupational therapist (or sometimes the physical therapist), but family members and others who are familiar with the child may also be knowledgeable about easy and effective strategies.

Movement Form and Function

Most motor disabilities start with an impairment in the brain or in the nerves, muscles, or joints of the body. When these impairments are present before or immediately after a child's birth, they may affect the development of the motor (or other) skills that occur so naturally during most children's early years and lead to lifelong motor disabilities.

Susan's motor disability affects not just her acquisition of motor skills, such as walking, but also speaking, eating, and toileting. Her limited skill performance, in turn, influences the ways in which she participates in activities and routines at home, at school, and in the community.

Most motor disabilities are not static; that is, they do not remain the same throughout an individual's lifetime. Some children may acquire motor skills later than would be expected for most children. A child, for example, may learn to walk at age five instead of at age one, which would have been more typical. By the time that a student has reached adulthood, walking may no longer be possible or preferred. The individual may have learned other more efficient and less taxing ways of getting around, such as using a power chair.

Every motor skill has both a form (i.e., the pattern and coordination of the movement, the way a person moves) and a function (i.e., the purpose of the movement). The purpose (the function) of walking is to enable a person to get around in the environment, to go from place to place. The form of walking differs based on individual circumstances. People may walk with their legs held far apart or close together, on their toes, with their knees held together, or using many other patterns. Children with motor disabilities may learn a motor skill but may use a different form or pattern to accomplish the same purpose or function. For example, the function of walking may be achieved by propelling a wheelchair or by using a power chair. Children with motor disabilities may move from place to place on their hands and knees or by using a walker. They may use a walker in their homes or classrooms but may use a wheelchair at the shopping center or when outside on the playground. The more severe the motor disability, the more likely a child will use different instead of typical ways of accomplishing motor functions. These different ways of accomplishing motor functions are likely to depend on adaptations, including assistive technology devices. If a child's hands are fisted and difficult to open for grasp and release, an adapted holder may help the child to hold objects in order to write, paint, or draw. However, creative expression, a function of writing, drawing, and painting, may be accomplished using a computer with a mouse and appropriate software. Children do not necessarily use assistive technology devices naturally or without instruction. Most often, the adaptations and assistive technology devices that help children accomplish basic motor functions, such as mobility, communication, or self-care skills, must be collaboratively taught by occupational and physical therapists, speech and language pathologists, teachers, family members, and others who are involved with the child. See Figures 9–1 and 9–2 and read the vignette about Susan that follows:

Susan's therapists worked with her family to purchase a gait trainer that allows her to help her dad wash the family car. When Susan was an infant, she

FIGURE 9–1
When positioned in a gait trainer, Susan is able to help her dad wash the car.

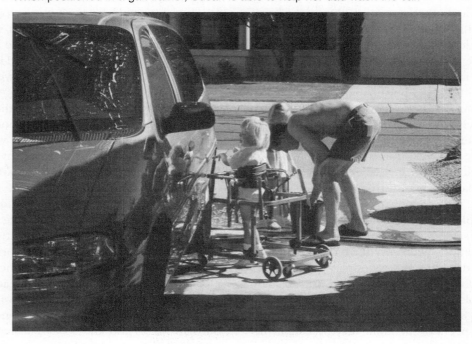

FIGURE 9–2
When Susan was an infant, she learned how to bear weight on her legs by being positioned in a stander.

learned how to put weight on her legs by using a stander while watching baby videotapes with her brother and sister.

Opportunities for individuals with motor disabilities to participate in activities and routines may be limited when the persons in those settings do not *expect* participation. Susan's father expected her to help wash the car and "created" opportunities for her to help. When adults, children's siblings, or peers do not create opportunities, the child with a disability may learn that nothing is expected, that it is better to be "helpless" (Seligman, 1975). On the other hand, when expectations and circumstances provide insurmountable challenges, the person may not be able to be successful and may have low self-esteem or an attitude of never being able to be "right" (Kunc, 1996). By using adaptations and assistive technology devices, a bridge is created between a child's abilities and the challenges present in the environment, which may result in the "just right" challenge where children can be successful. The goal is for the student to use movement as functionally as possible, even if the form is different from that used by typical peers. Adaptations and assistive technology are types of intervention that can facilitate successful participation.

The Importance of Weight Shifting to Movement Abilities

Posture describes the position of the body—sitting, standing, on hands and knees, lying down. *Alignment* describes the position of the body in relationship to the physical planes of space. For example, a person who is sitting in a chair and leaning backward against the back of the chair is in a sitting posture but is out of alignment. An aligned sitting posture in a chair occurs when the person sits straight, with feet on the floor and hips and knees bent at right (or 90°) angles. It is important to observe alignment when motor disability is present because the way in which the body is out of alignment is defined by the muscle tone differences, the acquired secondary motor disabilities, and the compensations that are being used to remain upright against gravity or comfortable in a position. Movement results when (a) the body is moved within the same posture, such as when a person reaches down to the floor but remains sitting or leans forward when sitting to reach an object that is past arm's length, or (b) when the body is moved through space, such as when rolling, crawling, walking, running, ice skating, or climbing steps.

All gross motor movements are made up of combinations of weight shifts of the body in different planes of space. Weight-bearing surfaces cannot move. To lean forward when sitting, the weight of the body must be shifted forward. To walk, body weight must be shifted from side to side and frontward. When weight is shifted, the weight of the body comes off of one part, resulting in an unweighting that allows movement of an extremity or body part that is not weight bearing. When a person is standing, for example, the weight of the body is on both feet. The weight has to be shifted off of one leg to allow the unweighted leg to move. The unweighted leg moves forward in front of the body, and then the weight has to be shifted forward onto that leg so that the back leg may be unweighted and move forward, resulting in walking.

Motor skills, such as walking, reaching, or getting into and out of positions, are made up of weight shifts. Particular weight shifts may be difficult for individuals with motor disabilities. A student with spasticity in the legs may have her pelvis and hips pulled backward by the spasticity and tightness in the hip or leg muscles and, therefore, may have difficulty shifting weight forward over the legs, which is a weight shift that is needed to stand up or be easily assisted into a standing position.

Spasticity in the hip and leg muscles was one of the problems that Mac had before her surgery, and spasticity is also an emerging issue with Susan, even though she is still young. Susan's therapists work to prevent the development of secondary disabilities in Susan's hips and promote opportunities for her to practice shifting her weight forward.

Weight shifts that are important for a child to learn and use should be incorporated into all routines and activities, including physical management routines.

For Susan, the desired motor skill of an anterior-to-posterior weight shift (i.e., moving the body forward and backward at the hips, such as in leaning forward or backward when sitting) was incorporated into as many physical management routines as possible so that, for example, when Susan was being moved from a chair, the person lifting her created an opportunity for her to practice the anterior-to-posterior weight shift by encouraging her to lean forward before lifting her. Susan needs to be lifted in order to be positioned in different types of equipment during kindergarten. When she comes to school in the morning in her wheelchair, her kindergarten teacher makes sure that Susan helps by leaning forward before she lifts her out the chair to position her on the floor for morning circle.

Barriers to Skilled Movement

The severity of the motor disability is dependent not just on the neurological or neuromuscular impairment, but also on the interaction between the limitations of the impairment and environmental challenges, circumstances, and expectations across the life span of the individual (Campbell, 1997). The degree of muscle tone and secondary motor disabilities are two barriers to performing skilled movement patterns (Stamer, 2000), while limited opportunity for learning and practice is another barrier (Larin, 2000).

Muscle Tone

Many individuals have motor disabilities that are related to atypical muscle tone. *Muscle tone* is a measure of the tension in individual muscles (or muscle groups). The term *postural tone* is also used to describe the degree of tension in muscles throughout the body. Normal postural tone provides sufficient tension in the muscles to hold the body up against gravity and to support coordinated movement into and away from gravity. Sufficient postural tone allows a variety of movements, such as reaching, which requires that the arm be held up against the influences of gravity, or rolling from the side onto the back, which requires controlled movement into gravity. Many functional movements are combinations of antigravity (away from gravity) and with-gravity (into gravity) movement. Standing up from a chair requires movement into gravity to lean forward and away from gravity to put weight on the feet and to stand up.

Some individuals with motor disabilities have *hypotonia*, or too little postural tone. This means that they may have difficulty with antigravity postures, such as sitting, or with antigravity movements, such as those required for moving from sitting to standing. Other motor disabilities involve too much tone, either in particular muscle groups (such as those in the legs) or throughout the body. The terms *hypertonia* and *spasticity* are used to describe the stiffness that results when the muscles have too much tension. Often, the body or an extremity (e.g., the arms, legs, or head) are pulled by the spasticity into the opposite direction of where the movement should occur. A student who is

sitting and who has significant spasticity in the arms may have the arms pulled backward behind the trunk by the spasticity instead of having the arms forward in front of the trunk, a position from which it would be possible to use the arms to reach outward. Combinations of atypical muscle tone are also possible. For example, muscle tone may be low in the head and trunk (hypotonic) and high in the arms and legs (hypertonic or spastic).

Muscle tone, particularly hypertonia, is influenced not just by the original brain impairment but also by environmental conditions, which may change tone to sudden stiffness throughout the body or in one or more extremities. An unexpected loud noise, for example, may cause a student to become even more spastic. Picking a student up from the floor without warning, for example, or using inappropriate techniques may activate spasticity (and make the motor disability even more difficult to manage). In contrast, appropriate physical management routines may maintain the student's muscle tone within more appropriate ranges, making the student more able to assist in the process and making the procedures safer and easier for the people supporting the student.

Secondary Motor Disabilities

A cycle that illustrates the ways in which posture and movement may become more abnormal over time is illustrated in Figure 9–3. The cycle shows the process that occurs when infants are born with abnormal tone or when atypical muscle tone is acquired through brain damage from accident or injury. Muscle tone, particularly in the head and trunk, is hypotonic for a majority of infants who are born very prematurely. Other infants with motor conditions may also have low tone in the head and trunk during their early development. Over time, many of these infants develop increased tone in the extremities and, to a lesser extent, in the head and trunk so that by school age they may demonstrate muscle tone that is described as hypertonic or spastic.

Various types of secondary motor disabilities, disabilities with which an infant was not born, can occur as a child gets older. The cycle of abnormal movement illustrates how children with abnormal muscle tone develop these secondary motor disabilities over time. First, reliance on body adjustments or on the arms to support antigravity postures may promote the use of compensatory movement patterns, leading to the practice of poorly coordinated movement patterns, which, in turn, may create secondary physical changes in the muscles and joint structures that may result in

FIGURE 9–3

Cycle of the Development of Abnormal Movement. This diagram illustrates the ways in which posture and movement develop abnormally over time. Deviations in postural tone result in postural adjustments that compensate for the inability of tone to hold the body upright against gravity. These adjustments, in turn, influence the kinds of movement that are possible.

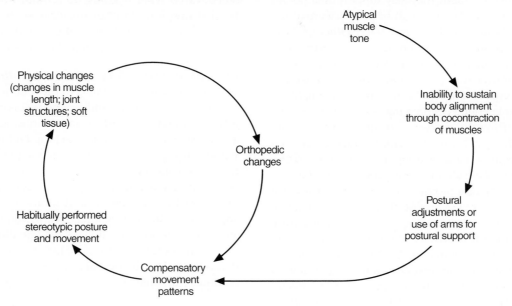

orthopedic deformities, which induce further development of compensatory patterns, secondary physical changes, and perhaps more orthopedic deformities. By the time many children with motor disabilities reach school age, secondary motor disabilities and orthopedic deformities have been added to the original motor disability that was present during their infant and early childhood years.

Secondary Physical Changes. *Secondary disabilities* include physical limitations in range of movement in the joints so that, for example, a child may not be able to fully straighten the arms. Limited range of movement may be related to another secondary disability that is present with spasticity, namely, muscle tightness. Tight muscles are those that do not easily stretch out to their full length, thereby maintaining a joint in a limited range of motion. For example, a student who acquires tightness and shortening in the muscles of the hips and knees so that they are in a bent position most of the time (as happens when children are positioned too often in sitting) may be unable, as an adolescent or adult, to straighten the hips and knees to stand, making it necessary for two people to move the student from a chair to the toilet, onto a school bus, into a car, or into any other position.

Some children have muscle tightness in the muscles on the inside of their legs that keeps their legs tightly together or sometimes even with one leg crossing over the other. It may be difficult for them or another person to move their legs widely apart or to turn their legs outward. Severe muscle tightness and limited range of motion may result in orthopedic changes. For example, children's leg bones may become dislocated from the pelvic bone when muscle shortening and tightness in the legs is severe. Muscles may also become overlengthened or overstretched. A child whose upper back is rounded may have muscle tightness in the shoulder muscles that pull the shoulders forward, thereby overlengthening the upper back muscles. Muscle weakness is another type of secondary disability that may develop from the limited use of certain muscle groups. Muscle weakness may be associated both with spasticity or with low muscle tone. Children with spasticity and underlying muscle weakness may still be unable to move well even after spasticity is reduced.

Compensatory Movement. Most infants and young children are intrinsically motivated to move; therefore, children with disabilities move in whatever ways are possible for them. Some of these ways of moving compensate for basic physical limitations. A common example among children with tightness in the leg muscles is that their knees are bent when sitting on the floor (instead of sitting with the legs straight out), or, if children have arm movement, they may support their bodies with their arms (see Figure 9-4a) or pull forward at the shoulders, as is illustrated in Figure 9-4b. Either of these floor sitting positions compensates for shortness or tightness in the leg muscles (in particular, the hamstring muscles). Another way of compensating is to use the arms to accomplish what the body muscles are unable to do. For example, young children may sit on the floor only when supporting themselves with their arms to compensate for the inability of the trunk muscles to maintain the body upright without arm support (see Figure 9-4c).

While each of the children in Figure 9-4 is achieving some degree of independent floor sitting, they are doing so at a high physical cost. The long-term negative outcomes from how each child achieves a sitting position may be forgotten when the immediate focus is on gross motor development or skill performance. The fact that a child has accomplished something independently should not outweigh concern over how this independence has been achieved. The child in Figure 9-4a shows increased tone (or spasticity) in the head and arms. This high tone is stiffening the top of the body so that the child is able to stay upright against gravity with the support of the adult. The child is not in alignment (or truly upright) against gravity but is tilted forward because of lack of sufficient extensor tone in the trunk. This extensor tone would straighten the trunk so that she was sitting on her hips (instead of forward of her hips, as is the case in the illustration). The preschooler in Figure 9-4b is able to sit on the floor without adult assistance, but does so with the upper back rounded forward, the head turtled or sunk into the shoulders, and the arms pulled forward to his chest.

The child in Figure 9-4c compensates with arms that are held out and away from the body for balance and stability. The sitting patterns of each of these children, while different from each other, all rely on adjustments of the body as well as use of the arms to compensate for low tone in the head and trunk. None of the children are upright and in alignment against gravity, although all of them are sitting. While these compensations make sitting possible, they also are associated with (a) increased muscle tone, so that the children are using spasticity to attain sitting; (b) posture that is not aligned against gravity; and (c) reliance on use of the arms to hold the body upright (making the arms

unavailable for functional activity, such as playing with toys or doing other things that would typically be done in a sitting position). Most children do not sit as an end in itself. Instead, they sit so that they can play with objects; watch what is going on around them; or move from sitting into another position, such as crawling, standing, or walking. These children with motor disabilities are able to sit, but are not able to sit functionally.

Preventing Secondary Motor Disabilities. A goal of therapeutic intervention is to prevent or limit the development of spasticity and secondary disabilities. From infancy, therapists work to maintain range of motion and muscle strength while teaching children to move without using spasticity. This is accomplished through proper positioning, therapeutic techniques such as active and passive range of motion, resistive exercises, or movement facilitation and motor learning–based approaches (Bly, 2000; Stamer, 2000). Even with the best attempts, secondary disabilities may be difficult to prevent. Thus, older children are likely to have movement that is limited by the primary disability, as well as by the secondary disabilities that have developed over time.

Even though Mac has received services since infancy, secondary disabilities were acquired. The amount of spasticity in her legs prevented her from being transferred easily from one position to another, so a recent surgical procedure was performed to decrease the spasticity in her legs and to allow her the possibility of learning to stand supported for a few seconds—long enough to be moved from one position to another. Even though the surgery has reduced the spasticity, Mac needs to practice using her legs for supported standing so that she can develop muscle strength and learn to stand as a part of moving from one position to another.

Adequate Opportunities for Learning and Practice

Sufficient opportunity to perform motor skills within the situations in which they are functionally used is necessary so that children can learn and practice movement. This means that a particular motor skill must be practiced often enough to become firmly established as "automatic." When a child is first learning to go up and down steps, for example, the required movements are thought out and made carefully and slowly. As the child goes up and down steps again and again, greater skill and precision result from the practice of repeating these movements. After much practice,

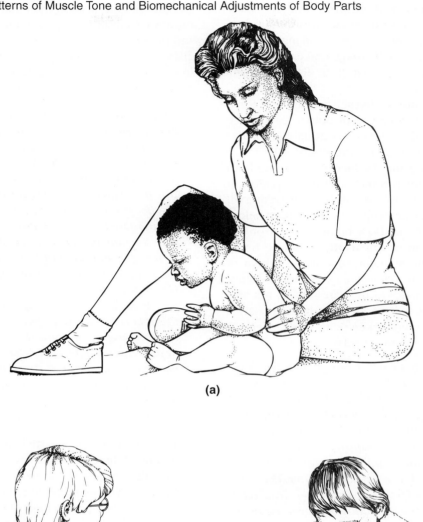

(a)

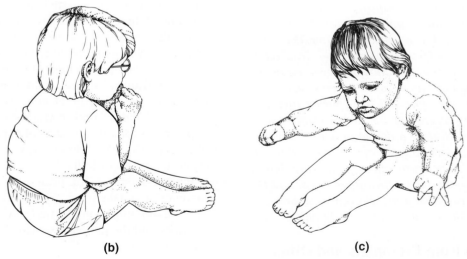

(b)

(c)

going up and down steps becomes automatic—a motor skill that is performed without even thinking. Many functional motor skills become automatic or are performed without conscious thought: walking, drinking from a glass, feeding oneself, riding a bike, playing volleyball, reaching for objects, washing dishes, or communicating with signs.

Individuals with motor disabilities can best learn new skills through practice. Opportunities for practice are provided by creating situations throughout the day where a child performs a specific motor skill. These practice opportunities may be incorporated into both physical management routines and participation in typical classroom activities. A child may be required, for example, to lift the arms up toward the adult before being picked up from the floor, before the tray on the wheelchair is put on or taken off, or before being moved out of a chair. By incorporating movement of the arms into many physical routines, an individual not only partially participates in the care routine but also uses the same motor skill (in this case, lifting the arms up) across routines, thereby practicing this movement numerous times throughout the day.

Susan's kindergarten teacher has created many additional practice opportunities. For example, she has all of the children lift their arms up many times during morning circle song, has incorporated this movement into the actions that children perform when listening to stories, and requires Susan to lift her arms up before putting on or taking off the smock that she wears during art and snack time. These natural opportunities for Susan to use her arms allow her to learn and practice functional arm use across a variety of situations. Because Susan's caregivers, teachers, and therapists all incorporate this arm movement into everything they do with Susan, more than 100 opportunities a day to practice lifting her arms are provided! This approach means that she will learn to lift her arms up more quickly than if she practiced only during therapy sessions, and she is less likely to develop muscle tightness and secondary disabilities in her arms and shoulders.

Getting Help from Therapists and Other Specialists: Working as a Team

There are people from many different disciplines who have specialized knowledge that may be helpful in planning how physical management routines will be implemented or in thinking of ways to promote participation in home, school, and community activities and routines. Helpful ideas may come from occupational and physical therapists; speech and language pathologists; assistive device specialists; and professionals from other disciplines, such as rehabilitation engineers, nurses, or respiratory therapists.

Susan's older brother Steven plays soccer in a community league. Susan has attended these games since she was an infant and may want to participate when she is old enough for the league. Although Susan will never run or kick a ball, there may be ways that she can participate in sports through the community league. Another sport may be easier to adapt for Susan's physical participation. For example, in baseball, she may be able to attempt hitting the baseball by using a T-ball support. Or she may be able to be on the swimming team, where adaptations will allow her to stay afloat and move her arms and legs. At the very least, if sufficient adaptations cannot be made to support her physical participation, she might be the scorekeeper, equipment manager, or timekeeper, or participate on the team in some way other than by playing the actual sport. Promoting her participation in a sports activity can occur when specialists team with families and coaches to promote participation in whatever ways are possible.

The activities that a particular person participates in are linked directly to settings in neighborhoods and communities where the individual spends time. When children are young, those activities are influenced by the decisions and preferences of their families, as well as by opportunity. Children who attend typical child care, preschool, or general education programs or adults who work in typical work settings have more opportunities for a wider range of experiences and social contacts than do children whose education occurs in special settings or individuals who are employed in sheltered workshops. The promotion of participation in activities that take place in everyday settings results from collaboration among the individual, the family, specialists, and the people associated with the particular activity or setting.

Susan wants to swim in the swimming program with her brother and sister in her neighborhood recreation center. For this to happen easily, collaboration must occur among the swimming instructor, Susan's family, and the specialists. The outcome of the collaboration is not to increase Susan's motor skills, necessarily, but to allow her to benefit from being in the swimming program (including the social benefits). Susan's participation will be facilitated through management routines for dressing, undressing, toileting, lifting, carrying, and positioning and potentially may require modifying the swimming setting or the typical swimming activities (see Box 9-1).

A Framework for Team Decision Making

Teams need a framework to guide decision making about children's participation and learning within the context of typical everyday activities and routines. Home, school, and community settings provide a context for specifically designed interventions. There are two general categories of intervention approaches that may be used for children with disabilities. One intervention approach relies on *accommodations and adaptations,* including assistive technology devices, for the purpose of making it possible for a student to participate in the activities and routines of home,

school, and community settings as successfully and fully as possible. The second intervention approach is designed *to teach new skills and abilities* by embedding specially designed special education and therapy intervention strategies (or techniques) into existing activities and routines. Both of these intervention approaches are more likely to be successful when there is a "fit" between the intervention and the requirements of the setting. Traditional therapy methods, for example, were designed for use within clinical or specialized educational settings where one therapist is working with one child at a time. These methods do not necessarily adapt easily or well to typical contexts where adult-to-child ratios may be larger and where the focus is on the activity as a whole instead of on individual student goals.

A first goal for all specialists is to ensure that a child is fully included in the activities and routines that characterize typical settings (Udvari-Solner, Causton-Theoharis, & York-Barr, 2004). This goal is generally best achieved through the use of accommodation and adaptation interventions that may not result directly

---

Box 9-1 Integrated Therapy

Until recently, most therapy services have been provided to students *directly;* that is, therapists work one-to-one with students in their classrooms, homes, or in other environments. In many instances, therapists establish their own goals (e.g., physical therapy goals) that may or may not be related to those established by a student's teacher or another therapist and then work with students individually or in small groups to provide the types of interventions that will assist the student to achieve therapy goals. More recently, therapists have begun to provide services to students by consulting or collaborating with individuals who spend the most time with a child, including teachers, family members, child care providers, and others to (a) promote a student's participation in home, school, and community settings, and (b) show others how to work on a child's or student's goals within these natural contexts.

Integrated therapy is a term that has gained increasing popularity as a way of describing an approach to providing therapy services for infants, toddlers, and students of all ages. Integrated therapy does not describe a particular model for providing therapy services but instead is a general term used to describe a variety of approaches, most of which share the following features:

- One set of functional goals are outlined on the individual family service plan (IFSP) or IEP, and various services or disciplines contribute their unique expertise and perspective to teaching and learning.
- Services are provided within the context of activities and routines that occur in various home, school, or community settings (i.e., students are not removed from typical activities to receive therapy services).
- All of the professionals in disciplines associated with a child's or student's needs collaborate together and with the family to determine priorities, plan and implement interventions, and monitor progress.

Other terms besides integrated therapy may be used to describe approaches with similar components, including *transdisciplinary, consultative,* or *collaborative teaming* (Orelove, Sobsey, & Silberman, 2004). Another term that is sometimes used is *coaching,* which emphasizes a therapist's role in helping other individuals, such as families or teachers, work effectively with students. Students who receive therapy services in an integrated manner appear to make greater gains in skill learning and have better skill generalization than do students whose therapy is provided totally through more traditional, direct one-to-one therapy in which services are provided outside of natural contexts (Giangreco, 1986). The important issue is not how an approach is labeled but instead that people collaborate and solve problems together so that individuals with motor disabilities may participate fully in life.

in a student's acquiring specific skills but that will allow successful participation in a particular activity or routine.

Susan's family enjoys and values sports. Each member of the family is involved in some sort of community sports activity, so it is logical that Susan's family would want to create opportunities for her to participate in sporting activities. Susan is interested in sports because she has attended sporting activities with other family members, and she likes to go swimming. However, it is not necessarily a goal for Susan to learn to swim or to be able to participate in swimming in ways that other children her age do. However, knowing the family's priorities and Susan's interest in swimming, specialists can develop the adaptation interventions that will let Susan to participate in the community swimming program with her family. Susan's therapists wanted her to learn to put her coat on independently, so they suggested that the kindergarten teacher use therapeutic techniques to help Susan put her arms into her coat sleeves before going out for recess and when leaving school. This approach did not work well within the kindergarten routine. Susan's teacher really did not have the time to focus only on Susan when so many children also needed help with their coats. Instead, Susan's mother purchased a poncho that could be put on easily by putting her head through the neck hole of the poncho. Having Susan wear a poncho instead of a coat was an adaptation that allowed her to participate successfully in a routine of getting ready to go outside.

A second goal is to use successful activities and routines of home, school, and community settings as contexts for individualized learning and practice. Routines or activities that are going well can provide a context into which specialized teaching or therapeutic strategies can be embedded.

One of Susan's goals was to reach forward. Opportunities for practice, as well as therapeutic interventions, were embedded into as many kindergarten activities and child care routines as possible. For example, in her "coat on" routine, once Susan was able to easily put her head through the hole of the poncho, her therapists showed her teacher how to use facilitation techniques to help Susan reach up and grasp the poncho and guide it over her head independently.

Specialists, families, and community program personnel can use the decision-making framework in Figure 9–5 to aid in making decisions about the best ways to meaningfully include students with a disability into their school and community, as well as to determine opportunities for addressing the individual's special learning and therapeutic needs. The process starts by identifying outcomes, which can be done by the student, family members, child care providers, peers and friends, teachers, or other people who spend time with the person. Person-centered planning processes such as the McGill Action Planning System, commonly known as MAPS (Vandercook, York, & Forest, 1989), or discussion with students and their family members also can help identify desired outcomes (refer to Chapter 3 for more on MAPS). Outcomes are not necessarily written as goals but often represent a broader context or framework for specific goals. For example, when parents and children identify desired outcomes, they are likely to use the context of their family's values, roles, priorities, and concerns as a framework. Outcomes may be expressions of what they would like to change (e.g., "I wish I understood better what John is trying to tell me" or "I'd like to be able to bathe Shawn more easily") or things that they would like to do (e.g., "We go skiing a lot and we want Stacey to be able to do this with us"). Outcomes generally fall into three categories: (a) participation in activities (e.g., go skiing), (b) better management of routines (e.g., bathe more easily), or (c) learning particular skills (e.g., communicate more clearly). When professionals identify goals for students, they, too, use their experiences with children as a contextual framework. This perspective typically emphasizes skills that come from developmental tests or other types of evaluations that they have used as a basis for understanding a child's needs. Professionals are more likely to identify outcomes and goals that are descriptive of skill learning (e.g., walk without support, eat with a spoon, communicate with peers), and if they use developmentally referenced tests as a primary way of identifying those goals, the skills may not necessarily be functional or necessary for a given student.

Mac was unable to hold a pencil or any writing instrument when she was younger and, therefore, was unable to independently do the seat work required in kindergarten. Her therapists identified holding a pencil as a goal, but then quickly revised this goal into a broader functional goal, namely, that Mac would

FIGURE 9–5

This diagram provides a framework for making decisions about whether and when to embed motor learning into activities and routines. A first step is to find out about activities and routines that may not be going well so that the routine or activity itself can be improved through adaptations or other means. Routines and activities that are going well provide opportunities for learning and a context in which to embed motor learning strategies.

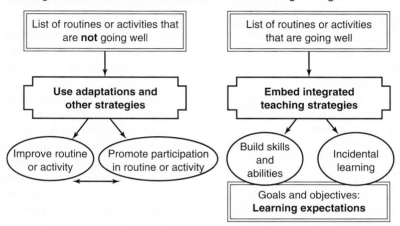

access a computer using a switch device so that she could do written work independently. Like other children, Mac did not learn to use the computer just because she was given a computer and a switch device. The best switch had to be identified and Mac needed to learn how to activate the switch and use different types of software; she also had to be given opportunities to practice. As she got older, different types of software were needed and, like others, she has needed instruction to use these new programs.

When Susan's family identified an outcome of participating in community swimming with family members, the school team working with Susan started by using the framework outlined in Figure 9-5 to solve problems regarding Susan's participation in swimming and to identify opportunities within swimming for her to learn and practice the goals and objectives included on her IEP. They viewed the swimming program as a setting with various routines and activities. The first step in their problem-solving analysis was to talk with the swimming program personnel to identify any activities and routines that were not going well. The second step was to use adaptation interventions (see Figure 9-6) so that Susan could participate as fully as possible in all of the swimming program activities and

routines. The third step was to identify activities and routines that were going well so that these could provide a context for Susan to learn specific skills. The fourth step was to decide which intervention techniques could be successfully embedded into these activities and routines so that Susan would have opportunities to learn and practice skills.

> *In Susan's swimming program, the routine for getting the children undressed, into their suits, into the pool area, and into the pool was somewhat chaotic for everyone. The specialists who were working with Susan talked to the swimming teacher and asked her to identify what was going well and not so well. The teacher thought that the swimming activities were going well but that the routine for getting into the pool was not going well. Susan's team then used the framework in Figure 9-6 to identify adaptation interventions to improve this routine and to promote Susan's participation.*

Adaptation Interventions to Promote Participation

The adaptation framework outlined in Figure 9-6 lists the types of accommodations and adaptations, including assistive technology, that can be designed to

FIGURE 9–6
Accommodation and Adaptation Framework. Accommodations and adaptations, including assistive technology devices, may be used to improve activities or routines that are not going well in classroom, school, home, and community settings with the goals of (a) improving the overall activity or routine for all children who are participating, and (b) promoting participation in the activity or routine of the person with a motor disability.

```
┌──────────────────────────┐
│  Use adaptations and     │
│  other strategies        │
└──────────────────────────┘
```

Environmental accommodations
    Adapt setup of environment
    Adapt/select "equipment"
    Equipment/adaptations for positioning
Adapt schedule
Select or adapt activity
Adapt materials and toys
Adapt requirements or instructions
Have another child help—peer sibling
    assistance
Have an individual child do something
    different (within the same activity)
Have an adult help a child do the activity
Have an individual child do something
    outside the context (with an adult)

promote children's participation in any activity or routine (Campbell, 2004). The framework begins at the top of the list with the least intrusive and generally easiest and least expensive interventions. These involve modifying the environment or setting where an activity takes place. For example, a student can be taught to maneuver around desks and other equipment in a classroom, or the classroom desks can be rearranged so that the student is able to maneuver independently. Other adaptations involve selecting or modifying materials used in the activity or altering the activity requirements or its schedule. When a student is provided with extra time to complete a math project, for example, the schedule of the activity has been modified. When a teacher provides a preschooler with easy-to-grasp crayon knobs, the materials necessary for art have been specially selected for that student. The framework ends with the most intrusive interventions, which are those that remove a student from either the activity or the setting (e.g., when a student is taken out of the classroom by a therapist in order to

work on learning to sit independently or when a student attends a special classroom).

While the adaptation framework may be used to promote participation in any activity or routine, it should always be used to guide decisions about improving routines and activities that are not going well. To apply the framework, teams begin at the top of the chart with environmental accommodations and work downward to the bottom of the chart so that students with motor disabilities are not removed from an activity or setting until all other strategies have failed.

Susan's special education teacher visited the swimming class and observed that all of the children and their caregivers did not necessarily get undressed and into their suits at the same time so that some children were ready and in the pool area before other children. The swimming teacher tried to have these children line up, but they became fidgety while waiting for those who were not yet ready. The special education teacher talked with the swimming teacher and they decided to try placing rubber mats next to the pool (environmental modification) so that each child would have his or her own mat and would sit down next to the pool when he or she was ready. In this way, children were not milling around, they were using a familiar routine (e.g., sitting on a mat), and they could still splash their feet in the water while waiting. The teachers also decided to have Susan come early to allow enough time for her to get into her swimsuit so that she was ready at the same time as the other children (adapting the schedule).

Individuals with motor disabilities may be prevented from participating in a variety of community programs when physical management needs are not easily met. For example, any difficulty in getting Susan undressed or dressed; managing her toileting needs; or lifting, carrying, and positioning her in the pool area or in the water may become obstacles to her participation in the swimming activity.

Susan's mother or babysitter dresses and undresses her in the locker room at the pool. The adult straddles the bench and sits Susan on the end of the bench between the adult's legs. By leaning forward, the adult is able to control the position of Susan's hips and pelvis, keeping them forward to prevent her legs from stiffening. (If her legs became too spastic, she would be difficult to control and might slip off the bench.)

In this position, the adult's hands are free to move Susan's arms and legs, using facilitation techniques taught by the physical therapist that make the activity of dressing or undressing one in which specific therapeutic intervention methods are used to promote the practicing of specific skills (e.g., reach forward, forward and backward weight shifts). After Susan's clothes have been removed and she is in her swimming suit, the adult places her arm under Susan's thighs and stands up, lifting Susan at the same time and positioning her so that she can be carried to the swimming pool. Susan's undressing is going so well that the therapist has suggested that Susan may be able to move her own arms out of the shirt sleeves when taking her shirt off or learn to stand up, assisted, from sitting on the bench so that she can walk a few steps assisted before being carried the rest of the way into the pool.

Only when routines are going well for a student can instruction or therapy techniques be embedded in that routine. For example, it would be very difficult to use the undressing routine as an opportunity for new skill learning if getting ready for swimming were not going well, not just for Susan but for all of the children in the swimming class.

The same process of identifying activities and routines within a particular setting (see Figure 9-5) and systematically designing adaptations (see Figure 9-6) was applied to resolve Mac's physical management needs during a Girl Scout troop outing.

When Mac was in fifth grade, her Girl Scout troop was going to visit a farm house—a hands-on museum about living on a farm. The two-story farmhouse had been built in the early 1900s, presenting innumerable architectural barriers to her participation. Many routines, such as positioning, lifting, and toileting, were going to be difficult in this situation. Obvious solutions were (a) having Mac miss the trip, or (b) having her mother go along so that someone would be available to lift, carry, and give assistance. Instead, Mac's mom and the scout leader used the process outlined in Figure 9-6 to identify adaptation interventions for promoting Mac's participation. First, they considered adapting the environment. While it was not possible to modify the farmhouse setting, it was possible to position Mac in her regular wheelchair, one that was lighter and smaller, instead of her power chair so that she could remain seated

and be moved easily around the first floor of the museum by another member of her troop (equipment/adaptations for positioning). The troop leader called ahead to tell the museum about Mac's abilities and ask about the activities that would take place at the museum so that materials and modifications could be brainstormed ahead of the visit. The troop made cookies in the farmhouse kitchen. Mac was able to slip her hand through the large handles of the old-fashioned cookie cutters and cut out cookies using a large breadboard that was placed across her knees (adapt materials). A partner used a spatula to move the cookies onto the cookie sheet. Fortunately, the farmhouse had a large bathroom on the first floor. Mac could be pushed into the bathroom and lifted onto the toilet. While she was not ideally positioned, the troop leader supported Mac from the front and then lifted her back into her chair (adult assistance). Mac is usually transported in her power chair in her family's van, which is equipped with a lift. For the farmhouse trip, she used a special adult-sized support car seat borrowed from a local equipment exchange program that her therapist knew about, and she rode in a regular car (equipment/adaptations for positioning).

For this field trip, Mac's needs were managed without her mother being required to attend and without total adult assistance. More lifting and carrying than normal were needed because all of the special equipment and adaptations that Mac uses were not available or possible at the farmhouse. Mac's therapist spent time one afternoon after school with the Girl Scout troop and showed the troop leaders how to lift and carry Mac easily and how to make sure that she was positioned well in her regular chair. This information was helpful for her troop leaders, who previously had not needed to lift or carry her because Mac attended the troop meetings in her power chair.

Specialists have information about ways to adapt environments or settings, as well as ideas about the positions that may work best for an individual with motor disabilities in particular circumstances. They also know how to adapt materials or change the sequence of steps in a routine or alter its requirements. Teachers, family members, and other adults who interact with students with motor disabilities may see specialists as sources of information and ideas that can help another adult manage physical needs easily and with limited effort. However, managing care routines easily and efficiently requires both adaptations and skillful use of techniques. Knowing how to lift a student, for example, is only one part of the process; the second part is carrying it out correctly. Many therapists have so many years of experience in using these techniques that they are able to do them automatically and with greater ease than a person who is just learning. When techniques seem difficult to implement, practice can help make them easier to use. Practicing any motor skill is important because it leads to competence, making the skill easier to use over time.

Many therapists are only now learning how to change their roles and to function as consultants to others (not just direct providers of one-to-one interventions). As consultants, therapists are collaborating with teachers and family members to make sure that students' physical needs are managed easily and efficiently. When specialists do not ask how routines are working or what activities are going well or not so well, teachers and parents must communicate this information and ask for assistance. In the absence of assistance, many families alter their activities because they can't figure out how to do them and include their child with a disability. When routines and activities are not going well, teachers and other professionals may view the situation as "unworkable" or "not possible," essentially excluding a child from participation. Another commonly used strategy is to ask for adult assistance in the form of a personal assistant for the student. In essence, adults have a natural tendency to start at the bottom of Figure 9–6 and work upward instead of starting at the top and working down. Teams of educators, family members, and specialists working with a particular student can focus on ways of making participation in typical environments possible. By sharing information and resources, collaborating, and using a problem-solving focus, the physical management routines of students with even the most severe motor disabilities may be managed easily and efficiently in practically all settings and environments.

When specialists help families determine how their children can participate on the playground or in the local park, suggest ways to go camping or what to do so that a child can go on the rides at an amusement park, or determine how a young adult can work for pay in an office setting or manage more independently in a restaurant, students' social and environmental experiences are broadened, as are their opportunities for learning. Similarly, when general education teachers share with specialists what is difficult within the context of their classrooms, specialists may contribute strategies that will make the situation successful instead of stressful. Problem solving by individuals with various backgrounds and expertise is important. Many of the issues that teams need to address do not have known solutions. Instead, the team may have to generate what seems to be an optimal solution (Rainforth & York-Barr, 1997).

Coordination of Services and Supports

Professionals from many different disciplines may be involved in working with and assisting individuals with physical disabilities. Physical and occupational therapists, speech and language pathologists, assistive technology specialists, vision or hearing specialists, adaptive physical educators, or recreation therapists are some of the specialists who may be involved with children with disabilities in addition to regular or special education teachers, paraeducators, child care providers, or other paid caregivers. One of the primary issues for families and people with disabilities is coordination of these services and supports, especially since the constellation of services and supports needed by individuals with motor disabilities of all ages is often provided by a variety of separate agencies, including schools, child care programs, or human services and home health agencies. Various team structures have served as a traditional way for coordinating services (Campbell, 1987; Downing, 2002; Giangreco, 1994; Rainforth & York-Barr, 1997), particularly in school settings. Coordination of services is required in publicly funded statewide systems for early intervention, but not for students in school settings. Service coordinators help families locate and use a variety of services and supports and coordinate these services so that they are provided in ways that help promote the progress of infants and toddlers with delayed development. In education, the teacher, special educator, school social worker, or the child's family may coordinate services. Plans such as the IFSP, used in early intervention; the IEP, required in education; or other plans, such as the individualized habilitation (or service) plan, which is for individuals beyond school age or those residing in various types of out-of-home living arrangements, help specify the ways in which services contribute to attainment of desired outcomes, goals, and objectives.

At times, conflicts arise because each professional discipline may view children's disabilities and development from a different perspective; sometimes these underlying perspectives result in different priorities or goals for children. For example, an occupational therapist who is approaching a child from a particular perspective, such as sensory integration (which focuses on ways in which the child is processing sensory information), may identify and view a child's skill limitations in terms of the processing of sensory information. The therapist in such a situation would likely establish goals to improve the integration of sensory stimuli as a means of enhancing a child's motor abilities. However, this same child's teacher may have as a priority teaching the child to write and may be more interested in adaptations, such as computer word processing programs that allow a child to write in spite of deficient motor abilities. The occupational therapist in this example is focused on improving performance, but the teacher is interested in improving participation in academic skills and access to the general education curriculum. Both professionals recognize the limitation in fine motor skills and the effect of this limitation on activities such as writing, but the occupational therapist is using a remedial approach to prepare the child to learn to write using a pencil and the teacher is addressing the issue from the standpoint of compensating for the fine motor deficits and writing limitations.

As Mac entered high school, the limitations that she had in writing became pronounced. Her writing was not easily intelligible and was very laborious, making it difficult for her to write as clearly and as quickly as was needed in her high school program. The occupational therapist wished to have her use a computer for writing but also wanted to spend individual therapy time working on fine motor coordination so that Mac's writing would ultimately improve. Her teacher wanted everything to be adapted so that Mac would not need to write at all and could participate in the academic curriculum via assistive technology. Each of these team members viewed the challenges presented by Mac's writing from a different perspective.

Sometimes different perspectives and approaches can coexist if professionals and families are working together. A physical therapist can work on unassisted walking as long as adaptations are in place that allow the individual to get around as independently as possible while acquiring the skills for walking.

Susan's family, teacher, and child caregivers needed her to be able to get from place to place without a great deal of assistance. Susan's physical therapist identified walking unassisted for short distances as a goal that Susan could attain and was reluctant to have too many adaptations used for fear that these would negatively influence her ability to walk. The physical therapist wanted Susan to be helped to walk without too much assistance, for example, when her parents were going from the house to their car or when Susan needed to move from one activity to another in kindergarten and child care. By talking with the family and Susan's teachers, the physical therapist learned about the importance of Susan's independence in mobility. She suggested using a gait trainer so that Susan could be independent in mobility at home and in school and also negotiated with Susan's parents to move the furniture in their family room closer together so that Susan could practice unassisted walking by moving from one piece of furniture to another.

The different viewpoints that may result from multiple perspectives need to be coordinated and integrated if students are to be maximally successful. Participation in typical activities and routines is critical, but participation is not enough to ensure improvement in current motor skills and abilities or the acquisition of new motor abilities. Motor competence provides a foundation for future development, learning, and participation and prevents the development of other disabilities that are secondary to the original disability and that occur as a child ages (Campbell, 1997).

While Susan may never learn to walk without assistance or use walking as her primary form of mobility, opportunities to practice walking are important so that she learns how to bear weight on her feet and move her legs to propel forward even short distances. When she is older, being able to walk with minimal assistance will be important as a way of moving her from one situation to another (e.g., moving her into an unmodified bathroom into which her wheelchair won't fit or into a stall in a bathroom or from one location in a room to another).

Many of the professionals who come into contact with individuals with motor disabilities do so for only short periods of time in that individual's life. One set of therapists and teachers may be replaced by a new set when a student moves from early intervention to preschool. Professionals may shift again each time a student moves within the educational system from elementary to middle to high school and then to postschool education or work. Families are the constant in their children's lives and are often the historical memory of what has occurred earlier in their child's life (Salisbury & Dunst, 1997). Families usually know what has worked or not worked, what has been tried with what result, and what may be easiest for their children. Professionals who develop positive and respectful relationships with parents and family members can learn a great deal about what has happened with the student before that professional entered the student's and family's life. Making sure that parents see themselves as "experts" with regard to their children is an important task for all professionals. Most motor disabilities are lifelong; they do not go away or decrease with age or programming. In many instances, motor disabilities become more limiting because of secondary changes that result from poor physical management, insufficient use of adaptive equipment or assistive devices, or overemphasis on independent performance of gross motor skills.

Proper Physical Management

The first goal of proper physical management is maintaining normal body alignment. Atypical muscle tone may allow the body to fall out of alignment with less-than-normal tone (hypotonia) or may pull the body out of alignment with greater-than-normal tone (hypertonus). The child previously illustrated in Figure 9–4b is being pulled out of alignment by spasticity in the shoulders and arms, as well as by spasticity in the hips. The hips have been pulled backward, causing the shoulders and arms to pull forward in order to allow the child to remain upright. The result is that his back is rounded and not straight (or aligned) over his hips. In contrast, the child in Figure 9–4c is out of alignment because she is falling into gravity. Holding her arms out to the side provides balance and stability so that she does not fall all the way forward. The result is that her spine is not in alignment over her hips and her back is rounded instead of straight (or upright)

against gravity. Postural alignment can be achieved with proper positioning and with handling that minimizes the effects of atypical muscle tone and maintains body alignment, as shown in Figure 9–4c.

A second goal of proper physical management is to encourage as much participation as possible by the individual and to prevent the development of secondary muscular and structural disabilities. Individuals who are being moved, fed, dressed, lifted, or positioned may become passive during physical management routines. Opportunities for an individual to physically participate in the physical management routine may be lost when full assistance in routines becomes automatic. Sometimes a major part of a routine may be difficult for an individual to perform and may take too long given the setting or situation in which the routine is being used. For example, a student may be able to walk to the bathroom with supervision, but it may require 30 minutes for the student to get to the bathroom. Students may participate within routines through communication, such as vocalizing that they are ready to be moved or using eye movement to look at the plate or glass to indicate what they might want next, or through small motor movements, such as opening their hands to have the spoon put in their hands before a hand-over-hand feeding routine or opening their mouths for the spoon or cup. There are many creative ways in which some participation can be incorporated into every physical management routine for every student (see Chapters 4, 10, and 12 for further discussion of participation in activities and routines). Many individuals remain dependent on others to physically move them because of the degree of their physical impairment. However, all individuals can learn the motor movement necessary to participate partially and meaningfully in one or more steps of a physical management routine.

The third goal of proper physical management is to move and position individuals in ways that allow desired motor skills to be used in as many situations as possible. Often there are one or more motor skills that are important for an individual to practice. These skills may be incorporated into several physical management routines so that many opportunities to practice are provided throughout the day. Incorporating motor skills into many routines is especially important for individuals with severe motor disabilities and for younger children who are just beginning to learn and practice these abilities. Students with severe disabilities are at great risk for developing secondary motor disabilities such as muscle tightness, limitations in range of motion, or orthopedic disabilities. Motor abilities such as range of motion can be maintained when children are expected to perform the movement numerous times throughout the day. For example, if a student has difficulty extending her arms the full length for reaching, if adults or peers hold or place objects away from the student, opportunities are created for the student to reach with her arm fully extended. For younger children who may be just learning a particular motor ability, opportunities for practice enable children to fully integrate the skill across various routines.

Physical Management Routines

Most adults lift, carry, or feed infants and young children without thinking how they are doing these things. When individuals have severe physical disabilities, however, caregivers must use specific procedures to promote participation, provide opportunities for practice, and prevent development of secondary motor disabilities. Thus, simple care activities become consistent physical management routines that, ideally, are used by all people involved in caregiving, including parents, teachers, paraprofessionals, therapists, sitters, nurses, siblings, friends, and peers.

Physical management routines should reflect both the environments in which the routines will be used and the physical needs of the individual. In developing these routines, the team of parents, friends, and professionals who are involved with the individual should also consider the efficiency with which the routines can be carried out (Campbell, 1995). In classroom or group settings, individual caregiving routines should not prevent students from participating in group activities or isolate students from their peers. Eating routines provide a good example. When a student's eating routine takes one hour at school and, therefore, the student eats in a classroom instead of a cafeteria, the social interactions that normally occur in conjunction with eating are lost, and the physical management routine isolates the student from his or her classmates. When even 15 minutes are required to reposition a child in adaptive equipment to allow participation in a kindergarten group activity, such as art or reading, the other children are likely to be completing the activity just as the student who has been repositioned is ready to join.

Ecological assessment strategies (see Chapter 3) can help teams establish the steps of a routine and the natural opportunities for participation (Baumgart et al., 1982; Campbell, 1997; Rainforth & York-Barr, 1997). Management routines are not isolated activities. They have beginning and ending points that link them with events occurring before and after.

Susan's team completed an ecological inventory (see Table 9-1) to help determine the ways in which Susan could participate in the eating routines in kindergarten and in her child care setting. The assessment process helped the team determine how Susan, who had been viewed as "needing to be fed," might be able to participate as fully as possible during lunch and snack times.

Physical management routines should be individualized according to a child's needs, but they also should include a series of steps that are incorporated into all routines (Stremel et al., 1990). These steps include the following:

1. Making contact with the individual
2. Communicating what is going to happen in a way that the individual can understand
3. Preparing the individual physically for the routine
4. Performing the steps of the routine in ways that require the individual to participate as much as possible

Making contact is important because many individuals with severe disabilities have disorders in vision, hearing, posture, and movement. Contact to prepare for a physical management routine may include touching, speaking, gesturing, signing, attracting the individual's attention visually, or a combination of these approaches. When individuals use specific communication systems, such as object cuing, an object may be used in conjunction with speaking to prepare the individual for the caregiving activity (Rowland & Stremel-Campbell, 1987). It is equally important to communicate what is going to happen next (e.g., "It's time to get on the bus and go home, so let's move to your wheelchair") in ways that the individual can understand. This may mean using speech and gestures; simple language; object cuing; or nonverbal systems, such as tactile or regular signing. A speech and language pathologist or others who know the best ways for a student to receive and understand language can help design optimal communication strategies.

TABLE 9–1

Ecological Inventory of Snack Time

Name: Susan		Environment: Classroom for 4 Year Olds			Activity: Snack Time
		Plan			**Observation**
Preschooler Inventory	**Inventory of Susan**	**Skills That Susan May Acquire**	**Skills That Susan *May Not* Acquire**	**Adaptation Possibilities**	**Assessment and Plan**
Children are at various learning centers and are cleaning up to prepare for snack time; children move to the snack table and seat themselves (time = 8 minutes).	Susan is standing in the stander at the art easel and is being cleaned up by the TA, who removes Susan from the stander, carries her to the snack table, and positions her in the snack chair (time = 10 minutes).	Use of a motorized chair to go to the snack table.	Transfer from the stander to the chair or walking device; walking; or moving chair with her arms.	Motorized chair	Equipment dealer has been contacted in order to obtain a loaner chair for Susan to try. Susan will be placed in a regular wheelchair and will vocalize to indicate that she would like to be pushed or moved and will point with arm movement to show where she wants to go. The TA will push Susan when she indicates and to where she points. Motorized chairs will be tried when available from the dealer.
Children wait while designated helper children pass out juice boxes, snack food, and napkins.	Susan is not yet to the snack table; her food is placed in front of the spot where she will sit.	Susan can get to the snack table on time if she starts out from the preceding activity earlier than the other children; she is already able to sit and wait.		Adapted chair is needed (and is already available); the chair sits on a wheeled platform.	The TA will start the transition from the learning centers to the snack area earlier so that time is available for clean up, transfer, and movement to the snack table and Susan is with the other kids.
Children insert straws in juice boxes, drink independently, and eat snack foods independently, requesting more if they would like additional juice or food.	Susan is unable to insert juice straw, drink from straw, or eat finger foods.	Eating using a spoon; drinking from a cup with a long straw (if held) for sipping; can vocalize to request more and can use large arm movement to indicate choice.	Using fingers to eat, especially with small foods; drinking from juice box using straw.	Try different cups; may be able to use Rubbermaid® juice box, which has large straw; needs shallow spoon with built-up handle; and a BIGmack® switch for requesting more.	Embed strategies to teach spoon feeding during snack time; work with teacher to have spoon-fed snacks instead of finger foods. Susan will use a BIGmack® switch to request more and large arm movement to indicate choice.
Children clean up after snack time by throwing juice boxes and napkins away; one helper child passes the basket.	Susan throws away her napkin (once she is able to grasp it) and can make large arm movements to wipe the table.			Toileting chair	

(continued)

360

TABLE 9–1 (*Continued*)

Name: Susan	Environment: Classroom for 4 Year Olds				Activity: Snack Time
Plan					Observation
Preschooler Inventory	Inventory of Susan	Skills That Susan May Acquire	Skills That Susan *May Not* Acquire	Adaptation Possibilities	Assessment and Plan
Children who need to use the restroom do so after snack time; others begin next activity.	Susan's diapers are either changed or removed if she is transferred to the toileting chair for training after snack time. These activities make her miss the next activity.	She may become toilet trained; learn to transfer from chair to toilet independently; and communicate her bathroom needs.			Wheel (or carry) her to the toileting chair and place her on the chair; undo Susan's clothes for her; sit her on the toileting chair for a maximum of 10 minutes, making sure that her muscle tone is relaxed. Encourage Susan to participate as much as possible. Give rewards for successes! Take Susan to the next activity.

Note: TA—Teaching assistant

Basic guidelines for each type of caregiving routine (e.g., lifting, carrying) that apply to all individuals with physical disabilities are discussed next. These guidelines must be individualized to suit a student's age, size, motor abilities, and ways of communicating, and the environments in which the routines are used. Table 9-2 is an example of a lifting and carrying routine written for Susan. This routine is implemented during kindergarten and at Susan's child care center in the afternoons each time that she is lifted and carried to another location. What works best for Susan's parents at home may not be as easily implemented by her teacher or the caregivers in her child care center (and vice versa because of the unique requirements of environments and people). Physical and occupational therapists are resources for individualized caregiving routines. Together with teachers and family members, written or picture instructions can be developed for how each individualized caregiving routine is to be implemented each time the routine is needed.

Mac's needs are addressed by a number of people, including her family and friends, people with whom she spends time in community activities, the paraeducator, and a number of teachers with whom she *interacts during a typical high school day. Mac carries her generic instruction plan (see Table 9-3) with her in the backpack attached to her wheelchair.*

Methods of Changing Position

Many different times during a day, individuals who are unable to move themselves independently may need to be lifted and moved from one position to another. Every attempt should be made to design routines that allow participation in whatever ways possible, however limited. A student who is unable to stand independently may still be able to stand briefly when being moved from a chair by using the feet as a point for pivoting the body from a wheelchair to a classroom chair or onto the toilet. A child who is unable to get to a sitting position by herself may be able to bend her neck and head forward to make it easier for the adult to move her into a sitting position and then pick her up from the floor.

Lifting. Several standard procedures are incorporated into any method for lifting to make the task physically easier for caregivers. All individually designed lifting programs, even those for infants and small children, should incorporate these procedures. In general, the rule is for adults to lift with the legs instead of with the

TABLE 9–2

A Routine for Lifting and Carrying

Name: Susan   **Date:** 5/11/99

Lifting and Carrying Routine

Follow these steps each time you pick Susan up from the floor or move her from one piece of equipment to another or move her in the classroom from one location to another.

Step	Activity	Desired Response
Contacting	Touch Susan on her arm or shoulder and tell her you are going to move her from _____ to _____.	Wait for Susan to relax.
Communicating	Tell Susan where you are going and show her a picture or object that represents where she is going. For example, show her coat and say, "We are going outside now to play."	Wait for Susan to respond with facial expressions and vocalizations. (Try not to get her so hyped that she becomes more spastic.)
Preparing	Make sure that Susan's muscle tone is not stiff before you move her. Use deep pressure touch with a flat hand on her chest area to help relax her.	Wait to make sure that Susan's body is relaxed and in alignment (as much as possible).
Lifting	Place Susan in a sitting position and lift her from sitting unless she is in the stander, where she will need to be lifted from standing. Tell her that you are going to lift her. Put your arms around Susan's back and under her knees and bend her knees to her chest so that you maintain her in a flexed position.	Wait for Susan to reach her arms forward toward you and facilitate at her shoulders if she does not initiate reach within 10 seconds.
Carrying	Turn Susan away from you so that she is facing away and can see where you are moving. Lean her back against your body to provide support and hold her with one arm under her hips with her legs in front. If her legs become stiff, use your other arm to hold her legs apart by coming under one leg and between the two legs to hold them gently apart.	Susan will be able to see where she is going and can use her arms to indicate location (grossly).
Repositioning	Put Susan in the next position that she is to use for the activity. Tell her what is happening: "Music is next, and you are going to sit on the floor so that you can play the instruments with Jilly and Tommy."	Susan is ready to participate in the next activity.

back by squatting down next to a person who is on the floor, holding the person, and then standing up. Lifting improperly may result in physical problems for parents, teachers, or other adults who perform this activity frequently. Back pain and more serious complications frequently result from the use of incorrect lifting methods. Younger children are lifted easily by one person. Older children or adults who are severely dependent may require two people in order to lift them safely.

A number of factors must be considered when determining methods for moving a student. These include the following:

1. The specific movements that the student is able to perform either independently or with assistance

2. The degree of discrepancy in postural tone (i.e., higher- or lower-than-normal tone)

3. The positions (postures) to be used for instructional activities and to which the student will be moved

4. The adaptive equipment being used to position the student

5. The number, size, and strength of the adults (or peers) who will be moving the student

6. The size and weight of the student

Individuals with severe discrepancies in postural tone (either very low tone or very stiff/hypertonic) are lifted more easily from the floor if they are placed in a sitting position before being lifted. Many children and adults are able to participate partially in a transition

TABLE 9–3
Generic Instruction Plan for Mackenzie

When Mackenzie's peers are participating in . . .	Mackenzie can . . .
Lessons at their desks	Be called on to participate Have a peer assist her in writing Use her computer Be involved in community-based instruction
Lunch	Eat with her peers in the lunchroom Be assisted by a peer to go through the lunch line (Mac needs help with reaching and grasping food items) Balance her cafeteria tray on her lap Use her eyes (eye-pointing skills) or vocalization to answer "yes" or "no" so that she can make choices Be assisted in eating and drinking by her friends Carol or Shawn
Changing classes	Use her motorized chair to get through the halls, especially if she leaves class a few minutes early Be accompanied by another classmate so that someone is available if she needs assistance
Using the bathroom	Use the bathroom on the first floor that has been specially adapted for her Be taken to the bathroom by a female student (Joanie and Susan are often available) Be taken to the bathroom by an aide Help when being transferred from her chair to the toilet (she needs a lot of physical assistance from an adult or another high school student) Use the toilet independently Assist in managing her clothing Wash her hands independently

Source: Plan modified from *Collaborative teams for students with severe disabilities: Integrating therapy and educational services* (2nd ed.), by B. Rainforth & J. York-Barr, 1997. Baltimore: Paul H. Brookes.

from stomach or back lying to a sitting position and may be able to hold on to the caregiver, maintain head position, or assist in other ways during lifting.

Many children are lifted from adaptive equipment, such as wheelchairs or specialized classroom chairs. Figure 9–7 illustrates the routine used to lift a preschooler with stiffness (hypertonus) throughout the body. The adult in this picture is kneeling beside the child, who is being lifted out of her adaptive chair. By kneeling next to the child, the adult does not need to bend over and place stress on the back. Instead, the adult will be able to easily pick the child up out of her chair and then stand up from the kneeling position. Physical and occupational therapists can work with teachers and parents to design individualized procedures for specific children.

Transfers. Many individuals with motor disabilities may not need to be lifted or may not require lifting in all situations. Standard methods are typically used to teach children and adults to move independently from one situation to another (e.g., from a chair to the floor,

from a chair to the toilet, from one chair to another). The specific methods used to move (or transfer) the individual depend on two factors: (a) the situation (the points between which the individual will be moving), and (b) the parts (or steps) of the routine that an individual can perform independently (Jaeger, 1989). For example, transfer is different from a bed to a chair than from a chair to the floor, and the ways used to accomplish this transfer would depend, for example, on whether the individual can use his or her arms to partially participate in the transfer.

Physical or occupational therapists should analyze home, school, and typical community environments to determine the most appropriate procedures for each environment and to help individuals achieve transfer as independently as possible. To be motorically efficient, transfer routines for each environment should achieve biomechanical advantage for both the person with a disability and the person helping, if help is needed. Two frequently used basic approaches are standing transfers and sliding transfers, both of which may be accomplished either independently or

FIGURE 9–7

Proper Lifting of a Small Child. Lifting a small child from a chair is easier when the adult kneels down next to the child so that the adult can pick up the child and then stand up by using one's legs instead of the back.

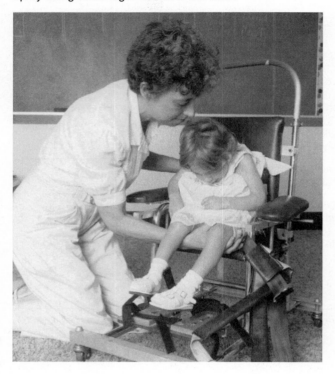

assisted by another person, depending on the extent of the motor disability. Standing transfers require a minimum of assisted weight bearing on the legs. Sliding transfers require the use of the arms for balance and support.

Carrying. Many younger children must be carried regardless of where they are. Infants are likely to be carried by parents and teachers more often than are school-age children or adults. Children with severe dysfunction in posture and movement can be difficult to carry for long distances, even when small in size. Instructional programs that focus on independent mobility are important to reduce the need for carrying as children get older and larger. Backpacks or "front-packs" can be used to carry infants, while strollers can be selected or specifically designed for infants, toddlers, and preschoolers. Wheelchairs and other types of adaptive seating can be designed for children who are older or extensively dependent.

There are several important guidelines for carrying infants and children:

1. The distance that any individual is carried should be as short as possible.
2. Routines should be designed to allow maximum individual participation, provide therapeutic management, and capitalize on biomechanical efficiency.
3. Children should be carried in ways that control muscle tone, achieve body alignment, and allow independent performance of selected movements.
4. Methods should be used that are appropriate for the size and strength of the adult, as well as for the situation(s) in which carrying is being used.
5. Carrying routines that require adults to use both arms for carrying do not work as well as those requiring one arm or use of the second arm intermittently because caregivers often need the second arm to open car doors or house doors, carry items (such as a diaper bag), or hold onto another child.

Carrying routines are best designed for the individuals who will use them and the settings where they will be used. Occupational and physical therapists can design strategies that will work for caregivers, teachers, and other personnel who will be carrying an infant or child. Illustrated examples of carrying routines can be found in reference texts (Finnie, 1975; Jaeger, 1989; Rainforth & York-Barr, 1997; Stamer, 2000). For example, a younger child with hypertonus (increased tone, spasticity) in the legs may be carried over one of the caregiver's hips to spread the legs and allow the legs to relax or become less stiff. A student with low tone and difficulty with head control may be easier to carry facing forward, with the legs held together and supported underneath by the caregiver's arm. When muscle tone is not controlled in some way, carrying children, especially for long distances, requires a great deal of strength and endurance on the part of the caregiver. Ideally, carrying routines capitalize on each child's individual ability to distribute his or her weight evenly and make carrying easier and more efficient.

Proper Positioning and Adaptive Equipment

The use of adaptive positioning equipment for proper positioning is an essential intervention for most individuals with severe motor disabilities. Well-aligned posture results from muscle contractions that maintain the body in positions against the varying influences of gravity. Increased muscle tone frequently occurs in response to gravitational effects on the body. An individual who is able to lie on the floor with reasonable postural tone may become hypertonic when placed in a sitting position or may slump. Such changes occur when the motor system is unable to coordinate tone and muscle contractions against the influences of gravity.

Proper positioning can help maintain body alignment and reasonable levels of postural tone by accounting for gravitational influences. Many individuals can be positioned to receive adequate postural support and alignment without the use of extensive adaptive equipment. However, most individuals with severe physical disabilities require at least some adaptive equipment to provide postural support (Breath, DeMauro, & Snyder, 1997; Rainforth & York-Barr, 1997; Trefler, Hobson, Taylor, Monahan, & Shaw, 1996). It is critical to take several precautions when using adaptive equipment:

1. Well-selected and well-fitted equipment can only maintain postural tone levels and body alignment, not produce normalized tone or proper body alignment.
2. Adaptive equipment maintains body alignment only when it is well fitted and when the individual has been placed properly in the equipment.
3. Adaptive equipment may not produce the specific results desired for each individual, so teachers, parents, and therapists must carefully observe the individual using the equipment over time and in a variety of situations to determine whether the desired function is being achieved.
4. Because many individuals with motor disabilities may lack the postural tone necessary to remain in static positions for long periods, the length of time that the individual is placed in equipment varies on an individual basis.
5. Restricting people to one position (even in equipment that fits well and is otherwise comfortable) can produce secondary problems, such as poor circulation or skin ulcerations, or secondary motor disabilities, such as muscle tightness or contractures that lead to deformity.

Teachers and parents should ask therapists to specify the length of time that each individual can be positioned in equipment. Some individuals can stand or sit comfortably for long periods of time (2 to 3 hours). Other individuals should be repositioned as frequently as every 20 to 30 minutes.

Positioning for Self-Care Routines

Positioning affects a child's ability to participate in eating, dressing, and toileting routines.

Eating. Well-coordinated contractions of the oral motor muscles result in appropriate use of the lips, teeth, tongue, and jaw for eating and drinking (Klein & Morris, 1999; Lowman & Murphy, 1999). Because the muscles in the oral-motor area are not able to contract in coordinated ways if the posture is misaligned severely, particularly in the head and shoulders, alignment through good positioning is the first step for implementing appropriate eating and drinking. Most individuals are fed in a seated position; therefore, alignment should start with the position of the pelvis and hips, which are the primary weight-bearing surfaces in sitting. The spine should align from the supporting base of the pelvis and hips to allow alignment of the head on an erect spine. Good alignment is achieved through proper positioning using specialized adaptive equipment where necessary. Only after a student is seated with good alignment will techniques specific to the oral-motor area be maximally effective (Lowman, 2004).

Toileting. Proper positioning is an essential component in effective toileting. Of particular importance are muscle tone, alignment, and postural control in the muscles of the pelvis, hips, and trunk. Reasonably normal degrees of tone must be attained for elimination. For example, individuals with hypertonus, particularly in the pelvis, hips, and legs, may have even greater increases in tone during toileting, thereby preventing elimination. An individual with low tone may lack the muscle contractions necessary for effective bowel and bladder elimination. Proper positioning can promote alignment while providing postural support. Therefore, as with other self-care routines, a first step is to make sure that the individual is properly positioned for the routine.

Adaptive equipment can assist a student to sit appropriately for toileting. Many types of toileting equipment are commercially available (see Figure 9–8 for one example). Additional modifications (e.g., towel roll supports or pads) may be necessary to ensure proper support and alignment when using commercial equipment. Most toileting areas in community buildings have been modified for use by people in wheelchairs through the installation of grab bars and high toilets to make independent transfer from a wheelchair easier

FIGURE 9–8
Adapted Toileting Chairs Position Students Securely and Comfortably for Toileting

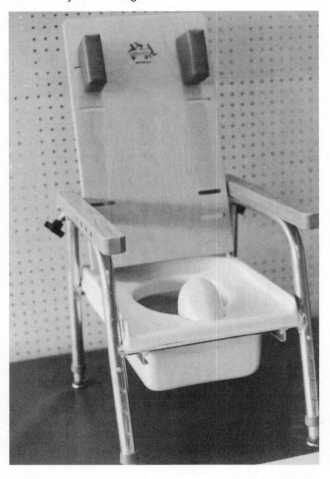

(or, in some cases, possible). These bathroom facilities, however, may not be easily used for children with severe motor disabilities who may need supports for sitting in addition to assistance in moving from their wheelchair to the toilet.

Mac is learning assisted transfer from her power chair (and her regular wheelchair) at school. One bathroom in her high school has been equipped with grab bars and with the special toilet adaptation that Mac needs in order to sit. Although she is able to lean forward and grasp the grab bars, she needs assistance to get out of the chair, turn, manage her clothing, and seat herself on the adapted toilet insert. Mac will probably never be fully independent in toileting because many of the places where she will need to

use the bathroom will not have the special adaptations and equipment that are required for her to become independent. However, as Mac learns to assist with the transfer, managing her toileting routine is easier for her caregiver. When Mac was much younger, her mother and her preschool teachers worked to teach her to communicate when she needed to use the bathroom. They used a BIGmack® switch, programming it to say "I need to pee" and making it available to Mac throughout the day. They also made sure that she drank a lot of liquids and that they knew approximately what times during the day she was likely to need to use the toilet. Then they asked her if she needed to go to the bathroom and prompted her arm movement onto the switch. As soon as Mac activated the switch, the adults lifted her from wherever she was positioned and carried her to a special toileting chair. They left her on the chair for a few minutes, using rewards and attention when she was successful.

Dressing. Typically, children above the chronological age of 12 to 18 months should be dressed and undressed in a sitting position. Sitting is a chronologically age-appropriate position from which to learn the necessary arm movements in a less passive position than back lying. Supported sitting, achieved either with equipment or with adult support, is necessary for individuals who are unable to sit independently or balance in a sitting position using the trunk muscles. Individuals who need to use their arms to hold themselves upright when sitting are unable to use their arms for movements in and out of clothing and should be supported by equipment or caregivers to allow arm movement.

A variety of adaptive equipment may be used to support students who are able to balance in a sitting position and move their arms and legs. Individuals who lack sitting balance or who require considerable guidance of arm and leg movements can be provided with postural support when positioned in sitting (e.g., on the floor or on a bed) with the adult positioned behind them. For example, by positioning a child in a sitting position on an adult's legs, the adult is able to provide postural support to maintain the child's muscle tone so that he or she does not increase muscle stiffening during dressing. Alternate positions that can be used for dressing and undressing can be designed by physical and occupational therapists, or examples are available in reference texts such as Best et al. (2004) and Finnie (1975).

Some activities, such as changing diapers and dressing or undressing infants, cannot be accomplished well with an individual in a sitting position. Changing diapers when infants or young children are lying on their backs is easiest. However, some children with spasticity may become stiffer when placed on their backs. Placing a small pillow under the head or applying pressure with the hands on the chest while bending the individual's hips and legs toward the chest may help reduce stiffness in the legs and make managing the diaper easier. Many children will be easier to lift and carry after diaper changing if moved first from a back-lying to a sitting position and then lifted and carried.

Selecting Adaptive Equipment

Equipment is available from a wide variety of commercial sources. Each piece of equipment varies in purpose, cost, and durability. Some individuals require equipment that is durable enough to last for several years. Others need positioning equipment only temporarily until they grow larger or their skills change. Because infants and young children are growing, their needs may be met most appropriately by equipment that is highly adjustable or low enough in cost to be replaced when they outgrow it. For example, an insert may be fabricated from triwall (e.g., cardboard used for an appliance carton) to help position an infant in alignment in a high chair. When this baby becomes a preschooler, a more substantial insert may be needed for the child to sit at the table for snack time at Sunday school.

When Susan was a toddler, she was easily able to be positioned in a wagon for transportation using two paper towel rolls to support her trunk (Figure 9-9). Now that she is in kindergarten, proper positioning is more difficult to attain. In Figure 9-10, Susan is sitting inside a laundry basket inside the wagon. Her position is so flexed that she is unable to use her arms well in this position.

Equipment must also be appropriate for the environment. Normal-appearing equipment enhances the

FIGURE 9–9
As an infant, Susan and her brother were transported in a wagon. Because Susan was not able to sit up independently, her mother positioned her in a laundry basket with paper towel rolls in order to keep her upright.

FIGURE 9–10

Now that Susan is older, she still sometimes rides in the wagon, but since she is bigger, she is able to fit in the laundry basket only in a position where her whole body is flexed (or bent). While she enjoys riding in the wagon, the amount of flexion in her body results in increased spasticity in her arms so that they pull in toward her chest for support and are not available for her to use for holding on in order to support herself.

social integration of an individual. Figure 9–11 shows a preschooler with severe disabilities who is learning how to ride in a motorized car to move around independently outdoors and in his preschool program. Another consideration is the extent to which a particular piece of equipment may result in the isolation of an infant or child from peers. Much of the currently available equipment for infants and young children has been designed for ease of use by adults or for use in classrooms or programs that are attended only by students or adults with motor disabilities. For example, wheelchairs such as Tumble Forms®, Carrie Chairs®, Snug Seats®, and travel chairs position young children so that the adults pushing them do not have to bend over. When such wheelchairs are used for activities other than just transportation, young children with physical disabilities are positioned higher than their peers and are physically isolated. Young children should be at the same level as their peers so that they can play and be together with children who do not have physical disabilities in child care, preschool, or community settings. Being familiar with major equipment vendors or with equipment available through catalogs can help keep teachers and therapists current on the features of various types of equipment that may be used easily in the community and in school.

Most individuals with severe motor disabilities receive equipment through a number of sources. Some physical and occupational therapists who work with the students in school settings suggest particular pieces of equipment and are responsible for securing and fitting equipment. Alternately, if an individual has been referred by a physician or therapist, seating clinics that are operated by hospitals and agencies in various states can prescribe equipment (all equipment or only seating devices). In other instances, equipment is purchased by families, therapists, or teachers who reviewed product literature and catalogs. Equipment that is paid for through insurance, medical health care plans, or federal medical programs (such as Medicaid) requires a physician's prescription. Some manufacturers and distributors help families and professionals secure the appropriate prescription and complete the necessary paperwork correctly. Seldom are individuals with severe physical disabilities able to use commercially available equipment without some adaptation. Parents may experiment with adaptations or may return to clinics or distributors to fit and adjust equipment. Physical and occupational therapists also may fit and adjust equipment. It is important to contact professionals when equipment does not position an individual adequately or when the body seems to be misaligned.

FIGURE 9–11
Young children who cannot walk can learn to use modified off-the-shelf child-sized cars to get around outside, on playgrounds, or in other open spaces. Michael's car was modified in order to allow him to operate it with a switch instead of the foot pedals that would be used by typical children.

The use of poorly fitting adaptive equipment may result in secondary motor disabilities, such as changes in muscle length or development of orthopedic deformities. When equipment is too big or too small, for example, the person being positioned is likely to be out of alignment. Being out of alignment may be uncomfortable and make it more difficult for the person to function, but misalignment also changes the length of the muscles or the position of the joints, resulting in the development of additional motor disabilities that were not present during infancy or the early years. The most common secondary deformities are those which involve the spine. Improper positioning may contribute to scoliosis (e.g., a "C" curve in the spine), kyphosis (i.e., a rounding of the shoulders), or lordosis (i.e., positioning of the pelvis in a tipped-forward position with a swayback).

The Purposes of Adaptive Equipment

Adaptive equipment has three major purposes:

1. Prevention of secondary motor disabilities, including deformities
2. Increasing the use of functional motor skills
3. Promotion of participation in activities and routines in home, school, and community settings

Sometimes, these purposes may be in conflict. For example, many individuals with severe motor disabilities are able to perform functional arm and hand skills best when in a sitting position, resulting in their being seated most of the time. Also, sitting may be the easiest position in which to manage a person with motor disabilities across many different environments, another factor that may contribute to sitting being selected as a preferred position. When Susan was beginning preschool, a

FIGURE 9–12

Wheelchairs are helpful for transporting children from one location to another but often do not work well for classroom positioning. Other chairs, like the one that Susan is sitting in, are adapted for good positioning and fit under tables or desk.

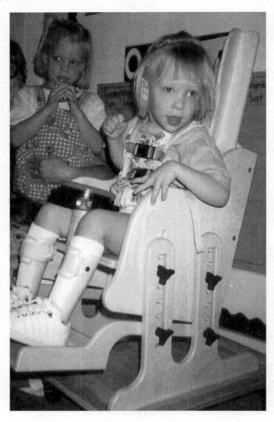

tions and types of equipment are necessary to place an individual in alternate positions to compensate and prevent secondary disabilities. Alternate positions for sitting are those that place the body muscles in an opposite pattern. Standing or side lying straightens the hips and knees and puts the muscles in the opposite position (extension) from sitting where the hips and knees are flexed. Alternate positions may require additional types of adaptive equipment. The functional appropriateness of a position in relationship to the setting and activity in which it will be used is of primary importance.

> *Positioning Mac, a high school student, in a side-lying position during art class is not socially appropriate, even though the position may work well for her and the equipment is available. Side lying is a good position to use for watching TV at home, for sleeping, or for just relaxing. Standing is the best alternative to sitting for a majority of settings.*

Most children with severe motor disabilities require several types of positioning equipment at home and as they begin child care or school. For example, they may need positioning for floor sitting, chair sitting, standing, mobility, and toileting. Many types of adaptive equipment are available for positioning; new types are produced every year (see Figures 9–8 and 9–13).

Physical and occupational therapists who are employed in clinic or hospital settings may not be fully aware of the environments in which adaptive equipment will be used. When equipment is acquired through a clinic or vendor, parents, teachers, and school-based therapists must describe these settings and the activities involved. Several pieces of equipment may appropriately position an individual; however, only one piece may be suited to a school environment, be transportable in the family's car or van, or work best in the home or in settings where a family spends time with their children. To find out after a piece of equipment has been purchased that it won't fit in the bathroom of the school or in the family car is unfortunate. Most pieces of equipment are quite costly, and seldom is their purchase fully covered by insurance or other health care programs; therefore, environmental factors must be considered before equipment is ordered, purchased, or fitted.

Increasing the Use of Functional Motor Skills

Teachers, therapists, and parents must select and use equipment that places individuals with motor disabilities

special adapted chair was obtained so that she would be functional in her school setting (see Figure 9–12). Even though sitting may appear to be the ideal position, when an individual spends most of the time in only one position, secondary disabilities may develop (even when equipment is well fitted and used appropriately). Changes in the length of muscles in the hips and legs occur frequently when an individual is in a sitting position most of the day. Tightness (or contractures) of the flexor muscles may result, causing the hips and knees to remain in a flexed (or bent) position, preventing them from straightening (or extending) in order to stand or lie with the legs straight. When any one position, such as sitting, is used in a particular setting such as school for most of the day, other posi-

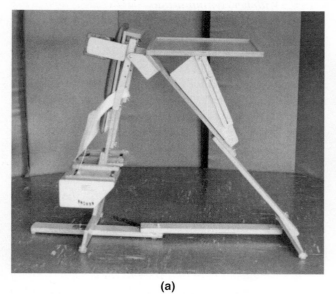

(a)

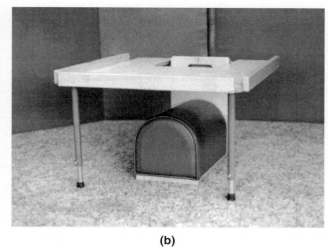

(b)

(c)

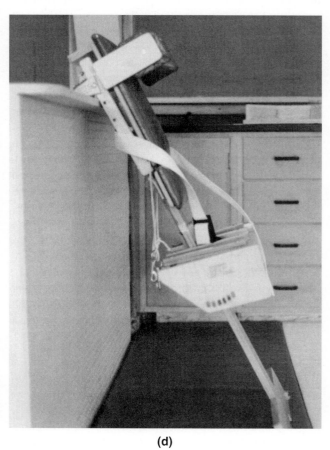

(d)

in positions where they can easily perform functional movements. When motor disabilities are severe, functional skills such as mobility, communication, eating, or class participation are likely to be limited by motor disabilities. Most individuals with severe motor disabilities will learn to perform these and other functional skills through the use of assistive technology devices. In many instances, arm and hand, head, or leg movements will be used to operate an assistive device.

Mac operates her power chair by using a switch interface device that is placed in her headrest. Her head movement activates and directs the movement of the chair.

Other types of switch interface devices, computers, communication aids, writing devices, adapted feeding equipment, or environmental control units are used by people with disabilities. Functional assistive devices enable a person to participate in the task or activity in spite of significant motor disabilities. There are many types of assistive technology devices that have been designed to provide an alternate way of performing a functional skill. Power wheelchairs, augmentative and alternative communication devices, environmental control units, or computers are examples of specially designed devices that use advanced technology to enable people with motor disabilities to be functional in many different settings. Usually, high-tech devices are not easily used without training, instruction, or practice in their use. In other words, a child does not just begin "talking" because he or she has been given an alternative communication device that uses voice output when activated. Low-tech devices (or adaptations) are as important as complex high-tech devices that are specially designed for use by people with disabilities, and they may be easier for a student to use, less expensive, and more useful across settings and activities. A power wheelchair, for example, is useful in many settings but will not fit onto an airplane or in many cars. Because of the limitations of high-tech devices, most individuals need a combination of high- and low-tech devices in order to perform functional skills across a wide variety of settings and activities.

Mac uses a communication device to express wants and needs and a computer, both of which are high-tech devices, but she removes printed paper from her printer by using a block of wood that she is able to grasp that has a substance to which the paper adheres. Mac is unable to pick up and grasp the paper with her

hand, but does so independently using this low-tech device. With her communication device, she is able to ask the paraeducator or the teacher to help her in the bathroom, and when she is positioned in her power chair, she can get to the bathroom independently; change classes by herself; and get to the cafeteria, the bus, and her after-school clubs and activities. Mac is not able to transfer to the toilet without assistance or manage her clothing, but managing her toileting routine is far easier because of the independence provided through her positioning equipment and other devices.

Susan uses a variety of communication aids, such as pictures and a single-switch interface, when on a class trip to the zoo (see Figure 9–14b). She also uses a simple device that holds her cup and allows her to move the cup toward her for drinking and out of the way when she is finished. She falls forward a lot in sitting, so when she is doing a painting activity, her teacher makes sure that she has an easel in front of her. Sometimes Susan stands to paint at an easel in the classroom and sometimes her teacher uses a cardboard tabletop easel that she has made by taping cardboard into a triangular shape.

Without sufficient trunk control to maintain an upright posture in sitting or standing equipment, many students may automatically use their arms to help hold the trunk upright. Using the arms for postural support inhibits them from being used for reaching or fine motor movement. A student may be unable to eat independently, manipulate learning materials, or even activate an assistive technology device when the arms are used to maintain an upright position (instead of being available for functional skills). Adaptive positioning equipment enables students to more easily perform functional skills, with or without the use of assistive technology devices, by supporting the trunk so that the head and arms are free for movement. Effective positioning (a) provides body alignment to prevent secondary motor disabilities, (b) allows for functional movement, and (c) promotes participation in an activity or routine.

When Susan wanted to paint at an easel or help to feed the fish in the kindergarten's aquarium, she was able to do so more easily in a standing position. The therapists and teachers decided that a gait trainer or supine stander would be most appropriate for this activity.

Standing equipment would probably *not* be best on the playground or when playing a game like baseball

FIGURE 9–14
Susan relies on different pieces of equipment and adaptations, including both low- and high-tech devices. When positioned in a walker, Susan can be close to the activity (see Figure 9–14a). In Figure 9–14b Susan is older and she communicates both by pointing to pictures pasted on her wheelchair tray and by accessing a high-tech communication device with voice output. She also uses a cup holder device so that she can drink from a cup when she is thirsty.

(a)

(b)

or when working with other children in a group table-top activity. Easel or mural painting, board work, or washing dishes may be more easily facilitated with standing than with sitting equipment, while independent mobility (moving from place to place) will be easier using adapted seating. A motorized or power chair enables a student to get from place to place but may not provide the best seating position when the student is doing class work with a computer; another type of adapted chair may promote better seating. Seating that transports a student safely to and from school may be inappropriate for classroom use because the student's movement, while restricted sufficiently to ensure safety when on the bus, may be too restricted to function in the classroom. Most individuals require a variety of positions and adaptive equipment not only to prevent secondary disabilities and deformities and maintain alignment, but also to promote functioning within the context of specific activities.

Promoting Participation

Many young children and school-age students receive services in schools and programs that are attended by peers and participate with their families and friends in many community activities. They may visit the firehouse with a Cub Scout troop, attend a birthday party at the home of a friend, swim at a community recreation center, attend church or religious classes, go shopping, visit amusement parks, go to day or overnight camps, see plays or movies, or participate in any number of other settings. In an ideal world, all environments and settings would be usable by individuals with motor disabilities. In reality, the necessary adaptations or devices may not always be available in all settings.

Mac can get to any bathroom independently in her power chair but often is unable to get through a standard doorway, which is likely to be too narrow to accommodate her chair. Sometimes when visiting a museum or another community building, she is unable to get in the building unassisted because of steps or ramps that are too narrow for her chair.

Because all settings are not fully accessible or don't accommodate all types of adaptive equipment, therapists and others need to design secondary strategies for overcoming these architectural barriers. Lifting and carrying routines may be needed in some settings even when individuals are independent in others. Partial or full independence in self-care routines such as toileting,

eating, bathing, or other care activities may be possible only through environmental accommodations, adaptive equipment for positioning (e.g., wheelchairs, toileting chairs, bathing chairs), assistive devices (e.g., grab bars around the toilet, adapted handles on the sink faucets, special plates and utensils, bars around a person's bed, a washcloth mitt), or other such aids. Students may be more dependent in a routine when the environment has not been designed or fully modified for individuals with physical disabilities or when needed equipment and devices are not available. When circumstances or settings are less than ideal, teams should problem solve for solutions.

When Mac needs to use a restroom in the community, her toileting routine is more difficult than when she is at home or at school. She still can communicate her needs with her communication device and, if in her power chair, get to the bathroom independently. Since her dorsal rhizotomy surgery, she can bear weight momentarily on her legs and feet, so it is possible to transfer her to a toilet using an assisted standing transfer, which can be managed by one adult. Before the surgery, her legs were so stiff and bent that Mac could not physically help in the transfer, and two people were needed to lift her onto or off a toilet. Once on the toilet, someone has to hold her in place, which is not necessary at home or in school, where she uses an adapted toileting chair.

Summary

Managing the physical care needs of individuals with severe motor disabilities requires teamwork, creativity, planning, and skill. Physical management routines include lifting, transferring, carrying, positioning, eating and drinking, toileting, and dressing. When these care routines accommodate the needs of each individual, they provide opportunities for participation and may also help prevent the development of secondary motor disabilities. Allowing individuals to participate in their own caregiving to the greatest extent possible may prevent learned helplessness, as well as make them less dependent on assistance from others.

Physical management routines need not yield full independence in a particular care activity; many individuals with severe motor disabilities require assistance in these activities throughout their lives. The purposes of these routines are to address care needs with dignity and in ways that promote participation, to manage routines efficiently, and to reduce the likelihood of secondary physical limitations and deformities.

Suggested Activities

1. At the beginning of each school year, work with therapists to assess whether each student's adaptive equipment is suitable for the student and is used properly. Answer the following questions:
   a. Does the equipment fit the student?
   b. Do the staff members place the student properly in the equipment?
   c. Does the equipment produce the desired function over time and across activities?
   d. How long should the student remain in the piece of equipment before being repositioned?
   e. Is the equipment suited to the student's chronological age and does it allow for a normalized appearance?
   f. Does the equipment isolate the student from an activity because of its size, height, or purpose?
2. Observe the typical routines that your students follow during their school day (e.g., arrival and departure on a bus, movement to and from scheduled activities in other locations, use of the restroom, change of diapers, change of clothing for physical education class, or use of the library). For students who are not independent in their movements or ability to communicate, check to see if the following four activities occur during these routines:
   a. The adult or peer makes physical contact with the student.
   b. The adult or peer communicates what is going to happen in a manner that the student can understand.
   c. The adult or peer prepares the student physically for the routine.
   d. The adult or peer performs the steps of the routine in ways that allow the student to have choices and require as much participation as possible from the student.

References

Batshaw, M. L. (2002). *Children with disabilities* (5th ed.). Baltimore: Paul H. Brookes.

Baumgart, D., Brown, L., Pumpian, I., Nisbet, J., Ford, A., Sweet, M., et al. (1982). Principle of partial participation and individualized adaptations in educational programs for severely handicapped students. *Journal of the Association for the Severely Handicapped, 7*(2), 17–27.

Best, S., Bigge, J. L., & Heller, K. W. (2004). *Teaching individuals with physical or multiple disabilities* (5th ed.). Upper Saddle River, NJ: Merrill/Pearson.

Bly, L. (2000). *Baby treatment based on NDT principles*. Tucson, AZ: Therapy Skill Builders.

Breath, D., DeMauro, G., & Snyder, P. (1997). Adaptive sitting for young children. *Young Exceptional Children, 1*(1), 10–16.

Campbell, P. H. (1987). The integrated programming team: An approach for coordinating professionals of various disciplines for students with severe and multiple handicaps. *Journal of the Association for Persons with Severe Handicaps, 12*(2), 107–116.

Campbell, P. H. (1995). Supporting the medical and physical needs of students in inclusive settings. In N. Haring & L. Romer (Eds.), *Welcoming students who are deaf-blind into typical classrooms* (pp. 277–305). Baltimore: Paul H. Brookes.

Campbell, P. H. (2004). Participation-based services: Promoting children's participation in natural settings. *Young Exceptional Children, 8*(1), 20–29.

Campbell, P.H. , Milbourne, S. & Wilcox, M. J. (2008). Adaptation interventions to promote participation in natural settings. *Infants and Young Children, 21*(2), 94–106.

Campbell, S. K. (1997). Therapy programs for children that last a lifetime. *Physical and Occupational Therapy in Pediatrics, 17*(1), 1–15.

Dormans, J. P., & Pellegrino, L. (1998). *Caring for children with cerebral palsy: A team approach*. Baltimore: Paul H. Brookes.

Downing, J. (2002). Working cooperatively: The role of team members. In J. Downing (Ed.), *Including students with severe and multiple disabilities in typical classrooms: Practical strategies for teachers* (2nd ed., pp. 147–162). Baltimore: Paul H. Brookes.

Finnie, N. (Ed.). (1975). *Handling your young cerebral palsied child at home*. New York: E. P. Dutton.

Giangreco, M. F. (1986). Effects of integrated therapy: A pilot study. *Journal of the Association for Persons with Severe Handicaps, 11*, 205–208.

Giangreco, M. F. (1994). Effects of a consensus-building process on team decision-making: Preliminary data. *Physical Disabilities: Education and Related Services, 13*(1), 41–56.

Jaeger, D. L. (1989). *Transferring and lifting children and adolescents: Home instruction sheets*. Tucson, AZ: Therapy Skill Builders.

Klein, M., & Morris, S. (1999). *Mealtime participation guide*. Tucson, AZ: Therapy Skill Builders.

Kunc, N. (1996, April/May). The right to be disabled. *Pennsylvania Early Intervention, 7*(7), 1, 4.

Larin, H. (2000). Motor learning: Theories and strategies for the practitioner. In S. K. Campbell, D. W. Vander Linden, & R. J. Palisano (Eds.), *Physical therapy for children* (pp. 170–197). Philadelphia: W. B. Saunders.

Lowman, D. K. (2004). Mealtime skills. In F. Orelove, D. Sobsey, & R. Silberman (Eds.), *Educating children with multiple disabilities: A collaborative approach* (4th ed., pp. 563–607). Baltimore: Paul H. Brookes.

Lowman, D. K., & Murphy, S. M. (1999). *The educator's guide to feeding children with disabilities*. Baltimore: Paul H. Brookes.

Mistrett, S. (2001). Synthesis on the use of assistive technology with infants and toddlers (birth through age two). Washington, DC: Division of Research to Practice, Office of Special Education Programs, U.S. Department of Education.

Orelove, F., Sobsey, D., & Silberman, R. K. (2004). *Educating children with multiple disabilities: A collaborative approach* (4th ed.). Baltimore: Paul H. Brookes.

Palisano, R., Rosenbaum, P., Walter, S., Russell, D., Wood, E., & Galuppi, B. (1997). Development and reliability of a system to classify gross motor function in children with cerebral palsy. *Developmental Medicine and Child Neurology, 39,* 214–223.

Rainforth, B., & York-Barr, J. (1997). *Collaborative teams for students with severe disabilities: Integrating therapy and educational services* (2nd ed.). Baltimore: Paul H. Brookes.

Rowland, C., & Stremel-Campbell, K. (1987). Share and share alike: Conventional gestures to emergent language for learners with sensory impairments. In L. Goetz, D. Guess, & K. Stremel-Campbell (Eds.), *Innovative program design for individuals with dual sensory impairments* (pp. 49–75). Baltimore: Paul H. Brookes.

Salisbury, C. L., & Dunst, C. J. (1997). Home, school, and community partnerships: Building inclusive teams. In B. Rainforth & J. York-Barr, *Collaborative teams for students with severe disabilities: Integrating therapy and educational services* (2nd ed., pp. 57–87). Baltimore: Paul H. Brookes.

Seligman, M. (1975). *Helplessness: On death, depression, and development.* San Francisco: W. H. Freeman.

Stamer, M. (2000). *Posture and movement of the child with cerebral palsy.* Tucson, AZ: Therapy Skill Builders.

Stremel, K., Molden, V., Leister, C., Matthews, J., Wilson, R., Goodall, D. V., et al. (1990). *Communication systems and routines: A decision making process.* Washington, DC: Office of Special Education Programs, U.S. Department of Education.

Trefler, E., Hobson, D., Taylor, S., Monahan, L., & Shaw, C. (1996). *Seating and mobility for persons with physical disabilities.* San Antonio, TX: Psychological Corporation/Therapy Skill Builders.

Udvari-Solner, A., Causton-Theoharis, J., & York-Barr, J. (2004). Developing adaptations to promote participation in inclusive environments. In F. Orelove, D. Sobsey, & R. Silberman (Eds.), *Educating children with multiple disabilities: A collaborative approach* (4th ed., pp. 151–192). Baltimore: Paul H. Brookes.

Vandercook, T., York, J., & Forest, M. (1989). The McGill Action Planning System (MAPS): A strategy for building the vision. *Journal of the Association for Persons with Severe Handicaps, 14*(3), 205–215.

10

Teaching Self-Care Skills

Martha E. Snell
Monica E. Delano

One of the first glimpses of personal independence comes when children start to participate in dressing and eating routines. When children learn to complete self-care routines, like using the toilet or getting dressed "all by themselves," there is often family celebration. For children and young adults with severe disabilities, the ability to manage personal care is also of paramount significance, even if there continues to be some reliance on others. A range of challenges, such as intellectual, physical, or behavioral disabilities, may slow, limit, or indefinitely postpone the development of basic adaptive skills. Sometimes lowered environmental expectations or poor instruction contribute to a lack of competence in self-care skills. Self-care skills can be more difficult to teach when students are older because of privacy concerns, social expectations, and competition with other learning objectives. Still, learning to be independent, or simply less dependent, in the

basic daily routines is a priority for all individuals with severe disabilities whether children or adults. There is clear evidence that, with instruction, students with disabilities can make progress in self-care skills and learn to demonstrate some level of independence from parents and other support providers. This chapter builds on Chapters 3 through 6, describing proven and socially acceptable methods specific to assessing and teaching the basic tasks of maintaining personal hygiene—dressing, eating, toileting, and grooming.

Before we begin, we'd like to introduce three students: Adrian, a kindergartener with autism; Toby, a third grader with an intellectual disability; and Patrick, a teenager with cerebral palsy who attends high school. Within the chapter sections on dressing, mealtime, toileting, and grooming, we will share the related issues faced by these three students and their educational teams.

✣ ✣ ✣ ✣ ✣   Adrian   ✣ ✣ ✣ ✣ ✣

Adrian is a five-year-old active kindergartner who has a love for computers and a diagnosis of autism. His early history of being a "failure to thrive" baby meant that he often refused to eat much and was overly picky with his foods through last year. Last summer, his parents enrolled

him in an intensive feeding program that greatly improved the amount and variety of foods he now eats. Adrian uses a daily schedule to structure his day and has learned to follow lists of steps that guide him through activities. He now participates actively in kindergarten activities, spending more than half of the day there. Like some of his peers, he struggles with handwriting. His special education teacher made a video to help him learn to sit on the rug with his peers during circle in kindergarten; he has now learned this skill. He used to be anxious about changes in the daily schedule until his team began posting pictures of who will be there that day (e.g., the occupational therapist, the physical therapist, the speech and language therapist) and what the lunch menu will be. Adrian checks this schedule several times a day, saying out loud who will be there and what is for lunch. He also eats lunch and attends library and P.E. with his classmates. Adrian spends part of each day in a resource classroom learning academic skills through a "structured work" procedure before using them in kindergarten. He is making progress in hand washing; following the kindergarten schedule; and using crayons and pencils to color, draw, and print. Toilet training is targeted for summer school.

✢ ✢ ✢ ✢ ✢   Toby   ✢ ✢ ✢ ✢ ✢

Toby is a bright-eyed, active third grader. At nine years old, Toby is diagnosed with an intellectual disability that resulted from seizures early in his life. He also has a primary diagnosis of autism and speech and language impairment. This is Toby's third year in an elementary school, where he spends a lot of his day in a classroom with other children who have severe disabilities. Toby uses the cafeteria line with peers, but all specials activities (P.E., art, and music) are taught separately from his peers. He is included with his nondisabled peers during recess, field trips, and assemblies. His weekly T'ai Chi classes include typical peers as well. Toby independently uses an object schedule to guide his day. He rides a bike around the school for daily exercise and gets and eats his lunch with minimal assistance. He does not communicate with words, but he is learning to choose tangible symbols to request preferred activities and to complete academic work using a structured work approach. He is making gradual progress toileting, washing his hands with sanitizer, and removing and hanging up his coat. Once a week, Toby walks with another classmate and a teacher to a local grocery store for community-based instruction. He has learned to walk to and from the store without sitting down on the way and to help push a cart. His mother now takes him shopping at the same store because she feels accepted there and the employees are accustomed to Toby. Toby will be moving in the summer and will attend another school in a different state. His educational team is working to make this transition smooth.

✢ ✢ ✢ ✢ ✢   Patrick   ✢ ✢ ✢ ✢ ✢

Patrick is in his second year in a post–high school program located on a university campus. At age 20, Patrick is tall with long arms and a big interest in others his age. Due to his cerebral palsy, he uses a wheelchair and communicates through a laptop computer with PixWriter™ and Speaking Dynamically™ Pro. Patrick attends several college classes, has a job delivering the college newspaper, and loves sports. He uses an adapted spoon and bowl at mealtimes and is learning to use a microwave oven to prepare his lunch. Patrick is in the maintenance stage of learning for several self-care skills, including as hand washing (verbal prompts to turn off the water and dry his hands), washing his face, and using a napkin. He lets his teachers know when he needs to use the toilet and does the transfer with assistance. His jacket hangs on a hook that he can reach and he is able to put his arms through the sleeves and flip the jacket over his head to get it on independently. His instructors support the maintenance of these skills by observing Patrick from a distance, providing him with natural opportunities to perform the skills, and using nonspecific verbal prompts as necessary.

General Teaching Considerations

This chapter is organized into five main sections: general teaching considerations and teaching the skills of dressing, eating, toileting, and grooming. In this first section, we address basic practices that cross all skill areas: (a) identifying what to teach, (b) planning how to teach, and (c) evaluating learning.

Identifying What to Teach

Self-care routines are part of all individuals' daily activities, and they have strong, lifelong influences on health and positive self-image. Family members often designate the activities of daily living as priorities for their children. If not performed by the student, these routines must be completed by someone else or medically managed if the person is to remain healthy. Progress in self-care skills provides a sense of self-control and accomplishment for students with disabilities. The attainment of proficiency in basic self-care skills (even with some necessary accommodation) allows students to be more independent and to meet their own personal needs.

Starting during the adolescent years, appropriate dressing and grooming skills are often necessary for acceptance in a peer group. The accommodations that are allowed and available during the school years often change when students leave school. Young adults who lack a high degree of independence in their daily hygiene may be excluded from many community, work, and living environments as a result. All of these facts point to teaching basic self-care skills during the early years. Identifying what to teach is the first step.

Team Input and Consensus

If you were Toby's new teacher, how would you identify what he needed to learn? His team members (including, of course, his family) and his current individualized education program (IEP) are the logical places to start. If his IEP happens to be one that the current team did not develop but instead "inherited" from another team or school, then its goals and objectives may need to be revisited by the current team. Skill selection is based on an inventory of the student's daily environments to determine which self-care routines and skills are the most important for the student to master and what the best schedule and settings are for instruction. The ecological inventory, described in Chapter 3, is the basic tool that teams use to identify needed skills and to select teaching methods. Ecological inventories use interviews with those who know the student and observations of the student to gather (a) information about the student's current performance on skills in expected routines (e.g., assist on most, assist on some, independent), and (b) opinions about skill priorities. Teachers, in collaboration with family members, related service personnel, general educators, paraprofessionals, and the student, use this information to choose which skills to target. They must pay close attention to the social, cultural, and age characteristics of the teaching procedures and the perspective of peers. The collaborative team makes many decisions about what to teach, how to teach, and how to improve teaching (Snell & Janney, 2005). A section of Toby's ecological inventory for self-care skills is shown in Figure 10–1.

Toby's teacher reviewed his ecological inventory with the team to identify priority skills. They discussed and

then reached agreement on several self-care skills. Because toilet training had not been successful in the prior year and Toby would be moving at the end of the school year, the team was intent on achieving this skill, along with pants up and down (Figure 10–2), and making progress on hand washing. These skills met their criteria for being high-priority skills (bottom of Figure 10–1).

Teachers. Special educators typically take the lead contacting parents and other team members to collaborate with them on the student's self-care priorities and current performance, writing task analyses, and measuring and keeping records of student progress on IEP objectives. Special education teachers also play a dominant role in providing training and oversight of the paraprofessionals who help implement self-care instruction. General education teachers must be involved as core members, too, because (a) their classroom activities and teaching schedule provide the context for assessment and teaching, and (b) classmates may be included as informal models for self-care.

Family Members. ~~Family~~ members and support providers can give the team perspectives that no professional members have, especially in the self-care domain. Involvement of the family or other support providers in instructional plans can encourage the student's use of the self-care routines where they are especially needed—in the home and the community—and thus facilitate skill generalization from the school to the home environment. Listening to the family as a valued team member gives others on the team an opportunity to learn about cultural preferences that the family may have, methods that have worked or failed, and difficulties that the family has experienced. Skills selected for teaching should meet *culturally appropriate criteria* (i.e., skills that family members value that are related to heritage, religious practices, and beliefs). These family preferences may influence the selection and performance of some self-care skills, particularly dressing and diet.

Adrian's parents were particularly concerned about his limited food choices. In preschool, he would eat only a narrow range of foods that his mother prepared or bought (e.g., Chicken McNuggets®); he refused to eat the snacks or lunches served at school. When the team understood the extent of the problem and its potential impact on his health, they identified an intensive feeding program at an area university outpatient clinic that he could attend to expand his food options. After two weeks at the clinic during

FIGURE 10–1

Dressing and Toileting Sections of Toby's Environmental Inventory

Student: Toby
Environment: School
Date: October 2010
Informants: Mother, teacher, teaching assistant
Methods: Interview and observation

Directions: First interview informants on the student's current skills in the domain and various environments. Then observe student, work with the team to target priority skills, and assess them against the criteria.

Domain: Self Management Environment: School	Performance Level			Component Skills					Comments
Subenvironment/ Activity	Assist on most steps	Assist on some steps	Independent	Initiates	Has related social skill	Makes choices	Terminates	Communicates	
Enter classroom									
Enters			X	X					Often with others
Takes off jacket		X					X		Accepts help from peer (Caitlin)
Hangs up jacket	X						X		Mom: This would be a useful skill
Greets peers/adults	X								Smiles when greeted by some; does not initiate greeting
Bathroom									
Toilets	X						X		Parents: We really want to target this skill
Pulls up pants		X					X		Parents: Would help if he could do this completely
Washes hands	X					X	X		Chooses hand sanitizer instead of soap
Brushes teeth (after lunch)	X					X	X		Hand-over-hand assistance; chooses brush and toothpaste Parents: Worried about cavities

Criteria Ratings on Target Skills

Criteria	Activity				Y = Yes N = No
	Takes jacket off and hangs it up	Toilets	Washes hands	Brushes teeth	Greets
Does the objective reflect the student's chronological age, culture, and preferences?	Y	Y	Y	Y	Y
Is the skill one that the student needs now and in the future across settings?	Y	Y	Y	Y	Y
Will this skill increase the student's independence?	Y	Y	Y	Y	Y
Do team members have consensus on the value of this skill?	Y	Y	Y	Y	Y

FIGURE 10–2
When Toby hooks his thumbs inside his waistband, he is successful pushing down and pulling up his pants.

(a)

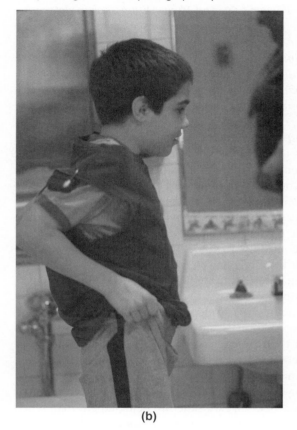

(b)

the summer, Adrian made significant progress. Teachers followed the clinic's suggestions for expanding the foods that he would eat at school. By November, he was eating school lunches.

Related Support Providers. When self-care skills are a priority, related services professionals make essential contributions for many students. Occupational therapists (OTs) have expertise in the activities of daily living and the fine motor movements required. OTs also can provide helpful assessment and input when students exhibit increased sensitivity to tactile or oral stimuli. Physical therapists (PTs) are sources of knowledge on adaptive equipment and positioning, which both influence skill performance. Speech and language therapists (SLTs) have expertise in oral musculature that may be useful in the evaluation of eating and oral hygiene activities. School nurses may confer with families or directly assess nutrition, bowel and bladder characteristics, and health concerns (e.g.,

seizure disorders, urinary tract infections, sensory limitations); they also may consult with the student's physician.

Most teams agree that related support services are best provided in an integrated, transdisciplinary model. Transdisciplinary services mean that decision-making and teaching roles are shared instead of having some team members make recommendations as experts. An integrated approach supports the assessment and implementation of therapy during natural self-care opportunities throughout the day (Cloninger, 2004). The integrated therapy model (a) has been shown to be effective for student learning, (b) may facilitate better skill generalization, and (c) is preferred by teachers and related services staff (Paul-Brown & Caperton, 2001; Scott, McWilliam, & Mayhew, 1999).

Toby's OT observes him during arrival and tries out methods for encouraging him to participate more in hanging up his coat. During team planning, ideas are discussed and adjusted so that they are feasible for all to use.

Patrick's OT and PT work together to determine the best way for him to use the rest room at his job site, at the football stadium, and at the two restaurants on campus that he frequents. They have advised building owners of ways to modify the bathrooms so that Patrick and other wheelchair users can access the toilets and sinks.

Paraprofessionals. Paraprofessionals, also referred to as teaching assistants, are crucial members of the student's educational team. Their role as instructors has continued to increase. Students who are not independent in self-care routines require assistance during the day that often is provided by paraprofessionals. While paraprofessionals with instructional experience can contribute to student progress, problems can also result from relying too much on them for instruction. For example, some studies have found that (a) paraprofessionals often lack the skills needed to be effective instructors; (b) students may become too reliant on paraprofessionals; and (c) students may be separated from their peers, have fewer opportunities to make choices, and have reduced personal control (Giangreco, Edelman, Luiselli, & MacFarland, 1997; Giangreco, Suter, & Doyle, in press). These difficulties are perhaps more likely when self-care skills are being taught than when academic, communication, or social skills are being taught because so many self-care skills must be taught in private. Thus, paraprofessionals are less easily supervised. There is agreement that the use of several team practices can reduce these problems (Giangreco et al., in press). First, paraprofessionals need training in order to be effective instructors, including such areas as general instructional principles, how to teach and support specific students, how to work on the team, and confidentiality (Doyle, 2008). Second, paraprofessionals can benefit from learning to respect students' preferences and to maximize students' personal control during self-care routines. This means teaching self-care routines while being mindful of the individaul student rather than "doing" self-care for the student. Improving paraprofessionals' involvement as team members allows them to contribute to program development, may improve their motivation for using teaching plans, and can provide information that is meaningful for team decisions (Doyle, 2008; Giangreco et al., in press; Riggs, 2004). Finally, paraprofessionals need and deserve regular supervision and feedback from teachers on their work with students; because self-care skill instruction

does not take place in the open classroom, observation times must be arranged. Sometimes, as a supplement to less frequent direct supervision, teachers can rotate their schedules so that they cycle through the schedules of their teaching assistants; this practice allows teachers to get another perspective on the teaching assistant's work, but does not create the scheduling difficulties caused by direct instruction.

Criteria for Selecting Self-Care Skills

Like all other domains of learning, the self-care skills that the team selects as IEP objectives for students must meet four criteria. Targeted self-help skills should be (a) skills that are judged as functional for a student and valued by the team; (b) suited to the teaching setting; (c) appropriate for the student's chronological age, peer standards, and culture; and (d) possible to acquire within a year.

Select Self-Help Skills That Are Functional for the Student. It is important that the assessment process (see Chapter 3) identifies those skills that a student needs. The scope and sequence charts in the Syracuse Curriculum break down self-care skills by typical age and location of performance, with shaded sections of the curriculum listing skills performed during nonschool hours (Ford et al., 1989, pp. 324–340); this organizational approach helps to pinpoint relevant self-care skill clusters. (The charts for hygiene and toileting are shown in Figure 10–3.) *Needed skills* are further defined through an ecological inventory as being important for a student to learn now or soon (see Figure 10-1). If too many skills are identified by the team as being needed, then team members must work together to prioritize them by necessity, asking a series of questions about each skill under consideration and then selecting those ranked more highly. Questions can include the following: Is this skill needed now? Will this skill be needed in the future? Can this skill be used across environments and activities? Will having this skill contribute to independence? Will this skill contribute to acceptance by peers? Will the absence of this skill contribute to being less accepted by peers? Is this a skill that the family rates as a top priority? Does this skill meet a medical need? Does the student have a positive attitude toward learning this skill?

The self-care priorities that are written into a student's IEP are those that are valued by all members, including the family; team members agree that the student would benefit from learning a particular skill over

FIGURE 10–3

Scope and Sequence for the Self-Management Home/Living Goal Area, Section on Hygiene and Toileting

Goal Areas	Kindergarten (Age 5)	Elementary School		Middle School (Ages 12–14)	High School (Ages 15–18)	Transition (Ages 19–21)
		Primary Grades (Ages 6–8)	Intermediate Grades (Ages 9–11)			
Hygiene and toileting (Instruction during school hours)	Use private and public toilets Wash hands and face with reminders Blow nose and dispose of tissue with reminders	Use private and public toilets Wash hands and face: Routine time (e.g., after toilet, before eating) Blow nose and dispose of tissue as needed	Use private and public toilets Wash hands and face: Routine times and for specific activities (e.g., food preparation) Follow acceptable hygiene practices	Use private and public toilets Wash hands and face: Routine times and for specific activities (e.g., food preparation) Follow acceptable hygiene practices Manage menstrual care	Use private and public toilets Wash hands and face: routine times and for specific activities (food preparation) Follow acceptable hygiene practices Manage menstrual care	Use private and public toilets Wash hands and face Follow acceptable hygiene practices Manage menstrual care
(Instruction during non-school hours)	Brush teeth Bathe Shampoo hair	Brush teeth Shower/bathe Shampoo hair	Brush and floss teeth Shower/bathe Shampoo hair Clean and clip nails	Brush and floss teeth Shower/bathe Shampoo hair Clean and clip nails Wear deodorant Shave	Brush and floss teeth Shower/bathe Shampoo hair Clean and clip nails Wear deodorant Shave	Brush and floss teeth Shower/bathe Shampoo hair Clean and clip nails Wear deodorant Shave

Source: Ford, A., Schnorr, R., Meyer, L., Davern, L., Black, J., & Dempsey, P. (1989). *The Syracuse community-referenced curriculum guide* (pp. 325–326). Baltimore: Paul H. Brookes.

another. Anderson and his colleagues developed a self-help skills inventory that provides a useful structure for teams to survey students' current performance of self-care skills (Anderson, Jablonski, Thomeer, & Knapp, 2007). A version of this inventory was used by Adrian's team (see Figure 10–4).

Adrian's team discussed and together completed a set of five questions on self-care skills that they thought would be functional to teach at school. His profile gave the team confidence that these skills were crucial.

Select Self-Help Skills That Are Suited to the Teaching Setting. Teams should select skills that are *suited to the teaching setting* so that there will be adequate opportunities for instruction. Sometimes teaching opportunities can be expanded so that teaching is more frequent and is integrated into ongoing routines. For example, Sewell and her colleagues taught preschoolers to dress and undress in the context of natural opportunities such as putting on and taking off smocks for painting, jackets for recess and arrival, and dress-up clothes at centers time (Sewell, Collins, Hemmeter, & Schuster, 1998). Dressing, showering, and hair care, if priority skills, can be taught in middle or high school following P.E. Certain self-care skills, such as toileting and brushing teeth, are best taught during the preschool years when natural teaching opportunities are easily arranged.

Select Self-Help Skills That Are Chronologically Age Appropriate. Self-care routines targeted for instruction, as well as the procedures for instruction and monitoring progress, should be age and culturally appropriate. Skills are *chronologically age appropriate* for a student if they are performed by others of the same age. The specific ways that skills are accomplished, as well as the materials and setting used, also can be influenced by a student's age. Using the flip-over-the-head method to put on a jacket might be

FIGURE 10–4
Questions That Help Teams Identify Functional Skills to be Taught

Identifying Functional Skills for Adrian to Learn Now	Coat On and Off	Pants Up and Down	Blow Nose	Toileting	Brush Teeth
1. Does the absence of the skill prevent Adrian from fully participating in activities with peers or siblings (e.g., inability to swim in public because not toilet trained)?	YES	YES	YES	YES	NO
2. Does not doing the skill for Adrian underscore his weaknesses and lead to his being less accepted by peers (e.g., requires help in the bathroom)?	YES	YES	YES	YES	NO
3. Is the skill necessary or important for teaching another skill (e.g., pulling pants up and down is important for toilet training)?	YES	YES	NO	NO	YES
4. Is this a still that must be performed independently in public (e.g., when Adrian becomes too old to accompany his mother into a public bathroom?)	YES	YES	YES	YES	NO
5. Is this a skill that, when absent, may create embarrassment for Adrian or his family?	YES	YES	YES	YES	YES
6. Is this a skill that, when absent, may result in noticeable messiness, unsanitary conditions, or create health concerns (e.g., not knowing how to blow nose)?	YES	YES	YES	YES	YES

(Adapted from Anderson, Jablonski, Tomeer, and Knapp, 2007, p. 22)

appropriate for preschoolers but is less so for older students; thus, teams need to decide if an "age bound" method should be selected temporarily or simply avoided. Whether a particular skill becomes a priority also may be determined by a student's chronological age. For example, *completely independent* toileting is not an appropriate goal for a preschool or kindergarten-aged child since typical children of this age receive assistance from parents or siblings in public toilets, with soap and towel dispensers, and even with getting on and off the toilet and manipulating doors because of the height, size, and novelty of the equipment. However, when students in elementary and middle school are still dependent on others for toileting, eating, and grooming assistance, their differences may isolate them from their peers.

Select Self-Help Skills That Can be Acquired in One Year. Predicting how long it will take for a student to learn a target skill relates both to the student's learning history and the student's current level of performance or stage of learning. Thus, to select skills that are *possible for a student to learn* within a year,

the team will identify IEP objectives that build on the student's present level of performance (PLOP) and then adjust the criteria so that the objectives are feasible to attain before the next IEP is written. (For most of the students that we are discussing in this chapter, this criterion means learning a skill within a year.) The four stages of learning include the following (see Chapter 4):

- *Acquisition:* Student performs less than 60% of the skill. Teaching focuses on learning enough of the skill to be an active participant instead of attaining mastery (e.g., completes the core steps of hand washing).
- *Maintenance:* Student carries out a skill routinely. Teaching focuses on performing the skill completely and habitually during daily scheduled opportunities (e.g., washes hands before lunch, after artwork, after toileting).
- *Fluency/Proficiency:* Student performs a skill smoothly at the right speed and without crucial errors. Teaching focuses on speeding up and perfecting performance (e.g., washes hands completely and without delay, playing in the water, or forgetting to dry hands with paper towel).

- *Generalization:* Student uses a skill across changing conditions (e.g., setting, people, materials, time of day). Teaching focuses on using the skill whenever and wherever it is needed (e.g., successfully uses the three different types of soap dispenser and two paper towel machines located in the elementary school bathrooms).

Sometimes priority self-care skills are age appropriate but are too difficult for a student to learn, such as shoe tying for many younger elementary school students. In such cases, the team may choose a goal of *partial participation* (Baumgart et al., 1982) instead of total participation in an ordinary manner. Partial participation refers to the process of teaching the student to do as much of a task as he or she can independently, while getting support for some steps through adapted materials, automated devices, changed sequences, or personal assistance. Partial participation goals should take less time to master, but still address active participation. For example, wearing shoes with VELCRO® fasteners instead of shoe strings allows a student to learn part of the task (putting on and taking off his or her shoes) without the need to learn shoe tying. Occupational and physical therapists often play an important role in the design of adaptations for partial participation. Common variations in partial participation include the following:

- Modified or adapted materials (e.g., toothbrushes, combs, forks, and cups that are designed for easier gripping; VELCRO® fasteners in place of buttons, hooks, or snaps)
- Adaptive switches or automated appliances (e.g., hair dryers activated by a pressure switch; battery-powered toothbrushes that provide scrubbing action automatically)
- Changed sequences within an activity (e.g., allowing a student to put her bathing suit on under her clothes before going to a public pool; sitting on the toilet for balance and then scooting underwear down)
- Personal assistance (e.g., giving a student with limited hand movement an electric brush with toothpaste already applied and letting her do the lateral motion up front, while the teacher completes the molars)

When a team decides to use partial participation with a student on a given task, any adaptations should be individually designed. Adaptations should be "only as special as necessary" (Janney & Snell, 2004) and

should meet the criteria of being age appropriate, nonstigmatizing, and practical (Ferguson & Baumgart, 1991).

Toby was unable to hang up his coat or get it from his locker until the custodian lowered the coat hook.

The team should take care that student participation is active and is meaningful to the function of the activity. As with all instructional strategies, ongoing evaluation of partial participation is needed to determine whether assistance can be faded and to ensure that modifications result in satisfactory outcomes. The goal is to get the task done while also empowering students.

Identify What Teaching Strategies to Use

The ideal teaching strategies to use are ones that are research-based, socially acceptable, and practical to use. Teams want uncomplicated and effective instructional methods. (Table 10–1 reviews teaching strategies that have been found to be effective for teaching self-care skills to students with severe disabilities.) In addition to using effective methods, we have found that the most "doable" program that works with an individual student is one that is developed by the team. Well-designed programs reflect input from all team members, are built on consideration of assessment results and the student's stage of learning, involve peers when appropriate, respect student privacy and preferences, are sensitive to the student's age and culture, and use proven teaching procedures.

Problems with Prior Self-Care Research

Even though self-care skills contribute to health, reduce dependence, and add to quality of life, much of the early research that has guided instruction of these skills was conducted in segregated settings. Some of these studies included aversive procedures as part of the intervention. Today, segregated placements and aversive procedures are not acceptable practices for students with disabilities. We understand the power that ordinary life experiences and typical peers can have for students with disabilities (Fisher & Meyer, 2002; Kraemer, McIntyre, & Blacher, 2003) and we have seen that more problems than solutions result from the use of aversive methods (Carr et al., 1999). Self-care instruction for today's students must rely on methods that will work in regular school settings and that team members find acceptable and can use with confidence.

TABLE 10–1

Effective Strategies for Teaching Self-Care Skills

Strategy	Research on Self-Care Skills	Notes for Teachers
Embed instruction during Natural Opportunities: Reinforce appropriate behavior in the context of typical routines. Embed teaching in these activities and encourage self-monitoring of performance.	Hobbs & Peck, 1985; Nelson, Cone, & Hanson, 1975; Riordan, Iwata, Wohl, & Finney, 1980, 1984; Smith, Piersel, Filbeck, & Gross, 1983	• Simple strategy, appropriate in most settings. • Embedding instruction appears to increase generalization. • Embedding involves distributed learning trials and natural stimuli, both of which seem to improve student motivation and generalization. • *Caution:* Many students need more information via prompts or other instruction to perform the behavior; having an opportunity is not enough.
Shaping: Reinforce successive approximation of the desired behavior.	Levine & Elliot, 1970; Luiselli, 1991, 1996; Marshall, 1966; O'Brien, Bugle, & Azrin, 1972; Richmond, 1983	• Allows student to experience success by reinforcing any improvements in performance. • May require extra materials or time to allow for gradually increased task demands.
Chaining: Total Task Teach all steps of a task at the same time in a forward order.	Batu, 2008; Cicero & Pfadt, 2002; Denny et al., 2000; Keen et al., 2007; Matson, Taras, Sevin, Love, & Fridley, 1990; Reese & Snell, 1991	• May be the most natural chaining approach because all steps are treated as learning opportunities. • Works best if chain is *not too long;* can subdivide into shorter task clusters and use total task on each cluster. • *Caution:* Learning may be faster when used after student has reached the end of acquisition phase (has learned one third to half of the task); thus might start with backward or forward chaining and then switch to total task when one third or so of the steps have been learned.
Chaining: Backward Chaining Do all but the last step for the student. Teach the final step(s) of a task until mastery; then teach the next preceding step(s) until mastery, expecting maintenance of last step, and so on.	Hagopian, Farrell, Amari, 1996; Luieselli, 1991	• Task is broken down into small teachable units for students who learn better with shorter sequences instead of receiving instruction through the entire task. • Begins instruction with completing the task, which can be naturally reinforcing.
Chaining: Forward Chaining Teach first step(s) of task until mastery, doing rest of the task for student on each trial. Then expect student to complete first step and shift instruction to the next step(s) until mastery (guide through rest of task) and so on. Follow reinforcement guidelines.[1]	Alberto, Jobes, Sizemore, & Doran, 1980; Bettison, 1982; Epps et al., 1990; Richman et al., 1984	• Breaks down tasks into small teachable units for students who are frustrated by being prompted through the entire task. • *Caution:* May be more difficult for student to understand function or outcome of performance, which may affect student's motivation.
Modeling or Observational Learning: Arrange students so that they can watch classmates being taught and then be provided direct instruction to complete the task. Teach in groups of two or three.	Biederman et al., 1998; Wolery et al., 1980; Wolery, Ault, Gast, Doyle, & Griffen, 1991	• May assist students to "learn by watching others," a useful self-instruction approach. • Allows for efficient instruction by grouping students. • *Does not provide for privacy.* • *Cautions:* Requires focused visual attention, memory, and ability to imitate. Not appropriate for instructor to perform some self-care tasks for observation (e.g., toileting, complete undressing).

TABLE 10–1 (*Continued*)

Strategy	Research on Self-Care Skills	Notes for Teachers
Video Modeling: Create a brief video of a peer (or the child) performing the target skill. Provide the child with daily opportunities to view the video. As the child makes progress, gradually fade the intervention.	Bainbridge & Myles, 1999; Keen, Brannigan, & Cuskelly, 2007; Van Laarhoven & Van Laarhoven-Myers 2006; Lasater & Brady, 1995; Murzynksi & Bourret, 2007; Norman, Collins, & Schuster, 2001; Rai, 2008	• Provides a consistent model. • May assist the child in focusing on the salient aspects of the task. • May reduce amount of direct instruction required for learning task. • *Caution:* If peers are used, little or no editing may be necessary; if the target student is featured, more time is needed to edit video so that the performance of the target skill is good.
Prompting: Simultaneous Prompting Cue the student to look at the task materials, give a task request, and immediately prompt student through each step of the task without a latency period.	Batu, 2008; Parrot, Schuster, Collins, & Gassaway, 2000; Sewell et al., 1998	• Low-error prompt system that is easier to use. • Provides maximal information about how to perform the task, especially for students new to the task, ensuring success. • *Caution:* May limit opportunity for students to perform some steps independently; some risk of providing "too much help." *Regular probes are necessary to determine when to fade prompts.*
Prompting: System of Least Prompts Select 2–3 prompts of increasing assistance. Give task request and pause a fixed latency period for student response (e.g., 3 seconds). If student is incorrect or does not respond, present the next least intrusive prompt and again pause. Repeat until the student is successful and reinforce.	Banerdt & Bricker, 1978; Horner & Keilitz, 1975; Young, West, Howard, & Whitney, 1986	• Provides opportunities for the student to perform each step independently or with the least amount of assistance required. • Strategy is easily implemented with multiple-step tasks. • *Cautions:* May work better once student has learned about a third or more of the task steps; start with a most-to-least system and then switch. May be time inefficient for students who require the most prompts at the most intrusive end of the hierarchy to perform the task correctly.
Prompting: Graduated Guidance and Decreasing Assistance Provide student with physical-verbal assistance on all steps to complete task. Gradually decrease the amount of assistance as the student begins to perform the task.	Albin, 1977; Azrin & Armstrong, 1973; Cicero & Pfadt, 2002; Denny et al., 2000; Keen et al., 2007; Matson et al., 1990; Reese & Snell, 1991; Simbert, Minor, & McCoy, 1977; Sisson, Kilwein, & Van Hasselt, 1988	• Provides maximal information about how to perform the task, especially for students new to the task, for students with physical disabilities or visual impairments, and for other students who respond positively to physical assistance. • Eliminates time going through prompt levels to which the student does not respond. • *Caution:* May limit opportunity for students to perform some steps independently or with less assistance; some risk of providing "too much help"; need a plan for fading assistance.
Prompting: Time Delay Over successive trials, small amounts of time are inserted between natural cues and instructional prompts. Prompts selected must be effective for the student.	Collins, Gast, Wolery, Halcombe, & Leatherby, 1991; Snell et al., 1989; Wolery et al., 1991	• Provides maximal assistance for student success. • Prompts are easily matched to individual student characteristics. • Delay allows student the opportunity to perform independently before receiving assistance. • *Caution:* Not for students who have difficulty waiting for assistance (progressive time delay may be more effective with these students).

[1]Reinforcement guidelines: When shaping or any of the prompting or chaining procedures are used, reinforcement follows a similar pattern: Give quick reinforcement (e.g., praise, smile, high five) for independent steps and for cooperating or performing the steps taught. Give more reinforcement or natural reinforcement at the end of the task. Reinforcement must be individualized.

Social Validity and Team Consensus

Social validity refers to the acceptability of procedures and outcomes according to social norms. The acceptability of teaching strategies to team members cannot be ignored. For example, overcorrection, or the repeated performance of the correct behavior after an error, was demonstrated years ago as a potentially effective component in the Azrin and Foxx (1971) toilet training program. In their procedure, a student who had a toilet accident was required to approach the toilet, pull down his or her pants, sit on the toilet, stand, and pull up his or her pants five times in rapid succession after each accident. While this procedure may indeed have been effective in reducing toileting accidents, there are many alternative strategies that are both effective and positive ways to improve toileting skills. Most team members view overcorrection as punishing, demeaning, stigmatizing, and intrusive, and thus unacceptable.

Team members should agree on the teaching methods that they will use. When selecting methods, it is useful for teams to compare their teaching methods to methods used to teach students without disabilities in similar settings and judge the appropriateness of the techniques. Family members should also evaluate the fitness of the technique for their son or daughter. Because of the personal and private nature of many self-care skills, it is even more critical that team members evaluate their comfort level with teaching plans. For example, in one study addressing how menstrual care might be taught, typical women in the community were surveyed to determine if instruction should be conducted using a doll rather than directly with the students themselves (Epps, Stern, & Horner, 1990). Women in the community indicated a preference for instruction using a doll, citing the intrusiveness of instruction on the student and the potential for the student to negatively react to such an approach.

Logistics of Teaching Self-Care Skills

When and Where to Teach. The guiding rule for teams is to teach students during as many natural opportunities for the target skill as possible (i.e., instruction is embedded within the natural opportunity for the skill). Embedding involves teaching in the locations and at the times when the skill is routinely used; embedding allows for peer modeling and promotes skill generalization (Batu, 2008; Sewell et al., 1998). The ultimate goal of instruction is to enable students to use self-care skills appropriately with as much independence as possible alongside others or in private at home, at friends' homes, at school, and in the community. Given this goal and the fact that students with severe disabilities have difficulty generalizing learned skills from one setting to another, there is clear support for instruction in natural settings and at times when all of the relevant conditions are present.

Embedding has applications to many skills and age groups. For example, there are a variety of functional settings for teaching self-care skills at school, such as the restrooms for toileting and grooming and the locker rooms for dressing and showering, but, as discussed next, the difficulty is in scheduling to preserve privacy. Much younger students will have more natural opportunities to practice eating, dressing, toileting, and grooming skills like brushing teeth at school. For example, teaching assistants in a day care setting were taught to embed instruction during a variety of daily routines in order to teach skills such as throwing a napkin in the trash after snack time, cutting with scissors, interactive play, and sitting in a circle of five preschoolers with severe intellectual disabilities (Shepis, Reid, Ownbey, & Parsons, 2001). The teaching assistants were taught on the job how and when to embed a system of least prompts to teach these skills. As the paraprofessionals mastered the ability to embed instruction, students developed independence in these skills.

Teachers and other team members must be sensitive to the fact that beyond preschool, typical peers will have acquired basic self-care skills and will not need further instruction. Thus, with many skills, *privacy* will be a critical consideration for when and where to teach. When peers see that a student beyond the preschool years requires instruction in toileting or basic grooming skills, it could be stigmatizing for the student with disabilities and uncomfortable for peers. Peers may perceive the student as less able in all areas of functioning. Thus, the team may decide to conduct instruction in a natural setting at a time when peers are not present (e.g., pulling students away from classroom activities to teach grooming) or in a location not used by peers for the activity (e.g. a bathroom by the nurse's office or eating in a classroom instead of the cafeteria). In addition, for some students like Patrick who has cerebral palsy, having privacy during instruction may allow a calmer environment to facilitate improved muscle tone for toileting and eating (Vogtle &

Snell, in press). While teaching in private does not mean teaching in isolated settings, it still requires precautionary practices so that students don't learn that it is acceptable to be exposed in public restrooms or that they should be compliant with any adults in any situations, which could make a student vulnerable to exploitation. The decision to teach a student in private away from peers must be made cautiously. We recommend that teams follow these guidelines when making this decision:

- If the targeted self-care activity is one that other class members perform openly at school (e.g., hand washing, combing hair, using a utensil at lunch, taking jackets off on arrival and putting them on for recess), then activity-based, non-isolated teaching may be appropriate.
- If the priority self-care activity is one that other class members do not perform openly at school, (e.g., brushing teeth, dressing), then isolated teaching may be best.
- If privacy is natural and appropriate to the task (e.g., toileting, menstrual hygiene, changing clothes for swimming), then any instruction should take place in private, although during expected times so that task completion leads to natural outcomes (e.g., swimming is preceded and followed by changing clothes).

Who Will Teach. When the skill is one that requires privacy and the student is beyond preschool, adults of the same gender as the child are the most preferred teachers. When this is not possible, female adults may be the next best option. In these cases, teams need to confer and consider the student's age and family and student preferences. For many self-care skills that do not require privacy, a variety of different team members should provide instruction to promote generalization; however, with multiple instructors, it is important to make sure that everyone is using the same teaching approach in a consistent manner.

Antecedent Strategies and Stages of Learning

As stated earlier in this chapter and in Chapter 4, skills selected for instruction must build on the student's present level of performance. Students who are true beginners in toileting, eating, and dressing will require teaching strategies that address acquisition learning, while other students who have some or many of the basics steps, but demonstrate performance problems

(e.g., fail to use the skill when needed, perform too slowly, or fail when the setting or materials change), will require different strategies. Different antecedent teaching methods are best suited to these various learning stages. Thus, teams will want to tailor their instructional methods to match the student's stage of learning.

Acquisition Stage Strategies. During the acquisition stage of learning, the student cannot complete the task without assistance. The goal of instruction during this stage is to provide maximal information to the student about how to perform the basic task steps in the routine. Prompting methods are used to promote low-error learning and reinforcement is fairly continuous, particularly early in this stage. Students in the acquisition stage perform between 0% and 60% of the task correctly on assessment probes. Students who have demonstrated performance above 60% are probably ready for a more advanced focus on fluency, maintenance, or generalization; acquisition strategies are replaced with reduced prompts, attention to natural cues, and minimal reinforcement. Most self-care studies have addressed skills in the acquisition stage of learning and thus have used some sort of physical prompting across steps in a task analysis.

While there are no rigid rules for deciding which instructional procedure is most effective at a given stage, there are "rules of thumb." For students who are completely new to a skill (in the acquisition stage), more intrusive prompts, such as *physical prompts* or *physical guidance,* may be best. This might mean using simultaneous prompting, graduated guidance, time delay with physical prompts, or a decreasing assistance prompt hierarchy. During the acquisition stage, many students initially cannot respond to minimal verbal or gesture cues and require models or physical assistance instead. Teaching time can be lost moving through two or more prompt levels in an increasing prompt hierarchy, such as a system of least prompts, especially when the least intrusive prompt used may not yet be meaningful.

During initial instruction for combing his hair, Toby's teachers did not verbally prompt him to "make a part" or even to "get the comb" because he did not understand these requests. Instead, his teachers relied both on Sam and Aaron as models (two typical fourth graders who were Toby's peer buddies) and on the physical assistance that the teachers gave when the peer models were not effective.

Students with motor disabilities also may need physical guidance initially to learn the movements necessary to perform skills. The exception is students who are less tolerant of physical prompting.

Maintenance Stage Strategies. When students begin to demonstrate some mastery of a task, teachers should select less intrusive strategies, provide more opportunities for students to perform independently, build skill performance into the schedule as a routine, fade any artificial reinforcement that may have been used, and eventually fade their presence altogether. Teachers can fade instruction and build routine performance in a number of ways, including the following:

- Stepping behind, then away from the student, and engaging in other tasks nearby while still monitoring the student;
- Leaving the task area at gradually increasing but unpredictable times (Dunlap & Johnson, 1985);
- Introducing peers into the instructional area so that teacher time and attention are divided among students and less focused on the target student;
- Eliminating intrusive prompts, such as physical guidance and modeling, and using instead simple pointing gestures, nonspecific verbal prompts (e.g., "What's next?"), verbal prompts that support the natural cue (e.g., "What do you do after you go to the bathroom?"), and natural cues (e.g., hands that are dirty after art);
- Encouraging self-correction, but using it carefully so as not to endanger or embarrass the student;
- Using picture task schedules (also called *between-task symbol schedules*) as permanent prompts for students to self-manage their daily self-care and chore routines, and involving students in selecting and arranging task photos in a schedule book each morning (Bambara & Cole, 1997; Irvine, Erickson, Singer, & Stahlberg, 1992; Mirenda, MacGregor, & Kelly-Keough, 2002) (Chapter 14 expands on self-prompting);
- Using video modeling or video self-modeling to increase a student's motivation for performance, as well as their awareness of the sequence of steps involved (Charlop-Christy et al., 2000); or
- Using visual supports such as social narratives, within-activity scripts as reminders of the task steps, and rule scripts as reminders of what is and what is not appropriate behavior for a given task (Mirenda et al., 2002).

Adrian's teeth are not healthy. He knows the basic steps of brushing teeth, but dislikes the task and often exhibits tantrums when pushed to engage in the activity. His parents want advice on how to make brushing teeth a positive experience and avoid the tantrums. The team identified several approaches that they will use to tackle this problem. First, they added brushing teeth to his visual schedule. Second, they identified a series of steps for teaching, which start by simply examining a variety of toothbrush materials outside the class bathroom; their plan is to gradually move instruction into the bathroom and to expect more and more active participation. Third, they have prepared a digital video that includes segments showing his teacher, his mom, and two peers brushing their teeth. Watching this video will be an optional activity during his computer breaks.

Teaching students to self-manage their dressing or grooming activities is a well-documented maintenance strategy. Several types of stimuli (e.g., pictures, picture checklists, tape-recorded messages, and videotapes) can be used to teach students to prompt and monitor their own performance of a series of self-care tasks that they already know how to accomplish in part. For example, Garff and Storey (1998) taught young adults to use a checklist to self-manage hygiene during work, and Lasater and Brady (1995) used video self-modeling to teach shaving. Material prompts like these may or may not be faded, depending on the student, but such prompts are designed by the team to be nonstigmatizing, easily carried, and independently used. For example, students can select and arrange pictures of morning routine tasks in a pocket-sized booklet to be used like a schedule or personal calendar. For other students, a booklet of task pictures (used initially during acquisition training) may be shortened to single-task photos that continue to remind students of task steps after teachers have faded their ongoing supervision. For students who are able to operate a small cassette tape recorder, the StepPad (Attainment Company, Inc., at http://www.attainmentcompany.com/home.php) can facilitate self-management. Teachers let students or peers record a series of prompting messages (e.g., brush teeth, shave, shower and shut curtain all the way, dress, comb hair, straighten bed, take medication, eat, pack lunch and get bus money). When a person presses the play button, the message plays. Pressing the fast-forward button plays the next step and pressing the replay button plays the previous step. Seventy-two seconds of recording time is available. Another device available from the Attainment Company, VoiceCue, allows up to five messages to be played at assigned times. For example, record the message "Brush teeth" and set the VoiceCue clock to play the message at 6:30 a.m. and 8 p.m. If the person does not hear the message, they can press the replay button to hear it again. More information on assistive technology and links to vendors can be found at the Alliance for Technology Access (http://www.ataccess.org/community/vendors. lasso) and by connecting to the assistive technology groups in your state (e.g., http://www.ataccess. org/index.php?option=com_content&view=article&id =16&Itemid=22).

Another antecedent method that is effective during the maintenance phase is *within-task scripts,* which remind students of the key steps of a routine (Mirenda et al., 2002).

> *Last year, when Patrick was sampling jobs, he spent a month working at a Pizza Hut® restaurant. The restaurant required him to wear a uniform shirt and he carried several things in his pack (a cap, a bus pass, his ID card, and his schedule). Because Patrick was challenged by getting ready, the team made the job preparation sequence an objective. Patrick had learned other skills quickly with within-task scripts and schedules so the team decided to use that approach. The teacher first assembled pictures of the key steps on a VELCRO® strip. Then she reviewed the sequence of steps with Patrick before the activity. While pointing at each picture, the teacher reviewed the steps: "It's time to get ready for work. First, you need to get your Pizza Hut® shirt and head to the bathroom. Then you need to take off your shirt and put on the Pizza Hut® shirt. Then you need to get your pack ready . . ." Finally, the teacher used each symbol to help prompt each step: "OK, let's get your shirt" (points to symbol, gives assistance). "Great, let's head to the bathroom" (points to picture). "Now, take off your shirt . . ." Within a few days, Patrick was able to use the picture strip (within-task schedule) on his own to complete the sequence.*

Rule scripts are like within-activity scripts except that they are created to "clarify the rules related to an activity rather than the sequence of steps that comprise it" (Mirenda et al., 2002, p. 195), somewhat like social narratives. Rule scripts are highly individualized with picture symbols and a simple script that teachers read to represent the rules for carrying out a task already partially mastered. For example, there are three rules for lunch:

1. Eat what is on your plate; do not eat what is on other peoples' plates.
2. Use your fork, knife, and spoon, to eat; do not eat with your fingers.
3. Eat slowly and take small bites/don't eat quickly or take large bites (Mirenda et al., p. 195).

Like within-task scripts, rule scripts are rehearsed before the activity, reviewed during the activity, used to reinforce successes with specific rules, and used to provide feedback about rule violations ("Oops, you forgot to use your fork—remember, do not eat with your fingers" [Mirenda et al., 2002, p. 195]). The symbols and rules are used as prompts and to augment teachers' feedback to students and thus have more value in the later stages of learning when most of the step sequence of a task is learned.

> *Adrian's teachers developed a rule script last September when teaching him to use the cafeteria line with his kindergarten classmates. The script was put into a book with pictures of him and his peers to illustrate each rule in the book (e.g., sit on the rainbow rug, take a place in line, walk to lunch but be quiet, take a place in line, get your tray and slide it along). The kindergarten teacher decided to use it with the whole class because Adrian was not the only one who needed to learn these rules.*

Fluency Stage Strategies. During fluency learning, students understand the task requirements but need more practice to perform the skill consistently and at an appropriate pace. Students need to be motivated to improve fluency. When students are near mastery of acquisition learning (more than 60% of the steps are correct), it is often time to revise a program, reduce prompts, and address motivation (e.g., shift from antecedent prompting tactics to consequences, making reinforcement contingent on faster or more perfect performance). Targeting more fluent performance in self-care routines often means emphasizing timed performance. Teachers or students might time their performance or students may learn to "beat the clock" to be ready for a preferred activity that follows the routine. Other strategies to increase student motivation for practicing and perfecting skill routines include self-monitoring performance, providing choices, recruiting peer support, and introducing more challenging or extended steps.

Sometimes the task steps need to be looked at and improved. When difficult steps are simplified or eliminated, or students are given extra practice on them, errors can be reduced and fluency enhanced. Fluency training in self-care routines may be necessary if adults are to let students use their skills independently. For example, in a busy family, parents may dress a child who takes too much time to dress by herself.

> *Toby's parents would like for him to be faster in putting on and taking off his coat. He is almost at 60% independent performance, but he does the steps so slowly that others tend to do the task for him. The team decides to institute a "beat the clock" approach that involves standing back and quietly cheering while peers perform alongside Tony at a pace that is just a little faster than his. They also lowered his coat hook so that it is easier for Tony to reach.*

Generalization Stage Strategies. During generalization and the other advanced stages of learning (i.e., fluency and maintenance), it is important to reduce prompting and to fade from artificial to natural consequences. To make school and community environments supportive of skills, teachers may involve peers and show them how to give more natural forms of reinforcement (e.g., "high fives," "All right!") and error correction (e.g., "Try it again," point to mistake). Environments should be arranged so that students can use their acquired skills regularly and obtain approval (or learn to give self-approval) for task completion at the end of a time period or after a cluster of related routines are completed (e.g., the three interrelated tasks of using the bathroom, hand washing, and returning independently to work). When students use self-scheduling photo books to plan their daily school schedule, self-reinforcement can be an added component of instruction.

Using multiple instructors (e.g., teachers, peers, therapists, parents) also enhances generalization because students learn that (a) who is present is less relevant than the task stimuli, and (b) they can complete the task despite differences between teachers. Generalization is facilitated when students are expected to use the target skill during all opportunities across multiple environments (e.g., eating in the school cafeteria, home economics room, and restaurants; using the toilet and washing hands in the classroom facility, the school restroom, the restaurant restroom, and the locker room). Teaching across multiple settings requires the student to adjust performance to apply the skills across (a) differences in materials, (b) changing background stimuli (e.g., noise, commotion, temperature), and (c) varying problems that may arise. For example, differences from one bathroom to another include the door into the toilet, the presence or absence of a stall, the type of lock on a stall, the height of the toilet, the presence or absence of wall supports, the location of the supports, the location and type of toilet paper dispenser, the height of the sink and faucets, the type of soap dispenser, the type of paper towel dispenser, and the location of the trash container. It is not unusual to have several different types of soap and towel dispensers in one bathroom! Even during the acquisition stage of learning, teaching across multiple task opportunities facilitates generalization, although learning may be slower initially.

> *Over the years, Patrick has used several different restaurants for lunch, but none without assistance. His OT and PT are working to develop a generic task analysis for team members to use that fits the seven fast-food restaurants that he frequents during community-based instruction or with his family. Their goal is to improve his independence by standardizing the steps, their cues, and the adaptations (e.g., having his order written out to give to the clerk, having a cup holder on his tray where his drink is to be placed, getting his lunch "to go" so that he does not need to deal with a tray).*

Consequent Strategies

Reinforcement. If reinforcement is to be effective, it must be individually planned. What is reinforcing varies from student to student. Some students may need concrete reinforcers (e.g., an object that represents the upcoming preferred activity) instead of a symbolic representation of the preferred activity (e.g., a picture). Some students may need frequent reinforcement (e.g., praise offered intermittently during the task) and others may only need a choice of an activity upon completion of the task. As discussed in Chapter 4, primary reinforcers such as sweets, drinks, and other edibles should be avoided. The only exception is if eating skills are being taught; then eating is natural to the task and more preferred foods can be used to reinforce the eating of less preferred foods. For most self-care tasks, it is better to reinforce students with enthusiastic, specific praise (e.g., point to clean hands, smile, and say "You have clean hands!") during instruction and follow instruction with a choice of short preferred activities that are suited to the student's age and interests. What reinforcers to use, how often, and how to represent the options need to suit a given student. (Chapter 3 described methods for identifying preferences.) The goal is to teach students to attend to natural reinforcers so that their performance is not dependent on artificial reinforcers.

- *Adrian's ability to fasten and unfasten his pants by himself means that he finishes faster, without frustration, and he can leave the boy's bathroom more quickly and head to the next activity.*
- *Toby's independent toileting is reinforced by having dry pants, increased independence (adults prompting him less often), privacy, and being more like his peers. Feeding himself without spilling is reinforcing because he can eat more quickly than when he is fed by others and there is less face washing after meals.*
- *Approval of peers and teachers is a strong reinforcer for Patrick. He shows pride in himself when he is able to complete a self-care routine on his own (e.g., putting his coat on, using the electric toothbrush at home).*

Still, during early instruction, especially if students have limited experience with natural reinforcers, the completion of self-care activities may not be very reinforcing. Teachers should be prepared to use artificial reinforcers (e.g., food, stickers) and then systematically fade them during the later phases of learning. *Now–Next visual supports* are simple displays of a picture or object to represent what a student is to do first on his schedule (e.g., get lunch, use the toilet, go to science class), followed by a picture or object representing a chosen, preferred activity that the student can engage in after completing the task. The Now–Next display is created just prior to the task with the student and is often taken along and used as a reminder of the reinforcing consequence to motivate performance. Teams want to arrange teaching so that students progress from a Now–Next structure to a more natural arrangement of a self-care task completed as part of a routine (e.g., eat in the cafeteria, use the bathroom; put jacket on and go outside), followed by a preferred natural activity (e.g., going outside) or a short, scheduled preferred activity (e.g., computer).

Error Correction. As described in Chapter 4, most systematic prompt methods have error correction built into the method. Regardless, the team's plan for handling a student's errors depends on the student and the stage of learning. During acquisition, it is important to gently interrupt errors with a prompt (e.g., when the student forgets to pick up the soap in the hand-washing task; Wolery, Ault, & Doyle, 1992). Then following this correction, the student could either be encouraged to continue performance of the rest of the task or be given an opportunity to perform the missed step again with a prompt that will likely result in a correct performance.

For students in later stages of learning, one or more approaches to errors can be selected:

1. Wait for self-correction with or without a cue ("What's next?"). Add prompts as needed.
2. Nonpunitively stop an error (physically, verbally, or with a gesture) and follow with option 1 or 3.
3. Direct attention to the relevant task stimuli (e.g., point to the missed button hole, orient the student toward the coat hook once the coat is off and the student hesitates for 5 seconds). Add prompts as needed.

In this stage (and earlier), it is always appropriate to *reinforce any self-correction* that the student makes (i.e., the student should be reinforced for demonstrating that he knew that there was an error and that he at least initiated a self-correction).

Apply Progress-Monitoring Procedures

Teams need to objectively judge student progress on target self-care skills based on student performance.

Adrian's team identified dressing and undressing as a priority (e.g., jacket, hat, shoes, socks, shirt, and pants). They wrote task analyses and designed a teaching plan (see Figure 10-5). They started by probing and graphing Adrian's baseline performance during natural opportunities for the skills. Then they drew an aim line (see Chapter 5) that which would help them judge Adrian's day-to-day progress. The four team members decided to use embedded instruction during all of the natural opportunities to teach the skills. They used intermittent probes during these natural opportunities to check how well he was doing. Adrian's rapid progress between February and April (shown in Figure 10-6) was celebrated by everyone.

FIGURE 10–5

Adrian's Probe and Teaching Data for Putting on Coat with Zipper

Dates P = Probe; 0 second, 4 second delay prompts	2/26 P	3/09 P	3/12 P	3/16 0s	3/26 0s	3/30 4s	4/02 4s	4/13 P	4/16 4s	4/20 8s
Instructional Cue: "Put your coat on"										
1. Grab the collar of your coat.	+	−	+	+	+	+	+	+	+	+
2. Put one arm in the armhole.	−	+	−	VP	+	+	+	+	+	+
3. Pull the coat up over your shoulder.	−	−	−	VP	VP	+	VP	+	+	+
4. Push hand out of hole and let go of coat.	−	−	−	VP	VP	VP	VP	+	+	+
5. Put your other arm in the armhole.	−	−	−	VP	VP	VP	+	+	+	+
6. Pull sides (to straighten).	−	−	−	VP	VP	+	VP	−	+	+
7. Grab the bottom zipper (both hands, one on each side).	+	−	−	VP	VP	+	+	+	+	+
8. Hook the zipper.	−	−	−	VP	VP	VP	VP	−	VP	−
9. Pull the zipper up (while holding the bottom).	−	+	−	VP	VP	+	+	+	+	+
Total correct (out of 9)	2	2	1	11	2	6	5	7	8	8
% Correct	22%	22%	11%	11%	22%	67%	56%	78%	89%	89%
P = Probe + = Independent VP = Verbal + physical prompt − = Error										

(Credit is given to Lindsey Rabideau for this figure.)

Performance can be measured under test or probe conditions (when no help or reinforcement is given to students), as well as measured during teaching when assistance and reinforcement are available to students. As detailed in Chapters 5 and 6, teams might *probe* students on target skills during the baseline phase (before teaching starts) and probe again periodically once teaching has begun. Probe data will give a more conservative picture of the student's learning because he or she is not getting ongoing assistance and praise; but probe data will identify when the student meets the criteria for an IEP objective or goal. In addition to the probe data, it also is important to record student performance during instruction (teaching data) and keep track of how much prompting occurs and how often errors occur (see Figure 10-5). Teams will use teaching data to make improvements in instruction. Graphs of student performance data can help team members easily view progress. Drawing an aim line on the graph helps teams monitor weekly graphed progress; while drawing a trend line helps determine if variable trends are ascending or not (see Chapter 5). (Figure 10-6 shows a graph of Adrian's progress on all of his dressing tasks with an aim line; there is no trend line because his ascending progress is evident.) Because data are valuable but time consuming to gather, teams must select methods and schedules that make data collection feasible and then must *use* the data to monitor students' progress and improve their instruction. (Figure 10-7 shows the plan that Adrian's teachers used to teach and probe dressing and undressing tasks.)

Special Considerations for Toileting

Learning to use the toilet is one of the most difficult self-care skills to teach because it requires a functional bladder (normal capacity, intact urethral sphincter, and mature nervous system), an awareness of internal stimuli (e.g., bladder fullness, bowel tension), and a lengthy

FIGURE 10–6
Graph of the Combined Data for All of Adrian's Dressing Skills (jacket, hat, shoes, socks, pants)

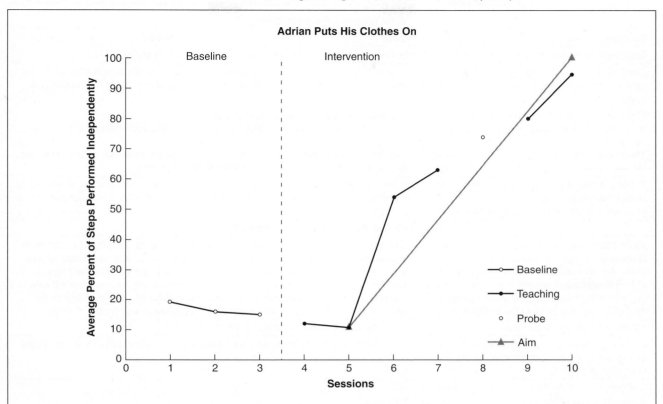

The aim line was drawn after several days of teaching; this line connects his early performance with the goal date (mid-April) and the goal criterion level (100% independent for dressing tasks) that his teachers have set for him. The slope of the aim line provides a rough guide for teachers to track the progress that he needs to make in order to reach the criterion by this date.

(Credit is given to Lindsey Rabideau for this graph.)

sequence of related skills (e.g., pulling up pants, flushing toilet) that must be learned in part or in its entirety for the skills to be useful. Although it varies by culture, studies of large samples of children in western countries found that attainment of daytime continence ("always dry") increased with age: age two (44%) and age three (86%) (Bax, Hart, & Jenkins, 1990). In the United States and in Great Britian, the expectation is that "a child will begin toilet training at 12–18 months and will be come clean and dry by the age of 3 years" (Harris, 2004, p. 773). But these norms for western cultures are later than those for some African, Iranian, and Bengali cultures, where babies may master daytime dryness by or even before a year old (Harris, 2004)! In western countries, boys tend to learn later (mean age 2.56 years) than girls (2.25 years) (Bloom, Seeley, Rathcey, & McGuire, 1993), while bowel control is typically mastered first for most children regardless of gender or age. Most children master daytime before nighttime control. This general pattern is also typically true for individuals with disabilities.

These facts, along with developmental sequences can serve as general guides for teaching toileting to most students with disabilities. However, intellectual disability may delay learning and neurological involvement (from cerebral palsy, brain injury, seizures, paralysis) may make daytime and nighttime control more difficult to attain. In a review of the toilet-training literature, Harris (2004) reported two frequent reasons for incontinence: bladder capacity that was too small for a child's age and dysfunctional voiding (i.e., an interrupted flow of urine that results from overactive pelvic floor muscles). Medical research informs us that "normal acquisition" of toileting skills by ages three to four years

FIGURE 10–7

Brief Teaching Program Guide for Adrian's Dressing and Undressing Skills

Brief Teaching Program Guide		
Student: Adrian	**School:**	**Start Date:** February 26, 2009
Teachers: Ruth (teacher), Lindsey and Carmen (teaching assistants), MaryAnn (OT)		**Aim Date:** April 20, 2009

Goal: Adrian will put on and take off his shirt, pants, jacket, hat, socks, and shoes; this does not include tying his shoelaces or doing fasteners other than zippers. He will put each clothing item on in 30 seconds or less and take each clothing item off in 20 seconds or less.

Objective(s):
First Objective: Adrian will take off his shirt, pants, jacket, socks, and hat (excluding fasteners).
Second Objective: Adrian will put on his shirt, pants, jacket, hat, and socks (excluding fasteners) and take each item off in less than 20 seconds.
Third Objective: Adrian will put on and take off his shirt, pants, jacket, hat, socks, and VELCRO shoes; this does not include fasteners. He will put each clothing item on in 30 seconds or less and take each clothing item off in 20 seconds or less.

Present level of performance: Adrian is able to put on and take off his coat and shirt with assistance because he is not able to zip or button the items. Adrian is not able to put on his hat, pants, shoes, or socks. Adrian is not toilet trained, although that is not part of this program; independent dressing is seen as a prerequisite for independent toileting.

Description of Assessment/Probe Procedure

Probes were completed during natural opportunities. During probe procedures, Adrian was given an instructional cue (varied according to clothing item) such as, "Put your coat on." The teacher then observed how he put the jacket on and recorded the data on the task analysis sheet. Adrian was never reinforced or prompted during probes. If Adrian asked for help he was told to try and complete the task himself. During baseline and intervention probes, a multiple-opportunity assessment was used. If Adrian performed a step incorrectly or if it took him longer than the 8-second latency period to initiate performance, then the assessor performed the step for him and marked it as an incorrect response for that step on the data table. Testing continued until the task was completed, regardless of the number of errors.

Stage of learning: Acquisition	**Grouping arrangement:** One-to-one	
Teaching times: During natural opportunities: before and after going outside, using the restroom, during P.E.	**Teaching days:** Mondays and Thursdays	**Test day:** Every fourth day

Setting: Special education classroom, restroom, gym

Instructional cue: "Put your _____ on" and "Take your _____ off"

Prompt(s)/prompt system and latency: Constant time delay with a verbal + physical prompt. First two teaching sessions 0-second latency period, followed by 3 training days with a latency period of 4 seconds, after which the latency was increased to 8 seconds for 5 days. Probes were given every 4 days.

Materials: VELCRO shoes, coat with zipper, winter hat, socks, pants with fasteners (button and zipper), and T-shirt

Reinforcers: Listening to music and computer time

Description of the Teaching Procedures

Adrian was always instructed during natural opportunities, which created natural reinforcement because Adrian usually wanted to put on or remove his clothing in order to prepare for the next activity, such as recess. Instruction began with the instructional cue and ended when Adrian had removed the entire clothing item or put on the item properly without the need for adjustments.

If Adrian performed an error, he was immediately prompted, with a verbal plus physical prompt, to repeat the step correctly. Reinforcement was faded as Adrian's abilities increased and the latency period was extended. For example, when an 8-second latency period was reached, Adrian was not provided with the option of selecting a song if he performed the task because there was not time for problem behavior since Adrian had moved into the fluency stage of learning.

After Adrian was able to complete all of the steps in a task analysis independently, he transitioned to the fluency stage of learning and the practicum student began to time Adrian during dressing procedures. For this reason, the latency period never exceeded 8 seconds and if Adrian's progress was decreasing during the extended latency period, then it was shortened to either 4 or 0 seconds.

How will you teach the next relevant stage of learning (generalization, maintenance, fluency)?:
Fluency: After Adrian mastered a specific skill (putting on or removing one type of clothing), he then transferred to the fluency stage. During this stage, he was timed with a stopwatch whenever he was dressing or undressing. All clothing items were to be removed in 20 seconds or less and to be put on in 30 seconds or less.

Maintenance: Adults should refrain from assisting Adrian when he is dressing or undressing. In order to entertain this concept on a regular basis, adults should allow extra time in the schedule for dressing and undressing so that Adrian will be able to complete these tasks independently. Probes should be given every 2 weeks in the beginning and faded to monthly after 2 months.

(Credit is given to Lindsey Rabideau for this guide.)

can be expanded to age five and beyond for children with disabiities of these types. At the same time, incontinence can have a damaging effect on the individual and lead to more personal stress and inconvenience in families (Macias, Roberts, Saylor, & Fussell, 2006). (See Chapter 7 for information on students who require specialized elimination procedures.)

If students are ready for toilet training, instructional plans should be balanced with the student's age and teaching setting. Ideally, students are taught these skills during the preschool years or at home. Toilet training gets more problematic when students move into the upper elementary grades and beyond. Teams should emphasize toilet training at younger ages when schedules are more flexible and social stigma is less likely. However, when older students still lack bladder control, teachers will want to work closely with team members to explore solutions for training the student using systematic methods and perhaps a more intensive approach. On the practical side, both time and money are saved when students are independent or, at the very least, when they are regulated in their bowel and bladder elimination. In this section, we discuss the process for (a) identifying what toileting skills to teach, (b) planning how to teach them, and (c) monitoring learning progress.

Identify What to Teach

For students who have toileting priorities, teams are likely to select objectives for elimination and for learning related skills (e.g., getting to the toilet, pants up and down, hand washing). Elimination objectives span from (a) bowel or bladder regulation (habit trained: student goes when taken and remains dry), to (b) self-initiated bowel/bladder, to (c) independent bowel/bladder. Objectives are selected based on elimination records and related skill performance data.

Record Keeping on Elimination

The first step in identifying what toileting skills to teach involves assessment. Team members need to determine if the student meets *three prerequisites* for toilet training:

1. A stable pattern of elimination
2. Daily one- to two-hour periods of dryness
3. A chronological age of two years or older

These characteristics are interdependent and are related to the maturity of the central nervous system and the muscle sphincters involved in elimination. Generally,

students who are ready for training have one bowel movement daily and three to five voidings occurring within predictable time periods, but many will differ from this pattern. Bowel responses and some urination responses should occur within predictable daily time periods, not randomly.

Efforts to teach Toby over the past six years had not been successful. His parents were hopeful that he could learn, but they worried that his brain damage at infancy from seizures was the explanation for his lack of progress. Toby also has a history of learning skills "slowly but eventually" when systematic teaching methods are used. His team decided that they would work together to carry out an extended baseline on his elimination patterns to confirm whether he met the first and second prerequisites. The OT, SLT, teacher, teaching assistants, and practicum students all worked in tandem to collect data on his elimination every 30 minutes throughout the school day.

A toileting record should be kept on a grid of days by time intervals. We recommend the use of 15- or 30-minute intervals. While these shorter intervals demand more staff time, they provide a more accurate picture of the student's elimination pattern. This information helps determine if students have prerequisites 1 and 2, and is crucial if a traditional toileting method is selected. Other considerations for the assessment of toileting include whether data will be collected across environments (e.g., at home, in the community, all school environments), the length of the day (e.g., an interval of the school day, the whole school day, all waking hours), and who collects the data.

To determine the natural pattern of elimination, check the student at the end of each time interval and record dryness, urination, or bowel movement. Figure 10–8 shows the data sheet used to track Adrian's eliminations during the baseline phase and one day of baseline data gathered during the two weeks of the baseline phase; one sheet was completed daily and the team studied these daily elimination records to determine his pattern.

During baseline, Adrian was checked every 15 minutes and prompted to the toilet every hour. Adrian was dressed in underpants with disposable pull-up diaper over them, so he and the staff could feel any wetness, but his outer pants would remain dry. When wet, he was changed without comment, but cooperated by disposing of the wet pants in the appropriate location. When he was outside the resource room, dry-pants

FIGURE 10–8
One of Eight Daily Data Sheets Used to Track Adrian's Daily Bowel and Bladder Eliminations

Adrian was checked every 15 minutes and prompted to the toilet every hour.

Student: Adrian   **Date:** 5/06/09 (Week 2 of baseline: 4/27–5/8)

Procedure: Dry-pants check every 15 minutes, prompt to the toilet every hour; he helps to change when wet, no comment.

Key: U = Urination **B** = Bowel movement **N** = nothing

Time	Dry-pants check (dry or accident)			Student was **prompted** to the toilet (success or non-elimination)			Student **self-initiated** sitting on toilet (success or non-elimination)		
8:30	(U)	B	N	U	B	(N)	U	B	N
8:45	U	B	(N)	U	B	N	U	B	N
9:00	U	B	(N)	U	B	N	U	B	N
9:15	U	B	(N)	U	B	N	U	B	N
9:30	U	B	(N)	(U)	B	N	U	B	N
10:00	U	B	(N)	U	B	N	U	B	N
10:15	(U)	B	N	U	B	N	U	B	N
10:30	U	B	(N)	U	B	(N)	U	B	N
10:45	U	B	(N)	U	B	N	U	B	N
11:00	(U)	B	N	U	B	N	U	B	N
11:15	U	B	(N)	U	B	N	U	B	N
11:30	U	B	(N)	U	B	(N)	U	B	N
11:45	U	B	(N)	U	B	N	U	B	N
12:00	U	B	(N)	U	B	N	U	B	N
12:15	U	B	(N)	U	B	N	U	B	N
12:30	(U)	B	N	U	B	(N)	U	B	N
12:45	U	B	(N)	U	B	N	U	B	N
1:00	U	B	(N)	U	B	N	U	B	N
1:15	U	B	(N)	U	B	N	U	B	N
1:30	(U)	B	N	U	B	(N)	U	B	N
1:45	U	B	(N)	U	B	N	U	B	N
2:00	U	B	(N)	U	B	N	U	B	N
2:15	U	B	(N)	U	B	N	U	B	N
2:30	(U)	B	N	U	B	(N)	U	B	N

Source: Adapted from *Self-help skills for people with autism: A systematic teaching approach* (p. 132), by S. R. Anderson, A. L. Jablonski, M. L. Thomeer, & V. M. Knapp, 2007, Bethesda, MD: Woodbine House.

checks were made in the kindergarten room toilet. A look at eight days of data indicated that Adrian seemed to be wet a lot when given the 15-minute dry-pants checks (approximately once every hour). He did not self-initiate. Five times over the eight days, he urinated in the toilet when taken and seemed pleased when he did. He showed displeasure with having wet pants. When at the toilet, he often self-initiated, pulling his pants up and down without physical prompts. Despite his rather frequent urination pattern, there were no medical reasons for not initiating toilet training and his participation in general education made toilet training very important. Thus, his team planned an individualized intensive program that they used during summer school when the class was small and there were no typical peers in attendance.

Dry-pants checks are done in private unless the child is very young or the setting is isolated. The following steps can be used during the baseline phase and the intervention phase, as well as to help the team gather reliable elimination data:

1. Tell the student that you are going to check to see if he or she has dry pants.
2. Place the student's hand in yours and together gently check the outside and then the inside of the pants to assess their condition (Anderson et al., 2007, p. 131). With small children, it may be helpful to use the toddler-training diapers with wetness sensors (pictures on the front that disappear when the diaper is wet) in place of feeling the pants.
3. When the pants are wet, use a neutral tone of voice to indicate to the student that he or she is wet and record this performance. Immediately change the student, then return to the previous activity. Having dry pants ensures that adults don't confuse recent accidents with earlier accidents and it is healthier for the student.
4. If the student is dry, reinforce him or her for being dry and record the performance on the data sheet.

To discover whether reliable toileting patterns exist and what those patterns are, most researchers recommend that baseline charting continue for a minimum of 2 weeks, with a possible extension to 30 days, if necessary (Anderson et al., 2007; Baker & Brightman, 1997; Fredericks, Baldwin, Grove, & Moore, 1975; Giles & Wolf, 1966). The longer elimination record is important (a) when a pattern is not quickly identified, and (b) to determine specific toilet-training times if a traditional method is used. (The traditional method, explained later, relies on taking students to the toilet when their bladder is likely to be full, thus baseline data help to identify those times.) This same record-keeping approach will be used initially to determine whether the student meets the prerequisites and finally to measure the student's elimination progress after toilet training begins. Record any eliminations in the toilet (e.g., U for urination and B for bowel movement) as correct (e.g., +U or +B), but indicate if the student was prompted or not (e.g., +U prompt, +B unprompted); record eliminations off the toilet as accidents (e.g., –U or –B) (see Figure 10–9 as an example of an elimination record over multiple days).

FIGURE 10–9

Toby's Elimination Record over a 7-day Intervention Phase Following Changes in His Toileting Program

Record in Pants or Toilet column: **U** = Urination, **B** = Bowel movement, **N** = Nothing (dry).
Circle the code for any self-initiated toilet trips with U or without (N).

Time	Monday 5/11 In Pants	Monday 5/11 **In Toilet**	Tuesday 5/12 In Pants	Tuesday 5/12 **In Toilet**	Wednesday 5/13 In Pants	Wednesday 5/13 **In Toilet**	Thursday 5/14 In Pants	Thursday 5/14 **In Toilet**	Friday 5/15 In Pants	Friday 5/15 **In Toilet**	Monday 5/18 In Pants	Monday 5/18 **In Toilet**	Tuesday 5/19 In Pants	Tuesday 5/19 **In Toilet**
8:30	Ⓤ	N	Ⓤ	N	N	N	N	N	Ⓤ	N	Ⓤ	N	N	N
9:00	N	N	N	N	N	N	N	N	N	N	N	N	N	N
9:30	N	N	N	N	N	N	N	N	N	N	N	N	N	N
10:00	N	N	N	N	N	N	N	N	N	N	N	N	N	N
10:30	N	N	N	N	N	N	N	N	N	N	N	N	N	N
11:00	N	N	N	N	N	N	N	N	N	N	N	N	N	N
11:30	U	N	N	N	N	N	N	N	N	N	N	N	N	N
12:00– 1:00	Ⓤ	Ⓤ	N	Ⓤ,Ⓤ	N	Ⓤ	N	ⓊB	N	Ⓤ	N	Ⓤ	N	ⓊB
INTENSIVE TRAINING 12:00–1:00: Record all urinations [5/18: If successful, 12-1 then end training day]														
1:30	N	N	N	N	N	N	N	N	N	N				
2:00	U	N	N	N	N	N	N	N	N	N				
2:30	N	N	N	N	N	N	N	N	N	N				

In the general education classroom, peers may become aware that a classmate is being assessed or toilet trained because of the frequency of removing the child to a nearby bathroom to check for dryness. If such issues arise, the team should handle them with care and perhaps as part of peer support efforts (Snell & Janney, 2005). The team must be sensitive to the student's right to privacy when selecting the location for baseline assessment and training. We suggest that records be easily accessible by team members who will be recording information, but still be kept secure and private. (Never tape toileting records to the bathroom wall or in any place where others can see them.)

Task Analytic Assessment

Task analysis will guide assessment (see Chapters 3 and 5) and later instruction. Teams need to develop a task analysis that reflects day-to-day conditions and the sequence of toileting skills that are likely to be targeted for a student.

Developing the Task Analysis. Tasks analyses should be individually designed to suit the student (e.g., age, ability, disability, preference, stage of learning) and the natural performance of the skill in the locations that are most often used. The goal is to develop a task analysis that is generic enough to be used with the variety of toilets that a particular student uses during the training period. This will require some discussion and an examination of the toileting locations the student will use at school and possibly in the community and at home. It is a good idea to develop the task analysis with team members, try it out with the focus student, and revise it as needed. (Refer to Chapter 4 for procedures for writing task analyses.) As Patrick's case illustrates, the toileting components, instructional cues, and student behaviors listed in the task analysis must be individualized.

> At home and at school, Patrick's parents and staff now use a one-person supported transfer, which involves Patrick being pulled to a standing position (he can bear weight), pivoted in place, having his pants lowered (by family/male staff member), and being lowered onto the toilet seat. Patrick is being taught this sequence and will use the grab bars for balance. School staff worked with the OT, PT, and family to modify their two-person transfer so that it can be safely executed by one person, making toileting at home and in job settings more feasible.

In addition to the elimination goal, the team will want to target skills in the toileting routine, such as getting to the toilet, lowering pants, wiping, or flushing; thus, these skills need to be added to the task analysis. The task analysis should be written so that it suits the bathrooms that the student typically uses; however, if the home bathroom is very different from the school bathroom(s) and instruction starts at school, the task analysis should reflect the school bathroom. For some students, teams may decide to postpone instruction on wiping or going to and leaving the toilet and instead prompt them through these steps without the goal of independence; these steps can still be a part of the task analysis but are simply performed by the adult and recorded that way. Putting all of the steps, including any "teacher steps," on the task analysis data sheet helps keep staff consistent. Depending on the student's current level of performance, more difficult skills can be added to the task analysis after the student is successful with the basic steps; these later skills can include latching a stall door, undoing and redoing pants fasteners, wiping, and hand washing.

Other considerations include adaptations made in the order of the steps in the task or in the way that a task is performed. For example, with younger children, a better method of teaching wiping requires the child to stand up and then wipe rather than to remain seated, while older students will sit and may learn to use premoistened wipes for easier cleansing (Stokes, Cameron, Dorsey, & Fleming, 2004). In addition, if skirts or dresses are worn, the "pants up and down" sequence obviously must be changed. Some students with physical disabilities will be more independent if they sit or lean on the toilet to lower their pants. The architectural characteristics of the bathroom (e.g., narrow doorways, sink access) and any adaptive improvements (e.g., grab bars, toilet height) in the bathrooms at school or at home will influence the way that the task can be performed and thus the task analysis. Simple or major bathroom modifications can make it possible for some students to attain independence (Schwab, 2006). Another consideration is the position for toileting for boys. The most typical urination position for boys is to stand and face the toilet. However, initially, boys usually are taught to use the toilet while sitting; later, boys who have adequate motor control will be taught to urinate while standing.

Task analytic assessment can be conducted in two ways: multiple- and single-opportunity methods. When a multiple-opportunity assessment is used, any steps that are not performed by the student during assessment are completed by the adult; this method allows student performance to be observed on all steps, but takes longer. (Figure 10–5 shows Adrian's coat-off performance using this method; refer to Chapter 5 for an explanation of task analytic assessment.) A single-opportunity task analytic assessment is fast and prevents errors, but does not give assessment information for each task step.

Toby was given a multiple opportunity assessment for the toileting task. If he skipped a step or performed it incorrectly, the teachers interrupted gently and performed it for him (e.g., pulling his pants down) and then marked it as having been performed incorrectly. Then he was given a 5-second latency period to initiate the next step. His team decided against using a single-opportunity procedure because this approach required that testing be stopped after the first error and they would learn less about his performance.

Selecting Learning Goals. When a student has the prerequisite skills or seems close, the team will examine both the student's elimination data and the task analytic assessment to identify reasonable objectives for elimination and for the related toileting skills (e.g., pants up and down, hand washing). Elimination objectives (and related skill objectives) will build directly on the skills that the student demonstrates in the baseline phase. Student objectives will align with one of three levels of performance, each requiring increasing ability:

1. *Regulated Toileting:* In regulated toileting, students learn to eliminate on a predictable schedule. These students acquire reliable patterns of bowel movements and urination and remain dry if someone else reminds them or assists them with going to the toilet at scheduled times. School staff can use a regular toileting schedule, as well as being alert to the student's signals that elimination is imminent and then prompt students to use the toilet. Keeping a predictable schedule with fairly stable eating and drinking patterns, paired with reinforcement for correct toileting behavior, helps students maintain regulated toileting, once acquired.

Toby currently has regular periods of dryness and elimination, but only rare eliminations in the toilet and no self-initiations. His current elimination objective is to become regulated so that his accidents are rare.

2. *Self-Initiated Toileting:* This level of toileting performance involves learning to determine the natural cues of bladder fullness (for bladder control) and pressure in the lower bowel (for bowel control) and to either request to toilet or simply to go to the toilet. During this stage, we want students to make a connection between these internal stimuli and the response of eliminating in the toilet. Noticing students' signals that elimination is imminent and prompting them to the toilet (or to request to go to the toilet), as well as giving positive feedback immediately upon elimination in the toilet, helps them make this connection. Once a student is sitting on the toilet, teachers may make regular checks and (depending on its appropriateness) listen or look for urination or defecation so that they can provide reinforcement with little delay. Whenever students signal a need to use the bathroom or simply initiate toileting on their own, staff must give enthusiastic praise and get them to a bathroom quickly with as little help as necessary.

When Patrick was learning to initiate the need for toileting five years ago, his pattern of elimination was very regular. But the team had problems with (a) Patrick being able to reliably signal others, (b) the staff learning to attend to Patrick's requests and act on them, (c) the staff efficiently providing assistance to get him to a toilet and make the transfer from wheelchair to toilet, and (d) Patrick learning to participate in the toileting components more quickly. First, classroom staff and Patrick worked with the OT and PT to improve the task analysis for getting to, on, and off the toilet. The teaching plan was then revised to focus on teaching Patrick to signal his need on a regular schedule and having all team members use consistent methods to get him to the toilet.

3. *Toileting Independence:* The final level of toileting performance is to attain generalized self-sufficiency. Independent students not only are aware of the need to toilet but also know how to manage clothing and have related cleanup skills (e.g., wiping, flushing, washing hands). Trainers will fade themselves out of the bathroom during routine toileting and shift the focus to skill generalization, fluency, and proficiency issues (e.g., speed, elimination of all accidents, social awareness), and routine performance.

Patrick is now working on independence: he self-initiates and has not had an accident at school for the past 6 months; he can assist in carrying out most of the related skills. His PT thinks that once the grab bars are repositioned properly, he will, with practice, be able to stand, pivot, and transfer to and from the toilet on his own. When Patrick wears athletic pants, he does not need help with fasteners and enjoys even more privacy.

Instruction on elimination and toileting skill objectives generally will be combined so that students are taught the targeted related skills at every toileting opportunity.

Identify Teaching Strategies

There are several approaches to teaching toileting: traditional, systematic schedule training, and intensive. The emphasis with all methods is on reinforcing students for eliminations in the toilet and for remaining clean and dry. The primary differences between traditional and intensive methods are toileting schedule and the intensity of training:

- *Traditional methods* rely on toileting students at the time that they are likely to experience bowel or bladder tension (when the bowel or bladder is naturally full). These times are identified from elimination records.
- *Systematic schedule training* involves the addition of one or more procedures associated with intensive methods (e.g., access to fluids, underpants not diapers, dry-pants checks) and increased regular toileting.
- *Intensive methods* require (a) access to fluids in order to create more frequent bladder tension; (b) dry-pants checks; (c) increased training time each day; (d) long periods in the bathroom; and (e) may include accident interruption, moisture-signaling devices, and request training. Consequences for accidents vary from neutral to negative.

Before describing these approaches, the team must address two issues, regardless of which approach they choose:

Diapers or Underpants?. First, teams need to discuss whether diapers or underpants will be worn by the student during training. Clothing students in training pants or ordinary underwear rather than diapers is recommended because it can facilitate detection of accidents during baseline and training phases (Dunlap, Koegel, & Koegel, 1986). This approach also allows learners to experience the naturally unpleasant feed-

back from wet or soiled clothing that modern disposable diapers have virtually eliminated; these naturally occurring, uncomfortable consequences of accidents can contribute to faster learning. Wearing diapers may lead to substantially more urinary accidents and fewer successful voids even when taken to the toilet regularly (Tarbox, Williams, & Friman, 2004) because they are more difficult to pull down or remove than underpants. However, without diapers, students' toileting accidents can be noticed by peers and be stigmatizing, especially beyond the preschool years.

Teams (including family members) must decide the appropriateness of having students wear diapers; teams may make exceptions to the no-diapers guideline with older students to avoid noticeable accidents. Training pants with disposable diapers over them may allow the student both privacy and feedback, although removal for toileting will likely require assistance. Anderson et al. (2005) recommend that when using more intensive methods, teachers and parents must "Get rid of the diapers" (p. 137) and use underpants. Thus, it is best to remove diapers with intensive or isolated instruction or if training occurs at home during summer vacation. Teams may decide that wearing diapers in school, even when training is under way, is the appropriate choice.

Communication and Visual Cues. Second, teams need to use communication modes that the student understands (e.g., gestures, photos, picture symbols, signs, words) and augment their spoken communication with the student's modes (e.g., show/point to the picture symbol for a toilet whenever the word "toilet" is spoken). For scheduled trips to the toilet, it may be appropriate to start with the student's picture or word schedule. For some students, Now–Next visual cues (first toilet, then computer), social narratives or Social Stories™ about toileting, and success charts can be valuable accompaniments to the toileting approach that the team selects. Others have reported better success when students viewed short toileting videos before every toileting opportunity, coupled with systematic instruction, than when only systematic instruction was given (Keen, Brannigan, & Cuskelly, 2007).

Traditional Toilet-Training Methods

Traditional toilet training begins with taking a child to the toilet at regular intervals throughout the day or when the student demonstrates the need to toilet (e.g., grabbing their crotch, increased movement). Students are praised for elimination in the toilet and remaining clean and dry. While these simple steps are successful for most typical students when they meet the prerequisites, this approach should be systematized somewhat to increase its success when student have disabilities (Anderson et al., 2007; Baker & Brightman, 1997; Fredericks et al., 1975; Linford, Hipsher, & Silikovitz, 1972; Schaefer & DiGeronimo, 1997):

1. Toileting times are selected based on the student's baseline elimination pattern. Identify all of the typical times when the student tended to eliminate on or off the toilet; this is likely to be two or three times during a full school day. Add other logical times, such as immediately upon arrival, following lunch, and before departure for home. The target times become the scheduled occasions when students are taken to the toilet. Some teams start with a few of the most likely target times and add more times with success.

2. When students are neither bladder nor bowel trained, continue the use of diapers and focus on bowel training first because it is easier to learn. Wet pants are changed in the bathroom without a fuss. When bladder training, training pants are better than diapers; however, the team needs to make that decision depending on the circumstances described previously.

3. Learn how the student signals the need to eliminate. Signals for bowel movements are more obvious (e.g., gets quiet, squats, strains, turns red in the face). Parents typically are very helpful in identifying these signals. Whenever these signals occur, even if it is not a scheduled time, take the student immediately to the bathroom urging speed and restraint ("Quick, let's go to the toilet!"), and then record these times on the record.

4. Establish a toileting schedule that includes the times identified in the baseline phase when elimination is most likely; follow it consistently. Adjust times only if the program is unsuccessful; make adjustments based on an analysis of the student's elimination pattern.

5. Use the regular toilet, with adaptations added only as necessary to (a) keep the student's feet flat on the floor or on a nonslip support, and (b) keep the student sitting securely (e.g., toilet seat inset). As in Patrick's case, specialized toilet chairs and support bars are sometimes needed, including toilet seat inserts if the child is younger than age five and

very small. If students are unstable while sitting, they will have trouble relaxing the sphincters that control elimination. When needed, team members should pool their talents to generate appropriate adaptations that are nonstigmatizing and practical.

6. Keep the toileting time positive but not distracting. Any rewarding activities beyond praise or brief reinforcers, such as stickers or food (if edibles are the only effective reinforcers), should take place after toileting and out of the bathroom. Unneeded conversation (e.g., social talk, singing, rhymes) is kept to a minimum, although talking about the toileting task in ways suited to the student is appropriate.

7. Take the student to the toilet according to a consistent schedule (and whenever a need is signaled), approximately (a) 15 minutes before the scheduled time for bowel training, and (b) 5 to 10 minutes before the scheduled time(s) for bladder training. The specific length of time for sitting on the toilet should be determined on the basis of individual student characteristics. The student should be placed on the toilet long enough to have the opportunity to eliminate, but not for so long that toileting becomes aversive. Of course, the student should never be left unsupervised.

8. Reinforce the student when elimination occurs. If elimination does not occur, return the student to the classroom for a 5- to 10-minute interval and then return to the toilet. Continue the alternating intervals until elimination occurs. Record any extra toileting times and the outcomes.

9. Continue elimination records so that the team can evaluate progress and adjust toileting times as needed.

10. Consider extending goals as the student is successful (e.g., add more times or more related skills, shift to self-initiation and then independence).

Systematic Schedule Training

When more traditional approaches are insufficient, teachers may consider a combination of several procedures: (a) increased reinforcement for successes, (b) more frequent scheduled toileting with underpants instead of diapers, (c) dry-pants checks, (d) natural consequences for accidents, (e) free access to fluids, (f) use of moisture-signaling devices, or (g) transfer of stimulus control. Teams also might simply begin by adding the first three procedures (a, b, and c) to a traditional method. Others recommend that teams make the traditional approach more systematic by scheduling toileting opportunities based on a student's elimination patterns (part of the traditional approach), getting rid of diapers, using dry-pants checks, and lengthening the time gradually between scheduled toileting opportunities (Anderson et al., 2007).

Regular Toileting. Without giving extra fluids, the number of times students are taken to the toilet can be increased using a regular interval across the day (e.g., every hour, every half hour). This approach may help when a student's baseline did not yield reliable periods of dryness over time and when the student is not showing progress with fewer target times. When the team decides to increase toileting trips, this means less time for instruction in other areas and plays havoc with time scheduled in general education classrooms. If regular toileting is the only change made to a traditional program that is not working, it may be inadequate.

Regular Toileting Without Diapers for Older Learners. As previously discussed, removal of diapers and replacement with training pants is recommended for younger students when intensive and even traditional methods are used. While there is limited testing for this approach to regular toileting without diapers for adults, its simplicity and limited success make it worth describing. It is likely that regular toileting without diapers is more appropriate for older students who have learned the basic toileting routine but continue to have accidents and wear diapers as a matter of convenience. Tarbox et al. (2004) tested this simple method with a 29-year-old adult with developmental disabilities who routinely wore adult diapers to his work setting. Two conditions were compared within a withdrawal design. First, the man's diaper was removed upon arrival at work and he was asked to use the toilet every 30 minutes, which he did independently and received praise for successful voiding. After six days, the man used adult diapers while at work and was still asked to use the toilet every 30 minutes. These two treatments (no diaper and diaper) were alternated several times for four to seven days each. Data were gathered on his daily occurrences of urinary accidents and his successful voids in the toilet. The findings showed that when the man did not wear a diaper, his urinary accidents decreased an average of 0.1 per day and his successful voids increased 1.8 per day; but when he wore a diaper, his accidents increased an average of 1.5 per day and his successful voids decreased an average of 0.5 per day. The findings

suggest that wearing a diaper may increase accidents and that negative reinforcement is involved: disposable diapers decrease the unpleasant sensation of wetness, others' awareness of accidents, and the need to use the toilet. Additionally, the extra social reinforcement for successful voiding may have helped increase his use of the toilet.

This approach is fairly straightforward, but it requires more supervision than simply having adults or students wear diapers. Additional replication of these findings will strengthen it as an option for reducing adult incontinence.

Dry-Pants Checks and Reinforcement. Somewhat like what was done during the baseline phase, dry-pants checks consist of assessing whether a student is wet or dry; however, during training, appropriate feedback (reinforcement for continence or signaling a need to change if wet) is provided. During the first two levels of toileting performance (regulation and self-initiation), pants checks serve to increase student awareness of being wet or dry. When using this approach, we recommend several changes from its original use (Azrin & Foxx, 1971; Foxx & Azrin, 1973). First, except for very young students or when training is conducted at home or in isolation, pants checks should be done in private, ideally in the bathroom. Before checking, teachers should approach the student and, using a tone that is nonjudgmental and a communication form that the student will understand (gestures, a picture, words), say "We are going to check to see if you have dry pants" (Anderson et al., 2007, p. 141). Place the student's hand in yours and together gently check the outside then the inside of the pants to assess their condition. If the student is dry, provide enthusiastic praise acknowledging the dry pants in simple language that he or she understands. A choice of a short preferred activity or a tangible item may be given as well. When students are wet or soiled, Anderson et al. recommend assisting the student to feel their pants again and saying in a firm, but nonpunitive voice, "You have wet pants." Using a neutral teacher–student interaction (neither punishing nor reinforcing) and no social interaction, immediately change students who are wet or soiled and return them to their prior activity. Teachers will record wetness or dryness after every check by the date and time. If a student is wet for most dry-pants checks, then the checking time needs to be more frequent (Anderson et al., 2007).

First his team got rid of the diapers and Adrian was dressed with regular pants and underpants (with a large supply of dry clothes to change into after accidents). While this approach meant that his accidents would become more apparent, the team viewed this as less of a problem during summer school because none of his peers without disabilities would be in attendance. Adrian tended to urinate every hour, so he was prompted to the toilet five minutes before the hour using his visual schedule (remove the toilet symbol from the schedule, take it to the bathroom door, and match/affix the toilet symbol to the symbol on the door). Once there, the teacher drew his attention to a within-task sequence of four pictures on the wall (pants down, sit, pee, pants up) as she prompted him with the symbol to carry out each step. Toilet flushing was added later. Hand washing was at the sink located outside the toilet where there was another set of six pictures (water on, wet hands, soap, wet hands, water off, dry hands) used to prompt him through each step. Team members added to the bottom of his picture schedule several toilet symbols for him to get (or be prompted to get) whenever he self-initiated or showed signs of needing to eliminate.

Dry-pants checks with several added steps continued during this teaching program: (a) staff prompted Adrian to feel his pants and asked him, "Are you dry?"; (b) if his pants were dry, staff smiled and said enthusiastically, "You are dry!" and praised him; (c) if his pants were wet, staff said, without smiling, "You are wet, you need to pee in the toilet" and pointed and took him there and then changed his pants. Soon during dry-pants checks, they could just ask him: "Are you dry?" He would shake his head and was accurate after several days of teaching. During summer school, staff intentionally used whatever bathroom in the school they were closest to in order to encourage generalization; he had no difficulty using different bathrooms. Every bathroom had the picture cues posted along with a supply of clean clothes and a disposal bag. Instruction was started on the first day of summer school and by the end of the four weeks Adrian eliminated 80% of the time when taken to the bathroom, reduced his accidents from three to five times a day to none, and had self-initiated several times during his last two weeks His parents began using the same procedures at home during the second week of summer school with similar success.

As was done by Adrian's team, other teams need to individualize their strategies: the specific length of time between dry-pants checks, their communication mode and vocabulary, the feedback given for wetness and dryness, and the reinforcement for continence. Feedback should always be directed toward increasing student awareness of being dry or wet; when wet, pants should be changed with little comment (simply, "You're wet," said in a neutral tone). Obviously, dry-pants checks are less accurate with disposable diapers than with training pants.

Toby's first instructional program in preschool up to age nine consisted of the traditional methods described previously with enthusiastic verbal praise whenever his pants were dry. When this was not successful, dry-pants checks every half hour in the bathroom were added, along with 60-minute scheduled toileting trips, an increase in team member involvement, and the use of moisture-signaling devices to indicate urination. Whenever the device was activated, he was rushed to the bathroom ("Hurry, you have to pee in the toilet!") and any elimination in the toilet was greatly praised.

Consequences for Accidents. When students are learning elimination control and are purposefully taken out of diapers, some accidents must be expected. Thus, a regular procedure for responding to accidents should be planned by the team. In most cases, extinction (planned ignoring) is an appropriate strategy; however, the team may consider several options:

1. *Extinction:* Following an accident, change the student's pants and clean the student in a neutral manner, with little socialization. Be careful not to provide any reinforcing activity too soon after an accident (Hobbs & Peck, 1985).
2. *Mild disapproval:* As soon as an accident is discovered, approach the student in a manner that respects his or her privacy, have the student feel and look at the pants, and express some age-appropriate form of disapproval in your words and facial expressions ("You have wet pants"; "Oh-oh, you have wet pants, you can't have music"). Change the student's pants as with the extinction procedure.
3. *Cleanup:* Use mild disapproval, but require the student to participate in washing him or herself with a damp cloth and changing clothes. Student cleanup should be implemented as a natural consequence, with little socializing and with no punitive talk or

handling. *Requiring the student to participate in an overcorrection procedure, that is, repeatedly practicing going to the toilet or doing more than required (e.g., mopping the entire floor where the accident occurred instead of just cleaning the soiled area) is aversive and should not be used.* Use the cleanup participation strategy cautiously, as students who require prompting to clean themselves may be reinforced by the extra attention for the accident or may become upset emotionally. In addition, some who clean themselves independently may find it reinforcing to leave classroom demands.

The approaches for handling accidents must be carefully matched to a given student. Note that if extinction is selected, neither disapproval nor student cleaning up of accidents should be used. However, disapproval and cleanup consequences may be used together, or disapproval may be used alone. Cleanup typically involves mild disapproval. Most experts and practitioners agree that it is the positive aspects of teaching that lead to learning new skills, not the negative consequences.

Moisture-Signaling Devices. One possible reason that students may not learn toileting is delayed feedback. Students who wear modern disposable diapers often feel little discomfort when they are wet, and teachers may be unable to identify if they are wet or exactly when elimination occurred. Learning to associate bowel or bladder tension with elimination (e.g., sphincter relaxation) is facilitated when students are quickly taken to the toilet during urination or bowel movement and receive approval for eliminating there. Moisture-signaling devices are used to signal the moment of elimination, either on or off the toilet.

Two types of moisture-detection or urine-signaling devices have been used, along with other teaching methods:

1. *Toilet alert:* This device can be built into a special toileting chair (for young students) or into a small toilet bowl that fits under the regular toilet seat and catches eliminations, triggering an auditory signal.
2. *Pants alert:* These special underpants or clip-on devices detect moisture when students eliminate in their clothing. Pants alerts involve a circuit and switch plan, somewhat similar to the toilet signal; the signaling device is attached to the pants, shirt, or vest pocket.

Both devices involve a low-voltage circuit being completed when moisture activates the switch for the auditory signal. The signal allows staff to provide students with appropriate feedback the moment that elimination occurs. Moisture-detecting switches connected to a toileting chair or toilet inset signal the moment of elimination and the time for positive reinforcement; moisture-detecting underpants signal the moment that an accident occurs and, thus, when the teacher should rush the student to the bathroom, urging that the student hold back (Cicero & Pfadt, 2002). These devices are available through the Sears® and JCPenney™ catalogs (Mercer, 2003) and are carried by many local pharmacies; pediatricians also can direct parents or teachers to suppliers. Other quick ways to access these devices are to conduct an Internet search for various brand names (e.g., Wet-Stop®).

> *Toby's initial intervention consisted of a dry-pants check every 30 minutes and being taken to the toilet upon arrival and on the hour. Wet pants were changed without comment; Toby put them into the laundry basket in the bathroom. A moisture-signaling device was put into his pants to alert staff to accidents in between dry-pants checks; when it was activated, he was quickly taken to the toilet.*

Despite the efficiency of signaling the moment of elimination, the disadvantages of moisture-signaling equipment in a toileting program are many. The equipment, which is noisy and fairly obvious (especially when it signals), can be quite stigmatizing to students who use it. If students spend time in regular education classes and in activities in the school and community, this equipment is not appropriate. Other problems with the device include expense, breakdown, or failure (Mahoney, Van Wagenen, & Meyerson, 1971; Smith, 1979), although newer devices are better. Teams should view moisture-signaling devices as an option for use in unusual situations in which toileting progress has been minimal; bladder control is relatively important for the individual; and training is conducted under more isolated conditions, such as during a summer program or at home.

Video Modeling. Several studies have applied video modeling with or without systematic instruction. Bainbridge and Myles (1999) demonstrated the use of "priming" to toilet train a child with autism. The student watched a five-minute video that showed children learning to use the toilet, along with accompanying songs. After each viewing of the video, the student was prompted to use the toilet. This approach, without additional training, resulted in increased self-initiations for toileting and dry diapers during checks, but not bladder control. (The video, *It's Potty Time* (Howard, 1991) is available at http://www.youtube.com.) Keen, Brannigan, and Cuskelly (2007) found that students with autism who received intensive training and viewed video models made more progress than those receiving intensive training alone. Video modeling appears to be a promising strategy for students who respond to visual cues and has been designated by some to be an evidence-based practice for individuals with autism (National Professional Development Center on Autism Spectrum Disorders, 2009).

Intensive Training Programs

Intensive toilet-training methods are rather complex training packages based primarily on the research of Azrin and Foxx (Azrin & Foxx, 1971; Foxx & Azrin, 1973, 1974) or of Van Wagenen, Mahoney, and colleagues (Mahoney et al., 1971; Van Wagenen, Meyerson, Kerr, & Mahoney, 1969; Van Wagenen & Murdock, 1966). Some components of the packages (e.g., dry-pants checks, moisture-detection devices) have already been discussed and can be used separately. Intensive training has been described as "rapid" because the program usually is delivered with high intensity and rapid changes in student performance have been reported. However, some of these older methods and their intensities conflict with today's emphasis on positive interventions. In addition, the speedy results have not been consistently replicated by researchers (see also Cicero & Pfadt, 2002). Typically, intensive approaches have been used with students in nonschool or institutional settings and have employed one or more of the following questionable practices: (a) fluid increases that may be dangerous, (b) removal of the student from all or most instruction other than toileting, (c) removal of the student from opportunities to participate with nondisabled peers, and (d) the likelihood of excessive punishment (i.e., see LeBlanc, Carr, Crossett, Bennett, & Detweiler, 2005, as a recent example of these negative characteristics).

In the past decade, several modified versions of Azrin and Foxx's intensive approaches have been tested. Some of these approaches continue the use of excessively long training periods in the bathroom and "positive practice" overcorrection for accidents, which is anything but positive! Some approaches have added new punitive methods: movement and response restriction (Averink, Melein, & Duker, 2005; Didden, Sikkema, Bosman, Duker,

& Curfs, 2001; Duker, Averink, & Melein, 2001), the requirement for a three-year-old to sit for 20 minutes on the toilet (Post-Kirkpatrick, 2004), and keeping students on the toilet until urination occurs (Luiselli, 2007).

Three versions of intensive approaches that do not use aversive methods will be described next in order of their intensity: (a) Richmond, 1983; (b) Cicero & Pfadt, 2002, and Keen et al., 2007; and (c) Anderson et al., 2007, and Chung, 2007. A summary of the components used in nonpunitive and punitive intensive methods is shown in Table 10–2. Intensive toileting approaches should be used only with total team support and if other less intrusive methods do not work after being implemented accurately and for a long enough period. Fortunately, if intensive methods are needed, there are enough effective, positive strategies from which teams can select; punitive intensive approaches should not be used.

Increasing or Regulating Fluids. Increasing the fluids that a student consumes will increase opportunities to urinate and thus to be taught and to obtain reinforcement. However, increasing fluids to boost the quantity of bladder-training sessions must be accompanied by certain precautions. When the intake of water or other liquids is forced or encouraged over an extended period, the balance of electrolytes in the body may be seriously endangered. Hyponatremia, or a low serum sodium level, while rare, may result and is associated with nausea, vomiting, muscular twitching, grand mal seizures, and coma (Thompson & Hanson, 1983). This condition "constitutes a serious medical emergency requiring prompt sodium replacement therapy and other medical support" (p. 140).

The decision to increase fluids requires approval by the family physician and should not be used with students on medications that increase urinary retention or those who have seizure disorders or hydrocephaly. If extra fluids are approved, the amount allowed throughout the day varies according to the size of the student. Children between 60 and 100 pounds can have *at most* a small serving every hour (one-third to one-half cup) during the school day; while adolescents and adults between 100 and 150 pounds can have *at most* up to two thirds of a cup of liquid every hour during the school day (Thompson & Hanson, 1983). These maximum limits allow increased opportunities for instruction without putting the students' health at risk. It is best to use water or noncaffeinated, low-sugar drinks (diluted fruit juice). Students should be offered drinks or given free access to drinks, but must not be

TABLE 10–2

Characteristics of Intensive Toileting Methods

Components of Intensive Toilet Training in School Settings	Nonpunitive Intensive Methods			Less Punitive, But Still Punitive: Do Not Use
	Intensive Toileting (Richmond, 1983)	Request Training and Accident Interruption (Cicero & Pfadt, 2002; Keen et al., 2007)	"Rapid" Methods Without Punishment (Anderson et al., 2007; Chung, 2007)	Averink et al., 2005; Didden et al., 2001; Duker et al., 2001
Scheduled, frequent toileting trips	Every 15, 30, 60, then 120 minutes over 4 weeks	Yes, every 30 minutes	Yes, every 30 minutes	Yes, every 30 minutes
Graduated guidance and total task sequence	Yes	Yes	Yes	No; least to most prompts
Positive reinforcement for successes	Yes	Yes	Yes	Yes
Free access to fluids	Yes	Yes	Yes	Yes
Underpants, no diapers, limited clothing	Yes	Yes	Yes	Yes
Training in 30-minute cycles in bathroom	No	Yes, then faded	Yes, then faded	Yes
Length of time seated or until elimination	Not stated	1–3 minutes	3 minutes; 20 minutes	5–20 minutes (varied)
Training primarily in the bathroom	No	Yes, then faded	Yes, then faded	Yes
Number of hours of training per day	Entire school day (morning)	Entire school day (5.5 hours)	4 hours; 3 hours per day	5.5–7 hours per day
Dry-pants checks	Yes	No	Yes	Yes
Urine-sensing equipment	No	No	Optional; No	No
Initiation request training ("Bathroom," by verbal or picture exchange)	Yes, but less formal	Yes	No	No
Accident interruption and rush to toilet with praise if elimination	No	Yes	Yes	No
Accidents followed by brief reprimand and simple correction (assistance in cleanup)	Yes	Yes	Yes	Yes
Video modeling and picture cues	No	No; Yes	No	No
Punitive methods: Response restriction (1-foot radius of movement) in toilet area, "positive" practice for accidents plus reprimand and time-out from reinforcers	No	No	No	Yes
Range of time to little or no accidents	4 weeks	7–11 days	Unclear	24–25 hours
Research support	Data presented for four preschool students with intellectual disability (ID), using single-subject design	Data for three students with autism, no experimental design; same but used an experimental design	No data presented; based on use in a program serving students with autism; Chung's single student with ID – mixed success	Data from three studies for 54 children to adults with ID; nonconcurrent multiple baseline across students

pressured to take fluids. Pressuring a student to drink when they express strong refusal will likely end up in a power struggle, which would be an obstacle to successful toilet training. Reinforcement should not be made contingent on drinking extra fluids.

This approach of using increased liquids plus a 30-minute toileting schedule and reinforcement for urinating in the toilet was successful when used with a 19-year-old woman with significant intellectual disability after 17 school days of training (Sells-Love, Rinaldi, & McLaughlin, 2002). In this study, the woman was "allowed to consume" 16 ounces of water (2 cups) in the morning and in the afternoon; however, because no information on seizure conditions or weight was reported, it is difficult to determine if this quantity was excessive, but the rate of consumption exceeded what is recommended.

Richmond's Rapid Procedure.

Four preschool children with profound retardation were successfully toilet trained with increased opportunities to use the toilet. Intervention consisted of four training phases (i.e., toileting every 15 minutes, every 30 minutes, every hour, every 2 hours), each lasting one week and followed by a posttraining or maintenance phase. Just before each toileting trip, the teacher made a dry-pants check. If no accident was detected, the child was praised for having dry and clean pants. The teacher then asked the child, "Do you need to use the toilet?" The child was prompted to respond and go to the restroom. In the restroom, the child was praised for engaging in the related toileting behaviors (e.g., pulling pants down and up). If necessary, graduated guidance was used to prompt these behaviors. Social praise and liquids were given for successful toileting, and no comments were made when accidents occurred. Extra fluids served both as reinforcers and to increase the frequency of urination. When an accident was detected, the teacher gave a brief reprimand and simple correction (i.e., the child was responsible for getting a clean set of clothes, removing the dirty clothes, washing soiled body areas, disposing of dirty clothes, and dressing). The morning preschool schedule continued even with the frequent toileting interruptions.

Richmond's results are encouraging news to teachers of younger children: Simple but intensive toileting methods applied in a consistent manner can be effective over a 9- to 15-week period without extreme techniques or schedule changes. The frequency of toileting, while important to learning bladder control, is problematic when students move into the elementary grades and beyond. Teams should emphasize toilet training at younger ages when schedules are more flexible and social stigma is less likely.

Cicero and Pfadt (2002); Keen et al. (2007).

In these two studies, request training and accident interruption were added to intensive training. Cicero and Pfadt included in their program three young children with autism (ages four, four, and six years) who all wore diapers and had urination accidents daily. Teachers carried out the training in a separate day school for children with autism, with all initial instruction taking place in the bathroom using 30-minute training cycles. Children were dressed in limited clothing and training pants and were encouraged to drink extra fluids with free access provided in the morning only. *Request training* started each 30-minute cycle. *Instead* of prompting students to request the use of the toilet by giving an instructional cue (e.g., "What do you want to do?"), teachers prompted them by using picture exchange with students who used picture symbols and verbal models ("bathroom" or "ba") with students who were verbal. Once students made the request, they were brought to the toilet and prompted to pull their pants down and sit. Eliminations were followed by prompts to stand and pull up their pants and flush, and then they were quickly reinforced with verbal praise and tangibles. When students did not eliminate, no reinforcers were given and the student was told, "OK, you don't have to pee."

Teachers were alert to noticing when students started to urinate off the toilet and used a nonaversive interruption procedure. This *accident interruption* method was used to startle the child and temporarily halt urination until the student could be quickly prompted to the toilet while the teacher lowered the student's pants ("No, no, no, hurry up, you pee on the potty"). If any urine was discharged in the toilet, the student was reinforced as before. The student's clothes were changed following each accident without any other consequence. No request training was given during accident interruption trials. The authors noted that these interruption procedures served as positive teaching opportunities not as negative consequences.

Once children made a spontaneous request to be taken to the toilet and then urinated there, requests were no longer prompted. Students then could request to be taken to the toilet, go on their own, or have an accident. Reinforcement and forward prompting through the task was continued. After 3 consecutive days of spontaneous initiations and no accidents, all other training components were faded, fluids were reduced to their usual amount, and the child's standard clothing returned. During this fading process, students were moved farther and farther from the bathroom, back to classroom locations and activities. All students learned to spontaneously request use of the toilet while reducing their accidents to zero following 7 to 11 days of training. Posttraining maintenance checks indicated skill retention at 6 months and 1 year, and generalization to the home.

Keen and her colleagues (2007) replicated Cicero and Pfadt's methods with five young boys with autism (ages six to nine), but they added *video modeling plus picture cues* and they used a multiple baseline across students design. A 6-minute color video with music and real and animated characters was shown prior to each scheduled toileting. Picture cues from the video were used to redirect children from places where inappropriate urination occurred. Picture cue redirection and giving students greater privacy when sitting on the toilet improved in-toilet urinations for three of the five students. The findings supported the addition of videos and picture cues to the intensive methods of Cicero and Pfadt (2002).

Anderson et al. (2007). This intensive approach is similar to the original Azrin and Foxx (1973) method in that it incorporates all of their positive approaches, but does not employ any of their punitive methods (e.g., full cleanliness training, overcorrection positive practice, or harsh reprimands). Thus, students have increased opportunities for toileting; wear underpants, not diapers, and minimal clothing; have increased fluid intake; are taught in toileting cycles of 30 minutes in the bathroom for up to 4 hours daily; have dry-pants checks every 5 minutes; are given systematic prompting (and fading of prompts) for steps in the chain; and receive positive reinforcement for success. Chung (2007) applied a similar approach with a 12-year-old boy with a seizure disorder and intellectual disability. After 2 weeks of school training at 3 hours per day, he urinated in the toilet reliably, but still experienced some accidents.

Whenever an intensive approach is used, it must be individually designed to suit the student and the team members who will be using it. Ongoing elimination data will serve to guide the team's evaluation of outcomes and any necessary program modifications.

After several months with little success, Toby's records (see Figure 10–9) showed that he either did not eliminate at all during school or he did so after noon. Several changes were initiated in May. First, Toby stayed in the bathroom between noon and 1:00 for intensive training. Second, during this hour, the staff set a timer and instituted (a) 4 minutes on the toilet with no interactions, and (b) 4 minutes off the toilet, sitting on a beanbag chair with a choice of a toy to play with or a book, and teacher interaction. These steps were repeated during the hour. Accidents were uncommon, but when they occurred, staff cleaned up with no comment; pull-up diapers were changed if wet. During this time, the moisture-signaling device was removed and Toby was dressed in a long T-shirt for privacy and his outer pants and underpants were removed. Initially, he wore a pull-up diaper with a hole cut in it for urination, which meant that the diaper could stay on so that getting on and off the toilet was faster, the beanbag chair was cleaner, he was less able to self-stimulate, and staff could see when he was starting to urinate. Once he eliminated in the toilet (or when it was 1:00), his pants were put back on and he returned to classroom activities. As shown in Figure 10–9, starting May 18, if he eliminated, training was discontinued for the rest of day, as he typically stayed dry. In late May, Toby was consistently urinating between noon and 1:00 and usually shortly after being taken to the toilet. At this point, the hour-long intensive toileting procedure was stopped and the pull-up diaper was replaced with underpants.

All three of these intensive methods are demanding on staff. Richmond's approach requires less time in the bathroom, but it has not been replicated. The training intensity and student's limited clothing in all three methods make instruction in school settings challenging. Staff involved in training and students spend little time outside of the bathroom. Teams must seriously evaluate if intensive methods are necessary before deciding to use them.

Special Considerations for Eating and Mealtimes

Eating is perhaps the most functional and frequently used of all self-care skills. In addition to filling our primary needs for nutrition, mealtimes are often a time for socializing. Mealtimes mean conversation, getting together with friends and family, sharing, and enjoying food. This should be true for students with disabilities, too. Pleasant and gratifying mealtimes can enhance the use of eating skills and the social and communication skills embedded in eating routines. Teams should structure mealtime and eating instruction so that learning and enjoyment result.

When developing individualized plans for teaching eating and mealtime behavior, teams focus on the general goals of healthy eating (e.g., meeting nutritional needs, eating without choking) and eating as independently as possible. This section addresses the elements of assessing and teaching basic mealtime skills to learners whose objectives are primarily independent eating. (See also Chapter 8 regarding nutritional monitoring and supplementation and non-oral feeding procedures; refer to Chapter 9 for specific positioning considerations for students with motor disabilities.)

Identify What to Teach

The educational team has several issues to consider in the process of selecting mealtime skills for instruction. First, does the child have the necessary prerequisites for instruction in eating independently? Next, the team reviews the family's preferences regarding eating routines and any cultural traditions related to mealtimes. The team will also gather information about the student's food preferences (specific foods and textures), dietary needs, food allergies, and any challenging behaviors that may impede instruction. Then the team reviews the developmental sequence of core eating skills and related mealtime skills. Finally, the team identifies priority skills, develops a task analysis, and collects baseline data.

Prerequisites for Instruction in Eating Independently

For students to be successful in learning to eat independently, they need an active gag reflex and the skills of sucking, maintaining closed lips, swallowing, biting, and chewing. Mastery of these basic skills greatly reduces the risk of choking. Before beginning assessment or instruction, students should be in the proper position for eating, even when they do not have extensive or obvious motor disabilities or high or low tone in their muscles. Proper position has a big impact not only on learning and success with eating, but also on the prevention of choking and the aspiration of food. The student's head must be stable, in midline, and with the chin and jaw as near to parallel with the floor as possible.

Family Interview

It is helpful to interview the student (when possible) and caregivers to learn about family routines and student needs (e.g., food preferences, allergies, dietary restrictions). Interviews also help the teacher to identify situations that may require expanding the educational team to include medical input or additional assessments. An informal observation in the home setting can also provide useful information regarding the student's mealtime skills (e.g., eating finger foods, drinking from a cup, using utensils, and displaying appropriate table manners).

Adrian's special education teacher visited his home and conducted a family interview. She learned that prior to this school year, Adrian ate a limited number of foods and rarely ate more than a few bites at one time. After participating in an intensive feeding program at a university hospital clinic, Adrian now eats a variety of foods. At home, Adrian's mother gives him an opportunity to eat every two hours during the day and tries to provide a preferred activity after each snack or meal. Adrian selects a picture of the activity that he would like to do when he is finished eating. He keeps the picture on the table during the meal. Adrian's teacher will use the same strategy and schedule a morning and afternoon snack for Adrian.

Sequence for Teaching Mealtime Skills

Core eating skills typically are taught in a general developmental sequence, beginning with various aspects of dependent feeding (e.g., anticipates spoon, uses lips to remove food from utensils), eating finger foods, eating with a spoon, drinking from a cup, using a fork, spreading and cutting with a knife, serving food, using condiments, and displaying good table manners. In general, targets should be both realistic in relationship to the current performance of students and immediately or subsequently relevant. Eating skill targets will be those that are prioritized by the family or teacher as being needed on a regular basis. Additionally, students must learn to eat a variety of foods because food refusal and food overselectivity can put students at risk nutritionally with regard to growth and health problems.

Not all eating skills, however, should be taught in a developmental sequence. Instead, teachers should tap extension skills (initiation, preparation, termination, problem solving) and enrichment skills (communication, choice, and social) that are relevant to the mealtime routine.

When Patrick was very young and dependent on others to feed him, parents and teachers taught him to initiate eating by vocalizing the "Eeee" and to look away when he was finished eating. Patrick's parents used graduated guidance to assist Patrick in bringing a spoon to his mouth.

Likewise, teaching skills in a functional order, even if not in the developmental order, may be the best option.

Toby, who is nine, spears food with a fork but does not use a spoon or knife or napkin unless prompted. He eats mainly with his fingers. Developmentally, he "should" master these first, but his team has decided that using a napkin and going through the lunch line are more functional, even if he bypasses spoon and knife use for now.

The team will review the family interview data and identify priority skills. The teacher will then develop a task analysis for each skill and collect baseline data.

Patrick enjoys going to the student union to have ice cream with his friends. He independently drives his wheelchair to the student union and navigates around the building. He is beginning to use a low-tech augmentative communication device (i.e., a folder with pages for different activities) when he is away from his computer. The targeted eating skills in this routine are appropriate spoon use and napkin use. Peers assist Patrick in obtaining and transporting the ice cream, as well as removing his adapted spoon from his backpack.

Identify Teaching Strategies for Eating and Mealtimes

A variety of methods have been successful in teaching mealtime skills (see Table 10–1). Specifically, shaping and physical prompting procedures (including physical prompts, time delay, and graduated guidance) have been shown to promote the acquisition of eating skills. Sometimes, these strategies have been combined with error correction, but positive procedures alone have proven to be adequate in other cases. Generally, graduated guidance and shaping are the recommended procedures for building basic eating skills and promoting independent eating during the acquisition stage.

Once students have learned the basic core eating skills (e.g., pick up spoon, scoop food), other teaching methods have been demonstrated as being more effec-

tive during the advanced stages. For example, skills can be maintained and made more fluent with simple reinforcement (e.g., praise and confirmation: "That's right!") and error correction. Procedures for correcting errors in these later stages may include teachers' or peers' verbal statements and models.

Eating Finger Foods

The first sign of independence in eating is the predictably messy stage of consuming finger foods. If the team's initial observations emphasize the need for utensil use *and* coordinating grasp, lift, and placement of finger foods in the mouth, finger food instruction should have priority over utensil use. At this early stage, students use pincer grasps and hand-to-mouth movements to pick up food in combination with the sucking, gumming, chewing, and swallowing of many soft foods, such as bananas and saliva-softened toast. Eating finger foods provides essential opportunities to improve the movements needed for later utensil use. Eating finger foods also allows opportunities for continued instruction in chewing. Working with the occupational therapist on the team, teachers can use mealtimes and snack times to introduce students to a variety of textures and tastes (Orelove, Sobsey, & Silberman, 2004).

Toby primarily eats with his fingers and still is messy. He often stuffs his mouth and does not use a napkin. Teaching him to use a spoon will be postponed until he makes more progress on eating more neatly with his fingers (see Figure 10–10).

FIGURE 10–10
Toby drinks from a straw, but eats mainly finger foods.

Drinking from a Cup or Glass

The earliest stage of learning involves students helping their parents or teachers hold the cup or glass and lift it to their mouth. At this early stage and when individuals first drink from a cup independently, they use both hands. When students have the potential to master drinking from a cup without assistance, straw use also may be taught, but typically this is not taught until after drinking from a cup is learned. For students who cannot learn independence in cup drinking, drinking liquids from stabilized, but age-appropriate, cups through straws is a good alternative means for becoming independent. Others can ask peers to assist on the steps that are too difficult to learn independently. Use of a straw also may be a functional skill for students in restaurants and cafeterias, where most people use them. As with eating with the fingers, the learning process is often messy.

Patrick asks a peer to help open his milk carton by touching the peer's arm and then pushing the milk carton toward the peer. He uses the same strategy to ask for help with putting a straw into the carton. The peer places the carton near Patrick's plate and he independently drinks from the carton.

The type of cup chosen for training may influence the initial success of students. Short, squat cups that do not turn over easily and can be held without difficulty are best to begin with. With preschool-age students, a weighted cup may be appropriate, although most cups of this style have a clear association with infants and are not age appropriate. Similarly, whereas double-handled cups are easier to hold, they also are not age appropriate in their design. However, plastic-handled coffee mugs (with or without the top) may be a good substitute. Durable plastic cups are obviously safer to use than are containers made of glass, brittle plastic, or paper. Spouted or nipple cups should never be used because they stimulate abnormal sucking and do not allow students to master the correct drinking response; however, sports cups with built-in straws are easily available and are often used by teens and adults. To reduce spilling, the amount of liquid in the cup should not be excessive, but also should not be so little that students need to tip their heads too much to drink, increasing the difficulty of the task. Adapted cups that are cut out on the upper side (to make room for the nose) can allow students with physical disabilities to drink all of the fluid without tilting their heads at all.

After students learn to drink holding handled cups or small glasses with both hands, teachers can begin to emphasize a reduction in spilling. Spilling may occur while drinking, but may also happen when a cup or glass is grasped, lifted, or placed on the table. As drinking from a glass improves, students should be reminded to lift glasses with only the dominant hand.

Using Utensils

Once students are able to grasp finger foods and move food from the table to the mouth with their fingers, along with the basic oral-motor responses (i.e., lip closure, chewing, and successful swallowing), teams can plan instruction on using utensils. At this time, observations should be made to assess the student's ability to pick up and eat from a spoon. Using utensils can be taught at the same time that drinking from a cup is taught.

Typically, utensil use is taught sequentially, from the easiest skill to the most difficult. Spoon use may be the simplest, followed in order of difficulty by eating with a fork, transferring spreads with a knife, spreading with a knife, cutting finger-grasped bread with a knife, and cutting meat with a knife and fork. The typical sequence is (a) spoon (with thicker foods, not thin liquids), (b) fork for spearing, (c) knife for spreading, and (d) knife and fork for cutting. Children may be able to eat using utensils in a palm-down finger or fist position. Teachers may use this grasp for initial instruction and teach the more mature, palm-up position after students have attained independence.

At age five, Adrian eats finger foods and uses a spoon to eat pudding. His team would like him to learn to use a fork for spearing his food.

Progress Monitoring

The instructional team will select the teaching schedule, setting, method, and progress monitoring procedure based on the characteristics of the student and the nature of the target skill. For example, a student who demonstrates food selectivity may be learning to accept new food items. During this learning process, the student may exhibit challenging behaviors during meals that include nonpreferred foods. Initially, the team may choose a private setting (e.g. resource classroom) to implement a feeding program. During instructional sessions, the teacher may collect data on the number of bites eaten of nonpreferred foods, the number of new foods accepted, and the rate of inappropriate behavior. After instructional sessions, the child may eat a preferred food item in the cafeteria with peers. For students with extensive support needs, mealtime instruction may require long mealtimes that interfere with instruction in other priority skill areas. In these cases, teachers may decide to teach and collect data for part of the meal and provide more assistance during the remainder of the meal. Task analytic data is useful for monitoring progress on skills that involve several steps (e.g., using a fork) and duration data may be useful for monitoring the pace of eating. Related and embedded skills may also be a focus for monitoring instruction. Chapter 5 describes measurement methods in detail and this information can assist the team in selecting a progress monitoring procedure that is appropriate for the target skill.

Addressing Problem Behaviors During Mealtime

Students with severe disabilities sometimes exhibit inappropriate behaviors related to mealtimes and eating. Often young, typically developing children are picky eaters and resist eating a variety of foods. Usually, with repeated exposure to a varied diet, children's diets become more diverse over time without intervention. However, children with severe disabilities may be highly selective in the foods that they will eat and this problem may persist for years. For example, a child may eat only foods in a particular food group or with a certain texture. Schreck, Williams, and Smith (2004) reported that children with autism ate a more restricted range of foods and had higher rates of food refusal than their peers. Medically fragile children sometimes receive treatments (e.g., suctioning, oral and nasal gastric tubes) that can lead to tactile defensiveness and oral hypersensitivity (Bailey & Angell, 2005; Comrie & Helm, 1997), which may play a part in the development of a resistance to eating and a restricted diet. Food selectivity can cause nutritional deficiencies and impede development. A systematic intervention may be necessary to ameliorate problem.

Much of the research on eating problems in chidren with disabilities has addressed food selectivity and food refusal (e.g., Ahearn, 2003; Levin & Carr, 2001; Wood, Wolery, & Kaiser, 2009). In this section, we describe approaches for addressing these challenges and supporting appropriate mealtime behavior. Eating problems, such as pica (i.e., eating nonedible substances) and excessive weight gain are not addressed here. Teams who are facing these problems may need to broaden the team membership to include medical input and to use additional assessment tools (e.g., functional assessment to study the conditions that seem to be maintaining the behavior, medical assessments, and health monitoring). (Chapter 7 addresses functional behavioral assessment; Chapter 8 discusses health monitoring.)

Food Selectivity and Refusal

Food refusal refers to the behavior of declining to eat a sufficient amount of food to maintain one's health. Food selectivity refers to eating a very narrow range of foods, often only a few foods and no others. Recent research describes several intervention procedures that may address these issues, including (a) antecedent strategies, (b) reinforcement, and (c) multicomponent treatment packages. Interventions may be implemented at school, at home, or both, depending on the child's needs and the family's preferences. Extreme cases of food selectivity may be treated in a clinic or hospital setting.

Antecedent Strategies. Antecedent strategies are those that concern the teaching arrangement, location, materials, teacher's directions, methods used to elicit student attention, and also prompt procedures used to get students to respond with few errors. In a teaching opportunity, antecedent methods occur before the student's response and thus influence how students respond to a teaching task. Ahearn (2003) illustrated the use of an antecedent strategy to address food selectivity in a child with autism in a multiple baseline design across different foods (vegetables). The results of an assessment of eating habits revealed that the child refused to eat vegetables but accepted at least one item from the fruit, protein, and starch food groups. He refused vegetables even when access to additional food was contingent on doing so. He preferred condiments (e.g., ketchup, barbecue sauce, salad dressing) and sometimes ate them without other food. Thus, the antecedent intervention consisted of presenting vegetables paired with a preferred condiment. This led to an increase in the variety and amount of vegetables that the child consumed. After the conclusion of the study, the child learned to use pictures to request specific condiments before meals and continued to eat vegetables.

Luiselli, Ricciardi, and Gilligan (2005) described a liquid-fading procedure implemented by classroom staff to increase milk consumption by a child with autism. The child refused milk, but would drink a blend of 50% PediaSure® (a nutritional supplement) and 50% whole milk. Gradually, classroom staff increased the milk to PediaSure® ratio across successive lunch sessions. When staff started the fading procedure, they reduced the amount of PediaSure® by one tablespoon and increased the quantity of milk by the same amount. When the student consumed at least 90% of this mixture during consecutive sessions, the ratio of milk to PediaSure® was increased again. When the fading procedure was completed, the child drank whole milk without PediaSure®. Together, these studies demonstrate that relatively simple strategies can help children overcome some forms of food selectivity and refusal.

Reinforcement Procedures.

Food selectivity has been successfully treated in some children by simple reinforcement of new choices (Najdowski, Wallace, Doney, & Ghezzi, 2003). Researchers determined student food preferences by observing their responses when presented with a variety of foods. The foods that students accepted were identified as preferred foods, and the foods that were refused were identified as nonpreferred foods. Children increased the variety and amount of food consumed when bites of nonpreferred foods were followed by bites of preferred foods, a method that is known as Premack's principle. When implementing this intervention, it is important to make reinforcement contingent on swallowing rather than accepting food (Najdowski et al., 2003). Although reinforcement procedures may be useful in addressing food refusal, often these procedures must be combined with antecedent procedures such as response prompts or visual supports in order to facilitate progress (Gentry & Luiselli, 2008). Reinforcement procedures also may be useful in supporting the maintenance of eating behavior after a more intensive intervention has been withdrawn.

As an infant, Adrian had a history of being a "failure to thrive" baby; this resulted in frequent refusals to eat and being highly selective with what he did eat. During the summer before kindergarten, his parents enrolled him in an intensive feeding program that greatly improved the amount and variety of foods he now eats. Over a six-week period, he was given meals with three foods and a drink twice a day and taught to take a bite of each food, followed by a drink (using a bite, bite, bite, drink pattern) in order to briefly watch a favorite DVD. When he returned to school, the classroom staff used a simplified version of this procedure, requiring that he eat his whole tray of food (at breakfast and at lunch) in a desig-

nated period of time and then was allowed to select and watch a DVD if he had eaten enough food and finished his drink. The program was highly successful and Adrian now eats almost everything in his school lunch alongside his peers (see Figure 10–11).

Multicomponent Treatment Packages.

Treatment approaches that address several variables (e.g., antecedents and consequences) are very effective in improving children's eating behaviors. Although researchers have investigated multicomponent treatment packages in home settings, the strategies employed in these studies may have useful applications in school settings as well. For example, Gentry and Luiselli (2008) combined antecedent and positive reinforcement procedures to increase the food consumption of a four-year-old boy with pervasive developmental disorder. The child ate a limited number of foods and only certain brands of some foods. Researchers interviewed the child's mother and identified a list of preferred and nonpreferred foods. The first intervention utilized a game spinner that was divided into eight sections, seven with a number and one with a question mark. The adult prompted the child to spin the arrow and when it stopped, to write the number on a chart that read, "I need to eat N bites of food." Then the adult presented a plate of food that was divided into three sections, two contained preferred foods and one contained a nonpreferred food. The adult said, "You have spun the number 2, that means you can eat 2 bites from this section, 2 bites from this section, and 2 bites from this section; then you can eat whatever you like." The child was also shown a reward chart with symbols representing preferred activities from which he chose an activity that he could do after he finished the meal. The adult prompted the child to take bites from the two preferred items first and then from the nonpreferred item. When the child ate the required number of bites of each food, he received verbal praise and was given the opportunity to eat the rest of the food on his plate, request additional food, or play. If he did not eat the required number of bites, he remained at the table for five minutes and then was asked to leave the table. If the arrow stopped on the question mark, the child received a toy from a gift box and was given only preferred food during the meal. Gradually, over time, the numbers on the spinner were increased to require the child to consume more food. During the second intervention phase, the game spinner was removed and the child was given a plate with a specific number of bites

FIGURE 10–11

Adrian has learned to line up with his peers, go to the cafeteria, use the lunch line, carry his tray, and sit down and eat. His teacher gives him word/picture cues when he forgets a step and provides a model for him to enter his lunch payment code.

of nonpreferred food. If the child consumed everything on the plate and refrained from inappropriate behavior, he was given access to a preferred activity. The number of bites of nonpreferred food was gradually increased. There was a steady increase in the amount of nonpreferred food consumed by the child. This procedure may need to be adapted as the negative consequence of staying for five minutes at the table when enough bites were not consumed may not be acceptable to team members.

Wood, Wolery, and Kaiser (2009) designed a treatment package that consisted of task direction, contingent reinforcement, physical prompts, and a procedure to introduce food gradually. This was the first investigation of a feeding intervention implemented with a child on a gluten-free/casein-free diet (GFCF). GFCF diets are an alternative treatment for autism and there is some concern that the use of a restrictive diet may further complicate the treatment of children with preexisting food selectivity. Prior to intervention, researchers conducted an assessment of the child's eating habits and identified five food categories. Categories were defined based on the child's response to the foods in each category. For example, food items in Category I were accepted 100% of the time when offered, while food items in Category III were rejected 50% of the time during the assessment. During intervention sessions, food was presented from selected categories. Foods from Category I were introduced in the initial sessions. These foods were eaten 100% of the time when offered. Category I bites were used as a reinforcer for consuming bites from the other categories. During intervention, a five-year-old boy with autism was presented with 10 bites of food. He was presented with a bite and was prompted to "Take a bite." He received verbal praise if he put the bite in his mouth. If the child did not pick up the spoon within 5 seconds, the adult used hand-over-hand physical assistance to put the spoon in the child's hand. After a 5-second latency period, if the child did not bring the spoon to his mouth, hand-over-hand assistance was provided. The food was left at the child's lips for 5 seconds. If the child did not consume the bite, the same steps were repeated with a half bite of food and then a quarter bite of food. If the child did not eat the quarter bite, he was prompted to use his tongue to touch the bite. This treatment resulted in an increase in the number and variety of food items that the child consumed.

Binnendyk and Lucyshyn (2009) evaluated the effects of a family-centered positive behavior support approach to addressing food refusal in a child with autism. The results of a functional assessment suggested that the child engaged in food refusal, self-injury, screaming, and aggression to escape the demand to eat nonpreferred foods and to sit at the table to eat preferred foods. A multicomponent Positive Behavior Support (PBS) plan was designed with the assistance of the child's mother. The plan consisted of 10 strategies, including (a) initiating a daily eating schedule, (b) use of general case programming, (c) gradually increasing the amount of nonpreferred food presented, (d) visual supports to illustrate the eating routine, (e) reinforcement contingency, (f) prompting and prompt fading, (g) contingent praise, (h) contingent access to preferred activity, (i) escape extinction procedures, and (j) de-escalation procedures. It is important to note that the escape extinction procedure involved holding a spoon of food up to the child's lips and repeating the prompt "Take a bite" every 30 seconds until the food was accepted. Some teams may find this strategy unacceptable; however, it was coupled with many highly positive teaching approaches. Initially, the therapist conducted training sessions with the child. Then the therapist trained the child's mother using behavioral procedures such as modeling, coaching, feedback, and self-monitoring. The child's mother then taught the child's father to implement the procedures. Following implementation of the behavior support plan, the child demonstrated high levels of food acceptance that were maintained over time. The child's eating behavior also generalized to new foods and to his father's supporting him during snack time.

Together, these studies suggest that multicomponent, but highly individualized PBS treatment packages are effective in treating food selectivity and these more comprehensive approaches may be necessary when less intensive interventions have failed.

Rapid Eating

Instruction aimed at pacing may be needed for some students in the fluency stage of learning, such as students who eat finger foods, use utensils, or drink from cups but do so either too quickly or too slowly. Pacing prompts have been used to slow down or speed up a student's rate of eating and to establish an appropriate eating speed. Assistive technology provides a means for students to learn to eat at an appropriate pace without the use of intrusive procedures. For example, Anglesea, Hoch, and Taylor (2008) used a vibrating pager to increase the duration of meal consumption in three teenagers with autism. Students were taught to take a bite only when the pager vibrated at predetermined intervals. The use of a vibrating pager enabled students to consume a meal at a pace that is comparable to that of a typical adult. Excessively rapid eating can be a serious problem because of social acceptability and potential health problems (e.g., vomiting, aspiration, poor digestion). It is critical for teams to address rapid eating, but it is important that the intervention selected fosters independence.

General Teaching Considerations for Dressing and Grooming

Participating fully or partially in dressing and grooming activities provides many opportunities for communicating preferences, interacting socially, making choices and exercising self-determination. Selecting colors and types of clothing, hairstyle, and accessories enable students to convey their individual style (Browder, 2001). Expressing fashion preferences may be especially important during adolescence when appearance and peer acceptance are often high priorities. Therefore, instruction should incorporate both skills (e.g., snapping, buttoning, brushing teeth) and personal preferences.

> *During the past year, Patrick has become more interested in his appearance. When he needs a haircut or wishes to buy clothing, he invites Caitlin, a friend from his history class, to go to the mall with him. She gives him advice and Patrick selects clothes and styles that appeal to him. His mother reports that Patrick has become more active in choosing his clothes each day. Like other parents of young adults, she sometimes does not like his fashion choices, but she is glad to see him developing his personal style.*

There are several challenges in providing this kind of instruction. First, teaching dressing and grooming skills in school settings is difficult because other students do not typically learn these skills at school. Nonetheless, instructional opportunities are available at school. For example, preschool and kindergarten children use dressing skills in playing dress-up (Sewell et al., 1998), while older students dress for P.E. classes and students in job training often need to change into uniforms. Arrival and departure routines often involve taking off and putting on jackets, sweaters, hats, or gloves. High school students often engage in a variety of grooming activities between classes (e.g., brushing hair, applying lipstick). Learning tasks under these natural conditions (e.g., time of day, location) is likely to increase the rate of learning (Freagon & Rotatori, 1982) and promote skill transfer and retention (Reese & Snell, 1991; Snell, Lewis, & Houghton, 1989). Teaching in natural settings and at natural times also allows peers to serve as models. When students with disabilities have friends of the same age and gender who are able to perform the skills that they are trying to master, learning by observing them and by getting their assistance may be a viable supplement or alternative to teacher-directed trials.

A second challenge in teaching dressing and grooming skills in school settings is that some students may require more intensive instruction than is possible during natural opportunities. Incorporating additional instructional opportunities may require scheduling longer and/or additional instructional sessions. These sessions may conflict with the activities scheduled in the child's classroom. In such cases, the instructional team must make decisions by balancing the individual student's need for intensive instruction in these areas with other instructional needs. It is important that all team members participate in this decision-making process and make adjustments to the child's schedule as needed. If time away from class is needed for a student to work on a dressing or grooming task, the classroom teacher needs both to understand why and also to give ideas on scheduling.

Finally, selecting target skills can be a challenging activity for the educational team. Typically, students perform certain skills (e.g., showering, shaving, shampooing) in the home environment. Yet, the student's family may identify these as priority skills. The team will need to decide how to support the student's development in such areas. For example, the team may develop strategies to assist the caregivers in teaching these skills during typical home routines. If the skills are a high priority, the team may consider artificial times and places for instruction. Collaboration throughout the school year will enable the team to address each of these challenges.

In this section, we discuss identifying and teaching dressing skills. Our focus is primarily on learners who will become actively involved or independent in their dressing. For more coverage of teaching tactics for students with motor disabilities, refer to Chapter 9 (see also Christiansen & Matuska, 2004, and Orelove et al., 2004).

Identify What to Teach

The dressing and grooming curriculum for students with severe disabilities encompasses routines that almost everyone engages in daily, from brushing teeth to evaluating one's appearance and making adjustments if necessary. The more difficult tasks in dressing and undressing include shoe tying and fastening and unfastening buttons, snaps, hooks, zippers, ties, and belts. Grooming skills such as bathing, showering, hand washing, brushing teeth, and menstrual care are critical for maintaining good hygiene. Grooming routines that are performed less frequently include clipping, filing, or painting fingernails; shaving face, under arms, or legs; and applying makeup. Shaving and makeup routines are specific to the student's gender, culture, and personal preference.

Preference Assessment

Identifying what dressing and grooming skills to teach involves several activities. First, a systematic preference assessment will help the teacher design instruction to support the student in developing his or her individual style (Browder, 2001; Lohrmann-O'Rourke, Browder, & Brown, 2000). (Also see Chapter 3.) The preference assessment will vary depending on whether a student uses symbols to communicate or not. For students who communicate with pictures, signs, or words, teachers can use catalogs, magazines, and the Internet to examine preferences in clothing style, colors, accessories, haircut, and makeup; and for those who use nonsymbolic communication, the teacher may create opportunities for the student to try various options (Browder, 2001). For example, the teacher may provide grooming material options (e.g., toothbrushes, toothpaste, combs, barrettes) and observe which items the student prefers. Peer participation in preference assessment activities will ensure that the choices are age appropriate and consistent with peer standards. Because self-care instruction is most effective when there is coordination between home and school, it is also important for teachers to involve caregivers. A conversation with caregivers will help the teacher understand current home routines and identify dressing and grooming skills that the family values.

Family Participation

It is always important to start with the caregiver to learn about the student's performance at home and to understand the family's preferences for instruction.

When Toby's mother was asked what dressing or grooming skills she would like to see Toby learn next, this was her response: "Like I said, putting on his jacket would be great. We'd also really like some help with brushing teeth so that he would start to do it. Being more consistent with hand washing would be helpful, too. Any progress that we can make in toileting would be wonderful, because he still wears diapers." (See Figure 10–12.)

FIGURE 10–12

Results of an Interview with Toby's Mother on Dressing and Grooming Skills

---

Student: Toby
Source: Ms. Kessler (Mother)
Domain: Dressing and Grooming Skills

Teacher: Ms. Gentry
Date: October 1, 2009

1. **Describe Toby's morning routine:** The morning is somewhat hectic at our house. My husband leaves for work before Toby gets up. I need to help Toby with dressing, breakfast, brushing his teeth, and getting to the bus stop. Toby can help on some steps—in putting on his pants and shirt—but I often just get him dressed because we're pressed for time. If I give him enough time, he puts his feet into his shoes, but I need to tell him to fasten the VELCRO. He is usually hungry in the morning so breakfast goes well. Because he is pretty slow with a spoon, I give him mostly finger foods. When the weather gets cold, it takes time to put on his jacket and gloves. I'm usually so rushed by then that I do it for him. He helps put his arms in the sleeves.

2. **What part of Toby's morning routine could he start to do independently? What could he do to help in the morning?** If he could just put on his jacket, then I could gather my papers for work and we would be set to leave. This would be very helpful to me.

3. **Does Toby choose his clothing for the day? Does he have any preferences related to color or style of clothing?** I try to select Toby's clothes in the evening to save time in the morning. I give him a choice of two shirts and he will touch one. I don't know if it's important to him, but he seems to like this. I have noticed that he prefers shirts without buttons and he does not like sweaters.

4. **Describe Toby's evening routine:** I have more time in the evening and Toby's dad often helps him bathe and get ready for bed. Toby does not really brush his teeth; he does not like to have them brushed. Given encouragement, he will briefly open his mouth and let us help him brush. If we stay with him and show him what he needs to do next, he'll wash himself in the bath. He needs help drying. He'll sometimes pull up his pajama bottoms and will help pull the top over his head, but he needs helps getting them on.

5. **Describe Toby's toileting skills:** He has made a great deal of progress recently in that he willingly goes when taken and he usually pulls down his pants if you lift his shirt. He sits on the toilet by himself. He usually pulls up his pants at least part way before leaving the bathroom. He doesn't flush the toilet. I don't think he likes the sound. He needs to be reminded to wash his hands and then he just partially does some of the steps. We keep hand sanitizer at all of the sinks—it is easier that way because then he doesn't need to dry his hands.

6. **What dressing or grooming skills would you like to see Toby learn next?** Like I said, putting on his jacket would be great. We'd also really like some help with tooth brushing so he would start to do it. Being more consistent with hand washing would be helpful, too. Any progress we can make in toileting will be wonderful, because he still wears diapers.

In addition to specific dressing or grooming skills, the teacher will work with the team to identify possible extension skills. Particularly relevant to dressing and grooming skills are the extension skills of making choices, initiating tasks, persisting through completion, and monitoring the speed and quality of the performance. Mastering problem-solving extension skills, such as identifying back and front and right and left in the context of dressing and grooming routines, are relevant for students in elementary school.

Adrian's grandmother mentioned that he sometimes puts his shirt on backwards. He is learning to use the tag to identify front and back.

The educational team will review the results of the preference assessment and caregiver interview. These data will assist the team in identifying priority dressing and grooming skills. The four criteria for target skills that were discussed earlier in this chapter can be used to ensure that the target skills are appropriate: (a) Does the objective reflect the student's chronological age, culture, and preferences? (b) Is the skill one that the student needs now and in the future across settings? (c) Will this skill increase the student's independence? (d) Have team members reached consensus on the value of this skill? As much as possible, the student should participate in the team's conversation and the list of priority skills should be skills that the student values and would like to improve. Adrian's team reviewed assessment data and identified priority skills for Adrian.

Adrian is unable to blow his nose, but he can wipe it when given a model prompt. When the teacher makes a blowing sound, he will hold the tissue to his nose and make the same sound! He can remove and hang up his jacket, as well as put it on when it is time for recess, but he needs instruction on how to use fasteners on his clothes. His team agrees that nose blowing and using fasteners are priorities.

Baseline Assessment

After priority dressing and grooming skills are identified by the educational team, the teacher will develop a task analysis for each target skill (see Chapter 4). The teacher will collect baseline data while observing the student perform each step of the task analysis (see Chapter 5). Baseline data serve several purposes. First, baseline data assist the teacher in identifying the specific steps of the task analysis that the student performs independently, as well as steps in which the student needs instruction and thus it is necessary to

write relevant goals and objectives. Baseline data also enable the teacher to identify the steps of the task analysis that may be appropriate for partial participation.

Baseline observations of Patrick's skills in putting on, taking off, and hanging up his jacket were valuable in designing a practical task analysis that avoided continued use of partial participation (see Figure 10-13).

Finally, baseline data help the teacher to identify the student's stage of learning for each task and consider whether the student demonstrates an acquisition deficit or a performance deficit. An acquisition deficit occurs when a student does not have a skill in his or her repertoire (e.g., a student has not mastered the steps involved in washing his or her face). A performance deficit refers to a skill that is in the student's repertoire, but not performed at the appropriate times (e.g., a student is able to wash his or her face, but fails to do so when his or her face is dirty). Knowledge of the student's stage of learning guides the teacher in the selection of teaching strategies. Specific teaching strategies are described in the next section.

When the team looked at Adrian's baseline probe data for putting his coat with a zipper on, they were clear on the specific steps that he could not perform on his own. (See Figure 10-5.) The data showed, without a doubt, that he was in the acquisition stage of learning with regard to this task. While Adrian never completed five of the nine steps during the baseline phase, he did perform four of the nine steps on his own at least once. Adrian had performance deficits on most of the dressing tasks. This helped the team agree that a systematic teaching approach was needed for all natural opportunities and that they might also create a few additional teaching opportunities each day.

Identify Teaching Strategies for Dressing and Grooming Skills

Specific instructional strategies, as well as materials to support instruction in grooming and dressing, will be described in this section. All instructional strategies discussed earlier in this chapter (see Table 10-1) have been used successfully to teach grooming and dressing skills. Graduated guidance, time delay, simultaneous prompting, and system of least prompts are effective in the acquisition stage of learning dressing and grooming skills. See Chapter 4 for directions on how to implement each of these teaching strategies.

FIGURE 10–13
With some changes in the height of the coat rack and a lot practice, Patrick has mastered taking off, hanging up, and putting his coat back on.

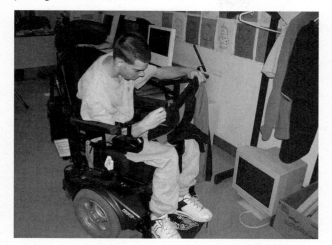
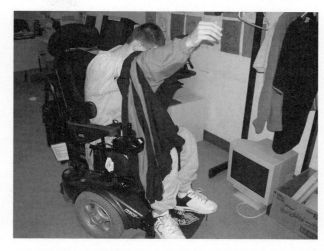

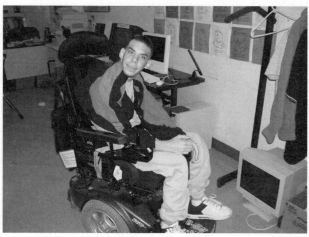

Strategies such as observation learning, video modeling, self-management, and social narratives or Social Stories™ are especially useful in enhancing performance, but may also support acquisition. These strategies, along with simultaneous prompting and forward chaining, are discussed in more detail in this next section of this chapter.

Observation Learning or Modeling

Several studies lend support to the practice of learning by watching others perform competently or by watching others being taught. This ordinary teaching approach has been called by different names: (a) observation learning (Shoen & Sivil, 1989; Wolery et al., 1992), and (b) passive modeling (Biederman, Fairhall, Raven, &

Davey, 1998). Biederman et al. (1998) demonstrated that for teaching hand washing and dressing skills, passive modeling was more effective than both interactive modeling (i.e., hand-over-hand instruction with ongoing verbal prompts and praise) and less rigorous verbal prompting.

Wolery et al. (1992) described an approach for using observation learning in small groups:

- Students who are addressing similar skills are taught in small groups of two or three.
- Students are asked or prompted to watch the individual who is being taught as he or she performs the skill.
- Students in the group take turns performing the target skill while others observe.

- One student can be taught half of the task, while others watch; instruction is then given to another student in the group for the other half of the task. Typically, students will learn some or all of the task steps that they have only observed.

Video Modeling

Video modeling is an evidence-based intervention that utilizes brief videos for instruction and is effective with students in early childhood through adolescence (Delano, 2007). Video modeling capitalizes on the potency of observational learning and can be implemented to teach a variety of skills (e.g., daily living, communication, academic). It may be used alone or in combination with other teaching methods. There is some evidence that video modeling may promote generalization and enable children with autism, in particular, to acquire skills faster than in vivo modeling (Charlop-Christy, Le, & Freeman, 2000).

There are four basic types of video modeling: (a) basic video modeling, (b) video self-modeling, (c) point-of-view video modeling, and (d) video prompting (Cox, Delano, Sturgill, Franzone, & Collet-Klingenberg, 2009). *Basic video modeling* is the most common form of video modeling and the one that teachers report as being the easiest to implement. The teacher films a peer or an adult performing the target skill (e.g., dressing or grooming). Typically, these films are brief and have little or no narration. Then the student watches the video prior to the teaching session. After watching the video, the student is prompted to perform the target skill. Most of the research on the use of video modeling with children on the autism spectrum has used this approach (e.g., D'Ateno, Mangiapanello, & Taylor, 2003; Nikopoulous & Keenan, 2003, 2004).

Self-modeling differs from basic video modeling in that a student observes him or herself performing the target skill. This form of video modeling may be very motivating for some students. There are two basic methods used to create self-modeling videotapes: role-playing and imitation (Buggey, 2009). Role-playing is useful for students who can follow directions and act out a script. In these cases, the student is prompted with the script while being videotaped. When using imitation, the camera is focused on the child and an adult provides prompts to help the child demonstrate the target behavior. During the editing process for either method, the prompts are removed so that the video shows the child performing the behavior "inde-

pendently." If a child has difficulty with role-playing and imitation, self-modeling tapes may be created by taping the child over a period of time and capturing examples of the target behavior (Buggey, 2009). However, creating these tapes may require more time for filming and more skill in video editing to piece together an example of a mastery performance. Sherer et al. (2001) compared basic video modeling in which a peer served as a model and video self-modeling. The results suggested that there was no difference in the rate of task acquisition between the two intervention conditions. Although more research is needed to determine which approach is most effective for which skills and which type of learners, using a model other than the focus student may be more efficient for some teachers because this approach typically involves less time filming and editing than the other approaches.

During the winter, Adrian had difficulty negotiating the end-of-the-day routine. He needed to put his chair on his desk; put on his coat, hat, and gloves; get his backpack; and get in line. He could perform each of these skills, but had difficulty completing the tasks in the appropriate sequence and required prompts to transition between tasks. Because he had mastered other skills through video modeling, his teacher decided to make a video of a peer completing this routine. She observed Adrian's peer, Juan, in the routine with his classmates, wrote a task analysis that also fit Adrian, and then taped the peer moving through the end-of-the-day routine. The tape needed no editing because Juan could complete all of the steps that Adrian needed to learn. The video, "Juan Gets Ready to Go Home," was made available for Adrian to watch. Adrian seemed to like the tape and chose this as one that he watched several times a day. The teacher also played it right before the routine at the end of the day. Adrian quickly made progress. His mother reported that Adrian was more independent in getting ready to leave the house in the mornings.

Point-of-view video modeling (Hine & Wolery, 2006) involves creating videos that demonstrate the task from the learner's perspective. In other words, the tape illustrates exactly what the child will see when successfully performing the task. Because the target student is not actually shown, another person performing the skill can be taped in point-of-view modeling. *Video prompting* is similar to other forms of prompting, except that the task and the taping is broken down into steps. Thus, each step of a task is filmed and later shown as a sequence of short video clips. The student watches the first step of the task and then performs the behavior. This process is continued until the student has finished the task. Rai (2008) used video prompting to teach three elementary school students with disabilities to clean sunglasses, put on a wristwatch, and zip a jacket. Cannella-Malone et al. (2006) compared the effectiveness of video prompting with video modeling to teach six adults with developmental disabilities daily living skills. Video prompting consisted of 10 separate video clips, one for each step of the task analysis. The video modeling tape showed all of the steps of the task analysis in one film. Video prompting resulted in rapid acquisition and video modeling was not effective. Interestingly, the video prompts were filmed from the perspective of the performer, much like point-of-view video modeling, but the video modeling tapes were filmed from the perspective of the spectator. Thus, the perspective from which the videos are filmed may impact the effectiveness of the intervention.

> *When Patrick goes to the restroom, a teaching assistant helps him transfer to the toilet. His teacher feels that Patrick has become dependent on verbal prompts to wash and dry his hands after toileting. Because Patrick enjoys watching videos, she decided to use video modeling to increase his independence. She filmed each step of the hand-washing routine (e.g., turning on the water, getting soap from the dispenser, washing hands) from Patrick's perspective. After just a few trials, Patrick was completing the routine without prompts (see Figure 10–14).*

These versions of video modeling can be useful strategies for teaching self-care and grooming skills. After teachers become comfortable creating videos, they report that video modeling is effective and implementation requires just a few minutes each day.

Social Narratives

A social narrative is a short story that describes the salient aspects of a specific situation that a child may find challenging; many variations of this approach are reported in the literature (e.g., Mirenda et al., 2002). Social narratives have been used to teach a variety of social, behavioral, and communication skills. There is some initial evidence that a specific type of social narrative, called Social Stories™, may be useful in teaching self-care skills (Bledsoe, Myles, & Simpson, 2003; Hagiwara & Myles, 1999). For example, Hagiwara and Myles (1999) taught two children with autism

FIGURE 10–14
Patrick is independently washing his hands when there is an accessible sink and the soap and towel dispenser are within reach.

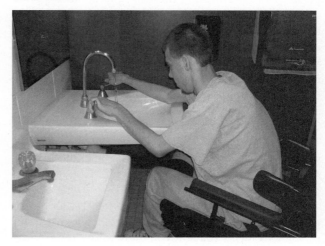

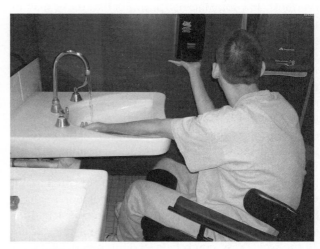

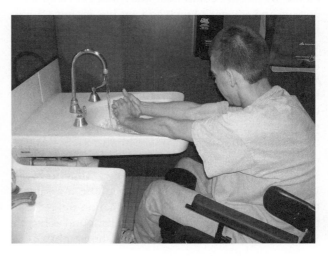

spectrum disorders a hand-washing task using computer-based Social Stories^{TM}. The computer-based stories contained the text of the stories, videos of the participants performing the task, and an audioplayer to present the story. Participants were taught to view the story, and did so once each day. Although the children demonstrated gains, the results were somewhat variable. Thus, practitioners should consider combining social narratives with additional interventions and strong reinforcement contingencies.

Self-Management

Teaching students to self-manage their dressing or grooming performances is a well-documented maintenance strategy. Several types of stimuli (e.g., pictures, picture checklists, tape-recorded messages, videotapes, and word lists) can be used to teach students to prompt and monitor their own performance of a series of self-care tasks that they already know how to accomplish in part. Material prompts like these may or may not be faded, depending on the student, but such prompts are designed by the team to be nonstigmatizing, easily carried, and independently used. For example, students can select and arrange pictures of morning routine tasks in a pocketsize booklet to be used like a schedule. For other students, a booklet of task pictures (used initially during acquisition training) may be shortened to single-task photos and continue to remind students of task steps after teachers have faded their ongoing supervision. For students able to operate a small cassette tape recorder, the StepPad (Attainment Company, Inc.) can facilitate self-management. Teachers let students or peers record step-by-step instructions (e.g., brush teeth, shave, shower, and shut the curtain all the way; dress, comb hair, straighten bed, take medication, and eat; pack lunch and get bus money). When the student presses the play button, the cue plays, but when the fast-forward button is pressed, the tape progresses to the next message. A given step of the instructions may be modified without affecting the other steps. VoiceCue (Attainment Company, Inc.) is a similar device, but adds a time component. The student or peer may record up to five messages and set the clock to play back messages at preset times. Each message can be assigned two playback times. For example, the student could record the message, "Time to brush your teeth" and set the clock to play the message at 6:00 a.m. and 8:00 p.m. More information on assistive technology and links to vendors can be found at http://www.attainmentcompany.com/xcart/home.php.

Prompts That Are Effective with Dressing and Grooming Skills

As shown in Table 10–1, a variety of systematic prompting approaches have been successful in teaching dressing and grooming skills. These general approaches are described in Chapter 4; here, we provide more detail on one method—simultaneous instruction. Simultaneous instruction or prompting of self-care skills involves ongoing physical prompting, with fading determined by student performance on regularly conducted probe trials. During probe trials, students are asked to perform the entire task without assistance, errors are ignored, and these steps are completed for the student without comment. Training trials involve cuing the student to look at task materials, giving a task request, and prompting and praising the student on each step of the task, with a choice of activity reinforcer offered at the end.

For example, Batu (2008) used simultaneous prompting to teach four children with developmental disabilities a variety of home skills, including dressing (e.g. tying shoes). Different materials were provided for each session in a multiple exemplar format. The prompting procedures for teaching wearing socks and tying shoes were modified to include modeling and verbal plus partial physical prompting. This procedure was effective in promoting acquisition and maintenance of skills. Participants also could generalize skills across trainers.

Sewell et al. (1998) used simultaneous prompting during activity-based routines to teach two preschoolers with developmental delays to take off shoes, socks, and pants, and to put on shirts, shoes, and jackets. Skills were taught in the context of routine activities that required the skill (e.g., taking off socks before dress-up play, sensory play, Pit Ball play, and rest time; putting shirt on for dress-up play, water play, and "messy" art activities). The teacher assessed student performance in a probe trial each morning and completed one-to-one instruction throughout various times of the day. The teacher first provided an attentional cue (e.g., "Look, [student's name]" or "Look at the [article of clothing]") and then gave full physical assistance and verbal directions and explanations throughout the task. The student received continuous verbal reinforcement as long as she allowed physical assistance. The students also performed a preferred task after the dressing skill was completed. The teacher used a variety of clothing to encourage generalization. Once students correctly performed a skill without assistance for three consecutive days, the teacher shifted to maintenance, withholding prompts and thinning continuous praise to praise following successful completion.

Toby's team members used simultaneous prompting to teach him to remove and hang up his jacket several times a day. Team members found this method easy to use. Figure 10–15 shows his mother withholding her help in order to probe his performance and assess how much he has learned. Once he gets the steps correct on a probe, he is not prompted on those steps again during training sessions.

Chaining

As explained in Chapter 4 and in Table 10-1, teachers may use three different chaining approaches to teach multiple-step tasks: (a) forward chaining, (b) backward chaining, and (c) total task. Forward chaining and total task are often used to teach dressing and grooming skills. In forward chaining, the instructor teaches the first step of the task analysis and helps the student through the remaining steps on each trial. When the student masters the first step, instruction shifts to the second step. The student is expected to complete the first step, receive instruction on the second step, and receive assistance on the remaining steps. This process continues until the student has mastered each step of the task analysis. Forward chaining has been used to teach menstrual care (Epps, Stern, & Horner, 1990; Richman, Reiss, Bauman, & Bailey, 1984). Epps et al. (1990) faded prompts by requiring students to return to the beginning of the task after errors until they performed without a prompt. Thus, whenever students made an error, they practiced the appropriate response with the prompt until they performed it correctly. Then, the students were taught to begin the task again, and no prompt was given. Richman et al. (1984) used an

FIGURE 10–15
Toby has learned to remove and hang up his jacket when he arrives at school.

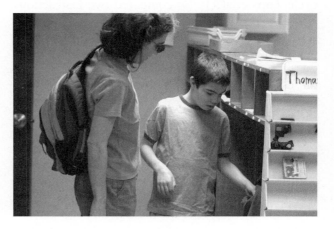

alternate forward-chaining approach to teach feminine hygiene. On the first trial, the women were prompted through the entire task. Then they were allowed to perform independently on the task until their first error. Errors were followed by having the women practice the missed step with verbal assistance until they could complete the step independently. Next, they were asked to begin the task again from the beginning. These forward-chaining strategies can be applied to a variety of grooming skills.

Dressing and Grooming Materials

In addition to specific teaching strategies, selecting dressing and grooming materials is an important aspect of instruction. When selecting materials for instruction, teachers should use real materials (e.g., clothing, toothbrushes, and deodorant) as much as possible. However, the use of larger clothing for initial instruction, faded over time to appropriate clothing sizes, has been demonstrated as a potent strategy (Diorio & Konarski, 1984; Reese & Snell, 1991). This may be best with students who are not as attuned to fashion or situations in which oversized clothes is the fashion or goes unnoticed (i.e., during dress-up in preschool or kindergarten).

To promote generalization of dressing and grooming skills to new materials and settings, students must learn to use a variety of materials and settings. Teams should decide what materials and what settings are most appropriate (e.g., nonstigmatizing, preferred, private) and most feasible (e.g., nearby, fits daily schedule). Sometimes in grooming instruction, teachers cannot use real materials and may supplement with artificial or simulated materials. For example, menstrual hygiene instruction for young women with severe disabilities takes longer than a single menstrual cycle. Epps et al. (1990) compared two instructional approaches, both of which involved simulation: (a) changing artificially stained underwear or a pad on oneself, and (b) using a doll and materials to practice these same maneuvers. Women taught using the dolls did not demonstrate generalization of their skills to themselves, but once they were given instruction on themselves, they were able to perform these same skills during their menses. When using task simulations to teach, match the simulation to the actual task as much as possible. The authors in this study agreed with this general practice. They noted that changing pads on dolls differs greatly from performing the same task on oneself. In addition, they found that when the simulated menstrual amount and stain was dissimilar from the woman's actual menses onset, generalization was worse than when the similarity was close. Their materials included examples of different colors and styles of underwear, underwear with stains in different locations, and underwear with no stains.

Team members have many proven teaching strategies to select from when addressing grooming and dressing IEP objectives. When planning how to teach, teams again must select methods that meet the principle of parsimony (Etzel & LeBlanc, 1979)—procedures that are both relatively easy to use and have been demonstrated to be effective with students who have severe disabilities.

Summary

Basic self-care skills, which include toileting, eating, dressing, and grooming skills, are areas where most students with severe disabilities will require some instruction. Teams will rely heavily on family members and information from physical and occupational therapists as they work to identify needed skills and write appropriate goals and objectives for the students' IEPs. Identifying the strategies for teaching these objectives requires that team members work together to identify evidence-based teaching methods that are suited to the student's age and preferences, as well as methods that can ethically and feasibly be used at school by team members. As with other priority skills, teams must identify an approach for measuring a student's present level of performance before instruction begins that will also allow for monitoring progress over time.

Suggested Activities

1. To become more aware of peer and cultural norms, pick an age level (e.g., elementary, middle, or high school) and interview three students about their preferred style of dress and grooming. Then conduct a systematic preference assessment with a same-age student who does not use speech and gather the same information. You may need to use photos or actual objects to supplement your questions. How alike and different are the students' preferences and personal styles? What did you learn that surprised you? How would you use the information that you gathered to assist you in teaching dressing and grooming skills?

2. Select a student who may benefit from video modeling (e.g., attends to video, is able to imitate). Identify a self-care skill from this student's IEP and collect baseline data. Write a task analysis for this skill. Select a type of video modeling (basic video modeling, video self-modeling, point-of-view video modeling, or video prompting) and create a video-modeling tape to teach the skill. Use the video to teach the student and collect data on the student's skill performance. Describe the process that you used to create the video. Did the student's performance change after you implemented video modeling? What other self-care skills would you consider teaching through video modeling?

3. Search the Internet for sites that sell adaptive materials for self-care tasks (e.g., adaptive eating utensils, drinking devices, clothing, toileting, and hygiene). Create a resource list for families that indicates the sites and the types of products available.

Note: For the student applications, we give thanks to Rachel Dickinson, Jeanne Pfaff, Diane Talarico-Cavanaugh, and Renee Hollinger Scott of Greene County, Charlottesville, and Louisville Public School System respectively and their students and parents.

References

Ahearn, W. H. (2003). Using simultaneous presentation to increase vegetable consumption in a mildly selective child with autism. *Journal of Applied Behavior Analysis, 36*(3), 361-365.

Alberto, P., Jobes, N., Sizemore, A., & Doran, D. (1980). A comparison of individual and group instruction across response tasks. *Journal of the Association for Persons with Severe Handicaps, 5,* 285-293.

Albin, J. B. (1977). Some variables influencing the maintenance of acquired self-feeding behavior in profoundly retarded children. *Mental Retardation, 15*(5), 49-52.

Anderson, S. R., Jablonski, A. L., Thomeer, M. L., & Knapp, V. M. (2007). *Self-help skills for people with autism: A systematic teaching approach.* Bethesda, MD: Woodbine House.

Anglesea, M., Hoch, H., & Taylor, B. (2008). Reducing rapid eating in teenagers with autism: Use of a pager prompt. *Journal of Applied Behavior Analysis, 41*(1), 107-111.

Averink, M., Melein, L., & Duker, P. C. (2005). Establishing diurnal bladder control with the response restriction method: Extended study on its effectiveness. *Research in Developmental Disabilities, 26,* 143-151.

Azrin, N. H., & Armstrong, P. M. (1973). The "mini-meal": A method for teaching eating skills to the profoundly retarded. *Mental Retardation, 11*(1), 9-11.

Azrin, N. H., & Foxx, R. M. (1971). A rapid method of toilet training the institutionalized retarded. *Journal of Applied Behavior Analysis, 4,* 89-99.

Bailey, R., & Angell, M. (2005). Improving feeding skills and mealtime behaviors in children and youth with disabilities. *Education and Training in Developmental Disabilities, 40*(1), 80-96.

Bainbridge, N., & Myles, B. S. (1999). The use of priming to introduce toilet training to a child with autism. *Focus on Autism and Other Developmental Disabilities, 14*(2), 106-109.

Baker, B. L., & Brightman, A. J. (1997). *Steps to independence: Teaching everyday skills to children with special needs* (3rd ed.). Baltimore: Paul H. Brookes.

Bambara, L., & Cole, C. L. (1997). Permanent antecedent prompts. In M. Agran (Ed.), *Self-directed learning: Teaching self-determination skills* (pp. 111-143). Pacific Grove, CA: Brookes/Cole.

Banerdt, B., & Bricker, D. (1978). A training program for selected self-feeding skills for the motorically impaired. *AAESPH Review, 3,* 222-229.

Batu, S. (2008). Caregiver-delivered home-based instruction using simultaneous prompting for teaching home skills to individuals with developmental disabilities. *Education and Training in Developmental Disabilities, 43*(4), 541-555.

Baumgart, D., Brown, L., Pumpian, I., Nisbet, J., Ford, A., Sweet, M., et al. (1982). Principle of participation and individualized adaptations in educational programs for severely handicapped students. *Journal of the Association for Persons with Severe Handicaps, 7,* 17-27.

Bax, M., Hart, H., & Jenkins, S. (1990). *Child development and child health.* Oxford, England: Blackwell Scientific.

Bettison, S. (1982). *Toilet training to independence for the handicapped: A manual for trainers.* Springfield, IL: Charles C. Thomas.

Biederman, G. B., Fairhall, J. L., Raven, K. A., & Davey, V. A. (1998). Verbal prompting, hand-over-hand instruction, and passive observation in teaching children with developmental disabilities. *Exceptional Children, 64,* 503-511.

Binnendyk, L., & Lucyshyn, J. (2009). A family-centered positive behavior support approach to the amelioration of food refusal behavior. *Journal of Positive Behavior Interventions, 11*(1), 47-62.

Bledsoe, R., Myles, B., & Simpson, R. (2003). Use of a social story intervention to improve mealtime skills of an adolescent with Asperger syndrome. *Autism, 7*(3), 289-295.

Bloom, D. A., Seeley, W. W., Rathcey, M. L., & McGuire, E. J. (1993). Toilet habits and continence in children: An opportunity sampling in search of normal parameters. *Journal of Urology, 149,* 1087-1090.

Browder, D. (2001). *Curriculum and assessment for students with moderate and severe disbilities.* New York: Guilford Press.

Buggey, T. (2009). *Seeing is believing: Video self-modeling for people with autism and other developmental disabilities.* Bethesda, MD: Woodbine House.

Cannella-Malone, H., Sigafoos, J., O'Reilly, M., de la Cruz, B., Edrisinha, C., & Lancioni, G. (2006). Comparing video prompting to video modeling for teaching daily living skills to six adults with developmental disabilities. *Education and Training in Developmental Disabilities, 41*(4), 344-356.

Carr, E. G., Horner, R. H., Turnbull, A. P., Marquis, J. G., McLaughlin, D. M., McAtee, M. L., et al. (1999). *Positive behavior support for people with developmental disabilities: A research synthesis.* Washington, DC: American Association on Mental Retardation.

Charlop-Christy, M. H., Le, L., & Freeman, K. (2000). A comparison of video modeling with in vivo modeling for teaching children with autism. *Journal of Autism and Developmental Disorders, 30,* 537-552.

Christiansen, C. H., & Matuska, K. M. (Eds.) (2004). *Ways of living: Adaptive strategies for special needs* (3rd ed.). Bethesda, MD: American Occupational Therapy Association.

Chung, K. (2007). Modified version of Azrin and Foxx's rapid toilet training. *Journal of Developmental and Physical Disabilities, 19,* 449-455.

Cicero, F. R., & Pfadt, A. (2002). Investigation of a reinforcement-based toilet training procedure for children with autism, *Research in Developmental Disabilities, 23,* 319-331.

Cloninger, C. (2004). Designing collaborative educational services. In F. P. Orelove, D. Sobsey, & R. K. Silberman (Eds.), *Educating children with multiple disabilities* (pp. 1-29). Baltimore: Paul H. Brookes.

Collins, B. C., Gast, D. L., Wolery, M., Halcombe, A., & Leatherby, J. G. (1991). Using constant time delay to teach self-feeding to young students with severe/profound handicaps: Evidence of limited effectiveness. *Journal of Developmental and Physical Disabilities, 3,* 157-179.

Comrie, J., & Helm, J. (1997). Common feeding problems in the intensive care nursery: Maturation, organization, evaluation, and management strategies. *Seminar in Speech Language Disorders, 18,* 239-261.

Cox, A. W., Delano, M. E., Sturgill, T. R., Franzone, E., & Collet-Klingenberg, L. (2009). *Video Modeling.* Chapel Hill: National Professional Development Center on Autism Spectrum Disorders, Frank Porter Graham Child Development Institute, University of North Carolina.

D'Ateno, P., Mangiapanello, K., & Taylor, B. (2003). Using video modeling to teach complex play sequences to a preschooler with autism. *Journal of Positive Behavior Interventions, 5*(1), 5-11.

Delano, M. (2007). Video modeling interventions for individuals with autism. *Remedial and Special Education, 28,* 33-42.

Denny, M., Marchand-Martella, N., Martella, R., Reilly, J. R., Reilly, J. F., & Cleanthous, C. C. (2000). Using parent-delivered graduated guidance to teach functional living skills to a child with Cri du Chat syndrome. *Education and Treatment of Children, 23,* 441-454.

Didden, R., Sikkema, S., Bosman, I., Duker, P. C., & Curfs, L. G. (2001). Use of a modified Azrin-Foxx toilet training procedure with individuals with Angelman syndrome. *Journal of Applied Research in Intellectual Disabilities, 14,* 64-70.

Diorio, M. A., & Konarski, E. A., Jr. (1984). Evaluation of a method for teaching dressing skills to profoundly mentally retarded persons. *American Journal of Mental Deficiency, 89,* 307-309.

Doyle, M. B. (2008). *The paraprofessional's guide to the inclusive classroom: Working as a team* (3rd ed.). Baltimore: Paul H. Brookes.

Duker, P. C., Averink, M., & Melein, L. (2001). Response restriction as a method to establish diurnal bladder control. *American Journal on Mental Retardation, 106,* 209-215.

Dunlap, G., & Johnson, G. (1985). Increasing the independent responding of autistic children with unpredictable supervision. *Journal of Applied Behavior Analysis, 18,* 227-236.

Dunlap, G., Koegel, R. L., & Koegel, L. K. (1986). *Toilet training for children with severe handicaps: A field manual for coordinating procedures across multiple community settings.* Huntington, WV: Autism Training Center, Marshall University.

Epps, S., Stern, R. J., & Horner, R. H. (1990). Comparison of simulation training on self and using a doll for teaching generalized menstrual care to women with severe mental retardation. *Research in Developmental Disabilities, 11,* 37-66.

Etzel, B. C., & LeBlanc, J. M. (1979). The simplest treatment alternative: The law of parsimony applied to choosing appropriate instructional control and errorless learning procedures for the difficult-to-teach child. *Journal of Autism and Developmental Disorders, 9,* 361-382.

Ferguson, D. L., & Baumgart, D. (1991). Partial participation revisited. *Journal of the Association for Persons with Severe Handicaps, 16,* 218-227.

Fisher, M., & Meyer, L. H. (2002). Development and social competence after two years for students enrolled in inclusive and self-contained educational programs. *Research and Practice for Persons with Severe Disabilities, 27,* 165-174.

Ford, A., Schnorr, R., Meyer, L., Davern, L., Black, J., & Dempsey, P. (1989). *The Syracuse community-referenced curriculum guide.* Baltimore: Paul H. Brookes.

Foxx, R. M., & Azrin, N. H. (1973). *Toilet training the retarded: A rapid program for day and nighttime independent toileting.* Champaign, IL: Research Press.

Foxx, R. M., & Azrin, N. H. (1974). *Toilet training in less than a day.* New York: Simon & Schuster.

Freagon, S., & Rotatori, A. F. (1982). Comparing natural and artificial environments in training self-care skills to group home residents. *Journal of the Association for Persons with Severe Handicaps, 7*(3), 73-86.

Fredericks, H. D. B., Baldwin, V. L., Grove, D. N., & Moore, W. G. (1975). *Toilet training the handicapped child.* Monmouth, OR: Instructional Development Corporation.

Garff, J. T., & Storey, K. (1998). The use of self-management strategies for increasing the appropriate hygiene of persons with disabilities in supported employment settings. *Education and Training in Mental Retardation and Developmental Disabilities, 33,* 179-188.

Gentry, J., & Luiselli, J. (2008). Treating a child's selective eating through parent implemented feeding intervention in the home setting. *Journal of Developmental and Physical Disabilities, 20*(1), 63-70.

Giangreco, M. F., Edelman, S. W., Luiselli, T. E., & MacFarland, S. Z. C. (1997). Helping or hovering? Effects of instructional assistant proximity on students with disabilities. *Exceptional Children, 64,* 7-18.

Giangreco, M. F., Suter, J. C., & Doyle, M. B. (in press). Paraprofessionals in inclusive schools: A review of recent research. *Journal of Educational and Psychological Consultation.*

Giles, D. K., & Wolf, M. M. (1966). Toilet training institutionalized severe retardates: An application of operant behavior modification techniques. *American Journal of Mental Deficiency, 70,* 766-780.

Hagiwara, T., & Myles, B. (1999). A multimedia social story intervention: Teaching skills to children with autism. *Focus on Autism and Other Developmental Disabilities, 14*(2), 82-95.

Hagopian, L. P., Farrell, D. A., & Amari, A. (1996). Treating total liquid refusal with backward chaining and fading. *Journal of Applied Behavior Analysis, 29,* 573-575.

Harris, A. (2004). Toilet training children with learning difficulties: What the literature tells us. *British Journal of Nursing, 13,* 773-777.

Hine, J., & Wolery, M. (2006). Using point-of-view video modeling to teach play to preschoolers with autism. *Topics in Early Childhood Special Education, 26*(2), 83–93.

Hobbs, T., & Peck, C. A. (1985). Toilet training people with profound mental retardation: A cost effective procedure for large residential settings. *Behavioral Engineering, 9,* 50–57.

Horner, R. D., & Keilitz, I. (1975). Training mentally retarded adolescents to brush their teeth. *Journal of Applied Behavior Analysis, 8,* 301–309.

Howard, B. J. (1991). *It's potty time* [Videotape]. Available from Duke Family Services, Learning Through Entertainment, Inc.

Irvine, A. B., Erickson, A. M., Singer, G. H., & Stahlberg, D. (1992). A coordinated program to transfer self-management skills from school to home. *Education and Training in Mental Retardation, 27,* 241–254.

Janney, R., & Snell, M. (2004). *Modifying schoolwork.* Baltimore: Paul H. Brookes.

Janney, R., & Snell, M. (2006). *Social relationships and peer support.* Baltimore: Paul H. Brookes.

Keen, D., Brannigan, K. L., & Cuskelly, M. (2007). Toilet training for children with autism: The effects of video modeling. *Journal of Developmental and Physical Disabilities, 19,* 291–303.

Kraemer, B. R., McIntyre, L. L., & Blacher, J. (2003). Quality of life for young adults with mental retardation during transition. *Mental Retardation, 41,* 250–262.

Lasater, M. W., & Brady, M. P. (1995). Effects of video self-modeling and feedback on task fluency: A home-based intervention. *Education and Treatment of Children, 18,* 389–407.

LeBlanc, L. A., Carr, J. E., Crosett, S. E., Bennett, C. M., & Detweiler, D. D. (2005). Intensive outpatient behavioral treatment of primary urinary incontinence of children with autism. *Focus on Autism and Other Developmental Disabilities, 20,* 98–105.

Levin, L., & Carr, E. (2001). Food selectivity and problem behavior in children with developmental disabilities: Analysis and intervention. *Behavior Modification, 25*(3), 443–470.

Levine, M. N., & Elliot, C. B. (1970). Toilet training for profoundly retarded with a limited staff. *Mental Retardation, 8*(3), 48–50.

Linford, M. D., Hipsher, L. W., & Silikovitz, R. G. (1972). *Systematic instruction for retarded children: The illness program. Part 3. Self-help instruction.* Danville, IL: Interstate.

Lohrmann-O'Rourke, S., Browder, D. M., & Brown, F. (2000). Guidelines for conducting socially valid systematic preference assessments. *Journal of the Association for Persons with Severe Handicaps, 25,* 42–53.

Luiselli, J. K. (1991). Acquisition of self-feeding in a child with Lowe's syndrome. *Journal of Developmental and Physical Disabilities, 3*(2), 181–189.

Luiselli, J. K. (1996). A case study evaluation of a transfer-of-stimulus control toilet training procedure for a child with a pervasive developmental disorder. *Focus on Autism and Developmental Disabilities, 11,* 158–162.

Luiselli, J. (2007). Single-case evaluation of a negative reinforcement toilet training intervention. *Child & Family Behavior Therapy, 29*(1), 59–69.

Luiselli, J., Ricciardi, J., & Gilligan, K. (2005). Liquid fading to establish milk consumption by a child with autism. *Behavioral Interventions, 20*(2), 155–163.

Macias, M. M., Roberts, K. M., Saylor, C. F., & Fussell, J. J. (2006). Toileting concerns, parenting stress, and behavior problems in children with special health care needs. *Clinical Pediatrics, 45,* 415–422.

Mahoney, K., Van Wagenen, R. K., & Meyerson, L. (1971). Toilet training of normal and retarded children. *Journal of Applied Behavior Analysis, 4,* 173–181.

Marshall, G. R. (1966). Toilet training of an autistic eight-year-old through conditioning therapy: A case report. *Behavior Research and Therapy, 4,* 242–245.

Matson, J. L., Taras, M. E., Sevin, J. A., Love, S. R., & Fridley, D. (1990). Teaching self-help skills to autistic and mentally retarded children. *Research in Developmental Disabilities, 11,* 361–378.

Mercer, R. (2003). *Several steps to nighttime dryness: A practical guide for parents of children with bedwetting.* Ashton, MD: Brookerville Media.

Mirenda, P., MacGregor, T., & Kelly-Keough, S. (2002). Teaching communication skills for behavioral support in the context of family life. *Families and positive behavior support: Addressing problem behavior in family contexts* (pp. 185–207). Baltimore: Paul H. Brookes.

Murzynski, N., & Bourret, J. C. (2007). Combining video modeling and least-to-most prompting for establishing response chains. *Behavioral Interventions, 22*(2), 147–152.

Najdowski, A. C., Wallace, M. D., Doney, J. K., & Ghezzi, P. M. (2003). Parental assessment and treatment of food selectivity in natural settings. *Journal of Applied Behavior Analysis, 36,* 383–386.

National Professional Development Center on Autism Spectrum Disorders. (2009). *Evidence-Based Practices for Children and Youth with ASD.* Chapel Hill: The University of North Carolina.

Nelson, G. L., Cone, J. D., & Hanson, C. R. (1975). Training correct utensil use in retarded children: Modeling vs. physical guidance. *American Journal of Mental Deficiency, 80,* 114–122.

Nikopoulous, C., & Keenan, M. (2003). Promoting social initiation in children with autism using video modeling. *Behavioral Interventions, 18,* 87–108.

Nikopoulous, C., & Keenan, M. (2004). Effects of video modeling on social initiations by children with autism. *Journal of Applied Behavior Analysis, 37*(1), 93–96.

Norman, J. M., Collins, B. C., & Schuster, J. W. (2001). Using an instructional package including video technology to teach self-help skills to elementary students with mental disabilities. *Journal of Special Education Technology, 16*(3), 15–18.

O'Brien, F., Bugle, C., & Azrin, N. H. (1972). Training and maintaining a retarded child's proper eating. *Journal of Applied Behavior Analysis, 5,* 67–73.

Orelove, F. P., Sobsey, D., & Silberman, R. K. (2004). *Educating children with multiple disabilities: A collaborative approach* (4th ed.). Baltimore: Paul H. Brookes.

Parrott, K. A., Schuster, J. W., Collins, B. C., & Gassaway, L. J. (2000). Simultaneous prompting and instructive feedback when teaching chained tasks. *Journal of Behavioral Education, 10,* 3–19.

Paul-Brown, D., & Caperton, C. (2001). Inclusive practices for preschool-age children with specific language impairment. In M. J. Guralnick (Ed.), *Early childhood inclusion: Focus for change.* Baltimore: Paul H. Brookes.

Post, A., & Kirkpatrick, M. (2004). Toilet training for a young boy with pervasive developmental disorder. *Behavioral Interventions, 19*(1), 45–50.

Rai, K. (2008). Technology to teach self-help skills to elementary students with mental disabilities. *Journal of the Indian Academy of Applied Psychology, 34*, 201–214.

Reese, G. M., & Snell, M. E. (1991). Putting on and removing coats and jackets: The acquisition and maintenance of skills by children with severe multiple disabilities. *Education and Training in Mental Retardation, 26*, 398–410.

Richman, G. S., Reiss, M. L., Bauman, K. E., & Bailey, J. S. (1984). Teaching menstrual care to mentally retarded women: Acquisition, generalization, and maintenance. *Journal of Applied Behavior Analysis, 17*, 441–451.

Richmond, G. (1983). Shaping bladder and bowel continence in developmentally retarded preschool children. *Journal of Autism and Developmental Disorders, 13*, 197–205.

Riggs, C. G. (2004). To teachers: What paraeducators want you to know. *Teaching Exceptional Children, 36*(5), 8–12.

Riordan, M. M., Iwata, B. A., Wohl, M. K., & Finney, J. W. (1980). Behavioral treatment of food refusal and selectivity in developmentally disabled children. *Applied Research in Mental Retardation, 1*, 95–112.

Riordan, M. M., Iwata, B. A., Finney, J. W., Wohl, M. D., & Stanley, A. E. (1984). Behavioral assessment and treatment of chronic food refusal in handicapped children. *Journal of Applied Behavior Analysis, 17*, 327–341.

Schaefer, C. E., & DiGeronimo, T. F. (1997). *Toilet training without tears* (Rev. ed.). New York: Signet Books.

Schepis, M., Reid, D., Ownbey, J., & Parsons, M. (2001). Training support staff to embed teaching within natural routines of young children with disabilities in an inclusive preschool. *Journal of Applied Behavior Analysis, 34*, 313–327.

Schreck, K., Williams, K., & Smith, A. (2004). A comparison of eating behaviors between children with and without autism. *Journal of Autism and Developmental Disorders, 34*(4), 433–438.

Schwab, C. (2006). Bathroom home modifications. *Exceptional Parent, 36*(7), 37–39.

Scott, S. M., McWilliam, R. A., & Mayhew, L. (1999). Integrating therapists into the classroom. *Young Exceptional Children, 2*(3), 15–24.

Sells-Love, D., Rinaldi, L. M., & McLaughlin, T. F. (2002). Toilet training an adolescent with severe mental retardation in the classroom: A case study. *Journal of Developmental and Physical Disabilities, 14*, 111–118.

Sewell, T. J., Collins, B. C., Hemmeter, M. L., & Schuster, J. W. (1998). Using simultaneous prompting within an activity-based format to teach dressing skills to preschoolers with developmental delays. *Journal of Early Intervention, 21*, 132–142.

Sherer, M., Pierce, K., Paredes, S., Kisacky, K., Ingersoll, B., & Schreibman, L. (2001). Enhancing conversation skills in children with autism via video technology: Which is better, "self" or "other" as a model? *Behavior Modification, 25*(1), 140–158.

Shoen, S. F., & Sivil, E. O. (1989). A comparison of procedures in teaching self-help skills: Increasing assistance, time delay, and observational learning. *Journal of Autism and Developmental Disorders, 19*, 57–72.

Simbert, V. F., Minor, J. W., & McCoy, J. F. (1977). Intensive feeding training with retarded children. *Behavior Modification, 1*, 512–529.

Sisson, L. A., Kilwein, M. L., & Van Hasselt, V. B. (1988). A graduated guidance procedure for teaching self-dressing skills to multihandicapped children. *Research in Developmental Disabilities, 9*, 419–432.

Smith, A. L., Jr., Piersel, W. C., Filbeck, R. W., & Gross, E. J. (1983). The elimination of mealtime food stealing and scavenging behavior in an institutionalized severely mentally retarded adult. *Mental Retardation, 21*, 255–259.

Smith, P. S. (1979). A comparison of different methods of toilet training the mentally handicapped. *Behaviour Research and Therapy, 17*(1), 33–34.

Snell, M. E., & Janney, R. E. (2005). *Practices for inclusive schools: Collaborative teaming* (2nd ed.). Baltimore: Paul H. Brookes.

Snell, M. E., Lewis, A. P., & Houghton, A. (1989). Acquisition and maintenance of toothbrushing skills by students with cerebral palsy and mental retardation. *Journal of the Association for Persons with Severe Handicaps, 14*, 216–226.

Stokes, J. V., Cameron, M. J., Dorsey, M. F., & Fleming, E. (2004). Task analysis, correspondence training, and general case instruction for teaching personal hygiene skills. *Behavioral Interventions, 19*, 121–135.

Tarbox, R. S. F., Williams, W. L., & Friman, P. C. (2004). Extended diaper wearing: Effects on continence in and out of the diaper. *Journal of Applied Behavior Analysis, 37*, 97–100.

Thompson, T., & Hanson, R. (1983). Overhydration: Precautions when treating urinary incontinence. *Mental Retardation, 21*, 139–143.

Van Laarhoven, T. & Van Laarhoven-Myers, T. (2006). Comparison of three video-based instructional procedures for teaching daily living skills to persons with developmental disabilities. *Education and Training in Developmental Disabilities, 41*(4), 365–381.

Van Wagenen, R. K., Meyerson, L., Kerr, N. J., & Mahoney, K. (1969). Rapid toilet training: Learning principles and prosthesis. *Proceedings of the 77th Annual Convention of the American Psychological Association, 4*, 781–782.

Van Wagenen, R. K., & Murdock, E. E. (1966). A transistorized signal-package for toilet training of infants. *Journal of Experimental Child Psychology, 3*, 312–314.

Vogtle, L., & Snell, M. E. (in press). Methods for promoting basic and instrumental activities of daily living. In C. H. Christiansen & K. M. Matuska (Eds.), *Ways of living: Adaptive strategies for special needs* (4th ed.). Rockville, MD: American Occupational Therapy Association.

Wolery, M., Ault, M. J., & Doyle, P. M. (1992). *Teaching students with moderate to severe disabilities*. White Plains, NY: Longman.

Wolery, M., Ault, M. J., Gast, D., Doyle, P. M., & Griffen, A. K. (1991). Teaching chained tasks in dyads: Acquisition of target and observational behaviors. *Journal of Special Education, 25*, 198–220.

Wood, B., Wolery, M., & Kaiser, A. (2009). Treatment of food selectivity in a young child with autism. *Focus on* Autism *and Other Developmental Disabilities, 24*(3), 169–177.

Young, K. R., West, R. P., Howard, V. F., & Whitney, R. (1986). Acquisition, fluency training, generalization, and maintenance of dressing skills of two developmentally disabled children. *Education and Treatment of Children, 9*, 16–29.

11

Supporting Peer Relationships

Erik W. Carter

Introduction

When asked about their experiences in school, children and youth are apt to talk about their friendships and activities with peers. Most conversations about school revolve around close friends; hanging out during homeroom, at lunch, between classes, and at recess; involvement in extracurricular activities with other classmates; and getting together with friends outside of school. If your own memories of school echo some of these same experiences, you already have a good grasp of what research has long affirmed. Peers play an instrumental role in the lives of children and youth—not only because of the enjoyment that relationships can bring, but also because of the important contributions that they make to childhood development and well-being. Studies that address the social lives of students can be summarized succinctly by a single statement: *Relationships really do matter.*

Most parents, educators, administrators, and other school staff are cognizant of the myriad ways in which students' relationships with their peers can promote learning, foster success in school, and enhance the quality of life. Although conversations about the purposes and practice of education often center on academic rigor and performance, supporting the development of successful and satisfying relationships among all students has long been recognized as an important element of high-quality educational programming (Brown et al., 1979; Wentzel & Looney, 2007). Indeed, the social opportunities afforded within general education classes and the wide range of other activities offered through school are often cited as being among the principal benefits of inclusive educational services (Carter & Hughes, 2006; Ryndak & Fisher, 2003).

At the same time, satisfying and durable peer relationships remain elusive or fleeting for substantial numbers of children and youth with severe disabilities. Instead of offering a sense of belonging, connections with peers, and shared learning experiences, schools often do not focus sufficient attention on providing students with severe disabilities the opportunities, skills, supports, and connections that enable them to interact and develop friendships with their peers. Put

Author's Note: Support for the writing of this chapter was provided in part by a grant from the Centers for Medicare and Medicaid Services, Medicaid Infrastructure Grant to the Wisconsin Department of Health Services (CFDA No. 93.768).

simply, many students with severe disabilities are missing out on opportunities to develop the friendships and other social connections that help make life enjoyable and that will prepare them to transition successfully to adulthood. This chapter focuses on the important role that relationships play in the lives of *all* students and describes recommended and evidence-based approaches for enhancing the social lives of children and youth with severe disabilities.

The social lives of students with severe disabilities are not a tangential concern. The efforts made—or not made—to support and foster peer relationships has direct implications for the lives of individual students with severe disabilities in every school across the country. Throughout this chapter, you will hear about three of these students—Elena, Samuel, and Aloura. Like other students their age, each has much to contribute to and benefit from interactions with their peers.

✢ ✢ ✢ ✢ ✢   **Elena**   ✢ ✢ ✢ ✢ ✢

Elena is a third grader at Kennedy Elementary School. Science, art, and music are just a few of her favorite classes and she loves attending a new after-school program. Like many of her classmates, she most looks forward to spending time with her friends at lunch, on the playground, and in her classes. Elena's teacher helped establish a peer network that provided an intentional avenue for her to meet new peers and develop new communication skills. Although Elena has severe intellectual disabilities and is unable to vocalize, she certainly has much to say. She uses an augmentative communication device to greet her classmates, request help from a peer or teacher, contribute her ideas to class discussions, and tell jokes from one of her favorite books. As her classmates have gotten to know Elena, they have realized that her facial expressions and gestures are another primary way that she lets others know what she wants and needs. Because Elena also has cerebral palsy, her peers are quick to help her navigate the hallways, lunchroom, and playground when needed.

Samuel is in seventh grade at Jefferson Middle School. As with many middle school students, Samuel can be quite shy when meeting someone for the first time and it takes a little while for him to feel comfortable around new people. Samuel also has autism and tends to repeat a few favorite phrases, avoid making eye contact, and hold fast to specific routines. However, when the topics of video games, movies, or comic books are brought up, his entire demeanor changes. Samuel absolutely loves

talking about magna comics, a new PlayStation® game, or the latest action film. Although these were once viewed as "obsessions" and perceived to be barriers to peer relationships, they are now the very interests that connect Samuel with a core group of peers. A paraprofessional, who himself collected comic books, knew of more than a dozen other students in the school who shared these interests in common. They started a weekly comic book club that met over the lunch period and occasionally after school. Samuel's new friends talk often about how much they have enjoyed getting to know, spending time with, and learning from Samuel.

Aloura is junior at Northside High School. Until last year, she knew few of her classmates and often felt alone at school. Aloura has moderate intellectual disabilities, a mild hearing impairment, and a severe physical disability for which she uses an electric wheelchair. In an introductory art class, she first met Kara and Nicole—two talented painters who the classroom teacher assigned to the same cooperative learning group. Through their growing friendship, Aloura discovered that she had a knack for abstract painting that features vibrant colors and bold lines. Kara encouraged Aloura to get involved in set design for an upcoming school play. Nicole—who was already involved in the art club—asked Aloura to come to the next meeting. Becoming involved in these activities offered Aloura an opportunity to become known for her gifts and talents, instead of for having a severe intellectual disability.

These experiences, along with those of thousands of other students, offer compelling reminders of the powerful roles that educators, parents, related services providers, and—perhaps most of all—peers can play in enhancing the opportunities that students with severe disabilities have to develop satisfying relationships and participate fully in the life of their school.

Contributions of Peer Relationships in the Lives of All Children

At first glance, it may seem unnecessary to spend time articulating the importance of relationships in the lives of children and youth with severe disabilities. After all, most of us can speak first hand to the importance of relationships in our own lives—the friendships through which we exchange emotional and social support; the neighbors who contribute to our sense of community; the coworkers and colleagues with whom we share our time at work; and the members of our congregations, organizations, or other community groups with whom we affiliate and recreate. However, when the topic turns to school and educational planning, attention typically focuses on academic outcomes, functional skill development, specific therapies, and transition services, sometimes to the exclusion of peer relationships. Yet, the absence of connections with peers for many students with severe disabilities suggests that a stronger case must be made for the central place that relationship development should have within educational services and supports.

Friendships Are Important in the Lives of All Students

From an early age, relationships with peers take on an important role in the lives of children. As they enter school, children spend an increasing amount of the day in the presence of other students in classes, at lunch, on the playground, and in other school activities. The interactions and relationships that students have with one another can contribute to their social and emotional development, promote positive adjustment, and affect their engagement and involvement in school (Gifford-Smith & Brownell, 2003; Rubin, Bukowski, & Laursen, 2009). It is within the context of these relationships that students exchange an array of important social supports, including emotional support, companionship, access to peers, information, practical assistance, and help with decision making (Kennedy, 2004a). Peers both learn from and teach one another and, through their exchanges, acquire and strengthen an array of academic, social, leisure, and other everyday life skills. Having friendships and being liked by others also represents an important protective factor for students, providing companionship and connections while offering a buffer against loneliness and isolation (Deater-Deckard, 2001). Most of all, meaningful interactions and close relationships make life enjoyable; promote well-being; and, simply put, bring children and youth—indeed all of us—happiness.

For Children and Youth with Severe Disabilities

For all of these reasons, relationships are important for students with severe disabilities. Through their interactions with their peers without disabilities, students learn, practice, and refine important social, academic,

self-determination, and other functional skills that can increase their independence, promote learning, and enhance their involvement in the life of their school (Collins, 2002; Weiner, 2005). Peers also represent an important source of social support for students with severe disabilities by modeling and reinforcing critical social skills, expanding students' social networks, and helping students learn peer norms and values (Carter & Hughes, 2005; Hunt & Goetz, 1997; Meyer, 2001). Research suggests that peers may be at least as effective as adults in promoting certain aspects of social competence (Prater, Bruhl, & Serna, 1998). As students with severe disabilities spend more time with their peers without disabilities, their own expectations of themselves and their aspirations for their future may be elevated. Finally, more so today than in years past, the peers who learn alongside their classmates with severe disabilities in school will also later work, live, recreate, and worship alongside them as adults. The relationships that students develop during school may have a long-term impact on the attitudes that they encounter, the supports that they receive, and the connections that they have into adulthood. Although close relationships with peers are no less important for children with severe disabilities, the absence of those relationships appear to be much more strongly felt.

For Peers Without Disabilities

The most satisfying relationships typically are considered to be mutually beneficial and bring shared enjoyment. Although some peers may initially express apprehension or hesitation toward interacting with or getting to know their classmates with severe disabilities (Siperstein, Norins, & Mohler, 2007), those students who have had these experiences are often quite articulate about the substantive personal benefits that they derive through these relationships (Copeland et al., 2004; Fisher, 1999; Jones, 2007; Kamps et al., 1998). Among the benefits that these students report are a deeper appreciation of diversity and individual differences, greater understanding of the value of inclusion, increased knowledge about specific disabilities, improved attitudes toward people with disabilities, acquisition of advocacy and support skills, greater self-confidence, a strengthened commitment to social justice principles, and personal growth. As future coworkers, employers, neighbors, friends, teammates, and fellow citizens, these early lessons can have a lasting impact and can reshape community attitudes toward and expectations of people with disabilities.

Moreover, providing social and academic assistance through peer support and other peer-mediated arrangements has been shown to convey substantial academic benefits to peers without disabilities (Bensted & Bachor, 2002; Cushing & Kennedy, 1997; McDonnell, Mathot-Buckner, Thorson, & Fister, 2001). Perhaps most importantly, peers often speak of the immediate enjoyment that they receive and the friendships that emerge from these interactions (Murray-Seegert, 1989; Staub, 1998). In other words, the reciprocal benefits associated with peers getting to know and learn alongside their classmates with severe disabilities reinforces the importance of making fostering friendships a central educational outcome.

Some of the students in Elena's class began spending time with her only after receiving an invitation from their teacher to be part of Elena's peer network. As these classmates came to know Elena, however, their initial motivations for spending time with her soon changed. Elena's peers are now quick to talk about their new friend and the fun they have together with her. Two students who sit next to and help support Elena during instructional times have found that they are more focused and attend more closely to the teacher as a result of their peer support roles. Other friends of Elena have learned about the importance of inclusion and are often seen advocating in small ways for those classmates who feel left out.

The Simplicity (and Complexity) of Peer Relationships

Although relationships can be difficult to define or quantify, their absence is easily recognized by adults and sharply felt by students. Like some other important educational constructs (e.g., citizenship, character, intelligence, self-esteem), it is not always clear that everyone describes peer relationships in similar ways. Indeed, even throughout this chapter, the phrase *peer relationships* is used broadly to refer to the wide range of associations and affiliations that students have with others.

Defining Relationships

What exactly is a peer relationship? As Kennedy (2004b) points out, the number of different answers offered to this question will likely depend on the number of people in the room. It is true that a certain subjectivity remains as to how we understand the various types of

relationships that students have with one another. At the same time, most of us "know them when we see them" and can easily recognize when they are absent in the life of a student. In general, *peer relationships* refer to the interactions and associations that students have with other children and youth who are of the same age (Rubin et al., 2009). Relationships typically are apparent through the interactions that students have, the connections that they feel, and the satisfaction that they bring. However, there is a difference between having a relation *to* someone and being in a relationship *with* someone. For example, peers may refer to a student with severe disabilities as being their classmate, lab partner, teammate, schoolmate, or neighbor—labels that describe the relation of one student to the other—without actually being in a relationship with that student. The most desirable peer relationships are evidenced when students do things together, interact with one another, attribute value to their association, and feel that their interactions are mutually enjoyable.

The Variety of Interactions and Relationships

What types of interactions and relationships do—or should—children and youth have during and beyond the school day? Peer relationships take many forms and vary along several dimensions. And each can offer different benefits and opportunities for students. Attending to the types of interactions and relationships that students with severe disabilities have with their peers can provide insight into the quality of their social connections and help educators, parents, and other members of the planning team identify areas that would benefit from additional support and focused intervention. Consider the following social experiences that students typically have.

Academic and Social Interactions
Within classrooms, teachers typically expect and encourage students to converse with one another about ongoing instructional activities, materials, projects, and related tasks. For example, students with and without disabilities might collaborate on a small-group activity, help each other with an assignment, demonstrate how to perform a task, discuss aspects of the course content, share notes, or study together for an upcoming quiz. Through these academic-focused interactions—which may occur incidentally or be planned within cooperative learning experiences—students learn important course content, provide and receive instructional support, and strengthen their capacity to work

collaboratively with others. Moreover, these interactions can promote engagement within the classroom and make learning more enjoyable. In many classrooms, these are the types of peer interactions that teachers most highly value and frequently reinforce.

Social interactions are those that address non-instructional topics, including conversations about peers, popular culture (e.g., television, movies, favorite Web sites), current events, extracurricular and after-school activities, or personal issues (Hughes et al., 2000). Students also joke with one another, offer personal support, and exchange social amenities (e.g., saying "Hi" in the hallway). These typically represent the primary focus of interactions that take place outside of the classroom, such as during lunch, at recess, in the hallway, or during club activities. At the same time, many of these social interactions also take place within classrooms, particularly before the class period starts, during transitions between activities, and after completing assignments or group work (Carter, Sisco, Brown, Brickham, & Al-Khabbaz, 2008; Schnorr, 1997). Even in the midst of ongoing instruction, students may be passing notes, gesturing to a peer, or laughing at a peer's joke. Thus, inclusive classrooms appear to offer rich opportunities to support a range of interactions among students.

Although the distinction between academic and social interactions may seem trivial, each is likely to set the occasion for the emergence of different types of relationships. Students who talk only about their schoolwork tend to describe their relationships very differently from those whose interactions are more social in nature. Yet, descriptive research suggests that the peer interactions that students with severe disabilities have in the classrooms often focus narrowly on academic topics (Carter, Hughes, Guth, & Copeland, 2005). Moreover, the nature of students' interactions with their peers without disabilities also is influenced by the manner in which students are asked to work together. Tutorial and instructional activities tend to foster instructional interactions, while recreational and leisure activities tend to promote social interactions (Breen & Haring, 1991; Hughes, Carter, Hughes, Bradford, & Copeland, 2002; McMahon, Wacker, Sasso, Berg, & Newton, 1996).

Samuel talks with a number of different students each day at school, but the nature of his relationships with these peers are quite varied. In his American history class, there are several students to whom Samuel can turn for assistance when he needs help with an assignment or his class project. These students help Samuel organize his class materials, answer his questions, and prompt him to pay attention when he seems distracted. Until recently, these were the only kinds of interactions that Samuel had. He certainly appreciated their help, but Samuel would not consider these students to be friends. As he has come to know more students through involvement in various extracurricular clubs, Samuel's teachers increasingly see him talking with peers about comic books, the newest television shows, or favorite movies. These are the interactions that Samuel looks forward to most each day.

Friendships

Research addressing the social lives of children and youth with severe disabilities has focused largely on increasing the quantity and quality of these discrete interactions (Haring, 1993; Webster & Carter, 2007). Certainly, it is important to encourage academic and social interactions, but they do not necessarily reflect evidence of or always translate into a friendship. At its simplest level, a friend is someone who a student knows and likes, someone who would also name the student as a friend (Berndt & McCandless, 2007). Mutuality, reciprocity, closeness, and companionship are attributes often associated with friendship. But friendships occur on a continuum, varying widely in both type and quality. Those peers who have relationships that are especially close and enduring are often referred to by children and youth as "best friends." Students sometimes differentiate between "close friends" and "good friends" when talking about peers who they see occasionally or with whom their ties are not quite as strong. The academic and social interactions that students with severe disabilities have with their peers can provide the initial encounters through which friendships initially emerge or offer the contexts through which friendships are sustained or deepened. However, interactions—even if quite frequent—should not serve as a substitute for real friendships.

At the beginning of the school year, Aloura would sometimes be greeted by peers passing in the hallway and she would occasionally eat with classmates at lunch. During her classes, she would periodically talk with her classmates while working on small group projects or when she needed help. But she had no real friendships. She was never invited to birthday parties and had no one to go with her to the homecoming football game. And when she went to the movies or the mall, it was usually with her parents or sister. It wasn't until she met and developed friendships with Kara and Nicole that Aloura really began looking forward to going to school each day.

Status Relationships

Early efforts to promote peer relationships within schools often involved establishing peer tutoring arrangements or structured friendship programs (Cole, Vandercook, & Rynders, 1988; Haring, Breen, Pitts-Conway, Lee, & Gaylord-Ross, 1987; Kishi & Meyer, 1994). Although these strategies have been quite effective at increasing social participation and the frequency of interactions, concerns have been raised about the types of relationships sometimes promoted through these efforts. For example, some researchers and advocates have noted that efforts among school staff to facilitate regular interaction among students with and without disabilities can inadvertently foster relationships that are characterized as unbalanced, nonreciprocal, or exclusively tutorial (Janney & Snell, 2006; Storey, 2007; Van der Klift & Kunc, 2002). When students with severe disabilities are primarily or exclusively placed in the role of tutee or the consistent recipient of support, real friendships may be less likely to materialize and negative perceptions among peers or stereotypes can be reinforced. Such supportive relationships are not all inherently undesirable because it is commonplace in schools to occasionally be on the receiving end of assistance and support from peers. But these should not represent the *only* type of relationship that students have with their classmates. Educators should look for indicators which suggest that a status relationship is pervasive, such as when (a) students with disabilities rarely initiate interactions and are always on the receiving end of requests and commands, (b) peer interactions more closely resemble those students have with their teachers (e.g., authoritative), (c) interactions are dominated by helping or caregiving behaviors, (d) roles that students assume (e.g., tutor/tutee, supporter/supported) remain static instead of rotate, or (e) relationships do not appear to be mutually enjoyable or voluntary for all students involved.

When Elena's peers first began to provide support to her in the classroom, it was clear that they saw themselves as mini-teachers. Almost all of their conversations were instructional and they did many things for Elena. Indeed, they were mirroring many of the ways in which they saw paraprofessionals and spe-

cial educators interacting with Elena. Although this was not what the classroom teacher had intended when she first began pairing students together, she realized that the students would need some extra guidance on the roles that they should and should not assume when working together.

Peer Groups and Social Networks

A friendship typically refers to a dyadic relationship between two people. However, the peer environment becomes broader and more complex as children enter and progress through school. Students' interactions and relationships become situated within larger, informal networks of peers (Brown & Dietz, 2009). Sometimes, these peer groups are organized around students who regularly spend time interacting and doing things together (i.e., cliques). For example, students may consistently spend time with some or all of a core group of friends during lunch, between classes, or after school and on weekends. Other times, the associations among students within a peer group are based primarily on reputation (i.e., crowds). For example, students may be associated with a larger network of peers based on some common defining feature, such as their interests, activities, abilities, social status, or cultural background. These associations may exist even if students do not regularly or ever interact with one another. Students can be part of multiple cliques and crowds, and these peer groups typically are more fluid than static. Because participation in a social network can offer an important source of companionship and social support—and the absence of these networks represent a source of considerable concern and loneliness—it is important for educators to create supportive opportunities for students with severe disabilities to be part of a peer group that brings them enjoyment and satisfaction.

Membership and Belonging

Within peer networks, classrooms, formal groups and clubs, or the broader school, a student's sense of belonging and membership is enhanced by the interactions that he or she experiences, the relationships that develop, and the contributions made. Students have a keen sense of who is—and whether they are—truly part of (rather than simply present in) a larger group. For example, Schnorr (1990, 1997) observed that being enrolled in an inclusive classroom does not automatically convey membership or a sense of community. Students with severe disabilities may still be viewed by others as a visitor within the classroom, a temporary guest, or the "inclusion" child, but not recognized as a full, contributing member. Although difficult to directly observe and measure, fostering a sense of belonging among all students represents a qualitative dimension of peer relationships that requires focused attention and intentional efforts.

Although it didn't happen overnight, Aloura now is definitely part of a peer group. Recognizing her interest and talent in art, Aloura's teachers helped connect her with the set design team for the high school's drama productions. Over the course of working closely with her peers on the fall musical, Aloura has become embedded in a network of students who share a common interest in the fine arts. As a member of the theater clique, she always has a group of peers with whom she can sit at lunch or hang out in between classes.

Romantic Relationships

As students enter adolescence, romantic relationships assume an increasingly prominent place in the lives and thoughts of most youth (Florsheim, 2003). Yet, dating, long-term relationships, falling in love, intimacy, and other romantic experiences remain among the most understudied and least supported aspects of adolescent relationships for youth with severe disabilities (Bambara & Brantlinger, 2002; Hingsburger & Tough, 2002; Valenti-Hein & Choinski, 2007). The limited attention given to this issue may reflect broader societal attitudes toward sexuality and individuals with disabilities (Brown & Pirtle, 2008). Just as with other adolescents, youth with severe disabilities may want to—and should be supported to—explore and pursue intimate relationships (Walker-Hirsch, 2007).

Relationships with Adults

In a chapter focused on supporting peer relationships, it is still appropriate to mention the prominent role that adults play in the lives of children and youth with severe disabilities. Adults still represent the primary or exclusive relationships experienced by many children and youth with severe disabilities. Students with severe disabilities spend a substantial portion of their school day in close proximity to paraprofessionals, special educators, related services providers, and other adults (Brown, Farrington, Knight, Ross, & Ziegler, 1999; Giangreco, 2010; Giangreco & Broer, 2005). Interviews with students with disabilities about their

relationships with school staff suggest several areas of concern (Broer, Doyle, & Giangreco, 2005; Hemmingsson, Borell, & Gustavsson, 2003; Skar & Tamm, 2001). For example, students often describe paraprofessionals and other paid staff as their primary friends, as protectors, or as caregivers. The appropriateness of such relationships is questionable and is of particular concern when adults are the only relationships that students have.

The Role of Context and Relationships

When it comes to peer relationships, both location and context play influential roles (Kennedy, 2001; Sheridan, Buhs, & Warnes, 2003). The interactions that students have with one another and the relationships that they experience can be affected by the settings in which they spend time together, the activities in which they participate, and the grade level in which they are enrolled. Within classrooms, some types of interactions are sanctioned or reinforced, while others are discouraged or punished. The interactions that are considered to be appropriate within cooperative learning groups look quite different from those encouraged during large-group instruction or independent seatwork. The conversations that students have during art class may look different from those that take place in math class, classrooms often look different from the settings in which extracurricular activities take place, and lunch may be altogether different from what takes place in the hallways between classes. Careful consideration should be given to the types of interactions and relationships that are encouraged within a setting, as well as how these interactions are valued by the students themselves. Students should be equipped with the supports and taught the skills that will enable them to participate meaningfully in these interactions within each of these contexts.

At the same time, the nature and focus of peer relationships typically evolve as students grow older. The importance of relationships does not diminish as students move through elementary, middle, and high school, nor does the supportive role that adults play in promoting relationships. However, the contexts within which students spend time together broadens, the roles of adults in facilitating relationships becomes less direct, the involvement of peers in providing social support becomes more prominent, and the influence and importance of peers become more pervasive. In *preschool* and *elementary school,* children spend most of their time in the same classroom with a smaller group of peers. Relationships are more dyadic and "best" friendships are more prominent. Children also may have more unstructured and play time during which socializing is a central goal (e.g., recess, play groups). Relationships that extend beyond the school day tend to be limited to other children living in their neighborhood or students with whom family members make arrangements to see. In *middle school,* students show an increased interest in opposite-sex friendships and romantic relationships may begin to emerge. Students often attend larger schools and change classes each period, encountering many different students. The influence of cliques and crowds becomes more prominent as the peer environment broadens. The expansion of extracurricular and after-school opportunities also introduce new contexts within which students spend their time and meet other peers. In *high school,* the complexity of interactions and relationships increases and the influence of peers intensifies. A driver's license and the expansion of school-sponsored extracurricular activities mean that relationships increasingly extend beyond the school day. Students rely on technology (e.g., cell phones, text messaging, e-mail, social networking sites) to stay in touch and make plans. For students with severe disabilities, the increasing importance of peer relationships, coupled with the complexity of these relationships; restricted participation in general education classes; communication difficulties; and challenges in accessing the same technological tools (e.g., texting, social networking Web sites) used by other youth can make these students particularly vulnerable to social isolation.

The Importance of Intentional Efforts to Foster Relationships

Even when students spend almost all of their day in the company of their peers, physical proximity does not necessarily lead to social interactions or translate into relationships. The social interactions and relationships of children and youth with severe disabilities have been the focus of extensive research over several decades (Carter & Hughes, 2005; McConnell, 2002; Odom & Ogawa, 1992; Webster & Carter, 2007). Collectively, these studies affirm that interactions and relationships among students with and without severe disabilities are likely to remain elusive apart from well-designed support strategies and intentional planning.

Interactions with Peers Who Do Not Have Disabilities

Even within inclusive classrooms and other school settings (e.g., lunchrooms, playgrounds, hallways), social interactions may be limited in frequency or quality unless meaningful opportunities and adequate supports are established. For example, Carter et al. (2008) spent more than 150 hours observing the social and academic participation of students in middle and high school with students with intellectual disabilities or autism within general education classrooms. Despite being enrolled in the same classroom, most (but not all) students with disabilities infrequently interacted with their classmates. Moreover, peer interactions were least likely to occur when students with disabilities were receiving one-to-one, direct support from paraprofessionals or special educators. This paucity of interactions has been found in classrooms across grades (e.g., Evans, Salisbury, Palombaro, Berryman, & Hollowood, 1992; Fryxell & Kennedy, 1995; Katz, Mirenda, & Auerbach, 2002; Kennedy, Shukla, & Fryxell, 1997). Although the cafeteria often represents the social epicenter of most schools, students with severe disabilities often sit at separate tables and few interactions occur with their peers without disabilities during lunch (Cutts & Sigafoos, 2001; Dore, Dion, Wagner, & Brunet, 2002). For example, Hughes et al. (1999) observed students with and without intellectual disabilities conversing less than 1% of the time during lunch in the cafeteria. Students' interactions on the playground, in the hallways, and during homeroom also seem to be somewhat limited and highly variable (Kemp & Carter, 2002; Ratcliffe & Cress, 1998).

Relationships with Peers Without Disabilities

Although much less attention has been focused on the friendships and social relationships of students with severe disabilities (Webster & Carter, 2007), two nationally representative longitudinal studies provide insight into this dimension of children's lives. The Special Education Elementary Longitudinal Study involved interviews with parents about the social experiences of their children (ages 6 to 13) who were served under each of the different special education categories (Wagner et al., 2002). According to these parents, 17% of children with intellectual disabilities, 21% of children with multiple disabilities, and 32% of children with autism had *never* visited with any friends (with or without disabilities) during the previous year. Half of the children with intellectual disabilities, 64% of children with multiple disabilities, and 81% of children with autism *never* or *rarely* receive telephone calls from friends.

The National Longitudinal Transition Study-2 focused on the social involvement of high school students with disabilities (Wagner, Cadwallader, Garza, & Cameto, 2004). Interviews with parents revealed that only 22% of youth with intellectual disabilities, 14% of youth with multiple disabilities, and 6% of youth with autism were reported to *frequently* see any friends outside of school. Forty-two percent of youth with intellectual disabilities, 63% of youth with multiple disabilities, and 84% of youth with autism *never* or *rarely* receive telephone calls from friends. And only 54% of youth with intellectual disabilities, 38% of youth with multiple disabilities, and 24% of youth with autism get together with friends outside of formal groups at least once each week.

Collectively, these research findings highlight the elusiveness of peer relationships and extend a compelling call for more direct intervention and support efforts toward this aspect of children's lives. Two points should be highlighted here. First, our focus on individual children should not be overlooked in these statistics. What matters most is not whether the majority of children with disabilities have friends or interaction opportunities, but whether Elena, Samuel, Aloura, or any of the other students with whom you work experiences a sense of belonging, knows and is known by his or her peers, and enjoys durable relationships with friends. Indeed, it is the focus on the individual needs of a child that is a defining characteristic of special education. Second, these research statistics should not be interpreted to suggest that restricted relationships are inherent to having a severe disability. Indeed, a fairly extensive body of research shows that with intentional efforts, relationships can and should be commonplace (Matheson, Olsen, & Weisner, 2007; Meyer, Park, Grenot-Scheyer, Schwartz, & Harry, 1998; Staub, 1998; Turnbull, Blue-Banning, & Pereira, 2000). In other words, peer relationships are not elusive because students with severe disabilities cannot participate in or benefit from them, but instead because intentional efforts rarely are made or the support and service delivery models often relied on in schools inadvertently hinder relationships.

Promoting Peer Interaction and Social Relationships

Efforts to promote interactions and relationships among students with and without severe disabilities should encompass four important themes:

1. Meaningful peer relationships should be the expectation for every student. When school staff prioritize social outcomes alongside other educational outcomes, they are more likely to seek out and support opportunities for students to interact with their peers throughout the school day.
2. Relationships and learning go together and enhance each other—they are not competing priorities. Research suggests that promoting relationships will strengthen, rather than detract from, efforts to improve academic rigor and performance (Rubin et al., 2009).
3. Fostering relationships usually requires intentional efforts. Although being present in the same classroom, lunchroom, or playground as other students is a prerequisite to interactions, mere proximity often is not enough to increase interactions and change peer attitudes. Adults must view peer relationships as a primary educational outcome and assume an active role in promoting this outcome (Turnbull, Pereira, & Blue-Banning, 2000).
4. Students should have relationships that are mutually beneficial and satisfying. Although every person has some relationships that are primarily one-way (e.g., tutors, teachers, work supervisors, service providers such as doctors or mechanics), this should not describe *all* of the relationships that students with disabilities have.

Creating Opportunities for Relationships

Although much is now known about the contexts within which peer relationship are most likely to develop and be maintained, friendships can form or falter for a variety of reasons. Facilitating relationships is perhaps more properly considered an art than a science. As you consider the following seven factors, reflect on your past school experiences as a student and consider which of these elements may have contributed to the relationships that you developed with your peers.

Shared Space
Among the most prominent barriers to peer relationships in schools is that students with and without severe disabilities are not spending time in the same places. Although increasing students' access to the general education curriculum has been a central theme of recent legislative initiatives, students with severe disabilities in most schools spend the majority of their day apart from their peers without disabilities

(U.S. Department of Education, 2009; Williamson, McLeskey, Hoppey, & Rentz, 2006). When physically included in classrooms, students with severe disabilities may still not be recognized by classmates or even by teachers as contributing participants for a variety of reasons, including the presence of paraprofessional support that inadvertently curbs interactions, physical isolation in a corner of the classroom, the unavailability of a communication system, and the use of instructional strategies in which the student with disabilities has few opportunities to respond. Even when inclusive approaches to the delivery of instructional services are used, students' experiences may be limited to participation in extracurricular and other school-sponsored activities. Descriptive research that compares inclusive and special education settings indicates that social opportunities are less available in self-contained classrooms (Freeman & Alkin, 2000; Fryxell & Kennedy, 1995; Hunt, Farron-Davis, Beckstead, Curtis, & Goetz, 1994; Kennedy, Shukla, et al., 1997). Yet, when asked about the primary barriers to developing friendships with students with severe disabilities in their schools, peers consistently emphasize that they are not enrolled in the same classes and had few opportunities to see each other in school (Copeland et al., 2004; Fisher, 1999; Han & Chadsey, 2004).

> *The few minutes of break between each class period, hanging out in the courtyard over lunch, and spending time catching up after the school bell—these are the times when most students at Northside get together with friends, talk about their day, and make plans for after school or the weekend. Until this school year, Aloura spent all of these times with school staff. She left each class a few minutes early to avoid the crowded hallways, she ate lunch with paraprofessionals and other students with severe disabilities at a table at the side of the cafeteria, and she went outside to catch the accessible bus 10 minutes before the last bell rang. She developed few friendships—not because she had severe disabilities—but because she so rarely had a chance to spend time with and get to know her classmates.*

Shared Activities

Although it seems obvious that interactions are unlikely to occur unless students are in the same place, at the same time, and doing the same things (Carter, Swedeen, & Kurkowski, 2008), much of what takes place in many schools belies recognition of this important element. It

is nearly impossible for students with disabilities to interact with their peers when they are not sitting near each other in classrooms, they are pulled out of class to receive related services, or they are learning completely different academic content. Similarly, it is difficult to spend time together when students with disabilities eat lunch in different areas of the cafeteria, travel the hallways at different times, and are not participating in the same extracurricular activities. Shared activities provide the context within which students interact with one another. And because relationships often develop over time, it is essential that students have sustained and recurring opportunities to engage in shared learning and social activities with their classmates.

> *Although Elena had always been enrolled in general education classes, she had not always been working on the same content objectives as her classmates. More often than not, Elena would be pulled to the side of the classroom with a paraprofessional to work on specific individualized education program (IEP) objectives, therapy goals, or altogether different learning activities. As a result, there were few opportunities for Elena to work with her peers and no compelling reason for her peers to talk to her. More closely aligning Elena's expectations and instruction with the rest of the class and embedding more cooperative learning activities provided a meaningful context for Elena to work with and meet her peers.*

Shared Interests

Relationships often begin—or deepen further—upon discovery of shared interests. The likelihood that students will want to spend time together may be influenced by their awareness of the interests, talents, experiences, and aspirations they hold in common. Students with severe disabilities have interests that—because of their communication challenges—often go undiscovered. Educators and families can play an important role in (a) highlighting the specific things that students with and without disabilities hold in common, (b) providing students with opportunities to develop age-appropriate interests that might provide a link between students, and (c) designing collaborative activities that incorporate students' individual interests (Turnbull, Pereira, & Blue-Banning, 1999).

> *A love for painting and creative expression was definitely what connected Aloura, Kara, and Nicole. Had Aloura never enrolled in art class, these friendships may never have had an opportunity to develop.*

Aloura's special education teacher definitely recognized this and began making extra efforts to discover the interests and talents of all of the students on her caseload. She then looked for opportunities within the school and broader community where her students could utilize those interests and talents in ways that might foster new relationships.

Instruction in Social and Communication Skills

High-quality instruction from educators, paraprofessionals, and other adults that focus on social and communication skills can enhance students' interactions and relationships with peers. Many students evidence substantial deficits in social skills and would benefit from learning how to start conversations with their peers (Hughes et al., 2000), greet their classmates (Nientemp & Cole, 1992), play cooperatively at recess (Harper, Symon, & Frea, 2008), comment on a classmate's work or content discussed in class, use an augmentative communication device (Cosbey & Johnston, 2006; Snell, Chen, & Hoover, 2006), and demonstrate other valuable social skills. Although much attention has been directed toward social skill intervention strategies (Bellini, Peters, Brianner, & Hopf, 2007; Brown, Odom, & McConnell, 2007), it should be emphasized that acquiring these skills should not be considered a prerequisite to having meaningful opportunities to interact with one's peers. Indeed, social and communication skills are best learned, practiced, and refined within the context of actual peer interactions and relationships.

Students with severe disabilities also must have access to a reliable and effective means of communication. Students cannot communicate effectively with their peers if their augmentative and alternative communication (AAC) devices are purchased but not used, signs and gestures are taught to them but not understood by peers, communication books are created but left in lockers, or AAC devices remain at school at the end of the day. In addition, it is important that the social skills that students are taught and the communication systems with which they are provided are flexible enough to reflect the full range of interactions that children have with their peers and are appropriate to the various settings in which they are spending time with their peers.

Before the school provided her with an AAC device, Elena was entirely dependent on her paraprofessional, Ms. Bauer, and other school staff to interpret her gestures and other communication attempts for classmates. Although Ms. Bauer knew Elena very well, she didn't always interpret Elena's initiations accurately. Other times, Elena's attempts to communicate with her peers were inadvertently overlooked. Gaining access to an AAC system changed everything. As Elena learned to use her speech-generating device, Ms. Bauer taught other students in the class how to support and encourage Elena's interactions.

Equipping Peers Without Disabilities

Some barriers to interactions and relationships are related to the attitudes and knowledge that peers possess (Copeland et al., 2004; Siperstein et al., 2007; York & Tundidor, 1995). For example, students without disabilities may have insufficient knowledge about disabilities or remain uncertain of how to interact with classmates who may communicate differently. Others may hold negative attitudes toward people with disabilities or initially be hesitant to interact with a classmate with severe disabilities. Sharing basic information with students can help alleviate any concerns that students may have, promote greater confidence, and lay the groundwork for future interactions (Kent-Walsh & McNaughton, 2005). Sometimes, the information provided to peers is very targeted, focusing on helping peers learn about a student's interests and talents or understand how the student communicates, participates in various activities, or benefits from specific supports. Schools can also take broader steps to promote awareness throughout the entire school by making sure that inclusion is a school-wide value, emphasizing relationships as an important element of their mission, and communicating information that helps to dispel myths or stereotypes about disabilities.

Promoting Valued Roles

Reciprocal relationships may be more likely to emerge when valued roles are identified for all students (Wolfensberger, 2007). If students with severe disabilities are perpetually identified as the recipients of help and assistance, they have few opportunities to demonstrate and become known for their strengths, interests, and contributions. Which roles are valued often is best determined by asking the students themselves. For example, being the timekeeper in a cooperative group, serving in a leadership position in an extracurricular activity, teaching a skill to others, and contributing ideas during group planning may all be considered high-status roles by students.

Samuel was used to always being the recipient of help. In his classes, he was almost always accompanied by an adult who sat next to him and provided one-to-one academic and behavioral support. Occasionally, he received extra assistance from a peer tutor or other classmates on specific academic tasks. Although he certainly benefited academically from the individualized help, he developed few friendships in his classes and felt like he was only known for what he couldn't do. But this was not the case in extracurricular activities. Samuel was clearly among the experts in the comic book club, where other club members admired Samuel for his considerable knowledge and often turned to him for answers to their questions. His gaming talents and expertise in programming landed him in the role of vice president of the computer club, which allowed him to work on interesting group projects with his peers.

Providing "Just Enough" Support

The manner in which school staff provides instruction and support to students with severe disabilities can inadvertently hinder opportunities for students with and without disabilities to get to know one another. The widespread reliance on individually assigned, one-to-one adults—usually paraprofessionals—to support students can discourage peers from interacting with these students or can diminish the need for students with disabilities to turn to peers for help (Carter & Kennedy, 2006; Carter, Sisco, Melekoglu, & Kurkowski, 2007; Han & Chadsey, 2004). The close proximity or intensive involvement of an adult also can make peers reluctant to initiate interactions and reinforce the perception that the focus student is different. These practices can send the message that conversations must always be channeled through a third person, particularly as students grow older and become accustomed to working more independently. In community-based work experiences, the excessive proximity of a job coach can yield similar effects among coworkers and customers. Giangreco, Edelman, Luiselli, and MacFarland (1997) highlighted several potential drawbacks associated with excessive one-to-one adult support, including (a) increased separation from classmates, (b) unnecessary dependence on adults, (c) reduced interactions with peers, (d) loss of personal control, (e) stifling of gender identity, and (f) insular relationships with adults. School staff should reflect carefully on the manner in which they provide direct support, providing "just enough" support to enhance participation, but

not more than is necessary. Instead of assuming that an adult should be the first line of support, Carter, Cushing, and Kennedy (2009) suggest first considering whether students can do an activity (a) on their own, (b) if given the right technology or adaptive equipment, (c) if provided some additional skill instruction, (d) if taught self-management strategies, (e) with help from a peer, or (f) with help from someone else in the setting. Just enough adult support is introduced only when these other avenues of support prove to be insufficient.

Evidence-Based Strategies for Supporting Relationships

With these elements in mind, the remainder of this chapter focuses on an array of promising and evidence-based strategies for increasing interactions and fostering relationships among students with severe disabilities and their peers in each of the four contexts in which students spend their day: (a) inclusive general education classrooms; (b) informal contexts; (c) extracurricular and school-sponsored activities; and (d) after school, on weekends, and during the summer. A wide variety of strategies for promoting social interactions and peer relationships have been described or evaluated in the professional literature. This chapter will focus on those that have strong evidence of efficacy and acceptability. *Efficacy* refers to the extent to which compelling research exists that an educational practice will produce the desired outcomes (Odom et al., 2005). *Acceptability* refers to the extent to which the strategies are feasible to implement in school; valued by teachers, students, and other stakeholders; and align well with other instructional and support practices (Snell, 2003). Educational practices that are both effective and socially valid are more likely to be used by practitioners and to benefit students.

Inclusive General Education Classrooms

As emphasized throughout this textbook, legislation, policy initiatives, advocacy efforts, and research findings are challenging schools to shift the contexts in which students with severe disabilities spend their school day (Individuals with Disabilities Education Improvement Act of 2004; Ryndak & Fisher, 2003). The general education classroom has clearly emerged as the recommended setting for providing access to a challenging academic curriculum, promoting involvement in relevant learning experiences, and fostering relationships among students (Spooner, Dymond, Smith, & Kennedy, 2006). Although inclusive classrooms offer numerous *potential* opportunities for students with and without severe disabilities to work together, interact with one another, and establish relationships with peers, those opportunities typically go unrealized unless intentional planning and well-designed supports are in place. Among the educational objectives that are addressed throughout the school day, it is essential that educators identify supportive and meaningful avenues through which students can get to know each other and learn alongside each other.

Peer Support Strategies

One of the most widely implemented approaches to supporting the classroom participation of students with severe disabilities involves the individual assignment of adults, such as paraprofessionals, special educators, or related service providers. Yet, an overreliance on one-to-one adult assistance can often (and inadvertently) limit the opportunities that students have to interact with and get to know one another (Carter et al., 2008; Marks, Schrader, & Levine, 1999). Peer support strategies offer a promising alternative to the exclusive reliance on adult-delivered support within inclusive classrooms. Broadly defined, peer support strategies involve arranging for students without disabilities to provide ongoing social and academic support to their same-age classmates with severe disabilities while receiving the necessary guidance and assistance from school staff (Carter et al., 2009). An array of peer-mediated approaches have been evaluated in the professional literature; these approaches vary widely with regard to their primary focus (e.g., social or academic participation) and intensity. For example, teachers might informally pair students together or implement more structured tutoring approaches. Peer support strategies have emerged as an evidence-based approach for increasing social interactions, expanding students' social networks, and promoting new friendships among students with and without disabilities within inclusive classrooms (Carter & Kennedy, 2006). Indeed, the active involvement of peers appears to be a critical element in meeting both the social and academic goals of students with severe disabilities.

Although peer support strategies should always be tailored to meet the individualized instructional and support needs of students with severe disabilities, the following steps typically are taken when establishing these arrangements:

1. Educators should begin by identifying students with and without disabilities who might benefit from involvement in peer support arrangements. Students with severe disabilities who need additional assistance to participate in class activities, experience few peer interactions during class, or have few friendships are especially likely to benefit from these support strategies. One or more peers without disabilities are then identified from within the same classroom to participate. Although there are no established criteria for who makes an effective peer support, educators often identify classmates who already know the student, have expressed interest in assuming these roles, have consistent attendance, share interests in common with the student, work well with others, and evidence a willingness to learn new skills. Although teachers tend to invite academically high-performing students to serve in peer support roles, research suggests that average- or low-performing students may benefit as much or more and are similarly effective in these roles (Cushing & Kennedy, 1997; Shukla, Kennedy, & Cushing, 1998). Moreover, students with disabilities—particularly during adolescence—should have a voice in determining from whom and how they receive support throughout the school day.

2. Students are oriented to their roles and responsibilities as peer supports. For example, peers may be provided with general information about a student's strengths, interests, and educational goals; basic strategies for supporting academic and social participation; strategies for supporting communication device or other technology use; ideas for promoting interactions with other classmates; suggestions for providing feedback and encouragement; and guidance on when to turn to adults for assistance. In peer support approaches that more heavily emphasize instructional arrangements, such as peer tutoring or academic coaching, peers may be taught more systematic approaches for providing instruction (Jameson, McDonnell, Polychronis, & Riesen, 2008; Kamps, Barbetta, Leonard, & Delquadri, 1994). When social participation is the primary emphasis, conversation-enhancing skills may be more relevant for students to learn (Hunt, Alwell, Farron-Davis, & Goetz, 1996; Kamps, Lopez, & Golden, 2002; Weiner, 2005). It is equally important to be sure that

students with severe disabilities know how to request and decline support from their peers, as well as understand the roles that peers will play. Equipping students with this initial information and these skills increases their confidence in and comfort with their new roles.

3. Students are provided with regular opportunities to work and interact within ongoing class activities. This involves first arranging for students to sit next to each other or within the same small group. As students work together, peers then support class participation and learning by sharing materials, assisting with in-class activities, reviewing the accu-

racy of work, sharing additional examples of a key idea, highlighting important concepts, and offering constructive feedback. At the same time, peers also support social goals by initiating interactions, reinforcing communication attempts, modeling social skills, offering social support, making introductions to other classmates, conversing about shared interests, and encouraging participation in class discussions. Typically, the specific avenues through which students will support each other are detailed in a written support plan at the start of the semester that is revisited as often as needed (Cushing, Clark, Carter, & Kennedy, 2005). For example, Figure 11–1

FIGURE 11–1
Example Support Plan for Inclusive Classrooms

Class: American history Teacher: Ms. Alameda		Student: Samuel Peers: Adrian and Thomas	
Typical Activities and Routines	**Expectations for all Students**	**Needed Adaptations and Supports**	**Roles of Peers in Providing Support**
Whole-class instruction	During lectures, students listen, answer questions, and take notes; during group discussion, students are expected to relate class topics to current events.	Samuel will receive guided notes prepared by the teacher; he will sit in the first two rows to minimize distractions.	Peers will help Samuel complete his notes, share their notes, and ask clarifying questions; peers will help Samuel research current events on the Internet.
Small-group instruction	During cooperative groups, students read case studies and answer application questions; students also work in teams to prepare for weekly debates that address historical issues.	Samuel will be part of the same group as Adrian and Thomas.	Peers will paraphrase aspects of the readings for Samuel, make connections to his experiences, and prompt him to contribute to group discussion; peers will help Samuel prepare for upcoming debates.
Independent work	Students use their textbook and other reading materials to answer worksheet questions.	Adapted worksheet questions will require short answers instead of essays; some worksheets will be reduced in length, as needed.	When finished with their work, peers will help Samuel record his answers and check his work for accuracy.
Homework and assignments	Students typically read one chapter of the textbook per week and turn in two homework assignments.	Samuel will have access to an electronic textbook with which he can listen to the readings.	Samuel will have access to a peer tutor during his fifth-period study hall when he needs additional assistance.
Needed materials	Textbook, notebook, weekly planner	None needed	Peers will help Samuel keep his assignments and class materials organized.
Other expectations	Students are expected to arrive to class on time, bring all of their needed materials, and actively participate in class activities.	None needed	Samuel will walk with his peers to and from class.

Adapted from *Modifying schoolwork* (p. 64), by R. Janney & M. E. Snell, 2004. Baltimore: Paul H. Brookes.

shows a completed support plan for Samuel. For each classroom routine, the team outlines the expectations for all students in the class, the adaptations and supports needed by the student with disabilities, and the roles that peers will play in providing some of these supports.

4. Fourth, adults within the classroom (e.g., general educators, special educators, paraprofessionals) monitor students' progress to ensure that they are benefiting socially and academically from their involvement. When additional support is needed for peer supports to feel confident in their roles, adults also provide it. For example, a paraprofessional might informally observe to determine whether students are remaining on task (engaged), interacting appropriately, and supporting one another effectively, as well as talk with the participating students to determine whether they have the information and direction that they need. As students with and without severe disabilities gain more experience working together, adults who previously provided one-to-one assistance gradually shift to a broader support role within the entire classroom. Because the manner in which peer support arrangements are established may influence the nature of the relationships that ultimately develop, it is important to pay close attention to the types of interactions that students have within these arrangements to ensure that they are mutually enjoyable, enhance membership, and lead to valued relationships.

Research offers strong evidence of the efficacy and acceptability of these intervention strategies (Carter & Kennedy, 2006). Peer support strategies can enhance the communication skills of students with severe disabilities, increase the frequency and quality of their interactions with peers, provide greater access to an array of social supports, expand their social networks, and lead to the development of new friendships (Carter et al., 2007; Kennedy, Cushing, & Itkonen, 1997; Laushey & Heflin, 2000). At the same time, classmates who serve as peer supports often report a substantial improvement in their attitudes toward and understanding of disabilities, improve their academic performance, and develop lasting friendships (Copeland et al., 2004; Kamps et al., 1998; Kishi & Meyer, 1994). Peer support strategies reinforce that students with disabilities can learn from their peers without disabilities and that such arrangements can be mutually beneficial.

Peer support interventions also are practical strategies that fit well within inclusive settings. Like other peer-mediated interventions, peer support draws on the one most readily available source of support in any classroom—other students. With some initial guidance, most students are quite adept at implementing basic academic and social support strategies, as well as brainstorming ways of enhancing their partner's active participation in class activities. These interventions also enable teachers to differentiate instruction and offer individualized support within heterogeneous classrooms without requiring broader changes in instructional delivery. For paraprofessionals, who often are given little direction regarding their roles within inclusive classrooms, these interventions define more clearly the avenues through which they can support students' success within the classroom.

Ms. Mosso, the special education teacher at Jefferson Middle School, took notice of the friendships that Samuel was developing through his extracurricular involvement. Yet, she also was aware that Samuel still knew few of his classmates and was often on the periphery of class activities. Samuel depended heavily on the paraprofessional who had attended all of his classes with him since elementary school. Ms. Mosso and several of Samuel's classroom teachers met to brainstorm ways of involving other students more directly in supporting Samuel's class participation. Several members of the computer and comic book clubs were enrolled in some of the same classes as Samuel, so the teachers invited them to serve as peer supports within each of Samuel's classes. Ms. Mosso invited students to meet with her over two lunch periods to talk about some of the ways that they could help Samuel participate more actively in class activities and introduce him to other classmates. As the students began working together, Samuel's paraprofessional continued to provide not only the additional support that Samuel needed, but also offered guidance to the peer supports as various needs arose. Over the course of the semester, Samuel began to feel more like a true member of his classes and his friendships with his peer supports deepened further.

Cooperative Instructional Arrangements

In many classrooms, particularly in middle and high schools, teacher-led instruction (e.g., lecture, large-group discussion) or independent seat work are among the primary avenues through which content is delivered. Establishing cooperative learning groups and other interdependent instructional arrangements have been shown to promote peer interaction among students with and without severe disabilities (Dugan et al., 1995; Piercy, Wilton, & Townsend, 2002). These interventions typically involve dividing the class into smaller groups of four or five students, establishing a set of common learning goals that each group works toward, delineating the specific and unique roles that each student within the group will assume (e.g., timekeeper, checker, facilitator, recorder, artist), and establishing clear expectations that all students must work together to accomplish (e.g., group accountability). Such arrangements provide regularly occurring interaction opportunities, establish interdependent contingencies that reward collaborative work, and create a socially supportive environment for all students. Often, peer support arrangements are embedded within cooperative learning groups by identifying one or more group members who receive additional information and guidance on how to support the active participation of a classmate with severe disabilities (Cushing, Kennedy, Shukla, Davis, & Meyer, 1997). Students may need explicit instruction on how to work together and support one another effectively (Cowie & Wallace, 2000). To this end, educators should establish clearly defined roles and responsibilities for students, as well as teach them to provide helpful feedback to each other in effective ways (e.g., providing positive feedback first, suggesting alternatives instead of providing directives, providing constructive responses).

Elena loved being in control! Mr. Bauer had always relied heavily on cooperative groups to promote learning within his classroom. But when he learned that Elena would be in his class, he wasn't exactly sure how to meaningfully involve her in small group activities. Mr. Bauer met with the special education teacher and speech-language pathologist to learn more about Elena's educational goals and brainstorm ways of involving Elena more fully. Several of Elena's goals focused on increasing her communication skills and AAC device use, as well as promoting social interactions with classmates. Mr. Bauer assigned Elena two important roles within the classroom. First, she was assigned the role of discussion facilitator, which meant that she decided who Mr. Bauer would call on when groups shared their answers with the rest of the class. The speech-language pathologist helped input the names of all of the classmates

into Elena's AAC device. This made her the most popular girl in the class because students who liked getting called on—and those who definitely did not—made sure to stay on Elena's good side. Second, Mr. Bauer assigned Elena and another peer the responsibility for managing materials for the weekly science lab. In order to complete their science experiments, every student had to interact with Elena and her peer. This gave Elena and her classmates a chance to get to know each other and provided a natural opportunity to practice using her AAC device.

Adult Facilitation Strategies

Although every classroom offers natural opportunities for students to interact with one another about both academic and social topics, these opportunities frequently are overlooked for students with severe disabilities (Carter, Hughes, et al., 2005; Evans & Meyer, 2001). Paraprofessionals, special educators, general educators, and other adults should be proactive by encouraging and reinforcing interaction and collaborative work among students with and without severe disabilities. However, adults often end up serving as "intermediaries" between students with and without disabilities instead of "bridge builders" or "facilitators" (Causton-Theoharis & Malmgren, 2005b). A number of simple but proactive steps can be taken to increase both the quantity and quality of the interactions that take place among students within the classroom, as well as during other aspects of the school day (Downing, 2005a; Ghere, York-Barr, & Sommerness, 2002). Examples of these supportive strategies include the following:

- Modeling ways for students to initiate, maintain, and extend conversations;
- Demonstrating how to converse with someone using an AAC device;
- Highlighting shared interests, strengths, experiences, or other similarities among students;
- Teaching and prompting critical social interaction skills (e.g., initiating a conversation, greeting classmates, requesting help, refusing support);
- Redirecting peers' questions and comments away from the adult and to the student with disabilities (and vice versa);
- Interpreting the communicative intent of nonverbal (e.g., gestures, signs, expressions) or challenging behaviors, as well as suggesting appropriate responses to those communication attempts;
- Highlighting students' strengths and contributions to small-group and other projects;

- Assigning classroom responsibilities that require frequent interaction, such as small-group assignments, cooperative projects, or activities that involve joint responsibilities;
- Relocating students so that they sit together and remain in close physical and social proximity; and
- Asking additional peers to provide occasional support as needed.

These discrete facilitation strategies can substantially increase the frequency of peer interaction by creating additional opportunities for students to converse, addressing attitudinal and other barriers to interaction, and communicating to all students the importance and value of getting to know one another (Causton-Theoharis & Malmgren, 2005b). However, the incidental lessons that adults communicate are equally important to consider. Peers often take their cue from the ways in which adults interact with their classmates with disabilities (Janney & Snell, 1997). When adults use affirming and age-appropriate language, model respectful interactions, and communicate high expectations for students with disabilities, peers may be more likely to echo these same postures. When peers observe patronizing or caregiving behaviors and childish language, they also are likely to follow suit.

It took a little time for Elena's classmates to feel comfortable and confident communicating with someone who used an AAC device. After all, this was a new experience for most of them. Ms. Bauer looked for opportunities to encourage interactions between Elena and her peers. When a classmate asked her a question about Elena, Ms. Bauer would respond, "I bet Elena can answer that question better than I can!" When Elena turned to Ms. Bauer for help, she would say, "Go ahead and compare your answers to Olivia's. She can check if your answers are correct." When peers appeared uncertain about how to ask for Elena's feedback, Ms. Bauer might say, "Try rephrasing it as a 'yes' or 'no' question; Elena is still learning to use her communication device." And when she learned that a classmate shared something in common with Elena, Ms. Bauer was quick to point it out, "I didn't realize you liked Harry Potter. You should talk with Elena . . . she is the biggest Harry Potter fan I know."

Self-directed Intervention Strategies

Recognition of the importance of fostering self-determination among children and youth with disabilities has led to the development, evaluation, and refinement of strategies that students with severe disabilities can use to expand their interactions with classmates. Students can learn to self-direct their own social behavior using a combination of self-management strategies, such as goal setting, self-prompting, self-instruction, self-monitoring, and self-evaluation (Lee, Simpson, & Shogren, 2007). For example, students may be taught to initiate interactions by using a picture book depicting conversational cues (Hughes et al., 2000), to use self-instruction to rehearse and start conversations in the hallways (Hughes, Killian, & Fischer, 1996), to self-monitor the extent to which they greet their classmates (Gilberts, Agran, Hughes, & Wehmeyer, 2001), or to self-monitor their use of important interaction skills (Morrison, Kamps, Garcia, & Parker, 2001). These self-directed strategies have been shown to have several potential effects: (a) increased independence, (b) decreased reliance on others to initiate conversations, (c) elevation of expectations for what students with severe disabilities can accomplish on their own, and (d) decreased extensive reliance on educators for constant support (e.g., Wehmeyer et al., 2007). Most importantly, these self-directed strategies are highly portable and can be used throughout the day.

Samuel was always forgetting to bring his book and other materials to class. And Mr. Franklin was tired of reminding Samuel or sending him back to his locker to retrieve his things. Mr. Franklin asked one of Samuel's classmates to show him the checklist that she kept in her folder that reminded her of everything she needed for each class. She helped him create his own checklist and soon Samuel came to love ticking off each item on his list. Mr. Franklin suggested a couple of additions to Samuel's checklist, including items related to greeting his peers, asking questions in class, and contributing to class discussions. Samuel referred to the list each day and gradually became less dependent on his teachers to participate actively in class activities.

Informal Contexts

Although students often spend five or more hours of their school day in the classroom, it is equally important to attend to those less structured times during which spending time conversing and "hanging out" with peers is a primary focus. Lunch, recess, breaks between classes, homeroom, and unstructured times before and after school typically offer numerous interaction opportunities. Observational studies, however, suggest that these may represent the school contexts during which students with severe disabilities remain most isolated from their peers without disabilities (Dore et al., 2002; Hughes et al., 1999; Kemp & Carter, 2002).

Lunch Group Strategies

In most schools, the lunch period offers a relatively unstructured context rich with opportunities for students to spend time together, converse socially, and meet with peers who they might not encounter during classes or outside of school. In some middle and high schools, students are free to spend lunch outside of the cafeteria, in the courtyard, hallways, classrooms, or even off-campus. Despite these potential opportunities, students with severe disabilities often spend their lunch period sitting at separate tables with other students with disabilities, eating exclusively with adults (e.g., special educators, paraprofessionals) or arriving at the cafeteria much earlier or later than the other students.

Intentional efforts to organize informal gatherings of students during lunch can reduce students' isolation and provide a natural avenue to expand their social networks (Breen & Lovinger, 1991; Kamps et al., 2002). Often referred to as a "lunch bunch" or lunch groups within elementary and middle schools, these interventions typically focus on increasing the social networks of an individual or a small number of students with severe disabilities. As with peer support strategies, students with disabilities should be asked about their interest in participating in a lunch group and be encouraged to suggest peers to invite. These interventions typically involve identifying regular times and locations where students will spend lunch together and inviting peers who already know or share a class with the focus student(s). Adults then organize initial introductory activities that help students to better get to know each other and help students define the primary focus of the group (e.g., eating lunch together, hanging out, playing games, planning activities related to shared interests). Peers are encouraged to invite other friends to join the group and, gradually, greater responsibility for maintaining the group is turned over to participating students. Adults are active in the organization and initiation of lunch groups and then assume a monitoring role. Adults should have as limited direct involvement in the group as possible, providing support only when absolutely necessary (e.g., interactions are inappropriate, challenging behavior occurs). Concurrently, it is advantageous to focus instruction on

relevant social, leisure, and other collateral skills (e.g., board, card, or computer games) outside of the cafeteria that will enhance the quality of the interactions that students with disabilities have within these groups (Gaylord-Ross, Haring, Breen, & Pitts-Conway, 1984; Haring, Roger, Lee, Breen, & Gaylord-Ross, 1986). Participating peers may also benefit from learning basic strategies for eliciting, responding to, and reinforcing the social and communication skills of the focus students.

Peer Network Strategies

As students progress through late elementary, middle, and high school, they begin to participate in a wider range of classes daily, each of which are led by different teachers and are made up of a different cadre of peers. Relationships that are evident in one classroom may not automatically extend to other classrooms or noninstructional contexts apart from deliberate programming because peers may be enrolled in different classes, follow different bell schedules, or participate in different extracurricular activities. Peer network interventions offer a promising approach for addressing social needs beyond the classroom and across the school day by establishing cohesive social groups around a particular focus student (Garrison-Harrell, Kamps, & Kravitz, 1997; Kamps, Dugan, Potucek, & Collins, 1999). Although peer networks are flexible approaches that should be tailored to meet the individualized needs of students, the following process is typically used to establish these networks (Haring & Breen, 1992).

Peer network interventions are implemented only after first talking with the focus student—as well as his or her parents—to determine an interest in participating and to solicit suggestions with regard to the focus and composition of the network. For example, peer networks might focus on a particular time of the day (e.g., recess, lunch), the broader school day (e.g., classes, extracurricular activities), after-school activities, or any combination of these. A small group of peers without disabilities—typically four to six students—are then invited to an initial meeting to organize the network. Peers who already know the focus student, attend classes together, share interests or experiences in common, have had prior interactions, and/or are themselves part of established social networks often are recommended as potential participants. Teachers, paraprofessionals, and other school staff who know the student well can be asked to suggest peers who fit these descriptions. However, the preferences of the focus student should always be sought and regularly revisited as part of any peer-mediated intervention.

During the first meeting with peers, the adult who is facilitating the group typically shares the rationale for the peer network, provides background on the focus student(s) (e.g., interests, hobbies, talents, preferences, school and community activities), offers guidance regarding the roles that students should and should not assume, and answers any questions that the peers have. The focus student typically is not present at this meeting. Next, participating students discuss their daily schedules, including the courses that they are taking; the extracurricular activities in which they are involved; and the places where they spend time between classes, at lunch, and before or after school. Based on their schedules, the students determine the times of day and the school activities (e.g., transitions between classes, lunch, extracurricular activities, other school-sponsored events) during which they will spend time with the focus student, as well as establish a regular meeting for the group. Although the goal is to identify at least one peer who the focus student will know and spend time with across different aspects of the school day, peers are encouraged to introduce the student to their own network of friends. The focus student is then introduced to this network and peers begin providing support. During subsequent meetings of the peers, the students adjust their schedules as needed; share ideas for providing social support, expanding the size of the peer network, and increasing the student's involvement in additional school activities; and collectively problem-solve any challenges that may arise. For example, peers might exchange ideas for conversation topics, engaging activities, or addressing challenging behaviors. Although an adult is present at these meetings of peers, their role should be to facilitate instead of lead the meeting and encourage students to assume increasing responsibility for sustaining the network.

When peer networks are established, students have been shown to engage in greater numbers of peer interactions across the day, increase their involvement in a range of structured and unstructured activities during and after school, and expand the size and quality of their social networks (Garrison-Harrell et al., 1997; Haring & Breen, 1992). Several factors appear to contribute to the efficacy of peer networks. Students with severe disabilities are introduced into an existing network of peers, each of whom makes introductions to other students in the school who they know. In addi-

tion, students receive the additional support and encouragement they may need to participate more independently and meaningfully in the everyday life of their school. Through these shared activities, they develop friendships with peers in their network and encounter additional students who they might not otherwise meet. Finally, the support and information available through the network meetings increase the peers' confidence in interacting with students who perhaps communicate in unfamiliar or unconventional ways.

Extracurricular and Other School-Sponsored Activities

Involvement in extracurricular activities (e.g., helping with the school yearbook, contributing to service activities, working on the homecoming float, competing in an athletic event, or performing in a drama production) becomes more prominent as students grow older and often is among the school experiences that students enjoy most. Supporting involvement in extracurricular and other school activities (e.g., assemblies, pep rallies, sporting events, dances, fine arts productions) enables students to meet new peers who share similar interests, promotes a sense of belonging and connection to a larger group, and creates a context in which students can develop new skills and interests that provide lifelong enjoyment (Mahoney, Harris, & Eccles, 2006). Although the Individuals with Disabilities Education Improvement Act of 2004 directs IEP teams to consider the aids, services, and other supports that students with disabilities need to "participate in extracurricular and other nonacademic activities" (§300.320(a)(4)(ii)), most students with severe disabilities have fairly limited involvement in these activities (Kleinert, Miracle, & Sheppard-Jones, 2007; Wagner et al., 2004). Indeed, these important contexts for developing relationships and increasing school involvement often are not explicitly addressed during educational planning.

Educators should be intentional about connecting students with disabilities to extracurricular activities and ensuring that they are equipped with the skills, supports, and opportunities needed to participate meaningfully in these school offerings and in ways that will foster relationships. Although there have been few empirical studies that address access to extracurricular activities for students with severe disabilities, the literature suggests several steps that planning teams might take (Carter, Swedeen, Moss, & Pesko, 2010; Hughes & Carter, 2008). These include

(a) identifying extracurricular opportunities that build on or expand students' interests and strengths; (b) determining the expectations and support needs associated with identified activities; (c) equipping students with information, skills, and supports that would enhance their participation; (d) preparing activity sponsors and peers to support the involvement and contributions of students; (e) keeping families informed about opportunities and logistical issues; and (f) reflecting regularly on the experiences that students have to ensure that the intended benefits accrue.

As with classroom-based peer support strategies, it can be advantageous to identify peers who already participate in club activities to provide social and practical support instead of automatically arranging for one-to-one assistance from a paraprofessional or other adult. Peers might be involved in assisting students with getting to and from club activities, helping students learn expected routines, supporting partial participation, making introductions to other peers, or working together on a specific club-related task. Club or activity sponsors can also take steps to foster positive relationships among all students by structuring team-building and other early opportunities for students to learn more about each other and work together on collaborative tasks.

In addition to expanding access to existing activities, schools may also establish new clubs or informal networks that engage students and create opportunities for students to get to know one another. For example, schools might create inclusive, social-focused clubs designed around recreational and service activities to encourage relationship-building and expand school or community involvement (e.g., a peer partners club). Or, educators might help students develop self-advocacy or disability-focused clubs in order to create a context in which youth with and without disabilities can develop new relationships, learn together about disability-related issues, and develop skills that enhance their self-determination.

Regardless of the avenue of extracurricular involvement, educators should consider logistical and support issues carefully, including the accessibility of activity events and locations, the availability of transportation, potential scheduling conflicts (e.g., interference with after-school jobs or other events), and the availability of needed adaptive equipment or communication devices. Conversations with families about extracurricular participation also are particularly important because parents may be hesitant to encourage involvement if

they have concerns about safety or worry that their child will not be welcomed by peers or well-supported in activities (Murphy & Carbone, 2008). Educators can strengthen family support for extracurricular involvement by keeping them informed of existing opportunities and upcoming activities, communicating the importance and value of extracurricular involvement, and sharing feedback on the contributions that their child is making in the group and the peer relationships that he or she is developing.

Aloura loved working on the "set team" for the school play. It gave her a chance to explore her creative side and an opportunity to meet other students with whom she didn't share any classes. Initially, Aloura's special education teacher, Ms. Horne, accompanied her to the first few after-school meetings. Ms. Horne tried to stay in the background, taking inventory of the types of support that Aloura might need to continue attending independently. Ms. Horne talked with the drama and art teachers to learn more about what the set team would be doing and to share some ways that Aloura might contribute to those efforts. They also discussed some of Aloura's medical issues and Ms. Horne shared an information sheet that described steps that should be taken if Aloura were to have a seizure. Ms. Horne asked if she could speak with several of the peers who would be working with Aloura in order to provide some background about her interests and strengths, as well as to answer any questions that they might have. Because many of the team's activities took place after school, Ms. Horne and Aloura's parents worked out transportation issues in advance. Aloura had a wonderful experience contributing to the success of the play and was thrilled to be recognized for her contributions to the design of the set on opening night.

After School, on Weekends, and During the Summer

As students become older, their interactions with peers increasingly extend beyond the school day. Involvement in sports and recreational programs; organized community groups (e.g., scouting, 4-H); activities offered through faith communities; summer camps; volunteering; and informal social events with friends (e.g., going to the movies, playing video games, shopping at the mall) represent just a sampling of the ways in which most children and youth spend their time outside of school. Although these out-of-school activities often are the contexts in which friendships develop, they rarely are addressed explicitly as part of educational planning and are accessed infrequently by children and youth with severe disabilities (Carter, Swedeen, & Trainor, 2009; Kleinert et al., 2007). Moreover, the research literature on promoting relationships that extend beyond the school day and the school year is much less well developed.

Mapping Inclusive Opportunities

Parents and practitioners often report a limited awareness of the inclusive activities that already exist or that might be developed within their communities (Trainor, Carter, Owens, & Swedeen, 2008). School staff and community members can collaborate to identify and create a "map" of the formal and informal programs and activities that might be accessed by children and youth with disabilities in their local community. Community resource mapping typically involves compiling information about both the disability-specific and generically available programs in a local community, along with the services and supports that could be drawn on in order to support participation (Crane & Mooney, 2005). Although many community activities and programs may not currently be inclusive, the professional literature offers guidance for refining programs and providing the needed supports within summer programs and camps, recreational activities, children's programs and youth groups sponsored by faith communities, and after-school programs (e.g., Carter, 2007; Rynders et al., 1993; Scholl, Smith, & Davison, 2005).

Intentional Planning

Efforts to address out-of-school time or the summer months within educational planning efforts can help ensure that students and their families have the information, supports, and connections needed to access a broader range of social opportunities in the community. Targeted discussions might focus on identifying inclusive recreation, leisure, and service opportunities; arranging potential school- and community-based supports; and addressing logistical issues such as transportation. For example, Carter, Trainor, Ditchman, Swedeen, & Owens (in press) evaluated the efficacy of intentional planning as part of an intervention package that focused on increasing the involvement of high school students with severe disabilities in summer work and community activities. Educators facilitated a planning process that involved identifying (a) a student's

goals for after high school, (b) summer experiences that might further those long-term goals, (c) individuals who might be able to help the student connect to those experiences, and (d) supports or resources that the student would need in order to participate meaningfully.

Collaborating with Families

Although the efforts that educators make to foster relationships during the school day set the stage for after school, families typically are the primary support for students beyond the doors of the school. Collaborating with families is an essential element of comprehensive efforts to foster relationships. Parents can play an important role in facilitating and supporting the interactions that take place beyond the school day by advocating for inclusion, supporting their child's participation in community activities, building and supporting friendship networks, and sharing information about their child (e.g., strengths, interests, commonalities) that will enhance participation (Turnbull et al., 1999). For example, parents might arrange play groups or other shared activities involving other children. They also can enroll their children in community programs and offer suggestions to staff for working with their child. In addition, they might arrange transportation or use existing supports such as respite dollars to support their child in community activities. It also is critical that schools inform families of inclusive recreation, volunteer opportunities, and other community programs in their communities.

Technological Connections

The emergence and rapid expansion of new technologies are transforming the avenues through which children and youth interact with one another and keep in touch. For example, digital encounters through social networking Web sites (e.g., Facebook®, MySpace®), online communities (e.g., chat rooms, Teen Second Life®), and other Web-based sites are quickly growing new avenues through which students first meet and learn about each other, discover peers with common interests, exchange information, and make social plans. Moreover, text messaging, e-mail, Web cameras, and other technologies are introducing new ways through which students can communicate with one another outside of the school day, regardless of transportation or geographical challenges. Ensuring that these new technologies enhance the social connectedness of students with severe disabilities—instead of isolate them further—will require careful planning. To date, there is limited research exploring how best to harness these emerging technologies in order to promote peer relationships (Jaeger & Xie, 2009; Kelly & Smith, 2008). Students with disabilities may benefit from systematic instruction in the use of social technologies, guidance on appropriate social skills within digital interactions, opportunities to practice their use at school and at home, and well-designed adaptations to ensure that technology remains accessible. Because peers often are more fluent in the use of these technologies, they may be more effective than adults at helping students with disabilities learn to access these avenues for communication.

Addressing Relationships Within Educational Planning Efforts

The strategies described in this chapter hold great potential to promote a sense of belonging, foster classroom membership, and develop friendships. However, it should not be presumed that these outcomes will accrue automatically simply because these strategies are implemented. Therefore, it is essential that these strategies be implemented upon a foundation that includes meaningful planning, ongoing assessment, and regular reflection.

Assessing Social Relationship and School Participation Opportunities

School-Wide Reflection

Sometimes, in the same school, there are rich interaction and relationship opportunities that exist in inclusive classrooms and other settings, alongside segregated classrooms and activities. Practitioners can begin by reflecting carefully on the opportunities that all students with and without severe disabilities currently have to spend time with and learn alongside one another in their school, as well as the approaches used to provide support and instruction that may be hindering or enhancing those opportunities. Such intentional reflection can guide schools in determining and prioritizing initial steps for expanding the quality and availability of opportunities and supports provided to students. For example, a small group of educators might begin a self-assessment process simply by listing all of the classrooms, clubs, and other settings where students typically gather in their school and determining whether students with and without severe disabilities are present together in these places at the same times and are involved in the same activities (see Figure 11–2). Involving a few students in this reflection process can be particularly insightful because educators and administrators who describe their

FIGURE 11–2
Tool for Reflecting on Social Opportunities Throughout the School Day

School Contexts	Are Students With and Without Disabilities . . .		
	In the Same Place?	At the Same Time?	Doing the Same Things?
Academic classes	N R S A	N R S A	N R S A
Related arts classes	N R S A	N R S A	N R S A
Elective classes	N R S A	N R S A	N R S A
Vocational classes	N R S A	N R S A	N R S A
Lunch	N R S A	N R S A	N R S A
Recess	N R S A	N R S A	N R S A
Hallways	N R S A	N R S A	N R S A
Extracurricular clubs	N R S A	N R S A	N R S A
Assemblies, pep rallies, spirit week, and other whole-school activities	N R S A	N R S A	N R S A
Athletics	N R S A	N R S A	N R S A
Dances, music or drama productions, and other school-sponsored activities	N R S A	N R S A	N R S A
School jobs (office assistant, library aide, school store)	N R S A	N R S A	N R S A
Other: _____	N R S A	N R S A	N R S A
Other: _____	N R S A	N R S A	N R S A

N – Never, R – Rarely, S – Sometimes, A – Always

schools as "inclusive" may be surprised to discover that students perceive the social environment of their school quite differently. For example, students with and without disabilities may be present in the same lunchroom, but rarely eat at the same tables; students with disabilities may be enrolled in physical education or elective and related arts courses, but absent from core academic classes; or students may be involved in extracurricular clubs, but those activities only involve other students with disabilities (e.g., Special Olympics, special recreation).

Several general and special educators at Aloura's high school were concerned that many students—both with and without disabilities—were disengaged from school and had few supportive friendships. Together, they began compiling a list of all of the extracurricular, service-learning, after-school, and other activities offered through their school. They also reflected on the ways in which various groups of students accessed these experiences and the barriers to student involvement that they might begin to address. They shared their findings with other teachers at a faculty meeting and prepared a small booklet to give to students and families that included brief descriptions of these activities. During annual planning meetings, teachers now talk with students about their interests and help them identify avenues through which they can explore these interests with their peers in school-sponsored activities.

Reflecting on a Student's Social Relationships

In addition to reflecting broadly on existing opportunities within the school, educators should gather more focused data on the interactions and relationships that their students have. An examination of the data is essential for determining a student's individualized instructional and support needs, as well as to evaluating the impact of any intervention efforts (see Chapter 5). Recognizing the inherent complexity of peer relationships, it is valuable to combine multiple approaches to assessing the social lives of students. Observations and interviews are two helpful approaches for informing this reflection.

Observations. Educators, paraprofessionals, or other school staff should periodically conduct formal or informal observations within classrooms, extracurricular programs, and other informal school activities to determine whether students interact with their peers and, if so, how. These observations can focus on a par-

ticular time of day (e.g., lunch, recess, reading, Ecology Club) or be spread across multiple contexts to obtain a more comprehensive picture of the social opportunities that students encounter and access. As with all assessments, it is important to clearly define the specific behaviors that are the focus of these observations so that data can be reliably collected and evaluated over time. The research literature reflects a wide spectrum of measures that offer indicators of the quality of students' relationships. Although Figure 11–3 includes examples of just a few of these social measures, educators should define these measures so that they meaningfully reflect the specific outcomes that are most important for a specific student.

In addition, the following set of overarching questions can help educators focus their observations (Carter et al., 2009; Downing, 2005b):

- Do students have a reliable means of communicating with their peers?
- Are they able to converse about the things that peers enjoy talking about?
- What do students' social interactions look like?
- With whom do these interactions occur?
- Where and when do these interactions take place?
- Are their interactions typical of those that usually take place among other students in these contexts?
- What are the indicators that students enjoy spending time with their peers?
- How are students supported in the classroom and in other school activities?
- What is the nature of the support that students with severe disabilities receive from their peers?

Direct observations can enable educators to understand the kinds of peer relationships that students already enjoy, identify additional avenues for expanding opportunities for interaction, determine the type of social and communication skills that would enhance students' interactions, and identify areas of potential concern that require more focused attention.

Interviews. The quality of students' relationships is as important to understand as is the extent to which students interact with their peers. Some relationships are highly valued by students, while others hold less importance. Students with severe disabilities can provide an important—albeit infrequently sought—perspective on the friendships that they have and the nature of their relationships with their peers (Broer et al., 2005; Matheson et al., 2007). Students should be

FIGURE 11–3

Examples of Social Outcomes

Social Outcome	Definition	Example
Social interactions	One student acknowledging another using verbal or nonverbal communicative behaviors, such as gestures, pointing, or using an AAC device	Elena used her AAC device to ask for help from her peers, comment on her group's project, and excuse herself from the classroom.
Initiation of conversation	New comments preceded by at least 5 seconds without an interaction or reflecting a change in conversational topic	Although she usually responded to her classmates when they ask her questions in science class, Aloura infrequently started conversations without prompting from her teacher.
Appropriate interactions	Interactions typical of other peers in the same setting, or responses generally corresponding to an initiation in meaning and tone	Samuel's conversations were occasionally inappropriate to the math class, particularly when he talked about children's television shows.
Positive affect	Smiling, laughing, relaxed body position, or making positive remarks	Elena's facial expressions suggested that she enjoyed her interactions with Oscar, but not with Thomas.
Quality of interaction	Overall judgment of interaction satisfaction on the basis of students' affect, reciprocity, and topics discussed, ranging from *low* to *high*	The art teacher described Aloura's interactions with her classmates as being of fairly high quality, although somewhat less equally balanced than those typical of other students in the class.
Interaction partners	People with whom the student is interacting, such as classmates, peer supports, other students with disabilities, paraprofessionals, or teachers	During lunch, Samuel tended to interact with three of his closest friends—Edgar, Lisa, and Carolyn.
Social contacts	Interactions in the context of an activity lasting at least 15 minutes	Although most of Elena's interactions were relatively brief, she typically had three or four extended interactions each school day.
Peers contacted	Total number of *different* peers involved in social contacts	Aloura primarily interacted with two students (Kara and Nicole) in art class, but she occasionally worked with Audrey and Kimberly.
Social support	Providing information, access to others, material aid, emotional support, help with decisions, or companionship	Samuel's peer supports primarily helped him complete his class assignments and encouraged him when he was having a tough day.
Peer proximity	Sitting directly next to or within 3 feet of a classmate	Although Elena sat directly next to two of her classmates for half of the class period, she worked with her paraprofessional for the rest of the time on one side of the classroom.
Social networks	The number of peers who are considered to be a "friend" by the student and with whom he or she has had contact in the recent past	Aloura has four friends with whom she spends most of her time.
Membership	Having access to valued social roles and the symbols of belonging	Samuel is considered by others to be a leader within the comic book club.
Social status	The number of classmates who identify a student as a close friend or "most liked" peer	More than half of her classmates consider Elena to be a friend.

Adapted from *Peer support strategies for improving all students' social lives and learning* (p. 88), by E. W. Carter, L. S. Cushing, & C. H. Kennedy, 2009. Baltimore: Paul H. Brookes.

asked to share their views on whom they enjoy spending time with, the types of interactions and school involvement that they would like to have, the ways in which they would prefer to work with their classmates, and the particular peers whom they would like to know better. Although the perspectives of younger children and students with significant communication challenges often are more difficult to discern, they are no less important to understand. Offering multiple avenues for students to express their preferences and perspectives—as well as observing students' affect as they spend time with peers—can provide important insight into these issues.

The perspectives of peers without disabilities also can provide valuable insight into the relationships that students with severe disabilities experience, the attitudes of other students in the classroom or school, and the broader peer culture (Copeland et al., 2004; Kamps et al., 1998; Schnorr, 1997). Educators can informally ask peers to share their views regarding factors that contribute to membership and a sense of belonging, describe their own relationship with a particular student, discuss the roles of students in facilitating friendships, and suggest specific information and supports that would enhance their relationships with their classmates with severe disabilities. Peers typically have unique insight into the barriers to relationships that exist in their school and creative recommendations for promoting greater social participation.

Ms. Barker sat down with Samuel to ask how things were going in American history class. Did Samuel enjoy working with and receiving support from his peers? Did he want to continue working with them? Were there other classmates he would like to get to know? Did Samuel think he needed other assistance that he was not currently receiving? In addition, Ms. Barker talked with both of Samuel's peer supports about their experiences. What aspects of the peer support arrangement were going really well? Were they comfortable with their responsibilities? What changes have they noticed in Samuel? How have they personally benefited from their involvement as a peer support?

Other teachers, paraprofessionals, and related services providers who work with a student during the school day can also be asked to describe the interactions and relationships that they have observed in different settings. These adults may be able to identify specific factors that promote or hinder interactions in specific school contexts, as well as speak to the benefits that students accrue through their relationships with peers. Finally, parents can be asked to share how their child describes his or her relationships at school and whether these interactions extend beyond the school day and, if so, how.

Collectively, observations and interviews can provide a clearer indication of whether students with severe disabilities experience peer relationships that provide companionship, promote learning, and bring

enjoyment. Moreover, regular data collection provides educators with the targeted information needed to determine whether students are affected by the intervention and the support that they receive and, if so, how. By regularly reflecting on the social opportunities that students with severe disabilities experience and the extent to which friendships emerge as a result, educators are better equipped to design high-quality educational plans that meet the individualized needs of their students.

Aloura's special education teacher, Mr. Haystie, was excited about the friendships that she had made so far this school year. But he also wanted to make sure that Aloura had opportunities to maintain and deepen those relationships over time. His conversations with Aloura revealed that she enjoyed being part of the set crew and liked spending time with her new friends. At the same time, she was interested in becoming involved in other school activities and getting together with Kara and Nicole outside of school. Mr. Haystie talked with Aloura's parents about arranging transportation for Aloura to weekend activities with her friends. Mr. Haystie also talked with Kara and Nicole about their friendship with Aloura. Both students suggested some social-related skills that might help Aloura fit in better with her peers. Based on his conversation, Mr. Haystie decided to involve Aloura in the social skills curriculum that he was teaching during the semester. Finally, he asked a paraprofessional to collect data on Aloura's peer interactions in her various classes. It became clear that Aloura was much less connected socially in her core academic classes than she was in her art class. All of this information was used by Mr. Haystie and other members of the IEP team to refine Aloura's educational goals and to arrange for more targeted supports in several of her classes.

Summary

Peer relationships can make an important difference in the lives of *all* students, including children and youth with severe disabilities. The services and supports that we provide to students should reflect our commitment to ensuring that every student has meaningful opportunities to experience a sense of belonging and enjoy satisfying relationships with their peers. This chapter described recommended and evidence-based strategies for promoting peer relationships within inclusive classrooms, informal school contexts, extracurricular activities, and after-school events. By implementing these strategies, educators, paraprofessionals, parents, and others can each play an influential role in equipping students with the skills and opportunities that they need to develop lasting friendships.

Suggested Activities

1. Think about the friendships that you had during elementary, middle, and high school. Where did you meet each other for the first time? How long did it take for your relationships to become friendships? What factors contributed to that transition? Next, consider the extent to which the students with severe disabilities with whom you work have these same opportunities. What steps could you take to create or expand these opportunities?
2. All interactions are not the same. Spend time observing, noting, and reflecting on the kinds of interaction students with severe disabilities have throughout the school day. With whom do they occur? Do they take place primarily with adults? Do they resemble those that other students have with their peers?
3. Consider your own relationships. Why are they important to you? What do you bring to and take away from your relationships with others? What steps could you take to ensure that students with severe disabilities are able to experience the same benefits from these types of relationships?
4. Use the tool shown in Figure 11-1 to reflect on the social opportunities that exist in your school. Are students with severe disabilities participating in these activities? What barriers hinder their involvement?

References

Bambara, L. M., & Brantlinger, E. (2002). Toward a healthy sexual life: An introduction to the special series on issues of sexuality for people with developmental disabilities. *Research and Practice for Persons with Severe Disabilities, 27,* 5-7.

Bellini, S., Peters, J. K., Brianner, L., & Hopf, A. (2007). A meta-analysis of school-based social skills interventions for children with autism spectrum disorders. *Remedial and Special Education, 28,* 153-162.

Bensted, E. A., & Bachor, D. G. (2002). The academic effects of low achieving or inattentive students providing peer support to students with moderate to severe disabilities in general education classrooms. *Exceptionality Education Canada, 12,* 51-73.

Berndt, T. J., & McCandless, M. A. (2007). Methods for investigating children's relationships with friends. In K. H. Rubin, W. M. Bukowski, & B. Laursen (Eds.), *Handbook of peer interactions, relationships, and groups* (pp. 63-81). New York: Guilford Press.

Breen, C. G., & Haring, T. G. (1991). Effects of contextual competence on social initiations. *Journal of Applied Behavior Analysis, 24,* 337-347.

Breen, C. G., & Lovinger, L. (1991). PAL (Partners at Lunch) Club: Evaluation of a program to support social relationships. In C. G. Breen, C. H. Kennedy, & T. G. Haring (Eds.), *Social context research project: Methods for facilitating the inclusion of students with disabilities in integrated school and community contexts* (pp. 106-128). Santa Barbara: University of California.

Broer, S. M., Doyle, M. B., & Giangreco, M. F. (2005). Perspectives of students with intellectual disabilities about their experiences with paraprofessional support. *Exceptional Children, 71,* 415-430.

Brown, B. B., & Dietz, E. (2009). Informal peer groups in middle childhood and adolescence. In K. H. Rubin, W. M. Bukowski, & B. Laursen (Eds.), *Handbook of peer interactions, relationships, and groups* (pp. 361-376). New York: Guilford Press.

Brown, L., Branston, M., Hamre-Nietupski, S., Johnson, F., Wilcox, B., & Gruenewald, L. (1979). A rationale for comprehensive longitudinal interactions between severely handicapped students and nonhandicapped students and other citizens. *AAESPH Review, 4,* 3-14.

Brown, L., Farrington, K., Knight, T., Ross, C., & Ziegler, M. (1999). Fewer paraprofessionals and more teachers and therapists in educational programs for students with significant disabilities. *Journal of the Association for Persons with Severe Handicaps, 24,* 250-253.

Brown, R. D., & Pirtle, T. (2008). Beliefs of professional and family caregivers about the sexuality of individuals with intellectual disabilities: Examining beliefs using a Q-methodology approach. *Sex Education: Sexuality, Society and Learning, 8,* 59-75.

Brown, W. H., Odom, S. L., & McConnell, S. R. (2007). *Social competence of young children: Risk, disability, and intervention.* Baltimore: Paul H. Brookes.

Carter, E. W. (2007). *Including people with disabilities in faith communities: A guide for service providers, families, and congregations.* Baltimore: Paul H. Brookes.

Carter, E. W., Cushing, L. S., & Kennedy, C. H. (2009). *Peer support strategies: Improving all students' social lives and learning.* Baltimore: Paul H. Brookes.

Carter, E. W., & Hughes, C. (2005). Increasing social interaction among adolescents with intellectual disabilities and their general education peers: Effective interventions. *Research and Practice for Persons with Severe Disabilities, 30,* 179-193.

Carter, E. W., & Hughes, C. (2006). Including high school students with severe disabilities in general education classes: Perspectives of general and special educators, paraprofessionals, and administrators. *Research and Practice for Persons with Severe Disabilities, 31,* 174-185.

Carter, E. W., Hughes, C., Guth, C., & Copeland, S. R. (2005). Factors influencing social interaction among high school students with intellectual disabilities and their general education peers. *American Journal on Mental Retardation, 110,* 366-377.

Carter, E. W., & Kennedy, C. H. (2006). Promoting access to the general curriculum using peer support strategies. *Research and Practice for Persons with Severe Disabilities, 31,* 284-292.

Carter, E. W., Sisco, L. G., Brown, L., Brickham, D., & Al-Khabbaz, Z. A. (2008). Peer interactions and academic engagement of youth with developmental disabilities in inclusive middle and high school classrooms. *American Journal on Mental Retardation, 113,* 479-494.

Carter, E. W., Sisco, L. G., Melekoglu, M., & Kurkowski, C. (2007). Peer supports as an alternative to individually assigned paraprofessionals in inclusive high school classrooms. *Research and Practice for Persons with Severe Disabilities, 32,* 213-227.

Carter, E. W., Swedeen, B., & Kurkowski, C. (2008). Friendship matters: Fostering social relationships in secondary schools. *TASH Connections, 34*(6), 9-12, 14.

Carter, E. W., Swedeen, B., Moss, C. K., & Pesko, M. J. (2010). "What are you doing after school?" Promoting extracurricular involvement for transition-age youth with disabilities. *Intervention in School and Clinic, 45,* 275-283.

Carter, E. W., Swedeen, B., & Trainor, A. A. (2009). The other three months: Maximizing summer opportunities for transition-age youth with disabilities. *TEACHING Exceptional Children, 41*(6), 18-26.

Carter, E. W., Trainor, A. A., Ditchman, N., Swedeen, B., & Owens, L. (in press). Evaluation of a multi-component intervention package to increase summer work experiences for transition-age youth with severe disabilities. *Research and Practice for Persons with Severe Disabilities.*

Causton-Theoharis, J. N., & Malmgren, K. W. (2005a). Building bridges: Strategies to help paraprofessionals promote peer interaction. *TEACHING Exceptional Children, 37*(6), 18-24.

Causton-Theoharis, J. N., & Malmgren, K. W. (2005b). Increasing peer interactions for students with severe disabilities via paraprofessional training. *Exceptional Children, 71,* 431-444.

Cole, D. A., Vandercook, T., & Rynders, J. (1988). Comparison of two peer interaction programs: Children with and without severe disabilities. *American Educational Research Journal, 25,* 415-439.

Collins, B. C. (2002). Using peers to facilitate learning by students with moderate disabilities. *The Behavior Analyst Today, 3*(3), 329-341.

Copeland, S. R., Hughes, C., Carter, E. W., Guth, C., Presley, J., Williams, C. R., et al. (2004). Increasing access to general education: Perspectives of participants in a high school peer support program. *Remedial and Special Education, 26,* 342-352.

Cosbey, J. E., & Johnston, S. (2006). Using a single-switch voice output communication aid to increase social access for children with severe disabilities in inclusive classrooms. *Research and Practice for Persons with Severe Disabilities, 31,* 144-156.

Cowie, H., & Wallace, P. (2000). *Peer support in action: From bystanding to standing by.* London: Sage.

Crane, K., & Mooney, M. (2005). *Community resource mapping (Essential tools).* Minneapolis, MN: National Center on Secondary Education and Transition.

Cushing, L. S., Clark, N. M., Carter, E. W., & Kennedy, C. H. (2005). Access to the general education curriculum for students with severe disabilities: What it means and how to accomplish it. *TEACHING Exceptional Children, 38*(2), 6-13.

Cushing, L. S., & Kennedy, C. H. (1997). Academic effects on students without disabilities who serve as peer supports for students with disabilities in general education classrooms. *Journal of Applied Behavior Analysis, 30,* 139-152.

Cushing, L. S., Kennedy, C. H., Shukla, S., Davis, J., & Meyer, K. A. (1997). Disentangling the effects of curriculum revision and social grouping within cooperative learning arrangements. *Focus on Autism and Other Developmental Disabilities, 12,* 231-240.

Cutts, S., & Sigafoos, J. (2001). Social competence and peer interactions of students with intellectual disability in an inclusive high school. *Journal of Intellectual & Developmental Disability, 26,* 127-141.

Deater-Deckard, K. (2001). Annotation: Recent research examining the role of peer relationships in the development of psychopathology. *Journal of Child Psychology and Psychiatry, 42,* 565-579.

Dore, R., Dion, E., Wagner, S., & Brunet, J. (2002). High school inclusion of adolescents with mental retardation: A multiple case study. *Education and Training in Mental Retardation and Developmental Disabilities, 37,* 253-261.

Downing, J. E. (2005a). Inclusive education for high school students with severe intellectual disabilities: Supporting communication. *Augmentative and Alternative Communication, 21,* 132-148.

Downing, J. E. (2005b). *Teaching communication skills to students with severe disabilities.* Baltimore: Paul H. Brookes.

Dugan, E., Kamps, D., Leonard, B., Watkins, N., Rheinberger, A., & Stackhaus, J. (1995). Effects of cooperative learning groups during social studies for students with autism and fourth-grade peers. *Journal of Applied Behavior Analysis, 28,* 175-188.

Evans, I. M., & Meyer, L. H. (2001). Having friendships and Rett syndrome: How social relationships create a meaningful context for limited skills. *Disability and Rehabilitation, 23,* 167-176.

Evans, I. M., Salisbury, C. L., Palombaro, M. M., Berryman, J., & Hollowood, T. M. (1992). Peer interactions and social acceptance of elementary-age children with severe disabilities in an inclusive school. *Journal of the Association for Persons with Severe Handicaps, 17,* 205-212.

Fisher, D. (1999). According to their peers: Inclusion as high school students see it. *Mental Retardation, 37,* 458-467.

Florsheim, P. (Ed.). (2003). *Adolescent romantic relationships and sexual behavior: Theory, research, and practical implications* (pp. 291-329). New York: Cambridge University Press.

Freeman, S. F. N., & Alkin, M. C. (2000). Academic and social attainments of children with mental retardation in general education and special education settings. *Remedial and Special Education, 21,* 3-18.

Fryxell, D., & Kennedy, C. H. (1995). Placement along the continuum of services and its impact on students' social relationships. *Journal of the Association for Persons with Severe Handicaps, 20,* 259-269.

Garrison-Harrell, L., Kamps, D., & Kravitz, T. (1997). The effects of peer networks on social-communicative behaviors for students with autism. *Focus on Autism and Other Developmental Disorders, 12,* 241-254.

Gaylord-Ross, R. J., Haring, T. G., Breen, C., & Pitts-Conway, V. (1984). The training and generalization of social interaction skills with autistic youth. *Journal of Applied Behavior Analysis, 17,* 229-247.

Ghere, G., York-Barr, J., & Sommerness, J. (2002). *Supporting students with disabilities in inclusive schools: A curriculum for job-embedded paraprofessional development.* Minneapolis: Institute on Community Integration and Department of Educational Policy and Administration, University of Minnesota.

Giangreco, M. F. (2010). One-to-one paraprofessionals for students with disabilities in inclusive classrooms: Is conventional wisdom wrong? *Intellectual & Developmental Disabilities, 48,* 1–13.

Giangreco, M. F. & Broer, S. M. (2005). Questionable utilization of paraprofessionals in inclusive schools: Are we addressing symptoms or causes? *Focus on Autism and Other Developmental Disabilities, 20,* 10–26.

Giangreco, M. F., Edelman, S., Luiselli, T. E., & MacFarland, S. Z. C. (1997). Helping or hovering? Effects of instructional assistant proximity on students with disabilities. *Exceptional Children, 64,* 7–18.

Gifford-Smith, M. E., & Brownell, C. A. (2003). Childhood peer relationships: Social acceptance, friendships, and peer networks. *Journal of School Psychology, 41,* 235–284.

Gilberts, G. H., Agran, M., Hughes, C., & Wehmeyer, M. (2001). The effects of peer delivered self-monitoring strategies on the participation of students with severe disabilities in general education classrooms. *Journal of the Association for Persons with Severe Handicaps, 26,* 25–36.

Han, K. G., & Chadsey, J. G. (2004). The influence of gender patterns and grade level on friendship expectations of middle school students toward peers with severe disabilities. *Focus on Autism and Other Developmental Disabilities, 19,* 205–214.

Haring, T. G. (1993). The context of social competence: Relations, relationships, and generalization. In S. L. Odom, S. R. McConnell, & M. A. McEvoy (Eds.), *Social competence of young children with disabilities: Issues and strategies for intervention* (pp. 307–320). Baltimore: Paul H. Brookes.

Haring, T. G., & Breen, C. G. (1992). A peer-mediated social network intervention to enhance the social integration of persons with moderate and severe disabilities. *Journal of Applied Behavior Analysis, 25,* 319–333.

Haring, T. G., Breen, C., Pitts-Conway, V., Lee, M., & Gaylord-Ross, R. (1987). Adolescent peer tutoring and special friends experiences. *Journal of the Association for Persons with Severe Handicaps, 12,* 280–286.

Haring, T. G., Roger, B., Lee, M., Breen, C., & Gaylord-Ross, R. (1986). Teaching social language to moderately handicapped students. *Journal of Applied Behavior Analysis, 19,* 159–171.

Harper, C. B., Symon, J. B. G., & Frea, W. D. (2008). Recess is time-in: Using peers to improve social skills of children with autism. *Journal of Autism and Developmental Disorders, 38,* 815–826.

Hemmingsson, H., Borell, L., & Gustavsson, A. (2003). Participation in school: School assistants creating opportunities and obstacles for pupils with disabilities. *Occupational Therapy Journal of Research, 23*(3), 88–98.

Hingsburger, D., & Tough, S. (2002). Healthy sexuality: Attitudes, systems, and policies. *Research and Practice for Persons with Severe Disabilities, 27,* 8–17.

Hughes, C., & Carter, E. W. (2008). *Peer buddy programs for successful secondary school inclusion.* Baltimore: Paul H. Brookes.

Hughes, C., Carter, E. W., Hughes, T., Bradford, E., & Copeland, S. R. (2002). Effects of instructional versus non-instructional roles on the social interactions of high school students. *Education and Training in Mental Retardation and Developmental Disabilities, 37,* 146–162.

Hughes, C., Killian, D. J., & Fischer, G. M. (1996). Validation and assessment of a conversational interaction intervention. *American Journal on Mental Retardation, 100*(5), 493–509.

Hughes, C., Rodi, M. S., Lorden, S. W., Pitkin, S. E., Derer, K. R., Hwang, B., et al. (1999). Social interactions of high school students with mental retardation and their general education peers. *American Journal on Mental Retardation, 104,* 533–544.

Hughes, C., Rung, L. L., Wehmeyer, M. L., Agran, J., Copeland, S. R., & Hwang, B. (2000). Self-prompted communication book use to increase social interaction among high school students. *Journal of the Association for Persons with Severe Handicaps, 25,* 153–166.

Hunt, P., Alwell, M., Farron-Davis, F., & Goetz, L. (1996). Creating socially supportive environments for fully included students who experience multiple disabilities. *Journal of the Association for Persons with Severe Disabilities, 21,* 53–71.

Hunt, P., Farron-Davis, F., Beckstead, S., Curtis, C., & Goetz, L. (1994). Evaluating the effects of placement of students with severe disabilities in general education versus special classes. *Journal of the Association for Persons with Severe Handicaps, 19,* 200–214.

Hunt, P., & Goetz, L. (1997). Research on inclusive educational programs, practices, and outcomes for students with severe disabilities. *Journal of Special Education, 31,* 3–29.

Individuals with Disabilities Education Improvement Act of 2004. (2004). P.L. 108–446, 118 Stat. 2647.

Jaeger, P. T., & Xie, B. (2009). Developing online community accessibility guidelines for persons with disabilities and older adults. *Journal of Disability Policy Studies, 20,* 55–63.

Jameson, J. M., McDonnell, J., Polychronis, S., & Riesen, T. (2008). Embedded, constant time delay instruction by peers without disabilities in general education classrooms. *Intellectual and Developmental Disabilities, 46,* 346–363.

Janney, R. E., & Snell, M. E. (1997). How teachers include students with moderate and severe disabilities in elementary classes: The means and meaning of inclusion. *Journal of the Association for Persons with Severe Handicaps, 22,* 159–169.

Janney, R. E., & Snell, M. E. (2006). *Social relationships and peer support* (2nd ed.). Baltimore: Paul H. Brookes.

Jones, V. (2007). "I felt like I did something good"—the impact on mainstream pupils of a peer tutoring programme for children with autism. *British Journal of Special Education, 34,* 3–9.

Kamps, D. M., Barbetta, P. M., Leonard, B. R., & Delquadri, J. (1994). Classwide peer tutoring: An integration strategy to improve reading skills and promote peer interactions among students with autism and general education peers. *Journal of Applied Behavior Analysis, 27,* 49–61.

Kamps, D. M., Dugan, E., Potucek, J., & Collins, A. (1999). Effects of cross-age peer tutoring networks among students with autism and general education students. *Journal of Behavioral Education, 9,* 97–115.

Kamps, D. M., Kravits, T., Lopez, A. G., Kemmerer, K., Potucek, J., Harrell, L. G., et al. (1998). What do the peers think? Social validity of peer-mediated programs. *Education & Treatment of Children, 21,* 107–134.

Kamps, D. M., Lopez, A. G., & Golden, C. (2002). School-age children: Putting research into practice. In H. Goldstein, L. A. Kaczmarek, & K. M. English (Eds.), *Promoting social communication: Children with developmental disabilities from birth to adolescence* (pp. 279–306). Baltimore: Paul H. Brookes.

Katz, J., Mirenda, P., & Auerbach, S. (2002). Instructional strategies and educational outcomes for students with developmental disabilities in inclusive "multiple intelligences" and typical inclusive classrooms. *Research and Practice for Persons with Severe Disabilities, 27,* 227-238.

Kelly, S. M., & Smith, T. J. (2008). The digital social interactions of students with visual impairments: Findings from two national surveys. *Journal of Visual Impairment and Blindness, 102,* 528-539.

Kemp, C., & Carter, M. (2002). The social skills and social status of mainstreamed students with intellectual disabilities. *Educational Psychology, 22,* 391-411.

Kennedy, C. H. (2001). Social interaction interventions for youth with severe disabilities should emphasize interdependence. *Mental Retardation and Developmental Disabilities Research Reviews, 7,* 122-127.

Kennedy, C. H. (2004a). Research on social relationships. In E. Emerson, C. Hatton, T. Thompson, & T. R. Parmenter (Eds.), *The international handbook of applied research in intellectual disabilities* (pp. 297-310). West Sussex, England: John Wiley & Sons.

Kennedy, C. H. (2004b). Social relationships. In C. H. Kennedy & E. Horn (Eds.), *Including students with severe disabilities* (pp. 100-123). Boston: Allyn & Bacon.

Kennedy, C. H., Cushing, L., & Itkonen, T. (1997). General education participation increases the social contacts and friendship networks of students with severe disabilities. *Journal of Behavioral Education, 7,* 167-189.

Kennedy, C. H., Shukla, S., & Fryxell, D. (1997). Comparing the effects of educational placement on the social relationships of intermediate school students with severe disabilities. *Exceptional Children, 64,* 31-47.

Kent-Walsh, J., & McNaughton, D. (2005). Communication partner instruction in AAC: Present practices and future directions. *Augmentative and Alternative Communication, 21,* 195-204.

Kishi, G. S., & Meyer, L. H. (1994). What children report and remember: A six-year follow-up of the effects of social contact between peers with and without severe disabilities. *Journal of the Association for Persons with Severe Handicaps, 19,* 277-289.

Kleinert, H. L., Miracle, S., & Sheppard-Jones, K. (2007). Including students with moderate and severe intellectual disabilities in school extracurricular and community recreation activities. *Intellectual and Developmental Disabilities, 45,* 46-55.

Laushey, K. M., & Heflin, L. J. (2000). Enhancing social skills of kindergarten children with autism through the training of multiple peers as tutors. *Journal of Autism and Developmental Disorders, 30,* 183-193.

Lee, S., Simpson, R. L., & Shogren, K. A. (2007). Effects and implications of self-management for students with autism. *Focus on Autism and Other Developmental Disabilities, 22,* 2-13.

Mahoney, J. L., Harris, A. L., & Eccles, J. S. (2006). Organized activity participation, positive youth development, and the over-scheduling hypothesis. *Social Policy Report, 20*(4), 3-32.

Marks, S. U., Schrader, C., & Levine, M. (1999). Paraeducator experiences in inclusive settings: Helping, hovering, or holding their own? *Exceptional Children, 65,* 315-328.

Matheson, C., Olsen, R. J., & Weisner, T. (2007). A good friend is hard to find: Friendship among adolescents with disabilities. *American Journal on Mental Retardation, 112,* 319-329.

McConnell, S. R. (2002). Interventions to facilitate social interaction for young children with autism: Review of available research and recommendations for educational intervention and future research. *Journal of Autism and Developmental Disorders, 32,* 351-372.

McDonnell, J., Mathot-Buckner, C., Thorson, N., & Fister, S. (2001). Supporting the inclusion of students with moderate and severe disabilities in junior high school general education classes: The effects of classwide peer tutoring, multi-element curriculum, and accommodations. *Education and Treatment of Children, 24,* 141-160.

McMahon, C. M., Wacker, D. P., Sasso, G. P., Berg, W. K., & Newton, S. M. (1996). Analysis of frequency and type of interactions in a peer-mediated social skills intervention: Instructional vs. social interactions. *Education and Training in Mental Retardation and Developmental Disabilities, 31,* 339-352.

Meyer, L. H. (2001). The impact of inclusion on children's lives: Multiple outcomes, and friendships in particular. *International Journal of Disability, Development, and Education, 48,* 9-31.

Meyer, L. H., Park, H., Grenot-Scheyer, M., Schwartz, I., & Harry, B. (1998). *Making friends: The influences of culture and development.* Baltimore: Paul H. Brookes.

Morrison, L., Kamps, D., Garcia, J., & Parker, D. (2001). Peer mediation and monitoring strategies to improve initiations and social skills for students with autism. *Journal of Positive Behavior Interventions, 3,* 237-250.

Murphy, N. A., & Carbone, P. S. (2008). Promoting the participation of children with disabilities in sports, recreation, and physical activities. *Pediatrics, 121*(5), 1057-1061.

Murray-Seegert, C. (1989). *Nasty girls, thugs, and humans like us: Social relations between severely disabled and nondisabled students in high school.* Baltimore: Paul H. Brookes.

Nientimp, E. G., & Cole, C. L. (1992). Teaching socially valid social interaction responses to students with severe disabilities in an integrated school setting. *Journal of School Psychology, 30,* 343-354.

Odom, S. L., Brantlinger, E., Gersten, R., Horner, R. H., Thompson, B., & Harris, K. R. (2005). Research in special education: Scientific methods and evidence-based practices. *Exceptional Children, 71,* 137-148.

Odom, S. L., & Ogawa, I. (1992). Direct observation of young children's social interaction with peers: A review of methodology. *Behavioral Assessment, 14,* 407-441.

Piercy, M., Wilton, K., & Townsend, M. (2002). Promoting the social acceptance of young children with moderate-severe intellectual disabilities using cooperative-learning techniques. *American Journal of Mental Retardation, 107,* 352-360.

Prater, M. A., Bruhl, S., & Serna, L. A. (1998). Acquiring social skills through cooperative learning and teacher-directed instruction. *Remedial and Special Education, 19,* 160-172.

Ratcliff, A. E., & Cress, C. J. (1998). Guidelines for enhancing reciprocal peer communication with adolescents who use augmentative/alternative communication. *Journal of Children's Communication Development, 20,* 25-35.

Rubin, K. H., Bukowski, W. M., & Laursen, B. (Eds.). (2009). *Handbook of peer interactions, relationships, and groups.* New York: Guilford Press.

Ryndak, D., & Fisher, D. (Eds.). (2003). *The foundations of inclusive education: A compendium of articles on effective strategies to achieve inclusive education* (2nd ed.). Baltimore: TASH.

Rynders, J. E., Schleien, S. J., Meyer, L. H., Vandercook, T. K., Mustonen, T. A., Colond, J. S., et al. (1993). Improving integration outcomes for children with and without severe disabilities through cooperative structured recreation activities: A synthesis of research. *Journal of Special Education, 26,* 386-407.

Schnorr, R. F. (1990). "Peter? He comes and goes...": First graders' perspectives on a part-time mainstream student. *Journal of the Association for Persons with Severe Handicaps, 15,* 231-240.

Schnorr, R. F. (1997). From enrollment to membership: "Belonging" in middle and high school classes. *Journal of the Association for Persons with Severe Handicaps, 22,* 1-15.

Scholl, K. G., Smith, J. G., & Davison, A. (2005). Agency readiness to provide inclusive recreation and after-school services for children with disabilities. *Therapeutic Recreation Journal, 39,* 47-62.

Sheridan, S. M., Buhs, E. S., & Warnes, E. D. (2003). Childhood peer relationships in context. *Journal of School Psychology, 41,* 285-292.

Shukla, S., Kennedy, C. H., & Cushing, L. S. (1998). Component analysis of peer support strategies: Adult influence on the participation of peers without disabilities. *Journal of Behavioral Education, 8,* 397-413.

Siperstein, G. N., Norins, J., & Mohler, A. (2007). Social acceptance and attitude change: Fifty years of research. In J. W. Jacobson, J. A. Mulick, & J. Rojahn (Eds.), *Handbook of intellectual and developmental disabilities* (pp. 133-154). New York: Springer.

Skär, L., & Tamm, M. (2001). My assistant and I: Disabled children's and adolescents' roles and relationships to their assistants. *Disability & Society, 16,* 917-931.

Snell, M., Chen, L., & Hoover, K. (2006). Teaching augmentative and alternative communication to students with severe disabilities: A review of intervention research, 1997-2003. *Research and Practice for Persons with Severe Disabilities, 31,* 203-214.

Spooner, F., Dymond, S. K., Smith, A., & Kennedy, C. H. (2006). What we know and need to know about accessing the general curriculum for students with significant cognitive disabilities. *Research and Practice for Persons with Severe Disabilities, 31,* 277-283.

Staub, D. (1998). *Delicate threads: Friendships between children with and without special needs in inclusive settings.* Bethesda, MD: Woodbine House.

Storey, K. (2007). Combating ableism in schools. *Preventing School Failure, 52,* 56-58.

Trainor, A. A., Carter, E. W., Owens, L., & Swedeen, B. (2008). Special educators' perceptions of summer employment and community participation opportunities for youth with disabilities. *Career Development for Exceptional Individuals, 31,* 144-153.

Turnbull, A. P., Blue-Banning, M., & Pereira, L. (2000). Successful friendships of Hispanic children and youth with disabilities: An exploratory study. *Mental Retardation, 38,* 138-153.

Turnbull, A. P., Pereira, L., & Blue-Banning, M. J. (1999). Parents' facilitation of friendships between their children with a disability and their friends without a disability. *Journal of the Association for Persons with Severe Handicaps, 24,* 85-99.

Turnbull, A. P., Pereira, L., & Blue-Banning, M. J. (2000). Teachers as friendship facilitators: Respeto and personalismo. *TEACHING Exceptional Children, 32*(5), 66-70.

U.S. Department of Education. (2009). *The 28th annual report to Congress on the implementation of the Individuals with Disabilities Education Act, 2006.* Washington, DC: Author.

Valenti-Hein, D., & Choinski, C. (2007). Relationships and sexuality in adolescence. In A. Carr, G. O'Reilly, P. N. Walsh, & J. McEvoy (Eds.), *The handbook of intellectual disability and clinical psychology practice* (pp. 729-755). New York: Routledge.

Van der Klift, E., & Kunc, N. (2002). Beyond benevolence: Supporting genuine friendship in inclusive schools. In J. Thousand, R. Villa, & A. Nevin (Eds.), *Creativity and collaborative learning: A practical guide to empowering students, teachers, and families* (2nd ed., pp. 21-28). Baltimore: Paul H. Brookes.

Wagner, M., Cadwallader, T. W., Garza, N., & Cameto, R. (2004). Social activities of youth with disabilities. *NLTS2 Data Brief, 3*(1), 1-4.

Wagner, M., Cadwallader, T. W., Marder, C., Newman, L., Garza, N., & Blackorby, J. (2002). *The other 80% of their time: The experiences of elementary and middle school students with disabilities during their nonschool hours.* Menlo Park, CA: SRI International.

Walker-Hirsch, L. (2007). *The facts of life... and more: Sexuality and intimacy for people with intellectual disabilities.* Baltimore: Paul H. Brookes.

Webster, A. A., & Carter, M. (2007). Social relationships and friendships of children with developmental disabilities: Implications for inclusive settings. A systematic review. *Journal of Intellectual and Developmental Disability, 32,* 200-213.

Wehmeyer, M. L., Agran, M., Hughes, C., Martin, J., Mithaug, D. E., & Palmer, S. (2007). *Promoting self-determination in students with intellectual and developmental disabilities.* New York: Guilford Press.

Weiner, J. S. (2005). Peer-mediated conversational repair in students with moderate and severe disabilities. *Research and Practice for Persons with Severe Disabilities, 30,* 26-37.

Wentzel, K. R., & Looney, L. (2007). Socialization in school settings. In J. E. Grusec & P. D. Hastings (Eds.), *Handbook of socialization: Theory and research* (pp. 382-403). New York: Guilford Press.

Williamson, P., McLeskey, J., Hoppey, D., & Rentz, T. (2006). Educating students with mental retardation in general education classrooms. *Exceptional Children, 72,* 347-361.

Wolfensberger, W. (2007). Social role valorization news and reviews. *The SRV Journal, 2*(2), 70-80.

York, J., & Tundidor, H. (1995). Issues raised in the name of inclusion: Perspectives of educators, parents, and students. *Journal of the Association for Persons with Severe Handicaps, 20,* 31-44.

12

Teaching Communication Skills

June E. Downing

Communication is the meaningful exchange between at least two people where a message is sent (expressed) by one person and understood (received) by another. The message can be expressed in a multitude of ways, about an unlimited number of topics, and for numerous reasons. Communication is an essential life skill for all individuals, regardless of age, gender, race, culture, or ability. Furthermore, it may be needed at any time and in any environment, and may be directed toward both familiar and unfamiliar persons. Instructional support for this critical skill cannot be relegated to any one environment or time period because it is a foundational support that is needed in order for a student to learn. When communication skills are interrupted, as is often the case with individuals who have severe disabilities, special attention must be paid to helping these individuals acquire the skills that they need through direct intervention. These skills cannot be left to chance or until the individual demonstrates some presumed prerequisite skills

because they impact every aspect of the individual's life. Communication skills allow individuals to request the things that they need or want, express feelings, share intimacies in order to develop closeness with another person, and obtain and provide information, as well as countless other critical aspects of a meaningful life. As such, everyone deserves to be able to communicate.

This chapter addresses the critical issue of communication, especially as it relates to students who have severe disabilities. Research that has demonstrated effective results will be shared, with examples provided of ways to implement recommended strategies in typical kindergarten through high school classrooms. The descriptions of three students of different ages and abilities who use augmentative and alternative communication (AAC) are presented next; these students will help clarify the issues presented in this chapter. Three students who use augmentative and alternative communication:

❖ ❖ ❖ ❖ ❖   **Ahmud**   ❖ ❖ ❖ ❖ ❖

Ahmud is a third grader who loves music, wrestling with his older brother, riding horses, playing with his dog, and swimming. He also loves amusement park rides,

especially those that spin around and go fast. He lives with his mother, grandmother, older brother, and baby sister. Ahmud is blind and does not make much use of

461

speech, although he knows a few words in Farsi (e.g., bathroom, water, dog, more). He understands simple directions in both Farsi and English. Ahmud primarily uses vocalizations, objects, parts of objects, and body movements to expressively communicate. He is learning to use a cane in an adapted manner to help him detect obstacles in his path. Ahmud uses his hands to explore items, identify them, and differentiate them from others. He loves being actively involved in activities and can become quite bored if subjected to prolonged verbal input only. When upset, Ahmud will scream, kick, and push people away. He has one or two friends at school, but has trouble making and maintaining friends in general.

Brandon

Brandon is a seventh grader who is a social butterfly. He loves going to school to be with his friends. He comes from a large, physically active family of eight, who are actively involved in activities after school and on the weekends. Brandon has a particular interest in anything related to sports. At school, he enjoys math, science, computers, and art. Brandon has severe athetoid quadriplegic cerebral palsy with limited and somewhat uncontrolled movement of his limbs. He uses an electronic wheelchair for the majority of the day, but also uses other positioning equipment during the day (e.g., wedges in P.E., a large bolster with support during computer time). Brandon also has mild to moderate intellectual impairment and communicates expressively via eye gaze at pictorial/written symbols presented alone or on a communication display/device. He has a DynaVox™ that he uses with a head pointer for most of his school communication, but he also uses body movement and facial expression with some vocalizations to convey unaided messages to familiar persons. Brandon appears to understand most of what is said to him and particularly enjoys joking with friends and family. He reads at an inconsistent grade one level.

Mara

Mara is a tenth grader who is passionate about crystals. This subject tends to occupy a large amount of her time. Mara lives with her mother and father and twin sister, Miranda, who has mild cerebral palsy. Mara has moderate intellectual impairment, as well as autism, and is nonverbal. She can become quite focused on a few things and then struggles to transition easily to something else. Mara has learned to recognize and use a number of pictorial communication symbols and has received some training in Picture Exchange Communication System (PECS), but she often uses loud, high-pitched vocalizations, going to get what she wants, hitting, biting, running off, and a number of other behaviors to express herself, especially when frustrated. She seems to work best with one or two other students and finds large-group instruction difficult. Her parents really want her to develop friendships at school and there are students who take different classes with her who would be very interested in getting to know her better.

The Fallacy of Prerequisite Skills

In the not too distant past, support existed for the expectation that individuals should display certain prerequisite skills prior to being provided with the necessary intervention to help develop communication skills (see Carter & Iacono, 2002; Cress & Marvin, 2003). These prerequisites often included such skills as establishing eye contact, understanding object permanence, imitating a model, and demonstrating intentionality. Such prerequisites denied intervention to those most in need of developing basic communication skills. Students could attend school for years and have instruction that targets these basic skills, but not specific skills in communication. The negative outcome of such thinking resulted in students beginning their final years of school without a reliable means for understanding what others wanted and lacking the ability to express their own thoughts in a fluent and effective manner.

A number of researchers and experts in the field of communication have since disproved the notion of prerequisite skills and instead support early intervention for any individual with complex communication needs (Cress & Marvin, 2003; Skotko, Koppenhaver, & Erickson, 2004; Snell et al., 2003). The National Joint Committee for the Communication Needs of Persons with Severe Disabilities (1992) created a communication *Bill of Rights* that states that all individuals have the right to be supported in their communication efforts. This *Bill of Rights* includes the right to request what is wanted;

reject what is not wanted; express preferences and feelings; get needed intervention; be spoken to and listened to with respect; and have communication that is clear, meaningful, and culturally and linguistically appropriate. In general, communication support should not wait for an individual to develop certain cognitive and physical skills, but should begin with the individual's needs and desires and support the individual to acquire the communication skills necessary for a high quality of life.

The Characteristics of Communication

While communication does not require a certain cognitive level, IQ score, or physical prowess, it does require that the individual have (a) some means to communicate, (b) some reason to communicate, (c) something to communicate, and (d) someone to communicate to (Beukelman & Mirenda, 2005). These are the four main characteristics of communication that will impact intervention strategies. All individuals, regardless of the severity of the disability, have or have access to these characteristics of communication. Therefore, all individuals can and do communicate. Helping to enhance these aspects of communication can strengthen and improve the skills of those at any age who struggle to express themselves.

Means or Modes of Communication

How individuals communicate with one another can manifest in many different forms or modes. Speech is the most common mode, but it is supplemented by several other forms of communication such as writing, texting, drawing pictures, tone of voice, facial expression, body language, and gestures. Individuals make use of these different modes of communication depending on the situation, the needs of both parties, and social dictates. For example, when giving directions to someone, drawing a map may add considerably to the receptive understanding of the person who is requesting assistance. During a meeting, individuals may use eye contact, facial expression, and write notes to express thoughts without interrupting the meeting. When addressing a large group, speech will be used, but will be supplemented with facial expression, gestures, tone of voice, and maybe a Microsoft® PowerPoint® presentation. In other words, different modes of communication are common for everyone. It is important to keep this in mind for students with severe disabilities who have complex communication needs.

When a disability is present that blocks access to a certain mode of communication (e.g., speech is blocked if the individual is deaf and print is blocked if the individual is blind), then alternatives to speech will be used (e.g., American Sign Language, braille). AAC is a system of communication which involves several different elements that support an individual's ability to communicate through means other than speech. The critical point of AAC is that the focus is on clear and effective communication and less on the means of communicating (Downing, 2005). The way that an individual communicates will depend on a number of variables, including both personal characteristics, as well as social and physical aspects. For example, in a particularly noisy environment where it is difficult to perceive speech, individuals will resort to visual means such as gestures and facial expressions. When an individual is unable to produce speech or understand it, then intervention will address alternative modes to support this person.

Ahmud's loss of vision makes it impossible for him to use picture symbols as an alternative to speech; however, he can and does use objects and parts of objects to make his needs known. He also uses these objects to better understand what others are saying to him.

Multiple Modes of Communication

A fundamental belief in the field of AAC is that any one individual (whether disabled or not) will make use of a variety of different modes of communication, depending on the situation, the audience, and the abilities of the individual (Beukelman & Mirenda, 2005; Cress, 2002; Downing, 2005; Hunt Berg, 2005; Light & Drager, 2007). Each of the three students presented at the beginning of this chapter use different modes of communication; some of these modes are symbolic in nature and some are not.

Ahmud uses objects, parts of objects, vocalizations, and body movements.

Brandon makes use of facial expressions, vocalizations, and an AAC device with pictures and voice output.

Mara uses pictures, facial expressions, vocalizations, and body movements to express herself.

Nonsymbolic and Symbolic Forms of Communication

Modes of communication can be unique and idiosyncratic to each person and somewhat difficult to interpret by others (e.g., stiffening of the body) or it can be generally understood by everyone with a clear relationship to one specific referent, which is characteristic of speech. *Nonsymbolic* or prelinguistic forms of communication do not have a clear and distinct referent, but could be interpreted in several different ways. Gestures, tone of voice, inflection, facial expression, body movement, and actual items that are part of an activity fall into this category.

> *When Ahmud, the third grader, grinds his teeth, those familiar with him know that this means that he is beginning to get frustrated with a situation and needs some support. Ahmud's grinding of his teeth is dependent on the context in which it occurs and on the ability of those around him to recognize the purpose it serves for him, based on past experience.*

Although not directly tied to a specific item or occurrence, nonsymbolic communication can be very effectively used by the individual and can serve a variety of different purposes for communication. Because all individuals use nonsymbolic forms of communication (e.g., facial expression, tone of voice, vocalization, movement) to add to their communicative exchanges, such expressions should be encouraged and supported for those having severe disabilities as long as these nonsymbolic expressions are socially acceptable.

Symbolic communication is the use of symbols that have specific referents; are not contextually bound or dependent; and can be used to communicate ideas about people, events, and feelings that are not constrained to the present time. Speech (in any language), written language, manual sign languages or systems, and specifically labeled pictures or parts of items are all examples of symbolic communication. Typically, the use of such symbols is clear to a very wide range of individuals who recognize and understand the specific meaning of the same symbols. (Obviously, communication would not occur if two people were speaking different languages, even though speech was involved.) The types of symbols that any one student might use is determined by that student's physical, sensory, and cognitive abilities, as well as by preferences, culture, native language, and the purpose of communication. See Table 12–1 for examples of both symbolic and nonsymbolic forms of communication and the communicative functions that they may serve.

Aided and Unaided Communication

Different modes of communication may also be aided or unaided. When an individual communicates without additional items or devices, the communicative exchange is considered to be *unaided.* Examples of unaided communication include nonsymbolic forms of gestures, facial expression, body movement, and vocal tone and inflection. Unaided communication also includes symbolic forms, such as speech and manual sign languages. With unaided forms of communication, the individual is always capable of communicating at any time and does not need to have additional tools to receive or convey messages.

Aided communication is any communication that occurs with the use of additional symbols, devices, or tools. Aided communication can be nonsymbolic when the individual uses the item within the activity and the use of this item is interpreted to mean that the individual wanted to engage in the activity. For example, when Ahmud is offered a drink, if he reaches up to take the

TABLE 12–1

Functions of Communication and Examples of Communication Forms

Function of Communication	Nonsymbolic Forms of Communication	Symbolic Forms of Communication
Rejecting an activity	Pushing away materials associated with the activity	Shaking head for "no"
Requesting a person	Grabbing the person's hand	Pointing to a photo of the person
Asking for information	Questioning facial expression	Using a picture/written symbol on a speech-generating device
Gaining attention	Loud vocalization	Using speech or sign to say, "Excuse me"
Making comments	Prolonged eye gaze at something of interest	Using a speech-generating electronic communication device to string symbols together in a statement or two about a topic
Confirming or denying	Not moving toward the location of the activity when asked if it was what had been requested	Signing "No, not that. I wanted something else"

cup, it is interpreted to mean, "Yes, that's what I want." The communicative exchange is obviously bound by the given context and situation to be meaningful. Aided communication also can be highly symbolic as in the use of AAC devices that have symbols and messages and require the speaker to make use of these symbols. Brandon has a DynaVox™, which is both an aided and symbolic form of communication. Mara also uses an aided form of communication—picture cards with written messages. These picture cards do not have a speech-generating component as does Brandon's DynaVox™, but they are symbolic and are effective in specific exchanges. Therefore, aided communication can be either very simple in nature or very complicated. Furthermore, while some fear that the use of a nonspeech mode of communication could hinder the development of speech, various studies have confirmed that the use of augmentative and alternative forms of

communication do not hinder speech, but can, in fact, support its development (Light & Drager, 2007; Millar, Light, & Schlosser, 2006; Schlosser & Wendt, 2008; Sulzer-Azaroff, Hoffman, Horton, Bondy, & Frost, 2009).

Low-Tech and High-Tech Options

Aided communication can be a very simple and low-tech, or electronic and quite complex. Several personal, social, and physical factors come into play when determining the type of AAC that may be needed. See Table 12–2 for a list of several low- and high-tech communication devices. Many different companies produce communication devices that represent a wide range of options. See Resources at the end of this chapter for a listing of several such companies. One of the advantages of electronic devices is the relatively large amount of symbols/messages that can be contained in one device. Some of these devices have

TABLE 12–2

Examples of High- and Low-Tech Communication Devices

Low-Tech Communication Devices	Features
Velcroed clipboard with pictorial symbols; converted VHS tape cover to hold symbols on Velcro strips	Easily removable symbols
	Static display
Small wallet-sized photo album with pictorial symbols	Portable
Pictorial symbols on a key ring	Can use many different types of symbols
Talking photo frames with picture symbols	Inexpensive

High-Tech Communication Devices	Features
DynaVox™ series (e.g., DynaMyte, EyeMax, DynaVox™ Xpress, Tango, DynaVox™ M³)	Dynamic display
	Pictorial symbols with speech output
	Scanning ability
	High portability
	Designed for a wide range of users
Vantage™, SpringBoard™, Pathfinder™, ECO™-14 by PRC	Dynamic display
	Pictorial symbols with speech output
	Drop-down menus
	Word prediction and next-word prediction
	Scanning ability
Smart/Series by AMDi	Various levels for different overlays
	Pictorial symbols with prerecorded voice output
	Scanning ability
	From 8 to 128 messages on one overlay
Optimist-3™ series by ZYGO Industries, Inc.	Dynamic display
	Lightweight
	Scanning
	Choice of speech synthesizers
MACAW® Family of Products and Talara-32® by ZYGO Industries, Inc.	From 32- to 128-message overlays
	Digital voice recording for messages
	Lightweight
	Scanning

FIGURE 12–1
A high school student uses his DynaVox™ with support from a peer tutor.

(Photograph by Antonia Pond)

dynamic displays that allow the individual to quickly move from one overlay to the next (like going from one window to the next on a computer). Such devices typically are able to support an individual's full communication needs (e.g., writing, speaking). Figure 12–1 depicts a high school student using his DynaVox™ to interact with a peer tutor during an eleventh-grade language arts class.

> *Brandon uses a DynaVox™, which has a dynamic display and allows him to move from topic to topic when conversing with peers by touching symbols on the display with a pointer attached to his head.*

Low-tech devices do not have the range of capabilities that high-tech devices do, but they have the advantage of being relatively easy to develop, inexpensive, and readily portable, and can use a variety of different symbols, depending on the student's needs and preferences and the specific situation. Low-tech devices need some kind of display (something that holds the symbols); symbols, which can be pictorial or tactile; and some kind of written messages for each symbol. Although low-tech devices typically don't have speech-generating potential (although some very inexpensive devices such as talking picture frames can), the messages should be written such that they represent the age, culture, and preferences of the student. Displays for low-tech devices can be almost anything (see Hodgdon, 1995, and Downing, 2005, for many different and creative ideas regarding low-tech communication aids). Examples of low-tech devices include

wallet-sized photo albums, CD holders, the boxes that VHS tapes come in, clipboards, simple cardboard sheets, purses or wallets, pictures or small objects attached to a key ring, or almost anything that will hold symbols for an individual to use. For example, Mara's low-tech device uses Boardmaker® picture symbols on small cards that she hands to someone in order to get her needs met. One student could have a number of different devices for different activities and environments. See Figure 12–2 for a sample communication tool that uses pictorial symbols and two messages that the student uses numerous times throughout the day. Because this student takes medication that makes him thirsty, he has a strong need for water, which he should always be able to request. He also becomes very frustrated at times and needs a quick way to remove or escape the stimuli that leads to his frustration. He chose the pictorial symbols used in this augmentative tool to which he always has access.

A Reason to Communicate

A reason to communicate is essential for all individuals. The purpose or function of communication will differ throughout the day, depending on the situation, the needs or desires that arise, interactions with others, and the specific interests of the individual. The need to control our environment is one reason to communicate (e.g., to obtain what we need or want through another person). If someone asks a question, the reason for the partner to communicate is to respond in some manner to that request. If the reason for communication is to convey friendship toward another, the individual might want to tease, joke, compliment, or share secrets. Many common reasons to communicate include

FIGURE 12–2
Low-tech communication aid always available to student.

I NEED A BREAK NOW!!!!!

Man I'm thirsty. Can I have some water.

(a) rejecting or requesting items, people, or activities; (b) requesting information, commenting, or sharing information with others; (c) greeting people; and (d) gaining and directing attention (Beukelman & Mirenda, 2005; Downing, 2005; Light, 1988). See Table 12–1 for examples of each of these different functions. Light (2003) categorized these reasons for communication into four general categories: (a) expressing needs and wants, (b) developing social closeness, (c) exchanging information, and (d) fulfilling the rules of social etiquette. The reasons to communicate will determine to some extent how one communicates or the mode of communication.

The Content of Communication (or What Students Will Talk About)

Another requirement of a communication exchange is that there is something to share between the sender of the message and the receiver. While this may seem overly basic, communication between individuals ceases when there is nothing to say. For individuals with typical life experiences, topics of conversation may be easy to come by. However, for individuals with severe disabilities, who may have reduced or limited life experiences, coming up with something to say may be more challenging. A lack of effective communication skills, such as an adequate means of expressing oneself, can compound this challenge.

Brandon, a seventh grader, really loves sports, but is very limited in what he can say about sports because of the limitations of his communication systems. Furthermore, the slow rate of speed when constructing a message, which is typical of most communication devices, makes it difficult for Brandon to say what he wants to say, when he wants to say it, and at the right moment. He may want to ask peers questions about certain players on certain teams, but unless this information is programmed ahead of time into his communication device, he is hindered in his ability to communicate what he wants to say.

When students don't have the symbolic communication skills that Brandon possesses, then communicating about certain topics becomes particularly challenging. To support a student's ability to discuss different topics, those around the student can help expand the student's life experiences and develop a means to assist the student to communicate about these experiences. Collecting artifacts and pictures from different experiences allows teachers and family members to support the student's communication around these experiences.

When Ahmud and his father go to a hardware store to purchase some items, his father makes sure that he feels the nuts and bolts that he enjoys and then these are used as symbols with messages to tell his mother about this experience. Ahmud's teacher and mother have been discussing using these nuts and bolts and other highly preferred materials to make tactile books for Ahmud. Tactile books would provide more opportunities for him to acquire the literacy skills of turning pages, feeling for the items, and recalling the experiences associated with the items in order to read the information.

The Social Requirements of Communication

It takes two to tango and it takes at least two to communicate. Most people have plenty of potential communication partners and the student with severe disabilities is no exception. The issue for students with severe disabilities is how to make it an effective interaction. Students with communication challenges will need support in order to interact meaningfully with students who do not experience such challenges. Students who both have the same severe communication challenges will have even more significant difficulty interacting. If one of the two individuals has fluent communication skills and strong social skills, then that partner can support and maintain the interaction. The importance of having competent and responsive communicative partners cannot be overestimated and will be discussed later in this chapter.

Receptive and Expressive Communication

Communication involves both receptive aspects (understanding what is conveyed by another) and expressive aspects (creating and conveying a message to another). A student may have significantly different skills and abilities in receptive and expressive communication, so each aspect needs to be considered in any assessment or intervention process. Students may use different modes of communication for receptive and expressive communication, depending on their strengths and limitations.

Ahmud, a third grader, understands spoken language in both English and Farsi and also makes use of objects and parts of objects to clarify what he is hearing. Expressively, Ahmud can say a few words in Farsi, but primarily uses vocalizations, body movements, and objects. Communication in a visual mode will not be effective with Ahmud because of his lack of vision. On the other hand, Brandon, the seventh grader, uses speech as his receptive mode of communication and uses graphic symbols (electronic or non-electronic), facial expressions, and vocalizations as his expressive modes.

Each student will be different and any communication system devised to support a student must consider both receptive and expressive needs. Furthermore, depending on the topic, student interest, the audience, and other factors, what may be effective for receptive or expressive communication in one situation may not be effective in others.

The tenth grader, Mara, can understand quite a lot of speech when it is about her favorite subject of crystals and other topics about which she has special interest or needs. However, when the information shared addresses areas that are highly abstract and are not of interest to her, she needs additional support to understand what is being said (e.g., pictorial symbols).

The Importance of Communication Skill Development

Communication is a skill that occurs across all settings and with all individuals who we encounter every day. Everyone communicates daily on a regular basis. Furthermore, communication is an important aspect of most typical activities and of all activities that have a social function. The importance of such a frequently occurring skill cannot be understated.

Communication for Relationship Building

Light (1997) stressed the importance of achieving social closeness with another person as one of the primary reasons for communication. While being able to effectively communicate is not a prerequisite for developing friendships, it is certainly supportive. Effective communication allows individuals to converse about any subject, about any time period, and during any time of the day. Han and Chadsey (2004) reported that the most frequently reported activity by middle school students was talking (for both male and female students). Yet students with severe disabilities often experience considerable difficulty conversing

with peers and, therefore, are often excluded from this critical friendship-building activity. Thus, learning different ways to communicate in different situations with different people can help to promote friendships and alleviate loneliness (Causton-Theoharis, Ashby, & Cosier, 2009).

Communication Skills for Emotional Development and Release

Being able to express one's feelings may help to relieve some of the emotion surrounding these feelings. Thus, sharing how we feel with another person may reduce the impact of negative emotions. Several researchers have investigated the relationship between challenging behavior and effective communication (Durand & Merges, 2001; Reeve & Carr, 2000; Sigafoos, 2000). Findings have revealed that there is a direct relationship between enhanced communication skills and decreased challenging behavior (see Chapter 7). However, helping students with severe disabilities and complex communication needs to use more conventional means of expressing their emotions may serve to decrease the need to engage in undesired behavior. In a study of self-determination skills and adolescents with severe intellectual disabilities, Carter, Owens, Trainor, Sun, and Swedeen (2009) found that students who display more challenging behaviors were deemed by their teachers and parents to have more self-determination skills. Carter et al. suggested that because of their limited conventional communication skills, these students were using the problem behavior as a means of asserting their choice and preferences, and letting their desires be known. While the problem behavior is negative, its communicative message is not, which highlights the need to teach more acceptable methods of communication.

Communication Skills for Learning

Teachers instruct through communication with their students. Typically, this is done through speech, but teachers also make use of different modes of communication such as eye contact, facial expression, gestures, tone of voice, and pictorial and actual object information. Any impairment in communication will compound the difficulties that a student with severe disabilities faces when learning meaningful skills and knowledge. In his seminal work, Vygotsky (1978) wrote of the strong linkage between language development and learning, stating that children use language to mediate what they know. Words open up new worlds, allowing individuals to expand on their knowledge.

Without effective communication of ideas, the student is prevented from asking questions and demonstrating what he or she knows. Such an inability to express oneself may result in lowered expectations for academic progress by teachers. In summarizing the state of the art in the communication field, Light and Drager (2007) concluded that expectations were low for early communicators, especially if the individual is older. Lowered expectations typically result in less instruction and, as a result, less learning and accomplishment. In investigating long-term outcomes for individuals who use AAC, Lund and Light (2006) stressed the connection between effective communication skills and educational achievement. White, Garrett, Kearns, and Grisham-Brown (2003) reported that students with deaf-blindness who had more proficient communication skills than other students with the same disability scored higher on alternate assessments. Language mediates learning, while its absence is a barrier to learning.

Communication Skills for a Higher Quality of Life

Self-determination is seen as one of the characteristics of a high quality of life (Agran & Hughes, 2005; Schalock, 2004; Wehmeyer & Palmer, 2003). Yet, students with severe disabilities appear to have limited skills in this area or lack the knowledge of the elements of self-determination and how to display it (Carter et al., 2009). Effective communication skills allow individuals to share their dreams with others, decide what will be needed and seek assistance, evaluate their progress toward meeting their goals, and discuss alternatives, as needed.

As adults, clear communication skills allow the individual with severe disabilities to make known their preferences of where he or she wants to live and with whom, if anyone. Communication skills play a major role when individuals are cohabitating and need to work through differences of opinion, as well as gain social closeness. Most work environments involve communication during the work day. Supervisors and coworkers need to have a successful means of interacting with one another to be efficient at their tasks. A lack of communication skills may serve to diminish future vocational outcomes; employment data indicate that only 15% of individuals with disabilities who use AAC are employed (Carey, Potts, Bryen, & Shankar, 2004). Finally, being able to communicate desires and

preferences aids in obtaining desired recreational activities. Interaction with community members often is needed to enter recreational sites and leisure activities may be much more enjoyable when shared with a friend. Essentially, every domain of life is affected by having effective communication skills in order to express one's thoughts, feelings, and needs, and to share special moments (Threats & Worrall, 2004).

Assessment

Assessing Communication Skills

Given the importance of communication skills in all aspects of life, it is critical to know the communication strengths and limitations of each student. While some standardized assessment tools will provide age equivalencies (e.g., receptive communication skills at a six-month level and expressive communication skills at a four-month level), such assessments often fail to recognize the unique characteristics, situations, and experiences of the student with severe disabilities (Cress, 2002; Ross & Cress, 2006; Snell, 2002). The results from such testing may seriously underrepresent the true abilities of a particular student. Under testing conditions, which are often in unfamiliar contexts and not a part of a familiar routine, students may not feel motivated to perform "on demand." They may not demonstrate what they are capable of doing unless placed in a situation that is familiar and motivating, and that supports optimal performance. For example, a student may seem somewhat unresponsive with few, if any, initiations in a special education room, but at a fun outing, the same student may initiate repeatedly, respond to questions, and demand attention and action. Formal assessment procedures with specific sequences of skills or checklists will not reflect this communication difference in performance. The unique interests of many students make it especially difficult to capture actual abilities and obtain the most promising picture.

Knowing a student's developmental level or mental age equivalency with regard to expressive and receptive communication skills is not nearly as important as knowing what the student wants to say or needs to understand in commonly frequented environments and within meaningful and regularly occurring activities.

Mara's results on standardized expressive and receptive language tests place her at a very young chronological age. Her parents worry that such results could lead to interventions that would reflect the skills and activities of a much younger person. Her teacher worries that these results could also lead to the development of AAC devices that would not be supportive of her actual chronological age. Mara's team recognizes that she is a high school student and needs to acquire skills that will enable her to best participate as a high school student in high school settings and activities. Treating her like a young child on the basis of standardized assessment scores will not teach her the skills that she needs as a young adult and will not enhance her self-esteem nor support interactions with others her age.

Obtaining Information from Significant Others

To obtain quality and comprehensive information, a recommended practice is to start with those who know the student the best (Bailey, Stoner, Parette, & Angelo, 2006; Cress, 2002; Downing, 2005, 2009). Talking with family members and others who have been involved with the student for some length of time can produce a rich and comprehensive baseline of student strengths and needs. Carefully constructed interview questions can assist the student's family members and friends in providing the most thorough and relevant information. As described in Chapters 2 and 3, input from the family and those close to the student is a critical consideration in the assessment process. Such input provides cultural, linguistic, religious, and ethnic perspectives that can be easily overlooked through the application of a standardized format.

Parents and other family members can be asked to describe the ways in which their child interacts with them—how he or she expresses certain desires and feelings. They can give examples of the ways in which the student initiates interactions with them and whether or not he or she responds appropriately. Family members can be asked with whom the student typically communicates and how effective the interactions are. Such information from those who know the student provides a solid foundation for further assessment, as needed, and highlights immediate needs for instruction.

Ahmud's family gave information on his likes, favorite activities, how he lets them know what he wants or dislikes, and what irritates him. They explained how they offer him choices by giving him different objects that represent the things that he likes to do. They feel that while they can understand a lot of what he wants to say, they wish that he could

communicate more effectively. They particularly expressed concern regarding his challenging behavior and felt that he was often frustrated. They want him to make friends and have social activities to do after school, especially with family members that he doesn't often see.

Analyses of the Communication Environment

Assessing how the individual communicates is highly dependent on environmental factors, both social and physical. Assessing the student in isolation, apart from any meaningful activity and environments, could quite conceivably produce a skewed depiction of the student's skills and needs. How the student communicates and for what purposes will be strongly affected by the social and physical environments. Students may not perceive any real need to demonstrate the skill that may be required during an out-of-context assessment. For example, once a second grader has greeted his teacher and classmates the first thing in the morning, the need for this communication skill is no longer in evidence for the rest of the day. Similarly, while lunchtime may call for high school students to order their food, this skill would not be expected or required in typical high school classes. As another example, students are expected to interact socially during lunch, recess, and before and after school. They are not expected to communicate socially when instructions are being given or during lectures, test taking, or sustained silent reading. Therefore, a comprehensive assessment of communication skills would necessarily involve assessing the environments and activities that are typical for the student at a certain age in order to accurately identify their communication expectations and demands.

Analysis of the communication environment must also look at the social aspect of communication and the potential communication partners for each student. The skills and expectations of communication partners will impact the type of communication intervention and supports that may be needed, but the partner's ability to understand the student's communication forms (e.g., gesturing and vocalizing but not using symbols, pointing to pictures, signing) also much be considered. For example, kindergarteners, although highly social, usually do not have strong reading skills. Therefore, aided communication that relies on the reading skills of the partner would not be very effective. Pictorial symbols will need to be used to assist these partners even when the target student may be unable to see and is using tactile symbols. Students of various ages may have unique forms of communication for greetings, to gain attention, or to share information. For example, texting and instant messaging are used frequently by young adults in order to share information, yet not by very young children. Students may greet each other with a "high five," a soft punch to the shoulder, knocking two fists together, a look, a thumbs up, a verbal "Hey" or "Yo," or a variety of other behaviors that are specific to an age range and culture.

Blackstone and Hunt Berg (2003) developed a formal communication inventory to assist in the gathering of information on the student's social environment. Through observation, the assessor obtains information on how the student communicates and with whom. Information is also collected on common topics of communication and the supports that the student need to be most successful during interactions. This type of assessment, which is observational and occurs without removing the student from natural and familiar environments, stresses the importance of the physical and social environments on communication skills.

An observational assessment of Ahmud's social skills and networks revealed that he rarely initiated interactions, but waited until someone approached him to ask a question. He had both extremely limited forms of communication and limited opportunities to interact outside of his family. His communication partners typically dominated the conversation and he usually just responded to yes/no questions. He primarily used sounds, body movements, and acting on objects to express himself.

Ecological Assessment of Communication Skills

When students do not fare well on standardized forms of assessment, observational assessment of the student in natural settings and engaged in typically occurring and age-appropriate activities may obtain the most authentic results of communicative competence (Blackstone & Hunt Berg, 2003; Siegel & Wetherby, 2006; Snell, 2002). Observations would occur across common activities when the student is engaged with familiar others. Information regarding how the student communicates (what different modes are used), the reasons that the student communicates, and with whom and about what topics are the focus of this type of observational assessment (Downing, 2005). Information also is obtained on whether the student initiates interactions, whether the interactions are successful (messages are expressed and understood by the partner), and the length of the inter-

action (e.g., the number of turns taken). Assessment information of this nature provides a direct link to needed interventions that will support the student's communication efforts in an age-appropriate manner (Blackstone & Hunt Berg, 2003).

Different strategies exist for collecting observational data. Snell (2002) describes a dynamic assessment of a student's communication skills that includes observation of the individual during familiar activities and during intentionally arranged environmental situations while documenting not only what the student can do, but also the level of supports needed and how those supports may change across activities. Including the support needs of the student in order to communicate as part of the assessment provides an optimal picture of what is possible for the student under different circumstances. This information also is helpful for the design of future intervention strategies. Suarez and Daniels (2009) recommend the use of digital video recordings as an effective means of sharing observational data with teachers, parents, and other team members. Video recordings of the student during typical activities can capture the unique and often nonverbal communicative behavior of students that could go unnoticed during a more standard form of assessment.

One way to complete an ecological assessment involves *discrepancy analysis*. In this process, the typical activities of a student's day are observed in order to identify not only what is expected in those activities, but also what skills the student is demonstrating and where discrepancies exist. This type of assessment does not remove the student from a natural environment in order to test the student on isolated communication skill development, but instead analyzes the student's performance on a number of different skills within typical and, hopefully, valued activities. Using activities that occur frequently for the student and, therefore, are representative of the student's day can provide meaningful assessment information for those who have the responsibility for supporting growth in communication and other critical skills. Figure 12–3 provides an example of one such discrepancy analysis of an activity. Such an analysis delineates the steps required for the activity; the natural cues that exist for any student involved in the activity; the communication skills required for each step; the actual performance by the student; the discrepancy and the rationale for the discrepancy, if any; and initial suggestions on how that discrepancy could be eliminated, or at least lessened. The form provided is only one way to gather this type of information and serves to remind the

FIGURE 12–3

Sample Ecological Assessment of Communication Opportunities, Skills, and Needs

Student: **Christee**	Grade: **6th**				
Class: **Science**	Activity: **Lab work: Compression & Expansion of Molecules**				

Steps in the Activity	Natural Cues That Prompt Behavior	Expressive (E) and Receptive (R) Skills Needed	Student Performance	Discrepancy Analysis (Why Student Isn't Doing the Step)	Initial Intervention Suggestions
Enter class while talking to peers	Knowledge of schedule Time Others talking	R: Understand peers talking E: Make comments/ask questions	−	Nonverbal Has no means to interact socially Doesn't recognize class	Give conversation book and teach her to use it Pair with one or two peers who will interact and help her get to class Provide a pictorial schedule
Find seat	Knowledge of assigned seat Knowledge of expected behavior		+		
Listen to teacher and take notes	Teacher talking Wanting/needing a reminder of the information	R: Understand what the teacher is saying	−	Material is too abstract Does not read or write conventionally	Provide pictorial and written information that is simplified and addresses "Big Ideas" Give one message with voice output of "I don't understand"
Get into lab groups while talking	Teacher's directions Others moving into groups Others talking	R: Understand the teacher E: Converse with peers	−	Does not know what group is hers No means to interact socially Nonverbal	One or two peers help her get with their group Provide message to request help from peers
Obtain needed equipment (cans, Bunsen burner, water)	Teacher's directions Not having what is needed for the lab	R: Understand teacher and peers' comments E: Ask questions, make comments, give directions	P	Helps get some material, but has no way to request help or ask questions	Provide pictorial and written list of needed materials Teach her to check off as each one is obtained Provide means to ask for help or ask what to do
Perform experiment (heat water in cans and then place in cold water) And talk about it	Written instructions Materials Stages of the experiment Others making comments and giving directions	R: Understand comments and directions of peers E: Make comments and ask questions	−	Does not understand science lab Nonverbal Has no means to make comments or as questions	Provide a pictorial sequence of the science experiment Provide means to ask what to do and request help Provide means to comment on experiment
Fill in science report on lab as a group	Teacher's directions Blank science form Knowledge of routine	R: Understand peers' comments and questions E: Make comments and ask questions	−	May not understand science behind experiment Nonverbal No means to add information	Provide pictorial and/or real items for her to select and add to the completion of the report
Clean up experiment while talking	Mess Teacher's directions Others talking	R: Understand peers' directions and comments E: Request help and make comments	P	Helps to clean up when directed by peers, but does not converse	Provide pictorial sequence of expectations and teach use
Return to seat	Teacher's direction Experiment over	R: Understand teacher	+		

+ Independent; − Cannot do; P Completes with prompt

FIGURE 12–4
Assessing the Communication Interaction

Student: **Mara**   Setting: **Lunch outside**

Potential Communication Partners: **Heather, Sophie, Dan, Karyn, and paraprofessional**

Mara has some PECS symbols and two different conversation books

Initiator	Responder	Modes of Communication	Function of the Behavior	Was the Interaction Understood?
Heather: "Mara."	Mara	Head turned toward peer	To say "What?"	Yes
Heather: "Whadcha do this the weekend?"	Mara	No response	Could mean she wants to be left alone or doesn't know what to say	Not clear
Heather: "Did you watch TV?"	Mara	Smiles	To say "Yes"	Yes
Dan: "Did you see *America's Funniest Home Videos*?"	Mara	Looks away	To say "No" or may want to talk with Heather and not Dan	Not clear
Sophie points to Mara's conversation book and asks, "What do you like to watch?"	Mara	Takes book and opens it but doesn't let them see	To say "I'm trying to think of what I want to say"	Probably

assessor of what information to collect during an observation. Analyses across a number of common activities for the student would be needed to obtain a thorough understanding of (a) the communication skills that the student possesses, (b) the typical expectations from different learning situations, and (c) the needs that the student demonstrates according to those typical communicative expectations. For instance, Figure 12-4 presents an observational assessment of one aspect of an activity that showed discrepancies in communication for Mara. Although Mara is fairly independent during lunch, the social interaction piece of this daily activity causes her some difficulty. A closer analysis of this one social step in the activity of lunch leads directly to intervention needs. No age-equivalency is obtained from such an assessment, but instead the focus is on age-appropriate expectations and alternate ways of meeting those expectations. (See Chapter 3 for more information on ecological assessment strategies.)

Intervention Strategies

The most effective means of intervention will rely heavily on a comprehensive and accurate assessment of a student's strengths and areas of need. The inter-

vention plan will be equally comprehensive and address where the intervention will occur, what skills will be targeted, how the skills will be taught, and who will provide the intervention. Each of these aspects of the intervention plan, with documentation from the research, will be discussed below.

Where Communication Intervention Will Occur

Teaching students to make use of existing communication skills and to develop new skills should occur within natural environments where the skills are most readily needed and expected. Instead of teaching communication skills in one environment with a unique set of stimuli, communication skills are best taught throughout the day where they typically occur or are expected to occur (Beukelman & Mirenda, 2005; Cress, 2002; Downing, 2005). For example, students can be taught to greet peers and teachers as they meet each other at the beginning of each day or in class or while passing in the hall. Students can be taught to make basic requests for water, food, or use of the restroom throughout the day as the need arises. Teaching students to request help or take a break when they are frustrated during the day may decrease the need to engage in problem behavior in order to accomplish these functions. Students are taught to respond to peers when classmates ask questions in small groups, engage in buddy work, or socially interact during recess or snack breaks. In general, opportunities for practicing skills occur throughout the day.

The rationale for teaching in natural environments where the skills are used and needed is to avoid the necessity of the student having to transfer skills acquired in one specific environment to other more natural environments. The difficulty of transferring skills from the learned to the natural environment for students with severe disabilities has been clearly recognized in the literature (Fox, 1989; Haring, 1988; Haring et al., 1985). If the learning environment is considerably different from the environment in which the skills are desired or expected, the student may have even more difficulty understanding when the skills are to be used. For example, if the room for instruction is small, quiet, with few distractions, and has only one adult present (as may be typical in some pull-out service delivery models), then the environmental stimuli present during periods of instruction may look and sound significantly different than in the more natural school and community settings. Students need to be able to communicate in noisy places with a great deal of visual and auditory stimulation. Therefore, the more closely the learning environment represents the typical environments in which the skills are to be used, the easier it is for the student to understand when the skills are required or expected.

In typical environments, unlike specialized settings, it may be somewhat difficult to control the number of possible conversational partners at any one time (as children come and go around the target student). An even greater challenge is to control the number and variety of different conversational topics that may be introduced to the student. The student must learn to interact in this type of environment if communication skills are to be truly effective for the student and to enhance his or her quality of life.

Because communication skills are taught during typical activities throughout the school day, it is important to recognize the demands of the class activities. Students are expected to listen to teachers and respond to their names being called for attendance, lunch count, and to answer questions and to contribute to the discussion. Students need to be able to respond to their peers and to initiate and maintain interactions with others. Intervention needs to address the expectations for communication that naturally arise during the typical school day and to ensure that

the student has the skills and/or tools to meet these expectations.

One very positive aspect of typical environments is the abundance of competent communication partners in the form of same-age peers. Students as communication partners will be discussed later in this chapter. However, we will mention that the research to date is supportive of the critical role that students without disabilities play in the development of communication skills (Carter & Hughes, 2005; Kamps et al., 2002; Von Tetzchner, Brekke, Sjothun, & Grindheim, 2005). Peers can serve as both role models for more effective communication and as responsive conversation partners.

What Skills to Teach

A very critical component of the intervention plan is to know exactly what skills are to be taught. Stemming from the information obtained as part of the assessment process, what the student is to learn will reflect the unique strengths of the student, as well as identified needs. The type of communication skills to be taught will incorporate the purpose (the function) of the communication exchange, the form the interaction will take (how it will occur), and what the message will look like (the content). These components of communication may look very different for each target student, depending on age, ability, sensory or physical limitations, cultural background, family preferences, and interests.

A speech-language pathologist once recommended teaching Mara to use signs to communicate. However, her parents did not want her to use a complex system that they would have to learn and were also concerned about others perceiving her to be deaf. Although Mara has the physical dexterity to learn signs, the family's preferences were considered more important. In addition, few of her classmates know how to sign, so that could further limit her social interactions with her peers.

Despite the need for individualized intervention, some general principles are recommended and will be presented in the following pages. Enhanced communication skills can involve the need to transition students from unintentional behaviors (e.g., gazing in an interested way at some object or action) to intentional communicative behaviors (e.g., reaching for the desired object and looking at the person holding it). Typically, this will mean learning more advanced forms of symbolic communication and when and how to use them.

Thus, educational team members will need to assist in the development and/or acquisition of augmentative forms of communication that can be used to support the student's current communicative behaviors.

Guiding the Student from Unintentional to Intentional Communication

Intervention support should consider the current behaviors of the student and work with the student to improve both the quantity and the quality of those behaviors to make them more functional for the student. Some students, regardless of their age, may not have learned intentional communication skills. Intentional communication occurs when the individual uses explicit behavior for the purpose of impacting the behavior of another person to obtain what is desired (McLean & Snyder-McLean, 1988). Individuals must act not only on a desired object, but also must include another individual in the intended message. Students with very significant cognitive needs may require assistance in learning to use simple behaviors for intentional communicative purposes. Typically, these students have very restricted movement and also may have severe visual disabilities and/or health impairments that have seriously impacted their ability to observe and imitate others in communicative acts. Carter and Iacono (2002) found that while those famil-iar with a student could understand the student's idiosyncratic behaviors, those who were not familiar were unable to interpret them. Therefore, those closest to the student can respond to what they see the student do as if the behaviors were intentional. Careful observation of the behaviors that these students use in perhaps an unintentional manner to convey thoughts and feelings can be shaped over time to become intentional communicative behaviors that will meet their basic needs. Once the student understands that slight behaviors are responded to by others in a particular way, the behaviors can be used purposefully to obtain desired items, people, and actions.

When a student communicates in a manner that is very unique and difficult for others to recognize and understand, Mirenda (2005) recommends the use of a communication dictionary. This individually devised dictionary lists the behavior demonstrated by the student, what the behavior typically means for the student, and what the conversation partner should do as a result of seeing the behavior. Behaviors are alphabet-ized and kept in a notebook that can be updated and expanded as needed. The communication dictionary can be used quite effectively to share information with all current team members, substitute teachers, and future team members. Following are some explanations of a few behaviors that appear in Ahmud's communication dictionary:

Behavior	Meaning	Consequence
Shrill, high-frequency squeal	Usually means that he is in pain (most likely a headache or a stomachache)	Tell him that you understand and that you will help him go to the nurse's office.
Swinging head back and forth	Usually means that he is bored or disinterested in the task	Tell him that you know that he is bored, show him how to request a change using his tactile/voice output device and offer him other options using tactile objects or parts of objects.
Tapping his throat	He is thirsty	Ask him if he is thirsty and show him his tactile symbol for requesting a drink. Offer him some water.

Consistently pairing the student's perhaps unintentional behavior with a specific result over time helps the student understand that the behavior can be used to intentionally convey the desire for this particular result.

Loreesha is a fifth grader who has profound intellectual disabilities and severe physical impairments that make it difficult for her to move her body. When she is shown something that she does not like, told *what it is, and it is placed alongside her arm (e.g., headphones to listen to music), she will tense up and move her arm slightly away from the item. Respecting this "request" not to listen to music by removing it and not carrying through with the activity will eventually allow her to understand that the way that she is saying "no" is being understood by others and can be used in other situations. On the other hand, when she does want something (e.g., being shown a book and being asked if she would like to read it), she relaxes and smiles. By responding positively to this "request" and supporting her in moving her arm toward the book, Loreesha will learn that such behavior will convey an intentional "yes" to her communication partners.*

Depending on the student and the communicative interaction, a considerable number of opportunities to practice these skills will be necessary to gain intentionality.

Developing Augmentative Communication Systems

While much information can be conveyed via nonsymbolic forms of communication (e.g., greetings and farewells, emotional states, confirmations or denials, gaining or directing attention), not having symbolic communication limits the ability to discuss topics of interest or concerns and to allow others to understand our thoughts and beliefs. Therefore, augmentative systems of communication that support symbolic communication are needed. As stated earlier, these can be highly complex and technological or quite simple and handmade. One device that supports symbolic communication will probably not meet all of the student's needs and a student may use different devices for different activities or settings in combination with nonsymbolic forms of communication.

Brandon uses his DynaVox™ when responding to peers' or teachers' questions. However, while passing in the halls, he prefers to smile, use body movements, and vocalize to interact with friends. In art class, he uses a laminated flat board with messages on it that takes up less space than the DynaVox™ and can be easily wiped clean.

Speech-language pathologists who have had training in AAC can be very helpful in assessing the student's needs in different environments, suggesting and obtaining communication aids, or designing communication aids and then evaluating their utility. Special educators also contribute to decisions about purchasing and using devices, as well as the creation of low-tech aids, and certainly to instructing how to use the device. Peers can contribute to the design and development of different AAC devices that are individually made for a particular student. Peers typically can suggest important words and phrases that "must" be on a student's device and can add digital voice recordings on certain devices. Family members also will have preferences

TABLE 12–3

Considerations in the Development and/or Purchase of a Communication Device

1. Are the symbols being used easily recognizable and preferred by the student?
2. Does the vocabulary meet the student's needs in different activities and environments? Does this include both academic and nonacademic activities? For learning? To have basic needs met? To make friends?
3. Is the device easy to access in terms of the student's sensory, physical, and cognitive limitations?
4. Is the device portable and readily available across different activities and settings?
5. Is the device personally appealing with regard to quality of voice output, appearance, weight, and cultural sensitivity?
6. Does the device support the student's literacy development?
7. Is the device easy to program?
8. Is the device expensive?
9. Does the device have a good maintenance record?

and suggestions with regard to the purchase of a commercial device or the development of a low-tech aid. Everyone's input is important as long as it supports the true needs and interests of the student. See Table 12–3 for considerations regarding the purchase or development of an AAC device.

Teaching a Broader Range of Communication Modes

While students may have developed a means of communication, helping students to expand their use of communication modes can enhance their ability to communicate with a wider range of individuals, about more topics, and in more diverse settings and activities. For instance, a student's communication dictionary shows that she uses facial expressions to show emotions, grinds her teeth and turns her head away to reject something, and vocalizes or moves her body to request more of some activity. Her team members have determined that she could benefit from learning to greet peers with a "high five" and to use objects or parts of objects to make requests and to initiate interactions.

Students can be taught to increase both nonsymbolic and symbolic modes of communication. Both can be very effective, depending on the situation. Students should be encouraged to use facial expression, common gestures, eye gaze, and vocalization to convey a number of messages in various situations. Because unaided communication does not depend on any additional equipment, supporting a student's use of nonsymbolic behaviors can be very effective (e.g., teaching a student to shrug her shoulders for "I don't know," raise a hand in response to the taking of attendance, or point when asked where she'd like to go).

In many situations, the use of symbols will be necessary. Therefore, teaching students to use symbols in addition to nonsymbolic behaviors would be a meaningful goal. Some students may use a few symbols (e.g., colored photographs) and need to learn a greater number of symbols, more abstract symbols, or learn how to put more than one symbol together to form a message.

Mara is learning to give a picture/word symbol to a teacher or peer to request help or ask for specific items. A next step for Mara is for her to combine a generic "want" symbol with a specific request (e.g., for help, for a music CD, or permission to feel a crystal pendant worn by someone). She will need to point first to the "I want" pictorial symbol and then to the pictorial representation of whatever it is that she is requesting.

Teaching Students to Use a Broader Range of Communication Functions

Often students have learned to clearly reject what is not desired (e.g., by pushing away, crying, stiffening their bodies) and to request what they need or want (e.g., by reaching toward, looking at, or pointing to objects or pictures). Considerable research exists to document that requesting is often the most frequently used and most easily learned communicative function by students with severe disabilities (Carter, 2003; Sigafoos & Mirenda, 2002; Snell, Chen, & Hoover, 2006). However, interacting with others is severely limited if the only functions that a student can engage in are requesting and rejecting. Such communicative functions do not lead to the development of social relationships. Students will need to learn a much wider range of communicative functions in order to be successful in most social interactions. Such functions may include gaining attention and initiating interactions, developing social closeness, requesting information, sharing information or commenting, and engaging in social niceties. There is no hierarchy to the teaching of such skills. Instead, the social situation, the expectations of the environment, and the needs or desires of students will determine the importance of teaching a broader array of communicative functions.

Gaining Attention and Initiating Interactions

Perhaps the most critical communication skill for any person is to be able to gain the attention of a communication partner in order to convey a message. Typically, students with severe disabilities who have complex communication needs assume the role of the responder in most social interactions (Cress & Marvin, 2003; Richardson, 2002). Although responding to another is an appropriate communicative skill, always waiting for someone to initiate an interaction places the student in a dependent and somewhat passive position. Students need to know how to initiate interactions in order to have as much control as possible over their social and physical environment.

Gaining another's attention can be done symbolically with speech, a speech-generating device, or handing someone a message, or can be done nonsymbolically with a vocalization, a wave of the hand, or just moving closer to someone. Often, unaided forms of communication are used for this purpose so that there is no dependence on an additional tool.

Although Brandon has a DynaVox™, which is a very complex electronic communication aid, he prefers to move his arm and vocalize to gain someone's attention. This is especially clear when he is transitioning from class to class and passing a number of students in the hall. He does not have time to communicate his message of greeting using his DynaVox™, which is in his backpack. Nor do his friends have time to wait for this device to be retrieved, turned on, positioned, and so forth. Instead, Brandon grins, moves his body, and vocalizes, which gets others' attention, who then greet him in return and continue on their way to class. His nonsymbolic behavior is very effective in this situation and is understood by those who know him.

Teaching the student to initiate an interaction requires that the following skills be taught: (a) approaching a potential partner or indicating an interest in talking, (b) obtaining the partner's attention, and (c) expressing the message. Students with limited physical skills may have great difficulty gaining someone's attention if they are unable to approach that person or if they cannot move a limb or vocalize. Such a student may need an aided tool (e.g., a speech output device or a single pictorial/message card) to obtain another's attention in order to begin a conversation.

Ahmud, because of his blindness, might make use of a single message with voice output that he taps to request the attention of someone near him. Mara, on the other hand, is learning to use a single message card that asks a question or makes a statement, or requests that she be allowed to approach someone and hand him or her the message.

Because even basic needs cannot be expressed without first initiating the interaction, learning how to gain another's attention in an efficient and socially acceptable manner is a very functional first step.

Developing Social Closeness

To more easily create friendships, students must be able to share age-appropriate information; tease; joke; and, in general, engage in behavior that is designed to bring people together. These types of social communication skills are difficult to acquire with limited or no symbolic communication. Therefore, those supporting these students need to teach these social skills, probably with the use of an aided and symbolic system. Hunt, Farron-Davis, Wrenn, Hirose-Hatae, and Goetz (1997) made use of conversation books for students with moderate to severe disabilities to enhance their social interaction skills. As a result of their teaching students with and without disabilities how to use the books with one another, students not only showed an increase in their interactions, but the students also demonstrated more initiation of those interactions. Furthermore, students made more use of comments with their peers instead of just requests or protests, making the interactions more socially balanced. Conversation books contain pictorial and, as needed, tactile artifacts with written messages from the student's perspective that convey information about interest, hobbies, experiences, and family.

One message from Ahmud's conversation book (see Figure 12-5) used both a picture and a tactile item (part of a rein). Both symbols were used because Ahmud's peers requested that the picture be added, while Ahmud feels the part of the rein to remind him about what that page means. Although Ahmud does not know Braille, both print and Braille are provided so that a sighted partner can read the message and Ahmud can feel that something is on the page that is connected to what the partner is reading.

The student is taught to gain another's attention and point, touch, or look at different messages (not in any particular order) to engage in a social interaction with a peer or adult. The peers also require instruction

FIGURE 12–5
Sample Page from Ahmud's Conversation Book

on how to use the book (e.g., encourage its use, respond to any communicative effort by the student, ask questions to keep the conversation going). Dyches, Cichella, Olsen, and Mandleco (2004) suggested the use of photographs with messages to help students express what is difficult to do so verbally. Students can be encouraged to take their own pictures or direct someone else to take pictures of certain items for this communicative purpose. One student could have several different conversation books or devices in order to discuss different ideas, and family members and peers can help in the development and modification of these aids. The end result of using such devices is not to obtain items (requests), but to achieve and maintain a personal closeness with others.

Requesting Information

Students have different interests and should be allowed to explore these interests without waiting for someone to recognize the interest and supply information. Helping students to ask questions may greatly affect their ability to build on what they know and obtain not only more information about the world, but also concomitant communication skills. Koegel, Camarata, Valdez-Menchaca, and Koegel (1998) investigated the impact of pivotal response training in the form of helping students labeled as autistic to ask questions. Using a time-delay procedure and items of high interest and value to the student, Koegel et al. were successful in teaching students with severe autism not only how to ask others the question "What's that?" but also in teaching additional vocabulary related to the item of interest.

Requesting information typically requires a symbolic mode of communication, although a puzzled facial expression can serve, at times, to get the communication partner to explain. When students use such a facial expression of inquiry, they should be immediately responded to and given feedback that the expression was seen and understood. Symbolic communication often adds clarity and specificity to the situation, so teaching students how to sign What? or Who? or using pictorial symbols with words (e.g., a picture of a questioning facial expression with a large question mark beside it for "Who?"), with or without voice output, may be the most effective practice.

Mara is learning to use a pictorial symbol of a woman shrugging her shoulders with a big question mark next to it and the written question, "What should I do?" Whenever Mara looks confused and is hesitant about beginning something, this pictorial symbol will be moved close to her in order to draw her attention. If she picks it up or touches it, the person supporting her responds by acknowledging her ("Oh, you don't know what to do") and will clarify or assist her to better understand expectations. If she doesn't touch it or pick it up, a series of prompts will be used to achieve this desired response so that she will learn how to request information when she needs it.

Sharing Information or Commenting

All students should be able to express how they feel about certain events or people and should be able to convey what they know about a particular topic or subject. This function of communication can be done with facial expressions, such as a scowl that means "I don't like it," or a smile that means "Great!" Therefore, students should be given the opportunity and encouraged to use their facial expressions to comment on various things (e.g., their art project, their peer's science project, the math lesson, the story, their lunch). However, more specific information is impossible without the use of symbols. Unfortunately, students with severe disabilities often are denied a means of conveying messages or making comments (no symbols or messages are provided as part of a communication tool in order to address this need).

When Ahmud starts to get irritated with an activity and it looks like he is going to become increasingly agitated, he is shown a small one-message voice output device that has a specific texture on it. When pressed, the message states "Gee, this is soooooo boring. I hate this!" in a young boy's voice with a very exaggerated tone. Ahmud seems to like this and usually stops his agitated behavior. Peers sometimes respond to him by whispering their agreement and an adult supporting him will take the hint to make some changes in the activity.

When asked questions in her classes, Mara needs to have pictorial symbols in front of her in order to respond. So, when the biology teacher asks her for the color of her hair, she needs to show him the appropriate color card from three different options. Her teacher then asks the rest of the class if it's possible for Mara to have one color of hair and her parents a different color and why. In this way, Mara is included in the group lesson and her response contributes to additional learning for the class.

Repairing Communication Breakdowns

Students with severe disabilities often experience communication breakdowns when attempting to convey a message (Halle, Brady, & Drasgow, 2004; Snell, Chen, Allaire, & Park, 2008). Communication breakdowns are interruptions in the sending and receiving of a message, such that the intent of the communication exchange is not understood by the communication partner. Communication breakdowns can result from an inadequate vocabulary, an inability to retrieve the necessary word(s), unintelligible speech, inadequate volume, misinterpretation of the intent by the conversational partner, or basically, anything that disrupts the effective exchange of a message. All individuals experience such communication breakdowns on a fairly regular basis and must make the necessary corrections to resolve the issue. When students with severe disabilities have limited communication skills, repairing communication breakdowns can be particularly difficult, resulting in either challenging behavior (Snell et al., 2008) or passivity, if the student typically tends to give up (Cress, 2002).

Ahmud often experiences communication breakdowns when his actions are misinterpreted or when he needs to say something but does not have the means to successfully share the message with others. At times, he is offered choices of activities using two different objects or parts of objects. Although he does choose one object and does want to engage in the activity, he may not want the adult to provide him with assistance. When he screams or pushes away, he is provided with other options using different objects. Unfortunately, his intended message is not that he doesn't want to do the activity, but that he doesn't want to do it with the adult. Such a breakdown in communication tends to increase his "challenging" behaviors.

Therefore, teaching students some strategies to deal with communication breakdowns and, essentially, to try another way is a critical communication goal (Cress, 2002). Students can be taught to repeat initial efforts or respond "yes" or "no" to suggestions made by partners to determine the message (e.g., "Did you mean to say ?"). Students also can be given different communication symbols to help the student to reformulate the intended message. Perhaps the best strategy for teaching communication repairs is to provide responsive and supportive conversation partners who clearly convey their interest in what the student has to say and who provide structure for a successful interaction.

Engaging in Social Niceties

In general, people like to interact with others who are polite and follow the social rules of interacting. People like to hear words like "please," "thank you," and "I'm sorry," and like to know that listeners are attending to what they are saying. For the beginning communicator, communication skills that will help the student attain the desired ends will probably be more easily taught and learned sooner than will be expressions of thanks or regret, or even casual greetings. The positive regard of others in reponse to the student engaging in social niceties may be an insufficient natural reinforcer for the student to understand the reason for using such expressions. However, modeling the use of social niceties, showing the modes of communication possible for this function (as determined by individual student characteristics), adding the expression to another function (e.g., requests), and praising their use are certainly recommended.

Brandon has symbols on each dynamic display on his DynaVox™ that say, "Hey, thanks" (which he chose over "Thank you very much") and "Please," so that he can fairly easily use them throughout the day. He also has these symbols on the arms of his

wheelchair so that he can access them when he is not using his DynaVox™. He often needs to be prompted to point to these symbols, but that doesn't make him that different from his peers.

A word of caution may be in order. Teaching a student with very limited communication skills, who does not have a firmly established means of obtaining desired or needed items, to engage in social niceties may be confusing to the student. The student may learn that the expression for "please" or "thank you" is the item or event requested. Students may resort to using the symbol for "please" or "thank you" in lieu of the appropriate referent. Such a misapplication of the social expression could result in very limited acquisition of needed vocabulary.

How to Teach Communication Skills

No single recipe or universal practice exists to teach students with severe disabilities to communicate. The strategies used should follow recommended practices in the field, but should also demonstrate consideration for individual learning styles, physical and sensory abilities, cultural beliefs and the wishes of family, cognitive skills, and the motivation of the student. Given the social nature of any communicative exchange, the quality of the partners plays a major role in any intervention.

The Characteristics of Supportive Conversation Partners and Teachers

When supporting someone who struggles to communicate effectively, the burden of a successful interaction will likely fall on the shoulders of the partner who has the stronger communication skills. This may happen in any interaction between very verbal people when visiting a foreign country and attempting to speak the native language. One person may have stronger skills in the foreign language and will thus be relied on to help the interaction continue. To support the exchange, those who have more advanced communication skills should be patient, wait expectantly, let the person know that you expect them to try while giving them a chance to create their message, anticipate what the person is trying to say, give them suggestions for saying it, and provide feedback as to whether the message was received clearly or not. Responsive partners follow the lead or interests of the student, respond immediately to their communicative efforts, and expand on them to help the student develop more advanced skills (Dennis, 2002; Kaiser & Grim, 2006).

> *Brandon loves sports and loves to be with his peers in seventh grade. He has a lot to say, but often his physical impairment, lack of strength, and the length of time that it takes to create messages on his DynaVox™ hinder his motivation to interact. He often resorts to facial expressions and body movements to communicate. His teachers and peers have all been told to talk about sports when appropriate (e.g., break, lunch, or embedded into content material), to wait for him to construct messages with his headpointer, and to encourage him to keep using the DynaVox™ because the device allows them to understand him better.*

Responsive partners do not dominate the interaction and provide sufficient time to allow the student to process information, formulate a response, and then engage in the desired communicative behavior. The quality of conversation partners can have a profound effect on the communication skill development of students, especially those who are just beginning to express themselves (Meadan, Halle, Ostrosky, & DeStefano, 2008). Unfortunately, beginning communicators, especially those who have unique and idiosyncratic forms of communication, may find that their initial efforts at communicating can go unnoticed (Arthur, 2003; Brady & Bashinski, 2008; Carter & Iacono, 2002; Finlay, Antaki, & Walton, 2007). Therefore, creating environments where potential social partners are taught to be responsive and supportive of a student's communicative efforts plays a significant role in any intervention strategy.

Naturalistic Approaches

Considerable research has looked at supporting a student's communication skill development within naturally occurring activities and familiar environments (Hamilton & Snell, 1993; Kaiser, Ostrosky, & Alpert, 1993; Meadan et al., 2008; Rodi & Hughes, 2000). Such approaches, often called *milieu* or *incidental learning*, are designed to take advantage of naturally occurring communicative opportunities throughout the student's typical day. Mancil (2009) reviewed the use of milieu teaching with students who have autism and found that in the eight studies that qualified for his research, students made progress with their communi-

cation skills and the majority generalized their communication skills to other settings and people.

Characteristics of milieu teaching (or teaching during typical activities in the natural environment) include (a) providing a model for the student of expected behavior, (b) giving a command (or direct instruction) and then modeling or correcting to obtain the desired response, (c) using time delay or waiting for the student to respond, and (d) incidental teaching based on the context and student interest (Yoder & Warren, 2002).

> *During a science lab, Shawntel, who is learning to ask "What?," is provided with several signed examples by the speech-language pathologist and peers with regard to the experiment. If the student doesn't sign "What?," then she is told to "Do this" (verbal prompt) and is provided with a model prompt. A wait time of three seconds is used between the verbal and the model prompts. Corrective feedback is provided, if needed. Then a response is immediately provided to her question. At the same time, when Shawntel becomes particularly interested in some aspect of the experiment (e.g., an interesting chemical reaction or strange rock shape or color), her facial expression, signs, and interest are all interpreted as her comments and are responded to and further elaborated. Other forms of incidental teaching are used to support her communication skills by creating needs in the environment (e.g., hiding something that she needs for the class, or doing something purposefully incorrect to elicit a reaction from her).*

Typically, the regular educational environment provides numerous opportunities for students to learn and practice communication skills. However, arranging the environment in different ways to create needs experienced by the student can increase the number of opportunities for the student to engage in communication skills. *Environmental arrangements* can take many forms: (a) having desired objects within visual range but beyond the reach of the student, (b) providing a minimal amount of something of interest to the student that will be insufficient, (c) creating unexpected situations that are novel to the student, (d) using intriguing materials that pique the interest of the student, and (e) offering choices throughout the day (Kaiser & Grim, 2006).

> *In the high school library, Mara typically goes to the section where she can find books on crystals, her*

favorite topic. In order to remove a book from the shelf, Mara needs to ask for help or ask someone to explain why the desired book is missing. An adult or peer would be present so that she could make the necessary request and not become overly agitated.

The third grader, Ahmud, is often provided with tactile choices throughout the day that let him decide which peer to sit by (by touching both peers), which materials to use in math, which task to do during science (by feeling representational items), or which reinforcer he wants to work for (e.g., listening to music or spinning a top). During lunch, Ahmud is often given a very small amount to drink so that he has several opportunities to request more if he is thirsty. He does this by grasping the cup offered and holding it up versus touching the napkin or food item.

Creating these adjustments to the natural environment ensures that students will have sufficient opportunities and be motivated to learn important communication skills.

Direct and Systematic Instructional Approaches

Regardless of where communication skills are taught, students with severe disabilities typically require instruction that is direct, systematic, and highly individualized. Supporting the student in communicating involves systematic teaching procedures founded on the field's knowledge of the behavioral strategies of prompting, shaping a response, fading, reinforcing, and providing corrective feedback. (See Chapter 4 for a review of systematic instructional strategies.) A systematic instructional plan should be in place for teaching communication skills so that all individuals involved in instruction can be consistent in implementing the plan. The plan will identify (a) the specific communication skills to be taught (whether an initiation, a response to a question, asking a question, making a comment, etc.), (b) the mode of communication to be taught, (c) the place it is to occur and with whom, and (d) the teaching strategy to be employed. Team members will specify in the teaching strategy the type and number of prompts to be used, how and when they are to be used, and the reinforcers that will be used. These decisions will depend on the skills to be learned, the situation, the characteristics of the learner, and whether the communication skills involve unaided or aided communication.

The Picture Exchange Communication System (PECS) (Bondy & Frost, 2002) is one direct instructional strat-

egy for teaching the use of pictorial/written symbols for requesting desired items, initiating interactions, and providing descriptions. Something that the student wants will be placed in front of him or her, along with the appropriate symbol card. An instructor in the role of the conversation partner will sit across from the student and wait, while a second instructor may physically prompt the desired response from behind the student (pick up the symbol card and give it to the first instructor). Upon receiving the symbol, the conversation partner (first instructor) gives the student what was requested. Although primarily targeting students who have autism, the strategy for teaching the symbol and its referent and the need to involve another person in the interaction in order to achieve a desired goal can be done with any student who has complex needs. Such explicit instruction for communication training can and should occur in natural settings and during typical activities. As an alternative to two adult instructors, the student's communication partner can be a student without disabilities with an adult (speech-language pathologist, general educator, special educator, or paraprofessional) providing prompts from behind the student.

When Mara is learning to initiate interactions with peers, a teacher, paraprofessional, or speech-language pathologist will prompt her toward a peer, who will be trained to wait for Mara to extend a pictorial/ written message card. The adult will provide a series of verbal and gestural cues to help Mara demonstrate the desired behavior, while the peer will wait until the initiation occurs from Mara and then will respond to her in a natural and positive way.

There are three general rules for any systematic approach to instruction: (a) prompts should only be used when necessary, (b) the least amount of prompting should be used, and (c) fading of prompts should occur as soon as possible (West & Billingsley, 2005; Wolery, Anthony, Snyder, Werts, & Katzenmeyer, 1997). The goal of instruction is for the student to display targeted skills independently without becoming overly dependent on prompts from an instructor. For example, one recommended practice in the field of augmentative communication is to allow and encourage students to play and experiment with their communication device, much like young children experiment with speech (McNaughton et al., 2008). They may need more systematic and direct instruction to make full use of the device in various situations, but they can also learn a lot about its use and effectiveness through exploration on their own.

Evaluating Instructional Practices

Any intervention needs to be evaluated to determine if it is, in fact, helping students to acquire skills that are considered important for them to learn. Certain questions need to be asked by the team to determine if their instructional practices should remain the same or if they need to be changed. Such questions include the following: Is the intervention effective in developing communication skills? Has enough time been given to the intervention to determine whether it is effective? Is everyone on the team implementing the intervention in the same manner? Could the student make better progress using a different strategy? Is the student generalizing skills to different environments, activities, and people? To answer such questions, careful data collection with regard to skills is needed.

Data Collection

While data may not be collected on every skill that the student is learning, the skills targeted in the individualized education plan (IEP) objectives should have supporting documentation in order to measure progress. To obtain such documentation, targeted communication skills should be explicitly described, as well as the

conditions under which they will occur and the criterion set for mastery against which they will be measured. Objective measurement should make sense with regard to the targeted skill, be specific to the skill, and of sufficient strength to ensure that the skill actually has been attained (Downing, 2008). The skill to be mastered should be specifically stated so that it is clear how the skill will be performed. For example, to say that a student will initiate or respond is insufficient. The means by which the student is to initiate or respond must be stated, as well as the conditions that must be present to have this occur. A revised objective might state that the student will initiate an interaction by pressing a voice-output message that asks someone to come over to talk within five minutes of sitting near a peer for lunch. Or after a peer has asked a question and pointed to the AAC device, the student will respond by opening the conversation book and pointing to a message. The communication skill must be clearly identifiable and observable for objective data to be gathered by different members of the team.

Sample goals and objectives that were written for the three students described at the beginning of the chapter appear in Table 12–4. Each goal and objective reflects the students' present level of performance, as well as assessment information from interviewing significant others in their lives and from observing them in typical educational environments. To measure progress, a data sheet has been developed for the first objective for each

TABLE 12–4
Sample IEP Goals and Objectives for Ahmud, Brandon, and Mara

Objective 1: When Ahmud needs assistance during class activities and with one verbal reminder, he will press a speech-generating device that asks for help without engaging in challenging behavior for 9 out of 12 consecutive opportunities.

Objective 2: When a peer sits next to or stands close to Ahmud at lunch and gives his tactile conversation book, Ahmud will initiate an interaction by touching the peer's arm and then touching a tactile symbol in his conversation book for 9 out of 12 consecutive lunch periods.

GOAL: Ahmud will initiate interactions with peers or adults using AAC at least 18 out of 24 opportunities during the school day.

Objective 1: During core content classes, Brandon will ask the teacher a question about the lesson using his DynaVox™ and sequencing at least four symbols for 12 out of 15 lessons.

Objective 2: When the teacher asks for ideas in any of his classes, Brandon will vocalize to gain her attention and will use at least four symbols on his DynaVox™ to make an appropriate comment for 12 out of 15 lessons.

GOAL: Brandon will add to the discussion of the lesson using at least four symbol messages on his DynaVox™ for 12 out of 15 lessons.

Objective 1: During lunch, Mara will initiate at least one interaction with a peer by touching his or her arm to gain attention and then showing at least one message in her conversation book without prompts for 14 out of 15 consecutive lunch periods.

Objective 2: During classes, Mara will respond to peers' questions and comments by pointing to or handing over at least one pictorial symbol per interaction for three interactions per day for 14 out of 15 days.

GOAL: Mara will use AAC to engage in social interactions with peers at least four times each day for 14 out of 15 days.

FIGURE 12–6

Sample Data Sheet on Communication Skills for Ahmud

Student: Ahmud

Objective: When Ahmud needs assistance during class activities and given one verbal reminder, he will press a speech-generating device (SGD) that asks for help without engaging in challenging behavior for 9 of 12 consecutive opportunities.

Date	Activity	Need for Help and Opportunity for Teaching	Behavior Used to Express Need	Response	Partner
4/07	Math: Determining which number of 2 or more is greater	Doesn't know what to do	Started to whine and fidget; physically prompted to use SGD	Physical P	Para
"	"	Dropped items on floor/can't find	None; physically prompted to use SGD	Physical P	Para
"	Science: Working with magnets in small groups	Peer asks him to hand her a magnet; He can't find one	Screamed; waited until quiet and then physically prompted to use SGD	Physical P	SLP and peers
"	Science: Putting away materials	Not sure what to do	Used device with verbal reminder	Verbal P	SLP and peer
4/08	Writing daily logs	Doesn't have items that he needs	Used device	Independent	VI teacher

Note: P = completes with prompt; VI = visual impairment.

This form would be kept with Ahmud's materials, and data collection would commence 2 weeks following initial instruction and thereafter during every class period. Ahmud would be shown his device, given the direction to make use of it should he need help, and then the support person would step away from him for a few minutes to observe what he does and record his behavior.

student. Information collected on the data sheet may be more extensive than what is actually specified for mastery in order to obtain additional information that may be helpful in future interventions. See Figures 12–6 through 12–8 for data sheets on each objective.

Data will be collected by all team members across the school day as the need for the communication skills arises. Collecting data should be relatively easy to do and should be part of the instructional routine. The collected data should be used to evaluate not only student progress toward targeted communication skills, but also the effectiveness of the instructional program. See Chapter 5 for more information on measuring student progress.

Who Provides Instructional Support?

With regard to communication, anyone who interacts with the student throughout the day can serve to support the development and expansion of communication skills. Students with severe disabilities need to learn to interact with a wide variety of individuals; the

variety of potential communication partners at any school easily provides such diversity. Communication partners can include a large number of adults who represent different roles, older or younger students, and same-age classmates.

Adults as Conversation Partners

At school, students interact with their teachers, both general educators and special educators; paraprofessionals; administrators; related service providers (e.g., speech-language therapists, occupational therapists, physical therapists, behavior specialists, vision specialists, etc.); school staff (e.g., cafeteria workers, janitorial crews, librarians, secretaries, bus drivers, playground monitors, etc.); and volunteers. While teachers and paraprofessionals will be the most frequent interactants, all other adults should be encouraged to also interact with the student. Therefore, they will need to know how the student communicates and what they should expect from the student during interactions.

FIGURE 12–7

Sample Data Sheet on Communication Skills for Brandon

Student: Brandon   **Classes:** Language arts, math, social studies, science

During core content classes, Brandon will ask a question of the teacher with regard to the lesson using his DynaVox™ and sequencing at least four symbols for 12 of 15 lessons.

Date	Class/Lesson	Was Question Asked?		Was Question Appropriate?	Number of Symbols Used	Were Pictures Put into Correct Sequence?
4/01	Math	Yes	(No)	–	–	–
4/01	Social studies	(Yes)	No	OK	2	Yes
4/01	Science	Yes	(No)	–	–	–
4/01	Language arts	(Yes)	No	No	3	Yes
4/01	Language arts	(Yes)	No	Yes	3	Yes
4/02	Math	(Yes)	No	No	2	Yes

Yes: Question asked was appropriate.

OK: Question was not directly related to lesson, but made sense (e.g., requesting help).

NO: Question asked was unrelated to lesson and off topic.

Note: Brandon will receive instruction on using his device and will be given appropriate symbols to use for each lesson. After 1 week of instruction, Brandon will be reminded at the beginning of each class to ask questions or volunteer information using his DynaVox™. This data form will be kept with Brandon's school materials and will be filled in each class by the person who is providing the instruction or by the teacher following the group lesson.

FIGURE 12–8

Sample Data Sheet on Communication Skills for Mara

Student: Mara   **Activity:** Lunch

Objective: During lunch, Mara will initiate at least one interaction with a peer by touching on the arm to gain attention and then showing at least one message in her conversation book without prompts for 14 of 15 consecutive lunch periods.

Date	Manner of Initiation	Message Used to Initiate	Was Initiation Successful?	With Whom	Message Used to Respond?	Was Message Appropriate?
4/13	None	None	No	Sherri	"Likes crystals"	OK
4/13	Looked briefly	Pushed book at peer (gesture cue)	Yes	Sherri	"Likes crystals"	No
4/14	Touched arm with point cue and verbal suggestion	"I like crystals, do you?"	Yes	Karyn	No response	No
4/14	Handed book to peer	None	Yes	Sidney	"Yes"	Yes
4/15	Touched arm with point cue	TV question page	Yes	Sidney	Smiled	No

Note: Mara will receive instruction for 3 weeks on initiating interactions with peers. Starting the fourth week of instruction, data will be collected using his form, which will be attached to the last page of the conversation book. Adult providing instruction or the peer tutor will collect data on her performance.

Even those adults who are familiar with the student with complex communication needs will need to learn how to be responsive communication partners, otherwise, many communicative efforts by these students may be ignored (Bloomberg, West, & Iacono, 2003; Brady & Bashinski, 2008; Cress, 2002; Porter, Ouvry, & Downs, 2001).

A Collaborative and Integrated Service Delivery Model

This chapter has emphasized the assessment of and the interventions used for communication skills that take place in typical environments for these students. The practice of using teaching and support staff in a collaborative manner to follow the student and provide services as needed and where they naturally occur complements this idea. This collaborative model of service delivery represents a unified and integrated approach among service providers for giving support (Cloninger, 2004). Instead of removing the student to work with a speech-language pathologist, for example, that specialist would work with the student on communication skill development during regular classes or other school activities (e.g., recess, lunch, social clubs). Times of the day when the student is expected to be interacting with others and has demonstrated deficiencies in this area would be targets for which the speech-language pathologists would deliver support services. Instead of removing the student from the environment in which the communication skills are needed, the therapist would embed his or her expertise into critical times for communication (Cross, Traub, Hutter-Pishgaki, & Shelton, 2004; Hunt, Soto, Maier, Muller, & Goetz, 2002). Because this expert is providing services within the classroom, other team members and students can witness the techniques used to support the student. By copying these techniques during times when the speech-language pathologist is not present, the student receives more consistent and ongoing support from numerous school personnel in order to develop critical skills.

Loriel, Ahmud's speech-language pathologist, provides direct instruction during small-group work for language arts on Tuesdays and during science groups or paired teams on Thursdays. When the group is working on identifying and using adjectives, for example, Loriel makes sure that Ahmud is an active member of the group. Certain adjectives are represented tactilely for Ahmud (e.g., soft, bumpy, rough, smooth, damp) and when he identifies the correct adjective from a field of two or three, his peers use the adjective in a sentence. She encourages his peers to interact with him, showing them what to do and how to read his responses and give him feedback. Ahmud is learning to respond to his classmates (e.g., a peer might say, "Ahmud, find the bumpy one") and his classmates are learning how to gain his attention (e.g., a touch to his forearm and saying his name), present the options in tactile form, and guide his hands (using the hand-on-hand technique) to the tactile options. Ahmud is also learning to grab a symbol and hold it out to someone so that he is sure that his message is being received. The speech-language pathologist provides prompts for Ahmud to interact with his peers and also provides feedback to his classmates on more effective strategies to use with him (e.g., "Don't just hold things in front of him because he can't see them").

Students as Conversation Partners

The most numerous potential partners for any student at school are the other students in attendance. These students may be younger, older, or the same age. They may also be siblings. Regardless of age, these students provide considerable stimulation for communication and serve both as competent role models, as well as responsive communication partners (Carter & Hughes, 2005; Kamps et al., 2002; Morrison, Kamps, Garcia, & Parker, 2001; Owen-DeSchryver, Carr, Cale, & Blakeley-Smith, 2008). In secondary schools, the student with severe disabilities may have the most frequent interactions with those students without disabilities in his or her class or classes, but all students at the school have the potential to provide the necessary encouragement and support.

Students introduce topics of interest to other students and provide age-appropriate models of words and phrases to use. Furthermore, students without disabilities can easily approach the target student, obtain eye contact, wait for and encourage a response, and model the use of AAC devices. Other students also may be interested in learning American Sign Language or other signed systems if that is what the target student uses. Seeing other students use alternative forms of communication can be particularly motivating for the student who depends on such alternative means for communicative interactions. In a study by McNaughton et al. (2008), parents were interviewed as part of a focus

FIGURE 12–9

Two fourth graders interact during class time.

(Photograph by Connie Zaragoza)

group on the topic of AAC for their child. Parents reported that peer support and involvement in the operation of the AAC device was critical for their child and that these peers need to encourage device use by their child. See Figure 12-9 for a picture of two fourth graders interacting during class. An added benefit for teachers and parents may be the willingness and ability of other students to help program electronic AAC devices.

Students serving as peer tutors also act in the role of conversational partners. Peer tutors may be the same age, but can often be older students who are earning school credit for serving as teaching assistants. Peer tutors can be particularly helpful in introducing the student who they support to their friends, increasing the potential number of social circles and social partners (Downing, 2005). In this way, more students who may not be directly involved with the target student can learn about the student's communication needs and skills and thus acquire skills that support interactions. Increasing the social circle around the student with severe disabilities provides more opportunities to practice communication skills with different partners.

Mara has a peer tutor for her fourth-period science class. This class occurs right before lunch, so the peer tutor, Elisha, walks with Mara to the lunchroom and invites her to join her group of friends for lunch. Elisha helps Mara order her food using her AAC device, which has various pictorial/written selections on it that have been geared toward lunchtime. Elisha also serves as a role model for her friends so that they know how to interact most effectively with

Mara (e.g., avoid overwhelming her with questions, point to her communication devices to direct her attention, and give her time to respond). A paraprofessional moves from student to student during this time to provide support and instruction as needed. She encourages Mara and her peers to make use of her pictorial conversation book in order to support her social interactions.

Training Needs

Regardless of the role served by peers, they are likely to need some instruction and feedback in order to provide the most effective communicative support (Hunt, Doering, Maier, & Mintz, 2009; Kent-Walsh & McNaughton, 2005). Students need information on how the target student communicates, what unconventional behaviors might mean, and how to respond. They need to feel comfortable using the student's modes of communication, including AAC devices, so that they can model the desired behavior and/or help program electronic devices. Students need to know how to be responsive partners in order to support communicative interactions (e.g., knowing the necessary wait time, looking expectantly, responding immediately and in a manner that allows the interaction to continue).

Carter, Cushing, and Kennedy (2009) offer a comprehensive approach to the effective use of peers to support their classmate who has severe disabilities. Their approach includes strategies for peer selection, training, and ways for adults to facilitate interactions and then fade themselves out. Peers who support their classmates with severe disabilities will need ongoing monitoring and feedback to ensure that they are assisting students with severe disabilities to communicate and develop more advanced skills. Serving in the roles of a conversational partner, role model, and buddy to a student with severe disabilities not only benefits the student, but also the peers serving in these roles (Carter, Hughes, Copeland, & Breen, 2001; Copeland et al., 2004; Weiner, 2005). (Chapter 11 provides more information on peer support.)

Summary

For students with severe disabilities, communication issues pose particular challenges in many aspects of life, including education, development of friendships, and sense of well-being and self-determination. Communication is a critical life skill that will need specific and individual attention for those who struggle to understand others and convey their own thoughts. Suggestions for both assessment and intervention have been presented in this chapter for those responsible for supporting these individuals.

A person-centered approach has been used as a premise for this chapter; the student's interests and motivation, the family's preferences, and the natural environment for a student in a particular age group provide guidelines for any type of communication assessment or intervention. Emphasis has been placed on developing multiple modes of communication for each student to use versus concentrating on one means of communication. In addition, helping the student to engage in an interaction with another person for a variety of reasons, other than just making a request, has been presented as a recommended strategy. Instead of waiting for the presumed prerequisite skills to emerge before teaching a greater variety of communication skills, these skills should be taught as the need arises, depending on the social situation for the student.

Given the very social nature of communication, the importance of ensuring socially responsive environments was stressed. Peers without disabilities can add considerably to a socially supportive environment for the benefit of student and peer alike. Everyone on the team and all others who interact with the student potentially play a role in the development of communication skills. Therefore, creating a highly social, responsive, and interactive environment for learning can help all students develop the critically important skill of communication.

Suggested Activities

1. To become more aware of how children at certain ages converse with one another and the range of topics that they discuss, pick two very different age levels and a social time for this age level (e.g., recess, lunch, transitioning in halls, after-school activities, group work). Position yourself close enough to hear the conversation, but not so close as to be obvious. Listen for 20 minutes or so and jot down phrases overheard and a list of topics discussed. Compare the two age groups and notice the differences. The purpose of this activity is twofold: (a) to obtain a better understanding of how a specific age group might express themselves, and (b) to incorporate this style of expression (words and phrases used) into any AAC device designed for a student of the same age.

2. Develop a simple, low-tech AAC device for a particular student who does not use speech. The device should contain at least four messages with accompanying symbols (pictorial or tactile) and be mounted on some type of display (e.g., book, wallet, CD holder, clipboard, etc.). Bear in mind the student's age, interests/motivations, culture, native language, physical and sensory abilities/limitations, and his or her most pressing needs. Also keep in mind the student's communication partners and what they will need to understand the message.

3. Search the Internet for pictures of AAC devices. Name one or two devices from about three or four different companies. Describe a particular student in need of an AAC device and list the pros and cons of each device researched for this student. The purpose of this activity is to become more aware of available technology and some of the decision making that must occur in the selection of a device for a particular student.

References

Agran, M., & Hughes, C. (2005). Introduction to the special issue on self-determination: How far have we come? *Research and Practice for Persons with Severe Disabilities, 30,* 105–107.

Arthur, M. (2003). Socio-communicative variables and behavior states in students with profound and multiple disabilities: Descriptive data from school settings. *Education and Training in Mental Retardation and Developmental Disabilities, 38,* 200–219.

Bailey, R., Stoner, J., Parette, H., & Angelo, M. (2006). AAC team perceptions: Augmentative and alternative communication device use. *Education and Training in Developmental Disabilities, 41,* 139–154.

Beukelman, D. R., & Mirenda, P. (2005). *Augmentative and alternative communication: Management of severe communication disorders in children and adults.* Baltimore: Paul H. Brookes.

Blackstone, S. W., & Hunt Berg, M. H. (2003). *Social networks: A communication inventory for individuals with complex communication needs and their communication partners.* Monterey, CA: Augcom Communication.

Bloomberg, K., West, D., & Iacono, T. A. (2003). PICTURE IT: An evaluation of a training program for carers of adults with severe multiple disabilities. *Journal of Intellectual and Developmental Disability, 28,* 260–282.

Bondy, A., & Frost, L. (2002). *A picture's worth: PECs and other visual communication strategies in autism.* Bethesda, MD: Woodbine House.

Brady, N. C., & Bashinski, S. M. (2008). Increasing communication in children with concurrent vision and hearing loss. *Research and Practice for Persons with Severe Disabilities, 33,* 59–70.

Carey, A. C., Potts, B. B., Bryen, D. N., & Shankar, J. (2004). Networking towards employment: Experiences of people who use augmentative and alternative communication. *Research and Practice for Persons with Severe Disabilities, 29,* 40-52.

Carter, E. W., Cushing, L. S., & Kennedy, C. H. (2009). *Peer support strategies for improving all students' social lives and learning.* Baltimore: Paul H. Brookes.

Carter, E.W., & Hughes, C. (2005). Increasing social interaction among adolescents with intellectual disabilities and their general education peers: Effective interventions. *Research and Practice for Persons with Severe Disabilities, 30,* 179-193.

Carter, E. W., Hughes, C., Copeland, S. R., & Breen, C. (2001). Differences between high school students who do and do not volunteer to participate in peer interaction programs. *Journal of the Association for Persons with Severe Handicaps, 26,* 229-239.

Carter, E. W., Owens, L., Trainor, A. A., Sun, Y., & Swedeen, B. (2009). Self-determination skills and opportunities of adolescents with severe intellectual and developmental disabilities. *Education and Training in Developmental Disabilities, 114,* 179-192.

Carter, M. (2003). Communicative spontaneity of children with high support needs who use augmentative and alternative communication systems II: Antecedents and effectiveness of communication. *Augmentative and Alternative Communication, 19,* 155-169.

Carter, M., & Iacono, T. (2002). Professional judgments of the intentionality of communicative acts. *Augmentative and Alternative Communication, 18,* 177-191.

Causton-Theoharis, J., Ashby, C., & Cosier, M. (2009). Islands of loneliness: Exploring social interaction through the autobiographies of individuals with autism. *Intellectual and Developmental Disabilities, 47,* 84-96.

Cloninger, C. J. (2004). Designing collaborative educational services. In F. P. Orelove, D. Sobsey, & R. K. Silberman (Eds.), *Educating children with multiple disabilities: A collaborative approach* (pp. 1-30). Baltimore: Paul H. Brookes.

Copeland, S. R., Hughes, C., Carter, E.W., Guth, C., Presley, J., Williams, C. R., et al. (2004). Increasing access to general education: Perspectives of participants in a high school peer support program. *Remedial and Special Education, 26,* 342-352.

Cress, C. J. (2002). Expanding children's early augmented behaviors to support symbolic development. In J. Reichle, D. R. Beukelman, & J. C. Light (Eds.), *Exemplary practices for beginning communicators: Implications for AAC* (pp. 219-272). Baltimore: Paul H. Brookes.

Cress, C. J., & Marvin, C. A. (2003). Common questions about AAC services to early intervention. *Augmentative and Alternative Communication, 19,* 254-272.

Cross, A. F., Traub, E. K., Hutter-Pishgaki, L., & Shelton, G. (2004). Elements of successful inclusion for children with significant disabilities. *Topics in Early Childhood Special Education, 24,* 169-183.

Dennis, R. (2002). Nonverbal narratives: Listening to people with severe intellectual disability. *Research and Practice for Persons with Severe Disabilities, 27,* 239-249.

Downing, J. E. (2005). *Teaching communication skills to students with severe disabilities* (2nd ed.). Baltimore: Paul H. Brookes.

Downing, J. E. (2008). *Including students with severe and multiple disabilities in typical classrooms: Practical strategies for teachers* (3rd ed.). Baltimore: Paul H. Brookes.

Downing, J. E. (2009). Assessment of early communication skills. In G. Soto & C. Zangari (Eds.), *Practically speaking: Language,* *literacy, and academic development for students with AAC needs* (pp. 27-46). Baltimore: Paul H. Brookes.

Durand, V. M., & Merges, E. (2001). Functional communication training: A contemporary behavior analytic intervention for problem behaviors. *Focus on Autism and Other Developmental Disabilities, 16,* 110-119.

Dyches, T.T., Cichella, E., Olsen, S. F., & Mandleco, B. (2004). Snapshots of life: Perspectives of school-aged individuals with developmental disabilities. *Research and Practice for Persons with Severe Disabilities, 29,* 172-182.

Finlay, W. M. L., Antaki, C., & Walton, C. (2007). On not being noticed: Intellectual disabilities and the nonvocal register. *Intellectual and Developmental Disabilities, 45,* 227-245.

Fox, L. (1989). Stimulus generalization of skills and persons with profound mental handicaps. *Education and Training in Mental Retardation, 24,* 219-229.

Halle, J., Brady, N. C., & Drasgow, E. (2004). Enhancing socially adaptive communicative repairs of beginning communicators with disabilities. *American Journal of Speech-Language Pathology, 13,* 43-54.

Hamilton, B., & Snell, M. E. (1993). Using the milieu approach to increase spontaneous communication book use across environments by an adolescent with autism. *Augmentative and Alternative Communication, 9,* 259-272.

Han, K. G., & Chadsey, J. G. (2004). The influence of gender patterns and grade level on friendship expectations of middle school students toward peers with severe disabilities. *Focus on Autism and Other Developmental Disabilities, 19,* 205-214.

Haring, N. G. (Ed.). (1988). *Generalization for students with severe handicaps: Strategies and solutions.* Seattle: University of Washington Press.

Haring, N. G., Liberty, K., Billingsley, F., White, O., Lynch, V., Kayser, J., et al. (1985). *Investigating the problem of skills generalization* (3rd ed.). Seattle: Washington Research Organization, University of Washington.

Hodgdon, L. A. (1995). *Visual strategies for improving communication: Practical supports for school and home.* Troy, MI: QuirkRoberts.

Hunt, P., Doering, K., Maier, J., & Mintz, E. (2009). Strategies to support the development of positive social relationships. In G. Soto & C. Zangari (Eds.), *Practically speaking: Language, literacy, and academic development for students with AAC needs* (pp. 247-264). Baltimore: Paul H. Brookes.

Hunt, P., Farron-Davis, F., Wrenn, M., Hirose-Hatae, A., & Goetz, L. (1997). Promoting interactive partnerships in inclusive educational settings. *Journal of the Association for Persons with Severe Handicaps, 22,* 127-137.

Hunt, P., Soto, G., Maier, J., Muller, E., & Goetz, L. (2002). Collaborative teaming to support students with augmentative and alternative communication needs in general education classrooms. *Augmentative and Alternative Communication, 18,* 20-35.

Hunt Berg, M. (2005). The bridge school: Educational inclusion outcomes over 15 years. *Augmentative and Alternative Communication, 21,* 116-131.

Kaiser, A. P., & Grim, J. C. (2006). Teaching functional communication skills. In M. E. Snell & F. Brown (Eds.), *Instruction of students with severe disabilities* (6th ed., pp. 447-488). Upper Saddle River, NJ: Pearson/Merrill.

Kaiser, A. P., Ostrosky, M. M., & Alpert, C. L. (1993). Training teachers to use environmental arrangement and milieu teaching with nonvocal preschool children. *Journal of the Association for Persons with Severe Handicaps, 18,* 188-199.

Kamps, D., Royer, J., Dugan, E., Kravits, T., Gonzalez-Lopez, A., Garcia, J., et al. (2002). Peer training to facilitate social interactions for elementary students with autism and their peers. *Exceptional Children, 68,* 173-187.

Kent-Walsh, J., & McNaughton, D. (2005). Communication partner instruction in AAC: Present practices and future directions. *Augmentative and Alternative Communication, 21,* 195-204.

Koegel, L. K., Camarata, S. M., Valdez-Menchaca, M., & Koegel, R. L. (1998). Setting generalization of question-asking by children with autism. *American Journal on Mental Retardation, 102,* 346-357.

Light, J. (1988). Interaction involving individuals using augmentative and alternative communication systems: State of the art and future directions. *Augmentative and Alternative Communication, 4,* 66-82.

Light, J. (1997). "Communication is the essence of human life": Reflections on communicative competence. *Augmentative and Alternative Communication, 13,* 61-70.

Light, J. C. (2003). Shattering the silence: Development of communicative competence by individuals who use AAC. In J. C. Light, D. R. Beukelman, & J. Reichle (Eds.), Communicative competence for individuals who use AAC (pp. 3-40). Baltimore: Paul H. Brookes.

Light, J., & Drager, K. (2007). AAC technologies for young children with complex communication needs: State of the science and future research directions. *Augmentative and Alternative Communication, 23,* 204-216.

Lund, S. K., & Light, J. (2006). Long-term outcomes for individuals who use augmentative and alternative communication: Part I— What is a "good" outcome? *Augmentative and Alternative Communication, 22,* 284-299.

Mancil, G. R. (2009). Milieu therapy as a communication intervention: A review of the literature related to children with autism spectrum disorder. *Education and Training in Developmental Disabilities, 44,* 105-117.

McLean, J., & Snyder-McLean, L. (1988). Applications of pragmatics to severely mentally retarded children and youth. In R. L. Schiefelbusch & L. L. Lloyd (Eds.), *Language perspectives: Acquisitions, retardation, and intervention* (pp. 255-288). Austin, TX: PRO-ED.

McNaughton, D., Rackensperger, T., Benedek-Wood, E., Krezman, C., Williams, M. B., & Light, J. (2008). "A child needs to be given a chance to succeed": Parents of individuals who use AAC describe the benefits and challenges of learning AAC technologies. *Augmentative and Alternative Communication, 24,* 43-55.

Meadan, H., Halle, J., Ostrosky, M. M., & DeStafano, L. (2008). Communicative behavior in the natural environment: Case studies of two young children with autism and limited expressive language. *Focus on Autism and Other Developmental Disabilities, 23,* 37-48.

Millar, D., Light, J., & Schlosser, R. (2006). The impact of augmentative and alternative communication intervention on the speech production of individuals with developmental disabilities: A research review. *Journal of Speech, Language, and Hearing Research, 49,* 248-264.

Mirenda, P. (2005). Augmentative and alternative communication techniques. In J. E. Downing, *Teaching communication skills to students with severe disabilities* (2nd ed., pp. 89-112). Baltimore: Paul H. Brookes.

Morrison, L., Kamps, D., Garcia, J., & Parker, D. (2001). Peer mediation and monitoring strategies to improve initiations and social skills for students with autism. *Journal of Positive Behavior Interventions, 3,* 237-250.

National Joint Committee for the Communication Needs of Persons with Severe Disabilities. (1992). Guidelines for meeting the communication needs of persons with severe disabilities. *ASHA, 34*(Suppl. 7), 2-3.

Owen-DeSchryver, J. S., Carr, E. G., Cale, S. I., & Blakeley-Smith, A. (2008). Promoting social interactions between students with autism spectrum disorders and their peers in inclusive school settings. *Focus on Autism and Other Developmental Disabilities, 23,* 15-28.

Porter, J., Ouvry, C., & Downs, C. (2001). Interpreting the communication of people with profound and multiple learning difficulties. *British Journal of Learning Disabilities, 29,* 12-16.

Reeve, C. E., & Carr, E. C. (2000). Prevention of severe behavior problems in children with developmental disorders. *Journal of Positive Behavior Interventions, 2,* 144-160.

Richardson, P. K. (2002). The school as social context: Social interaction patterns of children with physical disabilities. *The American Journal of Occupational Therapy, 56,* 296-304.

Rodi, M. S., & Hughes, C. (2000). Teaching communication book use to a high school student using a milieu approach. *Journal of the Association for Persons with Severe Handicaps, 25,* 175-179.

Ross, B., & Cress, C. J. (2006). Comparison of standardized assessments for cognitive and receptive communication skills in young children with complex communication needs. *Augmentative and Alternative Communication, 22,* 100-111.

Schalock, R. L. (2004). Quality of life: What we know and do not know. *Journal of Intellectual Disability Research, 48,* 203-216.

Schlosser, R. W., & Wendt, O. (2008). Effects of augmentative and alternative production in children with autism: A systematic review. *American Journal of Speech-Language Pathology, 17,* 212-230.

Siegel, E., & Wetherby, A. (2006). Nonsymbolic communication. In M. E. Snell & F. Brown (Eds.), *Instruction of students with severe disabilities* (6th ed., pp. 405-446). Columbus, OH: Pearson/Merrill-Prentice Hall.

Sigafoos, J. (2000). Communication development and aberrant behavior in children with developmental disabilities. *Education and Training in Mental Retardation and Developmental Disabilities, 35,* 168-176.

Sigafoos, J., & Mirenda, P. (2002). Strengthening communicative behaviors for gaining access to desired items and activities. In D. R. Beukelman & J. Reichle [Series Eds.] & J. Reichle, D. R., Beukelman, & J. C. Light (Vol. Eds.), *Augmentative and alternative communication series. Exemplary practices for beginning communicators: Implications for AAC* (pp. 123-156). Baltimore: Paul H. Brookes.

Skotko, B. G., Koppenhaver, D. A., & Erickson, K. A. (2004). Parent reading behaviors and communication outcomes in girls with Rett syndrome. *Exceptional Children, 70,* 145-166.

Snell, M. E. (2002). Using dynamic assessment with learners who communicate nonsymbolically. *Augmentative and Alternative Communication, 18,* 163-176.

Snell, M. E., Caves, K., McLean, L., Mollica, B. M., Mirenda, P., Paul-Brown, D., et al. (2003). Concerns regarding the application of restrictive "eligibility" policies to individuals who need communication services and supports: A response by the National Joint Committee for the Communication Needs of Persons with Severe Disabilities. *Research and Practice for Persons with Severe Disabilities, 28,* 70–78.

Snell, M. E., Chen, L., Allaire, J. H., & Park, E. (2008). Communication breakdown at home and at school in young children with cerebral palsy and severe disabilities. *Research and Practice for Persons with Severe Disabilities, 33,* 25–36.

Snell, M. E., Chen, L., & Hoover, K. (2006). Teaching augmentative and alternative communication to students with severe disabilities: A review of intervention research, 1997–2003. *Research and Practice for Persons with Severe Disabilities, 31,* 203–214.

Suarez, S. C., & Daniels, K. J. (2009). Listening for competence through documentation: Assessing children with language delays using digital video. *Remedial and Special Education, 30,* 177–190.

Sulzer-Azaroff, B., Hoffman, A. D., Horton, C. B., Bondy, A., & Frost, L. (2009). The Picture Exchange Communication System (PECS): What do the data say? *Focus on Autism and Other Developmental Disabilities, 24,* 89–103.

Threats, T. T., & Worrall, L. (2004). Classifying communication disability using the ICF. *Advances in Speech Language Pathology, 6,* 53–62.

Von Tetzchner, S., Brekke, K. M., Sjothun, B., & Grindheim, E. (2005). Constructing preschool communities of learners that afford alternative language development. *Augmentative and Alternative Communication, 21,* 82–100.

Vygotsky, L. (1978). *Mind in society: The development of higher psychological processes.* Cambridge, MA: Cambridge University Press.

Wehmeyer, M. L., & Palmer, S. B. (2003). Adult outcomes for students with cognitive disabilities three years after high school: The impact of self-determination. *Education and Training in Developmental Disabilities, 38,* 131–144.

Weiner, J. S. (2005). Peer-mediated conversational repair in students with moderate and severe disabilities. *Research and Practice for Persons with Severe Disabilities, 30,* 26–37.

West, E. A., & Billingsley, F. (2005). Improving the system of least prompts: A comparison of procedural variations. *Education and Training in Developmental Disabilities, 40,* 131–144.

White, M. T., Garrett, B., Kearns, J. F., & Grisham-Brown, J. (2003). Instruction and assessment: How students with deaf-blindness fare in large-scale alternate assessments. *Research and Practice for Persons with Severe Disabilities, 28,* 205–213.

Wolery, M., Anthony, L., Snyder, E. D., Werts, M. B., & Katzenmeyer, J. (1997). Training elementary teachers to embed instruction during classroom activities. *Education and Treatment of Children, 20,* 40–58.

Yoder, P. J., & Warren, S. F. (2002). Effects of prelinguistic milieu teaching and parent responsivity on dyads involving children with intellectual disabilities. *Journal of Speech, Language, and Hearing Research, 45,* 1158–1174.

Resources

Books on Communication for Students with Severe Disabilities

Beukelman, D. R., & Mirenda, P. (2005). *Augmentative and alternative communication* (3rd ed.). Baltimore: Paul H. Brookes.

Carter, E. W., Cushing, L. S., & Kennedy, C. H. (2009). *Peer support strategies for improving all students' social lives and learning.* Baltimore: Paul H. Brookes.

Downing, J. E. (2005). *Teaching communication skills to students with severe disabilities* (2nd ed.). Baltimore: Paul H. Brookes.

Hodgdon, L. A. (1995). *Visual strategies for improving communication. Vol. 1: Practical supports for school and home.* Troy, MI: QuirkRoberts.

Hughes, C., & Carter, E. W. (2008). *Peer buddy programs for successful secondary school inclusion.* Baltimore: Paul H. Brookes.

Koegel, R. L., & Koegel, L. K. (2006). *Pivotal response treatments for autism: Communication, social, and academic development.* Baltimore: Paul H. Brookes.

Light, J. C., Beukelman, D. R., & Reichle, J. (2003). *Communicative competence for individuals who use AAC: From research to effective practice.* Baltimore: Paul H. Brookes.

Quill, K. A. (2000). *Do-watch-listen-say: Social and communication intervention for children with autism.* Baltimore: Paul H. Brookes.

Roberts, J. E., Chapman, R. S., & Warren, S. F. (2008). *Speech and language development and intervention in Down syndrome and fragile X syndrome.* Baltimore: Paul H. Brookes.

Sigafoos, J., Arthur-Kelly, M., & Butterfield, N. (2006). *Enhancing everyday communication for children with disabilities.* Baltimore: Paul H. Brookes.

Soto, G., & Zangari, C. (2009). *Practically speaking: Language, literacy, and academic development for students with AAC needs.* Baltimore: Paul H. Brookes.

Augmentative and Alternative Communication Manufacturers

AbleNet, Inc.	http://www.ablenetinc.com
Attainment Company	http://www.attainmentcompany.com
Augmentative Resources	http://www.augresources.com, 1-877-471-1863
Communication Devices, Inc.	http://www.commdevices.com
Creative Communicating	http://www.creativecommunicating.com
Crestwood Communication Aids, Inc.	http://www.communicationaids.com
DynaVox™ and Mayer-Johnson	http://www.dynavoxtech.com
Enabling Devices	http://www.enablingdevices.com
PRC	http://www.prentrom.com, 1-800-262-1984
Words+	http://www.words-plus.com, 1-800-869-8521
ZYGO Industries, Inc.	http://www.zygo-usa.com, 1-800-234-6006

13

Teaching Academic Skills

John McDonnell
Susan R. Copeland

The acquisition of academic skills is a significant predictor of the employment, citizenship, and community living outcomes achieved by students with disabilities following school (Benz, Lindstrom, Yovanoff, 2000; Phelps & Hanley-Maxwell, 1997). Although ecological curriculum models for students with severe disabilities have historically recognized the importance of including academic skills as part of a student's educational program, they typically have emphasized the development of functional academic skills that have an immediate impact on a student's ability to participate successfully in home, school, and community settings (Browder, 2001a; Ford et al., 1989; Neel & Billingsley, 1989; Wilcox & Bellamy, 1987). By definition, a student's *ecological curriculum* includes life skills that are specifically referenced to the student's home, neighborhood, and community and may also involve employment and leisure activities readily available to that student. Examples of functional academic skills that often overlap with a student's ecological curriculum include learning to count money to pay for purchases in stores or reading the sight words necessary to ride the bus. Recently, the No Child Left Behind (NCLB) Act of 2001 and subsequent amend-

ments to the Individuals with Disabilities Education Improvement Act (IDEA) placed increased emphasis on the participation of students with severe disabilities in the general education curriculum, specifically in the areas of reading, math, and science. One of the challenges that currently face students, parents, and teachers is how to balance the need for students to learn academic content from both the general education curriculum and the ecological curriculum (see Chapters 3 and 6).

In this chapter, we briefly discuss the implications of current federal statutes for teaching academic skills to students with severe disabilities. Next, we will provide several guidelines that teachers can use to select appropriate academic skills for instruction. Finally, we describe specific strategies for teaching reading, math, and science skills to students.

Before we begin, we'd like to introduce you to Marcus and Jacob. Their specific circumstances illustrate the wide range of academic skills that students with severe disabilities may need to learn. In addition, they highlight the various instructional approaches that teachers may use to provide effective instruction on academic skills to students.

❖ ❖ ❖ ❖ ❖   **Marcus**   ❖ ❖ ❖ ❖ ❖

Marcus is a third-grade student in Mr. Garcia's general education class. Marcus has intellectual disabilities and requires extensive supports in order to participate in home,

school, and community settings. He wears glasses that provide him with normal vision. His hearing is also within normal limits. Marcus communicates using speech, but his articulation problems make it difficult for new communication partners to understand everything that he says. Marcus receives most of his special education support within Mr. Garcia's classroom, but is pulled out for one period a day for extra work on literacy skills with Ms. Carter, a special education teacher. He also receives speech and occupational therapy services on a weekly basis, usually within his general education classroom. Mr. Garcia and Ms. Carter regularly meet to plan how to adapt and modify instructional activities to meet Marcus's learning needs and also to enlist the help of his speech and occupational therapists in order to design instruction that allows him to acquire key content information, but in a manner that aligns with his learning needs. Because Marcus's reading skills are at an emergent stage, he does best in learning academic content when instruction involves hands-on learning activities, individualized visual supports, and peers to model and explain activities. He has a small but developing sight word vocabulary and is just beginning to use addition and subtraction in math. He needs many individualized modifications to the way that he receives content and the way in which he demonstrates learning, but with these in place, is acquiring some of the "big ideas" in the general curriculum. He especially loves working with peers in small cooperative learning groups and has developed some social and academic skills through these activities. For example, last week, the teachers selected the "big idea" from the upcoming science unit that they want Marcus to learn. They developed a hands-on small-group activity that allowed all of the students to discover some basic principles related to flotation. Marcus had a peer support within his group who helped him complete the steps of the activity for which he was responsible. When the group completed their lab log, another peer gave Marcus two choices for his assigned question (with pictures as visual supports) and asked him to select the choice that he thought was correct.

❖ ❖ ❖ ❖ ❖   **Jacob**   ❖ ❖ ❖ ❖ ❖

Jacob is a junior at Canyon High School; he has autism. His school is on an "A/B" block schedule. He has several classes on one day and has different classes on the next day. Jacob is enrolled in a number of general education classes, including theater design and construction, computer technology, adult roles and financial literacy, and foods and nutrition. In the remaining periods, he receives support from his special education teacher Mr. Karst and Ms. Jackson, Mr. Karst's paraeducator, to learn personal management activities like shopping for groceries and leisure activities like ice skating at the community recreation center. He also has a work-experience position at Smith's Food Center as a bagger. Jacob is able to participate in conversations with teachers and peers, but sometimes he perseverates on a topic and needs to be prompted to change the subject. He is able to read and understand simple stories, use the newspaper to get information about upcoming events, and access and use the Internet with some support. Jacob is able to add and subtract with a calculator and he can reliably count bill and coin combinations (10s, 5s, and 1s). However, he has difficulty understanding if he has enough money in order to buy something that he wants, as well as developing a plan to save money for something that he wants.

The Impetus for Teaching Academic Skills

The current emphasis on teaching academic content has been prompted by two movements: the expansion of inclusive education programs for students with severe disabilities and the standards-based reform of curriculum and assessment for all students (Hunt & McDonnell, 2007; McGregor, 2003). These movements have led to vigorous discussions in the field of severe disabilities about how to best utilize the general education curriculum and ecological curriculum in order to select academic content for students.

Inclusive Education

The number of students with severe disabilities being served in their neighborhood schools and in general education classes has steadily increased over the last decade (U.S. Department of Education, 2006). This has been driven by (a) strong advocacy efforts focused on achieving equal access and opportunity for students to participate in regular education classes (Lipsky & Gartner, 1997), and (b) research that supports the positive education and social benefits of inclusive education (Hunt & McDonnell, 2007).

While the initial focus of inclusion was on promoting social acceptance and increasing interactions between peers with and without disabilities, practitioners and researchers soon realized that these goals could not be achieved simply by placing students in general education classrooms. Achieving the full inclusion of students required that they actively participate in the instruction activities of the class (Giangreco, Dennis, Cloninger, Edelman, & Schattman, 1993). This logically led to efforts to validate instructional approaches and strategies that would allow students not only to learn functional academic skills, but also to access the content of the general education curriculum.

Standards-Based Reform

Another significant impetus for providing instruction on academic skills to students comes from the standards-based reform movement, which began in the 1990s (McGregor, 2003). A series of federal laws, culminating with the NCLB Act, required states to develop comprehensive academic content standards and academic achievement standards in the areas of reading, math, and science (U.S. Department of Education, December 21, 2007). Academic content standards ". . . specify what all students are expected to know and be able to do; contain coherent and rigorous content; and encourage the teaching of advanced skills" (U.S. Department of Education, December 21, 2007, p. 2). Academic achievement standards ". . . must include at least two levels of achievement (proficient and advanced) that reflect mastery of the material in the State's academic content standards, and a third level of achievement (basic) to provide information about the progress of lower-achieving students toward mastering the proficient and advanced levels of achievement" (U.S. Department of Education, 2007, pp. 2–3). Achievement standards provide the basis for the development of states' assessment systems and the systems must specify the "cut-off scores" that students must obtain at each level of proficiency. In addition, the states' assessments must be designed so that they allow for the determination of students' adequate yearly progress (AYP) toward achieving the academic achievement standards.

IDEA 2004 reinforces the NCLB Act mandates on curriculum and assessment by requiring individualized education plan (IEP) teams to address how students will participate and progress in the general education curriculum, regardless of their level of disability. In addition, it requires that students with disabilities participate in the state's assessment system, or an alternate assessment, that documents students' AYPs toward meeting the state's academic achievement standards.

All states have developed and begun implementing alternate assessments for students with significant cognitive disabilities. Regulations require that these assessments be aligned with the state's content standards but establish a different set of expectations for students. The content of the alternate assessments must be ". . . clearly related to grade-level content, although it may be restricted in scope or complexity or take the form of introductory or pre-requisite skills" (U.S. Department of Education, 2005, p. 26). This is accomplished by ". . . adapting or 'extending' those content standards to reflect instructional activities appropriate for this group of students" (U.S. Department of Education, p. 26).

Research suggests that states are struggling to achieve significant alignment among academic content standards, adapted or extended content standards, and alternate achievement standards (Browder et al., 2004; Flowers, Browder, & Ahlgrim-Delzell, 2006; Kohl, McLaughlin, & Nagle, 2006) (see Chapter 3). One significant barrier to achieving this alignment is that less than half of the states have developed alternate assessments that contain standardized assessment items to evaluate student progress in meeting academic content standards (National Center on Educational Outcomes, n.d.; Quenemoen, 2008). In most states, it is left to IEP teams to (a) identify the academic content standards in the general curriculum that students will be held accountable for, (b) adapt or extend those academic content standards so that they are appropriate for the student, and (c) develop alternate achievement standards that are consistent with state alternate assessment guidelines for determining whether the student has mastered the content.

This situation necessitates that IEP teams adopt planning procedures that will allow them to identify appropriate academic skills for students' IEPs that are aligned with their states' academic content standards (e.g., Browder et al., 2007). However, IEP teams also need to ensure that the skills selected for instruction allow students to participate successfully in home, school, and community settings (Bambara, Wilson, & McKenzie, 2007). The next section outlines some of the guidelines that members of the IEP team should take into account when selecting academic content for instruction and strategies that teams can use to develop academic IEP goals and objectives.

Selecting Academic Skills for Instruction

General Guidelines

A number of authors have argued that the expectations of parents, teachers, and administrators about the potential for students with severe disabilities to learn academic content have historically been low (Browder, Ahlgrim-Delzell, Courtade-Little, & Snell, 2006; Joseph & Seery, 2004; Katims, 2000a). In contrast, a growing body of research suggests that many students have the capacity to learn these skills when they are provided with systematic instruction and support (Browder & Spooner, 2006; Harrower, 1999; McDonnell, 1998). IEP teams should not make assumptions about the capacity of students to learn academic content based on their classification or assessed level of cognitive ability. For example, in the area of reading, the student's classification and cognitive scores have less impact on that student's ability to learn sound–symbol relationships than do a student's short-term memory, modes of communication, and personal experience (Connors, Atwell, Rosenquist, & Sligh, 2001; Katims, 2000a; Olson, Forsberg, & Wise, 1994). IEP teams should instead consider several more practical guidelines in developing appropriate academic goals and objectives for a student:

- *Select academic goals and objectives that build on a student's present level of performance in using symbols.* A critical factor in selecting academic goals and objectives for a student is how he or she will demonstrate mastery of the skill or concept being taught. Browder and her colleagues have suggested that there are three levels of symbol used, including presymbolic, concrete symbolic, and abstract symbolic (Browder, Ahlgrim-Delzell, Courtade-Little, & Snell, 2006; Browder et al., 2007). Students at the presymbolic level use objects or gestures to communicate knowledge and understanding; those at the concrete symbolic level use symbols such as pictures, logos, and drawings; and students at the abstract symbolic level use symbols such as letters, words, numbers, and mathematical function signs to demonstrate mastery of skills and concepts. In considering the student's symbol use, the IEP team may develop goals and objectives that focus on (a) the student's current level of symbol use in instructional or daily living activities (e.g., using pictures to demonstrate understanding of content in history

and science class, to locate items in the grocery store, or to monitor completion of job tasks at work); (b) expanding his or her use of symbols (e.g., learning to use new pictures in an instructional or daily living activity, or learning to apply known pictures in new instructional or daily living activities); and/or (c) teaching the student to use more complex symbols (e.g., identifying written vocabulary words in science or history, using a sight word list to locate items in the grocery store, and monitoring completion of job tasks at work). Thus, the way that the student uses symbols will impact how the IEP team aligns IEP goals and objectives with the state's academic content and achievement standards, and the strategies that the students will use to complete routines and activities in the home, school and community settings.

- *Align content with the student's ability to perform successfully in current environments.* The academic content selected for instruction should contribute to students' current quality of life and personal autonomy. This requires that the IEP team conduct an ecological inventory and then consider the potential applications of academic skills in the environments in which students are expected to perform on a day-to-day basis. Research suggests that many students will have difficulty generalizing the skills learned in school settings to typical performance settings without explicit instruction (Horner, McDonnell, & Bellamy, 1986; Rosenthal-Malek & Bloom, 1998). Consequently, goals and objectives should not only focus on the acquisition of academic skills, but also on the student's use of those skills in the routines and activities that the team regards as being a high priority. For example, a student might be taught to play a board game like *Trouble* with peers after learning to rational count ordered and unordered objects.

- *Align content with the student's long-term postschool goals.* While teachers are required under current federal law to select academic content that aligns with academic content standards, it is equally important to ensure that the skills selected for instruction contribute to the student achieving his or her long-term, postschool goals (Bambara et al., 2007). IEP teams need to carefully consider the information obtained from ecological inventories and/or ecological curriculum guides and evaluate how the academic skills selected as IEP goals and objectives will enhance the student's ability to work and live successfully in the community after the school years are over. This is especially important for high school and post–high school students who are transitioning from school to community life. For example, the skill of computing addition and subtraction programs using a calculator could contribute to a student achieving a number of employment, daily living, or leisure outcomes.

- *Select academic content that is suited to the student's chronological age.* The academic content selected for instruction should reflect the student's chronological age and grade level. Federal regulations require that the IEP team show how he or she will participate and progress in grade-level academic content standards that match his or her chronological age. When academic skills are selected from ecological inventories and/or ecological curriculum guides, the IEP team should ensure that the skills targeted for instruction will contribute to the student's performance of age-appropriate routines and activities.

- *Select academic content that has the potential to enhance inclusion in school and community settings.* Finally, the IEP team should consider whether academic content selected for instruction will increase the student's participation in the routines and activities of general education classes and the school. For example, learning to identify numbers could enhance a student's ability to eat lunch with his peers by allowing him or her to input a lunch code in the cafeteria. The same skill could help the student learn to use an automated teller machine (ATM) to get the money necessary to go to a movie with a friend.

Strategies for Developing Academic IEP Goals and Objectives

Achieving the intended outcomes for students who are participating and progressing in the general education curriculum requires that IEP teams ensure that there is a match among the state academic content standards targeted for the student, the adapted or extended academic content standards developed for the student, the alternate achievement standards identified to determine if the student is progressing toward proficiency on the adapted or extended academic content standards, and the instruction that the student receives (Flowers, Browder, Ahlgrim-Delzell, & Spooner, 2006). The most logical approach for achieving this align-

ment involves two steps: (a) using the IEP process to identify goals and objectives that are linked to the state's academic content standards and are structured to document a student's continuous progress toward mastering the content, and (b) developing IEP goals and objectives that are focused on learning academic content that is not aligned to the academic content standards but nonetheless are necessary for the student to perform successfully in home, school, and community settings. Meeting both of these needs requires that IEP teams use a comprehensive approach for developing IEP goals and objectives that target academic content.

Three general strategies have been described in the literature for developing academic IEP goals and objectives for students. These include (a) the standard-based approach that adapts or extends the state's academic content standards to accommodate a student's needs and symbol use (Browder et al., 2007; Flowers et al., 2006); (b) the standards-referenced approach that seeks to link the skills selected from ecological inventories and/or ecological curriculum guides with the state's academic content standards (Clayton, Burdge, & Kleinert; 2001; McGregor, 2003; Ward, Van De Mark, & Ryndak, 2006); and (c) the functional approach that selects skills from ecological inventories and/or ecological curriculum guides that will directly improve the student's ability to complete routines and activities in home, school, and community settings (Browder, 2001; McDonnell & Hardman, 2010). The decision facing IEP teams is which strategy, or combination of strategies, they will use to identify appropriate academic content for students and develop IEP goal and objectives that can guide the instruction provided to students during the school year.

The Standards-Based Approach

Several procedures have been proposed for assisting IEP teams to adapt or extend a state's academic content standards so that they accommodate a student's learning needs and symbol use (Browder et al., 2006; Kleinert & Thurlow, 2001; McGregor, 2003). Browder et al. (2006) suggests that the first step is to ask the general education teacher to identify the academic content standards that he or she would like all students in the class to master. For example, in a third-grade Language Arts curriculum, a general education teacher might identify the following standard—*Students understand, interpret, and analyze narrative and informational grade level text* (Utah State Office of Education, May 9,

2003)—as a priority standard for all students. Once these priority standards have been identified, the second step is to identify specific benchmarks or objectives that support priority learning outcomes for the student within the content standard. Continuing with our example, a priority objective or benchmark for a student within this standard might be *Applies strategies to comprehend text.* Next, the team identifies the indicators that describe how students demonstrate proficient levels of performance of the objective or benchmark. In our example, these indicators include statements like *Relate prior knowledge to make connections to text (e.g., text to text, text to self, text to world), generate questions about text (e.g., factual, inferential, evaluative), or make inferences and draw conclusions from text.*

In the final step, the IEP team adapts or extends the learning outcomes that are described by the standard, objectives/benchmarks, and indicators so that they match the student's needs and ability to use symbols (i.e., presymbolic, concrete symbolic, abstract symbolic) (Browder et al., 2007; Kleinert & Thurlow, 2001). For example, the expected learning outcomes of the indicator *Makes inferences and draws conclusions from text* might be restated for a student with severe disabilities as *Uses symbols/logos/words to predict what should or could happen next.* The team then uses the adaptation or extension of the standard to identify alternate ways that a student might demonstrate proficiency. So instead of reading a text passage and answering written questions that require the student to predict what the main character will do next, the team might identify an alternate achievement standard that matches the student's ability to use symbols such as *After listening to a story passage, the student uses pictures to predict what the main character will do next.* The adapted or extended academic content standard and the alternate achievement standard provide the basis for the development of IEP goals and objectives that can guide instruction for the student.

The Standards-Referenced Approach

A second strategy for developing goals and objectives that are aligned with state academic content standards is to identify priority skills based on ecological inventories and/or ecological curriculum guides (Browder, 2001; Ford et al., 1989; Giangreco, Cloninger, & Iverson, 1998; Neel & Billingsley, 1989; Wilcox & Bellamy, 1987) and then to identify appropriate grade-level academic content standards that match the critical functions of

the targeted skills (Clayton et al., 2001; McGregor, 2003; Ward et al., 2006). For example, a third-grade student's IEP team may have agreed to target the communication skills of *Makes requests* and *Follows instructions* as IEP goals after completing the Choosing Outcomes and Accommodations for Children (COACH) guide (Giangreco et al., 1998). The next step would be for the IEP team to link these skills to the third-grade academic content standards in reading, math, or science. For example, after reviewing the state's academic content standards, the team determined that the skills of *Makes requests* and *Follows directions* could logically be aligned to the state's third-grade reading/language arts standard *Students develop language for the purpose of effectively communicating through listening, speaking, viewing, and presenting* (Utah State Office of Education, May 9, 2003) and, more specifically, with the objective/benchmark *Develop language through listening and speaking.* Finally, the team agreed that the skill *Makes requests* could be aligned with the indicator *Speak clearly and audibly*, and the skill *Follows instructions* could be aligned with the indicator *Listen and demonstrate understanding by responding appropriately.* The team then develops IEP goals and objectives that are referenced to the standard, objective/benchmark, and indicators.

The Functional Approach

It is important to remember that not all academic skills taught to a student must be based on or aligned with the state's academic content standards. Frequently, it will be appropriate for teams to develop additional academic IEP goals and objectives that are specifically designed to improve a student's performance in home, school, and community settings. With this strategy, the IEP team would use ecological inventories and/or ecological curriculum guides to identify priority routines and activities for the student and the academic skills necessary for them to successfully complete them (Browder, 2001; Ford et al., 1989; Giangreco et al., 1998; Neel & Billingsley, 1989; Wilcox & Bellamy, 1987). Frequently, these academic skills will take the form of alternate performance strategies instead of the skills included in the state academic content standards. Alternate performance strategies are designed to simplify the cognitive, language, physical, or academic demands of routines and activities so that individuals who do not have these skills still can complete critical personal management, leisure, community, and work routines and activities. For example, an individual who cannot read could use pictures to locate items in the grocery store, or someone who cannot count money could take a large bill (e.g., $20 bill) to the store to pay for his or her purchases. With this approach, IEP goals and objectives are focused on the specific academic skills or alternate performance strategies that the student would need to learn to complete priority routines and activities.

Determining the Instructional Approach

Once students' IEP goals and objectives have been developed, the next important decision that faces teachers is selecting the instructional approach, or combination of approaches, that will be used to teach academic skills to students. Several options are available: (a) teaching academics within the typical instructional routines and activities, (b) teaching academics in parallel instructional activities, or (c) teaching academics in community-based activities.

Teaching Within Typical Instructional Routines and Activities

Recent research has validated a number of strategies for teaching academic skills within the typical instructional routines and activities of general education classes (Hunt & McDonnell, 2007). Some of the most promising strategies include universal design (Dymond et al., 2006), cooperative learning (Hunt, Staub, Alwell, & Goetz, 1994), curriculum accommodations and modifications (Janney & Snell, 2000), peer-mediated instruction (Carter & Kennedy, 2006), student-directed learning (Wehmeyer & Agran, 2006), and embedded instruction (McDonnell, Johnson, & McQuivey, 2008). Together, these strategies provide the basis for an empirically validated instructional technology that can support instruction on academic skills in general education classes (See Chapter 4 for additional discussion of these strategies).

As part of his Foods and Nutrition class, Jacob is learning about the food pyramid and dietary guidelines published by the U.S. Department of Agriculture. His IEP team decided that it was important for him to learn to read the key words from the nutrition facts panel on the back of packages (e.g., total fat, carbohydrates, sodium, sugars) and state the recommended daily allowance for each item so that he can make good decisions about the products that he buys at the store. To give Jacob enough practice in order to

learn this content, Mr. Karst developed an embedded instruction program that included constant time-delay, reinforcement, and error correction procedures, and a data collection form. Mr. Karst then trained Carrie, a peer who sits beside Jacob in class, to implement the program. Mr. Karst developed three sets of flash cards that contain three of the words from the nutrition facts label. Jacob was asked to read the word and then state the recommended number of grams of each item that should be consumed daily. Mr. Karst asked Carrie to present each word set to Jacob two times during the class period at times that would not interfere with the ongoing activities of the class.

Teaching Academics in Parallel Instructional Activities

It is often possible to focus instruction for students with severe disabilities on the same learning outcomes within the same learning activities as their peers. However, sometimes students may need instruction on functional academic skills that only partially align with the objectives of the instruction for students without disabilities or they may need instruction on skills that are completely different from those of their peers. For example, students may need to receive instruction in the same curriculum domain but on different skills. A student might be taught to match times on a clock face to the specific times on their daily schedule during math class while his or her peers are learning to tell time to the minute. This has been referred to as *multilevel curriculum and instruction* (Giangreco & Putnam, 1991). Another possibility is that students will need instruction on skills in other domains within the general education curriculum or skills selected from an ecological curriculum that are unique to the student's specific needs. For instance, during a shared reading activity that is focused on improving a student's oral reading, instruction for a student with severe disabilities might focus on learning communication skills such as labeling objects presented in the book's pictures or fine motor skills like learning to use a pincer grasp to turn the pages of the book. This is referred to as *curriculum overlapping* (Giangreco & Putnam). In addition to the strategies discussed above, teachers can also use one-to-one instruction, small-group instruction, and computer-based instruction to teach students skills that are specific to their educational needs (see Chapters 1 and 6).

Teaching Academics in Community-Based Activities

Another approach for teaching academic skills to high school and post–high school age students is to embed instruction on these skills in community-based learning activities. Studies have shown that embedding instruction of academic content within community-based instruction improves students' performance of skills such as reading community signs (Cuvo & Klatt, 1992; Schloss et al., 1995, using photographic grocery lists to locate items within stores (McDonnell & Horner, 1985), reading prices, selecting coins for use in vending machines (Browder, Snell, & Wildonger, 1988; Sprague & Horner, 1984), using the next-dollar strategy in stores and restaurants (McDonnell & Ferguson, 1988), and identifying numerals on an ATM (McDonnell & Ferguson, 1989).

> One of Jacob's IEP goals is to purchase healthy food items at the two grocery stores located in his neighborhood. Jacob goes to each grocery store once a week for instruction. Part of Jacob's instructional program is designed to teach him to identify the nutritional words on the labels of different brands and compare the products on the basis of their nutritional value. For example, if Jacob's list includes strawberry yogurt, he would be asked to find two different brands (e.g., Yoplait® and Kroger), find the word Sugars on each label, and identify the brand that has the least amount of sugar.

In addition to the absence of typical peers, one of the problems associated with only providing instruction in community-based settings is the limited number of instructional trials that are naturally available to students in order to learn a skill involved in completing an activity (McDonnell, 2010). For example, when a student is learning to purchase groceries, he or she will only have one natural opportunity during the session to pay for items. For most students, this will not be a sufficient number of instructional trials to result in efficient learning. One solution is to pair school-based instruction, either traditional table-top teaching formats or computer-based video instruction, with instruction in actual performance settings (Branham, Collins, Schuster, & Kleinert, 1999). Although we do not know the best way to pair school-based and community-based instruction, the small number of studies that have been completed to date suggest that pairing school-based instruction with community-based instruction on the same day produces better generalization than other strategies, such as

alternating school-based instruction and community-based instruction over successive days (Cihak, Alberto, Kessler, & Taber, 2004; Nietupski, Hamre-Nietupski, Clancy, & Veerhusen, 1985).

Literacy Instruction

Definition of Literacy

The increased emphasis placed on the participation of students with severe disabilities in the general education curriculum has spurred a national discussion of what constitutes literacy for this group of students (Browder, Wakeman, Spooner, Ahlgrim-Delzell, & Algozzine, 2006). Historically, literacy has been defined as conventional reading and writing. There is a growing consensus in the field of severe disabilities that *literacy* should be defined much more broadly to focus on obtaining meaning from printed materials, symbol systems, and other media (e.g., Alberto, Fredrick, Hughes, McIntosh, & Cihak, 2007; de Valenzuela & Tracey, 2007). There is also increasing recognition that literacy learning can continue over the life span rather than stopping after elementary school if a student has not become a conventional reader and writer (Morgan, Moni, & Jobling, 2004; Ryndak, Morrison, & Sommerstien, 1999).

Because individuals with severe disabilities may vary widely in their skill levels, it is important to also think broadly about the types of literacy instruction provided to them. One way to consider instruction is to think in terms of emergent literacy instruction, functional literacy instruction, and conventional early reading/writing instruction. It is also essential to think comprehensively when designing literacy instruction for these students. The components of a comprehensive literacy program include speaking (expressive communication), listening, reading (deriving meaning from print or graphics), and writing (communicating a message using print or some other form of written communication).

Teaching Emergent Literacy Skills

Emergent literacy includes children's reading and writing skills that will develop into conventional literacy (Sulzby, 1989). Emergent literacy learners have not yet acquired full understanding of written language but are developing the foundational skills on which conventional reading and writing skills will develop. Children's early literacy experiences have a considerable effect on their later literacy skill development (Whitehurst & Lonigan, 1998). All children, including those with and without disabilities, acquire understanding about written language by being surrounded by print, read to by adults, and having numerous opportunities to engage with print, such as by reading books and practicing writing using a variety of materials (Katims, 1994; Weikle & Hadadian, 2004). Many students with moderate or severe disabilities don't have the same early literacy experiences as their typically developing peers. This may be a result of various factors, such as parents placing literacy as a lower priority than development of other skills that they view as critical, or because of a lack of time or resources (Marvin, 1994; Weikle & Hadadian, 2004). Additionally, students may have cognitive, sensory, or physical issues that impede their development of literacy skills. The result is that they may not develop the emergent literacy skills that we would expect of typically developing young children, or we may see students in this phase of literacy development who are much older than we would typically expect (Browder, Trela, & Jimenez, 2007). Emergent literacy instructional practices are very useful in skill development for learners in this stage of literacy learning and can be adapted for older learners to ensure that the materials and methods are age appropriate.

Emergent Literacy Instructional Practices

Providing a literacy-rich environment is one way that children acquire a basic understanding of print (written language) and how it relates to oral language (Katims, 1994; Kuby, Goodstadt-Killoran, Aldridge, & Kirkland, 1999). A literacy-rich environment contains text, pictures, and graphics that are meaningful to the students in that setting. The teacher provides frequent opportunities for the students to communicate with peers and adults, interact with books and other engaging printed materials individually and in group play, listen and respond to stories adults read aloud to them, and experiment with writing and drawing about authentic topics that are related to their lives (Katims, 1994; Miranda, 2003; Neuman, 2004). These activities provide students with meaningful and sustained interactions with authentic literacy tasks and with others who are "literate models" (Kluth & Chandler-Olcott, 2008, p. 49). An important characteristic of these activities is that they actively engage the student and are drawn from students' own experiences.

Read alouds (sometimes called *shared reading* or *story-based lessons*) are a literacy practice in which an adult reads to one or more students; this may include reading a familiar story (*rereadings*). Students are often encouraged to retell the story or interact in other ways with the story during or after the read aloud. Read alouds are one way that emergent literacy learners can have access to quality literature and learn early literacy skills, such as acquiring concepts about print and developing deeper understandings of the way in which print maps spoken language. Read alouds came from reading instruction for typically developing children, but have been successfully adapted by researchers so that students with severe disabilities can participate and acquire emergent literacy skills (e.g., Browder, Mims, Spooner, Ahlgrim-Delzell, & Lee, 2009; Browder et al., 2007). Students can encounter interesting concepts and hear rich language through the use of read alouds.

Katims (2000b) suggested a variation of read alouds for both young children and older learners that is based on wordless books. The story in wordless books is represented almost entirely with pictures, making it ideal for use with learners with severe disabilities. Activities with wordless books develop (a) a knowledge of concepts about print, such as text features and meaning making from text and pictures; (b) vocabulary and expressive language skills; (c) listening comprehension skills, such as an understanding of narrative and story details, developing the ability to visualize, enhancing sequencing and prediction skills, and facilitating monitoring of understanding; (d) content knowledge (e.g., learning about the slave trade by reading *Middle Passage: White Ships, Black Cargo*, Feelings, 1995); and (e) writing skills (the ability to compose a message or story) (Katims, 2000; van Kraayenoord & Paris, 1996). Although many wordless books have been written for young children, there are books available that are more appropriate for adolescents or adults. Additionally, with digital formats, it is easy to create interesting and age-appropriate sequences of pictures taken of students during classroom or community-based instruction or pulled from the Internet. (Box 13–1 describes ways to use wordless books and provides resources.)

Teaching Functional Literacy Skills

Functional literacy is the ability to acquire information through varied modes, including words, symbols, and photographs, that can then be used to enhance participation in everyday activities (Alberto et al., 2007). Sight word instruction, the method most often used to teach

Box 13–1 Example of How to Create Wordless Book Activities, Including Resources for Wordless Books

Wordless Picture Book Activity

(Adapted from Katims, 2000b)

1. Select a wordless picture book that is appropriate for the group of students and the focus of the literacy lesson (e.g., the storybook called *Tuesday* (1991) to focus on prediction).
2. Work with the students in order to create a narrative (a story line) for the book. Begin by modeling this for several pages, stopping to ask the students questions or give prompts such as "What do you think happens next?"; "And then . . ." (allowing the students to fill in the blank); "When suddenly . . ."; "Finally . . .".
3. Write the students' suggestions on Post-it® notes and place these on each page, thereby keeping a record of the story that they create. Later, write the story on chart paper and have the students use this text for further word study (e.g., some students can identify letters, others words, others read the sentences). Students can type the handwritten text using computers and publish their stories.
4. Look for *teachable moments* during the activity in order to stop and discuss new concepts and vocabulary, and brainstorm *describing* or *action* words.
5. After students have become familiar with the process of "reading" wordless books, they can work in mixed-ability cooperative learning groups with other wordless books to create a story line. This is especially effective in inclusive classrooms where groups can include students with a range of literacy skill levels.

Follow-Up Activities

- Let the students "read" their favorite wordless books to a partner or to a younger child.
- Students might also want to create their own wordless book using the structure of the original text. For example, after reading and working with *Tuesday*, students might use the final drawing in the book as a springboard to create a book called *Next Tuesday*, featuring flying pigs.
- Plan an activity in which small groups of students use a camera to take pictures and create their own picture books. Publish these and put them in the classroom library for children to read during Silent Sustained Reading (SSR).
- Work with the speech-language pathologists to develop topics for books and related activities that will facilitate students' language skills.

Resources for Wordless Books:

- Web site shows examples of stories that children created after reading *Mysteries of Harris Burdick* (Van Allsburg, 1984). Also gives teachers ideas for using the book to develop students' writing skills. See http://www.houghtonmifflinbooks.com/features/harrisburdick
- Creative Writing Through Wordless Picture Books. See http://www.readwritethink.org/lessons/lesson_view.asp?id=130

functional literacy skills, involves directly teaching the association between the word (or symbol) and the item or idea that it represents. Sight words are not limited to functional words or symbols. All beginning readers (with and without disabilities) receive instruction in sight word recognition (Gunning, 2002). This is because the English language contains numerous high-frequency words with irregular spellings that are easier for beginning readers to learn through memorization than by trying to apply their decoding skills. Building a strong sight word vocabulary is critical for many students with severe disabilities because many of them will not acquire sufficient skills to make decoding a practical strategy for identifying words. It is also important to point out that building an initial sight word vocabulary can form the foundation on which more complex skills can be built. Some students who begin formal literacy instruction by learning functional sight words may be able to build on those skills and learn phonics skills that will expand their reading abilities.

Selecting Words for Instruction

Selecting words for instruction is the first important step in teaching sight words. This is a particularly critical decision when teaching students with the most severe disabilities. If a student is likely to master only a limited number of words or symbols, teachers must select these instructional targets with care so that the student learns the words that are most meaningful and useful to them. Thus, the words chosen will relate to the student's daily routines, academic activities, and preferences. For other students who are developing more conventional reading and writing skills, it may be helpful to select high-frequency words that will facilitate reading textbooks, stories, newspapers, and so on (e.g., the Dolch words, which are a list of the most frequently encountered words in all kinds of reading materials [Johns, Edmond, & Mavrogenes, 1977]).

An ecological approach to selecting words or symbols for instruction is helpful (Browder, 2001). Teachers choose words that would improve the student's successful participation in current or future environments. Alberto and colleagues (2007), for example, selected business logos to teach six elementary and middle school students with severe disabilities by first surveying the students' communities to see what business were represented there and then asking students' families to indicate which of these they routinely visited. This selection process ensured that the knowledge and skills gained from the instruction would be of genuine benefit to the students.

The following considerations may also be useful in selecting words for instruction. Select words that (a) are related to specific student interests (e.g., family members' names), (b) would increase participation in general education activities (e.g., classmates' and teachers' names; direction words; key content vocabulary, such as science or social studies terms) (e.g., Collins, Evans, Creech-Galloway, Karl, & Miller, 2007; McDonnell et al., 2006), (c) are found in the student's current environments (e.g., environmental print in the classroom or school), (d) are names of products that the student might wish to purchase (e.g., food or clothing products) (e.g., Mechling, Gast, & Langone, 2002), (e) would keep the student safe (e.g., walk/don't walk, exit), or (f) are related to the student's employment (e.g., Minarovic & Bambara, 2007). Other important considerations are the student's age and home language, if different from English. Sections of some communities may have many signs written in languages other than English, and it may be important to the student and his or her family that he or she learns to recognize these community words.

Ms. Carter and Mr. Garcia created a list of sight words for Marcus that included some functional words suggested by his family (e.g., favorite foods, the names of his brother and sister, and some safety words like "danger") and some key words in upcoming math, science, and social studies units (e.g., weather, cloud, ocean, add).

Instructional Methods

There are several well-supported instructional strategies for teaching sight words. The key for successful instruction is to carefully consider a student's learning characteristics and learning history before selecting a strategy and then monitor the student's progress in acquiring sight words and adjust instruction accordingly.

Response Prompting and Fading Procedures.

Response prompts are the actions of a teacher prior to the student responding or after an incorrect response that help the student give a correct response (Cooper, Heron, & Heward, 2007). These may include verbal cues, gestures, modeling, or even full physical assistance (e.g., guiding a student's hand toward the correct word in an array of three choices). The teacher can give prompts before a student responds or prompts can be given after a student responds in the form of feedback or following error correction (e.g., "That isn't correct. The word is *menu.*"). The response prompts provided by the teacher must be systematically faded if students are to read words independently. Strategies for fading response prompts include the system of least prompts, the system of most prompts, progressive time delay, constant time delay, and simultaneous prompting (Chapter 4 has a detailed explanation of how response prompt and fading procedures are used in instruction). Browder and colleagues (2006) conducted a meta-analysis of reading instruction research with individuals with significant disabilities and found that the use of response prompt strategies had a very strong evidence base for both students with moderate and with severe disabilities.

Embedded Instruction.

As more students with moderate or severe disabilities receive instruction in general education settings, it is important to utilize instructional strategies that match the learning needs of these students and do not stigmatize them or interfere with their participation in inclusive learning activities (Collins et al., 2007). Embedded instruction is a strategy that allows students with more extensive support needs to receive intensive, individualized instruction within the ongoing activities of the general education classroom (McDonnell et al., 2006). Although it has been used successfully to teach a range of skills (e.g., picture naming skills, play skills, sight words, vocabulary), it is especially useful for helping students with severe disabilities in general education classrooms acquire core content words (e.g., Jameson, McDonnell, Johnson, Riesen, and Polychronis, 2007; McDonnell, 2002). General education teachers and paraprofessionals have all successfully implemented embedded instruction within general education settings (Johnson et al., 2004). Research evidence also suggests that this method is as effective as massed trials instruction in teaching sight words to students with moderate or severe disabilities (Jameson et al., 2007; McDonnell et al., 2006). There is some initial evidence which indicates that students generalize information learned during embedded instruction to the typical materials used in the classroom (Riesen, McDonnell, Johnson, Polychronis, & Jameson, 2003).

Ms. Carter and Mr. Garcia selected four words in the current science unit to teach Marcus. They decided to use embedded instruction to teach the words because this method would not take Marcus away from routine class activities, yet it is very effective. Mr. Jones, the paraprofessional working in Mr. Garcia's class, had used embedded instruction to teach other students content vocabulary in the past, so the teachers asked him if he would work with Marcus on the science content words. Mr. Jones used a response prompt procedure to teach the target words during the 10-minute time period at the end of the science block when students were to be putting away materials and getting ready to go to the cafeteria. He printed each word on a separate flash card and used constant time delay to teach Marcus to read and define each term. At first, he presented a card, read the word, and gave a simple definition before asking Marcus to repeat what he had modeled. Once Marcus was responding consistently with this simultaneous prompt, Mr. Jones presented the card and said, "Read the word and tell me what it means"; he then paused for 3 seconds. If Marcus didn't respond within the 3-second delay, Mr. Jones modeled what to do and had Marcus repeat the information. If Marcus made an error, Mr. Jones corrected him and had him repeat the correct information. When Marcus responded correctly within the 3-second delay, Mr. Jones increased it to 5 seconds. Within 2 weeks, Marcus could read and give a basic definition for each content word, whether it was printed on a flash card or on a science worksheet.

Stimulus Prompts. Stimulus prompts are another effective method for teaching sign words. With this strategy, changes are made to the words themselves that facilitate the student's learning. For example, a set of words may be color coded (e.g., *school* is written in green, *exit* is written in red) or a word may be placed within a picture that represents the word (or the picture placed within a word).

Although teachers often like to place pictures next to the words that they represent to help students acquire sight words (external stimulus prompts), research findings that compare this procedure with other instructional strategies suggest that students pay attention to the picture instead of the word when these are paired (Sheehy, 2002). Students make an association between the spoken word and the picture, not the spoken word and the printed word. Thus, when the picture is removed, students often fail to identify the word alone because they were attending to the picture and not the printed word. In essence, the picture blocks the student's attention to, and thus identification of, the word (Didden, Prinsen, & Sigafoos, 2000).

Despite these cautions, researchers have found several effective methods for transferring stimulus control from the prompt (e.g., a picture superimposed over a word) to the printed word. *Stimulus fading* is a procedure in which the stimulus prompts are gradually reduced in size or intensity. In teaching sight words, this means that the picture cue is gradually faded over instructional sessions until only the word itself remains. Figure 13–1 demonstrates this strategy. This technique has been referred to using many different terms, such as *embedded picture prompts, integrated picture mnemonics* (e.g., de Graff, Verhoeven, Bosman, & Hasselman, 2007), or *picture fading* (e.g., Didden, de Graaff, Nelemans, & Vooren, 2006). Research has demonstrated its effectiveness in teaching letter sounds and sight words to children with moderate or severe intellectual disabilities (e.g., Hoogeveen, Smeets, & Lancioni, 1989; Sheehy, 2002) and to typically developing children (e.g., de Graff et al., 2007). *Picture Me Reading* is a commercial reading program that is founded on the use of stimulus prompts. The challenge for the teacher lies in the preparation of the materials.

Another variation in the use of stimulus prompts and fading is what Miller and Miller (1971) named *symbol accentuation*. With this method, a familiar picture is presented in initial trials. Over time, the picture is transformed to become the printed word. Figure 13–2

FIGURE 13–1
Stimulus fading to teach sight word recognition with each box representing increased fading of the stimulus prompt.

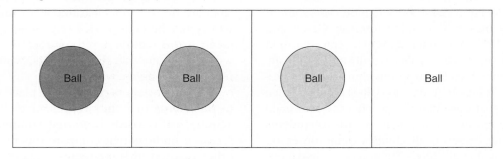

FIGURE 13–2
Example of symbol accentuation to teach sight words with each box representing increased abstractness.

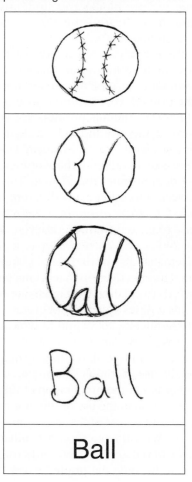

illustrates this method. Sheehy (2005) used a variation of this method by incorporating a morphing software application to teach sight words to eight students with severe disabilities who had no sight word vocabularies. Students learned six sight words using a word-only condition (words were presented on the computer and a series of response prompts were provided to teach the words) and six sight words using the morphing program. Under the morphing condition, students first saw the printed target word on the computer screen and were prompted to say it. The word was then gradually morphed into a photograph that represented the word and then was morphed back to the printed word. Five of the participating students acquired significantly more words using the morphing program than under the word-alone condition. The researchers emphasized the importance of individualizing the photographs chosen to represent target words, noting that students with severe disabilities may associate items with words in very idiosyncratic ways (e.g., a picture of a cup may represent *tea* to a student).

Stimulus shaping is another instructional method used successfully to teach sight words to students with moderate or severe disabilities. With this strategy, the target words remain unchanged, but the number and type of distractor words presented with them are gradually changed. This requires that the student make increasingly fine discriminations in selecting/reading the target word. Initially, a target word may be presented by itself; then it may be presented with a distractor word that is very different from the target word. Another distractor word that is more similar to the target may then be added and so on. The *Edmark Reading Program* is a published sight word reading program that is founded on this instructional strategy. Figure 13–3 shows an example of this type of teaching strategy.

FIGURE 13–3

Example of Stimulus Shaping to Teach Sight Words: Learning to Recognize the Word *book*. The teacher begins Trial 1 by showing the first row (blocking out the remaining rows with a piece of paper) and asking the student to point to *book*. In Trial 2, he or she shows the second row and asks the student to point to *book*. The teacher repeats this request with each row. The number of distracter words gradually increases, requiring the student to make increasingly more difficult discriminations among the words.

Trial 1	–	book	–
Trial 2	book	–	–
Trial 3	ball	–	book
Trial 4	–	book	ball
Trial 5	boat	ball	book
Trial 6	booth	book	boat

Promoting Generalization of Sight Words

It is important when teaching sight words to aim for generalization. That is, too often students acquire sight words in the classroom but cannot recognize those words in other settings at school, at home, or in the community. Using strategies such as *teaching with multiple exemplars* can enhance generalization. Multiple exemplars are examples that contain the critical stimulus or response features that students should pay attention to when learning a new skill. Teaching students to respond correctly to a range of relevant examples (stimulus exemplars) increases the probability that the student will be able to read the targeted word in the natural environment that contains all of the various ways that the word can be written or displayed. Teachers who use this method select a variety of teaching materials, being sure to vary both the relevant and irrelevant dimensions of target words so that students learn to recognize the words regardless of the font, size, or color used (e.g., that, that) or the type of text (e.g., a word printed on a card, on a sign displayed in the hallway, or on a restaurant menu).

Target words should also be taught in a variety of settings, not simply in the classroom, so that students learn to recognize the words no matter where they are encountered. *General case programming* is a generalization strategy that educators can use to teach students to transfer sight word learning across settings. This teaching method utilizes multiple teaching exam-

ples that sample the range of relevant stimulus situations and response variations. For example, teachers show the words printed in various fonts and sizes, and within varied texts, and ask students to respond in different ways (e.g., verbally reading a word, pointing to a word, or responding to a word). The instructor teaches these examples in various settings, across various persons, and within various activities. Mechling et al. (2002), for example, taught four school-aged students with moderate disabilities to identify grocery words on aisle signs and to locate the items represented by the words using a computer-based video program that incorporated video and photographs of overhead aisle signs from three grocery stores that were frequented by the students' families. After computer-based video instruction and multiple probes within the actual stores, students were able to successfully generalize their word-reading skills to locate items in a novel store.

Marcus's parents reported to his teachers that although Mr. Garcia said that Marcus had learned 10 new community sight words since school began, Marcus wasn't recognizing those words when he encountered them at home or in the community. Ms. Carter suggested that the staff reteach the words, but this time, instead of using response prompting with one set of flash cards to teach the words, they would create and use several sets of cards, written in different fonts, sizes, and colors. She also created several simple stories, using different fonts that incorporated the target words so that Marcus could practice reading the words in connected text. She asked a peer in Marcus's classroom to do a word treasure hunt with him. Marcus and Kate walked around the school, pausing in front of signs that Marcus was learning to read (e.g., School Office, Exit, Enter). Kate asked Marcus to read each sign as they came to it and helped him check off a box if he read it correctly. If he checked off all of the boxes, he and Kate got to have a treat when they returned to the classroom. After a couple of weeks of these activities, Marcus's mom called to say that Marcus had correctly (and proudly) read the Enter and Exit signs at the mall over the weekend.

To be truly functional for the student, sight word instruction must extend beyond merely learning to name words or symbols. This is accomplished by teaching *comprehension of target words* from the start of instruction. Instruction can include simple activities such as matching words to pictures or items, or being shown a word and asked to locate that item (e.g., being shown the word *cafeteria* and asked to find what it represents). It is also critical that students be taught to recognize and comprehend words in connected text if at all possible. For example, the teacher can construct simple two- and three-word sentences using the high-frequency or functional words that students are learning and have students practice reading these sentences and demonstrate comprehension of their meaning. This is especially appropriate for high-frequency words whose meanings may be very abstract unless they are taught within the context of a sentence (e.g., of, and, that). Even functional sight words, such as safety words, are most effectively taught when students learn what the words mean and the appropriate responses to such words (e.g., Exit).

Teaching Conventional Early Reading and Writing

Evidence is accumulating that some students with moderate or severe disabilities can acquire the literacy skills needed to be conventional readers and writers (Connors, 2003; Groen, Laws, Nation, & Bishop, 2006; Ryndak et al., 1999). Although much remains to be learned about the reading process for this group of learners, teachers have a responsibility to offer students an opportunity to acquire literacy skills beyond functional literacy. This means providing instruction in early reading skills, as appropriate, for individual students. Browder and colleagues' *Early Literacy Skills Builder* (2009), a published literacy program that focuses on comprehensive literacy instruction that utilizes the components of effective reading instruction identified by the National Reading Panel (2000), is an example of emphasis on building the early reading skills of students with more significant disabilities.

The National Reading Panel (2000) recommended instruction in five critical components of reading: phonemic awareness, phonics, vocabulary, comprehension, and fluency. The limited research available that examines these critical components of reading instruction with students with severe disabilities suggests that these students would benefit from instruction in these areas. Experts in the field advocate that teachers use instruction that has been verified with other student populations while additional research is being conducted (Browder et al., 2006; Mirenda, 2003). The next section details research-based instructional practices in each of these areas.

Instruction in Phonological Awareness and Phonics

Phonological awareness (PA) is the ability to recognize and manipulate the sounds in words (e.g., the ability to hear rhymes and segment syllables, and hear and manipulate individual sounds within words [phonemic awareness]). Children who are aware of the sound structure of language are better able to understand the alphabetic principle (i.e., understand that speech sounds can be represented by symbols and written down and read by themselves and others) (Torgeson & Mathes, 2000). Although there is less research on PA with children with more severe disabilities than with typically developing children, the research available suggests that just as with typically developing children, strong PA is linked with stronger reading abilities (Cupples & Iacono, 2000; Fletcher & Buckley, 2002; Saunders, 2007).

Phonics is related to, but is not the same skill as, PA. *Phonics* is the association between the sounds in a language and the letter(s) that represent the sound. Application of phonics skills to decode words requires both short-term memory and skill in manipulating sounds. To accurately decode the word *ball,* for example, a student must first isolate the individual sounds in the word (/b/, /a/, /l/), hold these in short-term memory, and then quickly blend the sounds back together to represent the word. These demands on auditory memory can be difficult for students with severe disabilities, and critics argue that learning decoding skills takes so much time for some individuals with severe disabilities that they may fail to gain other, more critical skills (Westling & Fox, 2004). Nevertheless, learning at least some decoding skills allows an individual to read novel words instead of relying only on words in his or her sight vocabulary (Saunders, 2007). Research shows that more students with severe disabilities are capable of learning and applying more decoding skills than was previously thought possible (e.g., Conners et al., 2006; Cupples & Iacono, 2000). Teachers and teams must thoughtfully consider which instructional outcome would best serve an individual student by increasing his or her active participation in family, community, school, and employment settings.

Phonics skills have been taught using an assortment of strategies (e.g., picture cues, response prompts, modeling, and published reading programs). Cohen, Heller, Alberto, and Fredrick (2008) used a constant time delay process to teach five students with mild or moderate intellectual disability to use a decoding procedure to read consonant–vowel–consonant (CVC) or consonant–vowel–vowel–consonant (CVVC) words. They taught students to (a) point to the target word, (b) slowly say each sound in the word, and (c) say the sounds in the word quickly (in order to blend them). All students learned the three-step procedure and were able to successfully decode the 12 target words, although the last step (blending) was the most difficult for them to master. The students who demonstrated the strongest decoding skills had the highest scores on a measure of phonological awareness, thus adding to prior findings that strong phonological memory is associated with stronger decoding skills.

Other researchers have utilized a published reading program based on systematic, explicit instruction to successfully teach decoding skills to students with moderate or severe disabilities. Bradford and colleagues (2006), for example, effectively used a direct instruction program to teach three students with moderate intellectual disabilities sound–letter correspondences, decoding words, and reading words in sentences and short paragraphs.

Conners et al. (2006) applied an intensive one-to-one instructional program to teach 20 children with intellectual disabilities to decode words. This program consisted of teaching the children to (a) blend sounds by first learning to blend syllables, then onsets and rimes, followed by vowel-consonants, and finally consonant-vowel-consonants; (b) learn six letter-sound correspondences using a combination of stimulus-fading and stimulus-shaping procedures combined with constant time delay; and (c) apply their sound blending and letter–sound knowledge to sound out words and nonwords. The researchers emphasized that decoding instruction for these learners must be "intense and well-targeted" (p. 133) and should include decoding instruction within a broad and comprehensive range of literacy activities to enhance development of comprehension.

Morgan and colleagues (2006) described a phonics instruction program for young adults with intellectual disabilities that included explicit instruction within instructional activities based on the students' interests and prior experiences, as well as their current abilities and skills. Some of the instructional activities within this program included creating alphabet books based on student interests (e.g., animals), using cards with ending sounds (e.g., rimes) to foster word recognition and develop writing vocabulary, and using cooking activities (a student's interest area) to extend knowledge of letter–sound correspondences and facilitate writing skills.

What seems to be important across these reading studies is that phonics instruction for this group of learners be systematic and explicit, and that it includes instructional activities that require active participation using game-like activities, manipulatives, and other instructional formats that promote dynamic student involvement (Mirenda, 2003). Figures 13–4 and 13–5 show an example of using visuals to teach letter–sound correspondences in a game-like format.

Ms. Carter used response prompts and visual cues to teach Marcus the letter-sound correspondences for five initial consonant sounds and two short vowels.

FIGURE 13–4
Sound Cards Illustrating Initial Sound of /p/. Students can match letters to picture cards, sort pictures by beginning sounds, or play an "odd one out" game in which four picture cards, three of which begin with the same sound and one of which begins with a different sound are displayed. The student selects the picture that does not begin with the same sound.

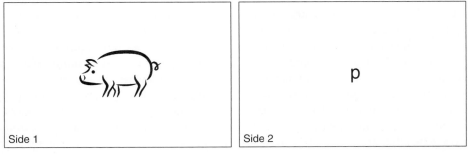

Source: Morgan & Moni, 2005.

FIGURE 13–5

Visual support for teaching letter/sound correspondence. Students place a letter card first in the Sound pocket and make the sound of the letter. Next, they place it in the Letter pocket and state the name of the letter.

She is extending his learning by helping him create "sound books" for each of the letter-sounds that he has mastered. She provides an array of three pictures of some of his favorite things and helps him to select the picture that begins with the targeted sound. He then glues the picture into his book and writes (or copies) the label for the picture, highlighting the targeted letter. Marcus shares his books with the kindergarten students that his class tutors each week, reinforcing their letter-sound knowledge, and takes his books home to read to his family.

Spelling

Like other areas of literacy instruction, students with moderate or severe disabilities have not always received instruction in spelling (Vedora & Stromer, 2006. Learning to spell facilitates literacy skills in other areas (e.g., reading) and extends written communication with others (Blischak & Schlosser, 2003; Heron, Okyere, & Miller, 1991; Vedora & Stromer, 2006. Heron et al. (1991) described three general instructional approaches for teaching spelling. These included a linguistics approach that is founded on the teaching of the phonological and morphological aspects of written language; a remedial approach founded on methods such as the Fernald technique, the Gillingham–Stillman method, the Horn method, and a phonovisual method; and a series of approaches that are primarily modifications of the other methods, such as teacher modeling,

constant time delay, teaching spelling rules, using distributed practice and interspersion of unknown words, and Copy-Cover-Compare. Some of these later approaches have been used to teach spelling to students with more significant disabilities. Vedora and Stromer (2006), for example, conducted two studies in which they taught two adolescents with intellectual disability to spell nine words using a computer program. The program included (a) writing words dictated by the computer, (b) writing words using letters from a choice pool when the words are dictated by the teacher and the youths are shown a picture of the object (anagram spelling), and (c) writing words when shown a printed word. After learning a set of words, students received a review of previously mastered words each day; they also copied the target words from a typed list three times per week in their classroom. Both students maintained their spelling skills over several weeks and were able to locate objects represented by words on a list.

Vocabulary Development

Vocabulary development is strongly related to the ability to read and is often an area of need for students with moderate or severe disabilities (Groen et al., 2006). Having a strong vocabulary contributes to increased reading comprehension and, at the same time, reading and encountering new words is an important way in which vocabulary development occurs. Research indicates that instruction in vocabulary improves students' word knowledge and also improves reading comprehension (Browder et al., 2006).

Students' vocabularies are composed of words that they understand and use in four different but related areas: listening, speaking (or using augmentative forms of communication), reading, and writing. Each vocabulary area affects a student's literacy abilities so it is important to systematically develop all four areas through instruction (Keefe, 2007). Just as with selecting sight words for instruction, it is useful to utilize an ecological approach to select words for vocabulary instruction. Words should come from the home, school, and community environments, as well as vocabulary from the general curriculum, which facilitates access to content knowledge (Keefe, 2007).

Effective vocabulary instruction, according to the National Reading Panel (2000), relies on a number of approaches: (a) direct instruction *and* context to teach word meanings, (b) incorporation of multiple forms of media during teaching activities, (c) utilization of

FIGURE 13–6

Target words were selected from a book the class read together. The teacher taught the word meanings using various strategies and created color-coded fill-in-the-blank worksheets. She typed the target words on file labels (color-coded) and asked the students to select the correct word for each blank. Students who couldn't write the words could peel and stick the labels containing the color-coded vocabulary words.

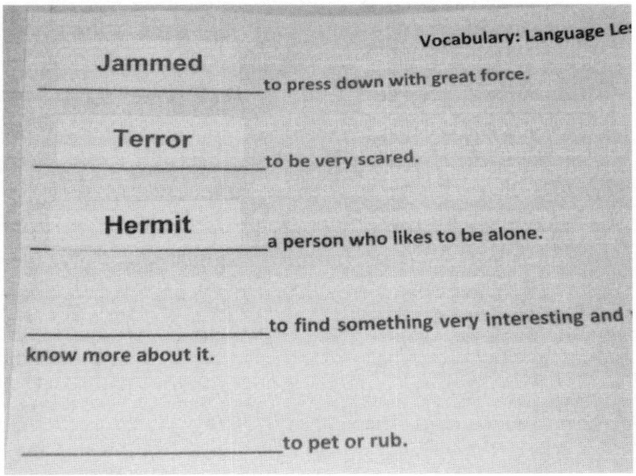

methods to enhance the association between new words and words that are already in a student's vocabulary, (d) opportunities to practice words to automaticity and to use them in multiple contexts, and (e) incorporation of active student response. Research on instructional strategies used to teach vocabulary to students with moderate or severe disabilities has examined several methods, each of which were successful: (a) embedded instruction (e.g., McDonnell et al., 2006), (b) response prompts and time delay (e.g., Collins et al., 2007), (c) computer-assisted instruction in order to teach sight word meaning (e.g., Mechling & Gast 2003), and (d) peer tutoring (e.g., Kamps, Locke, Delquadri, & Hall, 1989). Figure 13–6 shows an example of a vocabulary activity utilized in an inclusive classroom and adapted for students with severe disabilities.

Reading Comprehension

The goal of reading instruction is to understand what is read. Understanding must be taught from the beginning of instruction. Many experts suggest that since there is limited research on developing reading comprehension in students with significant disabilities that teachers utilize instructional strategies found to be effective with typically developing learners, taking into account students' current levels of literacy skills (Browder et al., 2006).

Reading comprehension for some students with severe disabilities involves understanding the meaning of single words or symbols. (Strategies to enhance sight word comprehension were discussed in a prior section.) Other students can work with connected text, even if it is only short sentences. Comprehension of connected text is a complex and active task that requires (a) recognizing and understanding the meaning of the individual words in the text; (b) activating any prior knowledge about the topic of the passage (i.e., relevant background knowledge) and knowledge of text structure; and (c) applying these skills to the text to facilitate comprehension while (d) constantly monitoring understanding to make the necessary understanding "repairs" if something doesn't make sense (Copeland, 2007a). Given the complexity of the task, it is not surprising that students with moderate or severe disabilities have difficulty with comprehension because they likely have difficulties with several of these four component skills. Effective instruction for these learners generally must include intervention in several areas of reading, such as working on underlying language difficulties *and* teaching specific strategies to use to facilitate comprehension.

It is useful to organize reading comprehension instruction according to strategies that target the before, during, and after phases of reading a text because there are specific tasks that successful readers utilize during each of these points in the reading process (e.g., Ehren, Lenz, & Deshler, 2004). One effective *before reading* strategy is setting a clear purpose or goal for reading. Individuals read for many different reasons and read many different types of texts (e.g., textbook, novel, grocery list). It is essential to use different kinds of texts during reading instruction and to use strategies such as *think alouds* (i.e., using self-talk to set a purpose for reading) to teach students to actively reflect on why they are reading a particular text. This helps students understand why they are engaging in the activity and how it relates to their interests or experiences (e.g., *We are reading a recipe today so that we can learn how to make a sandwich*). An *after reading* activity that is linked to the purpose makes this strategy even more effective. For example, making a sandwich and sharing it with a friend is a logical and engaging activity to follow the reading of a recipe. Pictures taken of the activity can be arranged in a wordless book (or computer-based book) and used to reinforce target reading objectives.

Activating prior knowledge and predicting are also effective *before reading* comprehension strategies. The National Reading Panel (2000) found strong evidence for using questions (i.e., *wh* questions) to activate prior knowledge and predict. Morgan et al. (2004), for example, taught six young adults with intellectual disabilities to improve their comprehension by using question words to access their prior knowledge and experiences before reading and then using prediction to help them make connections between their knowledge and experience and the stories being read.

There are a range of comprehension strategies that teachers can use *during reading* to help students monitor their comprehension. An example is an adapted maze exercise in which a text passage has blanks inserted at regular intervals and word choices listed beside the blanks to assist students in monitoring their comprehension as they read. Stopping to select a word (either by circling it, writing it in a blank, or pointing/using eye gaze) prompts students to think about the meaning of what they are reading so that they can make a word choice that makes sense (Copeland, 2007b). Foley and Staples (2007) suggest stopping students during reading to generate questions about the text that can then be put on sticky notes and examined later. They also suggest using graphic organizers such as KWL charts: (a) what I already *know* about a topic, (b) what I *want to know* about the topic, and (c) what I *learned* after reading about the topic) to organize information and events within the text.

Mr. Karst works with each of Jacob's general education teachers to identify the key concepts or terms that he needs to understand in each unit and for each reading assignment. In addition, he asks the teachers to identify several questions that they would expect students in the class to be able to answer after reading the assignment. Mr. Karst's paraeducator creates an audio recording of each reading assignment that Jacob can follow as he reads it at home. Mr. Karst then develops a guide for Jacob for each reading assignment that includes a list of the key concepts or terms that he needs to understand. He reviews each guide with Jacob before he goes home. Jacob uses the guide to identify the concepts or terms as he reads and then writes an explanation of the concept or a definition of the term in his own words. Mr. Karst reviews the guide with Jacob the next day and asks him the questions provided by his general education teachers to ensure that he clearly understands the material.

Story retellings (Morgan et al., 2004) and teaching story grammar (Katims, 2000b) are among the various comprehension strategies for *after reading* that have been used effectively with students with intellectual disabilities. The teacher can give picture cards to students to use in retelling activities to decrease the expressive language demand. For example, a student can select a picture from an array that represents the main idea of a short passage, or arrange a series of pictures that depict story events in the sequence in which they occurred.

Marcus and his peers in Mr. Garcia's class have been practicing recalling major points in a text and making and modifying predictions about forthcoming information. With Ms. Carter's help, Mr. Garcia has taught everyone in the class to use story grammar maps while they are reading in order to record key details from the stories and to make predictions. Marcus does not yet have sufficient reading skills to read a story independently, so Mr. Garcia has assigned him to work with a peer. The peer reads a story written at Marcus's listening comprehension level. He stops periodically to ask Marcus about details from the story and together they record these on a story map. Marcus participates by recalling details and events, and by selecting words that he can read from a choice pool to fill in the details on the story map (e.g., color words to describe the color of the dog in the story; see Figure 13–7). He also is learning to make predictions about what he thinks will happen next in the story. When they are done, Marcus retells the story to his peer support who prompts him if he forgets an essential event. Marcus then draws a

FIGURE 13–7

Example of a story map focused on character traits. Marcus filled in the story map as he read with peer support, using word choice boxes such as the one to the right to select words representing important details about the dog in the story.

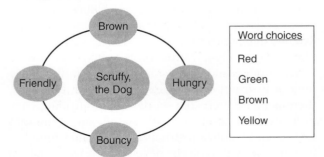

picture to represent the main events in the story and this, plus the story map he worked on with his classmate, is turned in to Mr. Garcia.

Fluency

Fluency is the ability to read words accurately and at an acceptable speed, using appropriate intonation and text phrasing (Keefe, 2007; Therrien, 2004). There is little research on fluency among students with moderate or severe disabilities (Browder et al., 2006; Saunders, 2007). Some of the successful instructional methods utilized with students with learning disabilities include paired reading (i.e., reading at the same time as a model) and repeated reading (i.e., re-reading a short passage several times) (Chard, Vaughn, & Tyler, 2002). Therrien conducted a meta-analysis of studies utilizing repeated reading as a fluency intervention. The results of a component analysis of the reviewed studies indicated the following as essential components for effective repeated reading interventions: (a) reading to an adult, (b) being provided with a cue to read faster and to try to remember what was read, (c) reading a passage multiple times (four or more times), and (d) being provided with corrective feedback until a criterion is reached.

Heller and colleagues (2007) examined and compared the effects of repeated readings with corrective feedback and paired reading (these authors called it *unison reading*) on the fluency of two elementary students with physical disabilities. Both students demonstrated higher rates of oral reading fluency after being provided with multiple opportunities to read a passage at their instructional level and receiving corrective feedback. Adding more reading repetitions (up to five more with one student) clearly increased student fluency rates. Adding unison reading as an intervention component was more effective than repeated readings and error correction alone, although this was examined with only one student. The researchers stressed that when teaching fluency to students with physical disabilities, teachers must provide appropriate adaptations that allow maximum access to the reading materials, including taking into account positioning needs and changes to materials such as increasing the font size.

Writing

Reading and writing are reciprocal processes: acquiring reading skills enhances writing skills and vice versa (Kay-Raining Bird, Cleave, White, Pike, & Helmkay, 2008). Being able to write has important social implications as well, because creating written texts is a form of communication that can increase participation in school, community, and vocational settings (Cohen, Allgood, Heller, & Castelle, 2001). The modest research available on writing instruction for students with moderate or severe disabilities suggests that it is an important part of a comprehensive instructional program (Joseph & Konrad, 2009; Kay-Raining Bird et al., 2008). Students with severe disabilities may encounter difficulty in learning to communicate in written form both because of their unique learning characteristics and because they may not have had expert, individualized instruction. However, learning to compose written text has several advantages for these students, including that written texts are permanent and can be revisited numerous times in order to increase understanding of the content of the text, as well as reorganized and revised in order to increase the clarity of its message (Farrell & Elkins, 1995; Sturm & Koppenhaver, 2000).

Sturm and Koppenhaver (2000) define *writing* as "a holistic and authentic process of communicating by construction of a meaningful text" (p. 75). Van Kraayenrood and colleagues (2002 emphasize that writing "involves constructing meanings by choosing and arranging symbols and understanding how these meanings change as a result of audience, context, and purpose" (p. 36). This broader interpretation of writing allows the inclusion of text composed of letters and words, pictures, graphics, or any combination of these.

Mr. Garcia knew that learning to compose written text is an important component of literacy instruction, but he was struggling to find ways to help Marcus with this area of literacy. He and Ms. Carter met to do some brainstorming. They came up with several ideas that they implemented over the next month. First, they created several options for Marcus to choose from during journal writing in the morning. Marcus now can choose to dictate what he wants to say on a topic to a peer support. His peer support prints what Marcus says and reads it back to him to check if that it is what Marcus wants to say, being sure that she runs her finger along the print as she reads it back. This helps Marcus develop his understanding of the concept of word, as well as deepening his understanding that print represents spoken language. Marcus can then use the computer to copy the entry or can copy it by hand to turn in. Another option that Marcus can choose for journal writing is to complete sentence frames using a word bank. It might say something like "I am going to

_____ *for Thanksgiving. I will get to eat* _____*." The word bank contains word choices that are also supplemented with pictures (e.g., the word turkey has a small picture of a turkey printed next to it). Marcus selects a word and copies it onto the frame. He can work on this independently or he can ask a peer to assist him.*

Mr. Garcia has taken these ideas of how to create access to composing text and has used them in other content areas throughout the school day. For example, in social studies, he has given Marcus a sentence frame summary to complete using a word bank of key content words supplemented with small pictures. He is also helping Marcus to create a book of stories that Marcus will publish and give to his parents as a holiday gift just as his classmates are doing. Mr. Garcia often helps Marcus get started on writing these by showing him pictures of things that Marcus is interested in or places Marcus has visited. He asks questions and copies down Marcus's answers. He then helps Marcus think about how to say what he wants and copies down his words onto a white board so that Marcus can see his spoken words represented in writing. Mr. Garcia reads the text back, being sure to let Marcus make revisions if he decides he wants to make a change in a word or add something. This process of writing and revising is helping Marcus to better understand how to communicate his thoughts and is helping him learn basic aspects of writing, such as punctuation. Marcus uses the computer to type his story (copying from Mr. Garcia's printing), he chooses pictures or graphics to illustrate his story, and he finally prints it out to include it in his book.

Effective writing instruction for students with severe disabilities begins with high expectations that students have something to say, providing numerous opportunities to utilize writing throughout the school day, selecting writing topics and purposes that are meaningful to the students, and providing the supports that many of these students require in order to express themselves by written means (e.g., specialized keyboards, assignments adapted to allow for the use of symbols or graphics instead of writing with letters) (Copeland, 2007b). Some specific instructional methods examined in research have included strategy instruction (e.g., Bedrosian, Lasker, Speidal, & Politsch, 2003; Konrad, Trela, & Test, 2006), computer-based instruction (e.g., Yamamoto & Miya, 1999), using the

FIGURE 13–8
Adapted journal writing using symbols instead of words. Students who don't write can select a picture symbol from the right side of the page to use in completing their fill-in-the-blank journal entries.

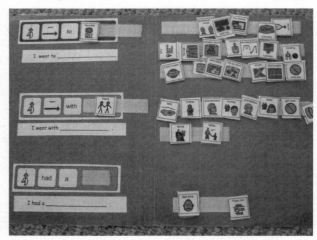

Four-Blocks literacy format (e.g., Hedrick, Katims, & Carr, 1999), and learning to compose a message using text/symbols (e.g., Foley & Staples, 2003). Figure 13–8 shows an example of a journal writing activity adapted for students who could not write and instead selected picture symbols to complete the journal prompts.

Selecting appropriate and engaging writing tasks is an important part of effective writing instruction. It is important to choose writing topics and activities that are meaningful to students (Copeland, 2007b). Tasks that are based on shared experiences, such as field trips or class projects, are examples of creating instructional opportunities that are meaningful to students and that increase their participation in their classroom and school. Foley and Staples (2003), for example, worked with five young adults with intellectual disability and autism who engaged in shared experiences such as trips to places in the community and then used a variety of writing tools (e.g., letter stamps, markers, computer writing software) to write about their experiences. Other possible writing activities include creating books and poetry through shared writing activities (e.g., Kahn-Freedman, 2001; Sturm & Koppenhaver, 2000) or using a language experience approach to write stories or other texts (Katims, 2000).

Handwriting

Handwriting requires fine motor skills, visual acuity, spatial and sequential ordering, and visual and kinesthetic memory (Rosenblum, Weiss, & Parush, 2003). Many students with severe disabilities struggle with handwriting because of their difficulties with these component skills, yet learning to write has many functional uses so it is an important area for instruction. Some researchers (e.g., Graham, Harris, & Fink, 2000) have linked handwriting to broader writing skills (e.g., composition), further indicating its importance in a literacy curriculum.

Students should have systematic instruction in handwriting and functional opportunities to practice writing within meaningful activities throughout the day (e.g., putting their name on the papers they turn in) (Graham et al., 2000; Oelwin, 1995). Students must be properly positioned before beginning instruction and have any adapted materials that they might need, such as a slant board, adapted writing implements and grips, and appropriate paper (e.g., paper with larger-sized manuscript lines or paper that contains raised lines in order to provide an additional tactual cue for where to begin or end a letter). An occupational therapist can be an invaluable resource for determining what materials might be most helpful to a student. Effective instruction includes the teacher or a peer modeling correct letter formation, students tracing and copying letters and words, and teachers or peers providing feedback to students (e.g., praising correct letter formation and requiring students to revise incorrectly formed letters). Batchelder, McLaughlin, Weber, Derby, and Gow (2009), for example, used hand-over-hand prompting and dot-to-dot tracing to help an adolescent with intellectual disability and autism learn to write the letters in his name. (See Figure 13–9 for an example of dot-to-dot tracing materials.) There are also a number of commercial programs available to teach handwriting that can be very helpful (e.g., *Handwriting Without Tears*® [Olsen, 2010], *The Sensible Pencil* [Becht, 1985]).

Foley and Staples (2007) point out that for students who struggle with the physical act of handwriting, so much energy and attention is focused on forming letters that the student may have few cognitive resources left over to do the critical tasks of composing what he or she wants to say. For students for whom handwriting is not an option, it is important to teach keyboarding, either with a standard or an adapted keyboard (Foley & Staples, 2007; Oelwein, 1995). Some experts recommend teaching both handwriting and keyboarding because in today's world students will likely need skills in both areas (Foley & Staples, 2007; Westling & Fox, 2009).

FIGURE 13–9
Illustration of using dot-to-dot prompts to teach handwriting skills.

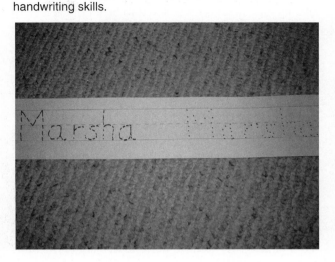

Students Whose First Language is Not English

As more students from linguistically diverse backgrounds enroll in schools, it is becoming more important for teachers to understand how students acquire a second language and how that process affects literacy learning. The process of second language acquisition in children with moderate or severe disabilities has not been thoroughly studied (Verhoeven & Vermeer, 2006), probably because of low expectations for literacy development in these students. Nonetheless, teachers must pay close attention to the language learning of English Learner (EL) students with more severe disabilities. It is easy to mistake second language learning difficulties for other learning problems and thus miss opportunities to provide effective language instruction. De Valenzuela and Tracey (2007) recommend that students receive a thorough assessment of their native language abilities by a competent bilingual specialist who has expertise in first and second language development and knowledge of the learning characteristics of students with severe disabilities. This information can then be used to build an appropriate literacy instructional program for these students. In general, EL students do best when instructed in early reading skills (e.g., phonological awareness) in their native language first, before receiving literacy instruction in English. There are few studies that examine literacy instruction of EL students with severe disabilities (e.g., Rohena, Jitendra, & Browder, 2002); this remains an area in need of much additional research that can guide teachers and families of students who are second language learners.

Math Instruction

Like literacy, math is considered to be a critical area of knowledge for all individuals in today's society. The math curriculum includes a number of domains, including numeracy and computation, money and consumer skills, and time and time management.

Numeracy and Computation

Research suggests that many students with severe disabilities are able to learn complex math skills when provided with systematic instruction and support (Browder, Spooner, Algrim-Dezell, Harris, & Wakeman, 2008; Butler, Miller, Lee, & Pierce, 2001). Several comprehensive curriculums for teaching math concepts and operations to students with severe disabilities have been developed (Ford et al., 1989; Resnick, Wang, & Kaplan, 1973). Table 13–1 illustrates the basic sequence of skills that students must master to be able to do basic addition and subtraction. This section presents strategies that teachers can use to teach key math skills, including counting and numerals, basic concepts and operations, money and consumer skills, and time and time management.

Counting and Numerals

Many students with severe disabilities can be taught to count and to identify and understand the values of numerals (Browder et al., 2008; Butler et al., 2001). The ability to count objects requires four types of counting. Students must (a) *rote count* (e.g., count from 1 to 10); (b) *rational count* (e.g., count how many pencils you have), which requires an understanding of one-to-one correspondence and the ability to count concrete moveable objects, fixed ordered objects (e.g., a line of boxes on a worksheet), and fixed unordered objects (e.g., a group of boxes randomly placed on a worksheet); (c) *count from a number to a number* (e.g., count from 6 to 10); and (d) *skip count* (e.g., count by fives to 30). Students also need to be able to use numerals and understand their values. This includes skills such as being able to identify a numeral from an array (e.g., "Point to 5"); match a numeral to an appropriate set of objects (e.g., matches the number 5 to the set with five objects in it); and write numerals when give a verbal cue (e.g., "Write the number 5"). The ability to count and use numerals are essential prerequisite skills to learning more complex math concepts, such as *more* and *less,* and the ability to complete basic operations such as addition and subtraction.

Several strategies have been shown to be effective in teaching these counting and numeral skills: response prompting and fading procedures, chaining, differential reinforcement, and systematic error correction (Browder et al., 2008; Butler et al., 2001). For example, Fredericks et al. (1976) recommended the use of verbal modeling and backward chaining to teach students to count from 1 to 10. Instruction begins with the teacher providing an instructional cue, "Let's count from 1 to 10." The teacher then models each number in the sequence 1 to 10 for the student. Once the student imitates the teacher's model for all of the numbers from 1 to 10, a backward chaining procedure is used to establish independent counting by the student. For example, the teacher would model the counting sequence from 1 to 9 and then provide the student with the opportunity to say the number 10. The teacher would provide differential reinforcement for correct responses and systematically correct the error if the student did not say 10. Once the student was able to say the number 10 without prompting, then the teacher would only provide models through the number 8 and the student would be expected to count the numbers 9 and 10. This procedure would continue until the student was able to count from 1 to 10 independently. Similar procedures can be used to teach other forms of counting and to teach students to identify numerals and state their values.

Computation

Once students have mastered the necessary prerequisite skills, they can move on to learning basic mathematical operations, including addition and subtraction. A number of strategies have been recommended for teaching these skills to students with severe disabilities.

Manipulatives. Students can learn to do addition and subtraction through the use of concrete objects that can be grouped into discrete sets (Flexer, 1989; Paddock, 1992). For example, a student might be presented with the written equation $(2 + 3 = \underline{\hspace{1cm}})$ and a group of 10 small blocks. To complete the problem, the student would read the equation (i.e., "2 plus 3 equals"), then place two blocks together in a set, place three blocks together in another set, count the two sets of blocks, write the sum next to the equal sign, and finally read the complete equation (i.e., "2 plus 3 equals 5"). Manipulatives can also be used to teach subtraction using similar procedures. The student would be presented with a written equation $(5 - 2 = \underline{\hspace{1cm}})$ and

TABLE 13–1
Sequence of Math Objectives

Units 1 and 2: Counting and One-to-One Correspondence[1]
A. The student can rote count.
B. The student can rational count moveable objects.
C. The student can rational count fixed ordered objects.
D. The student can rational count fixed unordered objects.
E. Given a numeral and a set of objects, the student can count out a specific number.
F. Given a numeral and several sets of fixed objects, the student can select a set that matches the stated number.
G. Given two sets, the student can pair objects and state whether the sets are equivalent.
H. Given two unequal sets of objects, the child can pair the objects and state which set has more.
I. Give two unequal sets of objects, the child can pair the objects and state which set has less.

Units 3 and 4: Numerals[2]
A. Given two sets of numerals, the student can match the numerals.
B. Give a numeral stated and use of printed numerals, the student can select the stated numeral.
C. Given a written numeral, the student can read the numeral.
D. Given several sets of objects and several numerals, the student can match numerals with appropriate sets.
E. Given two written numerals, the student can state which shows more (less).
F. Given a set of numerals, the student can place them in order.
G. Given a stated numeral, the student can write the numeral.

Unit 5: Comparison of Sets
A. Given two sets of objects, the student can count sets and state which has more objects or whether the sets have the same number of objects.
B. Given two sets of objects, the student can count sets and state which has fewer objects.
C. Give a set of objects and a numeral, the student can state which is more (less).
D. Given a numeral and several sets of objects, the student can select sets that are more (less) than the numeral.
E. Given a set of objects and several numerals, the student can select numerals that show more (less).
F. Given two rows of objects (not paired), the student can state which has more regardless of the arrangement.
G. Given three sets of objects, the student can count sets and state which has more (less).

Unit 6: Serration and Ordinal Position
A. Given three objects of different sizes, the student can select the largest (smallest).
B. Given objects of graduated sizes, the child can put the objects in order from smallest to largest.
C. Given several sets of objects, the student can put the sets in order from least to most.
D. Given ordered sets of objects, the student can name the ordinal position (first, middle, last) of the objects.

Unit 7: Addition and Subtraction (sums up to 10)
A. Given two numbers stated, sets of objects, and directions to add, the student can add the numbers by counting out two subsets and then combining and stating the combined number.
B. Give two numbers stated, set of objects, and directions to subtract, the student can count out a smaller subset from the larger set and state the remainder.
C. Given two numbers stated, a number line, and directions to add, the student can use the number line to determine the sum.
D. Given two numbers stated, a number line, and directions to subtract, the student can use the number line to determine the remainder.
E. Given addition and subtraction problems in horizontal (vertical form), the student can complete the problems.

Adapted from Task analysis in curriculum design: A hierarchically sequenced introductory mathematics curriculum, by L. B. Resnick, M. C. Wang, & J. Kaplan, 1973, *Journal of Applied Behavior Analysis, 6,* 685–886. Copyright 1973 by *Journal of Applied Behavior Analysis.* Adapted with permission.

[1]Unit 1 involves sets of up to five objects; Unit 2 involves sets of up to 10 objects.
[2]Unit 3 involves numerals and sets of up to five objects; Unit 4 involves numerals and sets of up to 10 objects.

a group of 10 blocks. The student would read the equation (i.e., "5 minus 2 equals"), then count five blocks into a set, remove two blocks from the set, count the remaining blocks, write the remainder next to the equal sign, and then read the complete equation (i.e., "5 minus 2 equals 3").

Number Line. A number line can also be used to teach students addition and subtraction (Cihak & Foust, 2008). In this procedure, the student is presented with a written equation $(2 + 3 = \_\_\_)$, he or she reads the equation (i.e., "2 plus 3 equals"), then the student would place his or her finger at 2 on the number

FIGURE 13–10
Illustration of addition using a number line. The student places his or her finger on the number line, designating the first number in the equation. Then he or she counts the number of spaces designated by the second number in the equation. Finally, he or she writes the number counted as the sum.

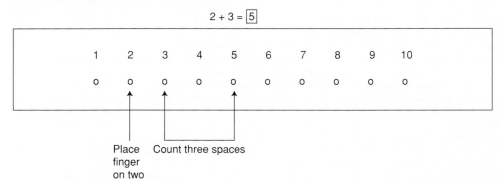

line, count three more spaces on the number line, then write the number that he or she said last next to the equal sign, and then say the complete equation (i.e., "2 plus 3 equals 5"). Figure 13-10 illustrates the use of a number line to complete an addition problem. The procedure would simply be reversed to teach the student to complete subtraction problems.

Touch Points. Another strategy for teaching addition and subtraction are touch points (Cihak & Foust, 2008; Kramer & Krug, 1973). In 1989, Bullock, Pierce, and McClellan refined this strategy into a commercial curriculum called *TouchMath* that teaches addition, subtraction, multiplication, and division using touch points. In this approach, dots representing the value of each number from 1 to 9 are embedded within the numeral (see Figure 13-11). The student touches the

FIGURE 13–11
Illustration of Touch Points

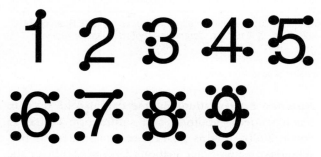

From A rationale and procedure for teaching addition, by T. Kramer & D. A. Krug, 1973, *Education and Training of the Mentally Retarded, 8,* 140–144. Adapted with permission.

dots once to count the value of each numeral. For example, for the equation 3 + 2 =, the student would count the dots embedded on the numeral 3 (i.e., one, two, three) and continue counting the dots on the numeral 2 (i.e., four, five) to arrive at the sum. Cihak and Foust (2008) taught three elementary students with autism to complete single-digit addition problems using either a number line or touch points. The results showed that two out of the three students learned addition using the number line and that all three students learned addition using touch points. However, touch points was a superior strategy to the number line for all three students.

> *Mr. Garcia has implemented touch-point math with Marcus and is beginning to see some improvement in Marcus' addition and subtraction skills. Marcus has struggled to understand basic addition and subtraction so Mr. Garcia and Ms. Carter have used lots of manipulatives with him and now have begun teaching him a touch-point system. Using the concrete "points" on the numbers seems to provide the supports that he needs in order to be successful.*

Calculators. Students with severe disabilities can also use calculators to complete addition and subtraction problems (Horton, 1985; Koller & Mullhern, 1977; Matson & Long, 1986). Researchers have demonstrated that students can extend their use of calculators to the next dollar (i.e., the one-more strategy) to purchase items in community settings or for budgeting skills (Frederick-Dugan, Test, & Varn, 1991; Matson & Long, 1986; Wilson, Cuvo, & Davis, 1986).

The emphasis on the participation of students with severe disabilities in the general education curriculum has prompted researchers to begin to examine strategies that can be used to teach more complex mathematical concepts and operations to this group of students (Jimenez, Courtade, & Browder, 2008; Morin & Miller, 1998; Neef, Nelles, Iwata, & Page, 2003). For example, Jimenez et al. taught three high school students with severe disabilities to compute the value of x in a standard algebraic equation (e.g., $\underline{5} + x = 15$). The researchers used concrete representations (i.e., spoons, pens, paper clips), a number line, a task analysis of the calculation steps, and a constant time-delay procedure to teach the students to complete the equations. The results showed that two out of the three students learned all of the steps of the task analysis and one was able to master eight out of the nine steps of the task analysis before the end of the study. The two students who learned to complete all of the steps of the task analysis were able to generalize the procedure across materials and maintained the application of the procedure on follow-up probes.

Although the emerging research on teaching complex mathematical concepts and operations to students is positive, much more study is needed to determine the best approaches for teaching these skills to students. Equally important, research is need to demonstrate how these concepts and skills can be integrated into students' daily routines and activities, and the impact that mastering these skills has on improving their quality of life.

Money and Consumer Skills

Being able to use and manage money are essential skills for successful community living. While developing basic math skills like adding and subtracting can enhance the ability of student to use and manage money, research suggests that even students without these skills can learn to use money to purchase goods and services, manage bank accounts, and use a budget in order to meet their immediate financial needs (Browder & Grasso, 1999; Xin, Grasso, Dipipi-Hoy, & Jitendra, 2005). In the following sections, we discuss strategies for teaching counting money, purchasing skills, and banking and consumer skills.

Counting Money. Historically, the general sequence for teaching money counting began with teaching students to count coins and then to count bills (see Table 13–2). This sequence is based on curricula for students

TABLE 13–2
Sequence to Teaching Money Counting

1. Count pennies to 10 cents (count by ones to 10).
2. Equate 10 pennies to one dime (both are 10 cents).
3. Count dimes to $1 (count by 10s).
4. Count quarters to $1 (count by 25s).
5. Equate two quarters plus dimes to $1 (count by 10s, beginning with 50).
6. Count nickels to $1 (count by fives).
7. Count quarters plus nickels (count by fives, beginning with 25, 50, 75).
8. Count dimes plus nickels (count by 10s and switch to counting by 5s).
9. Count quarters plus dimes (count by fives, beginning with 25, 50, 75).
10. Count quarters, dimes, and nickels (count 25, 50, or 75, then by 10s, and then by 5s).
11. Count $1 bills to $10.
12. Count $5 and $1 bills to $20.
13. Count $10 and $1 bills to $20.
14. Count $10, $5, and $1 bills to $20.
15. Use a calculator to compute the affordability of multiple purchases.

Adapted from *The Syracuse community-referenced curriculum guide for students with moderate and severe disabilities*, by A. Ford, R. Schnorr, L. Meyer, L. Davern, J. Black, & P. Dempsey, 1989. Baltimore: Paul H. Brookes.

without disabilities who typically begin with coin identification in kindergarten and move toward counting coin and bill combinations and giving change back from a purchase by third grade. This sequence is appropriate for young children, but it may not always be the most functional for older students, who lack basic counting and numeracy skills. In some cases, it may be more appropriate to teach students to count bills first in order to give students a strategy with which to participate more fully in community settings. Browder and Snell (2000) recommended an alternate sequence in teaching money counting to older students (see Table 13–3).

Research suggests that many students with severe disabilities can learn to count coins with explicit instruction (Browder et al., 2008; Xin et al., 2005). The procedures for teaching coin counting rely on the use of response prompting and fading procedures, differential reinforcement, and systematic error correction (Bellamy & Buttars, 1975; Lowe & Cuvo, 1976). Lowe and Cuvo taught students to tap coins in order to help them remember their value (e.g., quarter = 5 taps, dime = 2 taps, nickel = 1 tap). Students would count by fives in sequence for each time they tapped the coin.

TABLE 13–3
A Dollar-First Sequence for Teaching Money Skills

1. *$1 bill.* Use of $1 bill for small purchases (change can be saved in a personal bank at home and converted to dollars by caregivers).
2. *One to ten $1 bills.* Use of $1 bills needed for purchases up to $10 by the "one more than" strategy (e.g., $5.49, give five $1 bills and one more).
3. *$10 bill.* Use of $10 bills for large purchases. Use a number line of "one more ten than" strategy (e.g., for $36.59, give three $10 bills and one more $10 bill).
4. *Mixed $10 and $1 bills.* Student learns to count up to "one more than" using first 10s, then 1s (e.g., $36.59, give three $10 bills, six $1 bills, and one more dollar bill).
5. *Equivalence.* Students learn to use equivalent bills (e.g., $5 bill = five $1 bills; two $5 bills = $10 bill or ten $1 bills).
6. *Coins.* Teach coin counting once the use of bills is mastered. Teach counting by fives, beginning with nickels, following the strategy developed by Lowe and Cuvo (1976).

From *Instruction of students with severe disabilities* (5th ed.), by M. E. Snell and F. Brown, 2000, Upper Saddle River, NJ: Merrill.

The procedure began with the student organizing the coins from the largest to the smallest (e.g., quarter, dime, nickel, penny). Then he or she would begin to count by tapping and counting with the largest coin in the set. Pennies were counted last by having the student count from the last value they said by ones. For example, if a student was counting a dime, nickel, and three pennies he or she would begin with the dime tapping it twice and counting (i.e., 5, 10), then counting the nickel by tapping it once (i.e., 15), and then he or she would count the three pennies (i.e., 16, 17, 18). A similar strategy is to have the student use finger prompts to represent the values of the larger coins (e.g., quarter = 5 fingers; dime = 2 fingers; nickel = 1 finger).

Some students may not be able to master the counting and numeracy skills needed to successfully count coins. In this situation, it may be appropriate to identify an alternate performance strategy that would allow the student to be able to use money to buy goods and services. For example, research studies have examined the viability of strategies such as teaching students to obtain the amount of money needed to complete an activity before they do the activity (McDonnell, 1987; Schleien, Certo, & Muccino, 1984) or the use of coin cards (Browder et al., 1988; Sprague & Horner, 1984). Figure 13–12 illustrates a coin card that a student could use to purchase a soda from a vending machine.

The use of systematic instructional procedures is also necessary to effectively teach students to count bills. When students do not have the necessary prerequisite skills, IEP teams may need to consider alternatives such as taking a large bill (e.g., $20 bill) to purchase goods or services (Morse & Schuster, 2000) or the use of the next-dollar or one-more-than strategy (Colyer & Collins, 1996; Haring, Kennedy, Adams, & Pitts-Conway, 1987; McDonnell, Horner, & Williams, 1984; Test, Howell, Burkhart, & Beroth, 1993). The next-dollar or one-more-than strategy is designed for students who may have some counting and numeracy skills, but may not have the ability to count complex combinations of bills and coins. The student is taught to identify the dollar value on the cash register and/or cashier's request and then count out the next highest dollar value. McDonnell et al. (1984) taught students to say the dollar value shown on the cash register, say the next number, and then count out that number of $1 bills. So, if the price on a register was $5.67, the student would say "five," then say "six," and then he or she

FIGURE 13–12
Illustration of a coin card. The student would match coins to the pictures of the quarters and then use the coins to purchase a drink from the vending machine. The student could match coins either before or after going to the vending machine.

$1   1.00

would count out six $1 bills. The same procedure could be used to teach students to use bill combinations such as a single $5 bill and a single $1 bill. In a different variation of the strategy, Colyer and Collins (1996) taught students to count out the number of bills required for the dollar amount and one more for the cents. Using the above example, the student would count out five $1 bills and then say "one more for cents," giving the cashier one more $1 bill.

Purchasing Skills. As discussed earlier, students with severe disabilities often have significant difficulty using the skills learned at school in actual performance settings (Horner et al., 1986; Rosenthal-Malek & Bloom, 1998). Consequently, students may learn to count money proficiently at school, but may not be able to use these skills in order to purchase goods and services in stores, restaurants, or theaters.

Initial attempts to promote the generalization of money skills to community settings often focused on the use of classroom or school-based simulations (Horner et al., 1986). *Simulations* are training formats in which the natural stimuli found in the performance environment are represented through some alternate form or medium during instruction. Unfortunately, early studies on the use of simulations in order to promote generalization of money skills to actual performance settings had mixed outcomes for students. For example, McDonnell et al. (1984) taught students to use the next-dollar strategy using paper flash cards and photographic slides of cash registers to represent amounts. However, the results showed that neither the flash card nor the slides resulted in the students' generalized use of the next-dollar strategy to grocery stores. Only after pairing slide instruction with community-based instruction did the students' performance improve. Other studies found similar results, which reinforced the need for students to be provided community-based instruction in order to improve their generalized performance of money skills (Braham, Collins, Schuster, & Kleinert, 1999; Browder et al., 1988; Marholin, O'Toole, Touchette, Berger, & Doyle, 1979; McDonnell & Horner, 1985). In addition, these studies suggested that the level of generalization demonstrated by students was better if simulations were designed to approximate as closely as possible the stimulus conditions found at actual performance sites.

Recent improvements in computer and video technology have enhanced the ability of teachers to represent the actual stimuli found in community settings

at school. Several recent studies have shown that computer- and video-based instruction can improve students' ability to acquire generalized purchasing skills (Ayres, Langone, Boon, & Norman, 2006; Cihak et al., 2006; Hansen & Morgan, 2008; Mechling, Pridgen, & Cronin, 2005). For example, Hansen and Morgan (2008) use computer-based instruction consisting of DVD videos and CD-ROM screens to teach students with severe disabilities to go to the check-out area, stand in the shortest line, place items on the conveyer belt, pay for the items using the next-dollar strategy, respond to the request for "paper or plastic," and obtain the change. The students were able to master the skills using computer-based instruction, but more importantly, they were able to generalize the skills to three stores in the community.

> *Marcus's parents recently talked to Ms. Carter because they would like Marcus to be able to independently buy a snack or make a small purchase when the family goes out into the community. Because Marcus is still working on basic math skills, Ms. Carter decided to teach Marcus the next-dollar strategy in order to make small purchases and wait to teach making change until he has a stronger understanding of basic math skills. They practiced every day in the classroom during the math block using simulated activities. She and Marcus would use ads in the newspaper circular to select an item and then count out to the next dollar in order to pay for it. She also asked Marcus's parents to send money each week so that Marcus could practice the strategy while making an actual purchase. He went to the school store run by the PTA and bought small items. She then taught Marcus's mom and dad how to use the strategy and had them practice each weekend with Marcus when the family did their weekly shopping or family fun outings. After a few weeks, Marcus's family reported that he can now buy snacks by himself at the movie theater and at the local arcade.*

Consumer and Money Management Skills. Students with severe disabilities can learn a wide variety of consumer and money management skills, including using a calculator to determine whether they have enough money to purchase desired items (Frederick-Dugan et al., 1991; Matson & Long, 1986), writing checks and deposit slips (Bourbeau, Sowers, & Close, 1986; Davies, Stock, & Wehmeyer, 2003), using an ATM (Cihak et al.,

2004; McDonnell & Ferguson, 1989), and developing budgets (Wilson et al., 1986).

> *Mr. Karst is working with Ms. Davis, Jacob's adult roles and financial literacy teacher, to help him learn to use a personal financial program to develop and keep a budget. With support from his mom and dad, Jacob established budget categories and he is learning to enter the money he gets for doing chores around the house and to track his spending. The goal is to have Jacob become fluent at using the software before he gets a job, earns more money, and needs to manage more of his own expenses.*

Computer technology is increasingly being used to support individuals with disabilities so that they may meet the demands of daily living, including managing their own finances in the future. For example, Davies et al. (2003) describe the results of an exploratory study that compared the effectiveness of a computer software program and use of a traditional check register to allow adults with intellectual disabilities to write checks, record checks, and maintain their checkbook balances. The software program used icons to represent various tasks (e.g., write check) and payees (e.g., a house to represent paying the rent). The results showed that the rate of errors made by the study participants was significantly lower when they used the computer software than when they completed the tasks using a traditional check register.

Time and Time Management

When students have the skills required to tell time and schedule their activities, they are less dependent on others in home, school, work, and community settings. Some of the most important skills are (a) knowing when an activity begins and ends, (b) being able to follow a daily schedule, and (c) being able to plan weekly and monthly schedules in order to accomplish the activities that are necessary for successful daily living.

Telling Time. The act of looking at a clock or a watch and determining that it is 2:36 seems relatively simple, but telling time is a very complex operation that requires students to use a large number of counting and numeracy skills. However, with systematic instruction, many students with severe disabilities can learn to tell time using both analog and digital clocks. Several curricula for telling time have been developed to teach students to tell time using a traditional analog clock

TABLE 13–4
Illustrative Sequence to Teaching Telling Time with an Analog Clock

1. Responds to a familiar hand position on a clock as a specific cue for an event (e.g., 11:35 = lunch).
2. Tell time by the hour.
3. Tell time at 30 minutes past the hour.
4. Tell time at 15 minutes past the hour.
5. Tell time at 15 minutes before the hour.
6. Tell time at 45 minutes past the hour.
7. Tell time at 5-minute intervals past the hour.
8. Tell time at 5-minute intervals before the hour.
9. Tell time to the minute.

Adapted from *The Syracuse community-referenced curriculum guide for students with moderate and severe disabilities,* by A. Ford, R. Schnorr, L. Meyer, L. Davern, J. Black, & P. Dempsy, 1989. Baltimore: Paul H. Brookes.

face (Ford et al., 1989; Fredericks et al., 1976; O'Brien, 1974). Table 13-4 presents a typical sequence for learning to tell time using an analog clock. However, given the wide availability of digital clocks, watches, and other electronic devices with digital time displays (e.g., cell phones, computers), a student's IEP team should consider whether learning to tell time using an analog clock is actually the best option.

Developing and Following a Schedule. Learning to develop and follow a schedule can increase a student's ability to make choices and control his or her life. Students can learn to develop and follow daily and weekly schedules using a variety of formats, ranging from pictures and symbols (Bambara & Ager, 1992) to Personal Digital Assistants (PDAs) (Davies, Stock, & Wehmeyer, 2002). It is also important to note that students do not necessarily need to tell time in order to use a scheduling system. This can be accomplished by developing a picture or symbol system that designates the time (either analog or digital representations) when the activity is supposed to occur. The student is taught to identify the specific activity that the picture or symbol represents (e.g., Foods class) and is taught to match the time (e.g., 9:10) that the activity is supposed to occur with a clock face or digital clock (Wilcox & Bellamy, 1987). The schedule can be expanded to include self-management checklists that allow the student to gather the materials necessary for the activity (e.g., textbook, notebook, pencil) and/or to self-evaluate their performance in the activity (e.g., arrive to class on time, turned in homework assignment).

Jacob's Mom and Dad bought a new home computer this year. During Jacob's IEP meeting, his dad asked that Mr. Karst work with them to help Jacob learn to use to use Microsoft® Outlook® to develop a weekly schedule. Jacob and his parents came up with a list of household chores and leisure activities that Jacob would need to schedule on a regular basis. Mr. Karst is now teaching Jacob to use the calendar in Outlook® to set up his home schedule. Jacob begins with a list of known words that represent activities (e.g., trash, homework) that he has to get done each week and a list of activities that he can choose to do if he wants (e.g., computer game, go ice skating). Jacob's Mom and Dad came up with a set of guidelines that he can use to help him set up his schedule (e.g., how much time he needs to schedule in order to complete his homework and his chores, how much time he can watch TV and play on the computer, and when he needs to go to bed). Mr. Karst and Jacob's computer technology teacher have set up a teaching plan to help Jacob learn to use these rules to develop his weekly schedule.

In one of the earliest published studies on scheduling systems, Bambara and Ager (1992) taught three adults with severe disabilities to develop and follow a weekly leisure schedule. The study participants selected picture cards that represented specific activities that they wanted to complete, chose the day of the week on which they wanted to complete the activity, and placed the card into a schedule book. The participants were trained to follow the schedule during their typical daily routines. The results showed that all of the participants learned to self-schedule their leisure activities and follow the schedule without assistance, and they maintained use of the schedule system over time. Equally important, the use of the scheduling system resulted in an increase in the frequency and diversity of leisure activities completed by the participants each week.

Science Instruction

Science is one of the three areas of the general education curriculum that the NCLB Act and IDEA require that IEP teams address in developing a student's educational plan. Most state academic content standards are based on the National Science Education Standards developed by the National Research Council (1996). These standards address seven areas, including science as inquiry, physical science, life science, earth and space science, science and technology, science and social perspectives, and the history and nature of science.

Unfortunately, a limited amount of research has been conducted on approaches and strategies for teaching science content to students with severe disabilities (Courtade, Spooner, & Browder, 2007). Spooner, DiBiase, and Courtade-Little (2006) suggest that given the limited amount of research on teaching science content to students with severe disabilities, practitioners might do well to use the standards-referenced approach described above to look at how the functional skills that are important to a student's participation in home, school, work, and community settings can be aligned with science academic content standards. For example, teaching a student to read the weather report in the newspaper or from the Web to predict the type of clothing that he or she needs to wear that day could be linked to a standard such as *Evaluate weather predictions based upon observational data* (Utah State Office of Education, May 9, 2003). They assert that many functional skills are consistent with the principles laid out in the National Science Education Standards and could be justified legitimately as science content.

Some of the strategies that have been used to teach science concepts and skills to students have included the universal design of a science curriculum (Dymond et al., 2006), class-wide peer tutoring (Utley et al., 2001), and embedded instruction (Johnson et al., 2004; McDonnell et al., 2002). Dymond et al. (2006) conducted a study that focused on the application of universal design principles to a high school science course. A team composed of the general education teacher, a special education teacher who also taught the science course to students with mild disabilities, and the special education teacher for students with developmental disabilities worked collaboratively to restructure each science lesson using universal design principles. The team met weekly throughout the semester to restructure the traditional lesson plans so that they were accessible by all students in the class, including those with severe disabilities. The results suggested that structuring the course to meet the needs of all students had a number of benefits for both students with and without disabilities. For example, the researchers found that for students with disabilities, the process led to improved social interactions with their peers without disabilities and improved their participation in instructional routines and activities. The researchers noted positive outcomes for students without disabilities, including improved class participation; personal responsibility; and improved completion of work, grades, and end-of-year test scores.

Summary

Instruction on academic content is an essential for all students with severe disabilities. Current federal laws require that IEP teams demonstrate how students will participate and progress in three areas of the general education curriculum, including reading, math, and science. IEP teams must consider a number of factors in deciding whether goals and objectives should be selected from the general education curriculum or ecological inventories and/or ecological curriculum guides, or both. Research suggests that instruction on academic skills must be based on empirically validated strategies regardless of whether instruction occurs as part of typical learning activities in the classroom, in parallel instructional activities, or in community settings. Whatever approach is taken, teachers must ensure that students not only demonstrate mastery of the skills, but that they also demonstrate the ability to apply the skills in their daily lives. Finally, increased expectations for teaching academic content to students and rapidly developing technology in this area require that teachers be committed to keeping up with the research literature and developing their skills in order to teach complex academic content to students.

Suggested Activities

1. Imagine that you are the teacher of a first-grade student with multiple disabilities and complex communication needs. At the IEP meeting, you want to explain to the parents of the child and the rest of the team why you think that it is important to prioritize literacy learning for this student. What would you say? What examples might you give of how literacy instruction for this child might look?
2. Review your state's academic content standards in mathematics at the second, fourth, and sixth grades. Identify the critical functions of each standard and then pinpoint one functional skill that could be used to allow the student to demonstrate progress toward mastery of each standard.
3. Describe how embedded instruction could be used in general education classes in order to help Jacob

learn the key concepts and terms identified by his general education teachers for each unit.
4. Ms. Smith's first-grade class is working on the science standard that requires that students separate mixtures based on properties (e.g., by size or by substance [rocks and sand, iron filings and sand, salt and sand]). Create a lesson that teaches this standard and is adapted for Marisa, a child with autism, who has limited speech and uses the Picture Exchange Communication System (PECS) to communicate. For example, how could she participate in the lesson in a way that would help her gain an understanding of how to categorize items?

References

Alberto, P. A., Fredrick, L., Hughes, M., McIntosh, L., & Cihak, D. (2007). Components of visual literacy: Teaching logos. *Focus on Autism and Other Developmental Disabilities, 22,* 234–243.

Ayres, K. M., Langone, J., Boon, R. T., & Norman, A. (2006). Computer-based instruction for purchasing skills. *Education and Training in Developmental Disabilities, 41,* 253–263.

Bambara, L. M., & Ager, C. (1992). Using self-scheduling to promote self-directed leisure activity in home and community settings. *The Journal of the Association for Persons with Severe Handicaps, 17,* 67–76.

Bambara, L. M., Wilson, B. A., & McKenzie, M. (2007). Transition and quality of life. In S. L. Odom, R. H. Horner, M. E. Snell, & J. Blacher (Eds.), *Handbook of developmental disabilities* (pp. 371–389). New York: Guilford Press.

Batchelder, A., McLaughlin, T. F., Weber, K. P., Derby, K. M., & Gow, T. (2009). The effects of hand-over-hand and a dot-to-dot tracing procedure on teaching an autistic student to write his name. *Journal of Developmental and Physical Disabilities, 21,* 131–138.

Bedrosian, J., Lasker, J., Speidel, K., & Politsch, A. (2003). Enhancing the written narrative skills of an AAC student with autism: Evidence-based research issues. *Topics in Language Disorders, 23,* 304–324.

Bellamy, T., & Buttars, K. L. (1975). Teaching trainable level retarded students to count money: Toward personal independence through academic instruction. *Education and Training in Mental Retardation, 10,* 18–25.

Benz, M. R., Lindstrom, L., & Yovanoff, P. (2000). Improving graduation and employment outcomes of students with disabilities: Predictive factors and student perspectives. *Exceptional Children, 66,* 509–529.

Becht, L. (1985). *The sensible pencil: A handwriting program.* Birmingham, AL: EBSCO Curriculum Materials.

Blischak, D. M., & Schlosser, R. W. (2003). Use of technology to support independent spelling by students with autism. *Topics in Language Disorders, 23,* 293–304.

Bourbeau, P. E., Sowers, J., & Close, D. W. (1986). An experimental analysis of generalization of banking skills from classroom to bank settings in the community. *Education and Training of the Mentally Retarded, 21,* 98-107.

Bradford, S., Shippen, M. E., Alberto, P., Houchins, D. E., & Flores, M. (2006). Using systematic instruction to teach decoding skills to middle school students with moderate intellectual disabilities. *Education and Training in Developmental Disabilities, 41, 333-343.*

Branham, R., Collins, B., Schuster, J. W., & Kleinert, H. (1999). Teaching community skills to students with moderate disabilities: Comparing combined techniques of classroom simulation, videotaped modeling, and community-based instruction. *Education and Training in Mental Retardation and Developmental Disabilities, 34,* 170-181.

Browder, D. (2001a). *Curriculum and assessment for students with moderate and severe disabilities.* New York: Guilford Press.

Browder, D. (2001b). Functional reading. In *Curriculum and assessment for students with moderate and severe disabilities* (pp. 179-214). New York: Guilford Press.

Browder, D. M., Ahlgrim-Delzell, L., Courtade-Little, G., & Snell, M. E. (2006). General curriculum access. In M. E. Snell & F. Brown (Eds.), *Instruction of students with severe disabilities* (6th ed., pp. 489-525). Upper Saddle River, NJ: Merrill.

Browder, D., Flowers, C., Ahlgrim-Delzell, L. A., Karvonen, M., Spooner, F., & Algozzine, R. (2004). The alignment of alternate assessment content with academic and functional curricula. *The Journal of Special Education, 37,* 211-223.

Browder, D. M., & Grasso, E. (1999). Teaching money skills to individuals with mental retardation: A research review with practical applications. *Remedial and Special Education, 20,* 297-308.

Browder, D. M., Mims, P. J., Spooner, F., Ahlgrim-Delzell, L. A., & Lee, A. (2009). Teaching elementary students with multiple disabilities to participate in shared stories. *Research and Practice for Persons with Severe Disabilities, 33,* 3-12.

Browder, D. M., & Snell, M. E. (2000). Teaching functional academics. In M. E. Snell & F. Brown (Eds.), *Instruction of students with severe disabilities* (5th ed. pp. 493-543). Upper Saddle River, NJ: Merrill.

Browder, D. M., Snell, M. E., & Wildonger, B. (1988). Simulation and community-based instruction of vending machine with time delay. *Education and Training in Mental Retardations, 23,* 175-185.

Browder, D. M., & Spooner, F. (2006). *Teaching language arts, math, and science to students with significant cognitive disabilities.* Baltimore: Paul H. Brookes.

Browder, D. M., Spooner, F., Ahlgrim-Dezell, L., Harris, A. A., & Wakeman, S. (2008). A meta-analysis on teaching mathematics to students with significant cognitive disabilities. *Exceptional Children, 74,* 407-432.

Browder, D. M., Trela, K., & Jimenez, B. (2007). Training teachers to follow a task analysis to engage middle school students with moderate and severe developmental disabilities in grade-appropriate literature. *Focus on Autism and Other Developmental Disabilities, 22,* 206-219.

Browder, D. M., Wakeman, S. Y., Flowers, C., Rickelmann, R. J., Pugalee, D., & Karvonen, M. (2007). Creating access to the general education curriculum with links to grade-level content for students with significant cognitive disabilities: An explication of the concept. *The Journal of Special Education, 41,* 2-16.

Browder, D. M., Wakeman, S. Y., Spooner, F., Ahlgrim-Delzell, L., & Algozzine, B. (2006). Research on reading instruction for individuals with severe cognitive disabilities. *Exceptional Children, 72,* 392-408.

Bullock, J., Pierce, S., & McClellan, L. (1989). *Touch Math.* Colorado Springs, CO: Innovative Learning Concepts.

Bulter, F. M., Miller, S. P., Lee, K., & Pierce. T. (2001). Teaching mathematics to students with mild-to-moderate mental retardation: A review of the literature. *Mental Retardation, 39,* 20-31.

Carter, E. W., & Kennedy, C. H. (2006). Promoting access to the general curriculum using peer support strategies. *Research and Practice for Persons with Severe Disabilities, 31,* 284-292.

Chard, D. J., Vaughn, S., & Tyler, B. J. (2002). A synthesis of research on effective interventions for building reading fluency with elementary students with learning disabilities. *Journal of Learning Disabilities, 35,* 386-406.

Cihak, D. F., Alberto, P. A., Kessler, K. B., & Taber, T. A. (2004). An investigation of instructional scheduling arrangements for community-based instruction. *Research in Developmental Disabilities, 25,* 67-88.

Cihak, D. F., & Foust, J. L. (2008). Comparing number lines and touch points to teach addition facts to students with autism. *Focus on Autism and Other Developmental Disabilities, 23,* 131-137.

Clayton, J., Burdge, M., & Kleinert, H. L. (2001). Integrating alternate assessment with ongoing instruction. In H. L., Kleinert, & J. F. Kearns (Eds.), *Alternate assessment: Measuring outcomes and support for students with disabilities* (pp. 77-92). Baltimore: Paul H. Brookes.

Cohen, E. T., Allgood, M. H., Heller, K. W., & Castelle, M. (2001). Use of picture dictionaries to promote written communication by students with hearing and cognitive impairments. *AAC Augmentative and Alternative Communication, 17,* 245-254.

Cohen, E. T., Heller, K. W., Alberto, P., & Fredrick, L. D. (2008). Using a three-step decoding strategy with constant time delay to teach word reading to students with mild and moderate mental retardation. *Focus on Autism and Other Developmental Disabilities, 23,* 67-78.

Collins, B. C., Evans, A., Creech-Galloway, C., Karl, J., & Miller, A. (2007). Comparison of the acquisition and maintenance of teaching functional and core content sight words in special and general education settings. *Focus on Autism and Other Developmental Disabilities, 22,* 220-233.

Colyer, S. P., & Collins, B. C. (1996). Using natural cues within prompt levels to teach the next dollar strategy to students with disabilities. *The Journal of Special Education, 30,* 305-318.

Conners, F. A. (2003). Reading skills and cognitive abilities of individuals with mental retardation. *International Review of Research in Mental Retardation, 27,* 191-229.

Conners, F. A., Atwell, J. A., Rosenquist, C. J., & Sligh, A. C. (2001). Abilities underlying decoding differences in children with intellectual disabilities. *Journal of Intellectual Disabilities Research, 45,* 292-299.

Cooper, J. O., Heron, T. E., & Heward, W. L. (2007). *Applied Behavior Analysis* (2nd ed.). Upper Saddle River, NJ: Merrill/Pearson.

Copeland, S. R. (2007a). Reading comprehension. In S. R. Copeland & E. B. Keefe (Eds.), *Effective literacy instruction for individuals with moderate or severe disabilities* (pp. 79-94). Baltimore: Paul H. Brookes.

Copeland, S. R. (2007b). Written communication. In S. R. Copeland & E. B. Keefe (Eds.), *Effective literacy instruction for individuals with moderate or severe disabilities* (pp. 109–126). Baltimore: Paul H. Brookes.

Courtade, G. R., Spooner, F., & Browder, D. M. (2007). Review of studies with students with significant cognitive disabilities which link to science standards. *Research and Practice for Persons with Severe Disabilities, 32*, 43–49.

Cupples, L., & Iaconao, T. (2000). Phonological awareness and oral reading skill in children with Down syndrome. *Journal of Speech, Language, and Hearing Research, 43*, 595–608.

Cuvo, A. J., & Klatt, K. P. (1992). Effects of community-based, videotape, and flash card instruction of community-referenced sight words on students with mental retardation. *Journal of Applied Behavior Analysis, 25*, 499–512.

Davies, D. K., Stock, S. E., & Wehmeyer, M. L. (2002). Enhancing independent time-management skills of individuals with mental retardation using a Palmtop personal computer. *Mental Retardation, 40*, 358–365.

Davies, D. K., Stock, S. E., & Wehmeyer, M. L. (2003). Utilization of computer technology to facilitate money management by individuals with mental retardation. *Education and Training in Developmental Disabilities, 38*, 106–112.

de Graff, S., Verhoeven, L., Bosman, A. M. T., & Hasselman, F. (2007). Integrated pictorial mnemonics and stimulus fading: Teaching kindergartners letter sounds. *British Journal of Educational Psychology, 77*, 519–539.

de Valenzuela, J. S., & Tracey, M. (2007). The role of language and communication as a basis for literacy. In S. R. Copeland & E. B. Keefe (Eds.), *Effective literacy instruction for individuals with moderate or severe disabilities* (pp. 23–40). Baltimore: Paul H. Brookes.

Didden, R. de Graaff, S. Nelemans, M. Vooren, M., & Lancioni, G. (2006). Teaching sight words to children with moderate to mild mental metardation: Comparison between instructional procedures. *American Journal on Mental Retardation, 111*, 357–365.

Didden, R., Prinsen, H., & Sigafoos, J. (2000). The blocking effect of pictorial prompts on sight-word reading. *Journal of Applied Behavior Analysis, 33*, 317–320.

Dymond, S. K., Renzaglia, A., Rosenstein, A., Chun, E. J., Banks, R. A., Niswander, V., et al. (2006). Using participatory action research approach to create a universally designed inclusive high school science course: A case study. *Research and Practice for Persons with Severe Disabilities, 31*, 293–308.

Ehren, B. J., Lenz, B. K., & Deshler, D. D. (2004). Enhancing literacy proficiency with adolescents and young adults. In C. A. Stone, E. R. Silliman, B. J. Ehren, & K. Apel (Eds.), *Handbook of language and literacy: Development and disorders* (pp. 681–701). New York: Guilford Press.

Farrell, M., & Elkins, J. (1995). Literacy for all? The case for Down syndrome. *Journal of Reading, 38*, 270–280.

Feelings, T. (1995). *Middle passage: White ships, black cargo.* New York: Dial Books.

Fletcher, H., & Buckley, S. (2002). Phonological awareness in children with Down syndrome. *Down Syndrome Research and Practice, 8*, 11–18.

Flexer, R. (1989). Conceptualizing addition. *Teaching Exceptional Children, 21*(4), 21–24.

Flowers, C., Browder, D., & Ahlgrim-Delzell, L. (2006). An analysis of three states' alignment between language arts and mathematics standards and alternate assessments. *Exceptional Children, 72*, 201–213.

Flowers, C. P., Browder, D. M., Ahlgrim-Delzell, L., & Spooner, F. (2006). Promoting the alignment of curriculum, assessment, and instruction. In D. M. Browder & F. Spooner (Eds.), *Teaching language arts, math, and science to students with significant cognitive disabilities* (pp. 295–311). Baltimore: Paul H. Brookes.

Foley, B. E., & Staples, A. H. (2003). Developing augmentative and alternative communication (AAC) and literacy interventions in a supported employment setting. *Topics in Language Disorders, 4*, 325–343.

Foley, B. E., & Staples, A. (2007). Chapter 9: Supporting literacy development with assistive technology. In S. R. Copeland & E. B. Keefe (Eds.), *Effective literacy instruction for individuals with moderate or severe disabilities* (pp. 127–148). Baltimore: Paul H. Brookes.

Ford, A., Schnorr, R., Meyer, L., Davern, L., Black, J., & Dempsey, P. (1989). *The Syracuse community-referenced curriculum guide for students with moderate and severe disabilities.* Baltimore: Paul H. Brookes.

Frederick-Dugan, A., Test, D. W., & Varn, L. (1991). Acquisition and generalization of purchasing skills using a calculator by students who are mentally retarded. *Education and Training in Mental Retardation, 26*, 381–387.

Fredericks, H. D. Bud, Riggs, C., Furey, T., Grove, D., Moore, W., McDonnell, J., et al. (1976). *The teaching research curriculum for moderately and severely handicapped.* Springfield, Ill: Charles C. Thomas.

Giangreco, M. F., Cloninger, C. J., & Iverson, V. S. (1998). *Choosing outcomes and accommodations for children: A guide to educational for students with disabilities.* Baltimore: Paul H. Brookes.

Giangreco, M. F., Dennis, R., Cloninger, C., Edelman, S., & Schattman, R. (1993). "I've counted Jon": Transformational experiences of teachers educating students with disabilities. *Exceptional Children, 59*, 359–371.

Giangreco, M. F., & Putnam, J. W. (1991). Supporting the education of students with severe disabilities in regular education environments. In L. H. Meyer, C. A. Peck, & L. Brown (Eds.), *Critical issues in the lives of people with severe disabilities* (pp. 245–270). Baltimore: Paul H. Brookes.

Graham, S., Harris, K. R., & Fink, B. (2000). Is handwriting causally related to learning to write? Treatment of handwriting problems in beginning writers. *Journal of Educational Psychology, 92*, 620–633.

Groen, M. A., Laws, G., Nation, K., & Bishop, D. M. (2006). A case of exceptional reading accuracy in a child with Down syndrome: Underlying skills and the relation to reading comprehension. *Cognitive Neuropsychology, 23*, 1190–1214.

Gunning, T. G. (2002). *Assessing and correcting reading and writing difficulties* (2nd ed.). Boston: Allyn & Bacon.

Hansen, D. L., & Morgan, R. L. (2008). Teaching grocery store purchasing skills to students with intellectual disabilities using a computer-based instruction program. *Education and Training in Developmental Disabilities, 43*, 431–442.

Haring, T. G., Kennedy, C. H., Adams, M. J., & Pitts-Conway, V. (1987). Teaching generalization of purchasing skills across community settings to autistic youth using videotape modeling. *Journal of Applied Behavior Analysis, 20*, 89–96.

Harrower, J. (1999). Educational inclusion of children with severe disabilities. *Journal of Positive Behavioral Interventions, 1*, 215–230.

Hedrick, W. B., Katims, D. S., & Carr, N. J. (1999). Implementing a multimethod, multilevel literacy program for students with mental retardation. *Focus on Autism and Other Developmental Disabilities, 14*, 231–239.

Heller, K. W., Rupert, J., Coleman-Martin, M. B., Meei, P., & Calhoon, M. B. (2007). Reading fluency instruction with students with physical disabilities. *Physical Disabilities: Education and Related Services, 25*, 13–32.

Heron, T. E., Okyere, B. A., & Miller, A. D. (1991). A taxonomy of approaches to teach spelling. *Journal of Behavioral Education, 1*, 117–130.

Hoogeveen, F., Smeets, P., & Lancioni, G. (1989). Teaching moderately mentally retarded children basic reading skills. *Research in Developmental Disabilities, 10*, 1–18.

Horner, R. H., McDonnell, J., & Bellamy, G. T. (1986). Efficient instruction of generalized behaviors: General case programming in simulation and community settings. In R. H. Horner, L. H. Meyer, & H. D. Fredericks (Eds.), *Educating learners with severe handicaps: Exemplary service strategies* (pp. 289–314). Baltimore: Paul H. Brookes.

Horton, S. (1985). Computational rates of educable mentally retarded adolescents with and without calculators in comparison to normals. *American Journal of Mental Deficiency, 85*, 161–170.

Hunt, P., & McDonnell, J. (2007). Inclusive education. In S. L. Odom, R. H. Horner, M. Snell, and J. Blacher (Eds.), *Handbook on Developmental Disabilities* (pp. 269–291). New York: Guilford Press.

Hunt, P., Staub, D., Alwell, M., & Goetz, L. (1994). Achievement by all students within the context of learning groups. *The Journal of the Association for Persons with Severe Handicaps, 19*, 290–301.

Jameson, J. M., McDonnell, J., Johnson, J. W., Riesen, T., & Polychronis, S. (2007). A comparison of one-to-one embedded instruction in the general education classroom and one-to-one massed practice instruction in the special education classroom. *Education and Treatment of Children, 30*, 23–44.

Janney, R., & Snell, M. E. (2000). *Modifying schoolwork.* Baltimore: Paul H. Brookes.

Jimenez, B. A., Courtade, G. R., & Browder, D. M. (2008). Teaching an algebraic equation to high school students with moderate developmental disabilities. *Education and Training in Developmental Disabilities, 43*, 266–274.

Johns, J. L., Edmond, R. M., & Mavrogenes, N. A. (1977). The Dolch basic sight vocabulary: A replication and validation study. *The Elementary School Journal, 78*, 31–37.

Johnson, J. W., McDonnell, J., Holzwarth, V., & Hunter, K. (2004). The efficacy of embedded instruction for students with developmental disabilities enrolled in general education classes. *Journal of Positive Behavioral Interventions, 6*, 214–227.

Joseph, L., & Seery, M. (2004). Where is the phonics? A review of the literature on the use of phonetic analysis with students with mental retardation. Remedial and Special Education, 25, 88-94.

Joseph, L. M., & Konrad, M. (2009). Teaching students with intellectual or developmental disabilities to write: A review of the literature. *Research in Developmental Disabilities, 30*, 1–19.

Joseph, L. M., & Seery, M. E. (2004). Where is the phonics? A review of the literature on the use of phonetic analysis with students

with mental retardation. *Remedial and Special Education, 25*, 88-94.

Kahn-Freedman, E. (2001). Finding a voice: Poetry and people with mental retardation. *Mental Retardation, 39*, 195–200.

Kamps, D., Locke, P., Delquadri, J., & Hall, R. V. (1989). Increasing academic skills of students with autism using fifth grade peers as tutors. *Education and Treatment of Children, 12*, 38–51.

Katims, D. S. (1994). Emergence of literacy in preschool children with disabilities. *Learning Disability Quarterly, 17*, 58–69.

Katims, D. S. (2000a). Literacy instruction for people with mental retardation: Historical highlights and contemporary analysis. *Education and Training in Mental Retardation and Developmental Disabilities, 35*, 3–15.

Katims, D. S. (2000b). *The quest for literacy: Curriculum and instructional procedures for teaching reading and writing to students with mental retardation and developmental disabilities.* Reston, VA: Council for Exceptional Children.

Kay-Raining Bird, E., Cleave, P. L., White, D., Pike, H., & Helmkay, A. (2008). Written and oral narratives of children and adolescents with Down syndrome. *Journal of Speech, Language, and Hearing Research, 51*, 436–450.

Keefe, E. B. (2007). Chapter 7: Vocabulary development. In S. R. Copeland & E. B. Keefe (Eds.), *Effective literacy instruction for individuals with moderate or severe disabilities* (pp. 95–108). Baltimore: Paul H. Brookes.

Kleinert, H. L., & Thurlow, M. L. (2001). An introduction to alternate assessment. In H. L. Kleinert and J. F. Kearns (Eds.), *Measuring outcomes and supports for students with disabilities* (pp. 1–15). Baltimore: Paul H. Brookes.

Kluth, P., & Chandler-Olcott, K. (2008). *"A land we can share": Teaching literacy to students with autism.* Baltimore: Paul H. Brookes.

Kohl, F. L., McLaughlin, M. J., & Nagle, K. (2006). Alternate achievement standards and assessments: A descriptive investigation of 16 states. *Exceptional Children, 73*, 107–122.

Koller, E. Z., & Mulhern, T. J. (1977). Use of a pocket calculator to train arithmetic skills with trainable adolescents. *Education and Training in Mental Retardation, 12*, 332–335.

Konrad, M., Trela, K., & Test, D. W. (2006). Using IEP goals and objectives to teach paragraph writing to high school students with physical and cognitive disabilities. *Education and Training in Developmental Disabilities, 41*, 111–124.

Kramer, T., & Krug, D. A. (1973). A rationale and procedure for teaching addition. *Education and Training of the Mentally Retarded, 8*, 140–145.

Kuby, P., Goodstadt-Killoran, I., Aldridge, J., & Kirkland, L. (1999). A review of research on environmental print. *Journal of Instructional Psychology, 26*, 173–182.

Lipsky, D. K., & Gartner, A. (1997). *Inclusion and school reform: Transforming America's classrooms.* Baltimore: Paul H. Brookes.

Lowe, M. L., & Cuvo, A. J. (1976). Teaching coin summation to the mentally retarded. *Journal of Applied Behavior Analysis, 9*, 483–489.

Marholin, D., O'Toole, K. M., Touchette, P. E., Berger, P. L., & Doyle, D. (1979). I'll have a Big Mac, large fry, large Coke, & an apple pie—or teaching community skills. *Behavior Therapy, 10*, 236–248.

Marvin, C. (1994). Home literacy experiences of preschool children with single and multiple disabilities. *Topics in Early Childhood Special Education, 14,* 351-367.

Matson, J. L., & Long, S. (1986). Teaching computation/shopping skills to mentally retarded adults. *American Journal of Mental Deficiency, 91,* 98-101.

McDonnell, J. (1987). The effects of time delay and increasing prompt hierarchy strategies on the acquisition of purchasing skills by students with severe handicaps. *The Journal of the Association for Persons with Severe Handicaps, 12,* 227-236.

McDonnell, J. (1998). Instruction for students with severe disabilities in general education settings. *Education and Training in Mental Retardation and Developmental Disabilities, 33,* 199-215.

McDonnell, J. (2010). Instruction in community settings. In J. McDonnell, & M. L. Hardman (Eds.), *Successful transition programs: Pathways for students with intellectual and developmental disabilities* (pp. 173-202). Los Angeles: Sage Publishing.

McDonnell, J., & Ferguson, B. (1988). A comparison of general case in-vivo and general case simulation plus in-vivo training. *The Journal of the Association for Persons with Severe Handicaps, 13,* 116-124.

McDonnell, J., & Ferguson, B. (1989). A comparison of time delay and decreasing prompt hierarchy strategies in teaching banking skills to students with moderate handicaps. *Journal of Applied Behavior Analysis, 22,* 85-92.

McDonnell, J., & Hardman, M. L. (2010). *Successful transition programs: Pathways for students with intellectual and developmental disabilities.* Thousand Oaks, CA: Sage Publishing.

McDonnell, J., & Horner, R. H. (1985). Effects of in vivo versus simulation-plus-in vivo training on the acquisition and generalization of grocery item selection by high school students with severe handicaps. *Analysis and Intervention in Developmental Disabilities, 5,* 323-343.

McDonnell, J., Horner, R. H., & Williams, J. (1984). Comparison of three strategies for teaching generalized grocery purchasing to high school students with severe handicaps. *The Journal of the Association for Persons with Severe Handicaps, 9,* 123-133.

McDonnell, J., Johnson, J. W., & McQuivey, C. (2008). *Embedded instruction for students with developmental disabilities in general education classes.* Alexandria, VA: Division of Developmental Disabilities, Council for Exceptional Children.

McDonnell, J., Johnson, J. W., Polychronis, S., Riesen, T., Jameson, M., & Kercher, K. (2006). Comparison of one-to-one embedded instruction in general education classes with small group instruction in special education classes. *Education and Training in Developmental Disabilities, 41,* 125-138.

McGregor, G. (2003). Standards-based reform and students with disabilities. In D. L. Ryndak and S. Alper (Eds.), *Curriculum and instruction for students with significant disabilities in inclusive settings* (pp. 32-50). Upper Saddle River, NJ: Allyn & Bacon.

Mechling, L. C., & Gast, D. L. (2003). Multi-media instruction to teach grocery word associations and store location: A study of generalization. *Education and Training in Developmental Disabilities, 38,* 62-76.

Mechling, L. C., Gast, D. L., & Langone, J. (2002). Computer-based video instruction to teach persons with moderate intellectual disabilities to read grocery aisle signs and locate items. *The Journal of Special Education, 35,* 224-240.

Mechling, L. C., Pridgen, L. S., & Cronin, B. A. (2005). Computer-based video instruction to teach students with intellectual disabilities to verbally respond to questions and make purchases in fast food restaurants. *Education and Training in Developmental Disabilities, 40,* 47-59.

Miller, A. & Miller, E. E. (1971). Symbol accentuation, single-track functioning and early reading. *American Journal of Mental Deficiency 76,* 110-117.

Minarovic, T. J., & Bambara, L. M. (2007). Teaching employees with intellectual disabilities to manage changing work routines using varied sight-word checklists. *Research and Practice for Persons with Severe Disabilities, 32,* 31-42.

Mirenda, P. (2003). "He's not really a reader . . .": Perspectives on supporting literacy development in individuals with autism. *Topics in Language Disorders, 23,* 271-282.

Morgan, M., & Moni, K. B. (2005). 20 ways to use phonics activities to motivate learners with difficulties. *Intervention in School and Clinic, 41,* 42-45.

Morgan, M., Moni, K. B., & Jobling, A. (2004). What's it all about? Investigating reading comprehension strategies in young adults with Down syndrome. *Down Syndrome Research and Practice, 9,* 37-44.

Morgan, M., Moni, K. B., & Jobling, M. A. (2006). Code-breaker: Developing phonics with a young adult with an intellectual disability. *Journal of Adolescent & Adult Literacy, 50*(1), 52-65.

Morin, V. A., & Miller, S. P. (1998). Teaching multiplication to middle school students with mental retardation. *Education and Treatment of Children, 21,* 22-31.

Morse, T. E., & Schuster, J. W. (2000). Teaching elementary students with moderate intellectual disabilities how to shop for groceries. *Exceptional Children, 66,* 273-288.

National Center on Educational Outcomes (n.d.). *Special topic area: Alternate assessments for students with disabilities—Frequently asked questions.* Available at http://www.cehd.umn.edu/NCEO/TOPICAREAS/AlternateAssessments/altAssessFAQ.htm

National Reading Panel. (2000). *Report of the National Reading Panel: Teaching children to read. Reports of the Subgroups* (NIH Publication 00-4654). Washington, DC: National Institute of Child Health and Human Development.

National Research Council. (1996). *National science education standards.* Washington, DC: National Academy Press.

Neef, N. A., Nelles, D. F., Iwata, B. A., & Page, T. J. (2003). Analysis of precurrent skills in solving mathematics story problems. *Journal of Applied Behavior Analysis, 36,* 21-34.

Neel, R. S., & Billingsley, F. F. (1989). *Impact: A functional curriculum handbook for students with moderate to severe disabilities.* Baltimore: Paul H. Brookes.

Nietupski, J., Hamre-Nietupski, S., Clancy, P., & Veerhusen, K. (1985). Effects of minimal versus lengthy delay between simulated and in vivo instruction on community performance. *Education and Training of the Mentally Retarded, 20,* 190-195.

Neuman, S. B. (2004). The effect of print-rich classroom environments on early literacy growth. *The Reading Teacher, 58,* 89-91.

O'Brien, F. (1974). *Instruction in reading a clock for the institutionalized retarded.* Unpublished manuscript. Carbondale, Ill: Anna State Hospital and Southern Illinois University.

Oelwein, P. L. (1995). *Teaching reading to children with Down syndrome: A guide for parents and teachers.* Bethesda, MD: Woodbine House.

Olsen, J. (2010). *Handwriting without tears.* Cabin John, MD: Handwriting Without Tears.

Olson, R. K., Forsberg, J., & Wise, B. (1994). Genes, environment, and the development of orthographic skills. In V. W. Berninger (Ed.), *The varieties of orthographic knowledge I: Theoretical and developmental issues* (pp. 27-71). Dordrecht, The Netherlands: Kluwer Academic Publishers.

Paddock, C., (1992). Ice cream stick math. *Teaching Exceptional Children, 24*(2), 50-51.

Phelps, L. A., & Hanley-Maxwell, C. (1997). School-to-work transitions for youth with disabilities: A review of outcomes and practices. *Review of Educational Research, 67,* 197-226.

Quenemoen, R. (2008). *A brief history of alternate assessments based on alternate achievement standards.* Minneapolis, MN: National Center on Education Outcomes, University of Minnesota.

Riesen, T., McDonnell, J., Johnson, J. W., Polychronis, S., & Jameson, M. (2003). A comparison of time delay and simultaneous prompting within embedded instruction in general education classes with students with moderate to severe disabilities. *Journal of Behavioral Education, 12,* 241-260.

Resnick, L. B., Wang, M. C., & Kaplan, J. (1973). Task analysis in curriculum design: A hierarchically sequenced introductory mathematics curriculum. *Journal of Applied Behavior Analysis, 6,* 685-886.

Rohena, E. I., Jitendra, A. K., & Browder, D. M. (2002). Comparison of the effects of Spanish and English constant time delay instruction on sight word reading by Hispanic learners with mental retardation. *The Journal of Special Education, 36,* 169-184.

Rosenblum, S., Weiss, P. L., & Parush, S. (2003). Product and process evaluation of handwriting difficulties: A review. *Educational Psychology Review, 15* (1), 41-81.

Rosenthal-Malek, A., & Bloom, A. (1998). Beyond acquisition: Teaching generalization for students with developmental disabilities. In A. Hilton & R. Ringlaben (Eds.), *Best and promising practices in developmental disabilities* (pp. 139-155). Austin, TX: PRO-ED.

Ryndak, D. L., Morrison, A. P., & Sommerstein, L. (1999). Literacy before and after inclusion in general education settings: A case study. *The Journal of the Association for Persons with Severe Handicaps, 24,* 5-22.

Saunders, S. J. (2007). Word-attack skills in individuals with mental retardation. *Mental Retardation and Developmental Disabilities Research Reviews, 13,* 78-84.

Schleien, S. J., Cuvo, N. J., & Muccino, A. (1984). Acquisition of leisure skills by a severely handicapped adolescent: A data based instructional program. *Education and Training of the Mentally Retarded, 19,* 297-305.

Schloss, P. J., Alper, S., Young, H., Arnold-Reid. G., Aylward, M., & Dudenhoeffer, S. (1995). Acquisition of functional sight words in community-based recreation settings. *Journal of Special Education, 29,* 84-96.

Sheehy, K. (2002). The effective use of symbols in teaching word recognition to children with severe learning difficulties: A comparison of word alone, integrated picture cueing and the handle technique. *International Journal of Disability, Development, and Education, 49,* 47-59.

Sheehy, K. (2005). Morphing images: A potential tool for teaching word recognition to children with severe learning difficulties. *British Journal of Educational Technology, 36,* 293-301.

Spooner, F., DiBiase, W., & Courtade-Little, G. (2006). Science standards and functional skills: Finding the links. In D. M. Browder & F. Spooner (Eds.), *Teaching language arts, math, and science to students with significant cognitive disabilities* (pp. 229-243). Baltimore: Paul H. Brookes.

Sprague, J. R., & Horner, R. H. (1984). The effects of single instance, multiple instance, and general case training on generalized vending machine use by moderately and severely handicapped students. *Journal of Applied Behavior Analysis, 17,* 273-278.

Sturm, J., & Koppenhaver, D. A. (2000). Supporting writing development in adolescents with developmental disabilities. *Topics in Language Disorders, 20,* 73-92.

Sulzby, E. (1989). Assessment of writing and of children's language while writing. In L. Morrow & J. Smith (Eds.), *The role of assessment and measurement in early literacy instruction* (pp. 83-109). Upper Saddle River, NJ: Prentice Hall.

Test, D. W., Howell, A., Burkhart, K., & Beroth, T. (1993). The one-more-than technique as a strategy for counting money for individuals with moderate mental retardation. *Education and Training in Mental Retardation, 28,* 232-241.

Therrien, W. J. (2004). Fluency and comprehension gains as a result of repeated reading. *Remedial and Special Education, 25,* 252-261.

Torgeson, J. K., & Mathes, P. G. (2000). *A basic guide to understanding, assessing, and teaching phonological awareness.* Austin, TX: PRO-ED.

U.S. Department of Education (2005, August). *Alternate achievement standards for students with the most significant cognitive disabilities: Non-regulatory guidance.* Washington, DC: Author.

U.S. Department of Education (December 21, 2007). *Standards and assessments peer review guide: Information and examples for meeting requirements of the No Child Left Behind Act of 2001.* Washington, DC: Author.

U.S. Department of Education, Office of Special Education and Rehabilitative Services, Office of Special Education Programs (2006). *28th annual report to Congress on the implementation of the Individuals with Disabilities Education Act, 2006.* Washington, DC: Author.

Utah State Office of Education. (May 9, 2003). *Elementary core curriculum.* Salt Lake City, UT: Author.

Utley, C. A., Reddy, S. S., Delquardi, J. C., Greenwood, C. R., Mortweet, S. L., & Bowman, V. (2001). Classwide peer tutoring: An effective teaching procedure for facilitating the acquisition of health education and safety facts with students with developmental disabilities. *Education and Treatment of Children, 24,* 1-27.

Van Allsburg, C. (1984). *The mysteries of Harris Burdick.* Boston: Houghton Mifflin Harcourt Children's Book Group.

van Kraayenoord, C. E., Moni, K. B., Jobling, A., & Ziebarth, K. (2002). Broadening approaches to literacy education for young adults with Down syndrome. In M. Cuskelly, A. Jobling, and S. Buckley (Eds.), *Down syndrome across the life span.* (pp. 81-92). Philadelphia: Whurr Publishers.

van Kraayeroord, C. E., & Paris, S. G. (1996). Story construction from a picture book: An assessment activity for young learners. *Early Childhood Research Quarterly, 11,* 41-61.

Vedora, J., & Stromer, R. (2006). Computer-based spelling instruction for students with developmental disabilities. *Research in Developmental Disabilities, 28,* 489-505.

Verhoeven, L., & Vermeer, A. (2006). Literacy achievement of children with intellectual disabilities and differing linguistic backgrounds. *Journal of Intellectual Disability Research, 50,* 725-738.

Ward, T., Van De Mark, C. A., & Ryndak, R. L. (2006). Balanced literacy classrooms and embedded instruction for students with severe disabilities: Literacy for all in the age of school reform. In D. M. Browder & F. Spooner (Eds.), *Teaching language arts, math, and science to students with significant cognitive disabilities* (pp. 125-170). Baltimore: Paul H. Brookes.

Wehmeyer, M. L., & Agran, M. (2006). Promoting access to the general education curriculum for students with significant cognitive disabilities. In D. M. Browder & F. Spooner (Eds.), *Teaching language arts, math, and science to students with significant cognitive disabilities.* (pp. 15-38). Baltimore: Paul H. Brookes.

Weikle, B., & Hadadian, A. (2004). Literacy, development and disabilities: Are we moving in the right direction? *Early Child Development and Care, 174,* 651-666.

Westling, D. L., & Fox, L. (2009). *Teaching students with severe disabilities* (4th ed.). Upper Saddle River, NJ: Merrill.

Whitehurst, G. J., & Lonigan, C. J. (1998). Child development and emergent literacy. *Child Development, 69,* 848-872.

Wilcox, B., & Bellamy, G. T. (1987). *The activities catalog: An alternative curriculum for youth and adults with severe disabilities.* Baltimore: Paul H. Brookes.

Wilson, P. G., Cuvo, A. J., & Davis, P. K. (1986). Training a functional skill cluster: Nutritious meal planning within a budget, grocery list writing, and shopping. *Analysis and Intervention in Developmental Disabilities, 6,* 179-201.

Xin, Y. P., Grasso, E., Dipipi-Hoy, C. M., & Jitendra, A. (2005). The effects of purchasing skill instruction for individuals with developmental disabilities: A meta-analysis. *Exceptional Children, 71,* 379-400.

Yamamoto, J., & Miya, T. (1999). Acquisition and transfer of sentence construction in autistic students: Analysis by computer-based teaching. *Research in Developmental Disabilities, 20,* 355-377.

14

Building Skills for Home and Community

Linda M. Bambara
Freya Koger
Audrey Bartholomew[1]

Teaching skills for home and community are just as important in today's curriculum as they were in the late 1970s when Lou Brown (Brown et al., 1979) first brought to our attention the importance of teaching age-appropriate functional skills for current and future environments. Home and community instruction affords students with intellectual disabilities the skills needed to participate in daily family life and day-to-day routines; to be involved in their communities; and, eventually, to acquire autonomy and self-direction for full-fledged adulthood. However, approaches to home and community instruction have undergone important transformations as inclusion, standards-based reform, and self-determination are more fully understood.

Consider the transformations within the past three decades. In the 1980s, a large body of research emerged on teaching skills to individuals with intellectual disabilities for managing their homes and gaining access to their communities. Teachers focused on teaching skills in home and community settings, and students often spent large portions of their day away from the school building. In the 1990s, with the advent of

inclusion and the 1997 reauthorization of the Individuals with Disabilities Education Act (IDEA), instructional focus shifted from community access to promoting access to the general education curriculum. In the early 2000s, the focus on the general education curriculum was further strengthened by the reauthorization of IDEA 2004 and the No Child Left Behind Act (2002), which emphasized that the same content standards should guide the curriculum for all learners. Although efforts to increase access to the general education curriculum were not intended to downplay the importance of a functional curriculum (Wehmeyer, Field, Doren, Jones, & Manson, 2004), some saw the movement as being in conflict with a functional skills approach (Bouck, 2009). Furthermore, special education teachers often struggled with the trade-off between offering community instruction in "real" nonschool environments and encouraging students with intellectual disabilities to have a typical school day in general education classes while accessing the general education curriculum.

Fortunately, many educators (Basset & Kochhar-Bryant, 2006; Burcroff, Radogna, & Wright, 2003; Wehmeyer, Field, Doren, Jones, & Mason, 2004) now believe that teachers do not have to choose between an academic and a functional curriculum for students with intellectual disabilities. Students can have the benefit of

[1]We gratefully acknowledge Diane Browder's ever-present contribution to this chapter. This chapter is inspired by earlier versions of which Diane Browder was an author.

both curriculum approaches through careful planning of where, when, and how the curriculum is introduced and implemented. Presently, curriculum access is broadly defined to include academic content in general education and "access to the content inherent within participation in *all the experiences that comprise general education life*" [italics added] (Ryndak & Billingsley, 2004, p. 50). This definition applies to general education experiences inside and outside of school contexts that are important for school and community life. With this contemporary interpretation, instruction for home and community life is compatible with the general education curriculum if blended with general education experiences. Consider the case of Julia Romano.

❖ ❖ ❖ ❖ ❖   **Julia Romano**   ❖ ❖ ❖ ❖ ❖

Julia, a petite 14-year-old with moderate intellectual disabilities, is an active, happy eighth grader in middle school. Since Julia's earliest school days, her parents have insisted that she be included in general education classrooms and have full opportunity to participate in the school activities of her choice. Although Julia's eighth-grade schedule was difficult to design, she now attends an array of academic and nonacademic classes with her schoolmates. Julia is also a member of the middle school chorus and an after-school art club. As an active teen with tremendous school spirit, Julia loves to attend school games and dances with her friends.

Early in the school year, Julia's parents received an invitation to attend a transition planning meeting with the school's transition coordinator. This invitation took Julia's parents by surprise. Like many parents of young teens, they were more focused on Julia's current needs as a teenager than on her adult life. Julia had not thought much about her life as an adult either and her goals were uncertain. As they began to talk, both Julia and her parents expressed their dream for Julia to live in her own home someday, work in a job that she enjoys, and be active in her community as she has been at school. They recognized the importance of beginning to plan now.

Although the Romanos believed that it would be beneficial for Julia to begin learning the daily living and community skills needed for postschool life, they had one unsettling concern. They worried that preparing for adult living would take Julia away from what she loved most—her school classes, activities, and classmates. Julia's parents had worked hard in order for Julia to be fully included. They were not willing to sacrifice Julia's current needs as a middle school student in planning for her future needs, at least not at age 14. They feared that during the transition planning meeting, they would have to make a choice.

Questions for Planning and Instruction

1. How can Julia's instructional needs in home and community skills be addressed without detracting from typical school experiences?

2. What skills should be considered that could best address her current and future needs?

Promoting self-determination, which has become a best practice in the education of learners with disabilities (Wehmeyer et al., 2004), has also influenced home and community instruction. Martin and Marshall (1995) describe self-determined individuals as people who "know what they want and how to get it" (p. 147). In other words, self-determined people are empowered to follow their preferences and direct their lives in positive ways. This simple definition provides a value for making decisions about what to teach and how to teach in a way that encourages student empowerment and self-directed learning.

With regard to determining what to teach, skills for home and community living should be directly related to the student's and family's preferences and visions for the future. More than being functional in the eyes of professionals, instructional goals are personalized according to the individual's unique interests and needs. Almost any daily living or community skill could potentially enhance learner control; however, those that facilitate self-determination are useful and desirable from the learner's perspective (Bambara, Cole, & Koger, 1998; Wehmeyer, 2005). Home and community skills for Julia will take into account her current interests as an active teen as well her and her parents' vision for her to live independently in her own home some day. Skills for Rico Hernandez, which will be introduced later in this chapter, will differ not only because of the differences in the two students' preferences and goals for the future, but because of differences in their cultural heritage as well. Self-determination for most Anglo-Americans emphasizes independence and autonomy. In other cultures, including the Latino culture, interdependence and shared autonomy with other family members are typically highly valued (Rueda, Monzó, Shapiro, Gomez, & Blacher, 2005). While skills for independent living will be stressed in Julia's program, skills for shared homemaking while living with his extended family will be the targets for Rico.

Self-determination influences how we teach by encouraging student-directed learning and control. Within the conceptual framework of self-determination, the student is viewed as an instructional partner. To encourage self-determination, opportunities for learner control and self-direction are infused into instruction. This can take multiple forms, including offering opportunities for making choices; following the learner's spontaneous interests; and teaching specific strategies such as goal setting, problem solving, and self-prompting to encourage learners to do more for themselves and to learn in ways that they enjoy. Although self-determination encourages self-direction, not all acts need to be completely autonomous. Many learners with intellectual disabilities require some support from others because to their physical or cognitive limitations; however, they can partially participate in activities and still self-direct even if that self-direction guides others to assist them in participating.

Julia makes use of a personal assistant. After swimming lessons at her school, Julia turns the hair dryer on and off and blows the dampness from her hair, while her buddy Susan directs the tip of the dryer for final styling.

The point is, whether acting completely autonomously or partially participating in activities with the support of others, students with intellectual disabilities can and should be supported in expressing their self-determination by making things happen for themselves.

Guidelines for Planning Instruction to Enhance Skills for the Home and the Community

This chapter adheres to several contemporary values in describing how teachers can encourage students to gain skills for use in their homes and their communities. First, decisions on what and where to teach must be made in partnership with students and their families, honoring their values, preferences, and vision for the future. Second, instruction needs to be planned to encourage the student's self-determination skills by teaching choice making, honoring preferences, and encouraging self-directed learning. Third, instructional strategies need to be blended with typical general education experiences while encouraging interaction with peers. Fourth, home and community skills gain importance as students become older. While children rely mostly on their caregivers for daily living and community access, an important part of adolescents' transition to adulthood is their increased autonomy in their home (e.g., fixing their own breakfast) and community (e.g., meeting friends at a restaurant). In this section, we translate these values into specific guidelines for instruction and illustrate planning with three students: Julia (age 14), Rico (age 9), and Aaron (age 19).

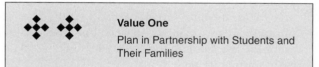

Value One

Plan in Partnership with Students and Their Families

Guideline One: Use Person-Centered Planning Strategies to Create a Vision

To enhance self-determination, the focus and methods of instruction must fit within the context of the student's and family's preferences, priorities, and future goals. Person-centered planning is a collaborative process that involves the student, family members, teachers, specialists, and, as needed, support personnel from nonschool services. Through problem solving and discussions among team members, person-centered planning aims to (a) describe a desirable future for the student, (b) delineate the activities and supports necessary to achieve the desired vision, and (c) mobilize existing resources to make the vision a reality (Michaels & Ferrara, 2006). From an instructional perspective, person-centered planning can help coordinate teaching with other forms of support and unify the goals of instruction with a person's own goals.

Several different person-centered planning processes have emerged over the past 20 years (Michaels & Ferrara, 2003) that guide educational teams through information gathering and planning to address the student's wants and needs. Some of these include Personal Futures Planning (Mount, 2000); Life Style Planning (O'Brien, 1987); Making Action Plans, or MAPS (Forest

& Pearpoint, 1992; O'Brien & Pearpoint, 2003); and Planning Alternative Tomorrows with Hope, or PATH (O'Brien & Pearpoint, 2003; Pearpoint, O'Brien, & Forest, 1992). Although each differs somewhat in format and focus, they guide teams to consider at least five essential questions:

1. *What is the student's history and current life situation?* Here team members contribute information that will paint a life history for the student. Both positive and negative events in the student's past and current life are noted.

2. *What are the strengths and gifts of the student?* The purpose of this question is to focus the team on building a vision based on the student's strengths and preferences rather than the student's deficits.

3. *What is the vision or dream for the student?* Team members discuss what an ideal life might be for the student for the next several years of childhood or as an adult. Team members think about what they want for the student and what the student would want for him or herself.

4. *What are the team's fears, obstacles, or challenges in building a better life for the student?* This question guides teams to consider fears about change and obstacles that may thwart the student's dreams with the aim of eliminating them.

5. *What are the priorities and goals for the future, and what will it take to make the vision happen?* Once a vision for the future has been established, team members focus on how to get there. They set priorities for achieving both short- and long-range goals, consider how to eliminate obstacles, and identify how to use supports to achieve desirable outcomes.

Because of their comprehensiveness, structured action plan approaches are useful when it is important to set new directions for the student, such as planning for the transition to postschool life or greater inclusion in school.

Mr. and Mrs. Romano were concerned about the transition planning process for their daughter, Julia. They feared that planning would result in a heavy vocational emphasis and take her away from the current school activities that she loved. Julia's parents were later relieved to discover that the transition coordinator selected MAPS to help them clarify what was important to Julia and to begin to think about her future as an adult. The MAPS process let them set priorities for the next three years (see Table 14-1). They decided that Julia will continue in general education classes, but her curriculum will be modified to reflect a stronger focus on home and community instruction. Instructional targets will include skills that will be useful now and in the future and that can be taught within general education classes. Julia, her mother, and Julia's teacher decided to meet periodically throughout the school year to target critical skills that Julia can learn at home (e.g., scheduling and self-initiating home chores). Julia will work with the community training specialist for one period, four days per week. Through the use of simulations in the school building and at actual community sites (e.g., the mall or music store), the community training specialist will teach Julia an array of skills that are appropriate for an active teen (e.g., how to use a cell phone, make purchases at fast-food restaurants, rent DVDs, shop for clothing) and, very importantly, how to keep safe in the community. Julia's family will explore options for home living, community, and employment supports. The transition coordinator will help Julia and her family connect with adult services for this initial planning.

TABLE 14–1
MAPS Outcomes for Julia

What is Julia's history?

Julia is a 14-year-old teen with intellectual disabilities.
Julia's parents have always felt strongly about inclusion.
Julia attended segregated preschool and school programs until age 8.
At her parents' insistence, Julia was fully included in a second-grade class.
She continued full inclusion through the eighth grade (her current grade).
Julia has had a happy childhood, doing activities typical for her age.
Grade 6 was bad for Julia. First year at middle school. New kids from other elementary schools ridiculed her, called her "retard." Problem solved after a school-wide intervention emphasizing friendships for all.

TABLE 14–1 (*Continued*)

Who is Julia?

Julia is a friendly, social girl who enjoys typical teen stuff.
She is very persistent, likes to be independent, and completes what she starts.
She is very methodical in her approach to things.
She laughs and giggles easily.
She's a "girl's girl": likes to primp, wear new clothes, have her nails done, wear makeup.
She likes to stay busy and go places; she loves to sing and draw.
She is somewhat gullible—easily led by peers she considers to be her friends.

What is your dream for Julia? What are your dreams for her as an adult?

In General:

For Julia to continue to be a part of her school.
For Julia to be happy, healthy, and safe.
To be able to pursue activities that she enjoys.
To have friends and people who care about her.

As an adult:

To live in an apartment with friends, family, or people who care about her.
To have her independence, but also the supports she needs to do what she wants to do.
To be involved in her community doing things she wants to do.
To have a competitive job that she likes.
To live in a community that will accept her for her gifts and talents.

What is your nightmare?

That Julia will be denied typical middle school and high school experiences.
That the focus on her "adult" needs will take her away from typical school activities.
That she will be lonely or unhappy.
That once she graduates, she will not be given the support she needs to achieve her goals.
That she will be put on a waiting list for adult services.
That once she graduates, the good life that she has built so far will stop: no more friends, no more activities, waiting for a job.

What are Julia's strengths, gifts, and abilities?

Julia is very persistent and will work hard at the things she enjoys or wants.
Julia has wonderful social skills; people are drawn to her.
She's easygoing.
Julia loves to be around people.

What are Julia's needs?

Julia enjoys attending, and therefore needs to attend, school with her same-age peers, doing typical school activities. Julia needs to continue with the school activities that she enjoys: swimming, chorus, and art.
Julia and her family need to begin exploring options for Julia's adult life.
Julia needs to develop daily living and community living skills that will enhance her independence now and in the future. Some areas are as follows:

• Basic cooking skills
• Community travel and safety skills
• Consumer skills (e.g., purchasing clothing, food shopping, ordering at restaurants)
• Use of communication tools (e.g., using the telephone, using newspapers and the Internet to access information)

Julia needs to develop personal care skills appropriate for her age (to help Julia to feel good about herself). Some areas are as follows:

• Skin care for a teen
• Teen grooming (e.g., styling hair, applying makeup and nail polish)
• Clothing selection and care
• Sex education

What would Julia's ideal day look like and what must be done to make it happen? *For at least the next 3 years:*

Julia will maintain her current level of participation in regular education classes and after-school activities.
Daily living and community living skills will be integrated within her regularly scheduled classes. For community-based instruction, Julia will meet with a community training specialist one period a day, four times per week.
Julia's weekly schedule will reflect her interests as well as her academic, social, and daily and community living needs (e.g., school chorus, swimming or gym, home economics, social studies, science, art, computers, community-based instruction).

Guideline Two: Coordinate Instruction with Families

Not all person-centered planning requires a comprehensive, structured approach. Sometimes, teams need to come together to problem solve with families on immediate issues, focusing on the goals and preferences of the student and the family. Although instruction is the primary responsibility of teachers, some parents may want to teach their children certain home and community skills or reinforce at home what has been learned in school. Furthermore, some families have access to therapeutic support staff through community-based behavioral health services who can assist with instruction or teach parents how to prompt new skills.

In situations such as these, teachers and other support staff can collaborate with families to help them plan and implement instruction at home. Specifically, teachers can help families target the critical skills for home and community that are most relevant to the family's needs, collaborate on the design of instruction, teach parallel skills at school, and provide information that will help parents teach at home. Inviting families to observe instruction at school is one way for teachers to share information on how to teach. Additionally, self-operated prompting systems (described later in this chapter), such as picture activity schedules and video models on portable DVDs used in school, can be easily adapted and provided to families to help them carry out instruction at home (Carothers & Taylor, 2004).

❖ ❖ ❖ ❖ ❖   **Rico Hernandez**   ❖ ❖ ❖ ❖ ❖

Rico Hernandez, a 9-year-old who has been diagnosed with autism, attends a third-grade class in his neighborhood school with the assistance of a full-time, one-to-one paraprofessional. He is performing close to grade level academically in most subject areas, but he requires behavioral support, which he receives through a community-based behavioral health services provider who specializes in autism, because of severe behavioral challenges and life-skill needs.

Mrs. Hernandez, Rico's mother, thought that she would never see the day when her son would be in a general education classroom. She and her husband are extremely proud of their son's accomplishments, yet at the same time, they were becoming increasingly concerned about Rico's display of challenging behaviors at home and his lack of participation in household and family activities. They asked for a team meeting, consisting of Rico's teachers, support staff, and behavior specialists from the behavioral health services, to address their concerns.

After conducting a functional assessment (see Chapter 7) and through many team discussions, it appeared that Rico's challenging behaviors, consisting of screaming, tantrums, and self-injury (face slapping), were most often associated with transitions or changes in routines or activities. The team speculated that from Rico's perspective, almost any activity not anticipated by him (e.g., being asked to put his toys away while watching TV, going to a different grocery store, having an unexpected visitor in the home) constituted a change of activity. As Rico's tantrums increased in frequency and intensity as a result of his physical growth, Mrs. Hernandez placed fewer demands on him to participate in household activities. With the family's hectic schedule, it was often easier to complete Rico's chores for him.

Mrs. Hernandez also feared bringing Rico with her into the community. She worried not only about the potential for challenging behavior but also for Rico's safety. Mrs. Hernandez reported that one day, while grocery shopping, she turned her back for a minute, only to find Rico walking aimlessly in a busy parking lot. With the growing concerns about Rico's safety and behavior, he has been spending most of his free time at home doing little else but watching television.

The team noted that Rico had experienced important successes at school. With the assistance of the paraprofessional, he was completing adapted class assignments and participating in activities. In contrast, Rico rarely interacted with his peers. Mrs. Hernandez expressed her concern to the team that her son was socially isolated at school and had no friends. Rico often sat alone at recess while his classmates played kickball and volleyball. Mrs. Hernandez said that she was worried that Rico was becoming increasingly dependent on the paraprofessional and could not function without her. She also wondered if the other children hesitated to play with Rico because he always had an adult nearby.

Questions for Planning and Instruction

1. How can Rico's participation in family routines and activities be enhanced while decreasing the instances of challenging behaviors?

2. How can Rico be encouraged to be more involved with his peers during leisure time at school and at home?

3. How can Rico's community access be encouraged? What supports will be needed with regard to his behavior and safety?

4. In what ways can Rico's teachers and home support work together to meet Rico's needs at home?

In Rico's case, Mrs. Hernandez, Rico's teachers, the behavior specialist, and the therapeutic support staff (TSS) from the behavioral health service, met to address Rico's team's four questions. The team members discussed how to coordinate their support for Rico and his family. The teacher agreed to design instructional strategies to meet priority objectives, teach as many as were relevant in school, and plan with the TSS so that the parents could learn how to teach these skills at home. The instructional targets selected were to teach Rico to (a) follow a picture schedule to enhance the predictability of activities at home and increase independence at school; (b) complete daily routines at home; (c) learn community travel skills (e.g., following his parents or classmates when traveling independently around the school or out in the community); and (d) master the basics of organized ball games, such as kickball and soccer. Instructional targets were integrated with other forms of support, including behavioral support, respite care, enrolling Rico in Junior League sports, and getting him involved in school recess.

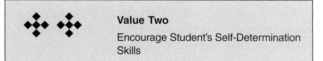

Value Two
Encourage Student's Self-Determination Skills

Guideline Three: Encourage Self-Determination Through Choice-Making, Self-Cuing, and Self-Management Skills

Self-determination is enhanced when instructional goals are matched to a student's preferences and his or her vision for the future. Self-determination is also enhanced when students learn to exert control and self-direct their own learning. Here we discuss three approaches to infuse self-directed learning into instruction for home and community settings: (a) choice, (b) self-cuing, and (c) self-management.

Choice

Choice, or the act of selecting among presented options, is both an expression of preference (students typically choose what they like) and control (students enjoy being in command). Not surprisingly, many studies have shown that when choice opportunities are incorporated during instruction, student participation and learning is enhanced (e.g., Cole & Levinson, 2002; Cooper & Browder, 1998; Dunlap et al., 1994; Mechling, Gast, & Cronin, 2006). For example, Taber-Doughty (2005) found that high school students with moderate intellectual disabilities performed better on community skills when given a choice of prompting systems to learn from. Furthermore, choice can reduce problem behaviors, especially when student protests or disruptions during instruction are related to low opportunities for student control (e.g., Bambara, Koger, Katzer, & Davenport, 1995; Carlson, Luiselli, Slyman, & Markowski, 2008; Cole & Levinson, 2002; Dunlap et al., 1994).

The choice diversity model (Brown, Belz, Corsi, & Wenig, 1993) is one approach for embedding choice opportunities into home and community instruction. In this approach, teachers first analyze steps or component parts of a routine or task and then identify choice options that can be made available at various steps. Teachers may consider providing between-activity choices to initiate an activity (e.g., in a home economics class, a teacher might ask, "Would you like to help prepare a shopping list or make a cake with this group for tomorrow's dessert?"), followed by any number of within-activity choices, such as choice of materials, sequence of activity, or choice of location to carry out the activity.

In a kitchen cleanup routine at home, Rico is offered the choice of clearing the table or stacking the dishes in the dishwasher. Then, once an activity is selected, Rico's mother gives additional options within the activity: (a) offers him a choice of materials (e.g., sponges, dish soap), (b) choice of sequence (e.g., cups or plates first), (c) choice of when to complete the activity (e.g., now or later), and (d) choice of partners (e.g., with or without help from Mom).

Two additional options, the choice to not participate and the choice to terminate an activity, are opportunities that must always be considered during instruction. If a student frequently refuses to participate, instructors should consider how to make the activity more enjoyable for the student in order to motivate learning.

When presenting choices, instructors also should consider how to best present options to match the learner's comprehension and indication skills (Bambara & Koger, 1996). With regard to comprehension, some learners benefit when options are presented with actual objects, and some respond better to pictures than to words. In addition, consideration should be given to the wording of choice prompts. Closed questions (e.g.,

TABLE 14–2
Examples of Choice Options According to Skill Level

Task Skill Level	Cooking Choices Offered Before Cooking Activity (Between Activities)	Choices Offered Within Dessert Activity
Beginner	Present bowls of ready-made Jell-O and pudding with the box for each displayed next to it. Teacher prompt: "Point to the one you want to make."	Options: • Two flavors of Jell-O (e.g., orange and cherry) • Two shapes to make Jell-O jigglers (e.g., star and circle)
Intermediate	Present student with three or four boxes of Jell-O and pudding that depict different flavors. Teacher prompt: "Would you like to make chocolate pudding, vanilla pudding, or cherry Jell-O?"	Options: • Three or four flavors of Jell-O • Mold or cookie cutters • Two or three different fruits to add
Advanced	Present student with picture recipe book that has several options for pudding or Jell-O. Teacher prompt: "Look through the recipe book. Which dessert would you like to make?"	Options: • Two or three different Jell-O desserts • Array of molds, parfait glasses, and cookie cutters • Array of items to add

"Do you want to iron in the living room or in the kitchen?") are useful when the student is unfamiliar with his or her options. Teachers may prompt choice by using open-ended questions (e.g., "What do you want to do now?") after the student has become familiar with the available options. With regard to indication, students may express their choice by labeling, pointing, grimacing, or moving closer toward a preferred object. Table 14–2 illustrates how teachers might present between- and within-activity choices to learners with different comprehension and indication skills. To enhance self-initiation of choice making, instructors are encouraged to respond to students' spontaneous choices whenever practical (e.g., "Thanks for telling me you want to wear your *blue sweater!*") and should expect that, as students learn the power of their choice making, spontaneous choices will increase.

Self-Cuing

Self-initiation and self-direction are hallmark characteristics of self-determination. Many learners with intellectual disabilities can become overly dependent on instructor prompts or cues and fail to learn how to initiate activities and complete tasks independently. To lessen reliance on instructor prompts, self-direction can be enhanced by teaching learners to respond to natural environmental cues and to use self-operated prompting systems and other self-management strategies.

Natural Cues

Ford and Mirenda (1984) describe ways to highlight natural cues during instruction by pointing out the salient features of the natural cue. For example, rather than saying, "Let's wash the dishes (instructional prompt), a teacher may point to the sink of dirty dishes (natural cue) and use a nonspecific prompt (e.g., "What's next?"). Sometimes, natural cues are not salient enough and need to be enhanced through adaptations, such as by (a) color-coding temperature controls on stove or oven dials; (b) using templates to highlight relevant buttons on telephones or microwaves; (c) using placement as a cue, such as hanging matching outfits together; (d) amplifying natural auditory cues, such as traffic sounds for pedestrian training; and (e) using unrelated, naturally occurring events to signal the onset of an activity (e.g., begin dinner when the television news starts or ends).

In cases where students make errors and the error does not pose a danger, teachers can encourage students to learn from their mistakes (natural cue) by pausing and allowing the student to self-correct, rather than immediately prompting a correct response. This requires that teachers modify their teaching approach so that correction prompts are withheld for a longer latency period after a student error has been made or replaced by gestures or questions that emphasize error cues.

If Julia forgets to get all of the items needed to bake a cake, the teacher may hesitate when Julia reaches the step requiring that item (mixing the batter with a spatula) and let her discover that the spatula is missing. If Julia somehow skips the step, the teacher might ask, "What did you forget?"

Such approaches probably work best once students have learned some of the task instead of in the early acquisition stage.

Self-Operated Prompting Systems

Many skills for home and community participation are quite complex, requiring lengthy response chains. As such, students with intellectual disabilities often have difficulty knowing when to initiate activities or what comes next in a routine or a multistep task even after they have been taught to respond to natural or adapted cues. In such cases, students may be taught to use a self-operated prompting system to guide their learning. Self-operated prompting systems consist of extra stimuli or cues, such as pictures, text, and audio and/or video recordings, that students operate to prompt their own learning. Once a skill is learned, self-operated prompting systems may be used as memory aids, similar to recipe books, appointment books, and to-do lists.

Conventional low-tech, self-operated prompting systems use pictures, audio recordings, and text to cue learner responses. Frequently employed picture-based systems provide an excellent form of graphic assistance for students with intellectual disabilities because of their versatility with nonreaders and their fit with visual learners; in addition, they are relatively easy and inexpensive to make. Typically, pictures or drawings that represent an activity or a step in a routine or task are placed sequentially in a photo booklet or on a chart. Students are then taught to "look and do," which means referring to the pictures as they complete each activity or step in a sequence.

Pictures of Rico's after-school home routine (e.g., put backpack away, make a snack, take out the trash, watch TV, set the table for dinner) are placed on a wall chart in the kitchen. Rico is guided to look at the chart, initiate the first activity, and return to the chart for the next activity once the previous activity has been completed.

Picture-based systems have been shown to be highly effective in teaching students with intellectual disabilities to conduct home and community activities involving multiple steps, such as cooking, making a snack, doing laundry, setting the table, using a computer, and shopping (Mechling, 2007). When used in the form of activity schedules, picture-based systems are also effective strategies for helping students initiate home activities (e.g., MacDuff, Krantz, & McClannahan, 1993); transition from activity to activity in school (e.g., Spriggs, Gast, & Ayers, 2007); and manage daily or weekly schedules for leisure activities, work, housekeeping, or grooming (e.g., Anderson, Sherman, Sheldon, & McAdam, 1997; Bambara & Ager, 1992; Bryan & Gast, 2000; Irvine, Erickson, Singer, & Stahlberg, 1992). As with most other self-operated prompting systems, a key advantage of using picture prompts is that they can help students to generalize tasks or routines to new settings. Once a student learns how to "read" pictures in one situation, the pictures may then be used in different settings to guide student performance on the same or similar tasks. For example, in a study conduced by Irvine et al. (1992), teachers helped students initiate activities at home (to the parents' delight) by sending the students home with the activity schedule used at school.

Self-operated audio prompting systems and word checklists are other low-tech options that can be tried. With audio systems, students operate (e.g., turn on, play, pause) a portable audio device such as a portable cassette or iPod® to listen and respond to step-by-step directions for completing a task. Like pictures, audio prompts have enhanced learners' generalization to different settings (Post & Storey, 2002). Word checklists, easily created with any word processor, also can effectively prompt students to complete home and work routines once sight words for specific tasks are taught and students learn how to "look and do" (Minarovic & Bambara, 2007).

New emerging high-tech forms of self-operated prompting systems make use of computer and video technologies. Handheld computers, such as personal digital assistants (PDAs) and pocket PCs, offer graphic, audio, and/or touch-screen technologies to prompt learners to initiate activity schedules (e.g., Cihak, Kessler, & Alberto, 2008; Ferguson, Myles, & Hagiwara, 2005) and complete multistep tasks such as cooking and cleaning (Cihak, Kessler, & Alberto, 2007). Several handheld computers and software programs developed specifically for people with disabilities are available commercially, such as the Visual Assistant®, which provides pictures and audio prompts for multistep tasks; the Schedule Assistant®, which uses icons and audio signals to prompt activity initiations; and the Community Integration Suite®, which uses pictures and audio messages to guide community travel; these devices are available through AbleLink Technologies (http://www.ablelinktech.com/). Because of their interactive nature and enhanced graphic and sound capabilities, handheld computers have many advantages over more conventional static picture or audio prompting systems; however, computer systems are complex and may require intensive instruction before learners can maneuver successfully through multilayered screens.

Lastly, teacher-made videos that show the student or someone else performing the steps of a task can be used as used as a high-tech, self-operated prompting system with the use of a portable DVD. For example, Mechling and Stephens (2009) taught students three cooking tasks by having them (a) watch a video segment on a DVD player, (b) press "pause," (c) perform the step, and (d) press "play" to resume the sequence. Although this form of self-directed prompting was found to be more effective than static picture prompts in teaching independent cooking skills, the researchers cautioned that the system may not be suitable for all learners. The "best system" is the one that best matches the task, the setting in which the prompting system is used, the student's skills, and the student's preferences for learning.

Self-Management

Another way to promote self-direction in daily routines is to incorporate self-management strategies in instruction. Broadly defined, *self-management* refers to the processes used by an individual to influence his or her own behavior (Storey, 2007). Technically speaking, the use of self-operated prompting systems are self-management strategies; however, to truly self-manage behavior, a combination of multiple components is needed, such as goal setting (setting personal performance goals), self-monitoring (recording progress toward goals), self-evaluation (evaluating the acceptability of performance outcomes), and self-reinforcement (rewarding oneself for a job well done).

A picture schedule was created for Rico that depicted each activity in his day; the schedule was placed in a binder on his desk. Each, day Rico selected the order of classroom activities whenever possible (goal setting). He monitored the completion of the activities by turning the page (self-monitoring). At the end of the day, he reviewed how well he did on each completed activity (self-evaluation).

Two methods of self-management—self-instruction and self-scheduling—have direct applicability for home and community use. In self-instruction, students are taught to use self-talk to move through the steps in a home, community, or leisure activity, and self-evaluate their performance as they go along. Hughes (1992) taught four students with severe intellectual disabilities to use self-instruction to solve task-related problems at home by identifying the problem (e.g., "the lamp is not plugged in"), stating the correct response (e.g., "I need to plug in the lamp"), evaluating the response (e.g., "I fixed it"), and self-reinforcing (e.g., "I did well"). Similarly, Bambara and Gomez (2001) used self-instruction to teach complex problem solving to adults with intellectual disabilities in their home. In this study, the adults were guided to consider more than one solution to a problem (e.g., "My toothbrush is missing. Look on the counter. Look in the cabinet. Ask for help.") and to evaluate their success (e.g., "I found it!").

FIGURE 14–1
This picture schedule was created for Jonathon, who is fully included in his high school. The picture icons, attached with Velcro, help Jonathan keep track of completed classes (by moving the icons from left to right) and see the classes that are next on his schedule. For example, he finished chemistry and is going to lunch. Picture icons were selected from The Picture Communication Symbols ©1981–2009 by Mayer-Johnson LLC. All Rights Reserved Worldwide. Used with permission. Boardmaker® is a trademark of Mayer-Johnson LLC.

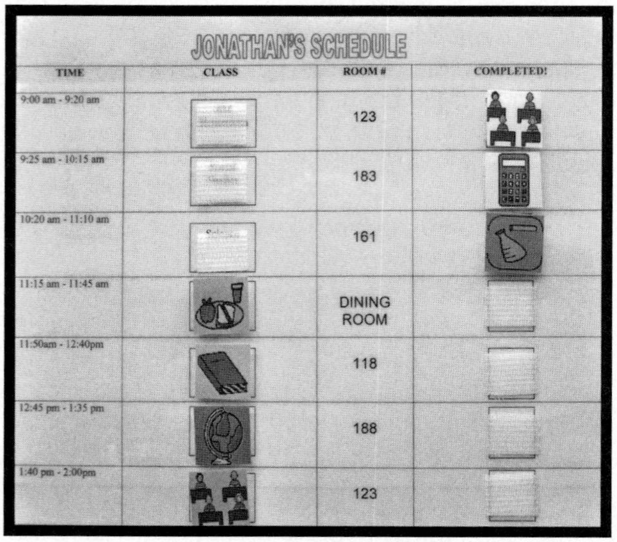

Self-scheduling can provide a way for learners to self-direct and control the multiple tasks needed for daily living. Learners are guided to select home, community, or school activities that are both enjoyable and necessary, plan when to do them that day or several days in advance, and use their schedule to initiate the planned activities (Anderson et al., 1997; Bambara & Ager, 1992; Bambara & Koger, 1996; Lovett & Haring, 1989). Like the activity schedules described earlier, self-scheduling systems can be (a) teacher made by using pictures, picture books, and calendar templates; or (b) supported through computer technologies. (See Figure 14–1.) Self-scheduling involves more than just following an activity schedule, however, the learner plans what to do and when.

Self-determination skills are important for learners of all ages, but they take on greater importance as students begin to transition of adult life. For someone like Aaron (the next case example), being in charge by setting learning goals; making daily decisions about what to do, how to do it, and with whom; and organizing, scheduling, and managing time is critical for having a quality adult life.

❖ ❖ ❖ ❖ ❖　　　　　　**Aaron Williams**　　　　　　❖ ❖ ❖ ❖ ❖

Aaron is a young man with intellectual and physical disabilities. Because of a stroke at age 8, he walks with an unsteady gait and has limited use of his right arm and hand. He walks with the assistance of a walker, but moves about freely in his automated wheelchair. He communicates with gestures, pictures, and a laptop computer.

At age 19, Aaron is nearing his last years of public school services. Aaron has completed several years of person-centered planning with his transition team, and his goals are clear. He wants to live in his own apartment with a roommate who shares his interests in music and sports. He also wants a job that pays well, but that gives him flexible or part-time hours because he tires easily. Because of his love of school and his desire to improve his career options, Aaron has been enrolled in his school district's postsecondary education transition program that is sited at a local university campus. Aaron wants to continue taking courses related to his personal (e.g., art, music) and career interests (computers) while exploring job opportunities and learning critical skills that will help him to be on his own. Partially resulting from his physical challenges, Aaron has not had many experiences doing things for himself or being on his own in community settings. Aaron has spent most of his time at home or at school. His family has worked hard to make their home accessible for Aaron but have found it difficult to find the resources (e.g., finances, physical assistance, transportation) to help Aaron spend time in the community. Aaron has had some community instruction and job sampling while in high school.

Aaron's eventual transition into a job and a home of his own will require the coordinated efforts of his planning team, which includes his parents, his school district's transition coordinator, a supports coordinator from developmental disability services, his teacher, and eventually representatives from adult supported employment and supported living providers. The team has begun to brainstorm ways to help Aaron meet his goals. For example, the supports coordinator will help Aaron and his family explore affordable housing options and connect with supported employment providers, while his teacher and transition coordinator will coordinate instruction and work experience opportunities on the college campus.

Questions for Planning and Instruction

1. What skills does Aaron need and want that will enhance his competence and help him maintain control over the direction of his life?

2. How can instructional support be coordinated across the multiple services (e.g., postsecondary education, supports coordination, home and community supports) that Aaron needs and wants?

Value Three

Select Instruction That Blends with General Education Contexts and Encourages Peer Interaction

Guideline Four: Select Appropriate Instructional Settings, Plan for Generalization, and Use Efficient Strategies

In order to maintain school inclusion and peer interaction, planning teams may need to give thought as to how skills for home and community settings can be taught. Here are some questions that can be asked in order to guide this planning:

- What setting will be used for instruction? Can the skills be embedded in typical school activities and routines? If not, will a simulated activity be feasible and effective, or is it best to schedule instruction in the settings where the skills are typically used?
- How can generalization be encouraged from school activities to actual home and community settings? How can we teach so that students will generalize across similar but different community settings? What strategies are needed in order for this generalization to occur?
- How can instruction be made more effective and efficient? Can peers be involved?

Choosing the Instructional Setting

The challenge in teaching skills to students for the home and community is that these settings differ greatly from typical school settings. Students may not generalize the skills taught in school to community contexts (Cihak, Alberto, Kessler, & Taber, 2004). Students also need general educational experiences even though the skills taught there may not address those needed in the home and community. To meet this challenge, teachers can consider three options for instruction: (a) embedding home and community skills in typical school routines and settings, (b) using school-based simulations of home and community settings, and (c) conducting in vivo instruction. If one of the first two school-based options is selected, some direct instruction in community settings and collaboration with families will help generalize the skills to these settings.

Embed Skills in Typical School Routines and Settings

In this option, the teacher considers how instruction for each priority skill can be incorporated in existing school or classroom activities. For example, Gardill and Browder (1995) taught purchasing skills using the school store, the cafeteria, and vending machines, as well as community settings. Similarly, food preparation might be incorporated in a general education unit in social studies when learning about other cultures or during a home economics class. Some housekeeping skills can be taught during cleanup time in the classroom where all students can share the responsibility for chores (e.g., emptying trash, cleaning a classroom

sink after art projects) and money-handling skills can be taught during math. Most middle and high schools have home economics suites that offer a context for all students to learn many home skills during their school day. This instruction may be incorporated into general education classes in home economics through team planning, or students may receive private tutoring during periods when the room is free. Embedded instruction is often ideal for teaching basic or foundational skills, such has learning how to follow a picture schedule, chopping vegetables, and counting money, that later can be applied to natural routines; however, in and of itself, embedded instruction is insufficient for teaching some students how to use these skills during actual home and community routines.

Use School-Based Simulations of Community and Home Activities

Many home and community skills cannot be embedded into typical school activities because the skills are so discrepant from the general education curriculum that instruction requires activities or materials not usually provided in schools. In cases where direct instruction in home and community settings is not always feasible or desirable given the focus of the student's curriculum, teachers can create simulations of natural routines in school settings where home and community skills can be taught. For example, in a classic study, Sowers and Powers (1995) implemented a community training program that included simulation to teach students how to purchase fast food. First, they developed a task analysis for making a fast-food purchase and then observed the students' performance at a local fast-food restaurant to target critical skills. Second, to teach the task analyses, the classroom teacher turned the school conference room into a simulated fast-food restaurant where the students could practice their skills in placing an order, paying for their purchase, and consuming it. The teacher had planned for instruction ahead of time by purchasing the desired food items for each student from the fast-food restaurant earlier in the day. The students then role-played placing an order with the teacher, after which they received the actual food items.

Once students had mastered the steps of the task analysis, the instructor invited the students' caregivers (e.g., parents or group home staff) to come to school to participate in the simulation. The caregiver watched the instructor give the student any needed assistance in the role-play of purchasing the food and then provided assistance on the second trial. They were also given a list of suggestions for encouraging the student to perform the steps for him or herself during outings to fast-food restaurants. Observations of the students demonstrated that they were able to generalize their skills from the simulated fast-food restaurant in the school conference room to community restaurants with both their teachers and caregivers.

Through the advancement of video and computer technologies, video-based simulations provide another way to teach home and community skills in classroom settings. Effective simulations can be created through *video modeling* and *video prompting,* either alone or in combination, shown via video players (e.g., VCR, DVD) or computers (desktop, laptop, handheld). In video modeling, the student watches a model (either an edited video of the student or of another person) independently performing the entire task in a natural setting. In the classroom, the student may view the video several times, discuss the video with the teacher, and/or practice the steps in the classroom before receiving instruction in community settings. For example, in a study by Alberto, Cihak, & Gama (2005), students watched a close-up video demonstration of a model (showing hands and arms only) withdrawing cash from an automated teller machine (ATM). While students watched the video, the teacher verbalized the required motor responses (e.g., "Press the arrow to withdraw from the checking account"). Students then received instruction in the community. The combined video modeling and community instruction were effective in teaching ATM use in natural settings.

In video prompting, instead of having the student watch a demonstration of a model performing the entire task, video segments are used to prompt specific responses from the student in a simulated activity, often presented in an interactive computer interface. When presented from a subjective viewpoint, students watch the video segments as if they were performing the task in an actual setting. Prompts embedded in the simulation can highlight naturally occurring cues (e.g., the video screen of an ATM machine showing "Enter your pin number"), instructor cues (e.g., "Press the green button"), and corrections (e.g., "Sorry, you have pressed an incorrect key, try again"). Hansen and Morgan (2008) combined video modeling and video prompting via CD-ROM instruction to teach the purchasing of groceries to high school students with intellectual disabilities. Video modeling showed students correct and incorrect ways of purchasing groceries. Video prompting via CD-ROM was used to teach four

steps: (a) choosing the shortest checkout line; (b) placing items on a conveyor belt; (c) making a payment using the dollar next strategy; and (d) taking the change, the receipt, and the groceries. During the CD-ROM instruction for each step, students watched a short video, then practiced the response through a simulated interactive learning game (e.g., moving the shopping cart to the shortest line). Following this instruction, the students showed increased purchasing skills in actual grocery stores.

Whether using actual items to recreate settings or using high-tech video modeling or prompting strategies, simulations have been shown to be highly effective in teaching students to generalize skills from the classroom to the home and community settings (Ayers & Langone, 2005; Cihak et al., 2004). However, in order for this generalization to occur, simulations must be carefully planned. To be effective, teachers must consider the following: *First, the simulation should carefully replicate the stimuli and responses found in the community or home setting where the student is expected to perform the target skill under natural conditions* (Nietupski, Hamre-Nietupski, Clancy, & Veerhusen, 1986). When recreating settings, this means using actual items from home or community settings, such as food and beverage containers, menus from area restaurants, city bus schedules, food cartons, and blank checks from a local bank. When actual items cannot be brought to a school setting, teacher-made replicas can be used. Browder, Snell, and Wildonger (1988) used photographs of actual vending machines when teaching vending machine use in the classroom. Each photograph was enlarged and glued to a stationary box to form a miniature machine. To make the simulation as real as possible, a "coin slot" was cut into the picture and students could hear a "clinking" sound as they dropped coins into the box. Additionally, the teacher pushed the food or drink out from under the box when the student pushed one of the buttons on the picture.

As demonstrated in Browder et al. (1988), students should practice the actual responses they will be required to use in natural settings. One advantage of video simulation is that it can more readily capture natural cues that cannot be closely replicated through other means. For example, using computer-based video prompting, Mechling, Pridgen, and Cronin (2005) taught students to respond to a cashier's questions (e.g., "Hi, can I help you?" "Is that for here or to go?") across several fast-food restaurants (McDonald's,

Wendy's, and Hardee's). Video segments showed actual cashiers behind their counters asking the questions and then waiting for a response.

A second consideration when planning simulations is to use multiple exemplars and stimulus variation. Specifically, teachers should consider the types of possible variations that a student may encounter in natural settings. For example, Neef, Lensbower, Hockersmith, DePalma, and Gray (1990) used multiple exemplars in simulated and in vivo instruction to teach laundry skills. In multiple exemplar training, the student either went to multiple laundromats or trained with multiple sets (several simulated box models) of washers and dryers. Interestingly, Neef et al. (1990) found that students generalized their laundry skills when introduced to multiple exemplars during classroom simulations. Variations in washing machines were achieved by using several different replicas of washing machines (i.e., exemplars) that the students might encounter in their community. Variations can also be achieved in video simulations in order to enhance generalization across different settings and materials. In the Mechling et al. (2005) example, students practiced answering a cashier's questions across different cashiers and variations in questions. Mechling, Gast, and Barthold (2003) used video simulations of different automated payment machines (APMs) to teach students to use a debit card when making purchases. Because of this variation, students were able to generalize their skills to actual community settings and across novel APMs not represented in the videos. When practicing across different exemplars, generalization is enhanced because students learn how to respond to variations that occur in home and community settings.

The third consideration when using school-based simulations is to include some opportunities to apply skills in actual community or home settings. As discussed, well-planned simulations can result in generalization to community contexts; however, generalization is not guaranteed for all students, all skills, or steps of a task (Cihak et al., 2004). When assessing generalization in the community, Mechling et al. (2003) found that students consistently made errors on the step requiring them to swipe the debit card in the APM. Interestingly, this was one of the few steps that was difficult to simulate, suggesting that no simulation can completely replicate environmental stimuli or the responses needed to be successful in community settings.

To ensure that students use their skills in natural settings, teachers should plan some community instruction

to supplement simulations. The advantage of using simulations is that community instruction may be scheduled much less frequently than would be needed if relying on community instruction alone (Cihak et al., 2004). At a minimum, teachers should assess whether students do generalize from school simulations to community settings and teach in actual settings if they do not. Also, when possible, schedule community instruction on the same day as simulated instruction for maximum effectiveness (Cihak et al., 2004). For home skills, collaboration with caregivers can help determine if skills performed at school are being used at home. A parent conference, similar to that in Sowers and Powers (1995), in which the caregiver sees and participates in the simulation, may be especially beneficial in encouraging this generalization.

Teach in Vivo

Not all skills can be simulated, and simulations can be difficult to create especially when multiple community and home skills are targeted for instruction. The third option for choosing instructional settings is to teach *in vivo*, meaning to teach directly and only in home and community settings. However, because this option can compete with and is logistically difficult to coordinate with general education inclusion, it may be best reserved for older students when time away from the school building is age appropriate and educational priorities shift from school to job training and community access. When students are past typical school age but still receiving educational services (i.e., ages 19 to 21), they are likely to receive instruction that is heavily, if not entirely, community based. Inclusion takes place in the community where many of their same-age peers now hold jobs, attend postsecondary schools, and recreate. During the transition years (around age 14 and older), students may also have direct community instruction for part of their school day, especially when (a) this is a student and parent priority, (b) this instruction can be scheduled as one or more periods of the student's class schedule and does not require the student to be removed in the middle of a general education class, and (c) other students leave school on a regular basis (e.g., to travel with school teams to sports events, work at a half-day job program, participate in honors activities, attend a vocational-technical center). At the elementary school level, direct community instruction is likely to be far less of a priority because it is more disruptive to peer interaction and the classroom routine. Sometimes, direct community instruction may be a strong student and parent priority (e.g., to teach safe street crossing) and may be less disruptive (e.g., in elementary schools that use a lot of individualized pull-out programs for music, sports, the arts, and other special interests).

Plan for Generalization: General Case Instruction

When teaching skills for home and community, it is important to plan for generalization from school to home and community settings. Carefully planned simulations, coupled with some community instruction, can achieve this goal. However, generalization *across* home and community settings is also important. Teaching a student to purchase fast food at McDonald's does not necessarily mean that the student will know how to make purchases at Burger King, Wendy's, and Taco Bell. Each setting is slightly different, requiring a different set of responses or skills. General case instruction is one way to maximize generalization across different community settings. Like multiple exemplar training, general case instruction teaches students to respond to different examples of materials and/or settings, but in general case instruction, the selection of exemplars is much more systematic to ensure that the full range of variation in community settings is presented during instruction (see Box 14–1). This approach has effectively taught students to generalize skills across different types of vending machines (Sprague & Horner, 1984), telephones (Horner, Williams, & Steveley, 1987), and restaurants (McDonnell & Ferguson, 1988), and request help across different community contexts (Chadsey-Rusch, Drasgow, Reinoehl, Hallet, & Collet-Klingenberg, 1993).

Consider how Rico's teachers use general case instruction to teach Rico how to purchase snacks at convenience stores with a companion:

First, an instructional universe is defined. Rico's teachers must answer several questions: Is the goal for Rico to be able to use all convenience stores in his neighborhood? In his region? In the United States? The teacher decides to focus on teaching Rico to use convenience stores in his region (the Lehigh Valley of Pennsylvania).

Table 14–3 shows the four convenience stores identified by the general case analysis.

Second, the teacher writes a generic task analysis for purchasing a snack at the store and then analyzes the stimulus and response variation in each store (see Table 14–3). Third, the teacher selects which stores will be used for training. The teacher chooses a 7-Eleven, a Penn Supreme, and the school cafeteria snack line (which offers snack foods like ice cream) because these three stores sample the range of variation in Rico's region. Nick's Market and Kate's One-Stop Shopping will be used to test for generalization to novel (never used for training) convenience stores. Rico will get daily instruction in the school cafeteria by his teacher and weekly instruction at a convenience store on Fridays by his TSS. Every fourth Friday, the TSS brings Rico to one of the novel convenience stores to check for generalization. This will continue until Rico demonstrates both mastery and generalization in all settings.

Efficient Teaching Strategies

For teachers, teaching efficiently is important particularly when trying to offset the extra time needed for community-based instruction. Teachers can teach efficiently by (a) using observational learning, (b) providing additional information while instructing, and (c) involving peers in instruction.

Box 14–1 General Case Instruction

General case instruction emphasizes selecting and teaching examples so that students learn to perform skills across the full range of settings and materials that they confront. Following are the five steps to set up general case instruction:

1. Define the instructional universe
2. Write a generic task analysis
3. Select teaching and testing examples that sample the range of stimulus and response variation
4. Teach
5. Test
6. Repeat steps 1 to 5.

TABLE 14–3
General Case Analysis

Generic Responses: Task Analysis (TA)	Instructional Universe: Convenience Stores in Lehigh Valley, Pennsylvania, Assessment Data: Sites to Sample Stimulus/Response (S/R) Variation (Parentheses Show S/R Variation for That TA Step in That Site)				Assessment Summary: Generalization
	Penn Supreme	Nick's	7–Eleven	Kate's	
1. Enter store	+ (electric door)	− (push)	− (pull)	− (push)	Push/pull door
2. Locate item	− (multiple aisles)	− (display case)	− (aisles)	+ (behind clerk)	Scan aisles and cases
3. Pick out item	+ (bottom shelf)	− (open case)	− (top shelf)	+ (clerk selects)	Shelf location and opening case
4. Take item to counter	+ (large counter)	− (small counter)	− (small counter)	N/A	Size/location of counter
5. Wait in line	+	+	+	N/A	Mastered
6. Pay cashier	− (clerk states price)	+ (clerk extends hand)	− (clerk states price)	− (clerk states price)	Verbal cue states
7. Take change/item	− (change with no bag)	− (no bag)	− (change and bag)	+ (bag)	Unbagged item, change cups
8. Leave store	+ (electric door)	− (pull)	− (push)	− (pull)	Push/pull door
Number correct/ Total Responses: Date of probe:	5/8 Nov. 3	2/8 Nov. 10	1/8 Nov. 12	3/6 Nov. 15	

Key: + = independent correct; − = incorrect or needed prompting, N/A = not applicable to that site.

Note: Reprinted from "Functional Assessment" by R. Gaylord-Ross and D. M. Browder, in *Critical Issues in the Lives of People with Severe Disabilities* (p. 58) by L. H. Meyer, C. A. Peck, and L. Brown (Eds.), 1991, Baltimore: Paul H. Brookes. Reprinted by permission.

Observational Learning

In an example of observational learning, Griffen, Wolery, and Schuster (1992) used a small group to teach students with cognitive disabilities to make a milkshake, scrambled eggs, and pudding. To maximize instruction, one student received direct instruction using prompting for each step of the task analysis with constant time delay. At the same time, the instructor prompted and reinforced the other two students to observe and follow instructions by turning the pages of a picture recipe. Although each student received direct instruction on only one of the three recipes, they learned most of the steps for all three.

Observational learning also may be facilitated through teacher demonstration and, as discussed, through the use of video models. Smith, Collins, Schuster, and Kleinert (1999) wrote about teaching high school students to clean tables using a task analysis and a least-prompts system. During each instructional session and after the students cleaned the tables, the instructor directed the students to watch him as he rinsed and put away the cleaning materials. Pre- and postassessments showed that through observational learning, the students were able to do most of the cleanup steps without direct instruction. Saving instructional time is a key advantage of observational learning. Critical steps not yet acquired by students can be taught directly, but teachers can still save time by not having to directly teach every step in a task analysis.

Additional Information

Instructional time may also be enhanced by providing additional information during the instruction of targeted skills. Taylor, Collins, Schuster, and Kleinert (2002) employed a system of least prompts to teach four high school students a routine for doing laundry. During instruction, they added extra information by inserting eight related functional sight words (e.g., detergent, normal, rinse, presoak, softener) printed on flash cards into the steps of the task analysis. As the student performed a step, the teacher praised the student and then pointed to and said the word before the student continued with the next step. Students learned the laundry task analysis and most of the words. Like observational learning, the sight words were acquired without direct instruction.

Involve Peers

Involving peers as tutors can enhance efficiency while also promoting interaction with classmates without disabilities. Collins, Branson, and Hall (1995) taught high school students from an advanced English class to teach recipe sight words to students with moderate cognitive disabilities. Students read each word and then found it in the recipe on the product's box or container. The advanced English students wrote about their teaching experiences as part of their English assignments. The students with intellectual disabilities learned to read the recipe words and could prepare the recipes when tested in the home economics room and at a nearby home.

Because many instructional procedures involve lengthy error correction strategies that can interfere with typical peer interactions, teachers might consider using less intrusive instructional procedures with peer tutors. Tekin-Iftar (2003) used simultaneous prompting with peer tutors who taught middle school students with disabilities to read community signs. A key advantage of simultaneous prompting is that the peer tutor needs only to model the response (in this case, say the word) and then wait for the student to respond. If incorrect, the peer tutor simply goes on to the next word or instructional opportunity. Although not used by the researchers in this way, peers can easily incorporate simultaneous prompting during typical peer activities without appearing overly teacher like. For example, community sight words can be taught as peers walk down the school hall together or participate on field trips (e.g., "This sign says 'women,'" "This sign says 'exit.'"). In the cafeteria, just before paying for lunch, peers could name the coins needed to make the purchase. Teachers would assess student learning at another time.

Value Four

Home and Community Skills Gain Importance as Students Become Older

Guideline Five: Use Transition Planning to Focus on Community-Based Instruction

Many of the skills described in this chapter are more suitable for adolescents and young adults in preparation for their transition to adulthood than for children. Adolescents may open their first bank account, prepare meals, and start going to the movies without their parents, while children may do chores, pick up their clothes, and fix snacks, but typically do not go to the movies alone. Thus, teachers may focus more on skills for the home and community during the transition years, around age 14 and older (IDEA 2004 requires transition planning to begin no later than age 16).

Julia, who is 14, will probably have more objectives related to domestic and community skills than Rico, who is 9 years old. Aaron's greatest instructional needs at age 19 are using community resources, obtaining a job, and establishing his own home. Many of the objectives for his individualized education program (IEP) will be related to community, employment, and home skills.

The transition years are a time for increased community-based and home instruction. Still, as Julia's and Aaron's programs show, individualization is important. Community-based instruction for Julia is carefully balanced with general education experiences in her high school. At age 14, maintaining relationships with high school buddies and being involved in the full range of high school activities (e.g., attending general education classes, pep rallies, school clubs) are important. In contrast, Aaron's program is entirely community based. At age 19, his peers have graduated from high school and are either attending college or working. Participating in high school activities is no longer age appropriate for Aaron.

In addition to traditional job training programs, many school districts are now offering postsecondary or commencement programs as an option for students between the ages of 18 and 21 (Morningstar & Lattin, 2004; Nuebert & Moon, 2006). Postsecondary programs are fully community based. Students attend graduation ceremonies with their peers but continue to receive services from their school district on transition-related IEP objectives until services are no longer needed or they turn 21. While some programs are housed in community buildings such as a storefront or apartment complex where students can have immediate access to the community, many school districts now offer services on a college campus, such as in a community college or a four-year university. Postsecondary programs in a college setting provide a unique benefit—students can receive community instruction and job training in an inclusive educational environment that provides opportunities for continuing education (i.e., attending college classes) and interaction with same-age peers in campus social, work, and educational activities.

Although postsecondary education programs vary, they share similar characteristics (Grigial, Neubert, & Moon, 2002a; Nuebert & Moon, 2006). Most postsecondary educational programs are staffed by school district personnel because public education will continue until age 21. In some college programs, students attend a self-contained "life skills" classroom with other students with disabilities for part of the day (e.g., for functional academics, self-determination skills, assessment) and then participate in college activities for community-based instruction, job training, or continuing education.

Other programs are highly individualized and inclusive; they do not involve a self-contained life skills classroom. Instead, a teacher or a transition coordinator plans instruction and supports on transition-related IEP goals across a range of campus and even community activities. Similar to the way that inclusion efforts are staffed in school settings, students who participate in campus and community activities receive support from multiple sources, such as school district teachers, paraprofessionals, and job coaches, as well as peers from college service organizations. If linkages have been established with adult disability services, instruction may also be delivered by supported employment job coaches and other home and community support workers.

Aaron's program, located on a state university campus, is individualized to his transition goals (see Figure 14-2). Aaron's schedule for the fall semester follows the format for creating an individualized college schedule as described by Grigal, Neubert, and Moon (2002b).

Aaron starts each day on campus meeting with his teacher or a school district paraeducator in a private room in the university library. There, Aaron receives instruction on home and personal management, including budgeting and money skills, and operating his PDA to schedule his daily and weekly activities. During the week, his time on campus involves

FIGURE 14–2
Aaron's curriculum matrix illustrates a sample of his activities on campus during the day. It identifies the specific activity, whom he will be with during the activity, and his targeted instructional goals during the activity.

Time	Monday	Tuesday	Wednesday
8:30–9:30	University library with instructor (scheduling, time-telling, and budgeting skills).	University library with instructor (scheduling, time-telling, and budgeting skills).	University library with instructor (scheduling, time-telling, and budgeting skills).
10:00–11:00	Use public transportation with instructor to travel to a preferred restaurant for lunch (vocational skills).	Attend art class on campus with college buddy (social and communication skills).	Use public transportation to go to bank and make a deposit or withdrawal with instructor (travel, communication, and budgeting skills).
11:30–12:30	Lunch at Hawk's Nest with college buddy (communication, social, and purchasing skills).	Computer lab with paraeducator to navigate the Internet (communication, vocational, and leisure skills).	Lunch at Mt. Top Campus with same-age peers (communication, social, and purchasing skills).
1:00–2:00	Go to university library with college buddy to locate preferred reading materials (social, purchasing, and communication skills).	Go to university gym with college buddy (social and communication skills).	Go to Barnes and Noble with instructor to select and purchase preferred reading material (social, purchasing, math, and communication skills).

attending an art class (with the support of a college student), receiving tutorials on accessing the Internet in the computer lab (with the support of a paraeducator) (see Figures 14-3 and 14-4), and working out in the gym with a peer buddy. Through the support of his school district job coach, he works three times a week in the university bookstore. Between these activities, he receives instruction from either his job coach or the paraeducator for independent travel and use of the ATM to withdraw money from his savings account. Because Aaron is unsure about the type of job that he might like, his job coach has arranged for him to sample other jobs on campus next semester where he can apply his computer skills (e.g., library desk, campus office).

Several times a week, Aaron has lunch with his peer buddy Jason, who attends football games with

FIGURE 14–4
Aaron uses the gym on campus with his college buddy on a regular basis.

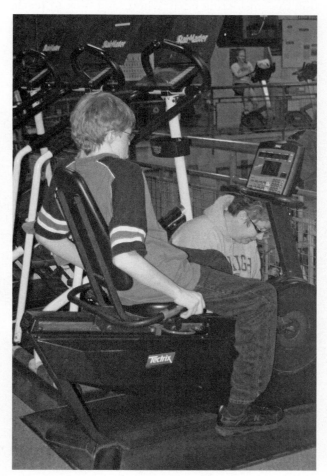

FIGURE 14–3
Aaron spends time in the computer lab at his university, learning new tasks on the computer: accessing his e-mail account, researching preferred topics, and updating his Facebook account.

Aaron on weekends. In addition to hanging out with friends during lunch, Aaron practices his purchasing and ordering skills at various food vendors on campus. Two times per week and the end of the day, Aaron receives instruction on menu planning and cooking meals in his family home by a support worker from an adult services agency. When he transitions to his new apartment, which will be fully accessible, home instruction will intensify.

Strategies for Teaching Home and Community Skills

To recap the discussion thus far, before teaching home and community skills, teachers need to plan instruction by considering what, where, and how to teach, while also honoring student and family preferences and students' ages, and selecting instructional strategies that are effective and efficient. In this next section, we will discuss specific ideas for teaching skills for use in home and community settings. We begin with skills for the home, and then we will review teaching skills in the community.

Skills for the Home

When you stop to think about it, myriad skills are needed to fully participate in one's home. Fortunately, many valuable commercially produced curriculum and supporting materials are available to help (e.g., http://www.attainmentcompany.com, http://www.stanfield.com). Food preparation; housekeeping, including home management; home safety; telephone use; and sexuality education are important areas of meaningful participation in household routines.

Food Preparation

Students are often highly motivated to participate in food preparation instruction because they can consume the results! In addition to its nutritional value, cooking has other social (e.g., cooking with family or friends), recreational (e.g., watching cooking shows on TV, joining a cooking class), and vocational (e.g., seeking a job in the food industry) benefits as well (Mechling, 2008). Finding the right location for instruction can be challenging because of the specialized equipment needed. In middle and high schools, home economics classrooms are ideal locations. In elementary schools, simple snack preparations can be done in

the classroom and lunchroom, and parents can be supported and encouraged to teach snack preparation at home. However, the bulk of cooking instruction is most likely to occur once students leave high school and have access to instruction that could be conducted in their homes or in a community cooking class.

Food preparation instruction has several components: planning, food preparation, safe food storage, and cleaning up. When teaching students to plan what foods to prepare, honor any dietary restrictions, respect both cultural and familial preferences (e.g., meatless or no pork), honor personal preferences, and encourage nutrition. Some students may benefit from learning recipe planning as described by Sarber and Cuvo (1983). In their study, adults with disabilities learned to plan meals using a board that had color cues for each food group. For example, peaches were cued for the fruits and vegetable group. Beef stew was cued as both meat and vegetables. After planning the menus, the adults learned to develop grocery lists for purchasing the necessary items. Arnold-Reid, Schloss, and Alper (1997) implemented the system of least prompts to teach participants to plan meals according to the four food groups: vegetables/fruit, meat, dairy, and breads/cereal. Because one participant had to limit sweets because of health concerns, these were listed in a column called the "Dreaded Other." Another student learned to have an item in the "Dreaded Other" column as an occasional treat. Students who do not have the academic skills to read or write food names in planning menus or self-monitoring their diet may benefit from a picture system. The Select-A-Meal Curriculum (Attainment Company, http://www.attainmentcompany.com) provides commercial materials that can be helpful for menu planning or restaurant use.

Besides teaching healthy menu planning, food preferences should be honored. Some students may be able to describe the foods that they want to learn to prepare. For students with more severe disabilities, preference assessment can be applied to determine which foods to select (Lohrmann-O'Rourke, Browder, & Brown, 2000). To conduct this preference assessment, the teacher might show the student an array of pictures or packages of food and wait for the student to select one by touching it, gazing at it, or making some other response. Or the teacher may offer samples of foods and then have students choose from among the samples.

Once the specific foods have been selected, consideration can be given as to how to teach the student to prepare the recipe. For young students, preparing snacks, such as making a drink, making a sandwich, or using the microwave oven to make popcorn or warm up pizza, can be taught directly via constant time delay or simultaneous prompting without the use of recipes to guide learning. Batu (2008) taught mothers to use simultaneous prompting, a relatively easy prompting system to use, to teach their elementary age children how to prepare simple snacks at home.

Older students are more likely to prepare meals involving more complex and multiple steps. When cooking meals, most of us rely on recipes to help us remember ingredients and what to do. Some students may be taught sight words in order to read directions on packages or to follow simple recipes or teacher-made instruction booklets using time delay or another prompting alternative (Browder, Hines, McCarthy, & Fees, 1984; Gast, Doyle, Wolery, Ault, & Farmer, 1991). Although sight words may be taught while the student learns the food preparation steps, some students may benefit from sight word instruction outside of cooking sessions (see Figure 14–5).

Picture recipes can be helpful to students who have difficulty reading words and remembering sequences (Mechling, 2008). Teachers can create their own by organizing photographs, drawings, or picture icons from commercially produced software, such as Boardmaker®

FIGURE 14–5
Rachael uses the instructions (i.e., pictures and words) on the back of the box to assist her in making muffins.

(available from http://www.mayer-johnson.com), to represent individual steps or clusters of steps in a cooking task analysis. Or, teachers may select from any number of commercially produced picture cookbooks such as *Visual Recipes: A Cookbook for Non-Readers* (Orth, 2000). Although commercially produced cookbooks are convenient, some students may have difficulty following steps that are not individualized to their learning needs.

High-tech, self-prompting systems such as video and handheld computers offer another recipe option for nonreaders (Mechling, 2008). Mechling and Stephens (2009) compared the use of static picture books versus video self-prompting via a portable DVD player to teach students with intellectual disabilities to independently complete multistep cooking tasks. Although students were able to complete recipes using both self-prompting systems, video self-prompting was more effective. Perhaps the sound and motion features of a video (students can listen to directions and follow a moving model) are an added benefit. Additionally, students can hit the replay button to watch any step that they missed or want to watch again.

As technology expands, more commercially produced options may become available. For example, Nintendo DS™ (a portable gaming system) offers a system called, *Personal Training: Cooking* (http://www.nintendo.com). Developed for anyone who can benefit from modeling and systematic instruction, the system offers a number of advantages for learners with intellectual disabilities. Once a user selects a pictured recipe, the system lists all of the necessary ingredients, which can then be used as a grocery list for shopping. When it is time to cook, the system prompts the user to gather all cooking materials and then gives step-by-step audio and video or picture directions to complete the recipe. The learner can hit the replay button at any time to repeat the audio directions or the model.

The teaching challenge is to design instruction so that it is efficient and effective, while also encouraging generalized use of self-prompting systems. Cooking supplies can be expensive, and often, instruction cannot be delivered in a one-to-one arrangement in school settings. Furthermore, rarely is it practical for each person in the group to perform all of the steps of the cooking task. If four students in a group each prepare a box of instant pudding, there will be 16 servings to consume! Teachers can have each student prepare part of the recipe while the others watch. The following guidelines help make instruction efficient while encouraging self-directed learning:

1. Where possible, teach food preparation in a small group of two or three, giving each person a chance to prepare part of the recipe while the others watch and follow the recipe using the package or a self-prompting system.

   In preparing a box cake mix, Sam adds the ingredients and prepares the pan using a picture recipe while Julia follows along using her own picture recipe. Then Julia uses the mixer and pours the mix into the pan and places it in the oven while Sam follows along on his picture recipe.

2. Use a prompt system, such as time delay or the system of least prompts, to teach students to follow the recipe steps or operate the self-prompting system.

   The teacher uses a verbal and gesture prompt: "Look at the next step and do it."

3. Consider including additional information about nutrition or safety within the cooking routine.

   The teacher consistently uses the same statement (e.g., "Use a protective mitt to keep from being burned").

4. Probe to assess learning.

   Ask Julia to make a boxed cheesecake by following the picture recipe and record the steps that she can do alone.

5. Probe for generalization.

   Give Sam and Julia untrained recipes with pictures similar to the cheesecake and other learned recipes. Can they use the pictures to follow the new recipes?

Housekeeping

To manage a home, individuals need strategies to keep pace with the ongoing demands of housecleaning and laundry. Even when chores can be shared, some household tasks still must be performed. As students make the transition from relying on their parents to clean the house and do their laundry, to caring for their own clothes and living space, they need to learn two important sets of skills: (a) how to perform housekeeping and laundry tasks, and (b) how to manage their time so that they can complete these tasks regularly.

Instructors typically use a task analysis of the skill and a prompting system (such as least intrusive prompts or time delay) to teach housekeeping tasks. Whether to teach the entire task (i.e., whole-task instruction) or some portion of it (i.e., chaining) will depend on the complexity of the task and the students' current skill level (see Chapter 4). For example, McWilliams, Nietupski, and Hamre-Nietupski (1990) taught students to make their bed using a system of least prompts and forward chaining in which steps of the task analysis were taught to mastery one at a time. In contrast, Snell (1982) used progressive time delay to teach the task of bed making, prompting students through the whole-task analysis during each teaching session: (a) make a partially unmade bed, (b) strip a bed, and (c) make up a bed completely.

Similarly, in teaching laundry skills, researchers have used the system of least prompts (Cuvo, Jacobi, & Sipko, 1981), time delay (Miller & Test, 1989), and most-to-least prompting (Miller & Test, 1989). For this task, McDonnell and McFarland (1988) found whole-task instruction to be more efficient than chaining, while Miller and Test (1989) found time delay to be slightly more efficient than most-to-least prompting. In applying these strategies to individual students, it is important to consider how the student learns best.

Another strategy is to encourage student-directed learning by using a self-operated audio-prompting system that because of its portability is well suited to cleaning tasks. Briggs et al. (1990) taught students with intellectual disabilities to operate a washing machine, clean a toilet, and clean mirrors using a taped script that they played while wearing a Walkman tape player. The script gave both verbal prompts and praise. The following sample from the Briggs et al. (1990) audiotape illustrates how the script contained prompting, self-checking of outcomes, seeking help as needed, and praise. When the bell sounded, the student turned off the tape and performed the step as follows:

> "Open the box and take out one set (two packets) of blue detergent. Put them in the washer." *[bell]*
>
> "Can you see the blue packets on top of the clothes? If you can't see them, call the teacher for help." *[bell]*
>
> "Good job! Now close the detergent box and put it back in the cabinet. Close the cabinet door." *[bell]*

Once students learn the basics of housekeeping, they need self-management skills to keep pace with the demands of these chores. Activity schedules suit this purpose. In a classic study, Pierce and Schriebman

(1994) taught children with autism to use pictures to self-manage chores. Students were given a photo album with one step on each page and a picture for that step of the task analysis. To make album pages easier to turn, felt dots were glued to the bottom of each page. Instructors taught in three phases. In the first phase, the instructor taught receptive labeling of all of the photos. In the second phase, students learned to choose a reinforcer, turn a page in the book, perform the response, and self-reinforce. In the third phase, the instructor faded her presence by saying, "Good work. I'll be back in a minute," and leaving the area while the student worked alone. Students were able to use the picture books to set a table, make a bed, make a drink, get dressed, and do laundry without an adult nearby.

Once students know how to follow a schedule, they can learn to self-schedule these activities. Lovett and Haring (1989) taught adults with intellectual disabilities to self-manage their daily living skills using self-recording, self-evaluation, and self-reinforcement. Tasks were divided into daily, weekly, and occasional schedules. Participants used a planning form to self-select these tasks. Using instructions, modeling, and feedback, the teachers taught participants to use the same form to self-record when each task was completed. If participants did not achieve 100% accuracy for self-recording, they were taught to self-reinforce (e.g., participate in a leisure activity) in order to improve their accuracy. After mastering self-recording, participants learned to graph their performance on a simple percentage chart and then determine whether they had made progress. Once they has become successful in self-evaluation, all participants learned to self-reinforce when tasks were completed on time.

The teacher helped Julia and her mother to identify Julia's chores, across school and home, and to determine flexible times for their completion. In a language arts class, the teacher and peers taught Julia to read the names of her chores and the days of the week. The teacher also taught her how to make check marks on the form by talking about what Julia had or had not done the night before at home. Once Julia could check off items on the form accurately, the teacher met with Julia and her mother to review how Julia could take charge of her own chores by using her charts and planning her list of "treats" for self-reinforcement. Julia then used her new self-management program at home with support from her mother as needed.

When doing housekeeping and laundry, students will encounter problems that prevent task completion unless they develop problem-solving skills. Hughes, Hugo, and Blatt (1996) taught students to use self-management strategies to solve several problems: (a) not having the right utensil in order to make toast, (b) trying to vacuum when the vacuum was unplugged, and (c) cleaning up when there were bread crumbs under the table or game pieces in the area to be vacuumed. The self-instruction strategy involved students learning to (a) state the problem, (b) state the response, (c) self-evaluate, and (d) self-reinforce. The instructor taught the strategy by modeling the problem-solving step, having the participant state what to do as the instructor performed it, and then having the participant do the step while saying the problem-solving strategy. For example, to cope with an unplugged vacuum, the participant would say the following:

1. "The vacuum won't run." (*State the problem*)
2. "Plug it in." (*State the response*)
3. "I plugged it in." (*Self-evaluate*)
4. "Great job!" (*Self-reinforce*)

Home Safety

Many skills contribute to being safe at home (Mechling, 2008), including recognizing and avoiding hazards (e.g., electric shock, hot burner), creating a safe home environment (e.g., locking doors, using matches appropriately), responding to emergencies (e.g., calling 911, evacuating a building), and using first aid (e.g., treating cuts and burns, responding to minor illnesses). Safety skills are taught like any other skill, but simulation and role-play may be needed to create "dangers" that are not typically present in everyday settings. Haney and Jones (1982) taught four school-age children to escape from a simulated fire in a home setting. Props were designed to make the training more realistic. For example, hot and cold pads were used to change the touch temperatures of doors and a tape recording of the home's fire alarm system was played. The instructor used a system of least prompts to teach the steps of the task analysis. Rae and Roll (1985) similarly employed a system of least prompts to teach evacuation. They also measured evacuation time to be sure that students could leave the building in the time recommended by the fire department. Sometimes, for students like Rico, school fire drills can be upsetting and confusing (see Box 14–2), and constructive steps must be taken to address interfering behaviors.

Box 14–2 How Rico Learned to Participate in Fire Drills

Whenever the school fire alarm sounded, Rico would begin to scream and slap his face. Feeling pressured to evacuate the students safely, the third-grade teacher and paraprofessional would plead with him to leave. They had even tried carrying him out of the building, but Rico became aggressive. The special education teacher designed a fire evacuation simulation training program for Rico. Each day, at a different time, the special education teacher or the paraprofessional asked Rico to choose two classmates from among those who had finished their work to practice a fire drill. In the first phase, the teacher rang a small buzzer briefly (a second) and used least prompts to teach Rico to follow the two chosen classmates to the school yard. Rico received continuous praise by the teacher and peers as he followed them without screaming or self-injury. When he returned to the classroom, he was given the choice of listening to a musical relaxation tape or looking at a book (activities which he liked and found calming). Over time, the teacher made the buzzer longer and louder until it was more similar to the school fire alarm. When the next fire drill occurred, the peers went to Rico and calmly asked him to follow them. Rico went with them, but wanted to hold their hands. He cried, but was not screaming. At the end of the fire drill, Rico returned and went directly to the relaxation tape just as he had done during simulations. The decision was made to continue the training program, but to fade to a weekly schedule.

Students also may encounter emergencies that require knowing first-aid skills. Spooner, Stem, and Test (1989) taught students to communicate an emergency, apply a bandage, take care of minor injuries, and respond to someone who was choking. The instructor used a group format followed by individual practice sessions with modeling and an intermittent probe of behavior acquisition. The task analyses used are shown in Table 14–4. These first-aid skills can also be taught with constant time delay (Gast, Winterling, Wolery, & Farmer, 1992), by using puppet simulations (Marchand-Martella et al., 1992a), or by peers who role-play having

TABLE 14–4
Task Analysis for First Aid

Communicating an Emergency	Applying a Plastic Bandage
1. Locate phone	1. Look at injury
2. Pick up receiver	2. Find bandages needed
3. Dial 9	3. Select proper size
4. Dial 1	4. Find outside tabs of wrapper
5. Dial 1	5. Pull down tabs to expose bandage
6. Put receiver to ear	6. Find protective covering on bandage
7. Listen for operator	7. Pull off by tabs, exposing gauze portion
8. Give full name	8. Do not touch gauze portion
9. Give full address	9. Apply to clean, dry skin
10. Give phone number	
11. Explain emergency	
12. Hang up after operator does	

Taking Care of Minor Injuries	First Aid for Choking
1. Let it bleed a little to wash out the dirt	1. Let the person cough and try to get object out of throat
2. Wash with soap and water	2. Stand behind victim
3. Dry with clean cloth	3. Wrap your arms around victim
4. Open plastic bandage	4. Make a fist with one hand, placing the thumb side of the clinched fist against the victim's abdomen—slightly above the navel and below the rib cage
5. Cover with bandage (hold by the edges)	
6. Call 911 if severe and no adult available	5. Press fist into abdomen; quick, upward thrust (repeat as needed)

Note: From "Teaching First Aid Skills to Adolescents Who Are Moderately Mentally Handicapped" by F. Spooner, B. Stem, and D. W. Test, 1989, *Education and Training in Mental Retardation, 24,* p. 343. Copyright 1989 by the Division on Mental Retardation and Developmental Disabilities, Council on Exceptional Children. Reprinted by permission.

wounds (Marchand-Martella, Martella, Christensen, Agran, & Young, 1992b).

To assess student performance when real injuries occur, teachers may need to rely on follow-up reports from parents (Mechling, 2008). Of course, our focus on independent or partial participation in any of these skills must never put a student in danger.

Video technology, either video modeling or video prompting, holds promise for providing real-life examples and simulated dangers that cannot be accomplished through traditional means (Mechling, 2008). Mechling, Gast, and Gustafson (2009) used video modeling to teach students three ways to extinguish kitchen fires: (a) scooping and releasing flour, (b) putting a lid on a pot or pan, and (c) using a fire extinguisher. During generalization probes in which the teacher started a small kitchen fire in an apartment rented by the school district, students were able to successfully extinguish the fire immediately after watching the video model. Although starting fires is not recommended(!), the study does show the potential power of video modeling combined with immediate practice in real settings. In addition to using simulations, safety skills can be taught by embedding opportunities in daily routines or during instruction of other skills. Safety skills also can be taught by adding safety steps to task analyses or routines.

> *After preparing a meal, Aaron is prompted, as part of his food preparation task analysis, to check that all appliances (e.g., coffeemaker, burner, oven) are turned off before he leaves the kitchen. When he enters his home with his community teacher, Aaron is taught to lock the door behind him before he hangs up his coat.*

In place of direct instruction, adding extra information is an ideal way of embedding safety skill information during instruction of home tasks or routines (Jones & Collins, 1997).

> *While teaching Aaron to use a microwave, his teacher tells him that if he sees smoke while cooking, he should quickly turn the microwave off. When Aaron reaches for his toast, his teacher says, "If the toast ever gets stuck, unplug the toaster, then use a rubber spatula to get the toast out."*

For critical safety skills, teachers should consider setting up mini-simulations to observe whether the student can apply the extra information when needed.

> *Aaron's teacher deliberately inserted folded bread in the toaster to see whether Aaron would unplug the toaster before removing the stuck toast.*

Telephone Use

Telephone use is related to many daily living skills (e.g., placing orders, getting information, and responding to emergencies) and social skills (e.g., calling friends). Because students may need many practice opportunities before mastering telephone skills, simulations are helpful. Emergency telephoning has been successfully taught to students with disabilities using task analyses and pictures of emergency situations to begin each simulated emergency call (Spooner et al., 1989). In a more recent study (Manley, Collins, Stenhoff, & Kleinert, 2008), teachers taught elementary students with intellectual disabilities to place a phone call and leave recorded voice mail messages using least-to-most prompting during in-class simulations. Teachers simulated voice message directions and beeps ("I'm not home right now, leave a message" *Beep*) through audio tapes. Students practiced across multiple exemplars of touch-tone phones, referring to a teacher-made phone book that depicts a picture of a person and the phone number. This strategy effectively taught students to make calls and leave voice mail messages, but students experienced difficulty generalizing to other settings, perhaps because the simulation did not include the full variation of stimuli present in other situations (e.g., different voice messages, setting distractions).

As more and more students use personal cell phones with technological adaptations, it may be less important to teach students how to dial different phones, or even dial for that matter (they can use speed dial instead), than it is to learn how to operate cell phones using technological adaptations for different purposes. For example, students can text message by using the "quick text" feature on their phone. General case instruction may be used to teach students to make different types of phone calls. Horner et al. (1987) applied general case instruction to teach generalized phone use to four high school students with moderate and severe intellectual disabilities. The instructional universe included frequently made and received calls. Training variations included the person calling or being called, and the topic of conversation (e.g., to leave a message, place an order). Once instructed on these variations, students learned to make a wide range of phone calls.

> *Using general case instruction to teach Julia how to make phone calls is an ideal strategy for her. As an active teen, she will need to use the phone for a variety of purposes like calling home to ask permission to visit a friend after school, calling friends to*

chat, and making emergency calls when she needs help. Julia's need to make a variety of phone calls can be addressed with a general case instruction approach.

Sexuality Education

Another relevant skill area for the home is sexuality education. Sexuality education is broader than just "sex ed." While sex typically refers to a sex act, sexuality refers to one's total being, including being male or female, feeling good about oneself, caring for others, and expressing oneself through intimacy. Fostering healthy sexual attitudes and behaviors are critical goals of sexuality education (Hingsburger & Tough, 2002). Unfortunately, sexuality education for learners with intellectual disabilities is typically overlooked or avoided. As a result, many adults with disabilities are uneducated about basic sex facts (e.g., names of body parts, knowledge of bodily functions, sexual acts) (McCabe & Cummins, 1996), are vulnerable to sexual abuse partially because of their lack of knowledge (Sobsey & Doe, 1991), and hold negative feelings about themselves and sexual issues (Garwood & McCabe, 2000). Others, acting on their sexual urges without proper education, may act inappropriately (e.g., engage in public masturbation, make sexual advances toward the wrong person) (Tarnai, 2006).

Feeling good about one's sexuality and having the opportunity to enter into intimate, loving relationships with others adds to personal happiness. To reverse the negative cycle of poor or no education, sexuality education should be viewed comprehensively and developmentally, focusing on (a) knowledge about basic sex facts, (b) skills (knowing how and when to act), (c) feelings (fostering positive attitudes), and (d) relationships (understanding and respecting others). Not everything can or should be taught at once. Some components will require the foundation of others, while all sexuality education must be age appropriate. Some guidelines about what to teach are offered by Schwier and Hingsburger (2000) in Table 14–5.

Commercial sexuality curricula are available to guide instruction (see Blanchett & Wolfe, 2002), but most curricula are limited because they rely on lecture, discussion, and line drawings to explain concepts. Many learners with severe disabilities may not comprehend the information presented in this way or know how to apply it. Commercial curricula can be useful for suggesting important sexuality topics, but teachers and parents need to teach the content so that it can be understood by and useful to the student.

TABLE 14–5
Sexuality Content Guidelines: What to Teach When

Age	Content
Early Years, 3–9	• Difference between boys and girls • Body names and functions • Public and private places • Modesty • How babies are born
Puberty, 9–15	• Hygiene (looking good, looking cool) • Physical changes • Menstruation • Wet dreams • Inappropriate touching and saying "no" • Social boundaries and social manners • Sexual feelings • How babies are made
Older Teens, 16 and up	• Dating preparation • Relationships (love vs. sex) • Handling sexual/emotional feelings • Laws/consequences for inappropriate touching • Sexual intercourse/other sex acts • Prevention of pregnancy • Prevention of STDs • Marriage/parenting

Adapted with permission from Schwier, K. M., & Hingsburger, D. (2000), *Sexuality: Your sons and daughters with intellectual disabilities* (p. 32). Baltimore: Paul H. Brookes which was adapted from: Maksym, D. (1990). Shared feelings: A parent guide to sexuality education for children, adolescents and adults who have a mental handicap. North York, Ontario, Canada: The Roeher Institute.

The best way to teach sexuality concepts is by infusing them into students' typical home or school routines and natural life experiences. For instance, body part names can be taught during dressing and bathing routines at home and, with parents' permission, at school when assisting the student to toilet or undress and dress for swimming. Learning anatomically correct names is critical for unambiguous communication (e.g., if abused, students can explain exactly where they were touched). Learning about public versus private areas of the home and school are important discriminations needed for acting sexually appropriate and for self-protection (Schwier & Hingsburger, 2000). During home routines, parents can label the bedroom and bathroom as private areas used for private activities such as dressing and masturbating. Private activities are not allowed in the public areas of the home. Furthermore, parents can teach their children that only certain people (e.g., friends, family members) may enter a private area of the house, but first they must ask permission (e.g., knock on the door). At school, teachers can encourage privacy by teaching students to close the bathroom door and to wrap a towel around themselves after showering.

Personal Hygiene. Personal hygiene is an important component of sexuality education. Research examples provide some guidance on how to teach menstrual care. For example, Epps, Stern, and Horner (1990) taught girls to manage their periods by using simulations and general case instruction. A training video, "Janet's Got Her Period™" (James Stanfield Publishing, http://www.stanfield.com), is a good resource to introduce the concept of menstrual care and can be followed up with parental instruction at home (e.g., Ersoy, Tekin-Iftar, & Kiracaali-Iftar, 2009). Personal hygiene should stress not only management of bodily functions but also looking good and feeling attractive. Wherever possible, teachers and parents can help students make the connection between their personal care routines and social activities. Getting ready for a party or a school dance, for example, can involve choosing nice clothes, styling hair in a special way, wearing special makeup, or choosing new perfume or cologne. Telling the student that he or she looks great, beautiful, or handsome can go a long way in bolstering the student's self-confidence and feelings of pride.

Social Boundaries. One area of sexuality education that can be especially appropriate for teaching in school and in the community is that of recognizing and respecting social boundaries. Students sometimes do not discriminate between who can be trusted with a hug and who cannot, or lack understanding about their personal versus public body parts or activities. The Circles Curriculum (James Stanfield Publishing, http://www.stanfield.com) provides videotapes and color coding to teach students to discriminate among different types of relationships. For example, the purple private circle is for the student alone. Some "circles" (relationships) welcome hugs, but some hugs should give the people space between bodies (friends versus lovers). People in the red zone (strangers) are not given physical or verbal contact. This program can be used to teach avoidance of sexual harassment and abuse and helps students to understand how relationships can develop from acquaintances into friendships. By selecting photographs of people who the student knows and color coding them, the discrimination can

be made more concrete. Students may need to practice their ability to discriminate when encountering people in the community. For example, the teacher might say, "What zone is Mr. Jones in? He's an acquaintance. What do we do? Just wave—no hugs." If a student makes inappropriate physical contact with a teacher or others, the teacher may use color coding on clothing to help the student know which zones are appropriate (e.g., a green patch on the arm to tap her for attention). Although not fully evaluated by research, reading Social Stories™ before going into the community may prime students about how to maintain appropriate social boundaries (Tarnai & Wolfe, 2008).

Protection from Abuse. Teaching protection from abuse is also critical. Sadly, people with disabilities are highly vulnerable to sexual abuse, with most abuse incidents occurring with *familiar* people, not with strangers (Sobsey & Doe, 1991). Teachers can teach students abuse protection responses at school, but practice and reminders at home are important if students are to report actual abuse incidents wherever they occur. The "No–Go–Tell" is one effective strategy. Lumley and colleagues taught adult women with disabilities how to respond to unwanted sexual advances that potentially could be made by their support staff (Lumley, Miltenberger, Long, Rapp, & Roberts, 1998). By presenting scenarios (e.g., "What would you do if staff touched your breasts?") and participating in role-play, the women learned a three-step sequence: No— Verbally refuse the lure or action, Go—Leave the situation, and Tell—Report the incident to a trusted adult. Discriminating between what are appropriate and inappropriate sexual advances is an important prerequisite. Combining the circles curriculum with No–Go– Tell may help students learn these discriminations (e.g., "Kissing [long and on the mouth] is okay with a boyfriend or girlfriend when you both like it, but kissing [like that] is never okay with a stranger, your teacher, or a member of your family").

Planning what sexuality skills to teach can be difficult. Collaboration between the teacher and the parents is important to honor the family's values and determine what information is most relevant for an individual student. Because of the highly individualized and comprehensive nature of sexuality education, Lumley and Scotti (2001) recommend a person-centered planning approach during students' transition years so that sexuality education and related non-instructional supports can be tailored to the student's needs and vision

TABLE 14–6

Planning for Aaron's Sexuality Education: Person-Centered Questions and Outcomes

What are Aaron's dreams for the future, and what are his interests in social relationships?	• Aaron wants to live in his own apartment and hold a part-time job while he attends college. • Aaron expresses interest in girls, but doesn't believe having a girlfriend is appropriate for someone like him.
What does Aaron need to know about sexuality? What skills are needed? Any concerns?	• Aaron's family is concerned about the potential for sexual abuse. • It's unclear what Aaron knows about sex, sexual relationships, or sexual abuse protection. • Aaron needs a healthier view about the possibilities of having a girlfriend and about his self-image.
What types of sexuality education and supports are needed?	• Basic sex education • Knowledge and skills for abuse protection • Awareness of disability and intimate relationships • Specific sexuality information and training regarding physical disabilities • Support and encouragement to seek social opportunities and date

How will support be provided? Who will provide it?	• Basic sexual education and abuse protection training
	• Mr. Burk, special education teacher
	• Parent support at home
	• Disability awareness:
	  • Attend program at the community college
	• Specific sexuality information regarding physical disabilities:
	  • Support for social opportunities
	  • Peer buddy
	  • Parents

for the future. Table 14–6 illustrates some relevant questions that can be incorporated into person-centered planning (Bambara, Koger, & Nonnemacher, 2002). Because of the highly sensitive nature of sexual issues, some questions are best discussed privately with the student and/or family instead of in the presence of an entire team. With the student's and parent's permission, information may be brought back to the team for planning, as is shown for Aaron in Table 14–6.

After Aaron's last transition planning meeting, Mr. Delaney, the transition coordinator, privately asked the Williamses if they had considered Aaron's sexual needs and the possibility of sexual relationships. The Williamses admitted that they had never considered the questions but did say that one of their greatest fears about Aaron's transition to supported living was that someone would sexually abuse him. They shared that they did not know how to talk to Aaron about sex. When Mr. Delaney spoke with Aaron privately, Aaron clearly expressed an interest in girls but seemed resigned to the idea that having a girlfriend was not for him. After further talk, Mr. Delaney

could not tell what Aaron knew or didn't know about sex. Once the Williamses thought about it, they were open to the idea that Aaron should have as normal a life as possible, including girlfriends and maybe even marriage some day. Together with Mr. Delaney and Aaron, they developed a plan for Aaron's sexuality education. First, his special education teachers would offer Aaron basic sexuality education and abuse protection education in a class format along with three other young men who needed similar training. Using slides, videotapes, discussions, and, where appropriate, role-play, basic sexual facts (e.g., body changes, sexual acts), sexually transmitted diseases and pregnancy prevention, and sexual abuse protection will be presented. The teacher will also invite Aaron's college Best Buddy and young adults from Aaron's university who did date-rape prevention training to talk about self-esteem and the body. Second, Mr. and Mrs. Williams agreed to discuss their values about sex with their son at home. The Williamses and Aaron will attend a continuing education class at a local community college on "Sexuality and Disability." At this program, several couples with physical disabilities will share their stories about overcoming obstacles to dating, privacy, and marriage. Third, Aaron's Best Buddy at his university agreed to help Aaron make social connections at school. They will look for social opportunities at school clubs and organizations where Aaron can meet girls, and encourage and support Aaron's social initiations (e.g., arrange for Aaron to meet a girl at the library, write phone numbers in his social book).

Skills for the Community

An important part of a student's transition to adult living is to acquire the skills needed for community settings, including public safety; mobility in the community; and the use of community resources like stores, banks, and restaurants. Younger students (elementary age) may also may receive some community instruction, depending on their individual needs and parental preferences.

Safety Skills

Community safety skills are critical. As students gain increased independence in the community, they are exposed to greater risks. Like home safety, community safety requires a wide variety of abilities, including recognizing and avoiding dangerous situations (e.g., walking away from strangers, avoiding certain streets), preventing hazards (e.g., safe street crossing), and knowing how to seek help when needed (e.g., going to a police officer, using the telephone). The same instructional strategies used for home safety may be applied when teaching public safety. These include role-play and simulations, and embedding direct instruction or adding extra information about safety during the instruction of other community skills. An additional strategy involves embedding problem-solving opportunities within community-based instruction. Based on procedures developed by Agran, Madison, and Brown (1995), Aaron was taught to travel to the bus stop after evening recreational activities at his community college.

As Aaron approached an unlit area of the campus, he was taught to ask and respond to the following questions: (a) "What is dangerous?" ("Walking on very dark streets"), (b) "Why is it unsafe?" ("I can get mugged"), and (c) "What can I do to make it safer?" ("I can go another way").

Some concepts of community danger and safety are abstract. Students may need to experience them before understanding how to respond. Using a No–Go–Tell strategy, Watson, Bain, and Houghton (1992) taught children with disabilities to refuse advances from a stranger, leave the area, and tell a trusted adult what happened. Once the children learned the sequence through role-play, people unfamiliar to the children were employed by the researchers to approach the children in the community to determine if the children had mastered the skills. Parental permission for this approach is, of course, essential.

In another example of making abstract safety concepts real, Taber, Alberto, Hughes, and Seltzer (2002) developed a three-phase program to teach middle school students with disabilities how to use a cell phone when lost in the community. The first phase of instruction took place in the school building where the students defined being lost (i.e., not being able to find the person with whom you arrived at a community location) and then pretended to be lost. While pretending, the students were taught via a task analysis and system of least prompts how to use their cell phone to call for assistance. Two important steps in the task analysis were staying put and describing landmarks in the immediate surrounding so that the students' locations could be identified by the person receiving the call. In the second phase, instruction took place in three community settings: the grocery store, the department store, and the public library. In these locations, the students were required to use the calling sequence as their instructor removed herself from the students' sight. If the student did not respond or make the call correctly within five minutes of being "lost," the instructor approached the student and reviewed the sequence. In the third phase, during typical community instruction in the same settings, the instructor on occasion left the students' sight to assess whether they would call under more natural situations. In both community phases, the students were always shadowed by another adult to ensure their safety.

In a replication study, Taber, Alberto, Seltzer, and Hughes (2003) modified emergency cell phone use for students who had difficulty dialing and/or trouble identifying when they were lost. The modifications included one-step speed dialing and answering a ringing cell phone when an adult discovered that the student was missing. When answering the phone, students were taught to provide relevant information about their immediate location (e.g., "What do you see?") so that they could be found.

Purchasing

Another important area of instruction is making purchases in the community (shopping). This may include purchasing groceries, clothing, dining and snacking, household goods, and personal care and leisure items. Teachers need to consider four questions before teaching students to make purchases:

1. Which stores does the student need to learn to use?
2. Is the goal to teach the student to make a purchase at a specific store, or a set of purchases in a variety of stores? That is, to what extent will generalization be taught?
3. To what extent will the student be taught to use money while making purchases versus using compensatory strategies (e.g., preselected amount of money)?
4. How can the student gain autonomy in making purchases?

If the goal is for the student to learn to purchase a short list of items in the grocery store that is used consistently by the student's family, the teacher might focus on teaching the skills needed for that one store. In contrast, if the goal is for the student to be able to use a variety of stores to make a range of purchases (e.g., clothing, leisure materials, groceries), training should focus on including variation in both school-based and community instruction (see Figure 14-6).

Generalization in Purchasing. When the goal is to teach generalized purchasing, general case planning can be used to infuse variation in simulations and in vivo instruction. McDonnell and Ferguson (1988) compared the relative effectiveness of general case in vivo instruction (variations that resulted by teaching in three different fast-food restaurants representing the range of stimuli) and general case simulations (variations were achieved by infusing a range of stimuli in school simulations). Because simulations should always include some community-based instruction, general case simulation was alternated each day with teaching in one community restaurant. After instruction, the students in both general case groups were assessed to see if they could generalize their purchasing skills to three new restaurants not used during instruction. Both general case in vivo and general case simulations were effective in teaching generalized purchasing skills. Students in both groups could apply their skills in novel restaurants without additional instruction.

FIGURE 14–6

Rachael selects a preferred recipe each week and prepares a picture grocery shopping list with the assistance of her instructor. She makes the purchase once she has located all the items that are necessary for carrying out the recipe.

The implication of this study is that when planning for generalized purchasing, teachers have some options. For older students whose instruction may be entirely community based, general case in vivo may make the most sense. For younger middle school or high school students, teachers may select either option, with consideration being given to student preferences for instructional settings, instructional costs, resources, and scheduling. For example, one advantage of choosing simulation is that it may be more practical for schools with limited transportation resources, and less travel time means more time in the school setting.

As an alternative, computer-based video simulations have been used to promote generalized purchasing skills with impressive results, including ordering across different fast-food restaurants (Mechling et al., 2005), checking out items across various grocery stores (Hansen & Morgan, 2008), and reading various aisle signs to locate items in a grocery story (Mechling & Gast, 2003; Mechling, Gast, & Langone, 2002). Mechling et al. (2002) videotaped three different grocery stores in order to teach high school students with moderate intellectual disabilities to read aisle signs and locate items in a grocery store. The videotapes illustrated travel throughout the stores, the location of aisle signs, and items within the aisle. To teach aisle sign reading, when a still photograph of an aisle sign appeared on a computer screen, selecting the correct word on the screen caused the computer to show movement down the aisle for a certain item. Students were taught to shop for items by identifying the correct aisle. The results showed that the video simulation consisting of video modeling and prompting taught students generalized reading of aisle signs (across different store examples) and the location of items in an actual store not used in the video instruction. With the assistance of a technology consultant, similar programs can be designed for schools so that older students could learn grocery shopping skills while taking computer classes with peers. Some community instruction time must be scheduled to ensure generalization.

Teaching Money Use. The demand for math skills involved in counting money can limit students' mastery of purchasing skills (Xin, Grasso, Dipipi-Hoy, & Jitendra (2005); therefore money-handling skills are an important instructional focus. For some students, the math skills needed during purchasing can be bypassed entirely by teaching students to (a) use a prescribed amount of money (e.g., always buy snacks with a five dollar bill), (b) use a template to match the correct coins or bills needed for an item, or (c) use a debit card (Mechling et al., 2003). For students with some math skills, other adaptations can be tried. For example, Cihak and Grimm (2008) used the "next dollar" and "counting on" strategies to teach high school students with intellectual disabilities and autism to make purchases. That is, for prices up to $5, students were taught to count out to the next dollar, using one dollar bills (e.g., for $3.50, count, 1, 2, 3, next 4). For prices between $5.00 and $9.99, students were taught to start with a five dollar bill, then count on to the next dollar; for prices between $10.00 and $14.99 or $15.00 and $19.99, students begin with a ten dollar bill or a ten and a five, respectively, and so on. Primary instruction took place in the high school resource room, using multiple examples for practice, followed by real opportunities to make purchases in the high school bookstore and during regularly scheduled opportunities for community instruction.

Comparison shopping is also important. Sandknop, Schuster, Wolery, and Cross (1992) taught students to select the lower-priced item from among similar groceries. Using constant time delay, students learned to look at two prices on a number line that was written vertically to determine which one was the lower price. Across training phases, students learned to compare not only the first digit of the price but then the second, third, and fourth digits. Frederick-Dugan, Test, and Varn (1991) developed a general case analysis of three types of purchases: food, clothing, and hygiene items. The instructor showed the students pictures of items from each category and a price up to $20. The students determined whether they could buy the items by using a calculator. The instructor used progressive time delay to teach the students to compare the price to the money that they had to determine whether they could make the purchase.

Social Skills. To be successful, students may need social skills while making a purchase. Westling, Floyd, and Carr (1990) taught these social skills as part of a purchasing program. These social skills are shown in Table 14-7 in a program designed for Julia to purchase items at discount department stores. By learning skills such as asking for help and being polite, Julia is more likely to have positive experiences when shopping alone or with friends.

Sometimes when shopping, people need to ask for help. Chadsey-Rusch et al. (1993) developed a general case approach to teach students to request help in community settings. For example, students might ask for help to negotiate curbs in getting into the store. Or, like Julia's example in Table 14-7, students may learn to ask for help across a variety of situations encountered in the store (e.g., finding the appropriate section of the store, finding the item on the shelf). With these social and communication skills, students can learn to navigate community routines like making purchases with no more teacher assistance than they need or want.

Community Leisure

There are many community leisure activities in which students can participate. These activities may include dining out, going to concerts or movies, participating in fitness classes, walking in the park, participating in clubs, and going to special community events. One challenge in leisure instruction is determining where and how to teach so that students can learn skills without losing the chance to make friends and have fun.

TABLE 14–7
Task Analysis of Shopping Skills

Student: Julia	Skill: Purchasing at discount department stores (e.g., K-Mart, Wal-Mart)
Purchasing Step	**Related Social Skill**
1. Enter door	Wait turn if needed
2. Go to correct store section	Ask help to find correct section Say "thank you" when given help
3. Find correct shelf	Ask help if can't find item on shelf Say "thank you" when given help
4. Select correct item(s)	
5. Go to register	Wait turn at checkout counter Keep cart from bumping others
6. Put item on counter	Greet cashier
7. Take out money	
8. Use "next dollar strategy"	
9. Give money to cashier	
10. Put change and receipt away	
11. Pick up purchased item	Say "good-bye" or "thanks"
12. Exit store	Wait turn at door to exit

Note: From D. L. Westling, J. Floyd., & D. Carr, 1990. Effects of single setting versus multiple setting training on learning to shop in a department store. *American Journal on Mental Retardation, 94,* 616–624. Copyright (1990) by American Association on Mental Retardation. Adapted with permission.

School and community extracurricular activities provide opportunities for inclusive leisure instruction. For example, many schools have music groups, pep clubs, computer clubs, and intramural sports. Important considerations for planning leisure activities include (a) assessing and honoring individual preferences for activities, (b) teaching individuals to self-initiate leisure activities, and (c) providing instruction or support for participation in inclusive settings.

Honoring Choice in Leisure Activities. An important aspect of leisure activities that makes them fun and relaxing is that they are optional. People choose what to do with their leisure time, including the choice to do nothing! Similarly, students with intellectual disabilities need the opportunity to choose how to spend leisure time. While some will be able to make these choices by telling others what they want to do or by initiating activities on their own, others need the opportunity to sample new leisure options to decide which to pursue. Sometimes these choices can then be expressed by selecting pictures of the activities or by using some other communication system (e.g., signing, communication board).

A challenge some teachers face is understanding the activity preferences of students who do not have a formal system of communication. Browder, Cooper, and Lim (1998) demonstrated how to teach students to select objects to indicate their choice of activity. In a three-phase study, these researchers first assessed participants' preferences for community activities by timing the duration of their participation in activities at each site. Once clear preferences emerged, they taught the participants to select an object to represent each activity. Using time delay, the instructor taught the participants to select a golf ball for golf, a library card to go to the library, a name tag for a club, or shoes for an aerobics class. This instruction occurred immediately before the leisure activity. Once the participants mastered associating the object with the activity, the third phase of the intervention was to give the participants a choice among the activities represented by the objects. Once a selection was made, the participant went to the community setting to strengthen the association between the object and the activity and to honor the participants' choice.

Teaching Self-Initiation of Leisure Activities. The second consideration in planning instruction for leisure activities is to encourage the students' self-initiations. Bambara and Ager (1992) taught adults with developmental disabilities to use pictures to self-schedule leisure activities for the upcoming week. The participants also initiated contact with support staff to request any necessary support (e.g., an escort or transportation). The pictures used were from the Attainment Company's *Plan Your Day Curriculum*. Devine, Malley, Sheldon, Datillo, and Gast (1997) also evaluated an intervention to teach adults to initiate leisure activities. Similar to Bambara and Ager (1992), they taught participants to use a calendar and pictures for self-scheduling. They also compared (a) having the participants put a reminder on their wall calendar with (b) giving participants a morning phone call to prompt the selected activity. Both prompting methods increased the participants' self-initiation of community leisure activities.

Instruction for Participation in Leisure Activities. Some students will benefit from direct instruction in how to participate in the leisure activity of their choice. For example, Zhang, Gast, Horvat, and Datillo (1995) taught students with intellectual disabilities "lifetime sport skills," including bowling, overhand throwing, and short-distance putting. Similarly, Bolton, Belfiore, Lalli, and Skinner (1994) taught adults with disabilities to putt in golf. They used stimulus fading by introducing guide boards for the golf ball that were then faded in size until the participant could get the ball in the hole with no guide.

Since many leisure skills are performed with family members or at home, it may also be beneficial to get interested family members involved in the instruction of leisure skills. For example, Wall and Gast (1997) taught caregivers (i.e., adult sibling, parent, houseparent) to teach leisure skills to adolescents. The caregivers learned to use task analyses and constant time delay to teach activities like horseshoes, checkers, croquet, board games, and turning the radio to a preferred station.

If developed well, leisure instruction can enhance inclusion with peers. Vandercook (1991) taught adolescents two activities that were popular with youth in their school (bowling and pinball). After determining the least intrusive effective prompt for each student, the teacher instructed the students in the bowling and pinball skills at the community bowling alley. Once a week, students bowled with their general education peers. During this weekly bowling time with their peers, the teacher did not interact with the dyad or prompt performance of bowling and pinball. As participants increased their bowling and pinball skills with the teacher, they generalized these skills to their weekly time with a peer. The peers also indicated a significant increase in their scores on their attitude toward individuals with disabilities. An alternative to this approach to facilitating inclusion is to teach peers to do the instruction.

Breen and Haring (1991) evaluated how important it was for the students with disabilities to have direct training in the leisure activity selected for peer inclusion. They selected eight computer games and provided intensive training in four of the games before setting opportunities for the adolescents with disabilities to play the games with their peers who were nondisabled. The instructor used a task analysis and least-prompts system to teach the four trained games. Using an alternating treatment design, they found that social initiations, game satisfaction, and peer satisfaction were all higher when playing the trained games versus the untrained games. This study and the work of Vandercook (1991) illustrate the potential need to provide intensive instruction as an adjunct to opportunities to engage in activities with peers.

To promote independence, it is sometimes important to teach the entire leisure routine (including initiating and terminating) and related social and communication skills, and not just only one component of the activity (e.g., the core steps of how to bowl) (see Chapter 3). Schleien, Certo, and Muccino (1984) illustrated how to teach an entire routine using a bowling alley to a student with intellectual disabilities. Instruction focused not only on how to bowl but also on how to purchase a drink and use the vending machine. The participant generalized these skills to three other bowling alleys without additional instruction. In another example, Taylor, McKelvey, and Sisson (1993) taught the entire routine for two skills (ordering a pizza and renting a video) to students with disabilities. For ordering the pizza, the skill cluster included using the phone, interacting with the delivery person, cutting and serving the pizza, and cleaning up. The students were also taught problem-solving skills. In renting a video, the students learned to ask the counter person to recommend a video if they could not find one that they liked or to help them find one on the shelf. Both skill clusters were taught in school simulations using a system of least prompts and props (e.g., pizza box, video boxes, phone) along with in vivo training in the community.

Banking

To participate in many community activities, students will need to acquire money-management skills such as paying bills and banking. LaCampagne and Cipani (1987) tested a method for teaching adults with disabilities to pay their bills. Instructional materials included a checkbook, check recorder, several real bills with their payment envelopes (e.g., electric company, credit card, telephone bill), and a calculator. The participants learned to perform the task-analyzed steps; (a) writing a check, (b) recording the amount in their checkbook, and (c) placing the payment in the payment envelope.

Because ATMs have essentially replaced the teller window banking for most of us, numerous research examples exist on how to teach students to use an ATM to withdraw cash or deposit money. ATM use can be taught whenever students are in the community through in vivo instruction (e.g., McDonnell & Ferguson, 1989) just before making a purchasing, or through combined simulation and community instruction to increase pratice opportunties. When creating simulations, teachers can construct a replica of an ATM (e.g., Bourbeau, Sowers, & Close, 1986) with plywood or cardboard and static enlarged picutures of ATM screens, or use modeling (e.g., Alberto et al., 2005) or video prompting in a computer environment (e.g., Davies, Stock, & Wehmeyer, 2003). Each of these simulation methods have been effective in promoting some geneneralization to actual ATM machines; however, mastery should not be considered complete until adequate performance in the community occurs.

Community Mobility

Community mobility involves pedestrian safety, being able to use public transportation, and finding locations in the community. The research on street crossing demonstrates that in vivo instruction has a clear advantage over classroom simulations (e.g., Marchetti, McCartney, Drain, Hooper, & Dix, 1983; Matson, 1980; Page, Iwata, & Neef, 1976), although some studies suggest that simulation can enhance efficiency (see Mechling, 2008), and one study found that simulated street crossing in a school gymnasium actually resulted in generalization to city streets by five students with intellectual disabilities (Batu, Ergenekon, Erbas, & Akmanoglu, 2004). Regardless of the potential advantages of simulation, street crossing is one skill in which community instruction and perhaps overpractice is essential because of safety concerns. Obviously, when

teaching street crossing in the community, there is little room for error! Teachers should consider using time delay, simultaneous prompting, or most-to-least prompting to avoid risky mistakes.

For some students, the most important street crossing skill to master is crossing streets with an escort (a partial participation goal). The task analysis would address walking or propelling a wheelchair near the escort, stopping at curbs, crossing when given a verbal or physical cue, and crossing without stopping in the street. For other students, the outcome is independent street crossing. When independence is the goal, it is important to take a general case approach to teach the variations of streets encountered in a particular community (Horner, Jones, & Williams, 1985). For example, the range of stimulus variation that the student may encounter includes the speed of cars, the number of cars, changes in lights, the types of pedestrian signal (e.g., words, pictures), the number of lanes, traffic directions (e.g., one way or two way), the angle of crossing (e.g., straight, diagonal), and the type of street (e.g., stop sign, traffic light). Horner et al. (1985) trained on 10 different streets daily and probed with untrained streets until it was clear that participants could cross a variety of streets safely.

In Aaron's pedestrian program, he is taught to (a) indicate when it is safe to cross; (b) choose to operate his motorized wheelchair alone or to request assistance, depending on the type of street and his own preference at the time; (c) steer his wheelchair safely near other pedestrians using the sidewalk; and (d) choose safe routes to travel.

Some individuals with intellectual disabilities need instruction to learn to walk from one location to another without stopping, wandering, or sitting down on the ground. For example, Spears, Rusch, York, and Lilly (1981) taught a boy to walk from his school bus to his classroom. They used pacing prompts (verbal reminders) to encourage the boy to keep walking without pausing. Teachers might consider having the student walk with peers to establish pacing. Another pedestrian skill is to find the way to a given location. Finding locations in some communities is complex and may require recognition of key landmarks. Singleton, Schuster, and Ault (1995) taught students to recognize community signs (e.g., "Barber," "Denny's," "KOA") and their meanings. For example, students learned that a barber gives a haircut. Although not a

TABLE 14–8
Task Analysis for Teaching Bus Riding with Simulation

Students: Julia, Tom, Sarah	Skill: Bus riding
Step of Task Analysis	**Video, Slide, or Picture Simulation**
1. Walk to bus stop	Pictures of nearby bus stops
2. Wait at bus stop	Show people waiting for bus
3. Identify correct bus	Pictures of buses that come to that stop
4. Signal bus to stop	Show person waving hand
5. Wait in line to enter bus	Show people in line
6. Enter front door of bus	Pictures of both bus doors
7. Give driver bus pass	Show driver and have real passes
8. Sit in empty seat or stand	Show seats that are empty and full
9. Identify destination	Pictures of landmarks
10. Pull cord for stop	Picture of cord
11. Exit rear door	Picture of inside bus doors
12. Move away from bus	Show person correct (moving away) and wrong (walking in front of bus)

focus of their instruction, recognition of community signs could be combined with teaching individuals a familiar route, such as walking to work or to the local community recreation center.

In some contexts, getting to these desired locations requires using public transportation, such as the bus or subway. Bus riding can be taught with some simulated practice. For example, slides taken in the local community can help students learn key landmarks to know when to get off the bus (Neef, Iwata, & Page, 1978; Robinson, Griffith, McComish, & Swasbrook, 1984). Such simulations, however, do not always produce generalization to actual buses (Coon, Vogelsberg, & Williams, 1981); in contrast, individuals with severe disabilities can learn bus riding when all instruction is community based (Sowers, Rusch, & Hudson, 1979). Table 14–8 provides a response sequence for teaching bus riding that uses simulations as an adjunct to community-based instruction. To practice bus riding, the teacher shows slides (or video clips) for each response in the task analysis.

When teaching Julia and some classmates to take the city bus to the mall, the teacher showed a video clip or slides of bus stops near the school. When the correct bus stop was shown, students were encouraged to raise their hands. The teacher asked one student to verbalize what they would do: "We get on the bus by

Jack's Diner." She then showed video clips or slides of the various buses that stop at that destination. When the bus that says "West Mall" was shown, students again raised their hands, and someone stated the appropriate step. This procedure continued until all of the steps had been rehearsed. Next, the students applied these skills in an actual trip to the mall.

Summary

This chapter describes how daily living and community skills can be taught in ways that honor and encourage self-determination and general education inclusion. Based on the research literature to date, some community-based instruction is needed to ensure that the skills learned through school opportunities or simulations generalize to real settings. For students who are beyond the typical school age, most of this instruction will probably take place in the community. Evidence-based procedures were described to teach skills for home and in the community that encourage student-directed learning, use technology, incorporate peer instruction and interaction when possible, and use powerful teaching strategies to promote acquisition of skills and generalization to everyday settings.

Suggested Activities

1. Families sometimes seek a teacher's assistance in increasing their child's independence in home routines. Based on your reading of this chapter, describe several ways that teachers can help support parents to promote greater independence at home. Identify specific teaching and collaboration strategies that teachers can use.
2. Choose a skill for community participation (e.g., purchasing, street crossing). Develop an instructional plan that involves in-school simulation and some in vivo instruction. Consider how you will create the simulation, how often you will teach in the simulated setting versus the community setting, and how you will evaluate student success in actual community settings.
3. Consider Aaron's instructional goals described in this chapter. If Aaron were enrolled in a postsecondary education program housed in your college, where might be the occasions for him to practice his instructional goals? Develop an individualized instructional schedule for Aaron as illustrated in Figure 14-2 using college activities and resources available on your campus. Consider how college peers might be used to support Aaron.
4. Compare the advantages and disadvantages of using low-tech picture cues with using more high tech-video prompts for teaching cooking skills? Are there certain situations (e.g., settings, learner characteristics) when it may be better to use one over the other? Are there additional skills that must be taught in order for learners to use picture cues or operate video technology?

References

Agran, M., Madison, D., & Brown, C. (1995). Teaching supported employees to prevent work injuries. *Journal of Vocational Rehabilitation, 5,* 33–42.

Alberto, P. A., Cihak, D. F., & Gama, R. I. (2005). Use of static picture prompts versus video modeling during simulation instruction. *Research in Developmental Disabilities: A Multidisciplinary Journal, 26*(4), 327–339.

Anderson, M. D., Sherman, J. A., Sheldon, J. B., & McAdam, D. (1997). Picture activity schedules and engagement of adults with mental retardation in a group home. *Research in Developmental Disabilities, 18,* 231–250.

Arnold-Reid, G. S., Schloss, P. J., & Alper, S. (1997). Teaching meal planning to youth with mental retardation in natural settings. *Remedial and Special Education, 18*(3), 166–173.

Ayres, K. M., & Langone, J. (2005). Intervention and instruction with video for students with autism: A review of the literature. *Education and Training in Developmental Disabilities, 40*(2), 183–196.

Bambara, L. M., & Ager, C. (1992). Use of self-scheduling to promote self-directed leisure activity in home and community settings. *Journal of the Association for Persons with Severe Handicaps, 17,* 67–76.

Bambara, L. M., Cole, C., & Koger, F. (1998). Translating self-determination concepts into support for adults with severe disabilities. *Journal of the Association for Persons with Severe Handicaps, 23,* 27–37.

Bambara, L. M., & Gomez, O. N. (2001). Using a self-instruction package to teach complex problem-solving skills to adults with moderate and severe disabilities. *Education and Training in Mental Retardation, 36,* 386–400.

Bambara, L. M., & Koger, F. (1996). *Innovations: AAMR Research to Practice Series—Opportunities for daily choice making.* Washington, DC: American Association on Mental Retardation.

Bambara, L. M., Koger, F., Katzer, T., & Davenport, T. (1995). Embedding choice in daily routines: An experimental case study. *Journal of the Association for Persons with Severe Handicaps, 20,* 185–195.

Bambara, L. M., Koger, F., & Nonnemacher, S. (2002, December). *Using a person-centered approach to support sexuality.* Paper presented at the 27th annual meeting of TASH [formerly known as the Association for Persons with Severe Handicaps], Boston.

Basset, D. S., & Kochhar-Bryant, C. A. (2006). Strategies for aligning standards-based education and transition. *Focus on Exceptional Children, 39* (2), 1–19.

Batu, S. (2008). Caregiver-delivered home-based instruction using simultaneous prompting for teaching home skills to individuals with developmental disabilities. *Education and Training in Developmental Disabilities, 43*(4), 541–555.

Batu, S., Ergenekon, Y., Erbas, D., & Akmanoglu, N. (2004). Teaching pedestrian skills to individuals with developmental disabilities. *Journal of Behavioral Education, 13*(3), 147–164.

Blanchett, W. J., & Wolfe, P. S. (2002). A review of sexuality education curricula: Meeting the sexuality education needs of individuals with moderate and severe intellectual disabilities. *Research and Practice for Persons with Severe Disabilities, 27,* 43–57.

Bolton, J. L., Belfiore, P. J., Lalli, J. S., & Skinner, C. H. (1994). The effects of stimulus modification on putting accuracy for adults with severe or profound mental retardation. *Education and Training in Mental Retardation and Developmental Disabilities, 29,* 236–242.

Bouck, E. C. (2009). No Child Left Behind, the Individuals with Disabilities Education Act and functional curricula: A conflict of interest? *Education and Training in Developmental Disabilities, 44*(1), 3–13.

Bourbeau, P. E., Sowers, J., & Close, D. W. (1986). An experimental analysis of generalization of banking skills from classroom to bank settings in the community. *Education and Training of the Mentally Retarded, 21,* 98–106.

Breen, C. G., & Haring, T. G. (1991). Effects of contextual competence on social initiations. *Journal of Applied Behavior Analysis, 24,* 337–348.

Briggs, A., Alberto, P., Sharpton, W., Berlin, K., McKinley, C., & Ritts, C. (1990). Generalized use of a self-operated audio prompt system. *Education and Training in Mental Retardation, 25,* 381–389.

Browder, D. M., Cooper, K. J., & Lim, L. (1998). Teaching adults with severe disabilities to express their choice of settings for leisure activities. *Education and Training in Mental Retardation and Developmental Disabilities, 33,* 228-238.

Browder, D. M., Hines, C., McCarthy, L. J., & Fees, J. (1984). A treatment package for increasing sight word recognition for use in daily living skills. *Education and Training of the Mentally Retarded, 19,* 191-200.

Browder, D. M., Snell, M. E., & Wildonger, B. A. (1988). Simulation and community-based instruction of vending machines with time delay. *Education and Training in Mental Retardation, 23,* 175-185.

Brown, F., Belz, P., Corsi, L., & Wenig, B. (1993). Choice diversity for people with severe disabilities. *Education and Training in Mental Retardation, 28,* 318-326.

Brown, L., Branston, M. B., Hamre-Nietupski, A., Pumpian, I., Certo, N, & Gruenewald, L. A. (1979). A strategy for developing chronological age-appropriate and functional curricular content for severely handicapped adolescents and young adults. *Journal of Special Education, 13,* 81-90.

Bryan, L. C., & Gast, D. L. (2000). Teaching on-task and on-schedule behaviors to high functioning children with autism via picture activity schedules. *Journal of Autism and Developmental Disorders, 30,* 553-567.

Burcroff, T. L., Radogna, D. M., & Wright, E. H. (2003). Community forays addressing students' functional skills in inclusive settings, *Teaching Exceptional Children, 35*(5), 52-57.

Carlson, J. I., Luiselli, J. K., Slyman, A., & Markowski, A. (2008). Choice-making as intervention for public disrobing in children with developmental disabilities. *Journal of Positive Behavior Interventions, 10*(2), 86-90.

Carothers, D. E., & Taylor, R. L. (2004). How teachers and parents can work together to teach daily living skills to children with autism. *Focus on Autism and Other Developmental Disabilities, 19*(2), 102-104.

Chadsey-Rusch, J., Drasgow, E., Reinoehl, B., Hallet, J., & Collet-Klingenberg, L. (1993). Using general-case instruction to teach spontaneous and generalized requests for assistance to learners with severe disabilities. *Journal of the Association for Persons with Severe Handicaps, 18,* 177-187.

Cihak, D. F., Alberto, P. A., Kessler, K. B., & Taber, T. A. (2004). An investigation of instructional scheduling arrangements for community-based instruction. *Research in Developmental Disabilities: A Multidisciplinary Journal, 25*(1), 67-88.

Cihak, D. F., & Grim, J. (2008). Teaching students with autism spectrum disorder and moderate intellectual disabilities to use counting-on strategies to enhance independent purchasing skills. Research in Autism Spectrum Disorders, *2,* 716-727.

Cihak, D. F., Kessler, K. B., & Alberto, P. A. (2007). Generalized use of a handheld prompting system. *Research in Developmental Disabilities: A Multidisciplinary Journal, 28*(4), 397-408.

Cihak, D. F., Kessler, K., & Alberto, P. A. (2008). Use of a handheld prompting system to transition independently through vocational tasks for students with moderate and severe intellectual disabilities. *Education and Training in Developmental Disabilities, 43*(1), 102-110.

Cole, C. M., & Levinson, T. R. (2002). Effects of within-activity choices on the challenging behavior of children with severe disabilities. *Journal of Positive Behavior Interventions, 4,* 29-37.

Collins, B. C., Branson, T. A., & Hall, M. (1995). Teaching generalized reading of cooking product labels to adolescents with mental disabilities through the use of key words taught by peer tutors. *Education and Training in Mental Retardation and Developmental Disabilities, 30,* 65-75.

Coon, M. E., Vogelsberg, R. T., & Williams, W. (1981). Effects of classroom public transportation instruction on generalization to the natural environment. *Journal of the Association for the Severely Handicapped, 6,* 46-53.

Cooper, K. J., & Browder, D. M. (1998). Enhancing choice and participation for adults with severe disabilities in community-based instruction. *Journal of the Association for Persons with Severe Handicaps, 23,* 252-260.

Cuvo, A. J., Jacobi, E., & Sipko, R. (1981). Teaching laundry skills to mentally retarded students. *Education and Training of the Mentally Retarded, 16,* 54-64.

Davies, D. K., Stock, S. E., & Wehmeyer, M. L. (2003). Utilization of computer technology to facilitate money management by individuals with mental retardation. *Education and Training in Developmental Disabilities, 38*(1), 106-112.

Devine, M. A., Malley, S., Sheldon, K., Datillo, J., & Gast, D. L. (1997). Promoting initiation of community leisure participation for adults with mental retardation. *Education and Training in Mental Retardation and Developmental Disabilities, 32,* 241-254.

Dunlap, G., DePerczel, C. S., Clarke, S., Wilson, D., Wright, S., White, R., et al. (1994). Choice making to promote adaptive behavior for students with emotional and behavioral challenges. *Journal of Applied Behavior Analysis, 27,* 505-518.

Epps, S., Stern, R. J., & Horner, R. H. (1990). Comparison of simulation training on self and using a doll for teaching generalized menstrual care to woman with severe mental retardation. *Research in Developmental Disabilities, 11,* 37-66.

Ersoy, G., Tekin-Iftar, E., & Kircaali-Iftar, G. (2009). Effects of antecedent prompt and test procedure on teaching simulated menstrual care skills to females with developmental disabilities. *Education and Training in Developmental Disabilities, 44*(1), 54-66.

Ferguson, H., Myles, B. S., & Hagiwara, T. (2005). Using a personal digital assistant to enhance the independence of an adolescent with Asperger syndrome. *Education and Training in Developmental Disabilities, 40*(1), 60-67.

Ford, A., & Mirenda, P. (1984). Community instruction: A natural cues and correction model. *Journal of the Association for Persons with Severe Handicaps, 9,* 79-88.

Forest, M., & Pearpoint, J. C. (1992). Putting all kids on the MAP. *Educational Leadership, 50,* 26-31.

Frederick-Dugan, A., Test, D. W., & Varn, L. (1991). Acquisition and generalization of purchasing skills using a calculator by students who are mentally retarded. *Education and Training in Mental Retardation, 26,* 381-387.

Gardill, M. C., & Browder, D. M. (1995). Teaching stimulus classes to encourage independent purchasing by students with severe behavior disorders. *Education and Training in Mental Retardation and Developmental Disabilities, 30,* 254-264.

Garwood, M., & McCabe, M. P. (2000). Impact of sex education programs on sexual knowledge and feelings of men with mild intellectual disability. *Education and Training in Mental Retardation and Developmental Disabilities, 35,* 269-283.

Gast, D. L., Doyle, P. M., Wolery, M., Ault, M. J., & Farmer, J. A. (1991). Assessing the acquisition of incidental information by secondary-age students with mental retardation: Comparison of response prompting strategies. *American Journal on Mental Retardation, 96,* 63–80.

Gast, D. L., Winterling, V., Wolery, M., & Farmer, J. A. (1992). Teaching first-aid skills to students with moderate handicaps in small group instruction. *Education and Treatment of Children, 15,* 101–124.

Griffen, A. K., Wolery, M., & Schuster, J. W. (1992). Triadic instruction of chained food preparation responses: Acquisition and observational learning. *Journal of Applied Behavior Analysis, 25,* 257–279.

Grigal, M., Neubert, D. A., & Moon, M. S. (2002a). Post-secondary education and transition services for students ages 18–21 with significant disabilities. *Focus on Exceptional Children, 34,* 1–11.

Grigal, M., Neubert, D. A., & Moon, M. S. (2002b). Postsecondary options for students with significant disabilities. *Teaching Exceptional Children, 35,* 68–73.

Haney, J. L., & Jones, R. T. (1982). Programming maintenance as a major component of a community-centered preventive effort: Escape from fire. *Behavior Therapy, 13,* 47–62.

Hansen, D. L., & Morgan, R. L. (2008). Teaching grocery store purchasing skills to students with intellectual disabilities using a computer-based instruction program. *Education and Training in Developmental Disabilities, 43*(4), 431–442.

Hingsburger, D., & Tough, S. (2002). Healthy sexuality: Attitudes, systems, and policies. *Research and Practice for Persons with Severe Disabilities, 27,* 8–17.

Horner, R. H., Jones, D. N., & Williams, J. A. (1985). A functional approach to teaching generalized street crossing. *Journal of the Association for Persons with Severe Handicaps, 10,* 71–78.

Horner, R. H., Williams, J. A., & Steveley, J. D. (1987). Acquisition of generalized telephone use by students with moderate and severe mental retardation. *Research in Developmental Disabilities, 8,* 229–248.

Hughes, C. (1992). Teaching self-instruction utilizing multiple exemplars to produce generalized problem-solving by individuals with severe mental retardation. *American Journal on Mental Retardation, 97,* 302–314.

Hughes, C., Hugo, K., & Blatt, J. (1996). Self-instructional intervention for teaching generalized problem-solving within a functional task sequence. *American Journal on Mental Retardation, 100,* 565–579.

Irvine, B. A., Erickson, A. M., Singer, G., & Stahlberg, D. (1992). A coordinated program to transfer self-management skills from school to home. *Education and Training in Mental Retardation, 27,* 241–254.

Jones, G. Y., & Collins, B. C. (1997). Teaching microwave skills to adults with disabilities: Acquisition of nutrition and safety facts presented as non-targeted information. *Journal of Developmental and Physical Disabilities, 9,* 59–78.

LaCampagne, J., & Cipani, E. (1987). Training adults with mental retardation to pay bills. *Mental Retardation, 25,* 293–303.

Lohrmann-O'Rourke, S., Browder, D. M., & Brown, F. (2000). Guidelines for conducting socially valid systematic preference assessments. *Journal of the Association for Persons with Severe Handicaps, 25*(1), 42–53.

Lovett, D. L., & Haring, K. A. (1989). The effects of self-management training on the daily living of adults with mental retardation. *Education and Training in Mental Retardation, 24,* 306–323.

Lumley, V. A., Miltenberger, R. G., Long, E. S., Rapp, J. T., & Roberts, J. A. (1998). Evaluation of a sexual abuse prevention program for adults with mental retardation. *Journal of Applied Behavior Analysis, 31,* 91–101.

Lumley, V. A., & Scotti, J. R. (2001). Supporting the sexuality of adults with mental retardation: Current status and future directions. *Journal of Positive Behavior Interventions, 3,* 91–101.

MacDuff, G. S., Kranz, R. J., & McClannahan, L. E. (1993). Teaching children with autism to use photographic activity schedules: Maintenance and generalization of complex response chains. *Journal of Applied Behavior Analysis, 26*(1), 89–97.

Manley, K., Collins, B. C., Stenhoff, D. M., & Kleinert, H. (2008). Using a system of least prompts procedure to teach telephone skills to elementary students with cognitive disabilities. *Journal of Behavioral Education, 17*(3), 221–236.

Marchand-Martella, N. E., Martella, R. C., Agran, M., Salzberg, C. L., Young, K. R., & Morgan, D. (1992a). Generalized effects of a peer-delivered first aid program for students with moderate intellectual disabilities. *Journal of Applied Behavior Analysis, 25,* 841–851.

Marchand-Martella, N. E., Martella, R. C., Christensen, A. M., Agran, M., & Young, K. R. (1992b). Teaching a first aid skill to students with disabilities using two training programs. *Education and Treatment of Children, 15,* 15–31.

Marchetti, A. G., McCartney, J. R., Drain, S., Hooper, M., & Dix, J. (1983). Pedestrian skills training for mentally retarded adults: Comparison of training in two settings. *Mental Retardation, 21,* 107–110.

Martin, J. E., & Marshall, L. H. (1995). ChoiceMaker: A comprehensive self-determination transition program. *Intervention in School and Clinic, 30,* 147–156.

Matson, J. L. (1980). A controlled group study of pedestrian-skill training for the mentally retarded. *Behavior Research and Therapy, 18,* 99–106.

McCabe, M. P., & Cummins, R. A. (1996). The sexual knowledge, experience, feelings, and needs of people with mild intellectual disability. *Education and Training in Mental Retardation and Developmental Disabilities, 31,* 13–21.

McDonnell, J. J., & Ferguson, B. (1989). A comparison of general case in vivo and general case simulation plus in vivo training. *Journal of the Association for Persons with Severe Handicaps, 13,* 116–124.

McDonnell, J. J., & McFarland, S. (1988). A comparison of forward and concurrent chaining strategies in teaching laundromat skills to students with severe handicaps. *Research and Intervention in Developmental Disabilities, 9,* 177–194.

McWilliams, R., Nietupski, J., & Hamre-Nietupski, S. (1990). Teaching complex activities to students with moderate handicaps through the forward chaining of shorter total cycle response sequences. *Education and Training in Mental Retardation, 25,* 292–298.

Mechling, L. (2007). Assistive technology as a self-management tool for prompting students with intellectual disabilities to initiate and complete daily tasks: A literature review. *Education and Training in Developmental Disabilities, 42*(3), 252–269.

Mechling, L. C. (2008). High tech cooking: A literature review of evolving technologies for teaching a functional skill. *Education and Training in Developmental Disabilities, 43*(4), 474–485.

Mechling, L. C., & Gast, D. L. (2003). Multi-media instruction to teach grocery word associations and store locations: A study of generalization. *Education and Training in Developmental Disabilities, 38,* 62–76.

Mechling, L. C., Gast, D. L., & Barthold, S. (2003). Multimedia computer-based instruction to teach students with moderate intellectual disabilities to use a debit card to make purchases. *Exceptionality, 11,* 239–254.

Mechling, L. C., Gast, D. L., & Cronin, B. A. (2006). The effects of presenting high-preference items, paired with choice, via computer-based video programming on task completion of students with autism. *Focus on Autism and Other Developmental Disabilities, 21*(1), 7–13.

Mechling, L. C., Gast, D. L., & Gustafson, M. R. (2009). Use of video modeling to teach extinguishing of cooking related fires to individuals with moderate intellectual disabilities. *Education and Training in Developmental Disabilities, 44*(1), 67–79.

Mechling, L. C., Gast, D. L., & Langone, J. (2002). Computer-based video instruction to teach persons with moderate intellectual disabilities to read grocery aisle signs and locate items. *Journal of Special Education, 35,* 224–240.

Mechling, L. C., Pridgen, L. S., & Cronin, B. A. (2005). Computer-based video instruction to teach students with intellectual disabilities to verbally respond to questions and make purchases in fast food restaurants. *Education and Training in Developmental Disabilities, 40*(1), 47–59.

Mechling, L. C., & Stephens, E. (2009). Comparison of self-prompting of cooking skills via picture-based cookbooks and video recipes. *Education and Training in Developmental Disabilities, 44*(2), 218–236.

Michaels, C. A., & Ferrara, D. L. (2006). Promoting post-school success for all: The role of collaboration in person-centered transition planning. *Journal of Educational and Psychological Consultation, 16*(4), 287–313.

Miller, U. C., & Test, D. W. (1989). A comparison of constant time delay and most-to-least prompts in teaching laundry skills to students with moderate retardation. *Education and Training of the Mentally Retarded, 24,* 363–370.

Minarovic, T. J., & Bambara, L. M. (2007). Teaching employees with intellectual disabilities to manage changing work routines using varied sight-word checklist. *Research and Practice for Persons with Severe Disabilities, 32,* 31–42.

Morningstar, M. E., & Lattin, D. L. (2004). Transition to adulthood. In C. H. Kennedy & E. M. Horn (Eds.), *Including students with severe disabilities* (pp. 282–309). Boston: Allyn & Bacon.

Mount, B. (2000). *Person-centered planning.* New York: Graphic Futures.

Neef, N. A., Iwata, B. A., & Page, T. A. (1978). Public transportation training: In vivo versus classroom instruction. *Journal of Applied Behavior Analysis, 11,* 331–344.

Neef, N. A., Lensbower, S., Hockersmith, I., DePalma, V., & Gray, K. (1990). In vivo versus simulation training: An interactional analysis of range and type of training exemplars. *Journal of Applied Behavior Analysis, 23,* 447–458.

Neubert, D. A., & Moon, M. S. (2006). Postsecondary settings and transition services for students with intellectual disabilities: Models and research. *Focus on Exceptional Children, 39*(4), 1.

Nietupski, J., Hamre-Nietupski, S., Clancy, P. L., & Veerhusen, K. (1986). Guidelines for making simulation an effective adjunct to in-vivo community instruction. *Journal of the Association for Persons with Severe Handicaps, 11,* 12–18.

O'Brien, J. (1987). A guide to lifestyle planning: Using the Activities Catalog to integrate services and natural support systems. In B. Wilcox & G. T. Bellamy (Eds.), *A comprehensive guide to the Activities Catalog: An alternative curriculum for youth and adults with severe disabilities* (pp. 175–189). Baltimore: Paul H. Brookes.

O'Brien, J., & Pearpoint, J. (2003). *Person-centered planning with MAPS and PATH: A workbook for facilitators.* Toronto, Ontario, Canada: Inclusion Press.

Orth, T. (2000). *Visual recipes: A cookbook for non-readers.* New York: DRL Books.

Pearpoint, J., O'Brien, J., & Forest, M. (1992). *PATH: Planning alternative tomorrows with hope.* Toronto, Ontario, Canada: Inclusion Press.

Page, T. H., Iwata, B. A., & Neef, N. A. (1976). Teaching pedestrian skills to retarded persons: Generalization from the classroom to the natural environment. *Journal of Applied Behavior Analysis, 9,* 433–444.

Pierce, K. L., & Schriebman, L. (1994). Teaching daily living skills to children with autism in unsupervised settings through pictorial self-management. *Journal of Applied Behavior Analysis, 27,* 471–481.

Post, M., & Storey, K. (2002). Review of using auditory prompting systems with persons who have moderate to severe disabilities. *Education and Training in Mental Retardation, 37,* 317–320.

Rae, R., & Roll, D. (1985). Fire safety training with adults who are profoundly mentally retarded. *Mental Retardation, 23,* 26–30.

Robinson, D., Griffith, J., McComish, L., & Swasbrook, K. (1984). Bus training for developmentally disabled adults. *American Journal of Mental Deficiency, 89,* 37–43.

Rueda, R., Monzó, L., Shapiro, J., Gomez, J., & Blacher, J. (2005). Cultural models of transition: Latina mothers of young adults with developmental disabilities. *Exceptional Children, 71,* 401–414.

Ryndak, D. L., & Billingsley, F. (2004). Access to the general education curriculum. In C. H. Kennedy & E. M. Horn (Eds.), *Including students with severe disabilities* (pp. 33–53). Boston: Allyn & Bacon.

Sandknop, P. A., Schuster, J. W., Wolery, M., & Cross, D. P. (1992). The use of an adaptive device to teach students with moderate mental retardation to select lower priced grocery items. *Education and Training in Mental Retardation, 27,* 219–229.

Sarber, R. R., & Cuvo, A. J. (1983). Teaching nutritional meal planning to developmentally disabled clients. *Behavior Modification, 7,* 503–530.

Schleien, S. J., Certo, N. J., & Muccino, A. (1984). Acquisition of leisure skills by a severely handicapped adolescent: A data-based instructional program. *Education and Training of the Mentally Retarded, 19,* 297–305.

Schwier, K. A., & Hingsburger, D. (2000). *Sexuality: Your sons and daughters with intellectual disabilities.* Boston: Paul H. Brookes.

Singleton, K. C., Schuster, J., & Ault, M. J. (1995). Simultaneous prompting in a small group instructional arrangement. *Education and Training in Mental Retardation and Developmental Disabilities, 30,* 218–230.

Smith, R. L., Collins, B. C., Schuster, J. W., & Kleinert, H. (1999). Teaching table cleaning skills to secondary students with moderate/severe disabilities: Facilitating observational learning during instructional downtime. *Education and Training in Mental Retardation and Developmental Disabilities, 34,* 342–353.

Snell, M. E. (1982). Teaching bed making skills to retarded adults through time delay. *Analysis and Intervention in Developmental Disabilities, 2,* 139–155.

Sobsey, D., & Doe, T. (1991). Patterns of sexual abuse and assault. *Sexuality and Disability, 9,* 69–81.

Sowers, J., & Powers, L. (1995). Enhancing the participation and independence of students with severe physical and multiple disabilities in performing community activities. *Mental Retardation, 33,* 209–220.

Sowers, J., Rusch, F. R., & Hudson, C. (1979). Training a severely retarded young adult to ride the city bus to and from work. *AAESPH [American Association for the Education of the Severely/Profoundly Handicapped] Review, 4,* 15–23.

Spears, D. L., Rusch, F. R., York, R., & Lilly, M. S. (1981). Training independent arrival behaviors to a severely mentally retarded child. *Journal of the Association for the Severely Handicapped, 6,* 40–45.

Spooner, F., Stem, B., & Test, D. W. (1989). Teaching first aid skills to adolescents who are moderately mentally handicapped. *Education and Training in Mental Retardation, 24,* 341–351.

Sprague, J. R., & Horner, R. H. (1984). The effects of single instance, multiple instance, and general case training on generalized vending machine use by moderately and severely handicapped students. *Journal of Applied Behavior Analysis, 17,* 273–278.

Spriggs, A. D., Gast, D. L., & Ayres, K. M. (2007). Using picture activity schedule books to increase on-schedule and on-task behaviors. *Education and Training in Developmental Disabilities, 42*(2), 209–223.

Storey, K. (2007). Review of research on self-management interventions in supported employment settings for employees with disabilities. *Career Development for Exceptional Individuals, 30*(1), 27–34.

Taber, T. A., Alberto, P. A., Hughes, M., & Seltzer, A. (2002). A strategy for students with moderate disabilities when lost in the community. *Research and Practice for Persons with Severe Disabilities, 27,* 141–152.

Taber, T. A., Alberto, P. A., Seltzer, A., & Hughes, M. (2003). Obtaining assistance when lost in the community using cell phones. *Research and Practice for Persons with Severe Disabilities, 28,* 105–116.

Taber-Doughty, T. (2005). Considering student choice when selecting instructional strategies: A comparison of three prompting systems. *Research in Developmental Disabilities: A Multidisciplinary Journal, 26*(5), 411–432.

Tarnai, B. (2006). Review of effective interventions for socially inappropriate masturbation in persons with cognitive disabilities. *Sexuality and Disability, 24*(3), 154–168.

Tarnai, B., & Wolfe, P. (2008). Social Stories for sexuality education for persons with autism/pervasive developmental disorder. *Sexuality and Disability, 26*(1), 29–36.

Taylor, J. C., McKelvey, J. L., & Sisson, L. A. (1993). Community-referenced leisure skill clusters for adolescents with multiple disabilities. *Journal of Behavioral Education, 3,* 363–386.

Taylor, P., Collins, B. C., Schuster, J. W., & Kleinert, H. (2002). Teaching laundry skills to high school students with disabilities: Generalization of targeted skills and nontargeted information. *Education and Training in Mental Retardation and Developmental Disabilities, 37,* 172–183.

Tekin-Iftar, E. (2003). Effectiveness of peer delivered simultaneous prompting on teaching community signs to students with developmental disabilities. *Education and Training in Developmental Disabilities, 38,* 77–94.

Vandercook, T. (1991). Leisure instruction outcomes: Criterion performance, positive interactions, and acceptance by typical high school peers. *Journal of Special Education, 25,* 320–339.

Wall, M. E., & Gast, D. L. (1997). Caregivers' use of constant time delay to teach leisure skills to adolescents or young adults with moderate or severe intellectual disabilities. *Education and Training in Mental Retardation and Developmental Disabilities, 32,* 340–356.

Watson, M., Bain, A., & Houghton, S. (1992). A preliminary study in teaching self-protective skills to children with moderate and severe mental retardation. *Journal of Special Education, 26,* 181–194.

Wehmeyer, M. L. (2005). Self-determination and individuals with severe disabilities: Re-examining meanings and misinterpretations. *Research and Practice for Persons with Severe Disabilities, 30,* 113–120.

Wehmeyer, M. L., Field, S., Doren, B., Jones, B., & Mason, C. (2004). Self-determination and student involvement in standards-based reform. *Exceptional Children, 70,* 413–425.

Westling, D. L., Floyd, J., & Carr, D. (1990). Effects of single setting versus multiple setting training on learning to shop in a department store. *American Journal on Mental Retardation, 94,* 616–624.

Xin, Y. P., Grasso, E., Dipipi-Hoy, C. M., & Jitendra, A. (2005). The effects of purchasing skill instruction for individuals with developmental disabilities: A meta-analysis. *Exceptional Children, 71*(4), 379.

Zhang, J., Gast, D., Horvat, M., & Datillo, J. (1995). The effectiveness of constant time delay procedure on teaching lifetime sport skills to adolescents with severe to profound intellectual disabilities. *Education and Training in Mental Retardation and Developmental Disabilities, 30,* 51–64.

15

Transitioning from School to Employment

David W. Test
Valerie L. Mazzotti

Case Studies

Serena is a 14-year-old female with autism spectrum disorder (ASD) who is enrolled in the eighth grade at an urban middle school. She was diagnosed with ASD at the age of four and has been served under the Individuals with Disabilities Education Act (IDEA) since preschool. She is verbal and has no major physical limitations. She lives with her parents and a younger sister in an urban community. Her parents are actively involved in her education and have a good relationship with Serena's special education teacher. The family participates in services and social events at their church, where the community welcomes Serena openly. Serena's mother states that Serena often helps out with chores at home and especially enjoys helping prepare dinner for the family.

Serena receives academic instruction in a self-contained setting with six other students with severe disabilities. Four of the students in the class have physical disabilities and two are nonverbal. The students participate in community-based instruction once a week. Serena participates in a school club called *Circle of Friends,* which is a school fundraising club that involves being paired with a peer without disabilities in order to raise money for the school through events like bake sales and car washes. Serena

indicates that she loves cooking and participates in an integrated home and consumer science class twice each week. She also participates in music and art classes with her peers without disabilities. Serena has a number of strengths, including using the "one more than" strategy to purchase items and reading more than 150 sight words. She also has a relatively good memory. If asked to run an errand composed of four different tasks, she usually remembers all of the tasks associated with the errand. Serena excels in her special education classroom when she works with an adult or a peer tutor from a general education classroom.

Serena struggles in social situations and tends to use a loud voice when speaking. She often discloses information that is socially inappropriate to the context in which she is involved. She also loves the color purple and insists on wearing purple clothing daily and coloring only with a purple crayon, pencil, or marker. She has been paired with a peer buddy without disabilities because she has difficulty transitioning from class to class in unstructured situations. Loud group settings, such as physical education in the gym and assemblies, are highly aversive for Serena. These environments often cause Serena to become anxious and agitated, resulting in her curling up on the floor and covering her ears in order to escape.

Serena's special education teacher has started working with her on becoming more aware of her strengths, needs, and disability as they relate to her in-school and postschool success. It is anticipated that in the area of future employment, Serena will need ongoing supported employment to work in a competitive employment environment. Recently, her teacher has started discussing

the idea of supported employment with Serena and her family. Upon graduation, Serena would like to be placed within her community in a job that best suits her abilities and preferences. Because of Serena's love of food and food preparation, she believes that she would like to work in the food service industry. In order to be trained on the work-related and social skills necessary to be successful with this job, a job coach would be beneficial for Serena.

✠ ✠ ✠ ✠ ✠   Rusty   ✠ ✠ ✠ ✠ ✠

Rusty is a 17-year-old student with severe disabilities. Rusty has a severe cognitive disability, is in a wheelchair, and has a speech impairment. He is a friendly, verbal, and attentive student who loves music. He has a functional vocabulary and can read a number of community sight words. Rusty likes to listen to music, watch movies, and enjoys going on family outings in the community. Rusty loves to watch *Dancing with the Stars* on television.

Rusty is an only child and lives at home with his mother and father who plan for Rusty to live at home until he is 20 years old. At that point, they will seek supported housing in a group home, or he will move in with a relative who is willing to care for him. Additionally, his parents feel that it is important for Rusty to spend his days working to the best of his ability so that he can gain skills and experience a sense of accomplishment in his life. It is important to his parents that Rusty receives instruction on life skills (e.g., cooking, money, personal hygiene, transferring from wheelchair to furniture) and self-determination skills (e.g., self-advocacy, choice making, goal setting) so that he can perform daily living and work tasks independently. Rusty's parents would also like additional information about finan-

cial planning and social security income to help them make informed decisions about Rusty's financial security in the future.

Rusty has participated in vocational training activities at school. Specifically, Rusty worked in a school-based enterprise where his duties included collecting inventory and assisting in ordering new supplies using the computer. Rusty's parents would like to see him pursue his computer interests after high school through customized employment. Rusty has indicated that he would like to start his own business in his community. Based on interviews with community business owners, there is a need for DVD and video production, Web site development, and Web sites that allow shopping online for groceries. Rusty's special education teacher has provided Rusty with information about these three jobs and intends to focus Rusty's community-based experiences in these three areas. Currently, Rusty has indicated that he would like to have his own business copying DVDs for local businesses. Rusty's teacher is working with a local record store and computer programmer to develop a paid internship position so that Rusty can receive job training in this area.

✠ ✠ ✠ ✠ ✠   Cassandra   ✠ ✠ ✠ ✠ ✠

Cassandra is a 19-year-old female with severe disabilities. She is attending her neighborhood community college where she participates in a public post–high school program for 18- to 21-year-olds that is preparing her for transitioning to adult life. The program includes instruction in "real life" and community settings. The focus of the program is to promote inclusion in the community and interaction with peers without disabilities. Additionally, she receives daily content instruction in functional reading and math. Cassandra also participates in vocational and daily living skills training, which is primarily community based. All of her coursework is delivered in individual and small-group

settings in the classroom and in the community, except for Digital Communications (a career technical course), which she has taken (using a modified curriculum) with the support of a one-to-one instructional assistant. Cassandra also participates in an on-campus work placement program by working in the school library.

Along with her family, Cassandra plans to stay in the program for 18- to 21-year-olds until she ages out at 21, which will provide her with 2 more years of services and additional instruction to prepare her for living and working as an adult. She lives at home with her mother, an 11-year-old sister, a 16-year-old brother, and her grandmother, who helps with her care. After receiving state-level mental health funding for personal care and 10 hours of one-to-one community-based services for the last 4 years, Cassandra was recently approved for Medicaid waiver-funded services. This funding source will provide Cassandra with an array of services to meet her needs, including (a) augmentative and alternative communication devices, (b) case management, (c) one-to-one community and home support, (d) personal care services, (e) respite, (f) specialized equipment and services, and (g) medical transportation. Funds will also be available for supported employment after high school graduation.

Cassandra has had a comprehensive transition component in place since she was 14. The development of a complete transition component was determined to be appropriate for Cassandra at an earlier age because of her complex needs and the length of time needed to obtain appropriate adult services. In preparation for transition planning, Cassandra has been administered speech, physical therapy, and occupational therapy assessments that focus on the skills and equipment needed for functioning in the home and the community. Cassandra's parents have completed Parent Transition Surveys and Cassandra has provided input by responding to picture choices in postschool domains.

Transition assessments indicated that Cassandra will need regular and extensive support in all areas of adult life in order to achieve her postschool goals. Additionally, she will need protection and advocacy services for managing money, legal issues, and self-advocacy.

It is anticipated that in the area of future employment, Cassandra will need ongoing supported employ-ment to work in a competitive employment placement. Cassandra enjoys interacting with other people, music, horticulture, computers, and clerical activities. She responds well to verbal praise and is able to stay focused on her tasks and activities for 20+ minutes with occasional verbal redirection. Cassandra has developed the skills needed to operate a variety of switch-activated devices (e.g., button maker, blender, etc.), use a paper shredder, and collate papers with a jig. Cassandra has worked successfully on an assembly line in the school-based enterprise and has held an on-campus job in the school library checking books in and out using a scanning system and shelving books with the help of a peer buddy.

Cassandra's residential plans for after graduation are uncertain. Cassandra is very happy at home and she indicated that she loves her family. Two of her classmates have moved into group homes and through classroom discussion and lessons on postgraduate residential options, Cassandra appears to have some understanding of becoming an adult and living more independently. Cassandra's mother would like to see her move into a group home or other supervised postschool living arrangement after high school. Cassandra has no understanding of money and does not provide input with regard to her health/medical care. She has been covered under her mother's work insurance policy, but she recently was approved for a Medicaid waiver program that will assist with medical care, equipment, and supplies. Cassandra's mother has guardianship of Cassandra and she has never received Supplemental Security Income benefits.

Although school is full of transitions—from preschool to elementary school, elementary to middle, and middle to high school—it is the transition from high school to adult life that is often the one that is most anticipated and anxiety provoking. It is at this point where students' and families' dreams for the future come face-to-face with the reality of being employed or getting a postsecondary education, or both. For students with severe disabilities, this reality is often harsh. In terms of employment, data from Wave 3 of the National Longitudinal Transition Study–2 (NLTS2) indicated while that 55.1% of all students with disabilities had a paid job outside the house a year or more out of high school, the percentages were lower for groups of students who might be considered to have severe disabilities. For example, only 33.3% of students with mental retardation, 37.2% of students with autism, and 39.4% of students with multiple disabilities were employed outside the home a year or more after leaving high school (NLTS2, 2009).

Clearly more must be done while students are still in school to improve these outcomes. Halpern (1992) defined a *transition* as "a period of floundering that occurs for at least the first several years after leaving school as adolescents attempt to assume a variety of adult roles in their communities" (p. 203). The purpose of this chapter is to provide readers with information so that their students with severe disabilities will avoid the floundering period and receive the transition services and supports needed for making a transition to employment and adulthood.

A History of Transitions

Given the low employment rates for students with severe disabilities once they leave high school, one might assume that transition services are a relatively new idea. Unfortunately, this is not the case. In fact, Halpern (1992) described three transition movements that occurred from the 1960s to the 1990s.

1960s: Cooperative Work/Study Programs

Work/study programs started in the early 1960s as a partnership between public schools and local vocational rehabilitation agencies. Work/study programs were designed to include academic, vocational, and social curriculums and were primarily designed to teach students with mild disabilities the skills that they needed to live in their community. Work/study programs typically involved having a classroom teacher also become a work coordinator who placed students in jobs as part of their high school course of study. Unfortunately, due to lack of funding and supervisory issues, work/study programs were ended in the mid-1970s. But as you can imagine, students' needs continued.

1970s: Career Education

Career education started in 1970 when Sidney Marland, then Commissioner of Education, declared career education as a top priority of the U.S. Office of Education (Halpern, 1992). While this vision of career education was originally considered to be a general education initiative, in 1977, the Career Education Implementation Incentive Act (P.L. 95-207) stated that students with disabilities were among those who were able to receive career education services. Although Congress repealed funding for Public Law 95-207 in 1982, by then, the Council for Exceptional Children had formed the Division of Career Development (today called the Division for Career Development and Transition), and with this new division, career education was expanded from a high school only movement to one dedicated to preparing students with disabilities for careers from elementary to high school.

1980–1990s: The Emergence of "Transition"

The 1980s and 1990s saw a rapid expansion of transition services brought on by four factors. First, from the mid-1980s to the mid-1990s, a series of studies were published that provided initial evidence that despite the free appropriate public education promised by Public Law 94-142, poor postsecondary outcomes

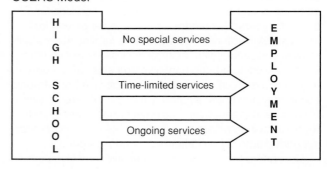

FIGURE 15–1
OSERS Model

for students with disabilities were the norm (Affleck, Edgar, Levine, & Kortering, 1990; Blackorby & Wagner, 1996; Hasazi, Gordon, & Roe, 1985). Second, in 1984, Madeline Will, the Assistant Secretary of the Office of Special Education and Rehabilitative Services (OSERS), U.S. Department of Education, published a paper that became known as the "transition bridges model" (see Figure 15–1. This model, which is still relevant, will be described in detail in the next section). The OSERS model described three "bridges" that students would take from high school to employment.

Third, with the knowledge that there is more to life than just work, Halpern (1985) expanded on the OSERS model by suggesting that a successful transition includes community adjustment. Community adjustment then included three pillars: residential, employment, and social and interpersonal networks (see Figure 15–2).

Finally, the transition movement was formally recognized on October 30, 1990, when Public Law 101-476, the Individuals with Disabilities Education Act (IDEA), was signed. By defining transition services and requiring that a transition component be added to a student's individualized education plan (IEP), transition planning was now a required part of the educational program of every student with disabilities. More information on the legal definition of transition will be provided later in this chapter.

History of Employment for Persons with Severe Disabilities

While the field of transition planning was evolving, so, too, were the employment options for adults with severe disabilities (see Figure 15–3). In the 1980s and 1990s, the mission of most community agencies serving individuals with severe disabilities was to provide

FIGURE 15–2
Revised Transition Model

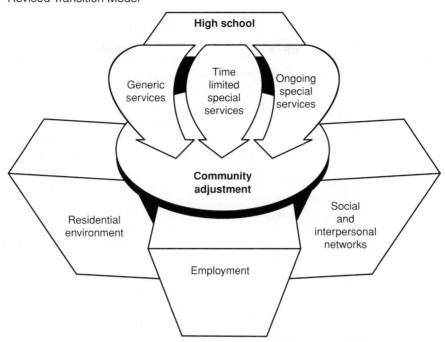

Note: From Transition: A look at the foundations, by Andrew S. Halpern, 1985, *Exceptional Children, 51,* 479–486. Copyright 1985 by The Council for Exceptional Children. Reprinted with permission.

FIGURE 15–3
Summary of Employment Approaches

Approach	Description	Impact/Outcomes
Work activity	Day program for daily living skills and limited exposure to work tasks	• Access to some instruction • A place to go during the day
Sheltered work	Segregated work setting in which the majority of the employees have disabilities	• Access to work tasks with limited earning
Supported employment • Crews • Enclaves • Individualized jobs	Employment in integrated settings with individualized support	• Increased earnings and integration compared with work activity and sheltered work
Customized employment	Employment roles negotiated carefully and specifically related to the interests and abilities of the person	• Employment tailored to the person, including individuals with the most severe disabilities
Self-employment	Small business owned or run by a person with a disability	• Potential for individualized work role and asset building as a business owner
Transition from school to work	Employment emphasized while in middle school and high school	• Increased probability of entering the workforce after completing formal education

Note: From Employment (pp. 390–409), by David Mank, 2007. In S. M. Odom, R. H. Horner, M. E. Snell, & J. Blacher (Eds.), *Handbook of developmental disabilities.* Copyright 2007 by The Guilford Press. Reprinted with permission.

a safe place for persons to go during the day in order to learn daily living skills (Mank, 2009). These types of placements did not identify work as an outcome. By the 1960s and 1970s, research emerged that demonstrated that individuals with severe disabilities could perform production tasks, albeit in segregated facilities (Bellamy, Horner, & Inman, 1979; Gold, 1973), and, furthermore, these individuals could perform real jobs in community settings (Wehman, 1981). This research led to the development of *sheltered workshops*. Sheltered workshops were, and still are, segregated places where individuals with disabilities go to work. However, because research in the 1980s continued to demonstrate that individuals with severe disabilities could get and keep community jobs with the support of a professional, a number of *supported employment* models emerged using enclaves, mobile work crews, and individual jobs (often called *job coaching*). By the 1990s and 2000s, research was clearly demonstrating that natural supports and coworker supports could be used to help individuals get and maintain community employment (Hagner & Cooney, 2003). Today, research on choice and self-determination have led to increased opportunities for employment through self-employment (e.g., small businesses run by individuals with disabilities) (Callahan, Shumpert, & Mast, 2002) and customized employment (i.e., tailoring jobs to talents, interests, and need for accommodation) (Luecking, Fabian, Tilson, Donovan, & Fabian, 2004).

Unfortunately, while the community employment choices for individuals with severe disabilities have increased, research indicated that not until 2002, for the first time in history, was the number of adults in supported employment (118,000) almost the same as in sheltered workshops (126,000); however, an additional 365,000 persons with severe disabilities were in adult day care and extended sheltered workshop programs (Rusch & Braddock, 2004). While one might argue that this difference is a result of students choosing segregated employment over supported employment, research indicates that when given a choice, individuals with severe disabilities choose community employment (Test, Carver, Ewers, Haddad, & Person, 2000; Test, Hinson, Solow, & Keal, 1993). The remainder of this chapter sets forth the information and strategies needed to help students with severe disabilities realize their postschool dreams of obtaining gainful, community employment.

The Definition of *Transition*

In order to fully understand the transition from school to adulthood for students with severe disabilities, it is necessary to examine how the definition of transition has evolved. In 1984, Madeleine Will, the Assistant Secretary of the Office of Special Education and Rehabilitative Services (OSERS), U.S. Department of Education, identified the transition from school to work for students with disabilities as a national priority and defined *transition* as

> *an outcome-oriented process encompassing a broad array of services and experiences that lead to employment. Transition is a period that includes high school, the point of graduation, additional postsecondary education or adult services, and the initial years of employment. Transition is a bridge between the security and structure offered by the school and the opportunities and risks of adult life. Any bridge requires both a solid span and a secure foundation at either end. The transition from school to work and adult life requires sound preparation in the secondary school, adequate support at the point of school leaving, and secure opportunities and services, if needed, in adult situations. (p. 2)*

Based on this definition, the *transition bridges model* was developed, which included three bridges to postschool employment for students with disabilities (see Figure 15–1). The first bridge, *no special services,* involved students moving from school to postschool employment without any services or with services readily available in the community (e.g., using the want ads, online job listings, friends, and family members). The second bridge, *time-limited services,* provided temporary services with the intent that individuals would become independently employed and services would end (e.g., vocational rehabilitation services). The third bridge, *ongoing services,* provided ongoing services for individuals with disabilities who would continue to need supported employment throughout their lives (e.g., supported employment services). The "transition bridges model" was an important first step in defining the transition from school to adulthood for individuals with disabilities because it moved the focus of postschool employment from segregated employment to supported employment where individuals with disabilities would have the same opportunities as individuals without disabilities to become gainfully employed.

While postschool employment outcomes for individuals with disabilities are important, the transition bridges model left out some key factors in the transition from school to postschool life. In 1985, Halpern expanded the transition model by suggesting that transition was not specifically about postschool employment, instead it was about quality of life and community adjustment. The revised transition model suggested by Halpern included three interrelated pillars that represented community adjustment (see Figure 15-2). The first pillar, *employment,* included various employment-related components (e.g., job networks, job search skills, wages, benefits). The second pillar, *residential environment,* included the quality of the community in which the individual lived (e.g., safety, community services, recreational opportunities). The third pillar, *social and interpersonal networks,* included the capacity to build and maintain relationships (e.g., daily interactions, self-esteem, family relationships and support, friendship). By expanding the model, transition from school to adulthood became more about overall quality of life and not just employment.

Although the transition movement expanded rapidly through the 1980s, it was not until 1990 that federal law recognized and mandated transition services for students with disabilities. The Individuals with Disabilities Education Act of 1990 (IDEA) (P.L. 101-476) was the first school-related federal mandate to formally recognize transition services for students with disabilities. Specifically, the law mandated that IEPs include a transition component for students with disabilities that would begin no later than age 16. Additionally, IDEA 1990 required that the transition services needs of students be met through coordinated planning that focused on movement from school to postschool life, emphasizing the role of family and adult services agencies in the transition planning process.

In 1997, IDEA was again reauthorized and the focus on transition services shifted from an educational process to an outcome-oriented process for students with disabilities (Cameto, 2005). Specifically, IDEA 1997 defined *transition* as

a coordinated set of activities for a student with a disability that is: (a) designed within an outcome-oriented process, which promotes movement from school to postschool activities, including postsecondary education, vocational training, integrated employment (including supported employment), *continuing and adult education, adult services, independent living, or community participation; (b) based upon the individual student's needs, taking into account the student's preferences and interests; and (c) includes instruction, related services, community experiences, the development of employment and other postschool adult living objectives, and, when appropriate, acquisition of daily living skills and functional vocational evaluation. (20 U.S.C. § 1400 [Sec. 602] [30])*

IDEA 1997 (P.L. 105-17) focused on aligning students' educational programs to meet their goals for postsecondary life. Additionally, it required that transition services for students with disabilities begin at age 14.

In 2004, IDEA was amended and went one step further to focus on accountability and results by defining *transition services* as

a coordinated set of activities for a child with a disability that is designed to be within a results-oriented process, that is focused on improving the academic and functional achievement of the child with a disability to facilitate the child's movement from school to postschool activities, including postsecondary education, vocational education, integrated employment (including supported employment), continuing and adult education, adult services, independent living, or community participation; is based on the individual child's needs, taking into account the child's strengths, preferences, and interests; and includes instruction, related services, community experiences, the development of employment and other postschool adult living objectives, and, when appropriate, acquisition of daily living skills and functional vocational evaluation. (20 U.S.C. § 1401 [Sec. 602] [34])

Unfortunately, in 2004, IDEA reverted to the 1990 requirement that transition services begin no later than age 16 for students with disabilities. However, each state still had the right to require an earlier starting point in their state and many states recognized that best practices suggest that the transition planning process begin as early as possible, so they kept the age at 14 (Test, Aspel, & Everson, 2006). Because of this, readers should check to see what is required by their state.

Transition Planning

In order to meet the requirements of IDEA 2004 and provide students with severe disabilities effective transition services that lead to successful employment, it is important to understand the key elements of the transition planning process. Effective transition planning ensures that students with disabilities have every opportunity to reach their postschool goals (Test et al., 2006). The transition planning process involves a number of stakeholders, including regular and special education teachers, the student with a disability, parents, outside services agencies, related services representatives, and anyone who is important in the student's life (Cameto, 2005). Transition planning provides students with disabilities and their families the opportunity to set goals for postschool life and make connections with adult services agencies in order to meet their postschool goals. Transition planning involves several steps, including (a) using transition assessment to identify students' strengths, needs, preferences, and present level of performance; (b) developing postschool goals and related annual IEP goals that reflect information obtained through transition assessment; and (c) identifying related transition services to help students attain postschool goals (Mazzotti et al., in press). This section will discuss components of the transition planning process, including (a) the requirements of the State Performance Plan/Annual Performance Report (SPP/APR), Part B, Indicator 13; (b) age-appropriate transition assessment; (c) person-centered planning; (d) self-determination and student involvement in the transition planning process; and (e) the role of teachers in the transition planning process.

Indicator 13 Requirements

To ensure that the states meet the requirements of IDEA 2004, the Office of Special Education Programs (OSEP), in coordination with OSERS, developed 20 SPP/APR performance indicators related to Part B (i.e., children with disabilities, ages 3 to 22). Of the 20 Part B indicators, four are directly related to secondary transition services for students with disabilities. The four indicators include (a) Indicator 1, improving graduation rates; (b) Indicator 2, decreasing drop-out rates; (c) Indicator 13, improving transition services; and (d) Indicator 14, improving outcomes for students

moving from secondary to postsecondary activities. Specifically, *Indicator 13* is defined as

> *appropriate measurable postsecondary goals that are annually updated and based upon an age appropriate transition assessment, transition services, including courses of study, that will reasonably enable the student to meet those postsecondary goals, and annual IEP goals related to the student's transition services needs. There also must be evidence that the student was invited to the IEP Team meeting where transition services are to be discussed and evidence that, if appropriate, a representative of any participating agency was invited to the IEP Team meeting with the prior consent of the parent or student who has reached the age of majority. (20 U.S.C. § 1416(a)(3)(B); OSEP, 2009)*

The National Secondary Transition Technical Assistance Center (NSTTAC) (2009), in collaboration with OSEP, developed an Indicator 13 checklist to help states collect data. The Indicator 13 checklist includes eight items and provides teachers and schools with guidelines for writing IEPs that meet the federal requirements of the indicator, as well as help facilitate the transition planning process, and meet the secondary transition needs of students with disabilities. The required items include the following:

1. *Is (are) there appropriate measurable postsecondary goal(s) in this area?* A student's postsecondary goals should be measurable (i.e., the behavior identified can be counted as having been completed or not) and should occur after the student graduates from high school. See Figure 15–4 for appropriate and inappropriate examples of measurable postsecondary goals.
2. *Is (are) the postsecondary goal(s) updated annually?* The postsecondary goal(s) should be updated annually and requires a yes/no answer from the teacher.
3. *Is there evidence that the measurable postsecondary goal(s) was based on an age-appropriate transition assessment?* There should be evidence in the student's IEP file that a transition assessment had been *conducted and was used to develop the student's postsecondary goal(s).*
4. *Are there transition services in the IEP that will reasonably enable the student to meet his or her postsecondary goal(s)?* Transition services (i.e., type of instruction, related service, community

FIGURE 15–4

Indicator 13 Examples of Appropriate and Inappropriate Measurable Postsecondary Goals

Examples of Appropriate Measurable Postsecondary Goals	Examples of Inappropriate Postsecondary Goals
Serena • Employment: After graduation, Serena will obtain a supported employment position in the food service industry. • Education: After graduation, Serena will take continuing education classes at the local community college. • Independent living: Upon completion of high school, Serena will independently prepare for work each day, including dressing, making her bed, making her lunch, and accessing transportation.	**Serena** • Employment: After graduation, Serena prefers to work at Mic's Taco Stand. *("Prefers" does not indicate an explicit behavior by the student that will occur after high school that can be observed as occurring or not occurring.)* • Education: Serena wants to learn more about cooking when she graduates from high school. *("Wants" does not indicate an explicit behavior by the student that will occur after high school that can be observed as occurring or not occurring.)* • Independent living: Serena enjoys cooking and wants to continue to help her mom in the kitchen after graduation from high school. *("Enjoys" and "wants" do not indicate an explicit behavior by the student that will occur after high school that can be observed as occurring or not occurring.)*
Rusty • Employment: After graduation, Rusty will receive job development services from vocational rehabilitation or a community rehabilitation program and will participate in supported self-employment within 1 year of graduation. • Education: After graduation, Rusty will participate in a compensatory education program and will take life skills classes (e.g., cooking, money and banking, self-advocacy, personal hygiene). • Independent living: After graduation, Rusty will participate in community-integrated recreational/leisure activities related to music, movies, and art, including events at movie theaters, concerts at the local community college, arts and crafts museums downtown, and the entertainment store at the mall.	**Rusty** • Employment: Rusty will apply for services through vocational rehabilitation to support his participation in a vocational center program. *(There is no indication that this will occur after high school.)* • Education: Rusty wants to improve his functional communication skills after high school. *("Wants" does not indicate an explicit behavior by the student that will occur after high school that can be observed as occurring or not occurring.)* • Independent living: Rusty wants to attend community dances sponsored by the local YMCA. *("Wants" does not indicate an explicit behavior by the student that will occur after high school that can be observed as occurring or not occurring; this is also an activity that could occur while Rusty is in school because there is no indication that it will occur after high school.)*
Cassandra • Employment: Within 3 months after graduation, Cassandra will obtain a supported employment position that allows her to work to her maximum stamina and incorporates the use of assistive technology for at least 10 hours per week. • Education: After graduation, Cassandra will participate in functional skills training through the Community Alternatives Program (CAP) services once per week at her home and in the community in order to develop her functional communication skills. • Independent living: After graduation, Cassandra will attend independent living classes at an adult day program and will participate in her daily care routine to the maximum extent possible at home with her parents.	**Cassandra** • Employment: Cassandra will express her preferences related to her postsecondary employment options, given picture symbols and the iTalk2, an augmentative communication device. *(This goal could be achieved while Cassandra is still in high school and does not reflect a postschool goal of employment.)* • Education: Cassandra will receive CAP services to work on functional communication. *(There is no indication of how Cassandra will improve her communication skills or that this goal will occur after graduation.)* • Independent living: Cassandra will communicate personal needs associated with daily care to her mother using picture symbols. *(There is no indication of how Cassandra will improve her communication skills in order to express her personal needs or that this goal will occur after graduation.)*

experience, development of employment and other postschool adult living objectives, acquisition of daily living skills [if appropriate], and provision of a functional vocational evaluation) should be included in the IEP in order to facilitate the student's movement toward his or her postsecondary goals.

5. *Do the transition services include courses of study that will reasonably enable the student to meet his or her postsecondary goal(s)?* A student's course of study should be aligned with his or her stated postsecondary goal(s).

6. *Is (are) there an annual IEP goal(s) related to the student's transition services needs?* The student's annual IEP goals should be related to the student's transition services needs and align with postsecondary goals.

7. *Is there evidence that the student was invited to the IEP team meeting when the transition services were discussed?* There must be evidence that the student was invited to participate in the IEP team meeting for the current year.

8. *If appropriate, is there evidence that a representative of any participating agency was invited to the IEP team meeting with the prior consent of the parent or student who has reached the age of majority?* Representatives from adult services agencies from outside the school (e.g., postsecondary education, vocational education, integrated employment [including supported employment], continuing and adult education, adult services, independent living, community participation) should be invited to participate in the development of the IEP. There must be evidence that the parent or the student with a disability (if he or she has reached the age of majority) has consented to inviting the agency representative.

IDEA (2004) mandates that a student's IEP include (a) all of the items on the Indicator 13 checklist, and (b) must be in effect beginning no later than age 16, or earlier, if required by your state or if deemed appropriate by the student's IEP team. Additionally, postsecondary goals must be updated annually and based on an age-appropriate transition assessment.

Age-Appropriate Transition Assessment

The transition assessment is a critical first step in the transition planning process and includes both formal and informal types of assessments (Mazzotti et al., in press). Often, students with disabilities are faced with difficult decisions in middle school regarding diploma track options, academic and employment preparation, and postschool goals; therefore, transition assessment should begin in middle school and be an ongoing process as students progress through high school (Neubert, 2003). IDEA (2004) mandates that age-appropriate transition assessment be used as part of the transition planning process in order to identify the strengths, preferences, needs, and interests of students with disabilities. Additionally, teachers of students with disabilities are required to use transition assessment as a basis for developing students' postschool goals. The Division on Career Development and Transition of the Council for Exceptional Children defined *transition assessment* as

> *the ongoing process of collecting data on the individual's needs, preferences, and interests as they relate to the demands of current and future working, educational, living, and personal and social environments. Assessment data serve as the common thread in the transition process and form the basis for defining goals and services to be included in the IEP. (Sitlington, Neubert, & Leconte, 1997, p. 70)*

When considering this definition, it seems logical that transition assessment would be the first step in the transition planning process because it provides the information needed to write postschool goals that reflect students' strengths, needs, preferences, and interests.

Transition assessment plays several roles in the transition planning process. First, it provides a method for identifying students' strengths, needs, preferences, and interests, which, in turn, allows students to make informed choices about their goals for postschool life (Neubert, 2003; Sitlington & Payne, 2004). Second, it provides information about students in order to help the IEP teams identify specific skills that students need in order to help them meet their postschool goals (Sitlington & Payne). Third, it helps students take charge of the transition planning process because it makes them aware of their self-determination skills (Field & Hoffman, 2007). Finally, transition assessment can provide information on a number of skill areas (e.g., self-determination, vocational, independent living, career exploration, achievement, behavioral) so the students' profile of skills needed to meet postschool goals can be identified for employment, education, and independent living (NSTTAC, 2007; Sitlington & Clark, 2007; Sitlington & Payne). When conducting transition assessment, three questions should guide the process:

1. Where is the student now?
2. Where does the student want to go?
3. How will the student get there?

In considering these three questions, it is important to be familiar with the types of transition assessment. Broadly, there are two types of transition assessment, formal and informal (NSTTAC, 2007), which can provide valuable information about students' strengths, needs, preferences, and interests. Using a variety of informal and formal assessments can lead to an overall picture of the student that will help facilitate the transition planning process.

Formal Assessment

Formal assessments are typically standardized instruments that have been evaluated for reliability and validity in order to support the effectiveness of the instrument (NSTTAC, 2007). Formal assessments can be used to learn about a wide variety of skills in a number of areas (e.g., vocational, academic, social) (see Chapter 3). Formal assessments can include various types, such as the following:

- *Adaptive behavior assessments:* Scales of Independent Behavior–Revised (SIB-R), Vineland Adaptive Behavior Scales, AAMR Adaptive Behavior Scales (ABS)
- *Aptitude tests:* Differential Aptitude Test (DAT), Armed Services Vocational Aptitude Battery (ASVAB), Bennett's Mechanical Comprehension Test
- *Interest and work inventories:* Career Interest Inventory, Levels One and Two; Self-Directed Search Forms R and E; Harrington/O'Shea System for Career Decision-Making
- *Intelligence tests:* Stanford-Binet Intelligence Scale, Form L-M (SBL-M); Wechsler Intelligence Scale for Children (4th ed.) (WISC-IV); Kaufman Brief Intelligence Test (K-BIT)
- *Achievement tests:* Woodcock–Johnson III, Basic Achievement Skills Inventory (BASI), Kaufman Test of Educational Achievement (2nd ed.)
- *Personality and preference assessments:* Personal Career Development Profile (PCDP), Student Styles Questionnaire (SSQ)
- *Employability assessments:* Career Decision Scale (CDS), Career Thought Inventory (CTI), Career Development Inventory (CDI)

- *Self-determination assessments:* ARC Self-Determination Scale (Adolescent Version), Self-Determination Assessment Battery, ChoiceMaker Self-Determination Assessment
- *Work-related temperament scales:* Work Adjustment Inventory (WAI)
- *Postsecondary support needs assessments:* Supports Intensity Scale (SIS)

Formal assessments are comprehensive and can provide detailed information about a student; however, they tend to be costly, time consuming, and difficult to score. Therefore, informal assessments may be an efficient alternative for teachers.

Informal Assessment

Informal assessments are nonstandardized assessments that are more subjective in nature and can focus on the individual in a variety of settings (e.g., classroom, employment, community) (Mazzotti et al., in press). Informal assessments include (a) observations in various settings (e.g., watching, listening, recording information about the student's behavior), (b) questionnaires (e.g., providing the student and persons involved in the student's life with the opportunity to report on areas such as the student's employment skills, independent living skills, self-determination), (c) interviews (e.g., structured or unstructured conversations with the student and persons involved in the student's life), and (d) curriculum-based assessments (e.g., task analysis, portfolio assessments, work sample analysis, criterion-referenced tests) (Test et al., 2006). Some popular informal assessments include the Transition Planning Inventory (TPI), the Life Centered Career Education (LCCE) Competency Assessment Knowledge and Performance Batteries, and the Transition Behavior Scale (Mazzotti et al., 2009).

Transition assessment is an ongoing and continuous process and should begin as early as possible in order to develop a well-rounded effective transition program that leads to positive postschool outcomes for the student with severe disabilities. Transition assessments have six relevant characteristics (Test et al., 2006):

1. *Should be an ongoing and continuous process.* Transition assessment starts with gathering information that allows a teacher to develop the student's IEP and should be ongoing as the student progresses through high school. It provides information so the student, teacher, and family can develop postschool goals and annual IEP goals, plan

the student's course of study, identify appropriate transition services, and evaluate the student's performance.

2. *Should be student centered.* Transition assessment should provide information about the student's strengths, needs, and desires for the future. It should be self-determined, and teachers and parents need to remember that it is the student's life.

3. *Occurs in many places.* Assessment should occur in a variety of natural environments in order to meet postschool goals. For example, as students learn new skills and begin to make choices about their options for postschool life, transition assessment should begin to occur in employment settings and community settings. By doing this, students are provides with options about postschool employment, education, and independent living so that he or she can may informed choices about life after high school.

4. *Must involve other people.* Transition assessment is a collaborative process that requires gathering information from a variety of people involved in the student's life (e.g., employer, special education teacher, general education teacher, parents, friends, case managers).

5. *Data must be understandable.* Data gathered from transition assessments must be useful and understandable not only to the adults involved in the student's life, but to the student as well. Therefore, it may be necessary to take steps to help the student interpret the information from transition assessments.

6. *Must be sensitive to cultural diversity.* Teachers and others need to understand five key elements in order to be culturally sensitive to diverse students when conducting transition assessments: (a) personal cultural and ethnic identities, (b) the personal values that underlie interpretation of the assessment data, (c) the role that the student and family's culture plays in the assessment process, (d) the differences between mainstream values and the cultural values of the student, and (e) the need to work as a team to help the student progress towards postschool goals.

Transition assessment encompasses all areas of transition and provides in-depth knowledge of the students' strengths, needs, preferences, and interests that can lead to specific skill development to allow the student to meet postschool goals in the areas of employment, education, and independent living. Once a transition assessment has been conducted, teachers are one step closer to developing effective transition components and meeting the needs of students as they progress through the transition planning process.

Serena

Serena's special education teacher has given her and her parents several informal transition assessments to identify her strengths, needs, and preferences related to employment, education, and independent living. Her teacher has used the Transition Planning Inventory (TPI) as the assessment tool. Serena completed a job-related interest and preference inventory which indicated that she would like to work indoors with other people. Specifically, she would like to work in the food industry and wear a purple uniform when she graduates from high school. The informal assessments also indicated that Serena wants to continue to participate in social events (e.g., bake sales, dances) at her church. Additionally, Serena participated in some community-based vocational training at a local bakery and indicated that she enjoyed the work and the people. While participating in the training, Serena did not engage in her problem behaviors (i.e., curling up on the floor, covering her ears) and indicated that she liked the job because sometimes they used purple icing on the cakes. This further substantiated that working in the food service industry was what she desired. Finally, Serena's parents expressed that they would like to see Serena take some cooking and life skills classes at the local community college.

Rusty

Reports from informal interviews and observations suggested that Rusty enjoys interacting with other people, music, dancing, and computers. During informal interviews, Rusty expressed a desire to continue working with computers when he graduated from high school. Other interest inventories conducted over the last few years have indicated that Rusty is interested in careers related to information technology. Rusty loves school and is always eager to learn new skills. He demonstrates a high level of motivation to please his teacher and his parents report that, even when he is sick, he begs to go to school. These behaviors are important to consider in the development of his postsecondary goals of self-employment and independent living. Additionally, Rusty completed the ARC Self-Determination Scale. Results from Section One (Autonomy) indicated that Rusty wants to be independent by completing his daily routines by himself (e.g., personal care and grooming) and that Rusty needs to continue to work on improving his self-determination skills.

Person-centered Planning

One method for facilitating the transition planning process is *person-centered planning*. The concept of person-centered planning dates back to 1979 and describes a variety of techniques that focus on recognizing the individual first instead of the disability (O'Brien & O'Brien, 2000). The idea behind person-centered planning involves understanding and supporting an individual with a disability so that the individual can become an actively engaged and contributing member of the community (Test et al., 2006). Person-centered planning focuses specifically on postschool outcomes and quality of life for the student with a disability (Michaels & Ferrara, 2005). The process encourages family and student participation in transition planning and involves communication and collaboration among team members. Person-centered planning allows the student to take a leadership role throughout the transition planning process (i.e., transition assessment, planning, delivery of services). Students are given the opportunity to think about their preferences and dreams when investigating options for postschool employment, education, and independent living (Lohrmann-O'Rourke & Gomez, 2001). As students take a leadership role in the transition planning process, the role of IEP team members is to support students and engage them in problem solving in order to allow students to move toward accomplishing postschool goals (Test et al., 2006).

The National Center on Secondary Education and Transition (NCSET; 2004) identified four steps that are commonly used in the person-centered planning:

- *Step 1: Choosing a facilitator.* This person can be a consultant, family member, school staff, or adult services provider who is a good listener, is willing to work to shape the dreams of the student, and understands the options available to the student within the community.
- *Step 2: Designing the planning process.* A preplanning meeting should be conducted during which the student's profile is developed. This meeting can take up to 2 hours and involves (a) identifying persons to be invited to the meeting who have knowledge of the student, have an ability to facilitate the process, and have connections to the community and adult services providers; (b) identifying a date, time, and place for the meeting; (c) discussing strategies to increase the participation of the student; (d) developing a personal history or life story of the student by sharing information about the student's life (e.g., medical problems, important relationships); (e) describing the quality of the student's life, including community participation and experiences, competence, choices, and rights; (f) discussing and describing the student's likes and dislikes; and (g) sending copies of the personal profile to meeting attendees.
- *Step 3: Holding the meeting: Implementing the person-centered planning process.* This includes (a) reviewing the student's personal profile and adding any necessary comments or observations; (b) identifying events or conditions that may affect the student's life goals; (c) sharing visions for the future than may increase opportunities for the student; (d) identifying barriers and opportunities that provide a real-life context for the student's vision; (e) identifying strategies and steps for facilitating the student's vision; and (f) developing a plan of action that includes steps that will be taken, when implementation will begin, and when the team will hold the next meeting.
- *Step 4: Planning and strategizing at the follow-up meetings.* Follow-up team meetings usually occur every 6 to 12 months and are an important component in the person-centered planning process because they ensure that the student is on track toward reaching his or her goals for ultimate life success. Follow-up meeting should include (a) celebrating student successes, (b) listing activities that have occurred since the last meeting, (c) listing barriers that have arisen since the last meeting, (d) discussing new ideas and strategies to assist the student, (e) identifying priorities for the next meeting, (f) establishing a

renewed commitment from team members, (g) developing 5 to 10 steps for each person to follow, and (h) determining the time of the next meeting.

There are several person-centered planning curricula available to teachers, including Making Action Plans (MAPS) (Sherlock, 2001), Group Action Planning (GAP) (Turnbull & Turnbull, 1995), and Planning Alternative Tomorrow with Hope (PATH) (Pearpoint, O'Brien, & Forest, 1993). Person-centered planning plays an important role in the life of a student with severe disabilities and should be a part of the transition planning process. It provides a model for increasing community experiences and participation for the student with the ultimate goal of improved quality of life.

Cassandra, her family, a family friend that works for the local parent advocacy center, the special education teacher, a representative from Vocational Rehabilitation, and a peer buddy attended Cassandra's most recent person-centered planning meeting. During the meeting, they discussed issues that would affect Cassandra's life goals (e.g., communication, personal care services, respite, medical transportation). The vision that emerged from this meeting was that Cassandra will continue to stay in school until she is 21 by participating in a program for 18- to-21-year-olds. Cassandra would then transition into an adult services program and supported employment. Several barriers to achieving her postschool goals were identified, including Cassandra's medical condition, her lack of communication skills, and her need for extensive support in all areas of adult life. Key stakeholders in Cassandra's person-centered planning team were identified and specific roles were assigned to help carry out the task developed. At the conclusion of the meeting, a plan was developed for Cassandra to enter the program for 18- to-21-year-olds, which will provide intensive community-based instruction in all life skill areas. Providers of adult services were identified to assist with the transition from school to postschool employment and life.

Self-Determination and Student Involvement in the IEP

Another critical component in the transition planning process is promoting student involvement (Blalock et al., 2003). While several definitions of self-determination exist throughout the literature (e.g., Field, Martin, Miller,

Ward, & Wehmeyer, 1998; Wehmeyer, 1995; Wehmeyer, Field, Doren, Jones, & Mason, 2004), Field et al. defined *self-determination* as "a combination of skills, knowledge, and beliefs that enable a person to engage in goal-directed, self-regulated, autonomous behavior" (p. 2). Self-determination is a complex construct with multiple components, including choice making, decision making, problem solving, goal setting, independence, self-observation, self-instruction, self-advocacy, internal locus of control, positive attributions of efficacy, self-awareness, and self-evaluation (Wehmeyer & Schalock, 2001). Teaching students self-determination skills allows them to take responsibility for their own life. Teaching self-determination skills to students with disabilities has been shown to be a significant predictor of postschool education, employment, and independent living outcomes (Halpern, Yovanoff, Doren, & Benz, 1995; Wehmeyer & Palmer, 2003; Wehmeyer & Schwartz, 1997). Therefore, it is extremely important that teachers provide students with opportunities to develop self-determination skills. Because of this, a primary goal for educators should be to teach self-determination skills to ensure that students with severe disabilities are prepared to lead self-determined lives (Cameto, 2005; Wagner, Newman, Cameto, Levine, & Garza, 2006). Unfortunately, self-determination is typically not included in school curricula (Test et al., 2004).

One way that has been used successfully to teach self-determination to students with disabilities is to get them actively involved in their IEP process, which allows them to practice various self-determination skills such as goal setting, problem solving, self-advocacy, and decision making (Test et al., 2004). Konrad (2008) identified five stages in which students can get involved in their IEP process: (a) Stage 1–developing background knowledge, (b) Stage 2–planning, (c) Stage 3–drafting, (d) Stage 4–meeting, and (e) Stage 5–implementation. Each of these stages includes specific elements to promote student involvement in the IEP process, which, in turn, can lead to improved self-determination skills. Konrad (2008) identified specific steps for each stage of the IEP process that teachers can follow to facilitate student involvement:

Stage 1: Developing Background Knowledge

1. *Use your resources.* Teachers should become familiar with available resources that help students learn about the IEP process, their disability, and what special education is about.

2. *Develop an IEP scavenger hunt.* Give students the opportunity to investigate their IEP by identifying certain components. Adjust the skill level to meet the needs of your student.

3. *Assign students the task of evaluating their IEP.* Provide students with a checklist to assess the components of the IEP. For students with severe disabilities, the checklist may simply include pictures and symbols that allow the student, with guidance from the teacher, to identify specific parts of the IEP.

4. *Have students read or read to them.* By reading books that include children with disabilities, students can identify the strengths and needs of the characters and possibly create mock IEP meetings that involve the characters in the books.

Stage 2: Planning for the IEP

1. *Work with students to help them develop vision statements.* This step allows students to begin to identify their postschool goals in the areas of education, employment, and independent living. Students can be prompted by having them complete the following sentence, "After high school, I plan to live _____, learn _____, work _____, and play _____" (p. 237).

2. *Get students involved in the transition assessment process.* Have students complete informal transition assessments, such as interest inventories. It may also be important to share with students information from formal transition assessments so that they can begin to identify their strengths, needs, preferences, and interests in order to help develop goals that meet their needs.

3. *Have students write letters to invite team members to attend.* For students with severe disabilities, these could be templates that students fill in on a computer.

4. *Use commercial programs.* For example, *The Self-Advocacy Strategy* (VanReusen & Bos, 1994) and *The Self-Directed IEP* (Martin, Marshall, Maxson, & Jerman, 1997) have been shown to be effective for teaching students to participate in the IEP process by identifying goals and needed services and accommodations.

5. *Involve students in preparing for the meeting.* This could involve making name tags for team members, discussing what to wear to the meeting, preparing a Microsoft® PowerPoint® presentation, and other aspects of preparing for the meeting.

Stage 3: Drafting the IEP

1. *Have students write about their IEP meeting.* For students with severe disabilities, this may include providing pictures and symbols, and allowing students to identify their strengths and needs.

2. *Once students have developed an idea of their strengths and needs, the needs should be changed into "I will" statements.* These "I will" statements can be used to develop the student's goals as they relate to the postschool outcome areas of employment, education, and independent living.

3. *Once the IEP has been drafted, students can meet with their parents in order to discuss their goals.* This will provide parents with the opportunity to see what goals the student has set and prepare both the student and the parent for the IEP meeting prior to the actual meeting.

Stage 4: Meeting to Develop the IEP

1. *Consider the range of options.* When involving students in the IEP process, the level of participation may vary. For example, younger students may attend the meeting, introduce the participants, and participate by actively listening. Whereas older students may actually lead the entire meeting by discussing their vision, strengths, needs, and goals.

2. *Provide opportunities for rehearsal.* Providing opportunities for students to verbally rehearse and role-play IEP meetings, in addition to prompting, leads to greater participation (Test et al., 2004).

3. *Consider using PowerPoint® presentations during meetings.* Using such presentations can provide a format in which students can express their goals. This also promotes student involvement by allowing students to develop and present their strengths, needs, and goals in a manner that expresses who they are.

Stage 5: Implementing the IEP

1. *Have each student create an IEP fact sheet.* A fact sheet will provide a summary for teachers and the student that includes the disability, strengths, needs, goals, services, and accommodations. This can serve as a reminder to students as they move through their school year.

2. *Teach students self-advocacy and self-recruitment skills.* Practice with students various ways to self-advocate by using role-playing and modeling.

3. *Provide students with access to their IEP.* Give students the opportunity to revisit their IEP to ensure that they are receiving accommodations, goals are being met, and any necessary changes are being made.
4. *Teach students to self-monitor and self-evaluate their progress.* Using self-management strategies with students with disabilities can help students meet their IEP goals.
5. *Have students develop person-first progress reports.* These can be used as a method for sharing progress toward goals with parents and IEP team members.

As students with severe disabilities are taught to be active participants in their IEP process, their self-determination skills will be strengthened. For students with severe disabilities, teachers may be more actively involved in developing these skills in order to support students as they become active participants in the IEP process.

> *Cassandra and her teacher developed a PowerPoint® presentation to facilitate her involvement in her IEP meeting. By developing a PowerPoint® presentation, Cassandra was able to participate in the development of her IEP. She began the presentation by introducing herself and showing pictures of herself with family and friends on the first couple of slides. She continued by sharing information about her disability and portrayed her school day through photographs that her teacher helped her take. After showing slides of her school day, she presented slides that expressed her likes (e.g., music, books) and dislikes (e.g., math, broccoli). Through the PowerPoint® presentation, Cassandra was able to indicate that she wants to work in a clerical position when she finishes high school and wants to have an apartment with a roommate, where she can live independently.*

Teaching Employment Skills

Because of the variety of possible careers and related employment skills, teaching employment skills to students with disabilities can be a daunting task. In this section, three important considerations for delivering employment skills instruction are discussed, including (a) where to provide instruction, (b) how to provide instruction, and (c) how to collect instructional data.

Where to Provide Instruction

While it would seem to make sense that employment skills should always be taught in the community instead of on a school campus, this may not always be possible. Fortunately, employment skills have been successfully taught in both school and community settings. So it is important to start by describing the advantages and disadvantages of both community-based and school-based employment instruction.

Community-based Instruction (CBI)

CBI has the distinct advantage of occurring in the real world with the natural variations that occur in life. This includes a variety of coworkers with different social and work skills and tasks that may change from time to time. This variety, combined with the use of real materials, will help promote skill generalization. However, in spite of these advantages, there are a number of disadvantages to CBI that must be considered, including transporting students to community sites, allocating staff to provide CBI, and coordinating school and business schedules. While these are potentially serious obstacles to providing CBI, potential solutions for each problem will be described later in "Where to Provide Instruction: Community-based Instruction Options."

School-based Instruction (SBI)

SBI has the advantage of being an easier environment to control. Transportation and scheduling are not typically an issue and school campuses tend to be a more forgiving environment for students who are learning how to perform job tasks, as well as how to behave appropriately. However, these advantages are offset by having to make sure that SBI is designed to incorporate strategies to promote generalization by using real materials and setting up the instructional environment to look as real as possible. In addition, SBI should help students build the stamina required for real jobs, as well as learn to work with little supervision and feedback. Thus, while logistically easier, SBI is often instructionally more challenging.

Given the advantages and disadvantages of CBI and SBI, one solution is to combine them. CBI provides students with access to real work settings, while SBI can provide opportunities to repeatedly practice skills that have not yet been mastered. However, it is important to not fall into the "readiness trap," in which student access to CBI is based on requiring them to master the prerequisite skills taught with SBI. When this happens, many students never get to CBI. Instead, students need CBI in order to support skill acquisition and generalization, and CBI should be provided as a critical and regular part of employment skills instruction.

Where to Provide Instruction: School-Based Instruction Options

Test et al. (2006) described four school-based instruction options for teaching employment skills, including (a) career–technical education, (b) school-based enterprises, (c) on-campus jobs, and (d) job clubs and vocational student organizations. Each of these four options is described below in more detail.

Career–Technical Education

Career–technical education (CTE) was defined by the Carl Perkins Vocational and Applied Technology Education Amendments of 1998 (P.L. 105-332) as

> *organized activities that offer a sequence of courses that provides individuals with the academic and technical knowledge and skills the individuals need to prepare for further education and for careers (other than careers requiring a baccalaureate, master's, or doctoral degree) in current or emerging employment sectors. Vocational technical education includes competency-based applied learning that contributes to the academic knowledge, higher-order reasoning and problem-solving skills, work attitudes, general employability skills, technical skills, and occupational-specific skills for an individual. (Title III, Section 3: Definitions, 20)*

CTE can play an important role in preparing students with severe disabilities for employment because courses are taught by CTE staff who have expertise in preparing youth for employment. All students with severe disabilities need access to CTE courses to help them develop career awareness and career preparation skills. Participating in CTE courses not only teaches students specific employment skills, it also gives them access to a variety of employment services, including vocational assessment, career counseling and planning, job training, and apprenticeships (Test et al., 2006).

While the Carl Perkins Act ensures that students with disabilities will have equal access to the full range of CTE programs available, some resistance may be encountered. Test et al. (2006) suggested eight

techniques for working with CTE staff, including the following:

1. Ensure that CTE teachers and special educators have joint staff development aimed at increasing the knowledge of each other's instructional areas and the laws directing these areas.
2. Develop a formal communication system to keep special education staff informed of student progress and provide CTE staff with consultative services for instructional issues and concerns.
3. Determine how CTE job responsibilities relate to the transitioning.
4. Determine how CTE career development plans can be interfaced with the transition component of the IEP.
5. Allow students with moderate to severe cognitive disabilities to take the same CTE course more than one time and receive credit each time. This allows students adequate time to cover the full range of skills taught in the course at a slower rate. The special education teacher and the CTE teacher should collaboratively identify which competencies will be worked on each year. These competencies should be clearly delineated so that coursework can be modified appropriately. Any end-of-course assessments for students who are taking the same course twice for credit can be designed individually to assess the competencies on which the students have focused.
6. Arrange for students to complete CTE internships for credit. Internships might be a viable option for CTE credit if students need additional hands-on employment preparation and/or the courses available on the school campus do not match the students' postschool outcome goals for employment.
7. Work closely with CTE staff to determine the types of accommodations that students will need to be successful in CTE courses.
8. Ensure that CTE is represented on all special education committees and advisory councils (e.g., community-level transition teams, school-level transition teams, IEP teams) and that special education is represented on all CTE committees and advisory councils.
9. Ensure that methods are in place to determine whether the CTE services being provided to students with disabilities are consistent with IEPs, and meet with IEP teams if, at any point, modifications need to be made.

10. Coordinate CTE recruitment activities (e.g., career day, job fairs) with a special education representative to ensure inclusion of students with disabilities.
11. Coordinate enrollment of students with disabilities in CTE courses to ensure that all guidelines for class size are met. Coordination should involve special education, CTE, student data personnel, guidance counseling, and school administration. The goal should be to honor students' choices regarding their vocational interests while ensuring that CTE classes are not overloaded with students with special needs to the point that students cannot receive adequate services and job skills training.

Rusty and his IEP team have decided that in order for him to pursue his interests in working with computers, he should enroll in a CTE course. After careful consideration, they chose a course titled "Careers in Computers." As part of Rusty's IEP, the CTE and special education teacher viewed the "blueprint" for this course, which contains 40 objectives, and selected the objectives that seemed to be most relevant for Rusty. These five objectives were then included in Rusty's IEP, which means that at the end of the course, these will be the only objectives used to evaluate Rusty's performance on any end-of-course assessments.

School-based Enterprises (SBEs)

A *school-based enterprise* has been defined as "any school-sponsored activity that engages a group of students in producing goods or services for sale or to be used by people, other than the student involved" (Stern, 1994, p. 3). While SBEs provide a simulated work environment, they do allow students the opportunity to develop and operate small businesses, perform work for area businesses, and/or complete tasks for volunteer organizations. (See Gamache and Knab, 2008, for an excellent description of how to plan, implement, and evaluate SBEs.)

SBEs can provide an environment in which students can learn the work habits (e.g., attendance, punctuality, organizing work, storing supplies), work behaviors (e.g., staying on task, following directions, assembly line work, tool use), and social skills (e.g., use of social amenities, social conversation, coworker interactions) needed to be successful in competitive employment. While working in an SBE, students are often involved in many procedures associated with operating a retail or service-oriented business, such as determining costs, ordering materials, maintaining equipment, marketing products/services, organizing tasks, and taking inventory. While creating an SBE might seem to be a simple task, there are many issues to consider, including funding, space, organization, and ensuring quality (Test et al., 2006). Box 15-1 provides a description of a working SBE.

Funding Considerations

Creating an SBE will require initial start-up funds for furniture (e.g., work bins, workstations, stools, file cabinets, work desks) and supplies (e.g., work aprons, safety glasses, work gloves) based on the type of work activities to be conducted. Funding can be obtained by using classroom instructional supply/equipment funds, grant/foundation funds, donations from civic groups, PTA/PTO funds, contributions from local businesses, profits from work performed through business contracts (after students are paid based on U.S. Department of Labor regulations), and fund-raising. Often, equipment can be obtained from or shared with the CTE department or donated by local businesses.

Space Considerations

An SBE can be implemented in an extra classroom, a large open instructional area, or a mobile unit. Size should be based on the number of students served and type of planned enterprise. For example, if finishing and/or painting furniture projects are planned, a large, well-ventilated area will be needed. If jewelry-making projects are planned, then smaller individual workstations could be used. If an SBE is going to be service oriented, such as a coffee and muffin shop, an

 Box 15–1 The Black Knight Coffee Shop Team

The Black Knight Coffee Shop

The Black Knights Coffee Shop was designed as an instructional program to teach students with moderate disabilities at Charlottesville High School domestic skills, community skills, vocational skills, and social interaction skills that will help prepare them for employment after high school. The program gives them an opportunity to operate a small nonprofit business at school and enhance their job experiences prior to leaving school.

The students participate in every aspect of the initiative. They named the coffee shop after our school mascot, "The Black Knight." They are responsible for planning, shopping, baking, coffee preparation, sales, serving, cleanup, restocking the cart, and financial accounting. Each day, the students put on their official uniforms and push the mobile coffee cart through the school, following a written delivery schedule. At each destination, they ask faculty and staff if they would like something from the cart. Next, they serve what was ordered. To simplify money handling, all items cost $1.00, including gourmet regular and decaffeinated coffee, hot chocolate, and assorted teas; applesauce spice muffins; big chocolate chip cookies; big oatmeal raisin granola bars; blueberry or peach muffins; and chocolate chip, cranberry, or raisin scones. Students also learn how to use a graph to keep a record of sales, count the money each day, and prepare it for deposit in the bank. Other activities include weekly trips out in the community to purchase the supplies needed for the coffee shop. While in the grocery store, students learn how to locate the items on the shopping list. They also learn basic estimation skills so that they can hand the cashier the correct number of dollar bills.

The skills taught as part of the Black Knight Coffee Shop include the following:

Personal Skills	• Dressing: Putting on a uniform • Hygiene: Hand-washing skills for food preparation/handling • Safety skills: Kitchen safety, awareness of working with hot foods/liquids
Housekeeping skills/domestics	• Cleanliness in the kitchen for food preparation • Washing/drying coffee pots, muffin tins, cookie sheets, and so forth • Laundering uniforms (learning to operate a washer and dryer) • Folding uniforms for daily storage • Clothing repair, as needed (sewing skills) • Following recipes for baking scones and muffins • Cleanup: Following a cleanup schedule to learn the task steps needed
Math skills	• Reading clocks • Using a timer for baking • Measuring liquid and dry ingredients • Taking orders and keeping inventory • Following steps (first, second, third, etc.)
Community-based instruction	• Preparation for shopping, including making a list and estimating how much money to bring • Shopping: Locating the items on the list at the store • Calculator skills for estimating the amount of money needed • Learning how to pay the cashier the correct number of dollars
Social skills	• Learning appropriate interactions with service personnel in the community • Learning appropriate interactions with school staff, faculty, and students
Vocational skills	• Experience acting as a cashier (collecting money, making change) • Learning how to serve food/coffee and follow customer requests • Delivery in a timely manner/keeping to a work schedule
Reading skills	• Following recipes • Reading and understanding orders • Reading shopping lists and aisle marker signs in grocery stores • Reading teachers' names from a list and matching them with names on the doors (for delivery)

Note: For more information, contact Mrs. Ellen Vigour, Special Education Teacher, Charlottesville High School, Ellen.Vigour@ccs.k12.va.us area equipped with kitchen equipment would be needed.

Organizational Considerations

An SBE should be organized to resemble a real work environment as much as possible. If a teacher has limited experience with business and industrial settings, consider contacting local industries and requesting the volunteer services of an industrial engineer to help design the SBE work area.

Next, consider how to set up and arrange the work area. At the same time, consider student abilities and needs to determine if work should be performed in an assembly line or start to finish. If possible, both options should be provided to increase the probability of skill generalization. Procedures should also be established for general work rules, appropriate dress, breaks, clocking in/out, evaluations, dismissals, layoffs, suspensions, and promotions. It is also important to develop an orientation process for all new student workers to teach them about policies/procedures when participating in the SBE. Just like in a real work place, students should be provided with written company policies and/or employee handbooks. Finally, opportunities should be made available in the SBE to experience different types of work, as well as to hold various positions, such as quality control supervisor, material handler, marketing director, inventory controller, accountant, and bookkeeper. Consider using these positions as a promotion and require that the student undergo an application and interview process.

Quality Considerations

The more realistic the SBE, the more likely that students will be able to successfully transfer the skills learned to jobs in the community. Keul (1991) developed a set of criteria to help ensure that SBEs are as realistic as possible:

1. Develop and use accurate task analyses that fully detail all steps for producing each service or product.
2. Develop and use simple methods for measuring the quality and speed of the student's work.
3. Following instructions, be sure that students (not teachers) perform the majority of the tasks.
4. Ensure that sufficient school resources and personnel are available to produce a quality product/service.
5. Guarantee that the SBE mirrors actual work demands in terms of stamina, endurance, and strength.

Finally, Keul (1991) suggested seven guidelines for determining products or services to be provided by an SBE:

Guideline 1: The service or product should be sellable in the community. Research market prices for services and products, quality/quantity demands, and consumer desires.

Guideline 2: The service or product should be feasible to produce within the SBE budget and time constraints, considering the school schedule, staff supervision, cost/benefits, storage, space, safety issues, and transportation of materials.

Guideline 3: The service or product should be beneficial to students in net profit (after expenses) and actual job skills gained. Are similar jobs available in the community?

Guideline 4: The service or product should be produced with minimal teacher intervention (other than initial training and ongoing supervision).

Guideline 5: The service or product should be valued and promote inclusion of students with disabilities. Consider joint projects with school clubs.

Guideline 6: The service or product should provide students with employment options for the future.

Guideline 7: The SBE should allow students to learn the work habits and work behaviors associated with success in real jobs.

The school-based enterprise created dessert trays for school and community gatherings. Serena was assigned the job of prep-cook, which included decorating the cookies with purple sprinkles for the dessert trays. In order for Serena to complete her assigned job, she needed specific skills, such as knowledge of safety and sanitation, following directions, time management, and following a recipe. These skills were addressed in Serena's annual IEP goals. Additionally, she was assigned a general education peer tutor to model and who would assist Serena in mastering the necessary skills for baking cookies.

On-Campus Jobs

Another school-based employment training option is on-campus jobs. On-campus jobs can be paid or unpaid work experiences in which students are placed in a real job on school grounds with supervision from a school employee. An on-campus job introduces students to a work environment that requires many of the same skills and same demands that they will encounter in community work settings. On-campus jobs can be part of a work-study program, which are designed for students with and without disabilities. NLTS2 found that almost 15% of students with disabilities held work-study jobs in a given school year (Wagner, Newman, Cameto, Levine, & Marder, 2003). Examples of on-campus jobs include cafeteria worker, office assistant, custodial assistant, teacher assistant, maintenance assistant, groundskeeper's assistant, bus maintenance assistant, physical education assistant, biology lab assistant, and art assistant.

While on-campus jobs can provide students with a variety of fairly realistic work settings, they should not take the place of community-based instruction. Nothing can take the place of work experience in the real world. On-campus jobs also offer the possibility of increasing student status if students with severe disabilities are seen by teachers and peers as providing needed school services, as well as opportunities to interact with their peers without disabilities in a work situation rather than in the classroom.

The transition planning process should be used to inform parents and students about the purpose and importance of on-campus job placements, as well as including them in the decision-making process. Making decisions and choices about on-campus job placements can provide opportunities for students to practice self-advocacy skills. The types of jobs, their duration, and training goals should be included in the transition component of the IEP. It is also a good idea to have parents and students sign a permission form for participating in an on-campus job to ensure that everyone is fully informed about performance expectations, compensation, duration of placement, and evaluation procedures.

Once on-campus job placements are identified, a job duties form listing all of the duties/tasks for each job should be developed. The job duties form can be used to assist the student and his or her work supervisor in understanding performance expectations. Task analyses can be prepared for individual job tasks listed on the job duties form if a student needs this level of instruction. In some cases, job task modification or accommodations will be needed for some students to participate in a particular on-campus job. For example, a student with limited language arts sills in a clerical assignment may need an alphabetizing guide to help with filing tasks. Finally, just like with a SBE, students will need an orientation session with each placement. During this session, the job duties form should be reviewed and a student contract documenting the student's agreement with the training placement, training, goals, performance expectations, and rules of behavior should be signed.

Job Clubs and Vocational Student Organizations

The final school-based employment training options are job clubs and vocational student organizations (VSOs). A job club can help students with disabilities develop job-seeking skills while providing systematic peer support for obtaining and maintaining a job. A job club can include students with and without disabilities. Although job clubs lack the national connections and occupational specificity associated with a VSO, these groups have greater flexibility to match local labor markets and student needs and interests.

Job clubs typically meet after school hours, once a week with a staff sponsor, and (a) provide peer support for job searches, (b) share job leads, (c) develop résumés and reference lists, (d) explore the local job market, (e) visit local businesses to meet with personnel directors, and/or (f) role-play job-seeking skills.

VSOs have similar goals, but their focus is often on helping students pursue the postschool training and education needed to obtain a career in a special occupational area. Examples of VSOs include Future Business Leaders of America, Future Farmers of America, Future Homemakers of America, Health Occupations Students of America, Technology Student Association, and Vocational Industrial Clubs of America.

Because Rusty has expressed an interest in developing and running his own business as a customized employment option, he has decided to join the Future Business Leaders of America (FBLA). This year, his school's FBLA club has decided to focus on the i-SAFE curriculum in order to learn about Internet safety during the fall semester. Then, he will work on the Practical Money Skills for Life *curriculum to learn about money management strategies during the spring semester. Both activities will help Rusty gain the skills and confidence that he needs to start his own computer business with the help of an employment specialist.*

U.S. Department of Labor Considerations for SBI

When scheduling school-based employment instructional activities, the U.S. Department of Labor's (DOL) guidelines must be followed for employment preparation for students with disabilities. The Fair Labor Standards Act (FLSA), which is administered by DOL outlines the rules and regulations governing minimum wage payments, overtime, equal pay, and record-keeping requirements for the payment of employees. School-operated employment preparation programs are not exempt from FLSA regulations and can be disciplined by DOL if labor regulations are ignored or violated. By following FLSA policies, school system personnel can be certain that program participants are treated in a fair and equitable manner and prevent the sanctioning of fines by DOL.

DOL standards provide greater latitude for employment preparation conducted on a school campus. Basically, DOL will not enforce FLSA with respect to minimum wages for students if a student is enrolled in a school-related employment preparation program as long as compliance with child labor provisions is ensured. However, school personnel must ensure that the purpose of the employment preparation activity is to benefit the student instead of meeting the labor needs of the school. For example, if a student is placed as a cafeteria assistant, the placement should be to learn about food service jobs and/or cashier skills (based on the student's needs) and not because the cafeteria needs additional help. In general, on-campus training should be limited to one period per day. Based on DOL policy, on-campus jobs can be viewed as unpaid employment preparation experiences unless the school district is contracting with a for-profit business for the service area in which the student is assigned. For example, if the school system is contracting with an outside lawn maintenance service, then a student cannot work with the groundskeepers unless he or she is compensated (Love, 1994). There are some exceptions to DOL's policy with regard to the application of FLSA to school campus employment preparation programs. For example, if a school is contracting with private businesses for students to perform work as a part of an SBE, then students must be paid at least minimum wage per hour unless the school has applied for and receive a subminimum wage certificate from DOL. Under no circumstances can students benefit private businesses by completing their work in an SBE unless students are compensated for the work performed.

Where to Provide Instruction: Community-Based Instruction Options

Community-based instruction (CBI) options can include paid and unpaid experiences, ranging from short-term job-shadowing/job-sampling assignments to long-term internships. The goal is to design an individualized instruction program that includes multiple options in order to meet the needs of all students so that as students get closer to graduation, training needs can change from exploring careers to developing specific employment skills.

According to Luecking (2009) and Test et al. (2006), there are six types of CBI options:

1. *Job Shadowing.* Job shadowing, sometimes called "work sampling," can be of short duration (1 to 3 hours) or an extended period of time (1 or more work days). The student follows an employee in a business as he or she performs his or her daily job. This can include "take your child to work" days. Job shadowing provides opportunities for students to try out a job by working alongside employees of area businesses and agencies, allowing them to develop a comprehensive understanding of the job duties associated with a particular position.

2. *Internships.* Internships allow students to spend an extended period of time at a single business in order to develop the specific skills and knowledge needed for that occupational area. Internships typically last for several weeks to months, can be paid or unpaid, and may involve earning high school credits.

3. *Apprenticeships.* Apprenticeships offer an opportunity to learn an occupation under the supervision of an experienced worker. Usually an apprenticeship lasts 3 to 4 years, with the student working part-time while in high school. Over time, the student assumes an increasing amount of responsibility on the job as more advanced skills are learned. Apprenticeships are paid work experiences and often high school credits are earned for participation. After graduation, the student continues to work with the company and can pursue additional postsecondary education/training related to the occupation. Apprenticeships can be sponsored by unions, public agencies, or a company/business. Examples of apprenticeships include furniture craftsperson, loom builders, and other highly skilled professionals who require on-the-job training and experience.

4. *Volunteerism/community service projects/service learning.* Individual or group volunteer projects can provide students with opportunities to learn and practice employment skills. All volunteer work should be recognized as such and should meet DOL guidelines for students with disabilities placed in volunteer settings. Students may never "volunteer" at for-profit businesses (Love, 1994).

5. *Mobile work crews or enclaves.* Mobile work crews or enclaves can provide a community-based instruction option for students who require more intensive supervision. Enclaves and mobile work crews involve a group of students who work for an area business or agency with continuous supervision. A mobile work crew moves from site to site, performing similar job tasks (e.g., landscaping, custodial). An enclave is stationed at one location with students working together to perform a set of job tasks. These employment preparation experiences may be paid or unpaid, but if actual work is performed for a business, then the student must be paid.

6. *Paid, competitive employment.* The opportunity to participate in paid employment experiences prior to graduation is a good predictor of a student's future employment success. These jobs can be scheduled during or after school, as well as during the summer.

Logistically, there are many issues to consider when planning CBI, including staffing, transportation, safety, insurance, and Fair Labor Standards Act (FLSA) regulations. A successful CBI program will have approved policies in place to ensure the ongoing, safe, affordable, and effective delivery of off-campus instruction for all students.

Staffing Considerations

CBI requires schools to rethink traditional methods of assigning staff and designing student schedules. The level and intensity of supervision required will be based on the type of training model used and students' needs. For example, during job shadowing and job sampling, employees at each business site can be used to train and supervise students. Also, job-shadowing sites are usually established for individual students versus groups of students, although a single site might provide multiple training options within a single location, in which case a school supervisor might be needed. If using mobile work crews, school staff will be needed

continuously to supervise a small group of students who need focused training and ongoing supervision.

Several resources can be used to staff CBI, including team teaching, the use of teacher assistants as job coaches, and integrating therapeutic support personnel into the program (Baumgart & VanWalleghem, 1986). Team teaching provides increased flexibility in scheduling classroom and community-based instruction by ensuring that both areas are covered by licensed staff. By training paraprofessionals (e.g., teacher's assistants) in safety issues, instructional strategies, transportation guidelines, and business relationships, they can assume a greater level of responsibility in the community.

Therapeutic support staff in the areas of physical therapy, speech therapy, and occupational therapy can provide valuable hands-on therapy in environments in which students will ultimately need these skills. Providing therapeutic support at a training site will result not only in additional staff for community-based training, but also increased skill generalization. In some cases, it is absolutely necessary to practice communication skills or mobility skills in real-life situations because the school environment cannot simulate community conditions (Baumgart, Johnson, & Helmstetter, 1990). For example, if a student is receiving mobility training or is learning to use a communication system, the best place to learn and practice these skills would be in a community work setting in which a student will ultimately work.

To help Cassandra choose which communication board with voice output to use in the workplace, her speech therapist has been coming to her community-based training site to provide her and her coworkers with practice using both italk2® and GoTalk 20+®. Her speech therapist started by helping to facilitate conversation during breaks and is now working with Cassandra's supervisor to teach them to interact about job-related duties. By doing this, Cassandra, her family, and coworkers can all help decide which augmentative communication system is best suited for the workplace.

Staffing resources can also be found outside of the school. For example, with proper orientation and training, volunteers (e.g., work buddies), college interns, and parents can assist with community-based training. If these options are not available and staffing is still a concern, the ways in which students are grouped and scheduled for CBI can be adjusted. Using a single site, combined with assistance from business employees, can reduce the number of school staff needed. For example, a large retail store can provide training sites for customer service, food service, stocking, clerical, plant or animal care, and custodial work all in one location. In this setting, students can be assigned throughout the business with designated employee supervisors. A single school staff person could then "float," supervising and instructing as needed. Hospitals, nursing centers, day-care centers, malls, and manufacturing plants are also good settings for multiple training options. Heterogeneous groupings can also be used to reduce the number of staff members needed by allowing cooperative learning and peer tutoring opportunities between students of varying abilities and students without disabilities (Baumgart & VanWalleghem, 1986).

Transportation Considerations

Without reliable and accessible transportation, a CBI program is not possible. Because of this, educators must consider the type of transportation that will be used, when transportation can be accessed, and the funding sources available to cover transportation costs. Transportation for CBI will require additional funds, but the actual cost will vary on the basis of the geographical characteristics of the school system and the type of transportation chosen. School staff should work closely with the system's Director of Transportation to ensure that staff are appropriately licensed to operate school-owned vehicles and that vehicles are available when needed.

Prior to establishing CBI sites, school personnel must know when and what transportation will be available. The most typical mode of transportation is school and activity buses. Other types of school-owned vehicles such as cars or vans might be appropriate, depending on state and local guidelines for transporting students during school hours. In an urban school system, public transportation can be used or students could walk to job sites. Finally, parents can be asked to provide transportation particularly, if the student is involved in competitive employment, which ends after school hours.

Safety Considerations

Educators and parents are always concerned about student safety. While classrooms located in a school building are perceived as being safe environments, they are not the most effective environment for delivering

employment preparation to students with severe disabilities. If students are expected to live, learn, work, and play in their community after graduation, then training in those settings must occur prior to graduation. As a result, the community must be viewed as an extension of the classroom for students with severe disabilities.

There are many methods for ensuring student safety while simultaneously protecting school staff from liability issues. It should be standard operating procedure for all parents and students to be fully informed about the various training components of a program, the types of community-based settings offered, and the expectations for behavior during CBI. This can be accomplished during IEP meetings when goals and objectives are written. Parents and students should sign written permission forms for all CBI activities. Even if the student is age 18 or older, it is still a good idea to involve parents in decisions about CBI. Parents should also be asked to provide medical information (e.g., medical conditions, allergies, medications, special care considerations, primary physician, health insurance) for their son or daughter and sign a permission form that allows their child to receive emergency medical care. These forms, along with basic contact information for each student, should be easily available to all CBI staff. In addition to easily accessible medical and health information, some other basic safety items include having students and staff wear ID tags at all times and having staff and students (if possible) carry cell phones. See Tabor, Alberto, Seltzer, and Hughes (2003) for a description of how six secondary school-aged students with moderate cognitive disabilities were taught to use a cell phone to call for assistance when lost in school or community settings.

Next, adequate training should be provided to students with regard to work safety before they participate in CBI. Because it cannot be assumed that students will engage in safe behavior at a job site, work-related safety skills should be included in the employment preparation curriculum (Pelland & Falvey, 1986). Work safety training should address identifying unsafe working conditions, practicing safe work behaviors, and responding appropriately to an accident. Because students with severe disabilities may also have medical conditions (e.g., seizures), sensory deficits, or motor impairments that can increase the likelihood of an accident, work safety should be considered a survival skill that is necessary for employment. Although businesses are responsible for ensuring a safe work environment, school personnel are also responsible for adequately training students in safety awareness skills. Otherwise, if a work-site accident occurs, liability issues might arise (Agran, Swaner, & Snow, 1998).

Insurance Coverage

Another factor that must be considered when planning a CBI program is insurance coverage (Test et al., 2006). Students should have some type of medical insurance coverage in case of an accident at the CBI site. Some students will have Medicaid and others may have private health coverage. One option is to have students covered through the school system's student insurance policy, which is usually available for a small annual fee. This ensures that students who are not otherwise covered will have a minimum policy in place.

Liability insurance for staff should also be provided. The school system's liability policy should be amended to provide coverage for employees who are conducting CBI activities as part of a student's educational program. Liability coverage should also be pursued for local businesses that sponsor training sites. In some cases, this type of insurance may already be in place for work-based training programs operated by the CTE department (e.g., cooperative education, apprenticeships) and can be extended for use by the special education program. Being able to offer liability insurance for businesses may encourage larger businesses and industries to host a training site.

Fair Labor Standards Act Considerations

As described above, child labor laws must be adhered to when delivering community-based instruction. Child labor laws fall under the Fair Labor Standards Act (FLSA), which governs several factors related to vocational training and competitive employment. CBI staff should be familiar with the federal regulations that govern the establishment of an employment relationship in order to prevent violations that could result in serious financial repercussions for the school system and its business partners. It is important to make sure that student participation in CBI is clearly for the benefit of the student and that it matches his or her postschool goals. In any case, where a student is benefiting a company or when an employer–employee relationship is established, a student must be compensated for his or her work.

In 1992, the U.S. Department of Labor (DOL) and the U.S. Department of Education (Education) jointly issued "Dear Colleague" letter that established guide-

lines for providing CBI to students with disabilities. These guidelines were designed to guarantee that when school systems implement training programs specifically aimed at student instruction, they are in compliance with federal guidelines in employment-related areas covered by the FLSA. The FLSA is administered and enforced by the DOL Wage-Hour Division and establishes minimum wage, overtime pay, equal pay, employment-related record-keeping requirements, and child labor regulations.

If *all* of the trainee criteria stated in the Departments of Labor/Education letter are met for each and every student at each and every community-based vocational training site, the school system should meet the requirements set forth in FLSA. School staff must ensure that students' needs are met first (over the needs of business), with the employer deriving no advantage, and that students are not being used to displace employees, fill positions, provide additional services, or relieve employees of regularly assigned duties. This means that a business cannot avoid hiring needed employees, use present employees to perform additional duties, or terminate employees because of the presence of community-based student trainees. When Pumpian, Fisher, Certo, Engle, and Mautz (1998) reviewed and analyzed litigation related to conducting unpaid, community-based training, they discovered that the courts examine four factors when determining employer benefit and the educational relevance of training. Based on these rulings, schools should evaluate training placements by asking questions regarding these same four factors:

1. Does the employer derive first and primary benefit?
2. Does the employer derive substantial benefit?
3. Does the trainee replace regular workers?
4. Is the experience educationally valid?

In addition, some of the reasons associated with a failure to meet FLSA criteria for establishing training situations include the following:

• Trainees are working at the convenience of the employer.
• Training is so poorly organized that the trainees receive no advantage.
• Trainees are being counted as staff members and are responsible for their own training.
• Employers are being allowed to review training performance prior to actually hiring the trainee for a paid position.

- The profit structure of the business is significantly improved by the presence of trainees.
- There is a reduction in the number of paid employees because of the work of the trainees.
- Trainees are responsible for learning skills through their own initiative.

Test et al. (2006) offer additional suggestions based on the FLSA for school systems to follow when designing and implementing vocational training programs:

1. The transition component of the IEP for each student involved in unpaid community-based vocational training should clearly state the goals and objectives for training. Training should be relevant to the student's postsecondary employment outcomes. Ideally, students should be given the opportunity to choose among a variety of training sites.
2. Prior to placement on a training site, student trainees should receive an orientation. Once students are at the work site, comprehensive training should be provided, and staff should assess student skills during the training period. Teacher checklists, anecdotal records, portfolios, rubrics, and performance graphs are all methods of evaluation that are appropriate for community-based training sites.
3. Training conducted at the work site should directly relate to the goals on the student's IEP. The IEP goals and objectives serve as the justification for student's placement at a particular site and confirm that the placement is to meet the student's needs.
4. Although the time limits set forth in the DOL/Education memorandum of understanding for vocational exploration, vocational training, and vocational assessment will not be the sole basis on which an employment relationship will be determined, these time frames should be followed as closely as possible. However, flexibility should be allowed because students learn at different rates.
5. All unpaid community-based vocational training should be conducted within normal school hours and should be founded on documented student needs.
6. Parental permission must be obtained for a student's participation in the community-based vocational training program. Parents may be kept informed of changes in the program and of the student's progress. The parental permission form should contain (a) a statement concerning student insurance, (b) an indication as to how the student's

performance at the training site will be used to determine grades or credits, (c) a clear statement indicating that the student will not be entitled to wages or to a job after the completion of training, (d) a statement concerning transportation arrangements, and (e) a statement granting permission for school staff to obtain medical care for the student in the event of an emergency at the training site.

7. A release-of-information form should be signed for each student so that relevant information about the student can be shared with appropriate representatives of the business at the training site.
8. Students should sign a written agreement concerning their participation in the community-based vocational training program. The student agreement should contain the following information: (a) how performance at the training site will affect grades or credits, (b) a clear statement indicating that there is no entitlement to wages or a job after completion of the training, (c) behavioral expectations, and (d) consequences for behavior problems related to the training site.
9. Signed written agreements should be in place between the school system and the local businesses and industries that are providing the training sites. These agreements should include the responsibilities of the local business, FLSA compliance issues, the responsibilities of the school, the schedule for community-based vocational training, and any other special conditions that are relevant to the training site.
10. There should be clearly designated supervisors for all students on community-based vocational training sites. If a member of the school staff is not going to be present at all times on the training site, an employee of the business should be designated as the students' supervisor. Also, a member of the school staff should be designated as the indirect supervisor and school contact for the training site.
11. Records (e.g., timesheets) should be maintained that indicate the dates and times that a student is involved in various community-based training experiences. Students should be given responsibility for maintaining these records and adult assistance should be provided if needed.

These guidelines can help ensure that the primary focus of the community-based training experience is on the needs of the student, not focused on the interests of the participating businesses (Test et al., 2006).

Because Cassandra was enrolled in general education classes in high school, she has not yet decided on a career. So, as part of Cassandra's program for 18 to 21-year-olds, her IEP team has worked together to develop a set of CBI experiences to help her make an "educated" choice. First, based on talking with Cassandra and her family, it was decided that she will have the opportunity to job shadow at three job sites, including the local public library; a small business that operates both a greenhouse and a plant store; and the local city hall, which includes many different types of clerical and office assistant opportunities. If Cassandra likes one or more of these options, as indicated by her input and her hours at the job site, she will then be able to spend longer periods of time at each site as a paid, or unpaid, employee. At the same time, she will receive mobility and transportation training to help her get to each site. Additionally, she will receive communication systems training for herself and her coworkers at each site. By having experience with a job, transportation, and communication at a variety of possible workplaces, Cassandra and her family will have multiple sources of information to use in order to help her choose a potentially fulfilling career.

How to Provide Instruction

When teaching employment skills in school and community settings, it is important to preserve the dignity of the student by not calling attention to him or her, while at the same time using effective instructional strategies. Therefore, it is recommended that when teaching employment skills, you use whole-task chaining, constant time delay, audio prompting, and/or self-instruction as your instructional strategies. (See Chapter 4 for further discussion of instructional strategies.)

Whole-Task Chaining

In whole-task chaining, training occurs in a forward manner (from the first step in the task analysis to the last step), and each step is performed by the student during every instructional session. The teacher provides assistance, as needed, and gives corrective feedback only on steps in which a student needs assistance. The whole task is taught to a predetermined criterion level (e.g., two whole sequences without assistance). Whole-task chaining (Certo, Mezzulo, & Hunter, 1985) has several advantages when teaching skills in the community. First, with whole task chaining, students practice each step in the task analysis every time a skill is

taught. Second, steps are taught and learned in the order in which they actually occur. Third, you do not have to continuously repeat a step (e.g., having to complete Step 4 three times without error before moving to Step 5) because multiple trial instruction of the same step can be boring. Fourth, practicing the whole task instead of part of the task makes the most efficient use of community instructional time because each time you train, the entire task is completed (e.g., a check is cashed, a sandwich is purchased, a job task is completed). However, if a student is not having success on a particular step in the task analysis, it can be helpful to remove that step from the task analysis and practice that step in isolation until the step is performed at an acceptable level.

Constant Time Delay

Time delay involves first providing a student with immediate prompts at the level required to ensure errorless learning (i.e., verbal, gestural, modeling, physical guidance) and then providing the same prompt only if the student does not perform the correct response. When this happens, the teacher should provide a prompt after a short waiting period in which the student is provided with an opportunity to respond independently. That is, if the student does not know how to respond, he or she should to be taught to wait and the teacher will provide him or her with the correct answer using the most effective prompt. There are two types of time delay. In *progressive* time delay, during each training session, the teacher gradually increases the wait interval before a prompt is given. In *constant* time delay, the wait interval remains the same during all training sessions.

Test, Walker, and Richter (2008) recommend constant time delay for teaching job skills because it has three advantages: (a) the prompt that always elicits a correct response from a student is used from the beginning, which should decrease training time; (b) time delay involves always using the single most effective prompt for an individual (rather than a series of prompts); and (c) having a single constant prompt time is easier to keep track of. As a result, constant time delay is usually the least intrusive prompting strategy. Although during initial training (at a 0-second delay), time delay might be intrusive depending on the level of prompt used. See Chapter 4 for a description of time delay.

Cassandra is learning to use her debit card in a vending machine during break time at her CBI site. After developing an appropriate task analysis, her teacher identified that the most effective prompts for Cassandra was to model the correct response. At the 0-second delay interval, the initial request is made, "Insert your card" (i.e., the first step in the task analysis), at the same time that the teacher models inserting the card, then immediately says, "Now you do it. Insert your card." Training should continue at the 0-second delay interval for all steps for the task analysis. After several successful instructional sessions using the 0-second delay interval, the teacher would then lengthen the delay interval to 4 seconds. During the 4-second delay interval, the initial request is made, "Insert your card." If Cassandra does not respond correctly within 4 seconds, or if she responds incorrectly, the most effective prompt (teacher model) is provided. Once a step is completed, the teacher then waits 4 seconds for Cassandra to start the next step in the task analysis before using the most effective prompt. If Cassandra correctly completes the step, then no prompt is given and the next step is attempted, and so forth, until the entire task is completed.

Audio Prompting

Because CD players, iPods™, and other electronic devices are now widely used by people in the community, using these devices to provide students with auditory prompts is a very unobtrusive strategy that can be used to facilitate skill generalization to other places or when the teacher is not there. Auditory prompting systems have been used when teaching vocational tasks (Grossi, 1998; Post & Storey, 2002). When using audio prompts to teach and/or facilitate generalization with community skills, Test et al. (2008) suggest using either a step-by-step instructional format or step-by-step instruction with inserted evaluation questions.

When using a *step-by-step instructional format, the whole task analysis* is read and recorded. The script should include instructions for successfully completing each step in the task analysis. Remember to leave enough time between instructions for the student to compete each step. While this process has been used to successfully teach new skills, Test et al. (2008) recommend that it be used after a student has learned how to do the task as a way to help the student remember how to successfully complete the task when the teacher is not present. For example, once a student has learned how to perform a job task, the task could be recorded and played each time the student needed to perform the task in their job.

Using *step-by-step instruction with inserted self-evaluation questions* is the same as the previous strategy except that at the end of the instructions, a series of self-evaluation questions are provided. For example, after completing a job task, the following questions might be heard: "Did you remember to complete all steps?" and "Did you ask for help if you got stuck?"

Self-Instruction

Because real-life workplaces are often busy, constantly changing places, if a student can learn to provide his or her own prompts, the chances of success should increase. Self-instruction is one strategy that can be used to facilitate this process and is appropriate for students who have some language, can attend to auditory and visual stimuli, and can initiate communication. Agran and Moore (1994) suggest that prior to initiating self-instruction training, a student should be provided with a clear explanation of the strategy, as well as its benefits.

Training sessions should use a model–practice–feedback–reinforcement format. All of the methods of self-instruction can be modified to use verbal labels, self-reinforcement, picture cues, self-monitoring, peer tutors, and group instruction in order to meet a wide variety of student needs. Before beginning self-instruction, a task analysis should be prepared and training sequences should be developed from the task analysis. Agran and Moore (1994) described four types of self-instruction strategies:

1. *Problem solving.* This method of self-instruction teaches students to identify and resolve problems in a workplace by stating the problem, coming up with a solution, and directing him or herself to perform the planned response. This approach can be used when running out of supplies/materials, misplacing a tool/item, and needing to ask a question.

   Serena is learning to follow a task analysis for making coffee. In Step 3, she must lay out the coffee filters because there will be times when the coffee filter container is empty. For this step, her teacher has taught her to ask, "Are there enough filters?" (If yes, do the next step, or, if no, get the container from the storage cabinet.)

2. *Did–Next–Now.* This method of self-instruction is useful with sequenced tasks and involves stating what task was just completed (Did: "I did . . ."), which task needs to be done next (Next: "Next, I . . ."), and directions to perform that task (Now: "Now, I . . .").

For example, Serena might say to herself, "I did lay out the coffee filters; next, I place one scoop of coffee on the filter."

This strategy can be used when students are performing sequenced job tasks such as cleaning a house, bulk mailing, packaging materials, and/or collating projects.

3. *What–Where.* This self-instruction strategy is appropriate for students who can already perform a task, but are not consistent or have difficulty with skill generalization. When using this strategy, the student reminds him or herself of what needs to be done (What) and where the task is to be performed (Where). This method can be used in jobs where the student is assigned to more than one area of a business (e.g., cleaning offices or motel rooms).

For example, since Serena prepares the coffee in the dining area, but must wash the coffee pot in the kitchen, she could be taught to remind herself, "I finished making coffee, now I need to wash the pot in the kitchen."

4. *Interactive Did–Next–Ask.* The final self-instruction strategy is appropriate for tasks that require social interactions in the area of customer service. Repeating the self-instruction aloud reminds the student about what to do while performing the task and interacting with another person, without making a negative impression on others. With the first verbalization (Did) a student is reminded of the task just completed. The second step (Next) directs a student to do the next step of the process. The third step (Ask) involves a student asking a question of the person with whom he or she is interacting. For example, a student can use this strategy when preparing a sandwich, taking a food order, checking in dry cleaning, assisting a customer in picking up a pre-ordered item, or gift-wrapping.

Serena is now working at the counter filling coffee orders for customers. To help her remember the task, as well as interact with the customers, she is taught to say, "I put coffee in your cup, next I need to find out what extras I need to add, would you like cream or sugar in your coffee?"

In conclusion, all CBI should be delivered with the understanding that ultimately the student must be able to perform the job skills independently even if a long-term job coach is going to be available. During training, the instructor must teach each student how to continuously assess his or her own performance and then seek out the natural job supports that will eventually lead to a level of independence comparable to that of coworkers without disabilities.

How to Collect Instructional Data

Because most employment skills are chained tasks, Test et al. (2008) suggest that task analytic-assessment strategies be used with the following modifications. First, use an upside-down or self-graphing format (see Figure 15-5 for an example). To make a self-graphing task analysis, start by putting the first step in the task analysis at the bottom of the page, with additional steps placed above it in reverse order. Step numbers are then placed in columns to the right of each written step. As a student completes the task, each correctly performed step is marked with an X. Incorrect responses are not marked. After the task is completed, the number of X's are counted and the number that represents the total number of X's is circled in that column. For example, on September 7, Cassandra correctly completed one step; on September 8, Cassandra correctly completed three steps; and, on September 9, she completed four steps correctly. A graph is then made by connecting the circled numbers. Since a graph depicting student progress is generated as data are collected, the self-graphing data collection strategy makes instructional decision making easy because you can see any problematic steps and use that information to make modifications the next time you teach the skill.

Second, Test et al. (2008) suggest that data do not need to be collected every time you teach a skill. In school, it is easy to collect data on every step that a student takes. However, when training in the community, they suggest using probes to gather student performance data. Using probes, the teacher can instruct for a while, then step back, watch the student perform the task without providing assistance, and collect the data. Data collection sheets could be kept out of sight in a pocket notebook during instruction and pulled out only during probes. If the task analysis is short, data can even be recorded at a later time. The idea is to collect only enough data to allow instructional decisions to be made in order to determine if the student is learning the skill.

Cassandra is prompted through the task analysis two or three times and then the teacher steps back and conducts a data collection probe using a self-graphing task analysis. This method is fast and provides useful data.

FIGURE 15–5
Upside-Down Task Analysis

Sample Self-Graphing Task Analysis: Cleaning Sinks and Mirrors						
Steps						
12. Put flowers back	12	12	12	12	12	12
11. Put soap dishes back	11	11	11	11	11	11
10. Wipe with paper towel*	10	10	10	10	10	10
9. Spray top middle part of mirrors	9	9	9	9	9	9
8. Rinse sinks	8	8	8	8	8	8
7. Turn on water	7	7	7	7	7	7
6. Wipe sink with paper towels	6	6	6	6	6	6
5. Wipe containers with paper towels	5	5	X̶	5	5	5
4. Spray sink with disinfectant	4	4	④	4	4	4
3. Spray containers with disinfectant	3	⊗	X̶	3	3	3
2. Take flowers out of containers	2	X̶	X̶	2	2	2
1. Take off soap dishes	⊗	X̶	X̶	1	1	1
Key:	9/07	9/08	9/09	9/10	9/11	9/12
X – Correct step O – Total No. Correct						

*Note: For step 10, wipe with paper towel, from side to side and from top to bottom until dry.

In order to gather enough data in an unobtrusive manner, consider the following: (a) conduct at least one data collection probe every day that you teach the skill, (b) once a skill is mastered (as per your criteria), switch to a once-a-week probe, and (c) after three weekly probes, switch to monthly probes.

Finally, Test et al. (2008) recommend teaching students to collect their own data. Having students learn to record their own performance (often called self-monitoring or self-recording) may itself increase the likelihood of independent and generalized performance. In addition, self-monitoring is unobtrusive because the student can record his or her own data and then review it with the teacher at a later time. (See Chapter 5 for additional measurement strategies.)

Using Assistive Technology

As technology advances, so do the possibilities for individuals with severe disabilities to live and work independently within the community. Mobility, communication, and environmental control devices are now available that open doors that were previously closed in the business world. In many cases, the only limits placed on accessing career possibilities through assistive technology are those of funding and staff expertise.

IDEA (2004) defines the term *assistive technology device* as "any item, piece of equipment, or product system, whether acquired commercially off the shelf, modified, or customized, that is used to increase, maintain, or improve the functional capabilities of a child with a disability" (Sec. 602 USC 1401). Assistive technology can be high-tech or low-tech. Low-tech devices are simple and low cost, including materials such as nonskid mats, VELCRO® attachments, reachers, and pencil grips. Many low-tech devices can be purchased in the community or can be designed from commonly available materials. High-tech devices are commercially manufactured by specialized vendors, expensive, and involve a high level of electronics or computerized components.

Because Cassandra has recently been approved for a Medicaid waiver, she has many options for both low-tech and high-tech assistive technology devices. Specifically, Cassandra's teacher and family have begun to use Pic Syms on a ring, a low-tech device that provides Cassandra with a simple tool to communicate her needs during community-based instruction. (For more information, go to http://assistivetech .sf.k12.sd.us/picsyms.htm.) They have also purchased a high-tech device, a talking photo album, for Cassandra. The talking photo album records up to 4 minutes of speech per page and will support Cassandra's independence, promote communication with her family and teachers, enhance her social capabilities, and facilitate communication at school and in community settings.

A major part of the transition process for students with physical, communication, and/or sensory disabilities should be to ensure that proper technological devices are accessible to students for use in all domains of their life. Usually, teachers, parents, and other persons involved in a student's transition from school to postsecondary life will seek to solve problems by using the simplest assistive technology devices first and work up the continuum to more complex devices if necessary to meet a student's needs (Geary, Griffin, & Hammis, 2006). Although assistive technology is not going to eliminate all barriers to employment, it should not be considered a luxury. For some individuals, assistive technology is a necessity that, unless used, will likely eliminate the possibility of competitive employment (Scherer & Galvin, 1996). Use of assistive technology in the workplace is often included in discussions on reasonable job accommodations for an individual with disabilities. Data from the Job Accommodations Network (JAN) indicates that most accommodations cost less than $500. More information is available at www.jan.wvu.edu

It is important to remember that the assistive technology devices that are used in school for instructional purposes may not be appropriate for community use. In school, trained educators and therapists are available to facilitate the use of devices, make adjustments/repairs to devices, and modify the environment to maximize the effectiveness of a device. However, in the community, the student will be involved in situations where the use of assistive technology is virtually nonexistent. Therefore, it is imperative that students receive a comprehensive assessment by a team of qual-ified professionals to determine the type of assistive device(s) that will be needed for the various work environments encountered during training and competitive employment. Test et al. (2006) offer suggestions for ensuring that a student's success at the work site is enhanced through the use of assistive technology:

1. Consider issues such as portability (i.e., the ease with which the device can be transported), expansion (i.e., the potential of the device to be expanded as a student's vocational needs change), maintenance (i.e., the ease with which the device can be maintained and repaired), adaptability (i.e., the ability of the device to be used in a wide range of environments and situations), and preference (i.e., what type of device is the student most at ease using).

2. Get specialists (e.g., physical therapist, speech therapist, occupational therapist) involved in the planning sessions.

3. Access the services of a rehabilitation engineer through Vocational Rehabilitation. Rehabilitation engineers can provide evaluation and assessment of the client, environment, and equipment; information about technology; recommendations for modifications, adaptations, and prototype development; and follow-up services to the individual to determine the ongoing effectiveness of the technology.

4. Identify possible funding sources, including traditional Medicaid, Medicaid waiver programs, Vocational Rehabilitation, public schools, private insurance, supplemental security income work incentives, and private pay.

5. Provide orientation periods in the work environment to evaluate the effectiveness of a device.

6. Ensure that the employer and key employees in the business understand the importance of the assistive device to the student's success and have been given strategies for supporting the student in the use of the device.

7. If school personnel have been primarily responsible for coordinating the purchase, upgrading, and maintenance of assistive devices for the student, measures must be taken prior to graduation to provide the student and the family with the knowledge needed to conduct these activities in the future.

Meeting Medical and Health Needs

Some students with severe disabilities who will be participating in employment training will have medical or health considerations that require advanced planning and accommodations. These may include conditions such as seizure disorders, metabolic disorders, bowel/urinary conditions, asthma, diabetes, and heart conditions. From an early age, the goal for students with medical/health needs should be to teach them about their conditions and to implement health care procedures (e.g., glucose monitoring, administration of medication, colostomy/ileostomy care, catheterization) as independently as possible. The first priority for a student with a medical problem is maintaining and improving his or her health. Preparing for future employment can actually enhance the health of an individual because of the emotional and psychological benefits associated with independence and community inclusion. Some practices and strategies to be considered when planning community-based training and job placement for students with medical/health conditions include the following:

1. Gather all information about a student's medical condition by obtaining signed releases from the student and/or the parent in order to obtain medical records, including names and contact information for all physicians and/or specialists, the student's medical history, prescribed medications, specialized medical procedures, physical restrictions, prognoses, and any other health-related information.

2. Help parents obtain a physician's opinion about the types of work environments and tasks in which the student might encounter difficulties.

3. Develop a packet for each student that contains parental permission for participation in community-based vocational training, specific instructions for performing all medical or health procedures, basic medical information (e.g., allergies, schedule for administering medication, side effects of medications, medical emergency information, physician contact information), parental permission for emergency medical care, and any work restrictions. Make work supervisors (school and/or business) aware of the information and where it is located.

4. Use transition planning sessions to help parents and students use physician recommendations, situational assessment results, and student interests to design employment preparation experiences that will lead to a job.

5. Provide training to enable the student to independently perform medical care procedures and self-administer medication.

6. Determine the types and amount of medical equipment and supplies that will be needed and a

method for ensuring their accessibility to the student while on the job site.

7. Teach students self-advocacy skills in order to coordinate their health care, including negotiating and problem solving with medical care professionals regarding changes in medical care that can facilitate employment, with adult services providers regarding services needed for employment, and with the employer regarding job accommodations and modifications.

8. Involve therapeutic support staff and school health professionals in planning for employment preparation activities and job placement.

Cassandra has spastic quadriplegic cerebral palsy, which requires her to use a manual wheelchair for mobility. The wheelchair has been adapted with trunk support and subasis bar. She uses her right hand to manipulate larger items and uses her left hand for stabilization. Cassandra receives physical therapy once each week for 30 minutes and has ongoing therapeutic services in the classroom including positioning on adaptive equipment. She wears ankle–foot orthotics for stability when using a stander and a left hand–elbow mobilizer. Cassandra's physical therapist would like for her to have a motorized wheelchair, but funds are not available. Cassandra also receives occupational therapy on a consultative basis. Her teacher and occupational therapist have been working on developing vocationally related jigs. Additionally, Cassandra has little intelligible speech other than single words and yes/no responses. She uses an iTalk2 to communicate simple needs and choices and is learning to use a GoTalk 20+. She does not use an augmentative communication device at home, but has a picture board that transitions with her among school, community, and home. Cassandra receives speech therapy twice a week.

Adult Outcomes and Meaningful Employment Outcomes

Developing employment skills in high school is key to preparing students with severe disabilities for postschool employment. In this next section, postschool employment opportunities are discussed, including (a) supported employment, (b) natural supports, and (c) customized employment.

Supported Employment

Beginning in the 1980s, supported employment emerged as an alternative employment model for providing individuals with severe disabilities employment options other than working in sheltered workshops (Wehman, Gibson, Brooke, & Unger, 1998). As youth with disabilities transition from school to work, it is important that they have the same employment opportunities as their peers without disabilities. Youth with disabilities should have the opportunity to move from school into integrated working environments and should be provided with the necessary supports to be successful in integrated work environments (Luecking, 2009). *Supported employment* was originally defined in the 1986 Rehabilitation Act Amendments (P.L. 99-506) as "competitive work in an integrated work setting with ongoing services for individuals with severe handicaps for whom competitive employment has not traditionally occurred, or has been interrupted or intermittent as a result of severe handicaps, or transitional employment for individuals with chronic mental illness." The purpose of supported employment is to assist individuals with disabilities in becoming and remaining competitively employed in integrated work settings (Wehman & Revell, 1997).

Data on the cost-effectiveness of supported employment as compared to sheltered workshops indicate that supported employment is more cost-effective for tax payers than sheltered workshops (Cimera, 2006). For example, in 2002, the cost of supported employment for the federal government was $108 million ($915.25 per person) versus $488 million ($1,010.35 per person) for sheltered workshops (Cimera, 2006). In addition to cost-effectiveness data, Test et al. (2000) found that individuals with disabilities who participated in supported employment were invariably satisfied with the supported employment jobs that they chose, as well as services provided by their job coaches. Additional benefits of supported employment have included higher wages, integration, ongoing support, and increased benefits for individuals with disabilities (Johnson, 2004; ODEP, 2009a). Supported employment includes the four models discussed below.

Individual Placement Model

This model involves one individual with a disability working in an integrated setting with a job coach to help the individual with a disability perform specific job tasks. Job coach responsibilities include on-the-job training and advocacy for the individual with a disability (Kellerman, 2001; ODEP, 2009a).

Mobile Work Crew Model

This model involves a group of individuals with disabilities (i.e., up to six) who move from job site to job site in order to perform job-related tasks (e.g., landscaping, gardening, painting) in various community settings. The crew is supervised by a job coach to ensure that they are performing the job-related tasks correctly at each job site (ODEP, 2009a; Test et al., 2006).

Enclave Model

This model involves a group of individuals with disabilities (i.e., 5 to 8) who work at one integrated job site and perform a variety of job-related tasks under the supervision of a job coach. The job coach provides ongoing support to the individuals with disabilities (ODEP, 2009a; Test et al., 2006).

Small Business Model

This model involves a group of individuals with disabilities (i.e., up to 6) and individuals without disabilities who operate a small business within a community setting. The business operates like any other small business would by providing work and paying employees like a typical business (ODEP, 2009a).

Natural Supports

The idea of natural supports was developed out of the supported employment concept. The Office of Disability Employment Policy (ODEP, 2009a) defines *natural supports* as "support from supervisors and co-workers, such as mentoring, friendships, socializing at breaks and/or after work, providing feedback on job performance, or learning a new skill together at the invitation of a supervisor or co-workers." There are several benefits to natural supports. First, natural supports provide social integration among the employer, coworkers, and the employee with a disability. Second, natural supports tend to be more permanent because they are readily available in the work place. Third, because natural supports are a part of the work environment, job retention tends to be more long term (ODEP, 2009a). Additionally, Cimera (2007) found natural supports to be significantly more cost-effective than supported employment because they reduce the cost of hiring job coaches.

When discussing the use of natural supports in the work place versus supported employment with a job coach, it is important to identify how natural supports work. Trach and Sheldon (1999) identified six categories of natural supports, including organizational, physical, social, training, community, and family/personal supports.

1. *Organizational supports* refer to preparing and organizing job activities in order to facilitate successful employment outcomes for the employee with a disability (e.g., work schedule, supplies, child care).
2. *Physical supports* refer to the design and function of physical objects in the job setting (e.g., computer equipment, accessibility ramps, assistive technology).
3. *Social service supports* include disability-related services to facilitate successful employment outcomes (e.g., personal assistant, residential services provider).
4. *Training support* involves training and instruction on specific job skills that are provided by the employer or a coworker(s). This may include providing the employee with a disability a task analysis for completing the job task or picture checklists.
5. *Community supports* involve identification of community agencies and services that can be accessed by the employee with a disability in order to facilitate movement to the job site and to improve employability skills (e.g., public transportation, compensatory education courses).
6. *Personal and family supports* involve networks of family and friends to help with the support needs of the employee with a disability (e.g., a self-advocacy group, family members to provide employment referrals).

Finally, Trach and Mayhall (1997) found that the key component in utilizing natural supports was an effective planning process that prepared individuals in the work environment to provide accommodations and supports to employees with disabilities.

Customized Employment

Although postschool outcomes for individuals with disabilities are improving, it is still true that individuals with severe disabilities are least likely to participate in postschool employment (Griffin, Hammis, Geary, & Sullivan, 2008; Wagner et al., 2006). In an effort to meet the employment needs of individuals with severe disabilities, the Office of Disability Employment Policy in 2001 began to fund projects that offered customized

employment to individuals with severe disabilities (Lueking & Lueking, 2006). *Customized employment* means "individualizing the relationship between job seekers and employers in ways that meet the needs of both. It is based on an individualized determination of the strengths, requirements, and interests of a person with a complex life" (ODEP, 2009b). Specifically, job tasks are developed based on the needs of the employer and the employee with a disability. Customized employment can benefit not only the individual with a disability, but the employer as well because it meets the vocational goals of the employee and the work-related needs of the employer (Elinson, Frey, Li, Palan, & Horne, 2008). There are four key elements in customized employment: (a) meeting the needs and interests of the individual with a disability, (b) utilizing a person to represent the individual with a disability (e.g., counselor, job developer, advocate, employment specialist), (c) successfully negotiating with the employer, and (d) developing a system of ongoing supports for the individual with a disability (ODEP, 2009b). Benefits of customized employment include competitive employment for individuals with severe disabilities, career advancement, competitive pay (i.e., at least minimum wage), job satisfaction, and integration (Fesko, Varney, DiBiase, & Hippenstiel, 2008).

Family Roles in Transition

When considering the transition to postschool life, family members play a key role in ensuring successful postschool outcomes for individuals with severe disabilities. Family involvement has been identified as one of the primary components of best practices in transitioning from secondary education (Kohler & Field, 2003). Families should be involved throughout the entire transition planning process and are often the determining factor in whether a student succeeds or fails in obtaining postschool employment (Test et al., 2006). However, eliciting family involvement is one of the greatest challenges that special educators face. It becomes the special educator's role to initiate family involvement and help families prepare their children to meet postschool goals. It is important for teachers to develop strong relationships with parents in order to support and promote successful transitioning from school to adult life for students with severe disabilities (Rowe, 2009).

Heslop and Abbott (2007) described four themes related to parents' perceptions of the transition planning process: (a) being connected with other families and professionals throughout the process provided social and emotional support with regard to the in-school and postschool needs of their children, (b) being proactive as they moved through the transition planning process helped facilitate their child's movement from school to postschool life, (c) receiving sufficient information with which to make informed choices about postschool options was extremely important, and (d) forward planning and adequate preparation time were extremely important in promoting successful transitions into adulthood for their children.

Parents can contribute to the transition planning process in several ways, they can (a) support their child's development of self-determination skills; (b) become actively involved in community-based employment preparation; (c) help their child obtain and maintain competitive employment; (d) act as a liaison as their child navigates through the adult services system; and (e) be a deciding factor in whether their child obtains his or her postschool goals for education, employment, and independent living (Test et al., 2006). However, as mentioned previously, eliciting family involvement can be a challenge for teachers. Test et al. (2006) identified 11 strategies to promote family involvement as students progress through the transition planning process:

1. Prepare elementary school teachers to be able to talk with families in the area of transition and employment for students with disabilities. By doing this, teachers can provide parents with information that will help them to begin thinking about self-determination, normalization, and person-centered planning when their child is at a young age. Teachers can also begin setting the expectation that their child will graduate from high school and move forward to postschool employment, education, and independent living options. Additionally, parents can assist students at an early age in developing the skills needed to attain postschool goals (e.g., reading stories about employment options, doing household chores, developing money skills by budgeting allowance).

2. Provide parent training opportunities to allow parents to develop the necessary skills to help their child with career choices. Parents can assist with job searches and job attainment. There are several ways in which to conduct parent training, including Webinars, podcasts, written products, family-night opportunities, and small-group or individual training sessions. Parent Training and Information Centers (also called Pacer Centers) are an additional source for information about family involvement. For more information, go to http://www.pacer.org

3. Keep parents informed by ensuring that they are included in all communications. Parents should be informed about how important a role they play in the transition planning process in that they have valuable information regarding their child that other team members lack.

4. Minimize, as much as possible, the emphasis placed on documents and forms at meetings because they can often be intimidating for parents. Additionally, avoid the use of jargon because it can make parents feel as if they are not members of the teams. Be sure that meetings are parent friendly and that all team members make parents feel that they are capable members who can understand the system, make informed and objective decisions, and be partners in their child's postschool preparation.

5. Be considerate and sensitive to cultural diversity issues that may arise while planning for the child's future.

6. Build a relationship with parents that helps them understand that you want their child to lead a successful postschool life. Become dedicated and involved with the student and parents as they dream about the child's future plans for education, employment, and independent living.

7. Establish a network of support for parents. By assisting in the establishment of parent networks and support groups, parents have the opportunity to interact with other families of youth with disabilities as they progress through the transition planning process. Such networks give parents the opportunity to express their fears and concerns with others who are in similar situations.

8. Encourage parents to be involved and talk with their child about their jobs and career paths. Parents can provide job-shadowing opportunities and can model strong work ethics for their child.

9. Help parents set reasonable and high expectations for their child. Often, parents of youth with severe disabilities do not recognize the opportunities that their child has for part-time or full-time employment once he or she graduates from high school.

10. Keep parents informed about all transition assessment information and be sure to include parents in the transition assessment process. They can provide valuable information about their child. Be sure that transition planning is based on the student's strengths, needs, and preferences to let parents know that decisions are based on their child's abilities. Also, interviews with parents can help identify natural supports within the student's family life that can assist the student with job development, job-shadowing opportunities, and mentoring.

11. Meet the needs of the family first as you support students as they enter postschool life. Families may need assistance with transportation, financial planning, understanding Supplemental Security Income and adult services agencies, and overcoming the fears associated with the student's transition from high school to postschool life.

In addition to these strategies, it is important to keep families informed about all aspects of the transition planning process (e.g., best practices, adult services agency roles, transition assessment, financial planning). Implementation of these strategies can assist schools in promoting active family involvement that can be very beneficial for the student with a severe disability.

Rusty's parents have researched various person-centered planning models and are excited about the process. They have committed to help his Case Manager facilitate the person-centered planning process because they understand the importance of collaboration not only with the school, but with agencies, as well, in order to help Rusty achieve his postsecondary goals. In the plan, several strategies were identified to facilitate family involvement, such as increasing teacher–parent communication, volunteering in the classroom, and working with agencies to ensure that Rusty will have the necessary services when he enters adult life. Rusty's teacher is going to provide his parents with task analyses for a variety of life skills (e.g., cooking, making purchases, safety, personal care) so that they can better practice these skills with Rusty at home. Additionally, Rusty's parents, in collaboration with the transition specialist, will identify community members for Rusty to work with to help achieve his dream of becoming an entrepreneur.

Interagency Collaboration

In terms of transition to employment, interagency collaboration refers to having key people, businesses, and agencies come together to plan and help students become successfully employed after leaving school. During the school years, the IEP planning meeting serves as the primary place in which collaboration occurs. Therefore, it is important for teachers to become familiar with IDEA requirements for agency notification and participation (Section 300.344f), as well as agency responsibilities (Section 300.348). In addition, teachers must also learn about the eligibility requirements and type of services provided by adult services agencies in their community. While the range of possibilities varies across communities, there are four types of community supports that are particularly important for students with severe disabilities, including (a) vocational rehabilitation services, (b) developmental disabilities services, (c) social security services, and (d) one-stop career centers.

Vocational Rehabilitation Services

Because vocational rehabilitation (VR) services are the primary resource for a student's transitioning to employment services, it is important to know what federal rehabilitation legislation says about employment and transitioning. First, the Rehabilitation Act Amendments of 1992 (p. 2, 102–569) and 1998 (Title IV, P.L.105-220, Workforce Investment Act of 1998) both include what is known as the *presumption of benefit*, "which is the assumption that all individuals can benefit from VR services unless the agency can demonstrate clear and convincing evidence that an individual cannot benefit from employment because of disability." (Test et al., 2006, p. 14). Second, both Acts define *transition services* using the same definition as IDEA. Third, VR counselors can use school assessment data as part of their eligibility in-take process as long as the assessments have been completed in the past year. Fourth, the individualized plan for employment (IPE) developed by VR services must be coordinated with the student's IEP. Finally, the VR system does not recognize (nor will it pay for) segregated employment as an outcome (Mank, 2009).

Possible Vocational Rehabilitation Services

The ranges of service that are potentially available to students through a VR agency can include, but are not limited to, the following (Luecking, 2009):

1. Assessment for determining eligibility for VR services
2. Vocational counseling, guidance, and referral services
3. Vocational and other training, including on-the-job training
4. Job placement and supported employment services
5. Transportation related to other VR services
6. Personal assistance services while receiving VR services
7. Rehabilitation technology services and assistive technology devices
8. Physical restoration and mental health services
9. Interpreter services for individuals with hearing impairments
10. Reading services for individuals with visual impairments

Finally, because VR services are typically a student's doorway to supported employment services, teachers must be aware that when students leave school, they are leaving the world of school entitlements and entering the adult world of eligibility. That is, while students are in school, they are entitled to special education services because of IDEA; however, once they leave school, they must be deemed eligible for services by each agency. Therefore, it is critically important for teachers to know—and to help students and families know—the eligibility requirements of adult services and to help students and families get on the waiting lists of employment services as early as possible.

According to Luecking (2009), to be eligible for VR services an individual must (a) have a physical or mental impairment that results in a substantial impediment to employment; (b) be able to benefit from employment (see the "presumption of benefit"); and (c) require VR services to prepare for, secure, retain, or regain employment. Finally, individuals who currently receive Supplemental Security Income or Social Security Disability Insurance are presumed to be eligible for vocational rehabilitation services.

Developmental Disabilities Services

Every community has a system for providing services to individuals with developmental disabilities, mental retardation, mental health issues, and substance abuse. Sometimes they are managed by local community service boards and sometimes they are managed by a state agency. In addition, in some states, VR services and supports are provided directly to individuals and, in others, they contract for services and supports through *community rehabilitation providers* (CRPs). Regardless of how services and supports are organized in your community, it is important to remember that these services are eligibility based and because waiting lists for services are often long, it is important to help families get their student on the list as early as possible.

Services that are provided by CRPs typically include, but are not limited to, case management, community housing and supported living options, counseling, family planning, personal health care, and mental health services. In terms of employment, CRPs should be involved in the transition planning process because they can provide both job development and job coaching services for youth while they are still in school, as well as also provide the long-term support services and funding needed for supported employment.

Social Security Administration

Probably the number one concern for students and families when a student with severe disabilities becomes employed is the possible loss of social security benefits (both financial and medical). Therefore, it is extremely important to help students and families get assistance with benefits planning. While it is not possible to describe detailed explanations of all benefits in this chapter, it is possible to provide an introduction to the topic and provide resources for more information. For transition-age students, the two most relevant programs are Supplemental Security Income (SSI) and Social Security Disability Income (SSDI). SSI is a Social Security Administration (SSA) "benefit program funded by Federal income tax and is a minimal monthly payment to people with disabilities or aged who are financially needy" (Brooke & McDonough, 2008, p. 62). SSDI is "an insurance benefit authorized under Title II of the Social Security Act for individuals who paid into the system through FICA taxes" (p. 62). Because eligibility criteria differ for both SSI and SSDI, consult the resources listed in Figure 15–6.

FIGURE 15-6
Web-based Resources for Social Security Administration Benefits

---

http://www.socialsecurity.gov
This Web site is the SSA's home page. There is a multitude of information to be found on this site related to disability benefits, applications for services, forms, and publications.

http://www.socialsecurity.gov/work
This SSA Web site is dedicated to employment supports for beneficiaries who want to work. Information is available on transition-age youth issues, the Ticket to Work Program, advocacy issues, and much more.

http://www.socialsecurity.gov/redbook
This SSA Web site provides a publication on disability benefits and how work affects those benefits. It is a general resource guide that is easy to understand and written for individuals with disabilities, families, teachers, and advocates. This book covers issues related to eligibility, employment, work incentives, and health care.

http://www.ssa.gov/ssi/links-to-spotlights.htm
This Web site provides SSA-developed handouts related to Supplemental Security Income (SSI) issues. These handouts encompass a multitude of topics, including Plans to Achieve Self-Support, Medicaid, trusts, and Student Earned Income Exclusion.

http://www.ssa.gov/pubs/10065.html
This SSA Web site serves as an easy-to-understand fact sheet on common questions and answers related to the Ticket to Work Program. At this site, you can find information related to how to use an SSA ticket, who provides services for ticket holders, contact information for employment networks, and much more.

https://secure.ssa.gov/apps10/oesp/providers.nsf/bystate
This SSA Web site provides information regarding Work Incentive Planning and Assistance Programs by state. Information is available regarding the services offered and contact information.

Note: From Web-based resources for Social Security Administration (SSA) benefits, by V. Brooke & J. T. McDonough, 2008, *Teaching Exceptional Children, 41,* 58–65. Copyright 2008 by The Council for Exceptional Children. Reprinted with permission.

Because the fear of losing benefits has kept many students with disabilities from pursuing competitive employment, the Ticket to Work and Work Incentives Improvement Act of 1999 (TWWIIA) (P.L. 106-170) was designed to remove many of these disincentives. While Figure 15–7 lists 10 SSI and SSDI employment supports, three of the most relevant incentives for transition-age students are described below.

Plan for Achieving Self-Support (PASS)
PASS allows individuals receiving SSI to set aside earnings in order to reach a specific employment-related goal. These savings are not counted when determining monthly benefit amounts. PASS plan goals must be preapproved by SSA, reasonable to achieve within a specified time period, and increase the chances of becoming financially independent. Examples of what might be purchased with PASS funds include "education tuition, job coaching, transportation, job-related items, or equipment to start a business" (Brooke & McDonough, 2008, p. 63).

Impairment-Related Work Expenses (IRWEs)
IRWEs are both an SSI and an SSDI work incentive. IRWEs are the cost of the services and equipment that a student needs to be able to work due to a disability. The IRWE costs are deducted from a student's earnings, resulting in increased SSI benefits. IRWEs have been used to pay for job coaching services, assistive technology, and personal assistants. IRWEs can also be prorated over time to allow for expensive purchases (e.g., wheelchairs, computers).

Student Earned Income Exclusion (SEIE)
SEIE is designed to allow individuals under the age of 22 who are receiving SSI and regularly attending school to exclude a certain amount of their employment earnings. According to O'Mara and Farrell (2006), this work incentive can allow many students to be employed without affecting their SSI cash benefit because the amount of earnings that can be excluded is so high. *Regularly attending school* is defined as (a) attending Grades 7–12 for a minimum of 12 hours per week, (b) attending a college or university for a minimum of 8 hours per week, or (c) attending an employment training course for a minimum of 12 hours per week (O'Mara & Farrell).

Finally, another important component of TWWIIA for transition-age youth is the National Benefits Planning, Assistance, and Outreach (BPAO) initiative (Brooke & McDonough, 2007). The BPAO program is designed to provide students and families with direct, individualized benefits planning on how work and different work incentives will affect SSA benefits. To find BPAO assistance near you, go to http://www.vcu-barc.org

In conclusion, social security benefits should not stand in the way of students with severe disabilities becoming employed. However, good transition planning must include benefits planning to help students and

FIGURE 15–7

SSI and SSDI Employment Supports: Work Incentives and Exclusions

SSA Benefit Program	Type of Work Incentive/Exclusion	Description of Work Incentive
SSI	1619(a)	Special SSI payments received by individuals when working over substantial gainful activity (SGA) level
SSI	1619(b)	Protects individuals' Medicaid coverage when earnings are high enough to result in the loss of the SSI payment
SSI	Blind Work Expense (BWE)	Expenses that individuals with blindness incur that are necessary in order to work
SSI	Plan for Achieving Self-Support (PASS)	Allows individuals to set aside the income and/or resources needed to reach a vocational goal, resulting in greater financial success
SSI	Student Earned Income Exclusion (SEIE)	Allows individuals under age 22 and regularly attending school to exclude up to $1,550 of monthly earnings and up to $6,240 of yearly earnings
SSI and Title II	Impairment Related Work Expenses (IRWE)	Expenses that individuals with disabilities incur that are deemed necessary to work, due to a disability, and are paid by the individual
Title II	Trial Work Period (TWP)	Period of at least 9 months during which individuals can work (at any earnings level) without losing cash benefits
Title II	Extended Period of Eligibility (EPE)	Period of 36 months immediately following the TWP when individuals receive cash benefits for any month in which earnings fall below the SGA level
Title II	Subsidies and special conditions	Support that individuals receive on the job, which results in greater pay than the value of the work performed
Title II	Unsuccessful Work Attempt (UWA)	Earnings that ended or fell below the SGA level after 6 months or less because of the individual's disabilities or the loss of the necessary supports needed to work

Note: From SSI and SSDI employment supports: Work incentives and exclusions, by V. Brooke and J. T. McDonough, 2008, *Teaching Exceptional Children, 41,* 58–65. Copyright 2008 by The Council for Exceptional Children. Reprinted with permission.

their families avoid the harm that can be caused when they are not aware of the effects that earnings can have on cash benefits and medical insurance (Brooke & McDonough, 2008).

One-Stop Career Centers

Established in 1998 by the Workforce Investment Act (P.L. 105-220), One-Stop Career Centers are places where youth and others can go to have easy access to career skills training. One-Stop Career Centers typically house multiple employment-related agencies and supports under one roof. Services include job search and career information and training (e.g., resume writing, interviewing), as well as job training and youth employment programs. Hoff (2002) stated that the three levels of services provided by On-Stop Career Centers are core, intensive, and training. Core services are available to anyone in the community and involve basic assistance in finding employment (e.g., job listings,

resume writing). Intensive services are available to certain job seekers, such as individuals who were recently laid off or who have a low income (Luecking, 2008). Training can include vocational assessments and career counseling and are designed for individuals who were not successful in using core or intensive services. Eligible persons may receive such intensive services as job-readiness training, on-the-job training, and adult education and literacy training (Luecking).

While it is early for Serena and her family to invite outside agency personnel to her transition/IEP meeting, her IEP team agrees that she will probably need both VR and CRP services to help her with future employment needs, whether this is an individual supported job or customized employment. In addition, they plan to get Serena on the waiting list for supported living through her county developmental disabilities services agency. Finally, they plan to invite a financial planner to discuss social security issues at their next meeting.

As Rusty moves forward with his plan to develop his own computer business, his IEP team continues to invite his VR counselor and the coordinator of a local CRP who specializes in customized employment to his meeting to help ensure that everything is on track for his graduation next year. Although he plans to live at home for a few more years, they plan to invite a developmental disabilities case manager to his next IEP meeting to begin exploring the residential options that are available in his community and to look at the implications of his future career plans on his social security benefits.

Because Cassandra will be going to the local community college next year to participate in her school systems' program for 18- to-21-year olds, her IEP team continues to invite representatives from VR and a local CRP, who currently provided her personal care, to her team meetings. Together, they have been very useful in helping plan Cassandra's sequence of community-based training activities and integrating them with her transportation, mobility, and communication training. Finally, although no longer needed at every meeting, her SSA financial planner has explained the use of PASS, IRWE, and SEIE, and is available to provide assistance as these benefits are needed in the future.

The Future: A Seamless Transition for All Students

Although recent data from the National Longitudinal Transition Study–2 (Wagner, Newman, & Cameto, 2004) indicate some improvement on postschool outcomes, students with severe disabilities continue to transition into segregated employment at unacceptable rates (Rusch & Braddock, 2004). This has occurred in spite of the increased availability of supported employment and customized employment, which were described earlier in this chapter and which are more cost-effective and preferred by individuals with severe disabilities. To solve this problem, recently, Rusch and Braddock and Certo, Luecking, Courey, Brown, and Mantz (in press) have suggested that all students be provided with the opportunity to leave high school already competitively employed or having been admitted to postsecondary education and having been ensured access to funding for coordinated, long-term supports. Together, this would increase the chances

of having all students successfully transition into integrated opportunities instead of segregated settings.

While some might consider the idea of a seamless transition for all students to be an impossible dream, recent events point to a much more encouraging future. First, the federal government has recently funded two projects designed to increase the number of students with disabilities enrolled in postsecondary education. The Center for Postsecondary Education for Individuals with Intellectual Disabilities was funded by the National Institute of Disability Rehabilitation Research to conduct research and disseminate information on promising practices that support individuals with intellectual disabilities so that they gain access to, and are successful in, inclusive postsecondary education. Next, the U.S. Department of Health and Human Services, Administration for Developmental Disabilities, funded the Consortium for Postsecondary Education for Individuals with Developmental Disabilities. The Consortium is designed to be the national resource for knowledge, training and technical assistance, materials, and dissemination about the participation of individuals with developmental disabilities in postsecondary education. For more information, go to http://www.ThinkCollege.net.

Second, Certo et al. (in press) described a model for providing a seamless transition to employment called the Transition Services Integration Model (TSIM). The TSIM allowed students to leave high school with a customized job and integrated community living activities linked with ongoing support from the same adult services agency. Data indicated that over a 5-year period, the postschool outcomes for employment for students supported by TSIM were above the national average for students with mental retardation.

Together, these projects should increase the chances that Cassandra, Serena, and Rusty will achieve their dreams of integrated employment. Working together, we can make these dreams become a reality.

Suggested Activities

1. Use the Indicator 13 checklist to evaluate a set of IEPs for high school students. Do they contain all required elements? If not, which elements are missed the most? Do you think that "compliant" IEPS are also "quality" IEPs?
2. Develop a four year transition assessment plan for one of the students in the chapter. Include the types

(and names if relevant) of assessments, a rationale for why the assessment is being used (e.g., for what purpose), and a timeline of when assessments will be given (used).

3. Develop a list of possible school-based and community-based work experience sites for a school in your community. List the pros and cons of each.

4. Develop a support employment/customized employment "Fact Sheet" for a high school (or parent) that includes (a) contact information for related adult service agencies, and (b) social security information and resources.

References

Affleck, J. Q., Edgar, E., Levine, P., & Kortering, L. (1990). Post-school status of students classified as mildly mentally retarded, learning disabled, or nonhandicapped: Does it get better with time? *Education and Training in Mental Retardation, 25,* 315–324.

Agran, M., & Moore, S. (1994). *How to teach self-instruction of job skills.* Washington, DC: American Association on Mental Retardation.

Agran, M., Swaner, J., & Snow, K. (1998). Work safety skills: A neglected curricular area. *Career Development for Exceptional Individuals, 21,* 33–44.

Baumgart, D., Johnson, J., & Helmsetter, E. (1990). *Augmentative and alternative communication systems for persons with moderate and severe disabilities.* Baltimore: Paul H. Brookes.

Baumgart, D., & VanWalleghem, J. (1986). Staffing strategies for implementing community-based instruction. *The Journal of the Association for the Severely Handicapped, 11,* 92–102.

Bellamy, G. T., Horner, R. H., & Inman, D. P. (1979). *Vocational habilitation of severely retarded adults: A direct service technology.* Austin, TX: PRO-ED.

Blackorby, J., & Wagner, M. (1996). Longitudinal postschool outcomes of youth with disabilities: Findings from the National Longitudinal Transition Study. *Exceptional Children, 62,* 399–413.

Blalock, G., Kochhar-Bryant, C. A., Test, D. W., Kohler, P., White, W., Lehmann, J., et al. (2003). The need for comprehensive personnel preparation in transition and career development: A position statement of the Division on Career Development and Transition. *Career Development for Exceptional Individuals, 26,* 207–226.

Brooke, V. A., & McDonough, J. T. (2007). The impact of employment on people with disabilities receiving social security administration benefits. In P. Wehman, K. J. Inge, W. G. Revell, Jr., & V. A. Brooke (Eds.), *Real work for real pay: Inclusive employment for people with disabilities* (pp. 323–338). Baltimore, MD: Paul H. Brookes.

Brooke, V., & McDonough, J. T. (2008). The facts ma'am, just the facts: Social security disability benefit programs and work incentives. *Teaching Exceptional Children, 41*(1), 58–65.

Callahan, M., Shumpert, N., & Mast, M. (2002). Self-employment, choice and self-determination. *Journal of Vocational Rehabilitation, 17*(2), 75–85.

Cameto, R. (2005). The transition planning process. *NLTS Data Brief, 4*(1). Retrieved May 22, 2008, from http://www.ncset.org/publications/viewdesc.asp?id=2130

Carl D. Perkins Vocational and Technical Education Amendments of 1998. (October 31, 1998). Title III, Section 3: Definitions (29).

Certo, N. J., Luecking, R. G., Courey, S., Brown, L., Murphy, S., & Mautz, D. (in press). Plugging the policy gap at the point of transition for individuals with severe intellectual disabilities: An argument for a seamless transition and federal entitlement to long-term support. *Research and Practice for Persons with Severe Disabilities.*

Certo, N., Mezzullo, K., & Hunter, D. (1985). The effect of total task chain training on the acquisition of busperson job skills at a full service community restaurant. *Education and Training of the Mentally Retarded, 20,* 148–156.

Cimera, R. E. (2006). The future of supported employment: Don't panic! *Journal of Vocational Rehabilitation, 24,* 145–149.

Cimera, R. E. (2007). Utilizing natural supports to lower the cost of supported employment. *Research and Practice for Persons with Severe Disabilities, 32,* 184–189.

Elinson, L., Frey, W. D., Li, T., Palan, M. A., & Horne, R. L. (2008). Evaluation of customized employment in building the capacity of the workforce development system. *Journal of Vocational Rehabilitation, 28,* 141–158.

Fesko, S., Varney, E., DiBiase, C., & Hippensteil, M. (2008). Effective partnerships: Collaborative efforts that support customized employment. *Journal of Vocational Rehabilitation, 28,* 159–168.

Field, S., & Hoffman, A. (2007). Self-determination in secondary transition assessment. *Assessment for Effective Intervention, 32,* 181–190.

Field, S., Martin, J., Miller, R., Ward, M., & Wehmeyer, M. (1998). *A practical guide for teaching self-determination.* Reston, VA: Division of Career Development and Transition, Council for Exceptional Children.

Gamache, P., & Knab, J. (2008). *School-based enterprise development, planning, implementing, and evaluating.* Tallahassee, FL: Bureau of Exceptional Education and Student Services, Florida Department of Education.

Geary, T., Griffin, C., & Hammis, D. (2006, September). Assistive technology at work. *E-info Lines: Employing People with Disabilities, 18,* 4–5.

Gold, M. (1973). Research on the vocational rehabilitation of the retarded: The present, the future. In N. Ellis (Ed.), *International review of research in mental retardation* (Vol. 6, pp. 97–147). New York: Academic Press.

Griffin, C., Hammis, D., Geary, T., & Sullivan, M. (2008). Customized employment: Where we are; where we're headed. *Journal of Vocational Rehabilitation, 28,* 135–139.

Grossi, T. A. (1998). Using self-evaluation to improve the work productivity of trainees in a community-based restaurant training program. *Education and Training in Mental Retardation and Developmental Disabilities, 33,* 248–263.

Hagner, D., & Cooney, B. (2003). Building employer capacity to support employees with severe disabilities in the workplace. *Work, 21*(1), 77–82.

Halpern, A. (1985). Transition: A look at the foundations. *Exceptional Children, 51,* 479–486.

Halpern, A. (1992). Transition: Old wine in new bottles. *Exceptional Children, 58,* 202–211.

Halpern, A. S., Yovanoff, P., Doren, B., & Benz, M. R. (1995). Predicting participation in postsecondary education for school leavers with disabilities. *Exceptional Children, 62,* 151–164.

Hasazi, S., Gordon, L., & Roe, C. (1985). Factors associated with the employment status of handicapped youth exiting high school from 1979–1983. *Exceptional Children, 51,* 455–469.

Heslop, P., & Abbott, D. (2007). School's out: Pathways for young people with intellectual disabilities from out-of-area residential schools or colleges. *Journal of Intellectual Disability Research, 51,* 489–496.

Hoff, D. (2002). Workforce Investment Act and one-stop career centers: Opportunities and ongoing challenges. *TASH CONNECTIONS, 28*(9/10), 23–26.

Individuals with Disabilities Education Act of 1990. P.L. No. 101-476.

Individuals with Disabilities Education Act of 1997. P.L. No. 105-17.

Individuals with Disabilities Education Improvement Act of 2004. P.L. No. 108-446, 20 U.S.C. 1400, H.R. 1350.

Johnson, D. R. (2004). Supported employment trends: Implications for transition-age youth. *Research and Practice for Persons with Severe Disabilities, 29,* 243–247.

Kellerman, T. (2009). What's a job coach? Retrieved May 3, 2009, from http://www.come-over.to/FAS/JobCoach.htm

Keul, P. (1991). *Consultation to school-based enterprises in Shelby City Schools.* Charlotte, NC: Supported Employment Training.

Kohler, P. D., & Field, S. (2003). Transition-focused education: Foundation for the future. *The Journal of Special Education, 37,* 174–183.

Konrad, M. (2008). 20 ways to involve students in the IEP process. *Intervention in School and Clinic, 43,* 236–239.

Lohrmann-O'Rourke, S., & Gomez, O. (2001). Integrating preference assessment within the transition process to create meaningful school-to-life outcomes. *Exceptionality, 9,* 157–174.

Love, L. (1994). *Applying the FSLA when placing students into community-based vocational education.* Phoenix, AZ: Arizona Department of Education.

Luecking, R. G. (Ed.). (2009). *The way to work: How to facilitate work experiences for youth in transition.* Baltimore: Paul H. Brookes.

Luecking, R. G., Fabian, E. S., Tilson, G., Donovan, M., & Fabian, E. S. (2004). *Working relationships: Creating career opportunities for job seekers with disabilities through employer partnerships.* Baltimore: Paul H. Brookes.

Mank, D. (2009). Employment. In S. M. Odom, R. H. Horner, M. E. Snell, & J. Blacher (Eds.), *Handbook of developmental disabilities* (pp. 390–409). New York: Guilford Press.

Martin, J. E., Marshall, L. H., Maxson, L. M., & Jerman, P. L. (1997). *The self-directed IEP.* Longmont, CO: Sopris West.

Mazzotti, V. L., Rowe, D. A., Kelley, K. R., Test, D. W., Fowler, C. H., Kohler, P. D., et al. (2009). Linking transition assessment and postsecondary goals: Key elements in the secondary transition planning process. *Teaching Exceptional Children, 42*(2), 44–51.

Michaels, C. A., & Ferrara, D. L. (2005). Promoting post-school success for all: The role of collaboration in person-centered transition planning. *Journal of Educational and Psychological Consultation, 16,* 287–313.

National Center on Secondary Education and Transition (NCSET). (2004, February). Person-centered planning: A tool for transition (Parent Brief). Retrieved May 4, 2009, from http://www.ncset.org/publications/viewdesc.asp?id=1431

National Longitudinal Transition Study–2 (NLTS2). (2009). NLTS2 Wave 3 2005 Parent/Youth Survey: Employment of youth out-of-secondary school a year or more (combined youth and parent items), table 332, estimates. Retrieved April 12, 2009, from http://www.nlts2.org/data_tables/tables/12/np3t7a_L7a_I2b.html

National Secondary Transition Technical Assistance Center (NSTTAC). (2007, November). Age-appropriate transition assessment guide, by Allison R. Walker, Larry J. Kortering, & Catherine H. Fowler. Charlotte, NC: NSTTAC.

National Secondary Transition Technical Assistance Center (NSTTAC). (2008). What is Indicator 13? Retrieved May 2, 2009, from http://www.nsttac.org/indicator13/indicator13.aspx

National Secondary Transition Technical Assistance Center (NSTTAC). (2009). Indicator 13 Checklist. Charlotte, NC: Author.

Neubert, D. A. (2003). The role of assessment in the transition to adult life process for students with disabilities. *Exceptionality, 11*(2), 63–75.

O'Brien, J., & O'Brien, C. L. (2000). The origins of person-centered planning: A community of practice perspective. Minneapolis, MN: Responsive Systems Associates.

Office of Disability Employment Policy (ODEP), U.S. Department of Labor. (2009a). Supported employment: What is supported employment? Retrieved May 3, 2009, from http://www.dol.gov/odep/archives/fact/supportd.htm

Office of Disability Employment Policy (ODEP), U.S. Department of Labor. (2009b). Customized employment: Principles and indicators. Retrieved May 3, 2009, from http://www.dol.gov/odep/pubs/custom/indicators.htm

O'Mara, S., & Ferrell, C. (2006). *Student earned income exclusion* (Fact Sheet). Richmond: Benefits Assistance Resource Center, Virginia Commonwealth University.

Pearpoint, J., O'Brien, J., & Forest, M. (1993). *PATH: A workbook for planning possible positive futures* (2nd ed.). Toronto, Ontario, Canada: Inclusion Press.

Pelland, M., & Falvey, M. A. (1986). Domestic skills. In M. A. Falvey (Ed.), *Community-based curriculum: Instructional strategies for students with severe handicaps.* Baltimore, MD: Paul H. Brookes.

Post, M., & Storey, K. (2002). Review of using auditory prompting systems with persons who have moderate to severe disabilities. *Education and Training in Mental Retardation and Developmental Disabilities, 37,* 223–234.

Pumpian, I., Fisher, D., Certo, N. J., Engel, T., & Mautz, D. (1998). To pay or not to pay: Differentiating employment and training relationships through regulation and litigation, *Career Development for Exceptional Individuals, 21,* 187–202.

Rehabilitation Act of 1973. 29 U.S.C. § 794 [Sec. 504] (1986).

Rowe, D. A. (2009). *Parent and family involvement annotated bibliography prepared for NSTTAC.* Retrieved June 10, 2009, from National Secondary Transition Technical Assistance Center, http://www.nsttac.org/products_and_resources/ParentInvolvementAnnotatedBibliography.aspx

Rusch, F. R., & Braddock, D. (2004). Adult day programs versus supported employment (1988–2002): Spending and service practices of mental retardation and developmental disabilities state agencies. *Research and Practice for Persons with Severe Disabilities, 29,* 237-242.

Scherer, M. J., & Galvin, J. C. (1996). An outcomes perspective of quality pathways to the most appropriate technology. In J. C. Galvin & M. J. Scherer (Eds.), *Evaluating, selecting, and using appropriate assistive technology.* Gaithersburg, MD: Aspen Publishers.

Sherlock, P. V. (2001). Making Action Plans: Student centered transitional planning. Retrieved July 23, 2009, from http://www.ric.edu/sherlockcenter/publications/MAPS.pdf

Sitlington, P., & Clark, G. (2007). The transition assessment process and IDEA 2004. *Assessment for Effective Intervention, 32,* 133-142.

Sitlington, P., Neubert, D. A., & Leconte, P. J. (1997). Transition assessment: The position of the Division on Career Development and Transition. *Career Development for Exceptional Individuals, 20,* 69-79.

Sitlington, P., & Payne, E. (2004). Information needed by postsecondary education: Can we provide it as part of the transition assessment process? *Learning Disabilities: A Contemporary Journal, 2*(2), 1-14.

Stern, D. (1994). *School-based enterprise: Productive learning in American high schools.* San Francisco: Jossey Bass.

Taber, T. A., Alberto, P. A., Seltzer, A., & Hughes, M. (2003). Obtaining assistance when lost in the community using cell phones. *Research and Practice for Persons with Severe Disabilities, 28,* 105-116.

Test, D. W., Aspel, N., & Everson, J. (2006). *Transition methods for youth with disabilities.* Columbus, OH: Merrill/Prentice Hall.

Test, D. W., Carver, T., Ewers, L., Haddad, J., & Person, J. (2000). Longitudinal job satisfaction of persons in supported employment. *Education and Training in Mental Retardation and Developmental Disabilities, 35,* 365-373.

Test, D. W., Hinson, K. B., Solow, J., & Keul, P. K. (1993). Job satisfaction of persons in supported employment. *Education and Training in Mental Retardation, 28,* 38-46.

Test, D. W., Mason, C., Hughes, C., Konrad, M., Neale, M., & Wood, W. M. (2004). Student involvement in individualized education program meetings: A review of the literature. *Exceptional Children, 70,* 391-412.

Test, D. W., Mazzotti, V. L., Mustian, A. L., Fowler, C., Kortering, L., & Kohler, P. (in press). Evidence-based secondary transition predictors for improving post-school outcomes for students with disabilities. *Career Development for Exceptional Individuals.*

Test, D. W., Walker, A. R., & Richter, S. (2008). Community functioning skills. In K. Storey, P. Bates, & D. Hunter (Eds.), *Transition to adult life for persons with disabilities: The road ahead* (pp. 131-150). St. Augustine, FL: Training Resource Network.

Trach, J. S., & Mayhall, C. D. (1997). Analysis of the types of natural supports utilized during job placement and development. *Journal of Rehabilitation, 63*(2), 43-48.

Trach, J. S., & Shelden, D. L. (1999). Natural supports as a foundation for supports-based employment development and facilitation. *American Rehabilitation, 25*(3), 2-7.

Turnbull, A., & Turnbull, R. (1995). A "Group Action Planning" cookbook for families, friends, and professionals. In P. Browning (Ed.), *Transition IV in Alabama: A profile of commitment.* Auburn, AL: Department of Rehabilitation and Special Education, Auburn University. Retrieved July 23, 2009, from https://fp.auburn.edu/rse/trans_media/08_Publications/02_Conf_Proceedings/Proceedings4/12a_TURNBULL.pdf

U.S. Department of Education. (2009). Special education and rehabilitative services: OSEP Parts B and C state monitoring and formula grants. Retrieved October 5, 2008, from http://www.ed.gov/policy/speced/guid/idea/monitor/index.html

VanReusen, A. K., & Bos, C. S. (1994). Facilitating student participation in individualized education programs through motivation strategy instruction. *Exceptional Children, 60,* 466-475.

Wagner, M., Newman, L., & Cameto, R. (2004). *Changes over time in the secondary school experiences of students wtih disabilities. A report of findings from the National Longitudinal Transition Study (NLTS) and the National Longitudinal Transition Study-2 (NLTS2).* Menlo Park, CA: SRI International. Retrieved December 9, 2008, from http://www.nlts2.org/pdfs/changestime_exec_sum_standalone.pdf

Wagner, M., Newman, L., Cameto, R., Levine, P., & Garza, N. (2006). *An overview of findings from Wave 2 of the National Longitudinal Transition Study-2 (NLTS-2).* (NCSER 2006-3004). Menlo Park, CA: SRI International.

Wagner, M., Newman, L., Cameto, R., Levine, P., & Marder, C. (2003). *Going to school: Instructional contexts, programs, and participation of secondary school students with disabilities. A report from the National Longitudinal Transition Study-2 (NLTS2).* Menlo Park, CA: SRI International.

Wehman, P. (1981). *Competitive employment: New horizons for severely disabled individuals.* Baltimore: Paul H. Brookes.

Wehman, P., Gibson, K., Brooke, V., & Unger, D. (1998). Transition from school to competitive employment: Illustrations of competence for two young women with severe mental retardation. *Focus on Autism and Other Developmental Disabilities, 13,* 130-143.

Wehman, P., & Revell, W. G. (1997). Transition into supported employment for young adults with severe disabilities: Current practices and future directions. *Journal of Vocational Rehabilitation, 8,* 65-74.

Wehmeyer, M. L. (1995). A career education approach: Self-determination for youth with mild cognitive disabilities. *Intervention in School and Clinic, 30,* 157-163.

Wehmeyer, M. L., Field, S., Doren, B., Jones, B., & Mason, C. (2004). Self-determination and student involvement in standards-based reform. *Exceptional Children, 70,* 413-425.

Wehmeyer, M. L., & Lawrence, M. (1995). Whose future is it anyway? Promoting student involvement in transition planning. *Career Development for Exceptional Individuals, 18,* 69-83.

Wehmeyer, M. L., & Palmer, S. B. (2003). Adult outcomes for students with cognitive disabilities three-years after high school: The impact of self-determination. *Education and Training in Developmental Disabilities, 38,* 131-144.

Wehmeyer, M. L., & Schalock, R. L. (2001). Self-determination and quality of life: Implications for special education services and supports. *Focus on Exceptional Children, 33*(8), 1-16.

Wehmeyer, M. L., & Schwartz, M. (1997). Self-determination and positive adult outcomes: A follow-up study of youth with mental retardation or learning disabilities. *Exceptional Children, 63,* 245-255.

Will, M. (1984, March-April). Bridges from school to working life. *Programs for the Handicapped.* Washington, DC: Clearinghouse on the Handicapped.

16

The Promise of Adulthood

Dianne L. Ferguson
Philip M. Ferguson

In his last year of high school, Ian Ferguson learned to fly. This was quite an accomplishment for someone labeled "severely mentally retarded" and physically disabled. As Ian's parents, we marveled at his achievement and worried about the law of gravity. Let us explain.

As part of Ian's final year as a student—nearly 20 years ago now—he enrolled in "Beginning Drama." Following his carefully designed transition plan, Ian spent most of the rest of his day out in the community working at various job sites, shopping at various stores, eating at various restaurants. But he began each day in drama class with a roomful of other would-be thespians. The logic behind Ian's participation in the class at the time was that it might lead somehow to his adult participation in some aspect or other of community theater. You see, while Ian's vision is poor, his hearing is great. In fact, he finds odd or unexpected sounds (human or otherwise) to be endlessly amusing. During high school, one of our more insightful friends bought Ian a set of sound effects tapes of the type used by theater groups (e.g., "Sound A-24, woman screaming, 27 seconds" [screaming ensues]; Sound A-25, man sneezing, 15 seconds . . .") as called for by various productions. Surely, we reasoned, Ian could learn to control his laughter long enough to help in such offstage

activities as the making of sound effects. Furthermore, the drama teacher at Ian's high school just happened to be quite active in community theater in our town. Our objective, then, was really to see if we could figure out how Ian might participate in community theater productions as an adult leisure activity, possibly networking with the drama teacher to gain an entrée into that group.

To our pleasure, Ian benefited in many more unexpected ways from his introduction to the dramatic arts: memorization, articulation, expressiveness, and social interaction. He also learned to "fly." A major part of the first few weeks of class involved Ian's participation in "trust" exercises. Some students fell off ladders, trusting their classmates to catch them. Others dived off a runway with the same belief that their friends would break their fall. The exercise that Joe Zeller, the teacher, picked to challenge Ian was called "flying." Seven or eight of Ian's classmates were to take him out of his wheelchair and raise him up and down in the air, tossing him just a little above their heads.

Now, the first time they tried this, everyone was very tense. Both Mr. Zeller and Leah Howard (Ian's support teacher) were nervous; it was an adventure for them as well. The students released Ian's feet from their heel straps, unbuckled his seatbelt, and, leaning over en masse, lifted him out of his chair. Joe and Leah positioned themselves at the most crucial locations on either side of Ian and slowly—together with the students—began to raise Ian's supine body with their hands. Now it was Ian's turn to be nervous. Ian's spasticity makes it impossible for him to break a fall by throwing out his arms. Several painful crashes have left him with a strong fear of falling at the first sensation of being off balance or awkwardly positioned. Like many folks who experience his kind of physical disability, Ian has a hard time trusting strangers to move the body that he has so little control over. As the students lifted him, he clutched nervously at the only wrist within reach of the one hand he can use, trying to find something to hold onto. His voice anxiously wavered, "Leah, Leah," seeking reassurance that this was, in fact, a wise course of action. It was pretty scary for Ian and pretty risky for everyone else. But the exercise went well. Months later, when the drama class repeated some of the same trust exercises, Ian greeted the suggestion that he "fly" with an eager response of "Out of chair! Out of chair!" That is how Ian learned to "fly" in his last year of school. The secret was building on his eagerness to be a true member of the class to learn to control his fear of falling. It is a lesson that has served us all well in the ensuing years.

We tell this story about "flying" in drama class because it also captures the simultaneous sensations of excitement and anxiety that we experienced as Ian finished high school and launched into adulthood. We were fairly certain that Ian had some mixed feelings as his old routines and familiar settings vanished and new activities and settings took their place. The people in Ian's social network of formal and informal supports and friendship also recognized the responsibility that enough hands be there to "catch" Ian if he started to fall. As Ian left the relative stability of public school, grounded as it is in legal mandates and cultural familiarity, we worried about the thin air of adulthood where formal support systems seemed to promise little and accomplish even less.

Ian turned 40 in September 2009. He lives in his own home, works at a job that he has enjoyed for nearly 20 years, and actively participates in a full schedule of household tasks, social engagements, parties, chores, weekends away, and an occasional longer vacation. He did participate as a member of the cast in a local production of *Oklahoma!* that was directed by

his high school drama teacher as we had hoped. He is supported in his adult life by a network of paid and unpaid persons, a personal support agent who also provides direct support, and our ongoing involvement to ensure that his life is more okay than not okay from his point of view most of the time.

Our journey through these years has been difficult, often confusing and frustrating, but also filled with many exciting achievements. We have all learned a good deal about how one young man can negotiate an adult life and the kinds of supports that this requires. Equally important, we have come to meet many other individuals (and their families) who have had similar experiences. Each journey is unique, but also is filled with a common mix of frustration and achievement. Moreover, all those with whom we have met continue to wrestle—to some degree or another—with a similar set of thorny questions. How can a family make sure that an adult-age child's life is really *his* life and not one that merely reflects the regulations, individual support plan procedures, agency practices, and other formal services trappings? How do we assure ourselves that our children are somehow authentically contributing to all of the choices that get made about what constitutes a good adult life for them? Over the past two decades or so—since Ian left school—families have helped create new options for a whole generation of people like Ian as they sought answers to these questions. We have also increased our understanding of what it means for someone who has a variety of severe disabilities to be an adult.

Exploring the Promise of Adulthood

In this chapter, we explore this status of adulthood and how it applies to people with severe disabilities. Our point is not that persons with severe disabilities who are over the age of 18 or 21 are somehow not adults; of course, they are adults. The problem is that our field has not spent enough time thinking through exactly what that means in our culture and era. Adulthood is more than simply a chronological marker that indicates that someone is over a certain age. As important as having a meaningful job or living as independently as possible is, adulthood seems to involve more than this. As one social commentator has framed this distinction, "In many ways, children may always be children and adults may always be adults, but conceptions of 'childhood' and 'adulthood' are infinitely variable" (Meyrowitz,

1984, p. 25). If it is our responsibility as the teachers and parents of students with severe disabilities to launch them as successfully as possible into adulthood, then it should be worthwhile to reflect on what promises such a role should hold. What is the promise of adulthood for people with severe disabilities?

We are not so bold as to think that we can fully answer that question in this chapter. Our efforts here will be to begin a discussion of the issue that we think needs to continue within the field of severe disabilities in general. We will organize our efforts into three main sections: (a) understanding adulthood, (b) denying adulthood, and (c) achieving adulthood. Finally, throughout our discussion, our perspective will be unavoidably personal as well as professional. We will not pretend to be some anonymous and objective scholars writing dispassionately about the abstraction of adulthood for people with severe disabilities. Our son, Ian, is one of those people and he is far from an abstraction to us. We will mention him throughout this chapter to illustrate some points that we make and to explain our perspective better. As mentioned, though, Ian is far from being alone with his story. So by way of comparison, we will also share stories about another young man named Douglas who we have known for more than 20 years, and whose journey as an adult with significant disabilities is both similar to and different from Ian's. While Douglas has never officially been placed along the autism spectrum, certainly a number of his responses to people and to his environment have raised that type of label as a possibility. For Douglas's family, it has been a long time since the specific labels have seemed particularly useful or important. For them, Douglas is Douglas.

✛ ✛ ✛ ✛ ✛   **Douglas**   ✛ ✛ ✛ ✛ ✛

We first met Douglas and his family a little more than 20 years ago when we started teaching each summer in Atlantic Canada at a local university. During the summer of 2009, he turned 38. For three weeks each July, our lives alternate among teaching classes to teachers, exploring the Maritime Provinces, and spending time with friends. Douglas's mother was a professor at the university and she invited us not only to teach, but to dinner, and through her we met, over the years, not just Douglas but the whole family. After the first year or two, we have come to appreciate as one of the best parts of our visit how Douglas greets us each time. He seems to be most excited to see Phil—especially now that they wear similar short beards—but we take his enthusiastic greeting as a welcome to us both. Douglas expresses himself clearly, but rarely with words that anyone but his family understands. He has a variety of health problems that have plagued him and his family over the years and he has an attention to order and detail that can be useful, but also annoying to live with. He is, nevertheless, a presence in his home, in his town, and in our memories of each of our summers in this part of Canada.

Finally, we will write not only as Ian's parents or Douglas's friend, but we also will draw on our own research and that of other professionals and scholars in disability studies to bolster our discussion as well. Such a mixture of the personal and professional perspectives does not only affect us as the writers, it should also affect you as the reader. You should read and respond to this chapter as a discussion of the concept of adulthood in general, but also as it fits (or does not fit) your own personal experiences with persons with severe disabilities.

Understanding Adulthood

The concept of adulthood is a fluid one that changes from era to era and from culture to culture (Ingstad & Whyte, 1995). For most European cultures, adulthood has a strong individualistic (or *egocentric* in anthropological terms) emphasis on personal independence and achievement. For many non-Western cultures, however, adulthood has a stronger emphasis on familial and social (or *sociocentric*) affiliations and connectedness (Klingner, Blanchett, & Harry, 2007; Rueda, Monzó, Shapiro, Gomez, & Blacher, 2005). Within a single culture, the status of adulthood might vary depending on the context. For example, a religious tradition might consider the beginning of adulthood to be at one age (e.g., age 13 in Judaism), while the legal status for the same person comes several years later (e.g., age 18), and the secular status might not be fully achieved until some time after that (say, age 21 or when undergraduate study has been completed). Even within our own American culture, the interpretation of adulthood has always undergone gradual historical shifts, influenced by all of the factors that go into our social profile; demographic trends, economic developments, educational patterns, cultural diversity, and even technology (think about how the availability of the automobile—both front and backseat—has changed the experience of adolescence). A quick historical review may help.

The Changing Status of Adulthood

The status of adulthood in our society is simple and complex, obvious and obscure. At one level, it is a straightforward matter of age. Anyone who is over the age of 18 (or, for some activities, 21) is an adult, pure and simple. The process is automatic: One achieves adulthood through simple endurance. If you live long enough, you cease being a child and become an adult. In legal terms, one could even be judged incompetent to manage one's affairs but still remain an adult in this chronological sense.

At an equally basic level, adulthood can mean simply a state of biological maturity. In such terms, an adult is someone who has passed through the pubertal stage and is physiologically fully developed. As with the chronological meaning, this biological interpretation also is still common and largely accurate as far as it goes: To be an adult, at least in the physical sense, is to be grown up, mature, fully developed.

However, it seems clear to us that the matter has always been more complicated than either chronology or biology (Blatterer, 2007; Kett, 1977; Molgat, 2007; Shanahan, 2000). These factors convey a sense of precision and permanence about the concept that simply ignores the process of social construction by which every culture imbues such terms with meaning (Blatterer, 2007; Ingstad & Whyte, 1995; Kalyanpur & Harry, 1999). Moreover, as Rueda and his colleagues (2005) have pointed out, cultures themselves are seldom homogeneous. So, conceptions of adulthood vary not only across cultures, but also within individual cultures.

For example, historically, we know that the beginning age for adulthood has been a surprisingly flexible concept even within the confines of Western culture (Modell, Furstenberg, & Hershberg, 1978). Philippe Aries (1962) has even argued that childhood itself, as a social distinction, was not discovered in Europe until the 16th century. Before then, he argues, children were treated as little more than "miniature adults"—much like they were portrayed in medieval art (Aries, 1962). Adolescence, for example, was reported in a 16th-century French compilation of "informed opinion" as being the third stage of life, lasting until 28 or even 35 years of age (Aries, 1962). On the other hand, in colonial New England, legal responsibility for one's personal behavior began at "the age of discretion," which usually meant 14 to 16 years old (Beales, 1985), and many children left home for their vocational apprenticeships as early as age 10 or 12 (Beales, 1985; Kett, 1977).

At the end of the 19th century in Europe and America and continuing today, a period of postadolescent youth emerged where the children of the upper and middle classes (mainly males at first, but now also females) could choose to postpone their adulthood by extending their professional training into their late 20s. The key distinction for this delayed adulthood was the extended status of economic dependency for these college students (e.g., Wohl, 1979). Taylor (1988) is even more specific: "Physically and psychologically adults, these individuals have not yet committed to those institutions which society defines as adult—namely, work, marriage and family" (p. 649). In many areas of the country, both urban and rural, this extended economic dependency continues to shape the cultural expectations of a successful transition to adulthood (Furstenberg, Cook, Eccles, Elder, & Sameroff, 1999; Magnussen, 1997). Most social historians seem to agree that after a period of compression and inflexibility in the decades following World War II, the "acceptable" time span for transition from childhood to adulthood has become a mosaic of psychological and sociological variations (Arnett & Tanner, 2006; Blatterer, 2007; Modell et al., 1978). The National Academy of Sciences has postponed the end of adolescence to age 30 in today's United States (cited in Danesi, 2003, pp. 103–104). If there ever was one, there is no longer a "standard" adulthood (Blatterer, 2007).

What remains is a curious interaction of fixed periods of institutional transitions (e.g., graduation, voting, legal status) with fluid patterns of social and structural change (e.g., economic separation, living apart from parents, sexual activity, postsecondary education) (Blatterer, 2007; Molgat, 2007). As America grows more diverse, it seems likely that the traditional cultural markers of adulthood will only become more problematic and situational (Molgat, 2007). Kalyanpur and Harry (1999), for example, point out that for many non-Anglo families, "it is assumed that the son will continue to live in the parents' home, regardless of economic or marital status, and that the daughter will leave after marriage only to move in with her husband's family" (p. 106). Rueda et al. (2005), in a study of Latina mothers of transition-age sons and daughters, found that "the notion of having one's young adult go off on his or her own was not part of the mindset of these mothers, irrespective of whether a developmental disability was involved" (p. 406). At the same time, many children from poor families feel early pressure to contribute to the economic survival of the family and their own material well-being. In many aspects of social life, teenagers engage in "adult" behavior at earlier and earlier ages (Furstenberg et al., 1999).

Given this cultural and historical variability, how might we elaborate on an understanding of adulthood that goes beyond age? How can we describe the social and cultural dimensions of adulthood? Finally, how do these social and cultural dimensions affect the experiences and opportunities of persons with severe disabilities? We will address these questions by examining some of the dimensions of adulthood and their symbolic significance.

The Dimensions of Adulthood

As Ian's parents, we naturally thought that it was important that Ian graduate from high school. More to the point, however, we felt that it was extremely important that he participate as fully as possible in his high school's commencement exercises. The graduation ritual itself seemed crucial to us. It took planning, coordination, cooperation, and compromise by a number of people to make that participation happen, but happen it did, as the picture of Ian in his cap and gown shows (Figure 16-1). Now, while Ian certainly enjoyed his graduation (especially the part where people applauded as he crossed the stage), we don't know if he fully appreciated all of the cultural symbolism attached to such events by many of the other participants. Missing the graduation ceremony would not have lessened the skills that Ian had learned in high school, threatened the friendships he had forged, or worsened his prospects for a smooth transition from school to work. In other words, the importance of Ian's participation in commencement was largely symbolic. It symbolized for us many of the same things that a son or daughter's graduation from high school symbolizes for most parents. We'll have more to say about Douglas's graduation later, but like Ian, his family valued the importance of his participation and for many of the same reasons.

Few events are as loaded with symbolism as a graduation ceremony. It is perhaps the closest that our particular society comes to a formal rite of passage from childhood to adulthood. Of course, other societies and traditions might have other symbols that are equally

FIGURE 16–1
Ian at His High School Graduation Ceremony

powerful that do not include anything related to ceremonies about finishing schooling. Much of what we are trying to capture in an understanding of adulthood occurs at this symbolic level of meaning. There are three important dimensions to this symbolic understanding as shown in Table 16-1.

The Dimension of Autonomy

Perhaps the most familiar and common symbols of adulthood in our society are those that convey a sense of personal autonomy. This dimension emphasizes the status of adulthood as an outcome or a completion. It is the *achieving* of adulthood that is the main focus; what happens throughout the adult years in terms of learning and growth or the physical changes that accompany aging are less the point. More specific features of autonomy can be seen in several aspects of life commonly associated with adulthood.

Self-Sufficiency. One of the most often cited features of adulthood is an expectation of self-sufficiency. At the

TABLE 16–1

The Dimensions of Adulthood

Autonomy:	Being your own person, expressed through the symbols of	
	Self-sufficiency:	Especially economic self-sufficiency, or having the resources to take care of oneself. Includes emotional self-sufficiency, or the ability to "make it" on one's own. Marks a shift from economic consumption to consumption and production.
	Self-determination:	Assertion of individuality and independence. The ability to assure others that one possesses the rational maturity and personal freedom to make specific choices about how to live one's life.
	Completeness:	A sense of having "arrived." A shift from the future to the present tense. No more waiting.
Membership:	Community connectedness, collaboration, and sacrifice as expressed through the symbols of	
	Citizenship:	Activities of collective governance—from voting and participation in town meetings to volunteering for political candidates; expressing your position on issues with money, time, or bumper stickers; or recycling to protect the shared environment.
	Affiliation:	Activities of voluntary association, fellowship, celebration, and support—from greeting the new family in the neighborhood with a plate of cookies to being an active member of the church, a participant in the local service or garden club, or a member of the local art museum.
Change:	Adulthood as an ongoing capacity for growth rather than the static outcome of childhood. Change occurs for adults as they change jobs, move to new apartments or houses, relocate to new communities, or go back to school to learn new jobs or hobbies. Change also occurs as old friends and family members move away and new friendships are formed.	

most fundamental level, this usually means economic self-sufficiency. Whether by employment, inherited wealth, or social subsidy, adulthood entails the belief that one has the resources to take care of oneself. This sense of self-sufficiency entails a transition from a primary existence of economic consumption and dependency to one of rough balance between consumption and production. Theoretically, even our welfare system works to preserve and enhance the self-sufficiency of individuals by providing temporary support and training.

However, self-sufficiency goes beyond this economic sense to also include elements of emotional adequacy. Adulthood usually brings the sense of having the emotional and economic resources to "make it on one's own." People who whine about trivial complaints are often told to "grow up" or "quit acting like a baby." Moreover, there are important gender differences in how our culture portrays emotional maturity. Still, in some sense or another, emotional competence in the face of life's adversities is presented as an expectation for adults.

Last year, Ian earned about $4,000 in his job at the university. This annual income has varied over time from a high of $4,500 to a low of $3,000 as his responsibilities changed, as supervisors changed, and as other parts of his life took precedence. While this job and these earnings are important to his life as an adult, they do not begin to cover his living ex-

penses, to say nothing of his recreational expenses. Even with the social services support dollars made available to him, the life that he is creating for himself exceeds his available economic resources too much of the time. However, Ian has a job and social services dollars to support his efforts. Many persons with severe disabilities have no such support, or what they do have is woefully inadequate. Poverty and disability have a long history, and self-sufficiency and poverty are incompatible.

One of the ongoing frustrations for Douglas and his family is that his employment has been episodic, with sometimes long periods of unemployment. In the last few years, for example, he has worked alongside a local man named John, who involves him in his jobs and activities around town, although without pay. But currently, he is again unemployed because John and a friend started up a new restaurant in a nearby town. Once the restaurant is operating smoothly, Douglas will join the team to assist with kitchen cleanup, stocking, and the other critical chores that are required for a small business. However, even then, the prospects are that this will also be on an unpaid basis for the foreseeable future.

Self-Determination. Self-determination and self-sufficiency are often treated as synonymous features of adulthood. However, while recognizing that the terms are closely related, we want to use the term *self-determination* to refer to a more active assertion of individuality and independence. An autonomous adult in this sense is someone who has the rational maturity and personal freedom to make specific choices about how to live his or her life. Autonomous adults make decisions and live with the consequences.

Certainly, from the perspective of childhood, this dimension of autonomy is probably the most anticipated. Self-determination involves all of the freedoms and control that seem so oppressively and unreasonably denied as we suffer through the indignities of adolescence. We can live where we want, change jobs if we want, make our own judgments about what debts to incur and what risks to take, and make our own decisions when faced with moral dilemmas. We can even stay up late if we want to or go shopping at 10:00 a.m. However, these new privileges are quickly coupled with new responsibilities.

For persons with severe disabilities, the concept of self-determination is challenging and promising and has become a relatively new focus of discussion and research (Priestley, 2001; Storey, Bates, & Hunter, 2008; Wehman, 2006). As a concept, self-determination changes not just what happens in the lives of persons with severe disabilities but, more fundamentally, how we think about such things as services, supports, interventions, and outcomes (Ferguson & O'Brien, 2005).

One example of the role of self-determination and the challenges faced in understanding and interpreting it for persons with severe disabilities first came to us wrapped in a Christmas Eve invitation.

Ian invited us to his house for Christmas Eve for the first time about 10 years ago. Previously, we had always celebrated holidays in our home, even after Ian moved into his own house. Of course, most families eventually face such a time when the location for holidays and other family rituals shifts from the parents' home to the children's. What is hard for us to unravel in our relationship with Ian, however, is just how this particular transitional invitation occurred. Did Ian somehow arrive at the determination that it was time to shift our holiday celebrations to his own home? Did his housemates, Robin and Lyn, who had been helping him can fruits and vegetables, make jam and breads, and decorate and arrange baskets for weeks, "support his choice" to invite us over or shape his choice? Did they somehow teach him how and why he might wish to request our presence at *this holiday celebration? Since this first invitation, we have had many more—sometimes for holidays, sometimes just for an ordinary Wednesday or Friday, sometimes for lunch, sometimes dinner. Whatever Ian's exact role in the decision to invite us, it is clear that he enjoys having us in his house in a quite different way than he seems to enjoy visiting ours.*

For individuals whose communication skills are limited and for whom our understanding of their preferences and point of view can be incomplete, it is sometimes difficult to figure out when they are making choices—determining things for themselves—and when it is the interpretations of others that shape the outcomes. At the same time, it seems better to try to guess at another's perspective and preferences than to ignore them altogether. At still other times, it may well be that no choice is made despite the opportunity.

"Do you want eggs, pancakes, or bagels for breakfast tomorrow?," we asked Ian recently during an overnight visit. "Bagels," was his prompt reply. "Do you want bagels, pancakes, or eggs?" Phil tried again, wondering if Ian was really listening and choosing. "Eggs," Ian just as promptly replied.

Over the years, we have tried various little tests like this to check whether Ian's answers are choices, humor, or just his effort to support the conversational exchange by repeating the last thing that he heard. Of course, questioning his apparent choices could seem to be unsupportive of his efforts to determine things for himself. Perhaps the admission that we question his responses is as important as whether he is really choosing. These are the essential questions and dilemmas of self-determination for Ian and others with similar disabilities.

Completeness. Perhaps completeness is the common element in all aspects of adulthood because autonomy is a sense of completeness. What one gains with self-determination and self-sufficiency is clearly more than the imagined pleasures of doing totally as one pleases. Adulthood brings no guarantee of living happily ever after. Instead of the rewards of choosing well and wisely, adulthood seems only to finally offer the opportunity to make those choices, from silly to serious, on one's own. Instead of working at learning all that one needs to know to be an adult, one now finally *is* an adult, presumably putting to use all that learning and preparation. Adulthood has to do with the feeling of knowing how to act and what to do, such as what to order and how much to tip in a restaurant. Most of us have felt the pain of youthful uncertainty in grown-up situations. We struggle to manage our youthful discomfort in the belief that each event will eventually bring the longed-for knowledge and confidence to cover all situations. In reality, of course, the completeness really comes with the ability to be comfortable with one's uncertainties.

Adulthood brings a sense of completeness—of preparation achieved—that is never there during childhood. The fact that many of us continue to feel uncertain in some situations well past middle age merely attests to the power of the notion of completeness to our understanding of adulthood. Even though as adults we continue to learn and grow, that learning is not in *preparation* for adulthood in the same way that most of our learning was before achieving adult status. Even if we are unsure in some situations, it is not so much because we aren't prepared to handle it, but instead because our knowledge and experience make the choice of an action more ambiguous.

A continuing struggle for us is to make sure that Ian's adulthood is complete in this way. Even though he has continued to learn many things since high school graduation, we have tried to make sure that his learning of new skills or information is not a requirement placed on Ian by his supporters for the achievement of adulthood. He is an adult even if he never learns another skill. It is a difficult balance to achieve. Ian—and all other adults—need to be afforded opportunities to continue to learn and grow, but without the trappings of preparatory training or schooling. If we think of life as a type of language, then adulthood as autonomy would seem to be a move from the future to the present tense.

The Dimension of Membership

Sometimes it seems as if we allow the dimension and symbols of autonomy to exhaust our understanding of adulthood. Adulthood, from this viewpoint, is essentially a matter of independence. This can create problems when we ask society to respond to all persons with severe disabilities as "fully adult" because many are limited by their disability from demonstrating such independence in ways that are similar to how others without disabilities demonstrate them. Indeed, for many people, this limited independence is precisely what the label of *disability* means in the

first place. However, we would argue that limiting our understanding of adulthood as "being able to do it by oneself" is problematic for all adults whether or not they have a disability. There is an equally important dimension in understanding adulthood that serves as a crucial counterbalance to the individualistic emphasis on autonomy. This dimension includes all of those facets of adulthood that involve citizenship and affiliation and that must be supported by the collaboration and sacrifice of others. We collectively refer to these facets as the dimension of membership. If adulthood as autonomy is a move to life in the present tense, then adulthood as membership recognizes that life is plural rather than singular, communal as well as individual.

If they needed a lesson in this importance of membership to emerging adulthood, Douglas's parents had one during his first year of high school. At one point, Douglas moved to a new high school that promised more openness in the inclusive program that his parents were determined to provide for him. However, the experience of moving from class to class in the new high school prompted Douglas to simply leave any time that the call of the activity in the gym was more appealing than what was going on in class. Waiting for a bell apparently seemed silly when the decision could be made so much more easily without the assistance of a bell! Expressing his self-determination in this way, however, was frowned upon by the adults in the school and the problem of getting up and leaving class became one to be solved by the professionals. The classroom teachers had few ideas, but the resource teacher decided that finding some ways for Douglas to "buddy up" with classmates might help. Soon a group of friends—one or more of whom were always in his class—simply looked out for Douglas to make sure that he got to the next place at the appropriate time. Invitations to movies, dances, and other social events followed and now, many years later, he still sees and spends time with some of these same friends who are all members of the community. One in particular—Lenny—is shown with Douglas in a favorite graduation picture (see Figure 16–2).

Citizenship. Anthropologists have probably contributed most to our understanding of the communal aspects of adulthood in most cultures, including our own. They have described in detail the rituals and responsibilities that societies attach to adult status. In a

FIGURE 16–2
Douglas and His Friend Lenny at High School Graduation

We have not pursued voting as a way for Ian to explore this aspect of membership, mostly because we fear that providing the assistance he would need might really just result in one of us having the advantage of two votes. However, there are other ways that Ian can exercise community responsibility. Stuffing envelopes, for example, passing out campaign information, or expressing an opinion through yard signs are ways that Ian can and does contribute to the political life of his community. Actively recycling by using his backpack instead of bags when shopping and expressing his political opinions on issues of accessibility with the "Attitudes Are the Real Disability" bumper sticker affixed to the back of his wheelchair are examples of ways in which Ian participates as a citizen of our community.

Affiliation. The communal dimension of adulthood is not only about a grudging performance of civic duties or even a cheerful altruism of civic sacrifice. An important aspect of communal adulthood lies in the various examples of voluntary association, fellowship, celebration, and support that adults typically discover and create. One of the most common signs of adulthood, for example, is the intentional formation of new families and the extension of old ones. Through formal and informal affiliations, adults locate themselves socially as well as geographically (see Figure 16–3). You might live on the east side of town, belong to the square-dance club, attend the Catholic Church, and have a spouse and two children. We might live in a

FIGURE 16–3
Ian Often Meets friends at One of the Local Pubs

very real sense, it is only with these rites of passage into adulthood that we become full members of our communities. In part, this involves an element of responsibility for others and the community in general. Voting and other acts of collective governance are the most obvious signs of this theme and perhaps seem the most daunting for some adults with severe disabilities. After the presidential election in 2008, a study conducted for the American Association of People with Disabilities (Schur & Kruse, 2009) showed that people with disabilities (of any kind or degree) voted in record numbers. Despite this improvement, the percentage of voting-age persons with disabilities who actually voted was still some 7% lower than the rate of people without disabilities who voted (compared to a 12% gap for the 2000 election). Obviously, there are additional considerations for some people with the most significant disabilities.

downtown condo, belong to the library patrons' society, participate in community theater, and volunteer at the local rape crisis center. The particular array of affiliations can differ dramatically. However, in the aggregate, those affiliations help define a community just as the community, in turn, helps define each of us as adults. Through their affiliations, adults support and define each other.

The definitional power of our affiliations seems to us to be very true for Ian and for other adults who require similar supports. Ian's life tends to reflect the people in his life. Right now, his two primary support people like to camp, give big parties, and garden. So Ian does, too. Moreover, Ian's community of Eugene, Oregon, is one that prizes such outdoor activities, and so there are many groups and opportunities to encourage these hobbies. When Ian was in his early 20s, dancing and the swimming pool were favorite pursuits of his supporters, and Ian obligingly enjoyed these activities just as much. Lately, one of his support providers has gotten involved in roller derby, and Ian enjoys the controlled chaos of these contests. At the same time, Ian has his own long-standing hobbies. He finds the lights and sounds of casinos especially enjoyable. Here, as well, it is not the singular pursuit of winning or losing that Ian enjoys so much as it is all of the people and the activity that fills the casino with noise and hubbub. All of us in Ian's life have had to find ways to join in the occasional excursions to nearby casinos, while keeping a close eye on the dollar amounts won and—more likely—lost (see Figure 16–4). Not only must Ian join in the interests and affiliations of friends and family, they must also join Ian in some of his choices as well. (For his 40th birthday, a trip to Las Vegas by Ian and a select group of friends and family was a grand success with concerts, games, and, yes, losing a few dollars at the penny slot machines.)

Douglas also illustrates this reciprocal relationship with those who support and befriend him. Lenny first became Douglas's friend in high school. He is married now and has his own children, but he and Douglas still see each other regularly. Sometimes Douglas helps around Lenny's house by splitting wood or doing yard work and gardening. Sometimes they go out to the bar or other places. Lenny's cousin owns a garage and sometimes they both go over to help out—Douglas is in charge of finding the right tools and making sure that everything gets put back in its correct place. Douglas is finicky about things

FIGURE 16–4
A Favorite Activity Is Playing the Slot Machines at a Nearby Casino

being in their proper places, whether it is in his parents' kitchen or the garage, and it is one of the personal traits that probably helps him build and grow his affiliations in the community through his friends and their friends.

The Dimension of Change

We said earlier that adulthood as autonomy could be described as a move from the future to the present tense. The dimension of adulthood as membership shows that the description requires a plural rather than a singular construction. Let us follow the logic in this final dimension of adulthood and argue that a dynamic approach to life demands that adulthood must finally be understood as a verb, not a noun. In the biological sense, adulthood may indeed represent a developmental maturity; in a social and psychological sense, it can also represent phases of continued growth.

Of course, this aspect of adulthood has been the focus of increased attention in developmental psychology since the seminal work of Erik Erikson (1950) on the eight "crises" or stages of the life cycle, four of which occur in adulthood. Subsequent psychologists have variously refined and revised this work (Erikson & Martin, 1984; Levinson, 1978; Vaillant, 1977). Sociologists and historians have added an important sociocultural perspective to these stages within the life span (Arnett & Tanner, 2006; Blatterer, 2007; Elder, 1998; Hareven, 1978). In general, however, these developmentalist writers help us to understand that adulthood has its own stages of growth, change, and learning. It is a period of both realization and continued transition.

Ian is now 40. He seems to have transitioned, along with his housemates, into the very beginnings of the ever-changing span of time we call "middle age." He is a different person than he was at 21. His tastes in music are still eclectic, but he seems to enjoy visiting his parents and singing along to old Paul Simon, Beatles, or Simon and Garfunkel CDs more than he did seven or eight years ago. He's gained some weight, and we've been told that he has a few early gray hairs (we haven't spotted them yet). He's getting a little arthritis in his knees. More than with just changes in his appearance, however, he approaches his 40s with a different demeanor. He can be serious or consoling when the occasion demands, although he might not describe the emotion in those terms. He has experienced the death of grandparents, lost friends and support workers, and learned how to be alone in ways that are different from when he lived with us.

His parents have moved to work in a new state. Although Dianne is still working in Eugene part time and is around for part of every month, Phil visits only a few times a year and talks to Ian a couple of times a week via video phone calls. These changes mark a new phase in all of our lives. We all miss living close to each other as Ian expresses clearly each time that he meets one of us at the airport with smiles, enthusiasm, and sometimes flowers. We worry about the distance, but, for now, Ian's adulthood is secure enough, even with all of the continuing challenges, to make this kind of change possible for all of us.

For many people with disabilities, these three dimensions of adulthood occur only partially, often as approximations of the symbols that the rest of us use to identify others and ourselves as adults. Table 16–2 illustrates some examples of these symbols that are present in many adult lives, although not in as many adult lives of people with disabilities. If we only assess

---

TABLE 16–2
Symbols of Adulthood: Some Examples

Symbols of Autonomy
- Having a source of income, a job, or wealth
- Making your own choices, both the big important ones and the little trivial ones
- No more waiting for the privilege of doing what you want, how you want, and when and with whom you want to do it

Symbols of Membership
- A voter registration card
- Membership cards for organizations and clubs
- An appointment calendar and address book
- Season tickets, bumper stickers, charitable contributions of time and money

Symbols of Change
- Marriage
- New hobbies
- Children
- A new job or a new home
- New skills
- New friends

---

the symbols we each can claim, however, we may make the mistake of denying the status of adulthood to people with disabilities. Symbols are important, but they are not the entire story. One way that we evaluate our success in supporting Ian's adulthood is to examine periodically just how each of these dimensions is visible in his life. How does the daily round of Ian's life reflect the ways of becoming a unique member of our community? Douglas's parents ask similar questions. Are Douglas's activities, affiliations, and ways of participating varied? Do Ian's and Douglas's preferences and choices change over time? Are those changes reflected in an evolving understanding among their circle of family, friends, and supporters? We will return to these questions later with examples that might help you see how these dimensions of adulthood can apply in the life of a person with severe disabilities. First, however, let us examine more completely why these notions have been so difficult to apply to this group of people.

Denying Adulthood

If the meaning of adulthood involves the dimensions of autonomy, membership, and change, then how have those dimensions affected our understanding of adults with severe disabilities? There are undeniable improvements over the past two decades in the movement of people with intellectual disabilities into community-based jobs and residences (Mank, Cioffi, & Yovanoff, 2003; Prouty, Alba, & Lakin, 2007). However, the evidence of continuing problems in the quality of life for many of these individuals is apparent even to the casual observer. Most states continue to have long waiting lists for residential and employment opportunities. According to one poll, only 35% reported being employed full or part time (cited in Grossi, Gilbride, & Mank, 2008, p. 108). The proportion of individuals in supported employment in all-day and work programs had dropped to 21% by 2006 (Braddock, Hemp, & Rizollo, 2008, p. 40). As of 2007, more than 80,000 individuals were estimated to be waiting for residential services outside of their family homes (Alba, Prouty, & Lakin, 2007, p. 42). Although the number of people with developmental disabilities who reside in large private or public institutions has dramatically declined over the past two decades, spending by federal and state governments still totaled more than $8.3 billion (for fiscal year 2006) to keep people in these large congregate care facilities (Braddock et al., 2008, p. 7). For more than 15 years, evidence has been mounting for the economic and social benefits of supporting employment for adults with developmental disabilities. Yet unemployment and segregated workshops and day programs still dominate the vocational services offered (DeLio, Rogan, & Geary, 2000; Mank, 2007; Wehman, 2006). For individuals with severe disabilities, in particular, this empirical evidence of a poor quality of life must also be understood in a historical context.

If you examine the history of adulthood for people with severe disabilities, you find a story not only of symbolic deprivation but also of economic deprivation. Indeed, at the heart of our discussion is the belief that the two are inextricably related. Symbols of adulthood accompany the practice of being an adult. Or, to reverse the logic, the denial of adulthood to people with severe disabilities has been symbolic as well as concrete. Recent movements to recognize the full range of rights and responsibilities of adults with severe disabilities can best be understood in light of this history of denial. Table 16–3 summarizes some of the symbols of the denial of adulthood across the dimensions that will be discussed next.

Unending Childhood

Wolfensberger (1972) not only helped popularize the principle of normalization as a basic orientation for

TABLE 16–3
Some Examples of Symbols of the Denial of Adulthood

Unending Childhood
- Childish, diminutive names like Bobby and Susie
- Enforced dependency that permits others to make all of the important choices
- Few life changes

Unfinished Transitions
- No more school but no job, home, or affiliations in the community
- Rituals for ending but not for beginning
- Acquisition of visible but empty symbols like beards and pipes, but no jobs, homes, or community affiliations

Unhelpful Services
- Clienthood: A focus on remediation and readiness that is determined through the mechanisms of professional preciousness (see later)
- Anonymity: Service standards and procedures that can obscure or even overwhelm individuality and uniqueness
- Chronicity: The professional decision to deny lifelong change because the client is not susceptible to further development

human services but he also deserves credit for raising our awareness of the symbolic dimensions of discrimination and stigma in the lives of persons with severe disabilities. In particular, he helped highlight how society referred to people with intellectual disabilities in terms and images that suggested a status of "eternal childhood." Nearly 40 years later, it is still frustratingly common to hear adults with severe disabilities described by the construct of "mental age": "Johnny Smith is 34 years old but has the mind of a 3-year-old." In an interview that we did some years ago (P. M. Ferguson, Ferguson, & Jones, 1988), a parent of a 40-year-old son with Down syndrome described him as a sort of disabled Peter Pan—one of the "never-never children." "This thing about normalizing will not happen . . . they'll always be childlike" (p. 109).

Fortunately, the myth of eternal childhood as the inevitable fate for people with severe disabilities is much less powerful than it was 10 or 20 years ago. We like to think that today's generation of young parents is less likely than our generation to hear from professionals that their sons and daughters are "never-never children." Increasingly, it seems that both professionals and the general public are aware of the stigmatizing assumptions built into childish terms of reference. Appearance and activities are more and more likely to avoid the most obviously childish examples (e.g., adults playing with simple puzzles or toys, carrying school lunch boxes to work). We are gradually moving away from our infantilizing images of the past.

Of course, if symbols are the only thing to be changed, then the true movement to adulthood will still be stalled. We remember working at a large state institution for persons with severe disabilities some 30 years ago. This institution closed in 1998, but at the time, a number of persons who worked there had apparently gotten only part of the message about treating people as adults. As a result, over a period of months, all of the adult men on one ward grew beards and smoked pipes. Nothing else changed in their lives to encourage their personal autonomy, much less their membership in the community. The beards and pipes were simply empty symbols of adulthood that had no grounding in the daily lives of indignity and isolation that the men continued to lead. Alternatively, allowing someone the choice of risking his or her well-being by not wearing a seat belt in the car or by eating three large pizzas for dinner in the name of autonomy and adult independence also misses the point, resulting instead in the limitation of adulthood, perhaps quite literally if that person's health is threatened by such risky choices.

Even at 40, Ian might choose to watch cartoons and always choose to drink chocolate milk or any number of other choices that might be more typical of a young child. Once in a while, these choices are fine. But as a steady diet, such choices do not communicate the full range of options that most adults enjoy. Part of truly supporting Ian's adulthood is making sure that he has enough experience with lots of different options in order to make adult decisions. He still does choose chocolate milk, but probably more often now he chooses Dr. Pepper or a beer. And his taste in beer has grown more sophisticated in the past decade. He even enjoys wine more than he used to. The point is not so much to deny revisiting the preferences of childhood but to offer the many more varied choices found in adulthood just as frequently.

Unfinished Transitions

An important part of the move away from the view of severe disability as an unending childhood has occurred in the increased programmatic attention paid to the transition period from school to adult life (Bambara, Wilson, & McKenzie, 2007; Storey et al., 2008; Wehman, 2006; Wehmeyer, Gragoudas, & Shogren, 2006). This focus on transition has certainly clarified the right of people with severe disabilities not to remain forever imprisoned by images of childhood. It has led to a heightened awareness on the part of the special education community that *what happens after a student leaves school is perhaps the most crucial test of how effective that schooling was.* In terms of program evaluation, the emphasis on transition planning in the schools has clearly identified adulthood as the ultimate outcome measure for the process of special education.

However, as a cultural generalization, an escape from unending childhood has not yet meant an entrance into full-fledged adulthood for many people with severe disabilities. Instead of eternal childhood, we see their current status as one of stalled or unfinished transition: a "neither–nor" ambiguity in which young people with severe disabilities are neither seen as children nor as adults. As with adulthood itself, however, transition, too, can be viewed symbolically. It is in this symbolic sense that people with severe disabilities can become embedded in a permanent process of incomplete transition.

Several scholars have suggested the anthropological concept of *liminality* as being most descriptive of this situation (Murphy, Scheer, Murphy, & Mack, 1988; Mwaria, 1990). Liminality refers to a state of being where a person is suspended between the demands and opportunities of childhood and adulthood. Many societies use various rituals of initiation, purification, or other transitions to both accomplish and commemorate a significant change in status. In many cultures where these rituals retain their original intensity, the actual event can last for days or months. During such rituals, the person undergoing the process is said to occupy a liminal (or "threshold") state. According to one author,

People in a liminal condition are without clear status, for their old position has been expunged and they have not yet been given a new one. They are "betwixt and between," neither fish nor fowl; they are suspended in social space without firm identity or role definition. . . . In a very real sense, they are nonpersons, making all interactions with them unpredictable and problematic. (Murphy et al., 1988, p. 237)

For too many adults with severe disabilities, one could say that the transition to adulthood is a ritual that once never began but now begins but seldom ends. Instead, they remain on the threshold of adulthood in a kind of permanent liminality—suspended in social space.

We see this liminality in the kinds of social responses to adults with severe disabilities that perpetuate social isolation in the name of autonomy. Professionals who tell parents that they need to "back off" from involvement in their newly adult son's or daughter's life so that he or she can begin to build a separate life apart from the ties of family and home sometimes end up isolating the new adult by removing the most effective advocates for an expanded membership in the community. Parents and professionals who conspire (usually with purely benevolent intentions) to create a facade of independence for adults with severe disabilities by allowing them trivial, secondary, or coerced choices instead of true self-determination (Ferguson & O'Brien, 2005) trap adults in the isolation of liminality in another way.

In still other instances, adults are given a plentiful supply of token affiliations and social activities with no attention to the symbols of self-sufficiency that are represented by a real job with a real income, making the illusion incomplete in yet another way. Such an ambiguous social status will continue to frustrate individuals in their efforts to define themselves as adults. Society, in general, will continue to feel uncomfortable in the presence of such people, not knowing how to respond.

Ian's own transition seemed to be at risk of an extended liminal status for the first few months after graduation. He continued to live in our home, and his only "job" was a volunteer job that he had begun when in high school. His personal agent and personal support staff created a schedule of personal and recreational activities to fill his days. While Ian certainly enjoyed this round of activity, it felt to us, and we think to him as well, like a kind of holding pattern. He was waiting for his chance to enter the routines and responsibilities of adulthood. The "meantime schedule" of activity was a substitute and one that, in the end, did not last long. We'll have more to say about Ian's adult life later and how his daily and weekly routines simply are his life and substitute or wait for nothing. For Douglas, the extended liminal status seemed to be more of a permanent condition, except for the fact that in a small rural community, with a chronic lack of services for adults with disabilities, community members and families find ways to circumvent the status of unfinished transition by relying on social networks and natural supports.

Unhelpful Services

Although the special education system must share part of the blame for unfinished transitions, much of the responsibility must fall on an "adult" services system that has been historically plagued with problems of poor policy, inadequate funding, and ineffective programs (P. M. Ferguson & Ferguson, 2001; Ferguson & O'Brien, 2005). There are significant exceptions to this generalization across the domains of residential programs (Felce & Perry, 2007, Stancliffe & Lakin, 2007), employment support (Grossi et al., 2008; Mank, 2007), and leisure and recreation (Miller, Bowens, Strike, Venable, & Schleien, 2009; Rynders, Schleien, & Matson, 2003), but for far too many, the promise of adulthood remains an unfilled promise.

Many analysts of the social services system continue to point to fundamental inadequacies in adult services (Bérubé, 2003; Drake, 2001; Ferguson, 2003; Fleischer & Zames, 2001; McKnight, 1995). Although each of these analyses has its own list of problems, they all include some basic complaints. We will briefly mention three of these issues that correspond to the three dimensions of adulthood that we have already set forth. These three issues are (a) clienthood, (b) anonymity, and (c) chronicity.

Clienthood

The traditional services system promotes "clienthood" rather than adulthood. Dependency unavoidably fosters the role of clienthood either explicitly or implicitly, and dependency is the status of many individuals "served" by the traditional services system. The role has many versions, but perhaps the most familiar is that which imposes a model of medical or behavioral deficit as the dominant rationale for services decisions. In this version, the essential orientation for the delivery of services is that the individual with the disability has something that needs to be cured or remediated. Just as patients are expected to follow the doctor's orders and take the prescribed medicine, so are people with disabilities expected to follow their "individual habilitation (or support) plans," work hard to improve themselves (Bickenbach, 2001; Drake, 2001; McKnight, 1995), and abide by the suggestions of their designated professionals (e.g., case managers, job coaches, residential providers).

This dependency is perhaps most familiar in those aspects of the welfare system (e.g., Supplemental Security Income, Social Security Disability Income, Medicaid) that can unintentionally create economic disincentives to vocational independence. But it is equally powerful at the more personal level through a tendency that Sarason (1972) has called "professional preciousness." Professional preciousness refers to the tendency of professionals to define problems in ways that require traditionally trained professionals (like themselves) for the solution. Thus, case managers sometimes define a client's needs according to what the system happens to provide (Drake, 2001; Taylor, 2001). Opportunities for meaningful employment are overlooked or not sought out unless they have been developed through the proper channels by certified rehabilitation professionals instead of untrained, but willing, coworkers (Ferguson & O'Brien, 2005). Those who find the penalties to be too high for participation in such a system can "drop out," but only at the risk of losing all benefits (especially health care), as well as official standing as "disabled" (P. M. Ferguson et al., 1990). By limiting the avenues for achieving jobs, homes, and active social lives to the "disability-approved" services offered through the formal services system, clienthood undermines autonomy (P. M. Ferguson & Ferguson, 2001; Williams, 2001).

We realize that we have drawn a pretty bleak picture. Our point is not that that all public policy is somehow bad or that it does not sometimes contribute in very real ways to realizing adulthood for many with disabilities. We are saying that people with severe disabilities will more often than not suffer less instead of more at the hands of the formal system. We and many other families have struggled to "tweak" and bend the demands of the formal system to allow it to better meet the needs of our sons and daughters. Our successes, when they occur, best serve to make our point that we need a system that doesn't require extraordinary effort to resist the clienthood, anonymity, and chronicity that too often describe our current system of services.

We have strived to create options for Ian that use the social services system but reject this status of clienthood, at least from Ian's point of view and, perhaps more important, from the point of view of his direct supporters. Although Ian's living situation is possible because of the official funding category of "supported living" and his job support dollars are provided through the category of "supported employment," we have redirected these dollars from the familiar residential or vocational programs to a process that allows Ian, his family, and supporters to

directly decide how to use these dollars. Along with a small number of friends and colleagues, we operate a nonprofit organization that does not decide for Ian or the six others whom we are currently also supporting, but instead manages the paperwork, rules, reports, and budgets that permit Ian and those most directly involved in his life to direct how the support dollars are best used to support his adulthood. Our collective efforts to support Ian's definition of his own life have allowed us to meet the necessary rules and regulations but protect Ian and his supporters from having to attend to them constantly. It has become the responsibility of Ian's personal support agent to make sure that the penalties of participation in the services system are minimized so that Ian may develop his own adult identity apart from that of social services system client.

Anonymity

The traditional system not only promotes dependency for many, but also creates a kind of bureaucratic isolation in which procedures replace people and standardization overwhelms context. Certainly, this is partly and simply a function of the size of the programs and the number of people involved. However, it goes beyond this to a style of centralization and control that pursues efficiency above all else. This style often leads to situations of sterility and isolation in programs that are ostensibly intended to increase a person's social integration. The need for efficient purchasing and supply can lead to so much similarity in the possessions and activities of clients that the individual becomes swallowed up in a collective that diminishes each member's uniqueness. It seems unlikely that the individuals in a dozen group homes and apartments operated by the same supported living agency all like the same brand of ice cream, prefer the same laundry detergent, and choose the same color of paper napkins, for example.

An even more powerful example involves the types of relationships many people with severe disabilities experience. One thing that seems to be important to the social relationships and friendships that most of us enjoy is "knowing each other's stories." The very process of developing a friendship usually involves learning about each other through stories about experiences and history that are shared in conversation.

When people enter Ian's life, we support the developing relationship by sharing much of Ian's story for him. If he lived in a community residential program, however, the constant turnover of staff and the demands for confidentiality might so limit what others know about his life that he is rendered virtually anonymous except for what can be readily observed and directly experienced. In a similar way, Douglas's friends, like Lenny, continue to introduce him to others in the community so that he has developed a very large network of people who know his "story" and his role in the community.

Chronicity

The final barrier that seems to be an unavoidable facet of the traditional support system is something we term *chronicity*. Chronicity is the officially delivered, systematic denial of lifelong change and growth. Chronicity is created by professional pronouncements that someone or some group is not susceptible to further development. Again, this barrier results from the dominance of what might be called a "therapeutic model" in the overall design of services. For those who "respond to treatment" in this model, there is a future of more treatment, more programs, and more clienthood. However, for those whose disability is judged as being so severe as to be beyond help (e.g., "incorrigible," "incurable," "hopeless," "ineducable"), there is a professionally ordained abandonment (Ferguson, 2002). The person becomes "caught in the continuum" (S. J. Taylor, 1988), whereby expansion of adult opportunities is denied as being premature while commitment to functional improvement is abandoned as unrealistic. For example, even service reforms such as supported employment that were initially developed specifically for people with severe disabilities have been denied to people with the most severe disabilities, who are judged to be "incapable of benefiting" from vocationally oriented training (D. L. Ferguson & Ferguson, 1986; Ferguson, 2002). In this orientation, the system presents full adulthood for people with severe disabilities as something that must be "earned," a reward handed out by professionals to people who are judged to be capable of continuing to progress. Failure to progress in the past justifies compressed opportunities in the future.

The Dilemma of Adulthood

All of this leaves those of us who wish to see the promise of adulthood fulfilled for people with severe disabilities with a frustrating dilemma: How can we help people with severe disabilities gain access to the cultural benefits of community membership and personal autonomy that are associated with adulthood without neglecting the continued need for adequate support and protection that did not end with childhood? How can we achieve this in the context of the current services system that can be more unhelpful than helpful? Let us offer a fairly minor example of this dilemma.

If someone asked Ian if he wanted to watch a Hannah Montana video or 60 Minutes, he would almost certainly choose Miley Cyrus. It's lively, has music that he likes, and recognizable voices. A Morley Safer interview just does not match up.

Concerned as we are with Ian's adult status, should we honor his choice as an autonomous adult and turn on the video even though we know it is an activity commonly associated with much younger people (mostly pre-teen girls)? Or should we override his choice in the belief that, in this case, the outcome (i.e., watching more adult entertainment) is more important than the process (i.e., allowing him to independently choose what he watches)? Perhaps we should not offer him the choice in the first place, confident that we will select a much more age-appropriate program. In the long run, we might argue, this will enhance Ian's image and expand his opportunities for affiliation and membership in a community of adults. Or is it okay to watch the Hannah Montana video once for every two or three times he watches Morley Safer? Finally, we might look at this example of his viewing habits as an area of learning for Ian and emphasize the dimensions of change for him. In so doing, we might honor Ian's choice for now while simultaneously exposing him to more options that might be equally appealing but less childish (perhaps Homer Simpson as a compromise between Morley Safer and Miley Cyrus).

Excessive emphasis on the symbols of autonomy might actually diminish a person's access to membership symbols. Having only a volunteer job is not the same as volunteering your free time after work at a paid job. Making sure that a young adult lives apart from family and previous friends in pursuit of an image of self-sufficiency, for example, may restrict the adult's involvement in activities and groups that his family and those very friends might help to access.

Similarly, excessive emphasis on change might perpetuate the liminal position of being permanently stuck on the threshold of full adulthood, spending one's days in endless preparation for life instead of actually living it. This is perhaps most common for those young adults who leave the preparatory experience of schools only to find themselves in a day program or residential service that continues a readiness training focus. Many young adults with severe disabilities still leave high school for the continued preparation of work training programs and sheltered workshops where many will labor for 30 to 40 years in a parody of productivity. We wonder how many adults "retire" from such programs when they reach their 60s without ever "graduating" to real jobs.

> *Douglas and his family have struggled with finding him real work since school ended. Services in his rural part of Atlantic Canada are quite limited and Douglas's support needs are significant despite his skills. One of the first jobs involved a family-operated business growing sprouts that were then sold to local grocery stores. Douglas learned to assist in growing the sprouts, but really liked packing the sprouts for sale, loading the van, delivering them to a round of local shops, and, yes, sometimes taking a break outside the sprout house (see Figure 16-5). Some of the people who he got to know through this job not only still know him, but make his daily presence in the community more secure and socially networked as he still sees and engages with them. The sprout business became a casualty of development. The smaller groceries gave way to one or two larger grocery chains that preferred to import their produce from large distributors in Ontario instead of purchasing from local farmers—and sprout growers. The business eventually became financially untenable and Douglas experienced the first of what would be several periods of unemployment.*

FIGURE 16–5
Douglas Takes a Break Outside the Sprout House

While sheltered workshops are less likely to include periods of unemployment, indirectly, such one-dimensional service offerings can deemphasize the importance of social reform to accommodate a broader range of acceptable adult behavior. Instead, we believe that a full understanding of the multidimensional aspects of adulthood in our tradition and culture allows a more productive and flexible approach to the dilemma of balancing self-sufficiency with support and social accommodation with personal development.

For us as parents, it seems that the professionals have done a good job of convincing society to recognize the importance of a transition from childhood but have not fully discovered what that process should be a transition to. We are, as it were, still in mid-journey on the trail toward adulthood for people with severe disabilities. As professionals, it seems to us that our field has not adequately understood the complexity of the journey or the character of its destination. Without such an understanding, the process of achieving adulthood—symbolically or otherwise—for people with severe disabilities will never reach a conclusion.

Having said that and having explored the dilemma of adulthood for people with severe disabilities, we must now turn to the good news. Answers are emerging. Perhaps we have moved past the midpoint of our journey, at least for some adults with severe disabilities. Our last section will explore some of these developments after we present a brief summary.

Achieving Adulthood

To summarize, the promise of adulthood in our society should be more than a job, a place to live, and being on one's own. A full understanding of the meaning of adulthood must look at the structure of symbols and imagery that surround this culturally defined role. In looking, we found that we could organize that symbolic structure around the three dimensions of autonomy, membership, and change. We further divided the dimension of autonomy into three elements (self-sufficiency, self-determination, and completeness) and membership into two elements (citizenship and affiliation). Then we discussed the ways in which our current services options often tend to deny full participation in these dimensions. Even though some of the symbols of autonomy, membership, and change might be attempted, too often the result for persons with severe disabilities is really an experience of unfinished transition or unhelpful services.

Despite recent and helpful moves within the field of special education and disability services to focus on the importance of the transition process from school to adult life, we argued that most adults with severe disabilities remain on the threshold of adulthood in the fullest sense of substantive participation in both the symbols and the substance of multidimensional adulthood. An unhelpful services system helps to perpetuate this unfinished transition by encouraging dependency, social isolation, and personal chronicity. This leaves us with the dilemma of how to surround people such as Ian and Douglas with resources that recognize their needs without denying their adulthood. The good news is that it really is possible. The bad news is that it is present for only a few so far. There is still much to do.

We believe that the solution to the dilemmas that we have raised about adulthood lies in the merger of a reformed support system with a multidimensional understanding of adulthood. In this section, we first outline some of the key themes of this new paradigm for support services that respond to the barriers to adulthood that the current system continues to create and maintain despite these new efforts. Next, we will look at how these themes are starting to emerge in terms of the three dimensions of full adulthood that we have discussed. We think that, taken together, these expanded versions of support and adulthood provide an inclusive approach to achieving a high quality of adult life for all people, even those with the most severe disabilities or intensive support needs. Finally, we freely admit that probably nowhere in our country could one find all of the elements of this new approach in place and fully functioning. However, we also believe that each of the elements does exist somewhere for some people right now, and for some, we are beginning to achieve several elements. There is increasing reason for optimism that systemic change is starting to occur. The challenge that we face is "simply" to fill in the gaps.

The Concept of Support

The significant reforms of the past 25 years in developmental disabilities have occurred mainly under the banners of deinstitutionalization and normalization. We need to recall the massive shift of people from large, segregated settings to more community-based arrangements that has occurred in less than three decades (Braddock et al., 2008; Lakin, Prouty, Polister, & Coucouvanis, 2003; Prouty et al., 2007). In the decade between 1995 and 2005, the percentage of individuals

with developmental disabilities receiving residential support who lived in homes of their own (either purchases or rentals) went from 13% to almost 25% (Lakin & Stancliffe, 2007, p. 154). In the past few years, even some of the money used to support these people has made a similar shift from institution to community (Braddock et al., 2008). However, while only partially achieved, normalization and deinstitutionalization now need to be joined (or perhaps even replaced) by a new banner if we are to revitalize the move toward continued restructuring of policy and practice (Ferguson, Ferguson, & Blumberg, 1997; McKnight, 1995; Nerney, 2008; O'Brien & Murray, 1997). It is increasingly possible to see the outline of an effort to move beyond the perceived limitations of deinstitutionalization and normalization as policy guidelines to an emphasis on support and self-determination.

The central feature of this new, and admittedly sporadic, effort to radically reorient adult services is an expanded understanding of the concept of "support" and its relationship to self-determination. One way of summarizing the conceptual model that seems to govern this effort is "supported adulthood." The supported adulthood approach is the result of an inductive process. Its unifying vision has emerged out of disparate reform initiatives from across several service domains, including supported employment, supported living, supported education, supported recreation, and supported families.

What Is Different about Supported Adulthood?

Supported adulthood is more than a simple commitment of the field to redress past institutional wrongs by eliminating segregated options. It is also more than an attempt to make people appear normal. The central theme is in the expanded interpretation of what is and is not supportive of a full adult life in the community. The common purpose is in the effort to recognize a dual sense of independence and belonging as the most basic benefits of social support programs. This enriched notion of *support* has indicated a way out of the conceptual dilemma whereby people with disabilities had to either earn their presence in the community with total independence and self-sufficiency or be inserted there with the type of bureaucratic arrogance so common to social welfare programs. In either case, the result was all-too-clustered isolation associated with the overlapping problems of perpetual clienthood and excessive individualism already described. The image of the 10-bed group home comes to mind, with residents separated from their neighbors simply by the size and regimentation of their house. It often became a place of work for direct care staff rather than a home where people lived. All too often, adults with severe disabilities were in the neighborhood physically but not socially; they were present but were not truly a part of their community.

What is different in the notion of supported adulthood is a guiding commitment to participation and affiliation instead of control and remediation. *Support* becomes an adjective, modifying and enriching an adult's capacity for participation in and contribution to his or her community. Support cannot be a predefined service that is available to anyone who meets the eligibility criteria. The real message of initiatives such as supported employment and supported living is—or should be—that all people do not have to be totally independent in terms of skills or fully competitive (or even close) in terms of productivity to be active, growing, valued adult members of their communities.

Components of Supported Adulthood

There are at least five features of this expanded approach to support for adults with severe disabilities and their families: (a) natural contexts, (b) informal supports, (c) user definitions, (d) local character, and (e) universal eligibility.

Natural Contexts

The traditional welfare approach to services for people with severe disabilities has been the creation of special settings, with special staff, and separate bureaucracies (e.g., institutions, self-contained schools, and sheltered workshops). Part of the economic irrationality of many of the current approaches is that funding tracks continue to direct financial resources into these settings even as the field increasingly recognizes their inadequacies. Certainly, the situation is improving because the states have finally tipped the balance in financial support toward community programs. The growing use of Medicaid waivers for community support (Braddock et al., 2008) has allowed the federal government to work more closely with the states in removing policy barriers that had previously kept Medicaid dollars from flowing into progressive community settings. All of these trends show a growing appreciation for the value of the natural context as the location of choice for people with disabilities regardless of the domain of life being discussed.

Supported adulthood requires a reliance on natural contexts in the design and location of its supports. *Support* must become an adjective or adverb that *modifies* an existing, natural setting instead of creating a separate one. This shift directly challenges the traditional belief that the more intensive the support needs, the more segregated the setting has to be (S. J. Taylor, 1988, 2001). Instead, the focus on natural settings allows the intensity of the support to be truly individualized from context to context instead of programmatically standardized along an arbitrary services continuum (American Association on Mental Retardation, 2002).

The supported adulthood approach brings progressively intensive support to those individuals who need it without abandoning the community setting. The assumption driving the design of services within this approach is that vocational programs for people with severe disabilities should occur in those settings within the community where the work naturally occurs, not in specially created sites or segregated settings (Mank, 2007). Homes should be in neighborhoods where other people live (Lakin & Stancliffe, 2007; Stancliffe & Lakin, 2007). A preference exists for the generic service instead of the specialized one whenever possible. The appeal of natural contexts, then, is twofold: (a) it returns to a reliance on the community setting, thereby combating the isolating tendencies of specialized programs; and (b) it encourages independence by placing people outside the protected environment of segregated programs.

A shift to natural contexts first began for Ian during his last years of high school. One of the community jobs that he explored—doing laundry at the local YMCA for the next day's fitness enthusiasts—continued as a volunteer job that earned Ian a free membership for a couple of years after he finished school. Now, all of his life and supports occur in natural contexts. He lives in his own home in a typical neighborhood much like that of his parents' (see Figure 16-6). His job for the past 20 years has been with the university food services part of the student union and involves him in traveling all over campus (see Figure 16-7). But even beyond these major components of his life, being part of the natural context over the years—for living, working, and recreation—has resulted in the emergence of natural supports, such as patrons who are familar with Ian and his paid support person, who come to the pub on High Street and who lend a hand with this chair when he

FIGURE 16–6
Ian's House and Front Yard

FIGURE 16–7
Ian at Work with Cart

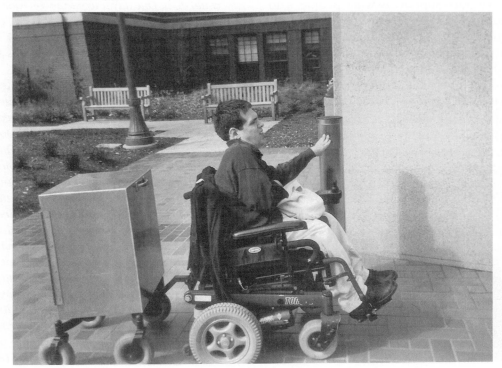

occasionally needs to use the bathroom that is up a couple of steps, or the concertgoers who are familiar with Ian's attendance at such events and let him break into the intermission refreshment line to join them and say hello.

For his part, Douglas also reflects this approach to adulthood, but with different specifics from Ian.

Douglas continues to live with his parents in the family home, but enjoys the relative independence and freedom that a familiar and comfortable setting provides in his small town. He does not work for wages, but has a number of volunteer activities in the community where his presence and participation are valued and encouraged. He has, in short, a life full of family, friends, and community membership with the type of embedded support envisioned by the paradigm of supported adulthood. And it continues to expand as it did when he first met his new nephew (see Figure 16–8).

Informal and Formal Support Resources

A second, related element is the recognition that support should be informal as well as formal. This element directly challenges the problems identified with the traditional client-based role for individuals with severe disabilities and their families. In practical terms, informal—or natural—support is what people who are not paid for their services provide (e.g., emotional support, practical assistance, moral guidance), such as the community members in the previous example. As we mentioned earlier, as long as a professional client model governs the provision of adult developmental disability services, then support, by definition, will be

FIGURE 16–8
Douglas Meets His New Nephew Patrick

organized and controlled by the formal services system. Efforts that most closely adhere to a supported adulthood approach are always bureaucratically flat, with little hierarchy, and are not necessarily oriented toward the direct provision of services. Such efforts recognize that the best support is that which is most natural and most embedded within the social relationships of the individual with disabilities. As with the element of natural contexts, this has the added benefit of economic prudence.

Before he moved to the Annapolis Valley where we met him, Douglas lived and went to school in the city. He and his family were offered the "funny bus" (in the United States, we often call it the "short bus") as part of the special education services. His mom, however, saw it as an opportunity to use the natural option—the city bus—and politely declined. Being an educator, she accompanied him on the bus through the transfer station to bus #9 and off at the school. After several days, she didn't stay on the second bus, but instead got in the car and drove to the school to make sure that he made it off the bus at the correct stop and went into the school instead of the much more interesting fire station next door. More days, more practice, even after the bus driver tried to assure Douglas's mom that all was well; he could do it! One day a woman who rode the same bus and made the same transfer offered to make sure Douglas made the transfer and got off at the school. Mom could release her support to this stranger who became Douglas's natural support.

All went well until the day that there was an extra first bus on the line with a different driver. This driver did not stop at the transfer station because no one rang the bell and he didn't know that Douglas needed bus #9. Because the bus didn't stop, Douglas simply stayed on the first bus and rode through the entire route. Of course, the school called his mom. Vowing not to panic, she called the bus system and found out about the extra bus and the new driver. When contacted, the driver reported that Douglas was still on the bus and he made it to the transfer station the second time around the route. Douglas got to school, albeit late. But, more importantly, his family learned that he had a good sense of where he was and where he was supposed to be. It has paid off throughout his adult life and it means that he can safely be home alone—an option that offers not only more freedom for the family, but more autonomy for Douglas.

Of course, natural support can take time to develop. Many members of the community have grown up not knowing much about disability and, because of the tradition of segregated services, they sometimes have not encountered people with disabilities. Even when they try to interact or be supportive, sometimes their efforts can fall short or simply be inappropriate because they have so little experience with people with disabilities. Some individuals with disabilities can be difficult to get to know or talk to, increasing the challenge for those who might provide natural supports. While natural supports can take time to develop and nurture, the presence of people with disabilities in natural settings as described is an important precursor to the development of these supports. Over time, with more community participation and visibility of people with all manner of disabilities, more and more community members will feel comfortable and will be able to lend a hand when it is needed (see Figure 16-9).

The critical outcome measure is no longer whether someone receives services, but instead whether someone's quality of life improves. The focus is on whether the individual finds the support needed regardless of where that support originates. The neighbor who decides at the last minute to invite Ian to accompany him to a ball game or over for dinner is just as supportive—if not more so—of leisure activity as the official recreational therapist with a scheduled swim time each week, and should be recognized as such. The point—at least from our perspective—is not that all formal support services should be withdrawn or avoided, but that

FIGURE 16-9
Ian and Lyn Enjoy Camping Trips at a Nearby Lake

they should be seen as only one source of the support that all of us need at one time or another.

User-Defined Supports

An emphasis on informal supports and natural contexts leads logically to a third feature of the supported adulthood approach. The individual receiving the support is the only one who can define what is or is not supportive. Again, this directly challenges the control of the bureaucratic structures to establish what services shall be available to an adult with a severe disability. Instead, the approach endorsed by all of the examples of supported adulthood is to empower the individual to make such determinations. For example, a young man with aggressive behavior might use his behavioral repertoire to indicate a clear preference for spending his residential support dollars to maintain him in a duplex with one other roommate instead of in the eight-person group home that was originally offered to him. In some situations, the "user" might be an entire family instead of any one individual. So, for example, parents might need to help define what type of services would be most supportive for a son or daughter or what balance of informal and formal supports would best match their own contributions to his or her lifestyle.

Local Character

A fourth common feature in examples of supported adulthood is recognition that support should be community referenced. The emphasis here is not only that individuals should define what is and is not supportive, but also that, once defined, that support should then take on the shape and texture of the local culture's traditions, values, and opportunities. The most obvious level of community referencing is the basic effort to "fit in." For example, using a group home model as the exclusive type of residential services arrangement may restrict the opportunities found in many urban community apartments. Recreational opportunities should support and (if needed) provide training in locally valued activities (e.g., making a good ski run in Colorado, making a good pastrami on rye in New York City) instead of rigidly adhering to some standardized agenda where all people with severe disabilities learn to bowl. Community referencing should draw on the traditions and values within a local culture. A tradition of resistance can also be supportive when identified as a valuable and important part of a local culture. What we are advocating by "local character" is not just nostalgia for some imagined era of the small-town simple life; tradition can include recognition of differences, even tension, which support for people with severe disabilities should not ignore in the pursuit of peaceful conformity.

> *Ian lives in Oregon in a city with an active tradition of strong minority voices and social activism. Environmental issues alone offer any number of opportunities for citizenship and affiliation, depending on the side you choose to support. Ian already contributes his voice to at least some environmental debates by his use of canvas bags or his backpack when shopping. During a public employees' strike a few years ago at the University of Oregon, Ian joined in support of his coworkers on picket lines. Ian may not have understood all of the issues involved in the strike, but he was aware that the routines were different and that the people he worked alongside were not at their posts. Joining the community expression of resistance, regardless of what he understood about the issues, not only allowed Ian to support his coworkers, but also increased their willingness to contribute to his support in other ways.*

There is also a strong disability rights organization in his community. Although individuals with intellectual disabilities have not always been well represented in the disability rights movement, and while Ian is not yet a member of the local group, he is assisted in contributing his support for disability issues. In the course of his job, Ian serves the university as a semiofficial "accessibility tester." During one period, he began to consistently run into trouble with one of the automatic doors at the same campus building. The building was the first on his morning route to deliver food supplies to cafés around campus. When he pressed the access panel to operate the door, nothing happened. Repeated calls by Ian's coworker to the physical plant resulted in frustration on all sides for a while. Whenever the repair team tested the panel, it worked, but the very next morning it would not work for Ian. Eventually, careful sleuthing by his coworker and others resulted in the discovery that during routine maintenance at night, the emergency switch was being turned off. After this incident, Ian was occasionally asked to try out a new door, entry, or ramp to test its effectiveness for someone with Ian's type of wheelchair and skills. Our point is that supported adulthood requires attention not just to local traditions of peace, harmony, and patriotism but also to the minority voices and social activism that might afford rich and preferred opportunities for community participation and contribution.

Universal Eligibility

Finally, a fifth feature of most of the emerging examples of supported adulthood—and perhaps the most controversial—is the principle of universal eligibility. Everyone who requires support to experience the full promise of adulthood should receive it. Unfortunately, since there are simply not enough formal resources for all who genuinely require them, only those who meet a more stringent test of poverty or extreme need, whether temporary or chronic, receive services. In Moroney's now classic analysis (1986), approaches that focus on a subgroup who are somehow "in most need" are described as reactive or residual. That is, such limited approaches perpetuate the problems of the welfare state programs that we summarized earlier. They tend to be stigmatizing, lack cost-effectiveness (because they are not preventative), and are destructive of personal independence and community membership (because they promote competition for services).

The customary rationale for this limited eligibility is inevitably tied to the professional–client orientation to support services. If we break away from that constraint, however, then the universalizing of disability policy seems much more feasible (Bickenbach, 2001; McKnight, 1995; O'Brien & Murray, 1997). For example, if formal support services are the only officially recognized, legitimate responses to an identified social need, then competition for scarce resources seems inevitable. If informal supports are included and existing natural contexts are preferred, then the available resources for support are dramatically multiplied. The addition of informal support to the equation automatically increases the total recognized resources. Equally important, formal support dollars become more cost effective when used to encourage this informal sector instead of paying the salaries of bureaucrats.

There is danger here as well, of course. The emphasis on informal supports can provide a "cover" for those politicians and administrators who simply want to avoid the expense and challenge of meeting their responsibilities. The legal protections embedded in such landmark legislation as the Individuals with Disabilities Education Act and the Americans with Disabilities Act remain necessary to prevent neglect of responsibility. Recognizing the value of informal supports should never become an excuse for not providing a formal social safety net for those who need it most.

Living the Promise

How might the elements of supported adulthood reveal themselves across the three dimensions of autonomy, membership, and change? We again use Ian's and Douglas's experiences to personalize our discussion. The years since graduation have been exciting and productive for Ian. He now enjoys many symbols of autonomy. Still, Ian will never be completely self-sufficient in many of the most important aspects of life. He will probably never be able to make independent and reliable decisions about some of the more fundamental areas of life: religious beliefs and abstract principles of moral behavior, long-term financial planning, or even when it is safe to cross a busy street corner. However, with appropriate support, he can attend church if he wants to (assuming that it is accessible), reciprocate the kindness of friends and strangers, help manage a small bank account, and even negotiate some intersections. Self-sufficiency certainly entails a number of discrete skills and resources that Ian will never be able to develop or discover on his own. However, self-sufficiency also conveys a pattern of life that goes beyond individual tasks or skills. In this expanded sense, Ian's autonomy is enhanced by appropriate types and levels of ongoing support.

Work life is perhaps the single area that is most commonly associated with personal autonomy. For Ian, the promises of supported employment have been exciting and rewarding. He has a great job—one that is uniquely suited to his skills and personality. Ian is a very outgoing guy who likes to be out and about, driving his wheelchair and meeting people. The food services located in the university's student union were decentralized by putting small cafés in a number of the classroom buildings around campus. However, space is at a premium, and the cafés can store only a few supplies. Ian's wheelchair offered a legal vehicle that could convey supplies throughout the center of campus. With the assistance of vocational rehabilitation, a carrier was designed that fits on the back of his wheelchair for carrying these supplies, and he enjoys a regular route that takes him all over campus, meeting and greeting lots of different people. His job has changed over the years: adding tasks like collecting the receipts or breaking down cartons that once held supplies, adding new stops on the route, and increasing his responsibilities for stocking supplies at the student union.

In March 1997, Ian moved into his own home. Several years later, he moved into a somewhat larger house in a different part of town, enjoying the new space, the larger yard, and the excitement of moving that this event offered. His housemates have changed as well in this time, but the couple who live with him now are about to celebrate their 13th year with him. With this stability has also come a regular routine. Weekdays always involve a morning at work (unless the university is on break), with the remainder of the day punctuated by haircuts, a massage every few weeks, swimming to maintain his range of motion and to combat the gradual weight gain that seems endemic to middle age, and Wednesday nights with an old friend from high school. Weekends are the time for dinner parties with us (we get invited over often!) or other friends, short weekend camping trips to the coast or the hot springs, working on a large variety of arts and craft projects—some of which become wonderful gifts for friends and family—as well as movies, a beer or coffee somewhere in town, or just a visit to the park to feed the ducks.

The year is punctuated with a round of parties and special events. The Easter egg hunt and Halloween haunted house draw larger and larger crowds from the neighborhood. The food is always good, the music and games are fun, and the atmosphere is celebratory. September brings some kind of theme party in honor of Ian's, his father's, and several other friends' birthdays—a Hawaiian luau has been one popular theme. Late summer usually involves a holiday— sometimes we all save up for something special like a trip to Reno or Las Vegas—but other times camping on the coast or the San Juan Islands of Seattle offers the needed respite from daily routine. Ian and his supporters are systematically exploring the accessibility of campgrounds in Oregon and Washington (see Figure 16-9). But then there's always gardening to be done, canning and freezing of vegetables, painting the living room, fixing up the craft room, cleaning the wheelchair, making bread, picking up Dianne or Phil at the airport when they come back from trips— all the comfortable routine chores and tasks that have become a regular part of Ian's daily, weekly, monthly, and yearly life.

Ian is benefiting from the increasing availability of supported living options within the services system. Simply put, supported living means that, despite Ian's limitations, he should be able to live where he wants (in his own home), with whom he wants, for as long as he wants, with the ongoing support needed to make that happen (O'Brien & Sullivan, 2005; Stancliffe & Lakin, 2007). For Ian, this support comes from Robin, his personal support agent, and Lyn, both of whom are his live-in companions; Jessica, Shane, and Andy, who support him during some parts of his week; and Susan, the manager of the supported living program that manages his income from the services system, along with other critical bureaucratic tasks. Ian receives several sources of income: the support dollars that come through mental health services that pay his supporters; his earnings from his job, along with Supplemental Security Income and Social Security Disability Insurance that pay for many of his personal needs and weekly expenses (food, some rent, spending money, haircuts, personal stuff, massages, swimming, gas for his van); and contributions from his parents that help cover his mortgage and utilities, as well as contributing to his vacations.

We know Douglas less well, of course, but his life, too, has been a full one since graduation. As noted earlier, his experiences at work have been less stable than Ian's. Around the time that the sprout business was ending, and during one of his evenings with Lenny at a local pub, Douglas met John. As John got to know Douglas and his family, he offered to have Douglas work with him in a series of jobs that he had as a general handyman in the community. He would arrive early at Douglas's house and together they would work through the morning routine of showers, dressing, and breakfast, and then head out for the day to work. Work varied from helping contractors lay flooring or carpeting to other renovations, including replacing roofs; eventually John and his network of subcontractors made a steady income "flipping" houses—buying houses that needed fixing up and then reselling them. These experiences greatly expanded Douglas's network of affiliations and contributed to his fitness as well.

We also think of ourselves as part of Douglas's affiliations—one that is just for fun. Douglas can be quirky at times, as we've said. One aspect of this is his commitment to things being in their proper place, orderly, and organized. He, like some others, always eats the food on his plate in order at mealtimes and without mixing—first, all the meat, then the vegetables, then the rice. We are not sure if he uses the same order each time, but he does finish one

food before moving on to the next. Of course, in Lenny's cousin's garage, this orderliness is a real asset and Douglas always leaves the garage perfectly organized. And it added to his usefulness and contribution working with John and his friends. And there is never a crooked picture on the wall in Douglas's house. All decorations on tables and shelves are precisely arranged and aligned—usually right to the edge, even if it is a family heirloom.

This commitment to order can also lead to less happy results. We often bring small gifts to the family when we come each summer and some years ago we brought one of those decorative corks for wine bottles. It was made of a turned wood that is popular in Oregon. For Douglas, however, corks, once they are out of the bottle, are finished and meant to be thrown away—which was exactly what happened to our decorative cork. Ever since that incident, we have enjoyed puzzling Douglas with gifts that challenge expectations and conventions. Mostly, we have done this with vases. The family has a large cutting garden, so bringing vases seemed appropriate. One year, we brought a vase that was plastic and collapsed flat. Douglas was puzzled, then intrigued. How could a plastic bag be anything but just that? Then another year we brought a ceramic vase that looked exactly like a small brown paper bag. Again, Douglas was incredulous and thwarted because he couldn't put it away with the paper bags, not to mention fold it flat. Then the round block of polished wood (with a small hole for a stem), and so on—each time bringing Douglas into the joke and the ritual of gift giving and receiving while poking gentle fun at his compulsive commitment to order. Douglas's curiosity was most recently piqued by a vase/planter that was shaped like a garden glove that has a hand in it, but doesn't. He opened it and laughed. We think that he's in on the joke now.

For us, as Ian's parents, it seems that the community is the safest place for him, for Douglas, and for others like them to be. The more hands that are there to catch him when he falls, the better. We firmly believe that the more deeply embedded Ian or Douglas is in the life of their neighborhoods, work places, and communities, the more people there will be who will notice if they are not there and will work to keep them there as a member of the community.

For both Ian and Douglas, life continues to grow and change. Supported change should not involve a lifetime of programs, interventions, training, and habilitation plans. However, it should encourage lifelong growth and development that will allow Ian and Douglas to change their preferences as they learn and experience new things. It should allow their relationships with people to evolve and develop without the frenzied impermanence of various paid staff who are here one month and gone the next. They should both be supported in activities that will create new levels of independence, but even more so in activities that will create new breadth of experience. Finally, Ian and Douglas should be helped to learn how to make their choices known in effective yet appropriate ways.

Many of these natural changes are occurring for Ian. His volunteer jobs have changed, as have his duties at his paid job. His first housemate, Faith, moved on to another phase of her own life, making it possible for Robin, who had worked for Ian some years previously, to come back into his life. New support people— Lyn, Alina, Kareem, Jennifer, Shane, and Jessica—each of whom has spent several years in Ian's life, have introduced him to new experiences and opportunities. Ian continues to learn. He is certainly talking more and about more things. His singing is better with the help of the Karaoke machine he got for Christmas a couple of years ago. He's added swimming twice each week to stay fit and continues to take an active part in the planning and preparation for the many parties that happen at his house for every possible occasion. He has finally made it onto the Oregon beaches with the help of a beach wheelchair rented from the Department of Parks and Recreation. He marked his 40th birthday with a trip to Las Vegas. While his life offers change and new opportunities, he also enjoys a comfortable and stable routine. It seems to be a good balance for everyone.

Through all of these changes, we learn more about how to engage Ian as the author of his emerging adult life. As we have watched Ian gradually separate his life from ours, our goal has not so much been one of self-determination in the particularly individual sense in which it is often applied to people with severe disabilities (Agran & Martin, 2008; P. M. Ferguson & Ferguson, 2001); instead, we have sought, with Ian, a good life. We can support Ian's autonomy, membership, and change. We can also support a growing self-sufficiency and completeness, but supporting self-determination has forced us to shift our thinking from Ian's individual

agency to our collective negotiations. We believe that Douglas's parents are doing the same.

Philosophers have long talked about the importance of *agency* in our understanding of what it means to be an individual. What they mean by that term is our personal ability to act on the world around us, to be our own agents of change. The challenge for Ian and others with even more significant cognitive (and physical, and sensory, and medical) disabilities is how close they seem to come to the absence of agency in key parts of their lives. We do not really know what Ian realizes about himself, though we would dearly love to know. Perhaps we should not assume that Ian finds meaning similar to our own experiences of the characteristics of self-regulation, empowerment, and autonomy so often cited as being central to self-determination. Certainly, we are all interdependent, but the truth of the matter is that the balance of interdependence in Ian's relationships is disproportionate in most matters in comparison with our own. He is more dependent. He requires more care. He determines fewer things in the course of a day, week, or year than each of us do. Yet he does contribute in some very important ways to what occurs in his life. Does he choose? Sometimes, and increasingly more so. But more often, he more indirectly influences people and events so that they end up being more okay than not okay from his point of view, even when we do not know, and perhaps cannot imagine, what his point of view is at the time. We want Ian to have a life that is more okay than not okay from his point of view most of the time.

One thing that we have found to be helpful in thinking of these issues is to borrow a couple of literary metaphors. Literary critics try to discover what a particular text means. Part of discovering the meaning of a text, or the "social text" of any person's life, is finding out what the authors of that text intended it to mean—to gather and take into account all possible meanings. That is never enough, however. The meaning of any text, including the social text of a life, belongs as well to the text itself and gets determined by each of us who "read" or participate in it. What even casual observers think about Ian's life contributes to his story and influences the next chapters.

Like many conventional texts, social texts often have multiple authors. Ian and others with limited communication skills can contribute as coauthors to the text. Even if they do not noticeably interpret any particular experience for themselves, in any strong sense of human agency, by shaping the collective story in whatever way others can comprehend, the social text is enriched by their contribution for others to interpret and elaborate on (P. M. Ferguson & Ferguson, 2001).

> *One Christmas, a few years ago, Ian made us bulletin boards—decorated around the edges with buttons and charms and pieces of old clocks. He gets help picking the colors and textures, and he helps with most of the gluing. In past years, he also made raspberry jam, marinated mushrooms, canned pears, and applesauce. He has also made refrigerator magnets, tree ornaments, and hand-painted mugs and plates. Over the years, he has gone shopping for socks, tea, coffee, really good chocolates, jewelry, winter scarves, and decorative candles. The results of his holiday efforts are certainly shaped by those that support his participation in the season. This is a part of the complexity of Ian's adulthood that we have come to understand. His taste and choices always reflect the people in his life. Our Christmas gifts come as much from them as from Ian. For our part, we have come to love the variety and choices that go into the content of Ian's gifts. Of course, we also cherish the self-satisfied smile that he always has when he hands us the present, which is something that is uniquely his.*

Multidimensional Adulthood

For us, the final key to understanding the full meaning of supported adulthood—indeed, of adulthood itself—is to recognize that it has no one single meaning. Autonomy is a very important dimension of adulthood, but there are others. Unfortunately, most attempts to describe the promise of adulthood for people with severe disabilities have tried to accomplish it by making careful discriminations in the meaning of autonomy and independence in order to account for the genuine limits in self-sufficiency that a severe disability might actually impose (this seems to be especially true of severe cognitive disability).

We believe that a multidimensional approach to adulthood allows a clearer way of interpreting the situation. Instead of trying to subsume everything that we want to include under the single rubric of independence, a multidimensional approach allows us to enhance our description of adulthood with the additional—but coequal—strands of membership and change that lead to the more accurate notion of adult "interdependence."

As we have described earlier, Ian's cognitive limitations and multiple disabilities are significant enough that the strand of autonomy in his version of adulthood may not be as strongly visible as his strand of membership. The situation is similar for Douglas even though he has a much different set of disabilities. The strand of personal change and growth may allow the balance between the other two strands to change over Ian's and Douglas's lifetimes. It seems to us that a full understanding of adulthood in our society would allow us to avoid the dilemmas of linear, one-dimensional thinking, where degrees of "adultness" occur on a single line of autonomy and independence. Adding other dimensions is not an excuse for limiting Ian's or Douglas's independence; it is an interpretation that expands their adulthood. Ian's adulthood is an expression of the relationships that he has with his parents, his paid supporters, his friends, and his neighbors who contribute toward determining what happens to him from day to day. Douglas's adulthood is an expression of a similar set of relationships with his large family, increasing numbers of nieces and nephews, his paid supporters, his friends, and his neighbors throughout his small community. To truly support Ian's, and Douglas's, adulthood, we are striving for relationships that nourish rather than smother, relationships that flourish rather than atrophy, and relationships that author rich stories of lives lived instead of reports of outcomes achieved.

A Cautionary Conclusion about Unkept Promises

Supported adulthood seems to provide an important clue as to how social services might accomplish a practical merger of personal independence and community support. However, claims of relevance and value for such ideas should always be chastened by the history of social reform efforts in our country. Too often, our optimism over reform has been followed by decades of unintended consequences that seem all too predictable in retrospect.

There is a definite danger that arguments in favor of the supported adulthood approach could overemphasize the cost-effectiveness of such elements as the use of natural contexts and the encouragement of informal supports. Some economic savings may, indeed, be available through natural contexts and natural supports. However, as the experiences of the deinstitutionalization movement have shown, effective community support can suffer if justified primarily on the basis of financial savings. The arguments for adopting supported adulthood must be careful not to imply any enthusiasm for underfunded social programs. The economic justification for the approach is that it rationalizes spending by tying it directly to valued outcomes, not that it saves money.

A second danger with supported adulthood is unintentionally justifying an even greater reliance on a charity model of social support. One of the risks in calling for procedures such as increased reliance on community-based responses that encourage informal supports is the creation of a one-sided, libertarian abandonment of the legitimate government responsibility to ensure the health and welfare of its citizens with disabilities. Of course, this move to the privatization of welfare gained popularity during the Reagan administration and seems to be enjoying continued appeal. The problem is that the charity model almost unavoidably accepts the systemic inequities that occasion the need for charity in the first place. An effective disability policy must challenge inequity and discrimination in our society with distributive and protective systems within the formal structure of social agencies. Supported adulthood should illuminate a comprehensive, egalitarian approach to a national disability policy, not just look for volunteers to step up in an age of social divisiveness that results from our class structure and continuing racial, gender, cultural, and religious discrimination.

A final danger in the approach is closely related to the potential overemphasis on charity. Just as the rediscovery of informal supports and natural contexts can be exaggerated into a privatized social policy of volunteers and cheerful givers, so can the concomitant deemphasis on traditional versions of formal supports lead to an overblown antiprofessionalism. Certainly, those within the field of disability services must recognize the value of properly focused expertise and technology in improving the quality of some person's lives. The contention that excessive professionalism has often encouraged a dependency role for disabled people should not entail the abandonment of all of the wonderful advances made in the behavioral and life sciences.

Despite these very real dangers of misapplication or distortion, the value of moving rapidly toward a vision of supported adulthood is worth the risk. To us it seems to represent the only hope that Ian's "flight" into full adulthood will be a smooth one. There are thousands of Ians and Douglases who are "taking off" every year in our society. There are thousands more making their way as adulthood moves from young adulthood to middle age and beyond. We have made implicit promises to all of them for as full and rewarding a lifetime as they can achieve. The true risk is the human cost of not doing everything we can to fulfill those promises.

Suggested Activities

Think about and discuss with your colleagues the ways in which you do and do not operate as an "adult" in terms of (a) self-sufficiency and (b) autonomy.

1. Think about and discuss with your colleagues all of the things, events, and supports you obtain from your own parents or other family members.
2. Inventory the services available for an individual with severe disabilities in your community. Try to obtain the following information about each agency or group that provides services:
   a. The mission and philosophy of those who provide the service;
   b. The role of the family in program design, monitoring, and improvement; and
   c. The role of the adult in program design, monitoring, and improvement.
3. Visit a residential or vocational program in your community that provides services for individuals with severe intellectual disabilities. Try to notice things that reveal the ways in which the people served and supported by the program or service think of themselves as adults and are thought of by others as adults.
4. Talk with someone who works directly with individuals with severe disabilities (e.g., in a vocational support agency or a residential program). Find out how he or she views adulthood for the people that they are trying to support.
5. Talk with a parent or a sibling of an adult with severe disabilities about his or her perspectives on how best to support the family member with the disability.

References

Agran, M., & Martin, J. (2008). Self-determination: Enhancing competence and independence. In K. Storey, P. Bates, & D. Hunter (Eds.), *Transition to adult life for persons with disabilities* (2nd ed., pp. 189–214). St. Augustine, FL: Training Resource Network, Inc.

Alba, K., Prouty, R. W., & Lakin, K. C. (2007). Services provided by state and non-state agencies in 2007. In R. W. Prouty, K. Alba, & K. C. Lakin (Eds.), *Residential services for persons with developmental disabilities: Status and trends through 2007* (pp. 37–42). Minneapolis: Research and Training Center on Community Living, Institute on Community Integration, University of Minnesota.

American Association on Mental Retardation. (2002). *Mental retardation: Definition, classification, and systems of supports* (10th ed.). Washington, DC: Author.

Aries, P. (1962). *Centuries of childhood: A social history of family life* (R. Baldick, Trans.). New York: Vintage Books. (Original work published in 1960)

Arnett, J. J., & Tanner, L. (Eds.). (2006). *Emerging adults in America: Coming of age in the 21st century.* Washington, DC: American Psychological Association.

Bambara, L. M., Wilson, B. A., & McKenzie, M. (2007). Transition and quality of life. In S. L. Odom, R. H. Horner, M. E. Snell, & J. Blacher (Eds.), *Handbook of developmental disabilities* (pp. 371–389). New York: Guilford Press.

Beales, R. W., Jr. (1985). In search of the historical child: Miniature adulthood and youth in Colonial New England. In N. R. Hiner & J. M. Hawes (Eds.), *Growing up in America: Children in historical perspective* (pp. 7–24). Chicago: University of Illinois Press.

Bérubé, M. (2003). Citizenship and disability. *Dissent, 50*(2), 52–58.

Bickenbach, J. E. (2001). Disability human rights, law, and policy. In G. L. Albrecht, K. D. Seelman, & M. Bury (Eds.), *Handbook of disability studies* (pp. 565–584). Thousand Oaks, CA: Sage.

Blatterer, H. (2007). Contemporary adulthood: Reconceptualizing an uncontested category. *Current Sociology, 55*, 771–791.

Braddock, D., Hemp, R., & Rizzolo, M. C. (2008). *The state of the states in developmental disabilities* (7th ed.). Washington, DC: American Association on Intellectual and Developmental Disabilities.

Danesi, M. (2003). *Forever young: The teen-aging of modern culture.* Toronto, Ontario, Canada: University of Toronto Press.

DeLio, D., Rogan, P., & Geary, T. (2000). APSE's position statement on segregated services: A background paper for advocates. *Advance, 10*(4), 1–2.

Drake, R. F. (2001). Welfare states and disabled people. In G. L. Albrecht, K. D. Seelman, & M. Bury (Eds.), *Handbook of disability studies* (pp. 412–429). Thousand Oaks, CA: Sage.

Elder, G. H., Jr. (1998). The life course as developmental theory. *Child Development, 69*, 1–12.

Erikson, E. H. (1950). *Childhood and society.* New York: W. W. Norton.

Erikson, V. L., & Martin, J. (1984). The changing adult: An integrated approach. *Social Casework: The Journal of Contemporary Social Work, 65*, 162–171.

Felce, D., & Perry, J. (2007). Living with support in the community: Factors associated with quality-of-life outcome. In S. L. Odom, R. H. Horner, M. E. Snell, & J. Blacher (Eds.), *Handbook of developmental disabilities* (pp. 410–428). New York: Guilford Press.

Ferguson, D. L., & Ferguson, P. M. (1986). The new victors: A progressive policy analysis of work reform for people with very severe handicaps. *Mental Retardation, 24*, 331–338.

Ferguson, P. M. (2002). Notes toward a history of hopelessness: Disability and the places of therapeutic failure. *Disability, Culture, and Education, 1*(1), 27–40.

Ferguson, P. M. (2003). Winks, blinks, squints and twitches: Looking for disability and culture through my son's left eye. In P. Devlieger,

F. Rusch, & D. Pfeiffer (Eds.), *Rethinking disability: The emergence of new definitions, concepts and communities* (pp. 131–147). Philadelphia: Garant/Coronet Books.

Ferguson, P. M., & Ferguson, D. L. (2001). Winks, blinks, squints and twitches: Looking for disability, culture and self-determination through our son's left eye. *Scandinavian Journal of Disability Research, 3*(2), 71–90.

Ferguson, P. M., Ferguson, D. L., & Blumberg, E. R., with Ferguson, I. (1997). Negotiating adulthood: Kitchen table conversations about supported living. In P. O'Brien & R. Murray (Eds.), *Human services: Toward partnership and support* (pp. 189–200). Palmerston North, New Zealand: Dunmore Press.

Ferguson, P. M., Ferguson, D. L., & Jones, D. (1988). Generations of hope: Parental perspectives on the transitions of their children with severe retardation from school to adult life. *Journal of the Association for Persons with Severe Handicaps, 13*, 177–187.

Ferguson, P. M., Hibbard, M., Leinen, J., & Schaff, S. (1990). Supported community life: Disability policy and the renewal of mediating structures. Journal of Disability Policy Studies, 1, 9–35.

Ferguson, P. M., & O'Brien, P. (2005). From giving service to being of service. In P. O'Brien & M. Sullivan (Eds.), *Allies in emancipation: Shifting from providing service to being of support* (pp. 3–18). South Melbourne, Australia: Thomson Dunmore Press.

Fleischer, D. Z., & Zames, F. (2001). *The disability rights movement: From charity to confrontation.* Philadelphia: Temple University Press.

Furstenberg, F. F., Jr., Cook, T. D., Eccles, J., Elder, G. H., Jr., & Sameroff, A. (1999). *Managing to make it: Urban families and adolescent success.* Chicago: University of Chicago Press.

Grossi, T., Gilbride, M., & Mank, D. (2008). Adult employment: Contributing through work. In K. Storey, P. Bates, & D. Hunter (Eds.), *The road ahead: Transition to adult life for persons with disabilities* (2nd ed., pp. 107–129). St. Augustine, FL: Training Resource Network, Inc.

Hareven, T. (Ed.). (1978). *Transitions: The family and the life course in historical perspective.* New York: Academic Press.

Ingstad, B., & Whyte, S. R. (1995). Disability and culture: An overview. In B. Ingstad & S. R. Whyte (Eds.), *Disability and culture* (pp. 3–32). Berkeley: University of California Press.

Kalyanpur, M., & Harry, B. (1999). *Culture in special education: Building reciprocal family-professional relationships.* Baltimore: Paul H. Brookes.

Kett, J. F. (1977). *Rites of passage: Adolescence in America, 1790 to the present.* New York: Basic Books.

Klingner, J. K., Blanchett, W. J., & Harry, B. (2007). Race, culture, and developmental disabilities. In S. L. Odom, R. H. Horner, M. E. Snell, & J. Blacher (Eds.), *Handbook of developmental disabilities* (pp. 55–75). New York: Guilford Press.

Lakin, K. C., Prouty, R., Polister, B., & Coucouvanis, K. (2003). Selected changes in residential service systems over a quarter century, 1977–2002. *Mental Retardation, 41*, 303–306.

Lakin, K. C., & Stancliffe, R. J. (2007). Residential supports for persons with intellectual and developmental disabilities. *Mental Retardation and Developmental Disabilities Research Reviews, 13*, 151–159.

Levinson, D. (1978). *Seasons of a man's life.* New York: Knopf.

Magnussen, T. (1997). Marginalised young men and successful young women? In J. Wheelock & A. Mariussen (Eds.), *Households, work, and economic change: A comparative institutional perspective* (pp. 187–194). Boston: Kluwer Academic.

Mank, D. (2007). Employment. In S. L. Odom, R. H. Horner, M. E. Snell, & J. Blacher (Eds.), *Handbook of developmental disabilities* (pp. 390–409). New York: Guilford Press.

Mank, D., Cioffi, A., & Yovanoff, P. (2003). Supported employment outcomes across a decade: Is there evidence of improvement in the quality of implementation? *Mental Retardation, 41,* 188–197.

McKnight, J. L. (1995). *The careless society: Community and its counterfeits.* New York: Basic Books.

Meyrowitz, J. (1984). The adultlike child and the childlike adult: Socialization in the electronic age. *Daedalus: Journal of the American Academy of Arts and Sciences, 113*(3), 19–48

Miller, K. D., Bowens, F., Strike, A-M., Venable, J. E., & Schleien, S. J. (2009). Something for everyone. *Parks and Recreation, 44*(2), 36–41.

Modell, J., Furstenberg, F. F., Jr., & Hershberg, T. (1978). Social change and transitions to adulthood in historical perspective. In M. Gordon (Ed.), *The American family in social-historical perspective* (pp. 192–219). New York: St. Martin's Press.

Molgat, M. (2007). Do transitions and social structures matter? How "emerging adults" define themselves as adults. *Journal of Youth Studies, 10,* 495–516.

Moroney, R. M. (1986). *Shared responsibility: Families and social policy.* Chicago: Aldine.

Murphy, R. F., Scheer, J., Murphy, Y., & Mack, R. (1988). Physical disability and social liminality: A study in the rituals of adversity. *Social Science and Medicine, 26,* 235–242.

Mwaria, C. B. (1990). The concept of self in the context of crisis: A study of families of the severely brain-injured. *Social Science and Medicine, 30,* 889–893.

Nerney, T. (2008). *Communicating self-determination: Freedom, authority, support, and responsibility.* Retrieved July 28, 2009, from http://www.centerforself-determination.com/docs/sd/COMMUNICATING%20SELF.pdf

O'Brien, P., & Murray, R. (Eds.). (1997). *Human services: Towards partnership and support.* Palmerston North, New Zealand: Dunmore Press.

O'Brien, P., & Sullivan, M. (Eds.) (2005). *Allies in emancipation: Shifting from providing service to being of support* (pp. 3–18). South Melbourne, Australia: Thomson Dunmore Press.

Priestley, M. (Ed.). (2001). *Disability and the life course: Global perspectives.* New York: Cambridge University Press.

Prouty, R. W., Alba, K., & Lakin, K. C. (Eds.). (2007). *Residential services for persons with developmental disabilities: Status and trends through 2007.* Minneapolis: Research and Training Center on Community Living, Institute on Community Integration, University of Minnesota.

Rueda, R., Monzo, L., Shapiro, J., Gomez, J., & Blacher, J. (2005). Cultural models and practices regarding transition: A view from Latina mothers of young adults with developmental disabilities. Exceptional Children, 71, 401–414.

Rynders, J. E., Schleien, S. J., & Matson, S. L. (2003). Transition for children with Down syndrome from school to community. *Focus on Exceptional Children, 36*(4), 1–8.

Sarason, S. B. (1972). *The creation of settings and the future societies.* San Francisco: Jossey-Bass.

Schur, L., & Kruse, D. (2009). *Fact Sheet: Disability and voter turnout in the 2008 elections.* Retrieved June 29, 2009, from http://www.nebraskaadvocacyservices.org/includes/downloads/lityvoterturnout08election.pdf?PHPSESSID=hgev26fubbo3ab1deqf7uigvs7

Shanahan, M. J. (2000). Pathways to adulthood in changing societies: Variability and mechanisms in life-course perspective. *Annual Review of Sociology, 26,* 667–692.

Stancliffe, R. J., & Lakin, K. C. (2007). Independent living. In S. L. Odom, R. H. Horner, M. E. Snell, & J. Blacher (Eds.), *Handbook of developmental disabilities* (pp. 429–448). New York: Guilford Press.

Storey, K., Bates, P., & Hunter, D. (Eds.). (2008). *The road ahead: Transition to adult life for persons with disabilities* (2nd ed.). St. Augustine, FL: Training Resources Network, Inc.

Taylor, S. J. (1988). Caught in the continuum: A critical analysis of the principle of the least restrictive environment. *Journal of the Association for Persons with Severe Handicaps, 13,* 45–53.

Taylor, S. J. (2001). The continuum and current controversies in the USA. *Journal of Intellectual and Developmental Disability, 26*(1), 15–33.

Taylor, T. (1988). The transition to adulthood in comparative perspective: Professional males in Germany and the United States at the turn of the century. *Journal of Social History, 21,* 635–658.

Vaillant, G. E. (1977). *Adaptation to life.* Boston: Little, Brown.

Wehman, P. (Ed.). (2006). *Life beyond the classroom: Transition strategies for young people with disabilities* (4th ed.). Baltimore: Paul H. Brookes.

Wehmeyer, M. L., Gragoudas, S., & Shogren, K. (2006). Self-determination, student involvement, and leadership development. In P. Wehman (Ed.), *Life beyond the classroom: Transition strategies for young people with disabilities* (4th ed., pp. 35–60). Baltimore: Paul H. Brookes.

Williams, G. H. (2001). Theorizing disability. In G. L. Albrecht, K. D. Seelman, & M. Bury (Eds.), *Handbook of disability studies* (pp. 123–144). Thousand Oaks, CA: Sage.

Wohl, R. (1979). *The generation of 1914.* Cambridge, MA: Harvard University Press.

Wolfensberger, W. (1972). *The principle of normalization in human services.* Toronto, Ontario, Canada: National Institute on Mental Retardation.

✤ Subject Index ✤